lonely

Brazil

DEC 2013

The Amazon
p563

Ceará, Piauí & Maranhão
p526

Pernambuco, Paraíba & Rio Grande do Norte
p479

Sergipe & Alagoas
p461

Mato Grosso & Mato Grosso do Sul
p358

Brasília & Goiás
p330

Bahia
p393

Minas Gerais & Espírito Santo
p160

São Paulo State
p215

Paraná
p260

Rio de Janeiro
p50

Rio de Janeiro State
p120

Santa Catarina
p284

Rio Grande do Sul
p309

THIS EDITION WRITTEN AND RESEARCHED BY

Regis St Louis,

Gary Chandler, Gregor Clark, Bridget Gleeson,

John Noble, Kevin Raub, Paul Smith

Contents

RIO DE JANEIRO P50

COPACABANA P57

VIVIANE PONTI / GETTY IMAGES ©

IAN TROWER / GETTY IMAGES ©

Contents

Contents

ON THE ROAD

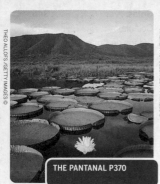

THE PANTANAL P370

MANAUS P600

Contents

OURO PRETO P172

JOHN W BANAGAN /GETTY IMAGES ©

Welcome to Brazil

Tropical islands, lush rainforests, marvelous cities and picture-perfect beaches set the scene for the great Brazilian adventure.

Landscapes & Biodiversity

One of the world's most captivating places, Brazil is a country of powdery white-sand beaches, verdant rainforests and wild, rhythm-filled metropolises. Brazil's attractions extend from frozen-in-time colonial towns to otherworldly landscapes of red-rock canyons, thundering waterfalls and coral-fringed tropical islands. Add to that, Brazil's biodiversity: legendary in scope, its diverse ecosystems boast the greatest collection of plant and animal species found on earth. There are countless places where you can spot iconic species in Brazil, including toucans, scarlet macaws, howler monkeys, capybara, pink dolphins, sea turtles and thousands of other living species.

Days of Adventure

Brazil offers big adventures for travelers with budgets large and small. There's horseback riding and wildlife watching in the Pantanal, kayaking flooded forests in the Amazon, ascending rocky cliff tops to panoramic views, whale watching off the coast, surfing stellar breaks off palm-fringed beaches and snorkeling crystal-clear rivers or coastal reefs, all are part of the great Brazilian experience.

Joie de Vivre

Brazil's most famous celebration, Carnaval, storms through the country's cities and towns with hip-shaking samba and frevo (music and dance style), dazzling costumes and parties that last until sun up, but Brazilians hardly limit their revelry to a few weeks of the year. Festas (festivals) happen throughout the year, and provide a window into Brazil's incredible diversity. The streets are carpeted with flowers during Ouro Preto's Semana Santa (Holy Week), while in the north, Bumba Meu Boi blends indigenous, African and Portuguese folklore. For a taste of the old world, hit Blumenau's beer- and schnitzel-loving Oktoberfest, the largest outside of Germany.

The Rhythms of Brazil

Wherever there's music, that carefree lust for life tends to appear – whether dancing with cariocas (residents of Rio) at Rio's atmospheric samba clubs or following powerful drumbeats through the streets of Salvador. There's the dance hall *forró* of the Northeast, twirling carimbó music of the Amazon, scratch-skilled DJs of São Paulo and an endless variety of regional sounds that extends from the twangy country music of the sunbaked *sertanejo* to the hard-edged reggae of Maranhão.

Why I Love Brazil

By Regis St Louis, Coordinating Author

The music, the beaches, the wildlife, and most importantly the people: it's hard not to fall for Brazil. Rio de Janeiro is one of my favorite cities: I never tire of watching the sunset from Arpoador, chasing the samba scene in Lapa or wandering the villagelike streets of Santa Teresa. But Rio is just the beginning, and in Brazil there really is no end. I have fond memories spotting wildlife (especially in the Pantanal and the Amazon), making friends in small towns and in general getting beneath the surface. There's really no other country that offers so much.

For more about our authors, see p736

Above: Beach, Boipeba (p431)

Brazil

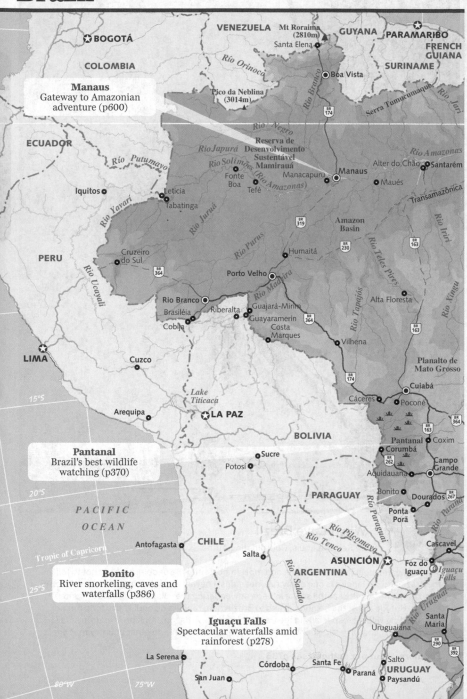

VENEZUELA
Mt Roraima (2810m)
Santa Elena
GUYANA
PARAMARIBO
FRENCH GUIANA
SURINAME

☆ BOGOTÁ

COLOMBIA

Río Orinoco

Boa Vista

BR 174

Serra Tumucumaque

Río Jari

Manaus
Gateway to Amazonian adventure (p600)

ECUADOR

Pico da Neblina (3014m) ▲

Reserva de Desenvolvimento Sustentável Mamirauá (Rio Amazonas)

Río Japurá

Río Amazonas

Alter do Chão

Santarém

Río Putumayo

Río Solimões

Fonte Boa

Manacapuru

Manaus

Maués

Iquitos

Leticia

Tabatinga

Tefé

Transamazônica

Río Yavari

Río Juruá

BR 319

Amazon Basin

Río Iriri

PERU

Río Ucayali

Cruzeiro do Sul

Río Purus

Humaitá

BR 230

Río Teles Pires

BR 163

Río Xingu

BR 364

Porto Velho

Río Madeira

Rio Branco

Riberalta

Guajará-Mirim

Alta Floresta

Brasiléia

Cobija

Guayaramerin
Costa Marques

BR 364

Río Tapajós

BR 163

LIMA

Cuzco

Vilhena

BR 174

Planalto de Mato Grosso

Lake Titicaca

Cáceres

Cuiabá

15°S

Arequipa

☆ LA PAZ

Poconé

BR 364

Pantanal
Brazil's best wildlife watching (p370)

Sucre

BOLIVIA

Pantanal

Coxim

Potosí

Corumbá

BR 262

Campo Grande

20°S

PACIFIC

Aquidauana

OCEAN

PARAGUAY

Bonito

Dourados

BR 267

Ponta Porã

Tropic of Capricorn

Antofagasta

CHILE

Río Pilcomayo

Río Paraná

Cascavel

Salta

Río Tenco

ASUNCIÓN ☆

Foz do Iguaçu

Iguaçu Falls

Bonito
River snorkeling, caves and waterfalls (p386)

25°S

Río Salado

ARGENTINA

Río Uruguay

Santa Maria

Iguaçu Falls
Spectacular waterfalls amid rainforest (p278)

Uruguaiana

BR 290

BR 392

La Serena

Córdoba

Santa Fe

Salto

URUGUAY

80°W

75°W

San Juan

Paraná

Paysandú

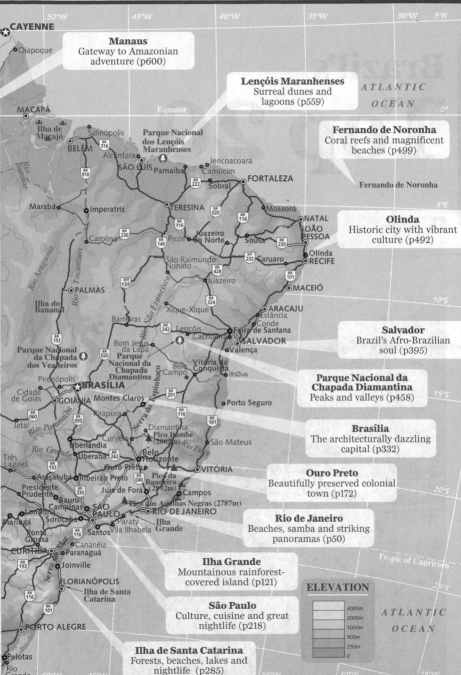

Manaus
Gateway to Amazonian adventure (p600)

Lençóis Maranhenses
Surreal dunes and lagoons (p559)

Fernando de Noronha
Coral reefs and magnificent beaches (p499)

Olinda
Historic city with vibrant culture (p492)

Salvador
Brazil's Afro-Brazilian soul (p395)

Parque Nacional da Chapada Diamantina
Peaks and valleys (p458)

Brasília
The architecturally dazzling capital (p332)

Ouro Preto
Beautifully preserved colonial town (p172)

Rio de Janeiro
Beaches, samba and striking panoramas (p50)

Ilha Grande
Mountainous rainforest-covered island (p121)

São Paulo
Culture, cuisine and great nightlife (p218)

Ilha de Santa Catarina
Forests, beaches, lakes and nightlife (p285)

ELEVATION

3000m
2000m
1000m
500m
250m
0

Brazil's
Top 20

1

Pão de Açúcar, Rio de Janeiro

1 Some say to come around sunset for the best views from that absurd confection of a mountain (p59). But in truth, it doesn't matter when you come; you're unlikely to look at Rio (or your own comparatively lackluster city) in the same way. From here the landscape is pure undulating green hills and golden beaches lapped by blue sea, with rows of skyscrapers sprouting along the shore. The ride up is good fun: all-glass aerial trams that whisk you up to the top. The adventurous can rock-climb their way to the summit.

Iguaçu Falls

2 No matter the number of waterfalls you've checked off your bucket list, no matter how many times you have thought to yourself you'd be just fine never seeing another waterfall again, Iguaçu Falls (p278) will stomp all over your idea of water trickling over the edge of a cliff. The thunderous roar of 275 falls crashing across the Brazil and Argentina border floors even the most jaded traveler. Loud, angry, unstoppable and impossibly gorgeous, Iguaçu will leave you stunned and slack-jawed at the absolute power of Mother Nature.

2

Salvador

3 The capital of Afro-Brazil, Salvador (p395) is famous for capoeira, Candomblé, Olodum, colonial Portuguese architecture, African street food and one of the oldest lighthouses in the Americas. Today's lively Bahian capital offers a unique fusion of two vibrant cultures. The festive music and nightlife scene culminates in February with one of Brazil's best Carnavals.

Ilha Grande

4 Thanks to its isolation, Ilha Grande (p121) served for decades as a prison and leper's colony. Spared from development by this unusual history, its jungle-clad slopes and dozens of beaches are some of the best preserved in all of Brazil. Days are spent hiking through lush Atlantic rainforest, snorkeling amid aquamarine seas and basking in crisp waterfalls. With no motor vehicles to spoil the party, this is one clean, green island – a true nature lover's paradise. It's also an easy day's journey from Rio.

PETER ADAMS / GETTY IMAGES ©

HARRIS PHOTOGRAPHY / GETTY IMAGES ©

Ouro Preto

5 The 18th-century streets of Ouro Preto (p172) veer between one baroque masterpiece and the next. You can admire the sculpted masterpieces of Aleijadinho, discover the 18th-century African tribal king turned folk hero Chico-Rei and gaze upon opulent gilded churches. The Holy Week processions are among the country's most spectacular.

Beers of Blumenau

6 Along with lederhosen and leberkäse, German immigration brought Reinheitsgebot, Germany's beer purity law, and these German-Brazilians aren't fond of sharing. That means with the exception of the once-micro Eisenbahn, good beers such as Schornstein Kneipe, Bierland and Das Bier don't fall far from the tree (p298).

Pantanal

7 Few places can match the wildlife watching experience provided by the Pantanal (p370), a remote wetland in the heart of Mato Grosso. From cute capybaras to stately storks, the animal life abounds and is easy to see in the open marshy surroundings. There's also no better place in South America to see the elusive jaguar! Above: jaguar (p617)

Fernando de Noronha

8 This archipelago (p499) of one 10km-long island and 20 smaller ones, 350km out into the Atlantic from Natal, has everything a tropical getaway should have – jaw-dropping scenery and seascapes, fine beaches, the best diving and snorkeling in the country, good surfing, memorable hikes and plentiful visible wildlife.

Jungle Trips

9 Needless to say, the best reason to visit the Amazon is to get out into the jungle (p601): to ply the winding waterways in a canoe, to hike lush leafy trails, to scan the canopy for monkeys, sloths and other creatures. The world's biggest and best-known rainforest has outdoor excursions of all sorts, and for all types of travelers: from easy nature hikes to scaling 50m trees, from luxury lodges to makeshift camps in the forest. Whatever your interest, experience, ability or budget, there's a jungle trip in the Amazon waiting to blow your mind. Above: canoeing, Rio Solimões (p626)

São Paulo Nights

10 Rivaling the frenetic pace of New York, the modernism of Tokyo and the prices of Moscow but swamping all of them in options, São Paulo city (p241) is home to a pool of 20 million potential foodies, clubbers and cocktail connoisseurs and nearly 30,000 restaurants, bars and clubs to satiate them. From the contemporary gourmet haunts of Itaim Bibi and Jardins to edgy offerings of Baixo Augusta to bohemian bars in Vila Madalena, it's a gluttonous avalanche of bolinhos, booze and beats that outruns the sunrise on most nights. Saúde! Above: bar, Vila Madalena (p245)

Brasília Architecture

11 What the city of the future really needed to back up its claim to be the harbinger of Brazil's 'new dawn' was an architect capable of designing buildings that looked the part. In Oscar Niemeyer they found the right man for the job. The 'crown of thorns' Catedral Metropolitana is a religious masterwork and the interplanetary Teatro Nacional is out of this world! Brasília is a city overloaded with architectural gems (p340) designed by a genius inspired by the concept of a better future.

Below: Catedral Metropolitana (p333)

Bonito

12 Bonito (p386) is beautiful! Book yourself onto a smorgasbord of aquatic adventures in the jaw-dropping surroundings of the Serra do Bodoquena and prepare for a wild wet-suited adventure like you've never experienced before. Whether you are taking your first foray into flotation on the Rio da Prata or journeying to the center of the earth at the Abismo de Anhumas, Bonito is packed with unique experiences that will rank among your most cherished memories of any trip to Brazil.

Below: Gruta do Lago Azul (p387)

VIVIANE PONTI / GETTY IMAGES ©

VIVIANE PONTI / GETTY IMAGES ©

Carnaval in Rio

13 Get plenty of sleep before you board the plane, because once you land, it's nonstop revelry (p35) until Ash Wednesday (sort of) brings it all to a close. With nearly 500 street parties happening in every corner of town, you will not lack for options. For the full experience, join a samba school and parade amid pounding drum corps and mechanized smoke-breathing dragons before thousands of roaring fans in the Sambódromo. Or assemble a costume and hit one of the Carnaval balls around town. The build-up starts weeks in advance.

Tiradentes

14 The colonial town of Tiradentes (p190) is so well preserved, and its natural setting so appealing, you could be excused for feeling like you've wandered onto a movie set. Cobbled lanes, flower-draped walls and some stunning colonial architecture make every step a delight – even more if you like to hike. The surrounding mountains are threaded with trails, Tiradentes' hyperactive restaurant scene serves up delicious traditional meals, and its charming guesthouses make a relaxing spot to recharge.

Parque Nacional da Chapada Diamantina

15 A pristine outdoor wonderland of rushing waterfalls, crystal-blue pools, rugged hiking trails and natural waterslides, Chapada Diamantina (p458) is an unspoiled national park off the beaten path – it's one of the only inland attractions in the beach-happy state of Bahia. Those who make the effort to explore the park, either on day trips from Lençóis or on the Grand Circuit with a local guide, often count the Chapada Diamantina as one of their top outdoor experiences in Brazil.

Lençóis Maranhenses

16 Of all Brazil's landscape spectacles, the most unexpected has to be the Lençóis Maranhenses (p559) in Maranhão – a 70km-long, 25km-wide expanse of high dunes resembling *lençóis* (bed sheets) spread across the landscape. From around March to September (best in July and August) the dunes are partnered by thousands of crystal-clear, freshwater lagoons from rainwater filling the hollows between them.

JON ARNOLD IMAGES / GETTY IMAGES ©

HOLGER LEUE / GETTY IMAGES ©

Recife & Olinda

17 These two contrasting Northeastern neighbors with an intertwined history and shared culture make a heady double act. Recife (p482) is the big-city big sister with skyscrapers and traffic, but also a fascinating historic center becoming more appealing through renovations and new museums and restaurants. Cute, tree-covered Olinda (p492) has tranquil winding lanes, colonial churches and artists' galleries. Their vibrant shared heritage comes together at Carnaval with riotous street festivities. Above: Carnaval (p492), Olinda

Alter do Chão

18 Alter do Chão (p592) truly has it all: a slice of Jericoacoara in the heart of the rainforest. Alter do Chão is best known for its beach: an island made entirely of fine white sand lapped by cool tea-colored water. But Alter do Chão also is a gateway to a major national forest, with massive *samaúma* trees and a chance to live with local rubber-tapper families. With so much to do, hotels for all budgets, and a great laid-back vibe, it's a place you'll want to to linger at for a while – and many travelers do just that.

Beaches of Santa Catarina

19 Santa Catarina (p285) is synonymous with the good life and that has a whole lot to do with its sun-toasted shores. Whether you hang out in Florianópolis, where an easy path to paradise boasts 42 idyllic beaches sitting within an hour's drive, or head south of the capital to Guarda do Embaú, one of Brazil's best surfing spots, or Praia do Rosa, the state's most sophisticated beach resort, a powerful punch of wow will greet you the first time you dig your toes into the state's unspoiled sands.

Paraty

20 No place in Brazil offers such an enticing blend of colonial architecture and natural beauty as Paraty (p127). Located in the picturesque Costa Verde, it has long been a favorite carioca getaway. Gorgeous beaches and a stunning mountain backdrop jostle for attention with the multihued, cobblestoned charms of the 18th-century town center. If you tire of sunbathing and sightseeing, cool off with a caipirinha, go hurtling down a natural waterslide nearby, or whip up a gourmet Brazilian meal at the local cooking school.

Need to Know

For more information, see Survival Guide (p696)

Currency
Real (R$)

Language
Portuguese

Money
ATMs widely available. Credit cards accepted in most hotels and restaurants.

Visas
Required for some nationalities, including Americans, Canadians and Australians.

Mobile Phones
Local SIM cards can be used in unlocked European and Australian phones, and in US phones on the GSM network.

Time
Brazil has four time zones. Rio and São Paulo are on Brasília time (GMT/UTC minus 3 hours).

When to Go

Manaus
GO Jul–Nov

Cuiabá
GO Apr–Sep

Salvador
GO Oct–Mar

Rio de Janeiro
GO Nov–Mar

Florianópolis
GO Nov–Mar

Desert, dry climate
Tropical climate, wet & dry seasons
Tropical climate, rain year round
Warm to hot summers, mild winters

High Season
(Dec–Mar)

➡ Brazil's high season coincides with the northern-hemisphere winter.

➡ It's a hot, festive time, though expect higher prices and minimum stays (typically four nights) during Carnaval.

Shoulder
(Apr & Oct)

➡ The weather is warm and dry along the coast, though it can be chilly in the south.

➡ Prices and crowds are average, though Easter week draws crowds and high prices.

Low Season
(May–Sep)

➡ Aside from July, which is a school-holiday month, you'll find lower prices and cold temperatures in the south.

➡ July to September are good months to visit the Amazon or Pantanal.

Websites

Embratur (www.visitbrasil.com) Official site of Brazil's Ministry of Tourism.

Insider's Guide to Rio (www.ipanema.com) Tips and planning info, with special sections on Carnaval and gay Rio.

Lonely Planet (www.lonelyplanet.com) Summaries on Brazil travel, the Thorn Tree bulletin board and other resources.

Rio Times (www.riotimesonline.com) English-language news and resources on Rio.

Brazzil (www.brazzil.com) Articles on the country's politics, economy, literature, arts and culture.

Gringoes (www.gringoes.com) Articles written by anglophones living in Brazil.

Important Numbers

Brazil country code	☑55
Ambulance	☑192
Fire	☑193
Police	☑190
International collect call	☑0800-703-2111

Exchange Rates

Argentina	R$1	R$0.41
Australia	A$1	R$2.04
Bolivia	B$1	R$0.32
Canada	C$1	R$2.10
Euro zone	€1	R$2.89
Japan	¥100	R$2.26
New Zealand	NZ$1	R$1.71
UK	UK£1	R$3.41
USA	US$1	R$2.21

For current exchange rates see www.xe.com.

Daily Costs

Budget: less than R$200

➡ dorm bed R$40-70

➡ sandwich and drink in a juice bar R$10-15

➡ long-distance buses R$10-15 per hour of travel

Midrange: R$200–400

➡ Standard double room in a hotel R$150-300

➡ Dinner for two in a midrange restaurant R$70-150

➡ Jungle trips R$200 per day

➡ Admission to night clubs and live music venues R$20 50

➡ One-way flight from Rio to Salvador/Iguaçu/Manaus from R$300/361/530

Top End: over R$400

➡ Boutique hotels R$500-800

➡ Upscale jungle lodges outside Manaus per night R$500-1000

➡ Dinner for two at top restaurants R$180-400

Opening Hours

Banks 9am–3pm Monday to Friday

Restaurants noon–2.30pm and 6–10:30pm

Cafes 8am–10pm

Bars 6pm–2am

Nightclubs 10pm–4am Thursday to Saturday

Shops 9am–6pm Monday to Saturday and 9am–1pm Saturday

Arriving in Brazil

Aeroporto Galeão (GIG; Rio de Janeiro) Premium Auto Ônibus (www.premiumautoonibus.com.br; R$10-12)

operates buses approximately every 20 minutes to Flamengo, Copacabana, Ipanema, Leblon and other neighborhoods. It takes 75 minutes to 2 hours. Radio taxis charge R$105 to Copacabana and Ipanema (45 to 90 minutes). Less-secure metered yellow-and-blue common (comum) taxis cost between R$50 to R$75.

Aeroporto Guarulhos (GRU; São Paulo) The Airport Bus Service (www.airportbusservice.com.br; R$35) is the most efficient way to/from GRU Airport, making stops at Aeroporto Congonhas, Barra Funda, Tiête, Praça da República and various hotels around Av Paulista and Rua Augusta. Guarucoop (www.guarucoop.com.br) is the only taxi service allowed to operate at the airport (R$116 to Av Paulista, R$125 to Vila Madalena).

Getting Around

Plane Useful for crossing Brazil's immense distances; can save days of travel; prices are generally high, but airfare promotions are frequent.

Bus Extensive services from *comun* (conventional) to *leito* (overnight sleepers) throughout the country, except for the Amazon. For timetables and bus operators, check out Busca Ônibus (www.buscaonibus.com.br).

Boat Slow, uncomfortable, but brag-worthy transport between towns in the Amazon, with trips measured in days rather than hours. You'll need a hammock, snacks, drinking water.

For much more on **getting around**, see p708

If You Like...

Beaches

Brazil has some of the finest beaches on earth: you'll find idyllic island getaways, vibrant big-city beaches and rainforest-backed sands all along the coastline.

Ilha Grande Enchanting island with dozens of gorgeous beaches, a welcome lack of cars and a laid-back island vibe. (p121)

Trancoso Cliff-backed beaches are a short stroll from this pretty Bahian village. (p447)

Jericoacoara Hip international beach scene with good activities, pousadas (guesthouses), restaurants and nightlife. (p540)

Ilhabela Dense jungle, waterfalls and picturesque beaches a few hours from São Paulo. (p254)

Ilha de Santa Catarina Protected dunes, and cliff- and forest-lined beaches, plus stunning lagoons in the interior. (p285)

Wildlife

Brazil is home to a staggering array of plant and animal species, with memorable wildlife watching in the rainforests, wetlands and along the coast.

The Amazon Manaus is still one of the top gateways for a journey into the mother of all rainforests. (p615)

The Pantanal You're likely to see a great many animal species in these wildlife-rich wetlands. (p370)

Fernando de Noronha World-class diving and snorkeling amid abundant marine life. (p499)

Praia da Rosa Watch southern right whales off the coast between June and October. (p306)

Parque Nacional de Monte Pascoal (p450) Part of the bio-rich Atlantic rainforest, this park lies just south of Salvador.

Scenery

Blessed with verdant rainforests, thundering waterfalls, craggy mountains and tropical islands, it's easy to see why Brazilians say 'Deus e Brasileiro' (God is Brazilian).

Rio de Janeiro The Cidade Maravilhosa (Marvelous City) lives up to its name with forested mountains and lovely beaches. (p50)

Fernando de Noronha Cliffs, rock pinnacles, beautiful bays and beaches all packed into one 10km-long island. (p499)

Iguaçu Falls Spread between Argentina and Brazil, these are some of the most spectacular waterfalls on earth. (p240)

Parque Nacional da Chapada Diamantina In the Bahian interior, you can hike across dramatic plateaus and swim in refreshing waterfalls. (p458)

Lençóis Maranhenses (p559) An otherworldly landscape of windswept dunes and sparkling blue lagoons.

Alter do Chã Startling white-sand beaches surrounded by jungle deep in the Amazon. (p592)

IF YOU LIKE... TRAIN RIDES

Hop aboard the *Serra Verde Express* for stunning views of mountain canyons and tropical lowlands en route between Curitiba and Morretes. (p268)

JOHN W BANAGAN / GETTY IMAGES ©

Food & Drink

Specialties in Brazil range from African-influenced stews to delectable Amazonian fish. Grilled meats, tropical fruits and international influences are all part of Brazilian gastronomy.

Ipanema & Leblon These twin beachfront neighborhoods have some of the best restaurants in Rio. (p91)

São Paulo With great pizzerias, sushi bars, and restaurants serving first-rate Brazilian and international fare, you won't go hungry in Sampa. (p254)

Vale dos Vinhedos This scenic valley in the south is the heart of Brazil's wine-growing region, and has top restaurants as well. (p244)

SENAC (p405) Take a cooking class or simply come for the buffet, which spreads all the great Bahian dishes.

Belém Sample lip-numbing *tacacá* (a soup) and many delicious Amazonian fish such as the prized Tucanaré (peacock bass). (p568)

4FR / GETTY IMAGES ©

Getting off the Beaten Path

Pre-Colombian rock art, deserted beaches, ends-of-the-earth fishing villages: these are just a few of the sights you can see by heading off the tourist path.

Parque Nacional da Serra da Capivara This dramatic rocky landscape contains thousands of prehistoric rock paintings. (p554)

Barra Grande This peaceful, bohemian village on the Bahian coast feels far removed from the tourist crowds. (p432)

(Above) Pelourinho (p398), Salvador
(Below) Kitesurfing

Itaúnas Charming beach town in little visited state of Espírito Santo, with a wild-life filled state park nearby. (p208)

Algodoal Isolated little village on the edge of wild beaches near the mouth of the Amazon. (p578)

Reserva Xixuaxú-Xipariná Magnificent rainforest reserve 500km north of Manaus. (p623)

São Miguel das Missões Gateway to the 17th-century ruins left behind by Jesuit missionaries. (p326)

Adventure

Brazil offers some memorable ways to experience its stunningly diverse landscapes, from multiday treks to snorkeling.

Trekking Take the three- to four-day journey across the spectacular Lençóis Maranhenses (p559) and see the dunes by moonlight.

Helicopter flight Contemplate the Brazilian version of the future (circa 1960) on a flyover of Brasília. (p337)

Ecotourism Bonito is a great spot for adventure, with river snorkeling, cave crawls, hiking and rappelling (abseiling). (p386)

Hiking The scenic high-country Parque Nacional do Itatiaia (p138) is a must for hikers and rock climbers.

Tree Climbing Get an intimate view of the rainforest canopy on an ascent inside the Amazon. (p592)

Slow-Boating String up your hammock and travel the old-school way on a riverboat trip between towns in the Amazon. (p580)

Kitesufari Go on a long-distance kitesurfing adventure near Jericoacoara. (p541)

History

You can delve into the past in Brazil's colonial centers, some of which are Unesco World Heritage sites.

Salvador Bahia's star attraction is packed with historic churches and Afro-Brazilian culture. (p395)

Ouro Preto One of Brazil's most alluring colonial towns, Ouro Preto is packed with 18th-century treasures. (p172)

Olinda Remnants of architecture left by the Portuguese as well as the Dutch. (p492)

Alcântara Fascinating town in Maranhão full of restored and abandoned mansions and churches. (p558)

Paraty Picturesque cobblestone village with beautifully preserved 18th-century buildings. (p127)

Museu Histórico Nacional (p70) One of the best places to learn about the presence of the Portuguese royals in Rio.

Festivals

Whether you prefer the colorful pageantry of Semana Santa (Holy Week) or the unbridled revelry of Carnaval, Brazil has you covered.

Carnaval Many cities throw a wild pre-Lenten bash, but Rio, Salvador and Olinda are among the most festive. (p34)

Gay Pride São Paulo hosts the world's biggest pride parade, with three to four million in attendance. (p2300)

Oktoberfest (p298) Experience Brazil's European roots at this beer- and bratwurst-loving bash in Blumenau. (p298)

Bumba Meu Boi São Luís erupts with color, music and dance in this June festival. (p550)

Semana Santa Colorful designs carpet the streets of Ouro Preto during this four-day fest. (p177)

Nightlife

Nightlife is electric, fueled by the nation's incredible music scene. Samba, Afro-Brazilian drumming, rock and hip-hop are all parts of the Brazilian soundtrack.

Lapa The epicenter of Rio's nightlife is packed with bars and samba clubs, and transforms into a street party on weekends. (p101)

Baixo Augusta Bars and clubs at this Paulista neighborhood attracts a wildly eclectic crowd. (p243)

Pelourinho Salvador's historic center is the place to hear drum corps like Olodum laying down the heavy rhythms. (p398)

Lagoa da Conceição Live music, lake views and top-notch DJs are the big draw of this town on Ilha de Santa Catarina. (p292)

Belo Horizonte Take in the lively arts scene and buzzing nightlife of the Minas Gerais capital. (p169)

Búzios Bask on the beach by day and hit the clubs by night at this stylish resort town. (p154)

Month by Month

January

Following the excitement of New Year's Eve, Brazil starts off the year in high gear, with steamy beach days and the buzz of pre-Carnaval revelry.

✵ Lavagem do Bonfim

In Salvador, on the second Thursday in January, this equal-parts Catholic and Candomblé fest features a ritual washing of the church steps followed by all-night music and dancing. (p405)

✵ Sommerfest

Blumenau's German-themed Oktoberfest is so popular that they also throw another version of it in mid-summer. Expect cheery crowds fueled by microbrews and hearty servings of bratwurst. (p298)

February

High season is in full swing, with people-packed beaches, sold-out hotel rooms and the unbridled revelry of Carnaval. It's a festive and pricey time to travel, and advance planning is essential.

✗ São Paulo Restaurant Week

South America's culinary powerhouse is well worth visiting during São Paulo restaurant week, when more than 100 top restaurants offer special menus and promotions (www.restaurantweek.com.br/sp). Dates vary, though it's held twice a year (February or March, then again in August or September).

✵ Festa de Iemanjá

On Praia Rio Vermelho in Salvador, Candomblé groups pay homage to the *orixá* Iemanjá, goddess of the sea and fertility on 2 February, followed by a lively street party. (p408)

✵ Carnaval

In February or March, for the five days preceding Ash Wednesday, the famous bacchanalian event happens nationwide, and is liveliest in Rio, Salvador and Olinda, with parades, costumes and round-the-clock merrymaking.

April

After Carnaval, prices dip, the intense heat subsides and the crowds dissipate, particularly in the north and northeast (when heavy rains continue through June). In Minas Gerais, however, Holy Week festivals keep things lively.

✵ Semana Santa

In Ouro Preto, Holy Week (the week before Easter) is a colorful event of processions and streets 'painted' with flowers. Sao João del Rei's Holy Week features parades accompanied by fabulous traditional orchestras. Other well-known Holy Weeks happen in Congonhas and Cidade de Goiás.

May

May is a quiet time for tourism with cooler temperatures beginning to arrive (particularly in the south) and heavy rains still falling in the Amazon.

✺✺ Festa do Divino Espírito Santo

Popularly known as Caval-hadas, this old-fashioned folk festival in Pirenópo-lis comprises medieval tournaments, dances and festivities, including mock battles between Moors and Christians. It takes place over three weeks around Pentecost, 50 days after Easter (May or June).

✺✺ Festival Internacional de Balonismo

The far southern beach town of Torres springs to life for five days in early May or late April when it hosts a colorful hot-air balloon festival (www.festivalbalonismo.com.br). Concerts, extreme sports, films and a country-style fair are among the attractions. (p328)

June

In the south, winter arrives (with cold weather the norm through August). Tourism-related activities remain curtailed (also through winter) in the north, south and northeast, though it's a good time to visit the Pantanal.

✺✺ Festas Juninas

Spanning the month of June, the feast days of various saints mark some of the most important folkloric festivals in Brazil. Expect concerts, food stands, fireworks and bonfires. Great places to be are Rio and Aracaju. (p85)

✺✺ São Paulo Pride

It's official, São Paulo throws the largest won

AFP / GETTY IMAGES ©

AWL / GETTY IMAGES ©

(Above) Gay Pride parade (p230), São Paulo
(Below) Bumba Meu Boi festival (p555), São Luís

earth in early June, attracting more than three million people to this massive parade.

✦ Rio das Ostras Jazz & Blues Festival

Located 170km east of Rio, in early June, Rio das Ostras boasts one of Brazil's best jazz and blues fests. (p154)

July

After months of rain, the dry season arrives in the Amazon, making it a good time to visit. Despite the cooler temperatures, Brazilians travel during July, which is a school holiday month.

✦ Festival Nacional de Forró

Music lovers wanting to get off the beaten track, should make their way up to the pretty beach town of Itaúnas, which hosts 10 days of concerts and dancing (to forró of course). (p209)

✦ Fest Itália

Italians have made many cultural contributions to the south, including this vibrant Blumenau fest featuring a week of wine, pasta and music in mid-July.

✦ Festival Literária Internacional de Parati

This important literary festival in early August brings together celebrated authors from around the world, plus film screenings, exhibitions and musical performances. (p130)

August

The tailend of winter is a quiet time in Brazil, with fewer tourists (and limited services) in the south and north. Temperatures are mild in the tropics and cold in the south.

✦ Festival de Gramado

The European-style town of Gramado hosts an important film festival each year, running for nine days in August. This long-running fest (around since 1973) is a showcase for Brazilian and other Latin American films. (p317)

September

It's a good time for wildlife watching with dry skies in both the Amazon and the Pantanal. The weather is mild from Rio north, but remains cool in the south.

✦ Rio International Film Festival

Rio's international film festival – Latin America's biggest – features more than 200 films from all over the world, shown at some 35 theaters from late September through early October. (p85)

✦ Bienal de São Paulo

This major art event occurs in even-numbered years (next in 2014 and 2016) between October and December and showcases the work of over 120 artists from around the globe. (p230)

October

The tourist masses and high-season prices haven't yet arrived, though the weather is starting to warm.

✦ Círio de Nazaré

Belém's enormous annual event on the second Sunday in October brings one million to the streets to take part in the procession of one of Brazil's most important icons. (p573)

🍷 Oktoberfest

This beerfest in Blumenau is the best place to connect to southern Brazil's German roots. Held in mid-October. (p298)

December

Summer marks the beginning of Brazil's most festive season (through February), with hot temperatures and ideal beach days. The crowds are growing and prices are rising.

✦ Carnatal

The country's biggest 'off-season Carnaval' is this Salvador-style festival held in Natal in the first week of December. It features raucous street parties and pumping *trios elétricos* (bands playing atop mobile speaker-trucks). (p516)

✦ Reveillon

Two million revelers, dressed in white, pack Copacabana Beach on 31 December, where music concerts and fireworks ring in the New Year. (p85)

Itineraries

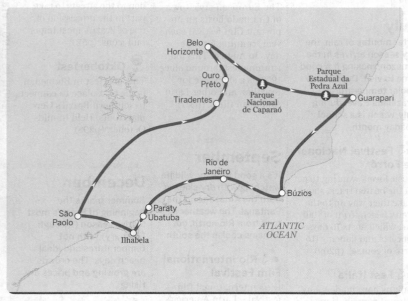

2 WEEKS · Rio & the Southeast

Gorgeous beaches, rainforest-covered islands and colonial towns are just some of the things you'll experience on this loop around the Southeast.

Spend a few days discovering **Rio** and its beaches, restaurants and incredible music scene before heading to **Paraty**, a beautifully preserved colonial town with rainforest hikes and stunning beaches nearby. Next, stop in **Ubatuba** with its jungle-clad mountains and spectacular coastal scenery. **Ilhabela** is a car-free island of beaches, forests and waterfalls. Stop in **São Paulo** for high culture, including the nation's best museums and restaurants.

Head next to exquisite **Tiradentes** and **Ouro Prêto**, some of Brazil's finest colonial gems. Afterwards, take in a bit of friendly Mineira hospitality, good restaurants and a burgeoning arts scene in **Belo Horizonte**.

Visit the hiker's paradise of **Parque Nacional de Caparaó**; further east, relish the dramatic beauty of **Pedra Azul** state park. Continue to the coast, for beach action and seafood in **Guarapari**. Further south you'll find the stunning beaches and high-end dining and nightlife of **Búzios**, which makes a great final stop before heading back to Rio.

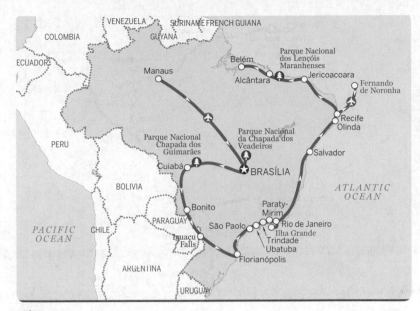

Best of Brazil

3 MONTHS

On this epic trip you'll experience the rhythm-infused towns of the Northeast, the jungles of the Amazon and the biodiversity of the Pantanal, with beaches, tropical islands and historic towns thrown into the mix.

From **São Paulo**, head east to Rio, stopping at glorious beaches such as **Ubatuba**, **Trindade** and **Paraty-Mirim**. Leave a couple of days for hiking the rainforest paths and basking on the beaches of **Ilha Grande**. Continue northeast to Rio, for a hearty dose of nightlife, beach culture and panoramic views.

From there head north, via bus or plane to **Salvador**, the country's Afro-Brazilian gem that's known for its colorful colonial center, drumming in the streets and lively (and numerous) festivals. Further up the coast visit historic and arts-loving **Olinda** then catch a flight from neighboring **Recife** to the spectacular archipelago of Fernando de Noronha, where you find pretty beaches, snorkeling, diving and a paradiselike setting.

Back on the mainland, travel north, stopping in the backpackers' paradise of **Jericoacoara** en route to the surreal dunes in the **Parque Nacional dos Lençóis Maranhenses**, a stark contrast to the colonial beauty of **Alcântara**. To the west lies **Belém**, a culturally rich city near the lush island of Ilha de Marajó. Catch a boat up the Amazon (or fly) to **Manaus**, where you can arrange multiday jungle trips.

From Manaus, fly to **Brasília** to take in its stunning architecture, then visit **Parque Nacional da Chapada dos Veadeiros**, for waterfalls, canyons and dips in natural swimming pools. Next head to **Cuiabá**, gateway to the breathtaking canyons of **Chapada dos Guimarães**. Spend a few days horseback riding, kayaking and hiking in the Pantanal, one of Brazil's best destinations for wildlife watching. Head south via Campo Grande (another Pantanal gateway) to **Bonito** for crystal-clear rivers, lush forests and caves. Continue south to the awe-inspiring **Iguaçu Falls**. Before completing the circle, explore the secluded beaches and charming Germanic towns around **Florianópolis**.

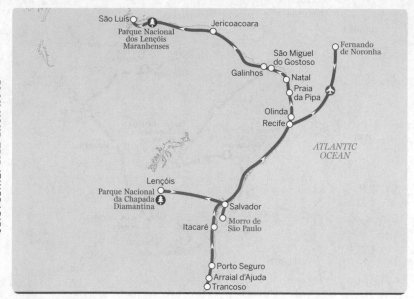

 6 WEEKS

Bahia & the Northeast

Those looking for the soul of Brazil would do well to focus on the Northeast. A confluence of music, history and culture amid spectacular natural scenery makes for an unforgettable journey.

Catch a flight to Porto Seguro, then quickly make your way to the pretty towns of **Arraial d'Ajuda** and **Trancoso**, both blessed with great guesthouses and restaurants, festive nightlife and access to walks on a seemingly endless cliff-backed beach. Continue north to **Itacaré**, a lively town with great surf and cove beaches reached via trails through hilly rainforest. Then head on to rhythm-filled **Salvador**, Bahia's most vibrant and colorful city. From there, catch a boat to **Morro de São Paulo**, an island with enchanting beaches and a laid-back vibe. Don't miss boat rides around the island – taking in mangroves, reefs, oysters and the quiet village of Boipeba.

Detour west to the tranquil diamond mining town of **Lençóis**, which has pretty outdoor cafes, cobblestone streets and caves, rivers and waterfalls nearby. From here, head into the **Parque Nacional da Chapada Diamantina** for crisp mountain streams, panoramic views and an endless network of trails. Back on the coast, go north to Maceió, a vibrant, youthful city with gorgeous beaches nearby. Keep going north to reach **Olinda**, one of Brazil's best-preserved colonial cities and a Unesco World Heritage site. From Olinda's buzzing neighbor **Recife**, fly out to **Fernando de Noronha**, an exquisite archipelago of rich marine life and splendid beaches.

Returning to the mainland, visit **Praia da Pipa**, then hit the coastline from **Natal** to **Jericoacoara**, including the coastal spots of **São Miguel do Gostoso** and **Galinhos**. In the sandy-street village of **Jericoacoara**, try your hand at sandboarding, kitesurfing and beachfront capoeira, and watch a memorable sunset. West of Jericoacoara, **Parque Nacional dos Lençóis Maranhenses** is a striking landscape of dunes, lagoons and beaches. Continue west to the reggae-charged **São Luís**, home to 18th-century buildings, seafood restaurants and buzzing nightlife. It's worth planning a trip around one of the town's folkloric fests. The last stop is the colonial gem of **Alcântara**.

Top: Parque Nacional da Chapada Diamantina (p458) Bottom: Praia do Parracho (p445)

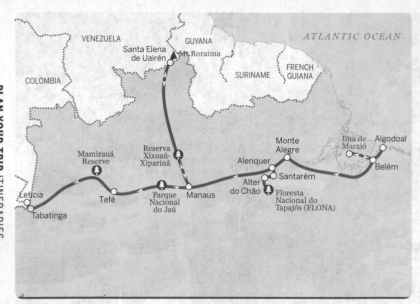

Waterways of the Amazon

Few places ignite the imagination like the Amazon. The largest forest on the planet has an incredible array of plant and animal life. These wetlands also contain historic cities, river beaches and one of the most important archaeological sites in South America.

Begin in **Belém**, a culturally rich city at the mouth of the great river. Explore the revitalized riverfront docks, visit the waterfront market, sample Amazonian dishes and catch a performance at the lavish Teatro da Paz. From here explore the forest-covered island of **Ilha de Marajó** which has bird-filled forests, friendly locals and itinerant water buffalo roaming the streets. Back in Belém, head northeast to **Algodoal**, a rustic fishing hamlet with windswept beaches and a remote feel.

Get a hammock and prepare yourself for a few hardy days of boat travel up the Amazon River. Stop in **Monte Alegre** to see ancient rock paintings, the oldest-known human creations in the Amazon, which are sprinkled among sandstone hills beyond town. Upstream is **Santarém**, a pleasant city with many nearby attractions. Across the river, **Alenquer** is near beautiful, rarely visited countryside, complete with scenic valleys, waterfalls and unusual rock formations. Also reachable is the virgin rainforest of the **Floresta Nacional (FLONA) do Tapajós**, where you can lodge with local families and take canoe trips on peaceful *igarapés* (inlets) while looking for wildlife. It's also worth stopping in **Alter do Chão**, a picturesque lagoon with startling white-sand beaches.

Continue upriver to **Manaus**, Amazonia's largest city. Visit the city's opera house, market, indigenous museums and nature parks, and the Encontro das Águas. From here, arrange jungle trips out into the rainforest or visits to the remote **Reserva Xixuaú-Xipariná**. You can also travel to **Santa Elena de Uairén**, Venezuela, for six-day treks up **Mt Roraima**. West of Manaus lies the fairly unexplored **Parque Nacional do Jaú**.

You'll see a variety of wildlife at the **Mamirauá Reserve**, outside of **Tefé**. From there, continue by river to **Tabatinga**, and into **Leticia** in Colombia for excursions into the **Parque Nacional Natural Amacayacu** or for stays at jungle lodges along the **Rio Javari**.

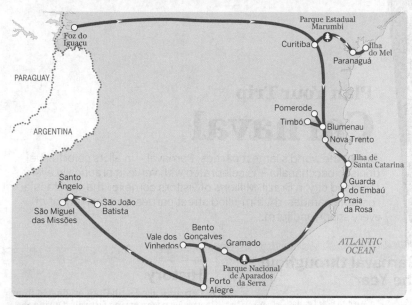

 Southward Bound

This trip through Brazil's southernmost states takes in forested islands and scenic beaches, mountainous national parks, historic missions and Bavarian-style towns.

Start in **Foz do Iguaçu** to gaze at the most impressive waterfalls on the planet. Take short day trips to Argentina and Paraguay to get a taste of lush rainforests before heading east (by overnight bus or quick flight) to **Curitiba**, a city with an intriguing environmentally friendly design, plus pretty botanic gardens and an Oscar Niemeyer museum. Visit **Parque Estadual Marumbi**, a lush setting with well-signed trails. Next, take the scenic train ride to **Paranaguá**, a sleepy waterfront town that's the jumping-off point to car-free **Ilha do Mel**. The forest-covered island has lovely beaches and low-key guesthouses, and is skirted by some pretty trails.

Next head to **Blumenau** and nearby **Vale Europeu**, where **Pomerode**, **Timbó** and **Nova Trento** boast Teutonic architecture, blond-haired residents and a local brew more Bavarian than Brazilian. Head back east to the coast and continue south to **Ilha de Santa Catarina**, a forest-covered gem of sand dunes, sparkling beaches, pretty lagoons and sleepy fishing villages. Keep going south to **Guarda do Embaú**, a seaside bohemian town with excellent surf. A short jaunt south is **Praia da Rosa**, which has pretty beaches and memorable whale watching.

On into Rio Grande do Sul, stretch the dramatic canyon and waterfalls of **Parque Nacional de Aparados da Serra**. Inland, it's worth heading further inland to **Gramado**, a charming mountain resort where gourmet chocolates, fondue and excellent infrastructure might make you feel like you've stepped into a Swiss portal. Continue west to **Bento Gonçalves**, gateway to the award-winning vineyards of the **Vale dos Vinhedos**, set amid the rolling hills of the Serra Gaucho.

Head south to **Porto Alegre** for transport links to **Santo Ângelo**, which leads on to the Jesuit missions. From there, visit **São Miguel das Missões**, **São João Batista** and other holy sites; true grail-seekers can cross into **Paraguay** or **Argentina** for a look at even more haunting Jesuit missions. Return to Porto Alegre for an onward flight.

Plan Your Trip
Carnaval

One of the world's largest parties, Carnaval – in all its colorful, hedonistic bacchanalia – is celebrated with verve in practically every town and city in Brazil. Millions of visitors come for the spectacular costume parades, rhythm-filled street parties, and merriment of every shape and form.

Carnaval throughout the Year

If you can't make it to Brazil during Carnaval, you can still join the party by hitting one of the so-called out-of-season Carnavals.

Carnatal

Natal's huge out-of-season Carnatal (p515) is the country's biggest and kicks off in the first week of December, with extensive street parties and Salvador-style *trios elétricos*.

Recifolia

Recife throws not one but two Carnavals (p486). The second happens late October or November.

Fortal

Half a million revelers celebrate Carnaval (p532) street-party style at Fortaleza's big bash in the last week of July.

Marafolia

The massive Salvador-style party (www.marafolia. com) in São Luís takes place in mid-October.

Maceió Fest

Maceió's Carnaval (p469) features drinking, dancing and music-filled trucks, and happens in the third week of November.

History

Carnaval, like Mardi Gras, originated from various pagan spring festivals. During the Middle Ages, these tended to be wild parties until tamed, in Europe, by both the Reformation and the Counter-Reformation. But not even the heavy hand of the Inquisition could squelch Carnaval in the Portuguese colony, where it came to acquire *índio* (indigenous) costumes and African rhythms.

Some speculate that the word *carnaval* derives from the Latin *carne vale*, meaning 'goodbye meat,' owing to the 40 days of abstinence (from meat and other worldly pleasures) that Lent entails. To compensate for the deprivation ahead, sins are racked up in advance with wild parties in honor of King Momo, the king of Carnaval.

Carnaval Dates

The following are the Carnaval dates (Friday to Shrove Tuesday) in coming years:
- **2014** February 28 to March 4
- **2015** February 13 to 17
- **2016** February 5 to 9
- **2017** February 24 to 28

Carnaval in Rio de Janeiro

If you haven't heard by now, Rio throws an exceptional party, with music and dancing filling the streets for days on end. The culmination of the big fest is the brilliantly colorful parade through the Sambódromo, with giant mechanized floats, pounding drummers and whirling dancers – but there's lots of action in Rio's many neighborhoods for those seeking more than just the stadium experience.

Out-of-towners add to the mayhem, joining cariocas in the street parties and costumed balls erupting throughout town. There are free live concerts throughout the city (near the Arcos do Lapa, on Largo do Machado and on Praça Floriano, among other places), while those seeking a bit of decadence can head to the various balls about town. Whatever you do, prepare yourself for sleepless nights, an ample dose of caipirinhas (cane-liquor cocktails) and samba, and mingling with joyful crowds spilling out of the city.

To get more information on events during Carnaval, check *Veja* magazine's *Veja Rio* insert (sold on Sunday at newsstands) or visit Riotur (p116), the tourist organization in charge of Carnaval.

Carnaval on the Streets

Joining the *bandas* and *blocos* (street parties) is one of the best ways to have the Carioca experience. These marching parades consist of a procession of brass bands (in the case of *bandas*) or drummers and vocalists (in the case of *blocos*) followed by anyone who wants to dance through the streets. Currently there are more than 400 street parties, filling every neighborhood in town with the sound of pounding drums and old-fashioned Carnaval songs – not to mention thousands of merrymakers. For many cariocas, this is the highlight of Carnaval. You can don a costume (or not), learn a few songs and join in; all you have to do is show up – and for Zona Sul fests, don't forget to bring your swimsuit for a dip in the ocean afterwards.

For complete listings, pick up a free *Carnaval de Rua* guide from Riotur. It's wise to confirm dates and times before heading out.

Banda de Ipanema (Praça General Osório, Ipanema; ☺4pm Sat of Carnaval and 2 Sat prior) This long-standing *banda* attracts a wild crowd, complete with drag queens and others in costume. Don't miss it.

Banda de Sá Ferreira (cnr Av Atlântica & Rua Sá Ferreira, Copacabana; ☺4pm Sat, Sun, Mon & Tue) This popular Copacabana *banda* marches along the ocean from Posto 1 to Posto 6.

Banda Simpatia é Quase Amor (Praça General Osório, Ipanema; ☺2pm 2nd Sat before Carnaval & Carnaval Sun) Another Ipanema favorite, with a 50-piece percussion band.

Barbas (cnr Rua Assis Bueno & Rua Arnoldo Quintela, Botafogo; ☺2:30pm Carnaval Sat) One of the oldest *bandas* of the Zona Sul parades through the streets with a 60-piece percussion band.

Carmelitas (cnr Rua Dias de Barros & Ladeira de Santa Teresa, Santa Teresa; ☺1pm Carnaval Fri & 8am Carnaval Tue) Crazy mixed crowd (some dressed as Carmelite nuns) parades through Santa Teresa's streets.

Céu na Terra (Curvelo, Santa Teresa; ☺3pm Carnaval Sat) Follows along the *bonde* (streetcar line) on a memorable celebration through Santa Teresa en route to Largo das Neves.

Cordão do Bola Preta (cnr Rua Evaristo da Veiga & Rua 13 de Maio, Centro; ☺8am Carnaval Sat) The oldest and biggest *banda* still in action. Costumes are always welcome, especially those with black-and-white spots.

Dois Pra Lá, Dois Pra Cá (Rua da Passagem 145, Carlinho de Jesus Dance School, Botafogo; ☺10am Carnaval Sat) This fairly long march begins at the dance school and ends at the Copacabana Palace.

Monobloco (Ave Rio Branco near Pres Vargas, Centro; ☺7am 1st Sun after Carnaval) Rise and shine! This huge *bloco* attracts upwards of 400,000 revelers who, nursing hangovers (or perhaps still inebriated) gather in Centro for a final farewell to Carnaval.

Suvaco de Cristo (Rua Jardim Botânico near Rua Faro, Jardim Botânico; ☺8am Sun before Carnaval) Very popular *bloco* (which means 'Christ's armpit' – in reference to the open-armed Redeemer looming overhead), it also meets on Carnaval Saturday, but doesn't announce the time (to avoid overcrowding), so ask around.

Samba-School Parades

The highlight of any Carnaval experience is attending (or participating in) a parade at the Sambódromo. There before a crowd of some 90,000 (with millions more watching on TV), each of 12 samba schools has its 80 minutes to dance and sing through the open Oscar Niemeyer–designed stadium. The pageantry is not simply eye candy for the masses. Schools are competing for top honors in the parade, with winners announced (and a winner's parade held) on the Saturday following Carnaval.

Here's what to expect: each school enters the Sambódromo with amped energy levels, and dancers take things up a notch as they dance through the stadium. Announcers introduce the school, then the lone voice of the *puxador* (interpreter) starts the samba. Thousands more voices join him (each school has 3000 to 5000 members), and then the drummers kick in, 200 to 400 per school, driving the parade. Next come the main wings of the school, the big allegorical floats, the children's wing, the celebrities and the bell-shaped *baianas* (women dressed as Bahian aunts) twirling in elegant hoopskirts.

Costumes are fabulously lavish, with 1.5m feathered headdresses; long, flowing capes that sparkle with sequins; and rhinestone-studded G-strings.

The whole procession is also an elaborate competition. A handpicked set of judges chooses the best school on the basis of many components, including percussion, the *samba do enredo* (theme song), harmony between percussion, song and dance, choreography, costumes, story line, floats and decorations. The dance championship is hotly contested, with the winner becoming not just the pride of Rio but all of Brazil.

The Sambódromo parades start with the *mirins* (young samba-school members) on the evening of Carnaval Friday, and continue on through Saturday night when the Group A samba schools strut their stuff. Sunday and Monday are the big nights, when the Grupo Especial – the 12 best samba schools in Rio – parade: six on Sunday night, and six more on Monday night. The following Saturday, the six top schools do it again in the Parade of Champions, which generally has more affordable tickets than on the big nights. Each event starts at 9pm and runs until 4am.

Most visitors stay for three or four schools, and come to see their favorite in action (every self-respecting carioca has a school they support, just as they have a favorite football team). If you're really gung-ho, wear your school's colors and learn the theme song (the words are found on each of the school's websites) so you can sing along when it marches through the Sambódromo.

Tickets

Getting tickets at legitimate prices can be tough. **Liesa** (http://liesa.globo.com), the official samba-school league, begins selling tickets in December or January, most of which get immediately snatched up by travel agencies then later re-sold at higher prices. Check with Riotur about where you can get them, as the official outlet can vary from year to year. At face value, tickets run from R$130 to R$550, though you'll probably have to pay about twice that (or more) if you buy just before Carnaval. The best sectors, in order of preference, are sectors 9, 7, 11, 5 and 3. The first two (9 and 7) have great views and are in the center, which is the liveliest place to be.

JOINING A SAMBA SCHOOL

Those who have done it say no other part of Carnaval quite compares to donning a costume and dancing through the Sambódromo before roaring crowds. Anyone with the desire and a little extra money to spare can march in the parade. Most samba schools are happy to have foreigners join one of the wings. To get the ball rolling, you'll need to contact your chosen school in advance; they'll tell you the rehearsal times and when you need to be in the city (usually a week or so before Carnaval). Ideally, you should memorize the theme song as well.

The biggest investment, aside from the airfare to Rio, is buying a *fantasia* (costume), which will cost upwards of R$600. If you speak some Portuguese, you can contact a school directly; many Rio travel agencies can also arrange this.

Top: School of Samba parade, Carnaval, Rio de Janeiro Bottom: Clown, Carnaval, Rio de Janeiro

By Carnaval weekend, most tickets are sold out, but there are lots of scalpers. If you buy a ticket from a scalper (no need to worry about looking for them – they'll find you!), make sure you get both the plastic ticket with the magnetic strip and the ticket showing the seat number. The tickets for different days are color-coded, so double-check the date as well.

If you haven't purchased a ticket but still want to go, during Carnaval you can show up at the Sambódromo at around midnight. This is when you can get grandstand tickets for about R$50 from scalpers outside the gate. Make sure you check which sector your ticket is for. Most ticket sellers will try to pawn off their worst seats.

And if you can't make it during Carnaval proper, there's always the cheaper Parade of Champions the following Saturday.

Open-Air Concerts

Lapa becomes a major focal point during Carnaval. In front of the Arcos do Lapa, the Praça Cardeal Câmara transforms into an open-air stage, with concerts running through Carnaval. About half a dozen different bands play each night (samba, of course) during this event, which is called Rio Folia. The music starts at 10pm and runs past 2am, though revelers pack Lapa until well past sunrise.

Samba-School Rehearsals

Around August or September, rehearsals start at the escolas de samba (samba schools or clubs). Rehearsals usually take place in the favelas (shantytowns) and are open to visitors. Mangueira and Salgueiro are among the easiest schools to get to.

Carnaval in Salvador

Although Rio's Carnaval hogs all the attention, Salvador hosts its own magnificent bash. In fact, this is one of the largest Carnavals in Brazil, attracting over two million revelers at last count.

Carnaval in Salvador usually kicks off Thursday night, with the mayor handing King Momo the keys to the city at Campo Grande (though in recent years it's happened at Praça Castro Alves). It all comes to an end on Ash Wednesday, with a handful of street parades giving a final afternoon send-off.

As elsewhere in Brazil, music plays a key role in the celebration, and in Salvador that means axé, an Afro-Bahian musical genre that incorporates a wide range of sounds, from samba-reggae and forró (a Northeastern two-step) to calypso and fast-passed frevo (a fast, syncopated, brass-band beat). It's the undisputed pop anthem during Carnaval in Salvador, and in many other parts of the Northeast.

Trios Elétricos & Blocos

The other integral element for the Salvadoran party is the trio elétrico – a long, colorfully decorated truck that's covered with oversized speakers. Small stages perch up top, with a band pumping out the rhythms as the trio slooowly winds through town. Hundreds of thousands line the streets of the parade route, packing in tightly – indeed, moving freely becomes a Sisyphean task.

Each trio is the centerpiece of a bloco, the gathering of revelers that surrounds the trucks. Those who want to be a part of the bloco pay anywhere from R$100 to upwards of R$700 (depending on the popularity of the bloco); this gives access to the cordão, the safer, roped-off area guarded by security personnel that surrounds the trio. Bloco members receive an abadá, an outfit (usually T-shirt and shorts) that identifies them as part of the group.

Those who don't want to pay to join a bloco can always choose to fazer pipoca (be popcorn) in the street. Once you get over the initial crush of the surrounding crowds, you can enjoy a wide variety of music and be spared the hassle involved with picking up the abadá.

You can also escape some of the madness by buying a day in a camarote, the walled-off, roadside bleachers with their own facilities. Head to the tourist office for information on camarote tickets.

Afoxés & Blocos Afros

Sprinkled between each of the blocos – and densely concentrated in the Pelourinho, where there are no trio elétricos – are afoxés, groups that parade to the rhythms, songs and dances found in Candomblé (the polytheistic Afro-Brazilian religion). Years ago, afoxé groups would perform a ritual in the *terreiro* (house of worship) before hitting the streets. Today, this is not mandatory, and in fact many *afoxé* members don't worship the *orixás* (the gods that the groups celebrate).

One of the most famous *afoxé* groups around today is the **Filhos de Gandhy** (Sons of Gandhi; www.filhosdegandhy.com.br), founded in 1949. Although Gandhi was not born in Brazil, the *bloco's* founding members felt he was an important symbol of peace; their nonviolent approach earned the *bloco* respect in the eyes of the authorities, which took a largely repressive stance toward Afro-Brazilian culture in the early 20th century. The *bloco* also helped pave the way for numerous other *afoxés*. Today, the Filhos are now the largest *afoxé*, with more than 10,000 members. They wear blue-and-white outfits with white turbans, shimmering sashes and blue-and-white beaded necklaces. Like some other *afoxés*, the group plays the serene rhythms of *ijexá*, and sprays the crowd with perfume.

The assortment of *blocos afros* also play an intrinsic role in the Carnaval festivities in Salvador. These are groups that celebrate African or Afro-Brazilian heritage in both costumes and themes. The most famous *bloco afro* performing today is **Olodum** (http://olodum.uol.com.br), a group widely credited for creating samba-reggae during Carnaval in 1986. Today the powerful drum corps parades with some 200 drummers, a handful of singers and thousands of costumed members.

Carnaval in Other Cities

Most foreign travelers tend to join the party in Rio or Salvador, but there are scores of other places to wrack up a few sins Brazilian-style before Ash Wednesday (or perhaps the week after) brings the revelry to a close.

➡ Recife: costumed re-enactments, diverse music, ample audience participation (bring a costume) and huge street parties, including the Galo da Madrugada, which gathers over 2 million celebrants on the official Saturday-morning Carnaval opening.

➡ Olinda: spontaneous, inclusive and playful; lasts 11 days and begins with a parade of more than 400 'Virgins' – men in drag.

➡ Porto Seguro: similar to Salavador's Carnaval; lasts a full week ending the Saturday after Ash Wednesday.

➡ Florianópolis: one of Brazil's most gay-friendly Carnavals (after Rio); the biggest and best bash in the South.

➡ São Paulo: while less riotous than most, Sao Paulo's Carnaval celebrations include a spectacular parade in its own Sambodromo; fewer crowds and lower prices are appealing.

Plan Your Trip
Outdoors

Brazil's coastline, its forests and mountainous interior set the stage for fresh-air adventures. Wildlife watching is world-class in the Pantanal and the Amazon. There are hundreds of great surf spots all along the Atlantic, while the chapadas (tablelands) are good destinations for hikes and treks. Other big draws include rock climbing, canyoning, paragliding and diving.

Top Activities

Watching
Seeing monkeys, macaws, capybara, caimans, toucans and dozens of other species on a wildlife-watching trip in the Amazon or the Pantanal.

Hang Gliding
Off Pedra Bonita in Rio de Janeiro.

Surfing
Ride the excellent breaks off Itacaré in Bahia.

Diving
Amid abundant coral and marine life off Fernando de Noronha.

Rock Climbing
Challenging routes surrounded by craggy peaks in the Serra dos Órgãos in Rio state.

Hiking
Taking the five- to eight-day Grand Circuit trek in the beautiful mountainous setting of Parque Nacional da Chapada Diamantina. Hiking to waterfalls set in a picturesque valley of the Parque Nacional da Chapada dos Veadeiros.

Snorkeling
The crisp rivers around Bonito.

Climbing

Climbing in Brazil is best in the cooler, drier months, from April to October. Brazil has many climbs, ranging from beginner level to the unconquered. Rio is the hub of Brazilian climbing, with some 350 documented climbs within an hour's drive of the city. You can even climb inside the city limits. The ascent up Pão de Açúcar has dozens of routes, from easy to challenging. Rio is also the best place to set up a climb if you're heading further afield.

Other places famous for rock climbing:

➡ **Parque Nacional Serra dos Órgãos**, Rio state

➡ **Parque Nacional de Itatiaia**, Rio state

➡ **Parque Nacional de Caparaó**, Minas Gerais

Diving & Snorkeling

The *mergulho* (diving) here doesn't match the Caribbean, but is worthwhile if you're keen. By far the best diving in the country is in the Fernando de Noronha archipelago. Here you'll find excellent visibility (up to 40m), warm seas and abundant marine life, including 15 coral species and more than 200 fish species. There are several reputable dive operators.

Other good places for diving including the following:

➡ **Arraial do Cabo**, in Rio de Janeiro state

➡ **Reserva Biológica do Avoredo**, near Porto Belo in Santa Catarina

➡ **Ponta do Seixas**, near João Pessoa in Paraíba

The snorkeling is good on Fernando de Noronha, including places where you can swim with sea turtles at high tide. Snorkel-by-boat excursions are available. For something different, nothing compares to the experience of snorkeling in the clear rivers around Bonito and seeing some of the Pantanal's most famous fish: pintados, pacus and dourados.

You can also go snorkeling on boat excursions from the following places:

➡ **Morro de São Paulo**, Bahia

➡ **Parque Nacional Marinho de Abrolho**, Bahia

➡ **Maceió**, Alagoas

➡ **Maragogi**, Alagoas

Fishing

The Rio Araguaia in Goiás and Tocantins states is known as a fishing paradise with a large variety of fish, including the pintado, dourado and the legendary *tucunaré* (peacock bass) – which unfortunately is heavily fished and faces declining numbers. Fishing for piranha is not undertaken by serious anglers, though is good fun. Fishing is brilliant in the Pantanal too, and is allowed from February to October.

Wildlife Encounters

Home to an astounding variety of creatures great and small, Brazil is one of the world's best places for seeing wildlife. A few top experiences for nature lovers:

➡ Spotting five species of monkeys, toucans, sloths, river dolphins and caimans at the Mamirauá Reserve deep in the Amazon jungle.

➡ Taking a day trip or overnighting at the Cristalino Jungle Lodge (p368), home to an awe-inspiring collection of wildlife.

➡ Swimming with sea turtles in the Fernando de Noronha (plane) archipelago.

➡ Watching hyacinth macaws and monkeys from the 25m observation tower at Pousada Araras Eco Lodge (p377) in the Pantanal.

➡ Snorkeling among 55 species of fish in the crystal-clear Rio da Prata near Bonito.

➡ Watching southern right whales – mothers and calves – from Praia da Rosa.

➡ Spying an amazing variety of birds on a boat trip around the Mangroves and Atlantic rainforest of Parque Nacional do Superagüi.

Hang Gliding & Paragliding

Probably one of the world's most scenic places to go hang gliding, Rio de Janeiro offers memorable tandem flights over tropical rainforest with views of the beach and island-filled ocean horizon.

Paragliding *(parapente)* can be arranged. Another place you can do a tandem hang-gliding flight is Rio da Barra.

Hiking

Hiking is best done in the cooler months of April to October. During summer, the tropical sun heats the rock to oven temperatures and turns the jungles into saunas. If you plan to hike in the Amazon, aim to come when the water levels are low (roughly August to December); at other times the forest is flooded and virtually all your activities will be by canoe.

There are great places to hike in Brazil, both in the national and state parks and along the coastline, and especially in the Southeast and South. Outstanding areas include the following destinations:

➡ **Floresta da Tijuca, Rio** Atlantic rainforest, peaks and ocean views inside the city limits.

➡ **Parque Nacional da Chapada Diamantina, Bahia** spectacular day hikes and multiday treks; Lençóis is a good base.

➡ **Parque Nacional da Serra dos Órgãos, Rio state** Hiking amid peaks and forest, several hours north of Rio.

➡ **Parque Nacional de Itatiaia, Rio state** Climbing, trekking, wildlife watching amid mountains and rainforest.

➡ **Parque Nacional da Chapada dos Veadeiros, Goiás** Vast, 650 sq km park in high-altitude cerrado with scenic day hikes taking in waterfalls, swimming holes, lunar landscapes.

➡ **Parque Nacional de Caparaó, Minas Gerais** Summit hikes to the highest mountains in the south, including Pico da Bandeira (2892m).

➡ **Parque Estadual Marumbi, Paraná** Well-signposted network of old pioneer trails.

➡ **Parque Nacional Serra do Cipó, Minas Gerais** Huge mountain park with lush river valleys, adventure activities, short and multiday hikes.

➡ **Parque Nacional de Aparados da Serra, Rio Grande do Sul** Stunning canyons, waterfalls, panoramas in the Serra Gaúcha

➡ **Serra de São José, Minas Gerais** Short hikes through protected Atlantic rainforest in the mountains near Tiradentes

Horseback Riding

In Minas Gerais you can ride stretches of the old gold road, the Estrada Real, or take a five-day horse trek from the state capital, Belo Horizonte, to its most famous historic town, Ouro Prêto.

Kayaking & Canoeing

There are some great places to get out on the water, paddle in hand, and take in the great Brazilian landscape. Foremost among them is the Amazon, where you can arrange dugout-canoe trips with many tour operators. You can also go kayaking off Ilha Grande, on the Lagoa da Conceição on Ilha de Santa Catarina, on excursions in the Pantanal, and from Itacaré and other beach destinations in the Northeast.

Surfing

There's surf virtually all along the coast, with particularly good waves in the South. The best surf beaches are in Santa Catarina state and the Brazilian championships are held here at Praia da Joaquina, on Ilha de Santa Catarina. São Francisco do Sul, Ilha do Mel, Ubatuba, Ilhabela, Maresias and the Boiçucanga area all serve up good waves.

There's also excellent surf just outside of Rio and a within a day's travel of the city in Saquarema, Búzios and Ilha Grande. The waves are best in the Brazilian winter (from June to August).

On other beaches surfing is still a way of life – even in Espírito Santo state with its breaks of 1m to 3m – boogie boarding is popular too. Renting boards can be difficult outside of popular tourist areas, though. If you plan to do a lot of surfing in less traveled places, you'll need to bring your own board.

Further to the north, Itacaré, Sítio, Porto de Galinhas and Fernando de Noronha are among the better spots.

SURFING VOCABULARY

Despite their reputation for aggressiveness in the water, once on land Brazilian surfers are fairly keen on meeting foreign surfers and hearing about their travels. Some are even willing to lend you a board.

body board – boogie board

onda – wave

Pode me emprestar sua prancha por favor? – Could I borrow your board please?

prancha – surfboard

quebrar – to break

surfista – surfer

Tem ondas? – Are there any waves?

Vamos pegar ondas. – Let's go surfing.

vento – wind

Windsurfing

Windsurfing has caught on in Brazil. In Rio you can rent equipment at Barra da Tijuca, but there are better conditions, and again equipment to rent northeast of Rio at Búzios. In São Paulo state there's good windsurfing at Ilhabela and around Boiçucanga. But Brazil's hardcore windsurfing mecca can be found much further north, along the Ceará coast, northwest of Fortaleza, where constant, regular, strong trade winds blow from July to December. Jericoacoara is one of the best spots in the country for windsurfing. Near Fortaleza, the beaches of Praia do Futuro and Praia de Iracema are also popular spots.

Plan Your Trip
Travel with Children

Long distances and high prices can make family travel challenging, but the rewards are considerable: endless fun on sun-kissed beaches, walks in rainforest, boat and train rides, and abundant wildlife-watching opportunities. Best of all is the warm reception from Brazilians themselves – who go out of their way to make kids feel welcome.

Brazil for Kids

Brazil is a family-friendly country that has a wide range of attractions for kids. Travel here with kids does require some advance planning, but most Brazilians will do their best to make sure children are well looked after.

Eating Out

Dining out isn't usually a problem even for fussy eaters. Ubiquitous per kilo places are a good place for a meal: children will have a huge range of options, and you can get in and out without a lot of fuss. Familiar food – pizza, burgers, ice cream – is widely available. Food courts in shopping malls are excellent spots for quick meals.

Juice bars are handy for snack breaks and serve up dozens of tangy flavors, as well as grilled burgers, sandwiches, *pão de queijo* (cheese-filled bread) and other bites.

Most sit-down restaurants will have a *cadeira alta* (high chair) though few have menus for kids. Portions however are huge, so kids can share what their parents order. Bring crayons, paper or other amusement, as Brazilian restaurants don't provide these things.

Best Regions for Kids

Rio de Janeiro state

Funicular rides and scenic views in Rio city, island-exploring on vehicle-free Ilha Grande, wandering cobblestone streets and taking schooner cruises off Paraty. You can even get a taste of mountain scenery in Parque Nacional de Itatiaia, and visit imperial sites in Petrópolis.

Minas Gerais

Time-travel to the 18th century in the colonial mountain town of Ouro Preto, which is near an old gold mine you can visit. You can also ride an old steam train from São João del Rei to Tiradentes.

Bahia

Lots of great food, music and street entertainment in Salvador. Catch the hydrofoil to car-free Morro de São Paulo for pretty beaches, a zipline and panoramic views from a hilltop lighthouse. Head inland for the canyons, waterfalls and swimming holes of Parque Nacional da Chapada Diamantina.

Transport

Given the great size of Brazil, transport presents challenges. You'll either spend long hours on buses or have to rely on pricier flights. Sticking to one or two regions is the best way to keep your holiday hassle-free.

Children typically pay 10% of the fare for flights if under two, and half fare if aged two to 12. On buses, it's all or nothing: they ride free if sitting on a lap and full fare if they take up a seat.

Children's Highlights

Coastal Highlights

Ilha Grande (west of Rio de Janeiro) A tropical rainforest-covered island, an old abandoned prison, boat trips, snorkeling, lovely beaches, howler monkeys – and all of it completely free from traffic.

Balneário Camboriu (Santa Catarina) This resort town has many attractions for kids, including an aerial tram, beaches, a roller coaster, with proximity to the Beto Carrero World (p303) amusement park.

Porto Belo (Santa Catarina) Another laid-back resort spot in the South, Porto Belo has lovely snorkeling, plus a scenic nature reserve and eco-museum at an island just offshore.

Arraial d'Ajuda (Bahia) This low-key beach-lovers' town has the usual coastal attractions, plus you can rent a buggy for exploring sandy coastal paths around the area.

Jungle Highlights

Foz do Iguaçu & Around (Paraná) The thundering waterfalls are quite family-friendly, with discount entry for kids to the falls, and kids stay and eat free all over town; there are also various wildlife adventures, boating activities, plus the jaw-dropping falls themselves.

JUNGLE LODGES

Many jungle lodges near Manaus offer fairly low-impact excursions, making them good for families with kids. High-water season may be best, as you do more canoeing than hiking. Black-water areas have far fewer mosquitoes and much lower risk of malaria.

Serra Verde Express (p268; Paraná) This memorable train ride traverses lush forests with sweeping views down to the coast.

Ecoparque de Una (p440; Bahia) Take a guided walk along a 2km trail that includes several tree-top canopy walkways in the wildlife-rich Atlantic rainforest.

Bonito (Mato Grosso do Sul) Bonito has caves, lush rainforests, tree-top canopy walks and crystal-clear rivers that you snorkel down.

Planning

For general advice on traveling with young ones, see Lonely Planet's *Travel with Children*. Don't forget to arrange visas (if needed) before you depart.

What to Bring

If you plan on renting a car, bring your own car seats with you as availability is unreliable with most rental agencies.

Diapers (nappies) are widely available in Brazil. You may not easily find creams, baby foods or familiar medicines if you are outside larger cities. Bring insect repellent, sunscreen and other essentials, as prices for these things, are much higher here.

Baby food is available in most supermarkets.

Health & Safety

If you are planning a trip outside of the main coastal cities, you'll need to enquire about vaccines and anti-malarial medications (particularly for the Amazon).

When to Go

To beat the worst of the crowds, but still enjoy warm beach weather, plan on coming from November through January or late March and April.

Accommodation

Many hotels let children stay free, although the age limit varies (typically up to the age of five). Cribs (cots) are not always available, so have an alternative plan before arriving.

Babysitters are readily available in most hotels.

Regions at a Glance

The great challenge of Brazil, with its vast size and incredible diversity, is deciding where to go. Rio figures high on most itineraries, with nightlife, beaches and scenery. Tropical islands and the historic colonial towns of Minas Gerais lie nearby. The Northeast offers a mix of picturesque towns, beaches and outdoor adventures, and its picturesque cities (Salvador, Olinda) offer a window into rich Afro-Brazilian culture. The south, meanwhile has notable European influence (Oktoberfests, vineyards, mountain towns) and stellar highlights such as Iguaçu Falls and the Ilha de Santa Catarina. For wildlife watching, the Pantanal and the Amazon are world-class destinations.

Rio de Janeiro

Scenery
Nightlife
Culture

Mountains & Beaches

Rainforest-covered peaks, sparkling beaches and a coastline dotted with islands – Rio is breathtaking, especially when seen from Corcovado or Pão de Açúcar.

Sounds of Samba

Rio's dizzying nightlife includes open-air bars, stylish nightclubs and old-school dance halls dominated by the addictive rhythms of samba.

Historic Treasures

At first glance, Rio's downtown is a bustling hive of business and commerce. Look deeper, and you'll discover landmarks, including 18th-century baroque churches, a former royal palace and an opera house.

p50

Rio de Janeiro State

Beaches
Outdoors
History

Sun, Surf & Sand

For easy access to dreamy beaches, Rio state is as good as it gets, from gleaming white dunes to island-studded bays backed by jungle-clad mountains.

Hiker's & Climber's Paradise

The crags of Itatiaia and the peaks of the Serra dos Órgãos are twin capitals of Brazilian rock climbing; hikers also thrill to the wild trails of Serra da Bocaina and Ilha Grande.

The Golden Road & Imperial Past

Near Paraty, the 18th-century Caminho do Ouro once brought gold from Minas Gerais, while Dom Pedro II's Petrópolis palace was the 19th-century seat of Brazilian imperial power.

p120

Espírito Santo & Minas Gerais

History
Food
Outdoors

Baroque Grandeur

With an incredible density of historical monuments, Minas's *cidades históricas* (historic colonial towns) are showcases for the uniquely Brazilian baroque style.

Bountiful Feast

From Espírito Santo's delectable seafood stews to Minas's hearty wood-fired ranch fare, this is foodie paradise. Don't forget the obligatory shot of smooth *Minas cachaça* (Brazil's best).

Wildlife & Waterfalls

Punctuated by natural pools and waterfalls, Minas's wide-open cerrado ecosystem is a hiker's dream. East toward the Espírito Santo border, awe-inspiring mountains rear their heads.

p160

São Paulo State

Food & Drink
Beaches
Landscapes

Culinary Powerhouse

São Paulo city holds its own with any gastronomic capital in the southern hemisphere. Cutting-edge Brazilian chefs such as Alex Atala (D.O.M.) and Helena Rizzo (Maní) have received worldwide acclaim.

The Green Coast

From the rainforest-lined coast of Ubatuba to the sophisticated getaway of Ilhabela, São Paulo's coastline is part of Brazil's Costa Verde (Green Coast), a world-class stretch of postcard-perfect beaches and islands.

Scenic Setting

Wide swaths of Mata Atlântica rainforest, modest but wonderful Serra de Mantiqueira peaks and sun-kissed sands: São Paulo is easy on the eyes.

p215

Paraná

Scenery
Nature
Architecture

Photogenic Panoramas

Besides the spectacular Iguaçu Falls, splendid scenery awaits on the car-free island retreat of Ilha do Mel, and the superb *Serra Verde Express* train, which snakes past lushly covered mountains from Curitiba to Morretes.

Waterfalls, Islands & Rainforest

Iguaçu Falls offers impressive hiking and adventure excursions amid subtropical rainforest; while Parque Nacional do Superagüi and Parque Estadual Marumbi boast abundant bird and plant life.

A Glorious Past

Morretes, Paranaguá and Curitiba's Largo da Ordem are cobblestoned glimpses into Brazil's colonial past.

p260

Santa Catarina

Beaches
Culture
Microbreweries

Seductive Shorelines

Whether you seek solitude, surf or social overload, Santa Catarina has the sands for you.

European Past

Nowhere is Brazil's rich melting pot more evident than throughout Santa Catarina's interior, where German enxaimel architecture, Italian and German food and distinctly European faces will leave you wondering if you've received a new passport stamp upon arrival.

Brew Culture

Brazil's best microbrews hail from Blumenau and its environs, offering the chance to sample beers unavailable in most other parts of the country.

p284

Rio Grande do Sul

Landscapes
Wine Tasting
Culture

Canyonlands

Parque Nacional Aparados da Serra and Parque Nacional da Serra Geral offer Southern Brazil's most striking landscape.

Venerable Vineyards

Around 90% of Brazilian wine comes from the Vale dos Vinhedos, a little touch of Tuscany in the heart of Cowboy Country that defies notions of typical Brazil.

Gaúcho Traditions

With its *chimarrão* (mate tea), *churrasco* (grilled meat) and traditional Farroupilha dress, Rio Grande do Sul's gaúcho culture lives on in this unique region; and Gramado is Brazil's most pleasant Alpine town.

p309

Brasília & Goiás

Architecture
Scenery
Culture

A Capital Idea

Niemeyer's genius proved that a few bags of concrete and a creative mind were all that it needed to make Brasília into a must-see for building buffs.

Striking Panoramas

The breathakingly beautiful cerrado is the perfect frame for heavenly sunsets on the planalto, especially at the otherworldly Vale da Lua in the Chapada dos Veadeiros.

Medieval Mischief

Pirenópolis converts itself from a kooky artist's enclave into a centre of historical re-creation, as the town goes medieval during the Festa do Divino Santo (Cavalhadas).

p330

Mato Grosso & Mato Grosso do Sul

Water Adventure
Wildlife Watching
Fishing

Surreal Snorkeling

Squeeze into your wet suit and let the current take you on a fish-watching adventure in the aquatic playgrounds of Bonito and Nobres.

Animal Encounters

The Pantanal has incredible wildlife watching, with capybaras, anacondas, macaws, capuchins and giant river otters just a few of many species you're likely to see.

Catch Your Dinner

Sling your hook for some of the world's best fishing in the waterways of Mato Grossoand maybe pick up a pacu!

p358

Bahia

Beaches
Outdoors
Culture

Bahian Beauty

Featuring more than 900km of coastline, the state of Bahia is rightfully renowned for its gorgeous beaches, from idyllic island getaways and surfers' hot spots to quiet fishing villages.

Hiking & Trekking

Head inland to see one of Brazil's finest national parks, Chapada Diamantina, which has great hiking and trekking, plus waterfalls, natural swimming holes and other idyllic spots to cool off.

Afro-Brazilian Star

Salvador is the center of Afro-Brazilian culture: capoeira and Candomblé, glittering churches, and pounding drums on the cobblestoned streets of the Pelourinho. Nearby Cachoeira is renowned for its woodcarving traditions.

p393

Sergipe & Alagoas

Scenery
History
Seafood

Coastal Allure

Alagoas' star attraction is its coastline, with its white-sand beaches and aquamarine waters. Top picks include Praia do Francês, Praia do Gunga and Maceió. The Galés marine reserve off the coast of Maragogi is a snorkelers' favorite.

Colonial Remnants

These neighboring states have a number of colonial highlights, including the churches of historic Penedo, cobblestone Laranjeiras and hilltop São Cristóvão.

Dining & Dancing

Seafood lovers won't want to miss the open-air restaurants of Aracaju, which specialize in fresh crabs; many also serve up live *forró* music, which make a great ending to crab feast.

p461

Pernambuco, Paraíba & Rio Grande do Norte

Beaches
Festivals
Outdoors

Endless Sands

The 1000km coast curving round Brazil's northeast corner is a succession of sandy beaches fronted by enticing tropical waters.

Carnaval, Northeastern Style

During Carnaval, head to the contrasting neighboring cities Recife and Olinda for their unbelievably euphoric explosions of color, music and fun.

Shoreline Adventures

This is the place for swimming, snorkeling, surfing, kitesurfing or buggy-riding. Fernando de Noronha, a tropical-archipelago getaway 350km offshore, has Brazil's best diving and snorkeling.

p479

Ceará, Piauí & Maranhão

Scenery
Outdoors
Cities & Towns

Dunes & Bays

The setting is spectacular: a sequence of long, dune-backed sweeps and small, palm-lined bays all along the tropical shoreline. There's also the unique dune-and-lagoon mosaic of the Lençóis Maranhenses.

Sun-drenched Adventures

You can do most things you've dreamed of in, on and beside the water, with steady winds providing some of the world's best conditions for kitesurfing.

Coastal Enclaves

Hang out at legendary Jericoacoara, enjoy the urban vibes of Fortaleza or head to end-of-road beach villages like Atins or Icaraí de Amontada for a tropical escape.

p526

The Amazon

Wildlife Watching
Adventure
Culture

Biodiversity Hotspot

The Amazon is a fabled setting for wildlife watching. You can stay in upscale rainforest resorts or community-run ecotourism outfits, both great bases for seeing wildlife.

Rainforest Experiences

The world's greatest rainforest offers memorable adventures, from tree-climbs through dense canopy, to silent canoe paddles across flooded forest. You can also take multiday boat trips between towns.

Amazonian Riches

Culturally rich cities like Belém and Manaus are the best places to sample Amazonian cuisine, hear unique musical styles and browse colorful markets.

p563

On the Road

Rio de Janeiro City

📞OXX21 / POP 6.3 MILLION

Best Places to Eat

➡ Zazá Bistrô Tropical (p94)
➡ Zuka (p94)
➡ Oro (p95)
➡ Meza Bar (p97)
➡ Espírito Santa (p101)

Best Places for Nightlife

➡ Rio Scenarium (p108)
➡ Casa Rosa (p109)
➡ 00 (Zero Zero) (p102)
➡ Bar Bukowski (p104)
➡ Democráticus (p108)

Why Go?

Planted between lush, forest-covered mountains and breath-taking beaches, the Cidade Maravilhosa (Marvelous City) has many charms at her disposal.

Although joie de vivre is a French invention (as is the bikini), it's the *cariocas* (Rio dwellers) who've made it their own. How else to explain the life-lusting zeal with which the city's inhabitants celebrate their days? While large-scale festivities such as Carnaval make Rio famous, there are countless occasions for revelry – Saturday at Ipanema Beach, a *festa* (party) in Lapa, football at Maracanã, or an impromptu *roda de samba* (samba circle) on the sidewalks of Leblon, Copacabana or any other corner of the city.

The spectacular landscape is another of Rio's shameless virtues. Verdant mountains and golden beaches fronting deep blue sea offer a range of adventure: surfing great breaks, hiking through Tijuca's rainforest or rock climbing up the face of Pão de Açúcar (Sugarloaf Mountain).

When to Go
Rio de Janeiro

°C/°F Temp — Rainfall inches/mm

Dec–Feb Steamy beach days and a packed festival calendar, including the Carnaval build-up.

Apr–May Cooler but sunny days, fewer crowds and lower prices.

Jun Low season and cooler temperatures, but still lively, especially during Festas Juninas.

Rio in Five Days

Start off on **Ipanema beach**. Have lunch on Leblon's restaurant-packed **Rua Días Ferreira**. Later, watch the sunset from **Praia do Arpoador**. Have dinner at one of Lagoa's **lakeside kiosks**. On day two, visit **Pão de Açúcar**, followed by a stroll around **Urca**. In the afternoon, explore bohemian **Santa Teresa**, followed by a night of samba in **Lapa**. On day three, go hiking in **Parque Nacional da Tijuca**. In the evening, dine at one of Ipanema's top **restaurants**. On day four, explore historic **Centro**, and join happy-hour crowds on **Travessa do Comércio**. On your last day, stroll **Copacabana beach**, then visit **Cristo Redentor** for outstanding views.

OLYMPIC FEVER

After winning the bid to host the Olympic Games in 2016, Rio is investing US$11.5 billion in the city (on top of the US$14 billion for the 2014 World Cup). The city is building dozens of new venues to host the events, adding thousands of hotel rooms, and upgrading existing stadiums, including Maracanã football stadium, which will play a starring role.

Transportation is also a critical factor: the metro will extend to Barra, and new bus lanes will create 'surface metros'. Barra aside (where the Olympic Village will be), other parts of Rio will also receive a makeover, including the port, which will see new museums, light rail and new parks and green spaces.

Neighborhoods at a Glance

➡ **Ipanema & Leblon** Beautiful people and beaches, great eating, drinking and shopping.

➡ **Lagoa** Lakeside kiosks, running/cycling track

➡ **Jardim Botânico** Botanical gardens, upscale dining.

➡ **Copacabana** Touristy, but attractive hotel-lined oceanfront; beachside kiosks, abundant restaurants

➡ **Botafogo** Local, lively bar scene

➡ **Urca** Scenic, village-like vibe; tram up Pão de Açúcar.

➡ **Flamengo & Around** Parque do Flamengo by the bay; west is leafy Laranjeiras and the cog train up Corcovado.

➡ **Centro** Busy downtown, but full of history, with good museums and baroque churches.

➡ **Santa Teresa** Bohemian district with aging mansions and worthwhile views.

➡ **Lapa** Buzzing nightlife, with samba clubs and a packed weekend street party.

➡ **Zona Norte** Maracanã and several royal sites.

➡ **Barra da Tijuca** Lovely beach, shopping malls.

SUNNY SUNDAY

Many museums in Rio are free on Sunday, making it a good day to pack in your sightseeing. If the weather is nice, head to the shore. On Sundays the beachfront road running from Leblon to Leme closes to traffic (until 6pm).

Fast Facts

➡ **Population** 6.3 million

➡ **Area** 1182 sq km

➡ **Telephone code** 0xx21

Resources

➡ **Insider's Guide to Rio** (www.ipanema.com) Tips and planning.

➡ **Riotur** (www.rioguiaoficial.com.br) Rio's tourism authority.

➡ **Rio Times** (www.riotimesonline.com) English-language news.

Must-Try Food & Drink

➡ **Açaí** Smoothie made from Amazonian berry.

➡ **Feijoada** Pork-and-black-bean stew, served Saturdays.

➡ **Acarajé** Bahian fritters, served at the Hippie Fair.

➡ **Agua de coco** Refreshing coconut water.

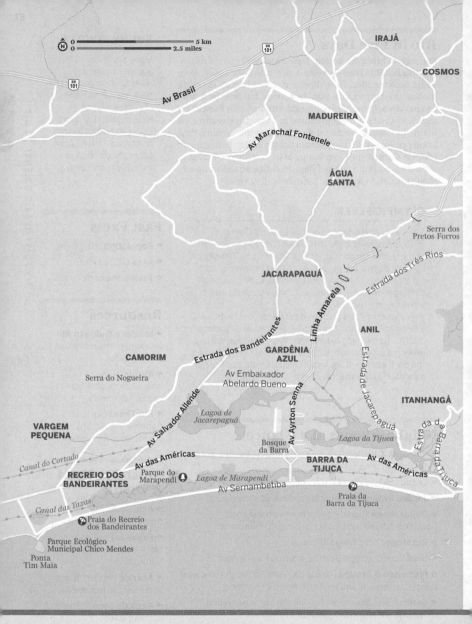

Rio de Janeiro City Highlights

❶ Frolic in the waves, while watching the passing people parade on lovely **Ipanema beach** (p54).

❷ Bask in the sunshine on **Copacabana beach** (p58), followed by drinks at an oceanfront kiosk.

❸ Take the cog train up Corcovado for stunning views beneath the open-armed **Cristo Redentor** (p61).

❹ Find the perfect beat at a samba club in **Lapa** (p105), Brazil's most musically charged neighborhood.

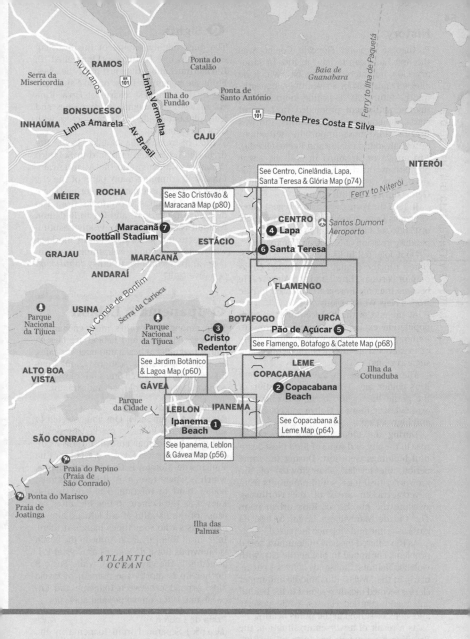

History

Portuguese explorer Gonçalo Coelho was the first European to land in Rio. In January 1502, he entered a huge bay, which he allegedly mistook for a river, thus bequeathing the future city its lasting moniker. Portuguese settlement proceeded in fits and starts, though by the 17th century, Rio was Brazil's third-most important settlement (after Salvador da Bahia and Recife-Olinda). African slaves streamed in and the sugar plantations thrived. Even more slaves arrived to work in the gold mines of Minas Gerais during the 18th century.

In 1807 the Portuguese prince regent (later known as Dom João VI) and his entire court of 15,000 set sail for Brazil to escape the impending invasion of Napoleon Bonaparte.

Dom João fell in love with Brazil. He declared Rio the capital of the United Kingdom of Portugal, Brazil and the Algarve. He became the only European monarch to rule from a New World colony.

At the end of the 19th century the city's population exploded because of European immigration and internal migration (mostly of ex-slaves from the declining coffee and sugar regions).

The early 1920s to the late 1950s were Rio's golden age. With the inauguration of the grand hotels, Rio became a romantic, exotic destination for Hollywood celebrities and high-society.

During the 1960s, modern skyscrapers rose in the city, and some of Rio's most beautiful buildings were lost. During the same period, the favelas (shantytowns) of Rio grew to critical mass with immigrants from poverty-stricken areas of the Northeast, swelling the number of Rio's urban poor. The Cidade Maravilhosa began to lose its gloss as crime and violence increased.

As Rio entered the new millennium, social problems continued to plague the city, with violence claiming thousands of lives – particularly in the favelas. Rio's middle and upper classes seemed mostly resigned to life behind gated and guarded condos, while poverty and violence surged in the slums nearby.

As a result of a worsening situation, the Brazilian government has invested in Rio's favelas improving sanitation, roads and healthcare. As of 2012 several dozen favelas have benefited from improvement schemes, with an eventual goal of reaching all 1000 of Rio's favelas by the year 2020, at a total estimated cost of R$8 billion.

◎ Sights

The once mighty 'capital of the Brazilian empire' (as one Portuguese king called it), Rio has much more than just pretty beaches. From the bohemian lanes of old Santa Teresa to the villagelike charm of Urca, Rio's colonial streets, magnificent churches and leafy plazas provide urban wanderers with days of exploration.

Rio's historic center, its lake (Lagoa Rodrigo de Freitas), the lush Jardim Botânico (Botanical Gardens) and the Atlantic rainforest still trimming many parts of the city make for some fascinating exploring. There are also the fantastic overlooks from Pão de Açúcar (Sugarloaf) and Cristo Redentor, tranquil islands in the bay, wildly beautiful beaches to the west, and vibrant markets, with vendors peddling everything from vintage samba recordings to tangy *jabuticaba* (a native fruit).

◎ Ipanema & Leblon

Truly among the world's most enchanting addresses, Ipanema and Leblon are blessed with a magnificent beach and open-air cafes, bars and restaurants scattered along tree-lined streets. Here you'll find a mix of wealthy *cariocas*, young and old, gay and straight.

Ipanema Beach   BEACH
(Map p56; Av Vieira Souto) One long stretch of sand, Ipanema beach is marked by *postos* (posts), which demarcate subcultures as diverse as the city itself. Posto 9, right off Rua Vinícius de Moraes, is Garota de Ipanema, which is where Rio's most lithe and tanned bodies tend to migrate. The area is also known as the Cemetério dos Elefantes because of the handful of old leftists, hippies and artists who sometimes hang out there. In front of Rua Farme de Amoedo the beach is known as Bolsa de Valores or Crystal Palace (this is the gay section), while Posto 8 further up is mostly the domain of favela kids. Arpoador, between Ipanema and Copacabana, is Rio's most popular surf spot.

Praia de Leblon   BEACH
(Map p56) Separated from Ipanema by the gardens and canal of Jardim de Alah, Leblon Beach attracts more families and has a slightly more sedate vibe than its eastern counterpart. Parents with little ones may want to check out Baixo Bebê, between posts 11 and 12, where you'll find other young families and a small playground on the sand.

Mirante do Leblon LOOKOUT

(Map p56; Av Niemeyer) A few fishermen casting out to sea mingle with couples admiring the view at this overlook at the western end of Leblon Beach. The luxury Sheraton Hotel looms to the west, with the favela of Vidigal nearby.

H Stern JEWELRY, MUSEUM

(Map p56; ☑2106-0000; www.hstern.net; Garcia D'Ávila 113; ◎9am-6pm Mon-Fri, 9am-2pm Sat) FREE The famous jeweler H Stern allows visitors to get a glimpse behind the scenes at the gemological headquarters. You can also ask to visit the small museum with its display of rare mineral specimens and a large collection of tourmalines. Following the tour, you'll meet with a sales rep, which some people find uncomfortable. A polite 'no thank you' will usually see you to the next level (the showroom) and on to the exit. Free shuttle service to and from any major hotel in Rio.

Museu Amsterdam Sauer MUSEUM

(Map p56; ☑2512-1132; www.amsterdamsauer. com; Garcia D'Ávila 105; ◎9am-7pm Mon-Fri, 9am-4pm Sat) FREE Next door to H Stern, the Amsterdam Sauer Museum houses an impressive collection of precious stones – over 3000 items in all. Visitors can also take a peek at the two replicas of mines.

Parque Garota de Ipanema PARK

(Map p56; off Francisco Otaviano, near Bulhões Carvalho; ◎7am-7pm) This small, scruffy park next to the Arpoador rock features a tiny playground, a concrete area popular with skaters and a lookout with a view of Ipanema beach.

Casa de Cultura
Laura Alvim CULTURAL CENTER

(Map p56; ☑2267-1647; Av Vieira Souto 176, Ipanema) Ipanema's beachside cultural center has a theater, a gallery space and a small cafe.

Elevador do Morro do Cantagalo VIEWPOINT

(Map p56; Barão da Torre & Teixeira de Melo) FREE Connected to the metro station off Praça General Osório, this elevator whisks passengers up to Cantagalo, a favela that's wedged between Ipanema and Copacabana. The sparkling sea views are quite fine, though local residents are happy simply to have a convenient way to get home that doesn't mean ascending hundreds of steps. From the top, keep heading uphill for even finer views over Ipanema and the lake.

As far as security goes, Cantagalo has been safe to visit since the police pacification units arrived in 2009. Recent high-profile visitors include Lady Gaga, Carla Bruni and even Brazil's president, Dilma Rousseff.

◉ Gávea, Jardim Botânico & Lagoa

Beginning just north of Ipanema and Leblon, these well-heeled neighborhoods front Lagoa Rodrigo de Freitas, a picturesque saltwater lagoon ringed with a walking/cycling trail and dotted with lakeside kiosks. The other big draw here is the royal garden (Jardim Botânico) that gave the neighborhood its name. Here you'll find stately palms, rare orchids and colorful flowering plants. Aside from its natural attractions, these neighborhoods have some excellent restaurants, trendy bars, a planetarium and the city's horseracing track.

Lagoa Rodrigo de Freitas LAKE

(Map p60) One of the city's most picturesque spots, Lagoa Rodrigo de Freitas is encircled by a 7.2km walking/cycling path. Bikes are available for hire (R$10 per hour) from stands along the east side of the lake, as are paddle boats (R$20 per half hour). For those who prefer caipirinhas (drinks made from sugarcane spirit, crushed lime, sugar and ice) to plastic swan boats, the lakeside kiosks on either side of the lake offer alfresco food and drinks, sometimes accompanied by live music.

Jardim Botânico GARDENS

(☑3874-1808; www.jbrj.gov.br; Jardim Botânico 920; admission R$6; ◎9am-5pm) This exotic 137-hectare garden, with over 8000 plant species, was designed by order of the Prince Regent Dom João (later to become Dom João VI) in 1808. Highlights of a visit here include the row of palms (planted when the garden first opened), the Amazonas section, the lake containing the huge Vitória Régia water lilies and the enclosed orquidário, home to 600 species of orchids. A pleasant outdoor cafe overlooks the gardens. Be sure to take insect repellent.

Planetário PLANETARIUM

(☑2274-0046; www.planetariodorio.com.br; Av Padre Leonel Franca 240; adult/child R$10/5; ◎9am-5pm Mon-Fri, 3-6pm Sat & Sun) The Planetário (Planetarium) features a museum, a praça dos telescópios (telescopes' square) and a

Ipanema, Leblon & Gávea

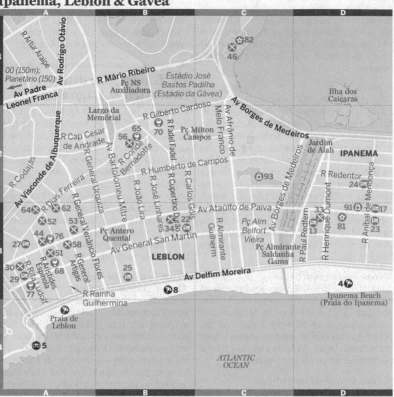

state-of-the-art operating dome, capable of projecting over 6000 stars onto its walls (40-minute sessions in the dome take place on weekends and holidays). Visitors can also take a peek at the night sky (R$20) through the telescopes on Tuesday, Wednesday and Thursday from 7:30pm to 8:30pm (6:30pm to 7:30pm in winter).

Parque Lage
PARK
(Map p60; ☑3257-1800, guided visits 3257-18721; www.eavparquelage.rj.gov.br; Jardim Botânico 414; ⊗8am-5pm) FREE This beautiful park, at the base of Parque Nacional da Tijuca, is about 1km from Jardim Botânico. It has English-style gardens, little lakes and a mansion, which has a cafe and hosts free exhibitions. Native Atlantic rainforest surrounds Parque Lage, and you can sometimes see monkeys and toucans among the foliage. This is the starting point for some challenging hikes up Corcovado.

Parque da Catacumba
PARK
(☑2247-9949; www.parquedacatacumba.com.br; Av Epitácio Pessoa; ⊗8am-5pm Tue-Sun) On the edge of the lake (but across the busy road), this park and sculptural garden added some new adventure activities in 2010, including a 7m rock-climbing wall (R$20), a zip line (R$20), rappelling down a rock face (R$100) and a canopy walk (R$30) through the tree-tops. It's operated by Lagoa Aventuras (☑4105-0079; www.lagoaaventuras.com.br). It's free to simply stroll through the park, and there's a short but steep trail (15 minutes' walking) to the Mirante do Sacopã, which offers scenic views from a height of 130m above Lagoa (also where the rappelling begins).

Museu Histórico da Cidade
MUSEUM
(☑2512-2353; www.rio.rj.gov.br/cultura; Estrada de Santa Marinha 505) Currently closed for renovation, the 19th-century mansion located on the lovely grounds of Parque da

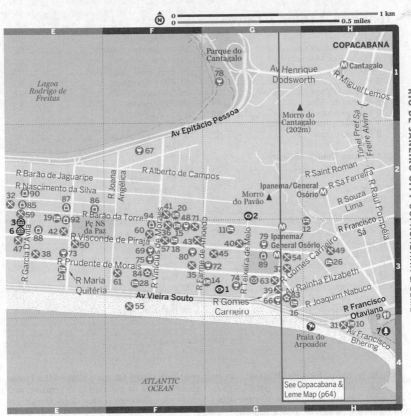

See Copacabana &
Leme Map (p64)

Cidade houses the City History Museum. In addition to its permanent collection, which portrays Rio from its founding in 1565 to the mid-20th century, the museum has exhibitions of furniture, porcelain, photographs and paintings by well-known artists. The park itself is free, open from 7am to 6pm.

Instituto Moreira Salles   CULTURAL CENTER
(☑ 3284-7400; www.ims.com.br; Marquês de São Vicente 476; ☉ 11am-8pm Tue-Sun) **FREE** This beautiful cultural center is next to Parque da Cidade and contains an archive of more than 80,000 photographs, many portraying old streets of Rio. The gardens, complete with artificial lake and flowing river, were designed by Brazilian landscape architect Burle Marx. There's also a craft shop and a quaint cafe here that serves lunch or afternoon tea.

Nirvana   DAY SPA
(Map p60; ☑ 2187-0100; www.enirvana.com.br; Jockey Club, Rua Jardim Botânico, near Praça Santos Dumont, Gávea; ☉ 10am-10pm Mon-Fri, to 8pm Sat) Inside the Jockey Club, this sunny full-service spa offers an enticing array of relaxing treatments, and you can also use the sauna. If you want to make a day of it, book a day-spa package, which includes a yoga class, lunch, exfoliating treatment, a selection of various treatments (reflexology, reiki, hot rocks massages etc) and aromatherapy bath.

⊙ Copacabana & Leme

Framed by mountains and deep blue sea, Rio's most beautiful beach curves 4.5km from end to end. No longer a symbol of Rio's glamour, Copacabana is a fascinating but chaotic place, its art-deco buildings, aging beachfront hotels and tree-lined side streets form the backdrop to a wildly democratic mix of tourists, elderly middle-class *cariocas*, and favela dwellers (who live in the hillsides surrounding the neighborhood).

Ipanema, Leblon & Gávea

Despite its faults, the neighborhood has its charms – old-school *botecos* (small, open-air bars), eclectic restaurants, vibrant street life, and the handsome beach still entrance many visitors.

Copacabana Beach
BEACH
(Map p64; Av Atlântica) A magnificent confluence of land and sea, the long, scalloped Praia de Copacabana always has a flurry of activity stretching its length: over-amped footballers singing their team's anthem, *cariocas* and tourists lining up for caipirinhas at kiosks, favela kids showing off their football skills, and beach vendors picking their way through the mass of bronzed bodies.

Museu Histórico do Exército e Forte de Copacabana
MUSEUM
(Map p64; ☑ 2521-1032; cnr Av Atlântica & Francisco Otaviano, Copacabana; admission R$4; ⊙10am-4pm Tue-Sun) Built in 1914, on the promontory of the former Our Lady of Copacabana chapel, the Forte de Copacabana (Copacabana Fort) was one of Rio's premier defenses against attack. You can still see its original features, including walls up to 12m thick, defended by Krupp cannons. The fort's

museum traces the early days of the Portuguese colony to the mid-19th century, and there are cafes overlooking Copacabana.

Forte Duque de Caxias
FORT
(Forte do Leme; Map p64; ☑ 3223-2034; Praça Almirante Júlio de Noronha; admission R$4; ⊙9:30am-4:30pm Tue-Sun) More commonly known as Forte do Leme, this military base is now open to the public, and visitors can walk to the top of Morro de Leme (Leme mountain) along a steep 800m trail that passes through Atlantic rainforest. At the top stands an 18th-century fort affording magnificent views of Pão de Açúcar (Sugarloaf mountain) and the Cagarras Islands.

◉ Botafogo

A largely middle-class residential area, Botafogo boasts some fine, small museums, several cinemas and some lively bars and restaurants.

Museu do Índio
MUSEUM
(Map p68; ☑ 3214-8736; www.museudoindio.org.br; Rua das Palmeiras 55; admission R$3; ⊙9am-5:30pm Tue-Fri, 1-5pm Sat & Sun) Featuring multi-

media exhibitions on Brazil's northern tribes, the small Museu do Índio provides an excellent introduction to the economic, religious and social life of Brazil's indigenous people. Next to native food and medicinal plants, the four life-sized dwellings in the courtyard were actually built by four different tribes.

Museu Casa de Rui Barbosa   MUSEUM
(Map p68; ☎ 3289-4663; www.casaruibarbosa.gov. br; São Clemente 134; admission R$4, free Sun; ◉10am-5:30pm Tue-Fri, 2-6pm Sat & Sun) The former mansion (completely restored in 2003) of famous Brazilian journalist and diplomat Rui Barbosa is now a museum housing his library and personal belongings.

◉ Urca

The tranquil, shady streets of Urca offer a pleasant escape from the urban bustle of other parts of the city. An eclectic mix of building styles and manicured gardens lines its streets, with local residents strolling among them. Along the sea wall, which forms the northwestern perimeter of Pão de Açúcar, fishers cast for dinner as couples lounge beneath palm trees, taking in views of Baía de Guanabara and Cristo Redentor off in the distance. Tiny Praia Vermelha, in the south, has one of Rio's finest beach views. A short but scenic walking trail begins from here.

Pão de Açúcar   MOUNTAIN
(Sugarloaf; Map p68; ☎ 2546-8400; www.bondinho. com.br; Av Pasteur 520, Urca; adult/child R$53/26; ◉8am-7:50pm) Seen from the peak of Pão de Açúcar, Rio is undoubtedly the most beautiful city in the world. There are many good times to make the ascent, but sunset on a clear day is the most rewarding.

Two cable cars connect to the summit, 396m above Rio. The first ascends 220m to Morro da Urca. From here, you can see Baía de Guanabara and the winding coastline; on the ocean side of the mountain is Praia Vermelha. Morro da Urca has its own restaurant, souvenir shops, a playground, an outdoor theater and a helipad (helicopter tours are possible).

The second cable car goes up to Pão de Açúcar. At the top, the city unfolds beneath you, with Corcovado mountain and Cristo Redentor off to the west, and Copacabana Beach to the south. The two-stage cable cars depart every 30 minutes.

Jardim Botânico & Lagoa

Those who'd rather take the long way to the summit should sign up with one of the granite-hugging climbing tours offered by various outfits in Rio.

Praia Vermelha
BEACH

(Map p68; Praça General Tibúrcio) Beneath Morro da Urca, narrow Praia Vermelha has superb views of the rocky coastline from the shore. Its coarse sand gives the beach the name *vermelha* (red).

Pista Cláudio Coutinho
WALKING TRAIL

(Map p68; ⊗ 6am-sunset) Everyone loves this paved 2km trail winding along the southern contour of Morro da Urca. It's a lush treed area, with the waves crashing on the rocks below. To get there, walk 100m north along the edge of Praia Vermelha (with your back to the cable-car station) and you'll see the entrance to the path straight ahead, just past the beach.

About 300m along the path, there's a small unmarked trail leading off to Morro da Urca. From there you can go up to Pão de Açúcar by cable car, saving a few reais. Pão de Açúcar can also be climbed – but it's not recommended without an experienced guide and climbing gear.

◉ Flamengo

Flamengo was once Rio's finest residential district, but lost its glitter after the tunnel to Copacabana opened in 1904. Along tree-shaded sidewalks, old-school restaurants and historic bars lie beside fragrant juice bars and Música Popular Brasileira–playing internet cafes. Flamengo also boasts the large Parque do Flamengo, which fronts a scenic beach (but it's too polluted for swimming).

Parque do Flamengo PARK
(Parque Brigadeiro Eduardo Gomes; Map p68)
Parque do Flamengo was the result of a landfill project that leveled the São Antônio hill in 1965, and now spreads all the way from downtown Rio through Glória, Catete and Flamengo, and on around to Botafogo.

Cyclists and rollerbladers glide along the paths, while the many football fields and sports courts are framed against the sea. On Sundays and holidays, the avenues through the park are closed (from 7am to 6pm).

Designed by famous Brazilian landscaper Burle Marx (who also landscaped Brasília), the park features some 170,000 trees of 300 different species. In addition there are three museums in the park: the Museu de Arte Moderna, the Monumento Nacional aos Mortos da II Guerra Mundial and the Museu Carmen Miranda.

Museu Carmen Miranda MUSEUM
(Map p68; ☑2334-4293; Av Rui Barbosa 560; ◉10am-5pm Tue-Fri, 1-5pm Sat & Sun) FREE
Peek at photographs, listen to recordings and watch a few film clips that highlight the legendary singer and actress.

◉ Cosme Velho

Cosme Velho lies west of Laranjeiras and is one of the city's most visited neighborhoods

– if only for the statue of Cristo Redentor soaring above its streets.

★ Cristo Redentor MONUMENT
(Christ the Redeemer; ☑2558-1329; www.corcovado.com.br; cog station, Cosme Velho 513; adult/child R\$46/23; ◉8am-7pm) Atop Corcovado (which means 'hunchback'), Cristo Redentor gazes out over Rio, a placid expression on his well-crafted face. The mountain rises straight up from the city to 710m, and at night the brightly lit, 38m-high statue is visible from nearly every part of the city – all 1145 tons of the open-armed redeemer.

Corcovado lies within the Parque Nacional da Tijuca. The most popular way to reach the statue is to take the red narrow-gauge train that departs every 30 minutes, and takes approximately 20 minutes to reach the top. To reach the cog station, take any 'Cosme Velho' bus: you can take bus 583 from Copacabana, Ipanema or Leblon.

If you want to take a vehicle up, vans depart every 15 minutes from Paineiras (around R\$25) and from the cog train station, from 8am to 7pm in summer (until 6pm otherwise).

Museu Internacional de Arte Naïf do Brasil MUSEUM
(☑2205-8612; Cosme Velho 561; adult/child R\$12/6; ◉10am-6pm Tue-Fri, to 4pm Sat; ◉180, 184, 583, 584) A short walk west from the Corcovado cog train station, this museum has a fascinating collection of colorful paintings made by artists often working well outside the establishment. Also known as primitivist, *arte naïf* paintings often deal with marginalized peoples – gypsies, sharecroppers, ghetto dwellers – and although small, the collection has pieces from 100 countries.

Highlights include a massive, much-reproduced painting by Lia Mittarakis, which depicts a vibrant Rio with Cristo Redentor as the focal point. Circling the room above it, 'Brasil, 5 Séculos' (Brazil, 5 Centuries), is one long canvas showing key points in Brazil's history from 1500 to the 1960s. Visitors receive a 50% discount by showing a ticket stub from the Corcovado cog train.

Largo do Boticário HISTORIC SITE
(Cosme Velho 822) The brightly painted houses on this picturesque plaza date from the early 19th century. Largo do Boticário was named in honor of the Portuguese gentleman – Joaquim Luiz da Silva Souto – who once ran a *boticário* (apothecary) utilized by the royal family.

1. Carioca da Gema (p108)
Samba music and dancing in this warmly lit club.

2. Ipanema beach (p54)
This long stretch of sand is very popular.

3. Santa Teresa (p72)
Cobbled streets and colonial architecture feature in Rio's most atmospheric neighborhood.

4. Cristo Redentor (p61)
Christ the Redeemer gazes over Rio with a placid expression on his face.

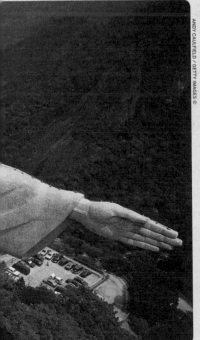

3

Copacabana & Leme

Cemitério
São João
Batista

Morro de
São João ▲
(240m)

Ladeira do Leme

R Euclides da Rocha

Ladeira dos Tabarajas

R Siqueira Campos

R Décio Vilares

R Figueiredo de Magalhães

R Maestro
Francisco Braga

16

17

Pç Edmundo
Bittencourt

R Anita Garibaldi

Siqueira
Campos

48

Cardeal
Arcoverde Ⓜ

Pç Cardeal
Arcoverde

R Tonelero

R República do Perú

R Paula Freitas

15

R Rodolfo Dantes

R Duvivier

11

10

27

58

5

41

38

32

12

56

20

36

COPACABANA

8

R Santa Clara

Túnel
Major Vaz

R 5 de Julho

R Dias
da Rocha

44

Pç Serzedelo
Correia

R Barata
Ribeiro

R Nossa de Copacabana

R Domingos Ferreira

R Hilário de Gouveia

Av Atlântica

Riotur ⓘ

42

45

1

R Pompeu Loureiro

R Constante
Ramos

R Barão de
Ipanema

25

53

R Leopoldo
Miguez

37

29

See Ipanema, Leblon
& Gávea Map (p56)

Cantagalo Ⓜ

28

54

47

R Bolívar

7

R Xavier
da Silveira

46

39

9

51

R Aires de Saldanha

R Miguel Lemos

▲
Morro do
Cantagalo
(202m)

R Djalma
Ulrich

34

21

52

55

Praia de Copacabana
(Copacabana Beach)

R Saint Roman

R Sá Ferreira

R Souza Lima

23

*ATLANTIC
OCEAN*

Av Atlântica

**Ipanema/General
Osório**

R Francisco Sá

R Bulhões de Carvalho

13

R Gomes
Carneiro

R Júlio de Castilhos

49

19

22

24

33

3

Ponta de
Copacabana

Av Rainha Elizabethe

R Joaquim
Nabuco

43

R Francisco Otaviano

57

4

18

Pç Coronel
Eugênio Franco

ARPOADOR

Praia do
Arpoador

Av Francisco Bhering

Parque Garota
de Ipanema

Praia de
Diabo

Ponta do
Arpoador

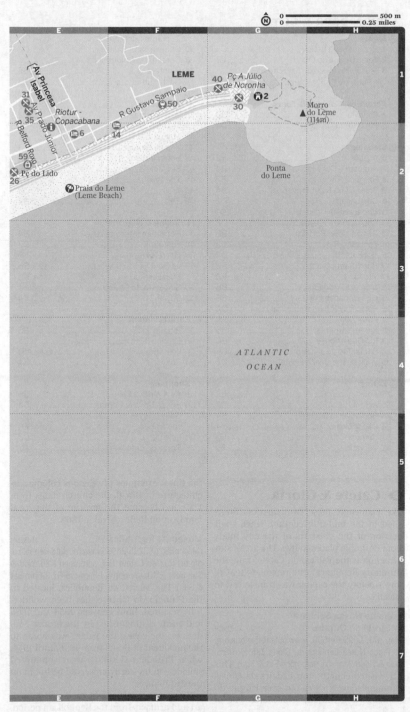

Copacabana & Leme

◉ Catete & Glória

Like Flamengo, these twin districts flourished in the mid-19th century, when their location at the outskirts of the city made them desirable places to live. The area's star attraction is the Palácio do Catete (now the Museu da República), the republic's seat of power before the capital was transferred to Brasília.

Igreja de Nossa Senhora da Glória do Outeiro   CHURCH
(Map p74; ☑ 2557-4600; www.outeirodagloria.org. br; Praça Nossa Senhora da Glória 135; ⊙ 9am-noon & 1-4pm Mon-Fri, 9am-noon Sat & Sun) This little-visited church atop Ladeira da Glória commands lovely views out over Parque do Flamengo and the bay. Considered one of the finest examples of religious colonial architecture in Brazil, the church dates from 1739 and became the favorite of the royal family upon their arrival in 1808.

Museu da República   MUSEUM
(Map p68; ☑ 3235-3693; www.museudarepublica. org.br; Rua do Catete 153; admission R$6, Wed & Sun free; ⊙ 10am-noon & 1-5pm Tue-Fri, 2-6pm Sat & Sun) The Museu da República, located in the Palácio do Catete, has been wonderfully restored. Built between 1858 and 1866 and easily distinguished by the bronze condors on the eaves, the palace was home to the president of Brazil from 1896 until 1954, when President Getúlio Vargas committed suicide – in the eerily preserved bedroom on the 3rd floor.

The museum also has a good collection of art and artifacts from the Republican period.

Museu de Folclore
Edison Carneiro MUSEUM
(Map p68; ☑2285-0441; www.cnfcp.gov.br; Rua do Catete 179; ⊙11am-6pm Tue-Fri, 3-6pm Sat & Sun) **FREE** Created in 1968, this small museum is an excellent introduction to Brazilian folk art, particularly from the northeast.

Centro Cultural Oi Futuro ARTS CENTER
(Map p68; ☑3131-3060; www.oifuturo.org.br; Dois de Dezembro 63; ⊙galleries 11am-5pm Tue-Sun, lobby to 8pm Tue-Sun) **FREE** With 2000 sq meters of exhibition space spread across six floors, this cultural space features multimedia exhibitions that run the gamut from architecture and urban design to photojournalism and video art.

In the auditorium, you can catch periodic concerts, plays and films.

◉ Centro & Cinelândia

Rio's bustling commercial district, Centro is a blend of high-rise office buildings, with remnants of its grand past still present in looming baroque churches, wide plazas and cobblestone streets.

Centro Cultural
Banco do Brasil ARTS CENTER
(CCBB; Map p74; ☑3808-2338; Primeiro de Março 66; ⊙9am-9pm Tue-Sun) **FREE** Housed in a beautifully restored 1906 building, the Centro Cultural Banco do Brasil (CCBB) hosts some of Brazil's best exhibitions. There is always something going on: exhibitions, lunchtime and evening concerts and film screenings.

Centro de Arte Hélio Oiticica MUSEUM
(Map p74; ☑2242-1012; Luis de Camões 68; ⊙11am-6pm Tue-Fri, 11am-5pm Sat & Sun) **FREE** This avant-garde museum displays permanent works by artist, theoretician and poet Hélio Oiticica, as well as bold contemporary art exhibitions.

Espaço Cultural
da Marinha MUSEUM & SHIPS
(ECM; Map p74; ☑2104-5592; ⊙noon-5pm Tue-Sun) **FREE** On the waterfront, you'll find a collection of ships and a small museum that provides insight into Brazil's naval past. Moored along the dock are the *Riachuelo* submarine and the *Bauru* (a small WWII destroyer), which have been turned into floating museums. You'll also find a 19th-century vessel used by Dom João VI, countless ship models, and maps and navigational instruments charting the history of imperial and Brazilian navigation. The boat tour to Ilha Fiscal leaves from here.

Casa França-Brasil CULTURAL BUILDING
(Map p74; ☑2332-5120; www.casafrancabrasil. rj.gov.br; Visconde de Itaboraí 78; ⊙10am-8pm Tue-Sun) **FREE** In a neoclassical building dating from 1820, the Casa França-Brasil sponsors changing exhibitions often dealing with political and cultural facets of *carioca* society. The classical revival building once served as a customs house. There's also a restaurant attached.

Ilha Fiscal ISLAND & HISTORIC BUILDING
(Map p74; ☑2233-9165; admission R$15; ⊙tours 12:30pm, 2pm & 3:30pm Thu-Sun) Looming large over tiny Ilha Fiscal (Fiscal Island) in the Baía de Guanabara, the lime-green, neo-Gothic palace (1889) looks like something straight out of a fairytale. Originally used to supervise port operations, the palace is famous as the location of the last Imperial Ball on November 9, 1889. Today it's open for guided tours three times a day from Thursday to Sunday; tours leave from the dock near Praça Quinze.

Igreja de Nossa Senhora
do Carmo da Antiga Sé CHURCH
(Map p74; Sete de Setembro 14; ⊙10am-4pm Tue-Sun) This beautifully restored church and former cathedral dates back to the 1770s, and played an important role in the imperial days of Rio. The elaborately gilded rococo-style interior witnessed royal baptisms, weddings and funeral rites, and several kings were crowned here – including Pedro I (in 1822) and his son Pedro II (1841); it is the only place in the New World where this occurred. The royal family used to sit in the balcony boxes overlooking the altar.

Igreja São Francisco da Penitência
& Convento de Santo Antônio CHURCH
(Map p74; ☑2262-0197; Largo da Carioca 5; admission R$2; ⊙church 8am-7pm Mon-Fri, 8-11am Sat, 9-11am Sun) Overlooking the Largo da Carioca is the baroque Igreja São Francisco da Penitência, dating from 1726. The church's sacristy, which dates from 1745, has blue Portuguese tiles and an elaborately carved altar made out of jacaranda wood. The church's **statue of Santo Antônio** is an object of great devotion to many *cariocas* in search of a husband or wife.

Flamengo, Botafogo & Catete

R Ar ao Reis

Túnel Santa Bárbara

34

Morro da
Nova Cintra
(267m)

R Pedro Américo

R Andrade Pertence

19

Catete

R Silveira Martins

4

5

14

R Bento Lisboa

R Correa Dutra

R Buarque
de Macedo

CATETE

Av Infante Dom Henrique

R Gen Mariante

R Erfurt

R Pereira da Silva

15

Parque
Guinle

Largo do
Machado

R Dois de Dezembro

1

R Machado Assis

25

FLAMENGO

Largo do
Machado

22

26

Praia do Flamengo

8

R das Laranjeiras

R Conde de Baependi

40

R São Salvador

38

R Ipiranga

33

21

Parque do
Flamengo

35

R Alice

LARANJEIRAS

R Coelho Netoga

R Paissandu

18

R Paulo IV

30

Pç David
Ben Gurion

R Pinheiro Machado

Flamengo

R Marquês de Abrantes

R Senador Vergueiro

R Barão
de Icaraí

R General Glicério

R Prof Luis Cantanheda

R Osvaldo Seabra

Morro
Mundo Novo
(128m)

R Juçana

R Jaguá

R Mundo
Novo

R Baro do Itambi

Praia de Botafogo

12

Av Osvaldo Cruz

Morro
da Viúva

Instituto
Fernandes
Figueira

2

R Marquês Olinda

Av dos Nações Unidas

R Assunção

R Bambina

R Muniz Barreto

39

Praia do
Botafogo

Enseada de
Botafogo

Pç Radial
Sul

R Barão
de Lucerna

32

R Prof Alfredo Gomes

3

R São Clemente

BOTAFOGO

Botafogo

13

Av Pasteur

R Dona
Mariana

R Sorocaba

16

17

36

37

Morro do
Pasmado

Av Pasteur

R da Palmeiras

R das Palmeiras

6

R Voluntários da Pátria

R Prof Álvaro
Rodrigues

R da Passagem

Av Lauro Sodré

Av Venceslau Brás

Universidade
Federal de Rio
de Janeiro

Beerjack
Hideout (125m);
Oui Oui (330m)

31

R São João Batista

R Visconde
de Caravelas

R Mena Barreto

R 19 Fevereiro

R Paulo Barreto

R General Polidoro

28

23

R Lauro Müller

Instituto e
Teatro
Benjamin
Constant

Meza Bar
(200m)

Oztel (525m)

R Álvaro Ramos

11

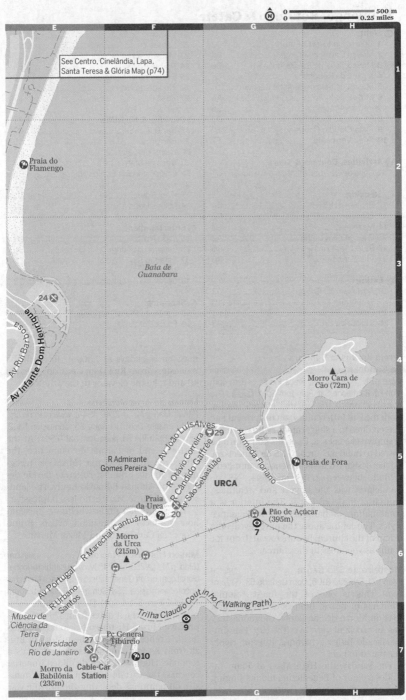

0   500 m
0   0.25 miles

See Centro, Cinelândia, Lapa,
Santa Teresa & Glória Map (p74)

Praia do
Flamengo

*Baía de
Guanabara*

24

Av Rui Barbosa

Av Infante Dom Henrique

Morro Cara de
Cão (72m)

Av João Luís Alves

29

R Admirante
Gomes Pereira

R Otávio Correira

R Cândido Gaffrée

Av São Sebastião

Alameda Floriano

Praia de Fora

URCA

Praia
da Urca

20

Pão de Açúcar
(395m)

7

R Marechal Cantuária

Morro
da Urca
(215m)

Av Portugal

R Urbano
Santos

Trilha Claudio Coutinho (Walking Path)

9

Museu de
Ciência da
Terra

Universidade
Rio de Janeiro

Pc General
Tibúrcio

27

Morro da
Babilônia
(235m)

Cable-Car
Station

10

Flamengo, Botafogo & Catete

Igreja de Nossa Senhora de Candelária
CHURCH

(Map p74; ☑2233-2324; Praça Pio X; ⊙8am-4pm Mon-Fri, 8am-noon Sat, 9am-1pm Sun) FREE The construction of the original church (dating from the late 16th century) on the present site was credited to a ship's captain who was nearly shipwrecked at sea. Upon his safe return he vowed to build a church to NS de Candelária. A later design led to its present-day grandeur.

Built between 1775 and 1894, NS de Candelária was the largest and wealthiest church of imperial Brazil. The interior is a combination of baroque and Renaissance styles. The ceiling above the nave reveals the origin of the church. Be sure to watch out for traffic as you cross to the church.

Mosteiro de São Bento
CHURCH

(Map p74; ☑2206-8100; Dom Gerardo 68; ⊙7am-6pm) This is one of the finest colonial churches in Brazil. Built between 1617 and 1641 on Morro de São Bento, the monastery has an excellent view over the city. The simple facade hides a baroque interior richly decorated in gold.

On Sunday, the High Mass at 10am includes a choir of Benedictine monks singing Gregorian chants; early risers can also hear mass on weekdays at 7:30am. To reach the monastery from Rua Dom Gerardo, go to No 40 and take the elevator to the 5th floor.

Museu de Arte Moderna
MUSEUM

(MAM; Map p74; ☑2240-4944; www.mamrio.org. br; Av Infante Dom Henrique 85; admission R$12; ⊙noon-6pm Tue-Fri, noon-7pm Sat & Sun) At the northern end of Parque do Flamengo, the Museu de Arte Moderna (MAM) is recognizable for its brutalist concrete facade designed by Alfonso Eduardo Reidy. The landscaping of Burle Marx is no less impressive.

The somewhat underwhelming museum houses pieces by Brazilian artists Bruno Giorgi, Di Cavalcanti and Maria Martins.

Museu Histórico Nacional
MUSEUM

(Map p74; ☑2550-9224; www.museuhistoricona-cional.com.br; off General Justo near Praça Marechal Âncora; admission R$8, Sun free; ⊙10am-5:30pm Tue-Fri, 2-6pm Sat & Sun) Housed in the colonial arsenal, which dates from 1764, the impressive Museu Histórico Nacional contains historic relics relating to the history of Brazil from its founding to its early days as a republic. Highlights include gilded imperial coaches, the throne of Dom Pedro II, massive oil paintings depicting the horrific war with Paraguay and a full-sized model of a colonial pharmacy. There's some attention paid to Brazil's indigenous population and curious pieces such as the quill that Princess Isabel used to sign the document abolishing slavery in Brazil.

Museu Nacional de Belas Artes   MUSEUM
(Map p74; ☑ 2219-8474; www.mnba.gov.br; Rio Branco 199, Centro; adult/student R$8/4; ☺ 10am-6pm Tue-Fri, noon-5pm Sat & Sun) Rio's fine-arts museum houses more than 18,000 original paintings and sculptures, some of which date back to works brought over from Portugal by Dom João VI in 1808. One of its most important galleries is the **Galeria de Arte Brasileira**, with 20th-century classics such as Cândido Portinari's *Café*.

Paço Imperial   HISTORIC BUILDING
(Map p74; ☑ 2215-2622; Praça XV (Quinze) de Novembro 48; ☺ noon-6pm Tue-Sun) FREE The former imperial palace was originally built in 1743 as a governor's residence. Later it became the home of Dom João and his family when the Portuguese throne transferred the royal seat of power to the colony. Today the building is used for free exhibitions, and there are several cafes on the main level.

Praça XV (Quinze)
de Novembro   HISTORIC SITE
(Near Rua Primeiro de Março) This square adjoining the former royal palace commemorates the day Brazil declared itself a republic on November 15, 1822.

Travessa do Comércio   STREET
(Map p74; Near Praça XV (Quinze) de Novembro) Beautiful two-story colonial townhouses line this narrow cobblestone street leading off Praça XV (Quinze) de Novembro. The archway, called **Arco de Teles**, leading into the area was once part of an old viaduct running between two buildings. Today, Travessa do Comércio contains half a dozen restaurants and drinking spots that open onto the streets. It's a favorite spot for *cariocas* after work.

Praça Floriano   PLAZA
(Map p74; Av Rio Branco) The heart of modern Rio, the Praça Floriano comes to life at lunchtime and after work when the outdoor cafes are filled with beer drinkers, samba musicians and political debate.

Real Gabinete Português
de Leitura   HISTORIC BUILDING
(Map p74; ☑ 2221-3138; Luís de Camões 30; ☺ 9am-6pm Mon-Fri) FREE Built in the Portuguese Manueline style in 1837, the gorgeous Portuguese Reading Room houses over 350,000 works, many dating from the 16th, 17th and 18th centuries. It also has a small collection of paintings, sculptures and ancient coins.

Theatro Municipal   THEATER
(Map p74; ☑ 2332-9220; www.theatromunicipal. rj.gov.br; Av 13 de Maio, Praça Floriano; guided tour R$10) Built in 1905 in the style of the Paris Opera, the magnificent Municipal Theater is the home of Rio's opera, orchestra and ballet. Its lavish interior contains many beautiful details. Hour-long guided tours are offered from Tuesday to Friday (at noon, 2pm, 3pm and 4pm) and Saturday (at noon and 2pm). It's also well worth coming here to see a performance.

⊙ Lapa

This former red-light district is the center of a vibrant bohemian scene in Rio, with dozens of music clubs, bars and old-fashioned restaurants scattered along its avenues.

On weekend nights, revelers pack the neighborhood's samba clubs, its streets and the wide plaza in front of the Arcos do Lapa, the neighborhood's prominent landmark.

Catedral Metropolitana   CHURCH
(Map p74; ☑ 2240-2669; www.catedral.com.br; Av República do Chile 24; ☺ 7am-6pm, museum 9am-noon & 1-4pm Wed, 9am-noon Sat & Sun) The enormous cone-shaped cathedral was inaugurated in 1976 after 12 years of construction. Among its sculptures, murals and other works of art, the four vivid stained-glass windows, which stretch 60m to the ceiling, are breathtaking.

★ Escadaria Selarón   LANDMARK
(Map p74; stairway btwn Joaquim Silva in Lapa & Pinto Martins in Santa Teresa) An ever-expanding installation, the **Escadaria Selarón**, leading up from Rua Joaquim Silva, became a work of art when Chilean-born artist Jorge Selarón, who died in 2013, decided to cover the steps with colorful mosaics. A dedication to the Brazilian people, the 215 steps are a vivid riot of color.

Arcos da Lapa   AQUEDUCT
(Map p74; Near Av Mem de Sá) The landmark aqueduct dates from the mid-1700s when it was built to carry water from the Carioca River to downtown Rio. In a style reminis-

HISTORICAL SITES

➡ **Paço Imperial** (p71) The former imperial palace was home to the royal family when they arrived from Portugal.

➡ **Praça XV (Quinze) de Novembro** (p71) Named after the date Brazil declared itself a republic (November 15, 1822), this plaza has witnessed a lot of historical action, including the crowning of two emperors and the abolition of slavery.

➡ **Travessa do Comércio** (p71) This narrow alley is a window into colonial Rio, with 18th-century buildings converted into bars and restaurants.

➡ **Museu Histórico Nacional** (p70) Set in the 18th-century royal arsenal, this museum houses Rio's best assortment of historical artifacts.

➡ **Jardim Botânico** (p55) Prince Regent Dom João VI insured the city would have no shortage of green spaces, and ordered this verdant garden planted in 1808.

➡ **Museu da República** (p66) Formerly known as the Palácio do Catete, this mansion was Brazil's presidential home from 1896 to 1954. Getúlio Vargas was the last president to live here, and committed suicide in one of the upstairs rooms.

➡ **Praça Floriano** (p71) Centro's picturesque main square has long been the meeting ground for popular demonstrations, including student uprisings against the military dictatorship in the 1960s and victory celebrations following World Cup finals.

➡ **Garota de Ipanema** (Map p56; ☎ 2523-3787; Vinícius de Moraes 49) The site of the famed drinking spot where Tom Jobim and Vinícius de Moraes penned 'The Girl from Ipanema,' whose international success introduced the world to bossa nova.

cent of ancient Rome, the 42 arches stand 64m high. It carried the *bonde* (tram) on its way to and from Santa Teresa until a tragic accident in 2011, after which the *bonde* was put out of service.

⊙ Santa Teresa

Set on a hill overlooking the city, Santa Teresa, with its cobbled streets and aging mansions, retains the charm of days past and is Rio's most atmospheric neighborhood. Currently the residence of a new generation of artists and bohemians, Santa Teresa has colorful restaurants and bars and a lively weekend scene around Largo do Guimarães and Largo das Neves.

Museu Chácara do Céu   MUSEUM
(Map p74; ☎ 3970-1126; www.museuscastromaya.com.br; Murtinho Nobre 93, Lapa; admission R$2, free Wed; ⊙ noon-5pm Wed-Mon) The former mansion of an art patron and industrialist, this museum has a small but diversified collection of modern art. Beautiful gardens surround the building.

Parque das Ruínas   VIEWPOINT
(Map p74; ☎ 2215-0621; Murtinho Nobre 169; ⊙ 10am-8pm Tue-Sun) **FREE** These ruins of a former mansion offers excellent views from

the viewing platform up top. There's also a small outdoor cafe-kiosk and terrace where concerts sometimes take place.

Centro Cultural Laurinda Santos Lobo   CULTURAL CENTER
(Map p74; ☎ 2224 3331; Monte Alegre 306, Santa Teresa; ⊙ 9am-5pm Tue-Sun) Built in 1907, this large mansion occasionally hosts exhibitions and open-air concerts.

⊙ Zona Norte

The north zone has a handful of attractions, including the Sambódromo, the Maracanã Football Stadium and the sprawling market amusement of Feira Nordestina. You'll also find the Quinta da Boa Vista, a large park containing the Museu Nacional and the Jardim Zoológico (zoo).

Maracanã Football Stadium   STADIUM
(Map p80; ☎ 2334-1705; Av Maracanã, São Cristóvão; admission R$15-100, sports museum R$20; ⊙ sports museum 9am-5pm Mon-Fri except game days) For a quasi-psychedelic experience, go to a *futebol* match at Maracanã, Brazil's temple to football (soccer). Matches here rate among the most exciting in the world, particularly during a championship game or when local rivals Flamengo, Vasco

da Gama, Fluminense or Botafogo go head-to-head. The stadium underwent a staggering R$900 million upgrade in preparation for the 2014 World Cup.

Games take place year-round and generally happen on Saturday or Sunday (starting at 4pm or 6pm) or on Wednesday and Thursday (around 8:30pm).

Quinta da Boa Vista   PARK
(Map p80; ☑2562-6900; ⊙9am-5pm) Quinta da Boa Vista was the residence of the Portuguese imperial family until the Republic was proclaimed. Today, it's a large and busy park with gardens and lakes. At weekends it's crowded with football games and families from the Zona Norte. The former imperial mansion houses the **Museu Nacional**, with a small zoo 200m away.

Museu Nacional   MUSEUM
(Map p80; ☑2562-6900; Quinta da Boa Vista s/n; admission R$3; ⊙10am-4pm Tue-Sun) The former imperial mansion houses the Museu Nacional. In addition to Etruscan ceramics, Egyptian mummies and stuffed prehistoric animals, the museum contains a small Brazilian section with relics from the country's early indigenous people.

Feira Nordestina   MARKET
(Map p80; ☑2580-5335; www.feiradesaocristovao.org.br; Campo de São Cristóvão; admission R$3; ⊙10am-6pm Tue-Thu, 10am Fri to 9pm Sun) This enormous fair showcases the culture from the northeast, with *barracas* (food stalls) selling Bahian dishes as well as beer and *cachaça* (cane liquor), which flows in great abundance here. The best time to go is on weekends, when you can catch bands playing *forró* (popular music of the Northeast). The vibrant scene runs nonstop from Friday morning through to Sunday evening. In addition to food and drink, you can browse the shops selling CDs, hammocks, snacks and handicrafts.

Sambódromo   ARENA
(Map p80; Marques do Sapucaí) The epicenter of Rio's Carnaval, the Sambódromo was designed by Oscar Niemeyer and completed in 1984.

⊙ Barra da Tijuca & Western Rio

Ten kilometers west of Leblon, Barra da Tijuca (Barra) is the Miami of Rio, with malls and shopping centers set against the tropical landscape. At 12km long, the lovely beach here is the city's longest. Beyond this, the region gets less and less urban. Some of Rio's most beautiful beaches lie out this way.

WORTH A TRIP

EXPLORING THE BAY

To the east of Centro lies Rio's scenic bay. Unfortunately, it's too polluted for swimming, but it makes a fine backdrop for the boat ride to Niterói or Ilha de Paquetá.

Ilha de Paquetá
This car-free **island** (☑ferry 0800-721-1012; www.grupoccr.com.br/barcas) provides a pleasant escape from the city's bustle. Transport is by foot, bicycle (with hundreds for rent) or horse-drawn carts. There's a certain decadent charm to the colonial buildings, unassuming beaches and businesses catering to local tourism. The place gets crowded on weekends. Boats leave from near the Praça XV (Quinze) de Novembro in Centro. The ferry takes 70 minutes and will cost you R$9 for a return trip. There are nine departures daily, the most useful being 7:10am, 10:30am and 1:30pm.

Niterói
East of Rio, the city of Niterói's principal attraction is the photogenic **Museu do Arte Contemporânea** (MAC; ☑2620-2400; www.macniteroi.com.br; Mirante da Boa Viagem, Niterói; admission R$6; ⊙10am-6pm Tue-Sun). The cruise across the bay, however, is perhaps just as valid a reason for leaving Rio. The ferry costs about R$9 return and leaves near Praça XV (Quinze) de Novembro in Centro; it's usually full of commuters. Once you reach the dock, the immediate area is a busy commercial district, full of pedestrians and crisscrossing intersections. From here catch bus 47B 2.1km south to the MAC – or get back on the ferry and head back.

Centro, Cinelândia, Lapa, Santa Teresa & Glória

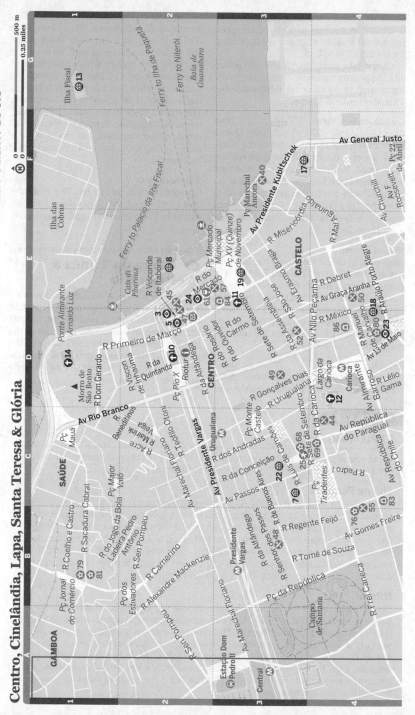

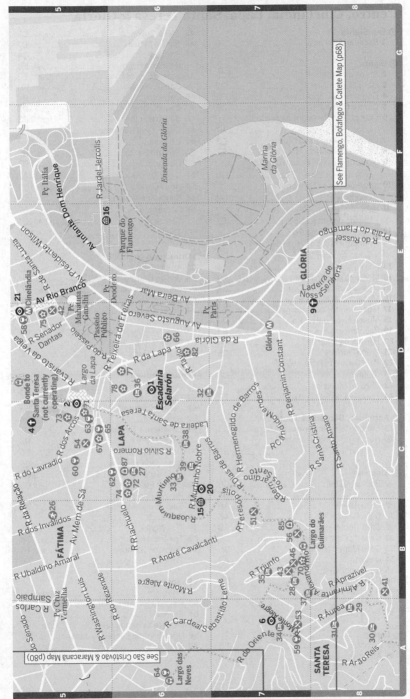

See Flamengo, Botafogo & Catete Map (p68)

See São Cristóvão & Maracanã Map (p80)

Enseada da Glória

Marina
da Glória

Praia do Flamengo
R do Russel

Parque do
Flamengo

GLÓRIA

Ladeira de
Nossa Senhora

Av Infante Dom Henrique

R Jardel Jercolis

Pç Itália

Av Presidente Wilson

R de Santa Luzia

Av Rio Branco

Cinelândia

R Senador
Dantas

Pç
Mahatma
Gandhi

Passeio Público

R do Passeio

Largo
da Lapa

R Teixeira de Freitas

R da Lapa

Av Beira Mar

Av Augusto Severo

Pç
Deodoro

Pç
Paris

R da Glória

Glória

R Benjamin Constant

R Evaristo da Veiga

Escadaria
Selarón

Ladeira de Santa Teresa

R Taylor

R Hermenegildo de Barros

R Cândido Mendes

R Bernardino
dos Santos

R Santa Cristina

R Santo Amaro

Bonde to
Santa Teresa
(not currently
operating)

R dos Arcos

LAPA

R Silvio Romero

R Murtinho Nobre

R Dias de Barros

R do Lavradio

R do Lavradio

FÁTIMA

R dos Invalidos

Av Mem de Sá

R Riachuelo

R Joaquim Murtinho

R Teresa

Largo do
Guimarães

R Ubaldino Amaral

R Washington Luis

R do Rezende

R André Cavalcânti

R Monte Alegre

R Cardeal Sebastião Leme

R do Oriente

SANTA
TERESA

Pç Cruz
Vermelha

R Carlos
Sampaio

R Triunfo

R Alexandrino

R Monte Alegre

R Almirante Alexandrino

R Aprazível

R Áurea

R Arão Reis

R do Senado

Largo das
Neves

Centro, Cinelândia, Lapa, Santa Teresa & Glória

Praia da Barra da Tijuca BEACH
(Av Sernambetiba, Recreio dos Bandeirantes)
The best thing about Barra is the beach.
It stretches for 12km, with the lovely blue
sea lapping at the shore. The first few kilometers of the eastern end of the beach are
filled with bars and seafood restaurants.

Sítio Burle Marx GARDENS
(✆ 2410-1412; visitas.srbm@iphan.gov.br; Estrada
da Barra de Guaratiba 2019, Guaratiba; admission
R$10; ☺ tours 9:30am & 1:30pm Tue-Sat, by ad-
vance appointment only) This 35-hectare estate
was once the home of Brazil's most famous
landscape architect, Roberto Burle Marx.
The estate's lush vegetation includes thousands of plant species, some of which are
rare varieties from different corners of the
globe.

Casa do Pontal MUSEUM
(✆ 2490-3278; www.museucasadopontal.com.br;
Estrada do Pontal 3295, Recreio dos Bandeirantes;
admission permanent collection/temporary exhibits R$10/4; ☺ 9:30am-5pm Tue-Sun) Owned
by French designer Jacques Van de Beu-
que, this impressive collection of over 5000
folk-art pieces is one of the best collections in Brazil. The assorted artifacts are
grouped according to themes, including
music, Carnaval, religion and folklore. The
grounds of the museum are surrounded by
lush vegetation.

🏃 Activities

Given the mountains, beaches and forests
in their backyard, it's not surprising that
cariocas are an active bunch. The coastline
brings an array of options: jogging, hiking,
walking, cycling and surfing. The mountains
offer their own allure: you can hang glide off
them or rock climb up them. Great hiking
trails through Atlantic rainforest lie just outside the city.

Walking & Jogging
Good walking and jogging paths in the
Zona Sul (southern neighborhoods between Flamengo and Leblon) include
Parque do Flamengo, which also has
workout stations. Around Lagoa Rodrigo
de Freitas, a 7.5km track provides a path
for cyclists and joggers. Along the seaside,
from Leme to Barra da Tijuca, there's a
bike path and footpath. On Sunday, the
road is closed to traffic from 7am to 6pm.
The road through Parque do Flamengo is
also closed on Sundays.

Hiking & Climbing
Aside from access to nearby national parks
such as Parque Nacional da Serra dos
Órgãos and Parque Nacional do Itatiaia,
Rio has many trails through the rainforest
of Floresta da Tijuca. Visitors can also take
part in hikes around Corcovado, Morro da
Urca, Parque Lage and other areas.

Rio is also the center of rock climbing in
Brazil, with hundreds of documented climbs
within an hour's drive. You can also try your
hand at the rock-climbing wall in Parque da
Catacumba (p56).

Jungle Me HIKING, GUIDED TOUR
(✆ 4105-7533; www.jungleme.com.br; tour R$150)
This top-notch outfit offers excellent hiking tours through Parque Nacional da Tijuca (p79) led by knowledgeable guides. The
peaks-and-waterfalls tour offers challenging
walks up several escarpments that offer stunning views of Rio followed by a refreshing dip
in a waterfall. The wild-beaches-of-Rio tour
takes you on a hike between scenic beaches
in Rio's little-visited western suburbs.

Rio Hiking HIKING
(✆ 2552-9204; www.riohiking.com.br; full-day tour
from R$150) Founded by a mother-son team
back in 1999, this popular outfit offers hiking trips ranging from easy to strenuous
and covering a variety of terrains around
Rio. You can also arrange kayaking, diving,
river rafting and numerous other adventure
sports here.

Rio Adventures HIKING
(✆ 2705-5747; www.rioadventures.com; hiking/
climbing/rafting tours from R$90/220/400) Offer-
ing a range of outdoor activities, Rio Adventures leads hikes through Parque Nacional
da Tijuca, including short treks up Pico Tijuca and more challenging ascents up Pedra
Bonito. They also run sightseeing tours, rock
climbs, rafting excursions (to Paraibuna River, 175km northwest of Rio) and parachuting
and paragliding trips.

Crux Ecoadventure ROCK CLIMBING
(✆ 9392-9203, 3474-1726; www.cruxecoaventura.
com.br) This reputable outfit offers a range of
climbing excursions and other outdoor adventures. The most popular is the ascent up
Pão de Açúcar (R$170), which isn't as daunt-
ing as it looks. Other possibilities include
rappelling down waterfalls, full-day hikes
through Parque Nacional da Tijuca, and
cycling and kayaking trips.

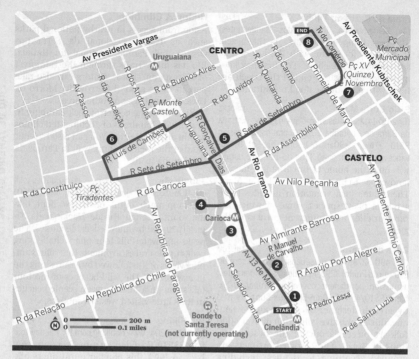

City Walk
Rio on Foot

START PRAÇA FLORIANO
END TRAVESSA DO COMÉRCIO
LENGTH 3KM, FOUR HOURS

A mélange of historic buildings and sky-scrapers, the center of Rio is an intriguing place to discover the essence of the city away from its beaches and mountains. This tour is best done during the week, as it gets rather deserted (and unsafe) on weekends.

Start at the ❶ **Praça Floriano** (p71), a scenic plaza set with several outdoor cafes. On the north side, the neoclassical ❷ **Theatro Municipal** (p71) is one of Rio's finest buildings, particularly after its recent R$65 million renovation. If you time it right, you can head inside on a guided tour.

Stroll north along Av 13 de Maio. You'll soon pass through the ❸ **Largo da Carioca**, a bustling area with a small market. Up on the hill is the ❹ **Igreja São Francisco da Penitên-cia** (p67), a 17th-century church with a jaw-dropping gilded interior. You can reach the church via stairs or elevator near the Carioca metro station.

After taking in the views, go back down and make your way over to narrow Rua Gonçalves Dias to reach ❺ **Confeitaria Co-lombo** (p99) for a dose of caffeine, pastries and art nouveau.

From Rua Gonçalves Dias, turn left on Rua do Ouvidor, following it to Largo de San Francisco de Paula. Continue one block further to ❻ **Real Gabinete Português de Leitura** (p71), a historic reading room that seems straight out of 19th-century Portugal.

Turn right when exiting and pass by Praça Tiradentes, before heading over to Rua Sete de Setembro. Follow it until it ends near the ❼ **Paço Imperial** (p121). Once the seat of the Portuguese rulers in Brazil, the building today houses intriguing art exhibitions as well as several cafes.

Leaving the Paço, cross Praça XV (Quinze) de Novembro and take the narrow lane be-neath the arch. You'll walk along one of Centro's oldest lanes, ❽ **Travessa do Comércio** (p71), with open-air restaurants and bars that draw crowds around happy hour. It's a fitting ending to the day's wander.

WORTH A TRIP

PARQUE NACIONAL DA TIJUCA

The Floresta da Tijuca (another name for Parque Nacional da Tijuca) is all that's left of the Atlantic rainforest that once surrounded Rio de Janeiro. In just 15 minutes you can go from the concrete jungle of Copacabana to the 120-sq-km tropical jungle of **Parque Nacional da Tijuca** (www.parquedatijuca.com.br; ☺ 8am-5pm) **FREE**. A more rapid and dramatic contrast is hard to imagine. The forest is an exuberant green, with beautiful trees, creeks and waterfalls, mountainous terrain and high peaks. It has an excellent, well-marked trail system, including the climb to the summit of **Pico da Tijuca** (1012m).

The heart of the forest is the Alto da Boa Vista area, which has many lovely natural and artificial features. Among the highlights of this beautiful park are several waterfalls (**Cascatinha Taunay**, **Cascata Gabriela** and **Cascata Diamantina**), a 19th-century chapel (**Capela Mayrink**) and numerous caves (**Gruta Luís Fernandes**, **Gruta Belmiro** and **Gruta Paulo e Virgínia**). Also in the park is a pleasant picnic spot (Bom Retiro) and several restaurants, which are near the **Ruínas do Archer**, the ruins of Major Archer's house. Tijuca wouldn't be the same without Archer – it was he who was tasked with replanting the forest in 1862 after years of clear-cutting for coffee and sugarcane plantations.

Pick up maps at the park entrance. It's best to get there by taxi, or go with an organized tour like those mentioned above.

Climb in Rio
ROCK CLIMBING

(☏ 2245-1108; www.climbinrio.com; half-day climb R$230) This respected agency offers half- and full-day climbing trips led by experienced guides. Navigating more than 400 routes around Rio de Janeiro and the state, this is an excellent pick to satisfy climbing junkies.

Cycling

There are over 300km of bike paths around Rio, with more planned in coming years. The best places to ride: around Lagoa Rodrigo de Freitas and along Barra da Tijuca and the oceanfront from Leblon to Leme. This last path also connects to Praia de Botafogo and Parque do Flamengo, running all the way to Centro. In the Tijuca forest, a 6km cycle path runs from a waterfall (Cascatinha) to a museum (Açude). On Sundays the beach road from Leblon to Leme closes to traffic, as does the road through Parque do Flamengo.

You can rent bikes from a stand along the east and west sides of Lagoa Rodrigo de Freitas for R$10 per hour. Another place to rent bikes is **Ciclovia** (Map p64; ☏ 2247-0018; Francisco Otaviano 55, Copacabana; per hr/day R$15/50; ☺ 9am-7pm Mon-Fri, 9am-4pm Sat, 10am-4pm Sun) One of several shops conveniently located on the cycle path between Ipanema and Copacabana.

Hang Gliding

If you weigh less than 100kg (about 220lb) and can spare R$250, you can do the fantastic tandem hang glide off 510m-high Pedra Bonita – one of the giant granite slabs that tower above Rio – onto Praia do Pepino in São Conrado. No experience is necessary; tandem riders are secured in a kind of pouch attached to the kite.

Flights typically last around 10 minutes, depending on weather and wind conditions. You can usually fly on all but three to four days per month, and conditions during winter are even better. If you schedule for an early flight, you have more flexibility to accommodate weather delays. Prices include pick-up and drop-off from your hotel. Travel agents also book tandem flights, but tack on their own fee. To cut out the middlemen, call direct.

Delta Flight in Rio
HANG GLIDING

(☏ 3322-5750, 9693-8800; www.riobyjeep.com/deltaflight) With more than 20 years' experience, Ricardo Hamond has earned a solid reputation as a safety-conscious and extremely professional pilot; he has flown more than 12,000 tandem flights.

Just Fly
HANG GLIDING

(☏ 2268-0565; http://justflyinrio.blogspot.com) Paulo Celani is a highly experienced tandem flyer with over 6000 flights to his credit.

São Cristóvão & Maracanã

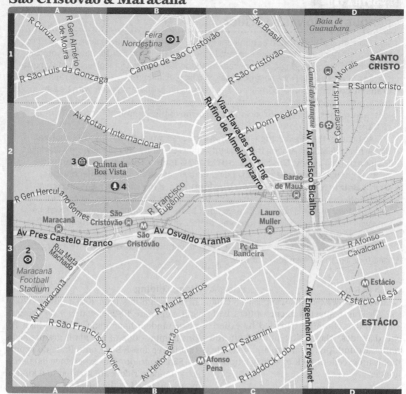

São Cristóvão & Maracanã

◉ Sights
1 Feira Nordestina................................B1
2 Maracanã Football Stadium A3
3 Museu Nacional....................................A2
4 Quinta da Boa Vista...........................B2

5 Sambódromo F3

✪ Entertainment
Maracanã Football Stadium..........(see 2)
6 Unidos da Tijuca...................................D2

SuperFly　　　　　　　HANG GLIDING
(☎3322-2286; www.riosuperfly.com.br) Founder Ruy Marra has more than 25 years of flying experience and is an excellent tandem glider pilot.

Tandem Fly　　　　　　HANG GLIDING
(☎2422-6371; www.riotandemfly.com.br) Two brothers – both very experienced pilots – run this outfit, and they also give lessons for those wanting to learn how to fly solo.

Surfing
Rio has some fine options when it comes to surfing, with some great breaks just outside the city. If you're not ready to leave the Zona Sul, Praia do Arpoador, between Copacabana and Ipanema, draws large flocks of surfers. Better breaks lie further west in Barra, Joátinga, Prainha and Grumari. Across the bay, Itacoatiara also has good breaks. For transportation to the western beaches, grab your board and hop on the **Surf Bus** (☎8702-2837; www.surfbus.com.br; 1 way R$4), a bright yellow-orange bus that makes four return trips daily (beginning at 7am) from Largo do Machado metro station (near Flamengo) to Prainha, with stops at beaches along the way.

If you don't have a board, you can hire or buy one in Arpoador at **Galeria River** (Map

**Casa de Dança
Carlinhos de Jesus**   DANCE
(Map p68; ☎ 2541-6186; www.carlinhosdejesus.
com.br; Álvaro Ramos 11, Botafogo) At this respected dance academy in Botafogo, Carlinhos and his instructors offer evening classes
in samba, *forró*, salsa and tango.

Centro Cultural Carioca   DANCE
(Map p74; ☎ 2252-6468; www.centroculturalcari-
oca.com.br; Sete de Setembro 237, Centro; ⊙ 11am-
8pm Mon-Fri) The cultural center offers one-
hour classes in samba, ballroom dancing
and the sensual lambada. Most classes
meet twice a week and cost around R$90
for a month-long course. The large dance
hall hosts parties on Friday at which samba
bands perform.

**Núcleo de Dança
Renata Peçanha**   DANCING
(Map p74; ☎ 2221-1011; www.renatapecanha.com.
br; Rua dos Inválidos 129, Lapa) A large upstairs
studio on the edge of Lapa, this dance
academy offers classes in *forró* and other
styles.

Rio Samba Dancer   DANCING
(Map p64; ☎ 8229-2843; riosambadancer.com;
Barata Ribeiro 261A, Copacabana; 90min private
lesson per person R$80) English-speaking
dance instructor Hélio Ricardo offers private one-on-one dance classes (in samba
or *forró*), as well as evening excursions to
dance places around town where you can
practice your new moves (R$120 per person
including lesson).

p56; Rua Francisco Otaviano 67, Arpoador; rental
per day R$30), a commercial center full of
surf shops and boutiques.

Beginners who want to learn to surf
can take classes through informal *escol-
inhas* (schools) off Ipanema Beach and off
Barra. You can also stay at the **Rio Surf 'N
Stay** (☎ 3418-1133; www.riosurfnstay.com; Rua
Raimundo Veras 1140, Recreio dos Bandeirantes)
in Recreio dos Bandeirantes, which offers
lessons (in English) and overnight accommodation.

🡒 Courses

Dance
Given the resurgent popularity of dance-hall
samba throughout the city, it's not surprising that there are a number of places where
you can learn the moves – then practice
them – in Lapa.

COOK IN RIO

At long last, travelers finally have the
opportunity to take a locally run cooking course, **Cook in Rio** (☎ 8761-3653;
www.cookinrio.com), which teaches
aspiring chefs how to make some of
Brazil's most famous dishes. Each
one-day class runs from 11am to 4pm
and includes the preparation of either
moqueca (seafood stew) or *feijoada
completa* (multi-dish black bean and
pork stew), along with appetizers and
side dishes, dessert and a master-
ful caipirinha. The best part is that
you'll get to devour your creations
afterwards. Courses cost R$150 per
person, including the cost of food and
drinks.

Football Fever

Rio's Maracanã stadium, recently refurbished for the 2014 World Cup, is hallowed ground among football lovers. The massive arena has been the site of legendary victories and crushing defeats. But no matter who takes the field, the 80,000-seat open-air arena comes to life in spectacular fashion on game day.

The Spectacle

A game at Maracanã (p72) is a must-see for visitors. Matches here rate among the most exciting in the world, and the behavior of the fans is no less colorful. The devoted pound huge samba drums, spread vast flags across great swaths of the stadium, dance in the aisles and detonate smoke bombs in team colors. You'll hear – and feel – the deafening roar when the home team takes the field, and the wall of sound and palpable air of near hysteria will surround you when a player slams the ball into the back of the net. Things are only slightly calmer since alcohol was banned inside the stadium back in 2003 (though with pressure from FIFA, an exception to the law was put in place for the 2014 World Cup).

The Clubs

Rio is home to four major club teams – Flamengo, Fluminense, Vasco da Gama and Botafago – each with a diehard local following. Apart from several short breaks for the Christmas–New Year holiday and Carnaval, professional club competitions go on all year. The major event in Rio's sporting calendar is the *classico*, when the four hometown teams play each other. Expect intense and bitter rivalry, matched in excitement only by Rio and São Paulo competitions.

1. Maracanã stadium (p72) 2. Spectators, Maracanã stadium 3. Football (p676)

BEACHES WEST OF RIO

Although Copacabana and Ipanema are Rio's most famous stretches of sand, there are many stunning beaches in the area, some in spectacular natural settings.

The first major beach you'll reach heading west of Leblon is Praia do Pepino in São Conrado. It's near where the hang-gliders land, but not the cleanest beach around. Further west is the small, lovely but well-concealed Praia do Joatinga, reachable by steep path down a rocky hillside. Be aware of the tides, so you don't get stranded.

Although it gets crowded on weekends, Recreio dos Bandeirantes is almost deserted during the week. The large rock acts as a natural breakwater, creating a calm bay. The 2km-long stretch of sand is popular with families.

The secluded 700m-long Prainha lies just past Recreio. It's one of the best surfing beaches in Rio, so it's always full of surfers. Waves come highly recommended here.

The most isolated and unspoiled beach close to the city, Grumari is quiet during the week and packed on weekends with *cariocas* looking to get away from city beaches. It is a gorgeous setting, surrounded by mountains and lush vegetation.

From Grumari, a narrow road climbs over a jungle-covered hillside toward Guaratiba. West of here is a good view of the Restinga de Marambaia (the vegetation-rich strip between the beach and the mainland), closed off to the public by a naval base. *Cariocas* enjoy eating lunch at several of the seafood restaurants in the area.

Tours

Favela Tours

Marcelo Armstrong CULTURAL TOUR
(☑ 3322-2727, 9989-0074; www.favelatour.com.br; per person R$65) The pioneer of favela tourism, Marcelo takes small groups to visit the favelas of Rocinha and Vila Canoas near São Conrado, where he does an excellent job explaining the social and political context of the favela in relation to greater Rio de Janeiro.

Paulo Amendoim CULTURAL TOUR
(☑ 9747-6860; pauloamendoim8@hotmail.com; tour R$65-75) The former president of Rocinha's residents association, Paulo seems to know everyone in the favela, and leads a warm and personalized tour that helps his visitors to see well beyond the gross stereotypes.

Be A Local CULTURAL TOUR
(☑ 9643-0366; www.bealocal.com; per person R$65) Offers daily trips into Rocinha (you'll ride up by moto-taxi, and walk back down), with stops along the way (R$65 per person). It also organizes a night out at a *baile funk* party in Castelo das Pedras on Sunday.

City Walking Tours
Longer guided hikes are also possible.

Lisa Rio Tours WALKING TOUR
(☑ 9894-6867; www.lisariotours.com; tours from R$110) Lisa Schnittger, a German expat who has lived in Rio for many years, leads a wide range of recommended tours. Some of her most popular excursions explore the colonial history of downtown, the bohemian side of Santa Teresa and Afro-Brazilian culture in Rio.

Cultural Rio WALKING TOUR
(☑ 9911-3829; www.culturalrio.com.br; tours from R$120) Run by the quirky Carlos Roquette, this tour offers visitors an in-depth look at the social and historical aspects of Rio de Janeiro.

Bay Tours

Marlin Yacht Tours BOAT TOUR
(☑ 2225-7434; www.marlimyacht.com.br; Marina de Glória, Glória; cruise R$60-95) Offers several daily tours aboard its large 30-person schooners to Cagarras Island, stopping for a beach swim along the way. It also offers sunset cruises, sailing and diving trips, and is known for its fishing tours.

Bem Brasil BOOZE CRUISE
(www.bembrasilrio.com; Marina da Glória, Glória; cruise R$50-70) Operates popular booze cruises in the bay from a two-floor sailboat soundtracked by well-known house DJ Andrew Gracie every Monday night at 11pm.

Other Tours

Most recommended outfits include round-trip transportation from your hostel/hotel in the price.

Be A Local   TOUR

(☎9643-0366; www.bealocal.com; per person R$80-90) Popular with backpackers, Be a Local offers favela tours, outings to football matches at Maracanã and trips to evening favela parties.

Brazil Expedition   TOUR

(☎9998-2907; www.brazilexpedition.com; city tours R$95) The friendly English-speaking guides from Brazil Expedition run a variety of traditional tours around Rio, including trips to Cristo Redentor, nightlife tours in Lapa, game-day outings at Maracanã and favela tours.

Helisight   SCENIC FLIGHTS

(☎2511-2141; www.helisight.com.br; per person 6-/15-/30-min flight R$210/520/720) Offering helicopter tours since 1991, Helisight has eight different itineraries, all giving gorgeous views over the city. There is a three-person minimum.

Jeep Tour   DRIVING TOUR

(☎2108-5800; www.jeeptour.com.br) Travels to the Parque Nacional da Tijuca in a large, open-topped jeep. The tour includes a stop at the Vista Chinesa, then on to the forest for an easy hike and a stop for a swim beneath a waterfall, before making the return journey.

Rio by Jeep   DRIVING TOUR

(☎3322-5750; www.riobyjeep.com) Another recommended outfit offering jeep tours.

★☆ Festivals & Events

Aside from Carnaval, there are many other exciting events happening throughout the year.

Festas Juninas   CULTURAL

(⊙ June) The June Festival is one of the most important folkloric festivals in Brazil. In Rio, it's celebrated in various public plazas throughout the month, primarily on June 13 (Dia de Santo Antônio), June 24 (Dia de São João) and June 29 (Dia de São Pedro).

Portas Abertas   CULTURAL

(www.artedeportasabertas.com.br; ⊙ a weekend in July) Santa Teresa's artists open their studios and the neighborhood becomes a living installation in this twice-yearly event.

Rio International Film Festival   FILM

(www.festivaldorio.com.br; ⊙ Sep & Oct) One of the biggest in Latin America, this film festival runs for 15 days from the last week of September through to the first week of October.

Reveillon & Festa
de Iemanjá   HOLIDAY, FESTIVAL

(⊙ December 31) New Year's Eve (Reveillon) in Rio is celebrated by millions of people. Tons of fireworks explode in the sky over Copacabana. New Year's Day coincides with the festival of Iemanjá, the sea goddess. Wearing white, the faithful carry a statue of Iemanjá to the beach and launch flowers and other offerings into the sea.

🛏 Sleeping

Rio has a wide mix of lodging options, including boutique hotels, hostels, B&Bs and plenty of cookie-cutter high-rise accommodations along Copacabana. If you want to be in the heart of the action and don't mind paying for it, stay in Ipanema or Leblon, with beautiful beaches and excellent restaurants, shopping and nightlife. If you don't want to pay a premium for those neighborhoods, opt for busier Copacabana, where you can find less pricey options while still being near the beach (and a short taxi or bus ride to Ipanema). For an alternative to beach culture, take a peek at Santa Teresa's colonial guesthouses – the neighborhood is also close

---

RIO FOR CHILDREN

Brazilians are very family-oriented. Some hotels let children stay free, although the age limit varies. Babysitters are readily available and most restaurants have high chairs.

There's plenty of good spade and sandbucket fun to be had on Rio's beaches, particularly Leblon's *posto* 12, known as Baixo Bébe for its mini-playground and all the moms and tots around. Other amusement for kids includes the shows and exhibits at the Planetário (p55), the impressive ships at Espaço Cultural da Marinha (p67), and the mechanized displays at the Museu de Folclore Edison Carnerio (p67). You can also hire bikes (including big, shaded four-seaters) and visit the playground near the bike stand at Lagoa Rodrigo de Freitas (p55).

LONG-TERM RENTALS

If you're planning to stay in Rio for longer than a few nights, you might consider renting an apartment, which is often a better value than staying in a hotel. Nightly rates start around R$200 for a studio apartment in Copacabana or R$350 in Ipanema; rates rise significantly during Carnaval and New Year's Eve.

Blame it on Rio 4 Travel (Map p64; ☑3813-5510; www.blameitonrio4travel. com; Xavier da Silveira 15B, Copacabana) Run by an expat from New York, this professional agency rents apartments and runs a full-service travel agency.

Copacabana Holiday (Map p64; ☑2542-1525; www.copacabanaholiday. com.br; Barata Ribeiro 90A, Copacabana) Specializes in Copacabana.

Fantastic Rio (Map p64; ☑3507-7491; http://fantasticrio.jimdo.com; Av Atlântica 974, Apt 501, Leme) Lists more than 200 apartments.

Rio Apartments (Map p64; ☑2247-6221; www.rioapartments.com; Av Rainha Elizabeth 85, Copacabana) A Swedish-run outfit with many apartment rentals in the Zona Sul.

to the nightlife of Lapa. Other neighborhoods along the metro line (Botafogo, Flamengo and Catete) generally have cheaper options than the beachside southern neighborhoods.

Hotel rates are 30% higher during summer (December to mid-March) and prices double or triple for New Year's Eve and Carnaval, when most places, including hostels, require four-day (or more) minimum bookings.

Keep in mind that many hotels add a combined 15% service and tax charge, though cheaper places don't generally bother with this.

🛏 Ipanema & Leblon

Ocean views with access to Rio's loveliest beaches, restaurants and bars make Ipanema and Leblon magnets for travelers. Not surprisingly, prices here are higher than elsewhere.

Che Lagarto Ipanema HOSTEL **$**
(Map p56; ☑2512-8076; www.chelagarto.com; Paul Redfern 48; dm/d from R$60/180; ❋@🛜)

Che Lagarto's Ipanema branch is a popular budget spot for travelers who want to be close to the beach. It's a five-story hostel, with spartan rooms and not much common space – aside from a bar on the ground floor.

Rio Hostel – Ipanema HOSTEL **$**
(Map p56; ☑2287-2928; www.riohostelipanema. com; Casa 1, Canning 18, Ipanema; dm/d from R$45/150; @🛜) This friendly hostel is set in a small villa on a peaceful stretch of Ipanema. It has clean rooms and an airy top-floor deck with hammocks. The same owners operate the respected Santa Teresa hostel of the same name.

Bonita HOSTEL **$$**
(Map p56; ☑2227-1703; www.bonitaipanema.com; Barão da Torre 107, Ipanema; dm from R$60, d without/with bathroom R$220/250; ❋@🛜🏊) This peacefully set converted house has history – it's where bossa nova legend Tom Jobim lived from 1962 to 1965 writing some of his most famous songs. Rooms are simply furnished, and most open onto a shared deck overlooking a small pool and patio.

Ipanema Beach House HOSTEL **$$**
(Map p56; ☑3202-2693; www.ipanemahouse.com; Barão da Torre 485, Ipanema; dm R$60, d without/with bathroom from R$180/200; @🛜🏊) This is one of Rio's best-looking hostels. It's set in a converted two-story house with crowded dorms. There are private rooms, indoor and outdoor lounge spaces, a small bar and an attractive pool.

Lemon Spirit Hostel HOSTEL **$**
(Map p56; ☑2294-1853; www.lemonspirit.com; Cupertino Durão 56, Leblon; dm R$70-80; ❋@🛜) Leblon's first hostel boasts an excellent location one block from the beach. The dorm rooms are clean and simple without much decor. There's a tiny courtyard in front, and a bar in the lobby.

Hostel Harmonia HOSTEL **$**
(Map p56; ☑2523-4905; www.casadaharmonia.com; Casa 18, Barão da Torre 175, Ipanema; dm/d without bathroom R$60/130; @🛜) Hostel Harmonia is one of the best choices on Ipanema's hostel row, with a good traveler vibe. The lounge and rooms have two-toned wood floors, and quarters are clean and nicely maintained with four to six beds in each room.

Z Bra Hostel HOSTEL **$**
(Map p56; ☑3596-2386; www.zbrahostel.com; General San Martin 1212, Ipanema; dm R$90, d without/with bathroom from R$240/295; ❋@🛜)

One of Rio's most stylish hostels, Z Bra has customized ultramodern dorm beds, with top-quality mattresses and thoughtful details (low lighting, reading lamps, big lockers). The small ground floor bar aims for retro cool and the owners have inside tips on great parties around Rio.

Margarida's Pousada POUSADA $$
(Map p56; ☎ 2239-1840; www.margaridaspousada.com; Barão da Torre 600, Ipanema; s/d/tr R$200/250/320; ❋ @) For those seeking a smaller, cozier atmosphere than the highrise hotels can provide, this excellently located Ipanema guesthouse is a good option. You'll find 11 pleasant, simply furnished rooms scattered about the low-rise building.

Hotel Vermont HOTEL $$
(Map p56; ☎ 3202-5500; www.hotelvermont.com.br; Visconde de Pirajá 254, Ipanema; s/d from R$310/350; ❋) The Hotel Vermont offers no-frills accommodations with small, clean but charmless rooms.

Hotel San Marco HOTEL $$
(Map p56; ☎ 2540-5032; www.sanmarcohotel.net; Visconde de Pirajá 524, Ipanema; s/d R$260/275; ❋ @ ☎) Offers small, but clean rooms with tile floors and a mint-green color scheme.

Ipanema Inn HOTEL $$
(Map p56; ☎ 2523-6092; www.ipanemainn.com.br; Maria Quitéria 27, Ipanema; d R$346-531; ❋) Ipanema Inn is a simple hotel whose rooms have off-white ceramic tile floors and simple wood furnishings; some are disappointingly small.

Arpoador Inn HOTEL $$
(Map p56; ☎ 2523-0060; www.arpoadorinn.com.br; Francisco Otaviano 177, Ipanema; r R$345, with view R$621; ❋ ☎) Overlooking Praia do Arpoador (Arpoador beach), this six-story hotel is the only one in Ipanema or Copacabana that doesn't have a busy street between it and the beach. The rooms are small and basic, but the brighter, prettier 'deluxe' rooms have glorious ocean views.

Ipanema Hotel
Residência SERVICED APARTMENTS $$
(Map p56; ☎ 3125-5000; www.ipanemahotel.com.br; Rua Barão da Torre 192, Ipanema; d from R$450; ❋ ☒) Set on one of Ipanema's lovely tree-lined streets, this high-rise has large apartments, with kitchen units, lounge areas and pleasant bedrooms.

Mar Ipanema HOTEL $$$
(Map p56; ☎ 3875-9190; www.maripanema.com.br; Visconde de Pirajá 539, Ipanema; d R$575-750; ❋) This reliable hotel in Ipanema has trim, modern rooms with decent beds, good lighting and an inviting color scheme. It's also in a great location, on Ipanema's lively shopping strip, just two blocks from the beach. The downside is the lack of a view.

Sol Ipanema HOTEL $$$
(Map p56; ☎ 2525-2020; www.solipanema.com.br; Av Vieira Souto 320, Ipanema; s/d R$505/560, with ocean view R$635/705; ❋ @ ☎ ☒) Occupying prime real estate facing Ipanema beach, the tall, slender Sol Ipanema features rooms decorated in creams and earth tones with dark-wood furnishings and good lighting. Pricier rooms have ocean views but are otherwise identical to the standard rooms.

★ **Casa Mosquito** GUESTHOUSE $$$
(Map p56; ☎ 3586-5042; www.casamosquito.com; Saint Roman 222, Ipanema; r R$660-1200) Opened by two French expats, the Casa Mosquito is a beautifully designed boutique guesthouse with luxuriously appointed rooms. The converted all-white 1940s mansion sits on a tranquil garden-filled property with scenic views of Pão de Açúcar and the Pavão-Pavãozinho favela. Meals available by request. More rooms and a pool are planned for the future. Casa Mosquito is located on a steep winding street about 10 minutes' walk from Praça General Osório.

Golden Tulip Ipanema Plaza HOTEL $$$
(Map p56; ☎ 3687-2000; www.goldentulipipanemaplaza.com; Farme de Amoedo 34, Ipanema; d from R$652; ❋ ☒) A top choice, the 18-story Plaza features nicely decorated rooms with tile floors, a muted color scheme and sizable windows to let in the tropical rays. You'll also find broad, comfortable beds, spacious bathrooms (with bathtubs) and a lovely rooftop pool. Some rooms overlook the ocean; others face the outstretched arms of Cristo Redentor.

Ritz Plaza Hotel SERVICED APARTMENTS $$$
(Map p56; ☎ 2540-4940; www.ritzhotel.com.br; Av Ataúlfo de Paiva 1280, Leblon; r from R$505; ❋ ☎ ☒) In one of Rio's most desirable areas, this stylish low-key hotel has attractive, uniquely designed rooms and common areas that give the Ritz a boutique feel. The best rooms have kitchen units and balconies – some with partial ocean views – and all are trimmed with artwork, good lighting and spotless bedrooms.

Marina All Suites
BOUTIQUE HOTEL $$$

(Map p56; ☑2172-1100; www.marinaallsuites.com. br; Av Delfim Moreira 696, Leblon; ste from R$865; ❋@⊛) Here you'll find beautifully decorated rooms, doting service and all the creature comforts. As per the name, it's all suites here, meaning that, between the comfy bedroom and living room, you'll have 39 to 75 sq meters in which to stretch out.

Hotel Fasano
HOTEL $$$

(Map p56; ☑3202-4000; www.fasano.com.br; Av Vieira Souto 80, Ipanema; d from R$1620; ❋@⊛⊠) Designed by Philippe Starck, the Fasano has 91 sleek rooms set with Egyptian cotton sheets, goose-down pillows and high-tech fittings. The best rooms have balconies overlooking the crashing waves of Ipanema beach, which lies just across the road. Rooms without a view simply don't justify the price.

⌸ Copacabana & Leme

Copacabana, particularly Av Atlântica, is packed with hotels. Quality and price varies considerably.

Pura Vida
HOSTEL $

(Map p64; ☑2210-8885; www.puravidahostel.com. br; Saint Roman 20, Copacabana; dm R$35-45, d without bathroom R$150-200; @) Pura Vida occupies a converted castle-like mansion (built in the 1920s) that was once the home of the Polish ambassador. Here you'll find huge dorm rooms with mostly single beds and polished wood floors, plus spacious common areas, including an outdoor veranda with bar.

Bamboo Rio
HOSTEL $

(Map p64; ☑2236-1117; www.bamboorio.com; Lacerda Coutinho 45, Copacabana; dm R$38-62, d R$120-180; ❋@⊛⊠) Yet another hostel set in a former villa, Bamboo Rio is a friendly, comfortable hostel with tidy air-conditioned dorm rooms (sleeping from five to 12), ample lounge space, a tiny pool and an inviting bar area.

Walk on the Beach Hostel
HOSTEL $

(Map p64; ☑2545-7500; www.walk-on-the-beach. com; Dias da Rocha 85, Copacabana; dm R$40-55; @⊛) Set in an unsigned two-story villa on one of Copacabana's rare quiet streets, this nicely designed hostel offers good-value fancooled dorm rooms (each with three to 12 beds). It has a lounge room and a small bar, and maintains a welcoming, low-key vibe.

Che Lagarto
HOSTEL $

(Map p64; ☑3209-0348; www.chelagarto.com; Barata Ribeira 111, Copacabana; dm R$45-60; ❋@⊛⊠) This popular full-service hostel has a friendly, party atmosphere. The small rooftop pool with adjoining bar is a good place to meet other travelers, and the hostel arranges loads of activities – boat parties, nights out in Lapa, BBQs and more. There are two other Che Lagartos in Copacabana and one in Ipanema.

Jucati
HOTEL $$

(Map p64; ☑2547-5422; www.edificiojucati.com. br; Tenente Marones de Gusmão 85, Copacabana; s/d/tr R$180/220/260; ❋@⊛) Overlooking a leafy park, the unmarked Jucati doesn't offer much in the way of atmosphere, though it does have large, simply furnished apartments with slate floors and small kitchens.

Hotel Santa Clara
HOTEL $$

(Map p64; ☑2256-2650; www.hotelsantaclara. com.br; Décio Vilares 316, Copacabana; s/d from R$240/260; ⊛) Along one of Copacabana's most peaceful streets, this simple three-story hotel has a mix of rooms. Those in back are a little gloomy; upstairs rooms are best (and well worth the extra reais), with wood floors and a balcony.

Augusto's Copacabana
HOTEL $$

(Map p64; ☑2547-1800; www.augustoshotel. com.br; Bolívar 119, Copacabana; s/d R$380/440; ❋@⊛⊠) Augusto's plays off the kitschy ancient Rome theme with murals of charioteers and lyre-playing toga-wearers. The rooms, however, are fairly straightforward with a light and airy feel, and modern bathrooms. Some rooms have balconies (but no views).

Hotel Ibis
HOTEL $$

(Map p64; ☑3218-1150; www.ibis.com; Ministro Viveiros de Castro 134, Copacabana; r not incl breakfast from R$269; ❋⊛) The international chain opened its first Copacabana branch in 2012, and offers good value for its small, modern rooms with comfortable beds, sizable windows, wood floors and reliable wi-fi.

Acapulco
HOTEL $$

(Map p64; ☑3077-2000; www.acapulcohotel. com.br; Gustavo Sampaio 854, Leme; s/d from R$385/410; ❋@⊛) The Acapulco hotel lies just a short stroll from the beach. Most rooms have a neat look about them with pressed-wood floors and colorful duvets and curtains.

Orla Copacabana　　　HOTEL **$$**
(Map p64; ☑ 2525-2425; www.orlahotel.com.br; Av Atlântica 4122, Copacabana; d R$450-600; ❋ 🛜 ☒) The Spanish-owned Orla Copacabana has attractive, understated rooms, but the beach-facing location is the real draw. The standard rooms are too dark and cramped to recommend, so it's not worth staying here unless you book one of the seafront deluxe rooms.

Rio Guesthouse　　　B&B **$$**
(Map p64; ☑ 2521-8568; www.rioguesthouse.com; Francisco Sá 5, Copacabana; d R$354-530; ❋ 🛜) On a split-level penthouse overlooking Copacabana beach, the Australian-Brazilian hosts open up their home and rent out several comfortable rooms to guests. The highlight is the outdoor patio with views over Copacabana.

Design Hotel Portinari　　　HOTEL **$$**
(Map p64; ☑ 3222-8800; www.portinarihotelrio. com; Francisco Sá 17, Copacabana; r R$423-590; ❋ @ 🛜) This 13-story hotel demonstrates real design smarts. The rooms have tile floors, good lighting and big windows, and each floor is decorated in a different style.

Mercure Arpoador　　　HOTEL **$$$**
(Map p64; ☑ 3222-9600; www.mercure.com; Francisco Otaviano 61, Copacabana; s/d R$503/665; ❋ @ 🛜 ☒) This dapper all-suites hotel is nicely located in Arpoador, giving easy access to both Ipanema and Copacabana. The suites have sleek white leather sofas that open into beds, modern kitchenettes, TVs with a stereo and a DVD player, ambient lighting and comfortable bedrooms.

Porto Bay Rio Internacional　　　HOTEL **$$$**
(Map p64; ☑ 2546-8000; www.portobay.com.br; Av Atlântica 1500, Copacabana; s/d from R$600/660; ❋ @ 🛜 ☒) One of Copacabana's top beachfront hotels, Porto Bay has stylish rooms painted in cool tones. Large white duvets, light hardwoods, elegant furnishings and simple artwork all complement each other nicely. Big windows let in lots of light, and most rooms have balconies.

Sofitel Rio de Janeiro　　　HOTEL **$$$**
(Map p64; ☑ 2525-1232; www.sofitel.com; Av Atlântica 4240, Copacabana; d from R$828; ❋ @ ☒) One of Rio's priciest hotels, the French-owned Sofitel does its best to impress. The excellent service, comfortable rooms, two lovely pools and beachfront location have earned many fans. All rooms have balconies

---

FAVELA CHIC

Favela sleeps are nothing new – intrepid travelers have been venturing into Rio's urban mazes for nearly a decade – but as more and more of Rio's favelas are pacified, hostels and pousadas are popping up faster than the rudimentary constructions that make up the favelas themselves.

Our favorites:

Maze Inn (Map p68; ☑ 2558-5547; www. jazzrio.info; Casa 66, Tavares Bastos 414, Catete; dm R$60, s/d from R$120/150) Owned by English renaissance man Bob Nadkarni, this pousada in Tavares Bastos favela is almost legendary. Don't miss the bimonthly jazz parties on the first and third Friday of every month.

Vidigalbergue (☑ /929-7999; www. vidigalbergue.com.br; Casa 2, Av Niemeyer 314, Vidigal; ❋ @ 🛜) Stunning seaviews are the coup at this friendly hostel at the bottom of Vidigal favela.

Pousada Favelinha (Map p68; ☑ 2556-5273; www.favelinha.com; Almirante Alexandrino 2023, Santa Teresa; dm R$45, d R$110; @) This European-run inn in Santa Teresa's Pereirão da Silva favela was the first...way back in 2004.

---

and are tastefully furnished. Deluxe rooms and suites have ocean views.

Copacabana Palace　　　HOTEL **$$$**
(Map p64; ☑ 2548-7070; www.copacabanapalace. com.br; Av Atlântica 1702, Copacabana; d from R$1150; ❋ @ 🛜 ☒) Rio's most famous hotel has a dazzling white facade that dates from the 1920s, when it became a symbol of the city. Today accommodations range from deluxe rooms to spacious suites with balconies. It has a lovely pool, excellent restaurants and fine service.

🛏 Botafogo

Though lacking beach access, Botafogo is an authentic slice of Rio, with old-school *botecos* and lively nontouristy restaurants hidden on the tree-lined streets.

Oztel　　　HOSTEL **$$$**
(☑ 3042-1853; www.oztel.com.br; Pinheiro Guimarães 91, Botafogo; dm R$55-75, d R$240-290;

✳@🛜) Evoking a Warholian aesthetic, Rio's coolest and most colorful hostel is like sleeping in an art gallery. The artsy front deck and bar is an inviting hangout lounge but the real coup are the R$270 private rooms: with a garden patio under the nose of Christo, you'll be hard-pressed to find a groovier room in Rio.

Stand Fast Hostel
HOSTEL $

(Map p68; 🗷 2553-7420; www.standfasthostel.com; 19 Fevereiro 52, Botafogo; dm from R$35, d without bathroom R$120; ✳@🛜) Once a Botafogo warehouse, then a private home, now an exciting new hostel run by a Dutch-born Brazilian-Scot named Cloud whose first language is American English (don't ask us, ask her). Everything here is spotless and top quality, including marble bathrooms and a sunny front porch. Dorm room 6 is the way to go: there's an expansive street-facing terrace.

El Misti
HOSTEL $

(Map p68; 🗷 2226-0991; www.elmistihostel.com; Praia de Botafogo 462, Casa 9; d without/with bathroom R$240/265; @🛜) El Misti is a popular budget spot among Brazilian and foreign travelers for its cheap dorm rooms and lively atmosphere. It's a short walk to the Botafogo metro station. Free airport pick-up if you book for four nights or longer.

Vila Carioca
HOSTEL $

(Map p68; 🗷 2535-3224; www.vilacarioca.com. br; Estácio Coimbra 84; dm/d from R$35/130; ✳@🛜) On a peaceful tree-lined street, this low-key and welcoming hostel has six- to 15-bed dorms in an attractively decorated house. The common areas are a fine spot to mingle with other travelers.

Brothers Hostel
HOSTEL $

(Map p68; 🗷 2551-0997; www.brothershostel. com; Farani 18; dm R$47-58, d R$140; ✳@🛜) In a handsomely converted house, Brothers Hostel was started by four well-traveled Brazilian brothers. Some of the rooms are cramped, but the rock-loving bar is a good place to meet other guests.

🛏 Santa Teresa & Lapa

A growing number of budget and midrange hotels have opened in Santa Teresa in recent years, drawing travelers to this intriguing, arts-loving neighborhood. Do take care when walking around, day or night, as crime is still an issue.

Books Hostel
HOSTEL $

(Map p74; 🗷 3437-3783; www.bookshostel.com; Francisco Muratori 10, Lapa; dm R$38-50, d without bathroom R$130-140; ✳@🛜) In the heart of Lapa and true to the nature of the neighborhood, this party hostel is the appetizer for your crazy night out. Dorms have graffiti art and there's a sociable barraca-style bar (rooms overlooking it don't allow for much sleep). All bathrooms are shared, and only some rooms have air-conditioning.

Terra Brasilis
HOSTEL $

(Map p74; 🗷 2224-0952; www.terrabrasilishostel. com; Murtinho Nobre 156, Santa Teresa; dm R$45-50, d R$200-230; @🛜) Near the Parque das Ruinas, this peacefully set guesthouse has a mix of dorm rooms and private doubles, all with wood floors and French doors that open onto a veranda overlooking the city. The breezy patio with bar is a fine place to nurse a drink in the afternoon.

Rio Hostel
HOSTEL $

(Map p74; 🗷 3852-0827; www.riohostel.com; Joaquim Murtinho 361, Santa Teresa; dm R$40-45, d R$150-160; ✳@🛜⊠) This Santa favorite is ideally placed for exploring Rio's most bohemian neighborhood. The backyard patio with pool is a great place to meet other travelers, and the hostel whips up different meals (for R$18) nightly.

Casa Mango Mango
GUESTHOUSE $$

(Map p74; 🗷 2508-6440; www.casa-mangomango. com; Joaquim Murtinho 587, Santa Teresa; r R$150-300; ✳@🛜⊠) In an atmospheric 19th-century mansion, this friendly guesthouse has a mix of uniquely designed rooms. The grounds have a small patio and pool, plus enormous 200-year-old mango trees.

Hotel Marajó
HOTEL $

(Map p74; 🗷 2224-4134; www.hotelmarajo.com.br; Joaquim Silva 99, Lapa; s/d R$100/120; ✳) A few paces from the Selarón steps, this basic hotel rents simple, fairly clean rooms, all with air-conditioning. It's perfectly located for taking advantage of Lapa's nightlife, if you don't mind the street noise.

Casa Áurea
GUESTHOUSE $$

(Map p74; 🗷 2242-5830; www.casaaurea.com.br; Áurea 80, Santa Teresa; dm R$75, s/d without bathroom R$140/180, s/d R$200/250) Set in one of the neighborhood's oldest homes (from 1871), the two-story Casa Áurea has rustic charm with simple but cozy rooms and a large covered garden where you can lounge on hammocks, fire up the barbecue or whip up a meal in the open-air kitchen.

Cama e Café HOMESTAY $$
(Map p74; ☑2225-4366; www.camaecafe.com; Paschoal Carlos Magno 90, Santa Teresa; r R$130-300; ⏱9am-5:30pm Mon-Fri, to 2pm Sat) Cama e Café is a B&B network that allow travelers to book a room from local residents. There are several dozen options, with accommodations ranging from modest to lavish – indeed, the best rooms are inside colonial homes with panoramic views and lush gardens.

★Casa Beleza POUSADA $$
(Map p74; ☑8288-6764; www.casabeleza.net; Laurinda Santos Lobo 311; r R$220-300; ✳🅰🛜🛏) This lovely property dates back to the 1930s and was once a governor's mansion. Tropical gardens overlook the picturesque pool, and you can sometimes spot toucans and monkeys in the surrounding foliage. It's a small and peaceful operation, with just four guestrooms. The kind family that runs the pousada lives onsite.

Casa da Carmen e do Fernando GUESTHOUSE $$
(Map p74; ☑2507-3084; www.bedandbreakfast rio.com.br; Hermenegildo de Barros 172; s/d from R$110/210; 🛜🛏) This familial eight-room guesthouse attracts a laid-back crowd who feel right at home in the century-old building. The colorfully decorated lounge is adorned with artwork (including paintings by one of the owners) and has a comfy, lived-in feel, making it a fine place to watch a film, play music or enjoy the fine view through the oversized picture window.

Out back is a small pool and rustic terrace with equally impressive views. Rooms are simply furnished but enlivened with bright colors, and some have fine views.

Casalegre GUESTHOUSE $$
(Map p74; ☑8670-6158; www.casalegre.com.br; Monte Alegre 316; s/d from R$140/240; 🛜) Casalegre has a rustic, art-loving bohemian vibe and its eight rooms are decorated with different works of art and vary in size (the cheapest two rooms share a bathroom). There's a strong communal vibe here, and the owners often host parties, yoga classes and other activities. It has an art gallery on the 1st floor and a small terrace in back.

Castelinho 38 HOTEL $$
(Map p74; ☑2252-2549; www.castelinho38.com; Triunfo 38, Santa Teresa; r R$207-426; ✳🅰🛜)

Another Santa charmer, Castelinho offers a range of spacious rooms with high ceilings, wood floors and a light, airy design. It's set in a mid-19th-century mansion and has an outdoor terrace with a garden and lounge space.

Casa Cool Beans GUESTHOUSE $$
(Map p74; ☑2262-0552; www.casacoolbeans.com; Laurinda Santos Lobo 136, Santa Teresa; d R$260-340; ✳🅰🛜🛏) Your expectations will easily be exceeded at this discreet 10-room B&B where the American owner's mantra focuses on personalized service. Each colorful room in the renovated 1930s Spanish-style villa was designed by a different Brazilian artist and it has a spacious sun deck and breakfast area. Book room 9 for the best views.

★Hotel Santa Teresa HOTEL $$$
(Map p74; ☑3380-0200; www.santa-teresa-hotel. com; Almirante Alexandrino 660, Santa Teresa; d from R$830; ✳🅰🛜🛏) Probably the finest boutique hotel in Rio, the Hotel Santa Teresa is set in a lavishly restored building with beautifully designed rooms, an award-winning restaurant, a stylish bar and a pool with fine views over the city.

🍴 Eating

Rio has an impressive array of restaurants, serving Brazilian regional cuisine along with international and fusion fare. In general, Ipanema and Leblon boast Rio's best dining scene, though every neighborhood has its gems.

Among Rio's quintessential dining experiences: feasting at a *churrascaria* (all-you-can-eat barbecued-meat restaurant), dining alfresco beside the lake in Lagoa, joining the fashion parade at a sidewalk cafe in Ipanema, chowing on local favorites at a neighborhood *boteco* and lingering over the views from a restaurant patio up in Santa Teresa.

Prices are high (it's not hard to spend R$100 or more on a meal for two). To eat on the cheap, try per-kilo places and juice bars. Self-caterers should check out Rio's many *feiras* (produce markets).

🍴 Ipanema

By day, Ipanema's busy cafes and juice bars fill with bronze bodies heading to and from the beach, while at night its tree-lined streets make a picturesque setting for open-air dining. Ipanema's Rua Garcia D'Ávila is packed with dining options.

Uruguai
SNACK STAND $

(Map p56; Posto 9, Ipanema beach; sandwiches R$8-12; ⊙noon-5pm) Of the many *barracas* (food stalls) on the beach, Uruguai is a long-term favorite, serving scrumptious chicken, beef or sausage sandwiches, which are grilled up fresh on the sands. Look for the blue-and-white striped Uruguayan flag flying high over the beach.

Polis Sucos
JUICE BAR $

(Map p56; ☑2247-2518; Maria Quitéria 70; juices around R$6; ⊙7am-midnight; ☑) One of Ipanema's favorite spots for a dose of fresh-squeezed vitamins, this juice bar facing the Praça NS de Paz has dozens of flavors, and you can pair those tangy beverages with sandwiches or *pão de queijo* (balls of cheese-stuffed tapioca bread).

Koni Store
JAPANESE $

(Map p56; ☑2521-9348; Maria Quitéria 77; hand roll around R$12; ⊙11am-3am Sun-Wed, to 6am Thu-Sat) With nearly two dozen branches in Rio, the Koni craze shows no sign of abating. The recipe is simple – *temaki* (a seaweed hand roll) stuffed with salmon, tuna, shrimp, roast beef or a combination – which can then be devoured at one of the tiny bistro tables. Other branches: **Ipanema** (Map p56; Farme de Amoedo 75); **Leblon** (Map p56; Av Ataulfo de Paiva 1174); **Copacabana** (Map p64; Constante Ramos 44; ⊙noon-3am Sun-Thu, to 5am Fri & Sat).

Vero
ICE CREAM $

(Map p56; ☑3497-8754; Visconde de Pirajá 260; small/medium/large ice cream R$9/12/15; ⊙11:30am-7:30pm) An instant hit after opening in 2011, this artisanal gelato maker whips up over two dozen rich and creamy varieties, including Amazonian fruits like *açaí* and *cupuaçu* and innovative combinations like *caramelo com flor de sal* (caramel with sea salt) and *figo com amêndoas* (fig with almond).

Galitos Grill
ROAST CHICKEN $

(Map p56; ☑2287-7864; Farme de Amoedo 62; mains R$14-36; ⊙noon-10pm) A handy spot in the neighborhood is this open-sided purveyor of roast chicken. Grab a seat at the counter and enjoy inexpensive nicely seasoned lunch specials (R$14 to R$17), whipped up in a hurry.

Delírio Tropical
BRAZILIAN $

(Map p56; ☑3624-8162; www.delirio.com.br; Garcia D'Ávila 48; salads R$11-15; ⊙11am-9pm Mon-Sat, noon-7pm Sun; ☑) Delírio Tropical serves a tempting array of salads, which you can enhance by adding on grilled trout, salmon carpaccio, filet mignon and other items. Go early to beat the lunchtime crowds.

Armazém do Café
CAFE $

(Map p56; ☑2259-0170; Rita Ludolf 87B; snacks R$5-10; ⊙9am-midnight Sun-Thu, to 1am Fri & Sat) Dark-wood furnishings and the fresh-ground coffee aroma lend of authenticity to this Leblon coffeehouse.

Yogoberry
FROZEN YOGURT $

(Map p56; ☑3281-1512; Visconde de Pirajá 282; small/medium yogurt R$7/9; ⊙10am-10pm) Ever popular, Yogoberry serves low-fat frozen yogurt in just three flavors: *natural* (plain), diet and *chá verde* (green tea), but the fresh fruit, cashews, chocolate chips and other toppings liven things up.

Laffa
KEBAB $

(Map p56; ☑2522-5888; Visconde de Pirajá 175; sandwich small/large R$13/19; ⊙11:30am-midnight) Harried staff whip up satisfying, piping hot grilled lamb or turkey shawarmas, falafel sandwiches or slightly more exotic inventions like strawberry and Nutella wraps.

Cafeína
CAFE $$

(Map p56; ☑2521-2194; www.cafeina.com.br; Farme de Amoedo 43; quiches R$7-9, sandwiches R$20-30; ⊙8am-11:30pm; ☎) In the heart of Ipanema, this inviting cafe (and its sidewalk tables) is a fine spot for an espresso while watching the city stroll by. You'll also find freshly made sandwiches, salads, quiches and some very rich desserts.

Gringo Cafe
CAFE $$

(Map p56; www.gringocafe.com; Barão da Torre 240, Ipanema; breakfast R$13-23, mains R$19-23; ☎) *Feijoada's* not sitting well? This American-run diner dishes up the homesick remedies in spades: waffles, pancakes, hash browns, mac and cheese, chili, tuna melts etc. It even smells like a US diner.

Terzetto Cafe
CAFE $$

(Map p56; ☑2247-3243; cnr Jangadeiros & Visconde de Pirajá; mains R$16-42 ; ⊙9am-midnight) Fronting Praça General Osório, Terzetto is a bright and bustling cafe with an assortment of prepared salads and antipasti as well as focaccia sandwiches, ravioli, bruschetta, grilled dishes, pizzas (after 2pm) and desserts. There's a pricier Terzetto next door, which isn't really worth the money.

Felice Caffè
CAFE $$

(Map p56; 2522-7749; Gomes Carneiro 30; mains R$26-50; noon-midnight Mon-Fri, 10am-midnight Sat & Sun) Felice has a small shaded front terrace and an air-conditioned interior, where locals and travelers enjoy gourmet sandwiches (grilled veggies, steak, thick burgers), grilled dishes, bountiful salads and, most importantly, rich Italian-style ice cream (R$10 for two scoops), pulled from the irresistible counter in front.

New Natural
VEGETARIAN $$

(Map p56; 2287-0301; Barão da Torre 167; per kg R$45; 8am-10:30pm;) New Natural was the first health-food restaurant in the neighborhood. Fill up on fresh pots of soup, rice, veggies and beans at the healthy lunch buffet.

Pintxo
SPANISH $$

(Map p56; 3586-4963; Gomes Carneiro 130; tapas R$6-14; 11am-10pm Mon-Thu, to 2am Fri & Sat) A short stroll east of Praça General Osório, tiny Pintxo serves creative Basque cooking amid a charming interior of old film posters and colorful ceramic-tile floors. Stop in at lunchtime for good-value two-course specials (R$17) or in the evening for tapas like the Amalur (foie gras with caramelized onions and mango), Txistorra (sausage, quail egg and spicy pepper) or less fussy slices of tortilla (Spanish omelet) or gazpacho.

All go down nicely with bottles of Estrella or Voll-Damm beer.

Benkei
JAPANESE $$

(Map p56; 2540-4829; Av Henrique Dumont 71; all-you-can-eat R$41-57; noon-4pm Tue-Sun, 7pm-midnight daily) Benkei does have a menu, though nearly everyone here comes for the all-you-can-eat sushi buffet, with a wide variety of rolls and sashimi, plus miso soup.

Frontera
BUFFET $$

(Map p56; 3289-2350; Visconde de Pirajá 128; per kg R$53-60; 11:30am-11pm) Frontera offers more than 60 plates at its delectable lunch buffet, featuring a mouthwatering assortment of grilled meats, baked casseroles, and seafood pastas, plus salads, fresh fruits, grilled vegetables and desserts. If you're famished, opt for the all-you-can-eat price (R$56).

Via Sete
INTERNATIONAL $$

(Map p56; 2512-8100; Garcia D'Ávila 125; mains R$28-56; noon-midnight) This restaurant on upscale Garcia D'Ávila serves big salads and grilled vegetable wraps, as well as heartier fare like grilled tuna and a high-end steak burger. Via Sete uses 100% organic ingredients (beef included). Go early to get a seat on the front-side patio.

Capricciosa
PIZZERIA $$

(Map p56; 2523-3394; Vinícius de Moraes 134; small/large pizzas around R$45/60; 6pm-1am) Inside this trendy high-end pizzeria, you'll find tasty thin-crust pizzas made with fresh ingredients. The price is high, but the chefs – working in an open kitchen next to the brick oven – are at least generous with the toppings.

Market
BRAZILIAN $$

(Map p56; 3283-1438; Visconde de Pirajá 499 ; mains R$30-50; noon-5pm Mon, 9am-midnight Tue-Sat, 9am-6pm Sun) Market serves inventive seafood dishes, grilled meats, creative salads and gourmet sandwiches. Hidden from the street, Market is reached by a narrow corridor to a shaded plant-trimmed patio and a cozy dining room beyond. Two-course lunch specials (R$31) are good value, and breakfast (waffles, eggs Benedict) is served until 5pm.

Brasileirinho
BRAZILIAN $$$

(Map p56; 2523-5184; Jangadeiros 10; mains R$34-57; noon-11pm) Facing Praça General Osório, this rustically decorated restaurant serves good traditional cuisine, including *carne seca* (jerked beef), *picanha* (rump steak) and *feijoada*.

Casa da Feijoada
BRAZILIAN $$$

(Map p56; 2247-2776; Prudente de Morais 10B; feijoada R$73; noon-midnight) Admirers of Brazil's iconic *feijoada* needn't wait until Saturday to experience the meaty meal. The casual Casa da Feijoada serves the rich black-bean-and-salted-pork dish every day of the week.

Azul Marinho
SEAFOOD $$$

(Map p56; 2513-5014; Av Francisco Bhering, Praia do Arpoador; mains R$62-100; noon-midnight) Below the Arpoador Inn, Azul Marinho serves an assortment of tasty seafood dishes, and the outdoor tables facing the ocean have the best beachside setting you'll find in the Zona Sul (there's no traffic between you and the sea, only palm trees and sand). Try one of the *moquecas* (seafood stews cooked in coconut milk) or the octopus vinaigrette salad.

Bazzar
INTERNATIONAL **$$$**
(Map p56; ☑ 3202-2884; Barão da Torre 538; mains R$48-70; ☉ noon-1am Mon-Sat, to 7pm Sun) Set on a peaceful tree-lined street, this nicely designed restaurant with relaxing front terrace serves creative, beautifully executed dishes. Recent hits include duck with crispy plantains, *cavaquinha* (a lobster relative) and inventive risottos. There's a smaller branch hidden with more of a bistro menu on the 2nd floor of Ipanema's **Livraria da Travessa** (Map p56; Av Rio Branco 44, Centro).

Zazá Bistrô Tropical
FUSION **$$$**
(Map p56; ☑ 2247-9101; www.zazabistro.com.br; Joana Angélica 40; mains R$51-65; ☉ 7:30pm-midnight Mon-Thu, 1:30pm-1am Fri & Sat, 12:30-6pm Sun) Inside an art-filled and whimsically decorated house, Zazá serves beautifully prepared dishes with Asian accents. Recent favorites include grilled squid and octopus with wild rice and lemon confit, flambéed prawns with risotto and grilled namorado served with caramelized plantains. Upstairs, diners lounge on throw pillows amid flickering candles. You can also sit at one of the tables on the front.

✕ Leblon

Rua Días Ferreira has an excellent selection of dining options.

Zona Sul Supermarket
SUPERMARKET
(Map p56; ☑ 2259-4699; Dias Ferreira 290; ☉ 24hr Mon-Sat, 7am-midnight Sun) Zona Sul supermarket has branches all over the city. The one in Leblon is the best of the bunch, with fresh-baked breads, imported cheeses and olives, wines, cured meats and other items. The adjoining pizza and lasagna counter serves decent plates. A handy **Ipanema branch** (Map p56; Prudente de Morais 49) is near Praça General Osório.

Vezpa
PIZZA **$**
(Map p56; ☑ 2540-0800; Av Ataúlfo de Paiva 1063; slice R$6-8; ☉ noon-2am Sun-Thu, to 5am Fri & Sat) Vezpa is a New York–style place, with brick walls and high ceilings, where you can order pizza by the slice. The crusts are thin and crunchy.

Bibi Crepes
CREPERIE **$**
(Map p56; ☑ 2259-4948; Cupertino Durão 81; crepes R$16-28; ☉ noon-1am) This small, open-sided restaurant attracts a young, garrulous crowd who enjoy the more than two dozen sweet and savory crepes available, as well as design-your-own salads.

Talho Capixaba
SANDWICHES **$**
(Map p56; ☑ 2512-8760; Av Ataúlfo de Paiva 1022; sandwiches around R$18-35; ☉ 8am-10pm) This deli and gourmet grocer serves excellent sandwiches (charged by weight) made from quality ingredients as well as pastas, salads and antipasti. Dine inside or at the sidewalk tables in front.

Vegetariano Social Club
VEGETARIAN **$**
(Map p56; ☑ 2294-5200; Conde Bernadotte 26L; lunch buffet R$30; ☉ noon-11pm Mon-Sat, to 5:30pm Sun; ✐) Vegetarians interested in sampling Brazil's signature dish should visit this small charmer on Thursday or Sunday when tofu *feijoada* is served. At other times, VSC serves a small lunch buffet, while the evening a la carte menu features risottos, yakisoba, heart-of-palm stroganoff and the like.

Prima Bruschetteria
ITALIAN **$$**
(Map p56; ☑ 3592-0881; www.primab.com.br; Rainha Guilhermina 95; bruschetta R$7-10, mains R$23-43; ☉ noon-1am) Prima showcases an Italian delicacy not often seen in these parts, with imaginative ingredients like goat's cheese, olive tapenade, prosciutto, smoked salmon and even caviar appearing atop its chargrilled bread.

Venga!
SPANISH **$$**
(☑ 2247-0234; Garcia D'Ávila 147; tapas R$15-30; ☉ noon-midnight) A festive spot to eat and drink, Venga! became Rio's first authentic tapas bar when it opened back in 2009. Classic wood details and a good soundtrack set the scene for noshing on *patatas bravas* (spicy potatoes), *pulpo a la gallega* (grilled octopus), *gambas al ajillo* (garlic prawns) and other Iberian hits. Match those small plates with a Spanish rioja. Also in Leblon.

Zuka
INTERNATIONAL **$$**
(Map p56; ☑ 3205-7154; Rua Dias Ferreira 233, Leblon; mains R$57-90; ☉ 7pm-1am Mon, noon-4pm & 7pm-1am Tue-Fri, 1pm-1am Sat & Sun) One of Rio's best restaurants, Zuka prepares delectable mouthwatering cuisine – zingy ceviche or the confection-like delicacy of Zuka's original foie gras to start, followed by rack of lamb with passion fruit, grilled fish of the day with *mandoquinha* (a kind of sweet root vegetable) purée, seared tuna over heart-of-palm tagliatelle and many other imaginative dishes. All the grilling action happens at the open kitchen to the right (you can sit at the counter and watch the chefs in action).

Sushi Leblon
JAPANESE $$$

(Map p56; ☑ 2512-7830; Dias Ferreira 256; mains R$50-70; ☺ noon-4pm & 7pm-1:30am Mon-Sat, 1pm-midnight Sun) Leblon's top sushi destination boasts a Zenlike ambience with a handsome dark-wood sushi counter setting the stage for succulent cuisine. In addition to sashimi and sushi, you'll find grilled *namorado* (a type of perch) with passion fruit *farofa,* sea-urchin ceviche and refreshing sake to complement the meal.

✗ Gávea, Jardim Botânico & Lagoa

During summer, live music fills the air at open-air restaurants around Lagoa Rodrigo de Freitas. Gávea has a few lively dining and drinking spots around Praça Santos Dumont, while Jardim Botânico has a sprinkling of eateries on Rua JJ Seabra and Rua Pacheco Leão.

DRI Cafe
CAFE $

(Map p60; ☑ 2226-8125; off Rua Jardim Botânico 414, Jardim Botânico; mains R$14-24; ☺ 9am-6pm) Inside the lush Parque Lage, this beautifully situated cafe serves tasty sandwiches, salads, quiches, pastas and desserts. On weekends it's a popular gathering spot for young families who come for the brunch (R$27 to R$32), which features fresh breads and jams, fruits, juices and the like.

Braseiro da Gávea
BRAZILIAN $$

(Map p60; ☑ 2239-7494; www.braseirodagavea. com.br; Praça Santos Dumont 116, Gávea; mains for 2 R$62-90; ☺ noon-1am Sun-Thu, to 3am Fri & Sat) This family-style eatery serves large portions of its popular *linguiça* (sausage) appetizers, *picanha* (rump steak) and *galetos* (grilled chicken). As the evening wanes, a younger crowd takes over, drinking late into the night.

Lagoon
BRAZILIAN $$

(Map p56; ☑ 2529-5300; www.lagoon.com.br; Av Borges de Medeiros 1424, Lagoa; mains R$30-60; ☺ noon-2am) This sparkling new eating and entertainment complex houses half a dozen restaurants as well as a cinema and a bar/ live music venue. The best tables are on the 2nd floor, and offer photogenic views over the lake. Italian, seafood, bistro fare and traditional Brazilian cooking are among the options – and no matter where you sit, you can order from any menu.

Arab Da Lagoa
MIDDLE EASTERN $$

(Map p60; ☑ 2540-0747; www.restaurantearab. com.br; Borges de Medeiros, Parque dos Patins; mains R$22-40; ☺ 9am-1:30am) This is one of the lake's most popular outdoor restaurants, serving traditional Middle Eastern specialties such as hummus, baba ghanoush, tabbouleh, kibbe and tasty thin-crust pizzas. You can hear live music from 9pm (cover charge is R$6) on weekdays, and 7pm on Saturdays and Sundays.

La Carioca Cevicheria
SEAFOOD $$

(☑ 2226-8821; Maria Angélica 113, Jardim Botânico; ceviches R$20-30; ☺ 6:30pm-1am) True to its name, this new Peruvian place specializes in ceviche, serving up over a dozen varieties of the tangy, tender seafood dish in small portions that are perfect for sharing. Have a seat on the inviting terrace in front and fortify yourself with fiery pisco or poetry (placemats bear a poem by Neruda).

Bráz
PIZZERIA $$$

(☑ 2535-0687; Maria Angélica 129; pizzas R$45-65; ☺ 6:30pm-12:30am) Perfect crusts and super-fresh ingredients are two of the components that make Bráz the best pizza place in town. This is no secret, so arrive early and plan on having a few quiet *chopes* on the front patio before scoring a table.

Guimas
BRAZILIAN $$$

(Map p60; ☑ 2259-7996; Rua José Roberto Macedo Soares 5, Gávea; mains R$42-60; ☺ noon-1am) An upscale *carioca boteco* with creative flair, Guimas has been going strong for over 30 years. Winning dishes include the *bacalhau à bras* (codfish mixed with potatoes, eggs and onions), shrimp risotto and the juicy *picanha no sal grosso* (grilled rumpsteak). There's outdoor seating in front.

Olympe
FUSION $$$

(☑ 2539-4542; Custódio Serrão 62, Lagoa; mains R$79-110; ☺ 7:30pm-midnight Mon-Sat, noon-4pm Fri) One of Rio's top chefs, Claude Troisgros mixes the old world with the new in dishes like duck with passion fruit, endive and foie gras or shrimp risotto with white truffle oil and mushroom foam. Set in a peaceful villa on a sleepy, tree-lined street.

Oro
BRAZILIAN $$$

(☑ 7864-9622; www.ororestaurante.com; Frei Leandro 20; three-/16-course dinner R$120/395; ☺ 7:30pm-midnight Mon-Sat) Felipe Bronze heads this acclaimed restaurant, which celebrates Brazilian produce and its cooking traditions while serving up some of the most imaginative plates in the city. The low-lit Zen-like interior contrasts with the culinary pyrotechnics on display in most dishes.

Utilizing the tools of molecular gastronomy (centrifuges, liquid nitrogen and other gadgetry), chefs whip up whimsical flavor-rich concoctions like compressed watermelon with sardine slices, pork belly with *jabuticaba* (an Amazonian fruit) and a shot of Jerez-infused vinaigrette, and elfin steak and pineapple sandwiches. If your holiday budget is particularly well-endowed, you can also order wine pairings with each course.

✖ Copacabana & Leme

Copacabana has everything from award-winning dining rooms to charming bistros from the 1950s. Although the open-air restaurants along Av Atlântica have nice views, the food isn't so hot, and things get a little seedy at night.

For fresh fruit, visit Copacabana *feiras* (produce markets), which happen on Wednesday on Rua Domingos Ferreira, Thursday on Rua Belford Roxo and Rua Ronald de Carvalho, and Sunday on Rua Décio Vilares. Supermarkets include **Pão de Açúcar** (Map p64; Av NS de Copacabana 497, Copacabana; ☺24hr) and the fruit-filled **Horti-Fruti** (Map p64; Av Prado Junior 277; ☺8am-8pm Mon-Sat, 8am-2pm Sun).

Cervantes   BRAZILIAN $
(Map p64; ☑2275-6147; Av Prado Júnior 335B, Copacabana; sandwiches R$13-21; ☺noon-4am Sun & Tue-Thu, to 6am Fri & Sat) A Copacabana institution, the late-night Cervantes gathers *cariocas* who come to feast on Cervantes' trademark meat and pineapple sandwiches. Around the corner, Cervantes' stand-up **boteco** (Map p64; Barato Ribeiro 7; ☺noon-4am Sun & Tue-Thu, to 6am Fri & Sat) serves up tasty bites in a hurry.

Boulangerie Guerin   BAKERY $
(Map p64; ☑2523-4140; Av NS de Copacabana 920, Copacabana; pastries R$8-10; ☺8am-9pm) Serving Rio's best croissants, *pains au chocolat* and eclairs, this classic French patisserie was an instant success upon opening in 2012. Prices for those delectable raspberry-covered tarts and creamy *mille-feuilles* are high, but so is the quality, and you can watch the bakers at work through the oversized windows adjoining the small bakery-cafe.

The Bakers   CAFE $$
(Map p64; ☑3209-1212; www.thebakers.com.br; Santa Clara 86, Copacabana; desserts R$7-10, lunch specials R$27-30; ☺9am-8pm) The Bakers is a fine spot for flaky croissants, banana Danishes, apple strudels and other treats. There are also salads, gourmet sandwiches (like prosciutto and mozzarella on ciabatta), quiches, and lunch specials.

Confeitaria Colombo   CAFE $$
(Map p64; ☑3201-4049; Forte de Copacabana, Praça Coronel Eugênio Franco, Copacabana; mains R$20-30; ☺10am-8pm Tue-Sun) Far removed from the hustle and bustle of Av Atlântica, this cafe has magnificent views of Copacabana beach. At the outdoor tables, you can sit beneath shady palm trees, enjoying cappuccino, pastas, salads or sandwiches as young soldiers file past. To get here, you'll have to pay admission (R$6) to the Forte de Copacabana (Copacabana fort).

Frontera   BUFFET $$
(Map p64; ☑3202-9050; Av NS de Copacabana 1144, Copacabana; per kg R$53-60; ☺11:30am-midnight) Frontera spreads an excellent lunch buffet. You'll find dozens of Brazilian dishes plus salads, individual counters for grilled meats, sushi, fried dishes and desserts. At night Frontera serves all-you-can-eat pizzas for R$22 to R$27 per person.

La Trattoria   ITALIAN $$
(Map p64; ☑2255-3319; Fernando Mendes 7A, Copacabana; mains R$28-55; ☺noon-midnight) Old photos, simple furnishings, hearty dishes and the constant din of conversation have made this trattoria a neighborhood favorite since 1976. Shrimp dishes are the Italian family's specialty – especially the *espaguete com camarão e óleo tartufado* (spaghetti with shrimp and truffle oil).

Santa Satisfação   BRAZILIAN $$
(Map p64; ☑2255-9349; www.santasatisfacao.com; Santa Clara 36C, Copacabana; mains R$20-42; ☺closed Sun) Oozing farmhouse charm, this always-packed bistro is worth forking over a bit extra for outstanding daily lunch specials of upscale Brazilian comfort food and sophisticated sandwiches.

Amir   MIDDLE EASTERN $$
(Map p64; ☑2275-5596; Ronald de Carvalho 55C, Copacabana; mains R$25-50; ☺noon-midnight Mon-Sat, noon-11pm Sun) Daytime crowds

come for the buffet (R$50 on weekdays, R$60 weekends), while at night the a la carte menu features platters of hummus, *kaftas* (spiced meat patty), falafel, kibbe and salads. There's a belly dancer Friday nights (at 9pm), while other nights you can smoke from a hookah if you snag a balcony seat.

Churrascaria Palace
CHURRASCARIA $$

(Map p64; 2541-5898; Rodolfo Dantas 16; all-you-can-eat R$70; noon-midnight) For the price, this is one of the best-value *churrascarias* in town. You'll find high-quality cuts of meat and attentive service at this elegantly set place. Waiters make frequent rounds with the goods; don't be shy about saying no otherwise you'll end up with more than you could possibly eat.

Le Blé Noir
FRENCH $$

(Map p64; 2267-6969; Xavier da Silveira 19A; crepes R$35-60; 7:30pm-midnight) Flickering candles and subdued conversation make this restaurant a real date-pleaser. Le Blé Noir offers over 50 different varieties of crepe, pairing rich ingredients like shrimp and artichoke hearts or Brie, honey and toasted almonds.

Capricciosa
PIZZERIA $$

(Map p64; 2255-2598; Domingos Ferreira 187, Copacabana; pizza from R$50; 6pm-2am) Like its better-known version in Ipanema, Capricciosa serves excellent thin-crust pizzas.

Azumi
JAPANESE $$$

(Map p64; 2541-4294; Ministro Viveiros de Castro 127, Copacabana; meals R$70-150; 7pm-midnight Tue-Thu & Sun, to 1am Fri & Sat) Some claim Azumi is the bastion of traditional Japanese cuisine in the city. This laid-back sushi bar certainly has its fans – both in the Nisei community and from abroad. Azumi's *sushiman* (sushi chef) masterfully prepares delectable sushi and sashimi, though tempuras and soups are also excellent.

Zot
CONTEMPORARY $$$

(Map p64; 3489-4363; Bolívar 21, Copacabana; mains around $40; 6pm-midnight Tue-Sat, from noon Sun) Set amid the bars of Baixo Copa, Zot is a sleek and stylish gastrobar featuring an inventive menu that showcases Brazilian ingredients and an excellent drink selection, including dozens of wines by the glass. On Tuesdays Zot hosts nights of live jazz (cover charge R$15).

Marius
BRAZILIAN $$$

(Map p64; 2104-9002; Av Atlântica 290; all-you-can-eat meat/seafood R$120/170; noon-midnight) Although the price is sky-high here, this spacious all-you-can-eat restaurant spreads a feast before a mostly tourist-filled dining room. You can opt either for grilled meats or a meat-and-seafood combination: with lobster, mussels, oysters, tuna, salmon, scallops and more brought to your table.

Siri Mole & Cia
BRAZILIAN $$$

(Map p64; 2267-0894; Rua Francisco Otaviano 50, Copacabana; mains R$75-140; 7pm-midnight Mon, noon-midnight Tue-Sun) Rated one of Rio's best Bahian restaurants, Siri Mole & Cia serves outstanding *vatapa*, *moqueca de camarão* (shrimp stew) and *ensopada de peixe* (fish and coconut milk stew). Stop in on Saturday (before 5pm) for the all-you-can-eat seafood buffet (R$75).

✕ Botafogo & Urca

Cobal do Humaitá
MARKET

(2266-1343; Voluntários da Pátria 446, Botafogo; 7am-4pm Mon-Sat) The city's largest farmers market also has cafes and restaurants on hand.

Meza Bar
TAPAS $$

(www.mezabar.com.br; Capitão Salomão 69, Botafogo; tapas R$10-25; 6pm-1am) Botafogo's see-and-be-seen hot spot serves up delectable, Brazilian-slanted tapas to a sophisticated and trendy crowd. Creative cocktails and delightful staff round out the fun here.

Emporium Pax
BRAZILIAN $$

(Map p68; 3171-9713; 7th fl, Praia de Botafogo 400, Botafogo; lunch buffet R$37-47; noon-midnight) One of many eateries at Botafogo Praia Shopping, Emporium Pax is a more polished affair than the adjoining food court and offers spectacular views of Pão de Açúcar and Baía de Guanabara. The big draw is the extensive lunch buffet, plus salads, sandwiches and quiches.

Garota da Urca
BRAZILIAN $$

(Map p68; 2541-8585; João Luís Alves 56, Urca; mains R$30-60; noon-1am Sun-Thu, to 2:30am Fri & Sat) Overlooking the small Praia da Urca, this neighborhood restaurant serves good-value weekday lunch specials, and you can enjoy views over the bay from the open-air veranda. By night, a more garrulous crowd converges for steak and *chope* (beer).

THE KIOSKS OF COPACABANA

The *quiosque* (kiosk) has long been a presence on the beachfront of Rio, doling out cold drinks and snacks to *cariocas* on the move, with plastic tables and chairs providing a fine vantage point for contemplating the watery horizon. In recent years Copacabana beach has seen a new crop of flashy kiosks replacing the old-fashioned wooden ones (angering traditionalists – not to mention a few disenfranchised kiosk owners). Now it's possible to get a decent meal (the kitchens are cleverly concealed underground), an ice-cold draft beer or gourmet snacks without leaving the sand.

The new kiosks are sprinkled all along the beach, with the most options between about Rua Siqueira Campos and the Copacabana Palace. Here are a few current favorites:

Três (Map p64; 4106-7185; www.tres-restaurant.com; Copacabana beach near Siqueira Campos; snacks R$3-19, sandwiches R$18-28) A top choice for foodies and Francophiles, Três whips up tasty crepes both savory (blue cheese and walnuts) and sweet (Nutella with strawberry and banana), as well as cheese and charcuterie plates, gourmet sandwiches, salads, milkshakes and appetizers (pan-fried shrimp with garlic).

Itaipava (Map p64; near Copacabana Palace; 9am-2am) A popular gathering spot, Itaipava serve up very cold *chope* and plenty of satisfying snacks – including cheese-covered *fritas* (fries).

Carioca Com Você (Map p64; near Praça Julio de Noronha; snacks R$12-20; 24hr) At the northeast end of Leme, elevated over the beach, this peacefully set kiosk serves small plates of sardines (six for R$12) as well as strong drinks. Nearby, you can watch fearless *carioca* kids diving off the seawall.

Miam Miam　CONTEMPORARY **$$**
(Map p68; 2244-0125; General Goés Monteiro 34, Botafogo; mains around R$50; 8pm-12:30am Tue-Sat) Exposed brick walls and a mishmash of retro furnishings set the scene for dining in style at Botafogo's culinary darling. Chef Roberta Ciasca serves up her own brand of comfort food, which means bruschetta with pesto and tapenade, codfish ragout and pumpkin curry with Morrocan couscous and other unique dishes. Don't miss the creative cocktail menu.

Oui Oui　FRENCH, BRAZILIAN **$$**
(2527-3539; Conde de Irajá 85, Humaitá; small plates R$32-36; noon-3pm Mon-Fri, 8pm-1am Tue-Sat) On a tranquil street in Humaitá, elegantly set Oui Oui serves innovative tapas plates designed for sharing – grilled trout with leeks and almonds, duck risotto, haddock croquettes and a zesty quinoa salad are a few recent hits. Several other good restaurants lie along the same street. Although evenings are best, Oui Oui also offers three-course lunch specials for R$33.

Zozô　BRAZILIAN **$$$**
(Map p68; 2542-9665; Ave Pasteur 520, Urca; lunch buffet R$55, mains around R$70; noon-4pm Tue-Sun & 8pm-midnight Tue-Sat) Next door to the cable-car station, Zozô serves a good lunch buffet that's popular with tourist groups. By night the elegant restaurant serves innovative cuisine (the head chef trained under Daniel Boloud in New York).

On weekends, Zozô transforms into a nightclub after dinner, attracting Rio's beautiful people. Come for dinner to ensure you can get in.

✖ Flamengo & Catete

On weekend nights, the restaurants and bars lining Rua Marquês de Abrantes crowd with neighborhood diners. In Catete, the streets near Largo do Machado have a few outdoor restaurants.

Tacacá do Norte　AMAZONIAN **$**
(Map p68; 2205-7545; Barão do Flamengo 35, Flamengo; Tacacá R$16; 9am-11pm Mon-Sat) *Tacacá*, a fragrant soup of manioc paste, lip-numbing *jambu* (a Brazilian vegetable) leaves, and fresh and dried shrimp isn't for everyone. But then again, neither is the Amazon. This simple lunch counter also offers savory bowls of *açai*, which is how folks in the Amazon eat it – and quite different from the sweet juice versions served everywhere else in Rio.

Armazem do Chopp BRAZILIAN $$
(Map p68; ☑ 2557-4052; Marquês de Abrantes 66, Flamengo; mains R$20-30; ⊗ noon-midnight) In a barnlike structure above the street, Armazem do Chopp is a neighborhood favorite for its tasty grilled dishes and traditional Brazilian fare. At night, its open-air front deck is a lively place for ice-cold drafts.

Estação República BUFFET $$
(Map p68; ☑ 2225-2650; Rua do Catete 104, Catete; per kg R$46; ⊗ 11am-midnight) Estação's buffet table is a neighborhood institution, featuring an extensive selection of salads, meats, pastas and vegetables. After 6pm the restaurant offers all-you-can-eat pastas, pizzas and crepes (R$20).

Lamas BRAZILIAN $$
(Map p68; ☑ 2556-0799; Rua Marquês de Abrantes 18A, Flamengo; mains R$20-40; ⊗ 8am-2:30am Sun-Thu, to 4am Fri & Sat) At this classic Brazilian restaurant (opened in 1874), you can't go wrong with grilled *lingüiça* (Brazilian sausage) or filet mignon with garlic. It's also a late-nate snack spot for filet mignon sandwiches.

Intihuasi PERUVIAN $$
(Map p68; ☑ 2225-7653; Barão do Flamengo 35D, Flamengo; mains R$30-57; ⊗ noon-3pm & 7-11pm Mon-Sat) Colorfully decorated with Andean tapestries and artwork, this Peruvian restaurant (a rarity in Rio) serves mouth-watering ceviches, *papas rellenas* (meat-filled potatoes), seafood soups and other Andean dishes.

Restaurante Kioto JAPANESE $$
(Map p68; ☑ 2225-5705; 3rd fl, Ministerio Tavares Lira 105, Flamengo; all-you-can-eat lunch/dinner R$40/50; ⊗ noon-midnight) Hidden on a street behind Largo do Machado, this simple, well-concealed restaurant (it's above a pool hall) has a decent sush buffet.

Porção Rio's BRAZILIAN, BARBECUE $$$
(Map p68; ☑ 3461-9020; Av Infante Dom Henrique, Flamengo; all-you-can-eat R$102; ⊗ noon-midnight) Set in the Parque do Flamengo with a stunning view of Pão de Açúcar, Porção Rio's is one of Rio's best *churrascarias*. Arrive early, both to score a good table and to see the view before sunset.

✗ Centro

Rio's busiest neighborhood has everything from greasy lunch counters to French bistros, not to mention ethnic and vegetarian fare, juice bars and *churrascarias*. Most restaurants open only for lunch on weekdays. Areas worth exploring include Travessa do Comércio just after work, when the restaurants and cafes fill with chatter. The cafes and restaurants around Praça Floriano are also popular gathering/quaffing spots.

Govinda VEGETARIAN $
(Map p74; ☑ 3549-9108; 2nd fl, Rodrigo Silva 6, Centro; lunch R$26; ⊗ 11:30am-3pm Mon-Fri) Amid artwork and decorations from India, the always welcoming Hare Krishnas whip up tasty vegetarian dishes made with care. It's tucked down a narrow lane just off Rua São José and is always packed, so arrive early to get a seat.

Bistrô do Paço CAFE $
(Map p74; ☑ 2262-3613; Praça XV (Quinze) de Novembro 48, Paço Imperial, Centro; mains R$14-30; ⊗ noon-7pm) On the ground floor of the Paço Imperial, this informal restaurant offers a tasty assortment of quiches, salads, soups and other light fare. Save room for the delicious pies and cakes.

Confeitaria Colombo CAFE $
(Map p74; ☑ 2505-1500; www.confeitariacolombo.com.br; Gonçalves Dias 34, Centro; pastries around R$7; ⊗ 9am-8pm Mon-Fri, to 5pm Sat) Stained-glass windows, brocaded mirrors and marble countertops create a lavish setting for coffee or a meal. Dating from the late 1800s, the Confeitaria Colombo serves desserts – including a good *pastel de nata* (custard tart) – befitting the elegant decor. Beyond the snack and dessert counters, the attached restaurant spreads an extensive buffet (R$70 per person).

Cedro do Líbano LEBANESE $$
(Map p74; ☑ 2224-0163; Senhor dos Passos 231, Centro; mains R$34-55; ⊗ 11am-5pm) Despite the gaudy interior – white tablecloths and plastic chairs and tables – this 70-plus-year-old institution serves first-rate kibbe, *kaftas* and lamb dishes.

The Line BRAZILIAN $$
(Map p74; ☑ 2224-6438; Travessa do Comércio 9; per kg R$36; ⊗ 11:30am-3:30pm Mon-Sat) In an atmospheric building on one of Centro's oldest streets, The Line spreads a good and reasonably priced lunch buffet. Stop in Saturday for all-you-can-eat *feijoada* (R$30 per person).

Café Arlequim CAFE $$
(Map p74; ☑ 2220-8471; Praça XV (Quinze) de Novembro 48, Paço Imperial, Centro; mains R$18-36;

⊗ 9am-8pm Mon-Fri, 10am-6pm Sat) In the middle of a book-and-music store, this small, pleasantly air-conditioned cafe is a fine spot to refuel, with Italian (Illy) coffee, sandwiches, salads, quiches, lasagna and desserts.

Brasserie Rosário
FRENCH $$

(Map p74; ☑ 2518-3033; Rua do Rosário 34, Centro; mains R$21-58; ⊗ 11am-9pm Mon-Fri, 11am-6pm Sat) Set in a handsomely restored 1860s building, this atmospheric bistro has a hint of Paris about it. The front counters are full of croissants, *pain au chocolat* and other baked items, while the restaurant menu features roast meats and fish, soups, baguette sandwiches and the like.

Ateliê Culinârio
BRAZILIAN $$

(Map p74; ☑ 2240-2573; Praça Floriano, Cinelândia; mains R$20-40; ⊗ noon-10pm Mon-Fri) Next to the Odeon cinema, this place serves up decent Brazilian fare on its open-air terrace. Ateliê opens onto the Praça Floriano, which is a lively gathering spot on weekday evenings. On weekends, it stays open during film screenings next door.

Bar Luiz
GERMAN $$

(Map p74; ☑ 2262-6900; Rua da Carioca 39, Centro; mains R$26-52; ⊗ 11am-10pm Mon-Sat) A festive air fills the old saloon (which opened in 1887) as diners get their fill of traditional German cooking (potato salad and smoked meats), along with ice-cold drafts – including dark beer.

Da Silva
PORTUGUESE $$

(Map p74; ☑ 2524-1010; 4th fl, Av Graça Aranha 187, Centro; all-you-can-eat R$50, after 2pm R$40; ⊗ noon-4pm Tue-Sat) Hidden inside the Clube Ginástico Português, this large, simply decorated restaurant spreads one of Rio's best lunch buffets. Portuguese in flavor, Da Silva has delicious salads, steaks and seafood, along with an enormous variety of addictive *bacalhau* (cod) dishes and many other dishes.

Cais do Oriente
CONTEMPORARY $$$

(Map p74; ☑ 2233-2531; www.caisdooriente.com. br; Visconde de Itaboraí 8, Centro; mains R$45-60; ⊗ noon-4pm Sun & Mon, to midnight Tue-Sat) Brick walls lined with tapestries stretch high to the ceiling in this almost-cinematic 1870s mansion. Set on a brick-lined street, hidden from the masses, Cais do Oriente blends elements of Brazilian and Mediterranean cooking, including a recommended cherne (grouper) with prawns, Brazil nuts and

roasted potatoes. There's a back courtyard and an upstairs concert space that hosts periodic concerts.

AlbaMar
SEAFOOD $$$

(Map p74; ☑ 2240-8378; Praça Marechal Âncora 186; mains R$60-80; ⊗ noon-5pm) AlbaMar has long been one of Rio's best seafood destinations. Top picks are fresh oysters, grilled seafood with vegetables and *moqueca* dishes. The old-fashioned green gazebo-like structure faces the Baía de Guanabara and Niterói.

✗ Santa Teresa & Lapa

Santa Teresa has superb views, while Lapa has an unrivaled music scene, and both are excellent places to discover a mix of new and old-fashioned eating and drinking haunts.

Cafecito
CAFE $

(Map p74; ☑ 2221-9439; www.cafecito.com.br; Paschoal Carlos Magno 121, Santa Teresa; sandwiches R$11-21; ⊗ 10am-10pm) A few steps above street level, this open-air cafe serves imported beers, desserts, cocktails (caipirinhas and mojitos), tapas plates and gourmet sandwiches (with ingredients such as smoked trout, artichoke hearts and prosciutto).

Nega Teresa
BRAZILIAN $

(Map p74; Monte Alegre; mains R$16-26; ⊗ noon-midnight Tue-Sun) This no-nonsense place serves up tasty and filling plates amid the banter of a mostly neighborhood crowd. The menu is as straightforward as the open-sided, thick-walled interior: salmon, *bife a cavalo* (steak with fried egg), fish filet or ribs and potatoes.

Santa Scenarium
BRAZILIAN $$

(Map p74; ☑ 3147-9007; www.santoscenarium. blogspot.com; Rua do Lavradio 36; mains R$20-36; ⊗ 11:30am-midnight Tue-Sat, to 5pm Mon) Angels, saints and other sacred images adorn the exposed brick walls of this atmospheric restaurant on Lapa's antique row. Grilled meats and other Brazilian staples are on offer at lunchtime, while at night *cariocas* gather for cold beer, appetizers and sandwiches. There's live music most nights.

Nova Capela
PORTUGUESE $$

(Map p74; ☑ 2552-6228; Av Mem de Sá 96, Lapa; mains for 2 R$60-90; ⊗ 11am-4am) This classic, old-time eating and drinking spot attracts a noisy mix of artists, musicians and party kids who fill the place till early into the morning. The *cabrito* (goat) dish is their most famous.

Bar do Mineiro BRAZILIAN $$
(Map p74; ☑ 2221-9227; Paschoal Carlos Magno 99, Santa Teresa; mains R$32-47; ☺noon-2am Tue-Sat, to midnight Sun) This much-loved old-school *boteco* serves traditional Brazilian cooking amid faded black-and-white photos and unfussy decor. The *feijoada* is tops (and a good value at R$33 for one), and served every day, along with appetizers, including *pasteis* (savory pastries). Strong caipirinhas will help get you in the mood.

★**Espírito Santa** AMAZONIAN $$$
(Map p74; ☑ 2507-4840; Almirante Alexandrino 264, Santa Teresa; mains R$42-60; ☺noon-midnight Wed-Mon) Espírito Santa is set in a beautifully restored mansion in Santa Teresa. Take a seat on the back terrace with its sweeping views or inside the charming, airy dining room, and feast on rich, expertly prepared meat and seafood dishes from the Amazon and the northeast.

Sobrenatural SEAFOOD $$$
(Map p74; ☑ 2224-1003; Almirante Alexandrino 432, Santa Teresa; mains for 2 around R$110; ☺noon-midnight Mon-Sat, noon-10pm Sun) The exposed brick and old hardwood ceiling set the stage for feasting on the *frutas do mar* (seafood). Lines gather on weekends for crabmeat appetizers, fresh grilled fish and flavorful platters of *moqueca*. During the week, stop by for tasty lunchtime specials. There's live music Monday, Wednesday, Friday and Saturday nights.

★**Aprazível** BRAZILIAN $$$
(Map p74; ☑ 2508-9174; Aprazível 62, Santa Teresa; mains around R$70; ☺7-11pm Tue-Sun) Hidden on a winding road high up in Santa Teresa, Aprazível offers beautiful views and a lush garden setting. Grilled fish and roasted dishes showcase the country's culinary highlights. Reserve ahead.

Térèze FUSION $$$
(Map p74; ☑ 3380-0220; Felicio dos Santos, Hotel Santa Teresa, Santa Teresa; mains R$70; ☺noon-3:30pm & 7:30-11pm) Inside Santa Teresa's finest hotel, Térèze serves inventive dishes (char-grilled octopus with couscous salad, black risotto with seafood, macadamia-crusted veal tenderloin) matched by superb views over the city. The design is green – ta-

---

TICKET MATTERS
....
When entering most samba clubs and live-music bars (plus self-serve restaurants), you'll be handed a ticket, which is used to track your consumption throughout the evening. When you're ready to move on, you'll pay a cashier for the goods (and possibly an admission fee). The cashier will then give you another ticket to pass onto the door attendant as you exit. It's all wonderfully Brezhnevian – but saves you the trouble of having to cough up every time you order a cocktail. Don't lose that ticket, as you may be charged R$100 or more. You'll see this system in many areas of Brazil.

---

bles and artwork are made from reclaimed lumber and recycled materials.

🍷 Drinking & Nightlife

Leblon and Ipanema offer flashy nightspots, as well as old-school watering holes. A youthful bar scene draws revelers to Gávea, while scenic Lagoa draws mostly couples. Centro's narrow pedestrian streets attract drinkers during weekday cocktail hours, while a mix of old and new clutters the streets of Lapa and Santa Teresa.

Flyers advertising dance parties can be found in music stores and clothing shops in Ipanema and Leblon, and in the surf shops in Galeria River shopping center, near Praia do Arpoador. Some clubs give a discount if you've got a flyer.

🍸 Ipanema & Leblon

Melt CLUB
(Map p56; ☑ 2249-9309; www.meltbar.com.br; Rita Ludolf 47; admission R$30-60; ☺10pm-4am Mon & Thu-Sat, 11pm-4am Tue & Wed) The Melt club gathers a young, attractive crowd in its candlelit main-floor lounge, sipping brightly colored elixirs. Upstairs, DJs break beats over the dance floor, with the occasional band making an appearance.

Bar Astor BAR
(Map p56; www.barastor.com.br; Veira Souto 110; ☺6pm-1am Mon-Fri, noon-3am Sat, noon-10pm Sun) Won't make it to São Paulo? No problem. One of Sampa's best bars has arrived in Rio in spectacular fashion. This gorgeous art

deco bar on prime Ipanema real estate does meticulously prepared caipirinhas, some 20 exotic flavors in all, and great food to help soak up the quality *cachaça* (cane liquor).

Barzin
BAR, LIVE MUSIC
(Map p56; Vinicius de Moraes 75; ⊙11am-3am Tue-Sun) Barzin is a popular spot for post-beach drinks, with an open-sided ground-floor bar that fills with animated chatter at all hours. Upstairs, you can catch a changing line-up of bands playing surf rock, hip hop and other popular Brazilian music (cover charge R$20 to $60).

Academia Da Cachaça
BAR
(Map p56; ☑2239-1542; Conde de Bernadotte 26G; ⊙noon-1am Sun-Thu, to 2am Fri & Sat) Along with traditional Brazilian cooking, this pleasant indoor-outdoor spot serves over 100 varieties of *cachaça*, and you can order it straight, with honey and lime, or disguised in a fruity caipirinha. For a treat, try the passion-fruit *batida* (*cachaça* and passion-fruit juice).

Delirium Cafe
BAR
(Map p56; ☑2502-0029; Barão da Torre 183; ⊙5pm-midnight Sun-Thu, to 2am Fri & Sat) This small cozy pub has more than 300 varieties of brew, with labels from across Europe, the US, Australia and beyond. If you've been to the original Delirium in Brussels, you might be a bit disappointed by its modest sister enterprise. Nevertheless, it's probably Rio's best destination for beer lovers.

Bar Veloso
BOTECO
(Map p56; ☑2274-9966; Aristides Espínola 44; ⊙11am-1am Sun-Wed, to 3am Thu-Sat) Named after the original bar (now occupied by Garota de Ipanema) where Jobim and de Moraes penned the famous song 'The Girl from Ipanema', the open-sided Bar Veloso attracts a young crowd who spill out onto the sidewalk on busy weekends.

Baretto-Londra
LOUNGE
(Map p56; ☑3202-4000; Av Vieira Souto 80; ⊙7pm-2am Mon-Thu, to 4am Fri & Sat) Cozy Baretto-Londra has an illuminated bar, leather armchairs and divans, and a DJ spinning world electronica. Drinks are pricey (cocktails around R$27), and unless you're a model (or have one draped over your arm), prepare for a long wait at the door.

Cobal do Leblon
BAR
(Map p56; ☑2239-1549; Rua Gilberto Cardoso; ⊙closed Mon) Leblon's flower-and-produce

market features a number of bars and restaurants, many of which open onto the large terrace in back. A vibrant, youthful air pervades this place, and it's a major meeting spot on weekends and on game days.

Devassa
BOTECO
(Map p56; ☑2522-0627; Prudente de Moraes 416; ⊙noon-2am) Serving some of Rio's best beer, Devassa makes its own creamy brews. The choices: *loura* (pilsner), *sarará* (wheat beer), *ruiva* (pale ale), *negra* (dark ale) and *Índia* (IPA). The food menu features well-prepared pub fare – burgers, steak, pastas, grilled fish and lots of appetizers.

Empório
BAR
(Map p56; ☑3813-2526; Maria Quitéria 37; ⊙8:30pm-late) A young mix of *cariocas* and gringos stirs things up over cheap cocktails at this battered old favorite in Ipanema. A porch in front overlooks the street – a fine spot to stake out when the air gets too heavy with bad '80s music. From Wednesday to Saturday you can catch live rock shows on the 2nd floor (entrance R$10 to R$20). Don't come early; Empório doesn't get lively until after midnight.

Jobi
BOTECO
(Map p56; ☑2274-0547; Av Ataúlfo de Paiva 1166; ⊙9am-5am) A favorite since 1956, Jobi has served a lot of beer in its day, and its popularity hasn't waned. The unadorned *botequim* (bar with table service) still serves plenty; grab a seat by the sidewalk and let the night unfold. If hunger beckons, try the tasty appetizers – the *carne seca* (jerked beef) and the *bolinhos de bacalhau* (codfish croquettes) are tops.

Shenanigan's
BAR
(Map p56; Visconde de Pirajá 112A; admission R$5 to R$25; ⊙6pm-2am) Overlooking the Praça General Osorio, Shenanigan's is an English-style pub with exposed brick walls, imported beers and a couple of tiny balconies perched above the street. Sunburnt gringos and the odd working girl mix it up over games of pool and darts to the occasional backdrop of live bands.

🍸 Gávea, Jardim Botânico & Lagoa

OO
LOUNGE, CLUB
(http://OOriodejaneiro.com.br/riodejaneiro.html; Av Padre Leonel Franca 240, Gávea; ⊙8pm-late)

Housed in Gávea's planetarium, 00 starts the evening as a stylish restaurant and transforms into a lounge and nightclub around midnight. Top-notch DJs spin at rotating parties here, and on Tuesday nights, Bem Brasil (p84) throws a bash for the hostel crowd – a good place to be if you want to mingle with other travelers.

Bar Lagoa   BOTECO
(Map p56; ☑ 2523-1135; Av Epitácio Pessoa 1674; ☻ 6pm-2am Mon-Fri, noon-2am Sat & Sun) With a view of the lake (but separated by a busy road), Bar Lagoa is one of the neighborhood's classic haunts. Founded in 1935, this open-air spot hasn't changed all that much since then: the bar still has surly waiters serving excellent beer to ever-crowded tables and, in spite of its years, a youthful air pervades.

Caroline Café   LOUNGE
(Map p60; ☑ 2540-0705; JJ Seabra 10, Jardim Botânico; ☻ 4pm-2am Mon-Sat) Caroline Café has long been a major draw for couples. There are a few outdoor tables, but inside is where you'll find most of the action, which here means a sizeable drink menu and an assortment of dishes (thick burgers, sushi and pizzas).

Bar do Horto   BAR
(Map p60; ☑ 3114-8439; Pacheco Leão 780, Jardim Botânico; ☻ noon-2am Sun & Tue-Thu, to 3am Fri & Sat) The decor is festive and kitsch: walls covered with shimmering fabric and an interior festooned with brightly hued paper lanterns, butterfly appliques, bottle-cap curtains and other recycled ephemera. On Thursdays to Saturdays, the sidewalk tables gather a festive crowd (largely couples).

Hipódromo   BAR
(Map p60; Praça Santos Dumont 108, Gávea; ☻ noon-1am) In an area known as Baixo Gávea, Hipódromo is one of several bars responsible for the local residents' chronic lack of sleep. Most nights, you'll find a college-age- and 20-something crowd celebrating here, with patrons spilling onto the facing Praça Santos Dumont.

Palaphita Kitch   LOUNGE
(Map p56; ☑ 2227-0837; www.palaphitakitch.com. br; Av Epitácio Pessoa s/n, Lagoa; ☻ 6pm-1am) A great spot for a sundowner, Palaphita Kitch is an open-air, thatched-roof wonderland with rustic bamboo furniture, flickering tiki torches and a peaceful setting on the edge of the lake. Come for the view and the creative (but pricey) cocktails.

♥ Copacabana & Leme

Copa's beach kiosks are also a fine destination for an afternoon or early-evening drink.

Fosfobox   CLUB
(Map p64; ☑ 2548-7498; www.fosfobox.com.br; Siqueira Campos 143, Copacabana; admission R$15-30; ☻ 11pm-4am Thu-Sat) This subterranean club is hidden under a shopping center near the metro station. DJs spin everything from funk to glam rock, and the crowd here is one of the more eclectic in the club scene.

Botequim Informal   BOTECO
(Map p64; ☑ 3816-0909; Domingos Ferreira 215, Copacabana; ☻ noon-1am) Botequim Informal is a lively drinking spot with an elevated open-sided deck, frothy drafts and tasty appetizers (including fried polenta with gorgonzola sauce). It lies amid half a dozen open-sided bars in a sub-neighborhood known as Baixo Copa.

Mud Bug   BAR
(Map p64; ☑ 2235-6847; www.mudbug.com.br; Rudolfo Dantas 16; ☻ 5pm-2am) Mud Bug is a warmly lit sports bar that has a rustic, all-wood interior where *cariocas* and foreigners mingle over football games, bar bites and a broad beer selection. There's also live music – typically classic rock on most weekends. A second Copacabana location is a few blocks west on Rua Paula Freitas.

Horse's Neck   BAR
(Map p64; ☑ 2525-1232; Av Atlântica 4240, Sofitel Rio de Janeiro, Copacabana; ☻ noon-2am) This bright and airy bar has potted palms, wood furnishings and ocean breezes that give it a tropical vibe. This is the place to come to nurse a Belgian beer, while taking in that magnificent stretch of coastline from one of the tables on the terrace.

Sindicato do Chopp   BAR
(Map p64; Av Atlântica 514, Leme) With a peaceful beachfront location, this casual bar is a relaxing and largely local spot to enjoy a draft or a filling meal.

Skylab   BAR
(Map p64; ☑ 2106-1666; 30th fl, Rio Othon Palace, Av Atlântica 3264, Copacabana; ☻ 7pm-midnight)

RIO DE JANEIRO CITY BOTAFOGO & URCA

GAY RIO

Rio has been a major destination for gay travelers since the 1950s. Back then the action was near the Copacabana Palace – and remnants of the past are still there (look for the rainbow-hued flag). Today, however, the party has mostly moved on, with the focal point of the GLBT (gay, lesbian, bisexual, transgender) scene, especially for visitors, in Ipanema. The gay beach sits at the end of Rua Farme de Amoedo (again, look for the rainbow flag), while bars and cafes of nearby streets – Rua Teixeira de Melo and Rua Farme de Amoeda – have a sprinkling of gay bars and cafes.

For more info on what's happening around town, check out www.riogayguide.com.

Cafeína (Map p56; ☑ 2521-2194; Farme de Amoedo 43, Ipanema; ⊗ 8am-11:30pm) A popular Ipanema cafe that attracts a mix of gays and straights.

Cine Ideal (Map p74; ☑ 2252-3460; www.cineideal.com.br; Rua da Carioca 62, Centro; ⊗ Fri & Sat) An old movie theater, and now an electronic music club, Ideal has an outdoor terrace with views of old Rio.

Fosfobox (Map p64; ☑ 2548-9478; basement, loja 22A, Siqueira Campos 143, Copacabana; ⊗ Tue-Sun) Small underground club that attracts a mixed crowd.

Galeria Café (Map p56; ☑ 2523-8250; www.galeriacafe.com.br; Teixeira de Mello 31, Ipanema; ⊗ Thu-Sat) This bar with a mixed crowd has lovely decor.

Le Boy (Map p64; ☑ 2513-4993; www.leboy.com.br; Raul Pompéia 102, Copacabana; cover R$10-30; ⊗ closed Mon) Open since 1992, Le Boy is Rio's gay temple. There are theme nights with drag shows and go-go boys.

Tô Nem Aí (Map p56; ☑ 2247-8403; cnr Farme de Amoedo & Visconde de Piraja, Ipanema; ⊗ noon-3am) On Ipanema's gayest street, this popular bar is a great after-beach spot.

The Week (Map p74; ☑ 2253-1020; www.theweek.com.br; Rua Sacadura Cabral 154, Centro) Rio's newest and currently best gay dance club has a spacious dance floor, excellent DJs and go-go dancers.

It's all about the view at this modestly decorated bar in the Rio Othon Palace. From 30 floors up, the coastline unfolds, allowing a glimpse of the Cidade Maravilhosa (Marvelous City) at its most striking.

🍷 Botafogo & Urca

Bar Bukowski CLUB
(Map p68; ☑ 2244-7303; Álvaro Ramos 270, Botafogo; admission R$35; ⊗ 10pm-6am Thu-Sat) Paying homage to the bohemian American writer, this club has a downstairs dance floor and bar, and an upstairs level for live bands playing rock, pop and blues. It's a great scene, and usually attracts a fun crowd. There's also a pool table, darts and you can have a go at one of the water pipes.

Casa da Matriz CLUB
(Map p68; ☑ 2266-1014; www.casadamatriz.com.br; Henrique de Novaes 107, Botafogo; admission R$15-30; ⊗ from 11pm, closed Tue & Sun) With numerous rooms to explore (lounge, screening room, dance floors), this old mansion embodies the creative side of the *carioca*

spirit. It usually attracts a student crowd. Check the website for party listings.

Cobal do Humaitá BAR
(Voluntários da Pátria 446, Humaitá; ⊗ 7am-2am Mon-Sat) A large food market on the western edge of Botafogo (technically in Humaitá), the Cobal transforms into a festive nightspot when the sun goes down, complete with live music and open-air eating and drinking.

Bar Urca BAR
(Map p68; ☑ 2295-8744; Cândido Gaffrée 205, Urca; ⊗ 9am-11pm Mon-Sat, to 8pm Sun) This simple neighborhood bar and restaurant has a marvelous setting near Urca's bayside waterfront. At night, young and old crowd along the seaside wall as waiters bring cold drinks and appetizers.

Champanharia Ovelha Negra BAR
(Map p68; ☑ 2226-1064; Bambina 120, Botafogo; ⊗ 5:30-11:30pm Mon-Fri) One of Rio's best happy-hour scenes, Ovelha Negra draws a local crowd who come for the lively conversation and 40 varieties of champagne and *prosecco* (Italian sparkling white wine).

Beerjack Hideout BAR

(📞 2226-0267; Martins Ferreira 71, Botafogo; ◉ 5pm-11pm Sun-Wed, to 2am Thu-Sat) Serious beer drinkers will want to toss their Skol cans aside and pay a visit to this fairly new addition to Botafogo, a classy but low-key bar set inside a converted two-story villa. You'll find over 200 varieties on hand, including some fine unique Brazilian microbrews (like the Diabólica Indian Pale Ale) as well as plenty of international choices.

O Plebeu BAR

(📞 2286-0699; Capitão Salomão 50, Botafogo; ◉ noon-4am Mon-Sat, to 9pm Sun) In the liveliest stretch of Botafogo, O Plebeu is a welcoming, open-sided two-story bar with tables spilling onto the sidewalk and a 2nd-floor balcony.

🍷 Flamengo & Catete

Belmonte BOTECO

(Map p68; 📞 2552-3349; Praia do Flamengo 300, Flamengo; ◉ 9am-3am) One of Flamengo's classic *botecos*, Belmonte serves up well-chilled *chope* until late into the night. When we went there Thursday was the liveliest night. Owing to its popularity, Belmonte branches are now found all over Rio.

Devassa BOTECO

(Map p68; 📞 2556-0618; Senador Vergueiro 2, Flamengo; ◉ noon-1am) A particularly inviting branch of the growing Devassa network, this bar is set on a shaded square, and serves the usual Devassa hits, including great drafts.

Herr Brauer BAR

(Map p68; 📞 2225-4359; Rua Barão do Flamengo 35; ◉ noon-midnight Tue-Sun, noon-4pm Mon) Dedicated to the great beers of the world, this cozy drinking den serves Brazilian microbrews and dozens of offerings from Belgium, Germany and beyond.

🍷 Centro & Cinelândia

Amarelinho BOTECO

(Map p74; 📞 2240-8434; Praça Floriano 55, Cinelândia; ◉ 11am-2am Mon-Sat, to midnight Sun) Easy to spot by its bright *amarelo* (yellow) awning, Amarelinho has a fine setting on the Praça Floriano, with the Teatro Municipal in the background. Its outdoor tables are popular lunch and after-work meeting spots.

Boteco Casual BAR

(Map p74; 📞 2232-0250; Travessa do Comércio 26, Centro; ◉ noon-midnight Mon-Fri, to 6pm Sat) Hidden in a narrow lane leading off Praça XV (Quinze) de Novembro, Boteco Casual is one of several photogenic open-air bars on Travessa do Comércio. The narrow pedestrian lane is a popular meeting spot and a festive air arrives at workday's end as *cariocas* fill the tables spilling onto the street.

🍷 Santa Teresa & Lapa

Barzinho NIGHTCLUB

(Map p74; 📞 2221-4709; Rua do Lavradio 170, Lapa; admission R$15-40; ◉ 6pm-2am Tue-Thu, to 4am Fri & Sat) New in 2012, Barzinho brings a touch more glamour to Lapa, courtesy of the celebrated DJ (and part owner) Rodrigo Penna who spins here one night a week and draws a dance-loving mostly Zona Sul crowd. Glittering chandeliers, colored wall-mounted light panels and artfully displayed kitsch (dolls, action figures, old-fashioned toys) lend a creative vibe, and you can head to a table on the upper level for a view over the long space.

Bar do Gomes BOTECO

(Map p74; 📞 2232-0822; Áurea 26, Santa Teresa; ◉ noon-midnight Mon-Sat, to 10pm Sun) Although the sign says 'Armazém do São Thiago,' everyone calls the place the Bar do Gomes. Regardless, this simple hole-in-the-wall has long been a favorite gathering spot, particularly on weekends, when young and old pack the few stand-up tables and bar front, spilling onto the sidewalk.

Bar dos Descasados LOUNGE

(Map p74; 📞 3380-0200; Almirante Alexandrino 660, Santa Teresa; ◉ noon-midnight) Inside Hotel Santa Teresa, this elegant bar with outdoor seating has lovely views. You can enjoy decadent cocktails (including a caipirinha made with tangerines grown on the property) and savory snacks (such as salmon tartare), while pondering the intriguing history that surrounds you (the building was once part of a coffee plantation and, later, a gathering spot for *descasados* – divorced men).

Boteco do Gomes BOTECO

(Map p74; 📞 2531-9717; Rua do Riachuelo 62, Lapa; ◉ 7am-1am) In Lapa, the Boteco do Gomes has the classical look of an old-time bar with brick walls, art-deco light fixtures, and tile floors. Patrons are a mix of musicians, students

Sounds of Rio

The city that gave the world Carnaval, samba and bossa nova offers dozens of ways to spend a sleepless night among the cariocas.

Samba

Samba, the great soundtrack of Rio, plays all across town, though if you're looking for its heart, you'll probably find it in the bohemian neighborhood of Lapa, where addictive rhythms spill out of old-fashioned dance halls, drawing music lovers from far and wide. Samba also takes center stage during Carnaval, with those percussive beats and singsong lyrics essential to the big fest. The top samba schools welcome visitors to their parties from September until Carnaval. These popular events are always a good time.

Bossa Nova & Jazz

Although bossa nova isn't much in fashion these days, there are still a few places where you can hear those rich, melancholic chords. Jazz also has its fans, and several venues around town have regular jazz nights.

Big Concerts

In addition to small bars and clubs, Rio has a few large concert halls that attract Brazilian stars such as Gilberto Gil and Milton Nascimento, as well as well-known international bands on world tours. During the warmer months, concerts are held periodically on the beaches of Copacabana and Ipanema, and the Marina da Glória is also a major venue.

1. Concert, Copacabana beach (p58) **2.** Drum players, Carnaval (p34), Rio de Janeiro **3.** Gilberto Gil

TOP LIVE MUSIC VENUES

➡ Samba: Democráticus (p108), Carioca da Gema (p108) and Rio Scenarium (p108)
➡ Bossa Nova: Vinicius Show Bar (p110)
➡ Jazz: TribOz, Maze Inn (p109)

and Lapa hangabouts, who gather for a quick drink at stand-up tables in front or at the roomier dining area in back.

Leviano Bar
BAR

(Map p74; ☑ 2507-5967; Av Mem de Sá 49; ⊘ 6pm-late) Near the entrance to Mem de Sá, the Leviano Bar is part of new crop of slightly more upscale drinking and dance spots. Watch the passing people parade – and take in the great view of the Arcos da Lapa – from outdoors in front before heading to the upstairs dancefloor where DJs mix house, electro-samba, soul and reggae.

Choperia Brazooka
BAR

(Map p74; ☑ 2224-3235; Av Mem de Sá 70, Lapa; ⊘ 6pm-2am Tue-Wed, 6pm-5am Thu-Sat) This popular four-story beer house has lots of nooks and crannies where you can while away the night over ice-cold drafts and tasty appetizers. The 20- and 30-something crowd packs this place, so arrive early to score a table.

Goya-Beira
BAR

(Map p74; ☑ 2232-5751; Largo das Neves 13, Santa Teresa; ⊘ 6pm-midnight Sun-Thu, to 2am Fri & Sat) Small but charming Goya-Beira is set on the peaceful Largo das Neves. Owner Rose Guerra prepares intriguing *cachaça* infusions as well as pizzas and appetizers. It's fairly sedate even on weekends.

Mike's Haus
BAR

(Map p68; ☑ 2509-5248; Almirante Alexandrino 1458A, Santa Teresa; ⊘ noon-midnight Sun-Thu, to 2am Fri & Sat) This German-style pub attracts a mix of expats and *cariocas* on weekend nights. It's a bit off the beaten path, so plan on staying for a while once you get there. Meals are served as well.

🍴 Barra da Tijuca

Nuth
CLUB

(☑ 3575-6850; www.nuth.com.br; admission men R$40-70, women R$20-30; ⊘ 9pm-4am) This club (pronounced 'Nooch') is one of the city's favorite dance spots, despite its location in Barra. Expect a friendly, well-dressed crowd grooving to electro-samba, house and hip-hop. If you don't like the venue, or the price tag, there are other bars nearby.

☆ Entertainment

Music & Dancing

Rio's music scene features talented performers playing in atmospheric settings to a democratic crowd. Lapa is the heart of samba, and its old clubs are a must-see for visitors. The widest assortment of music venues is along Av Mem de Sá.

Gafieiras (dance halls) are a big attraction in Lapa. Here you'll find restored colonial buildings hiding dance floors and large samba bands – along with their many admirers.

Lapa

Rio Scenarium
SAMBA

(Map p74; www.rioscenarium.com.br; Rua do Lavradio 20, Lapa; cover R$20-40; ⊘ Tue-Sat 7pm-4am) One of the city's most photogenic nightspots, Rio Scenarium has three floors, each lavishly decorated with antiques. Balconies overlook the stage on the 1st floor, with dancers keeping time to the samba that fills the air.

Carioca da Gema
SAMBA

(Map p74; www.barcariocadagema.com.br; Av Mem de Sá 79, Lapa; cover R$21-25; ⊘ 7pm-1:30am Mon-Thu, 9pm-3:30am Fri-Sun) Although it's now surrounded by clubs, Carioca da Gema was one of Lapa's pioneers when it opened in 2000. This small, warmly lit club still attracts some of the city's best samba bands, and you'll find a festive, mixed crowd filling the dance floor most nights. Catch free live music here from Monday to Friday around 8pm.

Democráticus
SAMBA

(Map p74; ☑ 2252-4611; Rua do Riachuelo 93, Lapa; admission R$25-50; ⊘ 10pm-3am Wed-Sat) Murals line the foyer of this 1867 mansion. The rhythms filter down from above. Follow the sound up the marble staircase and out into a large hall filled with tables, an enormous dance floor and a long stage covered with musicians. A wide mix of *cariocas* gathers here to dance, revel in the music and soak up the splendor of the samba-infused setting.

Lapa 40 Graus
LIVE MUSIC

(Map p74; ☑ 3970-1338; Riachuelo 97, Lapa; admission R$5-30; ⊘ 6pm-5am Tue-Sat) This impressive multistory music venue and pool hall has tables for lounging on the 1st floor, over a dozen pool tables on the 2nd floor, and a small stage and dancing couples on the top floor. Pop, rock, samba and *choro* kick off nightly around 7pm and 11pm.

Beco do Rato
LIVE MUSIC

(Map p74; ☑ 2508-5600; http://becodorato.com.br; Joaquim Silva 11, Lapa; ⊘ 8pm-3am Tue-Fri) **FREE** This tiny hole-in-the-wall bar hosts live groups playing to a samba-loving crowd.

The outdoor seating and informal setting are an unbeatable mix.

TribOz
JAZZ

(Map p74; ✆ 2210-0366; www.triboz-rio.com; Conde de Lages 19, Lapa; cover R$20-30; ⏰ 6-8pm & 9pm-1am Thu-Sat) Not for lazy ears, this avant-garde jazz house, a little hidden gem among the sonic cognoscenti, is unique in Rio for its serious approach to performances. Run by an Australian ethnomusicologist, it sits in a shadier part of old Lapa in a signless mansion, which transforms into a beautiful showcase space for Brazil's most cutting-edge artists.

It skews 30-plus and/or music aficionado, who come for the evening's three 45-minute sets and good-value Oz-inspired grub. Reservations are essential two days in advance by phone only.

Circo Voador
CONCERT VENUE

(Map p74; ✆ 2533-0354; www.circovoador.com.br; Rua dos Arcos, Lapa; admission R$50-80) Behind the Arcos da Lapa, Circo Voador hosts bigname Brazilian and international artists. The acoustics here are excellent, and after a show you'll find plenty of other musical options in the area. Check the website to see what's on.

Fundição Progresso
CONCERT VENUE

(Map p74; ✆ 2220-5070; www.fundicao.org; Rua dos Arcos 24, Lapa; admission R$25-40) This former foundry in Lapa, stages big-name acts like Manu Chao and Caetano Veloso, as well as theater, video arts and ballet. You can also study dance, *capoeira* and circus arts here.

Semente
SAMBA

(Map p74; ✆ 9781-2451; Joaquim Silva 138, Lapa; admission R$20-30; ⏰ 8pm-2am Sat-Thu) One of the few venues in Lapa that holds court on Sunday and Monday nights, Semente is small and intimate, with good bands and a crowd that comes for the music rather than the Lapa mayhem (note that it's closed Friday night).

Centro Cultural Carioca
SAMBA

(Map p74; ✆ 2252-6468; www.centroculturalcarioca.com.br; Rua do Teatro 37, Centro; admission R$30-40; ⏰ 7pm-1am Mon-Thu, 8:30pm-2am Fri & Sat) This carefully restored 19th-century building hosts an excellent musical line-up throughout the week. The scene here is slightly more sedate, which makes it a good choice for couples.

Other Locations

Studio RJ
LIVE MUSIC

(Map p56; ✆ 2523-1204; http://studiorj.org; Vieira Souto 110, Ipanema; admission R$20-60; ⏰ from 9pm Mon-Sat) Above Bar Astor, Studio RJ has given a much-needed jolt to Ipanema's dormant music scene. The spacious, acoustically fit music hall sees an eclectic line-up throughout the week, from old-school jazz nights (currently on Tuesdays) to innovative samba, Musica Popular Brasileira, hip hop and indie rock. Shows kick off around 9:30pm on weekdays and midnight on weekends, with DJs keeping the party going afterwards till the early hours.

Casa Rosa
LIVE MUSIC, CLUB

(Map p68; ✆ 2557-2562; www.casarosa.com.br; Alice 550, Laranjeiras; cover R$25-40; ⏰ 11pm-5am Fri & Sat, 5pm-1am Sun) Inside a former brothel, Casa Rosa hosts great parties. It has an eclectic musical line-up and a large outdoor patio for cooling off from the dance floor. Saturday is the best night to go, though Casa Rosa's Sunday *feijoada* and samba party is also a good time.

Bip Bip
LIVE MUSIC

(Map p64; ✆ 2267-9696; Almirante Gonçalves 50, Copacabana; ⏰ 6pm-midnight Sun-Fri) **FREE** Although it's just a hole-in-the-wall bar with a few scattered tables, Bip Bip has long been a musician's favorite. It hosts live samba on Thursday, Friday and Sunday, *choro* on Monday and Tuesday, and bossa nova on Wednesday. Music kicks off around 8pm.

Maze Inn
LIVE MUSIC

(Map p68; ✆ 2558-5547; www.jazzrio.info; Casa 66, Tavares Bastos 414, Catete; admission before/after 10pm R$30/40; ⏰ 10pm-3am, 1st Fri of month) Also known as the 'Casa do Bob' after owner Bob Nadkarni, this twice-a-month event is well worth attending if you're in town. It's set in the guesthouse of the same name high up in Tavares Bastos (one of Rio's safest favelas) and features live jazz and fantastic views.

Severyna de Laranjeiras
LIVE MUSIC

(Map p68; ✆ 2556-9398; www.severyna.com.br; Ipiranga 54, Laranjeiras; admission R$15; ⏰ 11:30am-1am) At this bar and restaurant (serving Northeastern fare), large percussive groups perform *samba,* MPB and *forró,* among other styles. Shows begin either at 7pm or 9pm.

Vinícius Show Bar
LIVE MUSIC

(Map p56; ☑2523-4757; www.viniciusbar.com.br; 2nd fl, Prudente de Morais 34, Ipanema; admission R$30-40) Billing itself as the 'temple of bossa nova,' Vinícius Show Bar has been an icon in the neighborhood since 1989. The intimate space makes a fine setting to listen to first-rate bossa nova (and occasional MPB and samba). Shows start between 9.30pm and 11pm.

Trapiche Gamboa
SAMBA

(Map p74; ☑2516-0868; Sacadura Cabral 155, Gamboa; admission R$15-20; ⊙7pm-midnight Tue & Wed, to 4am Thu-Sat) Trapiche Gamboa is set in a multistory colonial edifice in Gamboa (just north of Centro) and has a friendly mixed crowd and decent appetizers. It's a casual affair, with samba musicians gathering around a table on the ground floor, and dancers spilling out in front of them. It's best reached by taxi (R$40 or so from the Zona Sul).

Miranda
LIVE MUSIC

(Map p56; ☑2239-0305; mirandabrasil.com.br; Av Borges de Medeiros 1424, Lagoa; admission from R$40) New in 2012, Miranda is a classy but inviting bar and live-music venue that hosts a range of shows and events, including *feijoada* and live samba on Sundays (R$60), MPB groups and well-known Brazilian artists like Mart'nalia and BossaCucaNova (a group that blends bossa nova with electronica). It's located inside the Lagoon complex in Lagoa.

Classical Music, Theater & Dance

Classical music lovers should try to attend a concert held during the four-month-long **Música No Museu** (Music in the Museum; www.musicanomuseu.com.br). Held from January to April each year, this event features dozens of concerts (all free) held at museums and cultural spaces around the city.

The city's most lavish setting for a performance is the beaux-arts **Theatro Municipal** (Map p74; ☑2332-9195; www.theatromunicipal.rj.gov.br; Manuel de Carvalho). You'll find a more exciting repertoire of modern dance, theater and performance art at the excellent **Espaço Sesc** (Map p64; ☑2547-0156; www.sescrj.org.br; Domingos Ferreira 160, Copacabana). In Lapa the **Sala Cecília Meireles** (Map p74; ☑2332-9223; www.salaceciliameireles.com.br; Largo da Lapa 47, Lapa) is a splendid early-20th-century gem hosting orchestral concerts throughout the year.

Cinemas

Rio remains remarkably open to foreign and independent films, documentaries and avant-garde cinema. For listings and show times pick up *O Globo, Jornal do Brasil* newspapers or *Veja Rio* magazine. Ticket prices run R$20 to R$32. In addition to these cinemas, the major shopping centers also have cinemas.

Cine Santa Teresa
CINEMA

(Map p74; ☑2222-0203; www.cinesanta.com.br; Paschoal Carlos Magno 136, Santa Teresa) This small, single-screen theater is well located on Largo do Guimarães.

Estação Rio
CINEMA

(Map p68; ☑2226-9952; Voluntários da Pátria 35, Botafogo) This two-screen cinema in Botafogo has a cafe and bookstore inside.

Estação Botafogo
CINEMA

(Map p68; ☑2226-1988; Voluntários da Pátria 88, Botafogo) This small three-screen theater shows a mix of Brazilian and foreign films.

Estação Ipanema
CINEMA

(Map p56; ☑2279-4603; Visconde de Pirajá 605, Ipanema) A single-screen theater located in a small shopping complex in Ipanema.

Odeon Petrobras
CINEMA

(Map p74; ☑2240-1093; Praça Floriano 7, Cinelândia) Rio de Janeiro's 1920s landmark cinema shows a wide range of fare and sometimes hosts the gala for prominent film festivals.

Roxy
CINEMA

(Map p64; ☑2461-2461; Av NS de Copacabana 945, Copacabana) Copacabana's only cinema is a handy retreat for when the weather turns sour.

Spectator Sports

Rio's other football stadiums are Estádio Olímpico João Havelange and Estádio de São Januário.

Maracanã Football Stadium
STADIUM

(Map p80; ☑8871-3950; www.suderj.rj.gov.br/maracana.asp; Av Maracanã, São Cristóvão; admission R$15-100; ⊙9am-7pm; Ⓢ Maracanã) Following a R$900 million upgrade in preparation for the 2014 World Cup, Rio's famed stadium hosts spectacular matches. Don't miss the chance to see one of Rio's hometown teams (Flamengo, Fluminense, Vasco da Gama or Botafogo) take the field.

Games take place year-round and generally happen on Saturday or Sunday (starting at 4pm or 6pm) or on Wednesday and Thursday (around 8:30pm). You can always

SAMBA SCHOOLS

Starting around September, in preparation for Carnaval, most big samba schools open their rehearsals to the public. These are large dance parties, and provide a good chance to mingle with *cariocas*. Schools typically charge R$10 to R$30 at the door (prices are higher the closer you are to Carnaval).

Many samba schools are in the favelas, so use common sense when going.

You can visit the samba schools on a tour or you can go independently: you can catch a taxi there, and there are always cabs outside the schools waiting to take people home. It's a good idea to confirm that the rehearsals are on before heading out. The most popular schools for tourists are Mangueira and Salgueiro.

Beija-Flor (☑2233-5889; www.beija-flor.com.br; Praçinha Wallace Paes Leme 1025, Nilópolis; ⊙9pm Thu)

Grande Rio (☑2671-3585; www.academicosdogranderio.com.br; Wallace Soares 5-6, Duque de Caixas; ⊙9pm Tue)

Imperatriz Leopoldinense (☑2560-8037; www.imperatrizleopoldinense.com.br; Professor Lacê 235, Ramos; ⊙8pm Sun)

Mangueira (☑2567-4637; www.mangueira.com.br; Visconde de Niterói 1072, Mangueira; ⊙10pm Sat)

Mocidade Independente de Padre Miguel (☑3332-5823; www.mocidadeindependente.com.br; Av Brasil 31146, Padre Miguel; ⊙10pm Sat)

Portela (☑2489-6440; Clara Nunes 81, Madureira; ⊙9pm Fri)

Rocinha (☑3205-3318; www.academicosdarocinha.com.br; Bertha Lutz 80, São Conrado; ⊙10pm Sat)

Salgueiro (☑2238-0389; www.salgueiro.com.br; Silva Teles 104, Andaraí; ⊙10pm Sat)

Unidos da Tijuca (Map p80; ☑7590-1290; www.unidosdatijuca.com.br; Francisco Bicalho 47, Santo Cristo; ⊙10pm Sat)

Vila Isabel (☑2578-0077; www.gresunidosdevilaisabel.com.br; Av Blvd 28 de Setembro 382, Vila Isabel; ⊙10pm Sat)

buy tickets at the event. The ticket price is R$30 to R$60 for most games.

If you prefer to go in a group – which is, of course, more fun – a number of English-speaking tour operators organize game-day outings, including round-trip transportation. Leading big-group tours are **Brazil Expedition** (☑9998-2907; www.brazilexpedition.com) and Be A Local (p85). For something more small-scale, independent guide **Sergio Manhães** (☑9210-0119; futebolnomaracana.blogspot.com; per person R$110-120) takes up to four guests with him on game day.

Joquei Clube HORSE RACING
(Map p60; ☑3534-9000; www.jcb.com.br; Jardim Botânico 1003, Gávea; ⊙2-8pm Sat & Sun) One of the country's loveliest racetracks, with a great view of the mountains and Corcovado, the Joquei Clube (Jockey Club) hosts races on weekends and ocasionally on Mondays and Fridays. The big event is

the Brazilian Grand Prix (the first Sunday in August).

 Shopping

Rio has much in the way of shopping, from colorful markets to eye-catching Zona Sul boutiques. Some of the major strips in the city that make for window shopping include:

Av Ataúlfo de Paiva in Leblon, has boutiques sprinkled among cafes, bookshops and restaurants.

Rua Visconde de Pirajá is Ipanema's bustling shopping strip and **Rua do Lavradio** in Lapa contains a long row of antique stores.

Ipanema & Leblon

Toca do Vinícius MUSIC
(Map p56; ☑2247-5227; www.tocadovinicius. com.br; Vinícius de Moraes 129; ⊙10am-7pm

Mon-Fri, 10am-6pm Sat & Sun) Bossa nova fans shouldn't miss this store. In addition to its ample CD selection of contemporary and old performers, Toca do Vinícius sells music scores and composition books. Upstairs a tiny museum displays memorabilia of the great songwriter and poet Vinícius de Moraes.

Forum
CLOTHING
(Map p56; ✆ 2521-7415; www.forum.com.br; Barão da Torre 422; ⏰ 10am-6pm Mon-Fri, 10am-2pm Sat) Brazilian designer Tufi Duek reigns over this curiously designed flagship store. Here you'll find beautifully made pieces from his men's and women's collections.

Osklen
CLOTHING
(Map p56; ✆ 2227-2911; Maria Quitéria 85; ⏰ 9am-8pm Mon-Fri, 10am-7pm Sat, 11am-5pm Sun) One of Brazil's best-known fashion labels outside the country, Osklen is known for its stylish and well-made beachwear (particularly men's swim shorts and graphic T-shirts), sneakers and outerwear.

Gilson Martins
ACCESSORIES
(Map p56; ✆ 2227-6178; Visconde de Pirajá 462; ⏰ 9am-8pm Mon-Sat) Designer Gilson Martins transforms the Brazilian flag and silhouettes of Pão de Açúcar and Corcovado into eye-catching accessories in his flagship store in Ipanema. In addition to glossy handbags, wallets, passport covers, key chains and other iPad covers, the shop has a gallery in the back with ongoing exhibitions.

Maria Oiticica
JEWELRY
(Map p56; ✆ 3875-8025; Shopping Leblon, Av Afranio de Mello Franco 290, Leblon; ⏰ 10am-10pm Mon-Sat, 3-9pm Sun) Using native materials found in the Amazon, Maria Oiticica has created lovely handcrafted jewelry inspired by indigenous art. Seeds, plant fibers and tree bark are just some of the components of her bracelets, necklaces, earrings and sandals (there are even some striking handbags made from fish 'leather'), and her work helps support struggling local communities with craft-making traditions.

Isabela Capeto
CLOTHING
(Map p56; ✆ 2523-0052; Garcia d'Ávila 173; ⏰ 10am-8pm Mon-Fri, 10am-3pm Sat) One of Brazil's fashion stars, Isabela Capeto creates beautifully made clothing with seductive lines. Her Ipanema shop is a good place to see dresses and skirts that have earned her accolades from O Globo, Vogue and other publications.

Livraria da Travessa
BOOKS, MUSIC
(✆ 3205-9002; Visconde de Pirajá 572; ⏰ 9am-midnight Mon-Sat, 11am-midnight Sun) One of several branches around town, Livraria da Travessa has a small selection of foreign-language books and periodicals, with CDs upstairs. The buzzing 2nd-floor cafe (a branch of Bazzar) serves salads, sandwiches, quiches and desserts. There's an even larger Livraria da Travessa inside Shopping Leblon.

Havaianas
SHOES
(Map p64; ✆ 2267-2418; Xavier da Silveira 19, Copacabana; ⏰ 9am-8pm Mon-Fri, 10am-6pm Sat & Sun) The ubiquitous Brazilian rubber sandal comes in all different styles – sporting the flags of Brazil, Argentina, Portugal, England and Spain – plus snazzy designs for the ladies, and even logo-bearing bags, key chains and beach towels.

Aquim
CHOCOLATE
(Map p56; ✆ 2523-5090; Garcia D'Ávila 149; ⏰ 11am-7pm Mon-Sat) ✏ Stop by this jewel-box-sized store for rich truffles, macarons, chocolate cakes and mini tarts that look nearly too lovely to eat. Baristas whip up an excellent cappuccino, which you can enjoy at one of the two cafe tables out front.

Cavist
WINE
(Map p56; ✆ 2123-7900; Rua Barão da Torre 358; ⏰ 9:30am-midnight Mon-Sat) One of Rio's best-stocked wine shops, with a high-end attached restaurant, where you can try out any of the bottles in the shop.

Shopping Leblon
SHOPPING CENTER
(Map p56; ✆ 2430-5122; www.shoppingleblon. com.br; Av Afrânio de Melo Franco 290; ⏰ 10am-10pm Mon-Sat, 3-9pm Sun) There are plenty of tempting stores here that will drain your holiday funds, as well as good restaurants, a cinema and a well-placed Starbucks, complete with a live piano player in the evenings.

🛍 Gávea, Jardim Botânico & Lagoa

Dona Coisa
FASHION
(Map p60; ✆ 2249-2336; www.donacoisa.com. br; Lopes Quintas 153, Jardim Botânico; ⏰ 11am-8pm Mon-Fri, 10am-6pm Sat) One of Rio's top boutiques, Dona Coisa sells top labels by Brazilian and international designers, including one-of-a-kind pieces you won't find elsewhere (like snakeskin Converse by

Missoni). The multiroom design house also has original objects for the home – delicate ceramics by Heloisa Galvão, engraved wineglasses – in addition to skin and beauty products by Phebo and Granado.

🔒 Copacabana & Leme

Loja Fla CLOTHING, ACCESSORIES
(Map p64; ☑ 2541-4109; Av NS de Copacabana 219, Copacabana; ⊙10am-6pm Mon-Fri, to 4pm Sat) With more than 30 million fans worldwide, Flamengo is one of the most-watched football (soccer) teams in Brazil. This shop sells all the Flamengo goods, including jerseys, logo-emblazoned socks and soccer balls, posters and other memorabilia.

Bossa Nova & Companhia MUSIC
(Map p64; ☑ 2295-8096; Duvivier 37A, Copacabana; ⊙9am-7pm Mon Fri, 9am 5pm Sat) Here you'll find a decent assortment of bossa, *choro* and samba CDs and LPs, as well as musical instruments, coffee-table books, sheet music and biographies of top Brazilian composers.

Galeria River SHOPPING CENTER
(Map p64; Francisco Otaviano 67, Arpoador; ⊙10am-6pm Mon-Sat) Surf shops, skateboard and rollerblade outlets, and shops selling beachwear and fashions for young nubile things fill this shopping gallery in Arpoador. Shorts, bikinis, swim trunks, party attire and gear for outdoor adventure are in abundance. The shops here – like BoardsCo – are a good place to inquire about board rentals.

🔒 Botafogo & Urca

Botafogo Praia Shopping SHOPPING CENTER
(Map p68; ☑ 3171-9872; Praia de Botafogo 400, Botafogo; ⊙10am-10pm Mon-Sat, 2-9pm Sun) Botafogo's large shopping center has dozens of stores, featuring Brazilian and international brands. The 3rd floor is the best for top designers: check stores such as Philippe Martins, Gilson Martins, Osklen and Equatore. The mall also has a cinema and several top-floor restaurants with panoramic views.

🔒 Flamengo & Around

Pé de Boi HANDICRAFTS
(Map p68; ☑ 2285-4395; Ipiranga 55, Laranjeiras; ⊙10am-7pm Mon-Fri, 9am-1pm Sat) Although everything is for sale here, Pé de Boi feels more like an art gallery than a handicrafts shop, owing to the high quality of the wood and ceramic works, and the tapestries, sculptures and weavings.

🔒 Centro

Nova Livraria Leonardo da Vinci BOOKS
(Map p74; www.leonardodavinci.com.br; Rio Branco 185, Edifício Marquês de Herval, Centro; ⊙9am-7pm Mon-Fri, to 1pm Sat) Boasting one of Rio's best foreign-language book collections, da Vinci also has a wide range of art and photography books, as well as coffee-table books covering Rio's history and architecture. It's one floor down; follow the spiral ramp.

Arlequim BOOKS, MUSIC
(Map p74; ☑ 2220-8471; Praça XV (Quinze) de Novembro 48, Paço Imperial, Centro; ⊙9am-8pm Mon-Fri, 10am-6pm Sat) Bossa nova plays overhead at this charming cafe, bookstore and music shop. The menu features salads, sandwiches and, uh, chop suey.

Granado BEAUTY
(Map p74; ☑ 3231-6747; Primeiro de Março 14, Centro; ⊙8am-8pm Mon-Fri, 8am-2pm Sat) A classic-looking apothecary with a name that's been around since 1870, Granado incorporates Brazilian ingredients in its all-natural moisturizers, shampoos, soaps, scented candles and shaving products.

🔒 Santa Teresa & Lapa

La Vereda Handicrafts HANDICRAFTS
(Map p74; ☑ 2507-0317; Almirante Alexandrino 428, Santa Teresa; ⊙10am-8pm) Near Largo do Guimarães, La Vareda stocks a colorful selection of handicrafts from local artists and artisans. Handpainted clay figurines by Pernambuco artists, heavy Minas ceramics, delicate sterling silver jewelry and loosely woven tapestries cover the interior of the old store.

Plano B MUSIC
(Map p74; ☑ 2509-3266; www.planob.net; Francisco Muratori 2A, Lapa; ⊙noon-8pm Mon-Fri, to 6pm Sat) Only in Lapa will you encounter a place where you can pick through bins of old jazz records and new electronic mixes before stepping into the back room to get a tattoo, inspired perhaps by that old Elza Soares song playing overhead.

FOOD MARKETS

The *feiras* (produce markets) that pop up in different locations throughout the week are the best places to shop for *jabuticaba* (grape-like fruit), *acerola* (a type of cherry) and other fruits you won't find at home – not to mention delectable mangoes, papayas, passion fruit and more.

Cobal do Humaitá (p97) Flowers, veggies and fruits; there are also restaurants on hand for those looking for a bit more.

Cobal do Leblon (Map p56) Smaller than Humaitá's market, it doubles as an open-air eating-drinking spot in the evening.

Ipanema Monday on Rua Henrique Dumont, Tuesday on Praça General Osório and Friday on Praça NS da Paz.

Leblon Thursday on Rua General Urquiza.

Gávea Fridays on Praça Santos Dumont.

Jardim Botânico Saturday market on Rua Frei Leandro.

Copacabana Wednesday on Praça Edmundo Bittencourt, Thursday on Rua Ministro Viveiro de Castro and Rua Ronald de Carvalho, and Sunday on Praça Serzedelo Correia.

Leme Monday market on Gustavo Sampaio.

Urca Sunday on Praça Tenente Gil Guilherme.

Santa Teresa Friday on Rua Felicio dos Santos.

🏠 Barra da Tijuca

The Village
MALL

(☑ 3252-2999; www.shoppingvillage.com.br; Av das Américas 3900, Barra da Tijuca; ⊙ 11am-11pm Mon-Sat, 1pm-9pm Sun) New in 2012, this is Rio's most extravagant mall, with high-end retailers like Prada and Louis Vuitton.

Barra Shopping
MALL

(☑ 4003-4131; Av das Américas 4666, Barra da Tijuca; ⊙ 10am-10pm Mon-Sat, 1-9pm Sun) Rio's largest mall is an easy place to shop away a few hours or days as do 30 million shoppers each year. More than 500 stores clutter this 4km-long stretch, plus five movie screens, a kids' parkland and a wealth of dining options.

🏠 Markets

Rio's biggest market is found at the Feira Nordestina in São Cristóvão.

Hippie Fair
MARKET

(Map p56; Praça General Osório; ⊙ 9am-6pm Sun) Ipanema's Hippie Fair has artwork, jewelry, handicrafts, clothing and souvenirs for sale. Stalls in the southeast and northeast corners of the plaza sell tasty plates of *acarajé* (croquettes, with a sauce of *vatapá* and shrimp, R$7), plus excellent desserts (R$3). Don't miss it.

Av Atlântica Fair
MARKET

(Map p64; Av Atlântica, near Rua Djalma Ulrich, Copacabana; ⊙ 6pm-midnight Mon-Sat) Paintings, drawings, jewelry, clothing and a fair bit of tourist junk make up this Copacabana market. It's located on the median along Av Atlântica.

Feira do Rio Antigo
MARKET

(Map p74; ☑ 2224-6693; Rua do Lavradio, Lapa; ⊙ 10am-6pm 1st Sat of month) Although the Rio Antiques Fair happens just once a month, don't miss it if you're in town. The colonial buildings become a living installation as the whole street fills with antiques, and samba bands add to the ambience.

Praça do Lido Market
MARKET

(Map p64; Praça do Lido, Copacabana; ⊙ 8am-6pm Sat & Sun) This small Copacabana affair features handicrafts and souvenirs, soccer jerseys, jewelry stands and, from time to time, a man selling amazing slices of chocolate cake.

ℹ Information

DANGERS & ANNOYANCES

Rio has become slightly safer in recent years, although crime is still a problem, and tourists are sometimes targeted. To minimize your risk of becoming a victim, take some basic precautions. First off: dress down and leave expensive (or even expensive *looking*) jewelry, watches and sunglasses at home.

Copacabana and Ipanema beaches have a police presence, but robberies still occur on the sands, even in broad daylight. Don't ever take anything of value with you to the beach. Late at night, don't walk on any of the beaches. Lapa and Santa Teresa are other areas well worth visiting but have their share of crime. Avoid walking around empty streets; it's safest to stick to well-trafficked areas.

Buses are well-known targets for thieves. Avoid taking them after dark, and keep an eye out while you're on them. Take taxis at night (but never get into an unmarked car) to avoid walking along empty streets and beaches. That holds especially true for Centro, which becomes deserted in the evening and on weekends, and is better explored during the week.

Get in the habit of carrying only the money you'll need for the day, so you don't have to flash a wad of reais when you pay for things. Cameras and backpacks attract a lot of attention. Plastic shopping bags better disguise whatever you're carrying. Maracanã football stadium is worth a visit, but take only your spending money for the day and avoid the crowded sections. Some travelers prefer going with a tour group.

If you have the misfortune of being robbed, slowly hand over the goods. Thieves in the city are only too willing to use their weapons.

Scams

A common beach scam is for one thief to approach you from one side and ask you for a light or the time. While you're distracted, the thief's partner grabs your gear from the other side.

EMERGENCY

Report robberies to the **tourist police** (☏ 2332-4924; cnr Afrânio de Melo Franco & Humberto de Campos, Leblon; ☉ 24hr).

Other useful numbers:

Ambulance (☏ 192)
Fire Department (☏ 193)
Police (☏ 190)

INTERNET ACCESS

Internet cafes charge R$6 to R$10 per hour.

@Onze (Marquês de Abrantes 11, Flamengo; ☉ 9am-11pm) There's no Skype, but this peaceful spot serves up tasty sandwiches, salads, desserts and microbrews you can enjoy while browsing the web.

Fone Rio (Constante Ramos 22, Copacabana; ☉ 8am-midnight)

INTERNET RESOURCES

www.rioguiaoficial.com.br Riotur's comprehensive website.

www.riotimesonline.com Online English weekly for news and current events.

www.ipanema.com This website has good tips for first-time visitors.

MEDIA

Rio's main daily papers are **Jornal do Brasil** (www.jbonline.com.br) and **O Globo** (www. globo.com.br). Both have entertainment and event listings, particularly strong on Friday and Sunday. The national publication *Veja* has a *Veja Rio* insert, which details weekly entertainment options (it comes out on Sunday).

MEDICAL SERVICES

For medical emergencies, the best hospital for foreigners is the **Clínica Galdino Campos** (☏ 2548-9966; www.galdinocampos.com.br; Av NS de Copacabana 492, Copacabana; ☉ 24hr) with high-quality care and multilingual doctors.

There are scores of pharmacies in town, a number of which stay open 24 hours.

Drogaria Pacheco (Av NS de Copacabana 534, Leme; ☉ 24hr)
Drogaria Pacheco (Av NS de Copacabana 115, Copacabana; ☉ 24hr)
Drogaria Pacheco (☏ 2239-5397; Av Visconde de Pirajá 592, Ipanema; ☉ 24hr)
Farmácia do Leme (Av Prado Júnior 231, Copacabana; ☉ 24hr)
Farmácia Piauí (☏ 2274 8448; Av Ataúlfo de Paiva 1283, Leblon; ☉ 24hr)

MONEY

ATMs and banks can be found throughout the city. Banco do Brasil, Bradesco, Citibank and HSBC are the best banks to try when using a debit or credit card (HSBC charges the lowest withdrawal fees). Money changing is speedier at *casas de câmbio* (exchange offices) than at banks. At the airport, international ATMs and money exchange are located on the 3rd floor of arrivals.

In Ipanema you'll find *câmbios* scattered along Rua Visconde de Pirajá, about two blocks east and west of Praça NS de Paz. In Copacabana *câmbios* can be found on Av NS de Copacabana, near the Copacabana Palace hotel. There are banks and other ATMs on the main streets of Copacabana.

Banco do Brasil (Av NS de Copacabana 264, Copacabana)
Banco do Brasil (Av NS de Copacabana 1274, Copacabana) ATM.
Banco do Brasil (Senador Dantas 105, Centro) ATM.
Citibank (Av NS de Copacabana 828, Copacabana) ATM.
HSBC (Av Princesa Isabel 186, Leme) ATM.
Citibank (Rua da Assembléia 100, Centro)
Citibank (Visconde de Pirajá 459A, Ipanema) ATM.

HSBC (Vinícius de Moraes 71, Ipanema) ATM.

HSBC (Av Rio Branco 108, Centro) ATM.

HSBC (Praça Floriano 23, Centro)

POST

Most *correios* (post offices) open from 8am to 6pm Monday to Friday, and on Saturday until noon. Any mail addressed to Posta Restante, Rio de Janeiro, Brazil, ends up at the **main post office** (Map p74; Primeiro de Março 64, Centro).

Post Office (Map p68; Praia do Botafogo 324, Botafogo)

Post Office (Map p64; Av NS de Copacabana 540, Copacabana)

Post Office (Map p56; Prudente de Morais 147, Ipanema)

TELEPHONE

For local phone calls – and other calls within Brazil – you will need to buy a *cartão telefônico* (phone card; R$5 to R$20). These cards are available from newsstands. Many internet cafes offer international calling service, and Skype is also widely available.

TOURIST INFORMATION

Riotur (Map p74; ☑2541-7522; www.rioguiaoficial.com.br; Praça Pio X 119, Centro; ☺9am-6pm Mon-Fri) is the generally useful Rio city tourism agency. It operates a tourist information hot line, **Central 1746** (☑2271-7048, 1746; www.1746.rio.gov.br; ☺24hr). Press 8 for tourist info then 1 for English. Riotur's useful multilingual website, www.rioguiaoficial.com.br/en, is also a good source of information.

All of the Riotur offices distribute maps and the excellent (and updated) bimonthly *Rio Guide*, listing the major seasonal events.

You'll find information posts in Copacabana, on Copacabana Beach and at Galeão airport.

Copacabana (Map p64; ☑2541-7522; Av Princesa Isabel 183; ☺9am-6pm Mon-Fri)

Copacabana Beach Kiosk (Map p64; ☑2447-4421; Av Atlântica at Hilário de Gouveia ; ☺9am-8pm) Galeão airport **Terminal 1** (☑3398-3034; Domestic Arrival Hall, Galeão airport; ☺7am-11pm); **Terminal 2** (☑3398-2245; International Arrival Hall, Galeão airport; ☺6am-11pm)

TRAVEL AGENCIES

Andes Sol (☑2275-4370; Av NS de Copacabana 209, Copacabana) A good multilingual agency.

Blame It on Rio 4 Travel (☑3813-5510, in USA 917-254-4867; www.blameitonrio4travel.com; Xavier da Silveira 15B, Copacabana) Excellent travel agency run by a friendly and knowledgeable US expat.

Guanatur Turismo (☑2548-3275; www.guanaturturismo.com.br; Dias da Rocha 16A, Copacabana) Sells bus tickets to some domestic and international destinations.

ⓘ Getting There & Away

AIR

Most flights depart from Aeroporto Galeão also called Aeroporto Antônio Carlos (Tom) Jobim, 15km north of the center. Some flights to/from São Paulo and other Brazilian cities use Aeroporto Santos Dumont, east of the city center.

The table lists sample prices on Gol and TAM, Brazil's major carriers. Prices quoted are one-way and leave from Aeroporto Galeão. Given

TO/FROM RIO BY AIR

DESTINATION	AIRLINE	COST (R$)	FREQUENCY (DAILY)
Belém	Gol	535-900	7-10
	TAM	554-1067	7-10
Fortaleza	Gol	400-581	14-20
	TAM	448-750	6-12
Iguaçu Falls	Gol	361-620	6-8
	TAM	412-540	5-7
Manaus	Gol	530-672	6-8
	TAM	421-643	1-5
Recife	Gol	380-620	12-18
	TAM	432-686	12-18
Salvador	Gol	300-480	5-8
	TAM	312-497	5
São Paulo	Gol	135-360	20-35
	TAM	175-342	20-35

frequent specials and volatile prices, this information is subject to change.

Some airlines:

Azul (AD; ☑ 4003-1118; www.voeazul.com.br)

Avianca (AV; ☑ 4004-4040; www.avianca.com)

Gol (☑ 0300-115 2121; www.voegol.com.br; Aeroporto Galeão, Aeroporto Santos Dumont) All travel agents sell Gol tickets.

Ocean Air (O6; ☑ 4004-4040; www.oceanair.com.br)

TAM (KK; ☑ 4002-5700; www.tam.com.br)

BUS

Buses leave from the **Rodoviária Novo Rio** (Map p80; ☑ 3213-1800; Av Francisco Bicalho 1), about 2km northwest of Centro. Several buses depart daily from here to most major destinations, but it's best to buy tickets in advance. Very few travel agencies sell bus tickets, although Guanatur Turismo (p116) does sell bus tickets to main domestic and international destinations. It's worth paying Gunatur's small commission to avoid a long trip to the bus station to buy advance tickets.

If you arrive in Rio by bus, it's a good idea to take a taxi to your hotel, as the bus station is in a seedy area. To arrange a cab, go to the small booth near the Riotur desk, on the 1st floor of the bus station. Average fares are R$50 to the international airport and R$38 to Copacabana or Ipanema.

In addition to the main tourist destinations, buses leave Novo Rio every 30 minutes or so for São Paulo (R$76 to R$120, six hours) operated by **Viação 1001** (☑ 4004-5001; www.autoviacao1001.com.br) and **Itapemirim** (☑ 0800-723 2121; www.itapemirim.com.br).

ⓘ Getting Around

TO & FROM THE AIRPORTS

Rio's international airport, Aeroporto Galeão, is 15km north of the city center, on Ilha do Governador. Aeroporto Santos Dumont, used by some domestic flights, is by the bayside in the city center, 1km east of Cinelândia metro station.

Premium Auto Ônibus (www.premiumautoonibus.com.br; R$12) operates safe air-con buses from the international airport to Novo Rio bus station, Rio Branco (Centro), Aeroporto Santos Dumont, southward through Glória, Flamengo and Botafogo and along the beaches of Copacabana, Ipanema and Leblon to Barra da Tijuca (and vice versa). The buses run every 20 minutes or so, from 5:30am to 10:30pm, and will stop wherever you ask. Fares are R$12, and it takes anywhere from 90 minutes to two hours to reach the Zona Sul from the airport depending on traffic. You can also transfer to the metro at Carioca metro station in Centro.

Heading to the airports, you can catch the Real Auto bus in front of the major hotels, along the main beaches, but you have to look alive and flag them down.

From Galeão, radio taxis charge a set fare of R$105 to Ipanema, which takes about an hour depending on traffic. Less secure yellow-and-blue common *(comum)* taxis should cost around R$50 to R$70, depending on traffic.

Keep in mind that traffic can lead to excruciatingly long delays on the return journey to the airport. On bad days it can take almost two hours from the Zona Sul, so leave yourself plenty of time.

BOAT

Rio has several islands in the bay that you can visit by ferry, though you can also get fine views on the commuter ferry to Niterói.

Ilha de Paquetá (Map p74; ☑ 0800-721-1012; www.grupoccr.com.br/barcas) The ferry takes 70 minutes and costs R$9 return, leaving every two to three hours between 5:15am and 11pm. The most useful departure times for travelers are 7:10am, 10.30am and 1.30pm.

Niterói (☑ ferry 0800-704 4113; www.barcassa.com.br) The ferry leaves every 20 minutes from Praça XV (Quinze) de Novembro in Centro. Return tickets cost R$5.60 return.

CAR

Driving in Rio can be frustrating even if you know your way around. If you do chose to drive, it's good to know a couple of things: the first is that *cariocas* don't always stop at red lights at night because of the small risk of robberies at deserted intersections. Instead they slow at red lights and proceed if no one is around. Another thing to know is that if you park your car on the street, it's common to pay the *flanelinha* (parking attendant) R$2 for looking after it. Some of them work for the city; others are 'freelance,' but regardless, it's a common practice throughout Brazil, and you risk their wrath by not paying!

Hire

Car-rental agencies can be found at either airport or scattered along Av Princesa Isabel in Copacabana. At the international airport, **Hertz** (☑ 0800-701-7300; www.hertz.com), **Localiza** (☑ 0800-979-2000; www.localiza.com) and **Unidas** (☑ 2295-3628; www.unidas.com.br) provide rentals. In Copacabana, among the many are **Hertz** (☑ 2275-7440; Av Princesa Isabel 500) and **Localiza** (☑ 2275-3340; Av Princesa Isabel 150).

PUBLIC TRANSPORT
Metro

Rio's subway system (www.metrorio.com.br) is an excellent way to get around. It's open from

5am to midnight Monday through Saturday and 7am to 11pm on Sunday and holidays. During Carnaval the metro operates nonstop from Friday morning until Tuesday at midnight.

Both lines are air-conditioned, clean, fast and safe. The main line goes from Ipanema-General Osório to Saens Peña, connecting with the secondary line to Estácio (which provides service to São Cristóvão and Maracanã). More stations are planned in the coming years, with plans to integrate the rest of Ipanema and Leblon into the transport system.

A single ride ticket is called a *unitário* and it costs R$3.20. To avoid waiting in lines, you can purchase a *cartão pré-pago* (prepaid card) by paying a minimum of R$10; you can then recharge it (cash only, no change given) at kiosks inside some metro stations. If you're going somewhere outside of the metro's range (Cosme Velho or Barra for example) you can purchase a *metrô-expresso* (metro-express bus) pass (R$4.15 to R$4.35). Free subway maps are available from most ticket booths.

Bus & Van

Rio city buses (around R$3) are fast and frequent, and because Rio is long and narrow it's easy to get the right bus and usually no big deal if you're on the wrong one. Most buses going south from the center will go to Copacabana, and vice versa. The buses are, however, often crowded, stuck in traffic, and driven by speed-loving maniacs. They also have a bad reputation for robberies. In truth, such acts are rare and usually limited to outer-suburban areas where tourists are unlikely to travel. Do keep an eye on your belongings while riding, and don't travel by bus at night; taxis are generally a safer option.

Minibuses (*cariocas* call them '*vans*') provide a faster alternative between Av Rio Branco in Centro and the Zona Sul (along the coast) as far as Barra da Tijuca. The destination is written in the front window. The flat fare costs between R$2 and R$4.50. Call out your stop ('*para!*') when you want to disembark.

TAXI

Rio's yellow taxis are handy for zipping around town. Metered taxis charge around R$4.50 flat rate, plus around R$1.60 per kilometer – slightly more at night, on Sunday and the entire month of December.

Radio taxis are 30% more expensive, but safer. Many of the drivers lurking around

BUSES FROM RIO

DESTINATION	DURATION (HR)	COST (R$)	FREQUENCY (DAILY)	COMPANY
International				
Buenos Aires, Argentina	46	265	1	Pluma (☎ 0800-646-0300)
Santiago, Chile	62	350	1	Pluma (☎ 0800-646 0300)
National				
Belém	52	390	1	Transbrasiliana (www.transbrasiliana.com.br)
Belo Horizonte	7	65-135	8-14	Util (www.util.com.br)
Brasília	18	90-170	2	Util (www.util.com.br)
Buzios	3	46	8-16	Viação 1001 (www.autoviacao.com.br)
Curitiba	13	135-200	3	Penha (www.nspenha.com.br)
Florianópolis	18	200	1	Itapemirim (www.itapemirim.com.br)
Iguaçu Falls	23	235	2	Pluma (www.pluma.com.br)
Ouro Prêto	7	80-122	4	Util (www.util.com.br)
Paraty	4½	62	7-13	Costa Verde (www.costaverdetransportes.com.br)
Petrópolis	1½	20	15-30	Única-Fácil (www.unica-facil.com.br)
Porto Alegre	26	250	1	Penha (www.nspenha.com.br)
Recife	38	370	1	São Geraldo (www.saogeraldo.com.br)
Salvador	28	260-290	1-2	Aguia Branca (www.aguiabranca.com.br)
Vitória	8	88	4	Itapemirim (www.itapemirim.com.br)

the hotels are sharks, so it's worth walking a block or so to avoid them. A few radio-taxi companies include **Coopertramo** (☎ 2209-9292), **Cootrama** (☎ 3976-9944), **Coopatur** (☎ 2573-1009) and **Transcoopass** (☎ 2209-1555). In Rocinha and some other favelas, moto-taxis (a ride on the back of a motorcycle) are a handy way to get around, with short rides (usually from the bottom of the favela to the top or vice versa) costing R$2.

Rio de Janeiro State

POP 16 MILLION

Best Places to Eat

➡ Rocka Beach Lounge (p158)
➡ Restaurante Alcobaça (p142)
➡ Rosmarinus Officinalis (p137)
➡ Linguiça do Padre (p147)
➡ Bacalhau do Tuga (p152)

Best Places to Stay

➡ Samambaia Hostel (p141)
➡ Casa Búzios (p157)
➡ Hotel Solar dos Gerânios (p131)
➡ Quinta da Floresta (p131)
➡ Pousada Moriá (p137)

Why Go?

If you thought Rio was just a city, think again! Right next door, the equally enticing *state* of Rio de Janeiro is home to some of Brazil's greatest treasures, all within an easy drive of Rio.

Inland you'll find Itatiaia, Brazil's oldest national park, and the spectacular Serra dos Órgãos, whose whimsically shaped peaks test the mettle of international climbers and form the backdrop for the former imperial city of Petrópolis.

East along the coast are the dunes, lagoons, white sands and limpid blue-green waters of the Costa do Sol, an ever-popular playground for surfers, divers and suntan-seeking urban escapees.

West lies the Costa Verde, a patchwork of bays, islands, waterfalls and forest-draped mountains. Highlights include the 18th-century architecture of colonial Paraty and the vast island paradise of Ilha Grande, where dozens of hiking trails lead to more than 100 of Brazil's most secluded beaches.

When to Go
Buzios

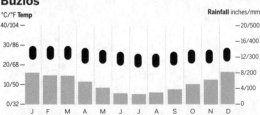

May Drier weather, perfect waves and lower prices.

Jul International authors and coffee *fazendas* (farms) during festivals in Paraty and Vassouras.

Dec–Feb Escape Rio's steamy heat in the mountain refuges of Petrópolis and Teresópolis.

History

The Tupí and other indigenous groups inhabited modern-day Rio state for over two millennia before Europeans arrived in the 16th century. Early Portuguese activity was focused along the coast, but the discovery of gold in the late 17th century prompted construction of Brazil's first major overland thoroughfare, linking coastal Paraty with the valley of the Rio Paraíba and continuing into Minas Gerais. Another important chapter in Rio state's development was the establishment of coffee plantations here in the early 19th century. The crop was taken by mule train to new ports along the coast, and these roads were the main means of communication until the coming of the railways after 1855.

Modern Rio de Janeiro state is one of Brazil's economic powerhouses, fueled by gushing oil, a burgeoning tourist trade and traditional industries such as steel and to shipbuilding.

❶ Getting There & Around

International and domestic flights fly into Rio de Janeiro's **Galeão** (✆ 021-3398-3034; Domestic Arrival Hall; ☉ 7am-11pm) and **Santos Dumont** airports, linking Rio state to cities throughout Brazil and the world. Rio's long-distance bus station is a hub for virtually every bus line in the country, with fast, frequent service to nearby towns via well-maintained modern highways.

COSTA VERDE

West of Rio city is a captivating stretch of coastline where jungled hillsides dotted with flowering trees dive precipitously into a blue-green sea. The sinuous shoreline here is perfect for meandering, and allows visitors to take time to appreciate the ever-changing panorama of bays, islands, peaks and waterfalls.

Ilha Grande & Vila Do Abraão

OXX24 / POP 6100

The fabulous island retreat of Ilha Grande owes its pristine condition to its unusual history. First it was a pirates' lair, then a leper colony and, finally, a penitentiary where political prisoners were held alongside some of Brazil's most violent criminals. All that remains of those days are some half-buried stone foundations, but the island's unsavory reputation kept developers at bay for a long time. Consequently, beautiful tropical beaches and virgin Atlantic rainforest (now protected as state parkland) abound on Ilha Grande, and there are still only a few settlements on the island.

Vila do Abraão, the island's biggest town, was itself a sleepy fishing village until the mid-1990s, when Ilha Grande's infamous penitentiary was destroyed and tourism on the island started in earnest. Over the years, a veritable thicket of pousadas (guesthouses), restaurants and bars has popped up, but this palm-studded beachfront town, with its tidy yellow church, is still incredibly picturesque, and remains small by mainland Brazilian standards. Except for Abraão's lone garbage truck, fire engine and police vehicle, cars are not allowed in town, so the only transport here is by foot or boat. The village comprises a few dirt roads, and everybody congregates down near the docks and beach at night. On weekends and during high season it can get a bit claustrophobic in Vila do Abraão, but you can easily escape the crowds by hiking a few steps out of town in any direction.

◉ Sights & Activities

The outdoor adventure options on Ilha Grande are endless. Posted around town are maps showing 16 different signposted trails leading through the lush forest to several of the island's 102 beaches. When visiting some beaches, it's possible to hike one way and take a boat the other. The most popular hike is the three-hour, 6.1km (each way) trek from Abraão to **Praia Lopes Mendes**. This seemingly endless beach with good surfing waves (shortboard/longboard rentals available on-site) is considered by some the most beautiful in Brazil. **Praia de Parnaioca** also ranks up there, accessible via a 16km trail that passes through **Dois Rios**, a picturesque beach where two separate rivers flow into the open Atlantic. Dois Rios itself served as the site of the **Colônia Penal Cândido Mendes**, Ilha Grande's last functioning prison, which was used to hold political prisoners during the military regime that took power in 1964, and which was finally destroyed (literally blown up!) by order of the state government in 1994. The reconstructed prison ruins now house the small but interesting **Museu do Cárcere** (✆ 2334-0939; ecomuseu@uerj.br; ☉ 10am-4pm Tue-Sun)

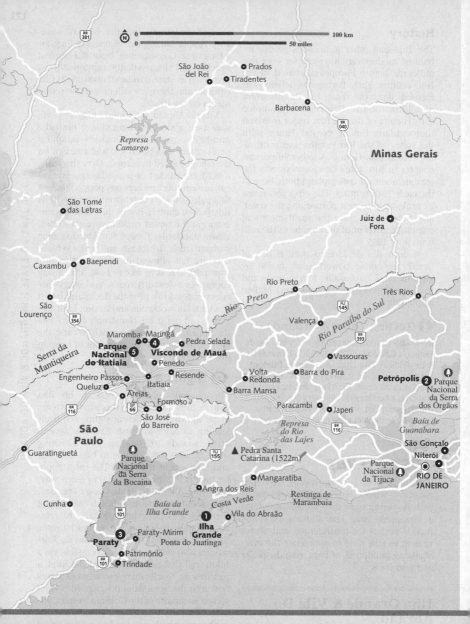

Rio de Janeiro State Highlights

1 On **Ilha Grande** (p121), surf the south shore's wild waves, or chill at the floating bar in a tranquil cove nearby.

2 Glide across the polished wood floors of the imperial palace in **Petrópolis** (p139), former home of Brazilian Emperor Dom Pedro II.

3 Snorkel, swim, slide down waterfalls or learn to cook gourmet Brazilian food in picturesque colonial **Paraty** (p127).

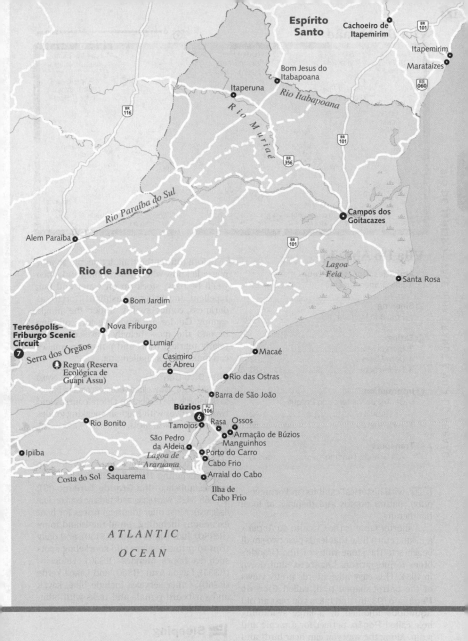

Espírito Santo

Cachoeiro de Itapemirim

BR 101

Itapemirim

Marataizes

ES 060

Bom Jesus do Itabapoana

Itaperuna

Rio Itabapoana

Rio Muriaé

BR 116

BR 101

BR 356

Campos dos Goitacazes

Rio Paraíba do Sul

Alem Paraíba

BR 101

Lagoa Feia

Rio de Janeiro

Santa Rosa

Bom Jardim

Teresópolis–Friburgo Scenic Circuit

Nova Friburgo

Serra dos Órgãos

7

Lumiar

Casimiro de Abreu

Macaé

Regua (Reserva Ecológica de Guapi Assu)

Rio das Ostras

Barra de São João

Búzios

RJ 106

Rio Bonito

6

Rasa

Ossos

Tamoios

Armação de Búzios

Manguinhos

São Pedro da Aldeia

Porto do Carro

Ipiíba

Lagoa de Araruama

Cabo Frio

Arraial do Cabo

Costa do Sol

Saquarema

Ilha de Cabo Frio

ATLANTIC OCEAN

4 Relax to the rhythms of rushing water in the idyllic hidden valley of **Visconde de Mauá** (p136).

5 Rappel up rocky Pico das Agulhas Negras in **Parque Nacional do Itatiaia** (p138).

6 Stroll at sunset, or party all night on breezy beachfront Orla Bardot in **Búzios** (p154).

7 Sample Alpine-style goat cheese amid spectacular mountain scenery along the **Teresópolis–Friburgo Scenic Circuit** (p147).

Vila Do Abraão

Vila Do Abraão

⊕ Activities, Courses & Tours
1 Ilha Grande Turismo.............................B2

⊜ Sleeping
2 Pousada Manaca D1

⊗ Eating
3 Biergarten..B2
4 Dom Mário B2
5 O Pescador B1

ⓘ Information
6 Centro de Visitante do Parque
   Estadual..A2
7 TurisAngra B1

ⓘ Transport
Ilha Grande Turismo.....................(see 1)

FREE, with historical exhibits (in Portuguese only), nature photos and displays of local handicrafts.

A shorter jaunt is the Circuito do Abraão, a 1.7km return hike that leads past two small beaches to the stone ruins of Ilha Grande's other former prison, **Lazareto**, shut down in 1954. This easy hike affords pretty views of the parrot-shaped peak called **Pico do Papagaio** (982m) and takes you past an old **aqueduct** adjoined by a large swimming hole called **Poção**, perfect for a picnic and a dip. Along the way you can hear birds and jungle creatures, and you may run into local kids jumping into the water on their way home from school. Beyond the aqueduct, a more challenging trail leads to **Cachoeira da Feiticeira**, a lovely 15m waterfall, before continuing to the beach at **Saco do Céu**.

Before hitting the trail, let people at your pousada know where you're going and when you'll be back, stock up on water and bug repellent and bring a flashlight (torch), as darkness comes swiftly under the jungle canopy. Guides are advisable for exploring beyond the most heavily traveled routes; poorly marked trails and poisonous snakes can make things challenging.

Elite Dive Center   DIVING
(☑ 3361-5501; www.elitedivecenter.com.br; Travessa Buganville, Vila do Abraão) Offers courses and two-tank dives with English-speaking guides in some fantastic spots.

☞ Tours

There are a dozen-plus tour operators in town, including the centrally located and long-established **Ilha Grande Turismo** (IGT; ☑ 3365-6426; www.ilhagrandeturismo.com.br; Rua da Igreja). Most offer identical prices for boat excursions including round-the-island tours (R$180), half-island tours (R$130), and daily trips to prime beaches and snorkeling spots such as Lopes Mendes (R$30), Feiticeira (R$35), Lagoa Azul (R$50) and Lagoa Verde (R$60). Other services include bike, kayak and surfboard rentals and treks with bilingual guides.

🛏 Sleeping

Vila do Abraão is swarming with pousadas. Note that we quote prices for high season (December to March). Prices drop by as much as 50% between April and November. Some locals also rent out rooms, especially in high season.

Holandes Hostel HOSTEL $
(Ilha Grande Hostel; ☑ 3361-5034; www.holandes
hostel.com.br; Rua da Assembléia s/n; dm R$58,
chalet R$160; @ 🖥) Uphill and inland from
the center of town, this shady, peaceful HI-
run retreat is the island's oldest hostel, with
banana trees, chirping parrots and a terrace
full of hammocks. Rooms are a bit musty,
but the location is lovely.

Che Lagarto HOSTEL $
(☑ 3361-9669; www.chelagarto.com; Praia do Canto; dm R$60, s/d R$120/140; @ 🖥) Prime waterfront location, live music nightly on the
atmospheric deck and a bar with free-flowing caipirinhas (cane-liquor cocktail) make
this Ilha Grande's party hostel; just don't
come expecting a good night's sleep! Some
boats from Conceição de Jacareí will drop
you at the Aquário hostel next door; otherwise, it's a 10-minute walk down the beach
from Abraão's town center.

Jungle Lodge GUESTHOUSE $
(☑ 9977-2405; www.ilhagrandeexpeditions.com;
Caminho de Palmas 4; r per person R$70-90; @)
Tucked away above town in the rainforest, this rustic, five-room guesthouse and
open-air chalet is run by a wild-haired Pantanal guide and his German wife. It's an entirely different experience than sleeping in
Abraão, a 1.5km hike away. The view from
the outdoor shower is miraculous.

Pousada da Cachoeira POUSADA $$
(☑ 3361-9521; www.cachoeira.com; Rua do
Bicão 50; s/d with fan R$170/200, with air-con
R$190/220; 🗷 @ 🖥) A five-minute uphill
trek from downtown Abraão, this peaceful
green oasis has beautifully maintained lawn
and garden spaces descending to a jungle-
fringed river with its own little swimming
hole. Four uphill rooms have air-con, but the
best of the bunch are the fan-cooled lower
units within earshot of the river.

Pousada Manaca POUSADA $$
(☑ 3361-5404; www.ilhagrandemanaca.com.br;
Praia do Abraão 333; r $220-250; 🗷 🖥) This
French-run beachfront pousada invites
guests to relax with TV-free rooms (many
facing the ocean), a sauna and two pleasant
patio areas. Rooms have minibars and solar
hot water. Owner Gerard speaks English,
French, Spanish, German and Portuguese.

Aratinga Inn POUSADA $$
(☑ 3361-9559; www.aratingailhagrande.com.br;
Rua das Flores 232; r R$275, chalet R$300; ⊘ closed

May, Jun & Sep; 🗷 🖥) 🖉 The affable Australian
owner at this cozy, environmentally and gay-
friendly pousada goes the extra mile to make
guests feel at home, offering complimentary
use of iPads, beach towels and thermoses, a
generous afternoon tea, and a 600-title mov-
ie library for rainy days. Rooms and chalets
all have 500-thread-count cotton sheets, si-
lent ceiling fans, top-of-the-line bathroom
fixtures and DVD players.

Pousada Naturalia POUSADA $$
(☑ 3361-9583; www.pousadanaturalia.net; Praia do
Abraão 149; r R$250; 🗷 🖥) Built among giant
boulders on a hillside just inland from the
beach, Naturalia offers 12 spacious rooms,
all with pretty ocean views and most with
solar hot water. Book ahead.

Asalem POUSADA $$$
(☑ 3361-5602; www.asalem.com.br; Praia da Crena
s/n; s/d/tr R$350/420/504; d/tr ste R$550/630;
🗷 @ 🖥) Despite its remote, immersed-
in-nature atmosphere, Asalem is only a
short boat ride from Abraão, or a 25-minute
walk via a scenic beachfront trail. Owned by
an internationally acclaimed photographer,
it commands gorgeous bay and forest views
from its hillside location. Price includes
pick-up and drop-off at Abraão pier, plus use
of kayaks, canoes and the hotel's library of
art books.

🍴 Eating

Restaurants abound along Rua da Praia,
Rua da Igreja, Rua Getúlio Vargas and the
small pedestrian street Travessa Buganville.
Some places offer – but don't prominently
advertise – a simple *prato feito* (dish of the
day) of fish, rice, beans and salad for R$15
to R$20; ask around. During busy periods
you'll see sweets carts being pushed about,
as well as entrepreneurial islanders selling
grilled seafood and caipirinhas.

Lua e Mar SEAFOOD $$
(Praia do Canto; mains for 2 R$45-99; ⊘11am-
10pm Thu-Tue) Candlelit tables on the sand
make a tranquil place to watch the waves
and scurrying crabs while you enjoy *moquecas* (fish stew), risottos and other seafood dishes. Solo diners will appreciate the
R$24 *refeições* (simple meals for one fea-
turing fried fish or beef served with rice,
beans and salad).

Biergarten SELF-SERVE, VEGETARIAN $$
(☑ 9839-9912; www.biergartenhostel.com; Getúlio
Vargas 161; per kg R$48; ⊘noon-10pm Wed-Mon;

▲) The self-serve buffet at this informal vegetarian-owned eatery includes everything from brown rice and soy protein to sushi and other seafood, with more vegetables than you'll see at most places around town. The owners also operate the Biergarten Hostel next door (dorm R$65 to R$70, d R$140).

Dom Mário
SEAFOOD $$
(☑ 3361-5349; Travessa Buganville; mains for 2 R$32-85; ⊙ 5-11pm Mon-Sat) Long-time local chef Mário cooks up seafood specialties like *filé de peixe ao molho de maracujá* (fish fillet with passion fruit sauce) and scrumptious desserts, including his trademark caramelized bananas.

O Pescador
MEDITERRANEAN $$$
(☑ 3361 5114; Rua da Praia; mains for 2 R$61-100; ⊙ 5pm-late) The Italian-run Pescador is one of the island's best choices for a fancy beachfront dinner, with mean caipirinhas and Mediterranean-style fish, meat and poultry dishes such as the *grigliata mista al salmoriglio* (fish, shrimp and calamari grilled with olive oil, lemon juice, garlic and oregano).

❶ Orientation

Ferries from the mainland (Angra dos Reis and Mangaratiba) dock at the cement pier on the west end of Abraão's beach. Private boats and most hydrofoils dock at a separate wooden pier about 150m east.

In between the two piers lies the heart of Abraão village, with its main street, the cobbled Rua da Igreja, curving to become Rua Getúlio Vargas. West of the piers is the road to Praia Preta and the ruined Lazareto prison. East of the piers, at the far end of the town beach, Ilha Grande's most popular hiking trail leads to Praia de Palmas, Praia dos Mangues and Praia Lopes Mendes.

❶ Information

There are no ATMs on the island, although many places accept credit cards and it's possible to change foreign cash in a pinch.

The **TurisAngra** (☑ 3367-7826; www.turisan gra.com.br; Rua da Praia; ⊙ 7am-7pm) tourist information office, at the foot of the wooden pier, offers general information about the island, including rudimentary maps of Abraão village and local trails. For more detailed state park information, a helpful scale model of the island and its trails, and displays on local history and culture, visit the **Centro de Visitante do Parque Estadual** (State Park Visitors Center; ☑ 3361-5540; falecompeig@gmail.com; Av Beira Mar s/n; ⊙ 8am-5pm), just west of the cement pier.

Internet service on the island tends to be extremely slow. A few hotels offer wireless connections, and there's a sprinkling of net cafes, including **Ilha Grande Turismo** (Rua da Igreja; per hr R$4; ⊙ 9:30am-midnight), with a dozen-plus computers, air-con and long hours.

❶ Getting There & Away

The most straightforward way to reach the island from Rio is via door-to-door van-plus-boat shuttle services such as **Easy Transfer** (www. easytransferbrazil.com) – these will pick you up at any hostel, hotel or pousada in Rio and deliver you straight to the island (R$75, 3½ to 4½ hours). Easy Transfer also offers a similar service from Paraty (R$50, 3½ hours).

Reaching the island via public transport is cheaper but slightly more complicated, as you have to choose from mutliple routes and buy two separate tickets (one for the bus, one for the boat).

Boats for Ilha Grande leave from three points on the mainland: Angra dos Reis, Conceição de Jacareí and Mangaratiba. Costa Verde runs buses from Rio to Angra (R$43, 2½ hours, hourly) and Mangaratiba (R$31, two hours, four daily). Any Angra-bound bus can also drop you in Conceição de Jacareí (R$43, two hours) *if* you tell the driver.

The most frequent boat crossings are from Conceição de Jacareí, where speedboats (R$25 to R$30, 25 minutes) and schooners (R$15 to R$20, 50 minutes) leave every hour or two between 9am and 6:15pm, returning from Abraão between 7:30am and 6:30pm.

More affordable are the daily ferries to Ilha Grande operated by **CCR Barcas** (www.grupoc cr.com.br/barcas), leaving from Angra dos Reis and Mangaratiba (R$4.80, 80 minutes from either port). Ferries depart Angra at 3:30pm weekdays and 1:30pm weekends, returning from Abraão at 10am daily. From Mangaratiba, ferries leave at 8am daily and 10pm Friday, returning from Abraão at 5:30pm daily. Extra ferries are sometimes added during high season; confirm locally before departure.

Ilha Grande Turismo (IGT; ☑ 3365-6426; www.ilhagrandeturismo.com.br) also runs fast catamarans (R$30, 50 minutes) between Angra and Abraão, leaving Angra daily at 8am, 11am and 4pm, and returning from Abraão at 9am, 12:30pm and 5pm. Buy tickets at the IGT offices inside Angra's bus station or just behind the church in Abraão.

Angra is the most useful port for those traveling west from Ilha Grande. Colitur buses leave Angra for Paraty (R$10, two hours) at least hourly from 6am to 11pm daily, departing from a stop midway between Angra's ferry and hydrofoil docks (a five-minute walk from either dock).

Paraty

✒ 0XX24 / POP 38,000

Set amid jutting peninsulas and secluded beaches, with a backdrop of steep, jungled mountains plunging into an island-studded bay, Paraty is one of Brazil's most appealing and exquisitely preserved historical gems.

Paraty's colonial center is remarkable not only for its centuries-old architecture, but also for its lack of automobile traffic. The irregular cobblestone streets are closed to motor vehicles, making it a delightful place to stroll about. Elegant white buildings adorned with fanciful multihued borders and latticed windows blend harmoniously with the natural beauty that envelops the town.

Dozens of pristine beaches are within a couple of hours of Paraty by boat or bus, while inland, the Parque Nacional da Serra da Bocaina provides protection for a lush remnant of Mata Atlântica (Atlantic rainforest). The Brazilian government has recognized Paraty as a National Historic Site since 1966.

Paraty is crowded and lively throughout the summer holidays, brimming with Brazilian and European vacationers. The town's cosmopolitan flavor is further enhanced by the large number of artists, writers and chefs, both Brazilian and foreign, who have settled here and opened shops, galleries and restaurants.

The historic center is small and easy to navigate, although street names and addresses can get confusing. Some streets have more than one name, and house numbers don't always follow a predictable pattern.

History

Paraty was inhabited by the indigenous Guaianás when Portuguese settlers first arrived here in the 16th century. With the discovery of gold in Minas Gerais at the end of the 17th century, Paraty became an obligatory stopover between Rio de Janeiro and the mines, as it was the only point where the escarpment of the Serra do Mar could be scaled.

As gold poured from the interior, Paraty became a busy, important port, and the wealthy built churches and fine houses. Paraty's glory days didn't last long. After the 1720s, a new road from Rio via the Serra dos Órgãos cut 15 days off the journey to Minas Gerais, and Paraty started to decline. In the 19th century, the local economy revived with

the coffee boom, but until the mid-20th century the sea remained the only viable commercial route to Paraty. In 1954 a modern road was built through the steep Serra do Mar, passing the town of Cunha, 47km inland. Then in 1960 the coastal road from Rio, 253km away, was extended to Paraty and 330km beyond to São Paulo, ushering in a new era of tourism-based prosperity.

◉ Sights & Activities

At the time of research, most of Paraty's historic churches were undergoing renovation and were closed to the public. Check with the tourist office for up-to-the-minute opening hours and prices.

Casa da Cultura   MUSEUM
(✒ 3371-2325; www.casadaculturaparaty.org.br; Dona Geralda 177; adult/student R$8/4; ⊙10am-6:30pm Wed-Mon) In a beautiful colonial mansion, Paraty's Casa da Cultura has a permanent exhibition documenting local culture through photos and videotaped interviews with residents. The museum also displays relics from Paraty's past, with signs in English and Portuguese. There are fabulous views of town from the main gallery upstairs.

Igreja NS do Rosário e
São Benedito dos Homens Pretos CHURCH
(cnr Dr Samuel Costa & Rua do Comércio; admission R$3) Built in 1725 by and for slaves, and renovated in 1857, the church has gilded wooden altars dedicated to Our Lady of the Rosary, St Benedict and St John. The pineapple-like chandelier base in the roof is a symbol of prosperity.

INDIGENOUS NAMES

Many place names in Rio state have their origins in indigenous words, including the following:

Geribá A kind of coconut palm.

Guanabara Arm of the sea.

Ipanema Place that gives bad luck or place of dangerous sea.

Itatiaia Many-pointed rock.

Mangaratiba Banana orchard.

Paraty A kind of fish.

Saquarema Lagoon without shells.

Tijuca Putrid-smelling swamp.

RIO DE JANEIRO STATE PARATY

Paraty

Paraty
Explorer
(350m)

R Orlando Carpinelli
R dos
Pescadores
17
Alameda Princesa Isabel
Rua São Pedro de Alcântara

R das Acácias

R Amaral
Gurgel
R Pontal
Av NS dos Remédios

Rio Perequê Açu

Praça da Matriz R Beira Rio
(Rua da Cadeia)
R da Capela
6
R da Matriz
R Dona Geralda

13
R Antônio de Oliveira Vidal
R Óseas Martins
de Alameda
R João Claudino
R João do Prado
Beco do Propósito
R Domingo
Gonçalves de Abreu
R Marechal
Deodoro da Fonseca
11
21

Largo do
Rosário 4
R Dr Samuel
Costa
18
2

R da Pedeira
R da Ferraria
10
R João Luis do Rosário
Praça do
Chafariz
22
8
19
R da Lapa

Av Roberto Silveira
23
R Patitiba
R do Comércio
R Santa Rita
12
20
25
R Manuel F dos
Santos Pádua
9
26
24
7
14
5

R José Vieira Ramos
Market
Market

BR-101 (1.5km);
Corumbé (7km);
Penha (8km);
Trindade (25km)
R Jango Pádua
R Aurora

27
R Aldmar
D Coelho
R Manuel Torres
R Valão
R Dr Derly Ellena
R Abel de Oliveira
R Floresta

Igreja Santa Rita dos Pardos Libertos
CHURCH

(Praça Santa Rita) Built in 1722, this was the church for freed mulattos (persons of mixed black and European parentage). It houses a tiny museum of sacred art and has some fine woodwork on the doorways and altars.

Capela de NS das Dores
CHURCH

(R da Capela btwn Dr Pereira & Fresca) This church of the colonial white elite was built

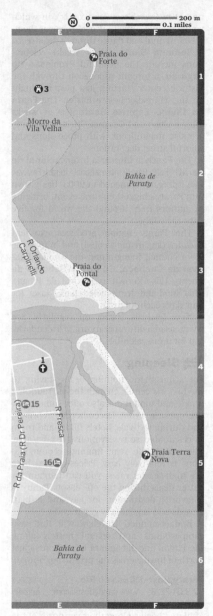

Paraty

Matriz NS dos Remédios CHURCH
(Praça da Matriz; admission R$2; ⊗9am-noon & 2-5pm Fri & Sat) Built in 1787 on the site of two 17th-century churches, this church holds art from past and contemporary local artists. According to legend, the construction of the church was financed by pirate treasure found hidden on Praia da Trindade.

in 1800 and renovated in 1901. It houses a small art gallery and a fascinating cemetery in the inner courtyard.

☞ Tours

Paraty Explorer OUTDOORS
(☎9952-4496; www.paratyexplorer.com; Praia do Jabaquara) ✐ This excellent Irish-run

agency specializes in hiking, sea kayaking and stand up paddle-board adventures around Paraty Bay. Paddy, the owner, has also opened Casa do SUP, a beachfront stand up paddle-themed hostel in Jabaquara.

Paraty Tours
OUTDOORS

(☎3371-1327; www.paratytours.com.br; Roberto Silveira 11) Next door to the tourist information office, this well-established agency offers hiking (R$100 to R$140, six hours), horseback riding (R$90, three hours), cycling (self-guided, R$9 per hour or R$45 per day) and diving (R$195 per day) adventures. Especially popular are five-hour schooner cruises, which cost R$40 and depart daily at 10am, 11am and noon, stopping at various beaches en route.

Paraty Adventure
OUTDOORS

(☎3371-6135; www.paratyadventure.com; Av Roberto Silveira 16) Just outside the historic center, this agency offers a wide variety of excursions.

✦✦✦ Festivals & Events

Carnaval here is a big street party – check out the Saturday procession of the **Bloco da Lama** (www.blocodalama.com.br), in which young people come in droves to cover themselves in mud and dance through the streets.

Semana Santa (Holy Week) celebrations include the beautiful **Procissão do Fogaréu**, a torchlit procession through the historic center starting just past midnight on the Thursday before Easter. The **Festa do Divino Espírito Santo** (seven weeks after Easter) and **Corpus Christi** (in June) are also magnificent, with processions and colorful street decorations.

The **Festival Literária Internacional de Parati** (FLIP; Paraty International Literary Festival; www.flip.org.br), launched in 2003, has grown into Paraty's biggest cultural event, bringing in authors from around the world for five days each July.

The Paraty region produces excellent *cachaça* (sugarcane alcohol) and in 1984 the town council inaugurated the annual **Festival da Cachaça, Cultura e Sabores de Paraty** (also known as Festival da Pinga). This food-and-drink-fueled party lasts for four days each August.

New festivals spring up regularly. See www.casadaculturaparaty.org.br/calendario.asp for a full calendar.

🛏 Sleeping

For atmosphere, nothing beats staying in the historic center, though the surrounding jungle and mountains also offer some enticing options. From December to February, and during festivals, hotels fill up and room prices double, so reservations are advisable. The rest of the year, finding accommodations is relatively easy. Prices quoted here are high-season rates; you can bargain for better deals during the off-season. Paraty is a favorite destination for gay and lesbian crowds and is generally gay friendly.

Budget-minded travelers will find two campgrounds and several hostels along the Pontal and Jabaquara beachfronts (just north of town, across the pedestrian bridge).

Paraty Hostel 'Casa do Rio'
HOSTEL $

(☎3371-2223; www.paratyhostel.com; Antônio Vidal 120; dm/d R$50/110; @ 🛜 ⛱) Paraty's HI-affiliated hostel, along the river north of the bus station, has dorms plus a couple of private rooms. A riverside deck and swimming pool, hammocks, a shady sitting area and laundry facilities give it a homey feel. The hostel also organizes boat excursions to local beaches (R$35) and van trips to the Caminho do Ouro and Tobogã waterslide (R$40).

DON'T MISS

CHEF FOR A DAY

Tired of eating out? How about cooking your own gourmet dinner tonight in Paraty's historic center, with the help of acclaimed local chef and cookbook author Yara Roberts?

Mixing theater with haute cuisine, chef Yara stages cooking classes in Portuguese, English, French and Spanish at her home-based culinary academy, the **Academia de Cozinha e Outros Prazeres** (☎3371-6025; www.chefbrasil. com; Dona Geralda 288; all-included dinner R$190). Guests learn about Brazilian regional cuisines, assist with the cooking (optional), then sit down to a leisurely dinner and an evening of lively conversation. Groups are often international – residents of over 60 countries have participated to date. The price includes cocktails, wine, desserts and recipes.

Hungry for more? Chef Yara also organizes multiday programs that combine cooking classes with visits to local producers. See the website for details.

DON'T MISS

ISLANDS & BEACHES

Paraty has some 65 islands and 300 beaches in its vicinity. To visit the less-accessible beaches, take an organized schooner tour; tickets average about R$40 per person.

Alternatively, you can hire one of the small motorboats at the port for a private tour. Local captains know some great spots and will take you out for R$50 to R$60 per hour, which is a good deal if you have a large enough group.

The closest fine beaches on the coast – **Vermelha**, **Lula** and **Saco da Velha** – are all east of Paraty, roughly an hour away by boat. Good island beaches nearby include **Araújo** and **Sapeca**; many other islands have rocky shores and are private. The mainland beaches tend to be better; most have *barracas* (stalls) serving beer and fish and, at most, a handful of beachgoers.

Back in Paraty, walking north across the river, the first beach you'll reach is **Praia do Pontal**. A cluster of open-air restaurants lines its shore, but it's not great for swimming. Another 2km further north is **Praia do Jabaquara**, a spacious beach with great views and shallow waters that's ideal for kayaking and stand up paddling.

★ Hotel Solar dos Gerânios   INN $$
(☑ 3371-1550; www.paraty.com.br/geranio; Praça da Matriz; s/d/tr R$100/150/200; @ 🕏) Run by the same family for decades, this rustic place on lively Praça da Matriz is the most affordable hotel in Paraty's colonial center. Wood and ceramic sculptures, stone walls and floors, columns and beamed ceilings, and a courtyard full of plants, cats and dogs all add character. Several rooms have balconies overlooking the square.

★ Quinta da Floresta   B&B $$
(☑ 9901-1600; quintadafloresta.com; Estrada Paraty-Cunha, km7, Penha; r with shared/private bathroom R$190/250, 🔁) 🐾 Monkeys and birds abound at this Atlantic rainforest hideaway 7km above Paraty. Rooms include a spacious upstairs double with veranda, a family-friendly downstairs unit and two less expensive doubles with shared bath. Guests love the sunny guest kitchen, laundry facilities, glass-walled, fireplace-equipped living room and two private river beaches flanked by giant boulders (secluded enough for skinny-dipping!).

Le Gite d'Indaiatiba   POUSADA $$
(☑ 3371-7174; www.legitedindaiatiba.com.br; Hwy BR-101, km558; r R$200, bungalow R$250, loft R$500; ❄ 🕏 🔁) In a gorgeous jungle setting 16km northwest of Paraty, well-traveled hosts Olivier and Valéria serve superb Franco-Brazilian cuisine and rent out five units with fireplaces and panoramic verandas, including two 'lofts' with air-con, large bathtubs and DVD players. Activities include horseback riding, jungle treks, and relaxing stints by the pool, waterfall and riverside sauna. See website for driving directions.

Estalagem Colonial   POUSADA $$
(☑ 3371-1626; www.paraty.com.br/estalagemcolonial; Rua da Matriz 9; r R$160, with shared bath R$100) This historic mansion in the heart of colonial Paraty features a sunlit downstairs common area, plus fantastic views from some upstairs rooms; book ahead for room 4, a super-spacious corner room, and room 5, with seven windows commanding views on three sides. Smaller rooms with shared bath also offer good value given the pousada's prime location.

Pousada Flor do Mar   POUSADA $$
(☑ 3371-1674; www.pousadaflordomar.com.br; Fresca 257; r R$225; ❄ @ 🕏) Hidden away on Paraty's beachfront, this simple little pousada has clean, spacious rooms, a pretty front courtyard with hammocks and couches, and one of the historic center's quietest locations.

La Pousada Arte Colonial   POUSADA $$
(☑ 3371-7347; www.pousadaartecolonial.com.br; Rua da Matriz 292; r R$260; ❄ 🕏) At this charming older house smack in the colonial center, each unique room has antique furnishings and plenty of character, and many get lovely natural light. There's a teeny pool out back.

Pousada Morro do Forte   POUSADA $$
(☑ 3371-1211; www.pousadamorrodoforte.com.br; Carpinelli 21; r R$270-350; ❄ 🕏 🔁) This modern pousada's incomparable vistas of the town and bay are well worth the uphill climb. Perched on the Morro do Forte, five minutes' walk from downtown, it has comfortable rooms with small balconies. The owners speak English and German.

PIRATES IN PARATY

Forte Defensor Perpétuo (admission R$2; ⊙ 9am-noon & 2-5pm Tue-Sun) was built in 1703 to defend against pirate raids on the gold passing through Paraty's port, then rebuilt in 1822 upon Brazil's independence from Portugal. It's a 20-minute walk north of town. To get there, cross the bridge over the Rio Perequê Açu, then climb the Morro da Vila Velha, the hill past Praia do Pontal. The fort commands sweeping views over the bay and houses a small museum with rotating cultural and historical exhibits.

Pousada do Ouro　　　POUSADA $$$
(☑ 3371-4300; www.pousadaouro.com.br; Rua da Praia 145; r from R$373-471, ste R$590; ✳ @ 🛜 🛋) It's easy to imagine bumping into Mick Jagger, Sonia Braga or Tom Cruise here – especially when you enter the lobby and see photos of them posing in front of the pousada! This centrally located hotel has everything – bar, pool, sauna and a gorgeous garden.

Pousada Arte Urquijo　　　POUSADA $$$
(☑ 3371-1362; www.urquijo.com.br; Dona Geralda 79; r R$410-650; 🛜 🛋) This cozy little pousada is obviously a labor of love for the artist owners. The downstairs sitting area features plush cushions, a stylish bar and a bubbling pool. Especially nice rooms are Sofia, with its deck, flowering tree and ocean view, and Xul, with its futon and floor-level window imparting a Japanese feel.

✗ Eating

Paraty has many pretty restaurants, but once your feet touch the cobblestones in the picturesque historic center, prices rise.

Sabor da Terra　　　SELF-SERVE $
(www.paraty.com.br/sabordaterra; Av Roberto Silveira 180; per kg R$36.80; ⊙ 11:30am-10pm) An affordable self-serve restaurant just outside the historic center, Sabor da Terra's tasty offerings include shrimp and fish.

Le Castellet　　　FRENCH $$
(☑ 8107-9909; www.lecastelletyveslepide.com.br; Dona Geralda 44; mains R$23-45; ⊙ 6pm-midnight) Chalkboard menus and low lighting contribute to the romantic ambience at this intimate, stone-walled eatery run by a French-Brazilian couple. The menu revolves around French favorites such as *salade niçoise, croque monsieur* and sweet and savory crepes. Marseillais owner Yves circulates among the diners, offering complimentary pre- and postmeal treats including home-baked bread, aromatic olive oils and cognac-infused grapes.

Casa do Fogo　　　BISTRO $$
(☑ 3371-3163; www.casadofogo.com.br; Rua da Ferraria 390; mains per person R$30-64; ⊙ 6pm-1am Thu-Tue) The name says it all here – everything's on fire! The menu focuses on seafood set ablaze with the local *cachaça,* and desserts don't escape a fiery death either.

Punto Divino　　　ITALIAN $$
(www.puntodivino.com; Marechal Deodoro da Fonseca 129; pizza R$23-42; ⊙ noon-midnight) This cozy Italian restaurant has wonderful thin-crust pizzas and pastas. Live music adds to the romance.

Cheiro do Camarão　　　SEAFOOD $$$
(☑ 9817-2411; Hwy BR-101, km569, Corumbé; mains per person R$30-60; ⊙ 10am-5pm Tue-Sun) Escape the crowds, wiggle your toes in the sand and enjoy some of the finest shrimp around at this informal family-run beachfront eatery 7km up the coast from Paraty in Corumbé.

Banana da Terra　　　SEAFOOD $$$
(☑ 3371-1725; www.restaurantebananadaterra.com.br; Dr Samuel Costa 198; mains R$65-79; ⊙ 6pm-midnight Mon, Wed & Thu, noon-4pm & 7pm-midnight Fri-Sun) Chef Ana Bueno's creative taste combinations and artistic presentation make this one of Paraty's classiest restaurants. There's also an excellent wine list.

🍷 Drinking & Entertainment

A slew of bars spill tables out onto the tree-shaded cobblestones of Praça da Matriz from late afternoon to the wee hours.

Paraty 33　　　LIVE MUSIC
(www.paraty33.com.br; Rua da Lapa 357) With an early evening happy hour featuring MPB (Musica Popular Brasileira) and bossa nova, and a late-night weekend mix of DJs and live acts, Paraty 33 is the historic center's liveliest nightspot.

Margarida Café　　　LIVE MUSIC
(☑ 3371-6037; margaridacafe.com.br; Praça do Chafariz; ⊙ noon-midnight) At the edge of the old town, this cavernous yet cozy cafe has great drinks and a nightly lineup of live mu-

sic including MPB, bossa nova, *forró* (popular music of the Northeast) tango and more, from 8:30pm onwards.

Teatro Espaço   THEATER
(☎3371-1575; www.ecparaty.org.br; Dona Geralda 327; admission R$50) Now entering its fifth decade, Paraty's internationally acclaimed Contadores de Estórias theater company presents puppetry, music and dance performances in this small playhouse.

❶ Information

Bradesco (Av Roberto Silveira) Multiple ATMs; more at Banco do Brasil next door.

CIT (☎3371-1222; Av Roberto Silveira s/n; ☉8am-8pm) Main branch just off highway BR-101; more convenient sub-branch at entrance to the historic center.

Internet Access (Av Roberto Silveira) Several places offer internet along this street just outside the historic center.

❶ Getting There & Away

The **bus station** (Rua Jango Pádua) is 500m west of the old town. **Costa Verde** (www.costa verdetransportes.com.br) offers frequent services to Rio de Janeiro (R$58, four hours, seven to 12 daily from 4am to 9pm). Colitur has buses to Angra dos Reis (R$10, two hours, at least hourly from 5am to 10:30pm) and **Reunidas** (www.reunidaspaulista.com.br) buses head to São Paulo (R$48, six hours, four to six daily between 8:30am and 11:30pm).

Around Paraty

The area surrounding Paraty is a nature-lover's paradise, offering some of southeastern Brazil's prettiest beach and mountain scenery. The region is also renowned for its excellent *cachaça*, and many *alambiques* (distilleries) in the area offer tours.

Paraty Islands & Beaches

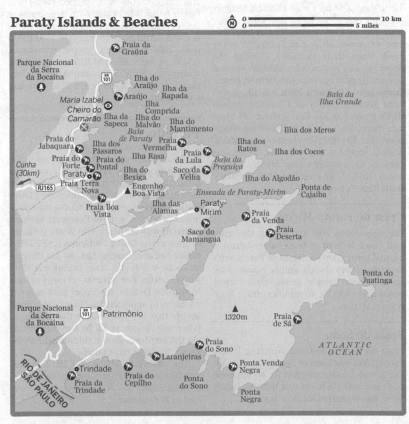

Cachoeira Tobogã

In the hills 8km inland, this natural water-slide is a blast! Take a local Colitur bus to Penha (R$3.70, 30 minutes), and get off at the white church. Follow signs 100m downhill to an idyllic pool surrounded by jungle, with a slick rock face that makes a perfect natural slide (once featured in the movie *The Emerald Forest*). Tourists who value their skulls should heed the posted warnings against surfing (ie standing instead of sitting), although local teenagers have mastered the technique and it's exciting (if terrifying!) to watch. Afterwards, grab a caipirinha at Bar do Tarzan, across the swinging bridge above the falls.

Praia da Trindade

About 25km south of Paraty, Trindade occupies a long sweep of stunningly beautiful coastline. Here you can lounge or hike along four of Brazil's most dazzling beaches (Cepilho, Ranchos, Meio and Cachadaço), with surging breakers, enormous boulders, vast expanses of mountain-fringed white sand, steep trails threading through the dense jungle, and a calm-watered natural swimming pool opposite the furthest beach, Cachadaço. The town itself has the somewhat scraggly quality of a frontier outpost that's grown up too fast (indeed, 20 years ago there was only a small fishing village here), but the sizeable cluster of pousadas, hostels, camping grounds and restaurants permits an overnight stay. Hourly Colitur buses (R$3.70, 40 minutes) serve Trindade from Paraty's bus station.

Praia de Paraty-Mirim

For accessibility, cost and beauty, this tranquil beach is hard to beat. Paraty-Mirim is a small town 17km southeast of Paraty, with an 18th-century church, and *barracas* (food stalls) serving simple meals. Colitur runs buses here (R$3.70, 40 minutes) from Paraty's bus station.

Praia do Sono

Praia do Sono is another stunning beach, about 35km southeast of Paraty. Catch a Colitur bus to Laranjeiras (R$3.70, 40 minutes) and then walk 1½ hours east to Sono. Paraty Tours has organized hikes to Sono.

Cachaça Distilleries

Paraty is renowned for its excellent *cachaça*, and many *alambiques* in the area offer tours. Among the best is **Maria Izabel** (☑ 9999-9908; www.mariaizabel.com.br; Sítio Santo Antônio, Corumbê), 10km north of town, which often places within the top 20 in nationwide competitions. Call at least 24 hours in advance to arrange a visit.

ITATIAIA REGION

Originally settled by northern Europeans, the Itatiaia region of northwestern Rio de Janeiro state is a curious mix of Old World charm and New World jungle. The climate is Alpine temperate and the chalets are Swiss, but the vegetation is tropical and the warm smiles are pure Brazilian. There are neatly tended little farms with horses and goats, and small homes with clipped lawns and flower boxes side by side with large tracts of dense forest untouched by the machete. This is a wonderful place to tramp around green hills, ride ponies up purple mountains, splash in waterfalls and hike trails without straying too far from the comforts of civilization: a fireplace, a soft bed, a little wine and a well-grilled trout!

Penedo

0XX24 / POP 29,000 / ELEV 600M

Originally started as a Finnish colony in the early 20th century, Penedo has grown into a vacation resort that embraces all things non-Brazilian. In the more developed lower section of town, you'll find tourist traps capitalizing on the region's European heritage mixed in with authentic Old World influences such as the **Clube Finlândia** (☑ 3351-1374; clubefinlandiablog.blogspot.com; Av das Mangueiras 2601), which still hosts traditional Finnish dances the first Saturday of every month. In Alto do Penedo, the upper part of town, it's easier to appreciate the luxuriant natural beauty that lies just outside the city limits. Wherever you go, you'll be sure to appreciate the emphasis on the traditional Finnish sauna, found at most hotels.

The **tourist office** (☑ 3351-1704; turismo@itatiaia.rj.gov.br; Av das Pedras 766; ⊙ 9:30am-5pm) has brochures and information in Portuguese.

Itatiaia Region

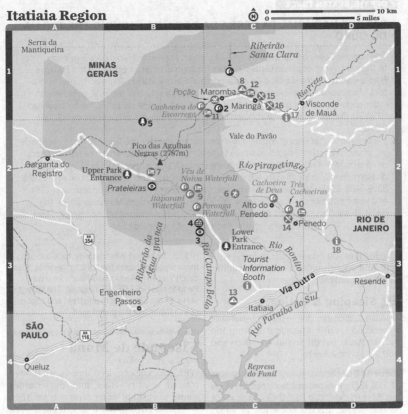

Itatiaia Region

◎ Sights
1 Cachoeira Santa Clara	C1
2 Cachoeira Veu de Noiva	C1
3 Lago Azul	B3
4 Museu Lago	B3
5 Parque Nacional do Itatiaia	B2

◎ Activities, Courses & Tours
6 Três Picos	C2

🛏 Sleeping
7 Abrigo Rebouças	B2
8 Fazenda Santa Clara Camping	C1
9 Hotel do Ypê	B2
10 Pequena Suécia	C2

11 Pousada Moriá	C1
12 Warabi Hotel	C1
13 Ypê Amarelo	C3

✖ Eating
14 Koskenkorva	C3
15 Le Petit	C1
16 Rosmarinus Officinalis	C1
Zorba Budda	(see 12)

ⓘ Information
17 Mauatur	C1
18 Tourist Office	D3

◎ Sights

Penedo's main attractions are the forest and waterfalls. Two especially worthwhile waterfalls are **Três Cachoeiras**, west of downtown Penedo along the main road just before it starts climbing to Alto do Penedo, and **Cachoeira de Deus**, about 20 minutes uphill from the bus turnaround in Alto do Penedo. Ask locally for directions, as signs are intermittent. About one hour of uphill **hiking** from the end of the asphalt in Alto do

PARQUE NACIONAL DA SERRA DA BOCAINA – HIKING THE TRILHA DO OURO

The historic Caminho do Ouro (Gold Trail), which connected Rio de Janeiro's coastline to the gold mines of Minas Gerais, passes through dramatic scenery in the **Parque Nacional da Serra da Bocaina** just north of Paraty. Paraty Tours and other operators offer two-hour day hikes covering a very small fraction of the trail, near Penha; independent travelers can also drive or take a bus from Paraty to the Penha trailhead (R$3.70, 8km uphill from Paraty) and hire the obligatory guide (per person R$20) there.

For a more challenging and unique experience, consider the Trilha do Ouro backpacking adventure, a three-day, 53km hike through the wildest reaches of the national park offered by **MW Trekking** (www.mwtrekking.com.br). This longer trek starts in São José do Barreiro in São Paulo state – most easily accessed by the **Viação Azteca** (☎0xx24-3359 0498; R$11; ☺90 min) bus from Resende near Parque Nacional do Itatiaia (p138) – and visits a number of spectacular waterfalls en route towards Mambucaba, on the coast 45 minutes northeast of Paraty. The R$396 price includes transport to the trailhead, park fees, food, simple lodging and excellent local guide.

Penedo takes you into very dense forest with trails and opportunities to observe wildlife, including monkeys.

🛏 Sleeping & Eating

Penedo is expensive, due to the large number of weekend tourists who come up from Rio and São Paulo, but the accommodations and food are above average.

Pequena Suécia   HOTEL $$
(☎3351-1275; www.pequenasuecia.com.br; Toivo Suni 33; s R$150-250, d R$250-495; ❄☎☻) A Penedo classic, this red house in the woods has provided luxurious amenities in a rustic setting for over half a century. The on-site restaurant serves Scandinavian and vegetarian food, the spa offers massage and shiatsu treatments, and the attached club features live jazz music on weekends. Single rate is available midweek only.

Koskenkorva   FINNISH, GERMAN $$$
(☎3351-2532; www.koskenkorva.visitepenedo.com; Av Três Cachoeiras 3955; mains R$35-60; ☺noon-4pm & 7:30-10pm) With a lovely outdoor seating area by a creek, Koskenkorva specializes in Finnish and German food. For a splurge, try Voileipäpöytä (R$110), a smorgasbord-like platter featuring smoked trout, marinated salmon, herring, trout pâté and much more. Leave room for the fruit dessert crepes.

ℹ Getting There & Away

Cidade do Aço (www.cidadedoaco.com.br) operates three buses daily from Rio to Penedo

(R$32, 3¼ hours). Alternatively, take one of its more frequent buses from Rio to Resende, then catch Viação Penedo's half-hourly Resende–Penedo bus (R$3.05, 45 minutes). The latter bus services the 3km-long main street and continues to the end of the paved road.

Visconde de Mauá

0XX24 / ELEV 1200M

With cozy chalets, deep forests, wildflower-fringed country lanes and the constant sound of rushing water, Visconde de Mauá is an idyllic river valley that feels like a world unto itself. Its isolation is largely thanks to the town's limited access routes; visitors must either switchback or precipitous mountaintops on the newly paved 27km route from Penedo, or take a series of rutted dirt roads from Liberdade, Minas Gerais.

The valley consists of three small villages a few kilometers apart along the Rio Preto. The road passes first through Mauá, the largest village, then heads uphill to Maringá, 6km to the west, and Maromba, 2km further on, before petering out at the edge of the national park. The entire stretch between Mauá and Maromba remains unpaved; expect a bumpy ride!

Maringá village actually straddles the Rio Preto; addresses here are marked 'RJ' or 'MG' to show whether they're on the Rio de Janeiro or the Minas side of the river.

◉ Sights & Activities

It's possible to kayak the rapids of Rio Preto, the cascading river dividing Minas Gerais from Rio state. The river also has several small beaches and natural pools. Two especially fine swimming spots are the **Poção**, a giant natural pool 1km west of Maromba, and the **Cachoeira do Escorrega**, a natural water slide culminating in another gorgeous pool 2km west of Maromba.

Horseback riding is also available from various private operators around town. Details are available at the tourist office.

Cachoeira Santa Clara   WATERFALL
Among the nicest and most accessible of Mauá's dozen or so waterfalls, this one is a 10-minute drive or a 40-minute walk northwest of Alto Maringá on the Ribeirão Santa Clara. Cross the bridge to Minas Gerais about 1km west of Alto Maringá, then continue another 1km over a hill to a left-hand fork marked with signs for the waterfall.

Cachoeira Veu de Noiva   WATERFALL
This very beautiful waterfall is 300m south of the main road, just west of Maromba.

🛏 Sleeping
The valley is jam-packed with cozy, chalet-style accommodations. Inexpensive, bare-bones rooms are also available near the bus stops in Mauá and Maromba; just ask around.

Fazenda Santa Clara
Camping   CAMPGROUND $
(☑3387-1508, www.viscondedemaua.com.br/camp ingsantaclaramaua.html; Estrada Maringá/Maromba, 1km; camping per person R$20) Occupying a grassy slope at the convergence of the Rios Preto and Santa Clara, this camping ground has a natural swimming hole, a snack bar and miniscule two-person A frames to rent (per couple R$60) for those without a tent. The bus stop across the river is accessible via a pedestrian bridge.

★Pousada Moriá   POUSADA $$
(☑3387-1505; www.pousadamoria.com.br; Estrada da Maromba s/n; d R$210, chalet R$170, with whirlpool tub R$280-310; 🐾) ⏃ At this idyllic end-of-the-road hideaway, eight chalets and three brand-new doubles with prime waterfall views straddle a hillside at the national park's edge. Cozy touches include fireplaces, electric blankets, a sauna, a DVD library and ample breakfasts served in a charming glass-walled cabin or on an outdoor deck within earshot of the waterfall. Owners are active in local reforestation efforts.

Warabi Hotel   POUSADA $$
(☑3387-1143; www.viscondedemauaturismo.com; Alto Maringá, RJ; r R$175-360) ⏃ Inviting features abound at this Japanese-Brazilian–run lodging just above Maringá: comfy futons, *ofuro* (Japanese bath) tubs and a spacious wooden deck overlooking the swimming pool, sauna and riverside lawn. Guests also appreciate the solar electricity, boats for floating downstream to a local swimming hole, and an on-site restaurant serving sushi, tempura, sukiyaki and other Japanese specialties (R$18 to R$48).

🍴 Eating
Since 1996, Mauá has hosted a May culinary festival, the **Concurso Gastronômico** (www.mauagastronomico.com.br), with special emphasis on the local trout and *pinhões*, giant nuts from the native *araucária* trees.

In Maringá, don't miss the Alameda Gastronômica (restaurant row), a street packed with restaurants for every taste along the Minas Gerais side of the Rio Preto. Here you'll find Italian and vegetarian eateries, a German beer garden, a jazz bistro and a restaurant whose menu revolves around local mushrooms.

Le Petit   BRAZILIAN $$
(☑3387-1554; Alameda Gastronômica, Maringá, MG; mains R$29-42; ⏱1-6pm Tue & Wed, to 10pm Thu, to 11pm Fri & Sat, to 7pm Sun) Founded in the 1980s as a place for locals to sip beer while waiting to use Maringá's lone public phone, this cozy eatery remains popular for its unhurried, convivial atmosphere and its inspired treatments of the valley's favorite fish; try the trout in sake sauce with coconut *farofa* (sautéed manioc flour).

Zorba Budda   PIZZERIA $$
(☑3387-1170; Alto Maringá, RJ; pizza R$29-59; ⏱8pm-1am Fri & Sat, to midnight Sun) A Mauá institution for over two decades, this pumpkin-colored pizzeria serves two dozen varieties of wood-fired, thin-crusted beauties. Try the *montanhesa*, with locally smoked trout.

★Rosmarinus
Officinalis   MEDITERRANEAN $$$
(☑3387-1550; Estrada Maringá, 4km; mains R$44-77; ⏱noon-5pm & 7-10pm Thu-Sat, noon-5pm Sun) Food and setting are equally divine at this sweet little house in the woods between Mauá and Maringá. Sporting a gorgeous new riverside deck, it's surrounded by meticulously tended gardens that

RIO DE JANEIRO STATE VISCONDE DE MAUÁ

provide veggies and herbs for some of Mauá's most memorable meals. Specialties include oatmeal-almond-breaded trout, brie-*pinhão* (giant pine nut) ravioli and a sweet tomato, basil and mascarpone dessert 'salad.'

ℹ Information

At the entrance to Mauá village, **Mauatur** (☎3387-1283; mauatur@viscondemaua.org; ☺10am-6pm Mon-Wed, 9am-6pm Thu & Sat, 9am-11pm Fri, 10am-4pm Sun) operates a tourist information hut with brochures and photos of area accommodations. Staff can help with room reservations upon request.

Wi-fi is very spotty and slow in the valley. There's an intermittent signal at the tourist information hut and a few pousadas.

ℹ Getting There & Around

Visconde de Mauá has no bus station. Buses stop at the top of Mauá's main street and in the center of Maringá before ending their run at Maromba's town square.

All public transport into Mauá passes through Resende, a city on the national park's eastern outskirts. The most useful buses, operated by Resendense, run three to five times daily from Resende to Maromba (R$6.80, two hours). Viação São Miguel also runs local buses from Resende but only goes as far as Mauá village (R$2.60, 1½ hours). at 8:30am, 1:40pm and 7pm Monday through Saturday, plus 8am and 7pm Sunday.

Cidade do Aço (www.cidadedoaco.com.br) runs one direct bus weekly between Rio and Maromba (R$56, 4½ hours), leaving Rio at 7:30pm on Fridays and returning from Maromba at 4pm on Sundays and holidays. Otherwise, catch one of Cidade do Aço's frequent Rio–Resende buses (R$30 to R$45) and transfer to a local bus in Resende. Note that long-distance buses arrive on the upper level of Resende's bus station, while local buses leave from the lower level.

Parque Nacional do Itatiaia

OXX24

Established in 1937, **Parque Nacional do Itatiaia** (☎3352-1292; icmbio.gov.br/parnaitatiaia; per day locals/foreigners R$11/22; ☺8am-5pm) 🖉 is Brazil's oldest national park, and one of its most ruggedly beautiful. Its lush, dark foliage contains more than 400 species of native bird and is also home to monkeys and sloths. Divided into upper and lower sections, the park features lakes, rivers, waterfalls, alpine meadows and primary and secondary Atlantic rainforests.

Don't let the tropical plants fool you; temperatures in the high country drop below freezing in June and, occasionally, the park even has a few snowy days! Bring warm clothes, even in summer.

◉ Sights & Activities

Each section of the park (upper and lower) has its own entrance station. Park headquarters and the adjacent **Muso Lago** are 9km north of Itatiaia town, in the park's lower, tamer section. From headquarters, a simple 400m walk takes you to **Lago Azul** (Blue Lake). A few kilometers up the road, short trails lead to the **Poronga, Véu de Noiva and Itaporani waterfalls** (lower section). For a longer hike in the low country, try the five-hour, 15km return trip to **Três Picos** (lower section; 1600m).

Climbing and trekking enthusiasts will want to pit themselves against the high country's more challenging peaks, cliffs and trails. The park's diminutive upper entrance station – almost two hours drive from Itatiaia town – is reached by way of a 15km extremely rugged unpaved road from a junction called Garganta do Registro, along Hwy BR-354 at the border between Rio and Minas Gerais states.

Prominently visible as you enter the park are the dramatic pointy profiles of **Agulhas Negras** (at 2787m, the area's highest peak) and, a bit further on, the boulders of **Prateleiras**. A guide is required for climbs to these peaks, or for the **Travessia Rui Braga**, a nine-hour downhill day hike that starts at the foot of Prateleiras and links the upper and lower parts of the park, allowing visitors to experience Itatiaia's alpine and Atlantic rainforest ecosystems in a single long day.

Contact the **Grupo Excursionista Agulhas Negras** (www.grupogean.com) 🖉, which organizes climbs throughout the year, or see the park's website (www.icmbio.gov.br/parnaitatiaia/guia-do-visitante.html) for a list of local guides; another excellent guide not on the park's list is **Levy Cardozo da Silva** (☎8812-0006; levy.ecologico@hotmail.com) 🖉.

🛏 Sleeping & Eating

Lodging inside the national park is generally upscale, with full board included at most hotels. Itatiaia town offers cheaper accommodations but a less inviting atmosphere.

Abrigo Rebouças HUT **$**
(☑ 3352-1292; reserva@abrigoreboucas.com.br;
dm per person R$10) This hikers' shelter in the
high country, with a gas stove and electricity, provides basic accommodations for up to
20 people but no food or other supplies. Reserve as far in advance as possible; the place
fills up fast!

Ypê Amarelo CAMPGROUND, POUSADA **$**
(☑ 3352-1232; www.pousadaypeamarelo.com.br;
João Mauricio Macedo Costa 352; campsite per
person with/without breakfast R$45/35, r per person R$65; 🛜 ➕) This combination pousada/
campground just north of the Via Dutra has
pleasant green grounds, hot showers, a pool,
a sauna and bicycles for rent. It's a 15-minute
walk west of the bus station (R$10 by taxi).

Hotel do Ypê HOTEL **$$**
(☑ 3352-1453; www.hoteldoype.com.br; s/d with
full board from R$260/330; 🛜 ➕) About 8.5km
north of the park entrance, near the end of
the road, the nicest of the lower park's three
hotels is close to several hiking trails, with
comfortable rooms and chalets for rent. Toucans and hummingbirds feed in abundance
outside the breakfast room window, and
Saturdays there's a great lunchtime barbecue (R$50 for nonguests) served outdoors
around the pool.

ℹ Getting There & Around

The village of Itatiaia is most easily reached from
the nearby city of Resende (the hub for buses
to/from Rio). Resendense and Penedo bus lines
run regularly between Itatiaia and Resende
(R$3.05, every 20 minutes on weekdays, every
40 minutes on weekends). Three daily buses
(R$2) run from Itatiaia village into the national
park, leaving Itatiaia's Igreja Matriz church at
7am, noon and 3pm. A taxi ride from Itatiaia
village to the end of the park road costs approximately R$40.

NORTH OF RIO DE JANEIRO

The mountains north of Rio rise up with
shapes so improbable and dramatic, they
catch your attention even from a great distance. Landing at Galeão international airport or surveying the northern skyline from
the top of Rio's Pão de Açúcar (Sugarloaf),
your eye is automatically drawn to the intriguing sawtooth ridge on the horizon. In
the 19th century, the allure of these mountains led Brazil's imperial family to set up
a summer residence in Petrópolis, and inspired the country's first Swiss immigrants
to choose Nova Friburgo as their New World
home.

More recently, climbers from all over the
world have become enamored of the vertiginous rocky faces of the Serra dos Órgãos
(Organ Pipe Range). To this day, the cooler
climate and recreational opportunities,
along with the region's imperial and immigrant legacy, continue to attract visitors
from Rio and beyond.

Petrópolis

☑ 0XX24 / POP 296,000 / ELEV 809M
A lovely mountain retreat with a decidedly
European flavor, Petrópolis is where Dom
Pedro II's imperial court spent the summer
when Rio got too muggy, and it's still a favorite weekend getaway for cariocas (residents of Rio city). The city center, with its
picturesque parks, bridges, canals and old-fashioned street lamps is easily explored on
foot or by horse and carriage.

◉ Sights & Activities

Most museums and other attractions are
closed on Monday.

A fun way to get oriented is by taking
a **horse and carriage ride**. Nineteenth-century *vitórias*, carriages of British design,
leave from in front of the Museu Imperial
and make 30- to 45-minute circuits of the
downtown area (R$50 to R$60).

★ **Museu Imperial** PALACE, MUSEUM
(www.museuimperial.gov.br; Rua da Imperatriz
220; admission adult/student R$8/4; ⊙11am-5:30pm Tue-Sun) Petrópolis' top draw is this
impeccably preserved 19th-century palace.
Felt slippers provided at the entrance help
protect the fine wood floors – great fun to
slide around in! Displays include the 1.95kg
imperial crown, with its 639 diamonds and
77 pearls, and the ruby-encrusted, feather-shaped gold pen used to sign the *Lei Aurea,*
which freed Brazil's remaining slaves in
1888.

Cervejaria Bohemia BREWERY
(www.bohemia.com.br/ceverjaria; Alfredo Pachá
166; adults/students & seniors R$19.50/9.50;
⊙11am-6pm Wed-Fri, 11am-8pm Sat & Sun) The
city's newest attraction is the self-guided
tour at this well-respected brewery, where
interactive exhibits trace the history of beer

Petrópolis

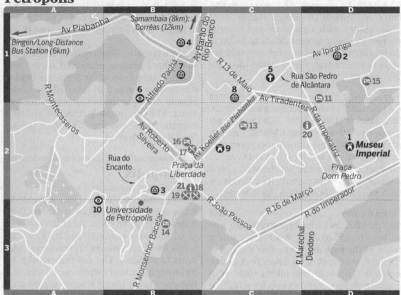

making and visitors can sample speciality beers (Escura, Weiss or Confraria) that are only brewed here. The on-site bar/restaurant is the only spot in Brazil you can get Bohemia on draft.

Catedral São Pedro de Alcântara   CHURCH
(Sao Pedro de Alcântara 60; ☉8am-6pm) Petrópolis' cathedral houses the tombs of Brazil's last emperor, Dom Pedro II, his wife Dona Teresa and their daughter, Princesa Isabel. The **bell tower**, which offers fine views of the city, was closed indefinitely at the time of research.

Palácio Rio Negro   PALACE
(Av Koeller 255; ☉10am-5pm Tue-Sat) **FREE** This grand yellow edifice, long a summer home for Brazil's presidents, has recently been opened for guided tours in English, Spanish and Portuguese.

Casa da Ipiranga   HISTORIC BUILDING
(☑2231-8718; casadaipiranga.blogspot.com; Av Ipiranga 716; admission R$8; ☉noon-6pm Wed-Mon) One of Petrópolis' finest mansions, the Casa da Ipiranga is open to visitors by guided tour. Other historical buildings can be viewed from the outside only, including the **Palácio da Princesa Isabel** (Av Koeller

s/n) and the **Casa do Barão de Mauá** (Praça da Confluencia).

Casa de Santos Dumont   MUSEUM
(Rua do Encanto 22; admission R$5; ☉9:30:am-5pm Tue-Sun) This charming house was the summer home of Brazil's diminutive father of aviation and inventor of the wristwatch. Photos and exhibits document Dumont's many inventions.

Palácio Cristal   HISTORIC BUILDING
(Alfredo Pachá; ☉9am-6pm Tue-Sun) **FREE** Built in France and imported in 1879, this ornate iron and glass structure was originally used as a hothouse for growing orchids. It's now a venue for evening cultural events.

Trono de Fátima   VIEWPOINT
Enjoy great views of Petrópolis and the surrounding hills from this 3.5m Italian sculpture of the NS de Fátima Madonna. To reach it, turn right as you leave the Casa de Santos Dumont and continue walking uphill, always taking the right fork.

Trekking Petrópolis   OUTDOORS
(☑2235-7607; www.rioserra.com.br/trekking) Organizes city tours, hikes, mountain-biking and bird-watching trips in the nearby Mata Atlântica rainforest.

Petrópolis

◎ Top Sights
1 Museu Imperial D2

◎ Sights
2 Casa da Ipiranga D1
3 Casa de Santos Dumont....................B2
4 Casa do Barão de Mauá..................... B1
5 Catedral São Pedro de
   Alcântara...................................C1
6 Cervejaria Bohemia............................ B1
7 Palácio Cristal................................... B1
8 Palácio da Princesa Isabel.................C1
9 Palácio Rio Negro C2
10 Trono de Fátima................................A3

◉ Sleeping
11 Casablanca Imperial..........................D1
12 Pousada 14 Bis F2
13 Pousada Imperial Koeller....................C2
14 Pousada Magister................................B3
15 Pousada Monte Imperial......................D1
16 Solar do Império B2

◈ Eating
Bordeaux......................................(see 2)
17 Leopoldina B2
18 Luigi B2
19 Restaurante Paladar B2

ℹ Information
20 Tourist Information (Centro
   de Cultura).................................D2
21 Tourist Information (Praça da
   Liberdade).................................B2

🛏 Sleeping

★Samambaia Hostel　　　HOSTEL, POUSADA **$**
(📞2242-3478; www.samambaiahostel.org; Estrada da Samambaia 138, Samambaia; dm R$65, d R$130-160, ste R$550; 🛜❄) 🅿 In an 18th-century mansion 8km outside Petrópolis, on the Burle Marx–designed grounds of his grandmother's estate, Swiss-Brazilian Jean-Charles has created this stunning hostel, pousada and environmental education center. Rooms in the main house ooze character, named after luminaries who once stayed there (Evita Perón, Brigitte Bardot, etc). Amenities include peacocks, ponies, bike trails, yoga classes, fireplaces and nature displays.

**Pousada Imperial
Koeller**　　　　　　　POUSADA **$$**
(📞2243-4330; www.pousadaimperialkoeller.com.br; Av Koeller 99; r R$195-315; @🛜❄) This gabled gem, dating back to 1875, is right in the heart of things, along architecturally stunning Av Koeller. Its sister hotel **Pousada Monte Imperial** (📞tel, info 2237-1664; www.pousadamonteimperial.com.br; José Alencar 27; r R$195-315; 🛜❄), in an old vine-covered house on the hillside above the Museu Imperial, shares the same rates.

Casablanca Imperial　　　HOTEL **$$**
(📞2242-6662; www.casablancahotel.com.br; Rua da Imperatriz 286; s/d with fan R$190/220, with air-con R$220/265; ❄🛜❄) Almost next door to the Museu Imperial, the Casablanca has a range of rooms – the best feature high ceilings, old-fashioned shutters, large bathrooms with tubs, and antique furnishings.

Pousada 14 Bis　　　　POUSADA **$$**
(📞2231-0946; www.pousada14bis.com.br; Buenos Aires 192; s/d with fan from R$90/175, with air-con R$150/250; ❄) On a quiet residential street near the downtown bus station, the restored colonial Pousada 14 Bis has handsome, well-appointed rooms with comfortable beds. The best offer lovely wood floors and balconies overlooking the mountains or the garden out back.

Pousada Magister　　　POUSADA **$$**
(📞2242-1054; www.pousadamagister.com.br; Monsenhor Bacelar 71; s/d from R$135/235; ❄🛜❄) This century-old mansion near the Casa de

Santos Dumont blends Old World elegance with modern amenities.

Pousada da Alcobaça
POUSADA $$$

(☑2221-1240; www.pousadadaalcobaca.com.br; Goulão 298, Corrêas; d from R$424; ✸ 🛜 ⊠) Midway between Petrópolis and Parque Nacional Serra dos Órgãos, this beautiful hotel has a pool, a sauna, a tennis court and lovely gardens crossed by a small river. There's also an excellent restaurant (p142).

Solar do Império
HOTEL $$$

(☑2103-3000; www.solardoimperio.com.br; Av Koeller 376; Fri & Sat r R$435-720, midweek R$398-635; 🛜 ⊠) Centrally located on Praça da Liberdade, with polished wood floors, 5m-high ceilings, grand fireplaces, a pool, sauna and spa, the meticulously restored Solar do Império will make you feel like a member of the royal family. The attached Leopoldina restaurant (p142) is one of the city's finest.

✖ Eating

Restaurante Paladar
SELF-SERVE $

(www.paladarpetropolis.com.br; Barão do Amazonas 25; per kg R$46.90; ☺11am-4pm Tue-Sun) Prices are higher than at your average per-kilo joint, but the atmosphere can't be beat at this classy converted mansion across from Praça da Liberdade. Watch the horse-drawn carriages clip-clop by as you enjoy classic Brazilian fare on the old-fashioned wraparound porch.

Bordeaux
INTERNATIONAL $$

(☑2242-5711; www.bordeauxvinhos.com.br; Av Ipiranga 716; fixed-price lunches R$20-26, mains R$24-60; ☺noon-5pm & 7pm-midnight Mon-Sat, noon-5pm Sun) On the picturesque grounds of the Casa da Ipiranga, these converted stables provide a pleasant backdrop for the menu of pastas, risottos, fish and meat dishes backed up by an extensive wine cellar.

Luigi
ITALIAN $$

(www.massasluigi.com.br; Praça da Liberdade 185; pizza R$19-49, pasta R$20-36; ☺11am-midnight) A charming Italian restaurant set in an old house with tall ceilings and creaky floors. The regular menu is supplemented by an antipasto bar (per 100g R$6.90) and an all-you-can-eat buffet (R$21.90). The pizzeria next door serves a *rodízio de pizza* (all-you-can-eat pizza, R$21.90) four nights a week.

★Restaurante Alcobaça
BRAZILIAN $$$

(☑2221-1240; www.pousadadaalcobaca.com.br/ingles/rest1ing.htm; Goulão 298, Corrêas; mains

R$45-69) 🍴 Verdant, flowery grounds and a gorgeous mountain setting enhance the mood of relaxed elegance in the lovely glass-walled dining room of Pousada da Alcobaça (p142), 12km outside Petrópolis. The locally sourced menu revolves around trout, steak, shrimp, chicken and pasta accompanied by fruit, veggies and herbs harvested from the pousada's own organic gardens. The Saturday *feijoada* (bean-and-meat stew) is truly legendary.

Leopoldina
BRAZILIAN $$$

(mains R$38-79) Tall windows flanked by murals of monkeys, capybaras and tropical foliage create a cheerful mood at this renowned restaurant attached to the Hotel Solar do Império (p142). Chef Nao Hara balances traditional recipes against more whimsical creations, using ingredients that range from lamb to lobster, figs to filberts. The midweek executive lunch (mains R$24.90) is especially good value.

ℹ Information

Bradesco (Rua do Imperador 268) One of many downtown ATMs.

Job Net (16 de Março 80; internet per hr R$6; ☺9am-8pm Mon-Fri, 9am-6pm Sat) Internet and Skype access.

Tourist Information (☑0800-024-1516; destinopetropolis.com.br) Two conveniently located offices at Praça da Liberdade (Praça da Liberdade; ☺9am-6pm) and at the Centro de Cultura (Praça Visconde de Mauá 305; ☺9am-6:30pm Mon-Fri), across from the Museu Imperial.

ℹ Getting There & Around

Única and Fácil buses from Rio (R$20, 1½ hours, half-hourly from 5:30am to midnight) drop you at the Leonel Brizola bus station in Bingen, 6km outside downtown Petrópolis. To reach the downtown bus station (Terminal de Integração), transfer to local bus number 100 (R$2.80, 30 minutes, every 10 to 15 minutes).

Vassouras

☑0XX24 / POP 34,000 / ELEV 434M

Vassouras, a now-quiet town 118km north of Rio, was the most important city in the Paraíba valley in the first half of the 19th century. Local coffee barons, with titles of nobility granted by the Portuguese crown, built huge *fazendas* in the surrounding hills. With the abolition of slavery in 1888, the depletion of the soil and the relocation of coffee production to São Paulo state, the importance of Vassouras diminished, but several historic buildings from the boom days still survive in the pleasant town center.

The area's biggest attractions are the coffee *fazendas* several kilometers outside of town, some of them on the scale of French châteaux and with gardens to match. To visit these, you really need your own vehicle; otherwise, you'll run up some hefty cab fares or calf muscles!

◎ Sights

The town's large central square, known as the **Campo Belo**, is a picturesque grassy slope dotted with palm trees and a fountain. Twin roosters crown the spires of the **Matriz NS de Conceição** church at the top of the hill.

The countryside around Vassouras teems with old coffee *fazendas* protected by historical preservation institutes. Most are still privately owned, so prior permission is required before touring them. The most popular are the imposing **Fazenda do Secretário** (☑2488-0150), **Mulungú Vermelho** (☑9829-3628; www.fazendamulunguvermelho.com), **Santa Eufrásia** (☑9994-9494; www.fazendasantaeufrasia.com), **Cachoeira do Mato Dentro** (☑9914-2286), **São Luiz da Boa Sorte** (www.fazendasaoluizdaboasorte.com.br) and **Cachoeira Grande** (☑2471-1264; www.fazendacachoeiragrande.com.br). The Casa de Cultura (p143) has detailed information and can help arrange visits.

Museu Casa da Hera   MUSEUM
(casadahera.wordpress.com; Dr Fernandes Jr 160; ◎10am-5pm Tue-Fri, 1-5pm Sat & Sun) FREE A few blocks from Vassouras' tourist office, this recently reopened museum displays antique hand-carved furniture and other colonial relics in the grand old home of aristocratic heiress Eufrásia Teixeira Leite. On-site guide Ramon Telles brings the building's history to life and sheds light on Vassouras' coffee-growing heritage with excellent free tours in English, French, German and Spanish.

✿ Festivals & Events

Spanning two weekends in April, **Café, Cachaça & Chorinho** celebrates Vassouras' triple heritage of coffee, *choro* (improvised samba) music and *cachaça* production, with concerts and tastings throughout the region.

For two weeks in late July, Vassouras buzzes with more than just coffee during the annual **Festival Vale do Café** (www.festival valedocafe.com). Daily concerts are scheduled, and some *fazendas* host dinners featuring period food and dress.

🛏 Sleeping & Eating

Mara Palace   HOTEL $$
(☑2471-1993; www.marapalace.com.br; Raul Fernandes 121; s/d from R$165/195; ❋�奈❃) A centrally located three-star with pools and a sauna. Rooms in the main building are preferable to the musty ones in the concrete annex out back.

Sabor do Vale   SELF-SERVE $
(Furquim 50; per kilo R$26.90; ◎11am-3:30pm) Locals favor this recently opened per-kilo lunch place one block below the main square, with a warren of high-ceilinged rooms and a wood stove laden with *comida mineira* – meat, fish, rice, beans, kale and other classic fare from the neighboring state of Minas Gerais.

Hipólito   BRAZILIAN $$
(☑2471-2805; Praça Barão do Campo Belo; mains per person R$28-56; ◎7-11pm Tue-Fri, noon-4pm & 7-11pm Sat, noon-4pm Sun) For fine dining and a good wine list, Vassouras' top choice is this grand 19th-century mansion with a pleasant back patio just above the tourist office on the main square.

❶ Information

Casa de Cultura (☑2471-2765; casadecultur aptn@gmail.com; Praça Barão do Campo Belo; ◎9am-6pm Mon-Fri, to 4pm Sat, to 2pm Sun) Displays photos and distributes information brochures (in Portuguese) about nearby coffee *fazendas*.

❶ Getting There & Around

From the **bus station** (☑2471-1055; Praça Juiz Machado Jr), **Útil** (www.util.com.br) runs five to six daily buses to Rio (R$43, 2½ hours). **Viação Progresso** (www.viacaoprogresso.com.br) also runs a 7:50am bus to Petrópolis (R$35, 2¾ hours) Monday through Saturday.

To get to the *fazendas*, you'll need your own wheels or a taxi.

Teresópolis

0XX21 / POP 164,000 / ELEV 871M

Do as Empress Maria Tereza used to do and escape from the steamy summer heat of Rio to the cool mountain retreat of Teresópolis, the highest city in the state, nestled in the strange, organ-pipe rock formations of the Serra dos Órgãos. The gorgeous winding road from Rio

ALE SANTOS / GETTY IMAGES ©

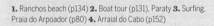

1. Ranchos beach (p134) **2.** Boat tour (p131), Paraty **3.** Surfing, Praia do Arpoador (p80) **4.** Arraial do Cabo (p152)

LONELY PLANET IMAGES / GETTY IMAGES ©

Beaches of Rio de Janeiro State

Amerigo Vespucci said it best: 'If there were an earthly paradise, it wouldn't be far from here!' Tiny Rio state offers a stunning variety of beaches. Whether you're into surfing, diving, bronzing your bod or strutting your stuff on a seaside dance floor, you'll find it here.

Ilha Grande

A nature-lover's vision of tropical paradise, Ilha Grande (p121) has more trails than motorized vehicles, and endless stretches of secluded sands. Circumnavigate the island on foot, or hop from beach to beach on the classic round-the-island boat tour.

Paraty

Paraty's (p127) spectacular mosaic of bays, islands, mountains, waterfalls and beaches would be reason enough to visit; the colonial center's whitewashed houses, kaleidoscopic latticework and picturesque cobbled streets are like icing on the cake.

Saquarema

Laid back and off the beaten track, Saquarema (p151) is best known to surfers, who flock here for international competitions; less-athletic types can admire its gorgeous 19th-century church, perched high on a promontory.

Arraial do Cabo

Even in Brazil, it'd be hard to find a cluster of beaches any prettier than this. Surrounded by prime diving and whale-watching spots, Arraial's (p152) white sands and blue-green waters are downright dazzling.

Búzios

If you'd like a few chic comforts and a little nightlife to go with that perfect tan, look no further than Búzios (p154). The preferred destination of Brazil's (and half of Argentina's!) beautiful people, this scalloped peninsula full of dreamy beaches is as luxurious and as decadent as it gets.

Teresópolis

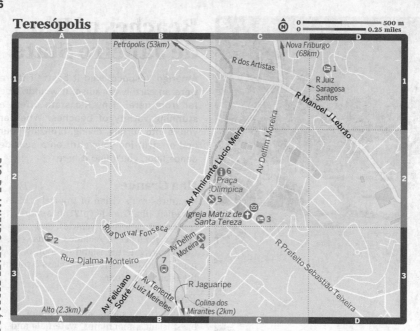

N 0 — 500 m
0 — 0.25 miles

Teresópolis

Sleeping

Eating

Information

Transport

to Teresópolis climbs steeply through a padded green jungle, with bald peaks towering dramatically overhead the entire way.

The Quebra Frascos, the royal family of the Second Empire, once resided here. Today the city's principal attraction is the surrounding landscape and its natural treasures.

For over three decades, Teresópolis's Comary neighborhood bore the distinction of being the training base of Brazil's national football squad but, as of 2013, plans were underway to move the team to a new training faclilty in Rio's Barra da Tijuca in preparation for the 2014 FIFA World Cup.

⊙ Sights & Activities

The area's main attraction is Parque Nacional da Serra dos Órgãos. The **Dedo de Deus** (God's Finger) is the town symbol, a dramatic rock spire visible from all over town. **Colina dos Mirantes**, in the southern suburb of Fazendinha, is an especially good place to view the city and its mountain backdrop. On clear days you can see as far as Rio's Pão de Açúcar and the Baía de Guanabara.

Many more attractions lie outside town along the road to Nova Friburgo (also known as the 'Estrada Tere-Fri'). For details, see the boxed text on p148.

🛏 Sleeping

Albergue Recanto do Lord HOSTEL $
(☎ 2742-5586; www.teresopolishostel.com.br; Luiza Pereira Soares 109; dm/s/d R$35/60/80; @ 🛜) Designed to look like an orange castle, this hostel commands amazing views of the Dedo de Deus and other nearby peaks from its hillside perch north of downtown. The friendly owners can provide a wealth of information about the surrounding area.

Várzea Palace Hotel HOTEL $
(☎ 2742-0878; hhotelvarzea@bol.com.br; Prefeito Sebastião Teixeira 41/55; s/d R$85/125, with shared bathroom from R$50/65; 🛜) This striking if

crumbling hotel, right off the main square, has been a Teresópolis institution since 1916. There are still plenty of atmospheric touches, including ornamental tiles, parquet wood floors, spacious rooms and high ceilings. The nicer suites have terraces.

Hotel Philipp
HOTEL **$$**

(☑ 2742-2970; www.hotelphilipp.com.br; Durval Fonseca 1333; s/d R$130/150; 🛜 ⛝) Uphill 1km west of the bus station, the Philipp feels a bit like a German mountain lodge, with a fireplace, pool and views of the mountains from the glass-walled breakfast room.

Hotel Rosa dos Ventos
HOTEL **$$$**

(☑ 2644-9900; www.hotelrosadosventos.com.br; Estrada Tere-Fri, km22.6; d incl breakfast from R$460, with full board from R$660; ⛝ 🛜 ⛝) Way up in the mountains, this luxurious Alpine-style resort has its own lake and network of hiking trails. Magnificent views abound from the many terraces and on-site restaurants. It's 22km out of town along the road to Nova Friburgo.

 Eating

Cheiro de Mato
HEALTH FOOD **$**

(☑ 2742-1899; Av Delfim Moreira 140; fixed-price lunches R$5.50-12; ⊙ 11am-3:30pm Mon-Fri) This is a good place for health food, including brown rice, salads and other vegetarian options. Three fixed-price plate sizes are available at very reasonable prices.

★ Linguiça do Padre
CHURRASCARIA **$$**

(☑ 2641-0065; Estrada Tere-Fri, km33; mains per person R$18-38; ⊙ 11am-3pm Mon-Sat) If you're touring the Teresópolis–Friburgo highway, don't miss this local favorite beside a rushing river. The menu ranges from R$5 *linguiça* (spicy Portuguese sausage) sandwiches to substantial country meals featuring trout, goat or roast suckling pig. Local strawberries also figure prominently on the menu, in fresh squeezed strawberry-orange juice (R$7 per pitcher) or served with whipped cream (R$7) for dessert.

Taberna Alpina
GERMAN **$$**

(☑ 2742-0123; Duque de Caxias 131; mains R$24-58; ⊙ 8am-midnight Tue-Sun) The Taberna's cozy interior room, sporting wooden benches with heart-shaped cutouts, is reminiscent of the Alps. So is the menu, featuring German mustard, brown bread, goulash, and smoked pork with sauerkraut.

❶ Information

HSBC (Av Delfim Moreira 746) One of several ATMs near the main square.

Tourist Office (☑ 2742-5561; www.teresopolis.rj.gov.br; Praça Olímpica; ⊙ 9am-6pm Mon-Sat, to 5pm Sun) In the town center.

❶ Getting There & Away

The **bus station** (Rua Primeiro de Maio) is south of the main square. **Viação Teresópolis** (☑ 2742-2676; www.viacaoteresopolis.com.br) runs buses to Rio (R$24, 1½ hours, hourly from 5am to 10pm), Petrópolis (R$15, 1½ hours, six daily between 7am and 7pm) and Nova Friburgo (R$17, two hours, five daily between 7am and 7pm).

DON'T MISS

THE TERESÓPOLIS–FRIBURGO SCENIC CIRCUIT

Pretty mountain vistas and European heritage are on full display along the **Circuito Turístico Tere-Fri** (www.terefri.com.br), a 68km scenic highway connecting the towns of Teresópolis and Nova Friburgo.

Starting from Teresópolis, highlights include the **Mulher de Pedra** (Woman of Stone) viewpoint at 12km, where a distant mountain really *does* look like a reclining woman; the **Fazenda Geneve** (www.fazendageneve.com.br) at 16km, where you can pet baby goats, buy local cheese, stroll the gardens or indulge in a fine French meal; the **Cachoeira dos Frades** turnoff at 21.5km, where an unpaved side road leads through an idyllic valley to a waterfall with a swimming hole; Hotel Rosa dos Ventos (p147) at 22.6km, one of many opulent hotels along the route; the Linguiça do Padre (p147) restaurant at 33km; and **Queijaria Suíça** at 49km, where a Swiss cheese factory sits adjacent to a small museum tracing two centuries of Swiss culture in the Friburgo area.

Additional points of interest are indicated on a handy map available throughout the region. It's easiest to drive the route in your own car, although local buses travel through here and will let you off wherever you like.

RIO DE JANEIRO STATE PARQUE NACIONAL DA SERRA DOS ÓRGÃOS

Parque Nacional da Serra dos Órgãos

Created in 1939, this national park covers 118 sq km of mountainous terrain between Teresópolis and Petrópolis. The park's most distinctive features are the strangely shaped peaks of **Pedra do Sino** (2263m), **Pedra do Açu** (2230m), **Agulha do Diabo** (2020m), **Nariz do Frade** (1919m), **Dedo de Deus** (1651m), **Pedra da Ermitage** (1485m) and **Dedo de Nossa Senhora** (1320m). With so many peaks, it's no wonder that this is the mountain climbing, rock climbing and trekking center of Brazil. The region has extensive trails, the most famous of which is the 42km, three-day traverse over the mountains from Petrópolis to Teresópolis. Unfortunately, most of the trails are unmarked and off the available maps. Hiring a guide, however, is easy. Inquire at the **national park entrance** (☑2152-1100; www.icmbio.gov.br/parnaserradosorgaos; admission Brazilians/foreigners R$11/22; ☉8am-5pm) ⬤ or with Trekking Petrópolis (p140). The best time for walks is from May to October (the drier months).

The main entrance to the national park is at the south edge of the town of Teresópolis, off Hwy BR-116 from Rio, about 4km from the center. Walking trails, waterfalls, natural swimming pools and tended lawns and gardens make this a pretty place for a picnic.

From the main entrance, the road extends into the park as far as Barragem Beija Flor. There are several good walks from near here. The highlight is the **Trilha Pedra do Sino** – a strenuous round-trip of about eight hours from the end of the park road (R$33 trail fee). The trail passes **Cachoeira Veu da Noiva**, the vegetation changes from rainforest to grassland, and the reward is a panoramic view stretching all the way to Rio de Janeiro and the Baía de Guanabara. For a shorter walk, head up to the **Mirante Alexandre Oliveira** (1100m), from where there is a good view of Teresópolis – it's about a one-hour round-trip from the park road.

There is another, secondary entrance down in the southeast corner of the national park, off the road from Rio. It also has an information center, walking trails and waterfalls.

ⓘ Getting There & Away

To get to the park's main entrance from the city center of Teresópolis, take the hourly 'Soberbo' bus (R$2.90). Alternatively, take the more frequent 'Alto' bus and get off at the Praçinha do Alto, from which it's a 10-minute walk south to the park's main entrance. Both buses can be caught at multiple stops along the town's main drag, Av Almirante Lúcio Meira. A taxi ride from town to the park entrance costs about R$25.

Nova Friburgo

OXX22 / POP 182,000 / ELEV 846M

In 1818, newly crowned Portuguese King Dom João VI started recruiting immigrants from Switzerland and Germany to help settle his vast Brazilian territory. The first 30 families to arrive, from the Swiss canton of Friburg, immediately set out to create a perfect little village reminiscent of their home country in the mountains north of Rio. Traces of Swiss and German heritage remain in modern Friburgo, in the local architecture, the town's passion for floral decoration and the fair-haired, blue-eyed features of some residents. Nowadays the local economy revolves around the lingerie industry, while tourism revolves around the region's resplendent natural attractions: waterfalls, woods, trails, sunny mountain mornings and cool evenings.

⊙ Sights & Activities

Most of the sights are a few kilometers out of town. Survey the surrounding area from nearby **Pico da Caledônia** (2310m), which offers fantastic views and launching sites for hang gliders. It's a 6km uphill hike from the Alto do Cascatinha neighborhood; to reach the trailhead, take a local bus marked Cascatinha-Interpass (R$2.90, 15 minutes).

Ten kilometers to the north of town, you can hike (trail fee R$6) to Pedra do Cão Sentado, a rock formation resembling a sitting dog that serves as Friburgo's town symbol. To the southeast, Lumiar (34km from Nova Friburgo and reachable by local bus) is a popular destination for Brazilian ecotourists, with cheap pousadas, waterfalls, walking trails and white-water adventures centered on the Encontro dos Rios, the tumultuous confluence of three local rivers. Guided adventure tours of the area can be arranged through the Alê Friburgo

Nova Friburgo

Hostel (p149) or **Lumiar Aventura** (☎8131-6768; www.lumiaraventura.com).

🛏 Sleeping

Alê Friburgo Hostel
HOSTEL $
(☎2522-0540; www.friburgohostel.com; Bizzotto Filho 2; dm/s/d R$40/60/120; @ 🛜 ⊇) This hostel, 2km straight uphill from Friburgo's town square, compensates for its remote location with friendly staff and great amenities, including a pool, sauna and nice mountain views.

Hotel Serra Everest
HOTEL $$
(☎2522-6443; www.hotelserraeverest.com.br; Adolfo Lautz 128; s/d/tr/q with fan R$99/156/198/250, with air-con R$120/180/230/270; 🌀🛜⊇) Perched on a steep hill a few blocks from the center, this hotel has a pool, pet peacocks and great views.

Hotel Auberge Suisse
HOTEL $$
(☎2541-1270; www.aubergesuisse.com.br; Rua 10 de Outubro, Amparo; s/d chalets from R$190/317;

Nova Friburgo

🛏 Sleeping
1 Hotel Maringá	C1
2 Hotel Serra Everest	C2

🍴 Eating
3 Crescente	B1
Dona Mariquinha	(see 1)
4 Quinta Rica	C2

ℹ Information
5 Tourist Office	C2

ℹ Transport
6 Local Bus Station	B1

🌀🛜⊇) The luxury chalets here, 12km northeast of Nova Friburgo, all have wi-fi and minibars; and most have fireplaces and DVD players. The pretty landscaped grounds include indoor and outdoor pools, a sauna and a small collection of farm

WORTH A TRIP

A BIRDWATCHER'S PARADISE IN RIO'S BACK YARD

Guapi Assu Bird Lodge (☑ 021-2745-3998; www.guapiassubirdlodge.com; s/d with full board R$320/520; ✿ @ ☎), only 80km from Rio's Galeão airport, is part of the non-profit **Regua nature reserve** (Reserva Ecológica de Guapi Assu; www.regua.co.uk), a 50-sq-km tract at the foot of the Serra dos Órgãos where Nicholas and Raquel Locke have dedicated their lives to restoring native ecosystems. Serious birders, or anyone who wants a genuine taste of Brazil's remarkable biodiversity, should head here. Volunteers from around the world are engaged in an ambitious reforestation project, while school kids from the local community are invited to use the reserve as a hands-on environmental education laboratory.

The comfy rooms have solar hot water, meals are served family-style around a big table and the library of nature books makes for great browsing, caipirinha in hand, after a long day of bird-watching. The artificial pond ecosystem next to the lodge draws in a stupendous array of birds, as well as families of capybaras. A network of trails surrounding the lodge offers opportunities to enter into deeper forest and visit other attractions, including a lovely waterfall. For details on reaching the lodge by bus, car or van shuttle, see the lodge's website.

animals, whose milk is used to make cheese for the excellent on-site restaurant specializing in traditional Swiss cuisine: raclette, fondue and trout.

✖ Eating

Friburgo's central grassy strip is lined with eateries for all budgets. A raucous youthful bar scene erupts nightly along Rua Monte Libano.

Quinta Rica   CHURRASCARIA $
(☑ 2523-3304; Praça Getúlio Vargas 104; per kilo R$29.90; ⏱ 10:30am-11pm) This restaurant serves a remarkably varied buffet featuring 150 dishes, including grilled meat.

Dona Mariquinha   BUFFET $$
(☑ 2522-2309; Monsenhor Miranda 110; lunch buffet R$34; ⏱ noon-3:30pm Tue-Sun, 7-9pm Mon-Fri) This friendly place features all-you-can-eat home cooking for R$34 at lunchtime and all-you-can-eat soup for R$10 in the evening. **Hotel Maringá** (☑ 2522-2309; hotelmaringa@yahoo.com.br; Monsenhor Miranda 110; s/d/tr R$80/140/175, with shared bathroom R$50/90/115; ☎) upstairs offers some of the most reasonably priced rooms in downtown Friburgo.

Crescente   FRENCH $$$
(☑ 2523-4616; www.elocrescente.com.br/crescente; General Osório 21; mains R$45-75; ⏱ 11:30am-11pm Thu-Sat & Mon, to 5pm Sun) This classy little place features French cuisine accompanied by wines from a dozen countries.

ℹ Information

Banco do Brasil (Praça Dermeval B Moreira 10) One of several ATMs downtown.

iFrog Cyber (Portugal 12; per hr R$4; ⏱ 8:30am-6pm Mon-Fri, 9am-1pm Sat) Internet access.

Tourist Office (☑ 2543-6307; circuito@ pmnf.rj.gov.br; Praça Dermeval B Moreira; ⏱ 8am-8pm Mon-Sat, to 6pm Sun) Has maps, complete lists of hotels and restaurants and excellent permanent staff, including the English-speaking Elaine and German-speaking Nair.

ℹ Getting There & Around

Nova Friburgo is a short jaunt from Rio, via Niterói, on bus line 1001. The ride is along a picturesque, winding, misty jungle road.

Nova Friburgo has two long-distance bus stations. From the **north bus station** (Rodoviária Norte; Praça Feliciano Costa), 2.5km north of the center, **Viação Teresópolis** (☑ 2522-2708; www.viacaoteresopolis.com.br) has buses to Teresópolis (R$17, two hours, five daily). From the **south bus station** (Rodoviária Sul; Ponte da Saudade), 4km south of the center, **Viação 1001** (☑ 2522-0400; www.autoviacao1001. com.br) has hourly buses to Rio (R$33 to R$39, 2½ hours) plus one direct bus to Cabo Frio on Saturday at 7am (R$43, 3¼ hours).

Local buses (R$2.90) connect both long-distance terminals to the central, **local bus station** just north of Praça Getúlio Vargas. Local buses also go to just about all the tourist attractions. Ask for details at the tourist office.

EAST OF RIO DE JANEIRO

East of Rio, the mountains recede and the coastal strip becomes flatter, punctuated by the sparkling lagoons of the Região dos Lagos (Lakes Region) and the dazzling white sands of the Costa do Sol (Sunny Coast). Some of Rio state's most beautiful beaches are found here. Only two hours from Rio by car, the area is a weekend playground for cariocas, with plenty of opportunities for nightlife and outdoor recreation.

Saquarema

0XX22 / POP 74,000

Straddling a spit of sand between a gorgeous lagoon and the open Atlantic, Saquarema is a laid-back little town 100km east of Rio. Polluting industries are forbidden in the municipality; the waters are clean, and fish and shrimp are abundant. Touted as the surfing capital of Brazil, its unmarred shoreline also attracts sportfishing enthusiasts and sun worshippers. The surrounding area is a horse-breeding and fruit-growing center; you can visit the orchards and pick fruit, or rent horses or a jeep and take to the hills. Most local pousadas can arrange these activities.

◎ Sights & Activities

The stunning white church of **NS de Nazaré** (1837), perched on the hill near the entrance to the lagoon, is the town's focal point. From this strategic spot you can survey the long, empty beaches, the lagoon and the mountains beyond. The mass held here on September 7 and 8 attracts around 150,000 pilgrims, second only to the Nazaré celebrations of Belém.

About 3km east of town is **Praia Itaúna**, Saquarema's most beautiful beach and one of the best surf spots in Brazil. National and international surfing competitions are held here each year, generally between May and October.

🛏 Sleeping & Eating

Most of the best places are near the Itaúna beachfront.

Pousada Canto da Vila   POUSADA $
(☑ 2651-1563; www.pousadacantodavila.com.br; Av Salgado Filho 52; d with fan R$116, with air-con R$158; 🕸🛜❄) This friendly beachfront place, just downhill from Saquarema's historic church, features bright, airy rooms, many with great views of surfers riding the waves.

Itaúna Hostel   HOSTEL $
(☑ 2653-8652; www.itaunahostel.com.br; Rua das Garoupas 100; dm/tw/d R$45/100/120; @🛜) A few blocks back from Itaúna beach, this small hostel offers spacious two- and five-bed dorms downstairs, two private rooms upstairs and an air-conditioned suite in the main house. Perks include hammocks and free use of bicycles.

Maasai Hotel Beach & Resort   HOTEL $$
(☑ 2651-1092; www.maasai.com.br; Travessa Itaúna 17; garden-view/ocean-view d R$250/350, ste R$420; 🕸@🛜❄) If you're looking for cushy digs, this place is a no-brainer. Maasai has a stunning beachfront location, comfy sitting rooms, a sauna and swimming pool and a pretty bar-restaurant overlooking the water (mains for two are between R$64 and R$98).

Garota da Itaúna   SEAFOOD $$
(☑ 2651-2156; Av Oceânica 165; mains per person R$24-45; ⊙11am-11pm Sun-Thu, to 1am Fri & Sat) The Garota's many attractions include a fabulous beachfront terrace and a wide variety of seafood specials. Enjoy the views but hang on to your beers – the wind can be vicious. It also rents simple rooms (single/double R$70/110).

Forno à Lenha   PIZZERIA $$
(☑ 2651-4088; Rua dos Mariscos 511; pizza from R$31; ⊙12:30pm-midnight Thu-Sun, from 5pm Mon-Wed) A few blocks back from Itaúna beach, this place has a cozy back room with a wood-burning oven, plus a front patio area where you can enjoy pizza and grilled meats.

ℹ Information

Centro de Atendimento ao Turista (☑ 2651-2123; turismo@saquarema.rj.gov.br; Av Saquarema; ⊙9am-5pm Mon-Fri, to 4pm Sat & Sun) Overlooking the lagoon, on the Itaúna side of the downtown bridge.

Lakes Shopping This tiny mall between downtown and Praia Itaúna has a Bradesco ATM downstairs and an internet place upstairs.

ℹ Getting There & Away

Viação 1001 (www.autoviacao1001.com.br) runs buses from Rio to Saquarema every other hour between 6:15am and 8:45pm, returning to Rio between 5:25am and 7:50pm (R$26, two hours).

Salineira (www.salineira.com.br) bus B145 runs direct from Saquarema to Cabo Frio four times daily between 6:30am and 10:40pm (R$4, one hour). The bus stop in Saquarema is on the ocean side of the bridge, one block from the main square in the town center.

Arraial do Cabo

0XX22 / POP 28,000

Arraial do Cabo, 45km east of Saquarema, is surrounded by gleaming white sand dunes and offers breathtaking beaches without half the touristy fuss of neighboring Búzios. Arraial is home to a working fishing port, Porto do Forno, which lends it a welcoming working-class demeanor. Some of the best beaches – pristine swathes of gorgeous sand and bright-green waters – are within an easy 15-minute stroll of the downtown bus station, while others are just a short boat ride away. Arraial is a renowned diving destination, and it's also a good place to observe humpback whales (*Megaptera novaeangliae*), whose migration routes pass directly offshore.

◉ Sights & Activities

Arraial's prime attractions lie along the shoreline. **Praia dos Anjos** has beautiful turquoise water but a little too much boat traffic for comfortable swimming. Just above the beach, look for the plaque commemorating Amerigo Vespucci's landing here in 1503. Vespucci left 24 men behind to start a settlement, making Arraial one of the first European toeholds in the Americas.

Favorite beaches within a short walking distance of town are **Prainha** to the north of town; **Praia do Forno** (accessed by a 1km walking trail from Praia dos Anjos) to the northeast; and the vast **Praia Grande** to the west, where wilder surf races in off the open Atlantic.

There are several other stunning beaches along the mountainous peninsula just south of town. For near-aerial views, and the best sunset in the area, climb up to **Pontal do Atalaia**, a popular viewpoint at the top of the peninsula that also makes an excellent spot for whale watching in July and Aug.

Ilha de Cabo Frio is accessed by boat from Praia dos Anjos (R$40 for the standard four-hour excursion). **Praia do Farol** on the protected side of the island is a gorgeous beach with fine white sand. From here it is a 2½-hour walk to the lighthouse. The **Gruta Azul** (Blue Cavern), on the southwestern side of

the island, is another beautiful spot. Be alert, though: the entrance to the underwater cavern is submerged at high tide.

Tour operators who organize dives in these waters abound – the tourist office keeps a complete list. Dependable agencies include **PL Divers** (☑2622-1033; www.pldivers.com.br; Peçanha 57), **Sandmar** (☑2622-5703; www.sandmar.com.br; Epitácio Pessoa 21), and **Ocean Sub** (☑2622-4642; www.oceansub.com.br; Luiz Corrêa 3).

🛏 Sleeping

Prices quoted here are for the high season. Discounts of up to 40% are common in the low season.

Marina dos Anjos Hostel　　HOSTEL $
(☑2622-4060; www.marinadosanjos.com.br; Bernardo Lens 145; dm/d with HI card R$55/160, without card R$65/185; @🔊) One block back from Praia dos Anjos, this hostel is a wonderful base from which to explore the area. The helpful staff rents bicycles, canoes, snorkels, surfboards and diving equipment, and organizes dune-buggy tours to surrounding beaches. The central courtyard, with hammocks and pillows for lounging, is the venue for spontaneous evening barbecues and jam sessions.

**Hotel Pousada
Caminho do Sol**　　HOTEL $$
(☑2622-2029; www.caminhodosol.com.br; Miguel Angelo 55; r from R$178; 🔊≋) Right on Praia Grande, this pretty resort hotel with a pool and beautiful views is a big hit with visiting Brazilians looking for a romantic weekend.

Capitão n'Areia Pousada　　POUSADA $$
(☑2622-2720; www.capitaopousada.com; Santa Cruz 7; r R$200-295, ste R$410-630; ❄🔊≋) All decked out in white walls and nautical decor, this classy place in the heart of Marina dos Anjos has a sundeck, a sauna, a very shallow pool, a gym and spacious rooms overlooking the boats in the harbor below.

🍴 Eating

★**Bacalhau do Tuga**　　PORTUGUESE, SEAFOOD $$
(☑2622-1108; Praia dos Anjos; mains per person R$25-58; ⊘6-11pm Wed-Fri, from 1pm Sat & Sun) From humble origins selling codfish fritters from a beachside stand in 2008, the 'Tuga' (Portuguese guy) has ridden a wave of popular acclaim to open this full-fledged restaurant on the sands of Praia dos Anjos. Super-fresh ingredients are incorporated

into Portuguese classics, from seafood stews to custard tarts, served alongside local specialties like *peixe com banana* (grilled fish with bananas).

Água na Boca   SELF-SERVE **$$**
(☑2622-1106; Praça da Bandeira 1; per kg R$42; ☉11:30am-5pm) A stone's throw from the bus station, this recommended self-serve place includes plenty of seafood in its daily offerings.

Saint Tropez   SEAFOOD **$$$**
(Praça Daniel Barreto 2; mains per person R$34-69) Just a block up from Praia dos Anjos, this French-run eatery with Asterix and Obelix murals is a good spot for fresh fish; from 6pm onwards, it also serves pizza (R$23 to R$39).

ⓘ Information

The **tourist office** (☑2622-1949; turismo@ar raial.rj.gov.br; ☉8am-5pm) at the town's formal entry portico, 3km from the center, has English- and Spanish-speaking staff, and provides a helpful map.

Just around the corner from the bus station, you'll find a **multibank ATM**. Av Getúlio Vargas is home to the **post office** (Av Getúlio Vargas 19) and several internet places.

ⓘ Getting There & Away

The Arraial do Cabo **bus station** (Praça da Bandeira) is situated in the town center. Direct buses operated by **Viação 1001** (☑2622-1488; www. autoviacao1001.com.br) run from Rio to Arraial every two hours from 5:15am to 9pm, returning with the same frequency between 3:40am and 7:20pm (R$49, 3½ hours).

An alternative is to catch a Salineira municipal bus to Cabo Frio (R$4), then transfer to one of the half-hourly Rio-bound buses leaving from the Cabo Frio bus station.

For Búzios, take Salineira bus 414 (R$4, 1½ hours, six to seven daily).

Cabo Frio
0XX22 / POP 186,000
Sandwiched between sand dunes, lagoons and the sparkling Atlantic, Cabo Frio's naturally gorgeous setting has been seriously stunted by industry and overdevelopment. Still, on weekends and summer holidays its bars and beaches continue to draw throngs of happy-go-lucky Brazilians, whose merrymaking spirit is the city's strongest attraction.

The twin focal points for tourists are Praia do Forte, a stunning stretch of white sand and green waters named after the fort at its eastern end, and the restaurant-fringed Canal do Itajuru, which links nearby Lagoa de Araruama to the Atlantic Ocean.

◉ Sights & Activities

There are three sand-dune spots in and about Cabo Frio. The dunes of **Praia do Peró**, a super beach for surfing and surf casting, are 6km north in the direction of Búzios, near Ogivas and after Praia Brava and Praia das Conchas. The **Dama Branca** (White Lady) sand dunes are on the road to Arraial do Cabo. The **Pontal** dunes of Praia do Forte town beach stretch from the fort to Miranda hill. Robberies can pose a danger at the dunes, so get advice from locals before heading out.

Forte São Mateus   FORT
(☉10am-5pm Tue-Sun) **FREE** Forte São Mateus, a stronghold against pirates, was built between 1616 and 1620 to protect the lucrative brazilwood trade. You'll find it at the eastern end of Praia do Forte.

🛏 Sleeping & Eating

Hotel Atlântico   HOTEL **$**
(☑2643-0996; www.hotelatlantico.tur.br; José Bonifácio 302; s/d/tr R$86/122/153; ❄☎🤶) Five blocks inland from Praia do Forte, the faded but comfortable Atlântico has large rooms with frigobar and cable TV.

Pousada Boulevard   POUSADA **$$**
(☑2643-1456; www.pousadaboulevard.com; Marechal Floriano 237; r R$240-270; ❄🤶🏊) Perfectly placed in Cabo Frio's canalside restaurant district, this newer pousada offers high-end amenities like satellite TV, a sauna and a plunge pool. The best five rooms have canal views.

Malibu Palace Hotel   HOTEL **$$**
(☑2643-1955; www.malibupalace.com.br; Av do Contorno 900; r from R$245, with ocean view R$336; ❄🤶🏊) For views and location, it's hard to beat this central place overlooking Cabo Frio's dazzling beachfront.

Restaurante do Zé   BRAZILIAN **$$**
(☑2643-4277; Blvd Canal 33; mains per person R$20-48; ☉noon-midnight) The sidewalk tables at this animated eatery overlook the canal, one of the most picturesque spots in town. The house specialty is *picanha na chapa* (sizzling grilled steak).

Tia Maluca SEAFOOD $$

(☑2647-4158; Blvd Canal 109; mains per person R$23-45; ☺11am-midnight) This canal-side favorite specializes in delicious seafood served at a sea of tables on the sidewalk.

❶ Information

HSBC (Av Assunção 793) One of several ATMs on this downtown thoroughfare.

Tourist Office (☑2647-1689; turismo@ cabofrio.rj.gov.br; Av Américo Vespúcio s/n; ☺8am-6pm) Directly across from Praia do Forte; English spoken.

❶ Getting There & Away

The **bus station** (Av Júlia Kubitschek) is 2km west of the center. Buses to and from Rio, operated by **Viação 1001** (☑2643-3778; www.auto viacao1001.com.br), leave at least hourly between 4:30am and midnight (R$53, 2¾ hours).

To Arraial do Cabo, catch **Salineira bus B150** (☑2643-8144; www.salineira.com.br) from the bus stop just to the left as you leave the bus station (R$4, 30 minutes). For Búzios, catch any Salineira bus marked 'Búzios' from the stop across the road (R$4, 45 minutes).

Búzios

OXX22 / POP 28.000

Beautiful Búzios sits on a jutting peninsula scalloped by 17 beaches. A simple fishing village until the early '60s, when it was 'discovered' by Brigitte Bardot and her Brazilian boyfriend, it's now one of Brazil's most upscale and animated seaside resorts, littered with boutiques, fine restaurants, villas, bars and posh pousadas. The Mediterranean touch introduced by the Portuguese has not been lost – indeed, the narrow cobblestone streets and picturesque waterfront contribute to Búzios' image as Brazil's St Tropez.

Búzios is not a single town but rather three settlements on the same peninsula – Ossos, Manguinhos and Armação de Búzios. Ossos (Bones), at the northern tip of the peninsula, is the oldest and most attractive. It has a pretty harbor and yacht club, plus a few hotels and bars. Manguinhos, on the isthmus, is the most commercial. Armação, in between, is the heart of town, with the most tourist amenities; it's here that you'll find Rua das Pedras, the hub of Búzios' nightlife, and Orla Bardot, the town's picturesque beachfront promenade.

◎ Sights & Activities

The biggest draws in Búzios are the natural setting plus its endless array of opportunities for relaxation, nightlife, shopping and ocean sports.

Cobblestoned **Rua das Pedras** (Rua das Pedras) is Búzios' main venue for shopping, dining and evening entertainment, overflowing with revelers on weekend nights. Its eastward continuation, **Orla Bardot**, is a delightful winding oceanfront promenade linking the two oldest and most picturesque sections of town (Armação and Ossos). As you walk along the beachfront, you'll notice several **statues** (Map p156) by sculptor Christina Motta, including representations of Brigitte Bardot and former Brazilian president Juscelino Kubitschek, plus some remarkably realistic-looking fishermen hauling in their nets.

☞ Tours

Several operators offer tours to local beaches and islands. If you'd rather explore at your own pace, Búzios' *taxis marítimos* (water taxis) are an attractive alternative, charging R$5 to R$12 per person to individual beaches around the peninsula (rates are posted on a board at Armação's main pier and elsewhere around town).

Tour Shop Búzios BUS TOUR

(Map p156; ☑2623-4733; www.tourshop.com.br; Orla Bardot 550; tours from R$50) This agency runs the Búzios Trolley, an open-sided bus that visits 12 of the peninsula's beaches daily. It also operates rafting tours and trips by glass-bottomed catamaran.

Buziosnautic BOAT TOUR, DIVING

(Map p156; ☑2623-9005; www.buziosnautic.com; Orla Bardot 712; boat tours R$40) Buziosnautic operates 2½-hour boat excursions from Armação, visiting 12 beaches and three islands, with stops for swimming and snorkeling at Praia João Fernandes, Ilha Feia and Praia da Tartaruga. It also has a dive center.

Casamar DIVING

(Map p156; ☑2623-8165; www.casamar.com. br; Rua das Pedras 242; 2-tank dives from R$150) Casamar offers day and night excursions for experienced divers, plus a full range of courses.

✷ Festivals & Events

To the north of Búzios, **Rio das Ostras Jazz e Blues** (riodasostrasjazzeblues.com) in late

Búzios

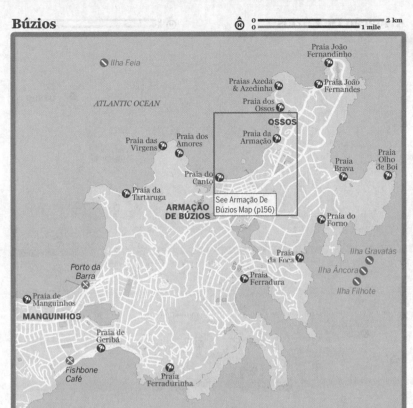

May/early June is one of Brazil's best music festivals.

🛏 Sleeping

Búzios caters to couples, so things can get pricey for solo travelers. Rates quoted here are for the high season: December through March, plus July.

Phoenix Hostel　　　　　　　HOSTEL $
(☎ 2623-1099; www.phoenixhostelbuzios.com; Hugo M Santos 8, Geribá; dm R$40-60, r with fan R$120-180, with air-con R$150-230; ❋ 🛜 🏊) With a laid-back atmosphere befitting its quiet residential location two blocks back from Geribá beach, this hostel sleeps a maximum of 32 guests in spacious four- and six-bed dorms with en suite bathrooms, plus three private rooms. The fenced yard encloses a pool and bar area that promote easy mingling, and friendly manager Jonas makes everyone feel at home.

El Misti Yellow　　　　　　　HOSTEL $
(☎ 2623-3174; www.elmistihostelbuzios.com; Rua da Mandrágora 13; dm R$40-62, r R$110-130; ❋ @ 🛜 🏊) Part of the Argentina-based 'Misti' hostel chain, this place has dorms in 4- to 15-bed configurations, plus private rooms from April to mid-December. It's a 15-minute walk from Rua das Pedras, or five from the main bus stop. Its sister hostel **El Misti** (☎ 2623-2383; www.elmistibuzios.com; Rua JV, No 7, Ferradura; dm R$40-63, d/tr R$198/262; ❋ @ 🛜 🏊), straddling a hillside garden with pool and banana trees, offers a more tranquil (if more isolated) alternative.

★ Nomad Búzios　　　　　　HOSTEL $$
(Map p156; ☎ 2620-8085; www.nomadbuzios.com. br; Rua das Pedras 25; dm R$60-90, tw R$180, d R$220-250; ❋ @ 🛜) Hands-down Búzios' best hostel, Nomad boasts a prime location in the thick of the Rua das Pedras nightlife zone. A slew of beautiful new doubles and even a

Armação De Búzios

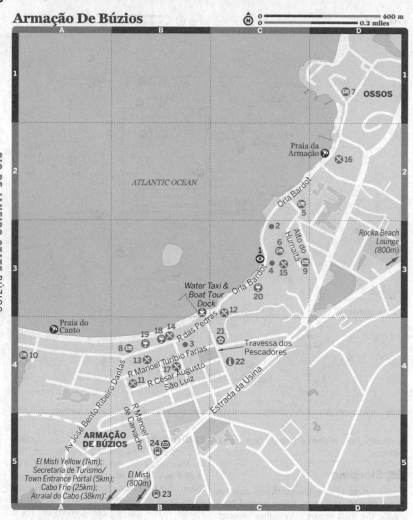

few split-level dorms enjoy gorgeous ocean views. The deck chairs and lounging bed on the beachfront terrace, coupled with R$6 caipirinhas in the stylish bar, reinforce the ritzy, decadent vibe.

L'Escale POUSADA $$
(Map p156; ☏ 2623-2816; www.pousadalescale. com; Travessa Santana 14, Ossos; r from R$240, with sea view R$290-330; ✴🛜) Book ahead for one of the three ocean-facing rooms with terraces and hammocks at this sweet, petite French-run pousada with a divine beachfront location in relaxed Ossos. Owners Syl-

via and Francis also operate the eponymous restaurant downstairs serving fish soup, seafood and French specialties including beef bourguignon, sweet and savory crepes, and profiteroles.

Pousada Saint Germain POUSADA $$
(Map p156; ☏ 2623-1044; www.saintgermain -buzios.com.br; Alto do Humaitá 5; r R$200-300; ✴🛜🅿) Although there's no ocean view, this pousada run by a Brazilian-American couple receives high marks for its prime location (100m to Orla Bardot, 400m to Rua das Pedras), tranquil hillside garden setting, and

Armação De Búzios

tasty breakfasts. In slower periods, excellent discounts can be negotiated – ask owner Paul for details.

★**Casa Búzios**　　　　　　POUSADA $$$
(Map p156; ☑2623-7002; www.pousadacasabuzios.com; Alto do Humaitá 1; r R$310-460; ❈ 🛜 ☒) In a dream location just off Orla Bardot, this lovely older home surrounded by a sweet hillside garden is now a French-run pousada, offering six spacious and unique suites with high ceilings, pretty shutters, and wood and tile floors. The poolside front patio affords picturesque views of boats bobbing in the harbor below.

Villa Balthazar　　　　　POUSADA $$$
(Map p156; ☑2623-6680; www.villabalthazar.com.br; Maria Joaquina 375; d R$345-435; ❈ 🛜 ☒) On a peaceful lane three blocks from Rua das Pedras, this stylish five-room pousada is a labor of love for youthful Swedish owners Petra and Felix, who have filled it with family heirlooms and homey touches inspired by their own world travels. Guests love the in-room DVD players, the swimming pool, and the delicious homemade breakfasts served on the pretty back deck.

Casas Brancas　　　BOUTIQUE HOTEL $$$
(Map p156; ☑2623-1458; www.casasbrancas.com.br; Alto do Humaitá 10; r R$700-1700; ❈ @ 🛜 ☒) If you're honeymooning or just won the lottery, head straight for this top-end place on Alto do Humaitá hill. Pampering touches include stupendous ocean views from the poolside terrace (and all but the most basic

rooms), massages in the on-site spa, and a choice of two restaurants: the upscale Atlântico and the chilled-out Deck Pizzeria.

🍴 Eating

Most of the better restaurants are in or near Armação. For good seafood at more affordable prices, check out the little thatched-roof places on Ferradura and João Fernandes beaches.

Three kilometers west of town at Manguinhos, the trendy food complex **Porto da Barra** (www.portodabarrabuzios.com.br) is also worth a look, featuring 14 bars and restaurants spread out along a tree-fringed waterfront boardwalk.

Chez Michou Crêperie　　　　CREPERIE $
(Map p156; ☑2623-2169; www.chezmichou.com.br; Rua das Pedras 90; crepes R$12-22; ⊙11am-late) Crowds flock here not only for the sweet and savory crepes, but also for the outdoor bar serving delicious piña coladas and the nightly DJ mixes (from 9pm).

O Barco　　　　　　　　SEAFOOD $$
(Map p156; Orla Bardot 1054; mains per person R$18-60; ⊙noon-11pm) More down-to-earth than most waterfront eateries, Barco stakes its reputation on well-made, reasonably priced fish dishes – from simple meals of fried fish with rice and salad, to full-on seafood stews. Eight tables on a cute little terrace plus a few extra sidewalk seats offer excellent people-watching and ocean views. In contrast to Buzios' many couples-oriented

DON'T MISS

BÚZIOS' BEACHES

With nearly two dozen beaches to choose from in and around Búzios, it's hard to know where to start. In general, the southern beaches are trickier to get to, but they're prettier and have better surf. The northern beaches are more sheltered and closer to the towns.

Going counterclockwise from south of Manguinhos, the first beaches are **Geribá** and **Ferradurinha** (Little Horseshoe). These are beautiful beaches with good surf. Next on the coast is **Ferradura**, which is large enough for windsurfing, followed by **Praia da Foca** and **Praia do Forno**, which have colder water than the other beaches. **Praia Olho de Boi** (Bull's Eye) is the area's only nude beach. It's reached by a little trail from the long, clean beach of **Praia Brava**.

On the north side of the peninsula, both **João Fernandinho** and **João Fernandes** are good for snorkeling, as are **Azedinha** and **Azeda**, reached by a short trail from Ossos. **Praia dos Ossos**, **Praia da Armação**, **Praia do Canto** and **Praia dos Amores** are lovely to look at, but a bit public and not so nice for lounging on. **Praia das Virgens** and **Praia da Tartaruga** are quiet and pretty. **Praia de Manguinhos** is another town beach further west.

Offshore, the islands of **Âncora**, **Gravatás**, **Filhote** and **Feia** are especially good diving destinations.

restaurants, Barco features plenty of *pratos individuais* (individual dishes), making this an attractive option for solo diners.

Fishbone Café SANDWICHES, BAR **$$**
(2623-7348; fishbonebuzios.com; Av Gravatás 1196, Praia de Geribá; sandwiches R$23, mains R$42-49; 11am-5pm) At this trendy beach club on Praia de Geribá, the menu features everything from sandwiches to salads to seafood, but plenty of people come just to drink, catch some rays and listen to some tunes on the waterfront outdoor deck.

Restaurante do David SEAFOOD **$$**
(Map p156; Manoel Turíbio de Farias 260; mains R$19-72) Still going strong after 40 years, David's serves high-quality seafood at little wooden tables with checkered tablecloths in the heart of town.

Bananaland SELF-SERVE **$$**
(Map p156; www.restaurantebananaland.com.br; Manoel Turíbio de Farias 50; per kg R$67.50; 11:30am-11pm) The best of several deluxe self-serve eateries on this street, Bananaland has something for everyone.

★ **Rocka Beach Lounge** SEAFOOD **$$$**
(2623-6159; www.rockafish.com.br; Praia Brava; mains R$57-86) Prime people watching and some of Búzios' most creative cuisine are the twin draws at this casual-chic seafood eatery perched directly above Praia Brava. Rocka is a full-day event for most visitors, who linger long after lunchtime on the lounge chairs

and beds, which are spread out on the terraces and grassy hillsides overlooking the beach. Reserve ahead for weekends, when things fill up fast.

Mistico Restaurante MEDITERRANEAN **$$$**
(Map p156; 2623-1217; www.abracadabrapousada.com.br; Alto do Humaitá 13; mains R$45-85; noon-10:30pm) Perched high on the hill between Armação and Ossos, this restaurant at the Abracadabra hotel enjoys one of the best panoramic views in Búzios, with poolside seating and an intimate glass-walled dining room. Since opening in 2012, it's won a loyal following for its enticing mix of pasta, seafood dishes and innovative creations such as watermelon gazpacho.

Bar do Zé MEDITERRANEAN **$$$**
(Map p156; 2623-4986; Orla Bardot 382; mains R$44-120; 6pm-midnight Mon-Fri, noon-2am Sat & Sun) This classy restaurant with an open-air deck facing Orla Bardot is famous for its well-mixed drinks (classic caipirinhas, freshly minted mojitos), served alongside grilled fish, risottos, steak and seafood.

Cigalon FRENCH **$$$**
(Map p156; 2623-0932; www.buziosdirect.com/cigalon; Rua das Pedras 199; menus R$55-67; noon-midnight) This fabulous French restaurant is right on the waterfront along Rua das Pedras. Candlelight dancing off the water and crisp white tablecloths set the elegant mood.

Drinking & Entertainment

Action on Rua das Pedras really gets going after midnight.

Patio Havana BAR
(Map p156; ☎ 2623-2169; www.patiohavana.com. br; Rua das Pedras 101; ⊙ 6pm-late Thu-Sun) This place is worth checking out if you're a fan of jazz, samba, salsa or bossa nova. Fabulous musicians from all over Brazil (and the world) regularly pop in.

Privilège CLUB
(Map p156; www.privilegenet.com.br; Orla Bardot 550; ⊙ Thu-Sun) For house music among the A-list crowd, head to this sleek nightclub with two dance floors and four bars on the Orla Bardot waterfront.

Pacha CLUB
(Map p156; ☎ 2633-0592; www.pachabuzios. com; Rua das Pedras 151; ⊙ 10pm-7am Fri & Sat) The epicenter of Rua das Pedras' nightlife, Pacha brings in top-name DJs from around the world nightly in summer and Saturdays throughout the year.

Gran Cine Bardot CINEMA
(Map p156; ☎ 2623-1298; www.viladomar.com/ cinebardot; Travessa dos Pescadores 88; admission R$20; ⊙ Thu-Sun) Shows movies on weekend nights, including some in English with Portuguese subtitles.

ℹ️ Information

Bradesco (Av José Bento Ribeiro Dantas 254) One of several downtown ATMs.

ClickNet (César Augusto São Luiz 254; per hr R$3; ⊙ 10am-11pm Mon-Fri, to 10pm Sat & Sun) Just off Armação's main square.

Hospital Municipal (☎ 2623-2419; Estrada Búzios-Cabo Frio) Just outside the town entrance portal along the road to Cabo Frio.

Multibank ATM (Praça Santos Dumont) Convenient but charges a hefty service fee.

Secretaria de Turismo (Map p156; www. visitebuzios.com) Two well-staffed offices distribute city maps and hotel information, at the town entrance portal (☎ 2633-6200; Av José Bento Ribeiro Dantas; ⊙ 8am-9pm Sun-Thu, to 10pm Fri & Sat) and just off the main square in Armação (☎ 2623-2099; www.visitebuzios. com; Travessia dos Pescadores 151, Armação; ⊙ 8am-9pm Sun-Thu, to 10pm Fri & Sat) .

ℹ️ Getting There & Around

The Búzios **bus station** (Map p156; Estrada da Usina 444) is a simple bus stop with no building attached, five blocks south of the Armação waterfront. **Viação 1001** (☎ 2623-2050; www. autoviacao1001.com.br) runs buses between Rio and Búzios (R$42, three hours) at least eight times daily between 6am and 8pm.

Municipal buses between Búzios and **Cabo Frio** (Map p156; Estrada da Usina 444; R$4; 45 minutes) make regular stops along Av José Bento Ribeiro Dantas and Estrada da Usina, including one directly opposite the Rio-bound bus stop.

Minas Gerais & Espírito Santo

Includes ➡

Best Places to Eat

➡ Xapuri (p168)

➡ Cantinho do Curuca (p211)

➡ Viradas do Largo (p193)

➡ Valsugana (p214)

➡ O Passo (p181)

Best Places to Stay

➡ Pouso do Chico Rei (p177)

➡ Hotel Solar da Ponte (p193)

➡ Pousada Santuário do Caraça (p203)

➡ Refúgio dos Cinco Amigos (p200)

➡ Mandala das Águas (p196)

Why Go?

For those seeking a tangible sense of Brazilian history, no state compares with Minas Gerais. The tortuous cobblestone streets and splendid baroque monuments of Minas' colonial mining towns have seen it all, from the horrors of slavery to the fervor of Brazil's 18th-century independence movement.

Minas' natural wonders are equally alluring. The Serra do Espinhaço, a Unesco Biosphere Reserve running the length of the state, is just one of many refuges providing exhilarating outdoor recreation opportunities and critical habitat for endangered species from the maned wolf to the woolly spider monkey.

Add to this the cosmopolitan charms of Belo Horizonte, the fabulous flavors of Minas' wood-fired cuisine, the intoxicating effects of Brazil's best *cachaça* (sugarcane alcohol) and the locals' legendary hospitality, and it's hard to resist Minas' seductive spell.

When to Go
Belo Horizonte

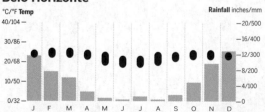

Mar–Apr Witness Brazil's most colorful Easter Week processions in Ouro Preto and São João del Rei.

May See America's largest primate, the woolly spider monkey as its favorite tree is flowering.

Jul Feel the heat at Itaúnas' *forró* festival, or chill out in Espírito Santo's 'wintry' mountains.

History

Espírito Santo, like much of the Brazilian coast, was colonized in the 16th century, but the focus quickly turned inland in the late 1600s, when gold was discovered in Minas Gerais. Brazilians began flocking to Minas, while Portuguese flocked to Brazil. Slaves were brought from Bahia's sugar fields and the savannas of Angola, and until the last quarter of the 18th century, Minas' mines were producing half the world's gold.

Minas set the gold-rush standard – crazy, wild and violent – more than 100 years before the Californian and Australian gold rushes. Licentious living, disease and famine were rampant. Much of the gold wealth was siphoned off to Portugal; among the few lasting benefits to Brazil was the creation of the beautiful, church-clad mining cities that still dot Minas' hills. Nowadays, the Estrada Real (Royal Road) that connected these *cidades históricas* has become the state's most popular tourist route.

In neighboring Espírito Santo, coffee plantations were the prime source of income up until the 1960s. They've since been superseded by mining, shipping and – in the capital city, Vitória – Brazil's most famous chocolate factory.

ⓘ Getting There & Around

Minas' capital city Belo Horizonte is the arrival point for most travelers. Pampulha and Confins airports handle domestic and international flights, while Belo's downtown bus station serves as a hub for ground transport. Direct buses from Rio and São Paulo also serve some of Minas' historic towns.

Vitória is Espírito Santo's largest city, with an international airport offering flights to major cities throughout Brazil. Buses run up and down the coastline, connecting Vitória with Bahia and Rio de Janeiro state, and also head inland to several cities in neighboring Minas Gerais.

MINAS GERAIS

POP 20 MILLION

Belo Horizonte

⤴ 0XX31 / POP 2.4 MILLION / ELEV 858M

Known to the locals as Beagá (pronounced 'bay-ah-gah', Portuguese for BH), Belo Horizonte was named for its beautiful view of nearby mountains. Urban sprawl makes it harder to appreciate the natural setting nowadays, but Brazil's third-largest city still has considerable charm. Walk down the buzzing cosmopolitan streets of the Savassi neighborhood on a Saturday evening, eat at one of the fine restaurants in Lourdes, stroll through the densely packed stalls at Mercado Central, attend a weekend street fair or a concert at the Palácio das Artes, or visit the Inhotim art museum west of the city, and you'll see that Belo Horizonte has countless dimensions. Add to all this the friendly, welcoming nature of Beagá's people and you've got a winning combination. Stick around a few days – you might grow fond of the place.

History

In the late 19th century, as the Brazilian Republic was coming into its own, mineiros (residents of Minas Gerais state) began planning a new capital to replace hard-to-reach Ouro Preto, which had fallen out of favor as a symbol of colonialism. Belo Horizonte sprang up as an art-nouveau city, influenced by the spirit of Ordem e Progresso (Order and Progress), the new slogan on the Brazilian flag.

In the 1940s, Belo expanded northward. Then-mayor Juscelino Kubitschek commissioned young architectural-school graduate Oscar Niemeyer to design the brand-new Pampulha district. These two men are largely responsible for the city's wide avenues, large lakes, parks and jutting skyline.

More than 100 years after its founding, Belo Horizonte still has the young, contagious energy of a community reinventing itself. The city underwent a major facelift in 2010, with several new museums opening in Praça da Liberdade and a slew of government agencies moving 20km north to the Cidade Administrativa, a futuristic complex designed by the centenarian Niemeyer shortly before his death in 2012.

Beagá's role as a host city for the 2014 FIFA World Cup and the 2016 Olympics has prompted a whole new round of infrastructure improvements, including modern high-speed bus lines, an expansion of Confins international airport, and remodeling of the city's venerable football stadium, Mineirão.

◎ Sights

Fans of modernist architect Oscar Niemeyer won't want to miss his creations dotted around a huge artificial lake in the Pampulha district, north of downtown. For information

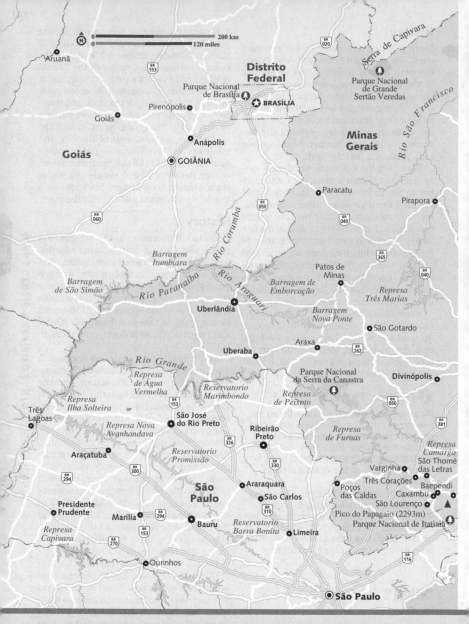

Minas Gerais & Espírito Santo Highlights

① Check out the 21 galleries of contemporary art at **Instituto de Arte Contemporânea Inhotim** (p172).

② Wander among the picturesque cobblestone streets and baroque architectural treasures of Ouro Preto (p172).

③ Climb Brazil's third-tallest mountain, the 2892m Pico da Bandeira in **Parque Nacional de Caparaó** (p203).

④ Catch a match at Mineirão football stadium in **Belo Horizonte** (p170), completely revamped for the World Cup.

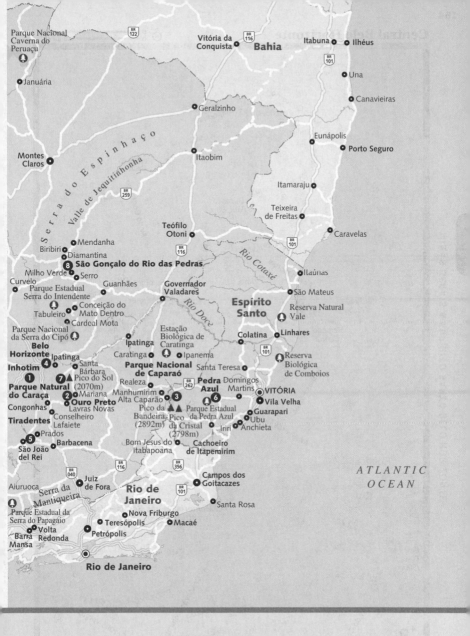

5 Take a ride on a historic *Maria-Fumaça* steam train from **Tiradentes** (p190).

6 Hold on to that rope as you scale the steep granite face of **Pedra Azul** (p214).

7 Wait by starlight for the maned wolves to appear at the old monastery at **Parque Natural do Caraça** (p203).

8 Get off the beaten track along the 18th-century Estrada Real outside **São Gonçalo do Rio das Pedras** (p200).

Central Belo Horizonte

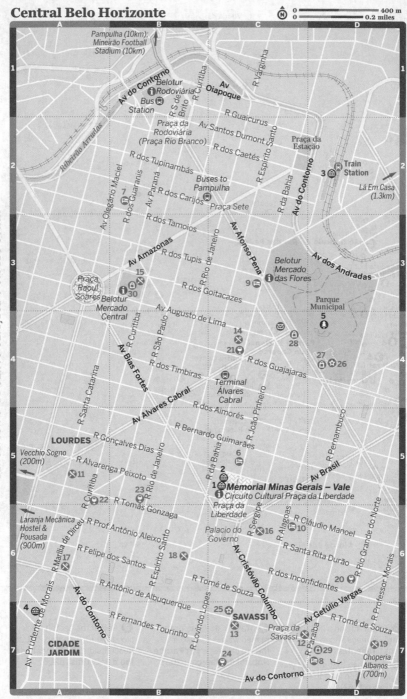

0   400 m
0   0.2 miles

Pampulha (10km);
Mineirão Football
Stadium (10km)

Av do Contorno

Belotur
Rodoviária
Bus
Station

R S de Brito

R Curitiba

Av Oiapoque

R Varginha

Praça da
Rodoviária
(Praça Rio Branco)

R Guaicurus

Av Santos Dumont

R dos Caetés

R Espírito Santo

Praça da
Estação

Av do Contorno

Train
Station

3

Lá Em Casa
(1.3km)

R dos Tupinambás

Av Olegário Maciel

R dos Guaranis

Av Paraná

R dos Carijós

Buses to
Pampulha

Praça Sete

R da Bahia

7

R dos Tamoios

Av Amazonas

R dos Tupis

R Rio de Janeiro

Av Afonso Pena

Belotur
Mercado
das Flores

9

Av dos Andradas

Praça
Raoul
Soares

15

30

Belotur
Mercado
Central

R dos Goitacazes

Parque
Municipal
5

R Curitiba

R São Paulo

Av Augusto de Lima

14

21

28

27   26

Av Bias Fortes

R Santa Catarina

R dos Timbiras

R dos Guajajaras

Av Álvares Cabral

Terminal
Álvares
Cabral

R dos Aimorés

R João Pinheiro

R Gonçalves Dias

R Bernardo Guimarães

Av Pernambuco

LOURDES

Vecchio Sogno
(200m)

R Alvarenga Peixoto

R Rio de Janeiro

R da Bahia

6

11

23

22   R Tomás Gonzaga

2

1 Memorial Minas Gerais – Vale
Circuito Cultural Praça da Liberdade

Av Brasil

Laranja Mecânica
Hostel & Pousada
(900m)

R Curitiba

R Prof Antônio Aleixo

Praça da
Liberdade

R Sergipe

16   10

R Cláudio Manoel

R Rio Grande do Norte

17

R Marília de Dirceu

R Felipe dos Santos

18

Palacio do
Governo

Av Cristóvão Columbo

R Santa Rita Durão

20

R Espírito Santo

R Antônio de Albuquerque

R Tomé de Souza

R dos Inconfidentes

R Professor Morais

4

Av Prudente de Morais

Av do Contorno

R Fernandes Tourinho

25

R Lovindo Lopes

SAVASSI

13

Av Getúlio Vargas

R Tomé de Souza

19

CIDADE
JARDIM

24

Praça da
Savassi
12

R Paraíba

29

8

Choperia
Albanos
(700m)

Av do Contorno

Central Belo Horizonte

on all of Praça da Liberdade's new museums, including some not covered here, visit the website **Circuito Cultural Praça da Liberdade** (circuitoculturalliberdade.com.br; Praça da Liberdade s/n).

◉ Praça da Liberdade & North

⭐ **Memorial Minas Gerais – Vale**   MUSEUM
(www.memorialvale.com.br; Praca da Liberdade s/n; ☺10am-6pm Tue, Wed, Fri & Sat, to 10pm Thu, to 4pm Sun) FREE The best element of Praça da Liberdade's 2010 makeover, this supremely cool contemporary museum chronicles Minas culture from the 17th to 21st centuries via three floors of cutting-edge interactive galleries and audiovisual installations.

Museu das Minas e do Metal   MUSEUM
(☎3516-7200; www.mmm.org.br; Praça da Liberdade s/n; adult/child R$6/3, free Thu & last Sun of month; ☺noon-6pm Tue-Sun, to 10pm Thu) Opened in 2010, this museum traces the economic, cultural and social history of mining in Minas Gerais, with multiple floors of mineral exhibits and some interesting interactive displays.

Parque Municipal   PARK
(Av Afonso Pena) One of Beagá's most appealing spots, this enormous sea of tropical greenery with artificial lakes and winding pathways is just 10 minutes southeast of the bus station. It's especially fun on Sunday, when everyone's out strolling and socializing.

Museu de Artes e Ofícios   MUSEUM
(☎3248-8600; www.mao.com.br; Praça Rui Barbosa; admission R$4, Sat & 5-9pm Wed & Thu free; ☺noon-7pm Tue & Fri, noon-9pm Wed & Thu, 11am-5pm Sat & Sun) Housed in Belo's historic train station, this museum displays a wide ranging collection of objects used in the daily lives of mineiros past and present. There are interpretive cards in English adjacent to each exhibit.

◉ Savassi, Lourdes & South

Museu Histórico Abílio Barreto   MUSEUM
(☎3277-8573; www.pbh.gov.br/cultura; Av Prudente de Morais 202, Cidade Jardim; ☺10am-5pm Tue-Sun, to 9pm Wed & Thu) FREE The centerpiece of this museum, southwest of Savassi, is a renovated colonial farmhouse, the solitary remnant of Curral del Rey, the rural village destroyed in the 1890s to make room for Belo. The adjacent building features rotating exhibits focused on the culture of Belo Horizonte.

◉ Pampulha

Igreja de São Francisco de Assis   CHURCH
(Av Otacílio Negrão de Lima s/n; admission R$2; ☺9am-5pm Tue-Sat, noon-5pm Sun) On the banks of Pampulha's artificial lake, Niemayer's striking modernist church is an architectural delight. Inside, the tiles and paintings by Portinari are equally striking.

OFF THE BEATEN TRACK

SABARÁ

Sabará, 25km southeast of Belo Horizonte, was one of the world's wealthiest cities in the 18th century, when it produced more gold in one week than the rest of Brazil produced in a year. Now just a workaday suburb, it still retains many churches, mansions, statues, fountains and sacred art from those gold-mining glory days.

All colonial attractions are signposted from central Praça Santa Rita. Most charge small admission fees, and all are closed Mondays.

Highlights include the triple-naved **Matriz de NS de Conceição** (Praça Getúlio Vargas; ☺9am-noon & 2-5pm Tue-Sun), finished in 1720, a fascinating blend of Asian and Portuguese baroque styles; the diminutive, jewel-like **Igreja de NS do Ó** (Largo NS do Ó; ☺9am-noon & 2-5pm Tue-Sun), decorated in gold, red and blue and dedicated to the Virgin Mary in her role as protector of pregnant women; **Igreja NS do Carmo** (Rua de Carmo; ☺9-11:30am Tue-Sun), where Aleijadinho's work predominates, especially in the faces of São Simão and São João da Cruz; **O Teatro Imperial** (Rua Dom Pedro II; ☺8am-noon & 1-5pm Tue-Sun), Sabará's elegant 1770 opera house, the **Museu do Ouro** (☎3671-1848; Rua da Intendência; admission US$1; ☺noon-5pm Tue-Sun), a 1730s gold foundry filled with historical artifacts; and the half-finished **Igreja NS do Rosário dos Pretos** (Praça Melo Viana; ☺8-11am & 1-5pm), started and financed by slaves, which now stands as a memorial to slavery's abolition in 1888.

Cisne (☎3672-1222) runs buses to Sabará (R$3.30, 40 minutes, every 15 minutes from 5am to 11pm) from a street corner on the south side of Belo's main bus station. Return buses leave from the bus stop on Av Victor Fantini in Sabará.

Museu de Arte da Pampulha   MUSEUM
(☎3277-7946; www.pbh.gov.br/cultura; Av Otacílio Negrão de Lima 16585; ☺9am-6pm Tue-Sun) **FREE** This art museum, with its cute garden designed by landscape architect Roberto Burle Marx, originally served as a casino and shows the obvious modernist influence of Le Corbusier.

Casa do Baile   MUSEUM
(☎3277-7443; www.pbh.gov.br/cultura; Av Otacílio Negrão de Lima 751; ☺9am-6pm Tue-Sun) **FREE** This former dance hall now holds all types of temporary art exhibits. Its lovely on-site cafe is a great place to take a break.

🛏 Sleeping

🛏 Praça da Liberdade & North

Lá Em Casa   HOSTEL $
(☎3653-9566; www.laemcasahostel.com; Eurita 30, Santa Tereza; dm R$32-40, d R$125, s/d with shared bathroom R$70/100; @☎) Owner Marília (sweeter than *doce de leite*) and her French husband Christophe (four languages between them) are consummate hosts at this welcoming hostel in a historic '30s townhouse in the bohemian neighborhood of Santa Tereza. You can bus here from Savassi or Centro in 10 to 15 minutes, though a

taxi (R$15) is more convenient for luggage-laden new arrivals.

Hotel São Bento   HOTEL $
(☎3271-3399; www.hotelsaobento.com.br; Guaranis 438; s/d/tr with fan from R$85/120/168, s/d/tr/q with air-con R$115/152/195/242; ❄☎) A few blocks south of the bus station, this is one of downtown's best-value budget hotels, provided you can avoid the claustrophobic interior rooms with windows facing the hallway.

Hotel Ibis   HOTEL $$
(☎2111-1500; www.ibis.com.br; João Pinheiro 602, Lourdes; r weekend/weekday from R$169/209; ❄@☎) Midway between downtown and Savassi, and just steps from leafy Praça da Liberdade, this ultra-convenient chain hotel has comfortable if predictable rooms in an ugly high-rise behind a pretty townhouse. The optional breakfast (R$14) and parking (R$15) cost extra.

Othon Palace   HOTEL $$
(☎2126-0000; www.othon.com.br; Av Afonso Pena 1050; r standard/deluxe from R$223/267; ❄@☎☀) The four-star Othon's many advantages include a great downtown location, multilingual staff, spacious rooms and spectacular views from the upper floors across the Parque Municipal. Don't miss the rooftop bar and pool, one of the best in

the city, and feel free to bargain – suites are sometimes offered for the price of a standard room.

🛏 Savassi, Lourdes & South

Laranja Mecânica
Hostel & Pousada HOSTEL **$**
(☑ 3291-0192; laranjamecanicahostelpousada.com; Rodrigues Caldas 703, Santo Agostinho; dm R$40, s/d R$85/125, with shared bathroom R$75/115) This attractive two-storey house with wood and marble architectural details features four-, six- and eight-bed dorms, an upstairs double with private veranda, and a downstairs unit with en-suite bathroom. It's in a residential neighborhood due west of Lourdes and Savassi, with good bus connections to downtown and the long-distance bus terminal (15 minutes).

Liberty Palace Hotel HOTEL **$$**
(☑ 2121-0900; www.libertypalace.com.br; Paraíba 1465, Savassi; r R$185-350; ✳ @ 🛜 ❄) This well-located Savassi business hotel has spacious rooms and big comfy beds, plus a pool, sauna, gym and an excellent restaurant. Weekend rates (30% cheaper than midweek) offer the best value.

Royal Savassi Hotel HOTEL **$$$**
(☑ 2138-0000; www.royalsavassi.com.br; Alagoas 699, Savassi; s/d midweek R$349/379, weekend R$170/210; ✳ @ 🛜) Well-positioned at Savassi's northern edge, just east of Praça da Liberdade, this business-oriented hotel is a good deal on weekends, when prices are slashed in half. Amenities include plush beds, big flat-screen TVs, minibars, a rooftop Jacuzzi, and the Amadeus restaurant downstairs, whose sumptuous lunch buffet is complemented by one of Minas Gerais' best-stocked wine cellars.

🛏 Pampulha

Pousada Sossego da Pampulha POUSADA **$$**
(☑ 3439-3250; www.sossegodapampulha.com.br; Av José Dias Bicalho 1258, Pampulha; s/d/tr/q with fan R$165/195/235/280, with air-con R$180/210/255/300; @ 🛜 ❄) A stone's throw from Pampulha's lake shore and the Mineirão football stadium, this pousada (guesthouse) is friendly, clean, well run and convenient for people arriving from the north. Amenities include a small pool and rooftop terrace with views of Belo Horizonte and the mountains. From Pampulha airport, 2km away, a taxi costs R$10.

🍴 Eating

Belo Horizonte is teeming with good food for every budget. The area between Praça Sete and Praça da Liberdade is best for cheap eats, with countless *lanchonetes* (snack bars), self-serve per kilo restaurants and fast-food places. Further south, the Savassi and Lourdes neighborhoods constitute the epicenter of the city's fine-dining scene.

The lion's share of the city's nonmineira restaurants specialize in Italian food, although you can also find a world of other flavors if you look around.

🍴 Praça da Liberdade & North

Casa Cheia MINEIRA **$**
(☑ 3274-9585; Shop 167, Mercado Central; daily specials R$18-23; ⊙ 10am-5:30pm Mon-Sat, to 1pm Sun) The name means 'full house'; visit on a weekend and you'll understand why. People line up by the dozen for a table at this long-established Mercado Central eatery, where a bevy of women cooks up traditional favorites on a giant stove. *Pratos do dia* (daily specials) include a not-to-be-missed Saturday *feijoada* (bean-and-meat stew served with rice; the Brazilian national dish).

Cantina do Lucas MINEIRA, ITALIAN **$$**
(www.cantinadolucas.com.br; Av Augusto de Lima 233, Centro; mains R$18-53; ⊙ 11:30am-2am Mon-Thu, to 4am Fri & Sat, to 1am Sun) Tucked off a busy downtown street on the ground floor of the Maletta building, this beloved local institution has been feeding belorizontinos into the wee hours for over 50 years. Vest-and-tie-clad waiters navigate through a landscape of checked tablecloths and wood paneling, hefting trays of mineira food and pasta. Especially popular after the Sunday hippie fair in nearby Parque Municipal.

🍴 Savassi, Lourdes & South

San Ro ASIAN, VEGETARIAN **$**
(Professor Moraes 651; per kg weekday/weekend R$36.90/39.90; ⊙ 11:30am-3pm; ☑) If you're not a carnivore, or just need a break from Minas' meat-heavy repertoire, make a bee-line for the buffet at this popular Asian-vegetarian, per-kilo place.

Marília Pizzeria PIZZERIA **$$**
(☑ 3275-2027; www.mariliapizzeria.com.br; Marília de Dirceu 189, Lourdes; pizzas R$31-59; ⊙ 6pm-late) With late hours and a floor-to-ceiling display of back-lit bottles at its fashionable

bar, Marília's has a trendy, youthful vibe and is routinely voted among the best pizzerias in Belo Horizonte.

Restaurante do Minas Tenis Clube
BUFFET $$

(☑ 3516-1310; Rua da Bahia 2244, Lourdes; all-you-can-eat buffet lunch weekday/weekend R$23/40; ☺ 11:30am-11pm Mon-Sat, to 7pm Sun) For atmosphere and price combined, it's hard to beat the midweek buffet at Belo's tennis club. Gorge to your heart's content in the spacious, parquet-floored dining room or on the palm-shaded back terrace overlooking the pool and water slides.

Baiana do Acarajé
BAHIAN $$

(☑ 3264-5804; Antônio de Albuquerque 473, Savassi; acarajé R$8-21, mains for 2 R$58-130; ☺ 6pm-midnight Tue & Wed, noon-midnight Thu-Sun) A small slice of Bahia just off Praça da Savassi, this bright, lively, informal bar-restaurant specializes in tasty *acarajé* (shrimp-stuffed brown bean fritters) served alongside pricier and more substantial dishes like *moqueca* (Bahian seafood stew). A popular spot for people-watching over late-afternoon beers.

Vecchio Sogno
ITALIAN $$$

(☑ 3292-5251; www.vecchiosogno.com.br; Martim de Carvalho 75; mains R$49-89; ☺ noon-12:30am Mon-Fri, 6pm-2am Sat, noon-6pm Sun) Repeatedly voted Belo's best restaurant (not just its best Italian one), Vecchio Sogno is worth the splurge. Mains range from duck and wild

rice risotto to shrimp flambéed in grappa. Reserve ahead.

A Favorita
INTERNATIONAL $$$

(☑ 3275-2352; www.afavorita.com.br; Santa Catarina 1235, Lourdes; mains R$49-95; ☺ noon-midnight) Everything's superb at this classy, high-ceilinged restaurant in the heart of the chic Lourdes district. Specialties include grilled meat, decadent desserts and home-made pasta dishes.

Dona Lucinha II
BUFFET, MINEIRA $$$

(☑ 3261-5930; www.donalucinha.com.br; Sergipe 811, Funcionários; all-you-can-eat buffet adult/child R$53/26.50; ☺ noon-3pm & 7pm-11pm Mon-Sat, noon-5pm Sun) The sumptuous buffet here features 50 traditional mineira dishes daily. It's fairly touristy, and prices have climbed thanks to the owner's publication of a best-selling cookbook, but the food is still outstanding.

✖ Pampulha

★ Xapuri
MINEIRA $$$

(☑ 3496-6198; www.restaurantexapuri.com.br; Mandacarú 260, Pampulha; mains R$36-55; ☺ noon-11pm Tue-Sat, to 6pm Sun) Dona Nelsa's local institution features fabulous mineira food served at picnic tables under a thatched roof, with hammocks close at hand for pre-meal children's entertainment or post-meal relaxation. The traditional wood stove blazes up front, while colorful desserts are attractively displayed in two long cases.

DON'T MISS

COMIDA MINEIRA: MINAS' FABULOUS FOOD

Ask any Brazilian what they like most about Minas Gerais, and they're sure to mention the food. Eating in Minas is an absolute treat. Wherever you go, you'll see signs advertising *comida mineira* – the hearty, high-calorie, and extremely flavorful local cuisine, traditionally cooked on a *fogão a lenha* (wood stove) and revolving heavily around pork, sausage, beans, rice and kale.

Don't miss these specialties, which you'll see throughout the state:

➡ **feijão tropeiro** – beans mixed with toasted manioc flour, crunchy pork rind, sausage, eggs, kale, garlic and onions

➡ **goibada** – sweet guava paste (like thick guava jelly) eaten as a dessert, often accompanied by cheese

➡ **gueijo Minas** – the traditional cow's milk cheese of Minas Gerais

➡ **tutu à mineira** – a thick puree of mashed beans with garlic and onion, usually served alongside pork loin, crunchy pork rind, kale and/or rice

➡ **pao de queijo** – chewy, cheesy and best enjoyed hot from the oven, Minas' famous cheese bread is made with tapioca flour, which accounts for its delightful consistency

Also legendary are Minas' *cachaça* and cheese – don't leave the state without amply sampling both of them. For more on *comida mineira*, and Brazilian food in general, see p681.

Drinking & Nightlife

Belo Horizonte is Brazil's self-proclaimed drinking capital, with thousands of *botecos* (neighborhood bars) sprinkled throughout the city. If you're visiting in mid-April to mid-May, don't miss the **Comida di Buteco festival** (www.comidadibuteco.com.br), in which dozens of places compete to see who makes the best bar food. Originating right here in 1999, it has since expanded to over a dozen other Brazilian ciites.

Late-night club- and pub-based nightlife gravitates toward Savassi, which is full of trendy dance clubs.

★ Café com Letras   CAFE
(☑ 3225-9973; www.cafecomletras.com.br; Antônio de Albuquerque 781; mains R$20-42; ☉ noon-11pm Mon-Wed, to midnight Thu-Sat, 5-11pm Sun) With live jazz Sundays and Mondays, DJs Thursday through Saturday, and a bohemian buzz between sets, this bookstore-cafe is a fun place to kick back over light meals and drinks, browse the shelves and enjoy the free internet. The cafe also sponsors jazz performances at the annual **Savassi Festival** (www.savassifestival.com.br).

Arcangelo   BAR
(2nd fl, Ed Maletta, Rua da Bahia 1148; ☉ closed Sun & Mon) The best bar of many inside the indie-intellectual Maletta building in Centro, with great views from its consistently-packed second floor open-air patio. Voted Beagá's best Happy Hour.

Choperia Albanos   PUB
(www.albanos.com.br; Pium-i 611, Sion; ☉ 6pm-1am Mon-Fri, 4pm-1am Sat & Sun) **FREE** This beloved, award-winning brewpub with its spacious tile-floored interior serves some of Beagá's best beer and is always buzzing at happy hour. There's a second branch in **Lourdes** (Rio de Janeiro 2076; ☉ 6pm-1am Mon-Fri, noon-1am Sat & Sun).

Bar Tizé   BAR
(☑ 3337-4374; Curitiba 2205, Lourdes; ☉ 5pm-1am Mon-Fri, noon-1am Sat & Sun) Since 1967, this strategically located corner bar with tables spilling onto a long island of sidewalk has been drawing crowds with ice-cold buckets of beer and award-winning *comida di buteco*.

Velvet Club   CLUB
(velvetclub.blogspot.com; Sergipe 1493, Savassi; ☉ 11pm-3am Wed-Sat) This club features a mix of DJs spinning electronica, rock and pop, plus occasional live bands.

2014 WORLD CUP VENUE: MINEIRÃO STADIUM

Belo's newly renovated, 64,000-seat **Mineirão** (www.minasarena.com.br/mineirao) stadium, 10km north of Centro in Pampulha, was chosen to host six 2014 FIFA World Cup matches, including one semifinal. It will also serve as a 2016 Olympic Games venue.

Improvements put in place for the World Cup include lowering the playing field by 3.4m for better visibility and increased seating capacity, a panoramic restaurant, a giant exterior esplanade accommodating 65,000 people for concerts, shopping and special events, and a brand-new football museum, the **Museu Brasileiro de Futebol** (Brazilian Football Museum; ☑ 3499-4300; www.minasarena.com.br; Av Antônio Abrahão Caram 1001, Pampulha; ☉ 9am-5pm Mon-Fri, to 1pm Sat & Sun) **FREE**. Among the 12 Brazilian World Cup host cities, Belo Horizonte was one of the first to complete its preparations.

A Obra   CLUB
(www.aobra.com.br; Rio Grande do Norte 1168, Savassi; ☉ 10pm-late Wed-Sat) One of Savassi's best dance clubs, A Obra hosts live rock and indie shows.

☆ Entertainment

Belo Horizonte is a cosmopolitan town with a vibrant arts scene and plenty of nightlife. Homegrown success stories include the dance troupe **Grupo Corpo** (www.grupocorpo.com.br), stage performers **Grupo Galpão** (www.grupogalpao.com.br), puppet theater **Grupo Giramundo** (www.giramundo.org) and musical ensemble **Grupo Uakti** (www.uakti.com.br).

Online entertainment listings are available at www.soubh.com.br and www.divirta-se.uai.com.br. Weekly entertainment calendars can also be found in the 'Divirta-Se' section of the *Estado de Minas* newspaper.

Theater

Palácio das Artes   PERFORMING ARTS
(☑ 3236-7400; www.palaciodasartes.com.br; Av Afonso Pena 1537) Near the southern end of Parque Municipal, this arts complex with multiple performance spaces and galleries is the hub of Belo's theater, dance, and music-concert scene. Current shows are listed in the

Art and Culture section of the free guide put out by Belotur, the municipal tourist bureau.

Live Music

Godofrêdo Bar Musical   LIVE MUSIC
(www.godofredog.com; Paraisópolis 738, Santa Tereza; ⊘ 6pm-late Tue-Sun) Locals pack into this intimate Santa Tereza bar every Friday and Saturday for live performances celebrating the legacy of the Clube da Esquina, Belo Horizonte's groundbreaking musical movement of the 1960s and 1970s. Sharing the stage are bar owner Gabriel Guedes and his friend Rodrigo Borges, son and nephew respectively of two of the Clube's revered co-founders.

O Alambique   LIVE MUSIC
(☑ 3296-7188; alambique.com.br; Av Raja Gabaglia 3200, Estoril; ⊘ 10pm-4am Tue-Sat) With a capacity of 1200, this venerable nightspot 6km south of the center has panoramic city views, five themed bars, 70 different *cachaça*-based drinks, and enough samba, *sertanejo* and *forró* (popular music of the Northeast) to keep things lively all night long.

Gamboa   LIVE MUSIC
(www.gamboabh.com.br; Sergipe 1236, Savassi; ⊘ 7pm-5am Wed-Sat) A relative newcomer in the heart of Savassi, this cabaret-style club draws a mixed crowd of locals and foreigners for live samba four nights a week.

Sports

Three football teams call Belo Horizonte home: **América** (www.americamineiro.combr), **Atlético Mineiro** (www.atletico.com.br) and **Cruzeiro** (www.cruzeiro.com.br).

🔒 Shopping

Don't leave Belo Horizonte without visiting its wonderful street markets. Locals also favor the many high-rise shopping centers downtown and Savassi's vibrant high-end boutiques.

Mercado Central   MARKET
(cnr Curitiba & Rua dos Goitacazes; ⊘ 7am-6pm Mon-Sat, to 1pm Sun) You'll find everything from parrots to perfume at this indoor market, a true Belo Horizonte institution. Sample the delicious local produce, socialize with locals at one of the bars or just roam the aisles aimlessly.

Feira de Arte e Artesanato   MARKET
(Feira Hippie; www.feirahippiebh.com; Av Afonso Pena; ⊘ 7am-2pm Sun) A Belo Horizonte classic, this Sunday street fair attracts massive crowds searching for clothing, jewelry, street food and more. Located between Rua da Bahia and Rua das Guajajaras, and bordered by the soothing greenery of the Parque Municipal, it's a fun place to wander and enjoy a slice of city life, even if you're not in a shopping mood.

Centro de Artesanato Mineiro   HANDICRAFTS
(☑ 3272-9516; Av Afonso Pena 1537; ⊘ 9am-7:30pm Mon-Fri, to 1:30pm Sat, 8am-12:30pm Sun) Inside the Palácio das Artes at the edge of Parque Municipal, this government-run store specializes in mineiro crafts. The selection is good, although prices are often higher than in the colonial towns.

Livraria Mineiriana   BOOKS
(☑ 3223-8092; www.livrariamineiriana.com; Paraíba 1419; ⊘ 9am-10pm Mon-Fri, to 5pm Sat) Excellent bookstore in Savassi.

ℹ Orientation

Central Belo Horizonte has a grid of large *avenidas* (avenues), with another smaller grid superimposed at a 45-degree angle. The boundaries of the original planned city are defined by the ring road called Av do Contorno. It's a hilly town, so trips are sometimes less straightforward than they appear on the map.

The main drag is Av Afonso Pena, which runs diagonally from northwest to southeast, starting at the bus station at the northern end of downtown and running past leafy green Parque Municipal. From northwest to southeast, there are three pivotal praças (squares): bustling Praça Sete, just southeast of the bus station; serene Praça da Liberdade, heart of the government-turned-museum district called Funcionarios; and trendy Praça da Savassi, the center of Belo nightlife and cafe society.

Outside of downtown, Pampulha (8km north) is the neighborhood with most cultural attractions and tourist amenities.

ℹ Information

EMERGENCY
Ambulance (☑ 192)
Fire department (☑ 193)
Police (☑ 190) For non-urgent matters, call 3330 5200.

INTERNET ACCESS
Internet places abound throughout the city.
Pró Terra (Shop 12, Av Augusto de Lima 134; per hr R$2; ⊘ 8am-10pm Mon-Fri) Centrally located, with fast connections and Skype.

MONEY

Banks with ATMs are clustered downtown between Praça Sete and Parque Municipal, and near Av do Contorno in Savassi.

Banco do Brasil (Rio de Janeiro 750)

Bradesco (Rua da Bahia 951)

HSBC (Rua da Bahia 932)

TOURIST INFORMATION

Belo Horizonte's municipal tourist bureau, Belotur, is among the best in Brazil. Its several offices distribute the free *Guia Turístico*, an exceptionally helpful trilingual (English, Spanish, Portuguese) guide cataloging the city's restaurants, museums, cultural events and other tourist attractions, with instructions on how to get there using local buses. The *Guia Turístico* also includes a city map, airline and bus company information, and everything else you wanted to know about Belo but didn't know how to ask.

Belotur (belotur@pbh.gov.br) Branches can be found at the bus station (☑3277-6907; Praça Rio Branco; ⊙8am-6pm); outside baggage claim at Confins airport (☑3689-2557; ⊙8am-10pm Mon-Fri, to 6pm Sat & Sun); on the ground floor of Belo's famous Mercado Central (☑3277-4691; ⊙9:40am-6pm Mon, 8am-4:20pm Tue, 8am-6pm Wed-Sat, 8am-1pm Sun); at Mercado das Flores (☑3277-7666; Av Afonso Pena 1055; ⊙8:30am-6:30pm Mon-Fri, 8am-3pm Sat & Sun), on the western edge of Parque Municipal; and on the lakeshore in the northern suburb of Pampulha (☑3277-9987; Av Otacílio Negrão de Lima 855; ⊙8am-5pm Tue-Sun).

Alô Turismo (☑3429-0405; ⊙24h) Belotur's tourist-inquiry hotline.

❶ Getting There & Around

AIR

Belo Horizonte has two airports. Most planes use the international **Aeroporto Confins** (CNF; 40km north), newly renovated and expanded for the 2014 FIFA World Cup. The **Aeroporto da Pampulha** (PLU; 10km north) is more convenient to the city center but only has domestic flights.

Flights from the two airports serve most locations in Brazil. A full list of airline offices, with phone numbers, appears in the front of the free Belotur guide.

AIRPORT BUSES

Expresso Unir (☑3663-8000; www.conex aoaeroporto.com.br) runs frequent, comfortable Conexão Aeroporto buses between downtown and Belo's two airports (Pampulha and Confins). The conventional bus (R$9.25 to either airport) leaves Belo's bus station every 15 to 45 minutes between 4:15am and 11:30pm. Travel time is approximately 30 minutes to Pampulha airport, 50 minutes to Confins. Buses return from Confins between 5:15am and 1:15am

Unir also runs an *executivo* bus to Confins airport (R$20.45, 50 minutes) from the **Terminal Álvares Cabral** (Alvares Cabral 387), just southwest of Parque Municipal, every 25 to 40 minutes between 3:15am and 11pm. See Unir's website for complete schedules.

BUS

Belo's **bus station** (Praça Rio Branco 100) is near the northern end of downtown. The free Belotur guide lists bus company phone numbers in the front pages.

During periods of peak travel, buses for Brasilia and the Northeast sometimes leave from alternate terminals; ask when buying your ticket.

See the table (below) for a list of destinations served.

LOCAL BUSES

Belo Horizonte's local buses, operated by **BHTrans** (www.bhtrans.pbh.gov.br), are color-coded. Blue buses (R$2.80) go up and down

MINAS GERAIS & ESPÍRITO SANTO BELO HORIZONTE

BUSES FROM BELO HORIZONTE

DESTINATION	COST (R$)	TIME (HR)	COMPANY
Brasília	123	11-12	União (www.expressouniao.com.br), Itapemirim (www.itapemirim.com.br)
Diamantina	76	5	Pássaro Verde (www.passaroverde.com.br)
Ouro Preto	26	2	Pássaro Verde (www.passaroverde.com.br)
Rio de Janeiro	74-107	6½	Útil (www.util.com.br), Cometa (www.viacaocometa.com.br)
Salvador	214	23	Gontijo (www.gontijo.com.br)
São João del Rei	47	3½	Sandra (www.viacaosandra.com.br)
São Paulo	96-160	8	Cometa (www.viacaocometa.com.br)
Vitória	85-118	9	São Geraldo (www.saogeraldo.com.br), Itapemirim (www.itapemirim.com.br)

main avenues in the city center, green express buses (R$2.80) only stop at select points, red-and-beige buses (R$3.40 and up, depending on distance) connect outlying suburbs to downtown, and yellow buses (R$2) have circular routes through the city.

For the 2014 FIFA World Cup, BHTrans also launched three new BRT (Bus Rapid Transport) lines designed to cut travel times in half through the use of exclusive new bus lanes. Downtown stops for the new BRT lines are on Av Paraná and Av Santos Dumont, with the main northbound line to Pampulha traveling along Av Antônio Carlos and Av Dom Pedro I.

TRAIN

Companhia Vale do Rio Doce (☑ 0800-285-7000; www.vale.com/brasil/EN/business/logistics/railways/trem-passageiros) operates a daily train to Vitória in Espírito Santo state (*econômica/executiva* class R$56/87, 13 hours), departing at 7:30am from the train station at Praça da Estação, just north of Parque Municipal. The return run leaves Vitória at 7am, reaching Belo Horizonte at 8:10pm.

Around Belo Horizonte

Three caves, all within two hours of downtown Belo, make great day jaunts.

Gruta da Lapinha   CAVE

(☑ 3689-8422; adult/child R$10/5; ⊗ 8:30am-4:30pm Tue-Sun) The highlight here is the Véu de Noiva, a crystal formation in the shape of a bride's veil. **Atual** (☑ 3271 8793) runs frequent buses to Lagoa Santa (R$6, 70 minutes); from there, bus 306 continues to the cave (R$3.50, 35 minutes, every 40 minutes from 7am).

Gruta do Maquiné   CAVE

(☑ 3715-1078; www.grutadomaquine.tur.br; Hwy MG-231, km7, Cordisburgo; adult/child R$16/8; ⊗ 8am-5pm) Some 120km north of Belo Horizonte, this is the largest, best known and most crowded of the caves in the area. Maquiné's seven huge chambers are well lit for guided tours. **Setelagoano** (☑ 3073-7575) runs buses there (R$35, 2¼ hours), leaving Belo Horizonte daily at 8:30am, plus 12:15pm on Sundays, returning at 4:20pm daily, plus 2:45pm on Sundays.

Gruta Rei do Mato   CAVE

(☑ 3771-5258; Hwy BR-040, km472, Sete Lagoas; adult/child R$10/5; ⊗ 8am-4:30pm) This is the most interesting of the three caves in the area around Belo Horizonte. Near Sete Lagoas, 70km north of Belo, it has prehistoric paintings and petroglyphs. From Belo Horizonte, take any Sete Lagoas–bound bus running along Hwy BR-040 (R$19, 70 minutes, hourly from 7am to 11pm) and ask the driver to drop you at the cave entrance.

Ouro Preto

☑ 0XX31 / POP 70,000 / ELEV 1179M

Of all the exquisite colonial towns scattered around Minas Gerais, Ouro Preto is the jewel in the crown. Significant historically as a center of gold mining and government, and as the stage for Brazil's first independence movement, the city remains vital in modern

---

DON'T MISS

GORGEOUS GARDENS & GARGANTUAN ART

The stunning **Instituto de Arte Contemporânea Inhotim** (☑ 3571-9700; www.inhotim. org.br; Rua B, 20, Inhotim, Brumadinho; adult/student R$20/10 Wed & Thu, R$28/14 Fri-Sun, Tue free; ⊗ 9:30am-4:30pm Tue-Fri, to 5:30pm Sat & Sun), a sprawling complex of gardens dotted with 21 world-class modern art galleries and numerous outdoor sculptures, lies 50km west of Belo Horizonte, near the town of Brumadinho. Much of the Brazilian and international artwork on view is monumental in size, with galleries custom-built to display it. The gardens, which opened to the public in October 2006 and are expanding constantly, boast over 4000 different species of plants (including the world's most extensive collection of palm trees), peacocks and lakes with swans. You can wander at will, or attend daily scheduled programs led by guides trained in visual arts and natural science. Ten on-site eateries serve everything from hot dogs to gourmet international fare. Tuesday's a great day to visit, as the museum is free; weekends can get crowded, but offer a wider range of guided tours.

From Tuesday through Sunday Saritur runs direct buses (R$32.50 round-trip, 1½ hours each way) from Belo Horizonte to Inhotim at 9:15am, returning at 4:30pm. Alternatively, take one of Saritur's three daily buses from Belo Horizonte to Brumadinho (R$16.35, 80 minutes), and catch a taxi to the museum (R$15).

times as a center for education and the arts, and as one of Brazil's most visited tourist destinations.

Built at the feet of the Serra do Espinhaço, Ouro Preto's colonial center is larger and has steeper topography than any other historical town in Minas. The narrow, crooked streets of the upper and lower towns tangle together and in places are too rough and precipitous for vehicles. Navigating the vertiginous cobblestone slopes on foot can be exhausting, but the views of 23 churches spread out across the hilly panorama are spectacular. The city is a showcase of outstanding mineiro art and architecture, including some of Aleijadinho's finest works.

History

Legend has it that a servant in an early expedition exploring Brazil's interior pocketed a few grains of an odd black metal he found while drinking from a river near the current site of Ouro Preto. It turned out to be gold, and the local deposits were soon discovered to be the largest in the New World.

Gold fever spread fast. In 1711, Vila Rica de Ouro Preto was founded, and in 1721 it became the capital of Minas Gerais. Gold bought the services of baroque artisans, who turned the city into an architectural gem. At the height of the gold boom in the mid-18th century, there were 110,000 people (mainly slaves) in Ouro Preto, compared with 50,000 in New York and about 20,000 in Rio de Janeiro.

In theory, all gold was brought to *casas de intendências* (weighing stations), and a *quinto do ouro* (royal fifth) was set aside for the Portuguese crown. The greed of the Portuguese led to sedition, as the miners found it increasingly difficult to pay ever-larger gold taxes. In 1789, poets Claudio da Costa, Tomás Antônio Gonzaga, Joaquim José da Silva Xavier (nicknamed Tiradentes, meaning 'Tooth Puller,' for his dentistry skills) and others, full of French Revolutionary philosophies, hatched an uprising against Portuguese colonization known as the Inconfidência Mineira.

The rebellion was crushed in its early stages by agents of the crown. Gonzaga was exiled to Mozambique and Costa did time in prison. Tiradentes was jailed for three years, then drawn and quartered in Rio de Janeiro. His head was paraded around Ouro Preto, his house demolished and its grounds salted to ensure that nothing would grow there.

In 1897 the state capital was shifted from Ouro Preto to Belo Horizonte, decisively preserving the city's colonial flavor. In 1980, Ouro Preto was enshrined as Brazil's first Unesco World Heritage site.

◉ Sights

There are virtually no 20th-century buildings to defile this stunning colonial town. As you wander, watch for informative historical plaques that have been placed on 150 houses around town to heighten visitors' curiosity and expand their knowledge of the city's treasures – part of a citywide cultural initiative known as Museu Aberto/Cidade Viva.

Ouro Preto is divided into parishes, each with its own Matriz (mother church). If you stand in Praça Tiradentes facing the Museu da Inconfidência, the parish of Pilar is to the right (west), the parishes of Antônio Dias and Santa Efigênia to the left (east).

For a panoramic view of the churches and rooftops, head northeast out of Praça Tiradentes and walk for five minutes along Conselheiro Quintiliano towards Mariana.

◉ Praça Tiradentes & Around

Praça Tiradentes is the heart of town, surrounded by some of Ouro Preto's finest museums and churches.

Museu da Inconfidência   MUSEUM
(Praça Tiradentes; adult/child R$8/4; ☺noon-5:30pm Tue-Sun) This historical museum is housed in Ouro Preto's old municipal headquarters and jail, an attractive building built between 1784 and 1854 on the south side of Praça Tiradentes. It contains the tomb of Tiradentes, documents of the Inconfidência Mineira, torture instruments and important works by Manuel da Costa Ataíde and Aleijadinho.

Museu do Oratório   MUSEUM
(www.museudooratorio.org.br; Adro da Igreja do Carmo 28; admission R$4; ☺9:30am-5:30pm) This museum features a fabulous collection of hand-carved *oratórios* – miniature home altars and portable devotional shrines dating back to the 17th century. It's housed in the Casa do Noviciado, a triple-level colonial building where Aleijadinho is said to have lived while working on the adjacent Igreja NS do Carmo.

Igreja NS do Carmo   CHURCH
(Brigadeiro Mosqueira; admission R$2; ☺8:30-11:30am & 1-5pm Mon-Sat, 10am-3pm Sun) Built

Ouro Preto

Map labels:

Bus Station

R Pe Rolim-ex-Merces

R Padre Jose Marcos Penna

Parque do Vale dos Contos

11

Igreja de São Francisco de Paula

18

R Gabriel Santos

Largo do Rosário

33 21

Igreja NS do Rosário

30

R Getúlio Vargas

R Antônio de Albuquerque

R Teixeira Amaral

R São José

R Camilo de Brito

17

Buses to Mariana & Minas da Passagem

31

2

15

R Cor Alves

R Senador Rocha Lagoa

9

Centro Cultural e Turístico da FIEMG

12

29

27

23

R Direita (Conde de Bobadela)

R Parana

25

32 26

34

1

24

R Claudio Manoel

35

20

28

16

Diogo de Vasconcelos

14

Travessa do Arieira

R Brigadeiro Musqueira

5 8

13

3

22

R do Pilar

6

R Costa Sena

R Sao Francisco de Assis

R das Merces

PILAR

Praça Barão do Rio Branco

Diogo de Vasconcelos

Av Vitorino Dias

Dr Pacifico Homem

R Xavier da Veiga

Lavras Novas (17km)

Ribeirão do Funil

R dos Inconfidêntes

Train Station

between 1766 and 1772, this lovely church was a group effort by the area's most important artists. It features a facade and two side altars by Aleijadinho.

Museu de Ciência e Técnica da Escola de Minas   MUSEUM
(Praça Tiradentes; admission R$6; ⊘noon-5pm Tue-Sun) This museum features gemstones from around the world. There's also an **astronomical observatory** (⊘8-10pm Sat).

MINAS GERAIS & ESPÍRITO SANTO OURO PRETO

Ouro Preto

⊙ Sights
Astronomical Observatory ....(see 9)
1 Casa de Tomás Antônio
   Gonzaga.....................................D3
2 Casa dos Contos.............................C3
3 Igreja de São Francisco de
   Assis D4
4 Igreja NS da Conceição de
   Antônio Dias E4
5 Igreja NS do Carmo D4
6 Matriz NS do Pilar..........................B4
7 Mina do Chico-Rei..........................F4
8 Museu da Inconfidência................. D4
9 Museu de Ciência e Técnica da
   Escola de Minas D3
Museu do Aleijadinho.................(see 4)
Museu do Oratório......................(see 5)
10 Oratório Vira-Saia..........................F4
11 Parque do Vale dos Contos.............C2
12 Praça Tiradentes...........................D3

⊜ Sleeping
13 Brumas Hostel D4
14 Goiabada com Queijo C4
15 Grande Hotel Ouro Preto.................C3
16 Pousada do Mondego D4
17 Pousada Nello Nuno.......................D2
18 Pousada São Francisco C2
19 Pouso Café com Arte E4
20 Pouso do Chico Rei.........................D3
21 Solar do Rosario.............................A2

⊗ Eating
22 René da Flauta D4
23 Café e Cia.....................................B3
24 Café e Livraria Cultural D3
25 Café Geraes...................................C3
26 Casa do Ouvidor............................D3
27 Chafariz.......................................B3
28 Chocolates Ouro Preto D3
29 Chocolates Ouro Preto B3
30 Hannah...B3
31 O Passo C3
32 Quinto do Ouro..............................D3

⊜ Drinking & Nightlife
33 Barroco e Barraco A2
34 Taberna Xagrille.............................D3

⊛ Entertainment
35 Teatro Municipal.............................C3

⊙ Antônio Dias Parish

**Igreja de São Francisco
de Assis**   CHURCH
(www.museualeijadinho.com.br; Largo de Coimbra s/n; admission R$8; ⊙ 8:30-noon & 1:30-5pm Tue-Sun) This exquisite church is Brazil's most important piece of colonial art, after Aleijadinho's masterpiece *The Prophets* in Congonhas. Its entire exterior was carved by Aleijadinho himself, from the soapstone medallion to the cannon waterspouts to the Franciscan two-bar cross. The interior was

painted by Aleijadinho's long-term partner, Manuel da Costa Ataíde.

Igreja NS da Conceição de Antônio Dias
CHURCH

(Rua da Conceição s/n; admission R$8; ⊙8:30am-noon & 1:30-5:30pm Tue-Sat, noon-5pm Sun) Designed by Aleijadinho's father, Manuel Francisco Lisboa, this church was built between 1727 and 1770. Aleijadinho himself is buried here, near the altar of Boa Morte.

Museu do Aleijadinho
MUSEUM

(www.museualeijadinho.com.br; Rua da Conceição; included in Igreja NS da Conceição ticket; ⊙8:30-noon & 1:30-5pm Tue-Sat, noon-5pm Sun) An homage to the life of Brazil's greatest Baroque artist, this museum behind Igreja NS da Conceição displays works by Aleijadinho and other 18th-century masters, including intricate crucifixes, elaborate oratories (niches containing saints' images to ward off evil spirits) and a vast collection of religious figurines.

Mina do Chico-Rei
MINE

(Dom Silvério 108; admission R$10; ⊙8am-5pm) Near Matriz NS da Conceição de Antônio Dias is the abandoned mine of Chico-Rei. There's little to see as you stoop through the low passageways, but it's the perfect place to meditate on the fascinating story of this famous king-turned-slave-turned-king-again (see p182).

Casa de Tomás Antônio Gonzaga
HISTORIC BUILDING

(Cláudio Manoel 61) This 18th-century building is the spot where Gonzaga and the other Inconfidentes conspired to put an end to Portuguese rule in Brazil.

◉ Pilar Parish

Matriz NS do Pilar
CHURCH

(Praça Monsenhor Castilho Barbosa; admission R$8; ⊙9-10:45am & noon-5pm Tue-Sun) On the southwest side of town, this is Brazil's second-most-opulent church (after Salvador's São Francisco). It has 434kg of gold and silver and is one of the country's finest showcases of artwork. Note the wild-bird chandelier holders, the scrolled church doors and the hair on Jesus (the real stuff, donated by a penitent worshipper).

Casa dos Contos
MUSEUM

(São José 12; ⊙10am-6pm Tue-Sat, to 4pm Sun, 2-6pm Mon) **FREE** This 18th-century treasury building doubled as a prison for members of the Inconfidência. The renovated mansion now houses displays on the history of gold – and money in general – in Brazil.

Parque do Vale dos Contos
PARK

(www.valedoscontos.com.br; ⊙7am-5pm) Built on the site of Ouro Preto's 18th-century botanical garden, this lovely, verdant public park snakes downhill along a creek from the bus station to the Pilar church, passing en route under the bridge adjacent to Casa dos Contos. It's a tranquil spot with pretty views, great for a break from the crowds and the cobblestones.

◉ Santa Efigênia Parish

Igreja de Santa Efigênia dos Pretos
CHURCH

(Santa Efigênia 396; ⊙8:30am-4:30pm Tue-Sun) Financed by gold from Chico-Rei's mine and built by the slave community, this mid-18th-century church honors Santa Efigênia, princess of Nubia. The exterior image of NS do Rosário is by Aleijadinho. Slaves legendarily contributed to the church coffers by washing their gold-flaked hair in baptismal fonts, or smuggling gold powder under fingernails and inside tooth cavities.

Capela do Padre Faria
CHURCH

(Rua da Padre Faria s/n; admission R$3; ⊙8:30am-4:30pm Tue-Sun) Built between 1701 and 1704 and named after one of the original *bandeirantes* (roaming adventurers who spent the 17th and 18th centuries exploring Brazil's interior), Ouro Preto's oldest chapel sits at the far eastern edge of town, behind a triple-branched papal cross (1756) representing the pope's temporal, spiritual and material powers. Because of poor documentation, the artists here are anonymous.

Oratório Vira-Saia
SHRINE

(cnr Barão do Ouro Branco & Ladeira de Santa Efigênia) This is the most famous of several *oratórios* built on street corners around town by early-18th-century Ouro Preto residents to keep evil spirits at bay. Others can be found on Rua dos Paulistas and Antônio Dias.

☞ Tours

AGTOP
WALKING TOUR

(⌨ 3551-2655; 4-/8-hr tour up to 10 people in Portuguese R$118/165, all-day tour in English, French or Spanish R$185) Official guided city tours are available at the tourist office. Note that prices quoted here are from the official ta-

SEMANA SANTA IN OURO PRETO

Semana Santa (Holy Week) is celebrated all over Brazil, but Ouro Preto's festivities are especially dazzling. For four days the town becomes a giant stage, starting with Thursday night's ceremonial washing of feet and the deposition of Christ from a giant cross in front of Igreja de São Francisco on Good Friday.

The most wonderful event is saved for the wee hours preceding Easter Sunday. Around midnight Saturday, locals begin opening bags of colored sawdust on street corners all over town, unleashing an all-night public art project in which 3km of Ouro Preto's cobblestone streets are covered with fanciful designs, a giant carpet marking the route for the following morning's Easter processions. Until the early 1960s, Ouro Preto observed the old Portuguese tradition of decorating Easter-parade routes with flowers and leaves. More recently, colored scraps of leather, sand, coffee grounds and sawdust have become the media of choice for these *tapetes coloridos* (colored carpets).

Tourists are welcome to participate in laying out the designs, but be prepared for a late night. Things really don't get going until well after midnight. Music and general merrymaking erupt unpredictably all night long, and a few stragglers stick around till dawn to put finishing touches on Praça Tiradentes, the last spot cleared of vehicle traffic. If you prefer your beauty rest, go to bed early Saturday evening, then wake up at 5am Sunday to see the magic that's unfolded while you slept. It's like awakening to a Technicolor snowfall!

The designs – some religious, some profane – change every year and only last a few short hours. Within moments of the procession's passing, the public works crew is out in force with brooms and shovels to clean the streets, until next year.

ble; you may be able to negotiate better rates with individual guides. The office can also help organize treks and horseback rides into the surrounding hills.

⭐ Festivals & Events

Thanks in part to Ouro Preto's huge student population, **Carnaval** (www.carnavalouropreto. com) (February/March) here is boisterous and fun. The town government hosts free live music on multiple stages in the historic center, while dozens of *blocos* (drumming and dancing processions) parade through the streets throughout the week; Balanço da Cobra and Bloco do Caixão are among the best.

Semana Santa (Holy Week; March/ April) processions in Ouro Preto are quite a spectacle (see p177).

Ouro Preto reclaims the symbolic role of state capital once a year, on **Tiradentes Day**, April 21. Other noteworthy cultural events are the literary festival **Forum das Letras** (www.forumdasletras.ufop.br) in late May/early June, the film festival **CineOP** (www.cineop.com.br) in mid-June, the month-long **Festival de Inverno** (winter festival) and the **Festival Tudo é Jazz**, which brings in jazz performers from Brazil and beyond for five days every September.

There are also festivities associated with Congado, the local expression of Afro-Christian syncretism (similar to Candomblé in Bahia or Quimbanda in Rio). The major **Congado celebrations** are for NS do Rosário (October 23 to 25, at the Capela do Padre Faria), for the New Year and for May 13 (the anniversary of abolition).

🛏 Sleeping

🛏 Praça Tiradentes & Around

Brumas Hostel   HOSTEL $
(☑ 3551-2944; www.brumashostel.com.br; Antônio Pereira 43; dm from R$35, s/d from R$90/130; 🅿 @ 🛜) In upgraded new digs behind the Museu da Inconfidência, this HI-affiliated hostel offers well-maintained dorms and private rooms in an unbeatable location. The small outdoor kitchen and lounge catches breezes off the surrounding hillsides.

★ Pouso do Chico Rei   INN $$
(☑ 3551-1274; www.pousodochicorei.com.br; Brigadeiro Musqueira 90; s/d from R$190/220, without bathroom R$90/160; ❄ @ 🛜) Easily Ouro Preto's best midrange option, this beautifully preserved 18th-century mansion directly opposite the Carmo church oozes colonial charm, with creaky wood floors and a breakfast room full of hand-painted antique cupboards. Each room is unique, and most

Colonial Towns of Minas Gerais

Minas' standout attraction, the *cidades históricas* (colonial towns) collectively constitute one of Brazil's most appealing and accessible tourist circuits. Baroque masterworks built with 18th-century mineral wealth, they all share a common ancestry, yet each has unique charms.

Ouro Preto

Ouro Preto (p172) tops the list as Minas' most magnificent and best-preserved colonial gem. Its two dozen churches and cobblestoned streets have benefited from more than 80 years of conservation efforts.

Mariana

A pearl inside the surrounding 21st-century oyster, Mariana (p182) is home to two of Minas' most harmonious squares and an 18th-century organ that still plays weekly concerts. Hop aboard the scenic train from Ouro Preto for a perfect day trip.

1. *The Prophets* (p185), Congonhas **2.** Cobblestone streets, Ouro Preto (p172) **3.** Igreja Matriz de Santo Antônio (p190), Tiradentes

Tiradentes

With winding alleys decked in flowers, a photogenic mountain backdrop, and atmospheric restaurants and boutiques on every corner, cute-as-a-button Tiradentes (p190) wins the prize for romantic charm.

Diamantina

Remote, rugged setting and unadulterated architectural integrity give Diamantina (p196) a 'lost in time' quality. Prefer something sleepier but just as picturesque? Follow the Estrada Real southeast to Serro, Milho Verde and São Gonçalo.

São João del Rei

A colonial-modern hybrid, bustling São João (p186) is peppered with enough 18th-century churches to hold their own against the encroaching high-rises.

Congonhas

Colonial Minas' ugly duckling, urbanized Congonhas (p185) remains a must-see thanks to Aleijadinho's brilliant sculptures of *The Prophets*, the crowning masterpiece of Minas' greatest baroque artist.

IAN TROWER / GETTY IMAGES ©

have period furniture and fabulous views. The two least-expensive rooms share a bathroom. Well worth booking ahead.

🛏 Antônio Dias Parish

Pouso Café com Arte   B&B $
(✆ 3552-2671; cafe.comarte@bol.com.br; Rua das Mercês 45; s/d R$75/85, with shared bath R$50/75, q R$180; 🛜) Dona Consuelo rents out a handful of simple rooms in her cheerful home, all with parquet wood floors and colorful embroidered wall hangings. It's a superb value given the prime location just below Igreja São Francisco.

Pousada Nello Nuno   POUSADA $
(✆ 3551-3375; www.pousadanellonuno.com.br; Camilo de Brito 59; s/d/tr R$110/140/175) In a quiet location northeast of Praça Tiradentes, this family-run pousada has clean and airy *apartamentos* (rooms with bathrooms) with artwork around a cute flagstoned courtyard. French and English spoken.

Pousada do Mondego   POUSADA $$$
(✆ 3551-2040; www.mondego.com.br; Largo de Coimbra 38; s/d from R$294/354, ste from R$495; @🛜) This classy inn – in an 18th-century colonial mansion with period furnishings, fine artwork and close-up views of Igreja de São Francisco de Assis – belongs to the exclusive international network Hotels de Charme. Potential downsides are the minuscule windows in the standard rooms tucked under the eaves, and late-night party noise from the adjacent *repúblicas* (student accommodations).

🛏 Pilar Parish

Goiabada com Queijo   HOSTEL $
(✆ 3552-3816; goiabadacomqueijohostel@gmail.com; Rua do Pilar 44; dm/r R$30/90; 🛜) Midway between Praça Tiradentes and the train station, this sweet and simple three-room hostel is a labor of love for well-traveled owner Liliane, who makes guests feel at home with her solid command of German and English and her enthusiasm for showing off Ouro Preto's hidden treasures.

Pousada São Francisco   HOSTEL, GUESTHOUSE $
(✆ 3551-3456; www.pousadasaofranciscode-paula.com.br; Padre Penna 202; dm/s/d downstairs from R$30/50/60, s/d/tr/q upstairs R$100/110/160/200; @🛜) Hidden away on a leafy hillside full of chirping birds, this hostel-like guesthouse has friendly multilingual staff and a guest kitchen. The two upstairs rooms with panoramic views are the best of the bunch. From the bus station, follow signs five minutes downhill, turning left just before Igreja São Francisco de Paula. Late-night arrivals should phone for an escort.

Grande Hotel Ouro Preto   HOTEL $$
(✆ 3551-1488; www.grandehotelouropreto.com.br; Rua das Flores 164; s/d/tr R$195/235/260, ste from R$230/290/360; @🛜🏊) Oscar Niemeyer's Grande Hotel is not as nice to look *at* as it is to look *from*. Very central, with a pool and bar area overlooking the town, it's the only modernist structure for miles and is something of an eyesore. The two-level suites offer views and are better value than the bland, rather cramped standard rooms.

Solar do Rosario   HOTEL $$$
(✆ 3551-5200; www.hotelsolardorosario.com.br; Getúlio Vargas 270; d/ste midweek from R$360/715, weekend from R$415/826; ❄@🛜🏊) With an enviable position facing the Rosário church, this four-star is the finest new hotel to open in Ouro Preto in recent years. Ample rooms in the original 18th-century mansion are complemented by luxurious suites in the colonial-style modern annex and countless amenities spread over pretty terraced grounds out back, including indoor and outdoor pools, a sauna and more.

🍴 Eating

There are plenty of budget eateries are clustered along lively Direita, São José and Praça Tiradentes.

🍴 Praça Tiradentes & Around

Café e Livraria Cultural   CAFE $
(✆ 3551-3239; Cláudio Manoel 15; snacks R$8.50-17; ⏰9am-7pm) Tucked away just below the tourist office, this laid-back little cafe with exposed stone walls has simple food, fancy coffee drinks, and an extensive beer and wine list. A good place to pore over the map and get your bearings.

Chocolates Ouro Preto   CAFE $
(✆ 3551-7330; www.chocolatesouropreto.com.br; Praça Tiradentes 111; snacks R$4-13; ⏰9am-7pm) Best known for its hot chocolate and other sinful indulgences, Ouro Preto's hometown chocolate factory also serves sandwiches, soups and a variety of other savory snacks. There's a **second branch** (Getúlio Vargas 66) that keeps the same hours and prices.

Quinto do Ouro   SELF-SERVE $
(Direita 76; per kg R$42; ⊘11am-3pm) Locals throng to this per-kilo spot, tucked below street level on Ouro Preto's main drag, for the quality and variety of its mineira food, including meat grilled to order.

Café Geraes   INTERNATIONAL $$
(✉3551-5097; Direita 122; mains R$29-52; ⊘ noon-midnight) Well-heeled students and artists favor this trendy spot to sip wine, talk shop and linger over creatively prepared salads, pasta, salmon and steak dishes. On weekdays, there's a good-value *prato executivo* lunch – main dish, salad, dessert and coffee for R$25. Their downstairs space **Escadabaixo** serves the exact same menu, but with more of a cellar beer-hall atmosphere.

Casa do Ouvidor   MINEIRA $$
(✉3551-2141; www.casadoouvidor.com.br; Direita 42; mains R$24-51; ⊘11am-3pm & 7-10pm) Just downhill from Praça Tiradentes, Ouvidor has garnered numerous awards for its *comida mineira*. At night, low lighting enhances the rustic charm of the ancient upstairs dining room. Definitely come with an empty stomach – portions are immense.

✖ Antônio Dias Parish

Bené da Flauta   INTERNATIONAL $$$
(✉3551-1036; São Francisco de Assis 32; mains R$29-79; ⊘noon-10pm) Directly below Igreja de São Francisco, this place occupies two levels of a gorgeous colonial *sobrado* (mansion). The open, airy atmosphere, the views and the wine list nicely complement the menu of trout, steak, pasta and mineira specialties, all presented with flair.

✖ Pilar Parish

Café e Cia   SELF-SERVE $
(✉3551-6515; São José 185; per kg R$41.90; ⊘11am-4pm) An old favorite with an airy back seating area overlooking the creek. The self-service lunch focuses on mineira fare.

★O Passo   ITALIAN $$
(São José 56; pizzas R$24-54; ⊘noon-midnight) In a lovely 18th-century building, this restaurant has intimate candlelit rooms, marbled walls and an extensive menu of pizza, pasta and salads complemented by a good wine list. Outside, the relaxed terrace overlooking the Casa de Contos is ideal for an after-dinner drink. On Tuesday nights, don't miss the *rodizio de pizzas* (all-you-can-eat pizza, R$29.90).

Chafariz   BUFFET $$
(✉3551-2828; São José 167; all-you-can-eat R$40; ⊘noon-4:30pm) Eclectically decorated with old photos, religious art, Brazilian flags and antiques, this local institution serves one of Minas' tastiest (if priciest) buffets. The menu showcases traditional local favorites such as *lombo* (roasted pork loin) and *feijão tropeiro*, followed by Minas cheese and *goiabada* (guava paste) for dessert. Post-meal shots of *cachaça*, coffee and *jabuticaba* liqueur are included in the price.

Hannah   JAPANESE, MIDDLE EASTERN $$
(www.hannahop.com.br; Getúlio Vargas 241; mains R$22-50; ⊘6pm-midnight) This newcomer to Ouro Preto's dining scene serves an unconventional but tasty mix of Japanese and Middle Eastern food, from tempura, *yakissoba* (fried noodles) and *temakis* (sushi cones) to lamb with couscous or *kofta* (meatballs) in tomato sauce. The *rodizio de comida japonesa* on Wednesday nights is a great deal, with all-you-can-eat sushi and other Japanese treats for R$44.90.

▼ Drinking & Entertainment

At night and on weekends, students assemble in Praça Tiradentes and crowd the bars along nearby Direita.

Barroco e Barraco   BAR
(www.barrocoebarraco.com.br; Gabriel Santos 16; ⊘2-10pm Mon-Thu, 4pm-late Fri & Sat) Locals convene at this artsy bar every afternoon and evening to sip wine and enjoy homemade bar snacks (R$15 to R$25), seated at sidewalk tables or on cushions along the stone wall overlooking Igreja NS do Rosário. The attached shop sells local artwork, and there's live music most Friday and Saturday nights.

Taberna Xagrille   BAR
(tabernaxagrille.com.br; Praça Tiradentes 64; ⊘6pm-late Tue-Thu, noon-late Fri-Sun) Tucked into a cozy 18th-century cellar just below Praça Tiradentes, this bar-restaurant hosts frequent jazz, tango, MPB (*música popular brasileira*) and other live performances.

Teatro Municipal   THEATER
(Casa da Ópera; casadaoperaop.blogspot.com; Brigadeiro Musqueira s/n) Built in 1769, this 280-seat theater is the oldest in Minas Gerais; it's open for occasional live performances.

ⓘ Orientation

Most streets in town have two names: the official one and another used by locals because the official one is too long. For example, Conde de Bobadela, the major thoroughfare descending from Praça Tiradentes, is commonly known as Direita, and Conselheiro Quintiliano, the road to Mariana, is also Rua das Lajes. Adding to the confusion, street names are rarely posted.

ⓘ Information

Banco do Brasil (São José 189)

Bradesco (Praça Tiradentes 44)

Centro Cultural e Turístico da FIEMG (☑ 3551-3637; www5.fiemg.com.br; Praça Tiradentes 4; ☺9am-7pm) Offers information in English, Spanish and French, including a leaflet listing museum and church hours and a rough town map.

Compuway (Praça Tiradentes 52A; per hr R$4; ☺8am-9pm Mon-Fri, 9am-6pm Sat) Internet in the heart of town.

HSBC (São José 201)

ⓘ Getting There & Away

BUS

Long-distance buses leave from Ouro Preto's main **bus station** (☑ 3559-3252; Rua Padre Rolim 661), a 10-minute uphill walk from Praça

Tiradentes at the northwest end of town. During peak periods, buy tickets a day in advance.

Pássaro Verde (www.passaroverde.com.br) provides service to Belo Horizonte (R$25, two hours, hourly from 6am to 8pm); **Útil** (☑ 3551-3166; www.util.com.br) goes to Rio (*convencional/executivo/semi-leito* R$76/107/119, 10am and 10pm daily) and São Paulo (R$129, 11 hours, 7:30am and 7pm daily); the São Paulo bus stops en route at São João del Rei (R$51, four hours).

To get to Mariana or Minas de Passagem, catch a local Transcotta (p184) bus (R$3.20, every 20 minutes from 6am to 11pm) from the local bus stop just northeast of Praça Tiradentes.

TRAIN

Ferrovia Centro-Atlântica (p195) operates a renovated historic tourist train on weekends between Ouro Preto and Mariana (one hour, one-way/round-trip R$40/50; with air-con R$60/80), leaving Ouro Preto's **train station** (☑ 3551-7705; Praça Cesário Alvim 102) twice daily Friday and Saturday, three times on Sunday. The 18km journey is pretty but slow, snaking along a river gorge the whole way. Best views are from the right side leaving Ouro Preto, and the left side leaving Mariana.

ⓘ Getting Around

Viação Turin runs a small bus (R$2) between the bus station and Capela do Padre Faria on the eastern side of town, making various stops in the historic center along the way.

Mariana

☑ 0XX31 / POP 54,000 / ELEV 712M

Graced with fine colonial architecture and two of Minas' prettiest squares, lovely Mariana, founded in 1696, was one of the state's earliest settlements and its first capital. Only 14km from Ouro Preto, Mariana makes an easy day trip or can even be used as a base to explore both cities. Its compact historical center is easier to navigate than Ouro Preto's, not only because of its smaller size, but also because the hills are less steep. The ground floors of many historic mansions have been transformed into stores, boutiques and artists' workshops where you're invited to wander at will.

⊙ Sights

All the sights are close together. Two blocks uphill from the tourist information office and the Ouro Preto bus stop, Praça Minas Gerais boasts one of the state's nicest arrangements of public buildings on a single square.

CHICO-REI

Brazil's first abolitionist was Chico-Rei, an African tribal king. In the early 1700s, amid the frenzy of the gold rush, an entire tribe, king and all, was captured in Africa, sent to Brazil and sold to a mine owner in Ouro Preto.

The king, Chico-Rei, worked as the foreman of the slave miners. Working Sundays and holidays, he finally bought his freedom from the slave master, then freed his son Osmar. Together, father and son liberated the entire tribe.

This collective then bought the fabulously wealthy Encardadeira gold mine, and Chico-Rei assumed his royal functions once again, holding court in Vila Rica and celebrating African holidays in traditional costume. News of this reached the Portuguese king, who immediately prohibited slaves from purchasing their freedom. Chico-Rei is now a folk hero among Brazilian blacks.

Igreja São Francisco de Assis
CHURCH

(Praça Minas Gerais; admission R$2; ☉9am-noon & 1-4pm Tue-Sun) Mariana's loveliest church was designed by Aleijadinho, whose work can also been seen in the pulpits and other interior details. The gorgeous ceiling panels in the sacristy were painted by Mariana's native son Ataíde, who lies buried here with 94 other lucky souls.

Praça Gomes Freire
SQUARE

One block downhill from Praça Minas Gerais, this leafy square is a gorgeous place to sit and watch the world go by, with a pond, a gazebo and park benches shaded by grand old trees.

Catedral Basílica da Sé
CHURCH

(☑3558-2785; www.orgaodase.com.br; Praça Cláudio Manuel; organ concerts R$24; ☉8am-6pm Tue-Sun, organ concerts 11:30am Fri, 12:15pm Sun) The star attraction at Mariana's cathedral is its fantastic German organ dating from 1701, painted with designs from the then-Portuguese colony of Macau and adorned with carved wooden angels. Organ concerts are held twice weekly.

Museu Arquidiocesano de Arte Sacra
MUSEUM

(☑3557-2581; Frei Durão 49; admission R$5; ☉8:30am-noon & 1:30-5pm Tue-Sun) Next door to the cathedral, this museum has sculptures by Aleijadinho, paintings by Ataíde, and other religious objects.

Cia Navegante Teatro de Marionetes
MARIONETTE THEATER

(☑3557-3927; www.cianavegante.com.br; Seminário 290; ☉9am-6pm) At this longstanding marionette theater founded by local artist Catin Nardi, you can see new puppets under construction, plus old ones that have appeared on Brazilian national TV miniseries.

Igreja NS do Carmo
CHURCH

(Praça Minas Gerais; ☉9-11:45am & 1-4pm) This church on Mariana's central square was severely damaged by fire in 1999, but still retains its original rococo chancel (the only element to have survived unscathed).

🛏 Sleeping

Hostel Mariana
HOSTEL $

(☑3557-1435; www.hostelmariana.com.br; Mestre Vicente 41; dm/s/d R$50/70/130; 🛜) A couple of blocks below the main square, Mariana's HI-affiliated hostel offers the best prices in town for its bland but clean dorms and private rooms, all with en-suite bathrooms.

Pouso da Typographia
POUSADA $$

(☑3557-1577; Praça Gomes Freire 220; s/d/tr Fri-Sun R$100/180/200, Mon-Thu R$180/260/300; 🛜) This pousada's central location on Mariana's prettiest square can't be beat, although front rooms can get noisy on the weekends. It's worth a peek just to see the antique printing presses in the foyer.

Hotel Providência
HOTEL $$

(☑3557-1444; www.hotelprovidencia.com.br; Dom Silvério 233; s/d/tr/q R$116/204/275/314; 🛜🏊) Guest rooms in this 1849 building, two blocks uphill from Praça Minas Gerais, are airy and inviting, with clean white sheets and lovely high ceilings. It shares a semi-Olympic-size swimming pool with the Catholic school next door.

🍴 Eating & Drinking

★ Lua Cheia
SELF-SERVE $

(☑3557-3232; Dom Viçoso 58; per kg R$27; ☉11am-3pm Mon-Fri, to 4pm Sat & Sun) Mariana's best per-kilo place, one block south of Praça Gomes Freire, offers a sumptuous buffet spread, along with atmospheric seating in a high-ceilinged colonial building or on the umbrella-shaded back patio.

O Rancho
BUFFET, PIZZERIA $$

(☑3558-1060; Praça Gomes Freire 108; all-you-can-eat buffet R$22, pizzas R$26-40; ☉11am-3pm & 6pm-midnight Tue-Sun) This cozy, low-key eatery specializes in hearty *mineira* fare, with soups bubbling on the wood-fired stove every night; there's also pizza for those needing a break from rice and beans.

Bar Scotch & Art
BAR

(Praça Minas Gerais 57; ☉6:30pm-2am Tue-Sun) Offering a wide selection of drinks and homemade snacks, this corner bar has cozy indoor seating plus a slate terrace overlooking lovely Praça Minas Gerais.

ℹ Information

Bradesco (Av Salvador Furtado) ATMs one block below the cathedral square.

Mundo Virtual Lan House (Praça da Sé 52; per hr R$2.50; ☉8am-10pm Mon-Sat, 9am-9pm Sun) Reasonably fast internet, plus Skype.

Post Office (Padre Gonçalves Lopes) Just below the cathedral.

Terminal Turístico (☑3557-1158; www.mariana.org.br; Praça Tancredo Neves; ☉8am-noon & 1:30-5pm) Just outside the historic center, in

---

WORTH A TRIP

MINAS DA PASSAGEM

Halfway between Ouro Preto and Mariana, this ancient **gold mine** (☑ 3557-5000; www.minasdapassagem.com.br; adult/child R$30/26; ⊙ 9am-5pm Mon & Tue, to 5:30pm Wed-Sun) opened in 1719. Guided tours descend in a rickety antique cable car, covering the mine's history and local gold-extraction methods, then visiting a subterranean lake and a shrine to the many black slaves who died here dynamiting into the rock. Any Ouro Preto–Mariana bus (R$3.20) can drop you here.

---

the square where buses from Ouro Preto stop. Offers city information and tours.

ℹ️ Getting There & Away

There are regular Transcotta (p184) buses between Ouro Preto and Mariana (R$3.20, 30 minutes, at least twice hourly from 6am to 11pm). In Mariana, the bus stop is across from the tourist information office on Praça Tancredo Neves; in Ouro Preto catch the bus from the local bus stop northeast of Praça Tiradentes.

Mariana's long-distance bus station, Rodoviária dos Inconfidentes, is located about 2km outside of town. Destinations served include Belo Horizonte (R$28, 2½ hours, several daily) and São Paulo (R$119, 11 hours, daily at 6:30pm). The Transcotta bus from Ouro Preto also stops here en route to downtown Mariana.

Mariana's picturesque peach-and-white-colored train station is just two blocks away from the local bus stop for buses to Ouro Preto. Trains (p195) leave Mariana for Ouro Preto twice daily Friday through Sunday. There's a museum and kids' playground to keep everyone occupied while you wait.

Lavras Novas

☑ 0XX31 / POP 1000 / ELEV 1510M

Lavras Novas, named for the new gold strikes discovered here in 1704, sits on a high plateau 17km from Ouro Preto. When the gold started running out in the late 18th century, this hamlet became home to a small community of freed slaves, and many of their descendants have remained to this day. Surrounded by wide-open mountain scenery, its cobblestone main street runs between colorful single-story houses to the town's focal point, the **Igreja NS dos Prazeres**.

The rapid influx of visitors over the past decade, coupled with the recent paving of Lavras' access road, have led to a small boom in new pousadas and ecotourism agencies; on busy weekends it can sometimes feel like outsiders outnumber locals. For lower prices and a taste of the town's traditional off-the-beaten-path tranquility, consider visiting midweek.

🏃 Activities

Several companies around town offer guided hikes and horseback-riding tours to local attractions, including the waterfalls **Três Pingos** and **Namorados**. An alternative resource for independent hikers is the rudimentary free trail map distributed at pousada Palavras Novas.

🛏️ Sleeping & Eating

Pousadas empty out during the week, but reservations are advisable on weekends and holidays, when there's often a two-night minimum.

Taberna Casa Antiga e Chalés Galo do Campo   CHALET **$$**
(☑ 9957-8189; www.lavrasnovas.com.br/galodocampo; Alto do Campo 213; d midweek R$180-220, weekend R$220-280) Nestled among trees at the edge of town are these cute chalets with views of horse pastures and mountains. The rustic-chic **restaurant** next door is filled with candlelight, cozy couches and curtain-draped nooks; it serves a varied international menu and hosts live blues bands on weekends.

Palavras Novas   POUSADA **$$**
(☑ 3554-2025; www.pousadapalavrasnovas.com.br; NS dos Prazeres 1110; d midweek/weekend from R$180/240, chalet with whirlpool tub midweek/weekend R$320/400; ☒) With fireplaces, afternoon tea, whirlpool tubs, in-room DVD players, a sauna, spa and heated pool, nice mountain views and live music on weekends, Palavras Novas caters to a luxury-minded crowd. The pousada leads group hikes every weekend.

ℹ️ Getting There & Away

Transcotta (☑ 3551-2385) runs daily buses to Lavras Novas (R$5.10, 45 minutes) from in front of the Ouro Preto train station (*not* the bus station). There are three departures in each direction Tuesday through Friday, four on Monday, and one each on Saturday and Sunday.

Congonhas

📍 0XX31 / POP 49,000 / ELEV 871M

This small industrial town has been saved from complete obscurity by the beautiful, brooding presence of Aleijadinho's extraordinary *The Prophets* at the Basílica do Bom Jesus de Matosinhos. The dramatic statues almost seem to be performing a balletic dance and it's a wondrous experience to be able to walk freely among them. They are Aleijadinho's masterpiece and Brazil's most famed work of art. It's worth taking the trouble to get to Congonhas just to see them.

Congonhas is 72km south of Belo Horizonte, 3km off Hwy BR-040. The city grew up with the search for gold in the nearby Rio Maranhão, and the economy today is dominated by iron mining in the surrounding countryside.

◉ Sights

Already an old man, sick and crippled, Aleijadinho sculpted *The Prophets* between 1800 and 1805. Symmetrically placed in front of the Basílica do Bom Jesus de Matosinhos, each of the 12 Old Testament figures was carved from one or two blocks of soapstone. Each carries a Latin message: some are hopeful prophecies, others warn of the end of the world.

Much has been written about these sculptures – their dynamic quality, the sense of movement (much like a Hindu dance or a ballet), how they complement each other and how their arrangement prevents them from being seen in isolation. The poet Carlos Drummond de Andrade wrote that the dramatic faces and gestures are 'magnificent, terrible, grave and tender' and commented on 'the way the statues, of human size, appear to be larger than life as they look down upon the viewer with the sky behind them.'

Before working on *The Prophets*, Aleijadinho carved (or supervised his assistants in carving) the wooden statues that were placed in the six little chapels below. The chapels themselves – also of Aleijadinho's design – and their placement on the sloping site are superb. The way the light falls on the pale sculpted domes against the dark mountain backdrop is truly beautiful.

Each chapel depicts a scene from Christ's passion, and several portray Jesus with a red mark on his neck. While little is known of Aleijadinho's politics, some local historians interpret this to mean that Aleijadinho intended

---

ALEIJADINHO

Antônio Francisco Lisboa (1738–1814), known worldwide today as Aleijadinho (Little Cripple), was the son of a Portuguese architect and a black slave. His nickname was given to him sometime in the 1770s, when the artist began to suffer from a terrible, debilitating disease. It might have been syphilis or possibly leprosy – either way, he lost his fingers and toes and the use of his lower legs.

Undaunted, Aleijadinho strapped hammers and chisels to his arms and continued working, advancing the art in his country from the excesses of the baroque to a finer, more graceful form known as Barroco Mineiro.

Mineiros have reason to be proud of Aleijadinho – he is a figure of international prominence in the history of art. He studied European baroque and rococo traditions through pictures, but went on to develop his own unique style, using only native materials such as soapstone and wood. Aleijadinho's angels have his stylistic signature: wavy hair, wide-open eyes and big, round cheeks.

For many years Manuel da Costa Ataíde, from nearby Mariana, successfully collaborated with Aleijadinho on several churches. Aleijadinho would sculpt the exterior and a few interior pieces, and Ataíde would paint the interior panels. With his secretly concocted vegetable dyes, Ataíde fleshed out many of Aleijadinho's creations.

Aleijadinho was buried in Ouro Preto's Matriz NS da Conceição de Antônio Dias, within 50 paces of his birth site. He was named patron of Brazilian arts by federal decree in 1973. *The Prophets* in Congonhas, the Igreja de São Francisco de Assis and the facade of the Igreja de NS do Carmo, both in Ouro Preto, were all carved by Aleijadinho, as were innumerable relics in Mariana, Sabará, Tiradentes and São João del Rei.

to draw parallels between the martyred Christ and slain independence fighter Tiradentes. Aleijadinho's sculptures of Roman soldiers lend support to this theory – they all have two left feet and sport ankle boots, a shoe style favored by the colonizing Portuguese.

⚜ Festivals & Events

Held from September 7 to 14, the **Jubileu do Senhor Bom Jesus do Matosinhos** is one of Minas' great religious festivals. Every year approximately 600,000 pilgrims arrive at the church to make promises, do penance, receive blessings, and give and receive alms. **Holy Week** (April/May) processions in Congonhas are also famous, especially the dramatizations on Good Friday.

🛏 Sleeping & Eating

It's possible to catch an early bus into Congonhas and another out that same afternoon. Since there's little to see beyond Aleijadinho's artwork, most people don't spend the night. One pleasure of staying over is the opportunity to see the statues in the early-morning light, when they're especially beautiful.

Hotel Colonial　　　　　　　　HOTEL **$**
(📞 3731-1834; www.hotelcolonialcongonhas.com.br; Praça da Basílica 76; s/d R$60/120; 🅰) Conveniently situated right across the street from Aleijadinho's masterpieces, this hotel still wears faded remnants of its former glory in the huge hallways and immensely high ceilings. Most rooms are spacious and the bathrooms surprisingly modern.

Cova do Daniel　　　　　　MINEIRA **$$**
(📞 3731-1834; Praça da Basílica 76; mains for 2 R$45-60; ⊙ 11am-11pm Tue-Sun, 9am-6pm Mon) This restaurant downstairs from Hotel Colonial specializes in mineira classics such as *feijão tropeiro* and *tutu à mineira*. It's a convenient lunch option for day-trippers.

❶ Getting There & Away

Congonhas is on the direct bus route between Belo Horizonte and São João del Rei, so these two towns make the best starting points for a day trip. **Viação Sandra** (www.viacaosandra.com.br) serves this route several times daily (R$21, 90 minutes from Belo Horizonte; R$26, two hours from São João).

❶ Getting Around

The long-distance bus station is on Av Júlia Kubitschek, across town from the sites of interest. From here local buses for the basilica and *The*

Prophets (R$2.45, 15 minutes) leave every 30 to 60 minutes. For the best approach and first view of the statues, get off just after the bus passes the church (as it heads downhill). The same bus returns you to the bus station, or you can take a taxi (R$15, 10 minutes).

São João del Rei

📍 0XX32 / POP 84,000 / ELEV 898M

Set between mountain ridges near the southern end of the Serra do Espinhaço, São João del Rei affords a unique look at a *cidade historica* (historic colonial town) that didn't suffer a great decline when the gold boom ended in the 1800s. Present-day São João has the unselfconscious urban vitality of a modern city, which can come as a welcome contrast to the preserved-in-amber quality of neighboring Tiradentes. Downtown there are plenty of high-rises and other trappings of 21st-century Brazil, yet around every corner lurk unexpected colonial surprises. The historic city center, which is protected by Brazil's Landmarks Commission, features two good museums, several of the country's finest churches and some gorgeous old mansions – one of which belonged to the late and still-popular never-quite-president Tancredo Neves. Floodlights illuminate the churches every night, adding to the city's aesthetic appeal.

São João is bisected by the Córrego do Lenheiro – really just a glorified creek in a concrete channel. Two lovely 18th-century stone bridges serve as convenient landmarks, roughly delineating the boundaries of the colonial center.

◎ Sights

Opening times vary widely. Monday is not a good day to visit, since most attractions are closed.

Igreja de São Francisco de Assis　　　　　　　CHURCH
(Padre José Maria Xavier; admission R$3; ⊙ 8am-5pm Tue-Sat, to 2pm Sun, to 4pm Mon) This exquisite 1774 baroque church, fronted by a palm-shaded, lyre-shaped plaza, is home to two **Aleijadinho sculptures** (second altar to the left) and one of Minas' finest facades, based on Aleijadinho's design. Out back, arrows lead to politician Tancredo Neves' grave, a pilgrimage site for Brazilians. The local Ribeiro Bastos orchestra and choir perform sacred baroque music Sundays at 9:15am.

Museu Regional São João del Rei   MUSEUM
(☑ 3371-7663; Praça Severiano Resende s/n; admission R$1, Sun free; ☺ 10:30am-5:30pm Tue-Fri, 1:30-5:30pm Sat & Sun) One of the best regional museums in Minas Gerais, this 19th-century colonial mansion houses three floors of antique furniture, sacred art and assorted cultural relics.

Museu de Arte Sacra   MUSEUM
(☑ 3371-7005; Praça Embaixador Gastão da Cunha 8; adult/reduced R$5/2.50; ☺ noon-5pm Mon-Fri, 9am-1pm Sat) In a building that served as the public jail between 1737 and 1850, this recently renovated museum has a small but impressive collection of art from the city's churches.

Igreja de NS do Carmo   CHURCH
(Getúlio Vargas; admission R$4; ☺ 8:30-11am & 1-5pm) This 18th-century church, dominating a lovely triangular *praça* (plaza), was designed by Aleijadinho, who also did the frontispiece and the sculpture around the door. In the second sacristy is a famous unfinished sculpture of Christ.

Catedral de NS do Pilar   CHURCH
(Getúlio Vargas; ☺ 8:30-11am & 1-8pm) Begun in 1721, São João's cathedral has exuberant gold altars and fine Portuguese tiles. Two of the city's famous orchestras can be heard here: on Wednesdays, the Lira Sanjoanense orchestra accompanies the 7pm Mass, and on Thursday and Friday it's the Ribeiro Bastos orchestra.

Igreja de NS do Rosário   CHURCH
(Praça Embaixador Gastão da Cunha; ☺ 8:30-10:30am) This simple church was built in 1719 to honor the patron saint who was protector of the slaves.

✯✯ Festivals & Events
Someone's always celebrating something in São João. There are literally dozens of festivals, both religious and secular – stop by the tourist office for a full calendar.

Semana Santa (March/April) processions are especially colorful, preserving centuries-old Portuguese traditions and incorporating the music of the city's two baroque orchestras, who have been performing here uninterruptedly since the 1700s. Locals also boast, credibly, that their **Carnaval** (February/March) is the best in Minas Gerais. The **Semana da Inconfidência**, from April 15 to 21, celebrates Brazil's first independence movement, culminating in a horseback procession between São João and Tiradentes.

🛏 Sleeping
Book ahead in December, when the town is filled with students sitting for exams, and during holidays such as Carnaval and Easter.

If saving money is your primary concern, São João offers more low-end options than Tiradentes.

Pouso Aconchegante   GUESTHOUSE $
(☑ 3371-2637; Bittencourt 61; r per person R$40-60) This grandmotherly place offers 10 very simple rooms, all with shared bathroom, in a family home full of colorful kitsch near the Carmo church.

Hotel Brasil   HOTEL $
(☑ 3371-2804; Av Presidente Tancredo Neves 395; per person R$45, with shared bathroom R$35; ☎) The management is as ancient as the infrastructure at this funky, rambling 19th-century relic with high-ceilinged, bare-bones rooms, some facing the river; it's straight across the pedestrian bridge from the train station. No breakfast.

Villa Magnolia Pousada   POUSADA $$
(☑ 3373-5065; www.pousadavillamagnolia.com.br; Ribeiro Bastos 2; s/d midweek from R$116/145, weekend R$156/195; ✳@☎☲) A delightful refuge just across from Igreja de São Francisco, this stylishly renovated 19th-century mansion features pure cotton bedding, oversized towels, spacious rooms, a large pool, shade trees and common areas filled with art books.

Pousada Beco do Bispo   POUSADA $$
(☑ 3371-8844; www.becodobispo.com.br; Beco do Bispo 93; s/d R$150/210; ✳☎☲) Tucked down a peaceful dead-end street a block from Igreja de São Francisco, this pousada has cheerful, ultra-comfy rooms with queen- and king-sized beds, fine cotton sheets, international TV channels and a pool with palm trees. Friendly multilingual owner Nitza has lived in Italy and the United States and enjoys sharing her love of São João with visitors.

Pousada Casarão   POUSADA $$
(☑ 3371-7447; www.pousadacasarao.com; Ribeiro Bastos 94; s/d R$100/170; ✳☎☲) In a refurbished mansion behind the Igreja de São Francisco, this pousada tastefully blends old with new; many rooms are decorated with antiques, yet all have modern bathrooms. The French doors in the breakfast room overlook the pool.

MINAS GERAIS & ESPÍRITO SANTO SÃO JOÃO DEL REI

São João Del Rei

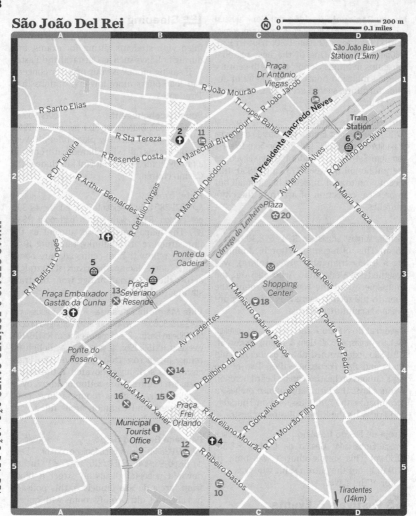

🍴 Eating

Restaurante Villeiros SELF-SERVE $

(☎3372-1034; Padre José Maria Xavier 132; per kg midweek R$29.90, weekend R$39.90; ⊙11am-3pm) A fabulous self-serve place with great variety near the Igreja de São Francisco, Villeiros is very popular with locals and has a cheerful patio out back.

Dedo de Moça BRAZILIAN $$

(Aureliano Mourão 101; mains for 2 R$23-48; ⊙6:30pm-midnight daily, plus noon-4pm Sun) This popular downtown spot is part bar, part restaurant, with a menu that offers in-

triguing new twists on traditional mineira cuisine. Local favorites include *acarajé mineira* – black-eyed pea fritters with various fillings including local cheese, sausage, *carne seca* (dried beef) and lemon grass – and *filé catauá* – steak with melted, grated Catauá cheese and fresh tomato-basil sauce.

Churrascaria Ramon CHURRASCARIA $$

(☎3371-3540; Praça Severiano Resende 52; mains for 2 R$39-66; ⊙10am-10pm) Ramon prides itself on perfectly cooked meats and all the traditional mineira favorites. For a bargain,

São João Del Rei

try the *prato feito* (meat, beans, rice, salad and potato salad) for R$16.

Monte Alverne　　　　INTERNATIONAL **$$**
(✆3371-7413; Praça Frei Orlando 26; mains R$30-40; ⏱6-11pm Mon-Sat, noon-11pm Sun) With nice views of the Igreja de São Francisco directly across the street, this centrally located eatery specializes in Brazilian cuisine with contemporary international flourishes. The menu includes salads, risottos, pasta, meat and fish dishes.

🍷 Drinking & Entertainment

Most of the city's nightlife is on the south side along Av Tiradentes.

Armazém　　　　　　　BAR
(Av Tiradentes 801; ⏱6pm-late) A cozy little place resembling a rustic cabin transplanted into the big city. Lots of people pack in here every night for delicious nibbles and drinks.

Del Rei Cafe　　　　　　BAR
(✆3371-1368; cnr Av Tiradentes & Gabriel Passos; ⏱9am-late) This busy corner bar, with numerous sidewalk tables, is great for people-watching. Locals congregate here daily for early-evening beers and late-night snacks.

São Jorge Bar Divertido　　　CLUB
(✆3371-2582; www.saojorgebardivertido.com.br; Balbino da Cunha 18; ⏱11pm-5am) Very popular with the 20- to 30-year-old crowd, who come to dance and flirt the night away to live rock, samba and more.

Teatro Municipal　　PERFORMING ARTS
(www.facebook.com/teatrosaojoaodelrei; Av Hermilio Alves) Constructed in 1893, this grand old theater in the heart of town stages occasional performances throughout the year (many free of charge).

ℹ Information

Bradesco (Av Hermilio Alves 200)
Municipal Tourist Office (✆3372-7338; cultura@saojoaodelrei.mg.br.gov; Praça Frei Orlando 90; ⏱8am-6pm) Opposite Igreja São Francisco de Assis.
RM 10 Serviços (Av Andrade Reis 120; per hr R$3; ⏱8am-6pm Mon-Fri, to noon Sat) Centrally located internet place.

ℹ Getting There & Away

BUS
São João's **bus station** (✆3373-4700; Rua Cristóvão Colombo) is 1.5km northeast of the center. See the table (p190) for a list of destinations served.

Frequent buses (R$3) connect São João and Tiradentes. See p190 for details.

TRAIN
The wonderful *Maria-Fumaça* tourist train (p195) runs on weekends and holidays between São João del Rei and Tiradentes. The train station is just east of the city center.

ℹ Getting Around

Local Presidente buses (gray with red letters) run between the bus station and the center (R$2.25, 10 minutes). Exiting the bus station, you'll find the local stop to your left and across the street (in front of the Drogaria Dose Certa).

Alternatively, catch a traditional taxi for R$15 or **motorbike taxi** (✆3371-6389) for R$4 just outside the bus station.

Returning from the center to the bus station, the most convenient local bus stop is in front of the train station.

MINAS GERAIS & ESPÍRITO SANTO SÃO JOÃO DEL REI

BUSES FROM SÃO JOÃO DEL REI

DESTINATION	COST (R$)	TIME (HR)	BUS COMPANY
Belo Horizonte	47	3½	Sandra (www.viacaosandra.com.br)
Caxambu	46	3½	Sandra (www.viacaosandra.com.br)
Congonhas	27	2	Sandra (www.viacaosandra.com.br)
Ouro Preto	52	4	Útil (www.util.com.br)
Petrópolis	60	4½	Paraibuna (www.paraibunatransportes.com.br)
Rio	68	5½	Paraibuna (www.paraibunatransportes.com.br)
São Paulo	80	7½	Gardénia (www.expressogardenia.com.br)

Tiradentes

⬛ 0XX32 / POP 7000 / ELEV 927M

Perhaps nowhere else in Minas do the colonial charm and picturesque natural setting blend so harmoniously as in Tiradentes. Quaint historic houses, fringed by exuberant wildflowers, stand out against a backdrop of pretty blue mountains threaded with hiking trails. If you can, visit midweek, when the town's abundant attractions are most easily appreciated. On weekends, the swarms of visitors who come to gawk at Tiradentes's antique stores and boutiques can make the place feel a bit like a theme park, and the sudden increase in horse-drawn carriages creates some strong aromas!

Tiradentes' center is a compact and photogenic cluster of cobbled streets. The town's colonial buildings run up a hillside from the main square, **Largo das Forras**, culminating in the beautiful Igreja Matriz de Santo Antônio. From the terrace in front of the church there's a stunning view of the terracotta-tiled colonial houses, the green valley and the towering wall of stone formed by the Serra de São José. For another picture-postcard view of town, climb the hill just above the bus station to the grassy square in front of **Igreja de São Francisco de Paula**.

History

Originally called Arraial da Ponta do Morro (Hamlet on a Hilltop), Tiradentes was renamed to honor the martyred hero of the Inconfidência, who was born at a nearby farm. In recent years, the town, which sits at the center of a triangle formed by Brazil's three largest cities, has become a magnet for artists and other urban escapees. Today the historic center is home to only a couple dozen

original Tiradentes families, intermingled with new arrivals from around the world.

⊙ Sights

At the time of research, Tiradentes' old town jail was being renovated to house the new **Museu de Sant'Ana** (cnr Direita & Rua da Cadeia), a museum featuring 270 images of St Ann in wood, stone and terracotta from the 17th century to the present. Conceived by the creator of Ouro Preto's Museu do Oratório, it's expected to open in 2014.

Igreja Matriz de Santo Antônio CHURCH
(Padre Toledo s/n; admission R$5; ⊘9am-5pm) Named for Tiradentes' patron saint, this gorgeous church is one of the last designed by Aleijadinho. The all-gold interior is rich in Old Testament symbolism. Noteworthy elements include the polychrome organ, built in Portugal and brought here by donkey in 1798, and the seven golden phoenixes suspending candleholders from long braided chains.The famous sundial out front dates back to 1785.

Igreja NS Rosário dos Pretos CHURCH
(Praça Padre Lourival; admission R$3; ⊘10:45am-5pm Tue-Sun) This beautiful stone church, with its many images of black saints, was built in 1708, by and for slaves. Since they had no free time during daylight hours, construction took place at night – note the nocturnal iconography in the ceiling paintings of an eight-pointed black star and a half-moon.

Chafariz de São José FOUNTAIN
(Rua do Chafariz) Constructed in 1749 by the town council, this beautiful fountain north of Córrego Santo Antônio has three sections: one for drinking, one for washing clothes and one for watering horses. The water

Tiradentes

⊕ N 0 _____ 200 m
    0 _____ 0.1 miles

Tiradentes

comes from a nearby spring, Mãe d'Agua, via an old stone pipeline.

Museu do Padre Toledo   MUSEUM
(Padre Toledo 190; admission R$10; ⊙10am-5pm Tue-Sun) Renovated and reopened in December 2012, this museum is dedicated to priest

and hero of the Inconfidência, Padre Toledo, who lived in this 18-room house where the Inconfidentes first met. It features regional antiques and documents from the 18th century, along with some fine ceiling paintings artistically reflected in floor-mounted mirrors.

🏃 Activities

At the foot of the Serra de São José there's a 1km-wide stretch of protected Atlantic rainforest, with several nice hiking trails. Most are not clearly marked, and locals advise against carrying valuables or trekking alone on the Caminho do Mangue. For up-to-date English-language information on trail safety, independent hiking opportunities and local guides, try John Parsons at the Hotel Solar da Ponte or Bia at Pousada da Bia. Several agencies around town also organize group hikes ranging in length from 2½ to 5½ hours.

Mãe d'Agua   TRAIL

Tiradentes' most popular and simple trail leads to Mãe d'Agua, the spring that feeds the Chafariz de São José fountain. From the top of the fountain square, cross through a gate (open 8am to 4pm) and follow the trail north for 10 minutes along the stone viaduct into the jungle. It's a magical spot, with sun-dappled glens and monkeys cavorting in the tall trees.

Calçada dos Escravos   TRAIL

(Trilha do Carteiro) This three-hour round-trip climbs through open fields to a windswept saddle with gorgeous views of the *serra*. It includes a section of the old stone-paved road built by slaves between Ouro Preto and Rio de Janeiro.

To reach the trailhead, climb from the bus station to Igreja de São Francisco de Paula, then follow the cobbled road north, continuing straight at the first intersection and bearing slightly left at the second, following the brown sign for Serra São José/Trilha do Carteiro. Shortly after passing Pousada Recanto dos Encantos on your right, take the right (uphill) fork and continue straight another few hundred meters; after passing house No 878 (left side), cross through a gate and look for a signpost indicating the Calçada dos Escravos. Fork left on the rickety bridge over the stream, then start climbing towards the saddle.

Caminho do Mangue   TRAIL

This two-hour walk, best undertaken with a guide, heads up the *serra* from the west side of town to Aguas Santas. There you'll find a mineral-water swimming pool and a simple Portuguese-owned restaurant.

🎊 Festivals & Events

Tiradentes is popular as a center for national events. Two of the biggest and longest established are the **Mostra de Cinema** (www.mostratiradentes.com.br), in the second half of January, and the **Festival de Cultura e Gastronomia** (gastronomiatiradentes.com. br), in the second half of August, respectively bringing international films and world-class chefs to Tiradentes. In late June, classic-motorcycle buffs pack the streets, celebrating **Bike Fest Tiradentes** (www.grupoberg.com.br) with beer, food, blues and rock and roll. Other recently launched events include the **Festival de Fotografia** (www.fotoempauta.com.br) in early March and a brand-new wine festival which saw its debut in June 2013.

🛏 Sleeping

Tiradentes caters to a well-heeled crowd and couples looking for romance. Budget-minded and/or solo travelers can save money by visiting midweek, when some pousadas grant discounts.

Pousada da Bia   POUSADA $

(☑ 3355-1173; www.pousadadabia.com.br; Ozanan 330; s/d midweek R$110/140, weekend R$110/160; 🛜🌀) Just outside Tiradentes' historical center, French- and English-speaking owner Bia runs this pleasant pousada with a sunny breakfast house, fragrant herb garden and relaxing pool area. Rooms to the right of the garden offer nicer views but less privacy than those on the left. There are also two spacious new deluxe rooms (R$180 to R$200 per couple, plus 30% per extra person).

Pousada Arco Iris   POUSADA $

(☑ 3355-1167; Ozanan 340; s/d R$70/120; 🌀) This simple pousada with a grandmotherly atmosphere offers the advantage of low price right on the edge of the historical center. Rooms out back are brighter and more spacious than those in the main house.

Pouso Alforria   POUSADA $$

(☑ 3355-1536; www.pousoalforria.com.br; Custódio Gomes 286; s/d R$225/285; @🛜🌀) This classy, secluded pousada, tucked up a flagstoned driveway five minutes' walk north of the center, features eight rooms in modern style, a reading room full of art books and some nice views of the Serra de São José. English and French are spoken.

Pousada do Ó
POUSADA $$

(☑3355-1699; www.pousadadoo.com.br; Chafariz 25; s/d R$160/180; ☎) This 18th-century house enjoys a privileged location two blocks below the church in the heart of colonial Tiradentes. The original pousada, featuring seven snug rooms around a small garden, is supplemented by four larger rooms in the building above. Rooms 8 and 11 are the best of the bunch.

Pousada Pé da Serra
POUSADA $$

(☑3355-1107; www.pedaserra.com.br; Nicholau Panzera 51; s/d weekday R$158/178, weekend R$178/198; ❄☎☀) This family-run place sits on a ridge just above the bus station. The nine small but spotless rooms have panoramic views – the location, garden and pool area make up for the otherwise simple decor.

Pousada Espaço Interior
POUSADA $$

(☑3355-1406; www.pousadaespacointerior.com.br; Santíssima Trindade 420; r R$180-280; ☎) If you like peaceful surroundings, don't require a pool, and don't mind a short trek out of town, this pousada 500m behind Tiradentes's Matriz church is a good bet. The rooms surround a vast garden, and most are palatial, with 3.5m-high ceilings, large windows and gorgeous mountain views. One suite features a fireplace.

★Hotel Solar da Ponte
POUSADA $$$

(☑3355-1255; www.solardaponte.com.br; Praça das Mercês; r midweek R$507-731, weekend R$676-975; ❄@☎☀) This magnificent re-creation of a colonial mansion is one of Brazil's finest hotels, with first-rate food and service across the board. The rooms have fresh flowers, beautiful antiques, and comfortable chairs and beds. There's a reading room, complete with fireplace, and complimentary afternoon tea is served in the garden.

Pousada Richard Rothe
POUSADA $$$

(☑3355-1333; www.pousadarichardrothe.com.br; Padre Toledo 124; r R$350-380; ❄@☎☀) On a picturesque street in the historic center, this stylish pousada has spacious suites, and an elegant reading room with fireplace, and a small protected forest out back where monkeys come to play at dawn.

✖ Eating

Divino Sabor
SELF-SERVE $

(Gabriel Passos 300; per kg R$32.90; ☺lunch Tue-Sun) Very popular with locals for its self-serve offerings, including grilled meats and the normal range of mineira specialties.

Estalagem do Sabor
MINEIRA $$

(☑3355-1144; Gabriel Passos 280; mains R$26-45; ☺noon-4pm & 7-9:30pm Mon-Fri, 11am-10pm Sat, to 4pm Sun) One of Tiradentes' finest restaurants, Estalagem specializes in meat and comida mineira supplemented by a good wine list.

Bar do Celso
MINEIRA $$

(Largo das Forras 80A; mains R$18-28; ☺11:30am-9pm Wed-Mon) On the main square, this locally run restaurant specializes in down-to-earth mineira fare at reasonable prices. Folks with less voracious appetites will appreciate the R$18 prato mini, a smaller plate designed for one person.

Empório Santo Antônio
BUFFET $$

(Belica 133A, Parque das Abelhas; all-you-can-eat R$30, mains R$20-44; ☺11:30am-4pm Wed-Fri, to 5pm Sat & Sun) Five minutes northeast of the main square, this is a great spot to eat well without the tourist hype. Best value is the delicious all-you-can-eat weekend buffet, with a wide selection of vegetables and salads, pastas, classic comida mineira and international offerings such as Portuguese-style codfish with potatoes and olives.

★Viradas do Largo
MINEIRA $$$

(☑3355-1111; www.viradasdolargo.com.br; Rua do Moinho 11; mains R$29-58; ☺noon-10pm Wed-Mon) Tucked down a peaceful lane far from the relative bustle of downtown Tiradentes, this is one of the region's standout restaurants for traditional mineira cuisine. Crowds pack into it on weekends, spilling over into the pleasant outdoor patio and garden area.

Tragaluz
REGIONAL $$$

(☑3355-1424; www.tragaluztiradentes.com; Direita 52; mains R$40-65; ☺7pm-late Wed-Mon) This restaurant prides itself on innovative home cooking served with artistic flair. Desserts here are especially divine; try the goiabada frita Tragaluz, guava paste mixed with cashews, fried and served on a bed of catupiry cheese with guava ice cream.

Pau de Angu
REGIONAL $$$

(Estrada para Bichinho Km 3; mains for 2/4 people from R$68.90/115.70; ☺11:30am-5pm Wed-Mon) In a peaceful country setting between Tiradentes and the artsy community of Bichinho, this is a great spot for homemade linguiça (garlicky pork sausage), hot sauces and all things mineira. Portions are huge and meant to be divided among two to five people.

🍷 Drinking & Nightlife

A trio of popular bars with outdoor seating and occasional live music vie nightly for visitors' attention on Largo das Forras.

Petruccio BAR
(Paolucci 20; ⊘6pm-late Wed-Sun) Grab a table under the spindly palms at this corner bar just east of the main square and sip a smooth Tabaroa *cachaça* (produced in nearby Bichinho), a double-strength caipivodka (the house specialty) or any of a dozen international beers.

Confidências Mineiras BAR
(🖉3355-2770; Gabriel Passos 26; ⊘6-11pm Wed-Fri, noon-11pm Sat, noon-6pm Sun) At this cozy, candlelit nightspot, compare notes on dozens of brands of artesanal *cachaça,* most of them locally distilled in Minas Gerais. Its **Ateliê de Cachaça** store just down the street at No 210A offers over 500 brands for sale.

ℹ️ Information

Bradesco (Passos 43) Multiple ATMs, near the main square.
Secretária Municipal de Turismo (🖉3355-1212; www.tiradentes.mg.gov.br; Resende Costa 71; ⊘9am-6pm Sun-Thu, to 8pm Fri & Sat) On the main square; provides maps, plus information on hotels and guided tours.

ℹ️ Getting There & Away

BUS

Tiradentes' **bus station** is just north of the main square, across the stream. Two companies, Presidente and Vale do Ouro, run regular buses (R$3, 30 minutes) between Tiradentes and São João del Rei. Thanks to this friendly rivalry, you'll never wait longer than 45 minutes for a bus during daylight hours. Between 7pm and 10pm, only Vale do Ouro operates, and departures are less frequent. If you miss the last bus, a taxi costs about R$50.

With advance planning, it's possible to catch a bus directly from Tiradentes to Rio. The morning **Paraibuna** (www.paraibunatransportes.com.br) bus originating in São João del Rei (8am Monday to Saturday, 10am Sunday) will pick up passengers in front of the Tiradentes train station (not the bus station), but you must buy your ticket in São João and indicate that you're boarding in Tiradentes. Coming from Rio, you can do the same thing in reverse – take Paraibuna's 7am bus Monday through Saturday (or the 2pm bus on Sunday) and indicate that you want to disembark in Tiradentes when buying your ticket; make sure to inform the driver as well.

TRAIN

For information on the tourist train that connects Tiradentes with São João del Rei, see the boxed text on p195. Tiradentes' train station is about 700m southeast of the main square.

Caxambu

🖉0XX35 / POP 22,000 / ELEV 895M

Long before Perrier hit Manhattan singles bars, Caxambu water was being celebrated on the international circuit, winning gold medals at the 1903 Victor Emmanuel III Exposition in Rome and the St Louis International Fair of 1904.

Caxambu remains the most venerable of several mineral spa towns in southern Minas – collectively known as the Circuito das Águas – although its turn-of-the-century glory has faded gradually toward dowdiness. Even so, it's a convenient transport hub for other southern Minas attractions, and worth a look for curiosity's sake if you're passing this way.

🏃 Activities

Parque das Águas PARK, SPRING
(admission R$5, plus individual attractions R$5-15; ⊘7am-6pm) A rheumatic's Disneyland, this vast park in the center of town has lovely gardens, tree-shaded canals, a geyser, a spring-fed outdoor swimming pool, a chairlift climbing 800m to the Christ statue atop Morro Cristo hill, and the ornate 1912-vintage **Balneário Hidroterápico**, where you can soak in a hot bath, take therapeutic showers or relax in a sauna.

🛏️ Sleeping & Eating

If you're in Caxambu outside peak holiday times you can get some good deals. The fancier hotels include meals, and many have spas and offer massages.

Locally produced honey, homemade fruit liqueurs and preserves are sold all over town.

Palace Hotel HOTEL $
(🖉3341-3341; www.palacehotel.com.br; Dr Viotti 567; s/d R$122/129, incl all meals R$170/189; 🛜🞔) This colonial establishment is one of the best deals in town. The pool out back has a waterslide, and the card-playing rooms downstairs exude 19th-century charm.

Apart-Hotel São José HOTEL $
(🖉3341-3133; www.aptsaojose.hpgvip.ig.com.br; Major Penha 264; s/d R$70/120; 🛜🞔) Quite a lot of amenities are offered at this budget location – including a pool and sauna.

DON'T MISS

SMOKING MARY

Sure, there are buses that will get you back and forth between São João del Rei and Tiradentes, but how can they compare with a trip on a 19th-century steam train in pristine condition? Jump aboard as this little engine hisses and belches its way through the winding valley of the Serra de São José to Tiradentes. The tracks pass through one of the oldest areas of gold mining in Minas and you'll see the remnants of 18th-century mine workings all around. Keep a sharp eye out for modern *garimpeiros* (gold panners) still hoping to strike it rich.

Built in the 1880s as the textile industry began to take hold in São João, the *Maria-Fumaça* ('Smoking Mary', as the steam train is locally known) was one of the first rail lines in Brazil. More history is available at the **Museu Ferroviário** (admission R$3, free with train ticket; ⊘9-11am & 1-5pm Wed-Sun) inside São João's **train station** (☑3371-8485; Av Hermílio Alves).

Now operated by the **Ferrovia Centro-Atlântica** (FCA; ☑0800-285-7000; www.trensturisticos.fcasa.com.br), trains run twice daily in each direction on Fridays, Saturdays, Sundays and holidays (R$40/50 one-way/round-trip, child six-12 half-price). When leaving São João the best views are on the left side. If you need more time in Tiradentes than the train schedule allows, you can always bus back (there are regular connections between the two cities).

A similar historic train travels between Mariana and Ouro Preto; for details, see p182.

Hotel Caxambu HOTEL **$$**
(☑3341-9300; www.hotelcaxambu.com.br; Major Penha 145; s/d incl breakfast from R$187/220, incl all meals R$272/320; ❄🐾🗗) The historic facade hides a slew of modern amenities. There's a pool and a good restaurant.

Coreto SELF-SERVE **$**
(Praça 16 de Setembro 59; per kilo R$23.90; ⊘11am-3pm) Organic salads and *mineira* cuisine cooked over the wood fire are the specialties at Caxambu's newest self-serve, which enjoys a nice location directly across from the bandstand in the town's central square.

Tarantella ITALIAN **$$**
(☑3341-2161; João Pinheiro 326; mains R$28-57; ⊘6-11pm) In addition to its classic Italian fare, this cozy restaurant with red-checked tablecloths specializes in smoked trout.

❶ Information

Bradesco (Dr Viotti 659)
Secretaria de Turismo (☑3341-5701; www.caxambu.mg.gov.br; Praça 16 de Setembro 24; ⊘8am-6pm Mon-Fri) In the town hall, adjacent to the Parque das Águas.

❶ Getting There & Away

The **bus station** is about 1km south of the center on Praça Cônego José de Castilho Moreira.

Expresso Gardénia (www.expressogardenia.com.br) offers service to Belo Horizonte (R$93,

six hours) at 8:10am daily and 10:40pm Sunday to Friday. **Cometa** (www.viacaocometa.com.br) goes to São Paulo (R$51, seven hours) four times daily. For Rio de Janeiro (R$47 to R$66, five hours) and Resende (R$22 to R$30, two hours), gateway to Parque Nacional de Itatiaia, **Cidade do Aço** (www.cidadedoaco.com.br) runs a daily *executivo* bus at 8am, plus a midnight service Sunday to Friday.

Aiuruoca & the Vale do Matutu

☑0XX35 / POP 6200 / ELEV 989M

About an hour east of Caxambu is the Vale do Matutu, a lush green valley flanked by waterfalls and mountains. Most prominent among the surrounding peaks is photogenic Pico do Papagaio (2293m), which forms the centerpiece of the **Parque Estadual da Serra do Papagaio**. There's some great hiking in the region. Access to the valley is via a very rough dirt road running 20km south from the small town of Aiuruoca. You could easily linger here for a few days, relaxing into the rhythms of nature, reading a good book, hiking and swimming.

◉ Sights & Activities

At the far end of the valley is the attractive century-old **Casarão do Matutu**, the headquarters of AMA-Matutu, a community organization dedicated to sustainable tourism. If somebody's home, it can give information about the valley and nearby hiking opportunities.

Guides are strongly recommended and can be arranged through the Casarão or through Mandala das Águas. Destinations include the nearby waterfall **Cachoeira do Fundo** (a moderate four-hour, 10km round trip, R$15-20 per person), or the valley's standout attraction, **Pico do Papagaio** (a challenging eight-hour, 13km round trip with 800m elevation gain, from R$60 per person).

Local outfitters offering hikes and horseback excursions include **Portal Matutu Ecoturismo** (www.facebook.com/portalmatutu) and **MMA Ecoturismo** (www.ajuru.com.br).

🛏 Sleeping & Eating

Throughout the valley, pousadas and hotels have sprouted like mushrooms in recent years; most serve meals.

Pousada Dois Irmãos　　　　POUSADA $
(☑3344-1373; Coronel Oswaldo 204, Aiuruoca; s/d R$50/100) This simple hotel is the best option if you arrive in Aiuruoca at night and just need a place to lay your head.

★**Mandala das Águas**　　　　POUSADA $$
(☑9948-5650; www.mandaladasaguas.com.br; Vale do Matutu, Km 15; s/d half-board weekday R$120/220, weekend R$140/240; 🛜) Near the valley's far end, the delightfully tranquil Mandala features spacious rooms, verandas with hammocks, panoramic views of Pico do Papagaio and trails to secluded swimming holes in the gorgeous river below. The American-Brazilian owners use produce from their garden in the hearty homemade meals.

Pousada Pé da Mata　　　　POUSADA $$
(☑3344-1421; www.pousadapedamata.com.br; Estrada Aiuruoca/Matutu, Km 12; r/chalet with full board R$170/200) Near a waterfall at the foot of Pico do Papagaio, this lovely pousada has sweeping views over the valley. Meals are cooked on a traditional *fogão à lenha* (wood stove).

★**Kiko & Kika**　　　　BRAZILIAN $$
(☑9927-4853; Estrada Aiuruoca/Alagoa, Km 1.8; mains R$30-50; ⊙noon-4pm & 7-9pm Thu & Fri, noon-9:30pm Sat, noon-4:30pm Sun) For fine dining in a rural setting, try this sweet little restaurant just 2km south of Aiuruoca. Run by a couple with roots in France and Switzerland, it specializes in trout – both fresh and smoked – along with earthy touches such as wooden utensils and fresh herbed lemonade.

ℹ Getting There & Away

Aiuruoca's bus stop is on the central Praça Côn José Castilho. Viação Sandra operates one daily bus (R$13.85, one hour) from Caxambu to Aiuruoca at 6:15pm, plus a 10am departure on weekdays only. Buses return to Caxambu at 5:20am and 11:10am on weekdays, 5:20am on Saturday.

To reach the more remote pousadas in the Vale do Matutu, you'll need your own car (beware the rough road) or a **taxi** (☑9944-1601, 3344-1601; www.ajuru.com.br/taxi; one-way from Aiuruoca R$120, from Caxambu R$190). Once settled in the valley, walking is the most pleasant way to get around.

Diamantina

📍0XX38 / POP 46,000 / ELEV 1113M

Isolated but fabulous, Diamantina is one of Brazil's best preserved and least visited colonial towns. Surrounded by desolate mountains, it was the most remote mining town in Minas and the starting point for the Estrada Real, the old road to the coast built with the sweat, blood and tears of thousands of African slaves. Diamantina's fine mansions and winding streets haven't changed much in the last 200 years. Designated a Unesco World Heritage site in 1999, this *cidade histórica* is also the birthplace of Juscelino Kubitschek, former Brazilian president and founder of Brasília.

As with most mineiro cities, Diamantina is built on precipitous slopes. The bus station sits high on a bluff, so the 500m descent into town can be tough on the knees, and the return climb is a true workout. The central square is Praça Conselheiro Mota, dominated by **Santo Antônio** cathedral – both colloquially known as Sé.

◎ Sights

Diamantina's churches (admission to each is R$2) are open variable hours throughout the year; check with the tourist office for the current schedule.

Casa de Juscelino Kubitschek　　　　MUSEUM
(☑3531-3607; São Francisco 241; admission R$3; ⊙8am-5pm Tue-Sat, to 1pm Sun) Casa de Juscelino Kubitschek, childhood home of the former president, is full of historical memorabilia that reflect his simple upbringing as the grandson of poor Czech immigrants. Kubitschek himself believed that his early life in Diamantina influenced him greatly.

Diamantina

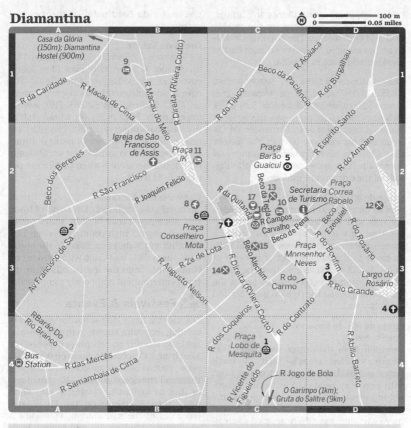

Diamantina

⊙ Sights
1	Casa da Chica da Silva	C4
2	Casa de Juscelino Kubitschek	A3
3	Igreja de NS do Carmo	D3
4	Igreja de NS do Rosário dos Pretos	D3
5	Mercado Municipal	C2
6	Museu do Diamante	B2
7	Santo Antônio Cathedral	C3

⊕ Activities, Courses & Tours
8	Biotrópicos	B2

⊜ Sleeping
9	Hotel Tijuco	B1
10	Pousada Capistrana	C2
11	Relíquias do Tempo	B2

⊗ Eating
12	Al Árabe	D2
13	Apocalipse Restaurante	C2
14	Casa Velha	C3
15	Deguste	C3

⊙ Drinking & Nightlife
16	Livraria Café Espaço B	C2
17	Recanto do Antônio	C2

Museu do Diamante   MUSEUM
(☑ 3531-1382; admission R$1; ⊙ 9am-5pm Tue-Sat, 9am-1pm Sun) Between Praça JK and the cathedral is the house of Padre Rolim, one of the Inconfidentes. It's now the Museu do Diamante, exhibiting religious art, old photos, furniture, weapons, and other relics of the diamond days.

Mercado Municipal   MARKET
(Municipal Market; Praça Barão Guaicuí) Built by the army in 1835, this public market is a popular community gathering place on

Friday evenings, when there's live music, and on Saturday mornings for the weekly food and craft market. The building's wooden arches inspired Niemeyer's design for the presidential palace in Brasília.

Casa da Chica da Silva   HISTORIC BUILDING
(☑ 3531-2491; Praça Lobo de Mesquita 266; ⊙ noon-5:30pm Tue-Sat, 8:30am-noon Sun) `FREE`
This fine colonial mansion was the home of diamond contractor João Fernandes de Oliveira and his longtime partner, the former slave Chica da Silva. Upstairs, paintings and poems (in Portuguese only) evoke the lifestyle of the extravagant mulatto.

Igreja de NS do Carmo   CHURCH
(Rua do Carmo) Adorned with rich, golden carvings and a gilded organ made in Diamantina, this is the town's most opulent church. Constructed between 1760 and 1765, its tower was reputedly built at the rear at Chica da Silva's request, so that she might sit in the front pews (Portuguese law at the time denied blacks the right to pass 'beyond the belltower').

Igreja de NS do Rosário dos Pretos   CHURCH
Downhill from the center you'll find Diamantina's oldest church, built by black slaves in 1731. Don't miss the tree out front with a cross embedded in its trunk; according to legend, it sprang up here as a divine sign to prove the innocence of an 18th-century slave who was falsely accused of stealing diamonds.

Casa da Glória   MUSEUM
(☑ 3531-1394; Rua da Glória 298; admission R$1; ⊙1-6pm Tue-Sun) Connected by a vivid-blue 2nd-story passageway, these two houses on opposite sides of the street were originally the residence of Diamantina's diamond supervisors and the palace of its first bishop. Currently housing Diamantina's Institute of Geology, the place has plenty of historical character, but exhibits are limited to a ragtag collection of old photos, mineral specimens and 19th-century German maps.

🏃 Activities

There are numerous interesting excursions near Diamantina, including the picturesque historical town of **Biribiri**, 14km north via a scenic dirt road through Biribiri State Park; along the way are some red-hued cliff paintings and a beautiful multilevel waterfall –

Cachoeira da Sentinela – with pools for swimming.

Gruta do Salitre   CAVE
(⊙9am-noon & 2-5pm Sat, 9am-noon Sun) This lovely spot is a quartzite cave 9km southeast near the village of Curralinho. The cave is administered by local environmental NGO **Biotrópicos** (☑3531-2197; www.biotropicos.org.br; Praça JK 25) ⌀, whose staff of professional conservationists can offer excellent advice on the area's natural attractions, recommend guides and occasionally offer tours themselves when they're not out doing field work.

Caminho dos Escravos   HIKING
Accessed via a trailhead 3km north of town, this stone-paved road built by slaves passes through rugged high country between Diamantina and Mendanha, 20km to the northeast. The walk is best done with a guide (get contact info from the tourist office), as the trail is intermittent and poorly signposted.

🎎 Festivals & Events

Diamantina has a long-standing tradition of evening serenades known as the **Vesperata**, held sporadically on Saturdays between late March and October. At 8pm on Vesperata night, dozens of local musicians parade into the small triangular *praça* at the north end of Rua da Quitanda, disappear into doorways, then re-emerge on the illuminated balconies of the surrounding mansions. A conductor standing in mid-square leads the performance. For the best seats in the house, pay for a table outside one of the bars bordering the square. Alternatively, watch for free from anywhere on the surrounding sidewalks. Hotels can fill up on Vesperata weekends, when many require a two-night minimum stay, so it's best to plan ahead. For a full list of this year's dates, contact the Diamantina tourist office.

🛏 Sleeping

For late arrivals who only need a convenient place to lay their head, there are several no-frills hotels directly across from the bus station.

Pousada Capistrana   POUSADA $
(☑3531-6560; www.pousadacapistrana.com.br; Campos Carvalho 35; s R$60, d R$120; P 🛜) Rooms here are a bit cramped, but the location smack in the middle of Diamantina's historic district is hard to beat. Parking is available.

Diamantina Hostel HOSTEL **$**
(☑3531-2003; www.diamantinahostel.com.br; Rua do Bicame 988; dm/d R$40/80) Diamantina's hostel sits on a residential hillside, 1km northwest of the bus station and within a 15-minute walk of the historic center. Dorms and doubles are very simple, but most come with ensuite bathrooms, and there are pretty views from the upstairs breakfast room and guest kitchen. Laundry facilities are also available.

Relíquias do Tempo POUSADA **$$**
(☑3531-1627; www.pousadareliquiasdotempo.com.br; Macau de Baixo 104; s R$140-180, d R$187-250, q R$295-399; 🛜) Take a trip back in time at this gorgeous historical house with fantastic views, antique furniture and local artwork. Afternoon tea in the rustic dining room is a real treat. There's also an old chapel and a small museum of historical artifacts downstairs.

Hotel Tijuco HOTEL **$$**
(☑3531-1022; www.hoteltijuco.com.br; Macau do Meio 211; s/d midweek from R$80/135, weekend R$130/170) The modernist Tijuco is a Niemeyer creation with spacious, airy rooms and efficient chain-hotel-style service. It's worth paying R$10 extra for a veranda with panoramic views. There are good photos of Juscelino Kubitschek along the staircase.

 Eating

Apocalipse Restaurante SELF-SERVE **$**
(☑3531-3242; Praça Barão do Guaicuí 78; per kg R$39.90; ⊙11am-3:30pm) Apocalipse serves an excellent international per-kilo lunch in an upstairs room affording views of the municipal market.

Al Árabe MIDDLE EASTERN **$$**
(☑3531-2281; Praça Dr Prado 124; sandwiches R$17, mains R$29-45; ⊙10:30am-11pm Mon-Sat; 🖋) From simple snacks (starting at R$4) to more elaborate dishes for two, Al Árabe's Lebanese-Brazilian chef offers an enticing line-up of Middle Eastern specialties, including many vegetarian options.

Casa Velha PIZZERIA **$$**
(Direita 106; pizzas R$26-47, mains for 2 R$49-51) Occupying the top floor of the home where Juscelino Kubitschek was born, this restaurant has wood floors, tall windows with cathedral views, and a menu that ranges from pizza to *comida mineira*. Don't miss the evocative collection of Kubitschek photos that adorn the walls.

Deguste CREPERIE **$$**
(Beco do Mota 31A; mains R$16.90-23.90; ⊙7pm-midnight Tue-Sun) With cheerful red and mustard-yellow decor, this rock'n'roll-themed eatery specializes in build-your-own crepes, salads and pasta dishes, accompanied by juices, milkshakes and ice-cream treats. It's hidden on a backstreet just above the cathedral.

O Garimpo MINEIRA **$$$**
(☑3531-1044; www.pousadadogarimpo.com.br; Av da Saudade 265; mains R$35-60; ⊙6-10pm Mon-Fri, noon-4pm Sat & Sun) Famous for its regional dishes, the restaurant at Pousada do Garimpo challenges the heftiest of appetites with its house specialty *bambá do garimpo*, a high-calorie concoction dating back to the diamond-mining days that includes pork chops, beans, rice, finely chopped kale and *angu* (corn porridge). There's also an occasional all-you-can-eat weekend buffet for R$35.

🍷 **Drinking & Nightlife**

On Friday evenings from 6pm onwards, visit Diamantina's Mercado Municipal for **Sexta Nossa**, a community happy hour where locals unwind with drinks and regional food, accompanied by live *chorinho* (informal instrumental music), samba and blues music.

Another classic weekend event is **Café no Beco**, held Sunday mornings from 8am to 1pm along the Beco da Tecla, a pedestrianized street between the cathedral and the market square. Locals sell baked goods, play live music and offer free coffee and tea to passers-by.

Livraria Café Espaço B CAFE
(☑3531-6005; Beco da Tecla 31; ⊙9am-midnight Mon-Sat, 11am-2pm Sun; 🛜) This bookstore-cafe is a relaxing spot to mingle with Diamantina's bohemian set. You can browse books (including a few in English), use the free wi-fi, and linger over coffee, tea, wine and light meals ranging from salads to pasta, trout and fondue.

Recanto do Antônio BAR
(☑3531-1147; Beco da Tecla 39; ⊙11am-3pm & 6pm-midnight Tue-Sun) With stone walls and wood beams, this cozy and convivial bar-restaurant features live music on weekends, and its *sanduiche de filé* (steak sandwich) is one of the tastiest bar snacks around.

ℹ Information

Banco do Brasil (Praça da Sé) Behind the cathedral.

Bradesco (Praça Barão do Guaicuí) Just below the Mercado Municipal.

Compuway (☑3531-9600; Beco Modesto de Almeida 80; per hr R$2.50; ⊙8am-9pm Mon-Sat) Internet and Skype access.

Secretaria de Turismo (☑3531-9532; turismo@diamantina.mg.gov.br; Praça Antônio Eulálio 53; ⊙9am-6pm Mon-Sat, to 2pm Sun) Distributes a Portuguese-language town map and guide.

ℹ Getting There & Away

From Diamantina's **bus station** at the top of town, Pássaro Verde (p182) runs seven daily buses to Belo Horizonte (R$75, five hours, from midnight to 6pm) and two to the neighboring historical town of Serro (R$22, 2½ hours). A taxi between the bus station and the center costs around R$12.

Diamantina's small airport, 7km west of town, had discontinued all commercial flights at the time of research.

Serro & Around

☑0XX38 / POP 21,000 / ELEV 781M

Founded in 1714, the charming colonial town of Serro snakes down a hillside in beautiful rural country south of Diamantina. While quite popular with Brazilians, this region remains little visited by foreigners and therefore retains a tranquí and traditional mineiro air. Its cheese is considered the best in Minas.

Heading north from Serro towards Diamantina, the tranquil high-altitude hamlets of **Milho Verde** and **São Gonçalo do Rio das Pedras** (less than 35km away) also make lovely stopovers, with access to some fabulous hiking opportunities, including some of the most scenic stretches of the original Estrada Real (the 18th-century 'Royal Road' that connected Diamantina to the Rio de Janeiro coast).

◎ Sights

Serro's main attractions are its historic buildings. In addition to the sights listed below, three other 18th-century churches keep regular hours and are worth a visit: the **Igreja de NS do Carmo** (⊙9am-5pm), the **Igreja do Bom Jesus do Matozinhos** (⊙1-5pm Mon-Sat) and the **Capela de NS do Rosario** (⊙1-5pm Mon-Sat). Admission to each costs R$2.

Capela de Santa Rita CHURCH
(⊙9am-1pm Mon-Sat) The most striking building in town is the graceful, single-steepled Capela de Santa Rita, straight uphill from the main square via a steep series of steps.

Chácara do Barão do Serro HISTORIC BUILDING
(⊙1-5pm Mon-Fri) **FREE** Just downhill from town, the Chácara do Barão do Serro is a lovely old mansion affording a glimpse of 19th-century baronial life in Serro.

✯ Festivals & Events

In early July, Serro hosts one of Minas' oldest festivals, the **Festa de NS do Rosário**, dating back to 1728. Townspeople representing Brazil's three traditional social groups parade through the streets in colorful attire: *caboclos* (the mixed descendants of indigenous peoples and Portuguese) beat out rhythms on bows and arrows, holding mock confrontations with sword- and guitar-wielding *marujos* (Europeans), while *catopês* (Africans) speak in ancient dialect and beat on instruments symbolizing empty plates.

🛏 Sleeping & Eating

Serro is full of low-cost eateries, most serving *comida mineira*, but its selection of hotels is limited. The towns of São Gonçalo and Milho Verde, with their rural tranquility, are nicer places to spend the night, and pousadas in both towns often include meals in their rates.

Pousada Riques Matriz POUSADA $
(☑3541-1770; Alferes Luiz Pinto 82; s/d R$30/60, s without bathroom R$25) Rooms in this historic house near Serro's Praça Matriz are quite basic, but the price is right.

★ **Refúgio dos Cinco Amigos** POUSADA $
(☑3541-6037; www.pousadarefugio5amigos.com.br; Largo Félix Antônio 160, São Gonçalo; r per person with breakfast R$50, with all meals R$70; 🖥) This charmingly rustic Swiss-run pousada next to the church green and bus stop has been welcoming guests to São Gonçalo for over three decades. Simple but delicious meals are cooked on the wood stove, and there's a spacious reading room with a fireplace for chilly nights.

Pousada do Capão POUSADA $$
(☑3541-6068; www.pousadacapao.com; Rua da Nascente 550, São Gonçalo; s/d with breakfast & dinner R$125/175, chalet R$175/220) Rooms and chalets encircle a spacious green area

A MYSTICAL RETREAT IN SOUTHERN MINAS

If you're into mysticism or superstition, or just looking for a cheap, fun and idyllic place to relax, consider a detour to the quaint village of **São Thomé das Letras** (population 7000, elevation 1291m, phone code ☑35). High on a plateau north of Caxambu, with a bird's-eye view of the surrounding farmland, São Thomé feels like a world apart. Perhaps this accounts for its reputation among Brazilian mystics as one of the seven sacred cities of the world, and the many sightings of flying saucers and extraterrestrials reported here.

The word 'Letras' in São Thomé's name refers to the puzzling inscriptions found in local caverns such as **Carimbado** and **Chico Taquara** (both 3km outside town) and the **Gruta de São Thomé**, a small cave in the heart of town. More down-to-earth attractions include the nearby waterfalls **Euboise** (3km), **Prefeitura** (7km) and **Véu de Noiva** (12km) and the town's buildings, made from beautiful slabs of quartzite. There are two nice churches: **Igreja Matriz de São Thomé** (1785), on leafy Praça da Matriz, and the raw-stone **Igreja de Pedra**, downhill towards the bus station. For great mountain views at sunset and sunrise, head up to the **lookout** 500m above town.

The town is filled with reasonably priced pousadas and restaurants. One block uphill from the Gruta de São Thomé, **Pousada Serra Branca** (☑3237-1200; www. pousadaserrabranca.com.br; João de Deus 7; s R$40, d R$70-90; ✷) offers bargain-priced *apartamentos*; just downhill, in an old stone building, **Pousada Arco Iris** (☑3237-1212; www.pousarcoiris.com.br; João Batista Neves 225; s/d from R$100/120; @ 🛜✷) is the prettiest of São Thomé's budget pousadas, with a sauna and pool. Centrally located eateries include the excellent per-kilo mineira cuisine at family-run **Restaurante da Sinhá** (☑3237-1348; Capitão Pedro José Martins 31; per kg R$24.90; ⊗11am-4pm Sun-Fri, to 10pm Sat), the wood-fired pizzas at **Ser Criativo** (☑3237-1266; Praça Getúlio Vargas 18; pizzas from R$25; ⊗6-10pm), and the more substantial mineira meals at **Restaurante das Magas** (☑3237-1344; Camilo Rios 2; mains for 2 R$35-48; ⊗11:30am-5pm & 7-10pm Thu-Tue), in a 180-year-old stone house.

São Thomé's **tourist information office** (☑3237-1276; turismo@saotomedasletras. mg.gov.br; José Cristiano Alves 4; ⊗9am-5pm) is just off the main square, Praça da Matriz. It provides a brochure in Portuguese with a rudimentary map of town and can point you to surrounding natural attractions.

During the third or fourth weekend in August the three-day **Festa de Agosto** draws lots of pilgrims with live music and other festivities.

From São Thomé's bus station, 1km north of the center, Coutinho runs once daily to/ from Caxambu along a rugged but scenic dirt road, in good weather only (R$19.10, 2¼ hours, leaving Caxambu at 2:15pm, returning from São Thomé at 9:15am). Alternatively, Trectur buses (R$10.65, one hour, six daily) connect São Thomé and the nearby town of Três Corações, where you can make onward connections to São Paulo (R$51, five hours) or Belo Horizonte (R$74, five hours).

at this lovely pousada hidden just outside São Gonçalo. Trained chef and American expatriate Peter and his Brazilian wife Marcia are consummate hosts, plying guests with superb homemade liqueurs, baked goods, international 'comfort food' and insiders' advice on local attractions, including hikes to the numerous nearby waterfalls.

ⓘ Information

Centro de Informações Turísticas (☑3541-2754; www.serro.tur.br; Praça João Pinheiro 154; ⊗8am-5pm) Hands out a useful map of Serro's old mansions and churches and also provides information about São Gonçalo and Milho Verde.

ⓘ Getting There & Away

Serro's bus station is one block downhill from the historical center. Destinations include Belo Horizonte (R$60 to R$81, six hours, four daily), Conceição do Mato Dentro (R$19, two hours, three to four daily) and Diamantina (R$22, 2½ hours, two to three daily).

Milho Verde and São Gonçalo do Rio das Pedras can be reached from either Serro or Diamantina. From Serro, TransFacil's two daily buses (R$5) pass first through Milho Verde (one hour) before continuing to São Gonçalo (1½ hours). From Diamantina, Diamantinense's lone daily bus (3pm Monday to Saturday, 6pm Sunday) goes first to São Gonçalo (R$10, two hours), then to Milho Verde (R$12, 2½ hours).

Parque Nacional da Serra do Cipó

📍 0XX31

Parque Nacional da Serra do Cipó (www.icmbio.gov.br) ✔**FREE**, 100km northeast of Belo Horizonte, is one of the most beautiful parks in Minas. Most of the park's vegetation is cerrado and grassy highlands, straddling the Serra do Espinhaço that divides the water basins of the São Francisco and Doce rivers. At lower elevations there are waterfalls and lush, ferny river valleys containing a number of unique orchids. Fauna here includes maned wolves, tamarin monkeys, banded anteaters, jaguars, bats and the small, brightly colored *sapo de pijama* (pyjama frog).

The park is vast, and the most popular trails involve multiday traverses of the *serra*. Information and trail maps are available at **park headquarters** (📞 3718-7151) a few kilometers southeast of the town of Cardeal Mota. Two especially worthwhile day hikes are the 16km round-trip from headquarters to a 70m waterfall called **Cachoeira da Farofa**, and the 24km round-trip to the 80m-deep gorge called **Cânion da Bandeirinha**.

Three recommended local tour operators offering hiking, rafting, horseback-riding and/or mountain-bike excursions to the park are **Bela Geraes Turismo** (📞 3718-7394; serradocipogeraes.com.br), **Cipoeiro Expedições** (📞 9611-8878; www.cipoeiro.com.br) and **Tropa Serrana** (📞 9983-2356; www.tropaserrana.blogspot.com)

🛏 Sleeping & Eating

Camping in the park is not permitted, but there are two campsites near the Véu de Noiva waterfall, on the main road 5km north of the park headquarters turnoff: **Grande Pedreira** (📞 3718-7007; www.pousadagrandepedreira.com.br; campsite per person R$25-30, d R$130-170) rents camping space on a grassy slope with nice (but distant) views of the waterfall, plus private rooms in their pousada up the hill; **Veu da Noiva** (📞 3718-7096; www.acmmg.com.br/veudanoiva.html; Hwy MG-010, km 99.5; campsite per person R$34; 📶💺) has a freshwater swimming pool, snack bar and direct access to the waterfall via a 200m footpath. Buses will drop you at the entrance to either place upon request.

Hotel Cipó Veraneio   HOTEL **$$$**
(📞 3718-7000; www.cipoveraneiohotel.com.br; Hwy MG-10, km 94; d incl meals from R$509; 💥📶💺) The most convenient place to stay if you're arriving by bus and want easy access to park headquarters, Cipó Veraneio is right on the road but has great facilities, including an acclaimed restaurant and a pool.

🛈 Getting There & Away

Serro and Saritur run buses to the park from Belo Horizonte (R$23, 2½ hours, several daily from 6am to 4pm). For park headquarters, get off at the Hotel Cipó Veraneio, then walk or hitch 3km east down the signposted dirt road on your right, just past the hotel but before the Rio Cipó bridge.

For camping, continue 5km further north through the town of Cardeal Mota.

Tabuleiro

📍 0XX31

North of Parque Nacional da Serra do Cipó, but still within Unesco's Serra do Espinhaço Biosphere Reserve, is the 273m **Cachoeira Tabuleiro**, Brazil's third-highest waterfall. Access is via the small town of Tabuleiro, approximately 180km north of Belo Horizonte.

Five kilometers east of the falls, the **Tabuleiro Eco Hostel** (📞 3654-3288; www.tabuleiroecohostel.com.br; Joaquim Costinha 1B, Vila do Tabuleiro; campsite R$30, dm R$50, d R$110-150; 📶) offers grassy terraces for camping, plus dorms and private rooms in a series of colorful buildings running down the hillside. Facilities include a DVD library, kitchen and laundry facilities and an onsite snack bar–restaurant. The hostel owners organize climbing excursions plus hikes and horseback rides to nearby cliff paintings, waterfalls, canyons and swimming holes. There are also some pousadas and simple restaurants in town.

To get to the falls, proceed west through downtown Tabuleiro approximately 3km to **Parque Estadual Serra do Intendente** (📞 3531-3919; admission R$5). From the entrance station, a well-marked 2km-long trail descends steeply to the river, then peters out, requiring you to boulder-hop the rest of the way upstream. The views of the waterfall are spectacular the whole way. During the dry season you can swim in the natural pool at the foot of the falls.

ℹ Getting There & Away

The first part is easy: take a Viação Serro bus from Belo Horizonte to Conceição do Mato Dentro (R$44, four hours, six daily from 6am to 4pm). The trick is getting from Conceição to Tabuleiro; local buses only leave at 3pm on Monday, Wednesday and Friday, and at 2pm on Saturday, returning from Tabuleiro at 8am the same days (R$5, one hour). A one-way taxi between Conceição and Tabuleiro costs R$70.

More convenient are the transfers offered (with advance notice) by the Tabuleiro hostel. From downtown Belo Horizonte or Confins airport, the trip to Tabuleiro costs R$300 for up to four people.

Parque Natural do Caraça

☑ 0XX31 / ELEV 1297M

Some 100km east of Belo Horizonte in the heart of the Serra do Espinhaço, the Parque Natural do Caraça is a blissful spot. Isolated from the rest of the world by a mountain ridge, the park encompasses 110 sq km of transition zone between the Mata Atlântica (Atlantic rainforest) and cerrado ecosystems. The park's centerpiece, nestled in a bowl-shaped valley, is a former monastery and boarding school attended by several Brazilian presidents. Now converted to a pousada, it's still owned and run by the Catholic congregation who use the neo-Gothic church for services.

The surrounding countryside includes several mountains – including **Pico do Sol** (at 2070m, the highest point in the Serra do Espinhaço) – as well as creeks forming waterfalls and natural swimming pools. The hillsides are lined with easily accessible hiking trails, all marked on a useful map provided at the park entrance. Most, including the four-hour round-trip to the gorgeous **Cascatona waterfall**, can be undertaken solo. Other, more treacherous trails require you to hike with a local guide (see www.santuariodocaraca.com.br/turismo/guias.php for a list of guides and their contact info).

🛏 Sleeping & Eating

★ **Pousada Santuário do Caraça** POUSADA $$
(☑ 3837-2698; www.santuariodocaraca.com.br; s/d/tr/q from R$157/218/323/399, s/d/tr with shared bathroom R$112/157/229; @ 🤖) 🖋
Rooms at this peaceful, one-of-a-kind pousada range from simple shared-bath *quartos* off the garden courtyard to larger *apartamentos*, the best of which are in the Ala do Santuário (Sanctuary Wing). All rates include three awesome mineira meals featuring local produce. The big highlight of staying here is the nightly feeding of the wolves. Advance reservations required.

Visit midweek if you can, as room rates are 10% cheaper, and it's easier to see the wolves and appreciate Caraça's isolation and tranquility without the crowds of weekend escapees from Belo. During less-crowded periods breakfast is served in the more intimate downstairs dining room, where you can fry your own eggs on the wood-fired stove.

ℹ Getting There & Away

The two towns nearest the park are Barão de Cocais and Santa Bárbara.

Pássaro Verde (www.passaroverde.com.br) operates frequent buses from Belo Horizonte to Barão de Cocais (R$27, two hours, every two hours from 6am to 8:30pm). From Ouro Preto, **Vale do Ouro** (☑ 3551-5679) runs two buses Monday through Saturday to Santa Bárbara (R$26, 2½ hours, 7:25am and 1:40pm).

Vale's daily Belo–Vitória train also makes a stop just outside Barão de Cocais, in Dois Irmãos (regular/*executivo* R$14/26, leaving Belo Horizonte at 7:30am and arriving at 9am).

From Santa Bárbara, Barão de Cocais or Dois Irmãos, the 30-minute taxi ride to Caraça costs around R$70. To reserve a taxi ahead of time, call **Célio do Táxi** (☑ 9689-3098). Note that the park gate is only open from 7am to 5pm (or to 9pm for pousada guests).

Parque Nacional de Caparaó

☑ 0XX32

This 250-sq-km national park contains southern Brazil's highest mountains, including **Pico da Cristal** (2798m), **Pico do Calçado** (2766m) and the third-highest peak in the country, **Pico da Bandeira** (2892m). Popular with climbers and hikers from all over Brazil, it affords panoramic views of the Caparaó Valley that divides Minas Gerais and Espírito Santo. The wide-open, rocky highlands that predominate here are complemented by a few lush remnants of Mata Atlântica (Atlantic rainforest) at lower elevations.

DON'T MISS

THE MANED WOLVES OF CARAÇA

The maned wolf – *lobo guará* in Portuguese – is South America's largest wild canine, living happily in the protected cerrado (savanna) environment of the Parque Natural do Caraça. A few years back, one of Caraça's priests had the idea of befriending the wolves, St Francis style. After two years of patient work gradually tempting them toward the church with offerings of food, he gained the wolves' trust.

Nowadays the feeding has become a nightly ritual, open to overnight guests at the Pousada Santuário do Caraça. After dinner in the monastery's old stone refectory, people drift out to the patio. The ceremonial tray of scraps for the wolf is placed on the flagstones just past sunset, while popcorn, herb tea, and *cachaça* are provided for the humans. Then the waiting begins.

Even on nights when the wolf never comes, the meditative pleasure of sitting under the stars, trading conversation and soaking up Caraça's tranquility is a magical memory that most visitors will carry with them for a long time. But wait patiently enough and you may be rewarded...with the patter of feet, the sudden hush rippling through the crowd, the scamper up the steps, the wild eyes of this beautiful creature come to steal a quick meal and then vanish again into the night.

The **park entrance** (www.icmbio.gov.br; admission R$11; ⊘7am-10pm) is 2km straight uphill from the nearest town, Alto do Caparaó. Between November and January there's lots of rain. The best time for clear weather is between June and August – although these are the coldest months. Bring warm clothes!

The classic hike to the summit of Pico da Bandeira can be made without climbing gear or a guide, as the trail is gradual and well marked. It costs between R$70 and R$80 for a taxi from town to the trailhead at Tronqueira campsite, 8km up a steep dirt road from the park entrance. Cars are prohibited beyond Tronqueira. From here, a gradual 9km climb leads to the summit. Most people go straight up and back to Alto do Caparaó the same day, but with your own tent, you can cross over to the Espírito Santo side of the park, camp overnight, and retrace your steps the following day. The drop-off from Pico da Bandeira on the Espírito Santo side is steeper than on the Minas side, making for some very dramatic views, and there are three waterfalls with idyllic swimming holes – **Farofa**, **Aurélio** and **Sete Pilões** – near the last campground, Macieira.

🛏 Sleeping & Eating

There are two official campsites on the Minas Gerais side of the park: Tronqueira and Terreirão, 4.5km beyond, which marks the halfway point of the 9km hiking trail from Tronqueira to the summit. On the Espírito Santo side of the park there are two additional campsites: at Casa Queimada,

4.5km down from the summit by trail; and Macieira, 4.5km further by dirt road. Bring all food and supplies with you, and reserve sites in advance by calling **IBAMA** (Instituto Brasileiro do Meio Ambiente e dos Recursos Naturais Renováveis; Brazilian Institute of the Environment and Renewable Natural Resources; ☑3747-2086; per site R$6). All sites have flush toilets and cold showers.

Pousada Querência Hostel   HOSTEL $
(☑3747-2566; www.picodabandeiratur.tur.br/querencia.htm; Av Pico da Bandeira 1061; r per person R$50, with shared bath R$40) 🍴 Despite its inconvenient location at the bottom of town, this friendly HI-affiliated hostel has good facilities, including a guest kitchen. It organizes rafting trips and sunrise hikes to Pico da Bandeira. The owners also run the affiliated **Rio Claro Hostel**, 14km away, which sleeps up to 10 people (per person R$30, bring your own food), with a waterfall supplying hydro power.

Pousada Vale Verde   POUSADA $
(☑3747-2529; Praça da Matriz 25; s/d R$30/60) This garishly green, family-run place offers simple rooms, near the bus stop on the main praça. Bargain-priced meals are available at the self-serve restaurant across the square.

Pousada do Bezerra   POUSADA $$
(☑3747-2628; www.pousadadobezerra.com.br; Av Pico da Bandeira; s/d incl breakfast R$119/168, incl half board R$146/208; ❄@🤙🏊) The lodging option closest to the park entrance has a sauna for soothing weary muscles and serves delicious trout at its attached restaurant. Half-board rates includes breakfast and lunch.

ℹ️ Getting There & Away

To reach Caparaó by bus from Belo Horizonte or Vitória (Espírito Santo), head first to the tiny town of Manhumirim, 25km outside the park. **Pássaro Verde** (www.passaroverde.com.br) operates three daily buses from Belo to Manhumirim (R$80 to R$88, six hours). From Vitória, **Águia Branca** (www.aguiabranca.com.br) runs a daily 6:30pm bus direct to Manhumirim (R$35, 4¼ hours).

Rio Doce runs nine daily buses from Manhumirim to Alto Caparaó (R$4.85, 45 minutes, from 6:30am to 8pm, returning 6:25am to 9:10pm). Alternatively, it's a half-hour taxi ride (R$50). Manhumirim's **Palace Hotel** (☑ 33 3341 2255; Av Lauro Silva 656; s/d R$55/90, with shared bathroom R$40/65; ❄ @ 🛜), diagonally across from the bus station, is perfectly adequate if you're stuck here overnight.

An alternate option from Vitória is Águia Branca's 7:20am bus to Manhuaçu (R$36, four hours), where eight daily Rio Doce buses connect to Alto Caparaó (R$9.70, 1½ hours).

ESPÍRITO SANTO

POP 3.5 MILLION

Vitória

☑ 0XX27 / POP 328,000

Espírito Santo's capital doesn't have much to show from its colonial past; indeed, the first thing visitors are likely to notice nowadays is Vitória's modern industrial port. Even so, the beaches east of the center are pleasant, the locals (known as capixabas) are warm and friendly, and the city has a flourishing economy, which means many bars, universities, nightclubs, restaurants and hotels.

The remnants of old Vitória, built on an island just off the coast, are connected to the mainland via a series of bridges. The city's best beaches are Canto and Camburí to the north, and the renowned Praia da Costa to the south, in the sister city of Vila Velha.

◎ Sights

◎ City Center

Anchieta Palace   PALACE
(☑ 3636-1032; www.palacioanchieta.es.gov.br; Praça João Clímaco; ⊙ 9am-5pm Tue-Fri, 10am-5pm Sat, 10am-4pm Sun) FREE Vitória's grandest historic building is this former Jesuit college and church, now the seat of state government. Guided 40-minute tours include the original 16th-century foundations, artifacts discovered during renovation, and the tomb of Padre José de Anchieta (1534–97), an early missionary hailed as the 'Apostle of Brazil'. Weekend tours (90 minutes) visit additonal rooms reserved for government functions on weekdays.

Parque Moscoso   PARK
(Av Cleto Nunes) Capixabas like to walk and relax in the leafy Parque Moscoso, just west of the city center.

◎ Vila Velha

Across the river and south of Vitória sits Vila Velha, the first place in Espírito Santo to be colonized.

Convento da Penha   CONVENT
(conventodapenha.org.br; ⊙ 5:45am-4:45pm) A must-see is this 16th-century convent atop the densely forested Morro da Penha. The panoramic city views are magnificent, and the chapel (founded in 1558) isn't too bad either. It's a major pilgrimage destination – around Easter expect massive crowds paying homage to NS da Penha, some climbing the hill on their knees.

Garoto   CHOCOLATE FACTORY
(www.garoto.com.br; Praça Meyerfreund 1, Vila Velha; ⊙ 9am-6pm Mon-Fri, 8:30am-2pm Sat) Brazil's best chocolate is made and sold right here, at Garoto's factory and store just off Rodovia Carlos Lindenberg – take bus 500 to Vila Velha, then transfer to bus 525 or 526. Hour-long **factory tours** (☑ 3320-1709; admission R$10) in English or Portuguese are available by advance reservation.

◎ Beaches

Praia da Costa   BEACH
This beach in Vila Velha is the city's nicest. It has fewer hotels and restaurants than Camburí, but you can swim and bodysurf. Keep a close eye on the horizon – huge supertankers often can pop up with surprising speed!

Praia do Camburí   BEACH
This 5km stretch of beach is punctuated by kiosks, restaurants, nightspots and midrange hotels. Don't swim near the bridge – it's polluted.

SAFE HAVEN FOR AN ENDANGERED PRIMATE

The *muriqui* (woolly spider monkey), largest primate of the New World, is a stunning creature. Adult males stand roughly 1.5m tall, and their movements and physical presence can be startlingly humanlike. The animal's photogenic qualities have made it a poster child for wildlife preservation in Brazil, but actually seeing one in the wild can be challenging. At the time of writing, there were only about 3000 left in the world – including only 900 of the rarer northern *muriqui* – down from an estimated 400,000 at the time of Portuguese colonization.

Three factors explain the *muriquis'* drastic drop in numbers: destruction of their native Mata Atlântica (Atlantic rainforest) habitat, their own docile nature (their Tupi name means 'easygoing folks') and the slow pace of their reproductive cycle. Female *muriquis* generally give birth to a single baby after a gestation period of eight months, and newborns stay with their mothers for up to three years, during which time no new mating occurs. *Muriquis* are slow-moving and less combative than most other primates – indeed, they spend most of their time eating, playing and hugging each other! So they've historically been easy targets for hunters.

Estação Biológica de Caratinga (www.preservemuriqui.org.br/estacao.htm) 🖉, a remote and little-visited nature reserve in eastern Minas, is the easiest place to spot *muriquis* in the wild. The reserve has played a critical role in rescuing the northern *muriqui* from extinction. In 1944 there were only eight *muriquis* on record here, when local coffee farmer Feliciano Abdalla committed himself to preserving a large chunk of the native Atlantic rainforest on his property. Forty years later, the Estação Biológica was established, and in the three decades since, research and preservation efforts have led to greater understanding of the *muriqui* and an impressive resurgence of its numbers. Today there are approximately 330 northern *muriquis* living within the reserve, representing roughly a third of the world's population.

🛏 Sleeping & Eating

Staying out at the beach is a much more attractive option than downtown, which is deserted after nightfall. Vitória receives a lot of midweek business travelers; on nonholiday weekends many hotels drop their rates. Decent budget options are scarce.

Make sure you try the regional specialty known as *moqueca capixaba*, a savory stew made from fish, shellfish, tomatoes, peppers and cilantro cooked in a *panela de barro* (earthenware casserole dish).

Cannes Palace Hotel HOTEL $
(☑3232-7200; www.hotelcannes.com.br; Av Jerônimo Monteiro 111; s/d R$99/119; 🕸@🛜) Not quite as decrepit as it looks from the outside, this aging high-rise is downtown's best budget option. Close to both the bus station and the Anchieta Palace, its rooms come with air-con and patterned wood floors.

Ibis Vitória HOTEL $$
(☑2104-4850; www.ibis.com.br; João da Cruz 385, Praia do Canto; r weekend/midweek R$139/159; 🕸@🛜) Well priced given its prime location, this chain hotel sits right at the edge of the Triângulo das Bermudas, Vitória's nightlife hub, and is only a few blocks from Praia do Canto. Breakfast costs extra. There's another Ibis 1.5km north on the Camburí beachfront.

Senac Ilha do Boi HOTEL $$$
(☑3345-0111; www.hotelilhadoboi.com.br; Bráulio Macedo 417; s/d from R$387/440; 🕸@🛜🗷) For a real night of luxury, this is an excellent choice. It's located on top of a hill with fabulous views of the surrounding bay. The service is impeccable and the amenities delightful, including a tennis court, solarium, piano bar, pools and saunas.

Pirão SEAFOOD $$$
(☑3227-1165; www.piraovitoria.com.br; Joaquim Lírio 753, Praia do Canto; mains for 2 R$85-170; ⊙11:30am-4pm & 6:30-11pm Mon-Fri, 11:30am-5pm Sat & Sun) With award-winning *moquecas* and *torta capixaba* (seafood frittata with olives and hearts of palm), Pirão has earned a reputation as one of the city's best restaurants over the past three decades.

Lareira Portuguesa PORTUGUESE $$$
(☑3345-0329; www.lareiraportuguesa.com.br; Av Saturnino de Brito 260, Praia do Canto; mains for 2 R$150-180; ⊙11:30am-3pm & 7pm-midnight Mon-Sat, 11:30am-4:30pm Sun) A gorgeous garden

Seeing the primates in their natural habitat is an amazing experience, and visitors have a better-than-average chance of a sighting, thanks to the expert skills of local guides. To arrange a day visit (R$120, including guide and rustic lunch), write or call the **park office** (33-3322-2540; preservemuriqui@gmail.com; Fazenda Montes Claros, Ipanema). Bring sturdy shoes for quick scrambles up the hillside, and don't wear red – *muriquis* take this as a sign of aggression. May is an especially good month to visit, as the *muriqui's* favorite food source, *Mabea fistulifera*, is in flower and the animals may linger in a single spot for long periods feeding on the nectar.

Ipanema and Caratinga are the transport hubs nearest the park. **Pássaro Verde** (www.passaroverde.com.br) runs two daily buses from Belo Horizonte to Ipanema (R$100, eight hours), and one early-morning bus from Ouro Preto to Caratinga (R$68, 5½ hours). **São Geraldo** (www.saogeraldo.com.br) also runs a direct service from Vitória (Espírito Santo) to Caratinga (R$48, 6½ hours, daily at 10:25pm).

From either Caratinga or Ipanema, take a Rio Doce bus (R$15, two hours from Caratinga; R$7, one hour from Ipanema) and ask to be let off at the Estação Biológica. From the bus stop, it's a 2km walk up a dirt road to park headquarters. With prior notice, **Antônio Bragança** (8882-6886; antonio_braganca@hotmail.com), the research station's field director, can sometimes provide a ride from Ipanema to the park.

Ipanema is your best bet for an overnight stay. The centrally located hotel **Italia Palace** (3314-1793; www.italiapalacehotel.com; Av 7 de Setembro 383; s/d with fan R$52/96, with air-con & minibar R$97/140;) offers excellent value.

Whether or not you visit the preserve, you can find out more about *muriqui* preservation efforts through **Preserve Muriqui** (www.preservemuriqui.org.br/ing/abraco.htm) .

and beautiful Portuguese tiles make this a sexy and sophisticated location. Delicious fish dishes form the backbone of the menu, but you'll also find Old World classics like roasted goat, plus plenty of Portuguese desserts.

Drinking & Entertainment

Capixabas like the nightlife – check out the Triângulo das Bermudas, a neighborhood packed with bars, eateries and nightclubs centered on the intersection of Joaquim Lírio and João da Cruz. Crowds also gather at Curva da Jurema, populated by shacks that serve snacks and food into the wee hours.

Theatro Carlos Gomes THEATER (www.secult.es.gov.br; Praça Costa Pereira) Drawing architectural inspiration from La Scala in Milan, this classy theater stages national-caliber productions at reasonable prices. See the website to see what's playing (click 'Espaços culturais' on the left-hand side).

Information

ATMs for several banks are clustered together inside the bus station.

PIT (www.vitoria.es.gov.br/turismo.php) Vitória's city government operates three tourist

information booths: in the arrivals hall at the airport (3235-6350; 7am-8:30pm), opposite track 6 at the bus station (3203-3666; 6am-8:30pm Mon-Fri, to noon Sat), and on the beachfront at Curva da Jurema (3382-3053; 7am-4pm Mon-Fri).

Getting There & Away

AIR
Eurico Salles airport (VIX; 3235-6300) is 10km northeast of the city center, in Goiabeiras. Flights leave regularly for Belo Horizonte, Rio, São Paulo and other Brazilian cities.

BUS
Vitória's teeming, modern bus station is just west of the old town center. See the table (p208) for a list of destinations served.

TRAIN
Companhia Vale do Rio Doce (p172) runs a daily train to Belo Horizonte (*econômica/executiva* R$56/87, 13 hours) from Estação Ferroviária Pedro Nolasco, 5km west of downtown Vitória in Cariacica.

Getting Around

Between the airport and the city center, take the local bus marked '*aeroporto/rodoviária*' (R$2.45).

Taxis from the airport cost around R$20 to Praia do Canto or R$30 to the city center.

Local buses (R$2.45) run from the various stops outside the bus station; the route is written on the side of each bus. For the center, catch any bus that goes along Av Vitória and get off after you pass the yellow Anchieta Palace on your left. For Praia do Camburí, catch any bus that goes along Av Dante Michelini. For Praia do Canto and Triângulo das Bermudas, take any bus that goes along Av Saturnino de Brito. To Vila Velha and Praia da Costa catch any bus marked Praia da Costa.

Itaúnas

📍 0XX27 / POP 2500

Surrounded by a majestic state reserve and encroaching sand dunes, 270km north of Vitória near the Bahia border, Itaúnas masquerades as a sleepy fishing village most of the year. However, around New Year's Eve and Carnaval (February/March), and again in July, it's a party-mad town filled with young Brazilians who come for the lively *forró* dance parties as much as for the beautiful surroundings.

Itaúnas is one of those rare places that manages to retain a low-key 'end of the road' feel despite the intermittent barrage of tourists. Many visitors fall under the town's easygoing spell and end up staying longer than they expected.

Fifty years ago, sand dunes engulfed the original village of Itaúnas, which was set about 1km closer to the ocean than it is now – these days the old church tower and other ruins lie completely buried in sand, marked only by a small sign.

◉ Sights & Activities

Parque Estadual de Itaúnas   PARK
The 36.7-sq-km Parque Estadual de Itaúnas extends for 25km along the coast and has impressive 20m- to 30m-high sand dunes that afford magnificent views of the Atlantic Ocean and the surrounding mangrove forest and wetlands. The wilderness here is home to monkeys, sloths, *jaguatiricas* (wildcats) and sea turtles, who come onshore from September to March to lay eggs.

The Itaúnas **park office** (📞 3762-5196; pei@iema.es.gov.br; ⊙ 8am-5pm) 🏍 is in the village next to the bridge over the Rio Itaúnas. It has a souvenir shop, as well as informative displays about the local flora, fauna and culture.

New in 2013, the **Trilha do Tamandaré** is an easy 700m nature trail that starts just across the bridge from the park office, weaving along the river and through the dunes to the beach. Birds and butterflies abound along this route. The other popular hike close to town is the 1km dunes trail, which crosses the dunes to a series of beachside *barracas* (stalls selling beer and seafood). From town, simply cross the bridge over the Rio Itaúnas, follow the dirt road until the dunes slope down to meet it, then start climbing. At the crest of the first dune, panoramic views of the ocean unfold.

More ambitious hikers can follow the beach 8km north to **Riacho Doce**, a small river that forms the border between Espírito Santo and Bahia. You'll know you've arrived when you see the handpainted sign on the other side 'Sorria – voce está na Bahia!' (Smile – you're in Bahia!). Here you'll find **Pousada do Celsão** (📞 9951-9834; r with fan/air-con R$90/100; ❄), whose attached restaurant serves tasty home-cooked meals for R$25. (Just beware the intrepid pet parrot – he'll try to climb in the hammock with you!) For the return trip, retrace your steps down the beach (best done at low tide), or hitch a ride with one of the pickup trucks or school buses that occasionally drive the 16km road back to town.

Casinha de Aventuras   OUTDOORS
(📞 3762-5081;   www.casinhadeaventuras.com.br; Av Bento Daher; ⊙ 9am-6:30pm daily Jan & Jul,

BUSES FROM VITÓRIA

DESTINATION	COST (R$)	TIME (HR)	BUS COMPANY
Belo Horizonte	78-95	9	São Geraldo (www.saogeraldo.com.br), Itapemirim (www.itapemirim.com.br)
Ouro Preto	67	7-8	São Geraldo (www.saogeraldo.com.br), Itapemirim (www.itapemirim.com.br)
Porto Seguro	85-121	9-11	Águia Branca (www.aguiabranca.com.br)
Rio	75-129	8	Águia Branca (www.aguiabranca.com.br)
Salvador	159	20	Águia Branca (www.aguiabranca.com.br)

9am–noon Tue-Sat rest of year) Near the bus stop in the center of town, this well-established outfit arranges kayaking trips along the Rio Itaúnas, horseback and dune-buggy excursions, bike rentals and more.

✹ Festivals & Events

For 10 days in late July, Itaúnas hosts the **Festival Nacional de Forró** (FENFIT; www. facebook.com/fenfit.itaunas). Big-name performers pour in from all over Brazil, and there's music and dancing all day and night. **Reveillon** (New Year's Eve) is an even bigger scene, drawing up to 10,000 visitors annually. Carnaval here also draws a festive, youthful crowd.

🛏 Sleeping

Casa da Praia POUSADA **$**
(☑ 3762-5106; Lage s/n; r R$110-150; ✱) This is one of Itaúnas' loveliest pousadas, on a backstreet with a deck overlooking the river. The owners take great pride in keeping the grounds and rooms spotless.

Pousada Ponta de Areia POUSADA **$**
(☑ 3762-5295, 9713-3170; itaunasbixao@gmail. com; Manoel Joaquim Junior; s/d R$50/80) This delightfully simple and welcoming pousada is hidden on a backstreet and not prominently signposted. To find it, ask locals for Bixão, the gracious and well-traveled owner, who is also an excellent resource for cyclists headed up or down the coast.

Pousada & Camping
A Nave POUSADA, CAMPGROUND **$**
(☑ 3762-5102; www.anave.tur.br; Ítalo Vasconcelos; campsites per person R$30, s/d from R$60/90; @) Rustic rooms with carved wooden doors abound at this attractive pousada, which is a labor of love for its sculptor/owner, Júlio. The attached camping ground, overlooking a mangrove forest and sand dunes, is also attractive.

Pousada Zimbaue POUSADA **$**
(☑ 3762-5023; www.guiaitaunas.com.br/zimbaue. html; Cabral da Silva 6; s/d/tr from R$80/100/150; ✱ @) This cheerful pousada just off the main square has clean white sheets, free bicycles for guests' use and a spacious common area with DVD player and internet access.

Pousada dos Corais POUSADA **$$**
(☑ 3762-5200; www.pousadadoscorais.com.br; Barcelos 154; d R$150-200; ✱ @ 🛜 ✈) If you're suffering from the heat, try this friendly pousada with its air-con rooms, comfortable sitting areas and pool.

✖ Eating

There are plenty of inexpensive eateries around Itaúnas. Especially appealing are the three *barracas* out at the beach – Sal da Terra, Tartaruga and Itamar – serving seafood and beer with ocean views. Note that hours are seasonal and prone to change.

Jack Dunas BURGERS **$**
(Av Bento Daher; snacks from R$8; ⊘ 11am-midnight) Previously known as McDunas (before the corporate lawyers from McDonald's came knocking), this is a convenient spot for burgers, juices and other quick snacks.

Dona Tereza SEAFOOD **$$**
(☑ 3762-5031; Leite da Silva; mains R$17-58; ⊘ 11am-midnight, to 8pm low season) This highly recommended restaurant with a breezy front terrace is a family affair; don't be surprised if the eight-year-old grandson takes your order! The *prato feito* (plate of the day, listed simply as 'pf' on the menu) is a great deal, including fish, rice and beans for only R$17. From the central square, go one block towards the river.

Dona Pedrolina SEAFOOD **$$**
(☑ 3762-5296; Linoria Lisboa Vasconcelos; mains R$17-58; ⊘ 11:30am-late, to 8pm low season) At this excellent family-run place, simple meals of fish, rice, beans and salad are very affordable, or you can splurge on *moqueca de camarão* (shrimp stew) – which feeds three people for R$115.

Restaurante Sapucaia INTERNATIONAL **$$**
(☑ 8143-9345; Barcelos; mains R$27-48; ⊘ 7-11pm Dec-Carnaval, Easter week & July) Open only in high season, this well-regarded restaurant has built its reputation on inventive seafood and pasta dishes such as *ravioli de camarão e banana* (ravioli stuffed with shrimp, ricotta and bananas); don't miss the house specialty – home-smoked fish carpaccio.

🍺 Drinking & Entertainment

During high season the pounding beats of *forró*, reggae and *axé* (an Afro-Brazilian pop style incorporating samba, rock, soul and other influences) spill from every open window and doorway in Itaúnas. Things don't really start swinging till after midnight, and the party lasts till dawn.

MINAS GERAIS & ESPÍRITO SANTO ITAÚNAS

GREEN DETOURS IN ESPÍRITO SANTO

Espírito Santo offers a handful of off-the-beaten-track attractions for nature lovers. All are easily accessible by car as day trips from Vitória, or can be combined into a longer itinerary progressing north towards Bahia.

Closest to Vitória, 82km northwest in the pretty mountain town of Santa Teresa, is the **Museu de Biologia Professor Mello Leitão** (☑ 0xx27-3259-1182; www.museude biologiamelloleitao.gov.br; José Ruschi 4, Santa Teresa ; admission R$2; ⊗ 8am-5pm Tue-Sun) 🍃. The museum celebrates the work of local ecologist Augusto Ruschi (1915–86), who conducted pioneering studies on the region's remarkable variety of hummingbirds and orchids and was a strong early proponent of environmental protection in Brazil. The verdant grounds are a peaceful oasis, and offer a chance to observe many local plant and hummingbird species.

Less than 100km further north, reached by a 23km dirt road from the city of Linhares, is the **Reserva Biológica de Comboios** (☑ 0xx27-3274-1209; www.tamar.org.br/cen tros_visitantes.php?cod=6; ⊗ 8am-noon & 1-5pm) 🍃, the Espírito Santo headquarters for the turtle conservation organization Tamar. Here you can observe giant sea turtles in the reserve's aquarium, or continue north 7km to visit the beach community of Regência, where residents earn their living from a combination of fishing and turtle conservation work.

Continuing 30km north from Linhares towards the Bahia border, the **Reserva Natural Vale** (☑ 0xx27-3371-9703; www.vale.com/EN/aboutvale/initiatives/natural-reserve; Hwy BR-101, km 121; ⊗ 8:30am-4:30pm) 🍃 is a privately protected 218-sq-km expanse of Atlantic rainforest whose tremendous biological diversity has earned it a place on Unesco's World Heritage list. Visitors can stay overnight at the reserve's simple but comfortable **lodge** (☑ 0xx27-3371-9797; s/d with full board from R$228/296; ❄ 🖳) and explore the surrounding network of trails.

Bar Forró LIVE MUSIC
(www.forrodeitaunas.com/bar-forro) The center of the action during New Year's, Carnaval and the Festival do Forró in July

Bar da Ponte BAR
Right next to the bridge, this place hosts live reggae and some samba during New Year, Carnaval and in July.

Bar da Ana BAR
(☑ 3762-5261; Rua Prof Deolinda Lage; ⊗ 6pm-late) This is a year-round backstreet hangout where locals go for drinks, occasional live music and unconventional snacks like shrimp-and-pumpkin cannelloni.

Buraco do Tatu LIVE MUSIC
(www.forroburacodotatu.com.br) Offers a mix of *forró* and reggae throughout the year.

❶ Orientation

The main road into town loops around the village square and back out again. Buses stop just a few yards from the square, and most stores, restaurants and pousadas are concentrated nearby. The beach is 1km east, across the bridge over the Rio Itaúnas. The village's handful of dirt streets are not signposted, but a pair of handy maps, posted on the square and near the bridge to the dunes, can help you get oriented.

❶ Information

Although many businesses accept credit cards, there are no banks in Itaúnas; bring some cash.

❶ Getting There & Away

The closest place you can make long-distance bus connections is in Conceição da Barra, 23km south. **Águia Branca** (www.aguiabranca.com. br) runs three buses daily from Vitória to Conceição (*convencional/executivo* R$49/65, five hours).

From Conceição a local Mar Aberto bus goes to Itaúnas (R$6.05, 40 minutes) at 7am, 12:30pm and 3:30pm daily, returning to Conceição at 8am, 1:30pm and 4:30pm. There's an additional 10:30am bus to Itaúnas on Monday and Friday throughout the year (returning at 11:30am), plus multiple extra buses in summer. If you get stuck overnight in Conceição, there are several pousadas to choose from.

To head north into Bahia, first catch an Águia Branca bus from Conceição out to São Mateus on the main highway (R$8, one hour). From there, buses run to Porto Seguro (six hours), at 6:15pm daily (R$55) and 12:25am Monday through Saturday (R$78).

Guarapari

0XX27 / POP 105,000

About an hour south of Vitória, Guarapari is a favored resort destination for Brazilians and, as such, retains a relaxed, fun and family-friendly atmosphere. There are 23 beaches in the municipality, each with an attractive mountain backdrop.

The center sits on a little peninsula, 500m south and across the bridge from the bus station; the beach is 200m further east.

◎ Sights

The best beach is **Praia do Morro**, north of the city (be aware that its so-called 'healing' black monazitic sand is, in fact, said to be radioactive!). Back in the center, from north to south, you'll find **Praia dos Namorados** (small but surrounded by rocks creating beautiful pools), **Praias Castanheiras** and **Areia Preta** (more radioactive sand but crystal-clear waters), **Praia do Meio**, aka Sir ibeira (great rock pools with gorgeous snorkeling), **Praia Enseada Azul** (a long stretch with lots of natural beauty) and **Praia dos Padres** (accessible only by trail from Enseada Azul, with stunning green waters). At the far southern end of town is **Meaípe**, best known for its beachfront eateries.

⎚ Sleeping

Camping Club do Brasil CAMPGROUND $
(3262-1325; www.campingclube.com.br/es_01. htm; Praia de Setiba; campsites per person/tent R$34.50/8.70) This camping spot a few kilometers north of town is just a stone's throw from lovely Setiba beach.

Hotel Atlântico HOTEL $$
(3361-1551; www.hotelatlanticoguarapari.com.br; Av Edísio Cirne 332; d with street/ocean view from R$230/250, ocean-view ste R$350; ❄@☎⚛) Just across from Praia dos Namorados in the heart of Guarapari, this well-equipped hotel offers comfy rooms with panoramic terraces, plus perks including a sauna, poolside bar and free beach umbrellas.

Porto do Sol HOTEL $$$
(3161-7100; www.hotelportodosol.com.br; Av Beira Mar 1; s/d from R$294/364; ❄@☎⚛) Surrounded by water on three sides, this high-end hotel has an unbeatable location between downtown and Praia do Morro. All rooms have panoramic ocean views, with wi-fi, DVD and whirlpool tubs in the deluxe suites. Sea turtles sometimes come up onto the rocks directly below the rooms.

✗ Eating

Up and down all the beaches, but particularly on Praia do Morro, you'll find dozens of *barracas* selling inexpensive fresh seafood and regional dishes. The classic spot to enjoy *moqueca capixaba* (Espírito Santo's famous seafood stew) is Meaípe, 10km south of town.

Restaurante João de Barro SELF-SERVE, MINEIRA $
(3262-8825; Getúlio Vargas 226; per kg midweek R$33.90, weekend R$35.90; ◷11am-4pm) Atmospherically decked out with bright murals, shelves of *cachaça* bottles, and an old wood stove, this high-ceilinged downtown self-serve specializes in fine *comida mineira*.

★Cantinho do Curuca SEAFOOD $$$
(3272-2009; www.cantinhodocuruca.com.br; Av Santana 96, Meaípe; mains for 2 R$49-165; ◷11am-10pm Mon-Sat, to 9pm Sun) The *moqueca* at this beachfront eatery in Meaípe has been voted the best in Brazil multiple times. Everything from fish to squid and shrimp to bananas finds its way into the dozens of clay pots bubbling away in the cavernous kitchen. Early arrivals can grab one of the limited front tables facing the water.

Restaurante Gaeta SEAFOOD $$$
(3272-1202; Av Santana 47, Meaípe; moquecas for 2 R$70-255) Jostling for the title of the region's best seafood restaurant, this beachside eatery offers a dazzling array of savory stews. Sizzling clay *panelas* (casserole dishes) come laden with everything from *moqueca de camarão pequeno* (featuring tiny shrimp) to the trademark *moqueca de banana* (invented here) to the house specialty *moqueca das três ilhas* (lobster, prawns and sea bass).

ⓘ Information

The **tourist office** (3262-8759; seltur@ guarapari.es.gov.br; Paulo de Águiar 68; ◷8am-6pm), in the center just west of the bridge, has maps and information in Portuguese. There are several banks with ATMs along Joaquim da Silva Lima in the center. Internet places are clustered in the center and along Praia do Morro.

MINAS GERAIS & ESPÍRITO SANTO GUARAPARI

ⓘ Getting There & Away

Planeta (☎ 3223-5761) runs buses from Vitória to Guarapari's **bus station** (João Gomes de Jesus 50) roughly hourly from 7:30am to 9:30pm (R$11.70, 1¼ hours).

Beaches South of Guarapari

☑ 0XX28

Within a 45-minute drive of Guarapari, you'll find a trio of beach communities worthy of an afternoon's jaunt: **Ubu**, (20km south of Guarapari), a sleepy little seaside town with a picturesque waterfront; **Anchieta** (8km further south), one of Espírito Santo's oldest settlements. with a 16th-century sanctuary founded by famed Jesuit priest José de Anchieta; and **Iriri** (8km south of Anchieta), an agreeable coastal getaway very popular with mineiros, who come in droves during the summer months (especially Carnaval), turning it into an up-beat, family-focused resort.

Every June, devoted followers of Padre Anchieta participate in the **Passos de Anchieta** (Steps of Anchieta) pilgrimage, a four-day, 100km walk along the beach from Vitória to Anchieta.

⊙ Sights

Praia de Ubu   BEACH
This long, picturesque stretch of sand has a cliff at one end and a mermaid statue marking the beach's midpoint.

**Santuário Nacional Padre
Anchieta**   CHURCH
(admission R$2; ⊙9am-noon & 2-5pm Tue-Fri, 9am-noon Sat & Sun) Dominating Anchieta town from its impressive hillside location, this striking blue-and-white church dates back to the 16th century. A graceful 150-year-old chestnut tree shades the pretty plaza out front. The adjacent museum contains relics uncovered during restoration, and highlights the evangelical work of Jesuit priest José de Anchieta among the *índios* (indigenous peoples).

Praia de Iriri   BEACH
Lined with beachfront eateries and pousadas, Iriri's pretty crescent-shaped beach is tucked into a sheltered cove flanked by rocky ledges on either side.

🛏 Sleeping & Eating

★**Recanto da Pedra**   POUSADA $
(☎3534-1599; www.recantodapedra.com.br; Av Beira Mar 16; s/d R$90/150; ✴ ⑳) Hands down the best value along this stretch of coast, Recanto da Pedra is picturesquely sited on rocks at the northern end of Iriri beach. Many rooms have terraces with bird's-eye views of the gracefully curving shoreline. The attached restaurant serves excellent food, and swimmers occasionally pop up out of the water for a quick drink at the bar.

Hotel Pontal das Rochas   HOTEL $$
(☎3534-1369; www.pontaldasrochas.com.br; Av Beira Mar s/n; d with street/ocean view from R$230/280; ✴ @ ⑳ ✴) On the point at the far end of Iriri's beach, this first-rate hotel offers fabulous amenities, including a panoramic restaurant, and a sauna and pool built into the rocks overlooking the water.

Restaurante do Português   SEAFOOD $$
(☎3534-1222; Alpoim 558; mains for 2 R$40-85; ⊙11am-9pm) Generous portions of tasty local seafood are served at this unpretentious eatery half a block from the beach, including a R$14 *prato individual* for solo diners. There are also a few bare-bones rooms upstairs (per person R$50) for penny-pinchers.

Moqueca do Garcia   SEAFOOD $$$
(☎3536-5050; www.peixadadogarcia.com.br; Praia de Ubu; mains for 2 R$68-174; ⊙10:30am-5pm, to 6pm Sat & Sun) Down by the waterfront in Ubu, celebrating half a century in business, this acclaimed restaurant serves top-notch capixaba cuisine, with a strong focus on *moquecas*.

ⓘ Getting There & Away

From Guarapari, Planeta runs half-hourly buses to Ubu (R$3.60, 30 minutes), Anchieta (R$5.05, 40 minutes) and Iriri (R$6.20, one hour).

Domingos Martins

☑ 0XX27 / POP 32,000 / ELEV 542M

The landscapes get more dramatic, the Old World influences more pronounced and the temperatures cooler as you leave Espírito Santo's coast for the mountainous interior. High season here is May to August, when Brazilians flock inland for a rare taste of winter comforts – chilly nights, fondue and a blazing fire.

Tucked into the highlands of the Serra Capixaba, this pretty little German-style town – also referred to as Campinho by lo-

THE GOITACÁ WARRIORS

Early European explorers reported encounters with the fearsome, long-haired, tall, robust and formidable Goitacá warriors, coastal dwellers of the Rio state–Espírito Santo border region. The tribe had long resisted invasions by rival Tupi nations and, despite the technological advantage of guns, the Europeans found the Goitacá almost impossible to capture. The Goitacá were excellent runners and swimmers, and seemed by all reports to be equally at home on land and in the water. When chased, they were so fast through the waters and jungle that nobody could catch them on foot, on horseback or by boat.

According to legend, a Goitacá could run after a wild deer and capture it with his arms, and could catch a shark using only a piece of wood. (This was accomplished by forcing a stick inside the shark's mouth to stop the jaws from closing, and pulling its guts out by hand until it died.) The Goitacá nation (around 12,000 people), never defeated in battle, was exterminated at the end of the 18th century by an epidemic of smallpox – a disease deliberately introduced by the Portuguese for that very purpose.

cals – makes a good base for exploring the nearby forests, streams and mountains. The town's Germanic roots are evident in the bilingual signs scattered around town, the German-influenced cuisine found on many local menus, and the orderly layout of the main square, a pretty gathering spot with benches, trees, well-tended flowers and an old Lutheran church.

Sights

Casa da Cultura   MUSEUM
(3268-2550; www.domingosmartins.es.gov.br; Av Presidente Vargas 531; 8am-5pm Tue-Fri, 9am-noon & 1:30-4pm Sat & Sun) FREE Opposite the first bus stop in town, this place serves as an unofficial tourist office, offering a wealth of advice about Domingos Martins and the surrounding area. The museum upstairs features photos, documents and household objects dating from 1847, when Pomeranians first settled this colony.

Instituto Reserva Kautsky   GARDENS
(3268-2300; institutokautsky.blogspot.com.br; by arrangement) FREE Flora lovers should head out to this lovely mountainside reserve, established by dedicated botanist Roberto Kautsky, who cultivated more than 100 species of orchids at his home at the southern end of town. To arrange a visit, phone weekdays between 8am and 5pm, or contact Cristine Feitosa at assessoria.ik@gmail.com.

Festivals & Events

In the second half of July, the **Festival Internacional de Inverno** is an annual 10-day gathering of Brazilian and international musicians who offer daily classes and nightly concerts on Domingos Martins' main square.

Sleeping & Eating

Solar da Serra   POUSADA $$
(3268-1691; pousadasolardaserra@hotmail.com; Gerardt 91; s/d with fan from R$90/150, with air-con R$130/200;) Up a steep hill a couple of blocks from the main square, this modern German-style pousada has spacious, clean rooms, the best of which offer pleasant views of the surrounding hillsides. Back rooms are a steal midweek, when prices drop 30% to 50% below weekend rates quoted above.

Sabor Café Expresso   CAFE $
(3268-3263; Lazer 54; strudel R$5, fixed-price meals R$8.50-12; 8:30am-10pm Mon-Sat, from 9:30am Sun) Homemade cakes, apple (or banana!) strudel, and hot chocolate are the specialties at this lively sidewalk cafe in the heart of the pedestrian zone. Inexpensive *pratos feitos* offer fantastic value.

Choperia Fritz Frida   GERMAN $$
(3268-1808; Av Presidente Vargas 782; mains from R$28; 10am-11pm Wed-Mon) This half-timbered building with a big upstairs window overlooking the main square serves pizza, beer and old German favorites. Half portions cost 70% of full portion price.

Getting There & Away

Ten buses daily Monday to Saturday and eight on Sunday make the 42km trip (R$10, one hour) from Vitória to Domingos Martins' **bus station** (3268 1243; Rua Bernardino Monteiro). Upon request, any bus between Vitória and Belo Horizonte will also stop on the main highway just outside the town entrance gate, where you can call a **taxi** (9928-3893) for the 3km, R$15 ride to the town square.

MINAS GERAIS & ESPÍRITO SANTO DOMINGOS MARTINS

Parque Estadual da Pedra Azul

This gorgeous **state park** ([📞]3248-1156; pepaz@ iema.es.gov.br; ⊙8am-5pm) 🏃**FREE**, 50km west of Domingos Martins along Hwy BR-262, is one of Espírito Santo's not-to-be-missed attractions. Towering dramatically above the surrounding green hills is the park's centerpiece, **Pedra Azul** (500m), a massive rock outcropping tinted by a bluish moss that changes color with the sun's shifting rays, making for some fabulous photo ops.

Rangers lead **guided walks** ([📞]27-9739-8005; walks R$10; ⊙9am & 1:30pm Sat & Sun; by arrangement midweek) to the rock's nine **natural pools**, a moderately difficult climb affording magnificent views of Pedra Azul and the surrounding forest and farmland. Bring a swimsuit and sturdy shoes – there's a short section where ropes are used to scale a steep rock face. The round trip takes three hours; book ahead, especially midweek when there are no set departure times. Independent climbing and camping are not permitted in the park.

Fjordland Cavalgada Ecológica ([📞]3248-0054; cavalgadapedraazul.com.br; 20/100min trail rides R$25/60) leads horseback excursions around the foot of Pedra Azul, on beautiful Fjorde horses from Norway.

🛏 Sleeping & Eating

The area is dotted with fancy resort hotels, many offering the option of full board.

Tre Fiori   CHALET $$
([📞]3248-1124; pousadatrefiori@gmail.com; Rota do Lagarto, km3. Aracê; d chalet midweek/weekend R$150/180) Tucked into a green valley at the foot of Pedra Azul, 3km from the main highway along winding Rua do Lagarto, these four simple duplex chalets and four additional rooms with panoramic terraces offer great views. The owner, with family ties to Italy's Trento region, recently opened the attached **Don Lorenzoni Due** restaurant (mains R$39 to R$69).

Pousada Pedra Azul   POUSADA $$$
([📞]3334-2420; www.pousadapedraazul.com.br; Rota do Lagarto, km1.5; d R$320-400, ste R$470-610; 🛜🏊) Set in lovely gardens only 500m from park headquarters, this high-end pousada is one of the region's oldest. The main brick-and-wood building with Alpinestyle balconies and pagoda-like roofs was designed by Brazilian architect Zanine. Amenities include a pool, sauna, tennis courts, lake and waterfall. The spacious guest rooms, completely renovated in 2013, have high ceilings, big tubs and armchairs.

★Valsugana   ITALIAN $$
([📞]3248-1126; off Hwy BR-262, km89.5; mains R$29-52; ⊙lunch Sat & Sun, dinner Sat year-round, plus dinner Fri Apr-Sep) Hearty Italian fare and pretty perspectives on Pedra Azul make this one of the area's nicest restaurants. Classics such as *saltimbocca* (prosciutto-and-sage-stuffed veal escalope) or spinach ravioli with ricotta and walnuts are interspersed with more inventive recipes, all featuring fresh local produce. The wine list is also excellent.

❶ Getting There & Away

Águia Branca buses pass within 2km of the park entrance. In Vitória, buy a ticket for Fazenda do Estado (R$19, two hours, 10 daily from 5am to 6:30pm), and ask to be let off at km88. The km88 bus stop is directly opposite Peterle's pousada and restaurant. From here, it's a 2km uphill walk to the park entrance along a lovely winding cobblestone road, Rota do Lagarto.

São Paulo State

Includes ➡

Best Places to Eat

➡ Maní (p237)

➡ Patuá da Baiana (p237)

➡ Mocotó (p241)

➡ Cantinho da Lagoa (p253)

➡ Baronesa Landscape (p247)

Best Places to Stay

➡ Hotel Emiliano (p234)

➡ Pousada Picinguaba (p253)

➡ We Hostel Design (p232)

➡ Na Mata Suites (p257)

➡ Guest 607 (p234)

Why Go?

Speaking of São Paulo state without using superlatives is difficult. The southern hemisphere's largest city! Its finest museums! Its best restaurants! Its worst traffic! (Well, you can't have everything.) São Paulo city – Sampa to locals – serves as Brazil's Boom Town, commercially, financially, industrially and culturally, and an explosion of sophisticated travelers descending on the city's extraordinary restaurants, art galleries, bars and cultural centers has catapulted the sprawling city into the continent's nouveau 'It' destination.

Inland from the cityscape, the Serra da Mantiqueira's 2500m peaks play the novel Alpine-esque getaway role, while Iporanga sits tucked away in pristine Brazilian Atlantic Forest. And out to sea, some of southeastern Brazil's finest beaches cling both to the mountainous stretch of rainforest-backdropped coastline near Ubatuba; and to nearby Ilhabela, which relishes its position as São Paulo's sophisticated island escape.

When to Go
São Paulo

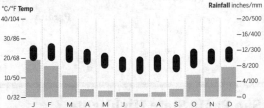

Dec–Feb Tropical downpours be damned, Sampa sizzles in summer nonetheless.

Mar & Sep Cooler temps, drier skies and São Paulo's best restaurants on sale for Restaurant Week.

Jun & Jul Jackets required in the mountains, but therein lies the novelty.

53°W · 51°W · 49°W

20°S

Mato Grosso do Sul

Mutum · BR 262 · Três Lagoas

Repressa Água Vermelha

Rio Grande

Reservatorio Marimbondo

BR 153

SP 310 · São José do Rio Preto

Represa Ilha Solteira

Represa Nova Avanhandava

Rio Tietê

Araçatuba

Reservatorio Promissão

SP 294 · SP 300

22°S · BR 267

Represa de Porto Primavaera

Presidente Prudente · SP 270

Tupã

Marília · SP 294 · Bauru · SP 300

Rio Paraná · Rio Paranapanema

Represa Capivara

BR 153 · Ourinhos · SP 280

Porto São José · BR 376

Avaré · SP 270

Paranavaí

Londrina · BR 369

Represa de Chavantes

Tropic of Capricorn

Maringá · Apucarana

Umuarama · Cianorte · Cruzeiro d'Oeste

24°S

Rio Ivaí · Itapeva

Campo Mourão

Parque Estadual do Alto do Ribeira

BR 369

Apiaí · 8

Rio Piquiri · BR 376 · BR 151

Paraná

BR 277 · Laranjeiras do Sul · Guarapuava · BR 373 · Ponta Grossa · Vila Velha · Serra do Mar · BR 116

53°W · 51°W · **CURÍTIBA** · 49°W

São Paulo State Highlights

❶ Driving one of the world's most stunning coastal routes along the Costa Verde from **São Sebastião** (p254) to Rio de Janeiro.

❷ Overwhelming yourself with cuisine, culture, cafe and craziness in **São Paulo** (p218) city.

❸ Gawking at the sheer endlessness of São Paulo city's eye-popping skyline from the top of the **Banespa** (p231) building.

❹ Seeking out wild, deserted beaches where mountains meet sea north of **Ubatuba** (p252).

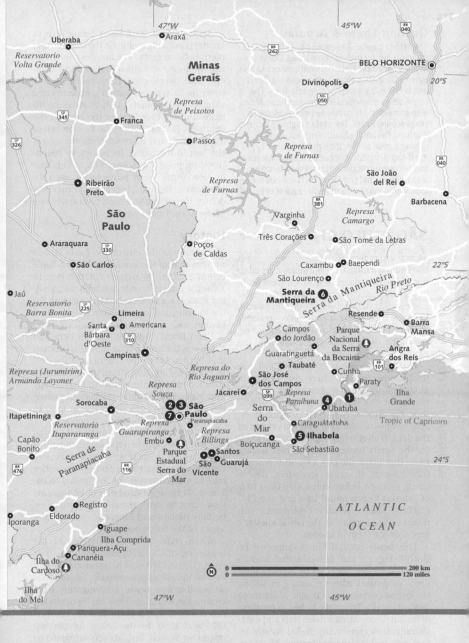

⑤ Escaping to **Ilhabela** (p255), São Paulo's idyllic island getaway for the rich and famous.

⑥ Hiking amid the green peaks of the **Serra da**

Mantiqueira (p247), São Paulo's Alpine wonderland.

⑦ Partying your *bunda* off in the legendary nightclubs of **São Paulo** (p241) city.

⑧ Going caving in pristine Brazilian Atlantic Forest in **Parque Estadual do Alto do Ribeira** (p256) near Iporanga.

Getting There & Around

The state's capital, São Paulo city, is Brazil's principal hub for international travel. Dozens of airlines have direct international services to São Paulo's Guarulhos airport, and there are direct bus services from neighboring countries. The city is also a major center for domestic air travel, with somewhat affordable airfares available to cities around Brazil. The state's highway system is among the best in South America, making driving a good option, though São Paulo city itself can be maddening because of poor signage and horrendous traffic. Alternatively, there are also frequent and good long-distance bus services, within the state and to other parts of Brazil.

SÃO PAULO CITY

☑ OXX11 / POP 11.3 MILLION (CITY), 19.9 MILLION (METRO) / ELEV 760M

São Paulo is a monster. Enormous, intimidating and, at first glance at least, no great beauty. It's a difficult city for the traveler to master and one that may not seem worth the sweat. Even the most partisan paulistano – resident of São Paulo city – will rail about the smog, the traffic, the crumbling sidewalks and the gaping divide between poor and rich.

But in the same breath they'll tell you they'd never live anywhere else. Let them guide you to their favorite haunts and the reason for this will begin to unfold. Maybe they will introduce you to the city's innumerable art-house cinemas and experimental theaters. If they're gourmands, you'll focus on the smart bistros and gourmet restaurants that make the city a world-renowned foodie haven. If they're scenesters, double up on espresso before embarking on a tour of raucous underground bars and the 24/7 clubbing scene. Whatever pleasures you might covet, Sampa – as the city is known – probably has them in spades.

This fertile cultural life is supported by Brazil's biggest and best-educated middle class and further enriched by literally hundreds of distinct ethnic groups – including the largest community of people of Japanese descent outside Japan, the largest population of Italian descendants outside Italy and a significant Arab community fueled mostly by Lebanese and Syrian immigration. There are one million people of German stock and, as well, sizable Chinese, Armenian, Lithuanian, Greek, Syrian, Korean, Polish and Hungarian communities. Sao Paulo also has the largest openly gay community in Latin America. Brazil's melting pot is quite hot indeed.

An estimated 20 million people live in greater São Paulo, making it the third-largest metropolis on earth. The numbers are dizzying: first-rate museums and cultural centers (150), world-class restaurants (12,500, covering 52 types of cuisine), experimental theaters and cinemas (420). Sampa's nightclubs and bars are among the best on the continent (15,000 bars make for one hell of a pub crawl) and its restaurants are among the best in the world. Its relentless, round-the-clock pulse – a close cousin of London's or New York's – can prove taxing even for the fiercest hipster. Then again, it may just deliver the charge you need to discover one of the world's great cities.

History

The history of the city of São Paulo largely mirrors that of the state. For the first three centuries after the arrival of Jesuits here in 1554, the city grew only gradually as a posting station for fortune hunters heading for the interior, and growers from nearby sugar plantations.

Upon Brazil's independence in 1822, São Paulo was declared a state capital, a decision that in turn led to the founding of the College of Law – arguably Brazil's first public institution of higher learning. An increasingly important political and intellectual center, the city was soon leading the fight both to end slavery and to found the republic.

The city's fortunes began to rise in the late 19th century when the region's planters began replacing sugar with the world's new, favorite cash crop: coffee. Some of the coffee barons' mansions still line Av Paulista today. The millions of descendants of immigrants who came to work those plantations – especially Italians and Japanese – are another legacy of the coffee boom.

When coffee prices plummeted at the beginning of the 20th century, there was enough capital left over to transform the city into an industrial powerhouse. Factory jobs attracted a new wave of immigrants from around the world, and the city's population practically doubled every decade between 1920 and 1980. In the 1980s, foreign immigration slowed, but laborers streamed in from the drought-stricken Northeast. Many found work building the city's new skyscrapers. Unfortunately, growth far outpaced investment in the city's infrastructure. Today's serious traffic congestion and poorly urbanized slums are the visible result.

In recent years, São Paulo's explosive population growth has slowed, though it is now firmly established as Brazil's banking, industrial and cultural capital. As such it has enjoyed the lion's share of Brazil's current economic boom, and is now seeing an influx of foreign job seekers looking to tap into the action. A 2014 FIFA World Cup host city, Sampa is making strides toward modernizing its infrastructure, including significant expansions of its metro, suburban train and highway systems. Traffic, crime and pollution still flummox city leaders and remain serious problems, but the dynamism of its culture and economy is still attracting the best and brightest from all over Brazil and beyond.

◎ Sights

The atmospheric old center of São Paulo, inventively titled Centro Velho, lies between Praça da Sé, Luz metro station and Praça da República. It's a pedestrianized maze offering a cornucopia of architectural styles (always look above the ground floor, where all charm has been lost to everyday shops).

◎ Praça da Sé & Around

The old heart of the city, **Praça da Sé** (literally, 'Cathedral Sq') has seen better days but still draws animated crowds, from street hawkers and nose-down business types to – unfortunately – more than its fair share of pickpockets and homeless people. Crowning the square is the domed **Catedral da Sé** (Map p222; ⊙ 8am-5pm), a huge neo-Byzantine concoction that, for better or worse, replaced the original 18th-century structure in the 1920s. Still, its lush interior is worth a gander. On the other side of Praça da Sé stands the more modest but also more authentic **Igreja do Carmo** (Map p222), which dates to the 1630s and still preserves its original high altar.

About 700m north of the cathedral, **Rua 25 de Março** is the traditional preserve of the city's Lebanese merchants and remains a lively, crowded wholesale shopping district where you can find remarkable deals on a variety of goods from clothing to electronics.

★ **Mercado Municipal**　　　　　MARKET
(Map p222; www.mercadomunicipal.com.br; Rua da Cantareira 306; ⊙ 7am-6pm Mon-Sat, to 4pm Sun) This covered market is a belle époque confection of stained glass and a series of vast domes. Inside is a delightful market special-

izing in fresh produce and dried goods. It's also a great place to sample a couple of classic Sampa delights: mortadella sandwiches and *pasteis* (pockets of dough stuffed with meat, cheese or fish and then fried).

Many Sundays there is live music, but note that approximately one Sunday per month, the market closes for maintenance. Unfortunately, there is no regular schedule for these closings.

Páteo do Colégio　　　　　LANDMARK
(Map p222; ☑ 3105-6899; www.pateodocolegio. com.br; Praça Páteo do Colégio; adult/student R$6/3; ⊙ 9am-4:45pm Tue-Fri, to 4:30pm Sat & Sun) Occupying the exact spot where São Paulo was founded in 1554 by Jesuit brothers José de Anchieta and Manoel da Nóbrega, this mission is actually a 1950s replica of the monastery that once stood here.

Inside, you'll find a nice little collection of original relics from the city's first days, as well as an interesting set of drawings that chart the city's growth over the last five centuries. The cafe at **Museu Anchieta** also makes for a tranquil pit stop.

Caixa Cultural　　　CULTURAL BUILDING
(Map p222; ☑ 3321-4400; www.caixacultural. com.br; Praça da Sé 111; ⊙ 9am-9pm Tue-Sun) FREE This cultural center, sponsored by Brazil's state-owned Caixa Economica bank, occupies a grand neoclassical-style building with an imperious facade of black marble. Temporary exhibits of major Brazilian artists are shown on the first two floors, and the executive office suite on the 6th floor has been turned into a museum of the bank's history.

Solar da Marquesa　　HISTORIC BUILDING, MUSEUM
(Map p222; www.museudacidade.sp.gov.br; ⊙ 9am-5pm Tue-Sun) FREE Down a set of narrow downtown side streets stands one of the city's last surviving 18th-century residences. This simple but delightful villa was once home to a lover of Emperor Dom Pedro I; now it houses the restrained **Museu da Cidade de São Paulo**, a multi-location museum devoted to the history of the city.

Igreja de São Francisco de Assis　　CHURCH
(Map p222; Largo de São Francisco) Built in the 17th and 18th centuries, this classic example of Portuguese baroque just west of the cathedral is one of the best-preserved colonial structures in the city (note that two churches stand adjacent to each other, each with the same name; the church to the right also

São Paulo

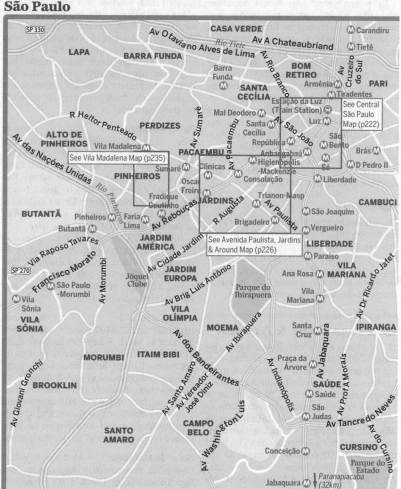

dates to the 17th century but is less architecturally important).

⊙ Triângulo & Anhangabaú

Just north of Praça da Sé lies the Triângulo, a triangle bounded roughly by Praça da Sé, Mosteiro São Bento and the Prefeitura (city hall). It has narrow, pedestrian-only streets and towering office buildings that in the late 19th and early 20th centuries served as the city's commercial heart. Even if Av Paulista and Vila Olímpia now attract the big

money, the Triângulo still does a brisk trade, thanks largely to the presence of Bovespa (Map p222; ☑ 3233-2000; www.bovespa.com.br; Rua XV (15) de Novembro 275, Centro; ⊙ 10am-5pm Mon-Fri) FREE, Latin America's largest stock exchange. There is no longer a live trading floor to visit, but the beautiful main lobby serves as a de facto museum, with small but often excellent temporary exhibits of Brazilian art which you can visit when there isn't a special event on.

Heading west from Praça do Patriarca, you'll cross the 1892 Viaduto de Chá, which crosses the Vale do Anhangabaú,

was begun in 1903 in the style of Paris' Palais Garnier. Its heavily ornamented facade seems to combine every architectural style imaginable, from baroque to art nouveau, and its interior is clad in gold and marble. The theater hosts the city's top classical-music, opera and ballet performances. Call ahead for free tour info.

Edifício Martinelli HISTORIC BUILDING
(Map p222; www.prediomartinelli.com.br; São Bento 405; ⊙tours half-hourly 9:30-11:30am & 2:30-4:30pm Mon-Fri, 9am-1pm Sat) FREE São Paulo's first skyscraper, in a gorgeous 1929 Beaux Arts building, features a mansion built on top of its 26th-floor viewing terrace. The terrace and its incredible views are now open for free visits. For tours, you must arrive on the half-hour during the above stated hours to gain entrance.

Centro Cultural Banco do Brasil CULTURAL BUILDING
(Map p222; www.bb.com.br/cultura; Álvares Penteado 112; cinema/exhibitions R$2-6; ⊙9am-9pm Tue-Sun) FREE Housed in an extraordinarily and lovingly restored Beaux Arts building, this cultural center holds innovative exhibitions of contemporary art as well as excellent film series and theater performances, some of which are charged for.

⊙ Praça da República & Around

Just a few blocks northwest of Anhangabaú lies **Praça da República**, an always lively square that turns into an open-air market on Saturday and Sunday, specializing in crafts, paintings, coins and gemstones. The area north of the square has become a center popular with the gay community, while to the south lies a dense nest of business hotels, huge office buildings and, especially along **Avenida São Luís**, what were once some of the city's most prestigious apartment buildings.

For Caetano Veloso fans, a visit to the corner of **Avenida Ipiranga** and **Avenida São João**, which features in his beloved song 'Sampa,' is mandatory. There are no sights to speak of, but the bustling intersection does do a good job of summing up the city.

Edifício Copan HISTORIC BUILDING
(Map p222; www.copansp.com.br; Av Ipiranga 200) Edifício Copan was designed by late modernist master Oscar Niemeyer. The build-

along with the **Viaduto Santa Efigênia** a little to the north and dating from the same era. Both of these elaborate cast-iron bridges were long synonymous with São Paulo's cultural and economic ascendancy. In the Tupi-Guarani language, Anhangabaú means Demon's Valley, and indigenous peoples believed evil spirits dwelled there. The area is dicey after dark.

★**Theatro Municipal** THEATER
(Map p222; ☑3397-0300; www.teatromunicipal.sp.gov.br; Praça Ramos de Azevedo) São Paulo's most splendid construction, this theater

Central São Paulo

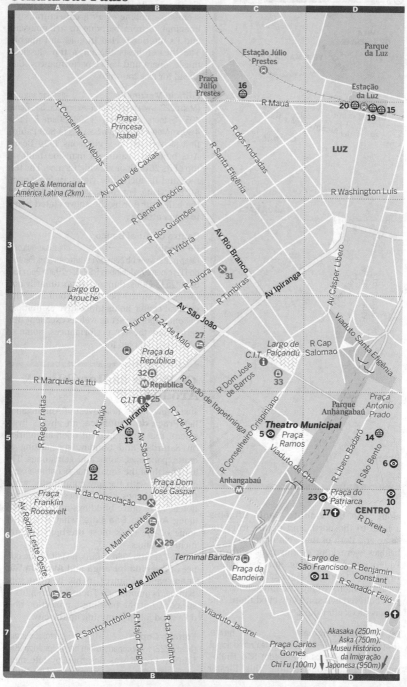

Parque da Luz

Estação Júlio Prestes

Praça Júlio Prestes

16

Estação da Luz

R Mauá

20 **19** **15**

LUZ

Praça Princesa Isabel

R Conselheiro Nébias

Av Duque de Caxias

R Santa Efigênia

R dos Andradas

R Washington Luís

D-Edge & Memorial da América Latina (2km)

R General Osório

R dos Gusmões

R Vitória

Av Rio Branco

R Aurora

31

R Timbiras

Av Ipiranga

Av Casper Libero

Viaduto Santa Efigênia

Largo do Arouche

Av São João

R Aurora R 24 de Malo

27

Largo de Paçandú

R Cap Salomao

C.I.T

Praça da República

R Marquês de Itu

32

Ⓜ República

R Barão de Itapetininga

R Dom José de Barros

33

Parque Anhangabaú

Praça Antonio Prado

R Rego Freitas

C.I.T **25**

R Araújo

Av Ipiranga

Av São Luís

R 7 de Abril

R Conselheiro Crispiniano

Theatro Municipal

5 Praça Ramos

14

13

12

Praça Franklin Roosevelt

R da Consolação

Praça Dom José Gaspar

30

Anhangabaú

Ⓜ

Viaduto da Chá

R Libero Badaró

R São Bento

6

23 Praça do Patriarca

10

17 **CENTRO**

R Direita

Av Radial Leste Oeste

R Martin Fontes

28

29

Terminal Bandeira

Praça da Bandeira

Largo de São Francisco

11

R Benjamin Constant

R Senador Feijó

26

Av 9 de Julho

R Santo-Antônio

R Major Diogo

R da Abolihto

Viaduto Jacarei

Praça Carlos Gomes

Chi Fu (100m)

Akasaka (250m); Aska (750m); Museu Histórico da Imigração Japonesa (950m)

9

Museu de Arte
Sacra (200m)

Pinacoteca
do Estado
4

R São Caetano

Terminal Tietê
Bus Station (5km)

Luz

R Paula Souza

Av Senador Queiroz

R Carlos de Souza

R da Cantareira

R Florencio de Abreu

R 25 de Março

R Barão de Duprat

C.I.T.
2
Mercado
Municipal

Rio Tamanduateí

3 Mosteiro São Bento
São Bento

Parque
Dom
Pedro II

Banespa
1

Praça
Ragueb
Chohfi

Praça
Fernando
Costa

Av do Estado

Parque Dom Pedro II

R Boa Vista

R Gen
Carneiro

R XV de
Novembro

21

R Dr Rodriguez

8
24

7

18

Av Angel Pestana

Memorial do
Imigrante (2km)

22

Sé

Praça
da Sé

R Anita Garibaldi

R de Carmo

R Tabatingüera

Choperia Liberdade (550m)

Central São Paulo

◉ Top Sights
1 Banespa	E5
2 Mercado Municipal	F4
3 Mosteiro São Bento	E4
4 Pinacoteca do Estado	E1
5 Theatro Municipal	C5

◉ Sights
6 Bovespa	D5
7 Caixa Cultural	E6
8 Casa da Imagem	E6
9 Catedral da Sé	D7
10 Centro Cultural Banco do Brasil	D6
11 College of Law	D6
12 Edifício Copan	A5
13 Edifício Itália	B5
14 Edifício Martinelli	D5
15 Estação da Luz	D2
16 Estação Júlio Prestes	C1
17 Igreja de Santo Antônio	D6
Igreja de São Francisco de Assis(see 11)	
18 Igreja do Carmo	E6
19 Memorial da Resistência	D2
20 Museu da Língua Portuguesa	D2
21 Páteo do Colégio	E6
22 Praça da Sé	E7
23 Prefeitura da Cidade de São Paulo	D6
24 Solar da Marquesa	E6

◉ Activities, Courses & Tours
25 SP Free Walking Tour	B5

◉ Sleeping
26 155 Hotel	A7
27 Hotel Marabá	B4
28 Novotel Jaraguá São Paulo	B6

◉ Eating
29 Estadão	B6
30 Ramona	B6
31 Rinconcito Peruano	C3

◉ Drinking & Nightlife
Alberta #3	(see 30)
Bar da Dona Onça	(see 12)
Café Floresta	(see 12)

◉ Entertainment
Sala São Paulo	(see 16)
Theatro Municipal	(see 5)

◉ Shopping
32 Feira da República	B4
33 Galeria do Rock	C4

ing's serpentine facade and narrow *brises soleil* (permanent sunshades) have become a symbol of the city. You can visit its snaking, sloping ground-floor shopping arcade, but the upper floors are made up of private apartments and thus off-limits.

Note that the leftist architect designed the building to bring together all classes by including sprawling apartments for the rich as well as tiny studios for the working poor – a real rarity in class-conscious São Paulo.

Edifício Itália   HISTORIC BUILDING, VIEWPOINT

(Map p222; ☑ 2189-2997; www.edificioitalia.com.br; cnr Avs São Luís & Ipiranga; ☉ 3-4pm Mon-Fri) **FREE** With 46 stories, this **skyscraper** just south of the Praça da República is the tallest in the city center. Its top-floor restaurant, **Terraço Italia**, offers some of the best views of São Paulo, though meal prices are high and the food only passable.

Views are free during the above stated window; otherwise, you'll need to shell out for an overpriced guaraná soda during restaurant-bar hours (noon to 10pm).

⊙ Luz

Located in a tough area just north of the city center, Luz has become an unlikely cultural hub thanks to major restoration of a series of grand turn-of-the-century buildings around the **Parque da Luz**. The park has also undergone a careful restoration, with spreading tropical trees, discreetly placed modern sculpture and a generous police presence.

Across the street from the park sits **Estação da Luz** (Map p222; Praça da Luz), a classic late-Victorian train station constructed with materials entirely shipped in from Britain and completed in 1901. It too has been returned to something close to its original splendor. It services São Paulo's extensive suburban lines, with a long tunnel linking it to Metrô Luz.

★ Pinacoteca do Estado   MUSEUM

(Map p222; www.pinacoteca.org.br; Praça da Luz 2; adult/student R$6/3, Sat free; ☉ 10am-6pm Tue-Sun) This neoclassical museum houses an excellent collection of Brazilian – and especially Paulista – art from the 19th century to the present, including works by big names such as Portinari and Di Cavalcanti. Renovations have made it a pleasant place to while away an afternoon, and there is an attractive cafe that faces the adjacent Parque da Luz.

Museu da Língua Portuguesa   MUSEUM

(Map p222; www.museulinguaportuguesa.org.br; Praça da Luz; adult/student R$6/3; ☉ 10am-6pm Tue-Sun) Half of Estação da Luz has been given over to this museum, with fascinating permanent exhibits documenting the rise of the Brazilian language as distinct from European Portuguese, as well as creative temporary installations celebrating Brazilian literature. Note, though, that all accompanying signs are (ironically?) in Portuguese only.

Estação Júlio Prestes   HISTORIC BUILDING

(Map p222; Largo General Osório 66) This grand turn-of-the-century Beaux Arts–style working railway station (actually completed in the 1930s) is the **Estação Pinacoteca** (☑ 3324-1000; www.pinacoteca.org.br; adult/student incl admission to Pinacoteca do Estado R$6/3; ☉ 10am-6pm Tue-Sun), an annex of the Pinacoteca do Estado hosting Sampa's three best contemporary art halls and an excellent permanent collection of modernist Brazilian art. Also here is the powerful **Memorial da Resistência** (Map p222; www.memorialdaresistenciasp.org.br; ☉ 10am-5:30pm Tue-Sun) **FREE**, occupying cells where dissidents were tortured during Brazil's military dictatorship.

Museu de Arte Sacra   MUSEUM

(Museum of Sacred Art; www.museuartesacra.org.br; Tiradentes 676; adult/student R$6/3; ☉ 10am-6pm, last admission 5:30pm Tue-Sun) The best of its kind in Brazil, this museum includes works by renowned 18th-century sculptor Antônio Aleijadinho, along with some 200 other ecclesiastical works from the 17th to the 20th centuries. The museum is housed in the 18th-century Luz monastery, which is one of São Paulo's best-preserved buildings of the period.

A new annex houses an amazingly large and elaborate Neapolitan manger scene, plus a collection of other manger scenes from around the world. It's 50m from Metrô Tiradentes.

⊙ Liberdade

Liberdade – a short walk south of Praça da Sé – has long been the traditional center of Sampa's massive Japanese community. Though most new Asian immigrants these days come from China and Korea, the gritty neighborhood is still lined with traditional Japanese shops and eateries and is full of hidden gems of Asian culture throughout its otherwise quiet streets.

SÃO PAULO STATE LUZ

Praça da Liberdade is the neighborhood's main square and also the location of its metro stop. It hosts an open-air market on Sunday. A short walk south on Galvão Bueno takes you past many Asian shops and restaurants as well as some rather neglected Japanese-style gardens.

Museu Histórico da Imigração Japonesa
MUSEUM

(Museum of Japanese Immigration; ✆3209-5465; www.bunkyo.bunkyonet.org.br; São Joaquim 381; adult/student R$6/3; ⊙1:30-5:30pm Tue-Sun) This modest but fascinating museum, on the 7th floor of a Liberdade office building, documents the arrival and integration of the Japanese community. Photos, period objects and a full-scale reconstruction of a typical immigrant's farm lodging tell a poignant story, from the arrival in Santos of the first 781 settlers aboard the *Kasato-Maru* in 1908 through to today. Bring ID.

◉ Higienópolis, Pacaembu & Barra Funda

Northwest of Av Paulista lies the leafy neighborhood of Higienópolis, one of the most traditional of the city's upscale neighborhoods and a good spot for a stroll. Praça Buenos Aires, a tree-filled, European-style square, serves as the neighborhood's lungs and playground. As you continue northwest, you pass through Pacaembu, a low-rise neighborhood of ramblingly luxurious homes reminiscent of upscale Los Angeles. Finally, you reach Barra Funda, a more workaday neighborhood that at night comes alive with some of the city's trendiest nightclubs.

Museu do Futebol
MUSEUM

(Map p226; www.museudofutebol.org.br; Praça Charles Miller s/n, Pacaembu; adult/student R$6/3, Thu free; ⊙9am-5pm Tue-Sun; 🚇) Tucked under the bleachers of colorfully art deco Pacaembu Stadium, the city's newest museum is devoted to Brazil's greatest passion – football (soccer). Its multimedia displays over two floors manage to evoke the thrill of watching a championship game, even for nonfans.

Catch bus 917M-31 'Morro Grande' on Av Dr Arnaldo at Cardoso de Almeida outside Metrô Clínicas and get off in front of Pão de Açúcar grocery store on Av Pacaembu.

Memorial da América Latina
MONUMENT

(✆3823-4600; www.memorial.sp.gov.br; Auro Soares de Moura Andrade 664, Barra Funda; ⊙9am-6pm Tue-Sun) FREE This Oscar Niemeyer creation is like a mini-Brasília, with a series of glass-and-cement structures in a beautiful if unsettling variety of shapes and sizes. While it looks uninviting at first glance, the sprawling complex has undergone renovations to make it more welcoming – and interesting – to visitors.

The Salão dos Atos is a ceremonial space where you can see Cândido Portinari's enormous painting *Tiradentes*. The perfectly round Galeria Marta Traba de Arte Latino-Americano displays contemporary art from around Latin America. And the Pavilhão de Criatividade displays a diverse collection of Latin American arts and crafts.

◉ Avenida Paulista, Jardins & Around

Once the domain of coffee barons and their sprawling manses, Avenida Paulista (often known simply as 'Paulista') began to go 'Manhattan' in the 1950s and today is lined with towering modernist office buildings. Though few of these buildings have much architectural merit, the sum of the parts is impressive. It's also a lively area both day and night, packed with restaurants, shops, theaters and cafes. Just off Paulista across from the Museu de Arte de São Paulo (MASP) lies Parque Siqueira Campos (Map p226; ⊙6am-6pm), a beautifully designed and maintained park that re-creates the Atlantic rainforest that was leveled to build São Paulo. It's a remarkably tranquil refuge just off the city's busiest street.

Along Rua Augusta north of Paulista, Baixo Augusta was São Paulo's traditional red-light district; however, the area has been commandeered over the last decade by a combination of gay, fashion-forward and alternative crowds (often all three), and its bars and nightclubs are packed after 10pm with the young, high-minded and multiply pierced.

On the southern slope of Paulista lies Jardins, the city's leafiest and most chic central neighborhood. This is where you will find some of the city's most over-the-top living and shopping and, above all, Rua Oscar Freire (Brazil's Rodeo Dr and the 8th most luxurious street in the world), with its showstopping series of boutiques and super-refined eateries.

Avenida Paulista, Jardins & Around

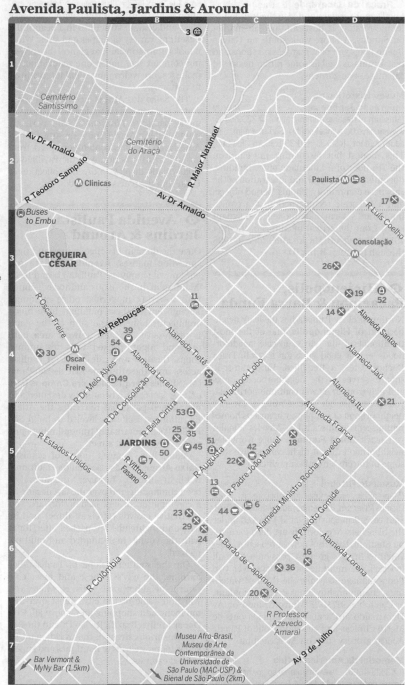

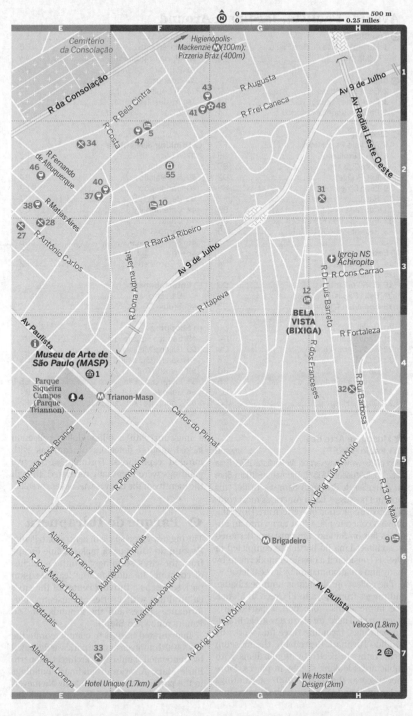

Avenida Paulista, Jardins & Around

★ Museu de Arte de São Paulo (MASP)
MUSEUM

(Map p226; www.masp.art.br; Av Paulista 1578, Bela Vista; adult/student R$15/7, Thu free; ⊙10am-6pm Tue & Thu-Sun, to 8pm Wed) Sampa's pride, this museum possesses Latin America's most comprehensive collection of Western art. Hovering above a concrete plaza that turns into an antiques fair on Sunday, the museum, designed by architect Lina Bo Bardi and completed in 1968, is considered a classic of modernism by many and an abomination by a vocal few.

The collection, though, is unimpeachable, and ranges from Goya to El Greco to Manet. The impressionist collection is particularly noteworthy. There are also a few great Brazilian paintings, including three fine works by Cândido Portinari. Regrettably, the museum seems rather neglected by its guardians, with public areas looking shabby in places. More shocking was the theft in 2007 of paintings by Portinari and Picasso, which revealed that a museum with a billion-dollar collection lacked motion detectors or cameras with infrared capabilities. Fortunately, the two paintings were eventually recovered, though the identity of the thieves was never revealed.

◉ Parque do Ibirapuera

The biggest green space in central São Paulo, Parque do Ibirapuera makes a fine escape from the city's seemingly infinite stretches of concrete. In addition, the leafy 2-sq-km park serves as a thriving center of the city's cultural life, with a series of museums, performance spaces and the grounds for São Paulo's renowned Bienal.

Inaugurated in 1954 to commemorate the city's 400th anniversary, the park was designed by renowned landscape architect Roberto Burle Marx. A series of landmark buildings in the park are the work of Oscar Niemeyer; most of them are linked by a long and distinctively serpentine covered walkway. At the north entrance stands Victor Brecheret's huge **Monumento Bandeiras**, erected in 1953 in memory of the city's early pioneers. A meandering duck pond takes up much of the western half of the park, and around it is arranged a series of shaded walks.

To get to the park, take the metro to Vila Mariana station and then bus 775-A 'Jardim Aldagiza.' There are lots of snack stands in the park, or you can get a full meal in the Museu de Arte Moderna, at **Prêt** (week/weekend R$49/56; ☺ noon-4pm Tue-Fri, 12:30-5pm Sat & Sun), which serves an excellent buffet in a light-filled, minimalist dining room.

Museu de Arte Moderna   MUSEUM
(www.mam.org.br; adult/student R$5.50/2.75, Sun free; ☺ 10am-6pm Tue-Sun) Brazil's oldest **modern-art museum** possesses a fine collection of Brazilian modernists such as Anita Malfatti and Di Cavalcanti as well as works by Miró, Chagall, Picasso and Dufy. However, the public spaces are devoted exclusively to temporary exhibits. Check the museum's website for current offerings.

✪ Pinheiros, Vila Madalena & Cidade Universitária

West of Jardins lies **Pinheiros**, a sprawling, mostly residential neighborhood of identikit high-rise apartments and excellent restaurants. At the heart of the larger Pinheiros neighborhood is the distinctly low-rise and pedestrian-friendly **Vila Madalena**. Long a Bohemian enclave, it has in recent years become a popular alternative to the high-end, attitude-heavy clubs and restaurants of nearby **Vila Olímpia**. The epicenter of the bar and restaurant scene is the corner of Rua Mourato Coelho and Rua Aspicuelta, which grow crowded at happy hour and, on weekends, stay that way until the wee hours. There are also a number of interesting shops, cafes and art galleries.

West of Pinheiros across the Rio Pinheiros lies Cidade Universitária, home of the prestigious University of São Paulo (USP). The quiet, tree-lined campus makes for pleasant strolling.

Museu de Arte Contemporânea da Universidade de São Paulo (MAC-USP)   MUSEUM
(☎ 3091-3039; www.mac.usp.br; Rua da Praça do Relógio 160, Cidade Universitária; ☺ 10am-8pm

Mon & Thu, to 6pm Wed & Fri-Sun) **FREE** Set amid the verdant University of São Paulo campus, this fine museum possesses what is arguably the country's best collection of Brazilian art since 1960, plus a smattering of works by international masters from Max Ernst to Robert Rauschenberg.

Casa da Xiclete   GALLERY
(Map p235; ☎ 2579-9007; www.casadaxiclet.com; Fradique Coutinho 1855, Vila Madalena; ☺ 2-8pm Wed-Sun) Occupying a ramshackle house at the edge of the neighborhood, Casa da Xiclete is the home and gallery of the artist of the same name, who runs a collective of other artists, many also in residence.

Fortes Vilaça   GALLERY
(Map p235; ☎ 3032-7066; www.fortesvilaca.com.br; Fradique Coutinho 1500, Vila Madalena; ☺ 10am-7pm Tue-Fri, to 6pm Sat) The traditional Fortes Vilaça displays the work of some of the city's most illustrious contemporary artists in a sprawling, cement-lined space.

Instituto Tomie Ohtake   MUSEUM
(Map p235; ☎ 2245-1900; www.institutotomie ohtake.org.br; Brigadeiro Faria Lima 201, Pinheiros; ☺ 11am-8pm Tue-Sun) **FREE** This cultural institute, founded by Ruy Ohtake, São Paulo's most prominent contemporary architect, is dedicated to his Japanese-born mother, one of São Paulo's most illustrious painters. An attractive gallery space features changing exhibits of prominent, mostly local artists.

✪ South & East of Jardins

Extra-wide Av Brigadeiro Faria Lima (called just 'Faria Lima') marks the southwestern edge of the Jardins neighborhoods. Faria Lima is also the main corridor connecting Pinheiros with the ritzy, though mostly uninviting, neighborhoods of **Morumbi**, **Vila Olímpia**, **Itaím Bibi** and **Moema**. All of these areas are composed largely of congested streets, forbidding luxury high-rises and glittering complexes that house the majority of the city's most profitable businesses, from banking to technology. That said, there are plenty of fine restaurants, nightclubs and shopping opportunities that diehards may want to seek out.

Museu da Casa Brasileira   MUSEUM
(☎ 3032-3727; www.mcb.sp.gov.br; Brigadeiro Faria Lima 2705, Pinheiros; adult/student R$4/2,

Sun free; ⊙10am-6pm Tue-Sun) Occupying an extravagant Palladian-style villa built by a local tycoon and his wife in the 1940s, the small but charming Museu da Casa Brasileira has a hodgepodge collection of Brazilian and European furnishings from the 17th to the 20th centuries and a newly renovated cafe-restaurant with lovely outdoor seating.

**Fundação Maria Luisa
e Oscar Americano**   MUSEUM, GARDENS
(✐3742-0077; www.fundacaooscaramericano.org.br; Av Morumbi 4077, Morumbi; adult/student R$10/5; ⊙museum & cafe 10am-5:30pm Tue-Sun) Home of the couple who developed the leafy, upscale suburb of Morumbi, this fine retreat hosts impressive gardens and a lovely collection of painting, sculpture and objets d'art from the 18th to the 20th centuries. The 1950s house-turned-museum is a small masterpiece of Brazilian modernism, and there's also a lovely cafe that serves traditional high tea for R$55.

Museu Paulista   MUSEUM
(www.mp.usp.br; Parque de Independência, Ipiranga; adult/student R$6/3, first Sun of month free; ⊙9am-5pm Tue-Sun) Set amid Versailles-like gardens in the eastern suburb of Ipiranga, this museum began its life as a memorial to Brazil's independence from Portugal. According to legend, Dom Pedro declared independence on the shores of a nearby stream. The gardens and palace are the real treat here, as are the fine vistas that its hilltop position affords.

🎓 Courses

Polyglot   LANGUAGE COURSE
(✐3744-4397; www.polyglot.com.br; Eng Luiz Carlos Berrini 96, Brooklyn) One of the most respected language schools for Portuguese.

CEL-LEP   LANGUAGE COURSE
(✐3743-7728; www.br.cellep.com) CEL-LEP specializes in English and Spanish but also offers Portuguese at a few locations throughout the city, including Av Paulista and Vila Madalena.

🧭 Tours

Flaviz Liz di Paolo   CULTURAL, SHOPPING
(✐98119-3903; www.flavializ.com) Personal guide Flavia Liz is an enthusiastic, multilingual São Paulo specialist who offers customized guiding services throughout the city and surroundings. Whether you want to dig into architecture, shopping, art galleries, museums, favelas (slums, shanty towns) or any other niche, she is your woman.

🎉 Festivals & Events

The city's two biggest events are the **Bienal de São Paulo** and the **Gay Pride events**. In 1997, São Paulo's first Gay Pride parade drew a meager 3000 people. In less than a decade, it has grown into the world's largest Pride event, attracting nearly three million.

Carnaval   CARNAVAL
(⊙Feb/Mar) The celebrations don't approach those of Rio, but there are parties throughout the city.

São Paulo Restaurant Week   FOOD
(www.restaurantweek.com.br; lunch/dinner R$34.90/47.90; ⊙Feb/Mar & Aug/Sep) More than 100 restaurants offer special menus and promotional prices for two weeks twice a year.

Virada Cultural   MUSIC
(www.viradacultural.org; ⊙late Apr/early May) A nonstop, free 24-hour party of cultural, especially musical, events around the city.

São Paulo International Art Fair   ART
(www.sp-arte.com; ⊙Apr) This national and international art fair is one of the world's largest.

Mostra Internacional de Cinema   FILM
(www.mostra.org; ⊙Oct) The country's largest film festival, with screenings throughout the city.

Reveillon   NEW YEAR
(⊙31 Dec) Av Paulista turns into a big outdoor party to ring in the new year.

🛏 Sleeping

São Paulo's only true traveler-like quarter is the bohemian *bairro* (district) of **Vila Madalena**, 6km west of Praça da Sé, which now boasts a bonafide hip hostel scene in addition to being the city's longstanding cradle of artsy boutiques, cutting-edge galleries and boisterous nightlife. The leafy, upscale district of **Jardim Paulista**, 5km southwest of Centro, is pricier but also very pleasant. There's a solid concentration of hostels around the residential neighborhoods of **Paraíso** and **Vila Mariana** off the southeastern end of Av Paulista – a little out of the way but near good metro connections. If you opt for Centro, the areas surrounding Estação da Luz train station and central downtown are rife with cheap hotels but also crime and prostitution – use extreme caution and don't walk

SÃO PAULO STATE SOUTH & EAST OF JARDINS

around at night. Stick to the safe-ish immediate area around Praça da República.

Be wary of lower prices luring you to neighborhoods like **Belem**, **Mooca** and **Parada Inglesa** – they might be cheaper, but you'll be a long haul from the action and sleeping in the city's two least desirable zones, North and East.

🛏 Central São Paulo

Akasaka   HOTEL **$**
(📞 3207-1500;   www.akasakahotel.com.br; Praça da Liberdade 149, Liberdade; d/tr/q R$135/150/210; 🌀📶) Conveniently located across from the metro, this newly remodeled budget option offers good value with no-frills but clean and just-modernized rooms. It's a convenient choice for those especially interested in the city's Japanese and Korean subcultures. Breakfast costs extra.

155 Hotel   BOUTIQUE HOTEL **$$**
(Map p222; 📞3150-1555; www.155hotel.com. br; Martinho Prado 173, Consolacão; d R$165, ste R$330; 🌀@📶) This gay-friendly, 76-room affordable boutique hotel between Centro and the alterna-hipster bars of Baixo Augusta is steeped in minimalist blacks and greys in the ultra-sleek suites; regular rooms aren't quite as hip but are still top-value all things considered, with tight bathrooms but hardwood floors and writing desks.

FREE SP!

There's no sugarcoating it: Brazil is expensive and São Paulo is the beast of the bunch. But that doesn't mean you can't have fun on a shoestring budget. Our favorite freebies:

Museu Afro-Brasil (www.museuafrobrasil.com.br; Parque do Ibirapuera, Moema; ⊙10am-5pm Tue-Sun) This hugely important, absolutely fascinating Parque do Ibirapuera museum features a permanent 3rd-floor collection chronicling five centuries of African immigration (and a nod to the 10 million African lives lost in the construction of Brazil) and hosts a rotating array of contemporary Afro-centric exhibitions on its bottom two floors.

Banespa (Map p222; João Brícola 24; ⊙10am-3pm Mon-Fri) For one of Sampa's best panoramas, head to the top of this 161m-high skyscraper, Brazil's version of the Empire State Building, completed in 1939. Ride free to the observation deck on the top floor for views of the city.

Note: you will need some form of ID to sign in. You will also have to wait in two lines, first to sign in and then for an elevator to the top. The five-minute maximum visit is enforced heavy-handedly, but the view will floor you.

Casa da Imagem (Map p222; 📞3106-5122; www.casadaimagem.sp.gov.br; Roberto Simonsen 136-B, Centro; ⊙9am-5pm Tue-Sun) Beautifully curated (and English signed!) from some 710,000 historical photographs, this newly inaugurated museum inside a restored colonial downtown mansion is a must for those interested in the São Paulo of days gone by. Themed exhibitions are changed every three months; and the building itself, where frescoes from the 1880s were uncovered in the restoration, is also worth a look-see.

Mosteiro São Bento (Map p222; www.mosteiro.org.br; Largo de São Bento s/n; ⊙6am-6pm Mon-Wed & Fri, 6am-8am & 11:30am-6pm Thu, 6am-noon & 4-6pm Sat & Sun) The austere but impressive Mosteiro São Bento, which is among the city's oldest and most important churches, dates to 1598, though its neo-Gothic facade dates only to the early 20th century. Step inside the church to view its impressive stained glass. Mass at 10am on Sunday generally includes Gregorian chanting.

SP Free Walking Tour (Map p222; www.spfreewalkingtour.com; ⊙11:30am Wed & Sat) Culls over 450 years of Sampa history into a long but fascinating 'Old Downtown' walk twice a week at 11:30am. The tour meets and ends next to the C.I.T. at Praça da República. A 'Paulista Ave' tour covers the modern city every Thursday and Sunday at 3:30pm, leaving from Banco do Brasil at the corner of Paulista and Rua Augusta on the Jardins side.

Hotel Marabá — HOTEL $$$

(Map p222; ☑ 2137-9500; www.hotelmaraba.com. br; Ipiranga 757, Centro; s/d R$350/420, ste from R$650; P ❋ @ 🖤) This refurbished office building just off Praça da República provides remarkable style and comfort. It isn't the deal it once was, but it's still an impressive choice in downtown's hippest and safest area. From quality bedding to chic lighting fixtures, Marabá was only just here before the hipsters but manages to come across as the neighborhood's Godfather of sleek.

Novotel Jaraguá
São Paulo — BUSINESS HOTEL $$$

(Map p222; ☑ 2802-7000; www.accorhotels.com. br; Martins Fontes 71, Centro; s/d R$525/555; P ❋ @ 🖤) The Accor chain has refurbished the old Hotel Jaraguá, which had long been central São Paulo's most chic hotel. Digs are spacious, plush and cheerfully done up in saturated hues. Rooms above the 20th floor have breathtaking city views. Prices can be slashed by 50% depending on occupancy.

🛏 Avenida Paulista, Paraíso & Vila Mariana

LimeTime Hostel — HOSTEL $

(Map p226; ☑ 2935-5463; www.limetimehostels. com; 13 de Maio 1552, Bela Vista; dm from R$35, r without bathroom R$120; @ 🖤) This superbly located, grafitti-slathered hostel sits within walking distance of Av Paulista, Metrô Brigadeiro and the airport bus stop at Hotel Maksoud Plaza. Power-equipped lockers and flat-screens give it a hi-tech edge, while the owner, a wild-haired DJ named Bebeto, is a perfect nightlife ambassador for the city. No breakfast, but there's one free caipirinha per night.

Pousada dos Franceses — POUSADA $

(Map p226; ☑ 3288-1592; www.pousadadosfranc eses.com.br; Rua dos Franceses 100, Morro dos Ingleses; dm R$50, s/d/tr from R$84/125/198; @ 🖤) On a quiet, almost suburban street, yet just a short walk to Av Paulista, this veteran hostel offers decent communal digs, bright and pleasant common areas, and private rooms of varying sizes and comfort.

★ **We Hostel Design** — HOSTEL $$

(☑ 2615-2262; www.wehostel.com.br; Morgado de Mateus 567, Vila Mariana; dm R$48-60, d without bathroom R$150-170; @ 🖤) Simply gorgeous, São Paulo's best new hostel popped up inside a beautiful 100-year-old historic white

🏃 City Walk
Sampa's Centro Velho

START/END PRAÇA DA REPÚBLICA
LENGTH 3.5KM; TWO HOURS

Downtown São Paulo is a vibrant living museum of architectural gems and glory days gone by. Head out on a weekday (weekends and nights are a little too dicey) on this pleasant Centro stroll.

Start at ❶ **Praça da República**, head down Av Ipiranga and then turn left onto Av São Luís to get a look at what's still one of the tallest buildings in town – the 46-story ❷ **Edifício Itália** (p109).Continuing down Av São Luís, check out the rather squat, grey building at the end of the small park on the left. It looks like a prison, but it's the ❸ **Mario de Andrade Municipal Library**, housing the largest book collection in the city.

Turning left onto Rua Xavier de Toledo, keeping the library on your left, follow the road downhill toward the Anhangabaú metro station a few blocks away. Follow Toledo until the ❹ **Theatro Municipal** (p221) appears – this baroque building, with its art-nouveau features, is the pride of the city. Opposite the theater, on the right, is the ❺ **Viaduto de Chá**, a metal bridge built in 1892 and named after an old tea plantation that used to be in the area. Pedestrian traffic became too heavy for the old bridge and a new one was inaugurated in 1938.

Crossing the bridge, look out over the ❻ **Parque Anhangabaú** on the left. At the other side of the bridge, enter ❼ **Praça do Patriarca** straight ahead. Here you'll find the ❽ **Igreja de Santo Antônio**, the central church of the settlement of São Paulo at the start of the 17th century, and rebuilt in the 18th century.

Turn right some 20 paces beyond on Rua São Bento, leading to ❾ **Largo de São Francisco**, a triangular plaza that is home to twin churches, both known as ❿ ⓫ **Igreja de São Francisco de Assis** (p219), and the well-respected ⓬ **College of Law**. Just beyond the controversial statue of a Frenchman kissing an indigenous woman in front of the College of Law is Senador Feijó, leading to the famous ⓭ **Praça da Sé** (p219). Soak up the joy-

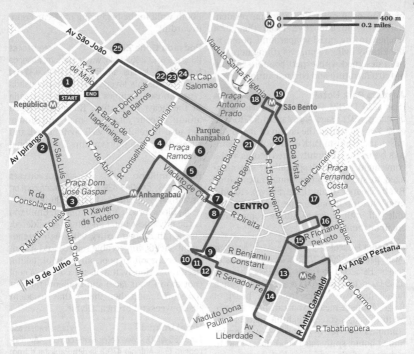

ous vibe in the square, but watch your pockets. Step inside the enormous ⑭ **Catedral da Sé** (p107).

As you exit the cathedral, head down the plaza and continue toward the ⑮ **Caixa Economica Federal**, home to the city's coffers and also a great cultural center (Caixa Cultural) that features Brazilian artists. Turning right onto Rua Floriano Peixoto, walk to the end and feast your eyes upon the pinkish-colored ⑯ **Solar da Marquesa** (p219). Follow the street around to the left to ⑰ **Praça Páteo do Colégio** (p219), the actual site where São Paulo was founded in 1554.

Directly in front of this plaza is Boa Vista. Following it away from Praça da Sé to the end, where you'll find ⑱ **Largo de São Bento**, home to the ⑲ **Mosteiro São Bento** (p231), a monastery and basilica built in an eclectic style and still putting on Gregorian-chant concerts.

Leaving the square, walk up the pedestrianized Rua São Bento to Av São João. Turn left at São João and another quick left at the next street, where on the right stands the art-deco ⑳ **Banespa building**. Head to the top floor for a sweeping view of São Paulo. Backtrack to São Bento and then keep heading straight down Av São João. On the left just past São Bento stands ㉑ **Edifício Martinelli** (p221). You are now crossing the Vale do Anhangabaú that you saw earlier from the Viaduto de Chá.

Head up São João as far as ㉒ **Largo de Paiçandú**. Behind the pretty ㉓ **NS do Rosário dos Homens Pretos** is the magnificent ㉔ **Monumento á Mãe Preta** (Monument to the Black Mother). This heartwrenching statue depicts an African slave woman suckling a white child, and the poem underneath gives voice to her lament for her own children who must go hungry.

To wrap up a long day, continue forward and you will end up at the ㉕ **intersection of Av São João and Av Ipiranga**, a corner that is considered the most famous in all of São Paulo and was immortalized in Caetano Veloso's beautiful ode to the city, 'Sampa.' Turn left and you will be back where you started at Praça da República.

mansion on a quiet Vila Mariana residential corner in late 2012. From the guest kitchen to the quasi-wraparound porch to the kitschy living room, everything here has been designed with expert connoisseurship of retro furniture and coveted antiques.

Augusta Park Hotel HOTEL $$
(Map p226; ☑ 3124-4400; www.augustapark.com. br; Augusta 922, Baixo Augusta; s/d R$210/248; ❄ @ 🛜 🞤) Set amid the action of Baixo Augusta, the Augusta Park offers some of Sampa's best-value if slightly dated rooms and a convenient location (especially if you managed to snag the promotional rates, some R$50 cheaper than those above). Rooms aren't luxurious but are perfectly comfortable, all with separate sitting rooms and small kitchens.

Pauliceia Hostel HOSTEL $$
(Map p226; ☑ 2503-2773; www.pauliceiahostel. com.br; Herculano de Freitas 250, Bela Vista; dm R$49-60, d/tr R$150/200; @ 🛜) This newish hostel just two blocks from the heart of Baixo Augusta means you can now tie one on in the city's coolest nightlife district and stumble home for free. Inside a well-maintained home, spiffy hardwood floors lead to a variety of six- and nine-bed dorms with shared baths and fans; and a couple of private suites.

Ibis Budget HOTEL $$
(Map p226; ☑ 3123-7752; www.ibishotel.com; Rua da Consolação 2303, Consolação; r R$180; ❄ @ 🛜) Large and somewhat soulless but with a great location and price, this chain hotel is worth considering. Rooms are spartan and rather dormitory-like but are perfectly adequate.

🛏 Jardins & Around

★ Guest 607 POUSADA $
(☑ 2619-6007; www.guest607.com.br; João Moura 607, Pinheiros; dm R$60, s/d/tr without bathroom from R$148/158/178; ❄ @ 🛜) This colorful six-room gastro-guesthouse is the brainchild of Cássia Saldanha, who lived in Italy and the UK before returning home and turning a two-story townhouse into a design-forward and food-centric spot to rest your weary head. Rooms are smallish, but the whole place is packed with personality and there's a sophisticated bistro serving three meals a day.

If your preferred aesthetic leans toward *Wallpaper*, look no further. It's just an 800m walk to the beginning of Oscar Freire in Jardins.

Pousada Dona Ziláh POUSADA $$
(Map p226; ☑ 3062-1444; www.zilah.com; Alameda Franca 1621, Jardins; s/d R$148/184; ℗ ❄ @ 🛜) A rare find, this lovely, briskly run pousada (guesthouse) occupies a Spanish-style villa in the heart of Jardins. Rooms, arranged around a courtyard, are small and simple but also tasteful and well maintained and sit above a lovely downstairs international bistro.

Hotel Emiliano BOUTIQUE HOTEL $$$
(Map p226; ☑ 3068-4399; www.emiliano.com.br; Oscar Freire 384, Jardins; d from R$1739; ℗ ❄ @ 🛜 🞤) Sleek, bright and minimalist, Emiliano is the city's best hotel all things considered, steeped in refined luxury, with high-thread-count sheets, impeccable service and a sun-drenched rooftop pool, all without taking itself too seriously. It nails the combo of cool (not too in your face) and opulent (but not too stuffy)...and then there's that decadent R$125 weekend brunch. Divine.

Hotel Unique DESIGN HOTEL $$$
(☑ 3055-4710; www.hotelunique.com.br; Av Brigadeiro Luis Antônio 4700, Jardim Paulista; d from R$1486; ℗ ❄ @ 🞤) Designed by Ruy Ohtake, the slice of watermelon–-reminiscent Unique is certainly the city's most architecturally ambitious hotel as well as a favorite of rock stars and fashionistas. Rooms, with their portal-like windows, are elegantly minimalist, and the rooftop bar and pool offer some of the city's very best views.

Hotel Fasano BOUTIQUE HOTEL $$$
(Map p226; ☑ 3896-4000; www.fasano.com. br; Vittorio Fasano 88, Jardins; d from R$1644; ℗ ❄ @ 🞤) This small but ultra-refined hotel seems to have been plucked straight from Milan, with muted gray marble set off with exquisite 1930s-era antiques in rooms and common areas, and a reserve and formality rare in Brazil. The Zen-like rooftop pool area alone is worth the price of admission. Many rooms have fine views.

Regent Park Suite Hotel HOTEL $$$
(Map p226; ☑ 3065-5555; www.regent.com.br; Oscar Freire 533, Jardins; s/d weekend R$345/373, week R$368/398; ℗ ❄ 🛜 🞤) A tony location plus fully equipped, one-bedroom apartments that are both plush and mutely stylish. Ask for a room on a high floor for views over the Jardins district.

🛏 Vila Madalena

Sampa Hostel HOSTEL $
(Map p235; ☑ 3031-6779; www.hostelsampa.com.
br; Girassol 519, Vila Madalena; dm from R$40, s/d/
tr R$95/120/180; @🛜) The best of Vila Ma-
dalena's newly founded hostel scene is also
the veteran, dating all the way back to 2008.
There're four- and eight-bed dorms, good-
value private rooms, a funky TV room and
kitchen facilities.

Vila Madalena Hostel HOSTEL $
(☑ 3034-4104; www.vilamadalenahostel.com.br;
Francisco Leitão 686, Vila Madalena; dm from R$40,
d without bathroom R$130; ✳@) This low-key
place is full of artistic touches and period
furniture. The eccentric owner is none too
keen on rowdy backpackers.

Casa Club Hostel HOSTEL $
(Map p235; ☑ 3798-0051; www.casaclub.com.br;
Mourato Coelho 973, Vila Madalena; dm from R$35,
d R$110; @) While the dorm-only facilities
are cramped and pack in as many as 16 beds,
this is Vila Madalena's most sociable hostel,
thanks to its courtyard bar that is open to
the general public. It's well located for the
neighborhood's nightlife and arts scene.

🍴 Eating

São Paulo's dining scene is as vast as the city
itself – and guaranteed to please all comers.
For the frugal, there are the ubiquitous *lan-
chonetes* – corner bars offering beer to the
thirsty and, for the hungry, full meals for under R$14. Plus, literally hundreds of ethnic
groups each have their offerings, from Lebanese to Uruguayan cuisine.

Although restaurants open by 7pm, most
don't fill up until 9pm or so on weekdays,
and later on weekends, when many kitchens
take orders to 1am or later. There are also
lots of very good 24-hour options for late-
night munchies.

🍴 Central São Paulo

Estadão FAST FOOD $
(Map p222; www.estadaolanches.com.br; Viaduto 9
de Julho 193, Centro; sandwiches R$10-22; ⊘24hr)
This classic Centro *lanchonete* serves working folk's meals at all hours, but its signature
pernil (pork loin) sandwich, smothered in
the cheese of your choice (provolone!) and
sautéed onions, is one of Sampa's gastronomic musts.

Vila Madalena 🔼 Ⓝ 0 ▬▬ 200 m / 0 ▬▬ 0.1 miles

Vila Madalena

◉ Sights
1 Casa da Xiclete	A1
2 Fortes Vilaça	A2
3 Instituto Tomie Ohtake	A3

🛏 Sleeping
4 Casa Club Hostel	A3
5 Sampa Hostel	A2

🍴 Eating
6 Bacio di Latte	B2
7 Feijoada da Lana	B2
8 Feirinha Gastronômica	B2
9 Julice Boulangère	A3
10 Lá da Venda	B2
11 Mercearia São Pedro	A1
12 Pitanga	B1

🍷 Drinking & Nightlife
13 Canto da Ema	A3
14 Coffee Lab	A2
15 Farol Madalena	B1
16 Filial	B2
17 São Cristóvão	A2
18 SubAstor	A2

Rinconcito Peruano PERUVIAN $
(Map p222; ☑ 8974-2965; Aurora 451, Centro; mains
R$13.70-32.80; ⊘noon-5pm Mon, to 11pm Tue-Sat,
to 9pm Sun) Great-value Peruvian classics

like *ceviche* and *lomo saltado* await adventurous travelers at this unsigned authentic 2nd-floor dive in downtown's dicey Peruvian neighborhood. You'll need to keep your guard up (it's more or less fine during the day, but keep in mind that this is Sampa's *Cracolândia*), but Peruvian cooks, waitstaff and clientele means it's the real deal.

Aska
JAPANESE $

(Galvão Bueno 466, Liberdade; mains R$12-16; ⏰11am-2pm & 6-9:40pm Tue-Sun) Steaming-hot bowls of pork ramen draws in legions at this Liberdade noodle restaurant that's entirely too cheap. It's practically Japan.

★ Ramona
BRAZILIAN, FUSION $$

(Map p222; www.casaramona.com.br; Av São Luís 282, Centro; mains R$33-49; ⏰noon-3pm & 8pm-late Mon-Fri, 1-4pm & 8pm-2am Sat; 🛜) This new República hot spot is on to something: contemporary downtown dining that is giving paulistanos a reason to venture into Centro at night. The legitimately retro space, fueled by a holier-than-thou indie soundtrack, excels at memorable dishes like the garlic-slathered sweet-potato appetizer and perfectly cooked *baru* nut-crusted catch of the day; great cocktails and delicious desserts as well.

SÃO PAULO BIENAL

Modeled on the Venice Biennale, the **Bienal de São Paulo** (www.bienal.org.br; Parque do Ibirapuera, Moema), founded in 1951, has grown into one of the world's most important arts events. Many of the participants are working artists who have been nominated by their home country. In addition, a guest curator chooses a theme and invites his or her own favorites. At its best, the Bienal offers the world a chance to view mind-bending contemporary art. Certainly it cannot fail to be impressive for its sheer size and diversity.

The event is held during even-numbered years, generally from October to December, in a sprawling pavilion designed by modernist master Oscar Niemeyer in the leafy Parque do Ibirapuera. In recent years, admission has been free, though this is subject to funding.

Chi Fu
CHINESE $$

(Praça Carlos Gomes, Liberdade; mains R$18-50; ⏰11am-4pm & 6-10pm Mon-Fri, 11am-5pm Sat & Sun) This seriously authentic Cantonese eatery near the Liberdade metro station appears pricy until the portions arrive: they can easily serve three and a small pony. The decor, the circular tables, the family-style seating and the staff – who barely have a grasp on Portuguese – are straight from the Motherland. Great spot, though smiling service isn't the priority.

✗ Avenida Paulista, Jardins & Around

Jardins is your place to splurge; it offers an incredibly dense collection of Brazil's most illustrious restaurants, plus some surprisingly reasonable choices to boot.

Bacio di Latte
GELATO $

(Map p226; ☎3662-2573; www.baciodilatte.com.br; Oscar Freire 136, Cerqueira César; scoops from R$8; ⏰noon-11pm Mon-Sat, to 10pm Sun; 🛜🍴) 🌿 A Scotsman and two Italians finally did what nobody outside Buenos Aires could previously do: produce amazing Italian gelato in South America. Voted the city's best in 2011 and 2012, it's Brazil's best as well. Also in **Vila Madalena** (Map p235; Harmonia 337, Vila Madalena; 🛜) and on **Bela Cintra** (Map p226; Bela Cintra 1829, Cerqueira César).

Maria Brigadeiro
SWEETS $

(Map p226; www.mariabrigadeiro.com.br; Capote Valente 68, Pinheiros; sweets R$3.50; ⏰9am-7pm Mon-Sat; 🍴) *The* place to come for *brigadeiro* (chocolate bonbons of condensed milk, butter and chocolate powder), served in sweet-tooth-satiating gourmet versions like pistachio, *doce de leite* (creamy milk and sugar concoction) with walnuts and *cachaça* (sugarcane alcohol). The adorable workshop, Brazil's first *atelier* dedicated to its most iconic sweet, serves espresso for those eating in, but it's a zoo of take-away chocolate ecstasy.

It's just a block away from Metrô Oscar Freire, 'scheduled' to open in 2013.

St Louis
BURGERS $

(Map p226; www.stlouisburger.com.br; cnr Batataes & Joaquim Eugênio de Lima, Jardins; burgers R$21-30; ⏰noon-3pm Tue-Sun & 6:30-10:30pm daily) As with its pizza, São Paulo is serious about its burgers (a full-on gourmet-burger war is raging). This intimate, unpretentious burger joint is one of the city's best, and the American-born owner has managed to perfect the char. Our favorite is the Pepper Crust (R$30). It's six blocks southwest of Paulista.

Benjamin Abrahão
PADARIA $

(Map p226; ☑ 3061-4004; www.benjaminabrahao. com.br; José Maria Lisboa 1397, Jardins; sandwiches R$9.70-22.30, buffet R$25.40; ☺6am-9:30pm; ☑) The French-born Brazilian running the show at one of the city's best *padarias* (bakeries) started making bread when he was 13, taught by Austrian, Swiss and German immigrants. You can't go wrong with sandwiches here, nor anything baked.

Asia House
SELF-SERVE, ASIAN $

(Map p226; ☑ 3064-0493; www.asiahouse.com. br; Augusta 1918, Jardins; per kg R$42.70; ☺11am-3:30pm Tue-Sat) For surprisingly good, fairly priced and lightning-quick (mostly farmed salmon) sushi, this per kilo buffet just off Av Paulista is a great option. You'll also find classic Japanese and Chinese dishes, from tempura to Kung Pao chicken.

Casa Santa Luzia
SELF-CATERING $

(Map p226; ☑ 3897-5000; www.santaluzia.com. br; Alameda Lorena 1471, Jardins; ☺8am-8:45pm Mon-Sat) Gourmet groceries and imported brands.

Bio Alternativa
VEGETARIAN $

(Map p226; ☑ 3898-2971; www.bioalternativa.com. br; Alameda Santos 2214, Jardins ; buffet R$27; ☺noon-3pm Mon-Fri; ☑☎) ✿ Just a block off Av Paulista lies this vegetarian oasis, which offers a buffet lunch with up to half a dozen hot dishes – some vegan and all made with carefully selected, largely organic ingredients.

Capim Santo
BRAZILIAN, SELF-SERVE $$

(Map p226; ☑ 3068-8486; www.capimsanto. com.br; Rocha Azevedo 471, Jardins; dinner mains R$48-98, lunch buffet weekday/Sat/Sun R$49/67/73; ☺noon-3pm & 7:30-midnight Tue-Fri, 12:30-4pm Sat, 12:30-5pm & 8pm-midnight Sun; ☎) ✿ Top chef Morena Leite turns out excellent regional Brazilian fare, with an emphasis on local and organic ingredients, served in a relaxed, beautifully Brazilian indoor-outdoor space. The weekday buffet is the affordable way to get yourself into this high-end spot.

Zena Caffé
ITALIAN $$

(Map p226; www.zenacaffe.com.br; Peixoto Gomide 1901; mains R$27-57; ☺noon-midnight Sun-Wed, to

1am Thu-Sat; ☎) Despite his mug being everywhere, including TV – on *Homens Gourmet* (*Gourmet Men*) – chef Carlos Bertolazzi remains a humble, immediately likable dude's dude. His menu, focused largely on the cuisine from his Ligurian bloodline, is homey and fiercely authentic Italian comfort food at prices that won't infuriate you. His gnocchi, focaccia and ragù are all outstanding, but you can't go wrong.

Z Deli
DELI $$

(Map p226; www.zdelisanduiches.com.br; Haddock Lobo 1386, Cerqueira César; sandwiches R$21-32; ☺noon-midnight Mon-Thu, to 1am Fri & Sat, to 11pm Sun) The servers can barely maneuver within this tiny real-deal deli that has capitalized on the city's odd combination of storied Jewish history but lack of the food that normally goes with it. Here you'll find awesome gourmet pastrami, roast beef and turkey sandwiches, bagels and lox – hell, we even saw an authentic cheesecake emerge at one point.

★ Maní
BRAZILIAN $$$

(☑ 3085-4148; www.manimanioca.com.br; Joaquim Atunes 210, Jardim Paulistano; mains R$49-72; ☺noon-3pm Tue-Sat, 8-11:30pm Tue-Thu, from 8:30pm Fri & Sat, noon-4:30pm Sun) Maní will astound you. This rustic-chic restaurant run impeccably by a Brazilian-Spanish couple is often touted as Sampa's best Brazilian restaurant, and rightly so. The inventive slow-cooked egg (1½ hours at 63°C) is more famous, but the deconstructed Waldorf salad and the house-cooked potato chips topped with filet Mignon are true culinary coups.

The contemporary Brazilian dishes are best savored when your taste buds acquiesce to the five-course seasonal menu (R$160) or the far more dramatic *degustação* (with/without wine R$450/310).

Patuá da Baiana
BAHIAN $$$

(Map p226; ☑ 3115-0513, 98312-5302; patuadabaiana@bol.com.br; Luis Barreto 74A , Bela Vista; meals R$75-100; ☺by reservation) It's expensive; we probably shouldn't even include it; but the experience at Bahian beauty Bá's 'secret' underground restaurant in her own home is just too priceless. You must call ahead and know someone who knows someone. If Bá digs your vibe, she greets you with open arms and treats you to a night of scrumptious Bahian specialties.

SÃO PAULO STATE AVENIDA PAULISTA, JARDINS & AROUND

Pizza Paulistana

Swarms of Italian immigrants settled in São Paulo in the late 19th century, giving the city one of the largest Italian populations in the world outside Italy and one of South America's best-kept culinary secrets. Locals say the pizza is so good, even the Italians are jealous!

Bráz Pizzaria

The experience at **Bráz** (www.brazpizzaria.com.br) will leave you thinking, 'Italy, schmataly.' Do as Brazilians do and order a Brahma draft beer (*chope*) followed by an appetizer of warm sausage bread (*pão de calabresa*) dipped in spiced olive oil, then let the feast commence.

Speranza

One of the oldest and most traditional pizzerias, **Speranza** (Map p226; www.pizzaria.com.br; Treze de Maio 1004, Bixiga; pizza R$33.50-61; ⊙6pm-1am Mon-Sat, to midnight Sun; ♨) in the Italian neighborhood of Bixiga, where the Famiglia Tarallo has been serving serious pizza since 1958. Perfect meal: the life-changing bruschetta appetizer followed by a fiercely traditional margarita pizza. No, wait: those calzones are insanely good, too.

Maremonti

This high-end pizza newcomer, **Maremonti** (Map p226; www.maremonti.com.br; Padre João Manuel 1160, Jardins; pizza R$33-89; ⊙lunch & dinner) is a little fancy, and the long list of pizzas on offer can be daunting, but it's notable for its four pizzas certified by the *Associazione Pizzaiuoli Napoletani* – the margarita will send you into a fit of indescribable satisfaction.

1. Maremonti 2. Bráz Pizzaria 3. Speranza

KEVIN RAUB ©

Acarajé (shrimp fritters made with a batter of black-eyed peas), moqueca (seafood stew) and bobó de camarão (shrimp with manioc sauce) – she chooses, not you – are most likely coming your way, and all the while Bá pulls off a one-woman show as a caipirinha extraordinaire as well. It's a night you won't soon forget.

Figueira Rubaiyat   STEAKHOUSE **$$$**
(Map p226; ☑3087-1399; www.rubaiyat. br; Haddock Lobo 1738, Jardins; steaks R$74-135; ⊙noon-3:30pm & 7pm-midnight Mon-Fri, noon-6pm Sun; ☎) Sprawling and luxurious like the massive limbs of the 150-year-old fig tree that spiders gracefully throughout its outdoor terrace, this top-of-the-line grill-restaurant serves up perhaps Sampa's best meat – go for Argentine or Brazilian picanha (R$103); you only live once – plus other delicacies from fresh oysters to Amazon river fish.

D.O.M.   BRAZILIAN, EUROPEAN **$$$**
(Map p226; ☑3088-0761; www.domrestaurante.com.br; Barão de Capamena 549, Jardins; 4-/8-course menu R$320/440; ⊙noon-3pm & 7pm-midnight Mon-Fri, 7pm-midnight Sat) Brazilian celebrity chef Alex Atala's small and deceptively casual contemporary Brazilian restaurant serves up some of the finest food in Sampa, which is saying a lot. Indeed, it placed sixth on the 2013 S. Pellegrino World's 50 Best Restaurants list, which foodies fawn over relentlessly.

For a blow-out, cutting-edge Brazilian meal, some say this is the spot, though we have never been personally blown away by it. Reservations mandatory.

Brasil a Gosto   BRAZILIAN **$$$**
(Map p226; ☑3086-3565; www.brasilagosto.com.br; Azevedo do Amaral 70, Jardins; mains R$52-98; ⊙noon-3pm & 7pm-midnight Tue-Thu, noon-5pm & 7pm-1am Fri & Sat, noon-5pm Sun; ☎) At once cozy and modern, this Jardins staple is one of the city's finest for homegrown cuisine, specializing in innovative takes on iconic ingredients and regional dishes from around Brazil.

Dalva e Dito   BRAZILIAN **$$$**
(Map p226; ☑3068-4444; www.dalvaedito.com.br; Padre João Manuel 1115, Jardins; mains R$48-125; ⊙noon-3pm & 7pm-late Mon-Sat, noon-5pm Sun; ☎) Chef Alex Atala's casual Brazilian gastro-den got off to a rough start in 2009, but the Saturday midnight galinhada (rice and chicken stew buffet; R$59) might have saved the beautiful space and heart-in-the-right-place kitchen. Limited to the first 80 folks who turn up (line starts at 11pm), this classic is served buffet-style along with a late-night samba.

✗ Baixo Augusta & Around

Madhu   INDIAN **$**
(Map p226; ☑3262-5535; www.madhurestaurante.com.br; Augusta 1422, Baixo Augusta; meals R$14.90-19.90; ⊙noon-10:30pm Tue-Fri, from 1pm Sat & Sun; ☎☑) Brazil's first Indian fast-food joint, this simple-with-a-dash-of-style spot serves up good curry and naan amid Augusta's bustle.

Gopala Hari   LACTO-VEGETARIAN, INDIAN **$$**
(Map p226; ☑3283-1292; www.gopalahari.com.br; Antônio Carlos 429, Consolação; 3-course meals R$25; ⊙11:30am-3pm Mon-Fri, noon-3pm Sat; ☑) Cheap and elegant with delicious food, this Indian vegetarian lunch place offers two set menus daily, including soup, main and dessert. Simple food but prepared and served with care.

★Tordesilhas   BRAZILIAN **$$$**
(Map p226; ☑3107-7444; www.tordesilhas.com; Bela Cintra 465, Consolação; mains R$42-75; ⊙noon-3pm & 7pm-midnight Tue-Fri, noon-5pm & 7pm-midnight Sat, noon-5pm Sun; ☎) Behind a thick tangle of plants inside a golden-yellow colonial mansion, chef Mara Salles creates some of the most authentic contemporary Brazilian cuisine in the city, including perfectly grilled Amazonian fish and sun-cured beef with hearts of palm.

✗ Vila Madalena & Pinheiros

Don't miss the incredible **Feirinha Gastronômica** (Map p235; www.feirinhagastronomica.com.br; Praça Benedito Calixto, Pinheiros; items R$4-20; ⊙11am-7pm Sun), a rousing artisanal gastro-fair mixing amateur and professional chefs every Sunday.

Mercearia São Pedro   BOTECO **$**
(Map p235; Rodésia 34, Vila Madalena; appetizers for 2 R$18-37; ⊙9am-1am Mon-Fri, from 10am Sat, 11am-6pm Sun) This independently minded boteco (traditional bar) five minutes' walk from Metrô Vila Madalena is slammed at night, when packs of sexy bohemians swill properly chilled bottled beer, fresh pastels (stuffed, fried pastries; R$4.50); and excel-

lent, down-to-earth fare like *picanha* (rump roast) with sauteed onions. You'll have a great time here without – as the Brazilians say – leaving your pants.

★ **Feijoada da Lana**   BRAZILIAN **$$**
(Map p235; Aspicuelta 421, Vila Madalena; feijoada weekday/weekend R$30/55; ⊙noon-3:30pm Tue-Fri, 12:30-5pm Sat & Sun) Lana, a journalist by trade, offers her hugely popular version of *feijoada*, Brazil's national dish, inside a smallish Vila Madalena house. Production here isn't as elaborate as at more expensive options or fancy hotels, but it's long on smiling service, hearty goodness and (included on weekends!) *batidinhas de limão*, a sort of strained caipirinha.

In our humble opinion – and Anthony Bourdain's! – it's the best *feijoada* for the buck in town and you don't have to wait until Saturday to enjoy it.

Pitanga   BRAZILIAN **$$**
(Map p235; ☑3816-2914; www.pitangarestaurante.com.br; Original 162, Vila Madalena; buffet Mon-Thu/Fri/weekend R$39/45/49; ⊙noon-3:30pm & 7pm-midnight Tue-Sat, noon-5pm Sat & Sun; ☑) Behind a screen of vines lies a colonial mini-villa that has been transformed into a quaint and airy restaurant. A creative and hearty daily Brazilian lunch buffet ranges from a showstopping buffalo mozzarella and basil ravioli to a signature shrimp *feijoada*.

Lá da Venda   BRAZILIAN, SWEETS **$$**
(Map p235; www.ladavenda.com.br; Harmonia 161, Vla Madalena; mains R$26-45; ⊙11am-9pm Mon-Fri, from 9am Sat, to 5.20pm Sun; ☑) ✐ Chef Heloisa Bacellar, who honed her pastry skills in France, runs this adorable kitschy homewares shop–restaurant-bakery. Excellent Brazilian comfort food (her *pão de queijo*, made with *canastra* cheese, is Sampa's most heralded cheese bread) and seriously sinister sweets – both often organic – are devoured by a high-style crowd who burn off the calories shopping for cutesy household items.

Julice Boulangère   BAKERY **$$**
(Map p235; ☑3097-9144; www.juliceboulangere.com.br; Lacerda Franco 536, Pinheiros; breakfast R$28.10-52.50; ⊙8:30am-8pm) Escape to France at this excellent bakery and social breakfast spot, voted the city's best in 2012. The delightful fresh breads just keep coming and coming; the cappuccinos are perfect; and the leafy, villa-like patio does its best to

teleport you from the southern hemisphere's biggest city.

✖ Greater São Paulo

★ **Mocotó**   NORTHEASTERN **$$**
(☑2951-3056; www.mocoto.com.br; Nossa Senhora do Loreto 1100, Vila Madeiros; mains R$22.90-36.90; ⊙noon-11pm Mon-Sat, to 5pm Sun) It's worth the trek to Zona Norte for a meal at this darling of regional restaurants, where the city's most likeable and impressive young chef took over his father's simple emporium and started churning out Northeastern specialties. Suddenly, Rodrigo Oliveira's kitchen found itself a destination restaurant for paulistanos who otherwise couldn't have told you where the hell Vila Madeiros was.

For weekend lunches, it's a full-on gastroparty, with everyone digging into seriously homey comfort food at friendly prices chased by hundreds of artisan *cachaças*. Take the metro blue line until the end at Tucuruvi; from there, it's a R$16 to R$20 taxi ride.

🍷 Drinking & Nightlife

Coffee in São Paulo is generally excellent by Brazilian standards, thanks largely to the city's Italian heritage. **Santo Grão, Café Suplicy** and **Café Floresta** serve some of

Brazil's best beans – mountain-grown arabicas, mostly from Minas Gerais.

Traditional bar neighborhoods are **Vila Madalena** (witness the corner of Aspicuelta and Mourato Coelho on weekends!), which skews mainstream; along Rua Mario Ferraz in **Itaim Bibi**, where the rich, bold and beautiful play; and **Baixo Augusta**, where the GLS scene (Portuguese slang for Gay, Lesbian and Sympathetics) mingles with artsy, alterna-hipsters in the city's edgiest-coolest nightlife district. **Avenida Paulista** is also very lively at happy hour along the sidewalk bars near Joaquim Eugênio de Lima.

Partying in Sampa isn't cheap: clubbing prices here rival those of New York or Moscow. Nightclubs don't open until midnight, don't really get going until after 1am, and keep pumping until 5am or later. Then there are the after-hours places. The hottest districts are **Vila Olímpia** (flashy, expensive, electronica) and **Barra Funda/Baixo Augusta** (rock, alternative, down-to-earth). Some clubs offer a choice between a cover charge averaging R$10 to R$40 and way on up (unless otherwise noted) or a pricier *consumação* option, recoupable in drinks. Most clubs offer a discount for emailing or calling ahead to be on the list. Keep the card they give you on the way in – bartenders record your drinks on it, then you pay on the way out.

If money is no object and you want to hit the most exclusive clubs in the city, almost all of them are located in Itaim Bibi. Expect cover charges pushing R$300. Try **Provocateur** (www.provocateurclubsp.com.br), **Black**

Calavados (www.clubbc.com.br) or **Disco** (www.clubdisco.com.br), to name a few that will probably all have fallen out of favor by the time you read this.

Time Out (www.timeout.com/sao-paulo) is now published in the city, with all of the requisite entertainment and cultural listings. You can also check out the Portuguese-language *Guia da Folha*, which has a website (www.guia.folha.uol.com.br) as well as a supplement in the Friday edition of *Folha de São Paulo* newspaper.

🍷 Central São Paulo

★ **Alberta #3**　　　　　　　　BAR
(Map p222; www.alberta3.com.br; Av São Luís 272, Centro; cover R$15-35; ⊙ closed Sun & Mon) Finally, a great bar arrives in Centro – this three-story hipster hideout off Praça da República draws inspiration from '50s-era hotel bars and lobbies and rides a soundtrack steeped mostly in classic rock, jazz and soul (DJs often spin vinyl on the small dance floor). No cover between 7pm and 10pm.

Bar da Dona Onça　　　BAR, BRAZILIAN
(Map p222; ☎ 3129-7619; www.bardadonaonca.com.br; Av Ipiranga 200, Centro; mains R$34-54; ⊙ noon-11pm Mon-Sat, to 5pm Sun; ☎) In the striking Copan building, Dona Onça is one of downtown's best bars, not only for the packed crowds and excellent drinks – lauded chef Janaina Rueda's kitchen here churns out extraordinary Brazilian-heart-

WORTH A TRIP

A TRAIN! A TRAIN!

Founded by the British-owned São Paulo Railway Company, the pretty town of **Paranapiacaba** may sit amid the Atlantic rainforest of the Serra do Mar, about 40km southeast of São Paulo, but it still retains distinctly English traits, right down to a rough replica of Big Ben. Because of its remoteness, the town has been remarkably well preserved, with a neat grid of streets populated by English-style buildings of wood and brick. The home of the railway's chief engineer, a classically Victorian wood construction known as 'Castelinho,' has been converted into the **Museu do Castelo** (Caminho do Mendes; ⊙ 9am-4pm Tue-Sun) **FREE**, a small museum with period furnishings and fine views. Paranapiacaba also makes a good base for day hikes into the **Parque Estadual Serra do Mar.**

The best way to arrive in Paranapiacaba is on the '50s-era **Expresso Turístico Paranapiacaba** (☎ 0800-055-0121; www.cptm.sp.gov.br; ⬚) tourist train, which runs from São Paulo's Estação Luz at 8:30am on Sunday to Estação Paranapiacaba. Definitely book ahead – trains are a novelty in Brazil and this one, the country's second-oldest locomotive in operation, is very popular, especially in summer. Trains do not run on the second Sunday of each month.

land fare (chicken with okra, a fabulous pork calf, some say SP's best *feijoada* on Saturday).

Choperia Liberdade KARAOKE
(Rua da Glória 523, Liberdade; consumação Sun & Tue-Wed R$10, Thu-Sat R$10; ☺7pm-4am) For karaoke the old-fashioned way, head to this kitsch classic, which is decked out in Christmas lights, party favors, plug-in paintings and glowing aquariums. The crowd runs the gamut: scenesters, serious Japazillion songsters, Brazilian baby boomers and curious twentysomethings on a birthday binge.

Café Floresta CAFE
(Map p222; www.cafefloresta.com.br; Av Ipiranga 200, Centro; ☺6:20am-1am) With its antique murals, excellent brew and location on the ground floor of Niemeyer's Edifício Copan building near Praça da República, this stand-up-only cafe is a favorite of traditionalists. The creamy espresso (R$3) here is indeed excellent.

☻ Avenida Paulista, Jardins & Around

★Veloso BOTECO
(www.velosobar.com.br; Conceição Veloso 56, Vila Mariana; ☺5:30pm-12:30am Tue-Fri, from 12:45pm Sat, 4-11pm Sun) Arrive early to this tiny, outstanding *boteco* a quick walk from Vila Mariana's metro station – crowds fight over the few tables here for some of the city's best caipirinhas, in exotic flavors (*jabuticaba*, starfruit with basil, tangerine with *dedo-de-moça* pepper; R$15-19), and shockingly good *coxinhas* (battered and fried shredded chicken, *catupiry* cheese and spices; R$20).

The house-made hot sauce is the best we've found in the country. Put your name on the list, but you'll be drunk and full before you get a table.

MyNy Bar COCKTAIL BAR
(☎3071-1166; www.mynybar.com.br; Pedroso Alvarenga 1285, Itaim Bibi; cocktails R$26-37; ☺noon-3pm & 6pm-late Mon-Fri, 8pm-late Sat) Easily Brazil's best cocktail bar; so much so, whole, racquetball-sized ice cubes are constructed to ensure they don't melt and spoil the serious mixology happening here. It's beautiful, too, decked out as a dark and sexy Prohibition-era speakeasy.

Drinks include resurrection cocktails, popular offerings like Penicillin (two types of whiskey, ginger extract, lime juice and honey) and one of only three drinkable bloody Marys we have ever found in South America.

★Santo Grão CAFE, BREAKFAST
(Map p226; ☎3062-9294; www.santograo.com.br; Oscar Freire 413, Jardins; coffee R$4.80-11.50, mains R$19-60; ☺10am-1pm Mon, 9am-1am Tue-Sat, to midnight Sun; ☎) São Paulo's most serious coffee haunt serves cappuccinos that are, quite simply, as good as those in Italy. Beans are toasted in back while the little terrace reverberates with caffeine-fueled conversation. A fab bistro menu serves eclectic fare, everything from *huevos rancheros* and waffles for breakfast to rarer mains like Thai baby beef and pistachio-crusted salmon. Insane people-watching.

Café Suplicy CAFE
(Map p226; ☎3083-0666; www.suplicycafes.com.br; Alameda Lorena 1430, Jardins; ☺7:30am-10pm) Refined industrial-chic feel and outrageously good coffee and pastries.

Suco Begaço JUICE BAR
(Map p226; www.sucobagaco.com.br; Haddock Lobo 1483, Jardins; juice R$5.90-12.50; ☺8am-6pm, from noon Sun; ☎) The city's best juice spot – this trendy cafe burns through 600 glasses daily, mixed with water, orange juice, tea or coconut water. Also offers awesome-value, build-your-own salads and sandwiches.

Skye BAR
(www.unique.com.br; Av Brigadeiro Luis Antônio 4700, Jardim Paulista; ☺noon-1am) Dress up a little for the rooftop bar on the top floor of the Hotel Unique, whose sleek design and unparalleled views make it the perfect place for a sundown cocktail.

Bar Balcão BAR
(Map p226; ☎3063-6091; Melo Alves 150, Jardins; ☺6pm-1am) With good wine, excellent light meals and a simple but elegant design built around a cleverly serpentine bar, this Jardins delight is especially popular with well-heeled designers, foreign correspondents and artists.

☻ Baixo Augusta

★Caos BAR
(Map p226; www.caos584.com.br; Augusta 584, Baixo Augusta; ☺8pm-late Tue-Fri, from 9pm Sat) Antique bicycles, hubcaps, household appliances, keychains – you name it, it's stuffed

WORTH A TRIP

EMBU

Founded in 1554, Embu spent most of its life as a quiet colonial village until, in the 20th century, it was swallowed up by São Paulo, whose center sits about 30km to the west. Yet Embu has managed to retain much of its colonial core, thanks largely to the hippies, artists and intellectuals who made the town their refuge from São Paulo's concrete jungle, starting in the 1970s. Today the town makes a popular weekend retreat for paulistanos, when local artisans offer their wares at the outdoor **feira** (market; Largo dos Jesuitas; ⏰9am-6pm Sat & Sun). The area around the *feira* is full of antique and crafts shops that make good browsing on other days of the week.

There is a **tourist office** (Centro De Atendimento Ao Turista; ☎4704-6565; Largo 21 de Abril; ⏰8am-5pm Mon-Fri, 9am-6pm Sat & Sun) just off the main plaza. **O Garimpo** (☎4704-6344; www.ogarimpo.com; Rua da Matriz 136; mains R$26-65; ⏰11:30am-10pm; 🐾) is a pleasant spot for the peckish, with a veranda, a colonial dining room, a beer garden, a pub and a huge menu ranging from German specialities to *moquecas* (Bahian seafood stews).

From São Paulo, catch the EMTU bus 033 'Embu' (R$3.35, one hour, about 15 minutes) from the stop at **Teodoro Sampaio 323** (Map p226), about 100m down the street from Metrô Clínicas.

inside this alternative hangout that's a microcosm of all that's great about the neighborhood: among the junkyard aesthetic, you get lip-locked lesbians, beer fiends downing Brazilian microbrews, hot-rod gearheads arguing pinstripe width and gringos taking it all in. Good times.

Beco 203   CLUB
(Map p226; www.beco203.com.br; Augusta 609, Baixo Augusta; cover R$15-30; ⏰from 11pm Tue-Sat) This straightforward Porto Alegre transplant is chock-full of teenage anarchists and pop fans on Tuesday, when it commandeers see-and-be-seen honors for the under-30 set. Other nights focus on indie rock.

Astronete   BAR, CLUB
(Map p226; www.astronete.com.br; Matias Aires 183, Baixo Augusta; admission R$20-40; ⏰10pm-5am Thu-Sat) A few years in and still a favorite among the counterculture: freaks, geeks and gaggles of *alternativos* gather over rock, electro, indie and soul could now be considered a Baixo Augusta classic.

Z Carniceria   BAR
(Map p226; www.zcarniceria.com.br; Augusta 934, Baixo Augusta; mains R$18-31; ⏰7pm-1am Tue-Wed & Sun, to 2am Thu-Sat; 🐾) Underground goes upscale at this Augusta staple, themed as butcher shop-chic, from the door handles fashioned from meat cleavers to the cow skulls on the wall. The indie-rockabilly crowd rules here, but others mingle in.

Volt   BAR
(Map p226; Haddock Lobo 40, Baixo Augusta; consumação R$30; ⏰9pm-2am Fri & Sat) Owner Facundo Guerra has decked out this trendy joint with the neon signs that used to light up the houses of ill repute on Augusta. Today the signs attract the young and well heeled like moths.

🎧 Barra Funda

D-Edge   CLUB
(☎3665-9500; www.d-edge.com.br; Auro Soares de Moura Andrade 141, Barra Funda; cover R$20-70; ⏰11pm-late Mon & Wed-Sat) With one of the city's most remarkable sound systems and a roster of world-famous DJs, this mixed gay-straight club is a 'don't miss' for fans of electronica.

🍽 Vila Madalena & Pinheiros

São Cristóvão   BOTECO
(Map p235; Aspicuelta 533, Vila Madalena; mains R$36-74) This wildy atmospheric *boteco* is spilling over with football memorabilia from the owner's collection, more than 3500 pieces in all.

Empório Alto de Pinheiros   BEER BAR
(www.altodospinheiros.com.br; Vupabussu 305, Alto de Pinheiros; mains R$18-41; ⏰noon-midnight Sun-Thu, to 1am Fri & Sat) This neighborhood secret started as a beer emporium and in-

volved into a full-on gourmet beer bar. *Cerveza* geeks fret nervously over which of the 400 bottled or an astonishing (for Brazil) 10 choices on draft, including rarer Brazilian microbrews, to choose from. You can drop anywhere from R$7 to R$515 here on brews.

★**SubAstor** COCKTAIL BAR
(Map p235; ☑3815-1364; www.subastor.com.br; Delfina 163, Vila Madalena; ⏲8pm-3am Tue-Thu, to 4am Fri & Sat) This dark and speakeasy-sexy bar sits below a *boteco* called Astor (extraordinarily great as well for food and caipirinhas), hence the name: SubAstor ('Below Astor'). Sincere mixology goes down here, from the ubiquitous but excellent *caju amigo* (*cachaça* and cashew juice) to more cutting-edge liquid art.

Filial BAR
(Map p235; www.barfilial.com.br; Fidalga 254, Vila Madalena; mains R$18-38; ☎) An extensive *cachaça* menu, creamy *chope* (draft beer) and fantastic Brazilian bar munchies (try the *bolinhos de queijo*, or fried cheese balls) served late draws swarms of the young and fun to this popular Vila Madalena *boteco*.

Coffee Lab CAFE
(Map p235; www.raposeiras.com.br; Fradique Coutinho 1340, Vila Madalena; coffee R$5-12; ⏲10am-7pm Mon-Fri, 11am-8pm Sat) Both caffeine junkie and international connoisseur, there are few brasileiras as crazy about coffee as the adorable Isabela Raposeiras, who runs this part cafe, part barista school. This is the spot to go for single-origin varieties as well as outside-the-box preparations.

Canto da Ema CLUB
(Map p235; www.cantodaema.com.br; Faria Lima 364, Pinheiros; cover R$16-28; ⏲10:30pm-4am Wed-Thu, to 5am Fri & Sat, 7pm-midnight Sun) For a break from São Paulo's danceterias, this relaxed club specializes in *forró universitário*, a more approachable version of the high-octane dance music of the Northeast.

☆ **Entertainment**

Live Music

★**Studio SP** LIVE MUSIC
(Map p226; www.studiosp.org; Augusta 591, Baixo Augusta; ⏲11pm-late Tue-Sat) This large, alt-bent cultural space is Sampa's hottest spot for live local music. Early sessions are free.

Bourbon Street Music Club JAZZ, SALSA
(☑5095-6100; www.bourbonstreet.com.br; Rua dos Chanés 127, Moema; cover R$35-65; ⏲10:30pm-late

Tue & Wed, from 11:30pm Thu, from midnight Fri & Sat) The top spot for live jazz and blues in Sampa, Bourbon Street has hosted the likes of BB King and Ray Charles.

Barretto MPB, JAZZ
(Map p226; ☑3896-4000; www.fasano.com.br; Vittorio Fasano 88, Jardins; cover R$37; ⏲7pm-3am Mon-Fri, from 8pm Sat) Hands down one of the best places to see live music in the world, this bar inside the Hotel Fasano recalls pre-war Milan and attracts top jazz and popular Brazilian musicians who normally play far larger venues.

Classical, Ballet & Opera

Theatro Municipal THEATER, OPERA
(Map p222; ☑3223-3022; www.teatromunicipal. sp.gov.br; Praça Ramos de Azevedo, Centro) Operas, classical ballets and symphonic music are held in São Paulo's most ornate theater. At the time of writing, the theater was closed for a major restoration. Check website for a progress report and alternative venues.

Sala São Paulo CLASSICAL
(Map p222; ☑3367-9500; www.salasaopaulo.art.br; Praça Júlio Prestes, Centro) Excellent classical-music venue, renowned for its fine acoustics, in refurbished train station Estação Júlio Prestes.

Sports

São Paulo's three biggest football teams are **São Paulo FC** (www.saopaulofc.net), which plays at the 67,428-capacity Estádio do Morumbi (a 2016 Olympic Games venue); **Palmeiras** (www.palmeiras.com.br), who will have moved to their new 60,000-capacity Nova Arena Palestra Itália, near Barra Funda, by end of 2013; and **Corinthians** (www.corinthians.com.br), who played at 40,199-capacity Estádio do Pacaembu at the time of research but moved to the new R$820-million Arena de Itaquera, 24km east of Centro, in late 2013. This new stadium, reachable from Metrô Corinthians-Itaquera, will host six 2014 FIFA World Cup matches.

🛍 **Shopping**

For remarkable bargains, head to Rua 25 de Março, just north of the historic center, where wholesalers sell a dizzying variety of deeply discounted goods from around the world. For high fashion and high-end home furnishings, wander Rua Oscar Freire and surrounding streets in the Jardins district. For high-end luxury shopping, **Shopping JK Iguatemi** (www.jkiguatemi.com.br; Juscelino

Kubitschek 2041, Vila Olímpia; ⊘ 10am-10pm Mon-Sat, 2-8pm Sun) in Vila Olímpia, opened in 2012, is South America's most luxurious and worth a stroll for the sheer opulence of it all.

Bookstores

Livraria Cultura   BOOKS
(Map p226; ☑ 3170-4033; www.livrariacultura.com.br; Av Paulista 2073, Bela Vista; ⊘ 9am-10pm Mon-Sat, noon-8pm Sun; ☗) Spread out over three stores on the ground floor of the Conjunto Nacional building, this is hands-down the city's best bookstore. There is a large selection of both English-language books and travel guides, plus a pleasant cafe.

Livraria da Vila   BOOKS
(Map p226; ☑ 3062-1063; www.livrariadavila.com.br; Alameda Lorena 1731, Jardins; ⊘ 10am-10pm Mon-Sat, 11am-8pm Sun) A gem of contemporary architecture as well as a fine bookstore.

Clothing & Shoes

Espaço Havaianas   SHOES
(Map p226; ☑ 3079-3415; www.havaianas.com; Oscar Freire 1116, Jardins; ⊘ 10am-8pm Mon-Sat, noon-6pm Sun; ☗) You will find flip-flops in every imaginable design and hue – and at quite reasonable prices – at the flagship store for Brazil's favorite beach footwear, boldly designed by Isay Weinfeld in a striking and minimalist space that is as beautiful to look at as the clientele inside.

Galeria Melissa   SHOES
(Map p226; ☑ 3083-3612; www.melissa.com.br; Oscar Freire 827; ⊘ 10am-7pm Mon-Fri, to 5pm Sat) This temple to high-end plastic footwear offers bold and unique designs by an international potpourri of creative folk like Vivienne Westwood, Zaha Hadid and Karim Rasheed, but is as notable for its consistently changing facade, which is a freestyle canvas for an ever-changing rotation of acclaimed Brazilian artists and designers – each new shoe line brings a completely new storefront.

Galeria do Rock   CLOTHING
(Map p222; ☑ 3223-8402; www.galeriadorock.com.br; São João 439, Centro; ⊘ 10am-6:30pm Mon-Fri, to 6pm Sat) This seven-floor shopping center is an anthropologically fascinating gathering point for São Paulo's underground communities, from punks to goths to metal heads. Hundreds of shops hawk everything from CDs and concert T-shirts to black capes and extreme piercing, divided up amongst three concepts: Art, Music and Attitude.

Galeria Ouro Fino   CLOTHING
(Map p226; ☑ 3082-7860; www.galeriaourofino.com.br; Augusta 2690, Jardins; ⊘ 11am-8pm Mon-Sat) From hip-high boots to camouflage club gear, this old-fashioned, three-story mall has been turned into ground zero for *alternativo* shoppers. Has 110 stores.

Salinas   SWIMWEAR
(Map p226; www.salinascompras.com.br; Melo Alves 344, Cerqueira Cesar; ⊘ 10am-7pm Mon-Fri, to 6pm Sat) Always dreamed of hitting the beach wearing virtually nothing? Salinas is one of the country's trendiest bikini brands. New collections range from R$188 to R$398, but upstairs you'll find days-gone-by bargains from R$40.

Markets

Feira da República   HANDICRAFTS
(Map p222; Praça da República; ⊘ 9am-5pm Sat & Sun) This open-air market specializes in handicrafts and painting.

Feira Benedito Calixto   ANTIQUES
(Praça Benedito Calixto, Pinheiros; ⊘ 9am-7pm Sat) Open-air market for handicrafts and antiques, plus food stalls and live music.

Souvenirs

★ Casa da Vila   HANDICRAFTS, HOME DECOR
(☑ 5575-2757; www.casadavila.com.br; Capitão Calvalcanti 82, Vila Mariana; ⊘ 10am-7pm Mon-Fri, to 4pm Sat) ✐ This gorgeously preserved 1929 mansion on a quiet residential street walking distance from Metrô Vila Mariana is Sampa's best spot for high-quality, affordable Fair Trade handicrafts. Over 3000 items from 27 Brazilian states fill each of the home's rooms by theme. A must.

🛈 Orientation

Because it grew at dizzying speeds and without a master plan, São Paulo has no single grid of streets but rather a hodgepodge of grids in more or less concentric circles that radiate out from the historic center. This, together with a dearth of easily identifiable landmarks, means it's easy to get hopelessly lost.

Sitting atop a low ridge and lined with skyscrapers, Av Paulista is the city's main drag, dividing its largely working-class Centro from tonier neighborhoods to the south. At its western end, Av Paulista is crossed by the corridor made up of Av Rebouças and Rua da Consolação, which roughly divides the city's eastern and western halves.

SERRA DA MANTIQUEIRA

About 180km northeast of São Paulo, the beautiful green peaks of the Serra da Mantiqueira are a hotbed of mountain biking and trekking for paulistanos, and are a hugely popular winter weekend getaway for paulistas who enjoy the novelty of wearing woolens. **Campos do Jordão**, Brazil's highest city, is a kitschy and comfortable base from which to explore the nearby peaks, which are home to some of the last remaining virgin *araucária* (Paraná pine) forests and proffer spectacular views of the Paraíba valley.

Popular attractions in the area are **Horto Florestal State Park** (☑ reception desk 3663-3762; admission per vehicle R$6; ☺ 9am-4pm), 14km east from Campos and home to the largest *araucária* reserve in the state, offers fine walks of varying levels of difficulty. One of the most popular climbs in the surrounding mountains is the 1950m **Pedra do Baú**. To explore the area on wheels, stop by **Desafius** (☑ 3664-6096; www.desafius.com.br; Frei Orestes Girardi 3159, Capivari) in Campos. **Altus** (☑ 3663-4122; www.altus.tur.br; Roberto Simonsen 1724, Vila Inglesa) organizes groups for hiking, rock climbing, mountain biking and other outdoor adventure activities.

Campos itself is a well-heeled getaway. The peak tourist period is July, when the town receives up to a million tourists (expect a minimum one-week stay at this time; there are steep discounts on weekdays and outside winter months). Budget travelers should gravitate to **Campos do Jordão Hostel** (☑ 3662-2341; www. camposdojordaohostel.com.br; Pereira Barreto 22; dm/d R$86/253; ☑ ☺), in a grand old building from the early 20th century. For Canadian-themed kitsch and coziness, try **Canadá Lodge** (☑ 3663-1697; www.canadalodge.com.br; Plínio de Godoy 403, Capivari; d from R$944; ☑ @ ☺); and for luxurious surrounds and service, the traditional **Grande Hotel Campos do Jordão** (☑ 3260 6000; www.grandehotelsenac.com.br; Frei Orestes Girardi; d incl full board from R$1190; ☑ ❋ @ ☺ ☒).

Campos fancies itself a bit of a gastronomic hub and in fact is second only to São Paulo for starred restaurants in the state, but dining out here is expensive and the majority of spots are more show than substance. **Baronesa Landscape** (☑ 3662-1121; www.baronesavonleithner.com.br; Alto da Boa Vista 3025; mains R$15-38; ☺ breakfast, lunch & dinner Thu-Sun), a wonderful cafe in a striking glass structure tucked away high above Campos on forested grounds, is worth the climb out of town. **Arte da Pizza** (☑ 3668-6000; www.grandehotelsenac.com.br; Grande Hotel, Frei Orestes Girardi, 3549, Capivari; pizzas R$35-81; ☺ dinner Thu-Sun Aug-Jun,lunch & dinner Jul), where pizzas are interrupted three times in the wood-burning oven to be slathered with olive oil so they don't dry out, and the award-winning **Harry Pisek** (☑ 3663-4030; www.harrypisek.com.br; Pedro Paulo 857; mains R$37.90-78.90; ☺ 11am-5pm Mon-Fri, to midnight Sat, to 6:30pm Sun; ☺), where Chef Pisek studied the art of sausage-making in Germany and is celebrated for his homemade productions, can be filed under expensive but worth it.

For tourist info, stop by **C.I.T.** (☑ 3663-1098; Praça João de Sá s/n, Capivari; ☺ 9am-8pm Mon-Sat, to 2pm Sun).

Campos is served by **Passaro Marron** (www.passaromarron.com.br), which goes to São Paulo (R$35.90, three hours, six daily) and direct to Guarulhos airport once daily at 8am (R$34.35, 3½ hours); and **1001** (www.autoviacao1001.com.br), which heads once daily to Rio de Janeiro (R$49, five hours, 3:45pm).

To the north of Av Paulista lies what is generally called Centro, including Praça da República and around; the traditionally Italian Bela Vista area (also known as Bixiga); Luz, a newly refurbished cultural hub; the traditionally Japanese Liberdade; and the old commercial and historic core around Praça da Sé and its cathedral, including Triângulo and Anhangabaú.

Extending for about 10 blocks south of Paulista is the leafy neighborhood known as Jardins (the neighborhood's official name is Jardim Paulista), which has the lion's share of the city's tony restaurants and boutiques. Further south is the leafy, low-rise and exclusively residential area known as Jardim Europa and also the slightly less exclusive Jardim America. Southeast of Jardim Europa is sprawling Parque do Ibirapuera, while to the west lie the upscale neighborhoods of Pinheiros and Vila Madalena. South of Jardim Europa lie the upmarket bastions of Vila Olímpia and Itaím Bibi, both of which are increasingly important business centers.

The *Guia São Paulo* is probably the best guide for navigating the city, with street maps, hotel and restaurant listings and bus lines. It has the clearest presentation of any street directory. Pick one up at any kiosk around town for about R$30.

Tourist offices also offer a free user-friendly map covering all of the city's most relevant neighborhoods.

❶ Information

EMERGENCY

Deatur Tourist Police (☎3257-4475; Rua da Consolação 247) A special police force just for tourists, with English-speaking officers.

MEDICAL SERVICES

Einstein Hospital (☎2151-1233; www.einstein. com.br; Albert Einstein 627, Morumbi) Located on a southwestern corner of Morumbi, Einstein is one of Latin America's best hospitals.

Sírio-Libânes Hospital (☎3155-0200; www. hospitalsiriolibanes.org.br; Dona Adma Jafet 91, Bela Vista) Another state-of-the-art hospital near Av Paulista.

MONEY

ATMs are widely available throughout the city. Bradesco, HSBC and Banco do Brasil are feeless and the most foreign-friendly. Note that most are closed from 10pm to 6am for security reasons. Always use ATMs inside banks to avoid cloning. *Always.*

POST

Correios (www.correios.com.br) locations are widespread throughout São Paulo.

SAFE TRAVEL

Crime is an issue in São Paulo, though the majority is limited to the city's periphery and tourists aren't often targeted unless you're the unlucky victim of an *arrastão*, when armed bandits rob an entire restaurant of patrons in the blink of an eye (a disturbing trend in the city of late). General rules of thumb include being especially careful in the center at night and on weekends (when fewer people are about) and watching out for pickpockets on buses, around Praça da Sé and on Linhas 1 (blue) and 3 (red) of the metro. Otherwise, maintain the same common-sense vigilance you would in other developing-world metropolises and you shouldn't fall victim to anything more than the traffic, crowds and pollution!

TOURIST INFORMATION

C.I.T (Map p222; ☎3331-7786; www.cidadede saopaulo.com; Praça da República) Airport (Terminals 1 & 2; ⏰6am-10pm) Mercado Municipal (Map p222; Rua da Cantareira 306, Rua E, Portão 4; ⏰9am-6pm Mon-Sat, 7am-4pm Sun) Paulista (Map p226; Av Paulista 1853; ⏰7am-6pm) Olida (Map p222; São João 473) Tietê Bus Station (Rodoviário Tietê, Santana; ⏰6am-10pm) São Paulo's tourist-information booths all have good city maps, as well as helpful walking maps for individual neighborhoods. It also offers a monthly events listing guide, as well as a guide specifically for the gay and lesbian community.

English is spoken, though the Paulista, Mercado Municipal and Olida locations are the most helpful.

VISAS

Polícia Federal (☎3538-5000; www.dpf.gov. br; Hugo Dantola 95, Lapa; ⏰8am-4:30pm Mon-Fri) For visa extensions, head to this office about 4km west of the Metrô Barra Funda.

❶ Getting There & Away

AIR

São Paulo is the Brazilian hub for many international airlines and thus the first stop for many travelers. Before buying a domestic ticket, check which of the city's airports the flight departs from, as the international airport also serves many domestic flights.

Guarulhos (recast as GRU Airport for the World Cup), the international airport, is 25km east of the center. Most domestic and all international flights depart from Terminals 1 and 2 in the main building, but Azul, Trip and Passaredo operate out of the new Terminal 4, 2km to the southwest. A free shuttle runs every four minutes, connecting the terminals 24 hours a day. At time of writing, plans were in place for additional domestic airlines to move to this terminal, so check ahead. A new and glamorous Terminal 3 was under construction at time of writing for a planned 2014 opening.

The domestic-only airport, Congonhas (CGH), 14km south of the center, services many domestic destinations, including the majority of flights to Rio (Santos Dumont Airport), which depart every half-hour (or less).

BUS

São Paulo has four long-distance bus stations, all accessible by metro. Each terminal tends to specialize in a certain set of destinations, but there are no hard-and-fast rules, unfortunately. If you need to check which terminal services your destination, check out the Consulta De Viagens section of **Socicam** (www.socicam. com.br).

GAY & LESBIAN SÃO PAULO

Latin America's largest and most visible gay community supports a dizzying array of options, day and night. There are not only gay bars and discos but also restaurants, cafés, even a shopping center – **Shopping Frei Caneca** (Map p226; ☑3472-2000; www.frei-canecashopping.com; Frei Caneca 569, Baixo Augusta; ⊙10am-10pm Mon-Sat, 2-8pm), known as 'Shopping Gay Caneca,' has a largely gay clientele. And **São Paulo Pride** (www.gaypridebrazil.org/sao-paulo), usually celebrated in mid-June, is by most estimates the largest gay gathering in the world. São Paulo is also the only city in Brazil where same-sex public displays of affection are a fairly common sight, at least in certain 'safe' neighborhoods. These include the area just north of Praça da República, which tends to be more working class; Rua Frei Caneca just north of Av Paulista, which attracts an alternative crowd; and Rua da Consolaçao in Jardins, largely the domain of Sampa's upscale gay guys and gals.

Don't miss the bars surrounding Praça Benedito Calixto (p246) in Pinheiros on Saturday afternoons after the street fair; the corner of Frei Caneca and Peixoto Gomide in Baixo Augusta, where the early-evening pre-party at the otherwise nondescript *lanchonete* (snack bar) **Bar da Lôca** (Map p226; cnr Frei Caneca & Peixoto Gomide, Baixo Augusta; ⊙6am-1am) spills into the streets; and **Bella Paulista** (Map p226; ☑3214-3347; www.bellapaulista.com; Haddock Lobo 354, Cerqueira Cesar; sandwiches R$23.90-33.90; ⊙24hr; ☎), the 24-hour restaurant where everyone ends up after the clubs close; and the mixed gay-straight D-Edge (p244).

Other gay and lesbian venues:

The Week (☑3868-9944; www.theweek.com.br; Guaicurus 324, Lapa; cover R$35-70; ⊙midnight-8am Sat, 5pm-midnight Sun) Both luxurious and cavernous, this club is the place to go if you like sweaty, shirtless, gym-hardened bodies. With two dance floors, three lounges, six bars, state-of-the-art light and sound, and an outdoor pool, it's like a big gay world unto itself.

A Lôca (Map p226; ☑3159-8889; www.aloca.com.br; Frei Caneca 916, Baixo Agusta; ⊙midnight-late Wed-Sun) Still the reigning queen of trashy chic, this sprawling club is the point of reference for Sampa's *alternativos* – gay, straight, male, female and various combinations thereof. Music varies from punk to electronica to classic disco.

Bubu Lounge (☑3081-9546; www.bubulounge.com.br; Rua dos Pinheiros 791, Pinheiros; consumação R$30-60; ⊙midnight-late Thu-Sat, open 1 Sun per month) Bubu is one-stop shopping: gays, lesbians, bisexuals and no shortage of straight (but obviously not narrow) folks fill this blockbuster club, one of Sampa's biggest and best. Lines extend down the block to get in, where the multilevel space hosts a soundtrack that includes live MPB and '80s flashback on Saturday.

Farol Madalena (Map p235; ☑3032-6470; www.farolmadalena.com.br; Jericó 179, Vila Madalena; cover R$12; ⊙7pm-1am Thu, to 2am Fri & Sat, to midnight Sun) One of the city's top lesbian bars, this smallish place packs in the young ladies for dinner (mains R$29 to R$37), then live music and DJs as the evening progresses.

Bar Vermont (☑3071-1320; www.vermontitaim.com.br; Pedroso Alvarenga 1192, Itaim Bibi; ⊙7pm-2am Thu, 9pm-5am Fri & Sat, 5pm-midnight Sun) If shirtless electroheads aren't your thing, this modern GLS venue offers a rare but interesting alternative. Upstairs, the usual (cocktails and DJs), but downstairs is more chilled with live samba, MPB and the like, along with dinner. The crowd here skews chic.

Fran's Café (Map p226; ☑3083-1019; www.franscafe.com.br; Haddock Lobo 586, Jardins; ⊙24hr; ☎) Fight the local boys for an outdoor table at this cozy and very gay branch of a classic Sampa cafe.

The main terminal and South America's largest, Terminal Tietê, 4.5km north of Centro, offers buses to destinations throughout the continent. Avoid bus arrivals during early morning or late afternoon – traffic jams are absolutely enormous.

Sample travel times and *executivo* fares (where applicable) from São Paulo appear in the table opposite.

Buses to Santos leave about every half-hour from a separate bus station – the Terminal Intermunicipal do Jabaquara, which is at the end of the southern metro line (Metrô Jabaquara). There is also Terminal Bresser,

---

OFF THE BEATEN TRACK

SÃO PAULO SEASHORE ESCAPES

There's a lot more beach on São Paulo's coast than our pages could possible cover. In addition to the beach towns we feature, consider escaping the city and digging your toes into these additional sands, several of which won't be quite so crowded.

Santos

Though it never receives a star for cleanliness, Santos is the closest beach to the city of São Paulo, just over an hour away on a good traffic day. Due to oil money, it's a fun town in its own right, with lots of great bars and restaurants. Locals consider Boqueirão, between canals 3 and 4, to be the city's best beach. Santos' beachfront garden, clocking in at 5335m, is in the record books for the largest in the world.

Cometa (www.viacaocometa.com.br) buses to Santos leave frequently from Terminal Intermunicipal do Jabaquara in São Paulo (R$20.50, 1¼ hours).

Guarujá

With its fine beaches along the stretch of coast closest to São Paulo, once-glamorous Guarujá has suffered from overdevelopment. Still, if you can't get further afield, it retains some charm as a quick getaway – even if concrete towers line the beaches, which get packed with weekend day-trippers. A recent cleanup of waters and sands has renewed interest in a town that was the extreme of chic back in the '70s. Surfers should note that there are good waves along Praia do Tombo and Praia do Éden, reached by a downhill trail from the road to Pernambuco or Iporanga beaches that's a good bet for beating the crowds.

Ultra (www.viacaoultra.com.br) buses to Guarujá (R$34, 1¼ hours) leave throughout the day from Terminal Intermunicipal do Jabaquara in São Paulo.

Boiçucanga & Around

The laid-back surfer town of Boiçucanga makes a good base to explore the stretch of coast that runs almost due west from São Sebastião. The variety of beaches, many backed by the steeply rising Serra do Mar, is remarkable, and there's good surf at nearby Camburi and Maresias, which have also developed into major party towns, and Juqueí is popular with families.

Boiçucanga is reached from São Paulo (R$42, four hours, six daily), Guarujá (R$26, two hours, three daily) and São Sebastião (R$10.25, 40 minutes, three daily) with **Litorânea** (www.litoranea.com.br).

Ilha do Cardoso

As wild as it gets in São Paulo state, this ecological reserve near the state's southern border with Paraná offers gorgeous natural pools, waterfalls and untouched beaches, and is home to only 400 residents and no cars. Dark sands and brownish-grey sea don't sway the nouveau hippies, who love these beaches due to their isolation.

Two **Intersul** (www.intersul-transporte.com.br) buses per day leave São Paulo's Barra Funda bus station for Cananéia (R$56, five hours), from where a number of private operators offer boat service to the island along the waterfront. Prices vary, but expect to pay around R$20 per person (four-person minimum). You can also reach Cananéia from Iguape (R$22.80, 1¾ hours) via Pariquera.

near the Memorial do Imigrante in the east-zone district of Brás, with services to the south of Minas Gerais state, and Terminal Barra Funda in the west zone, near the Memorial da América Latina, for destinations in São Paulo state, Paraná, including Iguape and Cananéia, and all buses to the Pantanal.

ⓘ Getting Around

TO/FROM THE AIRPORT

Passaro Marron (www.passaromarron.com.br) operates two airport buses. The **Airport Bus Service** (www.airportbusservice.com.br; R$38) is the most efficient way to/from GRU Airport, making stops at Aeroporto Congonhas, Barra Funda, Tiête, Praça da República and various hotels around Av Paulista and Rua Augusta. The *cheapest* way is to catch suburban Airport Service lines 257 or 299 to/from Metrô Tatuapé (R$4.60, 30 to 45 minutes; easily confused with the flashier aforementioned Airport Bus Service – they depart right next to each other outside Terminal 2), which departs every 15 minutes between 5am and midnight. To the airport, exit Tatuapé to the left towards Shopping Metrô Boulevard Tatuapé and the buses are on the street below to the left as you cross the pedestrian bridge.

Guarucoop (www.guarucoop.com.br) is the only taxi service allowed to operate from the international airport and charges vacation-spoiling prices to the city (R$115.97 to Av Paulista, R$124.80 to Vila Madalena).

For Congonhas, catch bus 875A-10 'Perdizes-Aeroporto' from Metrô São Judas or catch a regular taxi (R$30 to R$50 to/from most neighborhoods of interest).

BUS

São Paulo's immense public-transport system, run by **SPTrans** (☑ toll-free 156; www.sptrans.com.br), is the world's most complex, boasting 15,000 buses and 1333 lines. Buses (R$3) are crowded during rush hours, confusingly thorough and can be prone to pickpockets. Watch your valuables, especially phones in pockets or backpack side pockets. The city tourist-information booths are excellent sources of information about buses.

METRO

You can reach many places on the excellent **Metrô São Paulo** (www.metro.sp.gov.br), the city's rapidly expanding subway system. The metro is cheap, safe and fast and runs from 4:40am to midnight. A single ride costs R$3. Refillable **Bilhete Único** cards are worthwhile for discounts transferring between bus and subway. New Linha-4 (Yellow) stations set to open in 2013 include tourist-friendly spots like Rua Oscar Freire, Higienópolis and Morumbi stadium.

TAXI

Taxis are plentiful, though because of long distances and traffic they can be expensive. For example, a ride from Jardins to the historic center should cost around R$30 to R$40. All taxis should be metered – if your driver doesn't turn the meter on, be sure to mention it. If the

BUSES FROM SÃO PAULO

DESTINATION	FARE (R$)	TIME (HR)	COMPANY
Angra dos Reis	62	7½	Reunidas (www.reunidas.com.br)
Asunción (Paraguay)	159	20	Pluma (www.pluma.com.br)
Belo Horizonte	97	8	Cometa (www.viacaocometa.com.br)
Brasília	105	15	Real Expresso (www.realexpresso.com.br)
Buenos Aires (Argentina)	324.50	36	Pluma (www.pluma.com.br)
Curitiba	94	6	Cometa (www.viacaocometa.com.br)
Florianópolis	124	11	Catatrinense (www.catarinense.net)
Foz do Iguaçu	165	15	Pluma (www.pluma.com.br)
Montevideo (Uruguay)	310	32	Eucatur (www.eucatur.com.br)
Paraty	48	6	Reunidas (www.reunidas.com.br)
Pantanal (Cuiabá)	224	26	Eucatur (www.eucatur.com.br)
Pantanal (Campo Grande)	177	13½	Andorinha (www.andorinha.com)
Recife	388	45	Itapemirim (itapemirim.com.br)
Rio de Janeiro	99	6	1001 (www.autoviacao1001.com.br)
Salvador	291	32	São Geraldo (www.saogeraldo.com.br)
Santos	20.50	1¼	Cometa (www.viacaocometa.com.br)
Santiago (Chile)	355.50	54	Pluma (www.pluma.com.br)

driver still doesn't, ask to be let out. If you need to call a taxi, try **Ligue Táxi** (☑ 2101-3030; www. liguetaxi.com.br) or **Coopertax** (☑ 2095-6000; www.coopertax.com.br). However, the easiest, safest and coolest way to get a taxi in Sampa is via the 99Taxis app, the favorite among local taxi drivers.

PAULISTA COAST

São Paulo's coast, known in Portuguese as the Litoral Paulista, is most spectacular in its northern reaches, especially around Ubatuba, thanks to the jungle-covered peaks of the Serra do Mar that reach all the way down to the Atlantic.

Ubatuba

☑ 0XX12 / POP 79,000

Draped with the rich flora of the Mata Atlântica, the peaks of the Serra do Mar provide a dramatic, emerald-green backdrop to the winding Ubatuba coastline. This region has become a preeminent resort for well-heeled paulistanos, with its elegant beach homes and a number of stylish hotels and pousadas, especially south of the town. Heading north toward neighboring Paraty in the state of Rio de Janeiro, beaches tend to be harder to reach but also wilder and more pristine, and the little-visited Parque Nacional da Serra da Bocaina spans both São Paulo and Rio de Janeiro states.

The town itself, known simply as 'Centro,' is perhaps uninspiring, save for its handsome waterfront promenade, pretty bay views and a few small beaches, but there is no shame in basing yourself here while you explore the northern and southern coastlines – and there's plenty of action at night.

◎ Sights & Activities

The town's prettiest beaches are best reached by bike (Ubatuba is well equipped with bike lanes) and the scenic bay has become a popular spot for stand-up paddling (SUP). The real trick, though, is to get to the remote beaches and picturesque islands outside the city. The tourist office can also offer information about hikes and guided visits to the adjacent state park, with good hiking trails into the thickly forested coastal range.

Ubatuba is also a major birdwatching hot spot, especially in October.

Uba's Adventures BICYCLE RENTAL
(☑ 3282-3947; www.ubasadventure.com.br; per 24hr R$25) Rent bicycles from here.

Boat Trips

Boat trips leave from Itaguá for the most popular island trip, **Ilha Anchieta** (around R$60, three to four hours). This protected nature reserve offers rare glimpses of fish and birds undisturbed in their natural habitats, but there are loads more less explored choices as well. These minicruises offer enviable views of the coast and its beautiful, deep-green waters. You can make reservations at the tourist office or many hotels and guesthouses. Alternatively, deal directly with operators who set up tables along the promenade in front of Itaguá beach. Cruise operators also leave from the Enseada and Saco da Ribeira neighborhoods. You can also see the local **Projecto Tamar** (www. tamar.org.br), which protects native turtles and their eggs.

Beaches

Within the district of Ubatuba there are some 74 beaches and 15 islands spread across 100km. The best two beaches in town are **Vermelha** (good for surfing) and **Cedro** (more secluded), both reachable on foot or by bike.

Regular buses run along the coastal road. Some of the best beaches south of Ubatuba include **Praia Vermelha** (3km), **Enseada** (8km), **Flamengo** (12km, on the Ponta do Flamengo), **do Lázaro** (16km) and **Domingos Dias** (18km). The big, loud party scene is 6km south of Ubatuba at **Praia Grande**.

North of town, the beaches are hidden away down steep hillsides. They're harder to find but good for boogie boarding and surfing and well worth the effort. Among the best are **Vermelha do Norte** (9km), **Itamambuca** (15km), **Félix** (17km), **Prumirim** (23km), **Ubatumirim** (33km) and **Picinguaba** (43km).

🛏 Sleeping

If you're without a car, Centro is the most convenient place to stay. From here you can catch local buses (R$3) to the beaches.

Ecotrip Hostel HOSTEL **$**
(☑ 3833-4036; www.ecotriphostel.com.br; Dom Joao III 573, Centro; dm R$45-50, s/d R$100/140;

@ 🔊🗲) The *simpatica* and English-speaking Malu runs this welcoming Centro hostel, the best place in town to get your bearings and meet fellow travelers. Located just five blocks from the water, it's a simple but well-managed spot, with a nice outdoor kitchen, a small pool and, in season, breakfast fruits directly from Manu's secret fruit garden.

Hotel Solar das
Águas Cantantes   HOTEL $$
(🖉 3842-0178; www.solardasaguascantantes. com.br; Estrada Saco da Ribeireira 951, Lázaro; s/d R$270/300; ❋🗐🗲) With quarters ranged around a lush courtyard, this grand, whitewashed colonial affair run by the son of the original Austrian owner sits a short walk from the stunning (if crowded) Praia do Lázaro. The high-ceilinged rooms have an austere elegance. The hotel's starred restaurant, renowned for its seafood stews (mains for two R$79 to R$157), is excellent.

Torre del Mar   POUSADA $$
(🖉 3832-2751; www.pousadatorredelmar.com. br; Milton de Holnda Maia 210, Itagua; r R$265; ❋🗐🗲) This Mediterranean-white pousada tucked away a few blocks from the main drag receives rave reviews from travelers, who praise the accommodating English-speaking owners. The 18 rooms are smallish but well maintained and great common areas include a fabulous interior garden and perfect little rooftop pool and patio.

A Pousadinha   POUSADA $$
(🖉 3832-2136; www.ubatuba.com.br/pousadinha; Guarani 686, Itaguá; s/d R$180/200; ❋🗐) This former boarding house offers just seven small and simple but airily stylish rooms around a narrow, lemon-yellow courtyard, making for palpable value on this expensive stretch of coast.

★ Pousada Picinguaba   POUSADA $$$
(🖉 3836-9105; www.picinguaba.com; Picinguaba; r incl dinner R$950; 🗲) Tucked away in a small fisherman's village north of Ubatuba is one of the region's most charming pousadas, a nine-room gem run by a French-Portuguese couple. Everything here, from the original artworks and furniture to the outdoor poolside tables overlooking the calm bay, is subtle, meticulously curated and designed to instill a sense of place without going overboard.

It's a fabulous little hidden get-away-from-it-all perched just enough above an authentic fishing village. Brazil at its finest.

Itamambuca
Eco Resort   RESORT, CAMPGROUND $$$
(🖉 3834-3000; www.itamambuca.com.br; Praia de Itamambuca; campsites per person from R$72, d from R$556; ❋🗐🗲) 🐾 Surrounded by dense vegetation and a short walk to one of the area's most remarkable beaches, this resort is worth the splurge. Simple rooms are colorful and largely built from recycled wood and bamboo. Facility highlights include a well-done overwater spa, birdwatching excursions, kiddie distractions galore, an outdoor gym and wonderful kayaking on the tranquil river.

The excellent, if pricey, camping facilities on the property are top rate – complete with refrigerators and stoves! – and packed with regulars who plant themselves in for weeks at a time. Rustic chalets are also available (for two people low/high season R$135/218, big discounts for longer stays).

✗ Eating

Don't miss *azul-marinho,* a delicious local stew of fish and green bananas. There are a number of cheap eateries in the town center where you can get simple meals for R$12 to R$18.

★ Integrale   BAKERY $
(www.padariaintegrale.com.br; Esteves da Silva 360, Centro; sandwiches R$5.50-12; ⊘7:30am-8:30pm Mon-Sat, to 7pm Sun; 🗐🖉) 🐾 This beautiful natural bakery, said to be Brazil's first, is definitely a rare breed along this coast. Choose from a very long list of wholegrain, chemical and preservative-free breads (the French lunch chef spent 10 years with Cirque du Soleil), salads, sandwiches, quiches, snacks and strong organic coffee, then tuck into it all on the lovely and lush patio.

Cantinho da Lagoa   BRAZILIAN, SEAFOOD $$
(Prumirim; mains R$39-45; ⊘9am-8pm) The sophisticated dishes emerging from this excellent beach shack perched on top of the rocks at Prumirim Beach are the result of the owner's stint in London kitchens. Fabio, who's from the village, invented one of the best dishes on this coast, the *cajutapu* (palm-heart pasta with grilled shrimp and *juçara* fruit sauce).

Extra-friendly service and one of the region's prettiest beaches are gravy. Make a day of it.

Bardolino
ITALIAN $$

(www.restaurantebardolino.com.br; Esteves da Silva 18, Centro; mains R$28-74; ☺noon-1am) This classy spot, housed in one of the rare colonial buildings in the minuscule historical portion of Centro, specializes in fresh northern Italian pastas and seafood. It's one of the few kitchens here that both feels like a professional chef is running the show and where the prices (most dishes cost between R$30 and R$40) feel appropriately in sync with the quality.

Terra Papagalli
SEAFOOD $$$

(Xavantes 537, Itaguá; mains for 2 R$97-119; ☺noon-midnight Dec & Jan, closed Mon & Tue Mar-Nov) This intimate restaurant along the waterfront manages to be both the least touristy and the most creative along this string of mostly carbon-copy options. A few dishes each night are served, depending on the catch (we scored with *dourada* with a lovely tamarind sauce and Brazil-nut rice), and it all goes down very romantically among the candlelit tables.

Peixe com Banana
SEAFOOD $$$

(🖉3832-1712; Guarani 255, Itaguá; mains for 2 R$72-145; ☺11:30am-10pm) Don't be fooled by the plastic tablecloths or the touristy seafront location. This is one of the region's most popular seafood joints, famed for its excellent version of *azul-marinho* (R$103 for two), fresh fish and *moquecas*.

☆ Entertainment

Blues on the Rocks
LIVE MUSIC

(www.bluesontherocks.com.br; Chico Santos 17, Itaguá; cover R$5-15; ☺7pm-late Dec-Feb, closed Sun-Tue Mar-Nov) This wildly popular rock, blues and jazz venue is consistently voted the best live-music spot on the Paulista coast.

❶ Information

C.I.T. (🖉3833-9123; cnr Conceição & Iperoig, Centro; ☺8am-6pm) Housed inside the colonial blue-and-white Paço da Nóbrega building along the waterfront. Has useful maps of surrounding beaches and good local info.

HSBC (Conceição 85, Centro) Fee-less ATM one block north of Thomaz Galhardo.

❶ Getting There & Around

Ubatuba has two intercity bus stations. For São Paulo (R$54, four hours, 10 daily), São Sebastião (R$20, 70 minutes, hourly; change in Caraguátatuba) and other destinations within the state, head to **Litorânea bus station** (www.litoranea.com.br; Maria Victória Jean 381, Centro), located at the edge of the town center, about 1.5km from the tourist office and beach.

For buses to Paraty (R$11.20) and Rio de Janeiro (R$68), head to the **São Jose bus station** (Thomaz Galhardo 513, Centro), on the main street a few blocks from the beach.

Local buses (R$3, about hourly from 7am to 8pm) head up and down the coastal highway and come at least within hiking distance of most beaches. The main stop in the center is at Hans Staden 488, between the two long-distance stations.

São Sebastião

One of the only towns on the Paulista coast that has preserved a portion of its colonial charms, São Sebastião sits on a dramatic channel dividing the mainland from Ilha de São Sebastião (popularly known as 'Ilhabela'), a 15-minute ferry trip away. Prices in town are moderate by local standards, but for good reason. There are no beaches at hand, and the town is also a major oil depot, with huge tankers somewhat diminishing the natural beauty. Still, it makes a fine stopover if you're traveling to Ilhabela.

For tourist information, check out the **C.I.T.** (Secretaria de Turismo e Cultura; 🖉ext 203 012-3892-2620; www.saosebastiao.sp.gov.br/turismo; Altino Arantes 174; ☺9am-6pm Mon-Thu, to 10pm Fri & Sat, 1-7pm Sun) on the waterfront in the small colonial center of town.

🛏 Sleeping

Hotel Roma
INN $$

(🖉3892-4622; www.hotelroma.tur.br; Praça Major João Fernandes 174; tr/q R$165/205; 🅿✳@🛜) In the heart of the colonial quarter, Hotel Roma has no-frills triple and quadruple rooms with air-con arranged around a plain courtyard in the main colonial-style building. Outside of high season, it may offer doubles, but for those traveling in packs, it remains a solid choice in a great location.

Pousada da Ana Doce
POUSADA $$

(🖉3892-1615; www.pousadaanadoce.com.br; Expedicionários Brasileiros 196; s/d R$165/220; ✳🛜) With neat, cheerful little rooms arranged around a charming, plant-filled courtyard in the colonial center, this inn is the most charming in town, especially at such reasonable rates. Book ahead.

✖ Eating

Be sure to try the excellent locally made Rocha-brand *sorvete* (ice cream) and *picolês* (popsicles), available most famously at Altino Arantes 90. Flavors like *milho verde* (sweet corn), *côco queimado* (burnt coconut) and *banana caramelada* (caramelized banana) are unforgettable.

Atobá   BUFFET **$$**
(✆ 3892-4878;   www.atobarestaurante.com.br; Praça Major João Fernandes 218; per kg week/weekend R$39.80/45.30; ⏰ 11:30am-4pm; 🚗) In a colonial building on the town's main square, Atobá offers a high-quality per-kilo buffet for lunch. Small extras like a good selection of seeds and piles of roasted garlic give it a leg up in these parts.

❶ Getting There & Away

The bus station is located just off the main coastal highway and a short walk from the colonial center. **Litorânea** (www.litoranea.com.br) has frequent service to São Paulo (R$43.25, 3½ hours, 13 daily), as well as direct service to Guarulhos International Airport (R$40.80, four hours, four daily), Boiçucanga (R$10.25, 40 minutes, three daily) and other stops along the coast to Santos. **Util** (www.util.com.br) offers

service to Rio (R$85, seven hours, four daily), with a stop in Paraty.

Ilhabela

⬛ 0XX12 / POP 28,000 (WINTER), 120,000 (SUMMER)

Rising steeply from the narrow strait that divides it from the continent, the 350-sq-km Ilhabela (Beautiful Island) earns its name from its volcanic peaks, beautiful beaches, dense tropical jungle and some 360 waterfalls. Almost 85% of the island has been turned into a park and Unesco-protected biosphere, which shelters a remarkable profusion of plant and animal life, including toucans and capuchin monkeys. A haunt of pirates in the 16th and 17th centuries, its waters are scattered with shipwrecks, many of which make for excellent diving. The island also proffers jungle hiking, windsurfing and beach-lazing.

Be aware that in the height of summer the bugs are murder, especially the little bloodsuckers known as *borrachudos*. Use plenty of insect repellent at all times. Summer is also when the island is packed with vacationing paulistas. Also try to avoid arriving on Friday evening and/or leaving on Sunday evening, especially in summer, as traffic, the line for the ferry and spikes in accommodations prices can tarnish your experience of paradise.

WORTH A TRIP

TUDO BEM, Y'ALL?

When the South lost the American Civil War in 1865, Brazil's Emperor Dom Pedro II saw dollar signs. Offering cheap land to planters in exchange for the state-of-the-art techniques for growing cotton that they would bring with them, he lured as many as 10,000 Southerners to his country.

Most of the new immigrants settled in central São Paulo state, where they found growing conditions remarkably similar to those of the southern US. They planted pecans, peaches, corn and cotton just as they had in their native soil. They also made a concerted effort to stay aloof from Brazilian culture, venerating the Confederate flag and preserving their language and many of their customs. However, they did have to forgo one luxury: slavery, the institution they had fought so hard to defend. Research indicates that only a few former Confederates actually owned slaves in Brazil.

In the neighboring towns of **Americana** and **Santa Bárbara d'Oeste**, both about 100km northwest of São Paulo, you can still hear descendants of the *confederados* speaking English with a distinctly Southern lilt. And every year, the Fraternity of American Descendants – the community's main social institution – holds a picnic, complete with fried chicken, biscuits and peach pie.

Piracicabana (www.piracicabana.com.br) has direct services to and from São Paulo's Tietê bus station (R$33.55, two hours).

PARQUE ESTADUAL DO ALTO DO RIBEIRA (PETAR)

Nestled in the Vale do Ribeira in the hills near the São Paulo–Paraná border, Iporanga was founded in 1576 after gold was discovered here. Today, the surrounding region remains one of the least-disturbed stretches of the Brazilian Atlantic Forest and is of international importance for its biodiversity. It also makes a good base for visiting the **Parque Estadual do Alto do Ribeira**. This 360-sq-km state park, with its 280 cataloged caves, is known as Brazil's Capital das Grutas (Cave Capital).

PETAR's Núcleos de Visitação are well-set-up visitors' centers with information on cave trips, guides and campgrounds. There are four Núcleos: **Núcleo de Santana** (www.petaronline.com.br/petar.htm; per person R$9 plus per vehicle R$6), 18km northwest of town, has good facilities for visitors and campers, including a newly inaugurated coffee shop and exhibition hall, five caves and a 3.5km-long trek to a beautiful waterfall; **Núcleo Ouro Grosso** (13km northwest of town) has basic accommodations for groups and offers cooking facilities, two caves and a walking trail; **Núcleo Casa de Pedra** (9km by road plus 3km by walking trail, northwest from town) is the base for visiting the Casa de Pedra, famous for its 215m-high entrance and pristine Atlantic forest; and **Núcleo Caboclos** (www.petaronline.com.br/caboclos.htm; entrance/camping R$6/12), centrally located in the park, 86km by road from town, has good camping facilities, basic visitors' lodgings and several caves.

For information as well as camping and caving reservations, contact **PETAR** (Parque Estadual do Alto do Ribeira; ☑15-3552-1875; www.petaronline.com.br). The trustworthy **Ecocave** (☑15-3556-1574; www.ecocave.com.br) organizes expeditions to the caves, as well as hiking, rappelling and inner-tubing along the local river.

From São Paulo's Barra Funda bus station, **Transpen** (www.transpen.com.br) offers service to Apiaí (R$69, five hours, three daily), where you can catch a **Princesa dos Campos** (www.princesadoscampos.com.br) 3pm bus to Iporanga (R$4.60, 1¾ hours), returning at 7am.

◉ Sights

Vila Ilhabela, on the northwestern part of the island, has quite a few well-preserved colonial buildings, including the slave-built **Igreja NS da Ajuda** (founded 1532); the **Fazenda Engenho d'Agua** in Itaquanduba (founded 1582); and **Fazenda Santa Carmen** at Feiticeira beach. Two kilometers inland from Perequê beach (near the ferry terminal), **Cachoeira das Tocas** has various small waterfalls with accompanying deep pools and waterslides.

Beaches

Of the sheltered beaches on the north side of the island, **Praia Jabaquara** is recommended. It can be reached by car via a dirt road. On the eastern side of the island, where the surf is stronger, try beautiful **Praia dos Castelhanos** (good for camping and surfing), which is backed by the steeply rising jungle. From the town of Borrifos at the southern end of the island, you can take a four-hour walk to **Praia Bonete**, a windy surf beach lying on the southern side of the island that you will share mostly with a local community of fisher folk.

🏃 Activities

Maremar Aventura Turismo OUTDOORS
(☑3896-3679; www.maremar.tur.br; Praça Elvira Storace 12, Perequê) Near the ferry, this recommended agency organizes all kinds of outdoor activities, including schooner trips around the island (from R$50 per person), full-day trips to the idyllic fishing village and beach of Bonete (R$150) and Praia de Castelhanos (R$70); and rents bikes (per hour/day R$15/30).

🛏 Sleeping

Making a reservation is a good idea on weekends – mandatory on summer weekends. Prices are high, so some travelers choose to stay in São Sebastião, where rates are more reasonable.

Camping Canto Grande CAMPGROUND $
(☑3894-1713; www.cantogrande.com.br; Riachuelo 5638, Praia Grande; campsites per person R$35; P@🛜) Run by the kind Enzo, this grassy beachside campground approximately 6km south of the ferry landing offers hot-water showers, electric plug-ins (330 of 'em!), a gurgling stream, a simple restaurant, wi-fi, and beach chairs and umbrellas for hire.

★ Na Mata Suites POUSADA **$$**
(☎ 3895-8771; www.namatasuites.com.br; Benedicto Mariano Leite 690, Barra Velha; d R$160; P ✱ @ 🛜) Tucked away in a small thatch of lush neighborhood rainforest, you'll find an absolutely lovely four-bungalow trove of hospitality, courtesy of an Anglo-Brazilian couple and their two adorable kids. Tom and Silvia are consummate hosts, turning their own private jungle into a discerning getaway.

Each well-appointed bungalow comes with a rustic terrace that's perfect for breakfast (if you don't take it by the pool); and their select positioning insures privacy for all. Tom can set you up with sailing lessons, get you on a stand-up paddle board, or out on a mountain bike, but mostly they've just nailed the vibe.

Pousada Catamarã Brasil POUSADA **$$**
(☎ 3894-1034; www.pousadacatamarabrasil.com.br; José Batista dos Santos 273, Curral; d from R$220; ✱ 🛜 ❄) Hidden up an inauspiciously rutted side street, this colorful and pristinely maintained inn offers very comfortable rooms, plus a small but pretty pool hidden in a lush garden. Good value but little warmth or hospitality.

Bonns Ventos Hostel HOSTEL **$$**
(☎ 3896-5676; www.bonnsventoshostel.com.br; Benedito Serafim Sampaio 371, Perequê; dm/s/d/tr R$60/230/240/312; P ✱ @ ❄) Conveniently located about 500m from the ferry stop, this HI-affiliated hostel steeped in Zen punches above its weight class as far as hostels go, but stick to the four- and six-bed dorms (you'll find better-value privates elsewhere).

Pousada Mariola POUSADA **$$$**
(☎ 3896-4141; www.pousadamariola.com.br; Chico Reis 304, Saco da Capela; s/d from R$280.50/297; P ✱ 🛜 ❄) An engineer owns this fabulous choice implanted into giant granite stones perched high on a view-riffic hillside reached via a charming street with upright palms shooting straight from the cobblestones. The 12-room boutique inn offers spacious rooms with Asian aesthetics and patios that take full advantage of the expansive vistas of the sailboat-strewn sea below.

DPNY Beach BOUTIQUE HOTEL **$$$**
(☎ 3894-3000; www.dpnybeach.com.br; José Pacheco do Nascimento 7668; r week/weekend from R$730/820; P ✱ @ 🛜 ❄) Set right on the sands of Praia Curral, this über-trendy getaway for São Paulo fashionistas isn't subtle: the Mediterranean-on-overdrive aesthetic would be jarring if the crowd here didn't subscribe to the more-is-more line of trend-setting decorating.

Rooms are exquisitely appointed, with extra touches like Nespresso machines; there's a huge pool and harem-like spa that surely gets out of hand (in a good way) on busy nights. Miami-style ambient music pumps throughout the property. It is also home to Hippie Chic Beach Bar, the island's fanciest bar-lounge, and Tróia, its most gourmet restaurant (mains R$35 to R$109).

✖ Eating & Drinking

Note that some places tend to close early during low season when crowds are thin, so plan for a backup.

Cheiro Verde BRAZILIAN **$**
(☎ 3896-3245; www.cheiroverdeilhabela.com.br; Rua da Padroeira 109, Vila; meals R$19.20; ⏱ 11:30am-5pm Mon-Thu, to 10pm Sat & Sun; ♿) The best place in Vila for a generous *prato feito* (plate of the day) with grilled meat or fish, plus rice, beans and salad, this simple but clean and airy place attracts tourists and locals alike. Each day's menu awaits on a monitor by the door.

Cura BUFFET **$**
(☎ 3896-1341; Princesa Isabel 337, Perequê; per kg R$39.40; ⏱ 11:30am-4pm Mon-Fri, to 6pm Sat & Sun; ♿) The island's best per kilo restaurant, set in a large and homey space across from the sands of Perequê.

Capitano ITALIAN **$$**
(☎ 3896-5241; www.pastadelcapitano.com.br; Pedro Paula de Moraes 703, Saco de Capela; pastas R$36-52; ⏱ 7:30pm-1:30am Wed-Sun, daily Dec-Feb & Jul) Chef Fabio Piscioto hails from São Paulo's most traditional Italian neighborhood and was destined to return to his pasta-making roots after 30 years as a graphic designer. Everyone raves about the simple, clean pasta dishes here, and we, too, are in awe: the squid-ink tagliatelle with shrimp grew better as it aged on our plate.

Prainha do Julião SEAFOOD **$$**
(☎ 3894-1867; www.prainhadojuliao.com.br; Raichuelo 5370, Julião; mains R$28-58; ⏱ 10am-6pm; ♿) Hidden from the main road along the island's southside is this upscale beach shack, firmly planted into the sands of Ilhabela's best easily accessed beach, Julião. It does better-than-average seafood preparations with actual vegetables and serves them on a pristine stretch of beach dug into only by those in the know.

O Borrachudo
BURGERS, BAR $$

(☑3896-1499; www.borrachudo.com.br; Carvalho 20, Vila; sandwiches R$7.30-20.40; ⊙2pm-late) In a colonial building right on Vila's waterfront, this relaxed café-bar proudly serves excellent burgers of all kinds (including salmon, ostrich and Guinness-soaked top sirloin), as well as other gourmet sandwiches and over 125 beers.

Hippie Chic Beach Bar
LOUNGE

(www.dpnybeach.com.br; DPNY Beach, José Pacheco do Nascimento 7668, Curral; ☎) With quietly thumping lounge music, hip-tropical decor and table service on the sand, the island's fanciest bar attracts rich paulistas eager to show off this season's designer gear. Beers run around R$8 and specialty cocktails are R$22.

❶ Orientation

The ferry arrives from the mainland in the Barra Velha neighborhood, which blends seamlessly with the town of Perequê just to the north. About 7km north lies the historic town of Vila. Good roads run along the western coast of the island; however, the south and east coasts are reachable only by boat or on foot except for a rough road accessible by 4WD that reaches Praia dos Castelhanos on the west coast.

❶ Information

The **tourist office** (Sectur; ☑3895-7220; www. ilhabela.sp.gov.br; Praça Vereador José Leite dos Passos 14, Barra Velha; ⊙9am-6pm) is located about 100m from the ferry terminal in Barra Velha. You can also preview your visit at www.ilhabela.org, which includes history, hiking itineraries, listings for diving and other adventure activities – and more – in English.

For those bringing a car to the island, avoid huge lines waiting for the Dersa **ferry** (☑0800-773-3711; www.dersa.sp.gov.br) on summer weekends by booking in advance (R$83.10/124.60 weekdays/weekends return).

ATMs in Barra Velha, Perequê and Vila Ilhabela (Vila) accept international bank cards.

❶ Getting There & Around

The 15-minute ferry trip between São Sebastião and Ilhabela runs 24/7 every half-hour from 6am to midnight and hourly after that. Cars cost R$14.10 weekdays and R$21.20 on weekends, motorcycles cost R$7.10 weekdays and R$10.60 on weekends; pedestrians ride free. Returning to the mainland, you pay an environmental tax only (R$2 for motos, R$5 for cars).

A local bus (R$2.20, every 30 minutes, 5:35am to 1:40am) runs the length of the island, including a stop at the ferry. **Chame Taxi** (☑3895-8587) are usually waiting at the ferry.

A decent road runs the length of the western coast. Another unsealed road (22km) crosses the island. To get to the other side of the island requires either a 4WD, a boat or a good strong pair of hiking legs, though they are working on paving it.

Iguape & Around

☑0XX13 / POP 29,000

Founded by the Portuguese in 1538 to defend Brazil from the Spanish, Iguape is one of the oldest towns in Brazil and one of the few along São Paulo's coast to retain its colonial contours. An ongoing federal initiative is helping to restore the old city center, which had long been neglected. While beaches are a bit of a hoof, the town makes a tranquil base from which to explore the region.

◎ Sights

The town's colonial charms are clustered around the whitewashed main plaza, **Largo da Basílica**, and the 18th-century **basilica** (open 8am to 8pm). About 1.5km along the road to Barra do Ribeira is a turnoff to the **Mirante do Morro do Espia**, a lookout with a good view of the port and region.

Iguape looks across a narrow strait to **Ilha Comprida**, a long, skinny island (86km by 3km) that shelters Iguape from the open ocean. The island is covered with a combination of mangrove and Atlantic rainforest, and has an uninterrupted beach that stretches the entire Atlantic-facing length of the island. A toll bridge connects Iguape with the island.

🛏 Sleeping & Eating

There are a number of inexpensive pizzerias and other eateries on Largo da Basílica.

Silvi Hotel
HOTEL $

(☑3841-1421; www.silvihotel.com.br; Sandoval Trigo 515; s R$75-130, d R$115-170, tr R$150-210; ❀@☎) Humble but decent yellow-and-green, motel-style sleep. Rooms are plain but in perfect working order and the staff is both helpful and friendly. Downstairs, there is a decent restaurant with a reasonably priced buffet and a more expensive à la carte menu.

Pousada Solar Colonial POUSADA $$
(☑ 3841-1591; solarcolonial@terra.com.br; Praça da Basílica 30; s/d R$90/150; ☞) Occupying a handsome colonial building right on the town's main square, this inn offers simple but clean, refurbished rooms, plus breakfast in a bright room with French windows onto the main square. Rooms have fans only.

Panela Velha SEAFOOD $$$
(☑ 3841-1869; 15 de Novembro 190; mains for 2 R$77-170; ☺ 11am-11pm Tue-Sat, to 5pm Sun & Mon; ☞) Considered the best option in town, this trim, tiny, spotless little place specializes in simple but expertly prepared local seafood in the form of stews like *moquecas* and *caldeiradas*, grilled fresh from the sea or river (nothing farmed here) and *paella*. It's all good.

ℹ Information

Tourist information (☑ 3841-1016; Av Princesa Isabel 708; ☺ 8am-6pm) is run on concession inside a small crafts building near the main square. You'll find foreign-friendly ATMs behind the basilica.

ℹ Getting There & Around

Intersul (www.intersul-transporte.com.br) offers four daily buses from Iguape to São Paulo (R$52, 3½ hours). For Cananéia (R$22.80, 1¾ hours), switch in Pariquera-Açu. Local buses cross the bridge to Ilha Comprida. If you have a 4WD, it is possible to drive along the long, flat beach on Ilha Comprida and take the ferry across to Cananéia (per vehicle week/weekend R$9.10/13.70, passengers free), though you must time your trip for low tide.

Paraná

POP 10.4 MILLION

Best Places to Eat

➡ Manu (p263)
➡ Barolo (p263)
➡ Fim da Trilha (p273)
➡ Mar e Sol (p272)
➡ Vó Bertila (p277)

Best Places to Sleep

➡ Hotel das Cataratas (p276)
➡ Motter Home (p262)
➡ Hostel Natura (p274)
➡ Grajagan Surf Resort (p272)
➡ Curitiba Eco Hostel (p262)

Why Go?

Since its 1853 succession from São Paulo state, Paraná has been endlessly compared with its larger neighbor to the north. Indeed, the two share a slew of superlatives, rating among Brazil's highest standards of living and best educated populations.

With its efficient public transportation, innovative architecture and outstanding urban parks, the capital, Curitiba, exemplifies the state's successes. Though no tourism magnet, the city's air of European culture and excellent restaurants make for a nice dose of Brazil at its most developed. Sunbathers and surfers sigh for Ilha do Mel and Parque Nacional do Superagüi, where large swaths of unspoiled rainforest and pristine coastline make for some of the least developed and most idyllic beaches in southern Brazil.

But it's Iguaçu Falls that has always earned the wonder and admiration of travelers, from indigenous tribes to Jesuit missionaries to modern-day tourists. The awe it inspires cannot be overstated.

When to Go
Foz do Iguaçu

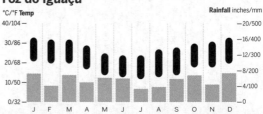

May & Sep Off peak prices and crowds coupled with tolerable weather at Iguaçu Falls.

Dec–Feb Peak season brings the sunshine at Iguaçu Falls and Ilha do Mel.

Aug Retreating cold and mugginess in Curitiba makes for comfortable days.

History

Like much of southern Brazil, Paraná was neglected by the Portuguese colonists; even a brief gold rush in the 17th century withered when bigger finds were discovered in Minas Gerais. When Paraná seceded from São Paulo in 1853, the economy was based on cattle and *erva maté* (tea), and the government encouraged Italian immigration to develop the economy. Waves of Germans, Ukrainians and Poles followed. With immigration and railroad construction, Curitiba developed into one of the country's richest cities.

ⓘ Getting There & Around

Curitiba is the state's transportation hub, with bus and air services to every major city in Brazil. A passenger train links Curitiba with the coastal town of Paranaguá. Foz do Iguaçu also has a small international airport and direct bus service to São Paulo, Rio de Janeiro and every big city in the South.

CURITIBA

⤴ 0XX41

While not necessarily sexy, Curitiba has long garnered praise for being one of the world's best models of urban planning. If it weren't for the bold initiatives of its three-term mayor, Jaime Lerner, whose daring moves in early 1970s – transforming a six-block length of the downtown into a pedestrian zone (done in secret under the cover of darkness), creating five express-bus avenues with futuristic tubular boarding platforms, encouraging recycling and sustainable design long before it was fashionable and planting trees and creating parks on an enormous scale – Curitiba would probably resemble any other Brazilian city. Instead, it's the envy of the urban planners the world over and Brazil's most efficient city. Today, it's easier to get around Curitiba than any other large city in Brazil. The city has also taken

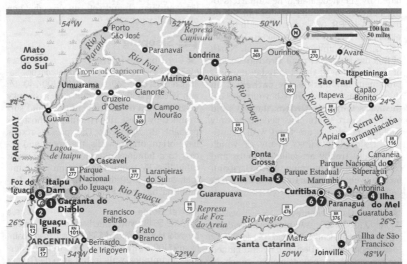

Paraná Highlights

❶ Experience Mother Nature's heart-stopping and thunderous roar from above and below **Garganta do Diablo** (p281) at Iguaçu Falls.

❷ Drench yourself under one of world's most magnificent waterfalls on an **Iguaçu Falls** (p281) riverboat trip.

❸ Ride the rails on the **Serra Verde Express** (p268) to Morretes, one of Brazil's last great train rides.

❹ Laze about the wild beaches and sandy trails of car-free **Ilha do Mel** (p270).

❺ Marvel at the ancient 'stone city' of **Vila Velha** (p267).

❻ Appreciate art and eye-popping architecture at Curitiba's **Museu Oscar Niemeyer** (p262).

❼ Indulge in a Michelin-level meal for a fraction of the price at Curitiba's **Manu** (p263), the South's hottest new restaurant.

❽ Marvel at the jaw-dropping engineering feat of **Itaipu Dam** (p283).

innovative approaches to urban ills such as homelessness, pollution and poverty. Today, the city ensures a quality of life unparalleled in Brazil. With its abundant green spaces, sophisticated population and well-heeled infrastructure, Curitiba is not a bad spot to recharge your batteries and soak in Brazil at its functioning best.

Curitiba will be one of several host cities for the 2014 FIFA World Cup. Well prepared for the huge sporting event with plenty of accommodations, there's little doubt that its citizens will be using their international spotlight to boast their city's best attributes.

◉ Sights & Activities

The focal point of Curitiba's downtown is **Rua das Flores**, officially known as XV de Novembro, a 500m pedestrian mall ideal for shopping and strolling. At its eastern end sits **Praça Santos Andrade**, dominated by the neoclassical headquarters of the **Federal University of Paraná**, home to **MusA-UFPR** (www.proec.ufpr.br; 15 de Novembro 695, 1st fl; ⊘9am-6pm Mon-Fri, 9am-1pm Sat) FREE, the university's museum. North of Rua das Flores is **Praça Tiradentes**, site of the founding of the city. Today its most prominent landmark is the **cathedral** on the northeast corner. Just beyond the cathedral is **Largo da Ordem**, the city's old colonial heart. Here, the pedestrian-only cobblestone streets are lined with beautifully restored buildings, many of which now house trendy art galleries, pubs and cafes. On Sunday morning, Praça Garibaldi hosts a lively **art and artisan market** (Praça Garibaldi; ⊘9am-2pm).

★ Museu Oscar Niemeyer   MUSEUM
(MON; ☑3350-4400; www.museuoscarniemeyer. org.br; Marechal Hermes 999; adult/child R$6/3; ⊘10am-6pm Tue-Sun) Designed by and named for the architect responsible for much of Brasília, this exotic, eye-shaped museum is painted with whimsical dancing figures in bold colors. Rotating exhibits highlight Brazilian and international artists of the 20th and 21st centuries; and there's an excellent permanent basement exhibit on Niemeyer himself.

Jardim Botânico   GARDENS
(☑3264-1800; www.jardimbotanicocuritiba.com.br; Eng Ostoja Roguski; ⊘6am-9pm Dec-Mar, 6am-8pm Apr-Nov) In the far south of the city, the Jardim Botânico is a vast, flower-filled expanse, studded with sculpture and criss-

crossed by walking paths. The centerpiece glass and metallic greenhouse is more interesting as a decorative showpiece than as a botanical wonder.

Oi Torre Panorâmica   LOOKOUT
(☑3339-7613; Castro Vellozo 191; adult/child R$4/2; ⊘10am-7pm, closed Mon Apr-Nov) For an overview of Curitiba, head to the 109m-high Torre Panorâmica, offering 360-degree views from its observation deck.

☞ Tours

Linha Turismo   CITY TOUR
(www.turismo.curitiba.pr.gov.br; tours R$27; ⊘every 30min 9am-5:50pm Tue-Sun Mar-Oct, every 15min 8:45am-6pm Nov-Carnival) This double-decker city tour bus is a great way to see the sights both inside and outside Curitiba's downtown. It starts at Praça Tiradentes and you can get off at any four of the 23 attractions and hop on the next bus. Stops are announced in English and Spanish and you can use your hop offs any day you wish.

🛏 Sleeping

★ Curitiba Eco Hostel   HOSTEL $
(☑3274-7979; www.curitibaecohostel.com.br; Tramontin 1693; dm R$40, s/d/tr R$80/100/140, d/q with air-con R$150/220; ✳@❀) In a swanky neighborhood on the edge of town and surrounded by forest, this HI-affiliated hostel is probably Brazil's nicest. The spacious rooms have bright-orange walls, tile floors and access to a fabulous outdoor deck and great cabin-like TV room. The location is a bummer, but it's a 20-minute ride on the 'Tramontina' bus from Praça Rui Barbosa.

Motter Home   HOSTEL $
(☑3209-5649; www.motterhome.com.br; Desembargador Motta 3574; dm R$38-40, r with shared bathroom R$100, r/q R$120/200; @❀) In leafy Mercês – 15 minutes' walk from Largo da Ordem – this newcomer makes artistic use of a striking canary-yellow, turret-style mansion from the '50s, with striking art, retro-sophisticated common areas, original hardwood floors and funky door handles.

The unwillingness to accommodate solo travelers privately without charging them for two, and fees for towels even in the most expensive private rooms, sours the fun here, but the place is gorgeous.

Curitiba Casa   HOSTEL $
(☑3044-7313; www.curitibacasahostel.com; Brasílio Itiberê 73; dm R$38-44, r R$110; @❀) Despite its

odd location 15 minutes east of the *rodofer-roviária* (bus and train station, this new hostel has more fans than *futebol*. Clean, colorful and classy.

Garden Curitiba Hotel
HOTEL $$

(☑3222-2524; www.gardencuritiba.com.br; Ébana Pereira 405; s/d/tr R$155/199/263; @ 🕾) Nothing fancy happens at this cozy little hostelry, but it is one of the more pleasant places to stay. Thanks to its small size and homey decor and very pleasant and helpful staff, the Garden Curitiba offers an air of small-town intimacy otherwise lacking in this big city. Prices generally land much lower than indicated here.

L'Avenue Apart Hotel
APART HOTEL $$

(☑3222-5525; www.lavenueaparthotel.com.br; XV de Novembro 526; s/d/tr R$170/190/230; ❄🕾) One of the few places to stay on Rua das Flores, this tasteful but not-too-trendy hotel has 63 suites, all with kitchenettes and sitting areas, some in better condition with better layouts than others. Great value.

San Juan Johnscher
BOUTIQUE HOTEL $$$

(☑3302-9600; www.sanjuanhoteis.com.br; Barão do Rio Branco 354; s/d R$280/330, ste from R$365; ❄🕾) Behind a beautiful neoclassical facade, this renovated hotel retains much of its original architectural detail, but does not skimp on modern amenities. Stained-wood floors, painted moldings and black-and-white photos give the 24 rooms an aura of understated elegance. The lobby, designed with a Jenga-like aesthetic of stacked *imbuia* (Brazilian walnut) wood support beams and fireplace, is a sight to see.

✖ Eating

Mercado Municipal (www.mercadomunicipal decuritiba.com.br; 7 de Setembro 1865; ⊙7am-2pm Mon, to 6pm Tue-Sat, to 1pm Sun), opposite the bus station, has Brazil's first organic food court; **Rua 24 Horas**, near Praça General Osório, is a pleasant street-turned-enclosed-food-court (not open 24 hours!). Local chain **Spich** does 10-dish buffets (R$4.95).

Bouquet Garni
SELF-SERVE $

(www.restaurantebouquetgarni.com; Carvalho 271; buffet midweek/weekend R$19/25; ⊙11am-3pm; 🕾☑) 🍴 Most of the ingredients at this all-organic vegetarian restaurant come from the owners' farm. The menu changes daily according to what's fresh and what's in season. Rock up on a bike for a 10% discount.

Yū
ASIAN $$

(www.yurestaurante.com.br; Praça Osório 485; per kg R$58.90; ⊙11:30am-3pm Mon-Fri, noon-3:30pm Sat & Sun) Reflecting Curitiba's significant Asian immigration, this pricier *por kilo* does outstanding Korean, Chinese and Japanese dishes, including sushi, sashimi and stop-you-in-your-tracks fantastic *lula apimentada* (spicy squid salad). Espresso is free.

Madero
BURGERS $$

(www.restaurantemadero.com.br; Kellers 63; burger & fries R$16.80-29.90; ⊙11:45am-2:30pm & 6:15-11:30pm Mon-Thu, 6:15pm-midnight Fri, 11:45am-midnight Sat, to 11:30pm Sun; 🕾) Chef of the Year, Restaurant of the Year...no, it's not a three-star Michelin eatery, it's a gorgeous, award-winning burger joint, even cheaper during the Monday to Thursday happy hour from 6:15pm to 7:45pm. Good local beers and a better-than-sex *doce de leite petit gâteau* insures your happy ending here.

The same chef runs **Madero Prime** (www.restaurantemadero.com.br; Jaime Reis 254; mains around R$35), voted the city's best steakhouse in 2012.

★ Barolo
ITALIAN $$$

(☑3243-3434; www.barolotrattoria.com.br; Av Silva Jardim 2487; mains for 2 R$51-100; ⊙noon-2:30pm & 7pm-midnight Mon-Sat, to 4pm Sun; 🕾) It's not located in Curitiba's touristy Italian neighborhood, but this upscale trattoria is the real deal indeed. The pastas – pick your type, then pick your sauce – served in cast-iron pans, are an absolute revelation. We went for Barolo (red pepper, cream, broccoli and tomato). Reservations are a good idea for dinner.

★ Manu
BRAZILIAN $$$

(☑3044-4395; www.restaurantemanu.com.br; Dom Pedro II 317; 4-/6-/8-course menu R$86/129/165, with wine R$161/244/297; ⊙8-11:30pm Tue-Sat; 🕾) Young buck Manoella Buffara is Curitiba's hottest chef and her pedigree backs up her impressive food. She did stints in two of the world's most famous kitchens, Noma in Copenhagen and Alinea in Chicago. Manu, in the trendy Batel neighborhood, offers three tasting menus in three price ranges nightly.

Classics like *bobó de camarão* (manioc paste flavored with dried shrimp, coconut milk and cashews; divine) or Sunday chicken, a sort of fowl pot roast, get unorthodox pairings with outside-the-box wines from

PARANÁ CURITIBA

Curitiba

PARANÁ CURITIBA

N

0 — 400 m
0 — 0.2 miles

R Marechal Deodoro
R Comendador Macedo
R Amaral
R da Paz
R General Carneiro
16
R Doutor Faivre
R Francisco Torres
R Nilo Cairo
R Benjamin Constant
R XV de Novembro
R Amintas de Barros
R Conselheiro Araújo
R Mariano Torres
R Tibagi
R Conselheiro Laurindo
R João Negrão
Av Presidente Afonso Camargo
Train Station
Rodoferroviária
P.I.T.
Vd Colorado
Curitiba Casa (650m);
Jardim Botânico (1km)
Afonso Pena
International
Airport (16km)
Av Silva Jardim

Passeio Público
Av Presidente Carlos Cavalcanti
Aeroporto Executivo Bus Stop
6
Praça Santos Andrade
Federal University of Paraná
1
5
R André de Barros
R Barão do Rio Branco
Av 7 de Setembro
Praça Eufrásio Correia
21

R Presidente Faria
R Riachuelo
Old City Hall
11
R Cândido de Leão
R Marechal Deodoro
R XV de Novembro (R das Flores)
R José Loureiro
R Pedro Ivo
12
20
Lourenço Pinto
R Visconde de Guarapuava

Museu Oscar Niemeyer (2km)
Cerro Azul
Largo da Ordem
R Barão do Cerro
Praça Tiradentes
4
9
R Monsenhor Celso
Av Marechal Floriano Peixoto
R Alameda Dr Muricy
R Westfalen
18
Travessa Frei Caneca

Ópera de Arame (5km)
R 13 de Maio
Praça João Cândido Garibaldi
P.I.T.
R do Rosário
2
8
14
R Ébano Pereira
10
19
7
R Voluntários da Pátria
Praça Rui Barbosa
Curitiba Eco Hostel Bus Stop
Av 24 de Maio
Barolo (1.5km)

Motter Home (1.3km);
Torre Panorâmica (2km)
Av Jaime Reis
15
R dez Clotário Portugal
Augusto Stellfeld
Alameda Cabral
R Saldanha Marinho
R Cruz Machado
R Carlos de Carvalho
17
13
R dez Ermelino de Leão
R Tibiriçá
Praça General Osório
Clube do Malte (550m);
Manu (950m)
R Vison de Nácar
Comendador Araújo
R 24 Horas
P.I.T.
Emiliano Perneta
R Doutor Pedrosa
Curitiba Eco Hostel (7km)

Curitiba

Greece or Morocco. This is the spot where gourmands gather and gaggle over subtle culinary feats, a two-star Michelin-quality equivalent for a lot less than €300! Reservations essential.

🍺 Drinking & Nightlife

On warm nights, revelers spill out of pubs and cafes onto the streets around Praça Garibaldi and Largo da Ordem.

Txapela   BAR
(☑ 3233-6810; www.txapela.com.br; Ébano Pereira 269; tapas R$4.76-60; ⊙ 5pm-1am, closed Sun) This Spanish-themed madhouse is Curitiba's *bar du moment*. Two locals ran off to Spain, returned with dreams of *tapas* and *jamón serrano* dancing in their heads, and voila! You have a line out the door at 6:30pm on a Monday.

Clube do Malte   BAR
(www.clubedomalte.cm.br; Des Motta 2200; ⊙ 11:30am-midnight Mon-Thu, to 1am Fri & Sat; 🛜) Beer hounds rejoice: a great spot for regional microbrews, with some 10 or so on tap at any given moment. Chase them with choices from the commendable pub grub menu.

Vox   CLUB
(Barão do Rio Branco 418; ⊙ 7pm-1am Wed-Thu, 8pm-6am Fri & Sat) With its colonial salmon facade and flower-strewn balcony, the space itself is gorgeous, but not half as much as the people inside. Downstairs, resident DJs rip pop and electronica, while the more intimate upstairs is all candlelight and antiques, an upscale lounge under the nose of reworked classical paintings.

Bar Triângulo   BAR
(Rua das Flores) Don't miss the people-watching at this 75-year-old bar.

☆ Entertainment

Opera de Arame   THEATER
(☑ 3355-6071; João Gava, Parque Pedreira Paulo Leminski; ⊙ 8am-10pm Tue-Sun) Constructed from wire with a glass roof, this theater is among Curitiba's most unusual and enigmatic landmarks. It is surrounded by the stone quarry park, which contains an outdoor stage hosting national acts throughout the year.

Sports

Curitiba's Arena da Baixada is undergoing a R$234 million renovation in preparation for the 2014 FIFA World Cup. Six public tours daily will resume in 2014 when the stadium reopens. It is the home stadium of **Atlético Paranaense** (www.atleticoparanaense.com).

ℹ Orientation

Curitiba's historic center is bounded in the east by Praça Santos Andrade and the nearby Passeio Público, a pleasant city park, and in the west by Praça General Osório and Rua 24 Horas. The two ends are joined by the lively, pedestrian-only Rua das Flores. Just to the north of Rua das Flores the city's colonial heart is Largo da Ordem, which is also its nightlife hub.

ℹ Information

Curitiba's tourist information offices are stocked with glossy brochures and maps and are well staffed with willing and helpful employees who speak a little English. The *rodoferroviária* tourist information booth is in the train station block behind the bus station – do not confuse it with the irrelevant *rodoferroviária* information booth in front of the bus station.

Internet cafes (LAN houses) are more and more scarce in Curitiba, but it would be odd if your chosen accommodations weren't wired.

Banco do Brasil (Praça Tiradentes 410)

HSBC (15 de Novembro) One of many pedestrian zone ATMs.

P.I.T. (Postos de Informações Turísticas, Tourist Information; ☑3352-8000; www.turismo.cu ritiba.pr.gov.br; Rua 24 Horas) Find branches at the airport (Airport Arrivals Hall; ☺7am-11pm), rodoferroviária (Rodoferroviária ; ☺8am-6pm), Praça Garibaldi (Praça Garibaldi 7; ☺9am-6pm Mon-Sat, 9am-4pm Sun) and Oi Torre Panorâmica (Castro Vellozo 19, Oi Torre Panorâmica; ☺10am-7pm, closed Mon Apr-Nov).

Polícia Federal (☑3251-7500; www.dpf.gov.br; Sandália Monzon 210 , Santa Cândida)

ℹ Getting There & Away

AIR

There are direct flights from **Afonso Pena International Airport** (CWB; ☑3381-1153; Av Rocha Pombo s/n, São José dos Pinhais), 18km southeast of Centro, to cities throughout Brazil.

BUS & TRAIN

Curitiba's long-distance bus and train stations form a single three-block complex called the **rodoferroviária** (☑3320-3121; www.rodofer roviaria.com.br; Av Pres Affonso Camargo 330), which sits 2km southeast of downtown and was getting a R$34 million World Cup–ready facelift during research. Bus companies for destinations within Paraná tend to be located around the back

of the second block. The train station block sits behind the two bus station blocks.

The train between Curitiba and Paranaguá via the Serra do Mar is one of the marvels of travel in Brazil.

ℹ Getting Around

URBS (www.urbs.curitiba.pr.gov.br) runs Curitiba's space-age bus system. City buses cost R$2.60 (R$1 on Sundays).

TO & FROM THE AIRPORT

An Aeroporto-Centro bus leaves every 30 minutes (R$2.60, 30 minutes) from Av 7 de Setembro. The classier **Aeroporto Executivo** (☑3381-1326; www.aeroportoexecutivo.com.br; R$10) goes direct every 15 to 20 minutes from 5:20am to 12:30am to select Centro stops, of which the bus station, Teatro Guaíra and Receita Federal are most convenient for tourists.

MORRETES

☑0XX41 / POP 16,000

Founded in 1721 on the banks of the Rio Nhundiaquara, this calm and collected colonial town rests on an emerald-green plain at the foot of the Serra do Mar. The loveliest colonial buildings are clustered around Praça Lamenha Lins and along Rua das Flores, the cobblestone walkway that runs along the river. The **tourist office** (☑3462-1024; Praça dos Imigrantes; ☺Sat & Sun) occupies a small kiosk just beside the riverbank near Pousada Nhundiaquara, and the grand **Igreja Matriz** (Mother Church) anchors one end.

BUSES FROM CURITIBA

DESTINATION	FARE (R$)	TIME (HR)	COMPANY
Asunción	144.50	14	Pluma (www.pluma.com.br)
Buenos Aires (AR)	321.50	34	Pluma (www.pluma.com.br)
Joinville	27	2	Catarinense (www.catarinense.net)
Morretes	18	1½	Graciosa (www.viacaograciosa.com.br)
Paranaguá	22	1½	Graciosa (www.viacaograciosa.com.br)
Florianópolis	65	4	Catarinense (www.catarinense.net)
São Paulo	94	6	Itapemirim (www.itapemirim.com.br)
Foz do Iguaçu	116	10	Catarinense (www.catarinense.net)
Porto Alegre	112	12	Pluma (www.pluma.com.br)
Rio de Janeiro	135	13	Penha (www.vendas.nspenha.com.br)
Santiago (CL)	382.50	54	Pluma (www.pluma.com)
Vila Velha	23	1½	Graciosa (www.viacaograciosa.com.br)

Fares are *executivo* fares (where applicable).

VILA VELHA

Located in Campos Gerais, 93km west of Curitiba, Vila Velha is known as the 'stone city'. The park's centerpieces are the 23 *aretinhas* (sandstone pillars), created over millions of years. The mysterious red-earth rock formations – some taking recognizable shapes such as boots and bottles – create striking silhouettes against the blue sky and green foliage.

Within the boundaries of the same park, visitors can witness another geological marvel: a series of *furnas* (craters) that are the result of underground erosion. A 90-minute bus tour stops first at the Lagoa Dourada, a lovely lagoon that attracts ample birdlife. The next stop features two yawning craters that reach depths of 54m.

From Curitiba, catch a **Princesa dos Campos** (www.princesadoscampos.com.br) bus to Vila Velha (R$22.80 1½ hours); any bus to Ponta Grossa will stop here, but the prevailing wisdom is that you should take the earliest buses at 6am, 7am, 8:15am or 9:45am to arrive early enough to see the whole park. Stop first at the **park center** (☎0xx42-3228-1138; Brazilians/foreigners R$18/25; ☉8:30am-5:30pm Wed-Mon), where you can watch an introductory video and buy tickets for the various tours.

The region's culinary gift to the world is *barreado*, a rib-sticking meat stew cooked in a clay pot. Originally, it served to keep revelers nourished over the course of several days of Carnaval (February/March), but you can test its sustaining qualities any time of year.

◉ Sights & Activities

The Rio Nhundiaquara is navigable by inner tube, which you can rent at the Pousada do Oasis (R$18 including transport), in the village of Porto de Cima.

Parque Estadual Marumbi　NATURE PARK
(☎3462-1155) Besides the quaint colonial center, the biggest attraction in Morretes is the Parque Estadual Marumbi, a paradise for rock climbers and nature lovers. It contains a network of old pioneer trails that were the only connections between the coast and the highland in the 17th and 18th centuries.

Calango Expedições　ADVENTURE TOUR
(☎3462-2600;　www.calangoexpedicoes.com.br; Estação Ferroviária; ☉9am-6pm Mon-Sat, to 4pm Sun) These ecocorrect adventure-tour specialists will get you out and about. Options include kayaking (R$60, 1½ hours), mountain biking (R$60, three hours) and Jeep tours (R$60, three hours) in the stunning surrounding scenery.

▦ Sleeping & Eating

Most of the restaurants are along Largo Dr José Pereira on the riverfront and are open for lunch only.

Hotel Nhundiaquara　POUSADA $
(☎3462-1228; www.nundiaquara.com.br; General Carreiro 13; s weekend/midweek R$80/60, r without

bathroom R$80, d/q R$120/200; ☎) Outside, the oldest building in town sits in pristine condition front and center on the riverfront; inside, plain, wood-paneled rooms with high ceilings and cramped bathrooms with low water pressure is what you get, but there's an antiquated air about the place among the warped flooring and apathetic breakfast.

The on-site restaurant is famous for its *barreado* (R$30), served on the breezy colonial-style terrace overlooking a lovely bend in the Rio Nhundiaquara – where you are *not* allowed to take your breakfast. Still, it's a hard place not to stay.

Pousada do Oasis　POUSADA $
(☎3426-1888;　www.pousadadooasis.com.br; Estradas das Prainhas, Porto de Cima; s/d R$90/140, chalets R$140-200; ✳@☎☲) A lush walkway leads to these sweet, spacious chalets surrounded by forest, flowering bushes and tropical goodness. It makes a great base for exploring the Parque Estadual Marumbi and you can also rent inner tubes here. Transport from Morretes is erratic – you're better off in a taxi (R$10 to R$15).

Estação Graciosa　BRAZILIAN $$
(☎3462-2009; Cons Sinimbú 271; mains for 2 R$45-80; ☉11am-4pm Tue-Fri, to 6pm Sat & Sun) Opposite the train station, Estação Graciosa occupies a blue clapboard house, decorated with folk art and mismatched furniture. A spacious porch overlooks the garden, where lemon trees bloom – an ideal setting to indulge in the local specialties.

Restaurante Casarão　BRAZILIAN $$
(☎3462-1314; www.barreado.com.br; Largo Dr José Pereira 25; mains for 2 R$39-87; ☉11am-3:30pm

PARANÁ MORRETES

Mon-Sat, to 5pm Sun) Restaurante Casarão is an upmarket place with a balcony on the river.

ℹ Getting There & Away

The Morretes train station is on a pretty square in the center of town. The Serra Verde Express (p268) runs to Curitiba daily at 3pm (4pm on Sunday).

The bus station is about 1km from the center of town. **Viação Graciosa** (www.viacaograciosa.com.br) buses run to Paranaguá (R$8, one hour) every half hour; and to Curitiba (R$15, 1½ hours, eight to 10 daily).

PARANAGUÁ

☎0XX41 / POP 140,500

This colorful old port, sitting serenely on the banks of the Rio Itiberê, has an appealing atmosphere of tropical decadence. Commercially important since the late 18th century, the city has some impressive churches and other public buildings, many of which are being carefully restored. For travelers, Paranaguá serves primarily as a point of departure to Ilha do Mel and Parque Nacional do Superagüi.

◉ Sights

The city's colonial churches are simple but striking. Several churches were constructed during the 18th century, including Igreja São Francisco das Chagas (XV Novembro s/n; ⊙9-11am & 2-6pm Mon-Sat, 2-6pm Sun) and Igreja de São Benedito (Conselheiro Sinimbu

s/n; ⊙7am-6pm), built specifically for the town's slaves.

Museu de Arqueologia
e Etnologia   MUSEUM
(Archeology & Ethnology Museum; ☎3721-1200; XV de Novembro 575; ⊙9am-6pm Mon-Fri, to 4pm Sat-Sun) FREE Housed in an 18th-century Jesuit college, this surprisingly great free museum displays indigenous artifacts, primitive and folk art, and old tools and machines.

Igreja de NS do Rosário   CHURCH
(Marechal Deodoro; ⊙8am-6pm) The oldest of the city's colonial churches is Igreja de NS do Rosário, parts of which date to 1578.

🛏 Sleeping & Eating

For a variety of cheap eats in a colonially draped food court, head inside the **Mercado Municipal del Café** (Carneiro 458; meals R$12-40; ⊙6am-6pm).

Hotel Ponderosa   HOTEL $
(☎3423-2464; Prescilinio Corrêa 68; s/d R$50/70, d with view R$80; ❋ ☎) Occupying a restored colonial building on a prominent corner, the Ponderosa evokes a grand past, with its high ceilings and wide-plank wood floors. The rooms facing the port are particularly pleasing, with lots of light and lovely views of the waterfront.

Hostel Continente   HOSTEL $
(☎3423-3224; www.hostelcontinente.com.br; Carneiro 300; dm R$38, s without/with air-con R$60/70, d R$80/95; ❋ @ ☎) This HI hostel has clean if cramped dorms and doubles in an enviable

---

DON'T MISS

ALL ABOARD!

The **Serra Verde Express** (☎3888-3488; www.serraverdeexpress.com.br; Estação Ferroviária) between Curitiba and Morretes offers sublime views of threatening mountain canyons, tropical green lowlands and the vast, blue Atlantic. As you descend, watch as the climate and environment change – the weather becoming hotter and muggier, the vegetation lusher and greener.

The train leaves Curitiba at 8:15am daily, descending 900m through the lush Serra do Mar to the historic town of Morretes, arriving at 11:15am and returning at 3pm Monday to Saturday and 4pm on Sunday. For Paranaguá, the train departs on weekends only at 7:30am, returning at 2pm. One-way economy/tourist-class tickets to either Morretes or Paranaguá cost R$57/74.

Views are most spectacular from the left side of the train (right side on the return trip), but the democratic computer ticketing system prevents requests – it takes turns between left and right (good luck!). Reservations are highly recommended during summer. Prices and times change frequently, so be sure to stop by the train station or check the website in advance.

Paranaguá

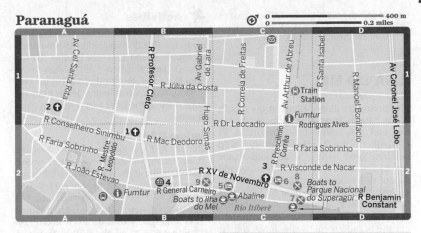

location across from the ferry dock. Facilities include laundry and communal kitchen, and it's the local watering hole of choice.

Gruta da Garoupa SELF-SERVE **$**
(☏3423 3896; XV de Novembro 120; per kg R$24.90; ☺11:15am-2:15pm Mon-Sat) This quality *por kilo* does a great variety of home-cooked mains – there's even brown rice! Coffee and dessert are free – if they are serving *chico balanceado*, a nasty-looking concoction of bananas, meringue *and manjar branco* (coconut pudding), dig in, despite its looks!

Danubio Azul BRAZILIAN, SEAFOOD **$$**
(www.restaurantedanubioazul.com.br; XV de Novembro 95; mains for 2 R$28-84, pizza R$25-40; ☺11am-3pm & 7pm-midnight Mon-Sat, to 3pm Sun) The town's best restaurant does excellent fish preparations and a tasty signature filet mignon among bland decor, but stretching water views, though you practically have to blackmail them to get them to cook a dish for one person. There are cheaper pizzas for more budget-conscious travelers.

ⓘ Information

Fumtur (☏3420-2940; www.fumtur.com.br; Av Arthur de Abreu 44; ☺8am-6pm Mon-Sat, 11am-2pm Sun) Paranaguá's municipal tourism information is well equipped with brochures, maps and Ilha do Mel info. There's another branch at the bus station (☏3420-2785; ☺8am-6pm).

HSBC (Faria Sobrinho 371) Feeless ATM.

Paranaguá

◉ Sights
1 Igreja de NS do Rosário B2
2 Igreja de São Benedito.......................A1
3 Igreja São Francisco das
  Chagas C2
4 Museu de Arqueologia e
  Etnologia B2

⊜ Sleeping
5 Hostel Continente...............................C2
6 Hotel Ponderosa C2

⊗ Eating
7 Danubio Azul C2
8 Gruta da Garoupa C2
9 Mercado Municipal del Café B2

ⓘ Getting There & Away

Abaline (☏ Pontal do Sul 3455-2616; www.abaline.com.br; Paranaguá Ferry Dock) runs boats to Ilha do Mel throughout the day (one way/round trip R$16/32), with stops at both Nova Brasília (1½ hours) and Encantadas (two hours). In high season, there are departures from Paranaguá at 8:30am, 9:30am, 11am, 1pm, 3pm, 4:30pm and 6pm (these dwindle down to 8:30am and 3:30pm in low season).

Boats to Parque Nacional do Superagüi (R$25, one hour) leave between 2:30pm and 3pm, from four docks northeast of Ilha do Mel's dock; and to Guaraqueçaba (R$20, 9am, two hours), an erratic access point for Superagüi, from three docks southwest of the Ilha do Mel dock.

From the **bus station** (☏3420-2925) on the waterfront, Viação Graciosa (p268) goes throughout the day to Curitiba (R$19, 1½ hours) and Morretes (R$4, one hour). The Serra Verde

Express (p268) goes all the way to Paranaguá (five hours) on Sunday only, departing Curitiba at 7:30am, returning at 1:30pm.

ILHA DO MEL

 0XX41 / POP 1100

This hourglass-shaped island at the mouth of the Baía de Paranaguá is the most pristine and picturesque beach resort in all of southern Brazil, offering mostly wild beaches, good surfing waves and scenic coastal walks. The island's tranquility and lack of development are thanks in part to its isolation. Accessible only by boat, Ilha do Mel is traversed by sandy paths and has not a single car, so traffic jams throughout the island's scenic sandy lanes consist of surfboard-toting Brazilians on bicycles and bedazzled foreigners in their new Havaianas.

The fatter, northern half of the island is an ecological preserve, closed to inland exploration. The hillier southern portion is the locale of three small villages: Nova Brasília and Praia do Farol near the isthmus; and Encantadas at the far southern tip. They can be rowdy during the summer holidays, when young crowds descend on the island. But for the most part, Ilha do Mel, or 'honey island,' is the territory of surfers, campers, beachcombers and other escapists in search of simplicity and serenity.

◎ Sights

The picturesque **Fortaleza de NS dos Prazeres** (Fort of Our Lady of the Pleasures), which dates to the 1760s, is a 3km hike from Nova Brasília via **Praia da Fortaleza**. Inspect the deserted fortress before climbing up to the lookout for an incredible vista of the bay.

The **Farol das Conchas** (Conchas Lighthouse), built in 1872 on orders from Dom Pedro II, stands picturesquely atop a hill at the island's most easterly point. From here you have panoramic views of the island, the bay and the Serra do Mar. It's a popular spot to watch the sun drop below the horizon – don't miss it.

Legend has it that the small caves at the island's southern tip, known as the **Grutas das Encantadas**, are inhabited by beautiful mermaids who enchant all who come near. Signs clearly mark the way to the caves from Encantadas and Praia da Fora.

⚡ Activities

You can hire boats to explore the nearby islands. For Ilha do Superagüi (R$400 return, 40 minutes) and Ilha das Palmas (R$400 return), **Táxi Náutico** (🕿 9128-9769) leaves from Praia do Farol; for Ilha das Peças, boats (R$300, four to five hours) leave from the same dock as the inter-island ferry in Nova Brasília.

Surfing & Swimming

Ilha do Mel has no shortage of beaches. Those facing the bay enjoy warm waters gently lapping at the white sand, while those facing the ocean boast the big surf. But almost all of them are unspoiled, marked only be windswept dunes, forested hills and rocky outposts. **Praia da Fora** and **Praia Grande** are a 20-minute walk (2km) from Nova Brasília and a 40-minute walk (4km) from Encantadas. According to local surfers, in winter these beaches have the best waves in Paraná.

The **Praia do Farol** is the long stretch of sand between the Nova Brasília dock and the Farol das Conchas. It is backed by the swampy, grassy protected area of the *retinga,* which also preserves the natural beauty of the beach. Surfers congregate at the base of the hill and ride the legendary **Ondas das Paralelas**.

If you didn't bring your surfboard, you might prefer the calmer, warmer waters of the beaches that face the shallow bay. In the north, **Praia da Fortaleza**, often nearly deserted, allows you to bathe in the shadow of the 18th-century Portuguese fort. The best beach near the settlement of Encantadas is **Praia da Fora**, which has big waves and a few stalls selling *cervejas* (beers) and *sucos* (fruit juices).

SUP Paradise   SURFING, STAND-UP PADDLE
(🕿 3426-8196; www.astraldailha.com.br; ⊙ 10am-6pm) The well-organized outfit based out of Pousada Astral da Ilha in Vila do Farol is the spot to come for surf lessons (per hr R$80) and stand-up paddle instruction (per hour R$120).

Cycling

Biking is a great way to beat the heat and land on the sand faster.

Eduardo   BICYCLE RENTAL
(🕿 3426-8076; per hr/day R$10/40) Rent a single-gear beach cruiser from Eduardo behind Mercearia da Trilha market near Vila do

Ilha do Mel

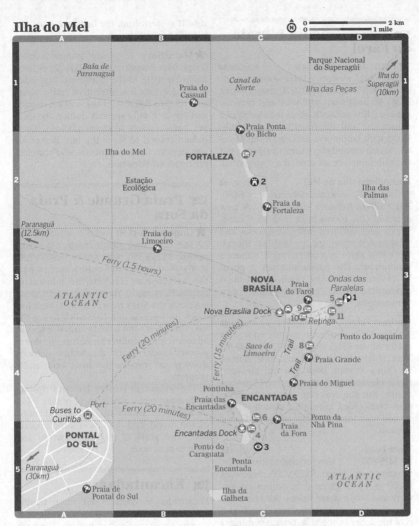

Farol. Note that you cannot take the bikes to Encantadas due to large rocks in the path.

🛏 Sleeping & Eating

To escape the summer crowds, head to the few **pousadas** (guesthouses) around Fortaleza, though you are a good one-hour, 3km hike from the Nova Brasília pier. Book ahead for holidays and any summer weekend. Expect discounts of 20% to 50% between April and November.

Ilha do Mel

⊙ Sights

🛏 Sleeping

🏠 Nova Brasília & Praia do Farol

⭐ **Pousada das Meninas** POUSADA $$
(☑ 3426-8023; www.pousadadasmeninas.com.br; r without/with bathroom R$170/230, chalets R$280; ❄️ 🌐) ✆ Built from driftwood and recycled material, this pousada offers the charm of a guesthouse and the friendliness of family. Hung with hammocks and chock-full of cutesy kitsch around every turn, the simple but tasteful rooms are set around a cozy garden.

Pousadinha Ilha do Mel POUSADA $$
(☑ 3426-8026; www.pousadinha.com.br; r R$90-260, r without bathroom R$80-120; 🌐) A new annex of chic rooms built from local hardwoods and outfitted with hammocks and solar-heated water are the best bet, though the whole place is a bit cramped, although comfortable. The Pousadinha has a popular **restaurant** serving pastas and seafood (mains R$58 to R$79 for two people) open to nonguests.

Marimar Farol HOSTEL $$
(☑ 3426-8032; www.hostelmarimar.com.br; dm R$60, r with fan R$175, with air-con R$210; ❄️ @ 🌐) This HI hostel is the first you come to from the Nova Brasília dock, offering pleasant, rustic, clapboard private rooms and four-bed dorms. But the real coup is the expansive deck overlooking a beautiful thatch of vegetation with the sea on the none-too-distant horizon.

Treze Luas POUSADA $$
(☑ 3426-8067; www.pousadatrezeluas.com.br; r without/with air-con R$200/300, beachfront R$350; ❄️ 🌐) Brightened by whimsical artwork and bold-colored linens, this charming pousada offers shiny stained-wood walls and cool tile floors (some have private verandas) and newer beachfront rooms. A common porch overlooks a makeshift Zen garden flocked by striking-red Brazilian tanagers. It'd be perfect were it not for the resistance that greets guests when their needs go beyond the bare minimum.

Enseada das Conchas POUSADA $$
(☑ 3426-8040; www.pousadaenseada.com.br; s/d/tr R$210/280/370; ❄️ 🌐) This quaint pousada has four spacious guestrooms painted in striking colors and decorated according to themes, such as 'Sunrise' and 'Sea Blue.' A wide deck is shaded by a thatch roof and scattered with lounge chairs and 12 or so cats. It is steps from the lighthouse and the island's best surf beach.

⭐ **Mar e Sol** BRAZILIAN, SEAFOOD $
(Praça Felipe Valentim; meals R$14-22; ⊙ 11am-10pm) En route to the lighthouse, Mar e Sol serves delicious fish, shrimp or crab *moquecas* (R$75 to R$120 for two), seafood risottos and cheaper daily specials. Junior, the local pet parrot, offers recommendations. Their defiant refusal to serve the best dishes for one person, however, means solo travelers are better off elsewhere.

🏠 Praia Grande & Praia da Fora

⭐ **Grajagan Surf Resort** POUSADA $$$
(☑ 3426-8043; www.grajagan.com.br; s/d without seaview R$253/390, with seaview R$400/620; ❄️ 🌐) ✆ Catering to wealthy surfers who like their creature comforts, the Indonesian-inspired Grajagan's rooms with ocean views are easily the Ilha's most luxurious: each has a private veranda and hammock facing the sea. Though it's the island's largest resort at 26 rooms, you wouldn't know it as you douse yourself under many clandestine outdoor showers or wander the lush, ecofriendly property.

The whimsical surfer's bar and upscale **restaurant** (great wholewheat pizzas; R$43 to R$59) is awash in intricately-detailed carved wood and an astonishing mosaic floor (two years of meticulous work) and open to nonguests.

🛏️ Encantadas

Encantadas is quieter and more family-oriented than Nova Brasília though there is a party scene on the beach itself. The walk from Nova Brasília to Encantadas is about 4.5km and is exposed to bright sun.

Hostel Encantadas Ecologic HOSTEL $
(☑ 9142-8087; hostel_ecologic@hotmail.com; Encantadas; dm R$30, camping with tent R$50, d with/without bathroom R$90/70; 🌐) ✆ The island's cheapest option is a colorful, sustainable choice, but poor email etiquette makes it hard to reserve.

Marimar Encantadas HOSTEL $$
(☑ 3426-9052; www.hostelmarimar.com.br; Encantadas; dm/s/d/tr R$60/150/175/245; @ 🌐) The island's best value, this popular hostel

facing Encantadas beach offers a generous breakfast, comfy common areas, a communal kitchen, a beachfront deck, and bike and surfboard rentals (per hour/day R$10/30).

O Recanto do Francês II POUSADA $$
(☑ 3426-9105; www.recantodofrances.com.br; s/d R$140/150; ☎) With an adorable garden setting, friendly French owners (and their crepes) and Whisky, a blind Yorkshire terrier with deft football skills, this pousada steps from Mar do Fora beach wins the charm-for-value race. Afternoon crepes are a big hit as well. The more economical **Recanto I** is 200m closer to the beach but not as charming.

★ **Fim da Trilha** POUSADA $$$
(☑ 3426-9017; www.fimdatrilha.com.br; s/d R$245/350; ✱@☎) ✎ Off the Grutas das Encantadas trail, an enticing winding path leads to this sustainable paradise. The spacious terrace is overflowing with blooming foliage and gurgling fountains; rooms are tastefully decorated. Here, the island's best **restaurant** welcomes nonguests and is a don't miss for its real deal spicy *paella* served – stop the presses! – in individual portions (R$37 to R$46).

Caraguatá POUSADA $$$
(☑ 3426-9097; www.caraguata-ilhadomel.com.br; Encantadas; d from R$320; ✱@☎) ✎ Just a few steps from the pier, Caraguatá's pretty chalets are adorned with flower boxes and greenery. Intimate rooms vary in size but they all have stained-wood ceilings, whitewashed walls and crisp linens. Run by an amicable Argentine-Brazilian couple, it's a rare top-end choice.

Praça de Alimentação SEAFOOD $
(Mar da Fora; mains R$15-40; ☺11am-6pm; ♨) This beachside restaurant complex located south of Encantadas serves simple, fresh and cheap dishes for lunch, along with a dose of *forró* (popular music of the Northeast) til late on Saturday nights.

Shams MIDDLE EASTERN $
(mains R$8-15; ☺1pm-midnight Sun-Fri, to 2am Sat) Yassir, a first generation Lebanese descendants threw down a couple of plastic tables in the sand and now churns out great shawarma, falafel, homemade burgers and – drum roll, please – banoffee pie!

ⓘ Orientation

Most of the hotels are clustered in the village of Nova Brasília, which occupies the isthmus

linking the two ends of the island, and Praia do Farol, the beach that stretches east from here. The landmark lighthouse sits atop a *morro* (hill) on its easternmost point. Another, smaller settlement, Encantadas, at the southern end of the island, is the closest point to the mainland. A 6km trail on the east coast links the two towns, traversing a series of undeveloped beaches including Praia da Fora, Praia do Miguel and Praia Grande.

ⓘ Information

There are no banks, ATMs or pharmacies on the island, so plan ahead. You'll find tourist information offices at the docks in both **Nova Brasília** (☑ 3254-1516; www.turismo.pr.gov.br; Arrival Dock, Nova Brasília; ☺9am-7pm) and **Encantadas** (Encantadas; ☺8am-6pm).

Ilha do Mel Online (☑ 3426 8065; www.ilhadomelonline.com; per hr R$9; ☺9am-9pm) This charming blue house is on the path between Nova Brasília and Farol das Conchas. It offers internet access, crepes, the island's best espresso, rooms for rent and information about the island.

ⓘ Getting There & Away

Abaline (p269) runs boats (R$32 return) at 8:30am, 9:30am, 11am, 1pm, 3pm, 4:30pm and 6pm in summer (these dwindle down to 8:30am and 3:30pm in low season) from the jetty opposite Paranaguá's tourist office, stopping first in Nova Brasília (1½ hours), and afterwards in Encantadas (two hours). Back to the mainland, boats depart for Paranaguá at 7:30am, 8:30am, 10:30am, 1:30pm, 3:30pm, 5pm and 6:30pm from Nova Brasília, a half hour earlier from Encantadas.

Alternatively, Viação Graciosa (p268) runs six daily buses from Curitiba to Pontal do Sul (R$28, 2½ hours), on the mainland opposite Encantadas, where you can embark for the 30-minute crossing to Nova Brasília or Encantadas (R$24 return). In high season, boats leave every half hour from 8am to 8pm from Pontal and 7am to 8pm from Ilha do Mel; in low season, every hour.

If you arrive with clunky wheeled luggage, a battalion of wooden cart-wielding sand porters have your back: from Nova Brasília, it's R$25 as far as Farol and R$35 to Praia Grande.

ⓘ Getting Around

It's a 1½-hour walk along the coast from Nova Brasília to Encantadas; otherwise, grab the island ferry from one village to the other (one-way/return R$8/15, 20 minutes, seven to nine daily). Be wary of snakes on the trails near Fortaleza and the Estação Ecológica – your devoted author was paralyzed by one blocking the trail for 45 minutes.

PARANÁ ENCANTADAS

IGUAÇU FALLS & AROUND

☎0XX45 / POP 256,000

Rising in the coastal mountains of Paraná and Santa Catarina, the Rio Iguaçu snakes west for 600km, picking up a few dozen tributaries along the way. It widens majestically and sweeps around a magnificent forest stage, before plunging and crashing in the tiered cascades known as Iguaçu Falls.

Thousands of years before they were 'discovered' by Europeans, the falls were a holy burial place for the Tupi-Guarani and Paraguas tribes. Spaniard Don Alvar Nuñes happened upon the falls in 1541, dubbing them 'Saltos de Santa María'. But this name didn't stick and the Tupi-Guarani name, Iguaçu (Great Waters), did. In 1986, Unesco declared the region a World Heritage site; a New Seven Wonders of Nature accolade followed in 2011.

Foz do Iguaçu

The Brazilian city of Foz do Iguaçu went through a period of frenzied growth during the 18 years that Itaipu Dam was under construction (completed in 1982), when the population increased more than fivefold. It was an edgy place then, but has settled down.

Tours

If you want to see both sides of the falls in a single day, taking an organized tour is the only way to make it happen without rushing about. Almost all the hotels in Foz do Iguaçu offer tours to Argentina for around R$130 (you'll save R$30 and a few hours if you opt to go independently).

Macuco Ecoaventura/ Safari BOAT TOUR, HIKING
(☎3529-9665, 3574-4244; www.macucosafari.com.br; Brazil) For boat tours and hiking on the Brazilian side.

Iguazú Jungle Explorer BOAT TOUR
(☎42-1696; www.iguazujungle.com; Argentina) Offers several river adventures on the Argentine side.

Sleeping

Av das Cataratas on the way to the falls is lined with chain and convention-style hotels. Don't be shy about trying to negotiate a lower price if the hotel is not full.

★**Hostel Natura** HOSTEL $
(☎3529-6949; www.hostelnatura.com; Av das Cataratas Km 12.5; camping/dm per person R$28/40, d/tr without bath R$105/110, tr R$150;) This hostel is set on a gorgeous piece of land, amid two small lakes and lush scenery. The rooms themselves are pleasant and tidy, and there's ample outdoor lounge space and a fun bar. Service is top-notch, including transportation, dinner and other perks. The hostel is 12km from town on the way to the falls.

Pousada Sonho Meu POUSADA $
(☎3573-5764; www.pousadasonhomeufoz.com.br; Mem de Sá 262; d/tr R$160/200; @) What from the outside looks like an administrative building becomes a delightful oasis barely 50m from the local bus terminal. Rooms are simply decorated with bamboo; there's a standout pool (complete with a mini *catarata*!), breakfast area and outdoor guest kitchen; and a warm welcome throughout. Cash only.

There are no singles in high season, but low-season solo travelers can sleep for R$80.

Favela Chic HOSTEL $
(☎3027-5060; www.favelachichosteliguassu.com; Raul de Mattos 78; camping per person R$18, dm from R$35, s/d R$90/110, with shared bathroom R$50/80; @) Warm-hearted Brit ex-pat Nick is the heart and soul of this artsy hostel, which boasts a social bar, full English fry-ups for breakfast and a downright cozy converted van in the backyard that sleeps two. *Seriously*. Newer private rooms are in hippie-chic, love-shack constructions.

Iguaçu Falls

Foz do Iguaçu

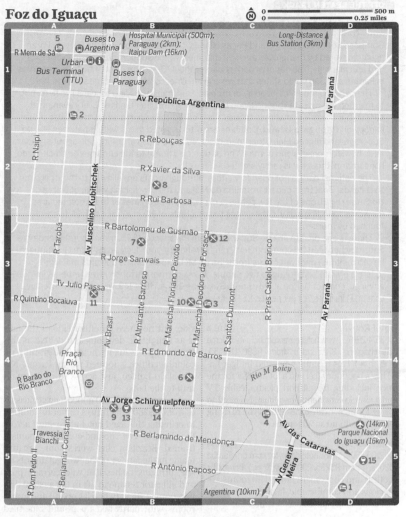

Foz do Iguaçu

Sleeping
1	Favela Chic	D5
2	Hotel Del Rey	A1
3	Hotel Rafain Centro	C3
4	Hotel Rouver	C5
5	Pousada Sonho Meu	A1

Eating
6	Beduinos	B4
7	Chef Lopes	B3
8	Famiglia Maran	B2
9	Oficina do Sorvete	B4
10	Trapiche	B3
11	Tropicana	A3
12	Vó Bertila	C3

Drinking & Nightlife
13	Capitão Bar	B5
14	Rafain Chopp	B5
15	Zeppelin Old Bar	D5

OFF THE BEATEN TRACK

PARQUE NACIONAL DO SUPERAGÜI

Composed of the Superagüi and Peças islands, this national park in the Baía de Paranaguá is covered by mangroves and salt marshes, which support an amazing variety of bird and plant life. The national park is part of the 4700 sq km of Atlantic forest reserves in Paraná and São Paulo states that were given Unesco World Heritage status in 1999.

The park is famous for its array of orchids. Hummingbirds and toucans live here, not to mention the roseate spoonbill and the stunning Brazilian tanager. Every evening at sunset, hundreds – sometimes thousands – of red-tailed parrots return to roost in the canopy on **Papagaio Island**. Dolphins are often sighted in the waters between Ilha do Superagüi and Ilha do Mel. Other mammals are more elusive, but include agoutis, pacas, deer, howler monkeys and pumas. The park is also home to the endangered black-faced lion tamarin, though it is rarely sighted.

The national park is not open to visitors, although boats are allowed to motor around the islands. Boat trips depart from Ilha do Mel and the tiny fishing village of **Barra do Superagüi**, one of the few settlements within the confines of the protected area. It's worth spending a day in the village to get a taste of life in a place still relatively untouched by tourism.

There is one boat to Ilha do Superagüi from Paranaguá ($25, three hours) Monday to Saturday between 2:30pm and 3pm; plus erratic, try-your-luck boats from Guaraqueçaba (45 minutes) and water taxis from Ilha do Mel. Expect prices upwards of R$250 to hire a private boat for up to five people. To make transportation arrangements in advance, contact Dalton at **Pousada Superagüi** (✆ 3482-7149; www.pousadasuperagui.com.br; Principal s/n; r per person R$40; @).

Hotel Rouver HOTEL $
(✆ 3574-2916; www.hotelrouver.com.br; Av Jorge Schimmelpfeng 872; s/d/tr from R$90/110/150; ❄@🛜❄) This recently renovated budget hotel has a boutiquey feel and a lot on offer for the price, including free airport pickup, cable TV and a simple continental breakfast. No need to spring for higher categories unless you're dying for a minibar and small terrace.

Hotel Del Rey HOTEL $$
(✆ 2105-7500; www.hoteldelreyfoz.com.br; Tarobá 1020; s/d from R$255/290; ❄@🛜❄) Friendly, spotless and convenient hotel. The rooms are spacious and comfortable, facilities are excellent and the breakfast buffet is huge.

Hotel Rafain Centro HOTEL $$
(✆ 3521-3500; www.rafaincentro.com.br; Deodoro 984; s/d R$270/345; ❄@🛜❄) More appealing than some of the megahotels around town, the Rafain is a renovated, four-star place with plenty of style, artistic detail and friendly staff. Rooms are simple with large balconies and there's a cracking pool and terrace. Prices can come down substantially.

★**Hotel das Cataratas** HOTEL $$$
(✆ 2102-7000; www.hoteldascataratas.com; r without/with waterfall views from R$1000/1405; ste from R$1530; ❄@🛜❄) You'll find spectacular views from the Sheraton on the Argentine side, but nowhere on either side of the falls is as delightful, delicious and deluxe as this Orient Express luxury hotel. The grand pink colonial edifice is located within Parque Nacional do Iguaçu, just across from the main trail to the falls.

A renovation in 2010 added a spa (massages from R$260) and fitness center in addition to bringing this aged hotel up to snuff across the board. The up-and-coming, Spanish-trained, Brazilian chef works some creative magic in the fancier of the two restaurants on site, bringing dishes like wild cerrado pork and alligator terrine to life in the austere dining room at Itapu (when it's open); and grand rooms with hardwood floors and blue-tiled bathrooms ensure complete comfort after a day in the park. If you're not tired of getting wet, the pool ain't too shabby, either.

🍴 Eating

True gourmands will find the best dining experiences – and service – in Puerto Iguazu in Argentina. Start with **La Rueda** (www.larueda1975.com).

Tropicana CHURRASCARIA $
(www.pizzariareopicana.com.br; Kubitschek 228; buffet R$22; ⊙11am-4pm & 7-11pm) This all-you-can-eat shoestring savior offers serious taste for money.

Famiglia Maran SELF-SERVE, BUFFET $
([phone]3027-1212; Barroso 1968; per kg R$19.20; [time]24hr) This bakery and cafeteria has something for everyone. Sandwiches, pastas and filling hot dishes will sate your hunger, as will the irresistible soup buffet (R$16.50, from 6pm to 5:30am).

Beduinos MIDDLE EASTERN $
(www.beduinos.com.br; Deodoro 755; mains R$7-19; [time]6pm-midnight Tue-Sun) Foz's Lebanese community is second in size only to São Paulo and this great Arab cheapie is a nice byproduct of that immigration. Great shawarma, a long line of *esfihas* (ground beef pastries with veggies and hummus are staples here. The decor isn't much, but there's a pleasant and popular patio.

Oficina do Sorvete CAFE $
(www.oficinadosorvete.com.br; Av Jorge Schimmelpfeng 244; per kg sandwiches/ice cream R$37.50/39.50; [time]1pm-1:30am; [icons]) Take a dive into nearly 50 colorful, beat-the-heat ice-cream flavors on hand, from traditional *(doce de leite)* to exotic fruits *(jabuticaba)* to edgy (Red Bull).

★**Vó Bertila** PIZZERIA $$
(www.vobertilla.com.br; Bartolomeu de Gusmão 1116; pizza R$17-57, pasta for 2 R$39-68; [time]6pm-midnight) This informal, family-run cantina churns out wood-fired pizza and authentic pastas in heaping portions. All homey and hardwoods, it's the kind of down-home Italian spot Brazil does so very well. Expect packed.

Trapiche BRAZILIAN, SEAFOOD $$$
([phone]3527-3951; Deodoro 1087; mains for 2 R$85-129; [time]5pm-1am Mon-Sat, noon-midnight Sun) Though inconsistency ails it, the *moqueca* and other outstanding seafood stews here are big enough to sate at least a couple of big appetites, and when the kitchen is on, they're damn good. The highest priced items include lobster and oysters (that have come a long way from the sea but are delicious nevertheless).

There's a substantial nightly seafood buffet (R$79.90) in case you just can't make up your mind amid this dizzying sea of options.

Chef Lopes BRAZILIAN $$$
(www.cheflopes.com.br; Barroso 1713; mains R$26-94; [time]11:30am-3:30pm & 6-11:30pm; [icon]) Intimate it's surely not, but this super-sized dining room churns out a *por kilo* lunch buffet (R$39.90) that locals rave about and, for dinner, it's the one destination in Foz that Hotel das Cataratas comfortably sends guests. The great-value menu is loaded with Argentine-cut steak options like *bife do chorizo* and non-farmed local fish like *congrio* and *surubi*.

🍷 Drinking & Nightlife

Nightlife is hopping along Av Jorge Schimmelpfeng, where you will find breezy beer gardens for early evening, lively outdoor patio bars and hot-to-trot nightclubs that stay open late. Good starting points inlcude **Rafain Chopp** (Av Jorge Schimmelpfeng 450; [time]4pm-3am ; [icon]) and **Capitão Bar** ([phone]3572-1512; www.capitaobar.com; Av Jorge Schimmelpfeng 288; pizza R$25; [icon]).

★**Zeppelin Old Bar** LIVE MUSIC
(www.zeppelinoldbar.com; Raul Mattos 222; cover R$4-20; [time]9pm-late Tue-Sat; [icon]) Outstanding bar serving up excellent cocktails and live music. The beautiful people congregate on Thursdays and Saturdays.

ℹ️ Orientation

Av Brasil is the main street, running north to south. The long-distance bus station is 4.5km to the northeast, but the local bus station – just north of Av República Argentina – serves the airport (15km southeast) and Parque Nacional do Iguaçu (17km southeast).

Just south of town, the junction of the Paraná and Iguaçu rivers forms the tripartite Paraguay–Brazil–Argentina border (marked by obelisks). The Ponte Presidente Tancredo Neves crosses the Rio Iguaçu about 6km from the center of town, connecting Brazil with the Argentine town of Puerto Iguazú. Just north of the center, the

---

ℹ️ IGUAZÚ/IGUAÇU TOURIST CORRIDOR

Mercosul (South American free trade zone) nationals can enter Argentina in the area around Iguazú Falls for less than 72 hours without a visa. Although citizens from most western European countries do not need a visa, citizens of the United States, Australia and Canada must pay a reciprocity tax in advance, even for day trips to the Argentine side of the falls. Conversely, if you need a visa for Brazil, you will need it to visit the falls from Argentina, even on an organized day trip.

See Getting to Argentina & Paraguay (p282) for specific detials.

PARANÁ FOZ DO IGUAÇU

Iguaçu Falls

Nearly nothing wows like the breathtaking roar of the Rio Iguaçu splicing the edge of Brazil and Argentina, creating the spectacular Iguaçu Falls. Encompassing some 275 individual falls occupying an area more than 3km wide and 80m high – it's wider than Victoria, higher than Niagara and more beautiful than both.

Brazilian Side

The main event of Parque Nacional do Iguaçu in Brazil is the Trilha das Cataratas, or 'Waterfall Trail.' This 1200m trail follows the shore of the Iguaçu river, providing innumerable photo ops and a grand overview of the falls along the way. It terminates at the bottom of Garganta do Diablo, or 'Devils'Throat,' the most spectacular part of the falls. A manmade walkway allows you to go out to the middle of the river so the force of rushing water seemingly surrounds you. Expect to be dazzled – and doused.

Argentine Side

Argentina's Parque Nacional Iguazú offers the single-most heart-stopping moment at Iguaçu Falls: As the 2km elevated plank walkway from Estación Garganta del Diablo culminates at the top of Garganta del Diablo, Mother Nature's absolute ferocity very suddenly and shockingly leaps from the stuff of legend to very real indeed. The sound and the fury is nothing short of electrifying.

Boat Trips

While admiring the falls from above, you will surely spot fearless adventurers experiencing the falls from below. You can get closer to Garganta do Diablo on

1. Iguaçu Falls
2. Boat trip, Iguaçu Falls
3. Swallowtail butterflies

boat tours on the Argentine side, but the Brazilian version is more elaborate and, a bit more expensive. Plus Brazilian boats have a backup motor and are Navy-inspected. See Macuco Safari (p281) and Iguazú Jungle Explorer (p274).

Outdoor Adventures

Parque Nacional do Iguaçu covers 550 sq km of rainforest, most of which is inaccessible to anybody but the wildlife. Hiking is more rewarding in the morning, when the weather is cooler and birds and animals are more active. Look for butterflies, parrots, parakeets, woodpeckers, hummingbirds, toucans, lizards and spiders, among more elusive creatures such as monkeys, deer, sloths and anteaters. Additional activities include tree-top adventures, rappelling and white-water rafting, all offered by **Cânion Iguaçu** (☑3529-6040; www.campodedesafios.com.br).

Aerial Views

While the Brazilian side gives the grand overview of the falls and Argentina the up close and personal look, no view is quite as memorable as fitting the entire motherload into one panoramic camera frame. Helisul, next to the entrance to Parque Nacional do Iguaçu, offers 10-minute helicopter tours of the falls for up to four people at a time.

ℹ BUENOS AIRES OR BUST

Note that when comparing the overnight Cama Suite service to Buenos Aires, it is considerably cheaper to catch the bus from Brazil rather than Puerto Iguazú on the Argentine side (R$210 rather than the peso equivalent of R$351), though the latter has more departures and levels of service.

Ponte da Amizade spans the Rio Paraná, crossing to the shabby Paraguayan town of Ciudad del Este aka Brazilian Shopping Paradise!

ℹ Information

Most hotels and hostels offer internet access on site and downtown Foz has a public wi-fi signal. Dozens of banks and money-exchange houses are all over town.

Banco do Brasil (Brasil 1377) ATMs and money exchange.

Correios (www.correios.com.br; Praça Getúlio Vargas 72; ☉9am-5pm Mon-Fri)

Hospital Municipal (☎3521-1951; Adoniran Barbosa 370; ☉24hr)

HSBC (Xavier da Silva 660) Feeless ATMs. There's another branch at Av Brasil (Av Brasil 1131).

Polícia Federal (☎3576-5500; www.dpf.gov. br; Av Paraná 3471)

PIT (☎0800-45-1516; www.iguassu.tur.br; Av das Cataratas 2330, Vila Yolanda; ☉7am-11pm) Provides maps and detailed info about the area. The main office is in Vila Yolanda, out of town on Av das Cataratas towards the falls, reachable on bus 120. Other branches are at the airport (☎0800-45-1516; www.iguassu.tur.br; Aeroporto Internacional de Foz do Iguaçu/Cataratas; ☉8am-10pm), long-distance bus station (☎0800-45-1516; www.iguassu.tur.br; Av Costa e Silva 1601; ☉7am-6pm) and local bus station (☎0800-45-1516; www.iguassu.tur.br; Kubitschek 1310; ☉7:30am-6pm).

ℹ Getting There & Away

AIR

Daily flights link Foz's **Cataratas International Airport** (IGU; ☎3523-4244), under renovation at time of research, to Lima, Rio, Salvador, São Paulo, Campinas, Curitiba and Porto Alegre. Sit on the left hand side of the plane on arrival for good views of the falls.

BUS

The **long-distance bus station** (☎3522-3336; Av Costa e Silva 1601) is 4.5km from the center of town.

Sample travel times and *executivo* (where applicable) fares from Foz are listed in the table (below).

ℹ Getting Around

Local bus fare costs R$2.90. The local transport terminal is known as **TTU** (Terminal Turístico Urbano; Av Juscelino Kubitschek).

TO/FROM THE AIRPORT

Bus 120 'Aeroporto/Parque Nacional' runs to the airport (R$2.90, 30 minutes) and the Brazilian side of the waterfalls (40 minutes) every 22 minutes from 5:25am to midnight. Catch it at the local bus terminal or any stop along Av Juscelino Kubitschek south of Barbosa. Bus 120 'Centro/TTU' goes from the airport to Centro (exit to the far left end and look for blue 'Ônibus' sign).

The official taxi booth in the arrivals hall charges R$45 to Centro and R$20 to the park.

TO/FROM THE BUS STATION

City buses 105 and 115 (R$2.90) cover the 6km between the long-distance bus station and the local terminal downtown (from TTU, catch it at Ala 3 for the correct direction). A taxi costs R$15.

TO/FROM THE FALLS

For the Brazilian side of the falls, catch the 'Aeroporto/P Nacional' bus (R$2.90) to the park entrance. You can catch it in the local bus terminal, or at stops along Av Juscelino Kubitschek and Av Jorge Schimmelpfeng.

PARANÁ FOZ DO IGUAÇU

BUSES FROM FOZ DO IGUAÇU

DESTINATION	FARE (R$)	TIME (HR)	COMPANY
Asunción	54	5	NSA (www.nsa.com.py)
Buenos Aires	210	19	Crucero del Norte (www.crucerodelnorte.com.ar)
Campo Grande	124	15	Eucatur (www.eucatur.com.br)
Curitiba	115	10	Catarinense (www.catarinense.net)
Florianópolis	140	12	Pluma (www.pluma.com.br)
Rio de Janeiro	230	23	Kalowa (www.expressokaiowa.com.br)
São Paulo	165	14	Kalowa (www.expressokaiowa.com.br)

To get to the Argentina side, catch a Puerto Iguazú bus (R$4, one hour) on Mem de Sá across from the local bus terminal. They pass every 15 minutes (30 minutes on Sunday) between 7:15am and 7pm (from 8am Sunday). At Puerto Iguazú bus station, **Río Uruguay** (www.rio uruguaybus.com.ar) services the falls (A$60 return, 30 minutes).

Parque Nacional do Iguaçu (Brazil)

You can't miss the shiny entrance to the **Parque Nacional do Iguaçu** (☑3521-4400; www.cataratasdoiguacu.com.br; admission foreigners/Mercosul/Brazilians R$41.10/32.85/24.60; ☺8:30am-5pm), which houses bathrooms, ATMs, lockers, souvenir shops and vast parking facilities. Once you buy your ticket, you will be directed to board a free double-decker bus.

To visit the falls, take the bus to the third stop, site of Hotel das Cataratas (p276). Here you can pick up the **Trilha das Cataratas**, or 'Waterfall Trail', a 1200m trail following the shore of the Iguaçu river, terminating at the **Garganta do Diablo**. From here, take the panoramic elevator to get a view of the falls from above. At the top, a short walk along the road leads to **Porto Canoas** station, where you will find a nice **restaurant** with an excellent lunch buffet (R$45) and a food court with less expensive options. Both have seating on a pleasant outdoor terrace overlooking the flats of the river.

Remember, it's always wet at the falls, and sunlight reflects off bodies of water. Pack rain gear *and* sunblock. Bug repellent is a must on the walking trails. Also note that lighting for photography is best in the morning on the Brazilian side.

Activities

Boat Trips

Many claim that the way to truly experience the falls is to feel their wrath raining down on you. Boats from both sides of the border take adventurous passengers under the falls. **Macuco Safari** (☑3574-4244; www.macucosafari.com.br; per person R$140) offers the Brazilian side's spectacular opportunity to get up close, personal and wet at the base of the falls. The excursion starts with a 3km ride through the jungle, with an English-speaking guide pointing out the park's flora and fauna. The second phase is a short hike (600m) to a small waterfall called Salto de Macuco, where

you can take a dip. Finally, climb aboard a Zodiac for a 4km journey over flat water and rapids, and under the falls known as the Three Musketeers. You *will* get soaked. The boat ride is 30 minutes, but the whole excursion takes about two hours.

Macuco Safari also offers a more sedate, 3½-hour boat trip along the flats above the falls.

To reach Macuco, get off the double-decker bus at the second stop.

Hiking

You can explore a few hiking trails in the company of a guide provided by the park (English-speaking guides are available). The **Trilha Poço Preto** (☑3529-9627; www.macucoecoaventura.com.br; per person R$135), run by Macuco Safari (p281), is a 9km trail that starts near the entrance (get off the bus at the first stop), and leads to the Lagoa do Poço Preto, a small lagoon that attracts birdlife. A quick boat ride and an optional paddle in a kayak complete the well-choreographed outing. The return trip is via the **Trilha das Bananeiras**, but you can get a lift.

Adventure Activities

For more excitement, stop off at the **Cânion Iguaçu** (☑3529-6040; www.campodedesafios.com.br) for Arvorismo (R$70), rappelling (R$70) and white-water rafting (R$80; Class II to III rapids depending on water levels). The entrance is at the third bus stop, opposite Hotel das Cataratas.

Parque Nacional Iguazú (Argentina)

The Argentine **park** (☑054-3757 491 469; www.iguazuargentina.com; adult/child AR$85/45; ☺8am-6:30pm, to 5:30pm Sep-Mar) has plenty to offer, and involves a fair amount of walking. The spread-out complex at the entrance has various amenities, including lockers, an ATM and a restaurant. The complex ends at a train station, where a train runs every half-hour to the Cataratas train station, where the waterfall walks begin, and the elevated walkway **Garganta del Diablo**.

Activities

Boating

Many claim that the way to truly experience the falls is to feel their wrath raining down on you. Boats from both sides of the border take adventurous passengers under the falls.

Iguazú Jungle Explorer (p274) offers two versions of this adventure. The Gran Aventura (A$310) is a one-hour excursion that includes an 8km ride through the jungle on the back of a jeep and a 6km ride down the Iguazú river. The trip culminates in an up-close-and-personal tour of Salto San Martin and Garganta del Diablo. This excursion departs hourly from the visitors center near the entrance.

If your primary interest is the so-called 'waterfall baptism,' you can opt for the abbreviated Aventura Nautica (A$150). The 12-minute trip departs from the dock opposite Isla San Martín (every 20 minutes), giving passengers a quick tour of the canyon and a sousing shower. Protective bags are provided for cameras and other gear; anything not contained therein – including you – will get wet.

Buy tickets just past the park entrance or at the Iguazú Jungle Explorer office near Estación Cataratas.

Hiking

To explore the rainforest in the national park, stop at the **Centro de Visitantes** (☑0xx54-3757-49-1445) near the entrance and inquire about the Sendero Macuco. This 7km trail is a rare opportunity to explore the park independently. Six interpretive stations explain the flora, including bamboo, palmitos and pioneer plants. The white-bearded manakin and toco toucan live in these parts, as does a troupe of brown capuchin monkeys. The trail's end point is the Arrechea Waterfall, a 20m cascade that has gouged out a lovely natural pool below.

Early morning is the best time for hiking. Departure before 4pm (3pm in winter) is required.

---

❶ GETTING TO ARGENTINA & PARAGUAY

Many nationalities can enter Argentina without a visa, but double-check before you arrive or at the **Argentine Consulate** (☑3574-2969; www.mrecic.gov.ar; Travessia Bianchi 26; ☉10am-3pm Mon-Fri). Overland-traveling citizens of the United States (10 years $160), Australia (single entry $100) and Canada (single entry/five years $75/150) must pay a reciprocity tax in advance through **Provincia Pagos** (www.migraciones.gov.ar); click on 'Pay Your Reciprocity Tax', follow the steps and print out your receipt to take along with you. For Paraguay, Americans ($100), Australians ($75) and Canadians ($65) need a visa (though not unless you go beyond Ciudad del Este). Get this in advance at home or from the **Paraguayan Consulate** (☑3523-2898; Deodoro 901; ☉8:30am-12:30pm & 1:30-4pm Mon-Fri) in Foz.

To Puerto Iguazú, Argentina

If traveling by bus, at Brazilian immigration in either direction, most bus drivers won't wait around while you finish formalities. You must get a pass from the driver, get your passport stamped, then wait and reboard the next bus. It's important you pay attention as drivers ask if anyone needs to stop at immigration on the Brazilian side – but in Portuguese (or Spanish), if at all. Many travelers miss it and end up with serious immigration hassles later (ie hefty fines).

On day trips to the Argentine side of the falls, do not forget your Brazilian entry card, you are officially leaving the country and will need to leave this with Brazilian authorities. You will be issued with a new one upon return. At Argentine immigration, the bus always stops and waits for everyone to be processed. Both borders are open 24 hours but bus service ends around 7pm. The last bus you can catch is the second-to-last bus back to Brazil. If you don't, there will be no bus coming after yours to scoop you up after you finish with border formalities.

To Ciudad del Este, Paraguay

Get a bus from Av Juscelino Kubitschek across from TTU (p280) – R$3.60, 30 minutes – or taxi to the border, get your passport stamped, then catch the next bus or a taxi to Ciudad del Este or walk across the Ponte da Amizade (Friendship Bridge). If traveling further into Paraguay, you'll need to complete formalities with Brazil's Polícia Federal and the Paraguayan immigration authorities at the consulate.

Itaipu Dam

On the Paraná river 14km north of Foz, **Itaipu Dam** (📞 0800-645-4645; www.turismoitaipu. com.br; Tancredo Neves 6702; panoramic/special tour R$22/56.10; ⊘ regular tour hourly 8am-4pm) trades jaw-dropping statistics with Three Gorges Dam in China for largest hydroelectric power plant on the planet accolades.

The statistics are startling. The dam's structures stretch for almost 9km and reach a height of more than 200m. The concrete used in its construction would be sufficient to build a two-lane highway from Moscow to Lisbon. At the height of construction, crews worked at a blinding pace, equivalent to building a 20-storey office building every hour. No wonder it cost US$18 billion. The plant provides 22% of the electric energy consumed in Brazil, and more than 90% of the energy consumed in Paraguay. Even more extraordinary is the massive size of the construction that spans the river, the palpable power of the water rushing out of the spillway, and the endless array of power lines emanating from the plant.

Construction of the dam was controversial. Critics estimate that 700 sq km of forest was lost or compromised in its construction. Several species of plant life have been driven into extinction. Many native Guarani and Tupi settlements were destroyed, as were the impressive Sete Quedas waterfalls. On the other hand, the dam's generating capacity is 14,000 megawatts of clean energy. To produce an equivalent amount in oil-burning thermoelectric plants, you'd need 434,000 barrels of oil per day. That's a lot of carbon dioxide emissions.

🛈 PESOS, POR FAVOR!

Credit cards are not accepted to purchase your entry ticket to Parque Nacional Iguazú (Argentina), nor dollars, euros or reais. Exchange in Foz or stop at the cash machine at the initial entrance gate to the park. There's a second ATM inside the park, but it's past the ticket takers.

For its part, the Itaipu Binacional – a joint Brazilian–Paraguayan agency that administers the dam – has been sensitive to criticisms. Innovative programs have relocated animals displaced by flooding, reforested the land along the reservoir's banks and compensated communities affected by the construction. Itaipu's public relations team is eager to publicize accomplishments, if not the downsides. So expect a barrage of propaganda when you take the regular tour *(visita panorâmica)*. A short film is followed by a visit to the central observation deck, providing a panoramic view of the complex. All information is in Portuguese and English. For a more technical tour, you'll want to indulge yourself in the truly fascinating **special circuit** *(circuito especial*; minimum age 14; 8am, 8:30am, 10am, 10:30am, 1:30pm, 2pm, 3:30pm and 4pm). This in-depth, two-hour tour is fascinating for anyone with engineering tendencies.

If you're wondering how this massive feat of engineering affected the local flora and fauna, check out the **Ecomuseu** (adult/student R$8.80/4.40; ⊘ 8am-4:30pm Tue-Sun).

To get to the Itaipu Dam, catch bus 101 or 102 (R$2.90, 30 minutes) which leave every 15 minutes from Foz do Iguaçu's TTU terminal (p280).

PARANÁ ITAIPU DAM

Santa Catarina

POP 6.25 MILLION

Best Places to Eat

➡ Bistrô Santa Marta (p293)

➡ Urucum (p307)

➡ Bar do Arante (p295)

➡ Basement English Pub (p302)

Best Places to Stay

➡ Janela de Márcia (p293)

➡ Pousada Natur Campeche (p294)

➡ Pousada La Roca (p306)

➡ Quinta do Bucanero (p307)

➡ Tucano House (p293)

Why Go?

Life's a beach. At least in sunny Santa Catarina, which boasts 560km of spectacular coastline. If you like your beach deserted, there is a spot of sand for you in the south of Ilha de Santa Catarina. If you prefer a party scene, head further north on that same island. If you're all about big surf, it's up in Guarda do Embaú and Praia do Rosa, two absolutely stunning surf villages south of Florianópolis.

Sun and sand aside, the inland regions are also where Santa Catarina exhibits the profound influence of its German ancestry, most evident during Oktoberfest, Blumenau's huge festival for folk dancing, accordion playing and beer drinking (mostly beer drinking). But the Alpine architecture and fresh-brewed beer are here to enjoy year-round.

Like the other southern states, Santa Catarina enjoys some of Brazil's highest standards of living, with sound infrastructure and a blonde-haired, blue-eyed population that often feels more European than latin.

When to Go
Florianopolis

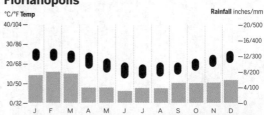

Jan, Feb & Oct Whether Sommerfest or Oktoberfest, Blumenau is awash in beer and brat.

Mar & Apr Post-Carnaval, the sun still shines in Florianópolis.

Jun & Jul Join the Brazilian celebration of winter kitsch in Santa Catarina's Serra Geral.

History

In the 1820s, an independent Brazil realized the importance of this region on the frontier between the Spanish and Portuguese Americas. The emperor invited German-speaking immigrants to develop the land and serve as a buffer against Spanish insurgency. The German immigrants – and Italians who followed – never adopted the plantation culture of the Northeast. Instead, the economy was based on family-owned farms, a legacy that lives on in the region's egalitarian politics and equitable distribution of income.

ℹ Getting There & Around

Florianópolis is the state's transportation hub, with direct bus and air services to every major city in Brazil. Joinville also has direct air services to São Paulo, with connections to other major cities. Most destinations within Santa Catarina are accessible from Florianópolis by bus service, which is extensive and dependable.

ILHA DE SANTA CATARINA

Ilha de Santa Catarina has a vibrant and varied coastline, from the calm, crowded bays of the north, to the wild, cliff-hugging beaches of the south. But it's not just the beaches that make this island so enchanting. A forest of protected pines shelters the east coast, while the dunes near Praia da Joaquina create a lunar landscape. The spine of mountains, luxuriant with the Mata Atlântica (Atlantic rainforest), drops precipitously down to the lovely Lagoa da Conceição.

Though technically speaking, the whole island is Florianópolis, it's downtown Floripa, known as Centro, that is the political capital of Santa Catarina, the cultural capital of southern Brazil and the gateway to the rest of the island. The island's *bairros* (districts) can feel like completely different towns with their own distinct personalities and infrastructure.

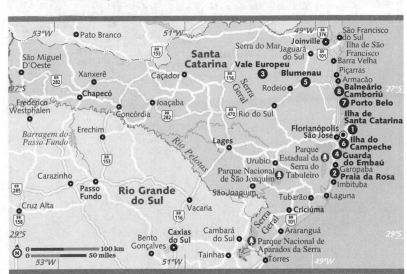

Santa Catarina Highlights

① Sun, surf and snorkel around the wild sands of beautiful **Ilha de Santa Catarina** (p285).

② Suck up the sophisticated surfer atmosphere in stunning **Praia do Rosa** (p306).

③ Drink your way through Santa Catarina's rich beer culture in the **Vale Europeu** (p304).

④ Join the parade of surfers and sun worshipers wading through the Rio da Madre to the stunning beach at **Guarda do Embaú** (p305).

⑤ Say *Prost!* to the world's third-largest Oktoberfest in **Blumenau** (p298).

⑥ Snorkel in the crystalline waters off **Ilha do Campeche** (p294).

⑦ Bounce about the lovely beach trifecta of **Porto Belo**, **Bombas** and **Bombinhas** (p307).

⑧ Beach-hop via the fun-packed Parque Unipraias in **Balneário Camboriú** (p302).

Ilha de Santa Catarina

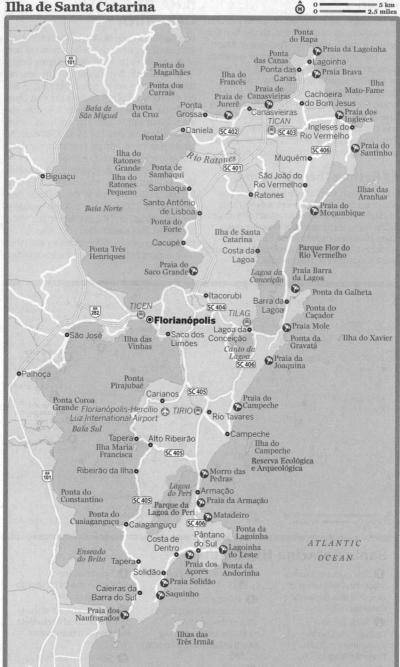

0 ___ 5 km
0 ___ 2.5 miles

Plan on big crowds and high prices between Christmas and early March. Prices can fall 20% to 40% outside peak times.

Florianópolis

OXX48 / POP 421.000

There are two sides to Florianópolis (Floripa). On the mainland, the industrial zone occupies the districts of Estreito and Coqueiros. Across the bay, the island holds the historic center and the chic district of Beira-Mar Norte. Two picturesque bridges link these halves. The old suspension bridge, the **Ponte Hercílio Luz**, is no longer open to traffic, but it still lights the night sky, acting as the defining feature of Floripa's spectacular skyline.

Florianópolis is a convenient transportation hub, with all of the island's 42 beaches within an hour's drive.

◎ Sights & Activities

The center of town is the inviting **Praça XV de Novembro**, with its shady walks and 100-year-old fig tree.

★ Museu Histórico de Santa Catarina   MUSEUM
(3028-8091; www.mhsc.sc.gov.br; Praça XV de Novembro 227; admission R$2; ☉10am-6pm Tue-Fri, to 4pm Sat & Sun) Formerly the colonial governor's palace, this gorgeous must-see building boasts ornate parquetry floors and outrageous 19th-century ceilings.

⎙ Sleeping

Florianópolis suffers from a lack of budget sleeping options, although prices drop dramatically outside high season (December to March), making many midrange places more affordable. Most folks spend little more than a night in the city, beelining instead for outlying beach districts.

Centro Sul Hotel   HOTEL $
(3222-9110; www.centrosulhotel.com.br; Praça Hercílio Luz, 652; s/d/tr R$98/129/159; ❄@ 🔊) CSH – as it is called – is a comfortable, kitschy budget-friendly option. Everything is a bit worn with age, but the rooms are clean and priced well, even in high season. The owner can be off-putting, but the rest of the staff is very helpful.

Floripa Hostel – Centro   HOSTEL $
(3225-3781; www.floripahostel.com.br; Duarte Schutel 227; dm R$50, d R$115; @🔊) On a

residential street, halfway between the city center and Av Beira-Mar Norte, this orderly HI hostel is an easy walk from either. The kitchen and shared bathroom facilities are spotless. Sturdy wooden bunk beds are lined up in the gender-segregated dorms. Unfortunately, solo travelers pay for two people in private rooms.

★ Cecomtur Executive   HOTEL $$
(2107-8800; www.cecomturhotel.com.br; Arcipreste Paiva 107; s/d R$164/194; ❄🔊❄) This efficient business hotel isn't fancy, but it's got everything you need: modern, spotless, spacious rooms; congenial, English-speaking service and a few perks besides. It's our pick for the best value, especially since in reality they charge about R$50 below their rack rate.

Florianópolis Palace   HOTEL $$
(2106-9633; www.floph.com.br; Artista Bittencourt 14; s/d R$176/202; ❄@🔊) The fanciest hotel in the historic center also goes by the rather goofy nickname 'the floph.' Rooms on the upper floors offer panoramic views of the city.

✖ Eating

Florianópolis has a little bit of everything, from safe bets for vegetarians to big plates of meat and seafood.

O Padeira de Sevilha   BAKERY $
(3025-3402; www.opadeirodesevilha.com.br; Esteves Júnior 2144; items R$2.50-10; ☉6:50am-8:30pm Mon-Fri, 7am-2pm Sat; 🔊) Considered one of the top 30 bakeries in Brazil, this social hotspot features an 11m-long communal table flanked by a self-serve cornucopia of fresh-baked artisanal breads and sweets selected from some 200 recipes.

Café Cultura   CAFE $
(www.cafeculturafloripa.com.br; Praça XV de Novembro 352; meals R$10-34.90; ☉9am-9pm Mon-Fri, to 7pm Sat; 🔊) Floripa's best coffee is served in this renovated neocolonial building, roasted in-house by an ex-Starbucks barista from California. Healthy breakfasts, salads, waffles and paninis round out the excellent fare. The executive lunch is a steal (R$22.90).

Central   SELF-SERVE $
(Vidal Ramos 174; per kg weekday/weekend R$39.90/45.90; ☉11am-3pm Mon-Fri; 🔊) This outstanding, award-winning por kilo buffet concentrates on a more subtle selection of

Florianópolis

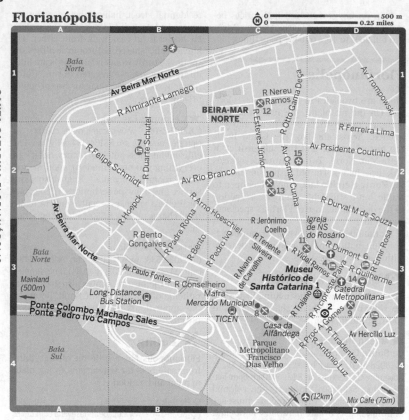

Florianópolis

daily dishes, each and all focused on high-quality, home-cooked goodness. Lines out the door: not uncommon. There's another branch on **Esteves Júnior** (Esteves Júnior 242; per kg week/weekend R$39.90/45.90; ⏱11am-3pm Mon-Sat).

★**Forneria Catarina** PIZZERIA $$
(☎3333-0707; www.forneriacatarina.com.br; Esteves Júnior 604; pizza R$30-57; ⏱6pm-midnight; 🎵) Considering it's located far, far outside São Paulo city limits, this upscale Sampa-style pizzeria does an absolute bang-up job

with *pizza paulistana* – at far more accommodating prices. We reckon half *rustica* (arugula, Parma ham), half *siciliana* (grilled eggplant, smoked mozzarella) is the perfect combination.

Box 32 SEAFOOD **$$**
(www.box32.com.br; Mercado Municipal; mains R$28.50-98; ☺10am-8pm Mon-Fri, to 3pm Sat) You'll often find local celebrities at this historic bar and restaurant in the Mercado Municipal, indulging in a happy hour of frothy house-brewed beer, fresh seafood and *pata negra* ham imported from Spain.

🍸 **Drinking & Nightlife**

While many people flock to Lagoa for its nightlife, Centro and around has a few hot spots too.

⭐ **Boteco Zé Mané** BOTECO
(Desembargador Pedro Silva 2360; mains R$14-25; ☺6pm-midnight Mon-Thu, to 1am Fri-Sat, to 11:30 Sun; 🐾) It's worth the trek to the mainland for this fantastic *boteco* (small open-air bar) in Coqueiros. Jazzed-up *caipirinhas* (cane alcohol cocktail; R$15) like bergamot, basil and pink peppercorn; and our fav, *jabuticaba* (a intense, native grapelike fruit), fuel the raging scene here in an revamped colonial house overlooking the waterfront. It's eight minutes away on buses 664 'Itaguaçu' or 665 'Abraão' (R$2.90) from TICEN.

Gato Mamado BAR
(www.gatomamado.com.br; Saldanha Marinho 351; ☺6pm-4am Tue-Fri) Revelers spill out into the sidewalk at this tiny (no, seriously, it's *small*) bar that is king in Centro for happy hour. Schornstein beer from Pomerode is on draft (rare to find outside the Vale Europeu; R$6) and the crowd tends toward bohemian. By happy hour, we mean the crowd doesn't swell before 9pm.

ℹ️ **Orientation**

The city's major sights, hotels and restaurants are just east of the long-distance and local bus stations. Some 2km north of the center, Av Beira Mar Norte runs along the coast of the Baía Norte. The waterfront promenade attracts runners, bikers and walkers, enjoying the breeze off the bay and a sweeping view across to the mainland.

ℹ️ **Information**

Change your cash at one of the money-exchange houses on Felipe Schmidt.

C.A.T (☎3228-1095; www.visitefloripa.com.br; Rodoviária; ☺8am-5:30pm Mon-Fri, 9am-6pm Sat & Sun) Florianópolis and Ilha da Santa Catarina maps are available from the friendly staff at the bus station.

HSBC (Schmidt 376) Feeless ATM.

Polícia Militar (☎3229-6000; www.pm.sc.gov.br)

ℹ️ **Getting There & Away**

AIR

Daily flights from **Florianópolis-Hercílio Luz International Airport** (FLN; ☎3331-4000; Rod Deputado Diomício Freitas 3393, Bairro Carianos), 12km south of Florianópolis, serve Buenos Aires, Brasília, Campinas, Porto Alegre, Rio de Janeiro and São Paulo, among others.

To reach the airport, bus 183 'Corredor Sudoeste' (35 minutes) and 186 'Corredor Sudoeste Semi-Direto' (25 minutes) leave from TICEN (p289) terminal frequently between 5:20am and 12:30am. Taxis cost R$28 to R$32.

BUS

The **long-distance bus station** (☎3212-3100; Av Paulo Fontes 1101) lies a few blocks west of the Praça XV de Novembro. Buses link Florianópolis with every major city in southern Brazil. There are buses to Asuncion daily at 3pm, Buenos Aires daily at 10:15pm and Santiago Tuesday at 12:35am. For Montevideo, buses depart at 12:45pm during the week and 2.30pm on Saturday and Sunday.

For sample travel times and *executivo* fares (where applicable) from Florianópolis see the boxed text (p290).

ℹ️ **Getting Around**

The city is the transportation hub for the rest of the island, all within a one-hour drive.

BUS

Local buses leave from the **TICEN** (Terminal de Integração Centro; Av Paulo Fontes s/n) terminal, one block east of Florianópolis' long-distance bus station. Connections to the island's beaches are made via three outlying terminals: TIRIO (Rio Tavares Terminal), TILAG (Lagoa Terminal) and TICAN (Canasvieiras Terminal).

For southern beaches, including Armação, Pântano do Sul and Costa de Dentro, catch bus 410 'Rio Tavares' then transfer at TIRIO to bus 563.

For eastern beaches, catch bus 330 'Lagoa da Conceição', then transfer at TILAG for a second bus to your final destination, for example bus 360 to Barra da Lagoa.

For Canasvieiras and northern beaches, catch bus 210 from TICEN to TICAN.

BUSES FROM FLORIANÓPOLIS

DESTINATION	FARE (R$)	TIME (HR)	COMPANY
Asunción (PY)	177	21	Pluma (www.pluma.com.br)
Blumenau	35	3	Catarinense (www.catarinense.net)
Buenos Aires	295	25	Pluma (www.pluma.com.br)
Curitiba	65	5	Catarinense (www.catarinense.net)
Foz do Iguaçu	138	14	Catarinense (www.catarinense.net)
Guarda do Embaú	11	1½	Paulotur (www.paulotur.com.br)
Garopaba	17.40	2	Paulotur (www.paulotur.com.br)
Joinville	44	2½	Catarinense (www.catarinense.net)
Montevideo (UY)	209	18	EGC (www.egc.com.uy)
Porto Alegre	82	6	Eucatur (www.eucatur.com.br)
Rio de Janeiro	178	17	Itapemirim (www.itapemirim.com.br)
Santiago (CL)	367	46	Pluma (www.pluma.com.br)
São Paulo	123	12	Catarinense (www.catarinense.net)

A single fare of R$2.90 (paid at the TICEN ticket booth) covers your initial ride plus one transfer. All of the above buses leave from Platform B.

CAR

Consider renting a car for easier exploration of the island's beaches. Beware that prices are generally high (from R$120 per day) and traffic can be deadly on weekends.

Localiza (☎0800-979-2020; www.localiza. com; Rodoviária; ☺6am-midnight) A reliable and expensive South American chain with counters at the airport and bus station.

North Island

From Praia de Jurerê to Praia dos Ingleses, the north of the island is designed for mass tourism: calm, family-friendly waters; newly widened roads that provide easy access to the international airport; and lots of anonymous hotels and restaurants.

Santo Antônio de Lisboa

On the west coast, Santo Antônio de Lisboa is among the oldest communities on the island. An old-fashioned, fishing-village atmosphere is complemented by cobblestone streets and Azorean architecture. The most prominent edifice is the **Igreja da NS da Necessidade**, dating from 1750.

Santo Antônio's seaside setting and fishing heritage guarantee that you can enjoy delicious seafood. Try **Marisqueira Sintra** (www.marisqueirasintra.com.br; XV de Novembro, 147; mains for 2 R$62-120; ☺noon-3:30pm & 7:30-11pm), which does wonderful things with octopus and Portuguese *cataplanas* (seafood stews) in a postcard waterfront setting.

Canasvieiras

Canasvieiras is not the most attractive place on the island, but it has easy access to **Praia de Jurerê** and **Praia de Canasvieiras**. Both beaches offer options for windsurfing, fishing and jet-skiing. Nightlife in town is hopping, as crowds of young people flock to the local bars and clubs. Outside the season, however, it's sleepy, and many hotels are closed altogether.

The vaguely institutional HI **Floripa Hostel – Canasvieiras** (☎3266-2036; Dr João de Oliveira 517; dm/d R$50/130; @☎) subscribes to all the hostel norms: friendly, English-speaking reception; bunk beds and lockers; shared bathrooms, kitchen and TV room. It's two blocks from the beach.

Praia da Lagoinha & Praia Brava

The northeastern tip of the island is a slender peninsula, accessed by slow-moving roads that wind around the hills to the beach. These towns are ritzier than their neighbors, though the beaches are still overbuilt. **Praia da Lagoinha** is a crescent-shaped patch of sand, surrounded on three sides by rocky cliffs that keep the water calm. Further south, **Praia Brava** has wilder waves that attract a steady stream of surfers.

🛏 Sleeping

Villabella Villaggio POUSADA $$
(☎ 3284-2017; www.villabellavillaggio.com.br; Av Epitácio Bittencourt 470, Praia Brava; d from R$250, chalets R$520; ※@🤙🛱) Santa Catarina's Italian heritage is lovingly showcased in the design and decor at the luxurious Villabella Villaggio. Every guestroom has an expansive view toward either Praia da Lagoinha or Praia Brava and the dark hardwood chalets (some fashioned from reforested eucalyptus) are dressed up in sophisticated country decor.

Pousada da Vigia POUSADA $$
(☎ 3284-1789; www.pousadadavigia.com.br; Cônego Walmor Castro 291, Lagoinha; d from R$300; ※🤙🛱) The pink Pousada da Vigia overlooks Praia da Lagoinha – and what a miraculous view it is! With only 10 guestrooms scattered around lovely gardens, service is attentive and reaches to the beach, which is accessible by a 200m footpath. Room 4 knocked us out.

Praia dos Ingleses & Praia do Santinho

Once among the island's finest beaches, **Praia dos Ingleses** has suffered from its popularity. It's now crowded with high-rise hotels and overpriced restaurants.

Further south, **Praia do Santinho** is quieter, thanks to the protected area of dunes behind it. Santinho is the north island's best surfing beach, acclaimed for its consistent waves and uncrowded conditions.

🛏 Sleeping

Pousada do Atobá POUSADA $$
(☎ 3269-2560; www.pousadadoatoba.com.br; Servidão Ipê do Costão 146; s/d/chalet R$210/230/260; ※@🤙🛱) Superb value awaits at this gem of a pousada (guesthouse) with airy, bright rooms looking onto well-kept gardens. The English-speaking family that runs the place takes exceptionally good care of guests. Bus 264 'Ingleses' from TICAN stops just 30m away.

Solar do Santinho POUSADA $$$
(☎ 3269-4168; www.pousadasolarsantinho.com. br; Estrada Vereador Onildo Lemos 2197 ; s/d R$200/350; ※🤙🛱) 🏖 A hands-on English-speaking couple hold court in this 14-room pousada tucked away in leafy surrounds 100m from the beach. Bilevel rooms are spacious, with kitchenettes, balconies and

tasteful art. Buddha statues are peppered throughout the property, which treats its own waste water and runs solar-heated showers.

East Coast

Facing the open ocean, the east coast boasts the island's cleanest waters, longest beaches and most challenging surf.

Barra da Lagoa & Around

In the north, **Praia do Moçambique** merges with **Praia Barra da Lagoa** to form a stunning, 14km strand. The beach is hidden from the road by a thriving pine forest. Surfing is sweet all along here: Praia Barra da Lagoa has gentle swells and shallow waters that are good for beginners, while the long stretch of Moçambique has more challenging peaks. Praia do Moçambique is protected, so the only construction is around the town of Barra da Lagoa. Restaurants, bars and pousadas are plentiful, but you'll need to go back to Lagoa town for a foreign-friendly ATM.

🛏 Sleeping

Backpackers Share House HOSTEL $
(☎ 3232-7606; www.backpackersfloripa.com; Servidão da Prainha 29; dm/d/tr R$50/140/195; @🤙) Across the pedestrian bridge from Barra

da Lagoa beach, that crazy white fortress with the souped-up motorcycle on the roof is the Backpackers Share House. It attracts an international party crowd with amenities including free use of surfboards and other beach toys, excursions and evening BBQs.

Floripa Hostel – Barra da Lagoa HOSTEL **$$**
(☑3232-4491; www.floripahostel.com.br; Inelzyr Bauer Bertoli s/n; dm R$58, d R$150; ☞) The nicest by far of the island's three HIs, this purpose-built hostel is just 150m from the beach and is a welcome respite from the high-priced Lagoa options. Well-equipped private rooms are a highlight here, with tasteful art and cable TV, and the numerous dorms sleep no more than four.

Pousada Oceanomare CHALET **$$**
(☑3269-7200; www.pousadaoceanomare.com.br; Rodovia João Gualberto Soares 8579; s/d R$250/ 300; ❄@☞☒) This new option north of Praia do Moçambique is perfect for families: a wonderful pool and sun deck and numerous distractions for the kiddos means adults here can enjoy the contemporary hardwood chalets that climb up the forested hillside worry-free.

A restaurant, small spa (with real sauna) as well as a nature trail that winds up and over to Canasvieiras round things out here nicely.

Praia Mole

Praia Mole is famous for its world-class waves and internationally heralded party scene, especially among the gay and lesbian community. The beach is absolutely beautiful, as are most of the bodies sunning and surfing. It does get crowded, but that's part of the appeal.

To take full advantage of the surf, sign up with **Nexus Surf Experience** (www.nexus surf.com; Rodovia Jornalista Manoel de Menezes 2031, No 6), which leads surf tours, provides instruction and books numerous outdoor adventure activities around the island.

Directly across from the beach, **Bangalôs da Mole** (☑3232-0723; www.bangalosdamole. com.br; Rod Jornalista Manoel de Menezes 1007; s/d R$160/180, bungalows R$260-300; ❄☞) has spacious suites and bilevel bungalows, all with cool tile floors and high ceilings.

Praia da Joaquina

About 3km south of Praia Mole, the huge white dunes of 'Joaca' are visible for miles.

These massive sandy mounds have inspired a new sport: sand surfing. Rent a sand board and haul it up to the top of the dune, from where it is a fast, dirty ride down.

Good old-fashioned surfing is still the number-one activity at Praia da Joaquina, which boasts long, fast, powerful waves that are up to 3m high. Stop in at the surf shop **Swell** (☑3232-0366; Estrada Geral da Joaquina 834; ☉9am-9pm) for more information and lots of gear.

There's a handful of places to stay along the road to Joaquina, including the simple veteran **Cris Hotel** (☑3232-5380; www. crishotel.com; Estrada Geral da Joaquina 1; d/tr R$190/260, with seaview R$240/380; ❄☞), which wins points for its prime beachfront location and contemporary touches that contrast nicely with the otherwise aging 30-year-old property.

Lagoa da Conceição

For spectacular scenery, exhilarating water sports or all-night parties, Lagoa da Conceição is a popular alternative to the beaches. Forested hills form a fabulous backdrop for the pretty lagoon. The town of Lagoa, often packed with tourists, sits on a sandbar that divides the two halves of the lagoon and is the island's action-packed center.

Get off the beaten track by hiking along the lagoon's undeveloped west coast. From the center of town, it is 6km to the tiny village of **Costa da Lagoa**, which is otherwise accessible only by boat.

🏃 Activities

Surfing, kitesurfing, diving and **stand-up paddle** outfits line the shores at Lagoa da Conceição as well as Barra da Lagoa on the island's eastern shore. Ecotourism is gaining a strong foothold as well – there are some wonderful treks around the island.

Reefifi SURFING, BICYCLE RENTAL
(Henrique Veras do Nascimento 151; ☉10:30am-10pm) A nice surf shop renting boards (per day R$35), bikes (per day R$35) and stand-up paddles (per hour R$35) and can arrange surf lessons (R$70).

Scuna Sul BOAT TOUR
(☑3232-4019; www.scunasul.com.br; trips R$50) Boat tours of the bay in Centro stop at some pretty 18th-century Portuguese forts; from Canasvieiras, the same company operates a pirate party ship.

🛏 Sleeping

Loads of pousadas are along the southern shore of the lake. Drive over the bridge and continue east on Rua das Rendeiras. Prices drop between 15% and 40% outside high season.

★ Janela de Márcia
B&B $$

(📞9958-1782; www.janelademarcia.com; Dr Alfredo Daura Jorge 131; s/d R$220/275; ❄ @ 🖙) Brazilian returnee Márcia and her big, hospitable personality run the show at this intimate B&B – don't call it a pousada! – hidden away in an upscale residential neighborhood five minutes walk from TILAG. A former Latin art curator in the US, Márcia's keen eye for design triumphs with restraint in her three cozy guestrooms.

A stay here is all about the intercultural exchanges in the common areas between consummate host and discerning guest – enjoy.

★ Tucano House
HOSTEL $$

(📞3207-8287; www.tucanohouse.com; Rua das Araras 229; dm R$50, r R$180, without bathroom R$160; ❄ @ 🖙 🖫) 🌿 Siblings Lila and Caio are your easy-on-the-eyes hosts at this eco-forward hostel in the heart of the Lagoa action. Their childhood home now features solar-heated showers, recycled rainwater cistern and amenities such as free use of bikes and surfboards and island adventures in a decked-out VW van. The small pool and front yard bar are constant sources of social buzz.

Pousada Ilha da Magia
CHALET $$

(📞3232-5038; www.pousadailhadamagia.com.br; Av Santiago 23; s/d R$220/260; ❄ 🖙 🖫) Across from the lagoon, these cute cottages come in a variety of styles, from Alpine to A-frame. mid-century modern–style Brastemp mini-bars add a wonderful retro touch.

🍴 Eating

Gelateria Max
ICE CREAM $

(Av Afonso Delambert Neto 619; ice cream R$5-9; ⊘12:30-8pm Mon-Fri, to 11pm Sat & Sun) Italian training and equipment ensure the creamy *gelato* produced here is some of Brazil's best. Killer flavors include pistachio, *doce de leite* and vanilla Madagascar (fava beans imported from the Motherland!).

Café Cultura
CAFE $$

(www.cafeculturafloripa.com.br; Severino de Oliveira 669; items R$6.50-36.90; ⊘9am-12:30am; 🖙)

Breakfast until 1pm, waffles, salads, paninis and sophisticated mains – there is something for everyone at Floripa's best cafe, brought to you by a Californian ex-Starbucks barista and his Brazilian coffee-heiress wife. It's packed open to close, though service can be unapologetically exasperating.

Black Sheep
SUSHI $$

(Av das Rendeiras 1956; rolls R$8-25; ⊘7-10:30pm Mon-Wed, to 11pm Thu, to midnight Fri & Sat) Among a sea of sushi, Black Sheep stands out: both the Japazillian chef and his Latvian wife/hostess honed their skills at Nobu (yes, *that* Nobu). You will find a grand total of *zero* items with cream cheese; but perhaps more surprising are the shockingly fair prices. Give the R$75 *omakase* (chef's menu) a go.

★ Bistrô Santa Marta
BRAZILIAN $$$

(📞3371-0769; www.bistrosantamarta.com.br; Laurindo Januário da Silveira 1350; mains R$25-65; ⊘7pm-1am Mon-Sat) Extraordinary value greets those willing to escape Lagoa town for Canto da Lagoa, the island's *Via Gastronomica*, a 4km stretch of 16 restaurants about 2km from town. This adorable, six-table contemporary bistro works with a limited but excellent menu (filet mignon, lobster, octopus, lamb) set to moody lounge music at perfect volume.

The honest-to-goodness hospitality is delivered by *gaúcho* (native of Rio Grande do Sul) couple Milene and Branco and English-speaking chef Barbara. As a trio, they'll leave you with a meal you won't soon shake from your consciousness.

🍸 Drinking & Nightlife

★ The Black Swan
PUB

(www.theblackswan.com.br; Manuel Severino de Oliveira 592; mains R$17.50-29.50; ⊘4pm-late Tue-Fri, noon-2am Sat & Sun; 🖙) A proper English-run pub pouring a wide range of proper pints – all R$19.50, all rarer than the pub's namesake – and serving up 10 televisions of your sporting heart's desire and live music from Thursday to Saturday. Hungry? It's all here, from fish and chips to English fry-ups. Salvation.

John Bull Pub
LIVE MUSIC

(www.johnbullfloripa.com.br; Rua das Rendeiras 1046; meals R$20; ⊘10pm-4am Tue-Sat Dec-Mar, closed Wed Apr-Nov) Famous for live music; with bonus views over the lagoon.

Confraria Club   CLUB
(☑7811-7705; www.confrariaclub.com.br; João da Costa 31; ☉11pm-5am Thu-Sat) It's hard to get hipper than this – if you can get in. Internationally famous DJs spin beats in a lavishly remodeled colonial-style house.

❶ Information

Banco do Brasil and Bradesco both sit at the corner of Moacyr Pereira Junior and José Henrique Veras.

ACIF (☑3232-8326; www.acif.org.br; Nossa Senhora da Conceição 30; ☉10am-2pm Mon-Fri) This private organization promotes tourism in Lagoa and is your best bet for well-rounded tourism information in the area.

Polícia Militar (☑3232-1490; www.pm.sc.gov.br; Av das Rendeiras 966) Police.

South Island

With white-sand beaches and mountains that drop into the sea, the south is the most pristine and picturesque part of the island. But south-island residents are engaged in the inevitable struggle between developers and preservers: the former see the potential for more tourists and big bucks; the latter fear that their piece of paradise will soon resemble the north. The balance is delicate and ever shifting.

For now, these towns retain their idyllic appeal. The beaches are less crowded (the hottest surf spots excepted) and the vibe is more laid-back than most other island destinations.

At the southern tip, **Praia dos Naufragados** is accessible only by hiking 4km on a flat, shady trail from the village of Caieiras da Barra do Sul. Your reward is a picturesque lighthouse and a fantastic vista of the islands in the vicinity.

Ribeirão da Ilha

More than any other town, the tiny village of Ribeirão da Ilha has preserved its Azorean heritage, evident in its cobblestone streets and colorful tile-roof houses. The main square centers on the lovely **Igreja NS da Lapa do Riberão**, which dates to 1806.

Given the village's location overlooking the tidal flats, it is no surprise that the local specialty is oysters – as plump, juicy and fresh as you'll find anywhere. Sit on the dock at incredibly atmospheric **Ostradamus** (☑3337-5711; www.ostradamus.com.br; Rod Bald-

icero Filomeno 7640; oysters R$33-38, mains for 2 R$83-168; ☉noon-11pm Tue-Sat, to 6pm Sun; ☎) and slurp a dozen or two.

Campeche

Campeche is a bohemian outpost, home to artists, massage therapists and other free thinkers, seeking to escape the crowds of the city and the tourist hot spots.

The 5km **Praia do Campeche** is protected, so the beach is completely undeveloped, but still those condo complexes have managed to creep in as close as the law allows. Desolate dunes and pounding surf – stretching for miles in either direction – offer relative solitude for swimmers and sunbathers. At the southern end of the beach, catch a boat (R$70 return) to **Ilha do Campeche**, an ecological reserve with opportunities for hiking and snorkeling; or, alternatively, save R$20 by catching one from the fisherman cooperative at Armação Beach.

The owner of the endlessly charming, socially aware **Pousada Natur Campeche** (☑3237-4011; www.naturcampeche.com.br; Servidão Familia Nunes 59; s/d from R$273/341; ❉☎❦) ✎ has traveled the world, foraging treasures to decorate the country-themed rooms. Exotic and steeped in carbon footprint-erasing touches like solar-heated showers, the unique rooms are spread deceptively about the property surrounded by hammocks, lush gardens and artistically fed common areas. It's just 100m from Praia do Campeche. Pretty perfect.

Armação

This little town dates to the 18th century, when it served as a whaling center. The impressive **Igreja Santa Ana** still stands from these days. While whaling is no longer practiced, the fishing industry still thrives here.

Armação provides access to three beaches, all excellent surfing spots. North of town, **Morro das Pedras** is popular for its consistent right, but you'll probably have to fight for a chance to ride it. Further south, **Praia da Armação** is a surfer's delight, especially at the north end of the beach. For a little adventure, follow a winding trail along the rocky coastline to the gorgeous **Matadeiro**, a near-deserted beach surrounded by lush greenery.

Inland from Armação, the **Lagoa do Peri** is a pretty lake surrounded by parkland. Lesser known and less visited than Conceição, it offers wonderful opportunities for swimming and hiking. The jumping-off point for the lake is about 1km south of Praia de Armação on the main road approaching the town – you can't miss the large park entrance.

🛏 Sleeping & Eating

Pousada Alemdomar   POUSADA $$
(☑3237-5600; www.alemdomar.com.br; Tulia de Olivera 403; s/d R$190/250; @ 🛜) After passing Hiper Bom Supermarket, follow the unpaved Euclides João Alves about 400m south from the Lagoa do Peri park entrance and take your first left to find this little plot of New-Age paradise. Six simple guestrooms evoke tranquility and harmony with nature. Behind the main house, guests can follow a woodsy trail all the way to Lagoa do Peri.

Nutri Lanches   DELI $
(Thomaz dos Santos 4615; sandwiches R$7-8.25; ⊙8am-8pm Tue-Sun) 🍴 'An overdose of health' is how Nutri Lanches lauds its healthy-leaning sandwiches, salads and pastries. The lunchtime buffet is an incredible array of homemade goodness (per kilogram R$24).

Pântano do Sul

Fishermen of Azorean descent still inhabit the village of Pântano do Sul, so its beach is dotted with fishing boats and seafood shacks. Ringed by mountains, the protected cove waters are calm, cool waters that are ideal for sunning and swimming.

From here, you can catch a lift from a local fisherman or hike about 1½ hours to the deserted beach of **Lagoinha do Leste**. The hike is hot, so leave early and bring plenty of water. Lagoinha do Leste offers some of the island's most consistent and powerful waves, so don't be surprised when surfers run past you on the trail.

The rustic seafood shack **Bar do Arante** (☑3237 7022; meals R$15-30) is the island institution, its walls covered with poetry and artwork that patrons have doodled over the years.

Costa de Dentro & Around

This is the end of the road, and it feels like it. These tiny towns are home to a handful of places to stay and eat, but they are left largely to their fishing and farming residents. Costa de Dentro has access to the lovely, calm waters of the **Praia dos Açores** –

making this a good escape from the surfing scene – or continue all the way to **Praia Solidão** or **Saquinho**.

🛏 Sleeping

Albergue do Pirata   HOSTEL $
(☑3389-2727; www.alberguedopirata.com.br; Ferreira s/n; camping/dm/r without bathroom per person R$20/35/50; @ 🛜) This spartan hostel offers economical sleeps about 500m from the beach.

⭐**Pousada Sítio dos Tucanos**   INN $$
(☑3237-5084; www.pousadasitiodostucanos.com; Ferreira 2776; d from R$230; @ 🛜) About 1.5km past Costa de Dentro, this multilingual, German-run pousada sits tucked away high up in isolated and peaceful farm country. Extremely cozy, it offers rustic but elegant rooms, most with balconies; common areas are flooded with light from tall French doors. If coming by bus 563, call ahead for pickup at the bus stop 800m away.

THE MAINLAND

North and south of Florianópolis, fine sand and big surf attract beachcombers, sunbathers and surfers. Inland, the Serra Geral runs parallel to the coast, protecting some of southern Brazil's most remote destinations. This is where Santa Catarina's German and Italian heritage endures most tenaciously.

Joinville

☑0XX47 / POP 515,000

While Joinville does not have the historic center (or the beer festival) of Blumenau, it does have its own claims to fame. It's the only city outside Moscow with a school of the Bolshoi Ballet, a coup that goes hand in hand with its annual **dance festival** (www.festivaldedanca.com.br), one of the largest and most renowned in the world; and relishes its own decidedly German roots. They are evident in the city's nouveau-Alpine architecture and well-manicured parks. The economy thrives on metallurgy, plastics and information technology, but this industrial activity is tucked neatly away from the eyes of visitors. The result is a big city with the good manners of a small town.

Joinville

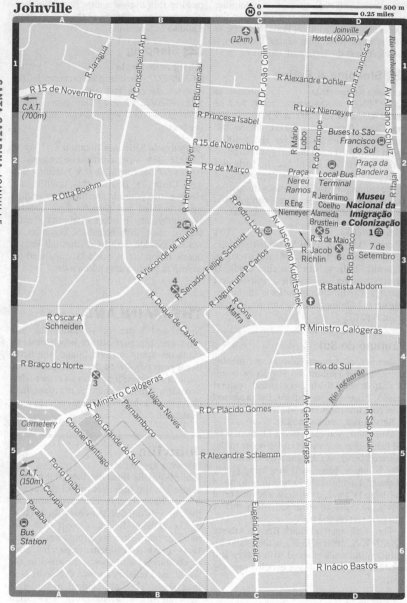

◉ Sights & Activities

To get a vista of Joinville and the Baía da Babitonga, head to the Morro do Boa Vista, about 10km east of the center. The 250m-high **Mirante** (Rua Saguaçu) is a tall tower with a circular staircase and a 360-degree panorama.

★ Museu Nacional da Imigração e Colonização
MUSEUM

(National Museum of Immigration & Colonization; ☎ 3433-3736; www.museunacional.com.br; Rio Branco 229; ⊘ 9am-5pm Tue-Fri, noon-6pm Sat & Sun) FREE In an elegant palace dating from

Joinville

1870, this museum documents the history of immigration to Santa Catarina. The impressive stand of palms along **Alameda das Palmeiras** will lead you there.

Barco Príncipe III   BOAT TRIPS
(☎3455-4444; www.barcoprincipe.com.br; adult/child incl lunch R$140/70; ◷tours 10am; ⊞) This famous boat cruise offers tours around the Baía da Babitonga, stopping in São Francisco do Sul for 1½ hours. It departs from the Espinheiros neighborhood, 10km from the center, but only when they have 100 people or more. Pricey, but everyone raves about it.

🛏 Sleeping

Joinville Hostel   HOSTEL $
(☎3424-0844; www.joinvillehostel.com.br; Dona Francisca 13/6; dm from R$55, s/d R$100/130, without bathroom R$90/120; @⊛) If you like your HI hostel to feel like home, this one, run by the immediately likable Kely, is for you. Boasting large green spaces, a little garden and a good bit more attention to detail and decor than the norm, Kely has created a homespun vibe just 10-minutes walk from Centro.

Hotel Tannenhof   HOTEL $$
(www.tannenhof.com.br; Visconde de Taunay 340; s/d from R$214.50/247.50; ✳@⊛⊠) This pleasant midrange offers more character than Joinville's myriad chain hotels, albeit of the old-fashioned German variety. Standard rooms are huge – no reason to upgrade – and come with headboards, minibars and closets dipped in paint-by-numbers European kitsch. Advantage here is you are on Joinville's liveliest street.

🍴 Eating & Drinking

Visconde de Taunay is Joinville's gastronomic strip, lined with great bars and restaurants. Undecided? Head instead to the gourmet food court at **Parque Opa** (Max Colin 1589), also the best place to indulge in Joinville's excellent hometown beer, Opa.

Tempeiro Crioulo   SELF-SERVE $
(3 de Maio 94; per kg R$23.90; ◷11am-2:30pm Mon-Sat; ⊛) This centrally-located *por kilo* restaurant serves a tantalizing spread of hearty Brazilian fare and salads – the *carne ensopada* (beef stew) is to die for.

Frankfurt Espresso Bar   CAFE $
(Alameda Brustlein 46; items R$2.50-5.90; ◷9am-10pm Mon-Sat; ⊛) This trendy cafe has a great patio staring straight at Joinville's imperial palms.

★**Biergarten**   BRAZILIAN $$
(www.biergarten.com.br; Visconde de Taunay 1183; mains R$25-68; ◷5pm-1am Mon, 11am-1am Tue-Sat, 1am-6pm Sun) The most agreeable restaurant in Joinville is a convivial spot to sample regional specialties like *marreco*, a kind of small duck; R$45.90), washed down with an Eisenbahn *chope* (draft beer). It draws a lively crowd, which fills up the good-time space of upscale rustic picnic tables, and service won't make you angry.

Delicatesse Viktoria   CAFE $$
(☎3422-0570; www.delicatesseviktoria.com.br; Felipe Schmidt 400; afternoon buffet per person R$29.50; ◷9am-8pm Mon-Sat, buffet from 3:30pm) This traditional classic is somewhat stuffy, but offers a welcoming light-filled porch with lace tablecloths and wicker furniture from which to enjoy afternoon *café colonial*, Brazil's version of high tea.

ℹ Information

C.A.T. (☎3433-5007; www.turjoinville.com.br; XV de Novembro; ◷8am-5pm) Joinville's tourist information booths are helpful, but most unhelpfully located around the town's outskirts. There are branches at the airport (☎3427-4409; Santos Dumont 9000; ◷7:30am-1:30pm & 4-10pm Mon-Fri, 11am-2:30pm & 4-8:30pm Sun), Casa Krüger (☎3427-5623; Rod SC301; ◷9am-5pm) and Baltasar Buschle (☎3453-0177; Ottokar Doerffel; ◷9am-5pm).
HSBC (Jerônimo Coelho 128) Feeless ATMs.

ℹ Getting There & Around

AIR
Joinville-Lauro Carneiro de Loyola Airport (JOI; ☎3481-4000; Av Santos Dumont 9000) is 13km north from the city; To reach the airport, catch

BUSES FROM JOINVILLE

DESTINATION	FARE (R$)	TIME (HR)	COMPANY
Blumenau	26	2	Catarinense (www.catarinense.net)
Curitiba	32	2	Catarinense (www.catarinense.net)
Florianópolis	47	2½	Catarinense (www.catarinense.net)
Foz do Iguaçu	124	16	Pluma (www.pluma.com.br)
Porto Alegre	94	9	Pluma (www.pluma.com.br)
Rio de Janeiro	152	16	Penha (www.vendas.nspenha.com.br)
São Paulo	98	8	Catarinense (www.catarinense.net)

bus 800/Iririú (R$2.90) and switch at Terminal Iririú for the Cubatão bus to the airport. Regular flights go to Campinas, São Paulo and Rio.

BUS
The **bus station** (☑ 3433-2991; Paraíba 769) is 2km southwest from the city center. Local buses go every 15 minutes to the city center. **Viação Verdes Mares** (www.vmares.com.br) runs regular buses to Ilha de São Francisco, both from the bus station (R$12), and more conveniently and cheaply, from Centro (R$8.25).

For sample travel times and *executivo* fares (where applicable) from Joinville, see the boxed text (below).

Blumenau
☑ 0XX47 / POP 309,000
Blumenau is not the only city in Santa Catarina that was founded by German settlers who transplanted their beer-brewing expertise and their taste for Alpine architecture to South America. But it is the best known, thanks in part to its uninhibited, over-the-top **Oktoberfest** (☑ 3326-6901; www.oktoberfestblumenau.com.br; Vila Germânica; admission per day R$20). The annual beer-drinking extravaganza is among Brazil's largest street parties, second only to Carnaval in Rio.

Oktoberfest is what makes Blumenau famous, but it is not what makes the city German. Throughout the historic city center, the architecture is dominated by Germanic themes. Local restaurants specialize in *jägerschnitzel* and bratwurst, and several beer brands are brewed locally. Most telling, perhaps, are the tall, fair population, many of whom still speak German in their homes.

◉ Sights
Blumenau's major festivals are held at **Parque Vila Germânica** (www.parquevilagermanica.com.br; Alberto Stein 199), part huge convention hall, part kitschy Alpine village, which is worth a look-see even when events aren't on as there are several good restaurants, bars, gourmet shops and a whole lot of *lederhosen*. To get there, catch bus '31 Proeb-Fonte via Caçadores' from Av Beira Rio.

Rua XV Novembro · NEIGHBORHOOD
Rua XV Novembro is home to the city's best examples of Germanic architecture, including the **Castelinho da XV**, now a Havan department store, a replica of the city hall of Michelstadt, Germany.

Museu de Família Colonial · MUSEUM
(☑ 3381-7516; Alameda Duque de Caxias 78; admission R$3; ◷ 10am-4pm Tue-Sun) Learn about Blumenau's beginnings at the Museu de Família Colonial, a group of houses that were occupied by the city's founder, Herman Bruno Otto Blumenau, in the 1850s. His daughter's cat cemetery – where lies interred Pepito, Mirko, Bum, Putzi, Schnurr and other beloved feline companions – is a nice spot of contemplation in the rambling backyard garden.

Museu da Cerveja · MUSEUM
(Praça Hercilio Luz; ◷ 9am-6pm Mon-Fri, to 5pm Sat & Sun) `FREE` If you are more interested in gastronomy than history, visit the small Museu da Cerveja.

⌘ Sleeping
Book accommodations well in advance if you plan to be in Blumenau during Oktoberfest or Sommerfest.

Ibis · HOTEL $
(☑ 3221-4700; www.ibishotel.com; Paul Herring 67; r weekend/weekday R$125/145; ❋ @ ☎) Yes, it's a chain, but this sleek 110-room hotel feels like a trendsetter in Blumenau. Rooms have all the mod-cons, have been meticulously maintained since its 2004 opening, and hardwood floors give it a contemporary feel. Breakfast costs R$14.

Blumenau

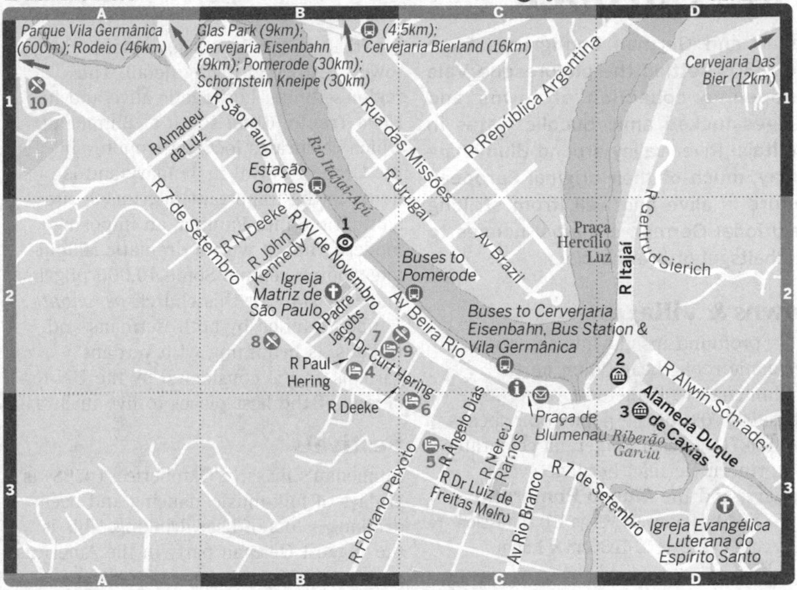

Hotel Hermann POUSADA $

(☎3322-4370; www.hotelhermann.com.br; Floriano Peixoto 213; s/d/tr R$64/105/145, with air-con R$80/115/155; ❄@📶) Optimal budget choice, inside a historic timber-frame home replete with creaky hardwood floors throughout. Rooms are simple but well maintained and the cozy feel of Blumenau of old permeates the entire premises.

★**Hotel Glória** HOTEL $$

(☎3326-1988; www.hotelgloria.com.br; 7 de Setembro 954; s/d/tr from R$125/160/210; ❄@📶) With its wood-paneled entrance, stained glass and traditional German *kaffeehaus* (coffeehouse) attached, this Blumenau classic modernized its fleet of rooms in 2012–13 but maintains its Old-World flair. Upgraded rooms boast restrained style and explosive showers. Breakfast is extraordinary.

Hotel Plaza Blumenau BUSINESS HOTEL $$

(☎3231-7000; www.plazahoteis.com.br; 7 de Setembro 818; s/d from R$275/306; ❄📶🏊) Of Blumenau's top hotels, you'll find the best value at this modern business hotel, with prices easily dropping 25% off the above rates even in high season. There's nothing particularly remarkable about it, but rooms are sizable and there's a 24-hour pool and fitness center.

Blumenau

Sights
1 Castelinho da XV ... B2
2 Museu da Cerveja ... D2
3 Museu de Família Colonial ... D3

Sleeping
4 Hotel Glória ... B2
5 Hotel Hermann ... C3
6 Hotel Plaza Blumenau ... C3
7 Ibis ... B2

Eating
8 Babilônia ... B2
9 Basement English Pub ... C2
Cafehaus Glória ... (see 4)
10 Don Peppone ... A1

Eating

Cafehaus Glória CAFE $

(☎3322-6944; www.cafehaus.com.br; 7 de Setembro 954; buffet from R$19; ⏱6am-8pm Mon-Sat) This old-world coffeehouse is a consistent madhouse, famous for its can't-miss *café colonial,* an afternoon buffet (per kilo R$36 Monday to Friday, R$26 all-you-can-eat Saturday; 3pm to 8pm) that features cakes, pastries and sandwiches similar to British high tea.

Vale Europeu

Italian and German immigrants from the 1830s settled the picturesque Vale Europeu, a collection of towns and villages tucked amid bucolic vistas in the Itajaí River valley around Blumenau. Today, much of their original European culture is alive and well, from striking traditional German *enxiamel* houses to Reinheitsgebot-brewed *biers*.

Towns & Villages

For a profound insight into the region's Germanic roots, head 30km north of Blumenau to Pomerode, where an estimated 70% of the population speaks German. The Festa Pomerana celebrates its northern German heritage every January, and the **Museo Pomerano** (☏3387-0408; Harmann Weege 111; admission adult/child R$2/1; ☺10-11:30am & 1-5pm Tue-Fri, 10am-4pm Sat & Sun) explores the town's history in loving detail. The region's Italian heritage is alive and in Nova Trento, 61km south of Blumenau, which celebrates local gastronomy in the Grape Festival in January and is home to the important pilgrimage site Santuário Santa Paulina, an imposing modern church with a dramatic slalom-like sloping ceiling. Some 40,000 pilgrims and tourists visit this church *per month*. Timbó, founded by both Germans and Italians, is brimming with verdant gardens and is considered by the UN to be one of the best places to live in Brazil.

Festivals

Blumenau's massive Oktoberfest (p298) is 17 days of folk music, dancing and beer drinking – lots of beer drinking. This is the 'biggest German party in the Americas'

(well, second biggest after Ontario, but who's counting?).

Outdoor Adventures

The Vale Europeu – like Europe itself – lends itself to beautiful countryside pedaling. See the Circuito Vale Europeu web site (www.circuitovaleeuropeu.com.br) for an excellent self-guided bike tour. The helpful website www.valeeuropeu.com.br, and the comprehensive booklet *Vale Europeu*, which can be picked up at the tourist office in Blumenau, both cover ecotourism opportunities in the valley.

Best Place to Stay

Good value and Deutsch-spun hospitality awaits in Pomerode at **Pousada Bergblick** (☎3387-0952; www.bergblick.com.br; Georg Zeplin 120; s/d R$155/255, s/d with balcony & Jacuzzi R$225/335; ❄️🛜), which has big rooms with mountain views.

Best Restaurant

The feast at **Abendbrothaus** (☎3378-1157; www.abendbrothaus.blogspot.com; Henrique Conrad 1194, Vila Itoupava; meals R$55; ⏱11:30am-3:30pm Sun) in Vila Itoupava, 25km north of Blumenau, is the most coveted table in Santa Catarina for *marreco* (stuffed Garganey, a kind of small duck).

Best Microbrewery

Schornstein Kneipe's (p304) pilsners, Indian pale ale, Weiss, bock and imperial stout all cure *homebeersickness*; and it has the best tasting room of the bunch as well. It's a must on the artisanal beer trail.

1. Joinville (p295) **2.** Cycling, Santa Catarina (p284) **3.** Bavarian brass band, Blumenau (p298)

STOCKBRAZIL / ALAMY ©

MARCELO RUDINI / ALAMY ©

MICHAEL FRITZEN / ALAMY ©

Lunchtime means a more traditional Brazilian buffet (per kilo R$29.50), while winter evening brings out the all-you-can-eat soup buffet (R$19).

★ **Basement English Pub** PUB $$
(☑3340-0534; www.basementpub.com.br; Paul Hering 35; mains R$14-38; ⊙6pm-midnight Mon-Sat; ☎) Easily one of Brazil's best bars, with its large selection of local beers (from R$5.50) and gorgeous authentic English pub atmosphere, but it's the gourmet pub fare that's arguably as alluring as its suds. Homesick-remedy grub like burgers, barbecued pork ribs and fish and chips hit the spot among a blitzkrieg of brats. Live music often.

Babilônia BRAZILIAN $$
(www.babiloniaonline.com.br; 7 de Setembro 1213, Shopping Neumarkt; mains R$16-48; ⊙11:30am-10:30pm Sun-Thu, to 11:30pm Fri & Sat; ☎) This Curitiba transplant is a Euro-style eatery inside Blumenau's best mall and it does great gourmet Brazilian bistro fare at pleasant prices, even more so on half-price sushi Mondays and Italian Tuesdays.

Don Peppone ITALIAN $$
(☑3322-9090; www.donpepponeexpress.com.br; 7 de Setembro 2013; mains for 2 R$53-83, pizza R$60-79; ⊙5pm-midnight; ☎) Fancier than its logo suggests, Dom Peppone is an upscale anecdote to sausages and sauerkraut and a fine example of Blumenau's 'other' ethnic cuisine.

🛍 Shopping

Blumenau produces high-quality crystal and glassware.

Glas Park CRYSTAL
(☑3327-1261; Rudolf Roedel 233; ⊙9am-6pm Mon-Fri, 9am-1pm Sat) An on-site crystal museum shows the history of the industry and the art, and fascinating demonstrations are given.

ℹ Information

Blumenau e Vale Europeu Convention & Visitors Bureau (☑3322-6933; www.blumenau.

com.br; cnr XV de Novembro & Nereu Ramos; ⊙9am-noon & 1-6pm Mon-Fri, 8am-noon Sat & Sun) Member-driven information about the Vale Europeu and town's most convenient tourist info.
Correios (Post Office; www.correios.com.br; Praça Dr Blumenau)
HSBC Feeless ATMs.

ℹ Getting There & Around

The **bus station** (☑3323-2155; 2 de Setembro 1222) is 6km west of the center. To get into the center of town, take bus '11 Aterro via 2 de Setembro' (R$2.90) from the far side of Av 2 de Setembro to Estação Gomes, or take a taxi for R$15. Heading back, the same bus leaves from Estação Dr Blumenau. Frequent buses go to Balneário Camboriú, Florianópolis, Joinville, and Curitiba.

For the Vale Europeu, hourly **Volkmann** (www.turismovolkmann.com.br) buses head from Av Beira Rio to Pomerode (R$4.45). From the bus station, **Expresso Presidente** (www.expresso presidente.com.br) has seven daily buses making the 30km jaunt from Blumenau to Timbó (R$8, 45 minutes). **Reunidas** (www.reunidas. com.br) has four buses from Blumenau to Nova Trento (R$17.50, two hours).

For sample travel times and *executivo* fares (where applicable) from Blumenau see the boxed text, below.

North of Florianópolis

Varied and inviting, the beaches along the coast north of Florianópolis are both its blessing and its curse. The blessing is the crystalline waters and fine sand, not to mention the endless days of sun. The curse is the high-rise hotels and condominiums that are more prominent than the forested hillsides and rocky outposts.

Balneário Camboriú
☑0XX47 / POP 108.000
Balneário Camboriú is considered a poor man's Rio – indeed it boasts a giant Christ statue, beautiful beaches, hopping nightlife

BUSES FROM BLUMENAU

DESTINATION	FARE (R$)	TIME (HR)	COMPANY
Balneário Camboriú	17	1½	Catarinense (www.catarinense.net)
Curitiba	37	4	Catarinense (www.catarinense.net)
Florianópolis	35	3	Catarinense (www.catarinense.net)
Joinville	24	2	Catarinense (www.catarinense.net)
Piçarras	19	2	Catarinense (www.catarinense.net)

SPRECHEN SIE DEUTSCH?

The first German immigrants arrived in the 1820s at the behest of Dom Pedro I. The southern part of the newly independent Brazil was still disputed by Argentina and Uruguay, and the emperor wanted to populate the region with loyal followers. Successive waves of immigrants arrived in the 1850s and the 1890s, then again around the two world wars. Contrary to popular imagination, most Germans who arrived in the 1940s were political and economic refugees, rather than Nazi leaders on the run.

For a century, German was the dominant language in many parts of southern Brazil. German speakers came from different regions of Germany and spoke different dialects, so they faced their own linguistic Babel. They often resorted to a kind of Creole, which incorporated Portuguese and local Indian languages. Italians facing a similar problem relied on 'Taliã,' an amalgamation of dialects based mainly on those of the Veneto region.

The 20th century took a toll on the German language in Brazil. The world wars led to the suppression of German in public institutions like schools and government. Industrialization and increasing economic integration brought the region into closer contact with Portuguese speakers. Finally, the arrival of radio and TV, dominated by national networks, reinforced the use of Portuguese, especially among the young.

In the town of Pomerode, a confluence of forces has ensured the preservation of the German language. Only in the last generation have decent roads linked Pomerode to Blumenau, so the town remained physically isolated from its neighbors. In addition, nearly all of its original settlers spoke the same dialect (Pomeranian), so there was no need to resort to Portuguese as a lingua franca. And the settlers were Lutheran, so German remained their language of worship. These days, a growing movement is preserving Brazil's bilingual communities.

and a long stretch of skyscraper-lined sand that suspiciously mirrors Copacabana right down to its name – Av Atlântica – all for for a fraction of Copacabana prices. Truth be told, Camboriú is really a carbon copy of Copacabana except for one caveat: it's much newer, so the city's infrastructure, from high-rise hotels to trendy street-level bars, is all in much better shape. Not a bad, deal, actually.

The summer population swells to nearly a million, as Argentines, Paraguayans and Brazilians flood in to enjoy one of Brazil's hottest party scenes. Camboriú is known for being as gay-friendly as Rio, and also for its *teleférico* (cable car) connecting a large central *morro* (hill) with not one, but two beaches – apparently the only one of its kind in the world. Families like Camboriú for its kid-friendly attractions and proximity to Beto Carrero World.

Tourist information (☑ 3367-8005; www. secturbc.com.br; ☺ 8am-6pm) is in the bus station, run by the municipality, and on Av Atlântica at Rua 51, run by **Beto Carrero World** (☑ 3261-2222; www.betocarrero.com.br; Inácio Francisco de Souza 1597; adult/child/senior R$80/70/44; ☺ 9am-6pm; ⓐ), though it's good for city info as well.

◉ Sights

★ **Parque Unipraias**   NATURE RESERVE
(☑ 3404-7600; www.unipraias.com.br; Av Atlântica 6006; ☺ 9am-8pm Dec-Feb, 9:30am-6pm Mar-Nov; ⓐ) Camboriú's pride and joy is this six-hectare urban reserve; in addition to 500m of walking trails, the real coup is its amusements: the **bondinho** (cable car; ☑ 3404-7600; www.unipraias.com.br; adult/child R$36/18; ⓐ), an Italian-built cable-car system that connects three stations between Barra Sul up to the 240m-high Morro da Aguada and back down to Praia Laranjeiras on a spectacular 3.2km, 30-minute ride over the Atlantic rainforest.

At the top, the park also operates the kid-tastic **Yoohooo!** (tickets R$20; ⓐ) roller coaster, which plunges 700m at 60km per hour, and **ZipRider** (tickets R$39), a thrilling 750m plunge to Praia Laranjeiras. Both are a blast! The park is mostly weekends only in June and August, so check ahead if you're coming through then.

Beaches   BEACHES
Praia Laranjeiras, the busiest and closest beach to town, and six beaches extending south along the Costa Brava have crystal-line waters and views of forested hills in the

DON'T MISS

EIN BIER, POR FAVOR!

Brazil's mainstream brews – Skol, Brahma and Antarctica – are fine for staving off the tropical heat, but let's face it: taste is not their strong suit. Luckily, the German immigrants of the Vale Europeu are here to help. There is a true beer culture here dating back to the mid-1800s, with real beer like pale ale, bock, wheat and pilsen. The following are some of the region's best breweries, all with tasting rooms in and around Blumenau.

Cervejaria Eisenbahn (✆3488-7307; www.eisenbahn.com.br; Bahia 5181, Blumenau; ◷4pm-midnight Mon-Sat,10am-1am Sun) Turth be told, given it's acquisition by big dog Schincariol, Eisenbahn could do more to beef up the visitor experience, but tours (R$5) are offered on the hour from 2pm to 7pm, and the brewery does garner the most world-wide recognition for its brewing efforts.

The small taproom features 12 beers, including Brazil's first organic pilsen, a rauchbier and Lust, a high-end beer brewed using the champagne method, and there are half-hearted nibbles to go with them. To get there, grab the bus marked 'Passo Manso' from the Estação Dr Blumenau stop on Av Beira Rio (R$2.90) and ask to get off at Eisenbahn.

Schornstein Kneipe (✆3333-2759; www.schornstein.com.br; Hermann Weege 60, Pomerode; ◷5pm-midnight Wed, from noon Thu-Fri, from 11am Sat & Sun; 🛜) This truly excellent microbrewery producers two types of pilsner as well as an Indian pale ale (our fave!), weiss, bock and an imperial stout. Call ahead to arrange a brewery tour. To reach the brewery, grab an hourly **Volkmann** (www.turismovolkmann.com.br) bus from Av Beira Rio to Pomerode (R$4.45)

Cervejaria Bierland (✆3323-6588; www.bierland.com.br; Gustavo Zimmermann 5361, Blumenau; ◷4:30pm-midnight Tue-Fri, 10am-midnight Sat) Don't judge a beer by its label – Bierland's brews are much better than their packaging. Eight in total are brewed here, including a pale ale, bock, golden ale and Viennese-style ale, with four on draft at any given time, along with finger foods to chase them with. It's 12km from Centro in Itoupava Central.

Cervejaria Das Bier (✆3397-8600; www.dasbier.com.br; Bonifácio Haendchen 5311, Gaspar; ◷5pm-midnight Wed-Fri, 3pm-midnight Sat, 11am-7pm Sun) Das Bier brews its two pilsens according to *Reinheitsgebot* (Germany's 1516 beer purity law) and follows those with a brown ale, weiss and pale ale. It also offers the most serious eats of the breweries listed here. Tours by appointment. Santa Terezinha runs seven buses per day from Blumenau to Gaspar (R$7.60).

background. Four kilometers north, on the road to Itajaí, **Praia dos Amores** has good surf conditions, as does **Praia Atalaia** in Itajai, 10km north of Camboriú.

Cristo Luz Statue
LANDMARK

(✆3367-4042; www.cristoluz.com.br; Indonésia 800; admission R$20; ◷4pm-midnight Mon-Sat, from 10am Sun) The 33m Cristo Luz statue holds a sombrero from which a spotlight illuminates the city at night, sometimes in streaming colors. During summer live music is often staged from 7pm.

🛏 Sleeping

Discounts range up to 50% outside of the packed summer months.

Rezende House
HOSTEL $$

(✆3361-1008; www.rezendepousada.com.br; Rua 3100, 780; dm/s/d/tr R$55/119/159/209; @🛜) In the middle of the beach and nightlife action, this hostel fills up fast in high season. It's a rare youth hostel with balconies in the dorms and good private rooms (there's even hairdryers!). There is an insistence on bank deposits from foreigners, so it's best to book through the HI web site.

Pousada Villa Atlântica
POUSADA $$

(✆3367-3821; www.villa-atlantica.com.br; Rua 3300, 415; s/d R$180/200; ✸@🛜) For something more quaint, this good-value pousada, just two blocks from the beach in Barra Sul, has simple but clean rooms accented in light colors and mod-cons like flat-screen TVs.

Mercure Hotel
HOTEL $$$

(📞3056-9500; www.mercure.com.br; Av Atlântica 2010; s/d R$498/572, with sea view R$590/659; ✳@🛜♨) The trendy Mercure is one of Camboriú hotspots, a top-end place to lay your weary head in the heart of the Praia Central action. Rooms are clean-lined and modern, a welcome respite from the somewhat gaudy turquoise hallways, and there are two pools, a fitness center, a spa and a pretty great restaurant. See-and-be-seen here.

Eating

Madero
BURGERS $

(www.restaurantemadero.com.br; cnr Av Atlântica & Rua 2900; burgers R$19.80-36.90; ⊙11:45am-12:30am; 🛜) Curitiba's top burger joint landed itself on some prime beachfront real estate for its trendy Camboriú outlet. Madero does great burgers between even greater buns; but save room for the sinister *doce de leite petit gâteau* dessert.

Sapore Speciale
SELF-SERVE, SEAFOOD $$

(www.spaorespeciale.com.br; Av Atlântica 2010; per kg R$53; ⊙9am-midnight, to 8pm Mar-Nov) Attached to the Mercure Hotel but independent, upscale Sapore is a high-quality *por kilo* for weekday lunch – you'll find an excellent variety of meat and seafood dishes – and turns into a lobster free-for-all buffet on weekends (R$87). At night, it sticks to a seafood-dominated à la carte (mains R$28 to R$125).

Bistrô Palatare
FRENCH/ITALIAN $$$

(📞3366-3699; www.balnear.com/palatare; Rua 2550, 699; mains R$36-68; ⊙7:30-midnight Fri & Sat) A hands-on couple run the best contemporary restaurant in town, specializing in Franco-Italian dishes that only hit their eight tables on Friday and Saturday nights. Zé Eduardo handles the kitchen, where mains like duck confit with gorgonzola polenta and grilled lemongrass and ginger shrimp hit the dining room, run by his wife, Margeret. Yes, you need reservations.

Drinking & Nightlife

Nightlife in Camboriú is king; the city boasts some of the world's most renowned clubs. Though they swing in and out of favor like a game of Pong, **Green Valley** (📞3360-8097; www.greenvalley.art.br; Rio Mamoré 1083) was the monster of the moment at time of research. Crowds here can swell to concert-level.

For something more low key, pop into any number of great bars lining Av Atlântica.

Taj Bar
BAR

(📞3264-0464; www.tajbar.com.br; Av. Atlântica 5710; cocktails R$12-26; ⊙6pm-late Tue-Sun; 🛜) Big, loungy and beautiful, this trendy bar is what would be if Buddha were Brazilian. No doubt inspired by the Parisian Buddha Bar brand, a night here moves from restaraunt to bar to *balada* as the night wears on. Creative cocktails and a solid Thai-Indian-Indonesian menu (mains R$28 to R$90) means you can easily call it a night.

Arrive early – getting in gets dicey after 10pm. DJs spin from 9pm.

Chaplin Bar
BAR

(📞3367-0250; Av Atlântica 2200; ⊙noon-4am) A classic for cold *chope* (from R$5.20) on the main drag of Av Atlântica.

ℹ️ Getting There & Away

Praiana (www.praiana.com.br) runs four to six buses a day to Bombinhas (R$13.50, 1½ hours), stopping in Porto Belo (R$10, one hour), but more frequent buses to Porto Belo leave from the intermunicipal bus stop on Santa Catarina next to the bus station (R$4.20). Hourly buses go to Florianópolis (R$21.50, 1½), Joinville (R$20, 1½ hours) and Blumenau (R$17.50, 1½ hours).

South of Florianópolis

The waves have put this stretch of coastline on the map. Long gone are the quiet fishing villages and near-deserted beaches that once dotted the coast south of Florianópolis. While the local population is still largely descended from Azorean fishermen, you'll be hard pressed to find them amid the suntanned surfers and bikini-clad beauties. The beaches that don't have big surf – and there are a few – are given over to fun-seeking families who show up every summer for their fix of sun and sand.

Guarda do Embaú
📞0XX48

Famous for its excellent left that breaks at the mouth of the river, Guarda do Embaú often makes the list of Brazil's best surfing beaches. But it's much more than that. When the river meets the sea in this laid-back, bohemian surf village it creates one of Southern Brazil's most postcard-perfect settings: Surfers and sun worshipers wading back and forth across the beautiful Rio da Madre between town and Guarda's gorgeous sun-toasted sands. It's an excellent destination for wave riders, backpackers and other bohemian types.

The tiny village has several restaurants, a lot of well-stocked surf shops and some jazzy boutiques. For more information on Guarda, see www.guardadoembau.com.br.

Sleeping & Eating

There are a half-dozen or so cocktail and sandwich *barracas* (stalls) on the beach. For nightlife, there is a decent option or two at the river.

Sun Hostel Pousada Magia da Guarda   HOSTEL $

(☑ 3283-2316; www.pousadamagiadaguarda.com. br; Estrada Geral 713; r per person R$40, with kitchenettes R$50; ☎ ▨) Casual, colorful and artsy, this laid-back spot just a few minutes walk from the beach is simple but friendly and criminally cheap. No breakfast.

Canto da Guarda   POUSADA $$

(☑ 3283-2375; cantodaguarda@bol.co.br; Inês Maria de Jesus; s/d from R$140/160, with air-con from R$160/190; ✳ ☎) A very cute and tasteful midrange choice offering just 10 rooms. There's little reason to upgrade above the bilevel standards, which are great value and perfectly comfortable with lovely hammockstrewn verandas.

Zululand   CHALETS $$

(☑ 3283-2093; www.zululand.com.br; Servidão Emerenciana s/n; d without air R$220, bungalows with air-con from R$330; ✳ @ ☎ ▨) Owned by well-known model/actor/surfer Paulo Zulu, Zululand is a collection of funky-shaped bilevel bungalows well equipped with tasteful art and flat-screen TVs, all set about a property flush with lush tropical foliage.

Big Bamboo   SEAFOOD $$$

(www.bigbamboo.com.br; Beira do Rio da Madre; mains for 2 R$46-89; ⊙ noon-midnight) A solid choice for seafood with organic leanings and good microbrews in a seaside setting with views of the river and beach. It's owned by the father of Brazilian footballer Fernando Prass, whose memorabilia decorates the bar.

❶ Getting There & Away

Paulotur (www.paulotur.com.br) has buses throughout the day from Florianópolis to Guarda (R$11, two hours). To continue south to Praia da Rosa, catch an hourly Paulotur bus in the village back to BR-101 (R$2.35, 10 minutes), flag down a Garopaba-bound bus (R$6, 30 minutes) from the southside bus stop near the underpass, and get off at the Praia da Rosa turnoff on the road to Garopaba and catch a local bus (R$2.60) to town.

Praia do Rosa
☑ 0XX48

Santa Catarina's swankiest seaside town, Praia do Rosa, is about 15km south of Garopaba. The beach here, all 3km of it, is the stuff of models and photo shoots – one of Brazil's storybook destinations, backed by small sand dunes and flanked by outcrops of lush Mata Atlântica. Besides the stunning beach, Rosa has two things going for it: A cultured, ecoconscious population; and waves that propelled the town, which sits high on a bluff above the beach, from a modest fishing hamlet in the '70's to one of Brazil's most sophisticated surf villages.

In winter, the bay becomes a breeding ground for southern right whales, and mothers and calves can be seen from the beach.

There are no banks in Praia do Rosa – Garopaba is the nearest ATM.

🕴 Activities

Turismo Vida Sol e Mar   WHALE WATCHING

(☑ 3355-6111; www.vidasolemar.com.br; Estrada Geral da Praia do Rosa; tours per person weekend/ weekday R$140/90; ⊙ tours 8am & 11am) 🏄 Every winter, between June and October, hundreds of southern right whales return to the Santa Catarina coast. For a close encounter, these ecologically sound whale-watching tours leave from Garopaba and last for 90 minutes or more, depending on the location of the whales. Each boat has an IBF scientist on board, but whale sightings are (obviously!) not guaranteed.

Sleeping

The highest road in town, Caminho do Rei, is home to accommodations options with sweeping views.

★ Pousada La Roca   POUSADA $$

(☑ 3355-7020; www.pousadalaroca.com.br; Caminho do Rei; s/d R$180/250; ✳ ☎) New Argentine owners have breathed new life into the bestvalue pousada along Caminho do Rei. Cool stone walls and shiny wood floors evoke an ecostylish atmosphere and the new and improved shared balcony – complete with stylish lounge furniture – offers ocean views from the upper floors, while the lower floors are engulfed in greenery.

Albergue Explorer   HOSTEL $$
(☑3355-7003; www.albergueexplorer.com.br; Francisco Marques; dm/d R$50/220; @✲) There are better-value privates out there, but the dorms here, all with private bath and one with a private kitchen, are in good shape. Enjoy expansive views from the common patio, a small pool with waterfall and the hospitality of Paulo and Francis, who speak English and Spanish, respectively.

No breakfast outside high season and holidays.

★ Quinta do Bucanero   POUSADA $$$
(☑3355-6056; www.bucanero.com.br; Estrada Geral da Praia do Rosa; d from R$705; ✲❋✲)

Built Bedrock-style literally in and around the rocky cliffside, Rosa's most charming option is a 10-room gem of hospitality in jungly surrounds. Rooms are dressed in light colors and feature five-star comforts and view-riffic patios. The gorgeous pool overlooks the lagoons and the beach below, while the pousada has it's own exclusive path and boat for beach access.

✗ Eating & Drinking

There are goods bars on the beach, but development has been restrained for the most part.

★Urucum   SEAFOOD $$$
(☑3355-7330; www.restauranteurucum.blogspot.com; Estrada Geral da Praia do Rosa; mains for 2 R$78-112; ◷1pm-midnight, closed Tue & Wed low

---

WORTH A TRIP

GO NORTH, YOUNG SUNSEEKER

While the stellar beaches south of Florianópolis might hog the most pristine sands and charming beach towns, it's no monopoly. The northern Santa Catarina coast has its own charms as well. Here are a few additional spots worth checking out.

Ilha do São Francisco
The lovely city of **São Francisco do Sul**, 45km east of Joinville, is Brazil's third oldest, founded in 1504 by the French (only Bahia and São Vicente are older). The historical center is on the Patrimônio Histórico (National Heritage list), for its decadent, colonial feel. The city acts as a gateway to the rest of the Ilha do São Francisco, a popular destination for sun-worshipers and surfers. **Viação Verdes Mares** (www.vmares.com.br) runs regular buses to Ilha de São Francisco from Joinville (R$8.25 to R$12).

Penha & Armação
These two villages are side by side along the north shore of a peninsula that juts out into the ocean, 110km north of Florianópolis. The crescent-shaped beach wraps around a bay dotted with colorful fishing boats. The idyllic village atmosphere changes slightly on summer weekends, however, when the main beachfront turns into one big *festa* (party). Regardless, these twin towns feel more like fishing villages than holiday resorts. **Catarinense** (www.catarinense.net) runs a few buses a day to Penha from Blumenau (R$20; two hours) and several from Joinville (R$17, 1½ hours), calling at Piçarras (6km north).

Porto Belo, Bombas & Bombinhas
A small peninsula fans out from Porto Belo about 60km north of Florianópolis. Here, clear, emerald-green waters offer some of the best diving in southern Brazil.

The town of **Porto Belo** is a developed fishing village, so its beach is dominated by a big dock and boats moored in the bay. The principal swimming beaches are **Praia Bombinhas** (9km from Porto Belo) and the adjacent **Praia Bombas** (3km). These sandy stretches are also lined with small-scale hotels and seafood restaurants.

From Balneário Camboriú, **Praiana** (www.praiana.com.br) runs four to six buses a day to Bombinhas (R$13.50, 1½ hours), stopping in Porto Belo (R$10, one hour). Frequent Porto Belo intermunicipal buses also depart throughout the day from Santa Catarina, next to Camboriú's bus station. **Viação Navegantes** (www.viacaonavegantes.net) also runs six buses per weekday from Florianópolis (R$13.50, 1¾ hours), less on weekends.

SANTA CATARINA SOUTH OF FLORIANÓPOLIS

SERRA GERAL

High in the mountains of the Serra do Rio do Rastro (an offshoot of the Serra Geral), **São Joaquim** is about 290km southwest of Florianópolis. This little town in the Rio Canoas valley is famous for its apple orchards, many of which were planted by the local Japanese population. São Joaquim's other claim to fame is its snowfall: come in early July for the annual Festival de Inverno. **Reunidas** (www.reunidas.com.br) has one daily bus from Florianópolis to São Joaquim (R$45, 5½ hours, 6:30pm).

Bom Jardim da Serra, founded in the 1870s by *gaúchos* (cowboys), is known as the 'capital of the water' and does indeed boast many lakes and waterfalls. About 45km south of São Joaquim, it also serves as the start of the hair-raising and spectacular winding road known as the **Estrada da Serrado Rio Rastro**, which switchbacks through high-mountain scenery toward the **Parque Nacional de São Joaquim**. The park boasts a breathtaking landscape of grassy highlands, thick *araucária* (Paraná pine) forests and Santa Catarina's highest peak, **Morro da Igreja** (1822m). The park lacks infrastructure, but hiking trails leading to panoramic lookouts and free-falling waterfalls. **Nevatur** (www.nevatur.com.br) has one 5:30pm bus to Bom Jardim da Serra (R$57, five hours, Monday, Wednesday, Friday and Sunday).

The nicest town is **Urubici**, 60km northeast of São Joaquim, famous for being near Morro da Igreja, where you'll find **Pedra Furada**, a large, naturally carved stone 30m in circumference. The area is a hotbed of adventure sports (hang gliding, rappelling) and cold weather – it recorded Brazil's chilliest day on historical record: -17.8°C in 1996! Reunidas also services Urubici twice daily (R$42, four hours, noon and 6:30pm).

season; 🛜) Chef Rafael Miralha hails from Espírito Santo and trained in Southern California before setting up shop in Rosa, *capixaba* recipes in hand. He specializes in *moquecas* (seafood stews) done up in the style of his home state (healthier and lighter than the Bahian version). Alongside eye-popping views, his scrumptious creations are served in well-worn clay cookware and do not disappoint.

Tigre Asiático   ASIAN **$$$**
(📋3355-7045; www.tigreasiaticorestaurante.com.br; Centrinho do Rosa; mains R$42-77; ⏱7-11pm; 🛜) Considered Santa Catarina's best beach restaurant outside Floripa, the Asian Tiger, located in town, is an Indonesian-Thai fusion trip by way of local Brazilian ingredi-

ents. In a romantic candlelit space with no shortage of Buddhas minding your menu choices, your best bets are the seasonal dishes; our fiery four-pepper octopus was a knockout. Skip the sushi.

Next door, **Tigre Cafe** (Centrinho do Rosa; snacks R$7-16; ⏱8am-10pm) is the town's best for sweets, coffee and smaller bites.

❶ Getting There & Away

Numerous local buses run to Garopaba (R$3.40, 40 minutes), from where you can continue on to Florianópolis (R$18.50, two hours) with **Paulotur** (www.paulotur.com.br); and to Imbituba ('Ibiraquera;' R$3.90, one hour), from where **Santo Anjo** (www.santoanjo.com.br) and **Eucatur** (www.eucatur.com.br) go to Porto Alegre (R$66, six hours) eight times per day.

Rio Grande do Sul

POP 10.7 MILLION

Includes ➡

Best Places to Eat

➡ Valle Rustico (p312)

➡ Belle du Valais (p319)

➡ Mamma Gema (p313)

➡ Casa di Paolo (p319)

➡ Atelier das Massas (p313)

Best Places to Stay

➡ Parador Casa da Montanha (p323)

➡ Pousada Borghetto Sant'Anna (p312)

➡ Jardim Secreto Pousada (p319)

➡ Pousada Corucacas (p323)

➡ Pousada das Missões (p327)

Why Go?

From the jaw-dropping forest-covered canyons of the national parks near Cambará do Sul, and cascading river valleys near cozy Brazilian alpine villages like Gramado, to the stunning Vale dos Vinhedos, where Italian-descended vintners produce wines to rival those of Chile and Argentina: the Rio Grande do Sul defies notions of typical Brazil.

Brazil's southernmost state is its most culturally distinct, home to an independently minded population steeped in cattle herding and cowboy culture. *Gaúchos*, as residents of Rio Grande do Sul are known, are a fiercely proud and traditional lot. In the countryside, it is not unusual to see old-timers sporting wide-brimmed hats and other traditional dress. Grilled meat, or *churrasco*, is still the state's favorite food, and everywhere – even in the cosmopolitan capital of Porto Alegre – locals suck down *chimarrão*, the distinctive, traditional tea made from the *maté* plant.

When to Go
Porto Alegre

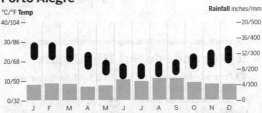

Jan–Mar Hot days and cool nights during harvest season in the Vale dos Vinhedos

May–Oct Prices are higher, but you might just see Brazilian snow in Cambará do Sul

Dec & Jun–Jul Gramado is in Alpine Wonderland mode for Christmas, then winter.

History

Living on land long disputed by the Spanish and Portuguese, the people of Rio Grande do Sul used the conflict to create an identity distinct from the rest of Brazil. The region even declared its independence during the ill-fated Guerra dos Farrapos, a decade-long civil war ending in 1845. A wave of immigrants, mostly German, Italian and Swiss, began arriving in the late 19th century, reinforcing the region's cultural differences.

ⓘ Getting There & Around

Porto Alegre is the state's transportation hub, with air and bus services to every major city in Brazil. Excellent roads and the efficient regional bus service makes traveling within the state relatively easy.

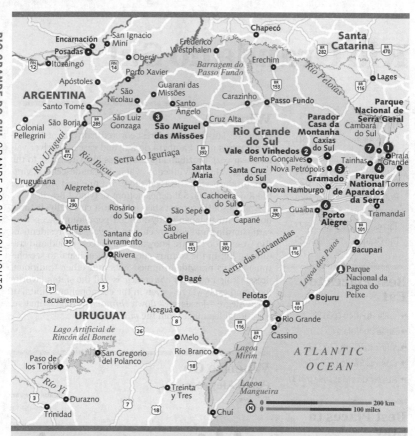

Rio Grande do Sul Highlights

❶ Peer over the edge of the Cânion da Fortaleza in **Parque Nacional da Serra Geral** (p322)

❷ Taste your way through the New World's emerging wine region in the gorgeous **Vale dos Vinhedos** (p244)

❸ Wander the stunning grounds of the ruined Jesuit mission at **São Miguel das Missões** (p326)

❹ Look skyward in wonder while tackling the stunning Trilha do Rio do Boi through **Parque Nacional de Aparados da Serra** (p322)

❺ Wander the carefree Swiss mountain village of **Gramado** (p317),

where fondue flows freely throughout a gorgeous Brazilian winterscape

❻ Learn to sip *gaúcho* tea with a *chimarrão mestre* in **Porto Alegre** (p311)

❼ Hole up in splurge-worthy tented luxury at the gorgeous **Parador Casa da Montanha** (p323)

PORTO ALEGRE

⬀ OXX51 / POP 1.4 MILLION

On the banks of the huge freshwater Lagoa dos Patos, Porto Alegre is southern Brazil's most important port city and a key player in Mercosul (the South American free-trade agreement).

The downtown area has benefited from a thoughtful approach to development, including the creation of transportation hubs and the preservation of much of its grand, neoclassical architecture. A long tradition of progressive politics has helped nurture vibrant arts and alternative music scenes, and the well-organized gay and lesbian community has won the right to register domestic partnerships.

Unfortunately, crime levels in the city have risen in recent years and the downtown area can be seedy. During the day, the city has a grittier feel than most southern Brazilian metropolises.

Porto Alegre will be a host city for the 2014 FIFA World Cup.

⊙ Sights

Praça 15 de Novembro, site of the 1869 Mercado Público (p313), is the centerpiece of the city. The old building bustles during daytime hours, when vendors sell fresh produce, meats and seafood, as well as the all-important *erva maté* for *chimarrão* (tea).

Three blocks south, the picturesque Praça da Matriz is dominated by the early-20th-century, neoclassical **Catedral Metropolitana**. On the northern side, you'll find the elegant mid-19th-century edifice of the **Teatro São Pedro** (⬀ 3227-5100; www.teatrosaopedro.com. br; Praça Mal Deodoro) and the sculpted facade of the **Biblioteca Público** (⬀ 3224-5045; www. bibliotecapublica.rs.gov.br; cnr Riachuelo & General Câmara; ⊙ 2-5pm Mon, 9am-7pm Tue-Fri, 2-6pm Sat).

Museu de Arte
do Rio Grande do Sul   MUSEUM
(www.margs.rs.gov.br; Praça da Alfândega; ⊙ 10am-7pm Tue-Sun) **FREE** A pedestrian promenade runs into Praça da Alfândega, the leafy square that is home to the Museu de Arte do Rio Grande do Sul. The neoclassical building is an impressive venue for regional artists. On the ground floor, the inviting Bistrot de MARGS takes advantage of the leafy setting, which is a lovely spot for lunch.

Museu Histórico Júlo
de Castilhos   MUSEUM
(www.museujuliodecastilhos.blogspot.com; Duque de Caxias 1205; ⊙ 10am-5pm Tue-Sat) **FREE** Near the Praça da Matriz is Museu Histórico Júlo de Castilhos, displaying *gaúcho* artifacts in a typical 19th-century home.

⊂⫐ Tours

Porto Alegre 10   BOAT TOUR
(⬀ 3211-7665; www.portoalegre10.com.br; Av Presidente João Goulart 551; adult/child R$20/10) One-hour cruises down the river (adult/child R$15/7.50; 10:30am, 4:30pm & 5:30pm during the week, hourly from 11:30am to 6:30pm on weekends). They depart from behind the Centro Cultural do Usino Gasômetro.

Linha Turismo   CITY TOUR
(www.portoalegre.travel; Travessa do Carmo 84; R$15; ⊙ 9am-5:30pm Tue-Sun) Offers 90-minute bus tours of local historical sites, including a *zona sul* (southern zone) tour that explores the southeastern periphery of the city.

⊨ Sleeping

Porto Alegre hotels fill up for Carnaval. Most budget travelers now stay in Cidade Baixa, where a healthy hostel scene has popped up.

★ Porto Alegre
Eco Hostel   HOSTEL $
(⬀ 3019-2449; www.portoalegreecohostel.com.br; Luiz Afonso 276; dm from R$37, s/d without bathroom R$70/100, d from R$120; @ 🛜 ⌨) 🞋 Down a quiet residential street in the heart of Cidade Baixa, this excellent hostel, chock-full of demolition wood furniture and eco-awareness, offers a lovely backyard garden in a pristine '30s-era home. Everyone speaks English.

Casa Azul   HOSTEL $
(⬀ 3084-5050; www.casaazulhostel.com; Gen Lima e Silva 912 ; dm R$35-45, r without bath R$100; ✴ @ 🛜) Say hi to your party hostel, in the thick of the Cidade Baixa action. A great front room bar serves as the preparty epicenter while the artsy decor, sweet management and a great rooftop kitchen round out the pluses here.

Lido Hotel   HOTEL $
(⬀ 3228-9111; www.lidohotel.com.br; Gen Andrade Neves 150; r week/weekend R$146/104; ✴ 🛜) A slick lobby gives way to basic but spacious rooms at this comfortable Centro option. Breakfast is R$10 extra.

Hotel Continental
Business   BUSINESS HOTEL $$
(⬀ 3027-1600; www.hotelcontinentalbusiness.com. br; Praça Otávio Rocha 49; s/d weekend R$145/157, week R$227/258; ✴ @ 🛜) Short on charm but

Porto Alegre

long on comfort, this towering hotel offers good-value rooms that are small but stylish, and the staff offers professional service.

★ Pousada Borghetto Sant'Anna
POUSADA **$$$**

(☎ 3453-2355; www.borghettosantanna.com.br; Linha Leopoldina 868; ste R$290, cottages R$350-380; ❄ @ 🐾) About 4km from Bento, perched above the Vale dos Vinhedos, this cluster of romantic stone houses gives a fantastic view of the valley below. Reminiscent of Tuscany, the lodgings mix rustic charm with sumptuous comfort and unobtrusive construction, right down to large portions of sedentary rock in the showers. Breakfast is disapointing, but the views make up for it.

Sheraton Porto Alegre
BUSINESS HOTEL **$$$**

(☎ 2121-6000; www.sheraton-poa.com.br; Olavo Barreto Viana 18; s/d from R$712/769; ❄ @ 🐾 ❄) The fanciest digs in town are 3km east of the center, in the upscale neighborhood of

Moinhos de Vento. Streets lined with quaint cafes and chic boutiques, plus the popular Parque Moinhos, make this a prime locale.

Eko Residence Hotel
APARTMENT, HOTEL **$$$**

(☎ 3215-7600; www.residencehotel.com.br; Av Des André da Rocha 131; s/d from R$384/440; ❄ @ 🐾 ❄) 🍃 This fresh, simple 97-apartment hotel near Parque Farroupilha offers solar-power showers, a vertical garden, rainwater toilets and a planned electricity-generating wind turbine. Steep discounts (as low as R$160) are easy to come by and long-term guests are attracted to in-room kitchenettes and the solid environmental sustainability program.

✗ Eating

★ Valle Rustico
BRAZILIAN **$$$**

(☎ 3459-1162; www.vallerustico.com.br; Linha Marcílio Dias s/n; 3-course prix-fixe R$68; ⊙ 6:30pm-midnight Wed-Sat, noon-3pm Sun; 🐾) 🍃 Wine

Porto Alegre

country's best restaurant sits down a lonely and dark dirt road - don't worry, it's open – where you'll find a atmospheric beamed wooden ceiling dining room in the basement of a house. Local chef done good Rodrigo Bellora offers two options nightly: An artisanal pizza *rodízio* (R$40); OK but skippable) and a three-course contemporary menu.

As many ingredients as possible are culled from the restaurant's own organic gardens and dishes like the mushroom risotto and the filet mignon with a dry chimmichurri are big hits paired with Vinhedos wines.

Sabor Natural   SELF-SERVE $
(Siqueira Campos 890; buffet R$15; ⊙11am-3pm Mon-Fri; 🖉) Vegetarians will delight at this all-organic, meat-free, all-you-can-eat buffet that caters to the downtown lunch crowd. Enjoy limitless soups, salads and other animal-friendly fare.

Tudo Pelo Social   BRAZILIAN $
(www.restaurantetudopelosocial.com.br;   João Alfredo 448; meals R$9-30; ⊙11am-2:45pm & 6-11:45pm Mon-Sat, till 2:45pm Sun) The giant Cidade Baixa dining hall is wildly popular for its award-winning working-class staples (simple grills, rice, fries and salad) served in astonishing portions for blink-worthy prices. It's always packed.

★ **Atelier das Massas**   ITALIAN $$
(Riachuelo 1482; mains R$21.80-41.90; ⊙11am-2pm & 7-11:30pm Mon-Fri, 11am-3pm & 7-11:30pm Sat; 🖥) Crammed as much with atmosphere as with artisanal pastas, put this dive-like pasta bar on your immediate to-do list. The walls are crammed with original artwork and funky photographs. The menu is no less creative, with an irresistible antipasti buffet and delectable homemade pastas.

Mamma Gema   ITALIAN $$
(www.mammagema.com.br; Estrada RS 444, Km18.9; mains for 2 R$56-62; ⊙noon-3:30pm Tue-Fri, til 4pm Sat-Sun) Unlike many of the trattoria's in the region, Mamma focuses on quality, not quantity. The owner, an ex professional footballer, harvests his own wild mushrooms for here and a second restaurant in Garibaldi; and the perfectly-executed pastas and risottos, such as the pumpkin-stuffed tortei bolognese, are outstanding.

The attached wine shop is a great place to pick up the best wines in the region in one spot.

Boteco Natalicio   BOTECO $$
(www.boteconatalicio.com.br; Genuíno 217; mains R$18.90-29.90; ⊙From 5pm Mon-Fri, from noon Sat; 🖥) The walls of this lively, bi-level *boteco* (open-air bar) straddling Centro and Cidade Baixa is covered in some 200-odd musings of comedians and locals, and packs a wild punch of *chope*-starved locals, here to preempt the beer with regional delicacies like honey-smoked pork ribs and crunchy shrimp sandwiches with *catupiry* cheese.

Mercado Público   MARKET $$
(www2.portoalegre.rs.gov.br/mercadopublico; ⊙7:30am-7:30pm Mon-Fri, til 6:30pm Sat) Porto Alegre's bustling public market offers a wealth of eats. Recommended options include **Banco 40** (www.banca40.com.br; Mercado Público; snacks R$4-14; ⊙8am-7:30pm Mon-Fri, til 6:30pm Sat), home of the incomparable *bomba royal* (a showy ice cream and fruit salad concoction; R$8.90); and **Gambrinus**

PROGRESSIVE POLITICS IN RIO GRANDE DO SUL

Rio Grande do Sul has a long history of contrariness. The state's *farroupilhas* (political extremists) revolted against the Brazilian emperor in the 1830s and 1840s, declaring a short-lived republic. In the late 1970s, strikes by *gaúcho* (cowboy) trade unions helped weaken the military junta ruling the country. In 2001, the city hosted the first World Social Forum (like a World Economic Forum for lefties). And, in March 2004, in a country that is overwhelmingly Catholic, the state's high court declared same-sex unions a civil right.

In progressive political circles, Porto Alegre is best known for its innovative approach to local politics called Participatory Budgeting (PB). In 1989 the Workers' Party instituted PB in an attempt to improve democratic institutions and to create citizen ownership. This radical reform is a complex system that gives residents a direct role in setting priorities and creating the municipal budget.

In principle, PB creates opportunities for poor, uneducated or otherwise disenfranchised citizens to get involved in the decision-making process. In practice, the trend has increased spending in lower-income neighborhoods. More generally, studies suggest that it results in greater government transparency and increased levels of public participation. Now, throughout Brazil, more than 180 municipalities are experimenting with PB, and it has also been replicated in other cities in Latin America and Europe.

PB has since been adopted by at least 140 Brazilian municipalities and is gaining traction worldwide, from North America (parts of Chicago, New York and Vallejo, California) to India (where a small Maharashtra village called Hiware Bazar turned its dire need of water, education and basic needs into model self-sufficiency with PB).

The region's success suggests that budgets by the people, for the people, just might be the wave of the future.

(www.gambrinus.com.br; Mercado Público; mains R$28-68; ⊗11am-9pm Mon-Fri, til 4pm Sat), an old-world Portuguese seafood restaurant (mains from R$28); and **Café Do Mercado** (www.cafedomcrcado.com.br; Mercado Público; ⊗8:30am-7:30pm Mon-Fri, 9am-5pm Sat), one of the city's best cafes.

Galpão Crioulo   CHURRASCARIA $$
(www.churrascariagalpaocrioulo.com.br; Parque Maurício Sirotsky Sobrinho; buffet lunch/dinner R$44.90/54.90; ⊗11:30am-3pm & 7:30-11:30pm) Serious *gaúcho* country means serious meat. Indulge yourself at one of Porto Alegre's best – and most touristy – *churrascarias*. The designated *Mestre do Chimarrão* (*chimarrão* master) guarantees the local specialty *maté* is memorable as well. The live entertainment is tacky but seemingly loved by patrons.

 Drinking

Cidade Baixa and upscale Moinhos de Vento are Porto Alegre's nightlife hubs. The city also has a very active gay and lesbian social scene – try **Casa do Lado** (☑9143-1401; www.casadolado.com.br; Rua da República 546; cover R$20-25; ⊗11pm-6am Fri-Sat), **Caba-**

ret (☑3307-8998; www.cabaretpoa.com.br; Av Independencia 590; ⊗11pm-7am) or **Vitraux** (☑3221-7799; www.vitraux.com.br; Conceição 492; ⊗from 11pm Fri & Sat, from 10pm Sun).

★**Dirty Old Man**   BAR
(www.dirtyoldman.com.br; Lima e Silva 956; cocktails R$8-10; ⊗From 6pm Tue-Sun) This awesomely named Cidade Baixa bar (a nod to Bukowski) is a must for those interested in *very* regional microbrews: Baldhead is on tap, served in real pints (R$8 to R$12), while the crowd swilling it down is as eclectic and rare as the beer. A must.

Apolinário   BOTECO
(www.apolinariobar.com.br; José do Patrocínio 527; items R$10-32; ⊗from 5:30pm Mon-Fri, from 7pm Sat; 🕿) This upscale beer *boteco* dangles the regional microbrew carrot to salivating beer hounds.

Chale da Praça XV   BRAZILIAN
(www.chaledapracaxv.com.br; Praça 15 de Novembro; mains R$20-48; ⊗noon-midnight) Housed in a pleasant, Victorian-style garden house and surrounded by a sprawling terrace, this Porto Alegre institution buzzes with activity. Great bet on Sunday.

☆ Entertainment

Cultural Centers

**Casa da Cultura
Mario Quintana** CINEMA
(☑ 3221-7147; www.ccmq.rs.gov.br; Rua dos Andradas 736; ☉ 2-9pm Mon, from 9am Tue-Fri, from noon Sat-Sun) The cultural center in this pink baroque building has a cinema and two busy cafés. The 7th-floor Café Santode Casa is a lovely place to listen to live music and watch the sunset over Lagoa dos Patos.

Sports

Grêmio (www.gremio.net) and **Internacional** (www.internacional.com.br) are the city's high-profile rivals, the latter of which calls Porto Alegre's 2014 FIFA World Cup venue home, despite the 2012 opening of Arena do Grêmio, one of the most state-of-the-art in South America. The renovated Beira-Rio Stadium, 4km south of the historic center, will hold 52,000 rabid fans. The expansion of Metrô Linha 2 will reach the stadium.

ℹ Orientation

The Mercado Público (Public Market) is the focal point of the city center and the transportation hub, with a metro station and a local bus terminal. Cidade Baixa, home to the best hostels and rowdy nightlife, is 2km south of Centro. The upscale shopping and nightlife district, Moinhos de Vento, is about 3km east of the Centro.

ℹ Information

EMERGENCY

Polícia Federal (☑ 3235-9000; Av Ipiranga 1365)

MONEY

Banco do Brasil (Av Uruguaí 185) Offers cash exchange and ATMs.
HSBC (Gen Câmara 250) Fee-less ATM.

TOURIST INFORMATION

C.I.T (☑ 0800-51-7686; www.portoalegre. travel; Praça 15 de Novembro; ☉ 9am-6pm Mon-Sat) Bus Station (Rodoviária; ☉ 8am-5:30pm) Airport (Arrivals Hall, Terminal 1; ☉ 8am-10pm) Cidade Baixa/Linha Turismo (Travessa do Carmo 84) Well-organized tourist information booths around town.

ℹ Getting There & Away

AIR

Terminals 1 and 2 of Porto Alegre's **Salgado Filho International Airport** (☑ 3358-2000; Av Severo Dulius) (POA), 6km from downtown, are connected by a free shuttle. The majority of airlines operate out of Terminal 1, but Webjet and Azul depart from Terminal 2. In addition to major destinations throughout Brazil, international destinations include Buenos Aires, Lisbon, Montevideo and Panama City. Take a taxi (R$25 to R$30, 15 minutes) or ride the metro (R$1.70, 30 minutes).

SAMPLE TIMES (WHERE APPLICABLE) FROM PORTO ALEGRE

DESTINATION	FARE (R$)	TIME (HR)	COMPANY
Buenos Aires	226	18	Pluma (www.pluma.com.br)
Cambará do Sul	32	5½	Citral (www.citral.com.br)
Canela	33	2½	Citral (www.citral.com.br)
Chuí	134	7	Planalto (www.planaltopassageiros.com.br)
Curitiba	162	12	Pluma (www.pluma.com.br)
Florianópolis	82	6	Santo Anjo (www.santoanjo.com.br)
Foz do Iguaçu	143	19	Unesul (www.unesul.com.br)
Gramado	31	2½	Citral (www.citral.com.br)
Montevideo	172	12	TTL (www.ttl.com.br)
Pelotas	64	3½	Embaixador (www.expressoembaixador.com.br)
Rio de Janeiro	247	24	Penha (www.vendas.nspenha.com.br)
Rio Grande	80	4½	Planalto (www.planaltopassageiros.com.br)
Sânto Angelo	117	7	Ouro e Prata (www.ouroeprata.com)
São Francisco de Paula	20	3	Citral (www.citral.com.br)
São Paulo	177	18	Penha (www.vendas.nspenha.com.br)
Torres	40	3	Unesul (www.unesul.com.br)

BUS

The busy **long-distance bus station** (☑ 3210-0101; www.rodoviaria-poa.com.br; Largo Vespasiano Julioveppo 70), 1.5km northeast of Centro, is accessible by metro; alternatively, a taxi downtown costs R$10. Two day and two overnight buses go to Chuí on the Uruguayan border; otherwise you can connect in Pelotas.

Getting Around

Porto Alegre's metro, **Trensurb** (www.trensurb. gov.br; R$1.70; ◷ 5am-11:20pm), has convenient stations at Estação Mercado (by the port), Estação Rodoviária (the next stop) and the airport (three stops beyond). For Cidade Baixa, catch bus T5 from the airport or 282, 2821 or 255 from the bus station (R$2.85). Both the metro and the bus stop sit between Terminals 1 & 2 (closer to 2). A shuttle is due in 2013 connecting the metro station with the terminals.

SERRA GAÚCHA

The scenic stretch of mountains north of Porto Alegre is known as the Serra Gaúcha. This lovely landscape – particularly beautiful between Nova Petrópolis and Gramado – is characterized by forested hillsides and unexpected rocky cliffs, often sparkling with waterfalls.

The region was first settled by Germans (beginning in 1824) and later by Italians (starting in the 1870s), and this heritage is still a source of pride and fascination. Although the mountains don't reach much more than 1000m, Gramado and Canela resemble Swiss villages in their architecture and atmosphere. In Bento Gonçalves and the nearby Vale dos Vinhedos, fountains flow with vino, as descendants of Italian immigrants foster gaining-momentum within the wine industry.

Bento Gonçalves

☑ 0XX54 / POP 107,200

Considering the region's Italian heritage and its dry, mountainous landscape, it makes sense that Rio Grande do Sul would be Brazil's wine epicenter. The command post for this burgeoning wine industry is Bento Gonçalves, 124km north of Porto Alegre, a distinctly indistinct middle-class Brazilian city that does not offer much beyond convenient access to the region's vineyards. The entrance to town leaves no doubt to its allegiances: a gigantic wine barrel known as Pórtico da Pipa straddles the street.

🛏 Sleeping & Eating

There is little reason to stay in Bento proper, with a wealth of beautiful inns in the countryside just steps away in the Vale dos Vinhedos. If you are dependent on public transportation, however, it is more convenient to stay in Bento.

Pousada do Chalé   POUSADA $

(☑ 3452-2763; www.pousadadochale.com.br; São Paulo 787 ; s/d from R$100/140, ste R$140/205; ❊ 🛜 🌊) Just over 1km from Centro, Bento's most charming option are the contemporary rooms in this yellow and brown wooden chalet-style property on well-manicured grounds on the city's northeast side.

Hotel Vinocap   BUSINESS HOTEL $

(☑ 3455-7100; www.vinocap.com.br; Barão do Rio Branco 245; s/d from R$90/125; ❊ @ 🛜) Perfectly agreeable, centrally located business hotel, which is well-equipped for wine tourism.

Canta Maria   ITALIAN $$$

(☑ 3453-1099; www.cantamaria.com.br; RST-470, Km217; Buffet R$49.50-62; ◷ 11:30am-3pm & 7-11pm Mon-Sat, til 3pm Sun) This Bento classic near Pórtico da Pipa features a brought-to-table buffet of *cappelletti* soup, salad, pasta, *galeto* (rotisserie spring chicken), *linguiça*, pork ribs, polenta and fried cheese that goes for R$49.50; tack on a *rodízio* (smorgasbord) of grilled meats and lamb for R$62 (necessary unless you got a real hankering). Call ahead for free transport.

ⓘ Information

C.A.T. (☑ 3453-6699; www.bentogoncalves. rs.gov.br; Marechal Deodoro 70; ◷ 10am-4pm Mon-Sat) Good tourism office with a must-have Vale dos Vinhedos map. There's another branch at Pórtico da Pipa (☑ 3453-2555; Pórtico da Pipa; ◷ 8am-5:30pm Mon-Fri, til 5pm Sat-Sun).

HSBC (Marechal Deodoro 30) Fee-less ATM.

ⓘ Getting There & Around

The **long-distance bus station** (☑ 3452-1311; www.rodoviariabento.com.br; Gomes Carneiro 19) is about 1km north of the center. Bento (p317) and **Ozelame** (www.ozelame.com.br) have hourly service to Porto Alegre (R$26.50, 2½ hours) and Caxias do Sul (R$7, 1¼ hours), respectively. For Canela, Gramado or Cambará do Sul, connect in Caxias. **Unesul** (www.unesul. com.br) has three daily buses Santo Ângelo (R$79, 7½ hours, 8:55am, 2pm & 7:55pm).

For Vale dos Vinhedos, **Transportes Monte Bello** can get you as far as Capela das Nevas on Via Trento four times a day (R$3, 30 minutes,

10:30am, 11:55am, 4:30pm & 6pm), which is walking distance from Casa Valduga, Pousada Borghetto Sant'Anna and a few other wineries, but renting your own vehicle or a local tour are best.

Pinto Bandeira

Sleepy Pinto Bandeira, just 15km northeast of Bento Gonçalves, is a separate wine appellation from the more established Vale dos Vinhedos but boasts soil arguably more suited for sparkling wines. It has its own fair share of charming places to sleep and taste.

Bento (www.bentotransportes.com.br) services Pinto Bandeira three times daily (R$8.30, one hour, 11am, 4pm and 5:35pm), passing the turnoffs for many of the wineries.

For more information of Pinto Bandeira, see www.asprovinho.com.br.

◉ Sights

Cave Geisse   WINERY
(🖉3455-7461; www.vinicolageisse.com.br; Linha Jansen s/n; tastings R$10-40; ⊙10am-5pm Sat & Sun) Founded by famed Chilean winemaker Mario Geisse, Cave Geisse produces Brazil's most internationally heralded sparkling wines and is a cult favorite abroad.

Don Giovanni   WINERY, POUSADA $$
(🖉3455-6294; www.dongiovanni.com.br; Linha Amadeus Km12; r weekend/week from R$275/200; ⊙9am-5:30pm Mon-Sat, til 1pm Sunday; ❀🛜🛏) Both a winery and a homey pousada, Don Giovanni is a one-stop shop in Pinto Bandeira. The eight rooms here are large and feed off a rustic upscale aesthetic, with expansive views of 50 hectares of vineyards. It's most famous for sparkling wines.

Gramado

🖉0XX54 / POP 32,200

Gramado isn't as sexy as Ipanema or as alluring as the Amazon, but this tiny mountain resort, which bills itself as 'naturally European,' is one of Brazil's finest. It does indeed feel like a Swiss mountain village – boutiques sell avant-garde glassworks and gourmet chocolate, local restaurants specialize in fondue, hotels are decked out like Swiss chalets – while infrastructure, safety and scenery all meet the standards of similar size towns in North America or Europe (pedestrian crosswalks are respected!). At times the insistence on *fahrvergnügen* crosses over into kitsch, but the overall affect is pleasant, and the standard of living in this little piece of Alpine paradise is on a completely different level to other Brazilian places.

In August, Gramado hosts **Festival de Gramado** (www.festivaldegramado.com.br), Brazil's most prestigious film festival.

◉ Sights & Activities

Três Coroas, 24km south of Gramado, is one of Brazil's whitewater-rafting hotbeds.

Lago Negro   LAKE
About 1.5km southeast of the center, Lago Negro is an attractive, artificial lake surrounded by hydrangeas and crowded with swan boats.

Aldeia do Papai Noel   PARK
(🖉3286-7332; www.papainoel.com; Bela Vista 353; ⊙10:30am-8pm Fri-Sat, 10:30am-6pm Sun & Wed) Closer to the center than Lago Negro, this Christmas theme park inside Parque Knorr offers inspiring views of the Vale do Quilombo.

CHEERS TO CHIMARRÃO

It was the indigenous Guarani who taught Spanish settlers the pleasures of *chimarrão* (tea from the *maté* plant) and how to sip it, not from a cup but through a *bomba* (straw) stuck into a hollowed-out *cuia* (gourd). Also known as *erva maté*, this tealike beverage is made from the leaves of the *maté* tree, which is native to the *pampas* (grassy plains) that extend from Argentina and Uruguay through southern Brazil.

The original *gaúchos*, the men who tended the region's vast cattle herds, quickly became addicted to *maté*'s pleasurable effects, which are at once energizing and calming. *Chimarrão* is an acquired taste and a serious addiction, but these days, this ancient tradition is getting a boost from scientists and pseudoscientists alike, who make claims about *maté*'s health benefits, from lower blood pressure to increased intelligence. Hard results are yet to come.

Anyone you meet with a gourd (read: that's nearly everyone!) will offer you some, or pop in Galpão Crioulo (p314) and begin your own personal case study!

Gramado

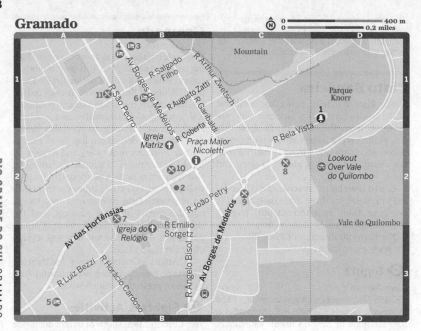

Gramado

◎ Sights
1 Aldeia do Papai Noel D1

✪ Activities, Courses & Tours
2 Passeio Panorâmico Gramado...........B2

🛏 Sleeping
3 Hotel Casa da Montanha B1
4 Hotel Vovó Carolina............................B1
5 Jardim Secreto Pousada A3
6 Pousada Metodista B1

✖ Eating
7 Belle du Valais.....................................B2
8 Cantina di Capo C2
9 Casa di Paolo C2
10 Josephina Café B2
11 Serra Grill A1

☞ Tours

Passeio Panorâmico
Gramado   CITY TOUR
(☑ 3286-9324; www.jardineiradashortensias.com.br; Av das Hortênsias 1710; tour per adult/child R$16/8; ⊙10am, 11:30am, 2pm & 4pm) This two-hour bus tour gives an overview of the town's history, architecture and nature highlights.

🛏 Sleeping

We list prices here for Gramado's high seasons – weekends in winter (June to August). Rates can rise significantly over Christmas and during the film festival.

Lanai Hostel Gramado   HOSTEL $$
(☑ 3295-1120; www.lanaihostelgramado.com.br; Rua dos Fontes 462; dm R$55, d/tr R$200/250; ✳@🛜) This new hostel, 1.5km from the main square, combines two spacious mansions surrounded by ample gardens. There is a range of private and dorm rooms, but the real coup is the stupendous views on offer from the common lounge and cinema rooms.

Pousada Metodista   POUSADA $
(☑ 3286-2299; Av Borges de Medeiros 2889; r per person R$85; 🛜) Seven rooms in the hallowed halls behind the Methodist church have big, industrial-style bathrooms; a recent remodeling has added new box spring beds and cozy comforters. If you're looking for hostel prices but with peace and quiet, you'll find salvation here.

Hotel Vovó Carolina   HOTEL $$
(☑ 3286-2433; www.vovocarolina.com.br; Av Borges de Medeiros 3129; s/d from R$180/217; ✳🛜) Right in the center, this 19-room hotel has

smallish, carpeted rooms, no-nonsense service and cake-laden breakfasts.

Aardvark Inn
POUSADA $$

(☎3286-0806; www.aardvarkinn.com.br; Mestre 18; s/d from R$280/300; @🛜) This residential small-scale inn tips the warm-and-fuzzy to value scale in your pleasant favor. Accented with refurbished wood throughout, rooms are large with whitewashed adobe walls and paraben-free amenities, and most have a private garden entrance. Off-season prices would feel like stealing if it weren't for prices elsewhere in the country (so it just feels like revenge!).

★ Jardim Secreto Pousada
POUSADA $$$

(☎3286-2023; www.pousadajardimsecreto.com.br; F G Bier 110; r from R$350; ❄🛜) An English-speaking, 20-something sibling threesome runs the hospitality at this triumphantly lovely pousada just 800m from the main square. Extensive gardens and fruit trees surround the property, which is dotted with gnomes, birdhouses and other rustic-chic knickknacks. If there's a downside, it's four-night minimums in high season and two-night weekend minimums otherwise.

Hotel Casa da Montanha
HOTEL $$$

(☎3295-7590; www.hotelcasadamontanha.com.br; Av Borges de Medeiros 3166; r from R$1053; ❄@🛜⊠) Resembling a rustic chalet on the outside and a luxurious Swiss hunting lodge on the inside, guestrooms here have fancy, old-fashioned flair. Other on-site amenities include a heated pool and romantic Jacuzzi; and La Caceria restaurant (mains R$43 to R$86), specializing in fresh trout and wild game.

✖ Eating

Gramado has no shortage of Italian, German and Swiss cuisine, reflecting the ethnic makeup of the region's original settlers. Rua Coberta is lined with sidewalk cafes. Many restaurants shut down for up to a month after Carnival and some are only open Thursday to Sunday outside peak season.

Serra Grill
SELF-SERVE $

(www.restauranteserragrill.com.br; São Pedro 567; per kg R$39.90; ⊘11am-3pm) People line up around the corner to get at this higher-quality buffet, which features an excellent, varied selection of grilled meats, well-done pastas and heartier regional mains.

Josephina Café
CAFE $$

(www.josephinacafe.com.br; Pedro Benetti 22; mains R$16.50-43.50; ⊘11:30am-11pm Tue-Sun; 🛜) Gramado's best cafe is short on forced touristy schtick, long on charm. Come for espresso and sweets or more sophisticated bistro fare.

Cantina di Capo
ITALIAN $$

(www.cantinadicapo.com.br; Av das Hortênsias 2174; mains for 2 R$61-92; ⊘11:30am-3pm & 7-11:30pm; ♿) As tends to be par for the course in southern Brazil, the *That's Amore!* of it all is overkill, but the food at this popular trattoria makes up for the green-and-red slap in the face. The Di Capo pasta (olive oil, filet Mignon, sage, basil, marjoram, sundried tomatoes and buffalo mozzarella) is an earthy, herbal delight.

Belle du Valais
SWISS $$$

(☎3286-1744; www.belleduvalais.com.br; Av das Hortênsias 1432; mains R$60-93; ⊘7pm-midnight, noon-3pm Sat-Sun Apr-Dec) Fondue is as common as the cold in Gramado, but this elegant hotspot is considered Brazil's best. The menu is rounded out by filets cooked on volcanic rocks and a wealth of impressive meat and fish preparations, all finely pairable from an excellent *Serra Gaúcha* wine list. Service? Impeccable. Reservations? Recommended.

Casa di Paolo
ITALIAN $$$

(www.casadipaolo.com.br; Garibaldi 23; buffet R$53; ⊘11:30am-3pm & 7-11pm) At this offshoot of Brazil's most famous *galeto* (rotisserie spring chicken) restaurant near Vale dos Vinhedos, you'll find the same succulent table-served buffet: endless *cappelletti* soup, salad, pasta, fried cheese, polenta and *galeto*. A must.

❶ Information

HSBC Fee-less ATM.

Tourist Information Office (☎3286-1475; www.gramado.rs.gov.br; Av Borges de Medeiros 1646; ⊘9am-7pm) Well-stocked tourist information office.

❶ Getting There & Around

The town is small enough to get everywhere by foot. From the **bus station** (☎3286-1302; Av Borges de Medeiros 2100), **Citral** (www.citral.con.br) runs buses to Porto Alegre (R$31, 2½ hours, 15 daily) and Canela (R$2.10, 20 minutes), which leave every 20 minutes.

Vale dos Vinhedos

Brazil isn't the first country that rolls off the palate of passionate oenophiles engulfed in wine-fueled debates, but those in the know are starting to rave about the outstanding award-winning sparkling wines, merlots and chardonnays produced in southern Brazil's Vale dos Vinhedos.

Wine Tasting

Hard work, innovation and cooperative earth has catapulted mostly Italian immigrant families from novelty winemakers in the 1870s to heralded vintners 150-years-later – Vale dos Vinhedos was named one of 2013's 10 Best Wine Travel Destinations by *Wine Enthusiast* magazine. More than 30 wineries, rural inns and restaurants dot the Estrada do Vinho and Via Trento, a picturesque loop.

Vinícola Almaúnica

Almaúnica's (⌨3459-1384; www.almaunica. com.br; RS 444, Km17.35; ☉8am-noon & 1:30-5:30pm Mon Fri, 10am-1pm Sat) ⟨FREE⟩ Syrahs and Quatro Castas blends are some of the region's most highly awarded reds; and the owner is often in the tasting room.

Casa Valduga

One of Brazilian wine's big guns, **Valduga** (⌨2105-3122; www.casavalduga. com.br; Via Trento 2355; tasting & tour R$20; ☉9:30am-6:15pm) offers free tastings as well as tours hourly from 9:30 to 4:30pm of its striking winery and pousada.

Vinícola Miolo

At **Vinícola Miolo** (⌨0800-970-4165; www. miolo.com.br; Estrada do Vinho, km21; tastings R$10; ☉8:30am-5pm Mon-Sat, 9am-4pm Sun) champagnes are notable, as well cabernet

1. Vineyard **2.** Wine tasting **3.** Wine barrels

sauvignon and merlot. The huge complex spreads out from a man-made lake and tours are run every half-hour.

Gastronomy

Valle Rustico (p313) sits down a lonely and dark dirt road – don't worry, it's open – where you'll find an atmospheric dining room in the basement of a local house. Local chef done good Rodrigo Bellora culls as many ingredients as possible from the restaurant's own organic gardens. Unlike many trattorias in the region, Mamma Gema (p313) focuses on quality, not quantity.

Tours

Vale das Vinhas (☎3451-4216; www. valedasvinhastur.com.br; Barão do Rio Branco 245; per person incl tastings from R$65; ☉7:30am-6pm) runs three-hour tours that visit three wineries in the Vale dos Vinhedos as well as a full day option. **Caminhos de Pedra** (☎3454-5702; www.caminhosdepedra. org.br; Erny Hugo Dreher 227, sala 10; per person R$10) organizes fascinating self-guided tours of architectural relics from the 19th century.

Best Places to Stay

This cluster of romantic stone houses at Pousada Borghetto Sant'Anna (p312) gives a fantastic view of the valley below. Reminiscent of Tuscany, the lodgings mix rustic charm with sumptuous comfort.

Hotel & Spa do Vinho Caudalie (☎2102-7200; www.spadovinho.com.br; RS 444, Km21; s/d from R$407/490, ste from R$840; ❊@🖤🏊) boasts unobstructed views of the vineyards. You can ogle the views from the hotel's pool and wine-barrel Jacuzzi to the upscale restaurant.

Cambará do Sul

0XX54 / POP 6500

Cambará do Sul is a dusty frontier town built on cattle ranching with an authentic *gaúcho* aura. Located 186km northeast of Porto Alegre, it serves as a base for both Parque Nacional de Aparados da Serra and Parque Nacional da Serra Geral, the national parks that are somewhat capriciously described as the 'Brazilian Grand Canyon.'

At an altitude of 1000m, Cambará receives more snowfall than any other destination in Rio Grande do Sul, making it a popular destination during winter months (May to October, when prices are higher).

Cambará do Sul claims to be the 'capital of honey,' and you can sample this local sweet all over town.

◉ Sights & Activities

Parque Nacional de Aparados da Serra   CANYON

(3251-1227; admission R$6; ⊙8am-5pm Tue-Sun) Located 18km from the town of Cambará do Sul, this magnificent park occupies 102.5 sq km on the border between Rio Grande do Sul and Santa Catarina states. It's here that vast, uninspired pasturelands give way to a series of stunning canyons, where the earth opens up and drops to depths of 720m.

The park preserves one of the country's last *araucária* (Paraná pine) forests, earning it its protected status. But the main attraction is the **Cânion do Itaimbezinho**, a narrow, 5800m-long canyon with sheer parallel escarpments, ranging from 600m to 720m. Two waterfalls drop into this incision in the earth, which was formed by the Rio Perdiz' rush to the sea.

Three trails wind through the park. **Trilha do Vértice** runs for 2km to an observation point for the canyon and the Cascata do Andorinhas. **Trilha Cotovelo** is a 3km trail (2½ hours round-trip) passing by the Véu de Noiva waterfall, with wonderful vistas of the canyon.

For a completely different perspective, **Trilha do Rio do Boi** follows the base of the canyon for 7km, from the Posto Rio do Boi entrance. This last route is most easily accessed from the town of Praia Grande in Santa Catarina. A professional guide is required for the challenging, loose, rocky trail. During rainy season it is closed because of the danger of flooding.

Parque Nacional da Serra Geral   CANYON

FREE Parque Nacional da Serra Geral, 23km from Cambará do Sul, contains canyons that rival Itaimbezinho. The **Cânion da Fortaleza** is an 8km stretch of escarpment with 900m drops. A gently inclining **Trilha do Mirante** leads about 7km to the edge of the canyon, yielding incredible views of the **Cachoeira do Tigre Preto** waterfall.

The **Pedra do Segredo** is a tower of rocks that balances precariously on this precipice. **Cânion Malacara** is formed by the river of the same name; the **Trilha Piscina do Malacara** leads to a natural pool with cool, crystal waters and wonderful views. At time of writing, the park had virtual no infrastructure, but there's talk of change on the horizon.

Cachoeira dos Venâncios   WATERFALL

(admission R$5) About 18km west of Cambará do Sul, the 4km Trilha da Cachoeira leads to a small but spectacular waterfall.

☞ Tours

Local companies provide transportation and guides for the canyons. Horseback riding and mountain-climbing expeditions are also available. Some agencies belong to ABETA, Brazil's strict ecotourism association.

Cânion Turismo   HIKING, ADVENTURE TOUR

(3251-1027; www.canyonturismo.com.br; Getúlio Vargas 1098; ⊙8am-noon & 1-6pm) Pop into this excellent agency and check out the scale model of the canyons for a much-needed perspective on the area. Guided treks like Trilha do Rio do Boi are around R$389 for one person, dwindling down to R$138 per person within a group of 10 people.

Guia Aparados Da Serra   HIKING, ADVENTURE TOUR

(3251-1173; www.guiaaparadosdaserra.com.br) Offers similar services.

🛌 Sleeping

Cambará has many economical, family-run inns, while higher-end options are outside of town. Camping in the parks is strictly prohibited, but the tourist-information office can help you locate municipal campgrounds.

Prices quoted here are for the high season (May to October). In other seasons, expect a discount of 25% or more.

Vila Ecológica   POUSADA $

(3251-1351; www.vilaecologica.blogspot.com.br; João Pazza 1166; s/d R$50/100; @ 🛜) If you

CANELA & PARQUE ESTADUAL DO CARACOL

While lacking Gramado's sophistication, neighboring Canela has a small-town charm of its own. Centered on a leafy green square, the village center is lined with shops and cafés and is anchored at one end by the impressive Gothic **Catedral de Pedra** (stone cathedral). Canela offers cheaper accommodations and more convenient access to the state parks, which are popular hiking spots.

The major attraction near town is the **Parque Estadual do Caracol** (⏩3278-3035; admission adult/child R$12/6; ☺8:45am-5:45pm), 7km northeast of Canela, and its spectacular **Cascata do Caracol**, a 130m free-falling waterfall. For tourist information, stop by **C.I.T.** (⏩3282-2200; www.canelaturismo.com.br; Largo da Fama 77; ☺8am-7pm) in central Canela.

Citral (www.citral.tur.br) runs buses to/from Gramado every 20 minutes (R$2.10, 20 minutes). Buses go to São Francisco de Paula (R$7.15, one hour), where you can connect to Cambará do Sul (R$12.35, 1½ hours), and to Caxias do Sul (R$12.60, two hours), where you can connect to Bento Gonçalves (R$7, 1½ hours) with **Ozelame** (www.oze-lame.com.br). Frequent buses go to Porto Alegre (R$32, 2½ hours). **Viação Canelense** operates three buses a day Parque do Caracol (R$2, 20 minutes) at 8:15am, 12:10pm and 5:30pm, returning to Canela at 8:35am, 12:25pm and 6pm Monday to Saturday; 8am, 1:30pm and 5:30pm, returning at 8:40am, 1:55pm and 6pm on Sunday.

judge a pousada by its facade, you wouldn't look twice at Vila Ecológica, sitting most ordinarily on a hill behind Casa do Turista. Inside, Cambará's best-value rooms are equipped with electric blankets, heaters and DVD players, and were constructed from ecologically savvy materials. A friendly couple handles everything, including the small and tasty restaurant (mains R$12 to R$25). There's even English. Touché!

Pousada Paraíso POUSADA $
(⏩3251-1352; Raupp 678; s/d R$80/120; ☎) Set on the edge of the village, this friendly two-story home can house 40 guests in its fresh, simple rooms. It's one of the best deals in town.

★ **Pousada Corucacas** POUSADA $$
(⏩3251-1123; www.corucacas.com; RS 020, Km1; s/d incl breakfast & dinner R$130/250; ☎) About 1km from town on the road to Ouro Verde, this working farm has rustic rooms and a big-sky setting, flush with lakes and *araucária* trees. Endless opportunities for horseback riding and hiking are just out the back door, and a fireplace heats up the common room in the evening.

Estalagem da Colina CHALET $$
(⏩3251-1746; www.estalagemdacolina.com.br; Av Getúlio Vargas 80; d R$227-269, q R$440; @☎) Offers 10 stylish wooden chalets, with Sky TV, minibars and heaters (some with hydro-bathtubs). In the main lodge, guests can congregate around the fire in winter, sipping on local fruit liqueurs.

Refúgio Ecológico Pedra Afiada LODGE $$
(⏩0xx51-3532-1059; www.pedraafiada.com.br; Priaia Grande; d incl meals R$250-780; @☎) Splendidly located within the Cânion Malacara in Praia Grande (Santa Catarina), this isolated inn boasts a gorgeous stone fireplace for chilly nights and a fabulous rooftop deck for clear days. Hiking, horseback riding, rafting and rappelling are all at your doorstep. There's a good bistro for lunch, which isn't included in the rates.

Parador Casa da Montanha CAMPGROUND $$$
(⏩3295-7575; www.paradorcasadamontanha. com.br; r incl afternoon tea R$380-780) Midway between Cambará and Itaimbezinho, the poshest place in the region is modeled after luxurious African safari camps. Overlooking *araucária* forest and a cackling waterfall, Brazil's only heated, elevated tents are perched amid postcard-envy scenery and combine creature comforts with rusticity to supremely tranquil effects.

✖ Eating

Dining options in Cambará are limited, though some cute cafés and bistros have sprung up.

Cabana Café CAFE $
(Dona Úrsula; items R$5-27; ☺11am-11pm Jan-Feb & July, 11am-4pm & 7pm-11pm Mar-Jun & Aug-Dec; ☎) Friendly owners and a chic, cabinlike

quality make this a fine place to pop in for a light dinner of crepes or savory pies.

★ O Casarão   BUFFET $$

(☑3251 1711; www.galeteriacasarao.com.br; João Francisco Ritter 969; buffets R$33.50-56.50; ⏱11:30am-3:30pm & 6:30-10pm Tue-Sun) Set amongst homey hardwoods, this excellent restaurant serves the homey food of Brazil's Italian colonists. A buffet of organic salads, house-made pastas and soups is standard but you'll want to add on house specialties like *galeto* (rotisserie spring chicken) or trout. Local wines and *grappas* are served as well.

Galpão Costaneira   BUFFET $$

(Dona Úrsula 1069; buffets R$20-30; ⏱11:30am-3pm & 7:20-10:30pm Mon-Sat, til 3pm Sun; 🛜) The town's other best restaurant is a rustic farmhouse serving a hearty buffet that's at it's best when you choose tabletop-cooked *picanha* (beef), spicy linguiça and colonial cheese.

❶ Information

Casa do Turista (☑3251-1320; www.cam-baradosul.rs.gov.br; Av Getúlio Vargas 1720; ⏱8am-6pm) On the far end of town on the road to Forteleza.

❶ Getting There & Around

The tiny **bus station** (Dona Úrsula TK) is right in town. **Citral** (www.citral.tur.br) offers one bus from Porto Alegre for Cambará do Sul (R$32, 5½ hours) at 6am Monday to Saturday. Returning, you must catch a 6:30am or 1:30pm bus to São Francisco de Paula (R$12.35, one hour) and switch there for Porto Alegre (R$20.30, 3 hours), Canela (R$7.50, one hour) or Gramado (R$8.45, one hour).

Expresso São Marcos (www.ex-pressosaomarcos.com.br) has two daily buses going to Caxias do Sul (R$22.50, 2½ hours, 7:30am Fri-Wed & 10:45am Mon-Sat), where you can connect hourly to Bento Gonçalves (R$7, 1¼ hours) with **Ozelame** (www.ozelame. com.br). There is one 9:45am daily bus to Praia Grande (R$9.15, 1¼ hours), an emerging ecotourism destination at the bottom of the canyons in Santa Catarina. If you are coming from the north, you can connect from Torres via Tainhas.

The parks are not serviced by public buses. A taxi to the national park costs R$60 round trip. Local tour companies are a reasonable alternative, especially if they can hook you up with a small group.

ROTA MISSÕES

Soon after the discovery of the New World, the Portuguese and Spanish kings authorized Catholic orders to create missions to convert the natives. The Jesuits were the most successful order, establishing a series of missions across Paraguay, Bolivia, Brazil and Argentina. At its height in the 1720s, this prosperous 'nation' claimed 30 mission villages inhabited by more than 150,000 Guarani people.

Today, all 30 missions are in ruins. Together, they form the Rota Missões, or 'Missions Route,' a network of pilgrimage sites for the faithful and the curious. Seven are in Brazil (in the northwestern part of Rio Grande do Sul), eight are in southern Paraguay and 15 are in northeastern Argentina. For an excellent overview of the Brazilian missions see the website of the **Rota Missões** (www.rotamissoes.com.br).

Santo Ângelo

☑0XX55 / POP 76,200

This small, pleasant city is the regional transportation hub and jumping-off point for exploring the Brazilian missions. The impressive cathedral, on **Praça da Catedral**, is a contemporary replica of the church at São Miguel das Missões. A few blocks north, the **Monumento ao Índio** remembers Sepé Tiaraju, the leader of the indigenous resistance during the Guarani War.

⛛ Tours

Without your own vehicle, it is difficult to visit all of the missions independently. An organized tour offers a reasonable alternative, but try to contact recommended companies well in advance.

Caminho das Missões   WALKING, CYCLING

(☑3312-9632; www.caminhodasmissoes.com.br; Antunes Ribas 984) Leads serious walking and biking tours of the missions, ranging from three to 14 days.

Marino Theobald   TOUR

(☑9961-3826; marino_theobald@yahoo.com.br; per day R$180) Marino organizes customized tours of the missions, including the three-day circuit of São João Batista, São Miguel das Missões and the Santuário de Caaró; as well as international missions in Argentina and Paraguay. He speaks Portuguese, Spanish and German and can arrange an English guide.

🛏 Sleeping & Eating

Turis Hotel
HOTEL $

(🖥 3313-5255; www.santoangeloturishotel.com; Antônio Manoel 726; s/d R$55/90, with air-con R$75/110; 🏢 🛜) Rooms vary widely, but none of them are going to win any design awards. Nonetheless, it's a solid budget option, just one block west of the Praça da Catedral.

Hotel Maerkli
HOTEL $$

(🖥 3313-2127; www.versarehoteis.com.br; Av Brasil 1000; s/d R$158/215; 🏢 @ 🛜) The nicer option in town, this hotel caters to business travelers and tourist groups, who appreciate the very friendly and attentive service. Standard rooms can be cramped, but the superiors offer spacious digs with large semicircular desks. It's on the main street, one block west of Praça Leônidas Ribas.

Kemper's Haus
CAFE $

(www.kempershaus.com.br; Marquês do Herval 1763; mains R$14-19; ⏱ 7:30am-8pm Mon-Fri, 8:30am-7pm Sat, 2-8pm Sun; 🛜) Pop into this new cafe for breakfast, decadent sweets and espresso, or a small but excellent menu of risottos, sandwiches and quiches. The best atmosphere in the region, bar none.

Quick
BRAZILIAN $

(cnr Av Brasil & Marquês do Herval; mains R$27-35, per kg R$30.90; ⏱ 11:30am-midnight; 🛜) A hearty lunchtime buffet until 2pm and an extensive late-night menu. It's simple food, but it's tasty and prepared with care.

ℹ Information

HSBC (Marechal Floriano Peixoto 1470) Fee-less ATM.

PARADISE LOST

In 1608, the governor of the Spanish province of Paraguay ordered the local Jesuit leader, Fray Diego de Torres, to convert the local Tupi and Guarani people. The Jesuits established missions across a vast region that encompassed much of southern Brazil, as well as portions of southern Paraguay and northern Argentina.

Unlike their brethren elsewhere in the New World, the Jesuits made a concerted effort to convert the indigenous people without destroying their culture or language. The missions became centers of culture and intellect, as well as religion. The missions flourished, combining elements of European and Guarani music and painting. Scholars created a written form of the Tupi-Guarani language and, beginning in 1704, published several works, using one of South America's earliest printing presses. The missions produced sophisticated sculpture, metallurgy, ceramics and musical instruments. In an age of monarchies and institutionalized slavery, the missions were an island of idealism, where wealth was divided equitably, and religion, intellect and arts were cultivated in tandem.

From the beginning, the missions faced threats from the outside world. In the 1620s they were harassed by Portuguese *bandeirantes*, bands of Paulistas who raided the interior in search of gold and *índios* (indigenous people) to enslave. Thousands of *índios* were captured, and the 13 missions of Guayra (present-day Paraná) were eventually abandoned. Beginning in the 1630s, the Jesuits consolidated their position in 30 sites across the northwest corner of present-day Rio Grande do Sul, as well as in Argentina and Paraguay. These sites, now in ruins, constitute the contemporary Rota Missões (Missions Route).

To a large part, it was the success of the missions that brought about their downfall. The independent-minded Jesuits became an embarrassment to Rome, and to the Spanish and Portuguese kings. In 1750 the Treaty of Madrid dictated that the sites be handed over to Portuguese rule, which would not protect the natives from enslavement. The Guarani were commanded to evacuate in 1754, but they refused to abandon their settlements and thus incited the Guarani War. In 1756 a combined Spanish-Portuguese army attacked the missions, killing more than 1500 Guaranis and selling many more into slavery, thus decimating the Guarani population. It was a tragic, bloody end to an amazing social experiment.

The missions were lauded by great thinkers from Voltaire to Montesquieu as a real incarnation of Christian utopia, which was destroyed by the very forces that created it. Robert De Niro and Jeremy Irons relive this story in the 1986 film *The Mission*, a moving, fictional account of these events.

❶ Getting There & Around

The **bus station** (☑ 3313-2618; www.rodoviari-asantoangelo.com.br; Sete Povos das Missões 419) is 1km west of the center. **Unesul** (www.unesul.com.br) has three daily buses to Bento Gonçalves (R$79, 7½ hours, 10am, 1:55pm & 9:35pm). For Foz do Iguaçu in Paraná, catch the 6pm **Tracisa** (☑ 3512-5544) bus to Santa Rosa (R$9.20, one hour), where you can switch for the 8pm Unesul to Foz (R$106.40, 12 hours). **Ouro e Prata** (www.ouroeprata.com.br)buses run frequently between Santo Ângelo and Porto Alegre (R$117, seven hours, up to 10 per day).

Antonello Turismo (☑ 3312-2184) has four daily buses to São Miguel das Missões (R$9, 1½ hours, 7am, 11am, 3:30pm & 4:45pm). Renting a car from **Pontual** (☑ 3313-6000; www.pontualautolocadora.com.br; Marquês do Herval 1845; per day from R$110; ☺ 8:30am-noon & 2-6pm Mon-Fri, 9am-noon Sat) is a good option for visiting the Brazilian missions.

GETTING TO/FROM URUGUAY

Located 245km south of Rio Grande, the border town of Chuí/Chuy is the end of the Brazilian line. The city is both Brazilian and Uruguayan, respectively. The main drag acts as the border: on the northern (Brazilian) side it is Av Uruguaí, while on the southern (Uruguayan) side it is Av Brasil. The Uruguayan side has grown over the last decade to be synonymous with duty-free shops, which are flooded with Brazilians from open to close. It's not interesting (unless you are Brazilian in need of some electronics!), but increased security in recent years means it's relatively safe as far as border towns go. Those who linger usually only do so to take advantage of cheaper accommodations when visiting Uruguayan attractions further afield. If you stay, the best value for money is at **Etnico Hostel** (☑ 548-4474-2281; www.etnicohostel.com.uy; Laguna Negra 200; dm UR$260, s/d UR$520/800; @ 🛜), three blocks into Uruguay, where trilingual host Rodrigo is eager to help, and homemade muffins and pastries at breakfast are a real treat.

Brazilian **immigration** (☑ 3265-2523; www.dpf.gov.br; BR-471, km650; ☺ 24hr) is on the main highway, several kilometers north of town. You do not need a visa or entry or exit stamp to visit the town; however, if you are continuing into Uruguay, you will need to tell the driver to stop at the border post for an exit stamp. In Uruguay, **immigration** (☑ 598-4474-2072; www.dnm.minterior.gub.uy; Ruta 9; ☺ 24hr) is 2.5km south of town. The bus will stop again for the Uruguayan officials to check your Brazilian exit stamp and Uruguayan visa (if you need one). Stop here for an exit stamp as well if you are entering Brazil.

Both **Brazil** (☑ 598-9-9904-5757; www.consbraschuy.org; Tito Fernandez 147; ☺ 9am-3pm Mon-Fri) and **Uruguay** (☑ 3265-1151; www.emburuguai.org.br; Venezuela 311; ☺ 9am-3pm Mon-Fri) maintain consulates on the Brazilian side of Chuí. Brazilian visas, required for citizens of Australia, Canada and the United States, among others, are processed in 48 hours. Most nationalities do not need a visa for Uruguay.

For Montevideo and other Uruguayan destinations, bus companies line Calle Leonardo Oliveira near Av Brasil on the Uruguayan side. **Rutas del Sol** (☑ 598-4471-2048; Leonardo Oliveira 121) (1am, 5am, 8am, 12:45pm, 6:15pm and 11:15pm) and **Cot** (☑ 4474-4697; www.cot.com.uy; Leonardo Oliveira 111) (11:30am, 8pm everyday, plus 4am Monday to Friday) are your best bets for Montevideo (UR$456, five hours). The Brazilian **bus station** (☑ 3265-1498; Venezuela 247) is about three blocks in from Av Brasil. **Embaixador** (www.expressoembaixador.com.br) has five daily buses to Pelotas (R$42, four hours) and two to Rio Grande (R$39, four hours, 7am & 3:30pm). **Planalto** (www.planaltopassageiros.com.br) goes to Porto Alegre (R$129, seven hours, 12:15pm & 11pm).

São Miguel das Missões

☑ 0XX55 / POP 7400

The best preserved and most moving of the Brazilian missions is **São Miguel Arcanjo** (adult/child R$5/2.50; ☺ 9am-noon & 2-6pm Mar-Sep, to 8pm Oct-Feb), located in the village of São Miguel das Missões, 53km southwest of Santo Ângelo. The elegant church, designed by an Italian architect who was also a Jesuit friar, earned Unesco World Heritage status in 1984. It is surrounded by the mystical ruins of the Jesuit settlement, which evokes the feeling of 'paradise lost.' On a beautiful day, snapping pics will drain your iPhone battery.

The archaeological site also includes the excellent little **Museu das Missões** (☑ 3381-1291; www.museudasmissoes.blogspot.com). Designed by Lúcio Costa, of Brasília fame, the museum contains an impressive collection of religious artifacts that were rescued from the ruins. A spectacular, if campy, **sound-and-light show** (São Miguel Arcanjo; adult/child R$5/2.50; ☺ 9:30pm Nov-Jan, 8pm Feb-Apr & Aug-Oct, 7pm May-July) illustrates the history of the missions.

🛏 Sleeping & Eating

The last bus to Santo Ângelo leaves before the sound-and-light show, so it's worth spending the night. A couple of casual restaurants are clustered around the bus station.

★ **Pousada das Missões** HOSTEL $
(☑ 3381-1202; www.pousadatematica.com.br; São Nicalau 601; dm/s/d/tr R$65/90/145/180; ✿ @ 🤝 🖭) Student groups utilize the dorm-style accommodation at this HI hostel, but more discerning travelers will be comfortable in the private rooms, each labeled with a Guarani name and accompanying explanation. It is located on well-manicured grounds just behind the archaeological site; follow signs from the entrance. There's also a decent restaurant for dinner only December to February.

Tenondé Park Hotel HOTEL $$
(☑ 3381-2000; www.tenonde.com.br; São Miguel 664; s/d R$156/220; ✿ @ 🤝 🖭) Boasting mission-style architecture, stylish rooms and good restaurant, this resorty hotel caters to more discerning pilgrims. Excellent facilities include tennis courts, a football field and a swimming pool.

ℹ Information

The **Secretary of Tourism** (☑ 3381-1294; www.saomiguel-rs.com.br; ⊙ 1:30-5pm Mon-Sat) offers tourist info near the entrance of the mission.

ℹ Getting There & Away

From the **bus station** (☑ 3381-1226) in Missões, **Antonello Turismo** has four buses to Santo Ângelo during the week (R$9, one hour, 6:30am, 8am, noon & 6:15pm), but service drops slightly on Saturday (8am, noon & 5:30pm) and by half on Sunday (8am & 5pm).

Other Brazilian Mission Sites

São João Batista RUINS
(⊙ 9am-5pm) FREE Midway between Santo Ângelo and São Miguel, little remains from the mission at **São João Batista**. With a little imagination, it is possible to make out the structures of the church, the cemetery and the school.

Santuário de Caaró CHURCH
(⊙ 7am-7pm) FREE About 20km west of São Miguel, the **Santuário de Caaró** is the place where the region's spiritual history is most alive. A modest monument honors three priests who were killed by *bandeirantes* in 1626. One of the victims, Roque González, has been canonized. This site attracts a stream of pilgrims, especially in November, around the anniversary of St Roque's martyrdom.

São Lourenço Mártir RUINS
(⊙ 9am-5pm) FREE In 1690, a group from the Argentine reduction of Santa Maria founded **São Lourenço Mártir**. It is located about 18km west of the turn-off to São Miguel, 9km north off the road to São Luiz Gonzaga (BR-285). The church, cemetery and school are still discernible and there is a small exhibit of findings from excavations. The most impressive find – the grand image of São Lourenço that once graced the church – is now held at the Museu das Missões (p326) in São Miguel.

São Nicolau RUINS
(⊙ 24hr) FREE About 120km west of Santo Ângelo, this mission was once an artistic center, producing painting, ceramics and wood sculpture. Today, all that remains at the archaeological site is the Jesuits' stone wine cellar and some sporadic ruins. There's a small exhibit on Jesuit-Guarani culture across the street at the **Secretary of Tourism**. (☑ 3363-1034; www.saonicolau.rs.gov.br; Salvador Pinheiro Machado; ⊙ 8am-11:30am & 1:30-5pm Mon-Fri)

Three recovered sacred images of Santo Antônio, Santo Izidro and Senhor dos Passos are displayed inside the modern-day Igreja Matriz, across the street from the ruins.

If you make it this far, you can spend the night with the friendly Diana, who's hospitality far outweighs the prices at **Pousada dos Jesuítas**, (☑ 9634-5411; pousada_dos_jesuitas@yahoo.com.br; Nilza de Moura Silva 1046; per person R$25; @ 🤝) 50m from the mission site.

LITORAL GAÚCHO

On paper, it sounds amazing: a 500km strip of Brazilian coastline that forms one seemingly endless beach, stretching from Torres on the Santa Catarina border, all the way to Chuí at the Uruguayan border. Unfortunately, the reality is less enticing. The water tends to be murky and the beaches are undistinguished, but there's good surf.

Torres

☑ 0XX51 / POP 34,600
On the border with Santa Catarina, Torres is the exception to the state's uninviting coastline. It's not thrilling, but the pleasant town, 205km north of Porto Alegre, has attractive (if crowded) beaches punctuated by basalt rock formations, vegetative dunes and a lively boardwalk – it's all vaguely reminiscent of a British seaside town.

Praia Grande, the town's main beach, is quite calm and is bookended by the smaller Prainha to the south and Praia dos Molhes to the north, a famous surf spot where the Rio Mampituba dramatically enters the sea. Praia da Cal, 2km south of Praia Grande, also draws serious surfers.

In winter, Antarctic currents bring cold, hard winds to the coast; the crowds disappear, and most hotels shut down from May to November.

Every year in April, Torres hosts **Festival Internacional de Balonismo** (International Hot-Air Balloon Festival; www.festivaldebalonismo. com.br) (hot-air-balloon festival), a spectacular sight.

◉ Sights & Activities

Parque Estadual
da Guarita
NATURE RESERVE

The gardens of Parque Guarita, 2km south of Av Beira Mar, make for a gorgeous natural setting while the nearby beach of the same name is considered the most beautiful in Torres.

Felipe Raupp
Escola de Surf
SURFING

(☑ 9991-4049; www.frsurf.com.br; 5-course packages from R$550) Internationally-renown Raupp is the man to get you up in Torres, offering serious, multiday surf courses.

⌖ Tours

Marina
BOAT TOUR

(☑ 3626-2933; www.barcosmarina.com.br; adult/ child R$40/25; ⊙ 11:15am, 3:15pm & 5:15pm Jan-Apr) Marina offers boat trips to Ilha dos Lobos, an ecological reserve that is home to a colony of sea lions between January and April. From the end of Av Silva Jardim, walk along the Rio Mampituba to Ponte Pênsil.

⌷ Sleeping

We've listed prices for summer (December to February) – expect discounts of 20% to 40% between March and November and a 25% hike during the hot-air-balloon festival.

★ Pousada da Prainha
HOTEL $$

(☑ 3626-2454; www.pousadadaprainha.com.br; Alferes Feirreira Porto 138; s/d R$108/168, with air-con R$128/188; ✱ ⚇) This amicable, colonial-style hotel is a block from the quiet beach at Prainha. It offers pretty shocking value for the price.

Solar Inn
POUSADA $$

(☑ 3626-3731; www.solarinn.com.br; Av Beira Mar 1713; s/d R$230/250, with seaview from R$320;

✱ ⚇ ⚇) Excellent beachfront location, Germanic architecture and a welcoming size (just 22 rooms); you can't beat this newish inn on Prainha beach.

✕ Eating

Doce Art
CAFE $

(Av Silva Jardim 295; sandwiches R$4-15; ⊙ 8am-10pm; ⚇) Come here for hot coffee, fresh juice and tasty pastries in the morning, or sandwiches and pastas at lunchtime.

Cantinho do Pescador
SEAFOOD $$

(www.cantinhodopescador.com; Av Beira Mar 210; mains for 2 R$27-83; ⊙ 11am-midnight; ⚇) Considered Torres' best, this partly open-air seafooder does a commendable job with local fish at the Praia dos Molhes end of town with panoramic Rio Mampituba views.

Restaurante A Prainha
SEAFOOD $$

(Joaquim Porto 151; mains for 2 R$49-135; ⊙ 11:30am-3:30pm & 7-11pm) Two blocks from the beach of the same name, this casual restaurant serves seafood and typical Brazilian platters on its pleasant, shady porch.

ⓘ Information

Casa do Turista (☑ 3664-1411 ext 710; www. torres.rs.gov.br; Av Barão do Rio Branco 315; ⊙ 8am-11pm) Excellent municipal tourism office.
HSBC (cnr Borges de Medeiros & Júlio de Castilhos) Fee-less ATM.

ⓘ Getting There & Around

The town is small and all conveniences are accessible by foot, including the **bus station** (☑ 3664-1787; www.rodoviariatorres.com.br; Av José Bonifácio 524). Destinations include Porto Alegre (R$39, three hours) and Florianópolis (R$43, five hours, six daily). For Cambará do Sul, **Expresso São Marcos** (www.expressosaomarcos.com.br) goes to the dusty one-horse town of Tainhas (R$18, 2½ hours, three daily) where you can connect on to Cambará just twice per day at 9:15am and 5:30pm (R$7, one hour). Alternatively, call *the* taxi, **Alex Offmann** (☑ 0xx54-8438-3200; Tainhas) (R$70, 30 minutes).

Rio Grande

☑ 0XX53 / POP 197,200

Located at the mouth of Lagoa dos Patos, Rio Grande was founded in 1737 to guard the disputed southern border of the Portuguese empire. The region's oldest city, it blossomed during the 19th century, when its port became a vital link in the profitable beef trade.

Rio Grande has a charming historic center that is home to some interesting colonial and neoclassical buildings. The excellent **Museu Oceanográfico** (☎3231-3496; www.museu.furg.br/museu_oceanografico; Capitão Heitor Perdigão 10; admission R$5; ☉9-11:30am & 2-6pm Tue-Sun) FREE is one of the best in Latin America.

🛏 Sleeping & Eating

★ **Paris Hotel**   HISTORIC HOTEL $
(☎3231-3866; www.hotelvillamoura.com.br; Marechal Floriano Peixoto 112; s/d R$62/100, with bathroom R$87.50/125; ☎) The oldest in Rio Grande do Sul, this hotel, built in 1826, exhibits a bygone grandeur in its high ceilings, antique furnishings and leafy courtyard. At this price, it would be silly not to sleep in an antique bed and lounge in a 19th-century patio that once hosted Dom Pedro II.

Marco's   SEAFOOD $$$
(www.restaurantemarcos.com.br; Av Silva Paes 400; mains R$40-88; ☉11:30am-2pm & 7-11:30pm Mon-Sat, 11:30am-2:30pm Sun; ☎) Tops in town, this higher-end seafooder has a strong menu of local fish and shrimp preparations.

❶ Getting There & Away

From the **bus station** (☎3232-8444; www.rodoviariariogrande.com.br; Vice-Almirante Abreu 737), buses connect Rio Grande with all major cities in southern Brazil. **Embaixador** (www.expressoembaixador.com.br) has two departures for Chuí (R$42, 4 hours, 7am & 3:30pm) on the Uruguayan border as well as Pelotas (R$10, one hour, every 30 minutes), which is the major transportation hub. **Planalto** (www.planaltopassageiros.com.br) has seven buses a day to Porto Alegre (R$84, 5 hours).

Brasília & Goiás

Includes ➡

Best Places to Eat

➡ Nossa Cozinha Bistrô (p339)

➡ Aquavit (p343)

➡ Chão Nativo I (p346)

➡ Pireneus Café (p353)

➡ Fazenda Babilônia (p352)

Best Places to Stay

➡ Villa do Comendador Eco-Resort (p352)

➡ Baguá Pousada (p357)

➡ Pousada do Ipê (p348)

➡ Pousada Tajupá (p352)

➡ Hotel Parque das Primaveras (p354)

Why Go?

Brasília was conceived as a workable, utopian answer to modern, urban chaos. The purpose-built city is lauded by many for its futuristic architecture and avant-garde design but knocked by detractors who bemoan the impracticality of the uberorganized, themed city blocks. As Brazil's seat of government, it's a city of bureaucrats, but it remains the only city in the world constructed in the 20th century to achieve World Cultural Heritage designation by Unesco.

Enveloping the Distrito Federal (DF), Goiás is Brazil's 'road less traveled,' though not for good reason: fiery red sunsets over the dramatic cerrado (savanna) landscape set the stage for unparalleled postcard-perfect views. Almost criminally overlooked by many tourists, Goiás is easy to get lost in for a few weeks. Major attractions include the picturesque colonial villages of Cidade de Goiás and Pirenópolis, and the rivers, waterfalls and forest trails of Parque Nacional da Chapada dos Veadeiros.

When to Go
Brasilia

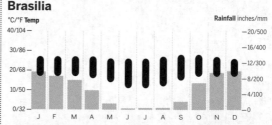

Semana Santa (Holy Week) Hooded *farri-cocos* take to the streets of Cidade de Goiás.

50 days after Easter Festa do Divino Espírito in Pirenópolis.

Nov & Dec When the breathaking cerrado is in full bloom.

History

On the heels of the gold discoveries in Minas Gerais, *bandeirantes* (groups of roaming adventurers who explored the interior) pushed further inland in search of more precious metals and, as always, indigenous slaves. In 1682 a *bandeira* headed by Bartolomeu Bueno da Silva visited the region. The indigenous Goyaz people gave him the nickname *anhanguera* (old devil) when, after burning some *cachaça* (sugarcane alcohol) – which the Goyaz believed to be

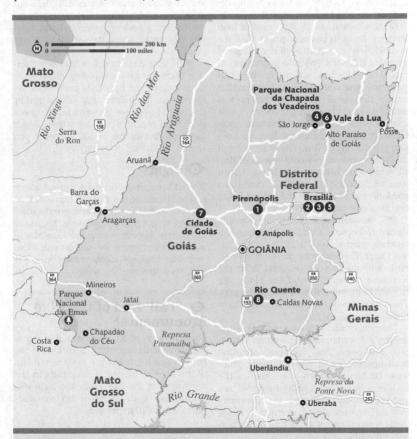

Brasília & Goiás Highlights

❶ Soaking up the alternative atmosphere in colonially cool **Pirenópolis** (p349).

❷ Cruising Brasília's futuristic architecture at night when the **Praça dos Trés Poderes** (p333) takes on an otherworldly glow.

❸ Stepping inside the ethereal **Santuário Dom Bosco** (p333) and watching your 'seen one church, seen them all' attitude adjusted on the spot.

❹ Trekking through the unique high-cerrado flora in **Parque Nacional da Chapada dos Veadeiros** (p355).

❺ Cleansing your soul or just taking a walk on the weird side at the **Templo da Boa Vontade** (p344).

❻ Rock-hopping the naturally formed lunarscape at **Vale da Lua** (p355).

❼ Lazily wandering the cobblestone streets of **Cidade de Goiás** (p347) in a sugar-induced coma.

❽ Curing your ills or, if you don't have any, just splashing about in the hot springs at the **Hot Park** (p355) in Rio Quente.

water – he threatened to set fire to all the rivers if they didn't show him where their gold mines were. Three years later, the old devil returned to his native São Paulo with gold and indigenous slaves from Goiás. Given the difficulties caused by the isolation of the region, its gold rush was essentially over before it had begun.

Goiás achieved official statehood in 1889 but went about its business quietly until the mid-1950s, when a portion of it was carved out to build Brasília. The concept of an inland capital dated back to 1823 and the Brazilian statesman José Bonifácio, who believed that moving the capital from Rio de Janeiro was central to capitalizing on the country's vast inland resources. The idea didn't gain many followers, however, until Dom Bosco, a Salesian priest living in Turin (Italy) prophesied that a new civilization would emerge in Brazil, somewhere between the 15th and 20th parallels. Suddenly it seemed like a good idea and land was allocated in the 1891 constitution for a new capital.

Still, it wasn't until 1955 that Brasília started to become a reality: President Kubitschek ordered work to begin, and architect Oscar Niemeyer took on the challenge. With millions of poor peasants from the Northeast working around the clock, the city was built, incredibly, in just three years. The capital was officially moved from Rio to Brasília on April 21, 1960.

The new capital became a symbol of the country's determination to become a great economic power and distracted attention from ongoing social and economic problems. Goiás too thrived, this time on the back of a 'green-gold' rush, a colossal soy and sugar boom, that made many farmers into millionaires almost overnight. Today, Goiás remains one of Brazil's most prosperous and comfortable states.

In 1989, due to the vastness of its borders, Goiás once again forfeited some of its land, when half of the state was split off to become the separate state of Tocantins.

BRASÍLIA

☑ 061 / POP 2.6 MILLION

Well into middle age, Brazil's once futuristic capital remains an impressive monument to national initiative. Brasília replaced Rio de Janeiro as Brazil's center of government in 1960 under the visionary leadership of President Juscelino Ku-

bitschek, architect Oscar Niemeyer, urban planner Lucio Costa and landscape architect Burle Marx.

From the air, Brasília's millennial design evokes the image of an airplane (or a hummingbird, if you prefer), with each of its architectural marvels strategically laid out along the Eixo Monumental (which forms the fuselage), and its residential and commercial blocks along its outspread wings (*asas*).

With long distances and harrowing six-lane highways connected by spaghetti junctions to negotiate, Brasília is not really a city for walkers. Though renting a car is trial by fire, the big picture becomes all the more clear from behind a steering wheel. To get the full effect of the layout, however, you should take a tour of the city by air.

⊙ Sights

Brasília's major edifices are spread along a 5km stretch of the Eixo Monumental. At the bottom end, in the 'cockpit' are the most interesting government buildings. Sights are listed here in order along the Eixo Monumental, beginning at the 'tail.' To visit them on public transport, combine local buses 104 and 108 with some long walks.

⊙ 'Tail' End of the Eixo Monumental

Though maps of Brasília invariably figure the airplane design with the cockpit at the bottom and the tail at the top, the tail end of the Eixo Monumental is actually in the northwest of the city. From the local bus station take buses 312, 331 or 343 from platforms C8 to C10 to get here.

Memorial JK MUSEUM
(Map p334; ☑ 3226-7860; www.memorialjk.com.br; Praça do Cruzeiro; adult/child R$12/6; ⊙ 9am-6pm) The tomb of JK (President Juscelino Kubitschek) lies underneath eerily beautiful stained glass by French artist Marianne Peretti inside the Memorial JK. The museum houses JK's 3000-book-strong personal library as well as a pictorial history of Brasília. Don't miss JK's 1973 Ford Galaxie just outside the back door.

Museu dos Povos Indígenas MUSEUM
(Map p334; ☑ 3223-3760; Praça Buriti; ⊙ 9am-6pm Tue-Sun) FREE Opposite the Memorial JK, in a Niemeyer building inspired by the

circular form of the indigenous Yanomani hut, is the Museu dos Povos Indígenas, a small but colorful display of indigenous artifacts put together by anthropologists Darcy and Berta Ribeiro and Eduardo Galvão. A sandy central courtyard is still used for tribal rituals.

Parque da Cidade — PARK
(Map p334; Eixo Monumental, Asa Sul; ☺ 5am-midnight) **FREE** A good park not far from the city center is the Parque da Cidade which has kiosks to grab a snack.

★ TV Tower — TOWER
(Map p339; Eixo Monumental; ☺ 8am-8pm) The 75m-high observation deck of the TV Tower gives a decent overview of the city, but it's still not quite tall enough to really get a sense of the city's airplane design.

★ Santuário Dom Bosco — CHURCH
(Map p334; ☎ 3223-6542; www.santuariodombosco.org.br; W3 Sul, Quadra 702; ☺ 7am-7pm) **FREE** Santuário Dom Bosco is made of 80 concrete columns that support 7500 pieces of illuminated Murano glass symbolizing a starry sky, which cast a blue submarine glow over the pews. The central chandelier weighs 2.5 tonnes and adds an amazing 435 light bulbs' worth of energy to the monthly electricity bill.

Bus 107 (platform E7 in the local bus station) passes here every 20 minutes.

◉ Complexo Cultural da República

As Niemeyer's original plans for Brasília continue to come to fruition, new attractions are popping up just west of Catedral Metropolitana.

Biblioteca Nacional — LIBRARY
(Map p334; ☎ 3325-6257; Esplanada dos Ministérios; ☺ 9am-9pm Mon-Fri, to 6pm Sat & Sun) The massive exterior of the new working national library, the Biblioteca Nacional, is long finished, but they still haven't loaded all the books.

Teatro Nacional — THEATRE
(Map p334; ☎ 3325-6105; ☺ 8am-6pm Mon-Fri) **FREE** The Teatro Nacional looks somewhere between a waterslide and a skateboard ramp.

★ Museu Nacional — MUSEUM
(Map p334; ☎ 3325-5220; Esplanada dos Ministérios; ☺ 9am-6:30pm) **FREE** A spherical half-dome by architect Oscar Niemeyer, the inside features a discreet mezzanine mostly held up by columns suspended from the roof. A signature curved ramp juts out from its base and runs around the outside like a ring of Saturn.

★ Catedral Metropolitana — CHURCH
(Map p334; ☎ 3224-4073; www.catedral.org.br; Esplanada dos Ministérios; ☺ 8am-6pm) **FREE** With its 16 curved columns and wavy stained-glass interior, the Catedral Metropolitana is heavenly viewing. At the entrance are the haunting *Four Disciples* statues carved by Ceschiatti, who also made the aluminum angels hanging inside.

◉ Setor Bancário Sul

Brasília's banking sector may not be the first place you would think of going for cultural enrichment, but there are a couple of museums here and guess what? They're free!

Caixa Cultural — MUSEUM
(Map p334; ☎ 3206-9450; SBS Q4, Lote 3; ☺ 9am-9pm Mon-Fri) **FREE** The lobby of the Caixa Cultural is a small museum of financial bits and pieces, ranging from old lottery tickets through to wooden safes. The exhibits themselves are of only passing interest, but the gorgeous stained-glass murals, each one representing a Brazilian state, make it worth the visit.

Museu de Valores — MUSEUM
(Map p334; ☎ 3414-2099; ☺ 10am-5:30pm Tue-Fri, 2-6pm Sat & Sun) **FREE** Numismatists may be interested in a visit to the money museum in the Banco Central do Brasil HQ. Cash from around the world is on show, as well as a complete set of Brazilian currency, including a 1,000,000-Cruzeiro note. You'll need to show your passport to get in.

◉ Praça dos Trés Poderes

Down in the cockpit, you'll find the most interesting buildings surrounding the **Praça dos Trés Poderes**. It's a synthesis of the ideas of architects Niemeyer and Costa, combining various monuments, museums and federal buildings. The space includes striking sculptures, including Bruno Giorgi's *Os Candangos,* Alfredo Ceschiatti's *A Justiça* and Niemeyer's *O Pombal* (which looks like a clothes peg), as well as a scale map of the city down the stairs in the **Espaço Cultural**

Brasília

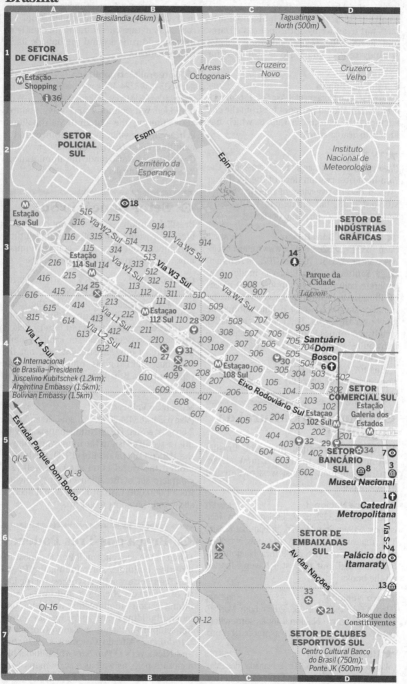

Brasilândia (46km)

Taguatinga North (500m)

SETOR DE OFICINAS

Estação Shopping
ⓘ36

Áreas Octogonais

Cruzeiro Novo

Cruzeiro Velho

SETOR POLICIAL SUL

Espm

Epin

Cemitério da Esperança

Instituto Nacional de Meteorologia

Ⓜ Estação Asa Sul

◉18

SETOR DE INDÚSTRIAS GRÁFICAS

516
316
715
914
913
914

Via W2 Sul
714
514

116
315

115
Ⓜ Estação
114 Sul 114
314
713
513

Via W5 Sul

14
⬦

Parque da Cidade

216
313
Via W1 Sul
312
311

910

Lagoon

416
215
113
112
311
510

Via W4 Sul
908
907

214 25
⊗

111
310

906

616
415

Ⓜ Estação
112 Sul 110 28

509

905

815
615
414
213
212
211

508
707
706

Santuário Dom Bosco

614
413
412
210

308
507
705
704

6 ⓘ

SETOR COMERCIAL SUL

Via L1 Sul
Via L2 Sul

613
612
411
410
209
26

307
506
505
504
503
502

611
610
409
208
207

Ⓜ Estação
108 Sul
106
107
306
305
304

Estação Galeria dos Estados
Ⓜ

Ⓐ Internacional de Brasília–Presidente Juscelino Kubitschek (1.2km); Argentina Embassy (1.5km); Bolivian Embassy (1.5km)

Via L4 Sul

408
407

206
105
205
204

Eixo Rodoviário Sul

104
303
302
301

608
607
606

405
404

103
Ⓜ Estação
102 Sul
102
101

203
202

SETOR BANCÁRIO SUL

201

Estrada Parque Dom Bosco

QI-5

QI-8

QL-8

605
604
603
602

403
402

32 ⊗
29
34 ✪

7 ◉

3 🏛

8 🏛

Museu Nacional

1 ⓘ

Catedral Metropolitana

QI-16

QI-12

⊗22

24 ⊗

SETOR DE EMBAIXADAS SUL

Av das Nações

Palácio do Itamaraty

Via S-2

4

13 🏛

33 ✪

21 ⊗

Bosque dos Constituyentes

SETOR DE CLUBES ESPORTIVOS SUL
Centro Cultural Banco do Brasil (750m);
Ponte JK (500m)

BRASÍLIA & GOIÁS

Brasília

Lucio Costa (Map p334; ☑ 3325 6244; Praça dos Trés Poderes; admission free; ◷ 9am-6pm) FREE.

It's worth visiting the *praça* during the day and again at night for two very different experiences. After dark, surreal lighting casts an eerie glow across the futuristic buildings, as though they are being lit up by the landing lights of an alien spacecraft. Robberies have been reported here at night, though, so have a taxi wait for you while you visit. Note that you will not be allowed to enter government buildings in shorts or sandals.

★ **Palácio do Itamaraty** GOVERNMENT BUILDING
(Palace of Arches; Map p334; ☑ 3411-8051; www.itamaraty.gov.br; ◷ 2-4pm Mon-Fri, 10am-3pm Sat & Sun) FREE Palácio do Itamaraty is home to the Foreign Ministry and one of the most impressive buildings – a series of arches towering over a reflecting pool and floating gardens landscaped by Burle Marx. Outside, the Bruno Giorgi sculpture *Meteor* consists of five marble blocks, each representing a continent.

Palácio da Justiça GOVERNMENT BUILDING
(Map p334; ☑ 3216-2025; ◷ 2-4pm Mon-Fri, 10am-3pm Sat & Sun) Water cascades between the arches of the Palácio de Justicia into a koi fish pond. Visits were suspended at the time of writing, which is a shame because there is a lovely garden inside.

★ **Congresso Nacional** GOVERNMENT BUILDING
(Parliament; Map p334; ☑ 3216-1771; ◷ 9:30am-5pm) FREE Featuring the photogenic 'dishes' and twin towers, the Congresso Nacional is one of the more interesting buildings on the inside as well. In addition to the color-coded chambers of the Senate (blue) and House of Representatives (green) there is an architecturally interesting Tunnel of Time and an exhibit of antique Senate benches and microphones from 1867.

The convex dome on the roof of the House of Representatives is supposed to signify that membership is open to all ideologies.

★ **Palácio do Planalto** PALACE
(Map p334; ☑ 3411-2042; ◷ 9:30am-2:30pm Sun) FREE The Palácio do Planalto is another Niemeyer design that's worth seeing, inside and out. From the curved lines of the exterior to the lustrous columns and sweeping curved ramp inside, it's one of the best examples of architectural Modernism in the world. The tour even lets you peek into the president's office.

There is a ceremonial changing of the guard outside the gates every hour on weekends and every two hours during the week.

Panteão da Pátria e da Liberdade Tancredo Neves   MUSEUM
(Map p334; ✍ 3325-6244; ⊘9am-5pm) **FREE** A newly opened tribute to the principal heroes of Brazilian history, including a set of vertiginous steps to an eternal flame in memory of Tancredo Neves, the elected president who died before he could assume power. The flame is slightly dangerous in a stiff breeze, but it's worth the risk for the aerial view of the Praça dos Trés Poderes.

Pavilhão Nacional   MONUMENT
(Map p334) On the first Sunday of the month the ceremonial changing of Brasília's tallest and largest flag, a 286-sq-meter banner on the Pavilhão Nacional flagpole takes place. Conceived by Sergio Bernardes, it consists of 24 separate flagpoles welded together, each one symbolising a Brazilian state.

◉ Setor de Clubes Esportivos (SCE)

★ Centro Cultural Banco do Brasil   GALLERY
(CCBB; ✍ 3310-7087; SCES, Trecho 2, Conjunto 22; ⊘9am-9pm Tue-Sun) **FREE** Brasília's most important contemporary museum houses fascinating exhibitions in two galleries, an indie cinema, a cafe and a bookstore. A free bus runs every 90 minutes (11am to 11pm) along the Eixo Monumental (look for the painted bus that says CCBB).

Behind the CCBB you can see the **Ponte JK** across Lago do Paranoá, a design presumably inspired by the Loch Ness monster.

★ Palácio da Alvorada   PALACE
(Palace of the Dawn; ✍ 3411-2317; SCEN; ⊘3-5:30pm Thu) **FREE** The official presidential residence, the Palácio da Alvorada is a Niemeyer building. It was the first edifice in the city to be inaugurated, in 1958, predating the inauguration of the city itself by two years. The name translates as 'Palace of the Dawn,' in reference to JK's description of Brasília as 'a new dawn in Brazilian history.'

The gates are marshaled by dapper Dragões da Independência (Dragons of the Independence) guards, from a special regiment of soldiers who date back to the War of Independence. Take bus 104 from platform A16 in the local bus station.

◉ North of the City

Parque Nacional de Brasília   PARK
(Map p334; ✍ 3465-2013; admission R$3; ⊘8am-4pm) In the northern reaches of the city limits, the 30-sq-km Parque Nacional de Brasília is a good place to relax. It has natural swimming pools and is home to a number of threatened animals, including deer, anteaters, giant armadillos and maned wolves. Bus 128.1 from the city bus station goes past the front gate.

The park is very popular on weekends and there's a visitors' center where you can get information.

☞ Tours

Esat Aerotaxi   SCENIC FLIGHTS
(✍ 9981-1917; with a 3-person maximum R$500) The quickest and most exhilarating way to make sense of Brasília's confusingly sensible layout is a breathtaking 10-minute helicopter flight with Esat Aerotaxi. Departures are from the airport.

Catedral Turismo City Tour   BUS TOUR
(Map p339; ✍ 3201-1222; www.catedralturismo.com.br; day tickets R$25) 'Brasília Tour' is the only authorised city tour bus, visiting the main attractions on a circuitous route. This is a good way to navigate the sights with a minimum of stress. Tickets on sale at a kiosk in front of Shopping Brasília (p338).

Billy Deeter   TOUR
(✍ 8112-3434; www.mrbrasilia.com) For themed multilingual tours, Billy Deeter, who was born in the USA but has lived in Brasília since he was a child, organizes group and/or private customized tours, which include some off-the-beaten-track points of interest.

🛏 Sleeping

The chain-hotel takeover of Brasília is nearing completion, so bank on spending more than you'd like to – 'budget' here means 'midrange' elsewhere. Characterless highrise formality is the norm, crammed into the central Setor Hoteleiro with its ubiquitous traffic noise. Those in the SHN (Setor Hoteleiro Norte) are more conveniently located for the shopping centers, but those in the SHS (Setor Hoteleiro Sul) are better value. Most hotels offer substantial discounts throughout the year when business is slow, so it's worth shopping around for the best deal.

Clandestine unlicensed budget pousadas (guesthouses) operate along Via W3 Sul despite a 2008 government blitz to shut them down. Hygiene and safety are not necessarily among their top priorities. Only licensed establishments are listed here.

Albergue da Juventude Brasília   HOSTEL $
(Map p334; ☑ 3343-0531; www.brasiliahostel.com. br; Camping de Brasília; s/d R$57/105; @) This 20-room hostel has big, open breezeways, spanking-clean rooms and individual lockers in dorms of six beds each (there are a few doubles as well). It's located just west of Asa Norte in Brasília's designated camping sector. Bus 143 runs between here and platform E2 of the city bus station.

Hotel Diplomat   HOTEL $
(Map p339; ☑ 3204-2010; SHN, Quadra 2, Bloco L; cabins/s/d from R$99/139/159; ✳ 🎱) Near the TV Tower, this otherwise uninspiring place wins votes for its ample breakfast, free wi-fi and substantial weekend discounts (basement rooms are the cheapest).

Econotel   HOTEL $$
(Map p339; ☑ 3204-7337; www.hoteleconotel. com.br; SHS, Quadra 3, Bloco B; s/d/tr from R$159/189/219; P ✳ 🎱) The closest thing to a budget hotel in the SHS, though the rooms are newer, fresher and better equipped than many of the other stagnant options in a higher range. No need to splash the extra cash on the 'luxury' rooms, either: the standard rooms are just as good.

América Bittar   HOTEL $$
(Map p339; ☑ 3034-3355; www.hoteisbittar.com.br; SHS, Quadra 4, Bloco B; s/d R$180/210; P ✳ @ 🎱 🅰) Now part of the Bittar chain, this hotel has undergone a facelift (and pricelift!). Modern, friendly and businesslike, it's still one of the better-value options in the SHS, though you'll pay for your wi-fi!

Aristus Hotel   HOTEL $$
(Map p339; ☑ 3328-8675; www.aristushotel. com.br; SHN, Quadra 2, Bloco O; s/d R$242/300; P ✳ @ 🎱) If you spend any time in Brasília you'll eventually get sick of elevators. The Aristus is comfortably squat with only two floors, so you won't need one. Rooms are fine, though some are a little dingy.

★ Kubitschek Plaza   HOTEL $$$
(Map p339; ☑ 3329-3333; www.kubitschek.com.br; SHN, Quadra 2, Bloco E; s/d R$680/810; P ✳ @ 🎱 🅰) The halls and lobby of this classic choice feature wonderful art by local artists and famous photographs of Juscelino Kubitschek's administration. Rooms on the upper floors include gorgeous hardwood floors and earth-toned pinstriped headboards. Don't be put off by the prices: they're slashed by 70% at weekends.

Royal Tulip
Brasília Alvorada   LUXURY HOTEL $$$
(☑ 3424-7000; www.royaltulipbrasiliaalvorada.com; SHTN, Trecho 1, Conjunto 1B, Bloco C; s/d R$320/370; P ✳ @ 🎱 🅰) The capital's most stylish hotel is a horseshoe-shaped complex overlooking Lago do Paranoá, right next door to the president's residence. Famed architect Ruy Ohtake designed a futuristic, open lobby with wavy hallways that climb up towards a wiry, Zeppelinesque ceiling. It's a haven for celebs, models and, of course, architects. The website offers a variety of special deals.

Phenícia Bittar Hotel   HOTEL $$$
(Map p339; ☑ 3704-6000; www.hoteisbittar.com. br/hoteis/phenicia/index.php; SHS, Quadra 5, Bloco J; s/d R$300/370; P ✳ @ 🎱) Third-floor nonsmoking rooms with ceramic floors are the nicest and brightest in this four-star hotel, which looks a bit like a giant egg box.

Torre Palace Hotel   HOTEL $$$
(Map p339; ☑ 3961-5555; www.torrepalace.com.br; SHN, Quadra 4, Bloco A; s/d R$340/390; ✳ @ 🎱) Despite an exterior that could do with a lick of paint, the spick-and-span air-conditioned rooms are functional if not exactly brimming over with character. Compensation comes in the form of the Lebanese Tanoor restauarant.

🍴 Eating

Brazilians may say that Brasília is boring, but foodies flock here with abandon – the capital has one of the highest concentrations of starred restaurants in the country. The best selections are around SCLS 209/210, 409/410 and 411/412, which forms a sort of 'gourmet triangle' (it is also home to the city's most lively nightlife). Another good selection of restaurants is clustered in SCLS 405. Here you'll find Tex-Mex, Portuguese, German, Thai, Japanese, Chinese and vegetarian eateries.

Elsewhere, Brazilians in need of sustenance head to the shopping malls. Three centrally located oases – **Shopping Brasília** (Map p339; www.brasiliashopping.com.br; Quadra 5, Asa Norte SCN), **Pátio Brasil** (Map p339; Asa Sul,

Central Brasília

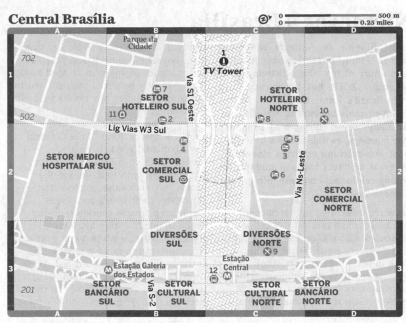

Central Brasília

W3 SCS) and **Conjunto Nacional** (Map p339; www.conjuntonacional.com.br; SDN CNB, Conjunto A) – all have food courts with enough variety to cater to most tastes. In the SCES, **Pier 21** (Map p334) has the largest concentration of restaurants, bars and nightclubs of all the malls but very few actual stores.

Marietta SANDWICHES $
(Map p339; ☑3327-3892; www.marietta.com.br; 2nd fl, Shopping Brasília; sandwiches R$11-19.90; ☺10am-11pm) This sandwich shop turns out the capital's best: a triangular triple-decker of arugula, buffalo mozzarella and sun-dried tomatoes. It has prizewinning juices and killer salads as well.

★Nossa Cozinha Bistrô FUSION $$
(Map p334; ☑3326-5207; www.nossacozinhabsb. blogspot.com.br; SCLN 402, Bloco C; mains R$27.50-38; ☺11.30am-3pm & 7.30pm-midnight, closed Sun; ☞) At this outstanding, near-makeshift bistro tucked away on Bloco C's backside, superb value awaits. The US-trained chef excels at gourmet treats like the signature pork ribs (velvety! chocolaty! tasty!). For Brazil, the check is a pleasant shock.

Mangai NORTHEASTERN $$
(Map p334; ☑3225-0186; SCES, Trecho 2, Loja 41; per kilo R$25; ☺noon-3pm & 6-10pm Mon-Thu, noon-10pm Fri-Sun) With culinary stars, this Bahian per-kilo offers a host of creative

Niemeyer's Brasília

Oscar Ribeiro de Almeida Niemeyer Soares Filho, passed away just 10 days short of his 105th birthday on 5 December 2012, but his legacy lives on in Brazil's futuristic capital. As the creative genius behind the 'free-flowing, sensually-curved' designs of Brasília's civic buildings, as well as some of Brazil's most eye-catching edificies elsewhere, the great architect had a unique gift for turning reinforced concrete into artistic masterpieces.

Niemeyer was visited in September 1956 by Brazilian president Juscelino Kubitschek who was an admirer of his work. With the words 'Oscar, we are going to build the capital of Brazil', a legendary partnership began and with the addition of Lucio Costa as the landscaper, the dream soon became a reality. The completion of the city took place remarkably quickly and Brasília was ready for business on 21 April 1960. Niemeyer later lamented the rush, but to the nonperfectionist, the results were still outstanding.

Though an atheist himself, the 'crown of thorns' form of the Catedral Metropolitana (p333) is widely recognised as one of his most cutting-edge designs, with long stained-glass panels 'to connect the people to the sky, where their Lord's paradise is'. The heavens theme continues nearby at the simple but stunning Museu Nacional (p333), a white dome with a circumnavigating ramp leading to the entrance that recalls Saturn and its rings. Less visually striking, the design of the domes on the roof of the Congresso Nacional (p336) represents an openness

of government to all political ideologies and reflected the optimistic future that Brasília would embody. Inspired by the words of Kubitschek 'What is Brasília, if not the dawn of a new day for Brazil?', Niemeyer created the modernist Palacio da Alvorada (Palace of the Dawn; p337) as the official residence of the president, its simplistic layout turning its nose up at the excesses of previous incumbents of Brazil's top job.

Niemeyer was politically leftist and designed Brasília along socialist principles, with similar apartment blocks to prevent the emergence of wealthy neighbourhoods. He was a friend of Fidel Castro, who once said 'Niemeyer and I are the last communists on this planet.' His political beliefs led to persecution under the military dictatorship of the 1960s and he was driven into exile, returning only when the country returned to democratic principles in the mid 1980s. Niemeyer continued to work right up to his death and lived to see Brazil finally beginning to fulfil the promise it promised with the building of Brasília.

Though he never cared for eulogies, it is hard to disagree with the words of President Dilma Roussef that marked his passing 'Brazil today lost one of its geniuses. It's a day for mourning'.

1. Congresso Nacional (p336) **2.** Catedral Metropolitana (p333) **3.** Palácio da Alvorada (p337)

JANE SWEENEY / GETTY IMAGES ©

RUY BARBOSA PINTO / GETTY IMAGES ©

ALAN WEINTRAUB/ARCAID / CORBIS ©

dishes served up by Natal chef João Pessoa at a startlingly low price. Try the *sovaco-de-cobra*, a kind of beef jerky with green corn. It's down by the Ponte JK and gets very busy at lunch.

Quitinete   BAKERY $$
(Map p334; ☑ 3422-0506; SCLS 209; pizzas R$17-33; ⊙ 7am-midnight) This chic deli-restaurant-bakery serves exquisite desserts – try the *tartellete de limão* (lemon tart) – and the best coffee in the city (roasted in-house). Pizzas are popular and delivery is available.

Mormaii Surf Bar   INTERNATIONAL $$
(Map p334; ☑ 3248-1265; SHIS, Quadra do Lago 10, Bloco E, Lote 8; sandwiches R$15-25; ⊙ 10am-1am) Locals park themselves on the outdoor lakeside patio every afternoon for tasty sandwiches and the house specialty, *açaí na tigela*, a refreshing sorbetlike meal of blended palmberries, guaraná syrup, bananas and honey. On weekends, the waterfront location (in the Pontão) attracts a roaring nightlife crowd as well.

ADDRESSES FOR THE LOGICAL MIND

Believe it or not, Brasília's addresses – a series of numbers and letters that pinpoint an exact location – are designed to make your life easier (once you know what all the acronyms mean!).

For example, the address SQS 704, Bloco Q, Casa 29. That means it's in Super Quadra South 704, *bloco* (building) Q, *casa* (house) 29. The first digit in the address (7) shows the position east or west of the Eixo Rodoviário (the main north–south arterial road) – odd numbers to the west and even to the east, increasing as they move away from the center. The last two digits (04) show the distance north or south of the Eixo Monumental. So the place you are looking for is four blocks to the south of the Eixo Monumental and four blocks east of the Eixo Rodoviário (1, 3, 5, 7). The higher the number of the Super Quadra, the further it is from the center.

Get to know these acronyms:

Asa Norte/Asa Sul The two 'wings' of the city, connected by main roads, *eixo rodoviários*. The N (Norte) or S (Sul) after an acronym indicates on which side of the Eixo Monumental it's located.

SBN/SBS (Setor Bancário Norte/Sul) The banking areas either side of the Eixo Monumental.

SCEN/SCES (Setor de Clubes Esportivos Norte/Sul) The main recreational zone on the shores of Lago do Paranoá.

SCLN/SCLS (Setor Comércio Local Norte/Sul) The main shopping blocks between the *superquadras*.

SCN/SCS (Setor Comercial Norte/Sul) The commercial office block areas next to the main shopping centers.

SDN/SDS (Setor de Diversões Norte/Sul) The main *conjuntos* (shopping centers) either side of the Eixo Monumental.

SEN/SES (Setor de Embaixadas Norte/Sul) The embassy sectors.

SHIN/SHIS (Setor de Habitações Individuais Norte/Sul) The residential areas around the lake. SHIN is reached on the Eixo Norte. SHIS is accessed via the bridges off Av das Nações.

SHN/SHS (Setor Hoteleiro Norte/Sul) The hotel sectors each side of the Eixo Monumental.

SMHN/SMHS (Setor Médico Hospitalar Norte/Sul) The hospital sectors each side of the Eixo Monumental, next to the SCN and SCS, respectively.

SQN/SQS (Super Quadras Norte/Sul) The individual *superquadras* in the main residential wings of the *plano piloto*.

Got it?!

Pizza à Bessa PIZZERIA $$
(Map p334; ☑3345-5252; www.pizzaabessa.com.
br; SCLS, Quadra 214, Bloco C, Loja 14; pizza rodízio
R$28.50; ☺6pm-midnight; 🏶) The *rodízio* (all-
you-can-eat) option here is excellent value
and the best way to try some inventive in-
gredients like pureed pumpkin, broccoli,
and an outrageous dessert pizza with a huge
scoop of ice cream. The *queijo coalho* (cured
white cheese) and *rapadura* (dried sugar-
cane juice) pizza is a masterpiece.

⭐ **Aquavit** CONTEMPORARY $$$
(☑3369-2301; www.restauranteaquavit.com;
SMLN, Trecho 12, Conj 1; menu R$95-135; ☺9pm-
2am Wed-Sat) A fascinating rotating menu of
six culinary masterpieces using ingredients
fresh from the cerrado and served on a picturesque balcony overlooking Lago Paranoá.
This is food art from award-winning chef
Simon Lau. Reserve in advance!

Universal Diner INTERNATIONAL $$$
(Map p334; ☑3443-2089; SCLS, Quadra 210, Bloco
B, Loja 30; dishes R$49-95; ☺noon-3pm & 7pm-
midnight Mon-Sat, 11am-5pm Sun) A junkyard-
chic aesthetic greets patrons at this eclec-
tic rock eatery (it's overflowing with funky
bric-a-brac and antique knick-knacks), an-
other of the city's Brazilicious culinary gems.
Mouthwatering tenderloin *au poivre* is the
way to go, served up on vinyl LP placemats.

Lagash MIDDLE EASTERN $$$
(Map p334; ☑3273-0098; SCLN, Quadra 308,
Bloco B, Loja 11/17; dishes R$30-75; ☺noon-4pm
& 7pm-midnight Mon-Sat, noon-5pm Sun) A mix
of Moroccan, Lebanese and Syrian cuisine
earns this sparsely decorated restaurant top
Middle Eastern food in town year after year.
Anything with lamb is delightful.

🍷 **Drinking & Nightlife**

Gate's Pub BAR
(Map p334; SCLS 403; cover R$15-20; ☺9pm-3am
Tue-Sun) Gate's claims to be the longest-es-
tablished bar in the city. True to its piano-
keyboard motif, there's live music most
nights with a rock, reggae and funk flavor,
then dance music until closing.

Bar Beirute BOTECO
(Map p334; ☑3244-1717; 109 Sul, Bloco A; light
meals R$5-32) This Brasília institution has a
massive outdoor patio packed with an edgier crowd than most spots. It's a GLS point –
the clever Brazilian acronym for gays, lesbians and sympathetics – but it's really a free-
for-all. There's no better spot for a cold Beira

– Beirute's own brand of beer! You can get
Middle Eastern food here as well.

Bar Brasília BAR
(Map p334; ☑3443-4323; SCLS, Quadra 506, Bloco
A, Loja 15A; ☺5pm-2am Mon-Thu, 11:30am-2am Fri
& Sat, 11:30am-midnight Sun) In the same vein
as the classic bars from Rio and São Paulo,
complete with a hardwood bar relocated
from a pharmacy in 1928, and antique tiled
floors. It's great for draft beer, but note that
staff will keep bringing you beer whether
you ask them to or not. Don't be afraid to
tell them to stop.

Bar Brahma Brasília BAR
(Map p334; ☑3224-9313; www.barbrahmasp.
com/brasilia; SCLS, Quadra 201, Bloco C, Loja 33;
cover R$20; ☺11am-late) As Brahma's plan for
world domination of the beer market chugs
along nicely, Bar Brahma Brasília is another
step towards a nationwide chain of bars promoting the brand. Live music most nights;
check the website for upcoming events.

Chiquita Bacana BAR
(Map p334; SCLS 209; ☺5pm-late) The *patricin-
has* and *mauricinhos* – as Brazil's beautiful people are affectionately called – spill
out onto Quadra 210 at this trendy open-
air *chopperia* (beer hall) complete with
whacky-hatted waiters. Undergoing renovations at the time of writing but promises to
come back stronger than ever.

☆ **Entertainment**

If you're after live music, check the listings in the 'Caderno C' section of the daily
Correio Brasiliense newspaper or the free
monthly booklet *Brasiliagenda*. If you
read Portuguese, www.candango.com.br is
a great online source of cultural and social
events in the city.

Arena Futebol Clube LIVE MUSIC
(Map p334; ☑3224-9401; SCES, Trecho 3, Lote 1;
cover R$10-15; ☺10pm-late Thu-Sat, 7pm-midnight
Sun) It's well worth the taxi fare to the Setor
de Clubes Esportivos Sul, southwest of Praça
dos Três Poderes, for this live-music mecca
that takes over the football (soccer) club
on weekends. Daughters of ministers and
politicos sweat it out to hip-shaking *forró*
(popular Northeastern music), samba and
samba-funk.

Bar do Calaf LIVE MUSIC
(Map p334; ☑3325-7408; www.calaf.com.br; SBS,
Quadra 2, Bloco S, Edifício Empire Center; cover

BRASÍLIA – CAPITAL OF THE 3RD MILLENNIUM

In 1883 an Italian priest, John Bosco, prophesied that a new civilization would arise between parallels 15 and 20, and that its capital would be built between parallels 15 and 16, on the edge of an artificial lake. Many consider Brasília to be that city, and a number of cults have sprung up in the area. If you tire of Brasília's architectural monuments, a visit to one of the cults may be part of your destiny.

About 45km east of Brasília, near the satellite city of Planaltina, you'll find the **Vale do Amanhecer** (Valley of the Dawn; ☑ 3388-0537; ☺ 10am-midnight), founded in 1959 by a clairvoyant, Tia Neiva. The valley is actually a small town where you can see (or take part in) Egyptian, Greek, Aztec, Indian, Roma, Inca, Trojan and Afro-Brazilian rituals. The mediums in the town believe that a new civilization will come during the 3rd millennium. The town's main temple was inspired by spiritual advice received by Tia Neiva. In the center is an enormous Star of David, which forms a lake, pierced by an arrow. Get there by bus 617 from the center of Brasília.

About 63km west of Brasília, near the town of Santo Antônio do Descoberto (Goiás), is the **Cidade Ecléctica** (Eclectic City; ☑ 3626-1391; ☺ 8am-6pm). Founded in 1956 by Yokanam, who was once an airline pilot, the group's aim is to unify all religions on the planet through fraternity and equality. You're welcome to attend its ceremonies, but there are strict dress regulations. Women cannot wear long pants (skirts only) and men cannot wear shorts. If you're not dressed suitably, you'll be given a special tunic to wear.

The **Templo da Boa Vontade** (Temple of Goodwill; Map p334; ☑ 3245-1070; www.boavontade.com; SGAS, Quadra 915, Lotes 75/76; ☺ 24hr) was created by the Legion of Goodwill in 1989 as a symbol of universal solidarity. It incorporates seven pyramids, joined to form a cone that is topped with a 21kg crystal. To view it, you must take off your shoes and walk along the spiraling inner circle via the black path. You must return on the white path (do not screw this up). It's all a bit dizzying. There is also an interesting Egyptian room for meditation (R$2) that will make you feel like King Tut (of course, they take all of this very seriously, so let's keep these jokes between us). Get there on bus 105 or 107 from the city bus station.

R$10-25; ☺ closed Sun) Though technically a Spanish restaurant, the food is an afterthought to the wildly mixed crowd, all of whom rate the excellent live samba, *pagode* (popular samba) and *choro* (improvised samba) over the paella. Monday is the biggest draw for samba-funk.

ⓘ Information

EMBASSIES & CONSULATES
Brasília has a large chunk of real estate devoted to embassies and consulates, most located between Quadras 801 and 810 in the Setor de Embaixadas Sul (Embassy Sector South).

EMERGENCY
Ambulance (☑ 192)
Fire Department (☑ 193)
Police (☑ 190)

MEDICAL SERVICES
De Base do Distrito Federal (☑ 3315-1200; SMHS 101)
Santa Lúzia (☑ 3445-6000; SHLS, Quadra 716, Conjunto E)

MONEY
There are banks with moneychanging facilities in the Setor Bancário Sul (SBS; Banking Sector South) and Setor Bancário Norte (SBN; Banking Sector North). Both sectors are close to the city bus station. All the major malls, bus stations and the airport have a variety of ATMs, most with Cirrus/MasterCard/Visa networking. Travel agencies will change dollars.

POST
Main Post Office (Map p339; SHS, Quadra 2, Bloco B; ☺ 9am-5pm Mon-Fri) There are also branches in the arrivals hall of the airport and at the main malls.

TOURIST INFORMATION
Information desks at the **airport** (☑ 3364-9102; www.vemviverbrasilia.com.br; Presidente Juscelino Kubitschek International Airport; ☺ 7am-10pm) and **Rodoviária Interestadual** (Map p334; Nova Rodoviária Interestadual; ☺ 7am-10pm) are your best bets for information, so take full advantage before you head to the city center. For a list of attractions, pick up a brochure from the front desk of any large hotel or travel agency. Though there is a scattering of

CAT information offices in the hotel district, they are typically either open sporadically or bereft of material.

TRAVEL AGENCIES

Any number of travel agencies in the **Hotel Nacional** complex and at the airport can help you book flights and rent cars.

ℹ Getting There & Away

Brasília has a large daily influx of sightseers and lobbyists, so the international airport connects with all major Brazilian cities. Most visitors fly in, but those who choose to go overland will cover some long distances. Brasília is a World Cup city and the new **Estadio Mané Garrincha** (Map p334) will host matches.

AIR

Brasília's **Aeroporto Presidente Juscelino Kubitschek** (BSB; ☑ 3364-9037; www.aeroportobrasilia.net), 12km south of the center, offers flights throughout Brazil as well as to Atlanta (USA), Lima (Peru), Lisbon (Portugal), Miami (USA) and Panama City (Panama). The easiest way to or from the airport is **Ônibus Executivo Aeroporto** (☑ 3344-2769; www.tcb.df.gov.br; fare R$8; ⊙ 6:30am-11pm), which runs between the Rodoviária Plano Piloto (local bus station) and the far right of the arrivals hall.

You can book flights through the travel agencies in the Hotel Nacional (p345) complex, but if you prefer to contact the airlines directly they all have offices at the airport.

BUS

From the flashy new long-distance bus station, **Rodoviária Interestadual** (Map p334; SMAS, Trecho 4, Conjunto 5/6), 3km southwest off the edge of Asa Sul, buses go almost everywhere in Brazil.

From platform E7 at the local bus station **Empresa Santo Antônio** (☑ 3328-0834; www.

grupoamaral.com.br) runs two daily services to Alto Paraíso (R$29, 4½ hours) at 7.15am and 1:30pm, with the later service continuing on to São Jorge (R$39, 5½ hours).

ℹ Getting Around

Estação Shopping of the **Metrô DF** (www.metro.df.gov.br; weekends/weekdays R$2/3; ⊙ 6am-11:30pm Mon-Fri, 7am-7pm Sat & Sun) connects the Rodoviária Interestadual with the local **Rodoviária Plano Piloto** (Map p339) bus station (Estação Central) in the city center, as does local bus 108.8 (R$2, 20 minutes). Otherwise the Metrô DF is only really useful for access to restaurants and bars in the Asa Sul. It runs from the city bus station to the huge suburbs of Ceilândia and Samambaia, with a predictably named station (102 Sul, 104 Sul, etc) every two blocks or so from the central station. Last service is at 11:30pm.

Despite horrendous delays, the official word is that the Brastram light-rail network will still be ready in time for FIFA World Cup matches in 2014, making Brasília the first South American city with a modern tramway. This willl eventually cover 23km of tracks, connecting the airport with the Asa Norte and with the aim to decrease pollution and traffic congestion by 30%.

Its (☑ 3224 8000; www.itsrentacar.com.br; SHS Quadra 1, Hotel Nacional; ⊙ 8am-6pm Mon-Fri, 8am-noon Sat) rents cars for as little as R$20 per day with a kilometer cap.

GOIÁS

POP 6 MILLION

Goiás is a vast and wild state of green hills and deep valleys, dominated by the picturesque cerrado so typical of central Brazil. Agriculture is big business here, with soya, biodiesel and ethanol industries making

BUSES FROM BRASÍLIA

DESTINATION	FARE (R$)	TIME (HR)	COMPANY
Belém	320	35	Transbrasiliana (www.transbrasiliana.com.br)
Cuiabá	162-169	20	Expresso São Luiz (www.expressosaoluiz.com.br), Eucatur (www.eucatur.com.br)
Goiânia	30-45	3	Viação Goiania (www.viacaogoiania.com.br), Araguarina (www.araguarina.com.br), Viação São Luiz (www.viacaosaoluiz.com.br), Eucatur (www.eucatur.com.br)
Porto Velho	347	42	Andorinha (www.andorinha.com)
Rio de Janeiro	160-229	17	Itapemirim (www.itapemirim.com.br
Salvador	185	22	Rápido Federal, Real Expresso (www.realexpresso.com.br)
São Paulo	161-228	14	Rápido Federal, Real Expresso (www.realexpresso.com.br)

BRASÍLIA & GOIÁS GOIÁS

this one of the wealthiest states in the country, albeit at the expense of the landscape. Fortunately, its unrelenting natural beauty is preserved in a series of jaw-dropping national parks, while a series of handsome colonial towns (www.cidadeshistoricasgoias.com.br) are perfect places to try the much-lauded regional cuisine.

ℹ Getting There & Around

The gateway to Goiás is Brasília, with daily flights to all major Brazilian cities. If you don't mind spending days on buses it's also possible to travel overland: from the coast via scenic Minas Gerais or from the Pantanal portals of Cuiabá and Campo Grande.

Goiás offers many attractions and is a popular stopover for travelers crossing the interior of the country. Regular bus services connect all the major towns and cities. Road conditions are generally good and renting a car is a viable option.

Goiânia

☎ 0XX62 / POP 1.3 MILLION

The capital of Goiás, Goiânia is the state's other planned city, predating Brasília by almost 30 years. Planned by urbanist Armando de Godói and founded in 1933, it's a pleasant enough combination of parks, leafy avenues and high-rise buildings laid out around circular streets. There's not much to see here, but it's a major transport nexus and if you're touring the state you'll inevitably find yourself passing through more than once.

🛏 Sleeping

There are a million places to stay for all budgets close to the gigantic bus station. Midrange and top-end hotels drop as much as 50% off their prices when business is slow.

Rodohotel   HOTEL $
(☎ 3224-2664; www.rodohotel.com.br; Rua 44 554; s/d with fan R$70/90, with air-conditioning R$90/120; ❄☎) Opposite the northern exit bus station, this almost-cheapie will do for an overnight stay before catching an early bus.

Goiânia Palace   HOTEL $$
(☎ 3224-4874; www.goianiapalace.com.br; Av Anhanguera 5195; s/d/tr from R$115/155/185; ❄☎) Pretty in pink! Art deco brick-and-wood *apartamentos* (rooms with private bathroom) with wardrobes and full-length mirrors. It's a good option and English is spoken.

Crystal Plaza Hotel   HOTEL $$
(☎ 3267-4500; www.crystalplazahotel.com.br; Rua 85 30, Setor Sul; s/d R$155/165; ⓟ❄@☎) Standard rooms at this centrally located hotel just off Praça Cívica are double the size of those elsewhere. There is a handy tourist agency on the premises.

✕ Eating & Drinking

There is some great regional food to try as well as some thriving nightlife.

★**Chão Nativo I**   GOIANA $$
(☎ 3233-5396; www.chaonativo1.com.br; Av República do Líbano 1809, Setor Oeste; fixed-price meals R$32.90; ⊙ 11am-3:30pm) Serve yourself from a bonanza of bubbling cauldrons of baffling Goiânian concoctions at this all-you-can-eat smorgasbord, repeatedly voted the city's best for local cuisine.

Piquiras   INTERNATIONAL $$$
(☎ 3281-4344; www.piquiras.com; Rua 146 464, Setor Marista; dishes R$41-96; ⊙ 11am-3pm & 6pm-late Mon-Fri, 11:30am-late Sat & Sun) A Goiânia institution serving great examples of local fare. South of downtown, the expansive outside deck is packed with the city's young and fun on weekends. Watch out for the R$17 cover charge on a la carte dishes!

Celsin & Cia   BAR
(☎ 3215-3043; Rua 22 475, Setor Oeste; ⊙ 5pm-late Mon-Fri, 11am-late Sat, 11am-5pm Sun) Goiânésians of all ilks drink in droves here, filling the 65 outdoor tables under illuminated almond trees day and night.

ℹ Information

Goiânia is clean, relatively safe and efficiently organized. If you're just passing through pretty much everything you are likely to need, from food to ATMs to a post office, is in the monster-size bus station-mall. If you're traveling on to the national parks or colonial towns, it is wise to get money here.

ℹ Getting There & Around

Aeroporto de Goiânia (☎ 3265-1500) is 6km northeast of the city center. You can fly to Rio, São Paulo and other major Brazilian cities, but it's usually cheaper (not to mention more convenient) to fly to nearby Brasília.

From the huge **bus station–shopping mall** (☎ 3240-0000), buses leave for Brasília (R$30 to R$45, three hours, hourly), Cuiabá (R$139, 16 hours, six daily), Caldas Novas (**Viação Estrela** (www.nacionalexpresso.com.br), R$28, 2½ hours, two daily), Pirenópolis (**Viação Goiânésia** (www.viacaogoianesia.com.br), R$14.50, 2½ hours, one daily 5pm), Alto Paraíso (Empresa São José, R$71, seven hours, one daily) and Cidade de Goiás (Empresa Moreira ; www.empresamoreira.com.br), R$25, three hours, hourly).

Many buses arriving in Goiânia stop first at the Campinas subterminal. If the station doesn't look ridiculously huge, then stay on board. You're not there yet!

Cidade de Goiás

⟋ 0XX62 / POP 24,700

Straddling the Rio Vermelho and surrounded by the rugged Serra Dourada, Cidade de Goiás is a sleepy town of lamplit cobblestone streets and whitewashed colonial homes. The former state capital, once known as Vila Boa (and briefly later on as Goiás Velho), was awarded Unesco World Heritage status in 2002. Its gorgeous baroque churches shine and the town's population swells during Semana Santa (Holy Week). Every July 25, the anniversary of the town's founding in 1727, the state governor visits Cidade de Goiás, which becomes the state capital for three days.

◉ Sights

Strolling through town, you quickly notice the magnificent 18th-century colonial architecture, much of which is home to narrow streets and low houses hawking the region's famous *frutas cristalizados* (sugar-coated fruit concoctions that come in a plethora of flavors). Fuel up and make your way around the town's seven churches.

★Museu das Bandeiras   MUSEUM
(⟋ 3371-1087; Praça Brasil Caiado; admission R$3; ⊙ 9am-6pm Tue-Sat, to 2pm Sun) The fascinating Museu das Bandeiras is an old jail (1766–1950) and also a former town hall that's full of interesting antiques and original furniture – the 1.5m-thick cell walls made of *aroeira* (pepper-tree) wood are a museum piece in themselves. Outside in the square, the **Chafariz de Cauda fountain** (1778) is perfectly preserved, save the water.

Museu de Arte Sacra   MUSEUM
(admission R$3; ⊙ 9am-5pm) In the old **Igreja da Boa Morte** (Praça Castelo Branco), this interesting museum has a good selection of 19th-century works by renowned Goiânian sculptor Viega Vale.

Casa de Cora Carolina   MUSEUM
(⟋ 3371-1990; Dom Cândido Penso 20; admission R$4; ⊙ 9am-4.45pm Tue-Sat, to 3pm Sun) The Casa de Cora Carolina is the birthplace and home of the area's renowned poet.

Palácio Conde dos Arcos   PALACE
(⟋ 3371-1200; Praça Castelo Branco; admission R$3; ⊙ 8am-5pm Tue-Sat, to 1pm Sun) The Palácio Conde dos Arcos is the restored colonial governor's residence.

Igreja São Francisco de Paula   CHURCH
(Praça Zaqueu Alves de Castro; ⊙ 1-5pm Tue-Thu, 9am-1pm Sat-Sun) FREE The most impressive of the town's seven churches is the oldest, built in 1761.

Espaço Cultural de
Goiandeira do Courto   ARTS CENTRE
(⟋ 3371-1303; Joaquim Bonifácio 19; admission R$3; ⊙ 9am-noon & 2-5pm Tue-Sat, 9am-1pm Sun) The Espaço Cultural de Goiandeira do Courto is well worth a visit. The art created here uses 551 varieties of sparkling colored sands found in the Serra Dourada, predating pixilation by decades (and done by hand, it should be noted).

✲ Festivals & Events

Semana Santa   RELIGIOUS
The highlight of the week before Easter is the Wednesday-night procession re-enacting the arrest of Christ. The streetlights are turned off and thousands march through the streets carrying torches, led by 40 eerie, pointy-hooded figures – the *farricocos* – whose colorful dress harks back to the days of the Inquisition. Those aren't klansman statues that you've been seeing around town!

Festival International de
Cinema Ambiental   THEATER
(International Environmental Film Festival) Over five days in early June, the festival includes film and video screenings, workshops, live shows, lectures and exhibitions – all environmentally themed. It was started in 1999 in an attempt to draw worldwide attention to the town.

▟ Sleeping

Cidade de Goiás is a popular getaway from Goiânia, so book ahead if you're arriving on a weekend. The town is packed during Semana Santa and for the Festival International de Cinema Ambiental, when prices rise.

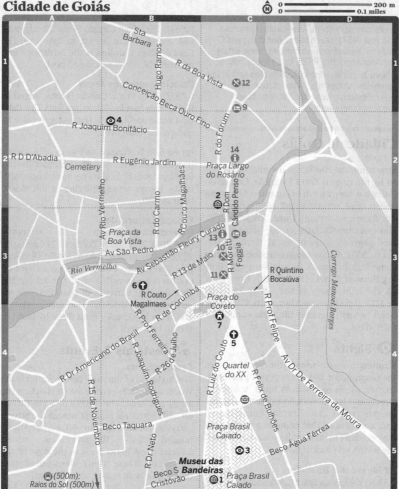

N 0 — 200 m
0 — 0.1 miles

★ **Pousada do Ipê** POUSADA **$**
(☏3371-2065; www.pousadadoipego.com.br; Rua do Forum 22; s/d apt R$111/127, chalets R$122/144; ❄🛜❄) The most charming place to stay, the pousada is a tranquil property set around a lush courtyard and swimming pool. Enjoy the sugar-laden breakfast of local jams and jellies in a room just off the old-style kitchen.

Raios de Sol HOTEL **$$**
(☏3371-3161; www.hotelraiodesol.com; Av Dario de Paiva Sampaio 6; s/d without air-con R$60/120, with air-con R$70/140; ❄) Maybe not the ray of sunshine you were looking for in your life, but this hotel next to the bus station is good value and saves you an uphill hike to the center if you arrive late.

Casa da Ponte HOTEL **$$**
(☏3371-4467; Moretti Foggia s/n; s/d R$70/150; 🅿❄@🛜) There's no accounting for taste with regard to the floral bedspreads, but this kitschy hotel is on a nice corner overlooking the Rio Vermelho.

✕ Eating

The *empadão* (savory pie filled with meat, vegetables, cheese, olives and sometimes egg) reigns here and is served everywhere. Equally ubiquitous are crystalized fruits.

Cidade de Goiás

◎ **Top Sights**
  1 Museu das Bandeiras..........................C5

◎ **Sights**
  2 Casa de Cora Carolina C2
  3 Chafariz de Cauda Fountain................C5
  4 Espaço Cultural de Goiandeira
    do Courto B2
  5 Igreja da Boa Morte............................ C4
  6 Igreja São Francisco de Paula.............B3
    Museu de Arte Sacra.................. (see 5)
  7 Palácio Conde dos Arcos...................C4

🛏 **Sleeping**
  8 Casa da Ponte C3
  9 Pousada do Ipê.....................................C1

🍽 **Eating**
  10 Casa do Doce C3
  11 Casarão C3
  12 Flor do Ipê..C1

ℹ️ **Information**
  13 CAT Tourist Office...............................C3
  14 Municipal Building C2

Casarão   GOIANA **$**
(☎9282-9826; Moretti Foggia 8; dishes R$8-10; ⊙9am-11pm) Up a rickety wooden staircase, this is the best spot in town to try piping-hot *empadão*, served in traditional ceramic crockery.

Casa do Doce   SWEETS **$**
(☎9651-5759; Moretti Foggia; sweets per kilo R$23; ⊙9am-10pm) If you don't mind a few bees, you'll find the colorful display of 28 crystallized fruits here too much to walk away from. Several branches are dotted around town. Eat your fill, then call your dentist.

Flor do Ipê   GOIANA **$$**
(☎3372-1133; www.restauranteflordeipe.com; Rua da Boa Vista; dishes for 2 R$23-50; ⊙noon-3pm & 7pm-midnight Tue-Sat, noon-3pm Sun) For lunch, there's a wealth of regional choices laid out in fiery-hot clay pots for R$27. In the evenings, the shady garden setting fills up quickly for excellent à la carte local dishes.

ℹ️ Information

Banco do Brasil (Av Sebastião Fleury Curado; ⊙11am-4pm Mon-Fri) Visa/MasterCard ATM daily until 10pm.

CAT Tourist Office (☎3371-7714; www.cidadedegoias.com.br; Moretti Foggia; ⊙7.30-11:30am & 1.30-5:30pm Mon-Fri) Operates irregularly and sometimes completely closed, in which case ask at the **municipal building** (Praça Largo do Rosário).

Post Office (Aguavi; ⊙9am-5pm Mon-Fri)

ℹ️ Getting There & Away

The bus station is 500m downhill south of Praça Brasil Caiado. Frequent buses run between Cidade de Goiás and Goiânia (R$25, three hours), from where you can connect to pretty much everywhere else in the state.

Pirenópolis

📞 0XX62 / POP 23,000

A curious mix of art deco and Portuguese colonial architecture first strikes visitors to 'Piri', but that's far from the only odd thing about this quirky town, on the Patrimonio Nacional (National Heritage) register since 1989. Set on striking red earth astride the Rio das Almas, it's another colonial gem with a history steeped in gold, though quite different from others in the state.

An alternative movement took hold here in the '70s and remains today. There is a New Age, vaguely hippie vibe to this laid-back spot and the streets are lined with artist workshops each trying to out-kook their neighbour. You'll be sick of waterfalls by the time you leave, but it's an excellent base from which to explore the 73 found around the area.

◎ Sights & Activities

Two interesting museums are devoted to the Festo do Divino Espírito Santo: the Museo do Divino and the Museu das Cavalhadas.

★ Museu do Divino   MUSEUM
(☎3331-1460; Bernardo Sayão; admission R$4; ⊙11am-5pm Wed-Sun) The municipal Museu do Divino exhibits the masks and costumes used during the Festo do Divino Espírito Santo. These masks were made by local craftsmen using methods passed down from generation to generation.

★ Museu das Cavalhadas   MUSEUM
(☎3331-1166; Direita 39; admission R$2; ⊙10am-5pm) The privately owned Museu das Cavalhadas is cluttered with bright and colorful artifacts brought to life in a guided tour from the owner. The sign says to ring the doorbell if the museum appears to be closed.

Pirenópolis

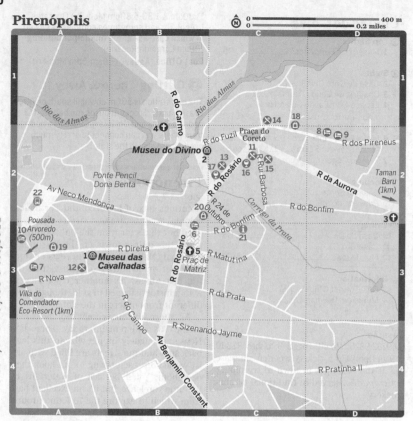

Pirenópolis

FESTA DO DIVINO ESPÍRITO SANTO

Pirenópolis is famous for performing the story of **Festa do Divino Espírito Santo**, a tradition begun in 1819 that is more popularly known as As Cavalhadas.

Starting 50 days after Easter, for three days the town looks like a scene from the Middle Ages as it celebrates Charlemagne's victory over the Moors. A series of medieval tournaments, dances and festivities, including a mock battle between the Moors and Christians in distant Iberia, takes place. Combatants ride decorated horses, kitted out in bright costumes and bull-head masks. The Moors are defeated on the battlefield and convert to Christianity, 'proving' that heresy doesn't pay in the end.

The festival is a happy one, and more folkloric than religious. If you're in the neighborhood, make a point of seeing this stunning and curious spectacle, one of the most fascinating in Brazil.

Igreja NS do Carmo & Museu de Arte Sacra
CHURCH, MUSEUM

(Rua do Carmo; admission R$2; ⊙11am-5pm Wed-Sun) Reopened in October 2009, the town's most famous church, Igreja NS do Carmo (1750), houses the Museu de Arte Sacra.

Igreja NS do Rosário Matriz & Museu da Matriz
CHURCH, MUSEUM

(Praça de Matriz; admission R$2; ⊙7am-5pm Thu-Mon) The town's oldest church, the 1732 Igreja NS do Rosário Matriz, was tragically gutted by fire in 2002 (arson is suspected). Inside, the Museu da Matriz explains the history and ongoing renovation. The new altar was restored and brought in from the former slave church, a necessary house of worship since slaves were banned from this one.

Igreja NS do Bonfim
CHURCH

(Rua do Bonfim) Full of charisma, the Portuguese-built Igreja NS do Bonfim (1750) is a simple, rectangular adobe church with wooden floors and ceiling, flanked by two lateral chapels. The gilded turquoise altar and wooden pulpit are worth a look, but the church interior is currently closed for repairs.

Santuário de Vida Silvestre – Fazenda Vagafogo
WILDLIFE RESERVE

(Vagafogo Farm Wildlife Sanctuary; ☑3335-8515; www.vagafogo.com.br; guided walk R$16; ⊙9am-5pm Mon-Sun) Six kilometres northwest of town, this is a 44-hectare private nature reserve. It's a great place to spot wildlife and even if you don't see much, the light hike is a welcome retreat from the heat (there are two natural pools for swimming). To walk here from town, head north along Rua do Carmo and follow the signs.

The cafe at the visitors' center does a ridiculously good weekend brunch (R$35; 9am to 4:30pm), with a rainbow coalition of homemade wild cerrado fruit preserves. Try them all.

Reserva Ecológica Vargem Grande
WATERFALL

(☑3331-3071; www.vargemgrande.pirenopolis. tur.br; admission R$20; ⊙9am-5pm) This 360-hectare park on private land contains two impressive waterfalls – **Cachoeira Santa Maria** and **Cachoeira do Lázaro**. There are small river beaches and natural pools for swimming. If you're here for waterfalls, these are the ones to see. The reserve is 11km east of town on the road to Serra dos Pireneus.

You don't need a guide to enter, but unless you have a car, you'll need a ride from one.

Parque Estadual da Serra dos Pireneus
PARK

Pireneus, 18km northeast of town, is a Brazilianization of the word 'Pyrenees' and the top spot in the state for bouldering and mountain climbing. There are waterfalls and interesting rock formations to see along the way, some dating back to Gondwanaland. You'll need an accredited guide to enter; ask at a local agency.

On the first full moon in July, locals celebrate the Festa do Morro with a procession to the Morro dos Pireneus (some to pray, some to play), where there is a small chapel on Pai. It's a modern tradition, more New Age than religious, and partying ensues.

🛏 Sleeping

You can't walk more than 100m without finding a pousada in Pirénopolis, but book ahead at weekends and during festivals (when prices can treble!).

Pousada SESC Pirenópolis
POUSADA $

(www.sescgo.com.br; Rua dos Pireneus 45; s/d R$118/150; ❋ ❄) If you can manage to book

BRASÍLIA & GOIÁS PIRENÓPOLIS

rooms 1 to 3, you've scored the best deal in town: well-appointed suites with a separate living room, very nice stone bathroom, and vaulted ceilings for the same price as a double. Reservations must be made through the website.

★ Pousada Tajupá
POUSADA $$

(☑ 3331-1305; www.pousadatajupa.com.br; Rua 4 Quadra 65; chalets R$180; P ❋ 🛜 ⁂) A short drag of your suitcase along a cobbled street from the bus station, these tastefully simple but sensational-value chalets are the perfect place to relax.

Pousada Arvoredo
POUSADA $$

(☑ 3331-3479; www.arvoredo.tur.br; Av Abercio Ramos Qd 17 Lt 15; weekend s/d R$250/280, week s/d R$120/140; ❋ 🛜 ⁂) ✐ This excellent-value pousada is steeped in sustainable tourism (all the bricks were recycled from old homes in Goiânia) and features lovely verandas and large rooms full of natural handicrafts.

Pousada O Casarão
POUSADA $$

(☑ 3331-2662; www.ocasarao.pirenopolis.tur.br; Direita 79; s/d R$170/250; ❋ 🛜 ⁂) The building is late-19th-century colonial, but the interior is that of an exquisitely modern and tasteful country retreat. Spacious, stately and cheap at the price.

Pousada Rio das Almas
POUSADA $$

(☑ 3331-2744; www.pirenopolis.tur.br/pousadariodasalmas; Rua dos Pireneus 81; chalets for 2 people R$200, additional beds R$50; P ❋ 🛜) Go country in the town centre in these rustic chalets set in green gardens on the Rio das Almas. Tranquil, homely and great value for groups.

Pousada Cavalhadas
POUSADA $$

(☑ 3331-1261; www.pousadacavalhadas.com.br; Praça do Matriz 1; per person week/weekend R$80/100; ❋ 🛜) Facing the Igreja Matriz, this is a basic, conveniently located option that won't win any awards. Its about the best (and most secure) of the cheapies around the *praça*.

★ Villa do Comendador Eco-Resort
RESORT $$$

(☑ 3331-2424; www.villadocomendador.com.br; GO 431, Km 1; s/d R$225/250, bungalows s/d R$450/580; P ❋ @ 🛜 ⁂) ✐ Opened in 2007 and situated 1km outside town, this is the first pousada in Pirenópolis to be sanctioned by national environmental watch groups as truly eco. It offers pools, playgrounds, horseback riding, volleyball and outstanding cerrado views. A haven for kids!

Taman Baru
BUNGALOWS $$$

(☑ 3331-3880; www.tamanbaru.com.br; Estrada dos Pireneus, Km 2; s/d apt R$270/370, bungalows R$360/410; P ❋ @ 🛜 ⁂) A romantic retreat with the occasional Balinese touch set inside a forest, located just east of town. The colorful bungalows and gorgeous infinity pool both offer outstanding views across the cerrado.

🍴 Eating & Drinking

Rua do Rosário, aka Rua do Lazer, is the main restaurant-cafe strip and turns into a pedestrianized free-for-all of outdoor tables and lively city dwellers on weekends. Cheaper buffet-type restaurants are mainly along Rua da Aurora. Most restaurants close on Monday, and some only open on weekends.

CAFÉ COLONIAL: THE FOOD OF THE TROPEIROS

After the *bandeirantes* swept Goiás clean of its gold, the *tropeiros* (the famed muleteers of Brazil) followed in their path, conquering the region and bringing slaves from Brazil's coast. Food was scarce en route, so the *tropeiros* adapted various foods from Afro-Brazilian, Portuguese and indigenous cultures to allow for the lengthy journey without refrigeration.

This long-lost subculture of Brazilian cuisine has been resurrected at **Fazenda Babilônia** (☑ 3331-1226; GO 431A, Km 24; ⊙ 8am-5pm Sat & Sun), a sugar plantation established in 1800 and *fazenda* (farm) on the Patrimonial Nacional (National Heritage) register since 1965. Every weekend this restored *fazenda*, 24km southwest of Pirenópolis, breaks out the historical gastronomy for a fascinating breakfast called **Café Colonial**. Hearty meats, cheeses and pastries highlight the near-endless options. *Carne de porco* (a succulent pork dish stored in its own fat for conservation), *mané pelado* (a sweet cake of grated manioc, eggs, cheese and coconut milk) and *matula galinha* (chicken with saffron, eggs, aromatic peppers and toasted corn wrapped in a corn husk) highlight an absolutely thrilling banquet that includes some 28 dishes that you're likely to have never seen before. The whole thing costs just R$25, including a fascinating tour of the *fazenda* itself.

★**Pireneus Café** CAFE $
(☑3331-3047; www.pireneuscafe.com.br; Rua dos Pireneus 41; sandwiches R$18-25) A sophisticated spot overlooking Praça do Coreto for life-changing grilled focaccia sandwiches and first-rate coffee.

Boca do Forno PIZZERIA $$
(☑3331-1790; Travessa Santa Cruz s/n; pizza R$28-47, rodízio R$20; ☺6pm-midnight Tue-Sun) The owner of this cozy pizzeria is from Brazil's pizza capital, São Paulo. If that means nothing to you, it will once you try the pizza. Wednesday's pizza *rodízio* (all you can eat) is a real treat.

Nori JAPANESE $$
(☑3331-1645; do Rosário 30; sushi R$10-15, mains R$20-28) Super sushi in a tent-like interior.

Restaurante Nena BUFFET $$
(☑3331-1470; Rua da Aurora 4; buffet R$25; ☺noon-4pm Fri-Sun) One of the nicer buffets you'll come across, with great regional food and a varied selection of salads. Get in early before the offerings are picked thin.

Bacalhau da Bibba SEAFOOD $$$
(☑3331-2103; Rua do Rosário 42; dishes for 2 people R$50; ☺10am-3pm & 7-11pm Fri & Sat, 10am-3pm Sun) Oh my cod! A restaurant that serves nothing but *bacalhau*! That's not the only thing that's slightly surreal about this place either. It doubles as an antiques shop!

🍷 **Drinking**

A Confraría do Boxea PUB
(☑3331-1518; Rua do Rosário 38; beer R$5-26; ☺from 5pm Tue-Thu, from noon Fri-Sun) If beer is your poison then you could spend a few nights working through the 35 types on the menu.

Seo Rosa Cachaçaria BAR
(☑3331-2046; Rua do Rosário 17; cachaça R$4-37; ☺from 4pm Sun-Thu, from 11am Fri & Sat) More than 300 different *cachaças* to choose from.

🛍 **Shopping**

Ruas Aurora and Rosário and Rui Barbosa are lined with places selling commercialized handicrafts from the region – everything from silver and ceramic pots to colorful cloths and statues of slaves. If you are looking for something more unique, then it's worth visiting the artist workshops on the Circuito de Criação (pick up a leaflet from the CAT office).

Adobe Ceramicas CERAMICS
(☑3331-1084; Rua dos Pireneus 67) The adobe pottery in Cristina Galeão's studio makes it one of the more interesting workshops.

Rosane Régis JEWELRY
(☑3331-3148; 24 de Outubro 20) Intent on proving that all that glitters is not gold, Rosane Régis has been working silver from the region for a quarter of a century.

Claudia Azeredo FASHION
(☑3331-1328; www.claudiaazeredo.com.br; Direita 58) If fashion is more your scene, visit Claudia Azeredo and peruse her creatively dyed fabrics.

ℹ **Information**

Banco do Brasil (☑3331-1182; Sizenando Jayme 1; ☺11am-4pm Mon-Fri) Visa/MasterCard ATM.
Bradesco (Sizenando Jayme 5)
CAT Tourist Office (☑3331-2633; www.pirenopolis.com.br; Rua do Bonfim 14; ☺8am-6pm)
Hospital Nossa Senhora do Rosário (☑3331-3309; Av Neco Mendonça 38)
Arena LAN House (Sizenando Jayme; per hr R$3; ☺9am-midnight) Internet access.

ℹ **Getting There & Away**

The **bus station** (☑3331-1080; Av Neco Mendonça) is 500m northwest of Igreja Matriz. There are buses to Brasília (R$21, three hours), one to Goiânia (R$12.50, three hours), leaving at 9:15am, and Anápolis (R$5.75, 1½ hours), where you can also catch a connection to Goiânia. Getting around town is easily done on foot or by moto-taxi.

Caldas Novas

☑0XX64 / POP 70,500
Suffering from high blood pressure after Brasília? Poor digestion after your visit to a truck-stop cafe in Minas? Exhausted after your extended Carnaval in Salvador? Then Caldas Novas, with more than 30 curative hot springs, may be just the place for you. Now an upmarket resort, the town's population swells to around 200,000 during holidays.

🏊 **Activities**

Nearly everyone in Caldas Novas has a thermal pool to cure what ails ya, but not all of them are open to the public. Besides the hotels and pousadas, there are a few good options in and around the city for day-use only. Working your way from the city center out, **SESC Caldas Novas** (s R$138-156, d R$188-216, tr R$258-29; ☺8am-8pm Mon-Sun) is the most conveniently located and favorably priced. The 11 thermal pools in the SESC complex are well maintained and within walking distance of Praça Matriz. A little further out is **di Roma Acqua Park** (☑3455 9393; Rua São Cristóvão 1110; ☺7am-5pm Mon-Sun), an all-out aquatic extravaganza featuring the world's first thermal wave pool, waterslides, lazy river, restaurants and numerous therapeutic waters.

🛏 Sleeping & Eating

During holidays and long weekends the town is packed, so reservations are advisable. Chain hotels dominate and rooms in all categories tend to be nearly identical – pick based on hot-springs action – and expect to break your budget in high season. It can be hard to find somewhere good to eat; most people eat at their hotels.

Hotel Parque das Primaveras   RESORT $$$
(☑3453-1355; www.hpprimaveras.com.br; Rua do Balneário 1; s/d R$405/625; P ❈ @ 🛜 🐾) Feisty macaws roam the jungly grounds at this lush pousada, the top digs in town. The four thermal pools feel more private than others.

Thermas di Roma   RESORT $$$
(☑3453-9393; www.diroma.com.br; Av Santo Amaro 1800; r R$678; P ❈ @ 🛜 🐾) A recently renovated megaresort a few kilometers out of town, di Roma has nine thermal pools and lots of action for kids (including a zip line!).

SESC Caldas Novas   RESORT $$
(www.sescgo.com.br; Av Ministro Elias Bufaiçal 600; s/d R$172/198; P ❈ @ 🛜 🐾) A large recreation area with 11 thermal pools. One of the best deals in town, but bookings must be made through the website.

Hotel Roma   HOTEL $$
(☑3453-1335; www.diroma.com.br; Praça Mestre Orlando 368; r R$345; ❈ 🛜 🐾) The six thermal pools, whirlpool and massive sauna skew a bit toward *On Golden Pond,* but the location on the main square is hard to beat.

Dodýs   GOIANA $$
(☑3454-5127; Praça Mestre Orlando; mains R$20-43; ☺noon-3pm & 7-11:30pm Tue-Sun) Dishes with a cerrado flavour, this is a reasonably priced and conveniently located place to pick a peck of pickled *pequis.*

Panneteria Famiglia Amoroso   PIZZERIA $$
(☑3453-6623; Rua Turismo Qd 4; pizzas R$25-42; ☺7-11pm Sun-Thu, to midnight Fri & Sat) This small bakery boasts 91 varieties of pizza cooked in a wood-fired oven.

ℹ Information

Banco do Brasil (☑3453-1186; Capitan João Crisóstomo 325) Visa/MasterCard ATM.

CAT Tourist Office (☑3454-3564; www.caldasnovas.com.br; Praça Mestre Orlando; ☺8am-6pm) Located on the main square, it can help with accommodations and hot-springs info. There is another small office at the bus station.

Post Office (☑3455-4107; Capitan João Crisóstomo 361)

ℹ Getting There & Away

The bus station is at the end of Rua Antônio Coelho de Godoy. In the high season buses run to São Paulo (R$130 to R$180), but at other times you'll need to travel through Goiânia (R$27, three hours).

Parque Nacional da Chapada dos Veadeiros

This spectacular national park in the highest area of the Central West showcases the unique landscape and flora of high-altitude cerrado across 650 sq km of pristine beauty.

With high waterfalls, raging canyons, natural swimming pools and oasis-like stands of wine palms, the park is a popular destination for ecotourists. In fact, the whole area is beautiful, with its big skies, exotic flora and dramatic hills rising up like waves breaking across the plains.

The sublime landscape, much of it based on quartz crystal and multihued sandstone, has also attracted New Agers who have established alternative communities and a burgeoning *esoturismo* industry in the area. It is also noticeably well maintained – you won't find a Skol beer can within miles.

Travelers visiting the park base themselves in one of two nearby towns: **Alto Paraíso de Goiás**, 38km from the park; or tiny **São Jorge**, 2km from the entrance. The best time to visit the park is between April and October, before the rivers flood during the rainy season and access becomes very slippery. You'll need two days to see the main attractions.

⊙ Sights & Activities

All visitors to the park (☎ 3455-1114; www.
chapadadosveadeiros.com; admission R$3; ☺ 8am-
6pm Tue-Sun, entry until noon only) must be accompanied by an accredited guide. Private
guides can be organized at the visitors' center,
through the local guide association, ACV-CV,
or at hotels in Alto Paraíso or São Jorge.

The guides run half-day tours (R$100) to
the park's three main attractions – *canions*
(canyons) and *cariocas* (rocks), which are
usually combined as they traverse the same
trail in the park, and *cachoeiras* (waterfalls).
The tours are included in the price of the
guide and can be divided by up to 10 people.

The **canions-cariocas tour** weaves along
the Rio Preto, which runs through the middle of the park. The river has cut two large
canyons (imaginatively named Canyon I and
Canyon II) through sandstone, with sheer,
20m-high walls on either side. It's a spectacular sight. There are natural platforms for
diving into the cold water at the bottom of
the rushing river. Canyon I is usually flooded
from September to May and inaccessible.
The **cariocas** (named for two girls from Rio
who went missing here in the '80s) picks
up at the end of the river valley on the trail
from Canyon II and leads to interesting rock
formations and a huge cascading waterfall.

The more difficult (and rewarding) **cachoeiras tour** takes in Salto do Rio Preto
I and II, two spectacular waterfalls (80m
and 120m, respectively) that cascade to the
ground just 30m apart. The falls are set in a
picturesque valley at the end of a trail that
weaves through a classic cerrado landscape
of meadows and gallery forests. There is a
small lake for swimming under II, where the
sun creates a dazzling celestial effect under
the water. Take loads of water and sunscreen; it's about a 6km ascent all the way
back and the sun can be brutal.

Vale da Lua   VALLEY
(Moon Valley; admission R$10; ☺ 7am-5:30pm)
A unique sight in the Chapada dos Veadeiros area is the Vale da Lua. Over millions
of years, the rushing waters of the Rio São
Miguel have sculpted rock formations into
a lunar landscape. An ethereal metacon-
glomerate of rocks containing quartz, sand
and clay reflect a rainbow of colours and the
chilly emerald waters add to the otherworldly atmosphere.

Vale da Lua is outside the national park,
so you don't need a guide, but flash floods

RIO QUENTE

The aquatic playground of **Rio
Quente**, 22km from Caldas Novas,
is home to the world's only thermal-
water river and enough water-themed
entertainment to ensure you'd rather
drown by the time it's all over. **Hot
Park** (☎ 3512-8040; www.hotpark.com;
adult/child R$105/79; ☺ 9:30am-5pm,
closed Thu in low season) is the epicenter of the fun, a sort of waterlogged
Disney World for bronzed Brazilian
beauties. Its 22,000 sq meters of
slippery amusement include a R$2.5-
million mega half-pipe imported from
Canada, the only one of its kind in
Latin America.

occur during the rainy season, so either get
one or check with locals before you head
off. Walk out on the road to Alto Paraíso
and take the first unmarked trail on the
right – from there it's a 4km hike (there
may not be a sign, as some guides remove
them to enslave you to their services). If
you miss this, it will be an 11km jaunt on
the main road. Take sunscreen and water
with you.

Alto Paraíso de Goiás

☎ 0XX61 / POP 7000

Crystals, dreadlocks and dirty feet are ubiquitous in Alto Paraíso, 38km from the park.
It is one of Brazil's kookiest towns, but besides unleashing your inner hippy, crystal
shopping or planning your trip to Chapada
dos Veadeiros, there is not much else to do
here except chill your boots.

⤢ Tours

Though most travelers stay in the village
of São Jorge, it is in fact easier (if ever so
slightly more expensive) to arrange visits to
Chapada dos Veadeiros in Alto Paraíso.

Travessia Ecoturismo   ADVENTURE TOUR
(☎ 3446-1595; www.travessia.tur.br; Av Ari Valadão
Filho 979; ☺ 8am-7pm Mon-Fri, 9am-2pm Sat & Sun)
An excellent eco-agency on the main road
in Alto Paraíso that can arrange everything
in Chapada, including more adventurous
canyoning and rappelling trips. Prices include transportation and English-speaking
guides.

UNIQUE CERRADO

Calling cerrado 'the South American savanna' is to oversimplify an extremely complex and varied ecosystem. True, it may look like bushy grassland for part of the year, but visit at the right time and it is converted into an immense flower garden of breathtaking scale and beauty. Nor is it strictly even grassland, in fact in some areas it is a type of forest. Confused? Let us explain!

Cerrado can be classified into four distinct types, each of which mesh together to form a mosaic of savanna-like habitat. *Cerradão* is dry cerrado forest, either in solid blocks or in small forest islands; *campo limpo* (clean field) consists entirely of grass; *cerrado sensu stricto* is composed of low, bushy vegetation with no grass at all; and *campo sujo* (dirty field) is a mix of all the other types into one. The different types are quite easily distinguishable to the naked eye even to non-specialists, but when you consider that the plant species that make up each of these broad classifications may differ dramatically from one area to the next, you begin to get an idea of the immense biodiversity that the cerrado harbors. In fact, of the 10,000 or more species of plants found in the cerrado, 44% are found nowhere else in the world.

But it's not just the plants that make the cerrado so important for conservation. Besides providing a home for some of Brazil's most spectacular and threatened mammal species such as the maned wolf, giant armadillo, pampas deer and giant anteater, it also protects a number of highly threatened and localized birds, such as the white-winged nightjar, dwarf tinamou, lesser nothura and the gorgeous yellow-billed blue finch, all of which depend on this unique habitat for their continued survival.

Sadly, that struggle for survival is getting harder with every passing year. Since the 1970s, vast tracts of native cerrado vegetation have been converted to soybean, rice, corn, wheat and cattle production – only 20% of the original vegetation is left. The rate of habitat loss makes it one of the world's fastest disappearing eco-regions, and the destruction shows no sign of abating.

Though the natural vegetation of most of Goiás state is cerrado, Parque Nacional Chapada das Guiamaraes and Parque Nacional da Chapada dos Veadeiros showcase it in dramatically beautiful surroundings, with the picturesque habitat framed against a stunning backdrop of rocky mountainsides and craggy cliffs.

🛏 Sleeping & Eating

Alto Paraíso has a wide range of accommodations, with several good options to rest and refuel here. Prices rise by 30% or more at weekends and in high season.

Pousada Veadeiros POUSADA $
(☑ 3446-1820; das Nascentes 129; s/d R$80/100; @) Cool kitschy little cabins not far from the bus station, each named after a native bird and decorated in its colors (you'll need a bit of imagination to associate the bird with some of them!). To get there, take the first right after the CAT (p357) office; if you pass a building that looks like King Arthur's castle then you are nearly there.

Pousada Camelot Inn RESORT $$
(☑ 3446-1581; www.pousadacamelot.com.br; GO 118 , Km 168; r/ste R$143/273; P ❄ @ 🌐 ⚊) Continuing the medieval theme, this replica castle is one you can actually stay in. In fact, it's more of a resort, with 20 hectares of gardens, themed suites, a sauna, outdoor pools and even a helipad! Try the Merlin Suite and see if it works its magic on you. It's at the entrance to town.

Oca Lila SELF SERVE $$
(☑ 3446-1006; Av João Bernardes Rabelo 449; lunch per kilo R$30, meals R$18-30; ⊙ noon-midnight, closed Tue; ☑) The all-natural vegetarian lunch-per-kilo place is highly recommended. Oca Lila turns à la carte for dinner (with excellent pizza) and there's a bit of *vida nocturna* in the evenings.

ℹ Information

Banco do Brasil (Av Ari Valadão Filho 690; ⊙10am-3pm Mon-Fri) Visa/MasterCard ATM.
CAT Tourist Office (☑ 3446-1159; www.altoparaiso.go.gov.br; Av Ari Valadão Filho s/n; ⊙8am-6pm) On the main street, 200m from the bus station. Helpful, but light on printed material.

ℹ Getting There & Away

From Goiânia there's a morning Empresa São José bus to Alto Paraíso (R$71, seven hours), with two daily buses doing the reverse leg on Monday, Wednesday and Friday.

Two daily buses leave platform E7 in the local bus station in Brasília for Alto Paraíso (R$30, 4½ hours, 7:15am and 1:30pm). The 1:30pm departure continues on to São Jorge, passing through Alto Paraíso around 6pm (R$9, one hour), but it can be pretty flexible in its arrival time so it pays to get there early. Returns to Brasília leave at 8:30am and 4:30pm.

São Jorge

⚐ 0XX61 / POP 1200

With sandy streets and a laid-back vibe, the former crystal-mining hamlet of São Jorge (2km from the national-park entrance) has the feel of a beach town, despite its inland location. Though logistically Alto Paraíso is more convenient for arranging trips to Parque Nacional da Chapada dos Veadeiros, many travelers prefer to stay in São Jorge because it is prettier, closer to the park and has more of a village atmosphere.

🛏 Sleeping & Eating

Quality pousadas are plentiful and usually very fairly priced, though prices rise considerably at weekends. Camping starts from around R$20 per person, with shady **Camping Taiuá** (☎9822-9666; per person R$20) at the entrance to town about the best of several similar options.

Pousada Flor do Cerrado POUSADA $
(☎3455-1059; s/d R$75/85; ❄❀) Small, cozy and the best of the cheaper options in town, with all wood furniture, earthy decoration and hammocks for lounging in the shade. You could be forgiven for feeling like you are robbing the owners at this price!

Pousada Bambu Brasil POUSADA $$
(☎3455-1004; www.bambubrasil.com.br; Rua 1 Quadra 1; week/weekend r R$140/190; ❂❀@ ❁❀) Great value for couples, this charming pousada with hand-painted furniture and poolside hammocks is a stylish place to relax. Children under 12 are not admitted.

★ **Baguá Pousada** POUSADA $$$
(☎3455-1046; www.baguapousada.com.br; Rua 1 Qd 16; bungalows R$420; ❂❀@❁❀) ⬤ Massive (82 sq meters!), breathtakingly classy bungalows at this designer eco-pousada have raised the bar on sophistication in Goiás, while safari-chic lounge furnishings in the common area should suit Brazil's fashion *cognoscenti*. It's closest to the park's entrance as well.

Lua de São Jorge PIZZERIA $$
(☎3455-1054; Rua 1 Qd 1; pizzas R$22-46; ⊙from 6pm Thu-Sun) Intensely researched conclusion: the best of the numerous wood-fired pizzerias in town.

ℹ Information

CAT Tourist Office (☎3455-1090; ⊙8am-6pm) There is a small tourist desk at the bus station at the entrance to town that can help you find a guide.

ℹ Getting There & Away

São Jorge has a tiny bus station at the entrance to town, but it doesn't really need one. There is a 1:30pm bus daily from platform E7 in the local bus station in Brasília to São Jorge (R$39, 5½ hours) via Alto Paraíso. The bus returns at 7am daily, leaving from the main street. Private transport to and from Alto Paraíso costs from R$120.

BRASÍLIA & GOIÁS SÃO JORGE

Mato Grosso & Mato Grosso do Sul

POP 5.5 MILLION

Best Places to Eat

➡ Avalom Grill (p385)

➡ Cantina Romana (p381)

➡ Pantanal Grill (p390)

➡ A Casa do João (p390)

➡ Da Mata Bistro (p366)

Best Places to Stay

➡ Pousada do Parque Eco Lodge (p366)

➡ Cristalino Jungle Lodge (p368)

➡ Pousada Araras Eco Lodge (p377)

➡ Bonito HI Hostel (p389)

➡ Turis Hotel (p379)

Why Go?

Mato Grosso was once Brazil's wild west, a land known only to explorers, indigenous hunters, poachers, gold seekers and naturalists. Today, some of Brazil's most cooperative wildlife and incredible scenery make it a prime destination for eco-tourists and anglers.

Though the Amazon has the glamor, it is the Pantanal that shines as Brazil's top destination for wildlife-viewing and bird-watching. One of the most important and fragile ecosystems on the planet it is home to an impressive concentration of spectacular animals. Cuiabá, Corumbá and Campo Grande are all gateways to this celebrated wetland, but the region's offerings certainly don't stop there.

In the far-north town of Alta Floresta, the cerrado (savanna) morphs into the Amazon; the Serra do Bodoquena near Bonito, is a breathtakingly beautiful, watery wonderland and, between the two, Parque Nacional da Chapada dos Guimarães boasts some of the most commanding views in Brazil.

When to Go
The Pantanal

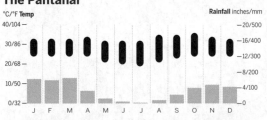

Feb Carnaval time in Corumbá; the biggest in the region.

Jun–Aug Top time for jaguar tours in the Pantanal.

Nov–Jan When Bonito is at its hottest and the water most inviting.

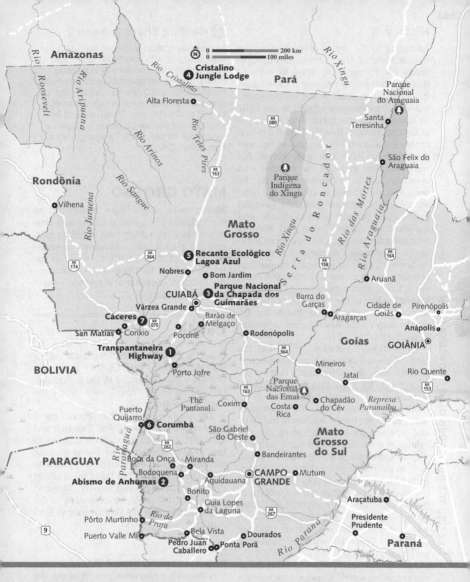

Mato Grosso & Mato Grosso do Sul Highlights

1 Gawk at incredible wildlife while driving the 145km **Transpantaneira 'highway'** (p375) in the northern Pantanal.

2 Journey to the centre of the earth at the **Abismo de Anhumas** (p388) near Bonito.

3 Watch the sunset over dramatic landscapes in **Parque Nacional da Chapada dos Guimarães** (p367).

4 Go bird bonkers at the twitcher's paradise **Cristalino Jungle Lodge** (p368) in the southern Amazon rainforest.

5 Snorkel with exotic fish in the crystal-clear water world at **Recanto Ecológico Lagoa Azul** (p368).

6 Dance in the streets in **Corumbá** (p383) during Carnaval, Mato Grosso style.

7 Sling a hook and hope for the best during the International Fishing Festival at **Cáceres** (p369).

History

According to the Treaty of Tordesillas, the remote state of Mato Grosso belonged to Spain, not Portugal. For years its exploration was limited to occasional expeditions by adventurers and Jesuit missionaries, but with the discovery of gold in the early 18th century, it was invaded by thousands of fortune hunters. Reaching Cuiabá meant crossing the lands of several indigenous groups, many of whom were formidable warriors. They included the *caiapó* (who even attacked the settlement at Goiás), the *bororo* of the Pantanal, the *parecis* (who were enslaved to mine gold), the *paiaguá* (who caused periodic panic in Cuiabá) and the *guaicuru* (skilled riders and warriors who gained many years of experience fighting the Europeans). As the gold rush tailed off however, Mato Grosso again slipped into obscurity and isolation, its inhabitants eking out a living from subsistence farming and fishing. As late as the 19th century, the only access to Mato Grosso from Rio de Janeiro was by ship via the Rio Paraguai, a journey of several weeks.

Mato Grosso's isolation helped fuel the birth of several separatist movements but, with the coming of the republic in 1889, the telegraph in the early 20th century and the opening of a few rough roads, it slowly reconnected with the world. The government policy of developing the interior in the 1940s and '50s and the construction of the new capital Brasília in 1960 brought waves of migrants from the Northeast and the South back to the region, participating in an agricultural boom that continues today. In 1979 the massive area of Mato Grosso was cut in half, creating the new state of Mato Grosso do Sul. Agriculture pays the bills in both states, with huge cattle, sugarcane, and soy plantations peppering whatever landscape isn't legally protected.

Mato Grosso is still home to many indigenous groups, several living as they have for centuries. The *erikbatsa*, noted for their fine featherwork, live near Fontanilles and Juina; the *nhambikuraa* are near Padroal; and the *cayabi* live near Juara. There are also the indigenous *cinta larga* of Parque Indígena Aripuanã and the tribes under the care of Fundação Nacional do Indio (Funai) in the Parque Indígena do Xingu, which was set up in the 1950s as a safe haven for several indigenous groups.

ⓘ Getting There & Away

The gateway cities to the region are Cuiabá and Campo Grande, with daily flights to Rio, São Paulo and Brasília. The majority of travelers coming from Bolivia take the scenic train journey from Santa Cruz to Quijarro and cross into the Brazilian town of Corumbá, which is connected by road to all points east. Mato Grosso do Sul also borders Paraguay to the south. There are regular bus services to the Paraguayan border from Campo Grande.

MATO GROSSO

Mato Grosso means 'thick forest.' Part of the highland plain that runs through Brazil's interior, it's a dusty land of rolling hills, endless plantations, abundant savannas and some of the best fishing rivers in the world. Three of Brazil's major ecosystems – the Pantanal, Amazon and cerrado – meet within its borders.

Cuiabá

☑ 0XX65 / POP 551,000

Cuiabá is a boomtown basking in the relentless Mato Grosso sun. The city is actually two sister cities separated by the Rio Cuiabá: Old Cuiabá and Várzea Grande (where the airport is located).

The town's name is an indigenous *bororo* word meaning 'arrow-fishing', though it was first gold and later agriculture that led to the city becoming one of the fastest-growing capitals in Brazil over the last 30 years. The population explosion has tailed off in recent times, but Cuiabá is still a lively place and a good starting point for excursions to the Pantanal, Chapada dos Guimarães and Bom Jardim.

History

In 1719 a Paulista, Pascoal Moreira Cabral, was hunting indigenous groups along the Rio Cuiabá when he found gold. A gold rush followed, but many of those seeking gold never reached the new settlement at Cuiabá. Traveling more than 3000km from São Paulo by river took five months; along the way, gold seekers found little food, many mosquitoes, dangerous rapids, lengthy portages, disease and incredible heat.

With the end of the gold boom and the decay of the mines, Cuiabá would have disappeared, except that the soil along the

Rio Cuiabá allowed subsistence agriculture, while the river itself provided fish.

By 1835 the town was the capital of Mato Grosso but, apart from a brief resurgence as a staging point for the war against Paraguay in the 1860s, it remained a backwater. Today, thanks mostly to the construction of Brasília and a massive agri-economy, Cuiabá has finally been propelled into the modern world. Cuiabá will be a host city for the 2014 FIFA World Cup.

◉ Sights

Museu Histórico
de Mato Grosso   MUSEUM
(☑ 3613-9234; museuhistoricodemt.blogspot.com; Praça da República 131; ☉ 8am-8pm Tue-Fri, 8am-3pm Sat) **FREE** Inside a restored colonial building, the museum is an interesting stroll through the state's history. Each room represents a different period and houses extensive collections of silver, military paraphernalia, and other historical odds and ends. Much of the history is illustrated in vibrant paintings by local artist Moacyr Freitas.

Some artistic license is involved though, for example in the *Destrução do Quilombo do Piolho*, where a North American bald eagle soars over the weary yet bemused slaves.

Museu Rondon   MUSEUM
(☑ 3615-8489; Av Fernando Correia da Costa; ☉ 7:30-11:30am & 1:30-5:30pm Tue-Sat, 9am-5:30pm Sun, 1:30-5:30pm Mon, zoo Tue-Sun) **FREE** The small Museu Rondon has exhibits on indigenous culture and is well worth a visit to check out the ornate headdresses and vicious weaponry. It is on the grounds of the Federal University of Mato Grosso (UFMT), which also has a small **zoo**.

To get there, catch a 103 Jd Universitário bus (R$1.85) on Av Tenente Coronel Duarte. Once you hit campus, the museum is behind the Aquatic Park and the zoo is directly across campus in the opposite direction. If you are there as the sun sets, hang around to watch the arrival of the flocks of herons and egrets that roost nearby.

Museu do Morro
da Caixa D´Agua Velha   MUSEUM
(☑ 3617-1274; Comandante Costa; ☉ 8am-noon & 1-5pm Mon-Fri) **FREE** Probably the city's oddest museum is the Museu do Morro da Caixa D´Agua Velha, which brings together a variety of frankly weird water-themed trinkets, from old tubes to shower heads. Far more interesting than the display is the construc-

tion itself, the city's former water tank dating from 1882 and built in the style of a Roman aqueduct.

Centro Geodésico
da America do Sul   MONUMENT
(Barão de Melgaço) An obelisk marks the Centro Geodésico da America do Sul, one of the exact centers of the continent according to the locals. There is of course only one real exact centre of South America, but inhabitants of Chapada dos Guimarães claim that it actually resides there. If you care enough to find out who is right, check Google Earth!

Mercado do Porto   MARKET
(☑ 3313-3332; ☉ 6am-6pm Mon-Sat, to noon Sun) Close to the municipal aquarium, the Mercado do Porto houses the fish market, with a variety of species, as well as a vegetable and spice market. It's a good place to check out what the region's fish look like before they arrive at your table.

☞ Tours

Cuiabá is an access town for the Transpantaneira road, Parque Nacional Chapada dos Guimarães and the aquatic attractions in the area around Bom Jardim. City tour operators invariably offer trips to all these places, see the Pantanal section, p373.

✯✯ Festivals

The **Festa de São Benedito** takes place during the first week of July at the Igreja NS do Rosário and the Capela de São Benedito. The holiday has a more Umbanda (white magic) than Catholic flavor; it's celebrated with colorful, traditional dances and regional foods such as *bolos de queijo* (cheese balls) and *bolos de arroz* (rice balls).

🛏 Sleeping

You may well be a bit disappointed by the accommodation options in Cuiabá, but on the bright side prices can be pretty reasonable. Reductions are common during the week and out of season (November to May).

Hostel Ecoverde   HOSTEL $
(☑ 3624-1386; www.ecoverdetours.com.br; Celestino 391; s/d without bathroom R$40/60; 🖝) A rustic pousada (guesthouse) in a 100-year-old colonial house with bags of character. Owner and local wildlife expert Joel Souza of Ecoverde Tours is one of the founders of ecotourism in the area and his quaint hostel is full of antique radios and books on the Pantanal.

Central Cuiabá

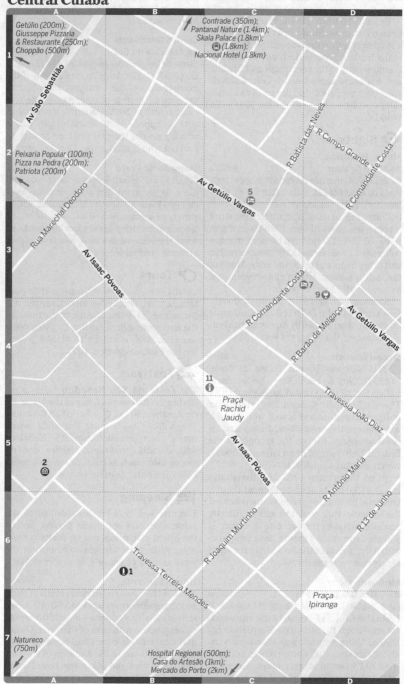

MATO GROSSO & MATO GROSSO DO SUL CUIABÁ

Getúlio (200m);
Giusseppe Pizzaria
& Restaurante (250m);
Choppão (500m)

Confrade (350m);
Pantanal Nature (1.4km);
Skala Palace (1.8km);
(1.8km);
Nacional Hotel (1.8km)

Peixaria Popular (100m);
Pizza na Pedra (200m);
Patriota (200m)

Av São Sebastião

R Batista das Neves

R Campo Grande

R Comandante Costa

Av Getúlio Vargas

Rua Marechal Deodoro

Av Isaac Póvoas

R Comandante Costa

R Barão de Melgaço

Av Getúlio Vargas

Travessia João Diaz

Praça
Rachid
Jaudy

Av Isaac Póvoas

R Antônio Maria

R 13 de Junho

R Joaquim Murtinho

Travessa Terreira Mendes

Praça
Ipiranga

Natureco
(750m)

Hospital Regional (500m);
Casa do Artesão (1km);
Mercado do Porto (2km)

0 ——— 200 m
0 ——— 0.1 miles

Central Cuiabá

There's also a small courtyard and garden, plus a washing machine and kitchen for guest use.

Skala Palace HOTEL **$**
(☎ 3621-3067; Av. Jules Rimet 26; s/d R$80/120; ❄ 🛜) Freshly revamped, bumping it up several notches in the style index, Skala Palace is the best bet of the row of hotels opposite the bus station, and ideal for a late arrival or early getaway

Gran Odara Hotel LUXURY HOTEL **$$**
(☎ 3616-2014; www.hotelgranodara.com.br; Av Miguel Sutil 8344, Ribeirão da Ponte; s/d R$242/340; P ❄ @ 🛜) With its exquisite reception area the Gran Odara makes an impact as soon as you walk in, and the tasteful rooms are along the same lines. Probably the best value in the city in this price range, but a little removed from the centre.

Amazon Plaza Hotel HOTEL **$$$**
(☎ 2121-2000; www.hotelamazon.com.br; Av Getúlio Vargas 600; s/d/tr R$315/435/493; P ❄ @ 🛜 ⛱) Jungle-themed four-star option with extra-large rooms and a kitschy pool area featuring jumbo-sized plastic coconuts. Just like the real Amazon!

Hotel Mato Grosso
HOTEL $$

(☏3614-7777; www.hotelmt.com.br; Costa 643; s/d/tr R$105/125/169; ⓟ✳🖙) For basic comfort in a central location, the simple but clean rooms here are good value for your real.

✖ Eating

The center is almost deserted at night, but there are good restaurants nearby on Av Getúlio Vargas.

Mistura Cuiabana
SELF-SERVE $

(☏3624-1127; Pedro Celestino; per kg R$21.50; ⊘11am-2:30pm Mon-Fri) An excellent buffet of regional selections for lunch (the fried bananas are divine). It's inside the orange colonial building on the corner.

Giusseppe Pizzaria & Restaurante
SELF-SERVE, PIZZERIA $$

(☏3027-3055; Praça Santos Dumont 59; lunch buffet per kg R$39, pizza R$29-41; ⊘11am-11pm) Bursting at the seams with local businessmen at lunch time because of its hugely varied and excellent value lunch buffet. Smiling, well-fed locals are always a good sign.

Choppão
BOTECO $$

(www.choppao.com.br; Praça 8 de Abril; mains for 2 R$50-80) Occupying an entire junction, this Cuiabá institution offers huge portions of meat and fish for two, all chased with frigid *chope* (draft beer) in specially iced tankards.

Getúlio
SELF-SERVE $$

(☏3624-9992; www.getuliogrill.com.br; Av Getúlio Vargas 1147; meals for 2 R$32-55; ⊘11am-2:30pm & from 5pm Tue-Sun) An upmarket bar and restaurant popular with young *cuiabános*. There's a respectable wine list, and DJs on the outdoor patio every night. On Saturday, the party moves upstairs for dancing.

Pizza na Pedra
PIZZERIA $$

(☏3622-0060; Praça Eurico Gaspar Dutra 45; pizza R$29-89; ⊘6pm-midnight Tue-Sun) A lively pizzeria right on 'Praça Popular'. It does an excellent pizza *rodízio* (all you can eat) on Tuesday and Thursday for R$28. Save room for the ridiculous sweet pizzas.

Peixaria Popular
SEAFOOD $$$

(☏3322- 5471; Av São Sebastião 2324; prix-fixe meals R$60; ⊘11am-3pm & 7pm-midnight Mon-Fri, 11am-5pm Sat & Sun) The lunch course for one will feed you plus a horse. It comes with three types of regional fish dishes and all the accompaniments. A must.

 ## Drinking & Nightlife

There are two main nightlife clusters in town, around the lovely Praça Popular (aka Praça Eurico Gaspar Dutra) and along Av Getúlio Vargas.

Tom Choppin
BAR

(☏3627-7227; www.tomchoppin.com.br; Rua das Laranjeiras 701; ⊘5pm-late Mon-Sat) Outstanding brews and views are the draw for Cuiabá's well-to-do at this cleverly named open-air MPB (Música Popular Brasileira) bar perched high above the city. Mondays get lively for *choro*, an informal, instrumental style of music. It's halfway between *centro* and the zoo.

Confrade
BREWERY

(☏3027-2000; www.confrade.com.br; Av Mato Grosso 1000; ⊘5pm-late; 🚻) A massive micro-brewery that offers *chope* laced with caramel, mint and syrup in addition to the usual suspects. Stick to the standards. There's live MPB every night of the week and even a play space for kids!

Bar Presidente
BAR

(☏3613-8500; Av Getúlio Vargas; ⊘8am-11pm Mon-Sat) A good central location for a few beers in none-too-shabby surroundings.

Conde de Azambuja
BAR

(Praça da Mandioca; ⊘7pm-late) If pretensions aren't your bag but drunk, dancing Brazilians are, then give this traditional bar in the old town a try. It's not easy on the eye, but let the Skols flow and you may find yourself having more fun than you expected. Live music from Thursday to Sunday.

🔒 Shopping

Casa do Artesão
ARTS & CRAFTS

(☏3611-0500; Rua 13 de Junho 315; ⊘8:30am-5:30pm Mon-Fri, to 1:30pm Sat) Seven themed rooms full of Mato Grosso handicrafts and sweets, including ceramics, woodcarvings, straw baskets and *pequi* créme liquor.

ℹ Information

EMERGENCY
Ambulance (☏192)
Fire Department (☏193)
Police (☏190)

MEDICAL SERVICES
Hospital Geral (☏3624-5284; 13 de Junho cnr Thogo da Silva Pereira)

MONEY

There are ATMs (open until 10pm) outside the airport for Visa/MasterCard withdrawals.

Banco do Brasil (Av Getúlio Vargas 915; ⊙11am-4pm Mon-Fri)

HSBC (Av Getúlio Vargas 346)

POST

Post Office (Praça da República 101; ⊙9am-5pm Mon-Fri, 8am-noon Sat)

TOURIST INFORMATION

CAT Tourist Office (Praça Rachid Jaudy; ⊙8am-6pm Mon-Fri) Closed for a refurb at the time of writing, but there is a small tourist-information booth in the arrivals hall of the airport and at the bus station.

Sedtur (☑3613-9300; www.sedtur.mt.gov. br; Voluntários da Pátria 118; ⊙2-6pm Mon-Fri) This office of the secretary of tourism has some helpful maps and brochures, but they are in Portuguese.

TRAVEL AGENCIES

Dreams (☑3027-5382; Av Isaac Póvoas 586) Helpful agency, west of downtown, for domestic and international flights.

❶ Getting There & Away

There are flights between Cuiabá and many airports in Brazil (with the notable omission of Corumbá in Mato Grosso do Sul) by **Gol** (☑0300-115-2121; www.voegol.com.br), **TAM** (☑3614-2555; www.tam.com.br), **Azul** (☑0800-884-4040; www.voeazul.com.br) and **Avianca Brasil** (☑4004-4040; www.avianca.

com.br). The latter and **Trip** (☑3682 2555; www.voetrip.com.br) fly to Alta Floresta.

Locally, frequent buses make the trip to Poconé (R$15, 2½ hours, six daily); the first leaves at 6am. For Chapada dos Guimarães (R$11, one hour) Expresso Rubi runs every hour from 6:30am; take an early bus if you're doing a day trip. For other destinations, see the table, below.

❶ Getting Around

Marechal Rondon airport (☑3614-2511) is in Várzea Grande, 7km from Cuiabá. Buses 24 and 55 (R$2.95) run from outside the Las Velas Hotel – turn left as you leave the airport and walk 100m to Av Getúlio Vargas. A taxi costs R$30. Buses back to the airport depart from Praça Ipiranga.

Cuiabá's **bus station** (☑3621 3629) is 3km north of the center on the highway towards Chapada dos Guimarães. From inside the bus station, you can get a Centro bus to Praça Alencastro (R$2.95). More frequent buses marked 'Centro' leave from outside the bus station and drop you along Av Isaac Póvoas; get off in front of the CAT office. A taxi from inside the bus station costs around R$20. Bus 7 runs between the airport and the bus station.

Referência (☑3682-6689; www.referencia. com.br) and **Localiza** (☑3682-7900; www. localiza.com.br) are a couple of reliable car rental companies with offices in the airport. The best car for the Pantanal is the Volkswagen Gol, but in the wet season (November to March) you'll need a 4x4 and off-road driving experience.

MATO GROSSO & MATO GROSSO DO SUL CUIABÁ

BUSES FROM CUIABÁ

DESTINATION	FARE (R$)	TIME (HR)	COMPANY
Alta Floresta	135-161	13½	Nova Integração (www.novaintegracao.com.br) Viagem Verde (www.viagemverde.com.br)
Brasília	140-169	15	Eucatur (www.eucatur.com.br), Expresso São Luiz (www.expressosaoluiz.com.br)
Cáceres	43-47	4	Eucatur (www.eucatur.com.br), Viagem Verde (www.viagemverde.com.br)
Campo Grande	82-102	11	Andorinha (www.andorinha.com), Eucatur (www.eucatur.com.br), Motta (www.motta.com.br), Nova Integração (www.novaintegracao.com.br), Viação São Luiz (www.viacaosaoluiz.com.br), Viação Ouro e Prata (www.viacaoouroeprata.com.br)
Goiânia	110-140	15	Eucatur (www.eucatur.com.br), Expresso São Luiz (www.expressosaoluiz.com.br)
Porto Velho	130-155	24	Eucatur (www.eucatur.com.br), Gontijo (www.gontijo.com.br), Rotas (www.nacionalexpresso.com.br)

Chapada dos Guimarães

⚑ 0XX65 / POP 17,800

The area around Chapada dos Guimarães is as little known as it is spectacular, reminiscent of the American Southwest and surprisingly different from the typical Mato Grosso terrain. The town is 800m above state capital Cuiabá and provides a cool and convenient base for exploring the surrounding areas. It is also home to one of the lushest central squares in Brazil.

The area surrounding the park has numerous attractions. On the way from Cuiabá to Chapada town, you pass **Rio dos Peixes**, **Rio Mutaca** and **Rio Claro**, which are popular weekend bathing spots for *cuiabános*; and three commanding valleys, **Vale do Salgadeira**, **Vale do Paciência** and **Vale do Rio Claro**. The sheer 80m drop called **Portão do Inferno** (Hell's Gate) is also unforgettable – it was formerly the town 'prison' in the early 1900s (use your imagination!).

In **Salgadeira**, 14km outside of Cuiabá, you can take a waterfall shower or grab a beer at one of the four restaurants that sit under the imposing cliffs. The whole thing is one long, drawn-out Kodak moment.

🛏 Sleeping & Eating

There is camping with good facilities at Salgadeira, just before the climb into the Chapada park. Otherwise Chapada town has plenty of accommodations.

Pousada Bom Jardim INN **$$**
(⚑ 3301-2668; www.pousadabomjardim.com.br; Praça Dom Wunibaldo; s/d with fan from R$75/100, d/tr with air-con from R$95/135; ❄ 🖥) There's no reason to spring for air-con at this cheapie right in the main square – the fans are high-octane. A favorite with backpackers.

Turismo Hotel HOTEL **$$**
(⚑ 3301-1176; www.hotelturismo.com.br; Fernando Corrêa da Costa 1065; s/d R$212/283; ❄ ☷) A spotless place run by a German family. The traditional breakfast spread is encased in glass – no flies!

★Pousada do Parque Eco Lodge LODGE **$$$**
(⚑ 3391-1346; www.pousadadoparque.com.br; Estrada do Parque Ecológico Km 52; s/d R$270/370; ❄ @ ☷) 🐾 This high-end eco-choice borders 150 hectares of newly preserved parkland and is the closest accommodations to the park's entrance (4.5km). All the wood used in the construction of this pousada came from recycled sources and the roofs are made of recycled milk cartons. Book in advance.

Pomodori ITALIAN, BRAZILIAN **$$**
(Caldas 60; mains R$22-32; ❂ from 4pm Mon-Fri, from noon Sat & Sun) Surely the cutest restaurant in the center, serving less than a handful of select Italian plates nightly and good stuffed pastries.

Felipe SELF-SERVE **$$**
(⚑ 3301-1860; Cipriano Curvo 596; meals per kg weekday/weekends R$30/33; ❂ noon-11pm) Fill your boots without emptying your pockets at this per-kilo extravaganza just off the main square.

★Da Mata Bistro CONTEMPORARY **$$$**
(⚑ 3301-3483; turnoff on Estrada do Mirante Km 1; dishes R$42-90; ❂ 8pm-2am Fri, 5pm-2am Sat, 11am-5pm Sun) A romantic bistro with stupendous views from the same owners as nearby **Morro dos Ventos** (also good – follow the sign!). It's high-class contemporary Brazilian cuisine 4km east of town along Hwy MT-251 in the direction of Campo Verde. The homemade pasta buffet on Sunday is worth telling your grandchildren about.

Restaurante Cachoeirinha INTERNATIONAL **$$$**
(⚑ 9216-3497; MT-251 Km 51; meals for 2 R$45-97; ❂ 8:30am-5pm) An outstanding restaurant on private parkland under the nose of two beautiful waterfalls. The pricy *pintado na telha* (catfish grilled on tiles) is unforgettable. Of the R$10 admission price, R$5 goes toward your check.

ℹ Information

If you're driving, drop by the official tourist office, **CAT** (⚑ 3301-2045; Penn Gomes s/n; ❂ 7am-6pm Mon-Sat), where a cartoonish map is available. You'll need it!

Banco do Brasil (Praça Dom Wunibaldo)
Bradesco (Fernando Corréia da Costa 868)
Post Office (Fernando Corréia da Costa 848) A block from the main square.

ℹ Getting There & Away

Expresso Rubi buses leave Cuiabá's bus station for Chapada town (R$11, 1¼ hours) hourly from 6:30am to 7:30pm. If you are only visiting Véu de Noiva, ask the driver to drop you at the park entrance, 10km west of town. The miraculous views are out the right-side window from Cuiabá.

In the other direction, the first bus leaves Chapada town at 5:45am and the last at 7:30pm. Chapada's bus station is two blocks from the main plaza (Praça Dom Wunibaldo).

Parque Nacional da Chapada dos Guimarães

🗸 OXX65

Only receiving national park status in 1989, the outstanding Parque Nacional da Chapada dos Guimarães remains under the mass tourism radar in the context of Brazil's most impressive national parks. Let us pray for status quo. There is a **visitors center** (☑ 3301-2045; www.chapadadosguimaraeas.tur.br; ⊙ 8am-5pm) FREE at the park entrance, but note that access to the attractions is controlled to avoid congestion. Try to visit during the week when it is quietest.

The two exceptional sights inside the park are the Véu de Noiva waterfall and the Cidade de Pedra. Frustratingly the colorful rocky outcrops of the Cidade de Pedra remain closed indefinitely due to lack of infrastructure. Véu de Noiva is the only part of the park you can visit independently. Otherwise a certified guide is required.

◉ Sights

Véu de Noiva   WATERFALL
(Bridal Veil) The impressive Véu de Noiva, an 86m free-falling waterfall, provides the park's characteristic postcard moment. A small trail leads to a magical lookout, perched on top of rocks with the canyon below. This is one of Chapada's most dazzling spots.

It is around 15km west of the town of Chapada dos Guimarães. You can get off the bus from Cuiabá and walk from the road, spend a couple of hours there, then flag down the next bus coming through to Chapada town. Start walking downhill over the bluff, slightly to your right.

Cidade de Pedra   MOUNTAIN
(Stone City) Cidade de Pedra provides Guimarães' most transcendent moment. Jagged sandstone rock formations reminiscent of stone temples jut up into the sky from the tops of enormous cliffs that drop down into the vast green valley below.

The best time to visit is sunset, when fiery red light illuminates the whole area in a monumental display of color and light. It's 20km north of Chapada town along the road to Água Fria.

Mirante de Geodésia   LOOKOUT
The *mirante* (lookout) is the unofficial geographic center of South America. It's a tad underwhelming, with nothing marking the occasion beyond a blank concrete slab that looks more like a manhole cover than a major geographical designator. That said, the views are magnificent!

Off to your right you can see the Cuiabá skyline, and beyond that, the flatlands that eventually become the Pantanal. It's outside the national park, 8km from town. Take the last road in Chapada on your right and go 8km; you'll see a dirt road. The rim of the canyon is a couple of hundred meters away.

☞ Tours

All the Cuiabá tour companies listed in the Pantanal section of this chapter (p373) run tours to the park. Most visitors join one of three tour circuits: **Circuito das Cachoeiras** (Waterfall Circuit; from R$110 per person – does not include Véu de Noiva); **Circuito Vale do Rio Claro** (Claro River Valley Circuit; from R$130 per person – does include Véu de Noiva); or the **Roteiro da Caverna Aroe Jari e Lagoa Azul** (Aroe Jari Cave Circuit; from R$130 per person plus R$20 cave admission), which includes Mirante de Geodésia and Brazil's largest sandstone cave. Trips begin by 9am and return by 6pm but should be reserved in advance, especially in July, August and September.

Chapada Explorer   ECOTOUR
(☑ 3301-1290; www.chapadaexplorer.com.br; Praça Dom Wunibaldo 57, Chapada dos Guimarães; ⊙ 8-11am & 2-5pm Mon-Fri, 8-11am Sat & Sun) 🖉 An excellent Chapada-based agency run by locals who have grown up around ecotourism. They are actively involved in teaching the benefits of low-impact tourism to locals. It runs excursions to all of the area's attractions in groups up to a maximum of 10.

Bring your own food; the price does not include admission costs.

Bom Jardim

🗸 OXX65

If you can't make it to Bonito then you can get a similar experience without the crowds by making a detour to the aquatic attractions at Nobres, 150km north of Cuiabá. Crystalline rivers overloaded with tropical fish, caves, waterfalls and macaws make this a rewarding place, whether you take a tour from Cuiabá or stay in Vila Bom Jardim.

MATO GROSSO & MATO GROSSO DO SUL

OFF THE BEATEN TRACK

CRISTALINO PRIVATE NATURAL HERITAGE PRESERVE

The uninspiring town of **Alta Floresta**, 873km north of Cuiabá, is the end of the road: beyond it to the north is the vast expanse of the Amazon jungle. The town itself has no attractions but there is one good reason for heading out here, and that is to visit the Cristalino Private Natural Heritage Preserve, considered one of Amazonia's best for spotting rare birds and mammals, including the endangered white-nosed bearded saki monkey, lowland tapir, giant otter and five species of macaw.

On the banks of the Rio Cristalino (39km north of Alta Floresta) in an area rich in Amazon flora and fauna, the **Cristalino Jungle Lodge** (☑3521-1396; www.cristalinolodge.com.br; s/d package per person from R$500/400) offers a 50m-high observation tower and 20km of good bird-watching trails (it is considered one of the top-50 spots in the world for birding). The new VIP bungalows ooze creature-comfort luxe. Rates include transfers, all meals, guides, excursions and insurance. Book well ahead if you want to stay in high season.

If you are short on time or money and can't spend the night at the Cristalino Jungle Lodge (the only way to see the abundant wildlife here unless you are on a fishing trip), **Floresta Tours** (☑3521 7100; www.florestatour.com.br; ☺8am-5pm Mon-Fri, to noon Sat) offers day trips into the Cristalino Private Natural Heritage Preserve for around R$200 per person. The trip takes nine hours and includes transfers, guides, excursions and lunch at the lodge. The agency is located at the **Floresta Amazônica Hotel** (☑3512 7100; www.fah.com.br; Av Perimetral Oeste 2001; s/d R$80/100; ✸@✸) in Alta Floresta. Advance reservations are required.

From Cuiabá the bus companies **Nova Integração** (www.novaintegracao.com.br) and **Viagem Verde** (www.viagemverde.com.br) run north to Alta Floresta (R$135-161, 13½ hours). Trip (p365) and Avianca (p365) have daily flights.

🅞 Sights & Activities

As in Bonito you'll need to be accompanied by a guide to visit the main attractions. Tour companies in Cuiabá run these excursions, but you can also contract a guide locally if you prefer to travel independently.

There is a **natural swimming pool** in Vila Bom Jardim to while away the hottest hours of the day.

Lagoa das Araras　　　　　　LAKE
(☺from 5pm) A 15-minute walk outside of Bom Jardim (ask for directions, it's easy to find) is Lagoa das Araras, where tourists gather at 5pm each night to watch the arrival of flocks of several species of colorful macaws that come noisily to roost each night.

**★Recanto Ecológico
Lagoa Azul**　　　　　　SNORKELLING
(snorkelling R$65) The number-one attraction, 8km from town, where you can snorkel in the 'Reino Encantado' (Enchanted Kingdom) or float leisurely along the 'Rio Triste' (Sad River). Nearby are some hidden caves (the guide will show you the way) complete with roosting bats and weird rock formations.

**Cachoeira da
Serra Azul**　　WATERFALL, SNORKELLING
(SESC Serra Azul, Rosario Oeste; snorkelling R$50) A 50m-high waterfall that plunges into an 8m-deep, vivid blue, natural pool. Predictably, there is a forest trail and some excellent *flutação* (flotation) to be had here as well.

🛏 Sleeping & Eating

Pousada Mangueiras　　POUSADA **$**
(☑3376-1345; www.pousadamangueiras.com.br; Av Getúlio Vargas 1501, Bom Jardim; s/d 70/150; ✸☎) A polished, economical option in Vila Bom Jardim with tasteful wooden furniture and an onsite travel agency.

**Pousada Rota
das Aguas**　　POUSADA **$$**
(☑3102-2019; www.rotadasaguas.tur.br; Rodovia 241 Km 65; r R$190; ✸☎✸) 🗘 Top accommodation both for its handsome setting and also for the fact that it is outside town and right on the doorstep of the area's major attraction, the Recanto Lagoa Azul. There is an excellent **restaurant** here as well (R$25 per person).

Vista da Serra SELF-SERVE, PIZZERIA $
(📱 9628-0014; Vila Bom Jardim; buffet per kg R$20)
Self-service buffet lunches and à la carte dinners and pizzas at this reliable choice.

❶ Getting There and Away

One bus a day runs from Cuiabá to Bom Jardim at 2:30pm (R$38, five hours) with the return leaving at 5am. Transport is included in guided tours from Cuiabá.

Poconé

📱 0XX65 / POP 32,000

The main entry point to the Pantanal for travelers heading south from Cuiabá, the 'pink town' of Poconé marks the beginning of the Transpantaneira 'highway.' Poconé still has a sleepy, frontier feel (as one local put it, 'In Poconé, even the restaurants close for lunch!'). The locals, many of whom are descended from the original tribe in the area, the *beripoconeses*, have a strong sense of tradition.

In May, Poconé celebrates the week-long **Semana do Fazendeiro e do Cavalo Pantaneiro** with a cattle fair and rodeos.

☞ Tours

Transpantanal TOUR
(📱 3345-2343; www.transpantanal.com.br; Av Aníbal de Toledo 1895; ⊙ 7:30am-6pm Mon-Fri, to noon Sat) The only agency in town that caters to serious fishers, Transpantanal offers seven-day fishing packages along the rivers Cuiabá, São Lourenço, Piquiri and Paraguai (minimum 12).

🛏 Sleeping

The best places to stay, especially if you're trying to organize a lift down the Transpantaneira, are a couple of kilometers out of town near the beginning of the road.

Pousada Pantaneira POUSADA $
(📱 3345-3357; www.pousadapantaneira.com.br; Rodovia Transpantaneira Km 0; s/d R$50/80) This simple pousada and *churrascaria* (barbecue restaurant) sits at the beginning of the Transpantaneira – a good base for organizing a reliable ride down the highway.

Hotel Skala HOTEL $
(📱 3345-1407; www.skalahotel.com.br; Praça Bem Rondon 64; s/d R$70/120; ❄ @) The best option in the center, with spacious, if slightly dark rooms and the most sophisticated restaurant in town, Tradição, right next door.

✗ Eating & Drinking

Cheiro Verde SELF-SERVE $
(📱 3345-3005; Praça Bem Rondon; buffet per person R$15) Simple home-cooked meals in spotless surroundings.

Atelier do Luizão BAR
(📱 3345-2733; Generoso Ponce 1101) A little bar in a huge craft shop of souvenirs and decorations all made on the premises. Unsurprisingly, most feature Pantanal wildlife designs.

❶ Information

Banco do Brasil (Campos Sales) Has a Visa/MasterCard ATM but don't bet your life on it working.

CAT Office (📱 3345-1575; Praça Menino Jésus; ⊙ 7am-1pm Mon-Fri) Has pousada information and a Transpantaneira map.

Post Office (Coronel Salvador Marques 335)

❶ Getting There & Away

Buses to/from Cuiabá first stop at the Poconé bus station about 10 blocks from the center of town, then continue on to Praça da Matriz; behind the Matriz church is the road that leads to the beginning of the Transpantaneira.

CÁCERES FISHING FRENZY

Every September anglers from across the globe descend on Cáceres, a quiet little town that hugs the banks of the Rio Paraguai for the **Festival Internacional de Pesca**. Recognized by the *Guinness Book of World Records* as the world's largest fishing festival, as many as 150,000 people attend, most of them toting fishing poles. Since 1979 the waters of the Rio Paraguai have been inundated by feverish fisherman from some 15 countries, all out to nab (and release) the largest pintado, dourado and pacu fish they can get their hooks on. Winners take home R$30,000 cars or boat motors. There are dance troupes by the river and local children – some 1500 strong – are taught the ecobenefits of catch-and-release fishing. Ask at the **Sematur** (📱 3223-3455; Rua Riachuelo 1; ⊙ noon-6pm Mon-Fri) office near the waterfront for more information. Head to the river and follow the road to the right as far as it goes.

There are buses from Cuiabá to Poconé (R$15, two hours, every three hours) from 6am to 7pm, and six in the opposite direction from 6am to 7:30pm. Alternatively, taxis leaving from the **Ponto de Taxi** (☎ 3345-1140) at Praça da Matriz will drop you at your final destination in Cuiabá for a mere R$30 per person if full.

THE PANTANAL

The Amazon gets the press coverage, but the Pantanal is a better place to see wildlife. The dense foliage of the Amazon makes it difficult to observe the animals, but in the open marshes of the Pantanal, wildlife is much easier to spot. If you like to see animals in their natural environment, the Pantanal should not be missed.

Located in the heart of South America, the world's largest wetland is 20 times the size of the famed Everglades in Florida – some 210,000 sq km. Something less than 100,000 sq km of this is in Bolivia and Paraguay; the rest is in Brazil, split between the states of Mato Grosso and Mato Grosso do Sul.

The Pantanal has few people and no towns. Distances are so great and ground transport so poor that people get around in small airplanes and motorboats; 4WD travel is restricted by the seasons. The principal access road that runs deep into the Pantanal is the **Transpantaneira**. This raised dirt road sectioned by small wooden bridges ends 145km south of Poconé, at Porto Jofre. The much-mooted road connection of Porto Jofre to Corumbá (at the border with Bolivia), long shelved due to ecological concerns and a lack of funds, now appears to be back on the negotiating table.

The **Parque Nacional do Pantanal Matogrossense** occupies 1350 sq km in the southwest of the region, but most of the Pantanal is privately owned. Cooperation between ecotourism and the landowners in the region (mostly cattle ranchers) has contributed to the sustainable conservation of the environment. By providing ranchers with an income that encourages their coexistence with the wildlife it covers the shortfall created by the seasonal flooding of the area, which would otherwise be covered by more intensive (and hence more destructive) ranching efforts. The national park and three smaller private nature reserves nearby were given Unesco World Heritage listing in 2000.

Geography & Climate

Although *pantano* means 'swamp' in both Spanish and Portuguese, the Pantanal is not a swamp but, rather, a vast alluvial plain. In geological terms, it is a sedimentary basin of quaternary origin, but its vastness led the early settlers to mistake it for a sea which they called the Xaraés. This began to dry out, along with the Amazon Sea, 65 million years ago.

The Pantanal – 2000km upstream from the Atlantic Ocean yet just 100m to 200m above sea level – is bounded by higher lands: the mountains of the Serra de Maracaju to the east, the Serra da Bodoquena to the south and the Serra dos Parecis and Serra do São Geronimo to the north. From these highlands the rains flow into the Pantanal, forming the Rio Paraguai and its tributaries (which flow south and then east, draining into the Atlantic Ocean).

During the wet season (November to March), the rivers flood their banks, inundating much of the low-lying Pantanal and creating *cordilheiras* (vegetation islands above the high-water level), where the animals cluster together. The waters reach their

---

CROSSING THE BORDER TO BOLIVIA

Besides fishing (see p369), the only other reason to come to Cáceres is to attempt the adventurous border crossing to the Bolivian outback town of San Matías. In Cáceres the little bus station is 10 blocks north of the riverfront. (Note that if you are coming from Cuiabá the bus stops first at the big station outside the city center in Vale do Araguaia, confusingly called the 'Terminal Rodoviario de Cáceres', stay on board!).

Two daily buses run to the Bolivian border at Corixio (R$21) at 4:30am and 10am, with the returns from Corixio at 7:30am and 12:30pm. You will be asked to show your passport to buy bus tickets. From Corixio a gaggle of minibuses ply the route to San Matías. Before you do anything though make sure you get your exit stamp from the **Federal Police** (☎ 3211-6330; Av Getúlio Vargas 2125; ☻ 8am-6pm) in Cáceres, 4km from town, close to the *prefeitura* (city hall).

The Pantanal

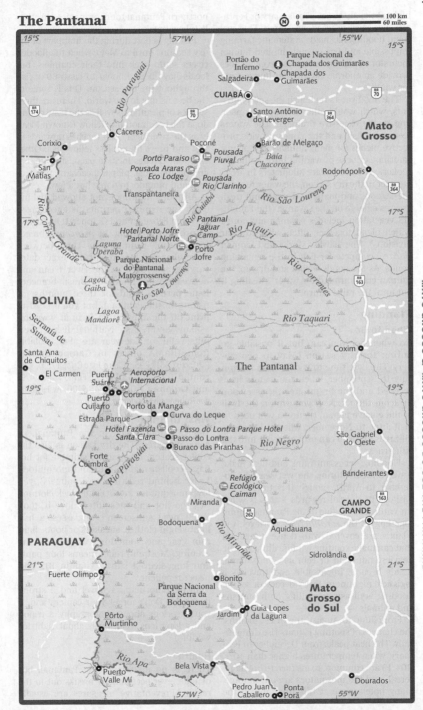

high mark – up to 3m – in January or February, then start to recede in March. This seasonal flooding has made systematic farming impossible and has severely limited human incursions into the area. However, it does provide an enormously rich feeding ground for wildlife.

The floodwaters replenish the soil's nutrients, which would otherwise be very poor, due to the excessive drainage. The waters teem with fish, and the ponds provide protective niches for many animals and plants. Enormous flocks of wading birds gather in rookeries several square kilometers in area.

Later in the dry season, the water recedes, the lagoons and marshes dry out and fresh grasses emerge on the savanna (the Pantanal's vegetation includes savanna and forest which blend together, often with no clear divisions). The hawks, storks and caiman (*jacaré*) compete for fish in the remaining ponds. As the ponds shrink and dry up, the caiman crawl around for water, sweating it out until the rains return.

Planning

When to Go

Go whenever you can, but if possible go during the dry season (May to September). The best time to watch birds is from July to September, when the waters have receded and the bright-green grasses pop up from the muck. If you are on the trail of the elusive jaguar, then you will need to visit June to November, when it is access-all-areas and you can probe deeper into the wilderness.

Flooding, incessant rains and heat make travel difficult during the wet season (November to April), though this time is not without its special rewards – this is when the cattle and wildlife of the Pantanal clump together on the *cordilheiras*. However, the islands are covered with dense vegetation that can make spotting wildlife difficult. The heaviest rains fall in February and March. Roads become impassable and travel is a logistical nightmare. Every decade or so, the flooding is disastrous, killing both humans and animals.

From June to August, the driest months, the chances of spotting jaguars rise dramatically. The heat peaks from December to February, when temperatures higher than 40°C (104°F) are common, roads turn to breakfast cereal, and the mosquitoes are out in force. Many hotels close at this time and in the northern Pantanal tour companies effectively take a break.

Fishing is best during the first part of the dry season (April to May), when the flooded rivers settle back into their channels, but locals have been known to lasso 80kg fish throughout the dry season. This is some of the best fishing in the world. There are three species of piranha, as well as the tasty dourado, a feisty salmon-like fellow (known locally as the river tiger) that reaches upwards of 9kg and preys on hapless fellow fish. Other excellent catches include pacu, suribim, bagre, piraputanga, piapara, cachara, pirancajuva and pintado, to name but a few.

Although hunting is not allowed, fishing (with the required permits) is encouraged between February and October. It is, however, prohibited during the *piracema* (breeding season) running any time between November and March with the exact dates varying according to the river basin and between years. Banco do Brasil branches issue permits valid for three months for fishing in the Pantanal, but you'll need to print off the application form at www.imasul.ms.gov.br first. National fishing permits valid for one year are also available from IBAMA offices in **Campo Grande** (☎ 0xx67-3317-2952; Padre João Crippa 753), **Corumbá** (☎ 0xx67-3231-6096; Firmo Matos 479) and **Cuiabá** (☎ 0xx65-3648-9100; Av Historiador Rubens de Mendonça 5250).

What to Bring

You can't buy much in the Pantanal, so come prepared. The dry season is also the cooler season. Bring attire suitable for hot days, coolish nights, rain and mosquitoes. Leave behind red (it scares animals), yellow (mosquitoes love it) and black clothing (it's too hot and mosquitoes love it, too). You'll need sunscreen, sunglasses, a hat, lightweight clothes, sneakers or boots, light rain gear and something warmer for the evening. Mosquito relief means long pants and long-sleeved shirts, vitamin B12 and insect repellent.

Bring binoculars, a towel and a strong flashlight. Don't forget your camera and, if you're serious about photography, a tripod and a long lens (300mm is about right for wildlife).

Health

There is no malaria in the Pantanal, but dengue fever occasionally breaks out in the region. Preventative measures are usually

PANTANAL CUISINE

Pantaneiros – the local Pantanal folks – make good use of regional ingredients in preparing their delicacies. You'll find lots of restaurants offering regional specialties on your travels in the area – stop in and try some.

In the northern Pantanal, the cuisine is decidedly fishy. Pacu, dourado and pintado are the most consumed fish, and they come *frito* (fried), *grelhado* (grilled), *assado* (baked) or *defumado* (smoked). Both dourado and pacu have lots of small bones, but they separate easily when baked slowly. Pacu is often baked and served with an *escabeche* sauce consisting of onions, tomatoes and peppers. Another favorite fish is pintado, excellent when spiced with rough salt and pepper and grilled. One specialty is *peixe à urucum*, where the chosen fish is served topped with spices, condensed milk, coconut milk and melted mozzarella. Piranha soup is another exotic favorite, considered an aphrodisiac by the *pantaneiros*.

On farms and in southern Pantanal, the dishes are more strongly influenced by the cattle and grains produced in the area. Specialties include *carne seca com abobora* (sun-dried beef with pumpkin) and *paçoca-de-pilã* (sun-dried beef with manioc flour), the latter eaten with bananas and unsalted rice. There's also *arroz de carreteiro* (rice with sun-dried beef served with fried manioc and banana) and *galinha caipira* – chicken served with white rice and *pequi*, a small yellow fruit of the cerrado. Don't bite into the *pequi* – its seed contains lots of spines! Pantanal desserts are sweet and tasty. Some popular ones are *furrundu* – a mixture of papaya trunk (not the fruit), sugarcane juice and coconut – and ice cream made from *bocaiúva*, another local fruit.

rapidly taken by authorities and the vector mosquito is, regardless, generally associated with urban areas and not the countryside. If you're concerned, consult a travel-health expert for the latest information before you leave home. For more on these and other travelers' health concerns, check out Lonely Planet's *Healthy Travel – Central & South America* by Drs Gheradin and Young.

There are medical services available in Cuiabá, Corumbá and Campo Grande.

☞ Tours

The principal access towns are Cuiabá in the north (for the Transpantaneira) and Campo Grande in the south (for the Estrada Parque), with Corumbá on the Bolivian border more of a sideshow these days. You can arrange guided tours from any of these three towns.

Tours from Cuiabá tend to be slightly more expensive, but more professional with smaller groups and better-trained guides than those from either Campo Grande or Corumbá. They also go deeper into the Pantanal. If time is a problem and money isn't, or if you'd just like a quality guide, contact **Focus Tours** (www.focustours.com) in the USA. Focus Tours specializes in nature tours and is active in trying to preserve the Pantanal.

☞ From Cuiabá

From Cuiabá, the capital of Mato Grosso, small tour operators arrange safaris along the Transpantaneira that include transportation, ranch accommodations on farms and guides. Guides are English-speaking and well-trained on the whole, and smaller groups increase your chances of seeing the shier animals. Fortunately, while there is healthy competition between tour operators in Cuiabá, it's not as intense as in Mato Grosso do Sul and some operators share the same Pantanal camps.

Tours here are well organized and quite comfortable, starting from around R$350 per day – if you are serious about seeing animals they are worth the extra money. Some companies also offer 'jaguar tours' for around R$700 per day, with an excellent chance of seeing this magnificent feline in the Porto Jofre area from June to November.

★ **Pantanal Nature**   NATURE TOUR
(☎ 00xx65-9994-2265; www.pantanalnature.com.br; Rua Professor Francisco Torres 48; per day high/low season R$700/450) Superb agency run by Ailton Lara that has quickly built up a sterling reputation for its professional tours and expert guides. It also runs a Panatal Jaguar Camp (p378) near Porto Jofre with excellent success rates in seeing the animal in the dry season.

Driving the Transpantaneira

In 1970 the government decided to push a road through the Pantanal from Cuiabá to Corumbá. After struggling as far as Porto Jofre, 145km from Poconé, they then made the wise choice of stopping and questioning the wisdom of traversing an area that was under water for six months a year. The result, or remnant, is the Transpantaneira, a raised dirt road that extends deep into the Pantanal, though the fanciful plans of completion still haunt the nightmares of local ecologists.

Wildlife is plentiful along the roadside and you'll see *jacarés* (caiman), capybaras and lots of birds. There are several places to stay along the Transpantaneira.

If driving from Cuiabá, head out around 4am to reach the Transpantaneira by sunrise, when the animals come to life. Weekdays are better for driving, as there's less traffic kicking up dust. The road officially starts in Poconé, though many consider the wooden sign and guard station 17km south as the beginning of the Transpantaneira. Fill up your tank in Poconé. Though you should be able to make it to Porto Jofre and back on one tank, better safe than sorry as the gas station at Hotel Porto Jofre charges twice the going rate if you miscalculate.

Heading south, you'll navigate over 125 little wooden bridges and around countless meter-wide potholes. Notice the interesting carved statue of Sào Francisco, Protector of Ecology, around Km18. He was installed by a priest in Poconé a few years back. Barara is a small bar at Km32, where you can stop for a beer and *galinhada* (boneless chicken and rice) or fried fish. You can also purchase a ticket here to go to the top of the lookout tower next door at Pousada Araras Eco Lodge (p377), a treat even if you're not staying.

After Km105, the landscape changes, with denser vegetation and an altogether wilder feel – it's jaguar country! Even if you don't spot one, you are rewarded for your efforts once you hit Campo do Jofre, just north of Porto Jofre.

1. Canoeing, the Pantanal 2. Caiman (p622) 3. Wooden bridge, the Pantanal

Pantanal Explorer NATURE TOUR
(☎ 0xx65-3682-2800; www.pantanalexplorer.com.
br; Av Governador Ponce de Arruda 670, Várzea
Grande) Owner Andre Von Thuronyi has
been working with sustainable tourism in
the area for 30 years and fights harmful government interference in the Pantanal with
ferocity. He is actively involved in saving the
hyacinth macaw and giant otter. Affiliated
with Pousada Araras Eco Lodge (p377).

Joel Souza Ecoverde Tours NATURE TOUR
(☎ 00xx65-9638-1614; www.ecoverdetours.com.br;
Pedro Celestino; per day R$370-400) Top-notch
company with 25 years of service and experienced guides. Working with local pousadas
towards an ecofriendly approach, Joel Souza
can guide you in English, German, French,
Portuguese or Spanish. You can find him at
Hostel Ecoverde (p361).

Natureco NATURE TOUR
(☎ 00xx65-3321-1001; www.natureco.com.br; Benedito Leite 570; per day from R$400) Another
time-tested Cuiabá agency, run by Munir
Nasr.

☞ From Campo Grande

Southern gateways to the Pantanal are the
cities of Corumbá, Campo Grande, Aquidauana and Miranda. Most backpackers
head to Campo Grande or Corumbá. Aquidauana and Miranda are popular with Brazilian anglers and high-end travelers.

Budget tour operators working in Mato
Grosso do Sul offer packages at camps along
Estrada Parque, a 117km stretch of dirt road
through the region known as Nhecolândia.
Estrada Parque is actually closer to Corumbá than to Campo Grande, but unless you're
traveling to or from Bolivia, there's no real
need to travel all the way to Corumbá to
join a tour. Most of the Corumbá agencies
also have offices in Campo Grande, a travel
hub and more convenient for onward travel
to other parts of Brazil. If you are visiting
Bonito, go to the Pantanal first as the tours
end in Buraco das Piranhas, closer to Bonito
than Campo Grande.

Campo Grande has tried to clean up its
act in recent years, with the opening of a
new bus station on the outskirts of town
that has reduced the mobbing and bullying
of disembarking tourists to a thing of the
past. Local government responded to the
barrage of complaints it had been receiving
from visitors by closing down the lodges that
didn't comply with ecological legislation and
tightening the screws on dodgy operators.
Problems persist, but things are moving in
the right direction. The cheapest tours are
rough-and-tumble affairs and groups are often large, but with prices starting at around

CHOOSING A GUIDE IN THE PANTANAL

Pantanal tourism is big business and in the past some companies have been guilty of
employing underhand tactics in the race to hook in clients. Though measures have
finally been taken to clamp down on the worst offenders, it is still worth bearing a few
suggestions in mind to have a safe and enjoyable trip.

➡ Resist making a snap decision, especially if you've just climbed off an overnight bus.

➡ Do not make your decision based on cost. Cheaper very rarely means better.

➡ Speak to other travelers. What was their experience like? In Campo Grande some of
the tour companies are quick to badmouth others. Get your advice straight from the
horse's mouth.

➡ Compare your options, but remember that the owner or salesperson is not always
your guide, and it's the guide you're going to be with in the wilderness for three to five
days. Ask to meet your guide if possible.

➡ Don't hand over your cash to any go-betweens or buy bus tickets that somebody
other than the person you give your money to is going to give you.

➡ If you are even remotely concerned about sustainable tourism, do not use operators
and lodges that harm this fragile environment. That means no picking up the animals for
photographs or touching them whatsoever.

➡ Group budget tours focus squarely on the spectacular and easy-to-see species. If you
are a serious wildlife-watcher you should be prepared to pay more for a private guide.
You won't regret it.

R$200 per day it is an economical way to see the Pantanal and its wildlife.

★**Pantanal Viagens & Turismo** NATURE TOUR
(☎00xx67-3321-3143; www.pantanalviagens.com. br; Joaquim Nabuco 200, loje 9 in old bus station) A nice agency working mainly with Pousada Passo do Lontra that has worked hard to maintain its excellent reputation. Caters for mid- to high-range budgets, but offers professional and reliable packages.

Pantanal Discovery NATURE TOUR
(☎00xx67-9163-3518; www.gilspantanaldiscovery. com.br; Dom Aquino 610, Hotel Nacional; per 3 days camping/r R$550/650) A perennial operator with a polished sales pitch; owner Gil is assertive and not without complaints but better reviewed than most budget operators in town.

☞ From Corumbá

Nearly all of the tour companies once in Corumbá have decamped to Campo Grande and some Campo Grande tour companies operate here under different names.

Canaã Viagens e Turismo NATURE TOUR
(☎0xx67-3231-3667; www.pantanalcanaa.com.br; Colombo 245) A recommended agency specializing in high-end fishing tours up the Rio Paraguai. It offers trips in two different barco-hotels (boat-hotels) and minitours of three days and two nights which leave twice a week. Prices include all meals, fishing, guides and transfers.

🛏 Sleeping

Pantanal accommodations are divided into three types: pousadas include all meals and range from simple to top-end; *fazendas* are ranch-style hotels that usually have horses and often boats for use; and *pesqueiros* cater for anglers and usually have boats and fishing gear for rent. If you have doubts about roughing it on the budget tours, it is better to spend a bit more money for basic comforts – a bed, running water and some hope of avoiding a million mosquito bites. It rarely costs much more and the investment is worth it for a good night's sleep.

If you travel independently, rates will usually include modest lodgings, three meals and at least one excursion per day. Drinks – even soda and water – are extra. Transportation is almost never included in the room rates and can take a sizable chunk out of your budget. From Cuiabá, transfers in and out, may require any combination of 4WD, boat, horseback and plane, depending on the season.

For this reason, it is almost always cheaper – not to mention logistically less stressful – to go in under the services of a tour operator. Transportation in and out is then included and they often have access to more remote lodges.

🛏 Along the Transpantaneira

Accommodations along the Transpantaneira are plentiful and offer a good variety of choices, from rustic to high end. They are listed here in north to south order.

Pousada Piuval POUSADA $$$
(☎0xx65-3345-1338; www.pousadapiuval.com. br; Transpantaneira Km 10; s/d with full board R$295/440; ❋@✿) It's a trade-off at the first pousada along the Transpantaneira: it's more commercial (feeding caimans) but also more comfortable. It sits on 70 sq km and is popular with Germans and bird-watchers. The pool is wonderful, as are sunset boat rides. It offers horseback riding, trekking and night safaris as well.

Porto Paraiso FAZENDA $$
(☎0xx65-3345-2271; www.portalparaiso.com.br; Transpantaneira Km 17; full board s/d R$190/310; ❋@✿) An excellent budget option on a small working buffalo and cattle farm near the beginning of the Transpantaneira. There are excellent camping facilities around the luxe pool area and some great bird-watching in the surroundings.

★**Pousada Araras Eco Lodge** POUSADA $$$
(☎0xx65-3682-2800; www.araraslodge.com. br; Transpantaneira Km 32; s/d R$469/674; ❋@☎✿) 🌱 This pioneering lodge offers the most comfort and luxury on the Transpantaneira. Rooms have lovely artisanal bedspreads and all feature nice patios with hammocks separated by bamboo curtains. There is a treetop tower for bird-watching (hyacinth macaws are always around) and an extensive bird list is available at check-in. Much of the food comes from its own farm.

Pousada Rio Clarinho FAZENDA $$
(☎0xx65-9977-8966; www.pousadarioclarinho. com.br; Transpantaneira Km 40; s/d incl meals & excursions R$180/340; ❋) An avian symphony

is your wake-up call at this rustic *fazenda* right on the Rio Clarinho (there's a small river platform for swimming). With an extensive area of forest, there are more than 260 species of birds on the property, as well as capybaras and giant otters. The food is authentic Pantanal. Rates include all excursions.

Hotel Porto Jofre
Pantanal Norte   LODGE $$$
(☎0xx65-3637-1593; www.portojofre.com.br; Transpantaneira Km 145; s/d R$370/622; ☺Mar-Oct; ✹@✍) Hotel Porto Jofre Pantanal Norte is a luxury hotel-lodge at the end of the road, catering mostly to sport fishermen on expensive packages. There's an airstrip, a marina and a nice restaurant, all in wonderful wilderness.

Pantanal Jaguar Camp   CAMP $$$
(www.pantanaljaguarcamp.com.br; s/d R$300/670; ☏) ✐ Six African-style tents with private toilets, comfortable beds and an onsite restaurant. This is a great Porto Jofre base for jaguar-seeking boat trips that is affiliated with Pantanal Nature (p373). Note that jaguar-seeking excursions are included in the accommodation price.

🛏 Around Miranda

There are several excellent, high-end hotel-*fazendas* in this area.

Refúgio Ecológico Caiman   LODGE $$$
(☎0xx11-3706-1800; www.caiman.com.br; s & d incl meals & 3 excursions R$1929; ✹@✍) ✐ An ecopioneering lodge 36km north of Miranda and a private Pantanal for a privileged few. There are three lodges: Sede, the main lodge, is the most luxurious; Cordilheiro, the most remote and rustic with a great lookout tower; and Baiazinha, a little more playful, with the best pool deck and position for spotting jaguars.

Multilingual guides who live on the *fazenda* lead tours. There are an estimated 40 jaguars and 300 macaws on the property. Prices include meals and numerous activities, from canoeing to horseback riding; there is a three-night minimum in high season.

🛏 Along Estrada Parque

Estrada Parque runs off the main Campo Grande–Corumbá road (Hwy BR-262) at Buraco das Piranhas, 72km from Corumbá and 324km from Campo Grande. The first stretch of Estrada Parque penetrates 47km into the Pantanal, before it dog-legs back toward Corumbá. At Porto da Manga, a barge ferries vehicles over the Rio Paraguai before Estrada Parque rejoins Hwy BR-262 at Lampião Aceso, about 12km from Corumbá.

To get to the Estrada Parque you can take the Campo Grande–Corumbá bus and arrange for your lodge to pick you up (for a small fee) by the Posto Florestal guard station at the Buraco das Piranhas intersection. At Passo do Lontra, 7km from Buraco das Piranhas, you cross Rio Miranda. There are lots of accommodations from here to Curva do Leque.

Hotel Fazenda Santa Clara   FAZENDA $$
(☎00xx67-3384-0583; www.pantanalsantaclara. com.br; 3-/4-day package camping R$350/400, dm R$550/650, r R$600/750; ✹✍) Shooting at a backpacker market, this is the principal budget lodge in the southern Pantanal. Visits are possible only as part of three- or four-day package tours booked through the office in the Campo Grande bus station. Expect large groups.

Passo do Lontra Parque Hotel   LODGE $$$
(☎0xx67-3245-2407; www.passodolontra.com.br; Estrada Parque Km 10; s/d R$345/390; ✹✍) ✐ A comfortable place with large *apartamentos* (rooms with private bathroom) and riverside chalets in an accessible location near the beginning of the Estrada Parque. Safaris along Rio Miranda are the focus.

❶ Getting There & Away

From Cuiabá, the capital of Mato Grosso, the main gateway to the Pantanal is Poconé. Campo Grande, the capital of Mato Grosso do Sul, is the principal southern launch point into the Pantanal, while Corumbá is a convenient point of access only if you are arriving from Bolivia and are pushed for time. The route to Corumbá from Campo Grande runs via Aquidauana and Miranda, part of the route being covered by the Pantanal Express Train (p383).

There are direct flights to Cuiabá and Campo Grande from Brasília and connecting flights from Rio and São Paulo. The airport at Corumbá receives only local flights these days and is connected to Campo Grande via Bonito.

❶ Getting Around

Roads in the Pantanal are unsurfaced, few in number and are are frequently closed by rain. Since the lodges are the only places to sleep, drink and eat, and public transportation is very limited, independent travel is difficult. Unless you have extensive off-road experience, hiring a car is an option in the dry season only. Only the Transpantaneira in Mato Grosso and Estrada Parque in Mato Grosso do Sul go deep into the region. Save yourself the stress and stick to a tour operator, or arrange transport in advance through a lodge.

MATO GROSSO DO SUL

Mato Grosso do Sul was created in 1977 when the military government decided it would be the best way to administer and develop such a large region (cynics claimed it was to provide more high-paying bureaucratic jobs for cronies). But even before the split, the area had a different economic and social makeup from the northern Mato Grosso.

In the late 19th century, many migrants from the south and southeast of Brazil arrived in the area, so the south has a greater number of smaller farms and a much more intensive agriculture when compared to the large farms and ranches in the north. All this is thanks to the rich, red earth, known as *terra roxa*.

The wealth created by the *terra roxa* has helped develop the state's modern agricultural sector. The main crop is soy, but there's also lots of corn, rice and cotton production and cattle farms. Mato Grosso do Sul also contains two-thirds of the Pantanal and the Serra da Bocaina, two wonderful natural areas that are popular with both Brazilian and foreign travelers.

Campo Grande

📞 0XX67 / POP 787,000

Known as the *Cidade Morena* not for its beautiful women but rather its red earth, Campo Grande is the capital of Mato Grosso do Sul, a modern city that is the major gateway to the southern Pantanal. Manganese, rice, soy and cattle are the traditional sources of its wealth, while education (there are four universities in the city), commerce and tourism are growing industries. Campo Grande lies 716km south of Cuiabá and 403km southeast of Corumbá.

Founded around 1875 as the village of Santo Antônio de Campo Grande, Campo Grande really began to grow when the railway came through in 1914. The city was declared the capital of Mato Grosso do Sul by decree of military president Ernesto Giesel in 1977.

◉ Sights

Until the new attractions under development at the Parque das Nações Indígenas begin to open, there's not much to see in the city itself, but it's a lively place, especially at night.

Aquario do Pantanal   AQUARIUM
(Parque das Nações Indígenas) Due for completion in June 2014, this ambitious aquarium/research centre promises to become the city's number-one attraction in a very short time. It will house 263 species of Pantanal fish and other native wildlife in gigantic walk-through tanks holding an incredible 6.6 million litres of water.

Museu das Culturas Dom Bosco   MUSEUM
(📞 3326-9788; Parque das Nações Indígenas; adult/child R$5/2.50; ⊙ 8am-6pm Tue-Fri, 1-6pm Sat & Sun) Relocated to a R$2 million building designed by Italian architect Massimo Chiappetta in the Parque das Nações Indígenas, this 3400-sq-meter expansion houses an excellent collection of over 10,000 insects and a beautiful exhibit of indigenous *bororo* headdresses and other artifacts from the indigenous *moro*, *karajá* and *xavante* groups.

Feira Central   MARKET
(📞 3324-8129; Av Calógeras & 14 de Julho; ⊙ 5pm-late Wed, Fri & Sat, 10am-late Sun) A great market worth a stroll is the Feira Central, a massive open-air food and shopping court lined with Japanese sobá-noodle joints and other food and merchandise stalls. It's packed with revelers on weekends.

⌖ Tours

For tours of the Pantanal from Campo Grande, see p373.

City Bus Tour   TOUR
(📞 3321-0800; www.campograndecvb.com.br/roteiros; Av Afonso Pena; tickets R$18; ⊙ Tue-Sun) City Bus Tour visits 42 sites of local interest. Buy your tickets at the CAT office.

🛏 Sleeping

The area immediately around the old bus station is seedy, so choose wisely.

★ Turis Hotel   HOTEL $
(📞 3382-2461; www.turishotel.com.br; Kardec 200; s/d/tr R$83/128/169; ❄ @ 🛜) Modern and minimalist, this excellent option is entirely too trendy for its location and is probably the best value in town.

Campo Grande

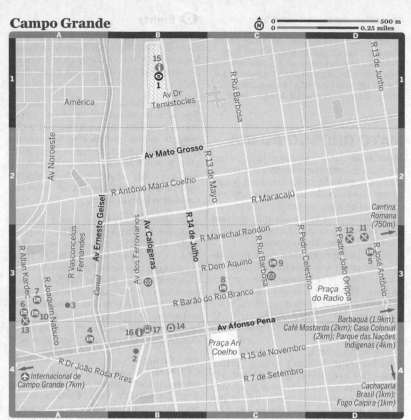

0 500 m
0 0.25 miles

Pousada Dom Aquino
INN $

(☎ 3384-3303; www.pousadadomaquino.com.br; Aquino 1806; s/d/tr with air-con R$75/105/126, s without air-con R$69; ❄ 🛜) A wonderful, relaxed pousada that is an oasis in the city and walking distance from nearly everything. The staff are very friendly and there's even international cable TV. Book ahead.

Alkimia Hotel
HOTEL $

(☎ 3324-2621; Av Afonso Pena 1413; s/d apt R$100/150; ❄ @) Two blocks from the old bus station in a slightly safer area. Rooms are spotless and the bathrooms are large. Discounts for cash.

Hotel Colonial
HOTEL $

(☎ 3382-6061; Kardec 211; s/d/tr with air-con R$80/120/140, s without air-con R$70 ; ❄ 🛜) Pokey rooms are compensated for by a monster breakfast and pool access at its more upmarket sister Hotel Internacional next door.

Hotel Nacional
HOTEL $

(☎ 3383-2461; www.hotelnacionalpantanal.com.br; Dom Aquino 610; s/d with air-con R$65/100, without air-con R$45/80; ❄ @ 🛜) A basic budget choice popular with Brazilian student groups.

Bahamas Apart Hotel
HOTEL $$

(☎ 3303-9393; www.bahamasaparthotel.com.br; José Antônio 1117; standard s/d R$236/306, luxury R$378/452; P ❄ @ 🛜 ❄) Sleek high-rise hotel with aquamarine window panes offering massive two-story *apartamentos* with kitchenette, living and dining areas and a small patio. By far the most luxury in town for the money.

Jandaía Hotel
HOTEL $$

(☎ 3316-7700; www.jandaia.com.br; Barão do Rio Branco 1271; s/d R$214/269; P ❄ @ 🛜 ❄) An upscale business hotel with plush rooms, marble floors and two decent restaurants. English is spoken and there is an on-site gym.

Campo Grande

Eating

Campo Grande boasts the third-highest Japanese population in Brazil and *sobá* noodles brought by Okinawan immigrants feature prominently on many menus. There is also a distinctly Paraguayan influence here. *Sopa paraguaia,* a savory cake made with eggs, corn, milk, cheese and onions, is popular, as is *tereré,* a cold and refreshing *maté* (tea).

Finding somewhere to eat on a Sunday night can be tough though, as most places close!

Galpão Gaucho   SELF-SERVE $
(☑ 3382-5108; Kardec 187; meals R$18) If you like the all-you-can-eat experience but don't have a wallet as big as your stomach, give this central cheapie a go. It has the added bonus of being open on a Sunday, too.

★**Cantina Romana**   ITALIAN $$
(☑ 3324-9777; www.cantinaromana.com.br; Rua da Paz 237; mains for 2 R$30-48; ⊙ 11am-2pm & 6-11pm Tue-Sun) Shock-value old school Italian cantina and pizzeria. Attentive service, mega portions and authentic surroundings

to pig out in. Try the *tagliarini alla cacciatora* for two (R$35).

Comitiva Pantaneira   SELF-SERVE $$
(☑ 3383-8799; www.comitivapantaneira.com. br; Dom Aquino 2221; per kg weekday/weekend R$34.90/39.90; ⊙ 11am-3pm) A massive perkilo swarming with locals digging into seriously good *pantaneira* cowboy cuisine.

Fogo Caipira   BRAZILIAN $$$
(☑ 3324-1641; www.fogocaipira.com.br; José Antônio 145; dishes R$28-65; ⊙ 11am-2pm & 7-11pm Thu-Fri, to midnight Sat, to 4pm Sun) The best dishes at this regional institution require an advance order, such as the *galinhada* (chicken stew, six hours, R$61) or *pacu recheado* (a tasty fish stuffed with manioc and spices, three hours, R$65). It's pricey, but as the only restaurant in the city with culinary stars, it's worth it.

Ceará   SEAFOOD $$$
(☑ 3321-3927; Dom Aquino 2249; meals for 2 R$48-80, lunch buffet weekday/weekend R$40/48; ⊙ 11am-3pm & 6-11pm Tue-Sun) One of the city's best *peixarias* (fish restaurants). The pintado in a tomato stew with banana *mandioca* (cassava) incites tears of culinary joy.

Casa Colonial   CONTEMPORARY $$$
(☑ 3383-3207; www.casacolonial.com.br; Av Afonso Pena 3997; mains R$45-70; ⊙ 11am-2:30pm Wed-Sun, 6:30pm-midnight Tue-Sun) The walk-in wine cellar is the first thing that catches your eye when you enter this sophisticated bar-restaurant, which positively oozes medieval romance.

Drinking

Campo Grande's nightlife knows no evening off, especially beyond the 3900 block of Av Afonso Pena, east of downtown where there is a cluster of happening bars.

Cachaçaria Brasil   BAR
(☑ 3313-6731; www.cachacariabrasilms.com.br; Av Fernando Correa da Costa 165; ⊙ 5pm-2am Mon-Sat) Samba, over 100 kinds of *cachaça* (sugarcane alcohol) and live *futebol* make this Campo Grande's in place for a crowd of all ages. With a bamboo beach-bar atmosphere, gigantic menu of food and drink, pool tables and live music every night, there is a little bit of something for everybody here.

Barbaquá   BAR
(☑ 3321-8576; Rio Grande do Sul 375; ⊙ 6pm-late Mon-Sat) A beautiful candlelit bar in a

restored house, full of local art. The intimate space attracts an artistic crowd, which comes for the live jazz and MPB nightly and upscale *tereré* (drinking).

Café Mostarda
BAR

(☎3301-9990; www.cafemostarda.com.br; Av Afonso Pena 3952; ☺6pm-late Tue-Sun) The rich and beautiful practically trip over themselves onto Av Afonso Pena at this trendy outdoor cafe, with live music nightly.

🛍 Shopping

Casa do Artes
ARTS & CRAFTS

(☎3383-2633; Av Calógeras 2050; ☺8am-6pm Mon-Fri, to noon Sat) Sells colorful indigenous ceramics, wooden crafts, sacred art and locally brewed liquor.

ℹ Information

EMERGENCY
Ambulance (☎192)
Fire Department (☎193)
Police (☎190)

INTERNET ACCESS
Matrix Cyber Café (☎3029-6706; Av Calógeras 2069; per hr R$2.50; ☺7:30am-7pm Mon-Sat)

MEDICAL SERVICES
Clínica Campo Grande (☎3323-9000; Marechal Rondon 1703)
Santa Casa (☎3322-4172; Rua 13 de Mayo)

MONEY
Banco do Brasil (Av Afonso Pena 2202; ☺11am-4pm Mon-Fri) Visa/MasterCard ATM and money exchange.
Bradesco (Av Afonso Pena 1828; ☺11am-4pm Mon-Fri) Visa/MasterCard ATM.

POST
Post Office (☎3389-5100; cnr Av Calógeras & Dom Aquino; ☺8am-5:30pm Mon-Fri, 8-11:30am Sat)
Post Office (☎3389-5137; Rui Barbosa 2810)

TOURIST INFORMATION
There are small tourist kiosks at the **bus station** (☎3314-4448; Rodoviária; ☺6am-10pm), **airport** (☎3363-3116; international airport arrivals hall; ☺6:15am-midnight) and the **Feira Central** (☎3314-3872; Feira Central; ☺6-10pm Wed-Sun).

CAT Morada dos Bais (☎3314-9968; Av Afonso Pena; ☺8am-6pm Tue-Sat, 9am-noon Sun) In a big cream-coloured colonial building, the Morada dos Bais, this is the best tourist office in the region and home to a museum dedicated to local miniature artist Lidia Bais. Friendly staff (most are tourism students) offer an excellent city map and an extensive database with information about the state. They won't recommend Pantanal tour companies though!

ℹ Getting There & Around

AIR
Aeroporto Internacional de Campo Grande (☎3368-6050; Av Duque de Caixas) is 7km from town; to get there, take the Indubrasil bus from the bus station (R$2.85, every 30 minutes). A taxi costs around R$30.

BUSES FROM CAMPO GRANDE

DESTINATION	FARE (R$)	TIME (HR)	COMPANY
Bonito	59	5	Cruzeiro do Sul (www.cruzeirodosulms.com.br)
Brasília	210-236	16	Motta (www.motta.com.br), São Luiz (www.expressosaoluiz.com.br)
Corumbá	81-103	6	Andorinha (www.andorinha.com)
Cuiabá	90-106	10	Andorinha (www.andorinha.com), Eucatur (www.eucatur.com.br), Motta (www.motta.com.br), Nova Integração (www.novaintegracao.com.br), São Luiz (www.expressosaoluiz.com.br), Viação Ouro e Prata (www.viacaoouroeprata.com.br)
Foz do Iguaçu	125	14	Nova Integração (www.novaintegracao.com.br)
Ponta Porã	62	6	Expresso Queiroz (www.expressoqueiroz.com.br)
Rio de Janeiro	204	23	Andorinha (www.andorinha.com)
São Paulo	146-173	15	Andorinha (www.andorinha.com), Motta (www.motta.com.br)

Daily flights with national airlines link Campo Grande to São Paulo, Cuiabá, Corumbá, Rio, Brasília and Porto Velho, and there is talk of a new route to Asunción, Paraguay.

BUS

Campo Grande's plush new **bus station** (☑ 3313-8707; Av Gury Marques 1215) is 6km outside the centre on the road to São Paulo. Local buses 061, 085, 087, 162, 165 and 189 (R$2.85) run from here to the centre. To use city buses you need to buy an an **Assetur** (☑ 0800-647-0060; www.assetur.com.br; Visconde de Taunay 345) *passe de ônibus* (bus pass) from news stands, pharmacies or bus stop kiosks. They come as one-time use *(unitario)* or rechargable *(recarregável)*. A taxi to the centre will cost around R$25.

Nondirect buses to Corumbá stop in Miranda and Aquidauana, and can drop you at the intersection with Estrada Parque. **Vanzella** (☑ 3255-3005; www.vanzellatransportes. com.br) run a direct minibus service to Bonito (R$80) which leaves from the airport at 1pm and 3pm.

TRAIN

Pantanal Express Train Bus (Trem do Pantanal; ☑ 3043-2233; www.traverdeexpress. com; Av Afonso Pena, Morada dos Bais; to Aquidauana R$120, to Miranda R$150) The *Pantanal Express* runs approximately monthly between Campo Grande and Miranda (11 hours) via Aquidauana (five hours). It's a scenic, if not particularly quick, way of making the journey. Departures are from the train station 18km from the centre. Transport to the station from the Morada dos Bais (p382) costs R$25.

It departs Campo Grande at 8am on a Saturday morning and returns from Miranda at 8am on a Sunday, with a lengthy lunch stop at Aquidauana en route.

Corumbá

☑ 0XX67 / POP 104,000

'Corumbaly' old Corumbá is a gracefully ageing port city close to the Bolivian border. Known as Cidade Branca (White City), it is 403km northwest of Campo Grande by road. The city sits atop a steep hill overlooking the Rio Paraguai; on the far side of the river, a huge expanse of the Pantanal stretches out on the horizon. Divided into two parts, the upper city contains most of the commerce, and the lower city is the old port area.

Founded in 1776 by Captain Luis de Albuquerque, by 1840 it had become the biggest river port in the world and boasted a dozen foreign consulates. The impressive buildings along the waterfront reflect the wealth that passed through the town in the 19th century. However, with the coming of the railway, Corumbá lost its importance as a port and went into decline.

These days, despite spending most of the year as a sleepy backwater, the city is home to the region's biggest **Carnaval** (www.carnavaldecorumba.com.br) during a long weekend in mid-February. The tradition was imported by naval officers, many from Rio, who found themselves stationed here and felt the need to liven things up.

◉ Sights & Activities

Corumbá's star attraction is the Pantanal; you can get a preview of it from the highest point in the area, **Morro Urucum** (1100m), 20km south of Corumbá. The Christ statue that overlooks the bus station on the hillside is the **Cristo Rei do Pantanal**.

Muhpan   MUSEUM
(Museu de História do Pantanal; ☑ 3232-0303; www.muhpan.org.br; Manoel Cassava 275; ⊙ 1-6pm Tue-Sat) **FREE** On the waterfront the city's glitziest attraction is Muhpan, full of interactive exhibits that tell the story of the formation of the Pantanal and the human struggles faced by its settlers. It is part of ongoing development in the port area that hopes to revitalize the city's flagging tourist industry.

Museu do Pantanal   MUSEUM
(Instituto Luiz de Albuquerque; ☑ 3231-5757; Praça da República; ⊙ 8am-noon & 2-5:30pm Mon-Fri) **FREE** The Instituto Luiz de Albuquerque houses the Museu do Pantanal, which contains a reasonably interesting collection of indigenous artifacts, local modern art and a library.

Forte Junqueira   FORT
(☑ 3231-5828; Cáceres 425; ⊙ 9:30-11am & 2-4:30pm Mon-Fri) Forte Junqueira is the only intact fort left near the city. It's a tiny hexagonal fort with 50cm-thick walls, though the real highlight is the excellent view of the Rio Paraguai and the Pantanal in the distance.

To get here, go east along Dom Aquino and turn left at the athletics ground. Once you hit the waterfront, continue east for another 10 minutes. The entrance is an unmarked door to the left of the main gate.

Art Izu   CULTURAL BUILDING
(Av Cuiabá 558; ⊙ 7-11am & 1-5pm Mon-Fri) Art Izu is home to one of Corumbá's premier

Corumbá

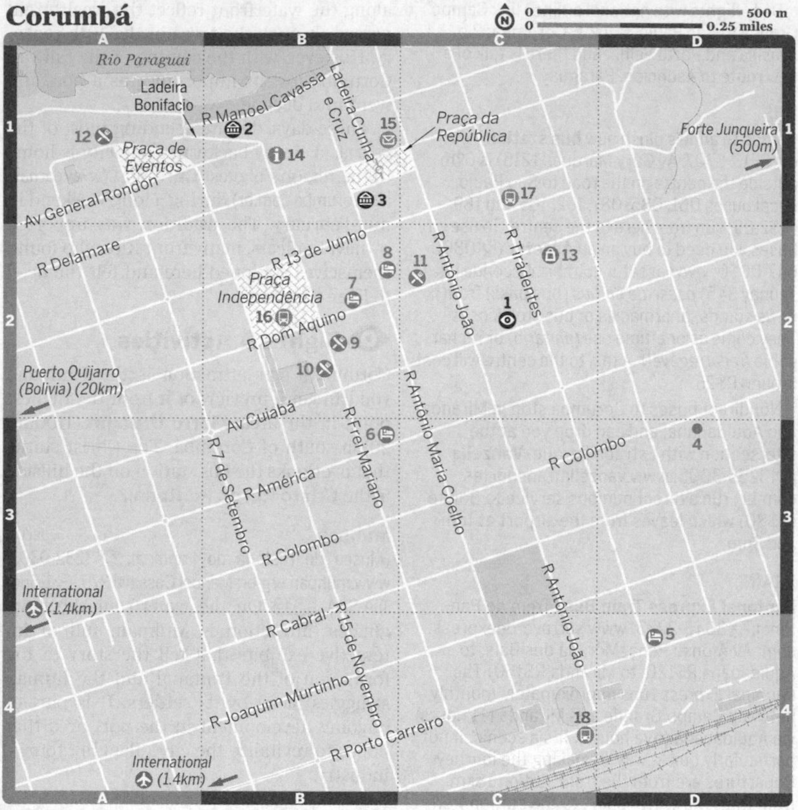

artists, Izulina Xavier. You can't miss it – the giant bird sculptures and bronze statue of São Francisco in the front yard are stunning and the crazy paving in front is, well, crazy.

Rio Paraguai Cruise BOAT TOUR
Between three and five hours long, cruises along the Rio Paraguai usually take in the Base Fluvial de Ladário, Brazil's first river arsenal, dating from 1872. Longer trips also stop for a little fishing. They can be booked through any travel agent, but require a minimum of 20 people.

Sleeping

There are some cheap hotels close to the long-distance bus station if you're just spending a night in Corumbá. Otherwise, there are better places closer to the waterfront and the restaurants and bars in the center of town.

Hotel El Dorado HOTEL $
(☎3231-6677; Porto Carreiro 554; s/d/tr R$100/148/160; ❄📶) A good option just off the corner of the bus station. The best value in town, all said and done.

Hotel Santa Rita HOTEL $
(☎3231-5453; www.santaritahotel.com; Dom Aquino 860; s/d/tr R$70/130/180; ❄📶) Cheapish central option with everything you are likely to need without being the sort of place that memories are made of.

Hotel Nacional HOTEL $$
(☎3234-6000; www.hnacional.com.br; América 936; s/d R$158/200; ❄@📶🏊) The rooms here are a bit nicer than the institutionalized hallways suggest. It's the top option in town.

Santa Mônica Palace Hotel HOTEL $$
(☎3234-3000; www.hsantamonica.com.br; Coelho 345; s/d R$136/185; ❄@📶🏊) A favorite

Corumbá

with tour groups, it's an aging building in the center of town. A makeover didn't quite stretch to replacing the telephones and mini-bars. They are like museum pieces!

✖ Eating

★ Avalom Grill INTERNATIONAL **$$**
(☑3231-4430; Frei Mariano 499; meals R$21-59; ☺11am-3pm & 7-11pm) Atmospheric, upscale Avalom bills itself as a culinary journey through the history of Corumbá, paying homage to the diverse groups of settlers, with indigenous, Portuguese, French, Spanish and Italian dishes on the menu. Streets ahead of the competition.

Peixaria do Lulu SEAFOOD **$$**
(☑3232-7855; Dom Aquino 738; meals for 2 R$35-50; ☺10:30am-3pm & 6:30-10pm Mon-Sat, 10:30am-3pm Sun) Lulu is the fried-fish king in Corumbá. Don't let the humble appearance fool you – Peixaria do Lulu offers superb regional fish dishes. It's a friendly, family-run place.

Vivabella ITALIAN **$$**
(☑3232-3587; Arthur Mangabeira 1; meals for 2 R$28-35; ☺5pm-late Mon-Sat) Vivabella is perched precariously on a hillside over the Rio Paraguai. Beautiful sunsets over the Pantanal and Bolivia beyond are the main draw on the outdoor deck at this small Italian restaurant and bar.

**Laço do Ouro
Churrascaria** CHURRASCARIA **$$**
(☑3231-7371; Frei Mariano 556; meals for 2 R$32-59, pizzas R$22-27; ☺10am-2am) *Corumbaense* flock to this bar-restaurant to beat the heat: extra large *garrafas* of beer line the outdoor tables, which fill up fast on weekends.

Shopping

Casa de Artesão ARTS & CRAFTS
(Dom Aquino 405; ☺8:30-11am & 1:30-5pm Mon-Fri) Here the old prison has swapped inmates for artists, who hawk their indigenous arts and crafts from former cells.

❶ Information

EMERGENCY
Federal Police (☑3231 5848; Praça da República 51; ☺8-11:30am & 1:30-5:30pm Mon-Fri)

INTERNET ACCESS
It's surprisingly hard to get online, with most places closing at 6pm.
M@b Cyber (Antônio Maria Coelho 192; per hr R$2.50; ☺8am-9pm Mon-Sat)

MEDICAL SERVICES
Hospital Santa Casa (☑3231-2441; 15 de Novembro 854)

MONEY
It seems shady business, but some shopkeepers on Rua 13 de Junho change reais, dollars, euros and bolivianos. All banks listed have ATMs that accept foreign cards.
Banco do Brasil (13 de Junho 914)
Bradesco (Delamare 1067)
HSBC (Delamare 1068)

POST
Post Office (Delamare 708; ☺8:30am-5pm Mon-Fri, 8-11:30am Sat)

TRAVEL AGENCIES
Pantanal tours, and boat and fishing tours of the Corumbá environs are available from all travel agencies or by consultation in the boat offices along the port road Manoel Cassava. For Pantanal tours from Corumbá, see also p373.

Mutum Turismo (☎3231-1818; www.mutum-turismo.com.br; Frei Mariano 17; ⊙8am-6pm Mon-Fri, to 1pm Sat) A reliable and long-established travel agency for Pantanal river cruises.

❶ Getting There & Away

Corumbá is primarily a transit point for travel to/from Bolivia. To get to Paraguay by river you'll need to strike a private deal with a boatman down in the port area. It won't be cheap!

AIR

Corumbá **international airport** (☎3231-3322; Santos Dumont, Bairro Aeroporto) is 3km west of the town center. Flights are limited these days and the only regular service is a Trip/TAM flight that links the city with Campo Grande via Bonito.

BUS

From the **long-distance bus station** (☎3231-2033; Rua Porto Carreiro), regular buses run to Campo Grande (R$81-103, six hours) but it pays to buy your ticket in advance. One **Cruzeiro do Sul** (www.cruzeirodosulms.com.br) bus a day meanders its way to Bonito (R$65, seven hours).

The centre is easily walkable from the bus station, or take a moto-taxi R$5.

❶ Getting Around

From the bus stop, located outside the long-distance bus station, the Cristo Redentor bus runs to the **local bus terminal** (Rua 13 de Junho), though its easy enough to walk it. From here you can catch the hourly **Popular Nova bus** to the airport.

A taxi from the centre to the airport costs around R$15 – make sure the taxi has a meter or establish a price before you get in, as some drivers like to play gringo rip-off.

Bonito & Around

☑0XX67 / POP 19,500

Bonito is *the* ecotourism model for Brazil. This small aquatic playground in the southwestern corner of Mato Grosso do Sul has few attractions of its own, but the natural resources of the surrounding area are spectacular, and local authorities have taken the high road in their regulation and maintenance. There are caves with lakes and amazing stalactite formations, beautiful waterfalls and incredibly clear rivers surrounded by lush forest where it's possible for divers to swim eyeball to eyeball with hundreds of fish.

Since Bonito exploded on the ecotourism map in the early 1990s, the number of visitors has risen dramatically every year, leading to the creation of the 76-sq-km Serra da Bodoquena national park in 2000. Though some of the attractions are within the park boundaries, the vast majority of the protected area is off-limits to visitors.

Bonito is a one-street show. Coronel Pilad Rebuá is a 3km stretch that's home to everything you are likely to need during your stay.

GETTING TO/FROM BOLIVIA

The **Fronteira** bus (R$2.50, 15 minutes) goes from Corumbá's Praça Independência to the Bolivian border every 25 minutes from 6am to 7pm. A taxi from the centre to the border is around R$27 while groups of two or less traveling light are better off using a moto-taxi (R$15).

All Brazilian exit formalities must be completed with the **Polícia Federal** (☎3234-7822; www.dpf.gov.br; ⊙8-11am & 2-5pm Mon-Fri, 9am-1pm Sat & Sun) at the border. Both countries work limited matching office hours, so be prepared to overnight in Corumbá if you are crossing outside of them. To enter Bolivia, most countries do not need a visa, but citizens of the United States must obtain a visa (US$135) from abroad or at the **Bolivian Consulate** (☎3231-5605; coliviancorumbams@hotmail.com; Porto Carrero 1650; ⊙8am-12:30pm & 2-4:30pm Mon-Fri) in Corumbá.

In Bolivia *colectivos* (B$3) and taxis (B$10) run the 3km between the border and Quijarro train station for onward travel to Santa Cruz. The *Tren Regional* is the slowest and cheapest and departs daily except Sunday at 12:45pm (21 hours, B$115). The fastest, most comfortable and most expensive train is the *Ferrobus* which departs at 7pm on Tuesday, Thursday and Saturday (14 hours, B$257). The intermediate *Expreso Oriental* leaves at 4:30pm on Tuesday, Thursday and Sunday (16 hours, B$127). Buy tickets in advance if you can.

The road from Puerto Quijarro to Santa Cruz is now much improved and an increase in bus traffic is likely over the coming years.

BONITO: A BEAUTIFUL WATER WORLD

If you bought a bunch of exotic fish and dumped them into your uncle's swimming pool, then jumped in with some goggles, you'd have an idea of what Bonito has to offer. But how did this happy accident of nature happen? The river waters spring from subterranean sources in a limestone base, almost entirely free of clay, which releases calcium carbonate into the water. The calcium carbonate calcifies all impurities in the water, which then sink to the riverbed (this is the reason you're asked to stay afloat and not touch the bottom during river tours). The result is an area filled with natural aquariums surrounded by lush forest – a beautiful environment in which to study the abundant and fascinating fish of the rivers and streams.

◉ Sights & Activities

There are few things to do around town, but taking a tour is mandatory to visit the more enticing attractions in the surrounding area.

Project Jibóia   SNAKE SHOW
(☑ 3255-2328; www.projetojiboia.com.br; Nestor Fernandes G10, admission R$25; ⊙ 7pm) Project Jibóia is a one-man crusade to change the world's opinion of snakes. Its an entertaining 90-minute show in Portuguese with plenty of audience participation and complete with boa constrictors that you nearly swap spit with by the end of the night. By the time you slither out you'll have a new respect for our scaly friends.

Aquario do Bonito   AQUARIUM
(Coronel Pilad Rebuá; admission R$20; ⊙ 9am-11pm) If you can't tell a pacú from a pirapu-tanga, wade through this makeshift aquarium of Pantanal *peixes*, with a remarkably unremarkable room full of rusty junk tagged on at the end.

Balneário Municipal   SWIMMING
(admission R$15; ⊙ 8am-6pm) The only natural attraction that doesn't need a guide or tour is the Balneário Municipal, a natural swimming pool on the Rio Formoso with clear water and lots of fish, 7km southeast of town. You can spend the whole day here mingling with locals and have lunch at the kiosks. A moto-taxi costs about R$7 one-way.

Villa Rebuá   ADVENTURE SPORTS
(Coronel Pilad Rebuá; per 40min R$30) Rock-climbing and *arvorismo* ('tree-top' trails) over a carpark, for a monkey's eye view of Bonito.

Taboa Fabrica   CULTURAL TOUR
(☑ 3255-2556; www.taboa.com.br; Flinto Muller; admission R$25; ⊙ 2-8pm) Its hard to get a handle on what the Taboa Fabrica really is, but

you'll see a bit of pottery, some handicrafts being made and at the end get a chance to sample some *cachaça*.

☞ Tours

If only everywhere in Brazil was as organized as Bonito, life would be a whole lot easier for travelers. The local government has strict regulations in place for visiting the area's natural attractions, partly because many are on private land and partly to minimize the impact on some pristine areas. Most attractions have a daily limit on the number of visitors they will accept, and an authorized, locally registered guide must accompany visitors at all sites. Not all guides speak English.

Countless travel agencies in Bonito offer a smorgasbord of different tours, but in truth it is easiest to arrange your trips through your hotel. Transport is usually only included in the cost when you book through a hotel, not an agency, but it sometimes depends on group size and you should ask in advance.

Snorkelling and *flutação* (flotation) in Bonito's incredibly clear waters are the main attractions, but remember that sunscreen is not allowed. Other adventurous diversions, include rappelling (abseiling), diving in underground lakes and some challenging *arvorismo* (treetop rope courses and sightseeing) will also get your adrenalin pumping. Many of the best tours take a full day and will include lunch.

In the high season, the most popular tours must be booked in advance. You'll need a solid three days to take in the best of Bonito.

Gruta do Lago Azul   CAVE
(half-day excursion R$36) A bargain attraction is the Gruta do Lago Azul, a large cave with a luminous underground lake and stalactite

MATO GROSSO & MATO GROSSO DO SUL BONITO & AROUND

Bonito

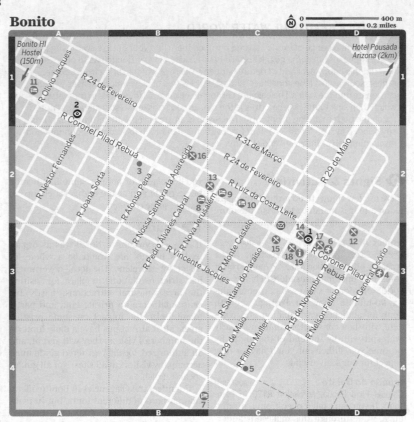

formations 20km west of Bonito. It's often the postcard view of Bonito, and is worth seeing, but it's only truly miraculous in late December and early January, when the sun shines in at just the right angle.

★ **Abismo de Anhumas** ADVENTURE TOUR
(www.abismoanhumas.com.br; rapelling R$460, scuba diving R$630) Abismo de Anhumas, 20km west of Bonito, is like a journey to Middle Earth. It's a 72m abyss culminating in an underground lake, home to incredible stalactite formations. The **rappelling training center** (Rua General Osório) is in town and you must successfully complete your training before 6pm on the day before your visit.

The tour involves rappelling down to the bottom and snorkeling or scuba diving in the lake (visibility is 30m). The whole thing is otherworldly – Bonito's most unforgettable attraction by a landslide, but it's limited to 18 visitors per day.

Nascente Azul SNORKELING
(www.nascenteazul.com.br; full day incl lunch R$140) Bonito's best kept secret is this fabulous new flutação attraction, 29km from town. It begins with a 1900m forest trek that culminates in your arrival at the breathtakingly beautiful *nascente* (spring), an indigo-coloured gateway to the centre of the earth. From here you leisurely float your way back to base along a crystal-clear forest stream teeming with fish.

Rio da Prata SNORKELING
(www.riodaprata.com.br; 5hr trip incl lunch R$198; ⏱6:30am-2pm) 🌿 The marvelous Rio da Prata, 56km south of Bonito, includes a trek through rainforest and some great snorkeling. The latter involves a 3km float downstream along the Rio Olha d'Agua, amazingly crystal clear and full of fish; and Rio da Prata, a little foggier but still fantastic for viewing massive pacu and big, scary dourado.

Bonito

This place should be near the top of your list. The afternoon 'contemplative' visit to Buraco das Araras (R$25), often tagged on, is forgettable, unless you are keen to see macaws.

Boca da Onça Ecotour   SWIMMING, WATERFALL
(☎3268-1711; www.bocadaonca.com.br; trekking incl lunch R$123, incl rappelling R$275; ◎9:30am-6pm) The Boca da Onça Ecotour, 59km northwest of Bonito, is a nicely manicured 4km trail through the forest to a series of 11 waterfalls, a few of which you can take a chilly dip in. It all culminates with the 156m Boca da Onça waterfall, an impressive cascading waterfall that takes the state's highest honors.

If you pass the course at their **training center** (Coronel Pilad Rebuá) you can also rapel from reportedly the highest platform in Brazil here. It's an 880-step climb back to the *fazenda*, where there is an excellent lunch and hang time by a fantastic natural riverwater pool, full of local fish.

**Reserva Ecológica
Baía Bonita**   SNORKELING, WILDLIFE RESERVE
(3hr tour R$152; ◎6am-7pm) Seven kilometers southeast of Bonito, this reserve is home to the Aquário Natural and the Trilha dos Animais. The half-day tour includes snorkeling in a beautiful natural spring with 30 varieties of fish and subaquatic vegetation, and then a short 900m flotation in the Rio Baía Bonita. The price includes wetsuits, snorkels and lunch.

You can also tack on an optional visit to the **Trilha dos Animais**, a zoo of regional animals including an impressive anaconda, a well-trained tapir and a cute little ocelot.

Rio Sucuri   SNORKELLING
(3hr trip R$138) The Rio Sucuri, 20km southwest of Bonito, is a 1500m snorkel with springs and a crystal-clear river with subaquatic gardens, surrounded by lush forest – but it's further out in the wild and is better for vegetation than for fish.

⌂ Sleeping

New accommodations continue to spring up in Bonito and though it is no longer as difficult as it was to find a room in high season, you should still book ahead to get the hotel you want at peak times. Out of season, higher-end options may slash their prices by as much as 50%. High season prices (December to March) are quoted throughout this section to help you avoid a nasty shock!

★**Bonito HI Hostel**   HOSTEL $
(☎3255-1462; www.ajbonito.com.br; Lúcio Borralho 716; dm R$50, apt with/without air-con R$150/100; ❋@⊕✱) ❡ One of Brazil's top HI hostels, this well-oiled backpacker paradise has a virtual monopoly on the budget end of the Bonito market. Hammocks, pools, kitchen, laundry, bikes for hire, multilingual staff – there is nothing they haven't thought of. Dorms come with private bathrooms, and the private rooms just around the corner from the main hostel are hotel standard.

Pousada Muito Bonito   POUSADA $
(☎3255-1645; www.hotelmuitobonito.com.br; Coronel Pilad Rebuá 1444; s/d/tr R$60/110/140; P❋@⊕) ❡ You will struggle to find better value than at this excellent budget pousada in the centre. Owner Mario Doblack speaks five languages and offers very well-appointed budget rooms around a small courtyard. He is also a mine of information on the area, being one of the first guides to establish themselves back before Bonito went mainstream. Its just three blocks from the bus station.

Pousada São Jorge INN **$**
(✆3255-4046; Coronel Pilad Rebuá 1605; s/d/tr R$70/120/180; ✳@📶) There's decent English spoken and a nice breakfast at this budget option, run by an extremely friendly couple. Some rooms are a little dark.

Wetiga Hotel de Natureza LUXURY HOTEL **$$**
(✆3255-5100; www.wetigahotel.com.br; Coronel Pilad Rebuá 679; s/d/tr R$324/374/488; P✳@📶🏊) ✎ The remarkable wood-and-stone architecture is more interesting than the rather simple rooms, which all overlook a nice courtyard and pool. Ask for a reduction during the off season.

Hotel Pousada Arizona CABIN **$$**
(✆3255-4190; http://hotelpousadaarizona.com. br; Águas Marinhas 680; s/d/tr R$241/353/490; ✳@📶🏊) Colorful, award-winning brick-and-wood bungalows surround the best pool (and poolside bar) in town at this 16-room retreat 2km from the main drag.

Pousada Remanso HOTEL **$$**
(✆3255-1137; www.pousadaremanso.com.br; Coronel Pilad Rebuá 1515; s/d/tr R$149/218/291; P✳📶🏊) Recently-remodelled, good-value, midrange option right in the heart of town, with leather hammocks, nicely maintained landscaping and a small pool.

Hotel Pousada Águas de Bonito POUSADA **$$**
(✆3255-2330; www.aguasdebonito.com.br; Rua 29 de Maio 1679; s/d/tr R$274/350/458; ✳@🏊) This pousada offers a little more character than others in town. Rooms are modern and spacious and the ones on the second level have pleasant patios.

✗ Eating

As you might expect for a tourist mecca there is a cosmopolitan selection of restaurants and quality is high.

Vicio da Gula Café SANDWICHES **$**
(✆3255-2041; Coronel Pilad Rebuá 1852; sandwiches R$7-22; ◷noon-2am) Popular corner spot for great burgers, fries and açaí na tigela (a berrylike fruit, in a bowl).

San Marino Pizza PIZZERIA **$$**
(✆3255-2656; Luiz da Costa Leite 1543; pizzas R$29-39; ◷6pm-midnight Wed-Mon) The four-cheese pizza from this outlet of the Campo Grande pizzeria of the same name is the best in town.

O Casarão SELF-SERVE **$$**
(✆3255-1970; Coronel Pilad Rebuá 1835; buffet R$24.90) Bouncing buffet joint on the main drag.

Tapera REGIONAL **$$**
(✆3255-1757; Coronel Pilad Rebuá 1957; portions for 2 R$40-60) Despite being one of the oldest restaurants in town, bright and breezy Tapera has had to work hard in recent years to gain a solid reputation for full-bodied fish dishes and bountiful beef platters.

Cantinho do Peixe SEAFOOD **$$**
(✆3255-3381; Coronel Pilad Rebuá 1437; meals R$27-60; ◷11am-3pm & 6-11pm Mon-Sat) Pintado (a type of catfish), fresh from Rio Miranda, ends up on plates 15 different ways at this simple, tasty spot just off the main drag. Try the pintado á urucum, a lasagna-like dish of pintado smothered in a tomato, condensed milk and mozzarella sauce.

★**Pantanal Grill** CHURRASCARIA **$$$**
(✆3255-2763; Coronel Pilad Rebuá 1808; meals for 2 R$28-60; ◷10am-11pm; ✳) ✎ Got a craving for capybara with bacon? What about peccary with pineapple? Make a beeline for Pantanal Grill. It's pricey but you'll find dishes here that you don't get in your local cafe. Don't worry, the meat is farmed, not wild.

★**A Casa do João** SEAFOOD **$$$**
(✆3255-1212; www.casadojoao.com.br; Nelson Felicio 664A; mains for 2 R$33-66; ◷11:30am-2:30pm & 6-11:30pm) ✎ Top spot in town for fish dishes, being especially famous for its traíra (a predatory fish) which comes in a range of sizes depending on your appetite. All the furniture here is made from recycled wood from fallen trees in the local area.

♟ Drinking

Taboa Bar BAR
(✆3255-1862; www.taboa.com.br; Coronel Pilad Rebuá 1837; ◷5pm-late) A graffiti-fueled institution on the main drag where locals and travelers converge over the house special: pinga (cachaça) with honey, cinnamon and guaraná.

ℹ Information

There is no official tourist information office in town, but there is no real need for one either. All hotels have all the tourist information you will need and will waste no time in telling you what your options are.

All travel agencies in Bonito are strictly regulated and all prices are fixed – so there's no use shopping around. Some, however, are more helpful than others. Regardless, most hotels can organize your tours for you at no extra cost.

Agência Ar (☑3255-1008; www.agenciaarbonito.com.br; Coronel Pilad Rebuá 1184; ☉24hr) Commercial all-purpose agency, handy if for no other reason than it's open 24 hours.

Banco do Brasil (Luiz da Costa Leite 2279; ☉9am-2pm)

Bradesco (Rebuá 1942)

Hospital (☑3255-3455; Pedro Apóstolo 201)

Post Office (Coronel Pilad Rebuá 1759; ☉8-11:30am & 1-4pm Mon-Fri)

ℹ Getting There & Away

Cruzeiro do Sul (p386) is the only bus company that serves Bonito. There are buses to Bonito from Campo Grande (R$59, five hours, five daily) and five in the opposite direction beginning at 5:30am, though only the 8am and noon services are direct. Additionally, Vanzella (p383) run a faster minibus service to Campo Grande (R$80) leaving Bonito at 7:30am and 10:30am, with hotel pick-up and drop-off. For Foz do Iguaçu it is easiest to head to Campo Grande and catch a direct bus from there.

One daily bus runs to Corumbá (R$65, seven hours, noon) for onward travel to Bolivia, and there is a daily noon service to Ponta Porã (R$52, five hours) for the border crossing to Paraguay.

Azul (p365) now flies between Bonito and São Paulo (Campinas) airport (from R$140, 1½ hours).

ℹ Getting Around

Unfortunately, many of Bonito's attractions are a fair hike from town, and there's no public transport. Hotels often provide transport, but not always and those booked through travel agencies rarely or never do. If you find yourself looking for transport, try the local shuttle service, Vanzella (p383), which will take you to any excursion provided there is a minimum of four people.

If you are part of a group, it might end up being more economical to hire a taxi for the full day (R$60 to R$150 depending on the distance) from any Ponto de Táxi. If you are on your own take your friendly neighborhood moto-taxi: to the Rio Sucuri (38km round-trip) and Gruta do Lago Azul (38km round-trip) and back to town costs R$45; to Rio da Prata (100km round-trip) costs R$90; and to Boca da Onça (120km round-trip) R$80. The drivers will wait around for the duration of the tour. As usual prices are fixed, so don't even bother trying to barter.

Ponta Porã

☑0XX67 / POP 78,000

It's a strange feeling to cross a street and change countries, but you can do just that in Ponta Porã, a bustling little border town divided from the Paraguayan town of Pedro Juan Caballero by Av Internacional. The beer changes from Skol to Pilsen and prices on electronics are slashed – other than that, it's hard to even notice there is a border here (Portunhol vernacular is rampant). There are only two reasons to come, because you are a member of the hordes of Brazilian bargain hunters, or because you are crossing to Paraguay. If you spend more than one night here, it had better be due to hospitalization.

It's not suburban Rio by any means, but it's a good idea to use extra caution, especially at night.

🛏 Sleeping & Eating

Hotel Guarujá　　　　　HOTEL **$**
(☑3431-9515; Guia Lopes 63; s/d R$70/135; ❇🛜) A bit tatty but still a good budget option with large *apartamentos*.

Pousada do Bosque　　　　POUSADA **$$**
(☑3431-1181; www.hotelpousadadobosque.com.br; Av Presidente Vargas 1151; s/d apt R$95/170; ❇🛜🏊) A little forested oasis just outside the center on the ritzy side of town. It's too nice for Ponta Porã, truth be told.

Hotel Barcelona　　　　　HOTEL **$$**
(☑3437-2500; www.hotelbarcelona.com.br; Guia Lopes 50; s/d R$135/165; P❇@🛜🏊) The nicest digs in the center, with big rooms (aged furniture free of charge) and a nice pool.

CROSSING THE BORDER TO PARAGUAY

Physically its as easy as walking over the road, legally it involves considerable messing around. Brazilian formalities take place at the **Federal Police** (☑3437-0500; Presidente Vargas; ☉9am-noon & 1-4pm Mon-Fri) in the town centre. Outside of working hours, if you can prove your need to travel is urgent (try 'I dont want to spend a night here!') they will stamp you up. The **Paraguayan immigration office** (☑3431-6312; Dr Francis; ☉7am-9pm) is 2km east of town in a big pink building next to Goodyear. They are open until 9pm, but there is no bell to ring if you are late.

From the bus station on Alberdi in Pedro Juan Caballero there are hourly buses to Asunción, (80,000-110,000G, seven hours) and Concepción (35,000G, four hours).

Mania de Pizza
PIZZERIA **$$**

(🖉 3431-2620; Tiradentes 754; pizza R$20-35; ⏺6pm-midnight) No fewer than 55 different toppings to choose from, with interesting combinations such as Korean and stroganoff, as well as a raft of dessert pizzas for those with a sweet tooth. Delivery available.

🛍 Shopping

Shopping China
SHOPPING CENTRE

(🖉 0xx36-74343; Ruta V c/Callejón Internacional, Pedro Juan Caballero; ⏺8:30am-7pm Mon-Sat, 9am-2pm Sun) Go see what all the fuss is about! This megastore has...well, *everything* and is teeming with wide-eyed Brazilians throwing down real after real for massive discounts on everything from Johnny Walker to Canon.

ℹ Getting There & Around

From the **bus station** (🖉 3431 4145), 4km from the center of Ponta Porã, **Expresso Quieroz** (www.expressoqueiroz.com.br) runs hourly to Campo Grande (R$62, six hours). There are three daily buses to São Paulo (R$190 to R$260, 25 hours) at 2:30pm, 4pm and 9pm with **Motta** (www.motta.com.br). Cruzeiro do Sul (p386) run direct to Bonito at 6:30am (R$10, one hour) and twice daily to Corumbá (R$120, 13½ hours) at 5am and 2pm. A local bus (R$2.85) runs between the main bus station and the central local bus station every 45 minutes until 10pm.

For Foz do Iguaçu, take a bus from the bus station on Alberdi in Pedro Juan Caballero (Paraguay) to Ciudad del Este (80,000-90,000G, eight hours, three daily), just across the border from Foz. You don't need a Paraguayan visa to transit through Paraguay on your way to Foz do Iguaçu but you do need an entry stamp.

Bahia

POP 13.5 MILLION

Best Places to Eat

➡ Maria Mata Mouro (p412)
➡ Portinha (p448)
➡ Caranguejo de Sergipe (p413)
➡ Cozinha Aberta (p457)
➡ Souza Bar (p426)

Best Beaches

➡ Trancoso (p447)
➡ Boipeba (p431)
➡ Caraíva (p448)
➡ Praia do Espelho (p448)

Why Go?

Africa meets South America in the staggeringly beautiful northeastern state of Bahia. The heady blend of two seemingly disparate cultures – classic Portuguese architecture and African drum beats, Catholic churches and Candomblé (Afro-Brazilian religion) – is unique, and for most travelers, truly intoxicating. Bahia's centerpiece is Salvador, a jewelbox colonial city with gilded churches, cobblestone streets, lively festivals, powerful percussion reverberating off old stone walls and capoeiristas (practioners of capoeira) battling against the backdrops of 16th-century buildings. But there's more to Bahia than its capital – with more than 900km of coastline, the state contains World Heritage listed sites, deserted beaches and paradisaical islands. In the south, idyllic coastal villages and a world-class underwater park attract sunbathers and divers, while inland, the Parque Nacional da Chapada Diamantina features waterfalls and quiet hiking paths waiting to be explored.

When to Go
Salvador

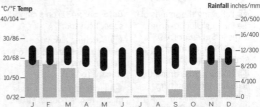

Dec–Mar Packed pousadas (guesthouses) and crowds in Salvador for February's Carnaval.

Apr–Sep Lovely warm weather, occasional rainy days.

Oct & Nov Minimal crowds and summery weather.

History

Prior to the Portuguese arrival, the region known today as Bahia had a wide variety of ethnic groups scattered inland and along the coast, speaking dozens of languages. Many of the tribes were wiped out by the Portuguese, though some – like the Pataxó – are still around today. The indigenous tribes

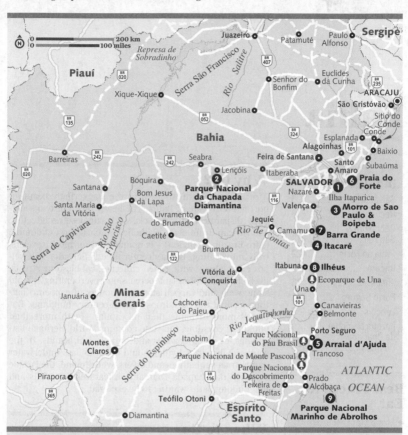

Bahia Highlights

❶ Following the sounds of the famous Olodum drum corps in **Salvador** (p395), Latin America's inspiring Afro-Brazilian capital.

❷ Hiking across dramatic plateaus and swimming in fresh waterfalls in the magnificent **Parque Nacional da Chapada Diamantina** (p458).

❸ Zooming around the island villages of gorgeous **Morro de São Paulo** (p428) and traditional

Boipeba (p431) on a classic speedboat tour.

❹ Catching a wave or taking a capoeira lesson on the sand in surfer-happy **Itacaré** (p433).

❺ Lingering over al fresco meals, taking coastal strolls and joining lively beach parties in **Arraial d'Ajuda** (p444).

❻ Watching tiny sea turtles hatch outside the TAMAR station in **Praia do Forte** (p422).

❼ Getting away from it all in the laid-back fishing village of **Barra Grande** (p432) on the Peninsula de Maraú.

❽ Tracing the footsteps of Brazil's literary great, Jorge Amado, in **Ilhéus** (p436).

❾ Diving beneath the deep to get face-to-face with tropical fish in the remote **Parque Nacional Marinho de Abrolhos** (p451).

practiced some form of agriculture, raising manioc, sweet potatoes and maize, and practiced hunting and fishing, while gathering fruits from the forests. Little else is known of the area's native population, who, for the most part, would disappear following the European arrival.

Portuguese sailors first made landfall near Porto Seguro in 1500, but it wasn't until one year later – All Saints' Day (November 1), according to legend – that Italian navigator Amerigo Vespucci sailed into Salvador's bay and named it Baía de Todos os Santos. Two generations later, in 1549, Tomé de Souza returned under orders of the Portuguese crown to found Brazil's first capital, Salvador da Bahia.

To fuel this new country, the colonists grew sugarcane and later tobacco in the *recôncavo* (region named after the concave shape of the bay) that surrounds the Baía de Todos os Santos. The Portuguese enslaved the indigenous people to work these fields, and when they proved insufficient, they brought over Africans in staggering numbers. From 1550 to 1850, at least 3.6 million slaves were brought from Africa to Brazil, and the majority ended up in the Northeast.

In such numbers, the slaves managed to maintain much of their African culture. When their own religious practices were prohibited, for instance, slaves moved their Candomblé *terreiros* (venues) underground and syncretized their gods with Catholic saints. African food and music enriched the homes of both blacks and whites, and the African culture deeply influenced the newly developing Brazilian culture.

Throughout the life of the colony, the Portuguese utilized a harsh plantation system that would keep African slaves tied to the land until their emancipation in 1888. In addition to sugar and tobacco, the Portuguese created cattle ranches, which spread inland, radiating west into the *sertão* (backlands) and Minas Gerais, then northwest into Piauí.

Primary products were shipped out, while slaves and European luxury goods were shipped in. Bahia was colonial Brazil's economic heartland, with Salvador da Bahia the capital of colonial Brazil between 1549 and 1763. The city was the center of the sugar industry, which sustained the prosperity of the country until the collapse in international sugar prices in the 1820s. During the gold and coffee booms in the south, Salvador continued its decline.

Industrialization in Bahia began in the mid-19th century and continued slowly, with developments in banking and industry, as new rail lines brought goods from the interior to Salvador's large port. Factories appeared and the economy, once a monoculture of the sugarcane industry, diversified. The most important event of the late 19th century was the emancipation of slaves, which brought freedom for many of Bahia's inhabitants.

In the 20th century, oil discoveries in the 1940s helped bring Bahia out of economic stagnation and contributed to the state's continued modernization. Today, Salvador remains an important port, exporting soy, fruit, cocoa, petrochemicals and sugarcane – which is once again achieving prominence for its role as a highly efficient biofuel. In recent decades, tourism has emerged as an important industry and, with the influx of cash, the state has invested in much-needed infrastructure and public-health projects.

🛈 Getting There & Away

Bahia's primary airport is located in its capital, Salvador, though Porto Seguro also has frequent and inexpensive flights.

Hwy BR-101 skirts the Bahian coastline but remains between 50km and 75km inland. It is the main thoroughfare through the state and the chosen route of most long-distance buses. There are good coastal highways only between Canavieiras and Itacaré and from Salvador north to the border with Sergipe.

🛈 Getting Around

Transportation is a snap in Bahia: there's always some way to get where you want to go. Aside from buses, Kombi vans and *bestas* (vans that run a specific route and will stop anywhere to drop off or pick up passengers) are common in rural areas, as are collective taxis.

SALVADOR

🎵 0XX71 / POP 2.68 MILLION

Salvador da Bahia has an energy and unadorned beauty that few cities can match. Once the magnificent capital of Portugal's great New World colony, Salvador is the country's Afro-Brazilian jewel. Its brilliantly hued center is a living museum of 17th- and 18th-century architecture and gold-laden churches. More importantly, Salvador is the nexus of an incredible arts movement. Wild festivals happen frequently, with drum

Salvador

0 — 1 km
0 — 0.5 miles

Terminal Marítimo
de São Joaquim (500m);
Mercado São Joaquim (500m)

Ladeira do
Baluarte

Praça de
Santo Antônio

R Direita de
Santo Antônio

SANTO
ANTÔNIO

Baía de Todos
os Santos

Av castelo Branco

Av de França

NAZARÉ

See Central Salvador Map (p400)

Vila
Olímpica

BARROQUINHA

Av Joana Angélica

TORORÓ

Av do Contorno

Av Marechal Costa Silva

Dique
do Tororó

Av Carlos Gomes

Av 7 de Setembro

CENTRO

R Forte de
São Pedro

BARRIS

R Theodoro
Sampaio

Av Vasco da Gama

Campo
Grande

Rua Leovigildo Figueira

VITÓRIA

CANELA

GARCIA

Av Reitor Miguel Calmon

Av Garibaldi

R da Graça

GRAÇA

FEDERAÇÃO

Av 7 de Setembro

See Salvador Barra Map (p404)

Av Centenário

R Ademar de Barro

BARRA

ONDINA

Av Almirante
Marques de Leão

Av Presidente Vargas

(27km)

(27km)

ATLANTIC OCEAN

Salvador

corps pounding out powerful rhythms against the backdrop of colonial buildings almost daily. At night, capoeira circles form on plazas and open spaces, while the scent of *acarajé* (bean and shrimp fritters) and other African delights fills the evening air. Elsewhere in town, a different spirit flows through the crowd as religious followers celebrate and reconnect with African gods at mystical Candomblé ceremonies. In fact, there's no other place in the world where descendants of African slaves have preserved their heritage as well as in Salvador – from music and religion to food, dance and martial-arts traditions.

Aside from the many attractions within Salvador, gorgeous coastline lies right outside the city – a suitable introduction to the tropical splendor of Bahia.

Chosen as one of Brazil's 12 host cities for the 2014 FIFA World Cup, Salvador is bracing for a major influx of visitors. Preparations have been slow to start, though. At the time of writing, construction was underway for an overhaul of the old Fonte Nova Stadium and city officials were discussing plans for improving the congested public-transportation system.

History

In 1549, Tomé de Souza landed on Praia Porto da Barra under Portuguese royal orders to found Brazil's first capital, bringing city plans, a statue, 400 soldiers and 400 settlers, including priests and prostitutes. He founded the city in a defensive location: on a cliff top facing the sea. After the first year a city of mud and straw had been erected, and by 1550 the surrounding walls were in place to protect against attacks from hostile *índios* (indigenous people). Salvador da Bahia remained Brazil's most important city for the next three centuries.

During its early years, the city depended upon the export of sugarcane and later tobacco from the fertile *recôncavo* region at the northern end of Baía de Todos os Santos. Later, cattle ranching was introduced, which, coupled with gold and diamonds from the Bahian interior, provided Salvador with immense wealth, as is visible in the city's opulent baroque architecture.

African slaves were first brought to Salvador in the mid-1500s, and in 1587 historian Gabriel Soares tallied an estimated 12,000 whites, 8000 converted *índios* and 4000 black slaves. The number of blacks eventually increased to constitute half of the city's population, and uprisings of blacks threatened Salvador's stability several times.

After Lisbon, Salvador was the second-most-important city in the Portuguese empire. It was the glory of colonial Brazil, famed for its many gold-filled churches, beautiful mansions and numerous festivals. It was also renowned as early as the 17th century for its bawdy public life, sensuality and decadence – so much so that its bay won the nickname Baía de Todos os Santos e de Quase Todos os Pecados (Bay of All Saints and of Nearly All Sins)!

Salvador remained Brazil's seat of colonial government until 1763 when, with the decline of the sugarcane industry, the capital was moved to Rio.

In 1798, the city was the stage for the Conjuração dos Alfaiates (Conspiracy of the Tailors) – the beginning of a wave of battles between Portuguese loyalists and those wanting independence. It was only on July 2, 1823, with the defeat of Portuguese troops in Cabrito and Pirajá, that the city found peace. At that time, Salvador numbered 45,000 inhabitants and was the commercial center of a vast territory.

For most of the 19th and 20th centuries the city stagnated as the agricultural economy foundered on its disorganized labor and production. Today, Salvador is Brazil's third-largest city, and it has only begun moving forward in the last few decades. New industries such as petroleum, chemicals and tourism have brought wealth to the city's coffers, but the rapidly increasing population is still faced with major economic and social problems.

BAHIA SALVADOR

◉ Sights

The Cidade Alta is packed with the city's most impressive sights, though you'll also find worthwhile museums in Vitória, a wonderfully scenic lighthouse in Barra and other fascinating attractions scattered about the city.

◉ Cidade Alta

Regardless of what the tourist information offices tell you, or even what's posted outside, the Pelourinho's churches keep sporadic opening hours – don't plan your day around getting inside one, or you may be disappointed.

★ Pelourinho   NEIGHBORHOOD

(Map p400) The centerpiece of the Cidade Alta is the Pelourinho, a Unesco-declared World Heritage site of colorful colonial buildings and magnificent churches. As you wander the cobblestoned streets, gazing up at the city's oldest architecture, you'll realize that the Pelô is not just for tourists. Cultural centers and schools of music, dance and capoeira pack these pastel-colored 17th- and 18th-century buildings.

The area has undergone major restoration work – which remains ongoing – since 1993 thanks to Unesco funding. Admittedly, the Pelô has lost a lot of its character in the process, but to say that it is now safer and better preserved is an understatement.

Igreja e Convento São Francisco   CHURCH

(Map p400; Cruzeiro de São Francisco; admission R$3) One of Brazil's most magnificent churches, the baroque Igreja e Convento São Francisco is filled with displays of wealth and splendor. An 80kg silver chandelier dangles over ornate wood carvings smothered in gold leaf, and the convent courtyard is paneled with hand-painted azulejos (Portuguese tiles). The complex was finished in 1723.

Forced to build their masters' church and yet prohibited from practicing their own religion, African slave artisans responded through their work: the faces of the cherubs are distorted, some angels are endowed with huge sex organs, while others appear pregnant. Most of these creative touches were chastely covered by 20th-century sacristans. The polychrome figure of São Pedro da Alcântara by Manoel Inácio da Costa shows a figure suffering from tuberculosis – just like the artist himself. One side of the saint's face

is more ashen than the other, so he appears to become more ill as you walk past him. José Joaquim da Rocha painted the entry hall's ceiling using perspective technique, a novelty during the baroque period.

Terreiro de Jesus   SQUARE

(Map p400; Praça 15 de Novembro) A colorful intersection of vendors, tourists, capoeiristas and colorful locals, the Terreiro de Jesus is a historic site of religious celebrations, and is ringed by four churches, as well as the 19th-century Faculdade de Medicina Building. The plaza feeds into the Cruzeiro de São Francisco, named for the cross in the square's center.

Museu Afro-Brasileiro   MUSEUM

(Map p400; ☑3283-5540; www.mafro.ceao.ufba. br; Terreiro de Jesus; adult/child R$6/3; ☺9am-5pm Mon-Fri) Holding one of Bahia's most important collections, the Museu Afro-Brasileiro exhibits wood carvings, baskets, pottery and other artwork and crafts linking Brazilian and African artistic traditions. The highlight of the museum is a room lined with 27 huge, breathtaking carved wooden panels by Argentine-born Carybé, who is perhaps Salvador's most renowned 20th-century fine artist.

The panels are stylized depictions of orixás (deities of the Afro-Brazilian religions), inlaid with shells and metals. There's also a worthwhile exhibit of photography, sacred objects and ceremonial apparel demonstrating the African roots of Brazilian Candomblé. At the time of writing, the museum was closed on weekends, though it plans to start opening on Saturday, as well.

Igreja da Ordem Terceira do Carmo   CHURCH

(Map p400; Largo do Carmo; admission by donation) The original church, founded in 1636, burnt to the ground; the present neoclassical structure dates from 1828. The nave has a French organ and a baroque altar with a scandalous statue of Nossa Senhora do Carmo. Church historians claim the statue was modeled in the likeness of Isabel II, daughter of Garcia d'Ávila, the largest landholder in the Northeast.

The artist, known as O Cabra (Half-Caste), was a slave with no artistic training, who was supposedly besotted with Isabel II. The Christ child cradled in the statue's arms has black features – could this be what O Cabra imagined their love child would look like? O Cabra took eight years to finish the life-size image of Christ (1630), with blood made from 2000 rubies. It's on display in the church's small museum.

Catedral Basílica CHURCH

(Map p400; Terreiro de Jesus; admission by donation) The Catedral Basílica dates from 1672 and is a marvelous example of Jesuit architecture. The interior is elegant and simple, with marble-covered walls and pillars that emphasize verticality. The sacristy has a beautiful carved jacaranda archway and a painted dome and floor.

Largo do Pelourinho SQUARE

(Map p400) The steep Largo do Pelourinho is a wide square that was once the site of the *pelourinho* (whipping post), where slaves were auctioned (historians disagree about whether slaves were publicly tortured here).

Museu da Cidade MUSEUM

(Map p400; ☑ 3321-1967; Largo do Pelourinho 1; admission R$3; ⊙ 9am-6pm Mon & Wed-Fri, 1-5pm Sat, 9am-1pm Sun) Rather like the city itself, Museu da Cidade contains an eclectic assortment of the old and the modern, the sacred and the profane. Exhibits include Candomblé *orixá* costumes, the personal effects of the poet Castro Alves (author of *Návio Negreiro*, or Slave Ship, and one of the first public figures to protest slavery), and traditional rag dolls enacting quotidian colonial life, as well as paintings and sculptures.

Igreja NS do
Rosário dos Pretos CHURCH

(Map p400; Largo do Pelourinho; admission by donation) The king of Portugal gave the Irmanidade dos Homens Pretos (Brotherhood of Black Men) the land for the periwinkle-blue Igreja NS do Rosário dos Pretos in 1704. Building in their free time, it took these slaves and freed slaves almost 100 years to complete it. The rococo facade includes design elements pertaining to Candomblé and tiled towers with indigenous flavor.

Fundação Casa de
Jorge Amado MUSEUM

(Map p400; ☑ 3321-0070; www.jorgeamado.org. br; Largo do Pelourinho; admission R$3, Wed free; ⊙ 10am-6pm Mon-Fri, to 4pm Sat) Literary types shouldn't miss a quick visit to the Fundação Casa de Jorge Amado, where visitors get an overview of the life of one of Brazil's best-known writers. A wall of Amado's book covers in every major language demonstrates his widespread popularity.

Praça da Sé SQUARE

(Map p400) The slick, L-shaped Praça da Sé has cool fountains and the fenced-off ruins of the foundations of its namesake church. At the far end of the plaza, the 1874 funicular railway **Plano Inclinado Gonçalves** (Map p400) used to send 30-passenger cars between Cidade Alta and Cidade Baixa on terrifyingly steep tracks – it's been out of service since 2011, though plans to restore the train are in the works.

★ Elevador Lacerda HISTORIC BUILDING

(Map p400; ☑ 3322-7049; fare R$0.25; ⊙ 7am-11pm, extended hr summer weekends & Carnaval) The beautifully restored, art deco Elevador Lacerda connects the Cidade Alta with Comércio via four elevators traveling 72m in about 30 seconds. The Jesuits installed the first manual rope-and-pulley elevator around 1610 to transport goods and passengers from the port to the settlement. In 1868 an iron structure with clanking steam elevators was inaugurated, replaced by an electric system in 1928.

Facing the elevator are the impressive arches of the Câmara Municipal, the 17th-century city hall, which occasionally puts on cultural exhibitions.

Praça Municipal SQUARE

(Map p400; Praça Tomé de Souza) Once the political seat of colonial Brazil, the Praça Municipal is now a lively place to people-watch and see panoramic views over the bay. Overlooking the plaza, note the impressive **Palácio Rio Branco** (Map p400; ☑ 3322-7255; Praca Municipal), reconstructed in 1919; the original 1549 structure housed the offices of Tomé de Souza, Brazil's first governor general.

Museu de Arqueologia
e Etnologia MUSEUM

(Archaeology & Ethnology Museum; Map p400; ☑ 3283-5530; www.mae.ufba.br; Faculdade de Medicina, Terreiro de Jesus; admission R$6; ⊙ 10am-5pm Mon-Fri) Below the Museu Afro-Brasileiro, the Museu de Arqueologia e Etnologia exhibits indigenous Brazilian pottery, bows and arrows, masks and feather headpieces. Also tucked between the building's arching stone foundations is 19th-century glass and porcelain found during the excavations for the metro.

Ladeira do Carmo MONUMENT

(Map p400) Leading away from the Pelourinho, the steep Ladeira do Carmo provides access to the **Escadas do Carmo**, a wide set of

BAHIA CIDADE ALTA

Central Salvador

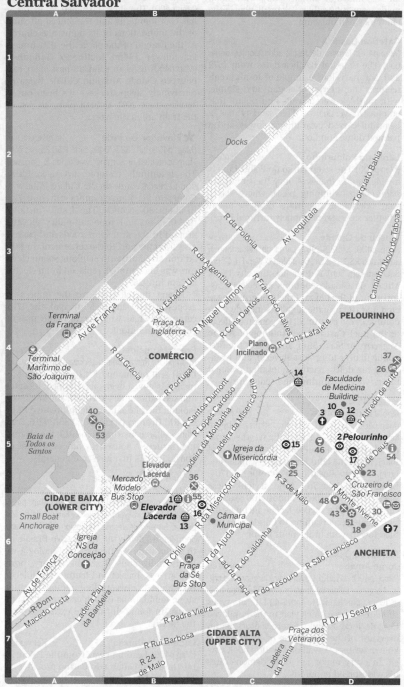

BAHIA SALVADOR

Docks

Torquato Bahia

R da Polônia

Av Jequitaia

R da Argentina

Av Estados Unidos

R Miguel Calmon

R Cons Dantos

R Francisco Galvea

Caminho Novo do Taboão

Terminal
da França

Av de França

Praça da
Inglaterra

PELOURINHO

R Cons Lafaiete

Terminal
Marítimo de
São Joaquim

R da Grécia

COMÉRCIO

R Portugal

Plano
Incilnado

37

26

R Alfredo de Brito

14

Faculdade
de Medicina
Building

40

53

R Santos Dumont

R Lopes Cardoso

R da Montanha

Ladeira da Misericórdia

3

10

12

R João de Deus

Baía de
Todos os
Santos

Igreja da
Misericórdia

15

46

2 **Pelourinho**

17

54

Elevador
Lacerda

36

25

23

Cruzeiro de
São Francisco

Mercado
Modelo
Bus Stop

1

55

R 3 de Maio

48

30

**CIDADE BAIXA
(LOWER CITY)**

*Elevador
Lacerda*

16

13

Câmara
Municipal

R Monte Alverne

43

51

18

7

Small Boat
Anchorage

R da Misericórdia

R da Ajuda

R do Saldanha

ANCHIETA

Igreja
NS da
Conceição

R Chile

*Praça
da Sé
Bus Stop*

R São Francisco

Av de França

R Dom
Macedo Costa

Ladeira Pau
da Bandeira

R do Tesouro

R Dr JJ Seabra

R Padre Vieira

**CIDADE ALTA
(UPPER CITY)**

Praça dos
Veteranos

R Rui Barbosa

R 24
de Maio

Ladeira
da Palma

steps that were the setting of *O Pagador de Promessas* (1962). This was the first Brazilian film to win a Cannes film festival award. They lead to the eternally 'closed for renovation' **Igreja do Santíssimo Sacramento do Passo** (1737).

◉ Cidade Baixa

Interspersed between the Comércio's modern skyscrapers is some fantastic 19th-century architecture in various stages of decay.

Mercado Modelo   MARKET
(Map p400; www.mercadomodelobahia.com.br; Praça Cayru; ⊙9am-7pm Mon-Sat, to 2pm Sun) The original 1861 Customs House was partly destroyed in a fire in 1986. After reconstruction, it was transformed into a tourist market, the Mercado Modelo. When shipments of new slaves arrived into port, they were stored in the watery depths of this building while awaiting auction. Night guards report all sorts of phantasmic activity after closing hours.

Live music and free capoeira demonstrations often occur out back – be sure to ask the price before snapping photos of the capoeiristas. There's a touristy but fun cafe-restaurant, Camafeu, on the upper level; the terrace, looking over the bay, is ideal for a shopping break.

Solar do Unhão   HISTORIC BUILDING
(Map p396; Av do Contorno; ⊙1-7pm Tue-Fri & Sun, to 9pm Sat) This wonderfully preserved 18th-century complex served as a transfer point for sugar shipments: legend says it's haunted by the ghosts of murdered slaves. Today, the building houses the **Museu de Arte Moderna** (Map p396; ☎3117-6139; www.mam.ba.gov.br; Contorno s/n; adult/child R$6/3; ⊙1-7pm Tue-Fri & Sun, to 9pm Sat) FREE, with a changing display of avant-garde exhibits.

The museum hosts Saturday-evening jazz and bossa nova concerts, while the hillside sculpture garden, with bay views, is stunning at sunset. Take a taxi – the place is off bus routes and the desolate walk is known for tourist muggings.

◉ Vitória

The main artery of this leafy suburb is a well-traveled boulevard between Barra and the Pelourinho.

BAHIA CIDADE BAIXA

Central Salvador

Museu Carlos Costa Pinto　　MUSEUM
(Map p396; ☑ 3336-6081; www.museucostapinto. com.br/museu.asp; 7 de Setembro 2490; admission R$5; ⊙ 2:30-7pm Mon & Wed-Sat) This lovely two-story mansion houses some of Salvador's finest decorative art, from the collection of the patrician couple Carlos de Aguiar Costa Pinto and his wife Margarida, both born in Bahia in the late 19th century. Displays highlight gold, crystal, porcelain and silver pieces, as well as beautifully carved coral jewelry and tortoiseshell fans. Don't miss the outdoor cafe.

Museu de Arte da Bahia　　MUSEUM
(Map p396; ☑ 3117-6902; 7 de Setembro 2340; adult/child R$5/3; ⊙ 1-7pm Tue-Fri, 2-7pm Sat & Sun) Set in an attractive neocolonial build-

ing, the Museu de Arte da Bahia showcases works from Bahian artists, with paintings by José Teófilo de Jesus (1758–1817) and drawings by Argentine artist Carybé.

⦿ North of the Center

To reach these sights north of the center, take a taxi or a Ribeira or Bomfim bus from the base of the Elevador Lacerda.

★**Igreja NS do Bonfim**　　CHURCH
(☑ 3316-2196; Praça Senhor do Bonfim; ⊙ 6:30am-noon & 2-6pm Tue-Thu & Sat, 5:30am-noon & 2:30-6pm Fri & Sun) This famous 18th-century church, located a few kilometers north of Comércio on the Itapagipe Peninsula, is the source of the *fitas* (colored ribbons)

you see everywhere in Salvador, a souvenir of the church and a symbol of Bahia itself. Bonfim's fame derives from its power to effect miraculous cures, making it a popular shrine.

In the Sala dos Milagres (Room of Miracles) on the right side of the church, devotees leave photos, letters and *ex votos* – wax replicas of body parts representing those that were cured or need curing.

Due to Candomblistas' syncretization of Jesus Christ (Nosso Senhor do Bonfim) with Oxalá, their highest deity, Bonfim is their most important church. Huge services are held here on Friday, Oxalá's favorite day of the week.

If you tie a *fita* around your wrist, you are making a commitment that lasts for months. With each of the three knots a wish is made, which will come true by the time the *fita* falls off. Cutting it off is inviting doom.

Mercado São Joaquim MARKFT
(⊙9am-6pm) **FREE** The die-hard market fan will enjoy Mercado São Joaquim, a small city of sketchy waterfront stalls about 2km north of the Elevador Lacerda. Puddles of green slime, a meat neighborhood capable of converting the unprepared into a devout vegetarian, and bar stalls where rough hands grip glasses of rougher *cachaça* (sugarcane alcohol) let you know this is the real thing.

◉ Barra

Barra's busy waterfront has three jutting points of land, occupied by the colonial forts of **Forte São Diogo**, **Forte Santa Maria** and the most impressive of the bunch, **Forte de Santo Antônio da Barra** (Map p404). Built in 1698, Bahia's oldest fort is more commonly called the Farol da Barra for the lighthouse – South America's oldest – within its walls. Today the striking structure houses the excellent nautical museum listed below. As you join the locals gathering to catch the sunset from the grassy ledge behind the fort, notice how Salvador's peninsula is the only location in Brazil where the sun appears to set over the ocean.

★**Museu Náutico da Bahia** MUSEUM
(Nautical Museum of Bahia; Map p404; ☑3264-3296; www.museunauticodabahia.org.br; Largo do Farol da Barra s/n, Forte de Santo Antônio da Barra; adult/student R$10/5; ⊙8:30am-7pm Tue-Sun, daily Jan & Jul) In addition to having superb views, the Forte de Santo Antônio da Barra

contains this excellent nautical museum, with relics and displays from the days of Portuguese seafaring, plus fascinating exhibits on the slave trade. All information is offered in both Portuguese and English – a rarity in Bahia. Sunset is delightful at the museum's gorgeous terrace cafe.

Beaches

Praia Porto da Barra is rather like the Pelourinho: small, picturesque, usually crowded, loaded with vendors selling everything imaginable, and roughly half those present are foreigners. The bay's waters are clear and calm, and the people-watching is fantastic. To the left of the lighthouse, **Praia do Farol da Barra** has a beach break popular with surfers. Barra's waterfront is lined with bars and restaurants and is well lit at night, but it gets a bit sleazy in the later hours.

Smaller crowds and an unpolluted Atlantic are about 40 minutes' bus travel east from the center (or more with traffic), but it's worth it. Calm seas lap on flat white sands with *barracas* (stalls) and swaying palms at popular city beaches **Piatã** (25km) and **Itapuã** (27km). As you reach the beaches of **Stella Maris** (31km) and **Flamengo** (33km), the waves get progressively stronger, *barracas* begin to space out, and sand dunes and more greenery create a more natural setting. Catch an Itapuã, Aeroporto or Praia do Flamengo bus, making sure it goes up the coast *(via orla)* and as far as you are going.

⚑ Courses
Capoeira, Dance & Percussion
Classes in capoeira, African dance and percussion are easily arranged through hostels and pousadas in the Pelourinho. Course prices vary depending on season, availability, and the number of people in your party, but generally you can expect to pay around R$30 per hour for a class.

Associação Artística e Cultural Diaspora DANCE
(Diáspora Art Center; Map p400; ☑3323-0016; 3rd fl, Cruzeiro de São Francisco 21; prices vary; ⊙10am-6pm Mon-Fri) Stop in to inquire about the latest schedule of classes in traditional and contemporary Afro-Brazilian dance, capoeira and percussion.

★**Associação Brasileira de Capoeira Angola** CAPOEIRA
(Map p400; ☑9266-7881; www.capoeirabrasil bahia.com; Gregório de Mattos 38; 1-hr class R$30,

BAHIA BARRA

Salvador Barra

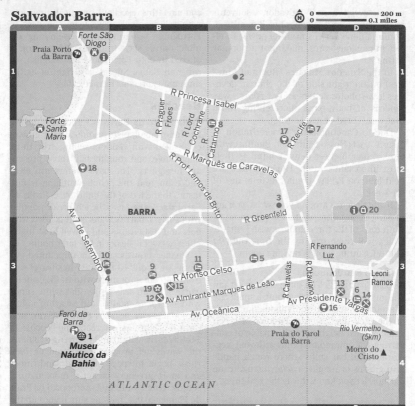

Salvador Barra

discounts for longer commitments; ⊘classes 1-3pm Tue & Wed; 🖭) This friendly capoeira association runs biweekly classes open to all ages (including children five and older). Be sure to wear comfortable, loose-fitting pants you can move around in.

Atelier Mestre Lua Rasta MUSIC
(Map p400; ✔3488-3600; www.atelierlua.com.br; Acciole 3; price varies) To set up a percussion class, pass by this shop of instruments handmade by the *mestre* (master) himself; Mestre Lua can also set you up with a capoeira class and provide overnight accommodation (R$25 per person).

Fundação Mestre Bimba CAPOEIRA
(Map p400; ✔3322-5082; Gregório de Mattos 51) A school run by the son of the founder of Capoeira Regional, Mestre Bimba.

Cooking

SENAC COOKING
(Map p400; ✔3186-4000; www.ba.senac.br; Largo do Pelourinho 13-19; from R$30; ⊘ 9-11am & noon-5pm Mon-Sat) A must-see for foodies, SENAC is a Bahian culinary school where both locals and tourists take cooking classes – one course focuses solely on the preparation of popular street foods like *acarajé*. Inside this lovely colonial building, there's also a free museum dedicated to Bahian gastronomy, and a pair of eateries – the student-run *buffet típico* (p411) is particularly excellent.

Language
Hostels and pousadas in Salvador can recommend language courses – a minimum one-week commitment is common – and private teachers. Contact the schools for the latest prices.

Diálogo LANGUAGE
(Map p404; ✔3264-0007; www.dialogo-brazil-study.com; Dr João Pondé 240, Barra; ⊘9am-6pm Mon-Sat) Language classes here get mixed reviews from travelers, though some teachers are reportedly excellent. Benefits include language exchange with Brazilian students, city excursions and samba classes.

Idioma Escola de Português LANGUAGE
(Map p404; ✔3267-7012; www.portugueseinbrazil.com; Greenfeld 46, Barra; ⊘8am-6pm Mon-Fri) Convenient if you're staying in Barra, this language school offers group classes and private sessions in addition to cultural excursions such as Bahian cooking workshops and scuba-diving classes.

Tours

Salvador Bus TOUR
(Map p404; ✔3356-6425; www.salvadorbus.com. br; Av 7 de Setembro s/n; adult/child R$45/30; ⊘9:30am-6:45pm Mon-Sat) If you're short on time, climb aboard the open-air Salvador Bus at Farol da Barra, the Mercado Modelo or a number of other downtown destinations; the hop-on, hop-off sightseeing bus offers multilingual tours and has stops as wide-ranging as Rio Vermelho and Igreja do Bonfim. The Barra office doubles as an internet cafe (open 9am to 9pm, R$6 per hour) and travel agency offering handy excursions to hard-to-reach destinations like Mangue Seco.

Toursbahia TOUR
(Map p400; ✔3320-3280; www.toursbahia.com. br; Cruzeiro de São Francisco 4, Pelourinho; ⊘9am-6pm Mon-Sat) Toursbahia is an extremely professional multilingual agency offering local and national tours.

🎉 Festivals & Events
Salvador delights in its wild festivals, which have links to both Catholicism and Candomblé. Although Carnaval steals the show, there are numerous festivals, particularly in January and February.

Processão do Senhor Bom Jesus dos Navegantes RELIGIOUS
(⊘ Jan 1) A maritime procession transports the image of Bom Jesus from Igreja NS da Conceição in Cidade Baixa north along the bay to Igreja de NS da Boa Viagem. A festival ensues on Praia da Boa Viagem.

Festas de Reis RELIGIOUS
(⊘ Jan 6) On the Dia de Reis, a procession of the *reis magos* (wise men) statues travels to a crèche in the Igreja da Lapinha.

Lavagem do Bonfim RELIGIOUS
(⊘2nd Thu in Jan) Salvador's biggest festival outside of Carnaval honors the saint with Bahia's largest following – Senhor do Bonfim, associated with Candomblé. A procession of *baianas* (women dressed as Bahian 'aunts') in ritual dress carrying buckets of flowers walks 6km from Cidade Baixa to Igreja NS do Bonfim.

There, they perform a ritual *lavagem* (washing) of the church steps, overseen by Catholic priests and *mães de santo* (Candomblé priestesses). The rowdy street party afterwards lasts into the night.

BAHIA BARRA

Capoeira

Combining elements of the fight, the game and the dance, capoeira was developed by Afro-Brazilian slaves more than 400 years ago as a means of maintaining a ready self-defense against their masters. Today, it remains a uniquely Bahian art form.

Origins

Capoeira is said to have originated from a ritualistic African dance. Capoeira was prohibited by slave owners and banished from the *senzalas* (slave barracks), forcing slaves to practice clandestinely in the forest. Later, in an attempt to disguise this act of defiance from the authorities, capoeira was developed into a kind of acrobatic dance. The clapping of hands and striking of the *berimbau*, a one-string musical instrument that looks like a fishing rod, originally served to alert fighters to the approach of the boss and subsequently became incorporated into the dance to maintain the rhythm.

As recently as the 1920s, capoeira was still prohibited. In the 1930s, Mestre Bimba changed the emphasis of capoeira from a tool of insurrection to a form of artistic expression that's become an institution in Bahia.

Traditions & Variations

Today, there are two schools of capoeira: the slow and low Capoeira de Angola, originally led by Mestre Pastinha, and the more aggressive Capoeira Regional, initiated by Mestre Bimba. The former school believes capoeira came from Angola; the latter says it was born in the plantations of Cachoeira and other cities of the *recôncavo* region.

1. Capoeira performers, Salvador 2. Capoeira dancer, Itacaré

The movements are always fluid and circular, the fighters always playful and respectful as they exchange mock blows. Capoeira is typically practiced by two fighters at a time inside a *roda* (circle) of spectators/fighters who clap and sing. In addition to the *berimbau*, other instruments such as the *pandeiro* (tambourine), *agogô* (bell) and *atabaque* (drum) provide musical accompaniment. Capoeira gains more followers by the year, both nationally and abroad. Throughout Brazil – particularly Bahia – you will see people practicing their moves on the beach and street *rodas* popping up in touristy areas.

Watching Capoeira

At night in the Pelourinho, you'll hear music spilling out of capoeira studios clustered in the area of Teatro San Miguel Santana. Take a peek inside and don't be surprised if you're asked to pay a small fee to observe – you're supporting the studio. It's more authentic than the capoeira you'll see in touristy areas: linger to watch the performers in the Terreiro de Jesus and the ground level of the Mercado Modelo, and you'll be hustled for cash within moments. More professional capoeira is on proud display in folkloric shows like Salvador's famous Balé Folclórico da Bahia.

Capoeira Classes

In Salvador, capoeira classes are held in the Pelourinho. Elsewhere in Bahia, capoeiristas often advertise lessons at youth hostels. Expect to pay around R$30 for a one-hour class; wear comfortable, loose-fitting pants you can move around in.

Baía de Todos os Santos & Recôncavo

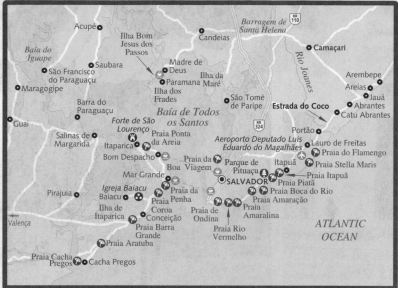

Festa de Iemanjá
RELIGIOUS

(⊙Feb 2) Perhaps Candomblé's most important festival, the event pays homage to the *orixá* Iemanjá, goddess of the sea and fertility. Devotees descend on Praia Rio Vermelho in the morning, where ceremonies are held to bless offerings of flowers, cakes, effigies and bottles of perfume. The ensuing street festival is packed with people and some of Salvador's best bands and lasts into the night.

Festa de São João
RELIGIOUS

(⊙Jun 22-25) Pyrotechnics and street parties spring up all over town and *genipapo* (local fruit) liqueur flows like water.

Festa de NS da Conceição
RELIGIOUS

(⊙Dec 8) Candomblistas honor the saint's *orixá* alter ego, Iemanjá, with a procession and ceremonies in Cidade Baixa.

Passagem do Ano Novo
NEW YEAR

(⊙Dec 31) New Year's Eve is celebrated with all the zest of Carnaval, especially on the beaches.

🛏 Sleeping

Staying in Cidade Alta means being close to the action, but the beach suburbs are mellower (and just a short bus or taxi ride away from the Pelourinho). Santo Antônio is a peaceful neighborhood with classy pousadas in renovated old buildings just a short walk from the Pelourinho. Reservations during Carnaval are essential.

🛏 Pelourinho

★ Hostel Galeria 13
HOSTEL $

(Map p400; ☑3266-5609; www.hostelgaleria13. com; Accioli 23; dm/d from R$35/140; 🌡🛜🖼) Located in an old colonial house complete with a swimming pool, Moroccan-style lounge, and tapas bar, this hostel is a huge success with backpackers. Though there's no communal kitchen, breakfast is served till noon – and the location can't be beat. It's affiliated with the excellent Bar Zulu, just around the corner.

Pousada Terra Nossa
INN $

(Map p400; ☑3321-5267; www.pousadaterran ossa.com; Leovigildo de Carvalho 3; dm/d/tr from R$40/120/140; 🌡🛜) This cozy pousada offers private rooms and dorm-style accommodations; both have high ceilings and exposed brick walls that remind you that you're on one of the city's most historic blocks. A bit noisy at night, but the atmosphere is warm.

Hostel Solar dos Romanos   HOSTEL $
(Map p400; ☑ 3321-6812; www.hostelsolardosromanos.com; Portas do Carmo 14; dm R$40-50, d R$120; ❄ ☎) This clean and affordable hostel boasts an unusual combination: both a location in the heart of the Pelourinho and a terrace with bay views. Doubles are simple; perks include 24-hour kitchen access.

Laranjeiras Hostel   HOSTEL $
(Map p400; ☑ 3321-1366; www.laranjeirashostel. com.br; Ordem Terceira/Accioli 13; dm R$41, d with/without bathroom R$140/116; ❄ @ ☎) The highest-quality and most attractive Pelô hostel, noisy, busy Laranjeiras has high-ceilinged dorm rooms with triple bunks, and good bathrooms. The private rooms are overpriced. Price drops after Carnaval. An HI discount is offered.

Albergue do Pelô   HOSTEL $
(Map p400; ☑ 3242-8061; www.alberguedopelo. com.br; Rua do Passo 5; dm R$30; ❄ ☎) This long-running hostel has basic rooms with dorm beds, a small but comfy lounge, laundry facilities and a central location in the Pelourinho.

Bahiacafé Hotel   BOUTIQUE HOTEL $$
(Map p400; ☑ 3322-1266; www.bahiacafehotel. com; Praça da Sé 22; d from R$190) This chic but low-key boutique hotel has 10 fashionably outfitted rooms and an excellent location close to the center of the action in the Pelourinho. The lobby cafe, filled with locally produced artwork and open to the public, is the perfect spot for a quick cappuccino during an afternoon of sightseeing.

★Casa do Amarelindo   BOUTIQUE HOTEL $$$
(Map p400; ☑ 3266-8550; www.casadoamarelindo.com; Portas do Carmo 6; s/d R$378/420, d with balcony & view R$530-630; ❄ ❄) Inside a 19th-century colonial mansion on a historic block, this charming boutique hotel is truly a gem. Ten impeccably outfitted guest rooms have first-class bedding, rainfall showers and huge windows; there's an adorably petite rooftop swimming pool, a popular bistro and a small fitness center. No children under age 14 are permitted.

Hotel Villa Bahia   BOUTIQUE HOTEL $$$
(Map p400; ☑ 3322-4271; www.lavillabahia.com; Largo do Cruzeiro de São Francisco 16; d R$530-730; ❄ ☎) ❂ Occupying a pair of restored Portuguese-style colonial houses, this sustainably run boutique hotel (practices include recycling and employment of local craftsmen) has 17 rooms with hard-wood floors, shuttered windows and antique furnishings from heavy armoires to twinkling chandeliers. There's a panoramic terrace and plunge pool, plus a good organic restaurant that's open to the public.

🛏 Carmo & Santo Antônio

Hostel Cobreu   HOSTEL $
(Map p400; ☑ 3117-1401; www.hostelcobreu.com; Ladeira do Carmo 22; dm R$26-30, d without bathroom R$130-150; @ ☎) Colorful Cobreu offers basic dorms and private rooms, plus a DVD library, balconies overlooking the quaint Ladeira do Carmo, interiors done by a well-known local graffiti artist, and the cool Cafe Alquimia (p413) downstairs. Travelers rave about the helpful staff but complain about the stuffy temperatures in summer.

Pousada Baluarte   POUSADA $$
(Map p396; ☑ 332/-0367; www.pousadabaluarte. com; Ladeira do Baluarte 13; s/d R$140/160; ❄) Run by a friendly French-Brazilian couple, Baluarte feels like a B&B, with a welcoming, homelike ambience and just five rooms with hard-wood floors and beautiful block prints by a local artist. A delicious breakfast is served on the veranda; the Pelourinho is a 10-minute walk away.

Pousada do Boqueirão   POUSADA $$
(Map p400; ☑ 3241-2262; www.pousadaboqueirao.com.br; Direita de Santo Antônio 48; d/tr from R$210/280, s/d without bathroom from R$120/150) Two early-20th-century houses have been joined together to form this elegant pousada, tastefully decorated with antiques and artwork. Spacious common rooms back onto a porch with a fantastic bay view, where a lovely breakfast is served.

Studio do Carmo   BOUTIQUE HOTEL $$
(Map p400; ☑ 3326-2426; www.studiodocarmo. com; Ladeira do Carmo 17; d/tr/q R$300/390/450; ❄) Above an art gallery, this boutique offers gorgeous guest rooms – each set with polished wood floors, big windows, artwork and fresh flowers. All have small kitchen units, and a delightful breakfast is brought to your door.

Pestana Convento do Carmo   HOTEL $$$
(Map p400; ☑ 3327-8400; www.pestana.com/en/pestana-convento-do-carmo; Rua do Carmo 1; d

from R$550; ❄🛜🍴) Set in a restored 17th-century convent, this magnificent hotel has elegantly furnished rooms with old-world details and modern comforts, and even more impressive common areas. There's a stone chapel and arched walkways around the cloister.

🛏 Barra & Coastal Suburbs

Of all the beachside suburbs, happening Barra attracts the majority of visitors due to its proximity to the Pelourinho.

★Open House Barra
INN $
(Map p404; ☎3264-0337; www.openhousebarra.com; Catarino 137, Barra; dm/s/d R$44/77/110, d with shared bathroom R$88; 🛜) This fantastically colorful and homey place is hosted by Alex and Jacqueline, professional artists with deep connections with the local music, dance and film community. Musicians and capoeira demonstrations periodically take place at the hostel, especially during Carnaval, when the pousada offers one of Salvador's most memorable party experiences.

Pousada O Ninho
POUSADA $
(Map p404; ☎3264-6952; www.pousadaoninho.com.br; Afonso Celso 371, Barra; s/d/tr R$125/145/180; ❄🛜) This relaxed but classy pousada occupies an elegant building just two blocks from the beach; the atmosphere is quiet but friendly. Because of the excellent value, it can be difficult to score a room: if you can, book well in advance.

Âmbar Pousada
INN $
(Map p404; ☎3264-6956; www.ambarpousada.com.br; Afonso Celso 485, Barra; dm/s/d R$53/130/155; @🛜) 🍴 A favorite among budget-minded travelers, this easygoing and ecofriendly pousada has a welcoming atmosphere. Dorms are quiet, and doubles are small – note that some of the private bathrooms are only separated by a partition, not a door – but there's ample public space, and it's a two-minute walk to the beach.

La Villa Françaíse
POUSADA $
(Map p404; ☎3245-6008; www.lavilafrancaise.com; Recife 222, Barra; dm R$45, s/d/tr from R$80/120/150; ❄🛜) Travelers rave about the peaceful atmosphere, tasty breakfast and kind owners at this cozy French-influenced guesthouse. The kitchen is open for guest use and the shared spaces are inviting.

Che Lagarto
HOSTEL $
(Map p404; ☎3235-2404; www.chelagarto.com; Av Oceânica 84, Barra; dm R$44-48, d R$142; ❄🛜) Occupying a coveted spot of real estate just across the street from the beach, this spacious branch of the Che Logarto hostel chain is a good place to meet other travelers. But let the buyer beware: travelers complain about poor service and the ongoing need for better maintenance.

Pousada Noa Noa
POUSADA $$
(Map p404; ☎3264-1148; www.pousadanoanoa.com; Av 7 de Setembro 4295, Barra; d from R$160; ❄🛜) The oceanfront terrace and bar – an ideal spot from which to watch the sunset with a caipirinha in hand – is the key selling point of this welcoming guesthouse. Of 16 simply furnished guest rooms, only a few have ocean views, but the attractive common areas make good use of the property's lovely seaside location.

Pousada Estrela do Mar
HOSTEL $$
(Map p404; ☎3264-4882; www.estreladomarsalvador.com; Afonso Celso 119, Barra; s/d R$135/155, s/d with veranda R$180/215) This white stucco house with dark-blue shutters – very Portugal-meets-the-tropics – is surrounded by greenery, while inside, plain white walls set off bright Bahian paintings and vibrant blue tilework. The location is close to the beach on a mellow, tree-shaded street.

🍴 Eating

Dining out is a delight in Salvador. Traditional Bahian cuisine has a heavy African influence, featuring ingredients like coconut cream, tomato, seafood, bell pepper and spices of ginger, hot peppers and coriander.

🍴 Pelourinho

The Pelourinho is packed with restaurants; some feel uncomfortably touristy, while others are wonderfully charming.

A Cubana
ICE CREAM $
(cones R$6 to R$12; ⏱9am-10pm) **Pelourinho** (Map p400; ☎3321-6162; Rua Alfredo de Brito 12; cones R$6-12; ⏱9am-10pm) **Praça Municipal** (Map p400; ☎3322-7000; Praça Municipal; cones R$6-12; ⏱9am-10pm) One of Salvador's oldest and best ice-cream shops, with two popular locations in the Pelourinho.

SALVADOR'S CARNAVAL

Carnaval in Salvador is billed as 'the world's largest party.' It's a debatable distinction, but as the organizers explain, while Rio de Janeiro's Carnaval may draw more people, Salvador's Carnaval occupies more physical space (several kilometers at a time) than its sister party in A Cidade Maravilhosa. Either way, it's a huge party, attracting upwards of two million revelers for six straight days of revelry before Ash Wednesday. Each day, the festivities kick off around 5pm every afternoon and wind down around 5am.

The focus is on music, namely nationally famous city bands playing *axé* and *pagode* (Bahia's pop music) atop creeping *trios elétricos* (long trucks loaded with huge speakers). Between them march a few *blocos afros* (groups with powerful drum corps promoting Afro-Brazilian culture) and *afoxés* (groups tied to Candomblé traditions). A *trio elétrico* (drum corps), together with its followers grouped in a roped-off area around it, form a *bloco*. People pay big bucks for the *abadá* (outfit) for their favorite band, mostly for prestige and the safety of those ropes. Choosing to *fazer pipoca* (be popcorn) in the street is still a fine way to spend Carnaval, as you'll see a variety of music and be spared the hassle involved with picking up the *abadá*.

There are three major parade circuits: Dodô, between Barra and Ondina along Av Oceânica, Osmar or 'the Avenidas,' between Campo Grande and Praça Castro Alves along Av Sete de Setembro, and Batatinha in the Pelourinho.

Crowds clearing (in order to escape a fight) pose the greatest threat during Carnaval, so be aware of your surroundings. A large police presence helps to keep violence to a minimum. On the Barra–Rio Vermelho circuit, avoid the section where the coastal road narrows near the Morro do Cristo – the tension heats up there.

Otherwise, if you're planning on spending Carnaval in Salvador, the best thing to do is to plan ahead: many hostels and pousadas offer packages, but they tend to fill up quickly. It's advisable to look closely at a city map before committing to anything: some city neighborhoods can be so noisy during Carnaval that you wouldn't be able to sleep if you wanted to. Many locals living in the Barra neighborhood clear out completely for Carnaval, renting out their apartments and houses to tourists, which is another accommodation option if you're up for the adventure.

For more information and details on specific events and schedules, log onto the official online portal for Salvador's Carnaval at www.carnaval.salvador.ba.gov.br. For English-language background on the music at the center of the event, check out the helpful page at www.bahia-online.net/Carnival.htm.

BAHIA PELOURINHO

★ **Bar Zulu** INTERNATIONAL $$
(Map p400; Laranjeiras 15; mains R$14-28; ☉ 11am-1am; 🛜📖) This laid-back corner bar and eatery has outdoor tables and serves a wide range of Spanish tapas, Bahian classics and international dishes, plus Argentine wine (R$10 a glass) and cocktails like the 'Galeria 13,' made with lemon, watermelon and *cachaça*. The house burger and chocolate brownie with ice cream are favorite picks; vegetarian stand-outs include Thai curry and lasagne.

O Coliseu BAHIAN $$
(Map p400; 📞 3321-5585; www.ocoliseu.com.br; 2nd fl, Cruzeiro de São Francisco 9; mains R$18-42; ☉ 11:30am-4pm & 7-8:30pm Mon-Sat; 📖) This vegetarian-friendly restaurant offers a spread of regional dishes – buffet-style for lunch, and à la carte in the evening,

when the dinner hour precedes the popular Topázio (p415) folkloric show, which begins at 8:30pm.

★ **Restaurante do SENAC** BUFFET $$
(Map p400; www.ba.senac.br; Largo do Pelourinho 13; buffet R$40; ☉ 11:30am-3:30pm) With the best Bahian buffet in town and a convenient location in the center of the Pelourinho, the cooking school SENAC spreads a tempting array of regional dishes, including several varieties of *moqueca* (a spicy stew of coconut milk, pepper, and seafood or meat) and traditional desserts you won't find elsewhere. The *buffet típico* is on the top floor, not to be confused with the street-level self-service restaurant (per kilo around R$29.)

Ristorante La Figa ITALIAN $$
(Map p400; 📞 3322-0066; www.ristorantelafiga. com; Laranjeiras 17; mains R$25-50; ☉ 11am-

midnight Mon-Sat, noon-5pm Sun) A Pelourinho classic, this well-loved Italian restaurant specializes in traditional homemade pastas enhanced with Bahia's fabulously fresh seafood. The setting is casual but elegant.

Jardim das Delicias BAHIAN $$$
(Map p400; ☑ 3321-1449; João de Deus 12; mains R$35-65, mains for 2 R$100; ⊙ 11:30am-4pm & 6-11pm Tue & Fri-Sun, lunch only Mon & Wed) This stylish yet pleasantly old-fashioned eatery is a foodies' favorite. The flower-bedecked central courtyard is a dreamy place to sample a traditional *moqueca* or to just relax with a citrusy cocktail while musicians serenade the small crowd.

★ Maria Mata Mouro BRAZILIAN $$$
(Map p400; ☑ 3321-3929; www.mariamatamouro. com.br; Accioli 8; mains for 2 R$60-100; ⊙ noon-11pm) The picture-perfect garden patio and elegant dining room are fine settings to enjoy one of Pelô's top menus. You'll find Bahian classics, fresh seafood and Portuguese dishes prepared with a gourmet twist, plus a varied wine list and a talented bartender shaking up unique cocktails.

Pelô Bistrô BRAZILIAN $$$
(Map p400; www.casadoamarelindo.com; Hotel Casa do Amarelindo, Portas do Carmo 6; mains R$41-59; ⊙ 8am-10pm) The lovely bistro at Hotel Casa do Amarelindo (p409) is a sure thing for an elegant breakfast (R$24 per person) or a gourmet lunch or dinner – the seafood-focused menu features grilled salmon with passion fruit and sauteed shrimp with pineapple rice, plus a good South American wine list.

✕ Carmo

★ Cafélier CAFE $
(Map p400; ☑ 3241-5095; www.cafelier.com.br; Carmo 50; snacks & light meals R$5-20; ⊙ 2:30-9:30pm Thu-Tue) This quaint hideaway cafe, located inside an antique house that's positioned dramatically on a cliff top over the ocean, is one of a kind. Come for the views, plus beautifully prepared cappuccino, rich chocolate cake, wines by the glass, and festive caipirinhas served in old-fashioned glass goblets.

✕ Cidade Baixa

In the Comércio, cheap *lanchonetes* (snack bars) and self-service restaurants abound. For something more memorable, head south along the bay, where there are several fine (if expensive) restaurants with views over the water.

Camafeu BAHIAN $$
(Map p400; ☑ 3242-9751; Mercado Modelo, Praça Cayru; mains R$18-45; ⊙ 9am-7pm Mon-Sat, to 4pm Sun) A standard Bahian menu is avail-

---

A NIGHT OUT IN RIO VERMELHO

The coastal neighborhood of Rio Vermelho has always been culturally significant to the city of Salvador: Portuguese sailors wrecked their ship offshore in 1510, famed writer Jorge Amado lived here and the important Candomblé festival Festa da Iemanjá (p408), honoring the goddess of motherhood and fertility, takes place on its shores. But in recent years, the neighborhood has also emerged as a hub of nightlife.

Arrive around sunset and take your pick from the sea of plastic tables and chairs set up on the lively plaza of **Largo de Santana**. Several casual bars serve cold beer to these outdoor tables, but the real attraction is the traditional street food prepared by colorfully dresed Bahian women at stands around the square. Particularly legendary are the *acarajé* (balls of dough fried in *dendê* oil and served with spicy sauces and shrimp) served nightly at the **Casa da Dinha** stand.

On any given evening, there are cultural events and free concerts at the cultural center Casa de Mãe Iemanja (p415) and the waterfront market **Mercado do Peixe**. Afterward, go for drinks at nearby Póstudo (p414), then follow the DJ-spun house music over to **Borracharia** (Conselheiro Pedro Luís 101A, Rio Vermelho; admission women/men R$15/20; ⊙ 11:30pm-5am Fri & Sat), a tire-repair shop that morphs into one of the city's coolest nightspots after dark, although it suffered badly at the hands of a fire and was yet to re-open at the time of writing.

Rio Vermelho is about a thirty-minute walk along the coast – or a short bus ride from Barra on any bus marked 'Orla' (waterfront).

able at this casual spot on the upper terrace of the Mercado Modelo. Though it's touristy and the food isn't particularly notable, many shoppers or travelers waiting to take the ferry to Morro stop here for coffee, juice, snacks, *moqueca* or cold beer with lovely views over the bay.

✕ Barra & Coastal Suburbs

Many restaurants in the coastal suburbs have superb tropical ambience – dining with outdoor tables and sea views. Budget-minded travelers will find plenty of self-serve eateries, sandwich shops, tapioca stands and supermarkets in Barra, too.

Light House SELF-SERVE $
(Map p404; Afonso Celso s/n, Barra; per kg R$30; ⊙11:30am-3:30pm Mon-Sat; 🅿) Tucked away on a quiet block around the corner from the beach, this laid-back eatery does a self-serve lunch buffet with a range of seafood and vegetarian dishes; there's appealing outdoor seating under the shade of tall trees.

★Caranguejo de Sergipe SEAFOOD $$
(Map p404; ☑3248-3331; www.caranguejodesergipe.com.br; Av Oceânica & Fernando Luz, Barra; mains R$22-45; ⊙11am-late Tue-Sun, from 4pm Mon) A local favorite, this always-packed eatery is known for fresh crabs and platters of grilled seafood and vegetables. Don't miss the expertly prepared *maracujá* (passion fruit) caipirinha – perhaps the most delicious drink on the beach.

Cabana da Cely SEAFOOD $$
(Map p404; ☑3035-0514; www.cabanadacely.com.br; Marques de Leão 183, Barra; mains R$18-44; ⊙11am-midnight Mon-Sat, to 5pm Sun) You'll have to battle for a sidewalk table at this popular casual restaurant where local couples and families come for cold beer and fresh fish. Do as the Bahians do with a pot of piping-hot *lambreta* (clams) or a pile of fresh garlic shrimp.

Caranguejo do Porto SEAFOOD $$
(Map p404; ☑3245-9197; www.caranguejodoporto.com.br; Av Oceânica s/n, Barra; mains R$22-38; ⊙noon-late Mon-Sat) Another of Barra's seaside hot spots for traditional Bahian food – think *moqueca*, fresh crabs, *pasteles* (empanada-like pastries stuffed with meat and other savory fillings), cold beer and caipir-inhas – this lively eatery transitions into a casual bar scene as the night rolls on.

Paraíso Tropical BAHIAN $$
(☑3384-7464; www.restauranteparaisotropical.com.br; Rua Edgar Loureiro 98B, Cabula; mains R$30-55; ⊙noon-11pm Mon-Sat, to 5pm Sun) Though it's far off the beaten path in the residential neighborhood of Cabula, foodies don't mind the detour to Paraíso Tropical: the classic Brazilian restaurant has long been considered one of Salvador's top choices for beautifully prepared Bahian cuisine with a gourmet twist. Come for a leisurely lunch; expect long waits on weekends.

🍷 Drinking & Nightlife

The Pelourinho is Salvador's nightlife capital: bars with outdoor tables and live music spill onto the cobbled streets. It's the place to be every week on Terça da Benção (Blessed Tuesday), when street parties kick off after evening Mass.

In Barra, find relaxed ambience and music along Av Almirante Marques de Leão and the waterfront around the Farol da Barra; Rua Recife and the Morro do Cristo also have some popular bars. Bohemian Rio Vermelho has by far the hottest nightlife scene along the Atlantic shore and a reputation for drawing all types. Its Largo de Santana and Largo de Mariquita are lined with outdoor restaurants and bars that fill up nightly.

🍷 Pelourinho & Carmo

Many restaurants and cafes on the side streets of the Pelourinho offer live music at night.

Casa do Amarelindo Bar COCKTAIL BAR
(Map p400; ☑3266-8550; Hotel Casa do Amarelindo, Portas do Carmo 6; ⊙noon-late) The chic tropical-style bar at the lovely Pelô Bistrô (p412) at Casa do Amarelindo is the ideal spot for a nightcap; better still is the panoramic terrace where a skilled bartender shows up after dark to mix classic cocktails.

Bar Cravinho BAR
(Map p400; Terreiro de Jesus 3; ⊙11am-11pm) Decorated with barrels and packed with a lively mix of locals and tourists, this neighborhood bar specializes in flavored shots of *cachaça*, including its trademark clove-infused variety.

Café Alquimia BAR

(Map p400; ☑3326-4079; Ladeira do Carmo 22; ⊙5pm-late) Located on the quaint cobblestoned hill leading up to Largo do Carmo (on the ground level of Hostel Cobreu (p409)), this bluesy cafe-bar is a happening spot for young travelers, musicians and artistic types. Arabic finger foods are on the menu alongside inexpensive cocktails and cold beer.

Odoyá BAR

(Map p400; ☑3322-4397; www.odoya.com.br; Praça Anchieta 1; ⊙11:30am-late) Drinks are standard, and you'll have to deal with an endless stream of panhandlers sitting at these outdoor tables, but the views at night – several gorgeously illuminated churches surround you – are memorable as you relax with a caipirinha or two.

Barra & Coastal Suburbs

★**Pereira** BAR

(Map p404; ☑3264-6464; Av 7 de Setembro 3959, Barra; ⊙noon-4pm & 5pm-1am Tue-Sun) Up a staircase from the seaside road that curves around the tip of Barra, Pereira is a stylish watering hole featuring a Japanese restaurant and wine bar. Excellent *chope* (draft beer) is on tap and the sunset views over the ocean are beautiful.

Barravento BAR

(Map p404; ☑3247-2577; www.restaurantebar ravento.com.br; Av Oceânica 814, Barra; ⊙10am-2am) Right on the sand in Barra, this classy waterfront bar and restaurant, with a long cocktail list and a menu of Bahian staples, is a choice spot for a sundowner. There's ample seating and it's open almost around the clock, so it's also a solid option if the restaurants nearby are jam-packed.

Póstudo BAR

(☑3334-0484; João Gomes 87, Rio Vermelho; ⊙noon-3pm & 6pm-late Mon-Sat) This perpetually cool bar and restaurant, right in the middle of Rio Vermelho nightlife action, has ocean views and a long drink menu.

Floripa BAR

(Map p404; ☑3267-4386; Rua Recife 86, Barra) In an area of lively bars, this relaxed spot attracts a festive crowd for cold beer and cheap prices – several similar indoor-out-door bars on the block make Rua Recife a hot spot for casual bar-hopping.

☆ Entertainment

Bars and clubs tend to come and go in Salvador, so ask around to see what's hot at the moment, or log onto the agenda of parties, concerts and performances at **Festa da Semana** (www.festadasemana.com.br/salvador).

Live Music

Salvador is the pulsing center of an incredible music scene, where a blend of African and Brazilian traditions has produced mind-blowing forms of percussion that *salvadorenhos* mix into their reggae, pop and rock, *pagode* and *axé*. The city has also produced unique styles such as *afoxé* and sambareggae. Since hardly a bar or restaurant in the city lacks live music at least one night of the week, catching some of Salvador's talented artists isn't hard.

During the high season, there are almost nightly concerts in the inner courtyards of the Pelourinho, with cover charges ranging from free to R$30. Take a stroll by the following places and find out what's on for the evening: Largo de Tereza Batista, Largo do Pedro Arcanjo and Praça Quincas Berro d'Água (usually free). There are also occasional concerts on the Terreiro de Jesus. You can also frequently hear drum corps, which rehearse by walking through the Pelourinho, blocking traffic and gathering a following as they go.

Traditional groups (characterized by strong Afro drum corps) to be on the lookout for include Ilê Aiyê (the first exclusively black Carnaval group), the all-female Dida, Muzenza and Male Debalê. More pop and with strong percussion sections are world-famous Olodum – a Tuesday-night Pelourinho institution – Araketu and Timbalada, brainchild of master composer and musician Carlinhos Brown. The queens of Salvador pop music – Margareth Menezes, Ivete Sangalo and Daniela Mercury – also often 'rehearse' publicly.

If you aren't going to experience Carnaval in Salvador, don't worry: the two months leading up to it are the next best thing. *Ensaios* (dress rehearsals or auditions) showcase secret big-name guests; and clubs around the city put on special balls.

For the biggest acts, keep your eye on Salvador's finest venue, the **Teatro Castro Alves** (Map p396; www.tca.ba.gov.br; Praça 2 de

Julho, Campo Grande) – its amphitheater has weekly concerts throughout summer.

⭐ **Jam no MAM**　　　　　LIVE MUSIC
(Map p396; www.jamnomam.com.br; Contorno s/n; cover R$3-6; ◷ 6pm Sat) Saturday-evening jazz and bossa nova at MAM (Museu de Arte Moderna (p401)) is a must for music lovers. Go early to see the museum first, and catch the views at sunset. Though the venue is located within walking distance of the Pelourinho, muggings are common along the quiet stretch; taking a taxi is recommended.

Casa de Mãe Iemanja　　　　LIVE MUSIC
(☑ 3334-3041; Guedes Cabral 81, Rio Vermelho; ◷ 2pm-2am Fri-Sun) FREE Named after the Yoruba goddess of the sea, this Rio Vermelho bistro–cultural center is a great space to hear live music.

Fundo do Cravinho　　　　LIVE MUSIC
(Map p400; www.clubedosamba.com.br; Terreiro de Jesus 5, Pelourinho; cover R$5; ◷ 4-11pm) Live samba nightly starting around 8pm, down an alley behind the eponymous bar.

Sankofa　　　　　　LIVE MUSIC
(Map p400; ☑ 3321-7236; www.sankofabrasil.com; Ladeira de São Miguel 7, Pelourinho; cover R$10-15; ◷ 9pm-3am Tue, 7-11pm Wed, 9pm-3am Fri & Sat) This centrally located bar hosts live salsa, samba, and DJs who mix everything from reggae to Congolese rumba.

Bahia Café Hall　　　　LIVE MUSIC
(☑ 3371-0664; www.bahiacafehall.com.br; Parque de Pituaçu, Paralela; tickets from R$50; ◷ show times vary) This busy concert venue – out of the way, but worth it – hosts major music festivals like Forró da Amizade and big-name acts like Seu Jorge.

Folkloric Shows & Capoeira
The chance to see a folkloric performance that showcases the unique range of Bahian music and dance – including live percussion and vocals, the dances of the *orixás*, *maculêlê* (stick dance), samba and capoeira – shouldn't be missed. You can also catch some authentic capoeira in the Pelourinho, where studios charge a few reais for watching a class (often called a 'show') and for taking pictures.

⭐ **Balé Folclórico da Bahia**　PERFORMING ARTS
(Map p400; www.balefolcloricodabahia.com.br; Matos 49, Teatro Miguel Santana; admission R$40; ◷ shows 8pm Mon-Sat) The most astounding professional show is put on by this world-renowned folkloric ballet company.

Topázio　　　　PERFORMING ARTS
(Map p400; www.capoeiratopazio.com.br; 2nd fl, Cruzeiro de São Francisco 9; ◷ 8:30pm Mon-Sat) The popular show that used to be staged at the Solar do Unhão now happens after dinner at O Coliseu (p411).

🔒 Shopping

For most visitors, shopping opportunities in Salvador fall into one of two camps: the artisan crafts and traditional Bahian souvenirs of the Pelourinho and the Mercado Modelo, and large shopping centers such as **Shopping Barra** (Map p404; ☑ 3264-4566; Av Centenário 2992, Barra, SAC) and **Shopping Iguatemi** (Av Tancredo Neves s/n, Iguatemi), across from the bus station, busy with Brazilian fashionistas and bustling food courts.

Mercado Modelo　　　　HANDICRAFTS
(Map p400; www.mercadomodelobahia.com.br; Praça Cayru, Cidade Baixa; ◷ 9am-7pm Mon-Sat, to 2pm Sun) This two-story market – once the site where slaves were held – has dozens of tourist-oriented stalls selling local handicrafts, plus food stands frequented by locals.

GAY & LESBIAN VENUES

Salvador's gay nightlife scene may be subdued compared to those of other Brazilian capitals, but these off-the-beaten-path venues are worth seeking out.

Art mavens and a young, gay friendly crowd flock to **Beco dos Artistas** (Artist's Alley; Map p396; Av Cerqueira Lima, Garcia), a lively alley with several bars popular for pre-clubbing drinks. Take a taxi and enter from Rua Leovigildo Filgueira. After midnight, the party gets started at **Queens Club** (Map p396; ☑ 3328-6220; Theodoro Sampaio 160, Barris; ◷ 11:30pm-6am Fri & Sat) – expect throbbing electronic beats, go-go boys and a dark room.

In Barra, near the beach, **Off Club** (Map p404; ☑ 3267-6215; www.boiteoffclub.com.br; Dias D'Ávila 33, Barra; ◷ 10pm-6am Thu-Sun) is another hot spot for dancing, bringing in top-name DJs – log onto the website to see the agenda and get your name on the list.

OLODUM

Walking around in Salvador, the bold symbol of a red, yellow and green peace sign is everywhere: it's the iconic symbol of Olodum, an Afro-Brazilian cultural group founded in 1979 by percussionist Neguinho do Samba. Originally, the objective was to curb racism and create opportunities for Bahia's marginalized youth. The organization still works towards these aims, primarily through music: the Olodum school is famous for developing its leader's signature style of 'bloco afro' or samba reggae, which takes inspiration from the musical styles of Caribbean reggae, salsa and Brazilian samba.

Today, Olodum runs a school, and the official band records music with big-time Brazilian musicians; during Carnaval, Olodum features prominently on the musical lineup. The colorful band of percussionists has also made waves in the international pop-culture scene: Michael Jackson filmed his 1996 music video for the single 'They Don't Care About Us' with the Olodum troupe in the streets of the Pelourinho. Log onto www.olodum.com.br for more on the organization, or take a peek into the **Escola Olodum** (Map p400; Laranjeiras s/n) in the Pelourinho.

Bahia Online   MUSIC
(Map p400; ☎ 3321 0536; www.bahia-online.net; João de Deus 22, Pelourinho; ⊙ 10am-10pm Mon-Sat) This music store has a fantastic selection of Bahian artists; the website is also an excellent resource for anyone interested in the region's music culture.

ⓘ Orientation

Salvador sits at the southern tip of a V-shaped peninsula at the mouth of the Baía de Todos os Santos. The city can be difficult to navigate as there are many one-way, no-left-turn streets that wind through Salvador's hills and valleys. The center of the city is on the bay side of the peninsula and is divided by a steep bluff into two parts: Cidade Alta (Upper City) and Cidade Baixa (Lower City).

The heart of historic Cidade Alta is the Pelourinho (or Pelô), which is also the heart of Salvador's tourism and nightlife. This roughly refers to the area from Praça da Sé to Largo do Pelourinho.

From Praça Castro Alves, Av 7 de Setembro runs through the Centro to the wide Praça Campo Grande, then continues southwest through the well-to-do Vitória neighborhood, and down to the mouth of the bay. Here, at the tip of the peninsula, is the affluent Barra district, with its lighthouse, forts and popular beach.

A main thoroughfare, which constantly changes names (one being Av Presidente Vargas), snakes east from Barra along the Atlantic coast. It passes through middle-class coastal suburbs such as Rio Vermelho, and a chain of beaches all the way to Itapuã.

Cidade Baixa contains the Comércio (the city's commercial and financial center), the ferry terminals and port. North, the land curves around the bay to create the Itapagipe Peninsula, including the Bonfim and Boa Viagem neighborhoods. The suburbs along the bay are poor, and the level of poverty generally increases with the distance from the center.

ⓘ Information

EMERGENCY
Delegacia do Turista (Tourist Police; ☎ 3116-6817; Cruzeiro de São Francisco 14, Pelourinho) Any crime involving a tourist must be handled by the city's tourist police. A few speak English or French.
Pronto Socorro (Ambulance; ☎ 192)

INTERNET ACCESS
It's easy to get online in Salvador. Internet cafes are everywhere (R$4 to R$6 per hour); most pousadas and many restaurants offer wi-fi.
Baiafrica Internet Café (Praça da Sé 8, Pelourinho; per hr R$4) Fast internet and flat-screen monitors, each outfitted with Skype and a webcam.

MEDICAL SERVICES
Hospital Espanhol (Av 7 de Setembro 4161, Barra)

MONEY
Banco do Brasil (Cruzeiro de São Francisco 11, Pelourinho) Also in the airport and scattered around Barra.
Bradesco (Mattos s/n, Pelourinho) With international ATMs in the Pelourinho, Barra, the bus station and the airport.
Toursbahia (☎ 3320-3280; www.toursbahia.com.br; Cruzeiro de São Francisco 4, Pelourinho) Changes cash or traveler's checks; nearby oufits do the same .

SAFE TRAVEL

In the center, tourist police maintain a visible presence, particularly in the Pelourinho. Crime in the Pelô increases during the high season (especially around Carnaval) and on crowded Tuesday nights, and pickpocketing is common on buses and in crowded places where tourists are easily singled out. To minimize risks, dress down, keep jewelry to a minimum, carry just enough cash for your outing and only a photocopy of your passport, and try to be roughly oriented before you set out.

If you must carry a bank card, take only one – and use ATMs inside banks instead of freestanding machines that are more susceptible to hackers.

The Pelourinho shifts quickly into sketchy areas, so avoid wandering off the beaten path. Cidade Baixa is deserted and unsafe at night and on weekends, and the *ladeiras* (steep roads) that connect it to Cidade Alta should never be taken on foot.

On the beaches, keep a close eye on juvenile thieves – or *capitães d'areia* (captains of the sand) – who are quick to make off with unguarded possessions.

Don't hesitate to use taxis after dusk or in areas where you feel apprehensive, although taking buses in the evening is not necessarily unsafe.

TOURIST INFORMATION

You can also find plenty of tourist information at the many travel agencies spread throughout the city.

Bahiatursa/SAT (www.bahiatursa.ba.gov. br) airport (☑3204-1244; ☻7:30am-11pm) bus station (☑3450-3871; Av Antônio Carlos Magalhães, Iguatemi, bus station) Mercado Modelo (☑3241-0242; Mercado Modelo, Praça Cayru) Pelourinho (Map p400; ☑3321-2463; Rua Francisco Muniz Barreto 12; ☻8:30am-9pm Mon-Thu, to 10pm Fri-Sun) Porto da Barra (Map p404; ☑3264-5440; Av 7 de Setembro, Instituto Mauá, Porto da Barra) Shopping Barra (Map p404; ☑3264-4566; SAC, Shopping Barra) The tourism authority is friendly if not terribly organized. The Pelourinho office, which has maps and listings of what's happening around town, is your best bet. Also see www. bahia.com.br.

Quatro Cantos Turismo (☑3264-2000; Marquês de Caravelas 154, Barra; ☻9am-6pm Mon-Fri) If you're staying in Barra, this travel agency is a helpful stop for maps, tourist information, and trip planning; the agents can also help you buy plane tickets or make reservations for bus travel.

Disque Bahia Turismo (Dial Tourism Bahia; ☑3103-3103) Round-the-clock tourist information or help (in English).

Emtursa Lacerda (Map p400; ☑3321-3127; www.emtursa.salvador.ba.gov.br; Elevador Lacerda, Cidade Alta) The city's tourism office can be helpful; as with Bahiatursa, these agents slip up sometimes, so it's best to reconfirm (with the relevant organization) any important information they give you.

Grupo Gay da Bahia (Map p400; ☑3322-2552; www.ggb.org.br; Ladeira de São Miguel 24, Pelourinho) A cultural center for gays, lesbians and transgenders.

❶ Getting There & Away

AIR

Aeroporto Deputado Luis Eduardo do Magalhães (SSA; ☑3204-1010; São Cristóvão) is served by **Gol** (☑3204-1603; www.voegol.com. br; airport), **TAM** (☑3365-2324; www.tam.com. br; airport), and **Azul** (www.voeazul.com.br). There are daily flights to any Brazilian destination, but multiple stops are common.

TAP (Air Portugal; ☑3204-1531; www.flytap. com; airport) connects Salvador with Europe and **American Airlines** (www.aa.com) now offers a direct flight to Miami (USA). Generally speaking, though, flights to international destinations go via São Paulo or Rio.

BOAT

Boats to Morro de São Paulo and points on Baía de Todos os Santos leave from the **Terminal Marítimo Turístico**, behind the Mercado Modelo, and the **Terminal Marítimo de São Joaquim** (Map p400; ☑3633-1248; Av Oscar Pontes), a 10-minute taxi ride north.

BUS

Though foreigners generally can't purchase tickets online, as Brazilians can easily do, many bus companies sell their tickets at outlets and travel agencies throughout the city. In summer, it pays to buy your tickets ahead of time. When in doubt, ask the staff at your hotel or hostel: they're often willing to help make travel arrangements.

❶ Getting Around

TO/FROM THE AIRPORT

The airport is located about 30km east of the center. Transportation options to the center are surprisingly limited and expensive. Most travelers take a taxi: going to Barra or the Pelourinho, you'll pay R$107 in advance at the airport – the taxi stands inside the arrivals hall accept credit cards, which is convenient if you're not carrying local currency. You'll pay slightly less if you hail a taxi outside, though you might not see any available cars.

There are also buses (R$6, running 7:30am to 8pm) that head to the center, winding along the beach road and ending up in the Pelourinho about a 1¼ hours later, depending on traffic. They're marked 'Praça da Sé/Aeroporto' – note that they're only recommended if you're not carrying much luggage.

Buses to the airport depart regularly from the so-called Praça da Sé bus stop, a block southeast of Praça Municipal. Supposedly they leave every 30 minutes, but the schedule isn't fixed, so leave plenty of time. You can pick up the same bus in Barra. In light traffic, the ride takes about an hour; with traffic allow 1¾ hours.

TO/FROM THE BUS STATION

Salvador's **bus station** (☑ 3616-8300) is 8km east of the city center. A taxi to Cidade Alta or Barra runs R$25 to R$35. Buses (R$6) marked 'Praça da Sé' go to the center from in front of Shopping Iguatemi, just across the footbridge in front of the bus station. Going to the bus station, any bus that's labeled 'Iguatemi' will get you to the vicinity.

PUBLIC TRANSPORTATION

Linking Cidade Alta and Cidade Baixa are the **Elevador Lacerda** (☑ 3322-7049; fare R$0.15; ☺ 24hr).

Public buses crisscross the city; note that passengers board the bus through the rear door (and pay the attendant seated there), then disembark from the front door of the bus (near the driver). There are two main city bus terminals in the center that can serve as destinations or transfer points: Terminal da França in the Comércio, and Lapa, behind Shopping Lapa and Shopping Piedade. If heading north to the Igreja NS do Bonfim, catch a bus from the stop at the base of the Elevador Lacerda.

Taxis can be taken at meter price (legal) or negotiated, but you might not get to choose which.

RECÔNCAVO

A region of green, fertile lands surrounding the Baía de Todos os Santos, the *recôncavo* brought riches to Salvador (and the Portuguese crown) with its sugar and tobacco crops. The profits reaped off these lands also spurred the growth of once-rich towns like Cachoeira, which is resplendent with colonial architecture and history.

Cachoeira & São Félix

☑ 0XX75 / POP 46,400

Cachoeira, affectionately known as the jewel of the *recôncavo*, is a sleepy place, full of colorful, mostly preserved colonial architecture uncompromised by the presence of modern buildings. The town sits below a series of hills, strung along the banks of the Rio Paraguaçu in a face-off with its twin, São Félix – the two towns are connected by a striking British-built bridge divided for cars and pedestrians. A steady trickle of tourism flows through the area, attracted by Brazil's best tobacco, its reputation as a renowned center of Candomblé and a strong woodsculpting tradition. If you get an early start, it's possible to see both Cachoeira and São Félix on a day trip from Salvador.

History

Diego Álvares, the father of Cachoeira's founders, was the sole survivor of a ship bound for the West Indies that was wrecked in 1510 on a reef near Salvador. This Portuguese Robinson Crusoe was saved by the indigenous Tupinambá of Rio Vermelho,

BUSES FROM SALVADOR

DESTINATION	TIME (HR)	FARE (R$)	FREQUENCY	COMPANY
Aracaju	4-6	50-98	8-14 daily	Bomfim (☑ 3460-0000)
Ilhéus	7-8	74-129	7 daily	Águia Branca (☑ 4004-1010)
Lençóis	7	59	4-5 daily	Real Expresso (☑ 3450-2991)
Maceió	11	92-140	2-3 daily	Bomfim
Natal	21	159-182	2 daily	São Geraldo (☑ 3450-4488)
Penedo	9	70	daily	Bomfim
Porto Seguro	11	150	2 daily	Águia Branca
Recife	12	140-159	daily	Itapemirim (☑ 3450-5644) & Penha (☑ 0800 646 2122)
Rio de Janeiro	28	190-236	2 daily	Águia Branca & Itapemirim
São Paulo	33	280	3 daily	São Geraldo
Vitória	19	140-208	3 daily	Águia Branca

who dubbed the strange white sea creature Caramuru, or 'Fish-Man.' Álvares lived 20 years with the *índios* and married Catarina do Paraguaçu, the daughter of the most powerful Tupinambá chief. Their sons João Gaspar Aderno Álvares and Rodrigues Martins Álvares killed off the local indigenous people, set up the first sugarcane *fazendas* (ranches) and founded Cachoeira.

By the 18th century, tobacco from Cachoeira was considered the world's finest, sought by rulers in China and Africa. The 'holy herb' also became popular in Brazil, taken as snuff, smoked in a pipe or chewed.

⊙ Sights & Activities

Cachoeira is one of Candomblé's strongest and perhaps purest spiritual and religious centers. The *terreiros* are in small homes and shacks in the hills, where long ceremonies are usually held on Friday and Saturday nights. Travelers who are especially interested in learning more should contact the tourist office for information about local guides who take visitors to ceremonies.

The town has maintained a tradition of wood carving with a heavy African flavor. Stop in on the *ateliers* (studios) of two of the best sculptors in town, **Doidão** (cnr 25 de Junho & 7 de Setembro, Cachoeira) and **Louco** (Rua 13 de Maio, Cachoeira), to get a sense of the local style; they operate roughly from 10am to 4pm Monday to Friday.

Note that, as elsewhere in Bahia, churches are sometimes closed even when their posted opening hours indicate otherwise. Admission is by donation.

Igreja da Ordem Terceira do Carmo CHURCH
(Praça da Aclamação, Cachoeira) The Igreja da Ordem Terceira do Carmo has a gilded baroque altar, paneled ceilings and *azulejos*, and dates from 1702.

Igreja Matriz NS do Rosário CHURCH
(Nery s/n, Cachoeira) The church dates to between 1693 and 1754. It has beautiful *azulejos* and a ceiling painted by Teófilo de Jesus. On the 2nd floor, the Museu das Alfaias contains remnants from the abandoned 17th-century Convento de São Francisco do Paraguaçu.

Igreja de NS da Ajuda CHURCH
(Largo da Ajuda, Cachoeira) Cachoeira's oldest church is the tiny Igreja de NS da Ajuda, built in 1595 when the town was known as Arraial d'Ajuda.

Casa da Câmara e Cadeia HISTORIC BUILDING
(Prefecture & Jail; Praça da Aclamação, Cachoeira; ⊙8am-4pm Mon-Fri) FREE At the Casa da Câmara e Cadeia, organized criminals ran the show upstairs and disorganized criminals were kept behind bars downstairs. The building dates to 1698 and served as the seat of the Bahian government in 1822.

Museu Hansen Bahia MUSEUM
(☑3425-1453; 13 de Maio, Cachoeira; ⊙9am-5pm Tue-Fri, to 2pm Sat & Sun) FREE The birthplace and former home of Brazilian heroine Ana Nery, who organized the nursing corps during the Paraguay War. Today, it houses powerful block prints and paintings on the theme of human suffering, depicting primarily prostitutes and Christ, of German-Brazilian artist Hansen Bahia.

Museu da Boa Morte MUSEUM
(13 de Maio, Cachoeira; admission by donation; ⊙10am-6pm) The exclusively female Boa Morte (Good Death) religious society began as a sisterhood of slaves that assured dead slaves a proper burial and bought old slaves their freedom. This small museum was closed for renovations at the time of writing.

Museu Regional da Cachoeira MUSEUM
(☑3425-1123; Praça da Aclamação 4, Cachoeira; admission R$2; ⊙8am-noon & 2-5pm Mon-Fri, 8am-noon Sat & Sun) Housed in an 18th-century colonial mansion, the humble Museu Regional da Cachoeira displays colonial furnishings and priestly vestments.

Centro Cultural Dannemann MUSEUM
(☑3438-4308; www.centroculturaldannemann.com.br; Salvador Pinto 29, São Félix; ⊙8am-noon & 1-5pm Tue-Sat) FREE In São Félix, this riverfront cultural center has modern art displayed throughout a converted warehouse. In a large room in the rear of the building, heavy with the rich smell of tobacco, women dressed in white with flowered head wraps sit at antique wooden tables rolling *charutos* (cigars), as has been done here since 1873. Dannemann cigars are considered Brazil's finest.

BAHIA CACHOEIRA & SÃO FÉLIX

Cachoeira

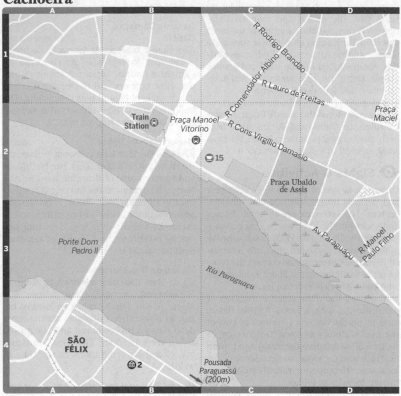

✨ Festivals & Events

Festa de São João   FOLKLORIC
(☉ Jun 22-24) The largest popular festival of Bahia's interior, celebrated with folklore, music, dancing and a generous amount of food and drink.

Festa de NS do Rosário   RELIGIOUS
(☉ mid-Oct) Another religious festival featuring great music and food.

Festa de NS D'Ajuda   RELIGIOUS
(☉ mid-Nov) Features a ritual *lavagem* of the church and a street festival.

🛏 Sleeping & Eating

On Cachoeira's waterfront plazas, vendors sell everything from cold beer and popcorn to regional treats like *caldo de cana* (sugarcane juice).

Pousada do Convento do Carmo   POUSADA $
(☎ 3425-1716; www.pousadadoconvento.com.br; Praça da Aclamação, Cachoeira; s/d from R$72/105; ❄ 🛜 ♨) The 18th-century convent attached to the Igreja da Ordem Terceira do Carmo has been converted into a comfortable pousada, with no loss of atmosphere. Rooms are spacious, with tall ceilings and heavy wood floors. The classy on-site restaurant, A Confraria, is open to the public (11am to 10pm).

Pousada Paraguassú   POUSADA $
(☎ 3438-3369; www.pousadaparaguassu.com.br; Salvador Pinto 3, São Félix; s/d from R$75/105; ❄ 🛜) Located on the riverfront in São Félix, Paraguassú has basic, cozy rooms surrounding a small garden. The riverside terrace is a breezy place to enjoy the ample breakfast buffet, or, at night, Bahian food or pizza in the pousada's restaurant.

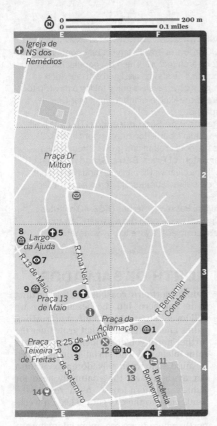

serve you (in other words, service is painfully slow.)

Gruta Azul   CAFE
(☑ 3425-1295; Praça Manoel Vitorino 2, Cachoeira; ⊙ 11am-8pm Sat & Sun) This cool, darkened cafe, popular with locals, features a beautiful tiled bar; it's an ideal spot for a cold drink or a bite to eat while you wait for your bus. Unfortunately, it keeps irregular opening hours.

❶ Information

Both São Félix and Cachoeira have banks with ATMs. For more information on the towns' history, river excursions, or church visits, stop into the helpful **tourist office** (Nery 7; ⊙ 8am-noon & 2-5pm Mon-Fri, 9am-noon Sat & Sun) in Cachoeira.

❶ Getting There & Away

These twin towns are served by nearly identical bus stations, positioned directly across the river from each other at each base of the bridge: most trips commence on the São Félix side, stopping to pick up passengers in Cachoeira before continuing out of town.

Numerous daily buses operated by **Transporte Santana e São Paulo** (☑ 3450-4951) run to Salvador (R$20, two hours, 5:30am to 7pm), stopping in Santo Amaro (R$8, one hour) along the way.

To make connections north, south or west, you can also catch one of Transporte Santana's various daily services to Feira de Santana (R$7, 1½ hours, 12 daily).

Aclamação Restaurante   BRAZILIAN $
(☑ 3425-3428; Praça da Aclamação 2, Cachoeira; mains R$4-38; ⊙ 11am-10pm) This busy corner eatery offers a range of great-value sandwiches, acai, and traditional Bahian dishes. Try the sandwich named after the nearby river, Rio Paraguaçu, piled high with bacon, cheese, grilled chicken, beef, tomatoes and lettuce – at a mere R$6, it's a steal.

Pizzaria Shambhalah   PIZZERIA $
(☑ 3425-3414; Rua Inocência Bonaventura, Cachoeira; mains R$12-25; ⊙ 6-10pm) This popular pizzeria has brick walls, a varied menu and nicely lit tables with views onto the plaza. It fills up in the evening with groups of students and local couples and families.

Baiana's Point   BAR
(☑ 3425-4967; Virgílio Reis, Cachoeira; ⊙ 5-10pm) Perched on scenic stilts over the river, this place makes a great setting for an early-evening drink – if you can get anyone to

BAHIA CACHOEIRA & SÃO FÉLIX

WORTH A TRIP

ILHA DE ITAPARICA

The Baía de Todos os Santos, occupying 1000 sq km, is Brazil's largest bay, containing 56 islands rich with lush vegetation and historic architecture. The most popular escape for residents of Salvador is the island of Itaparica. The shores are lined with vacation homes, and while the beaches are only average, many travelers enjoy taking a day trip to the bars, restaurants and relaxed atmosphere of the likable island town of Mar Grande, 9km south of the transport hub of Bom Despacho.

Guarding the northern tip of the island, the **Forte de São Lourenço** (1711) was built by Dutch invaders and figured prominently in Bahia's battle for independence in 1823. In the center of the island, a huge tree wraps its roots around and grows through the ruins of the **Igreja Baiacu** church. The clear waters of **Praia Barra Grande**, in front of the village, is Itaparica's finest public beach. It has clear water and weekend homes, and lies in front of its namesake village. Plenty of casual restaurants, clustered near the ferry dock, serve Bahian-style seafood with bay views.

The boat journey from Salvador is half the fun. Passenger ferries (R$3, 40 minutes, every 30 minutes from 6am to 6pm, to 6:30pm on weekends) run between Salvador's Terminal Marítimo Turístico and Mar Grande's terminal. It's wise to buy your return ticket ahead of time on summer days.

Santo Amaro

☑ 0XX75 / POP 58,000

Santo Amaro is a friendly colonial sugar town that sees very few tourists and has an unpretentious charm. It is most well known for being the hometown of the brother-sister pair Caetano Veloso and Maria Betânia, two of Brazil's most popular singers (who often put in an appearance during Carnaval). The center bustles with people, especially around the small outdoor market. Paper production has replaced sugar as the major industry, visible in the invasion of bamboo on the hillsides where sugarcane once flourished, and a large paper mill outside of town.

The decrepit sugar-baron mansions along the old commercial street, Rua General Câmara, and the numerous churches are reminders of Santo Amaro's prosperous days. The ornate **Matriz de NS da Purificação** (1668) is the largest church, with *azulejos* and a painted ceiling. Unfortunately, a gang of thieves stole most of the church's holy images and exported them to France.

The **Lavagem da Purificação** (January 23 to February 2) is celebrated by a procession and ritual washing of the church steps by *baianas* in traditional dress, before bands and *trios elétricos* take over the streets.

Buses leave Salvador for Santo Amaro (R$12, one hour) almost every 30 minutes from 5:30am to 7pm. Most continue on to Cachoeira/São Félix (R$8, one hour).

NORTH OF SALVADOR

Bahia's northern coast is not as startling as its southern, but the beaches here are still lovely, boasting tall bluffs with rustling palms and white sands (that grow finer the further north you go), which front a mix of calm inlets and wild surfable breaks. Keep in mind that when salvadorenhos want a day at the beach, they naturally head for Bahia's northern coast. As a result, the sands close to the city get packed on weekends. To escape the crowds, head further north, where there are many kilometers of deserted pristine shoreline.

The Estrada do Coco (Coconut Hwy) runs as far north as Praia do Forte, where the Linha Verde (Green Line) picks up, continuing all the way to the Sergipe border. You may feel that you are going against the grain if you are trying to access this coast heading north to south. Grassy medians in the highways require buses to pass town entrances and then double back, so few do. Instead, they drop passengers on the highway, leaving you to walk or pick up other transportation into the small towns and fishing communities along this stretch of coast. Traveling from south to north is a much smoother process.

Praia do Forte

☑ 0XX71

Beloved by tourists, upmarket Praia do Forte is an attractive and somewhat ecologically sensitive beach village overflowing with stylish restaurants and shops. The main drag, Alameda do Sol, is a pedestrian walkway that leads to an incredibly picturesque and pint-sized church, a sea-turtle reserve and fantastic, palm-lined beaches with sparkling white sands that fill up on weekends. Surrounding the village are castle ruins, a lagoon for canoeing and the Sapiranga forest reserve, which has hiking and biking trails and a zip line. If you can, time your visit for the full moon and walk along the beach past the resort at sunset, when the sun turns the waters of the Rio Timeantube red as the moon rises over the sea.

◉ Sights & Activities

Castelo do Garcia d'Ávila RUINS
(☑ 9985-3349; www.fgd.org.br; Alameda do Farol s/n; admission R$10; ☺ 8:30am-6pm) Dating from 1552, the Castelo was the first great Portuguese edifice in Brazil. Desperate to colonize, the king of Portugal granted lands to merchants, soldiers and aristocrats; a farmer named Garcia d'Ávila, endowed with this tract of land, chose this oceanview plot for his home. Today, it's an impressive ruin with sweeping views. It's 7km outside of town – take a taxi.

Reserva da Sapiranga HIKING
(☑ 9985-3349; www.fgd.org.br; admission R$10, guided hikes R$5-15; ☺ 8am-5pm) A turn-off from the road to the castle leads down a dirt track to the Reserva da Sapiranga, where local student guides take visitors along trails skirting through 600 hectares of secondary Atlantic rainforest. Hikes range from 30 minutes to five hours, with one of the more popular hikes leading down to the Rio Pojuca (bring your swimsuit).

☞ Tours

Worthwhile tours in the area include hiking and birdwatching treks, canopy tours, kayaking and whale watching (in season). A handful of professional outfitters such as Portomar (☑ 3676-0101; www.portomar.com.br; Rua da Aurora 1; ☺ 9am-7pm) handle these trips and run popular excursions at low tide to nearby *piscinas naturais* (natural pools), where you can snorkel or scuba dive around a colorful coral reef.

🛏 Sleeping

Praia do Forte has an abundance of attractive midrange guesthouses that fill to capacity on summer weekends. Rua da Aurora, parallel to Alameda do Sol, has a handful of more affordable pousadas.

Praia do Forte Hostel HOSTEL $
(☑ 3676-1094; www.albergue.com.br; Aurora 3; dm/d with fan R$52/130, d with air-con R$145; ❀ 🤍) The popular HI hostel has a convenient location, clean rooms facing onto a grassy courtyard, and a good breakfast spread. Rental bikes and surfboards are available, too.

Pousada Montreux POUSADA $
(☑ 3676-1494; www.praiadofortepousada.com.br; Rua Aurora 22; d with fan/air-con R$150/180; ❀) One of Forte's better deals, Montreux is a friendly Swiss Brazilian–run guesthouse with clean, pleasant rooms with balconies.

Pousada dos Artistas POUSADA $$
(☑ 3676-1147;www.pousadadosartistas.tur.br;Praça dos Artistas s/n; d/tr R$168/218; ❀ 🤍) This friendly pousada – run by a dancer and a painter-sculptor, as the name suggests – offers lovely colonial-style rooms (each with a private balcony and hammock) looking out over a lush tropical garden.

Casa Verde Apart APARTMENT $$
(☑ 3676-1531; www.praiadoforteapart.com.br; Peixe Espada 100; apt for 3/4 people R$180/220; ❀ 🤍) In a leafy setting near the beach, these six attractive and spacious apartments are complete with well-equipped kitchens and balconies with hammocks. The place is managed by a gracious couple – breakfast is available on request, for an extra fee.

Pousada Ogum Marinho POUSADA $$
(☑ 3676-1165; www.ogummarinho.com.br; Alameda do Sol s/n; d/tr R$250/312; ❀ 🤍) One block from the beach, Ogum Marinho has attractive rooms with stone-slab floors, comfortable furnishings and private decks strung with hammocks.

Pousada Tia Helena POUSADA $$
(☑ 3676-1198; www.tiahelenapraiadoforte.com.br; Alameda das Estrelas s/n; s/d with fan R$130/180; 🤍) Tia Helena offers clean, simple rooms, a warm welcome and prices that make her guesthouse a firm favorite among budget travelers.

Tivoli Ecoresort RESORT $$$
(☑ 3676-4000;www.tivolihotels.com;Av do Farol s/n; s/d incl half-board from R$825/990; ❀ 🤍 ✦) ⚑ It's all luxury at this excellent resort, where walkways wind through groomed gardens

BAHIA PRAIA DO FORTE

Candomblé

The wild and little-understood Candomblé religion is deeply rooted in Bahian culture and connects countless Afro-Brazilians to a long line of West African ancestry.

African Origins

Candomblé is the most orthodox of the religions brought from Africa by the Nago, Yoruba and Jeje peoples. Candomblé is an African word denoting a dance in honor of the gods. Afro-Brazilian rituals are directed by a *pai de santo* or *mãe de santo* (literally saint's mother or father – the Candomblé priests) and practiced in a *casa de santo* or *terreiro* (house of worship). The ceremonies are conducted in the Yoruba language.

Orixás

The religion centers around *orixás,* or deities. Like the gods in Greek mythology, each *orixá* has a unique personality and history. Candomblé followers believe that every person has a particular deity watching over them – from birth until death. A person's *orixá* can be identified when a *pai* or *mãe de santo* makes successive throws with a handful of *búzios* (shells), in a divination ritual known as Jogo dos Búzios (Casting of Shells). The position of the shells is used to interpret one's luck, one's future and one's past relationship with the gods. Although *orixás* are divided into male and female types, there are some that can switch from one sex to the other, such as Logunedé, son of two male gods, Ogun and Oxoss.

Candomblé in Practice

To keep themselves strong and healthy, followers of Candomblé give food or other offerings to please their respective *orixás*. For example, to Iemanjá, the goddess or queen of the sea, one should give perfumes, flowers, combs and mirrors. Oxúm, god of fresh waters and waterfalls, is famous for his vanity, and is honored with earrings, necklaces, champagne and honey. In Bahia and Rio, followers of Afro-Brazilian cults turn out in huge numbers for the festival held during the night of December 31 and on New Year's Day – and in Salvador, on February 2. Millions of Brazilians go to the beach at this time to pay homage to Iemanjá. Flowers, perfumes, fruits and even jewelry are tossed into the sea to please the mother of the waters, or to gain protection and good luck in the new year.

Attending a Candomblé Ceremony

Ceremonies take place in richly decorated halls called *terreiros*. Drummers pound out powerful rhythms while the mostly female dancers, chanting in Yoruba, glide in a counterclockwise circle, representing the rolling back of the centuries, as they reach out to their ancestors. A festive, celebratory atmosphere prevails, with the *mãe de santo* or *pai de santo* presiding. The chiming of bells conjures the spirits: when a spirit arrives, those dancing may take on the attributes of the *orixá* in question. A good list of *terreiros* can also be found at www.bahia-online.net/Candomble.htm.

JAN SOCHOR / ALAMY ©

1. Candomblé devotees
2. Festival of Yemanjá
3. Women dancing, Festival of Yemanjá

LATINCONTENT / GETTY IMAGES ©

LATINCONTENT / GETTY IMAGES ©

past eight swimming pools to the beach. Rooms all have verandas, the cuisine is top-notch and the spa offers a wide range of treatments. Although there's nothing particularly 'eco' about the design, the hotel does contribute to social and educational programs.

✗ Eating

Countless attractive eateries line the town's pedestrian walkways, but prices are high and the food is nothing special. For the best atmosphere and value, explore side streets and the casual cafes around the central plaza, where cold beer flows freely at night.

Exkinão do Lanche
SANDWICHES $

(Av do Farol s/n; mains R$9-13; ⊗11am-10pm ; ✐) This popular deli does made-to-order sandwiches – choose between *pernil* (pork), *picanha* (steak) or one of the vegetarian options. Take your sandwiches to the beach, or dine at one of the well-positioned outdoor tables and watch the beach crowd come and go.

★ Souza Bar
BAHIAN $$

(✐9987-8638; www.souzabar.com.br; Alameda do Sol s/n, Tamar Project station; small plates R$10-15, mains for 2 R$40-70; ⊗10am-1am) The festive Souza Bar now has two locations in town. The original, inside the Tamar Project station, has a dramatic setting along the rocky coastline. The newer location, near the bus drop-off, hosts live music. Both are a sure bet for fresh clams, crispy *bolinho de peixe* (fried fish balls) and caipirinhas.

Casa da Nati
BUFFET $$

(✐3676-1239; www.casadanati.com.br; Alameda do Sol s/n; mains R$18-42; ⊗11am-late Mon-Fri, from 8am Sat & Sun) A longtime Praia do Forte favorite, Casa da Nati spreads an excellent self-serve lunch buffet, with tasty à la carte dishes by night and breakfast service on weekends. The glow of lanterns illuminates the pretty outdoor dining area.

Vila Gourmet
BRAZILIAN $$$

(✐3676-1088; www.sobradodavila.com.br; Alameda do Sol; mains for 2 R$62-95; ⊗8am-10pm) This stylish tropical-style eatery (connected to the centrally located Pousada Sobrado da Vila) serves regional cuisine that's a cut above the rest – thanks to organic vegetables and eggs sourced from a private farm.

ℹ Orientation

Buses stop at the northern end of the main pedestrian thoroughfare, Alameda do Sol (also called Av ACM). Though beaches are crowded in front of the plaza and church, find a peaceful spot under the palm trees by walking south along the coast for five to 10 minutes.

ℹ Information

Several ATMs are located near the bus stop. At the time of writing, the nearby tourist information office was closed indefinitely. In the meantime, get the details on area excursions and acitivities at any of the travel agencies around town.

ℹ Getting There & Around

Praia do Forte is 3km off the highway. **Linha Verde** (✐3460-3636) has regular departures to Praia do Forte from Salvador's bus station (R$8.25 to R$9, 1¾ hours, 14 daily between 5am and 6pm). Buses make the return journey frequently between 7am and 6:30pm. Informal Kombi vans make the same trip to Salvador for R$7 – wait near the bus stop for pick-up.

Praia do Forte to Sítio do Conde

Imbassaí is a rustic beach town 16km north of Praia do Forte. A tall sand dune and the peaceful Rio Barroso, which runs parallel to the beach, separate the village from a pretty beach with rough surf. Most guesthouses in town are midrange and top-end options, though **Lujimba Eco Hostel** (✐3677-1056; www.imbassaihostel.com.br; dm/d from R$31/80; 🔊) offers good value for its pleasant wooden-floor rooms in a rustic, thatched-roof guesthouse amid greenery. Hammocks, fruit trees and excursions add to the allure.

A few kilometers north of Imbassaí, along the river, lies the more rustic town of **Diogo**, which sees fewer visitors and retains the charm of village life. For those looking to unwind, the relaxing **Too Cool Na Bahia** (✐9952-2190; www.toocoolnabahia.com; d from R$135; ✱) is a destination in itself: the pousada has eight colorfully designed chalets with verandas overlooking the lush surroundings. The friendly owner can arrange kitesurfing, kayaking, horseback riding and other activities.

To reach most places between Praia do Forte and Sítio do Conde, take a **Linha Verde** (✐3460-3636) bus from Salvador's bus station (almost hourly between 5am and 6pm) and alert the driver to your destination.

Sítio do Conde

🔊 0XX75

Wet lowlands full of cattle surround this quiet, working-class beach retreat. While there's little to the town itself – just a few main streets and a sleepy central plaza – Sítio has a lovely beach with pounding surf (located 1km from the plaza). North or south along the coast quickly leads to a deserted shore with churning seas and flat sands backed by bluffs topped with coconut trees.

Pousada Talismã (🔊 3449-1252; www. pousadatalisma.com; s/d R$70/100) offers simple accommodation, plus ocean views and a lovely restaurant. **Zecas & Zecas** (🔊 3449-1298; Praça Arsênio Mendes 51; mains for 2 R$24-48; ☺ noon-10pm Mon-Sat), on the main square, is a popular seafood restaurant serving the town's best *moqueca*. Travelers rave about the personalized attention (in English) and paradise-like setting at **B&B Bela Bahia** (🔊 3449-7037; www.bela-bahia.com; Poças; d/tr R$190/250), a few kilometers outside of town and run by a laid-back Belgian-Brazilian couple.

Direct transportation to Sítio do Conde is infrequent: the meandering trip can take four or more hours from Salvador on bus lines São Luís and Oliveira (R$45, seven to eight daily). You can also catch a bus directly to Conde, then take a *topique* (van, R$3) or taxi (around R$25) for the 8km trip on to Sítio. If you're in a hurry, some area pousadas, like B&B Bela Bahia, offer private transportation from the Salvador airport (R$500 round-trip per carload).

Mangue Seco

🔊 0XX75

Mangue Seco is a tiny, beautifully rustic riverfront village at the tip of a peninsula formed by the Rio Real, which delineates the Bahia–Sergipe border. The town itself is just a scattering of simple dwellings along sandy paths, a tiny church and plaza, a modern lighthouse (yielding lovely views for intrepid climbers) and a few friendly guesthouses and restaurants. The town ends at the edge of an enormous expanse of tall white sand dunes, beyond which the wide, flat sands of the Bahian coast stretch to the south. Mangue Seco's remote location prompts most visitors to come on guided day tours, preventing rapid growth and leaving nights decidedly quiet. It's about a 1.5km walk to the ocean, which has a handful of simple *barracas* strung with hammocks.

🛏 Sleeping & Eating

Mangue Seco's culinary specialty is *aratu*, a tiny red shellfish sometimes prepared in *moquecas*. In addition to the pousadas' excellent restaurants, visitors can sample sea-

DON'T MISS

THE SEA TURTLES OF TAMAR

There are only five remaining species of sea turtle left in the world – and all of them live on the Bahian coast. A true highlight of any trip through the region is a visit to the sea-turtle reserve that's dedicated to protecting loggerhead, hawksbill, olive ridley and green turtles – and their adorably tiny babies.

One of 18 stations run in Bahia by the nonprofit organization **Projeto TAMAR** (🔊 3676-0321; www.tamar.org.br; admission R$16; ☺ 9am-5:30pm) – the name is an abbreviation for the Portuguese word for sea turtle, *tartaruga marinha* – the Praia do Forte is perhaps the most impressive, exhibiting pools with marine turtles of various sizes and species, as well as urchins, eels and other sea life.

Outside the station itself, the most important action happens on the shoreline during the turtles' nesting season (September to March). Tamar researchers protect around 550 nests a year along 50km of coast close to Praia do Forte. The moist, leathery, ping-pong-ball-size eggs are buried in the sand when laid and either left on the beach or brought to the hatcheries for incubation. When they hatch, the baby turtles are immediately released into the sea. Though this system allows some 500,000 baby turtles to hatch each year in Bahia, only several hundred will reach adulthood.

A trip to the reserve, located just behind the church on Praia do Forte's main square, is interactive and family-friendly; take your time and have an outdoor lunch beside the ocean at Souza Bar (p426), located inside the project station.

food at low-key outdoor eateries along the riverbank.

Pousada Suruby
POUSADA $

(📞3445-9061; www.pousadasuruby.com.br; d from R$130; ❀) This simple, fan-cooled rooms face onto a walkway lined with hammocks, and the breezy restaurant serves seafood (mains R$27 to R$45). To get to Suruby, exit the dock and follow the riverfront to the left, toward the beach.

★Pousada O Forte
POUSADA $$

(📞3445-9039; www.pousadaoforte.com; bungalows for 1/2/3 people from R$200/250/310; ❄🎔🏊) 🏊 Located just outside the village center on the riverfront, on the way to the beach, this eco-friendly French Brazilian–owned pousada occupies an isolated spot overlooking the river. With pretty bungalows and a lovely swimming pool, it's family-friendly, too.

Recanto de Dona Sula
CAFE $

(📞3445-9008; snacks R$6-15; ⊗8:30am-8:30pm) 🏊 At this local favorite, homemade candies, ice creams and liqueurs are made from regional fruits; the coffee is excellent, too. Both charming and environmentally conscious (recycling is a priority), this sweet cafe is located next to the church.

❶ Getting There & Around

Mangue Seco is remote; unless you're hiring private transportation or coming on a day trip from Salvador, getting here requires a combination of bus, taxi and boat.

Most travelers arrive in Mangue Seco as follows: from the south, a **Bomfim** (www.bomfim.com.br) bus from Salvador (R$40 to R$57, three daily) to Estância, or from the north, a Bomfim bus from Aracaju to Estancia – but note that the company was running irregular service on the Aracaju–Estancia segment at the time of writing. A taxi from Estancia to Pontal (R$60) takes you to the speedboat between Pontal and Mangue Seco (around R$40 for up to four people). If you can catch one, vans also make the trip from Pontal (R$8, 90 minutes) to Estância.

Especially if you're traveling with others, it's worthwhile to ask your pousada in Mangue Seco if they offer more direct transportation. Pousada O Forte, for example, offers service from Salvador (R$350 to R$400 for up to four people) and Aracaju (R$190 for up to four people).

SOUTH OF SALVADOR

Morro de São Paulo
🗹 0XX75

As postcard-pretty as any Mediterranean island village, Morro de São Paulo has long been a favorite weekend getaway for travelers and Salvador locals alike. Though Morro is overtly touristy, many visitors don't care, since it's also a fabulous tropical paradise with sandy lanes, calm waters and a candle-lit nightlife scene.

Remotely perched at the northern tip of the Ilha de Tinharé, Morro's appeal stems from its relaxed pace – no cars are allowed on the island – and unique geography: three jungle-topped hills on a point at the meeting of the mangrove-lined Canal de Taperoá and a clear, shallow Atlantic.

During the high season the village booms, dozens of vendors mix fresh-fruit caipirinhas on the sand, and lighthearted dancing and music enliven the beaches every night.

◉ Sights & Activities

The town's icon is a 17th-century carved-stone **fortress gate**, which welcomes each arrival from its position above the dock.

Around the corner at the point are the **fort ruins** (1630). Catching the rare sight of the sun setting over the river and mangroves from the fort is a visitor ritual. The **lighthouse** (1835) above the fort affords a fantastic view over Morro's beaches.

Down a sandy lane from the main square, the **Fonte Grande** (Great Fountain), in operation since the 17th century, is a good example of an old urban water supply system in Bahia.

The waters of Morro's four conveniently named main beaches are mostly calm, shallow and warm, and their sands are narrow and swallowed by the high tides. Tiny **Primeira Praia** is lined with pousadas, occasionally hosts lively football matches on the sand, and has a decent surf break. Deep **Segunda Praia** (500m) is the 'action' beach, with pousadas, restaurants, nightclubs and a sea of tables and chairs. Pousadas and anchored boats dominate one end of **Terceira Praia** (1km). Once you pass a pair of restaurants, **Quarta Praia** (2km) is a long, lovely stretch of sand graced by tall, swaying palms. For even more isolated peace, continue on at low tide to **Praia do Encanto** (5km) or further down the island to **Garapuá**, which has one pousada.

☞ Tours

A boat trip around the island (R$80), with stops at the Garapuá and Moreré offshore reefs and the villages of Boipeba and historical Cairu, is obligatory. You'll fly over waves in a 10-person speedboat past gorgeous beach and mangrove scenery, swim, snorkel and stop at a floating oyster bar. Horseback riding and guided hikes are easily arranged at the island's many local agencies. Scuba enthusiasts can log onto the website or stop into the local office of **Companhia do Mergulho** (☑ 3652-1200; www.ciadomergulho.com; Prainha s/n, Primeira Praia), located on the path to the beach.

🛏 Sleeping

Reservations for Morro's numerous pousadas are required for all major holidays, especially Carnaval and the days before and after. Be forewarned that staying on Segunda Praia during summer means sleeping to the nightclubs' pounding beats; the least expensive pousadas are in town.

Pousada Caravelas   POUSADA $

(☑ 3652-1350; www.caravelaspousada.com; Rua da Fonte Grande; d/tr R$140/170; ❈ ☎) This small, simple pousada, just around the corner from the historic fountain, offers a first-rate breakfast served on your balcony – it's a rare pleasure to enjoy coffee and homemade pastries while watching hummingbirds flitting through the lush courtyard.

Pousada Primeira Praia   POUSADA $

(☑ 3652-1002; www.pousadaprimeirapraia.com.br; Rua da Prainha s/n; d R$140; ❈ ☎) As the name suggests, this pousada is one of only a handful on the mellow Primeira Praia. With an emerald and turquoise color scheme and simple rooms – some with private balconies – its a popular choice in a slightly quieter stretch of the waterfront.

Pousada Ninho da Águia   INN $

(☑ 3652-1201; www.pousadaninhodaaguia.com; Caminho do Farol s/n; d from R$130; ☎) On the hill above the dock, the tranquilly set Ninho da Águia is indeed at eagle's-nest heights: a privilege you'll earn with a steep uphill hike. It's a friendly, family-run affair with tidy, simple rooms (upstairs rooms have great views).

Che Lagarto Hostel   HOSTEL $

(☑ 3652-1018; www.chelagarto.com; Fonte Grande; dm R$32-50, d R$128-185; ☎) Convenient to the ferry dock and local nightlife, yet with a middle-of-the-jungle feel thanks to its forest-shrouded wooden sundeck, this chain hostel is geared to those looking for a youthful party vibe.

Pousada Colibri   POUSADA $$

(☑ 3652-1056; www.pousada-colibri.com; bungalows R$145, ste R$170-225; ❈ ☎ ≋) In a marvelous hilltop position, the lushly landscaped Colibri has pretty cabins and suites with verandas and hammocks. Surrounding jungle assures quiet, but it's a bit of a hike from the beach – luckily, rates include round-trip baggage transfer from the harbor. To reach it, take the path to the spring, then turn right up a quiet forested lane.

O Casarão   POUSADA $$

(☑ 3652-1022; www.pousadaocasarao.com; Praça Aureliano Lima 190; d/bungalows from R$200/280; ❈ ☎ ≋) Reigning over the main plaza, this beautifully renovated colonial mansion – dating from 1906 – has lovely rooms with classical furnishings and large windows, plus hillside bungalows with private balconies. Amenities include two swimming pools: one, with a bar, for adults, and another for children. The atmospheric restaurant on the terrace (mains R$24 to R$51) is open to the public for dinner.

Pousada Natal   POUSADA $$

(☑ 3652-1059; www.pousadanatal-msp.com.br; Caminho da Praia s/n; d R$160; ❈ ☎) This laid-back main-street budget spot has basic rooms and friendly staff; it's well positioned between the harbor and the beaches. To get here, just follow the crowds heading to the beaches from the port – it's about midway between the plaza and Primeira Praia.

Pousada Paraíso do Morro   POUSADA $$

(☑ 3652-1121; www.paraisodomorro.com.br; Terceira Praia; d without/with sea view R$180/230; ❈ ☎) This charming guesthouse is all about peace and tranquility: colorful, stylish rooms overlook the sea or a small garden. It's just around the corner from the action on Segunda Praia, but far enough away that you're unlikely to be kept awake by beach parties and nightlife.

Pousada Ilha do Sol   POUSADA $$

(☑ 8871-1295; www.minhapousadailhadosol.com.br; Rua da Prainha, Primeira Praia; d R$180-220; ❈ ☎) At the base of the steep road leading to the ocean, this well-established guesthouse is good value for its open two-room suites catching the ocean breeze, and porches for prime people-watching.

Villa das Pedras
POUSADA $$$

(☑ 3652-1075; www.villadaspedras.com.br; Segunda Praia; d R$450-610; ❄🛜🏊) This eye-catching pousada, with vibrant hues and clean, modern lines, wins the most style points on busy Segunda Praia. The lavish breakfast spread, swimming pool and bar, and location directly across from the beach make it worth the splurge; the downside to the central location is that the area can be loud at night.

🍴 Eating & Drinking

Restaurants in Morro are priced for well-off vacationers, and quality varies – not to mention that most eateries price their main dishes for two, making eating out expensive for solo travelers. Luckily, casual dining options abound on the island. Sample crepes and *pasteles* and freshly squeezed juices at the food stands along the beaches. The path leading from the main square to Fonte Grande is lined with good-value bakeries and lunch spots. At night, Segunda Praia is alive with restaurants competing for your business – it's a prime opportunity to dine with the sand between your toes.

After dark, don't miss dexterous vendors along Rua Caminho da Praia and on Segunda Praia mixing delicious caipirinhas – made with a wide range of fresh fruits, many of which you've probably never heard of. Outdoor bars are scattered along Segunda Praia.

★ Pedra Sobre Pedras
CAFE $

(Segunda Praia; mains R$8-15; ⊘ 24hr) This little cafe is on a wooden deck perched high over Segunda Praia, just off the pedestrian walkway. Pull up a stool and enjoy crepes, well-mixed caipirinhas and gorgeous views over the beach action.

Tia Lita
BAHIAN $

(www.pousadatialita.com.br; Rua da Prainha, Terceira Praia; mains R$15-30; ⊘ noon-11pm) This casual and popular down-home restaurant serves grilled fish, chicken or beef with rice and salad, plus sandwiches and *moqueca*. It's located down a narrow lane off Terceira Praia.

Minha Louca Paixão
BRAZILIAN $$

(www.minhaloucapaixao.com.br; Terceira Praia; mains R$28-62; ⊘ 5-11pm) Well-prepared seafood dishes served at elegant (and quiet) waterfront tables make this sophisticated eatery one of the more romantic dining options along the beaches. It's a great option for a special occasion.

Café das Artes
BRAZILIAN $$

(☑ 3652-1057; Praça Aureliano Lima; mains R$10-60; ⊘ 11am-11pm) This pretty cafe-restaurant doubles as an art space; the patio overlooking the square is a sweet spot for a little night music. House specialties include seafood risotto and shrimp cooked in green coconut sauce.

Bianco e Nero
PIZZERIA $$

(☑ 3652-1097; Caminho da Praia; mains R$18-45; ⊘ noon-11:30pm Tue-Sun, from 5:30pm Mon) This fashionable Italian pizzeria and eatery is hugely popular for its fresh seafood pastas, oven-fired pizzas, rich Italian desserts and wines by the glass, all served on a large terrace above the main pedestrian thoroughfare. Service can be lax; you're paying for the stylish atmosphere.

Sabor da Terra
SEAFOOD $$

(Caminho da Praia; mains R$16-45; ⊘ noon-11pm) Excellent seafood is prepared simply or with Bahian spice; fish *moqueca* and *casquinha de siri* (shredded crab meat) are excellent. Part of the appeal is people-watching and hearing live music from nearby eateries at these tables lining the pedestrian walkway.

ℹ Orientation

Unless arriving by charter flight, all visitors disembark on the northern tip of the island (visitors pay a R$12 tourist tax on arrival, and another R$0.62 tax on departure).

At the dock, wheelbarrow valets wait to help you transport your luggage and lead you to your pousada, which is especially useful for travelers with rolling luggage (be sure to negotiate the price beforehand).

Uphill lies the main square (Praça Aureliano Lima) in the Vila, with an information office and a few restaurants. To reach the beaches, take a left at the square; this passes along the main street, Rua Caminho da Praia, and is lined with restaurants and shops. Continue downhill to access the shores, reaching Primeira Praia (First Beach), then Segunda Praia, and so on. Heading right from the main plaza, you'll go through an archway down Rua da Fonte and pass the spring-fed fountain that was once the village's freshwater source.

ℹ Information

There are a few ATMs on the island, but it's wise to bring necessary funds with you from the mainland, especially during high season, when tourists deplete the ATMs' cash supply. Many establishments also accept credit cards. Pharmacies and internet cafés are plentiful (R$4 to R$7 per hour).

At the top of the hill up from the dock, **Centro de Informações ao Turista** (☑3652-1083; www.morrosp.com.br; Praça Aureliano Lima; ☺8am-10pm) sells boat and domestic airline tickets, organizes excursions and distributes maps. Travel agencies scattered around the island provide similar services.

ⓘ Getting There & Away

A handful of operators run catamarans and *lanchas rapidas* (speedboats; R$80) between Morro and the Terminal Marítimo Turístico in Salvador. There are at six to seven daily departures each way. For reservations, contact **Biotur** (☑3641-3327; www.biotur.com.br), **Farol do Morro** (☑3652-1083; www.faroldomorrotour. com), **IlhaBela** (☑in Salvador 0xx71-9195-6744; www.ilhabelatm.com.br) or **Lancha Lulalu** (☑75-9917-1975), or stop into a travel agency on the island. The ride can be rough – come with Dramamine if you're especially prone to seasickness – and it's common for passengers to get wet on smaller boats.

If you're heading directly to Salvador's airport from Morro, contact **Cassi Turismo** (☑71-9111-111; www.cassiturismo.com.br). The agency sells a transfer package (R$100, two daily) involving a short boat ride to Bom Jardim combined with an overland bus journey to the airport.

If coming from the south, frequent passenger ferries travel upriver to Morro from Valença (R$8.70, 1½ hours). *Lanchas rapidas* (R$16, 40 minutes) make the trip even faster.

Two small airlines have daily flights between Salvador and Morro (R$200, 25 minutes). Contact **Aerostar** (☑in Salvador 0xx71-3377 4406; www.aerostar.com.br), **Addey Taxi Aéreo** (☑in Salvador 0xx71-3204 1393; www.addey.com.br) or a travel agency.

Boipeba

☑0XX75

South of the Ilha da Tinharé, across the narrow Rio do Inferno, sits the Ilha de Boipeba. The village of Boipeba, on the northeastern tip of the island, is quiet, rustic and said to be what Morro was 20 years ago – though this is slowly changing as more travelers hear about this little paradise. The island's coastline is pristine, with more than 20km of beautiful, deserted beaches, including **Ponta de Castelhanos**, known for its diving.

🛏 Sleeping & Eating

Expanding tourist infrastructure has brought several new pousadas to Boipeba; most have charming tropical-themed bars and restaurants that are open to the public. More eateries serving fresh seafood line the beach where the river meets the sea.

Pousada Pérola do Atlântico   POUSADA $$
(☑3653-6096; peroladoatlanticoboipeba@hotmail. com; Rua da Praia s/n; s/d/tr R$140/180/210; ❄ 🛜) On the beach, this welcoming guesthouse has lush gardens with winding pathways leading through the tranquil setting. Guest rooms offer private patios with hammocks.

Pousada Santa Clara   POUSADA $$
(☑3653-6085; www.santaclaraboipeba.com; Travessa da Praia 5; d R$170-220; ❄❄ 🛜) A 10-minute walk from the town center, this restful pousada truly feels like a getaway. Santa Clara has lush foliage and large, cheerful rooms; the wonderful breakfast and on-site restaurant (open to the public Tuesday to Sunday), both using local produce, are particularly beloved by repeat guests.

ⓘ Getting There & Away

From Morro de São Paulo, a boat leaves for Boipeba at 9:30am and then leaves Boipeba for the return journey to Morro at 2pm (both R$75, 2½ hours). You can also negotiate a ride to Boipeba with one of the many tour companies running day trips.

Alternatively, you can arrive by jeep. **Bahia Terra** (☑75-3653-6017; www.boipebatur. com.br) (R$75, four daily) transfers leave from Segunda Praia in Morro; the one-hour jeep ride connects you to the short boat ride (R$20) to Boipeba.

From Valença's ferry dock, catch a speedboat (R$35, one hour, hourly between 9am and 5pm) to Boipeba.

Valença

☑0XX75 / POP 88,700

Valença is a colonial fishing town on the banks of the Rio Una, historically the site of Portuguese struggles with both indigenous tribes and the Dutch. For most it is simply the gateway to Morro de São Paulo, but locals know it as a center of shipbuilding: 15th-century techniques have been so well maintained that the town was chosen to produce a replica of the Spanish galleon *La Niña* for the American epic film

1492 (1992) about Christopher Columbus' journey.

To see the building of *saveiro* fishing boats in action, wander to the far end of the port, where the smell of sap and sawdust, old fish and sea salt mingles with the wonderful odor of nutmeg drying in the sun. For a good walk and a beautiful view, follow the river's left bank upstream toward the Igreja NS de Amparo (1757) on the hill.

From the port, walk straight uphill to reach the pedestrian center of town. Keep going straight up along this main street, Rua Governador Gonçalves, to reach the bus station, about 1km from the port. There are several banks and internet cafes around town.

Sleeping & Eating

Casual outdoor bar–snack stands are scattered along the riverfront near the bridge.

Hotel Guaibim   HOTEL $
(3641-4114; www.guaibimhotel.com.br; Praça da Independencia 74; d R$100; ❄️ 🛜) A simple hotel with friendly staff and clean, colorfully painted rooms with mini-refrigerators. The on-site restaurant offers self-serve Bahian food during the day, and *feijoada* (bean-and-meat stew) on Saturday night.

Hotel Portal Rio Una   HOTEL $$
(3641-5050; www.portalhoteis.tur.br; Maestro Barrinha s/n; d R$185-285; ❄️ 🛜 🏊) This large, attractive hotel has Valença's finest restaurant and rooms, each with verandas overlooking the river. It's 1km from the river, on the opposite side of the port.

Mega Chic   BRAZILIAN $
(www.restaurantemegachic.com.br; Maçônica 11; mains R$18-35; ⏰ 11:30am-4pm) Across the bridge from the center, Mega Chic offers a self-serve buffet and an à la carte menu of pastas, salads, sandwiches and cocktails.

ⓘ Getting There & Away

There are daily boat services to Boipeba, Gamboa and Morro de São Paulo from the port in the center.

The **bus station** (3641-4894) is a 1km hike from the port (or a R$15 taxi ride). Águia Branca buses go to Porto Seguro (R$67 to R$75, nine hours, one or two daily) and Camamu (R$11, 1½ hours, three to five daily). For Salvador, take a bus to Bom Despacho (R$16, two hours) on the Ilha de Itaparica, and then a ferry across the bay.

Camamu

0XX73 / POP 31,055

On the mainland, shielded from the open ocean by the Peninsula de Maraú, Camamu is primarily the jumping-off point for Barra Grande. The town is the port of call for the many tiny fishing villages in the region and overlooks a maze of mangrove-filled islets and narrow channels. The beautiful Açaraí Waterfalls are 5km away, accessible on foot or by taxi. If you need to spend the night, there are a few inexpensive, family-run pousadas and simple cafes around the boat dock.

There is no real bus station here; buses stop near the port. Cidade Sol (www.viacao cidadesol.com.br) and Aguia Branca (3255-1823; www.aguiabranca.com.br) run to and from Bom Depacho several times daily (R$25 to R$28). Aguia Branca also goes to Ilhéus (R$18, three hours, two daily) and Ubaitaba (R$10, 1¼ hours, three daily), where connections south can be found.

Barra Grande

0XX73

Deliciously off the beaten path on the northern tip of the Peninsula de Maraú, laid-back Barra Grande is a remote fishing village with sandy streets, tree-shaded magic and a tiny, picturesque center. Though it remained a relatively desolate paradise for decades, it's slowly becoming more of a vacation getaway for Brazilian families. The village remains a great place from which to explore the rest of the peninsula.

Separating the peninsula from the mainland is the island-riddled Baía de Camamu, Brazil's third-largest bay. One long, bumpy dirt road (often impassable after rain) heads down the peninsula, providing access to stunning beaches with crystal-clear water, such as Praia Taipús de Fora (7km, rated among Brazil's top beaches), and a handful of very small fishing villages. Pricey excursions to Lagoa Azul, viewpoints, bay islands and down the Rio Maraú are offered by local providers.

Other lovely destinations are accessible on foot from Barra, though visitors should note that, although the town center is small, the surrounding area is not: many beaches are a hike from the pousadas.

At the base of the village, where the boats arrive from Camamu, is the 2km-long Barra Grande beach, where the calm waters are fine for swimming and those traveling with children. A short walk along the beach leads to the **Ponta da Mutá**, the northeastern point of the peninsula, with a lighthouse marking the bay's entrance. Around the rocky point, you access a long stretch of coast, with **Praia da Bombaça** the next notable beach (3.5km from Barra Grande), before reaching Praia Taipús de Fora (located 3.5km further).

⊨ Sleeping & Eating

A range of new pousadas have opened to accommodate the influx of visitors: it pays to shop around before committing to one. There are several supermarkets around the main plaza and a string of casual beach bars serving food and drinks along Praia Barra Grande. Note that hours listed below are for the high season; opening hours are more limited in the low season.

★ Flat Barra   APARTMENT $
(☎3258-6124; www.flatbarra.com.br; Jose Melo Pirajá s/n; apt for 2/3 people R$124/144; ❉ 🖢 🌊) Staying at this lovely property is like renting your own beach apartment. The place looks like a pousada – complete with tropical foliage, a lavish breakfast spread and a swimming pool – but instead of regular guestrooms, these accommodations have full kitchens, private balconies and separate sleeping and living areas.

Pousada Don Pepe   POUSADA $
(☎3258-6326; www.pousadadonpepe.com.br; Maraú 1003; d/tr R$140/170; ❉ 🖢) On the road leading out of the village towards the northern tip of the peninsula, this friendly pousada offers simple but comfortable accommodations in a cheerful yellow house.

Ponta do Mutá   POUSADA $$
(☎3258-6028; www.pousadapontadomuta.com.br; Anjo s/n; s/d without sea view R$280/330, with sea view R$290/350; ❉) 🏊 This welcoming pousada's primary selling point is its location right on the beach, near the boat dock, and its grassy lawn dotted with chaise longues facing the water. Pleasantly decorated rooms each feature a veranda and hammock; many have sea views.

Pousada Porto da Barra   POUSADA $$
(☎3258-6349; www.pousadaportodabarra.com.br; Vasco Neto 13; d/tr without sea view R$270/340, with sea view R$304/380; ❉🖢) Another pousada near the dock, Porto da Barra offers standard rooms with tile floors and hammocks strung outside the doors. The sea

breezes and leafy, palm tree–dotted grounds, just steps from the beach, are the main draw.

Pousada Barrabella   POUSADA $$
(☎3258-6285; www.pousadabarrabella.com.br; Vasco Neto 3; d R$236; ❉ 🖢🌊) This pretty pousada, decorated with furnishings made by local craftsmen, offers tranquil rooms with sea or bay views and private balconies, an excellent restaurant, an inviting swimming pool with a waterfall, and a cocktail bar that overlooks the ocean.

★ Praça da Taínha   BRAZILIAN $
(Av Jose Melo Piraja; mains R$9-32; ⊙5pm-late) This grassy open-air plaza is home to several casual, budget-friendly eateries – look for crepes, pizzas, sandwiches, tapioca, *moqueca*, ice cream and cocktails – and a stage where live musicians often perform. The pretty lights and festive atmosphere make the place extremely appealing at night.

A Tapera   BAHIAN $$
(☎3258-6119; www.atapera.com.br; Doutora Lili s/n; mains for 2 R$30-60; ⊙1-11pm) Just off the plaza, this traditional Bahian restaurant – considered by many to be the best on the peninsula – serves fresh seafood, including an unforgettable squid *moqueca*. Dine outside under the trees for the best ambience.

❶ Information

Get funds before going to Barra Grande, as there are no banks. There's a tourist-information kiosk near the entry to the boat dock on Praia Barra Grande; check www.barragrande.net for the complete lowdown on the area.

❶ Getting There & Around

Passenger ferries (R$6, 1½ hours, five to six daily from 7:30am to 5pm) and *lanchas* (R$30, 20 to 30 minutes, three to five daily) travel between Barra Grande and Camamu. Heading to or from Itacaré, you will need to negotiate a ride with a tour provider (around R$75 per person).

Four-wheel-drive *jardineiras* (R$10) park near the main plaza in town, and leave for the beaches as soon as they have a full load.

Itacaré

☎0XX73 / POP 27,000

Beautiful Itacaré has long been sought out by hippies and surfers mesmerized by wide stretches of virgin Atlantic rainforest, picturesque beaches and reliable surf breaks. Countless pousadas and restaurants now pack the streets; still, a mellow, youthful vibe prevails, surf culture reigns supreme, and many establishments in the area are committed to environmentally friendly practices (look for the Carbon Free Tourism sign proudly posted around town).

🏃 Activities

The closest beach to town is **Praia da Concha**. Though not overly remarkable, it features the most services – beach cabanas serve drinks and food and rent lounge chairs – and calm waters ideal for those traveling with children.

The lovely coast south of Itacaré is characterized by rough surf, better for surfing than for swimming. **Resende**, **Tiririca** and **Ribeira** beaches are set in coves separated by rainforest-covered hills. Offering palm-tree shade and basic services, they're located within 1.5km of town – just follow the signs (and the parade of surfers.)

Slightly beyond these is the idyllic **Prainha**, reachable by trail from Praia do Ribeira, and further, the paradise-like **Engenhoca**, **Havaizinho** and **Itacarezinho** beaches, located 12km south of town. Many travel agencies offer day trips to the are, as well as a range of excursions: canoe trips upriver, rafting, mountain biking, rappelling, hiking and horseback riding. A popular excursion is the day-long adventure up to the Peninsula de Maraú (R$70), with stops at **Lagoa Azul** and **Praia Taipús de Fora**.

Surfboard rentals and surf lessons are easily arranged through outfitters around town.

Brazil Trip Tour
OUTDOORS
(🖉9950-9577; www.braziltriptour.com; Pedro Longo 239) One of several reliable agencies offering excursions, surf lessons, transfers and tours, Brazil Trip Tour specializes in English-speaking guides and eco-minded tours.

Easy Drop
SURFING
(🖉3251-3065; www.easydrop.com; João Coutinho 140; 1-day class R$215, weekly package incl lodging from R$2225) This well-established surf camp, offering a week-long surfing experience with classes and accommodation, gets great reviews from travelers.

🛏 Sleeping

The majority of guesthouses are scattered along Rua Pedro Longo. For a quieter stay that's still close to the action, try the pousadas in Condomínio Conchas do Mar.

Backpackers and budget-minded travelers should shop around: new hostels are opening all the time in this town to cater to the steady stream of surfers who come and go.

⭐ Pousada Ilha Verde
POUSADA $
(🖉3251-2056; www.ilhaverde.com.br; Ataíde Setúbal 234; s/d from R$100/140; ❋🛜🞉) 🏊 In a lush setting, Ilha Verde has uniquely decorated rooms inspired by the owners' world travels. Features include private patios, an inviting swimming pool, abundant outdoor lounge space for luxuriating in the greenery, and a fair-trade shop with handicrafts made from Brazilian straw and shells.

Casa Zazá
GUESTHOUSE $
(🖉3251-3022; www.casazaza.com; Condomínio Conchas do Mar; d/tr R$135/165; ❋🛜🞉) Run by a welcoming Dutch owner, this pretty guesthouse has a warm, homey feel with nicely furnished rooms and a veranda with hammocks. There's also a pool bordered by a wooden deck, a tree-shaded backyard and plenty of relaxing lounge space.

Pousada Maresia
POUSADA $
(🖉3251-2338; www.maresiapousada.com.br; Pedro Longo 388; d/tr R$100/150; ❋🛜) 🏊 Simple rooms and a lush garden courtyard – a memorable setting for breakfast – are part of the charm of this budget-friendly pousada that's focused on sustainable tourism. It's well positioned between the beach path and the heart of the action in the village.

Pousada Nainas
POUSADA $
(🖉3251-2683; www.nainas.com.br; Praia da Concha; d R$120; ❋🛜) Set around a pretty garden, Pousada Nainas has uniquely designed rooms with romantic canopied beds and vibrantly colored decor. All have private verandas strung with hammocks for soaking up the tropical vibe.

Concha Tropical Flat
APARTMENT $
(🖉3251-3426; www.conchatropical.com.br; Rua B, Praia da Concha; apt for 2/4 people R$130/190; ❋🛜) Ideal for self-caterers, these modern apartments are equipped with kitchens, flat-screen televisions and private balconies with ocean views. There's no breakfast included; communal facilities include a barbecue area.

Casarão Verde Hostel
HOSTEL $
(🖉3251-2037; www.casaraoverdehostel.com; Castro Alves s/n, Praia da Coroa; dm/s/d R$38/80/110; ❋🛜) Budget travelers rave about the friendly reception and pristine, spacious rooms

at this lovely colonial house – painted pale green, as the name suggests – that's been smartly converted into a hostel.

Pousada Casa Tiki
POUSADA $

(☑9810-6098; www.casa-tiki.sitew.com; Praia da Concha; dm/d R$40/100, d without bathroom R$90; 🐾) The home-away-from-home vibe is what makes this small pousada special: there are only four rooms (one that has a few dorm beds); leisurely breakfasts happen around a communal table; and the owners, a young English-speaking couple, mix potent cocktails and offer travel advice.

Pousada Navio
Albergue Camping POP
CAMPGROUND $

(☑3251-2305; www.pousadanavio.com.br; Praia da Concha; camping per person R$20, dm/d with fan from R$30/80) This friendly backpacker's haven offers shady campsites close to the beach; amenities include decent showers, laundry facilities and a cafe-bar. There are also fan-cooled rooms if you're traveling without a tent.

Albergue O Pharol
HOSTEL $

(☑3251-2527; www.albergueopharol.com.br; Praça Santos Dumont 7; dm/s/d R$28/90/120; ✳@🐾) A favorite among backpackers, this centrally located and low-key hostel has tidy rooms, some with private balconies. There's a shared kitchen and a guest laundry area; the only downside is that there's no breakfast.

Itacaré Hostel
HOSTEL $

(☑3251-2510; www.itacarehostel.com; Barbosa 19; dm/d with fan R$40/110, with air-con R$48/130; ✳@🐾) In the heart of the action, this HI hostel has small, tidy rooms fronted by hammocks and a narrow courtyard with a pool. The communal kitchen and tour desk are particularly useful.

Pousada Burundanga
POUSADA $$

(☑3251-2543; www.burundanga.com.br; Condomínio Conchas do Mar; d/tr R$198/245; ✳🐾✖) This boutique hotel has beautifully furnished rooms, hung with local artwork and uniquely decorated with tropical woods and textures. Common to all rooms are private wooden decks overlooking the greenery.

🍴 Eating & Drinking

A browse up and down Itacaré's main thoroughfare is the best way to discover what's on offer – look for pop-up burger stands and makeshift caipirinha stands at night.

Tio Gu Cafe Creperia
CREPES $

(www.tiogu.com.br; Pedro Longo 488; mains R$12-20; ☺noon-11pm; 🐾) 🌿 This ecoconscious surfers' hangout has a loyal local following thanks to its perfectly prepared crepes (including delicious dessert options such as chocolate and kiwi) and healthy fruit and vegetable infusions.

Alamaim
VEGETARIAN $

(www.restaurantealamaim.com.br; Pedro Longo 377; mains R$12-30; ☺2:30-10pm Mon-Sat; 🗷) Get your hummus fix here: this cool but casual catery specializes in vegetarian Arabic food, from falafel to couscous, and has relaxing lounge space where you can kick back after a day of surfing or swimming.

Tapiocaria Bem Bahia
BAHIAN $

(Praça Santos Dumont 32; mains R$10-22; ☺noon-11pm) This casual eatery on the main square specializes in delicious tapioca pastries stuffed with your choice of fillings: with a few outdoor tables, sandwiches, fresh juices and caipirinhas, it's a great budget pick for lunch or dinner.

Manga Rosa
BRAZILIAN $$

(www.restaurantemangarosa.com.br; Pedro Longo 350; mains R$22-45; ☺noon-11pm Mon-Sat, from 5pm Sun) This open-air restaurant, right in the center of the action, has a tropical, easygoing feel that makes it appealing at any time of day: stop in for a mint-infused lemonade (R$5) on the way back from the beach, or dine on fresh dishes like squid ceviche with mango (R$32).

Boca de Forno
PIZZERIA $$

(Almeida 108; pizzas R$18-35; ☺6-11pm) This place serves pizzas everyone raves about (try the one with *carne seca*, or cured beef) in a flower-bedecked outdoor setting.

Estrela do Mar
SEAFOOD $$

(☑3251-2230; Praia da Concha; mains R$25-48; ☺noon-11pm Mon-Sat; 🖤) Overlooking the beach, elegant Estrela do Mar serves expertly prepared seafood, pastas and salads. There's a children's menu and a decent wine list, too.

Mar e Mel
BAR

(☑3251-2358; www.maremel.com.br; Praia da Concha; mains R$18-35; ☺7pm-12:30am) This is the place to hear (and dance to) live *forró* four nights a week (Tuesday, Thursday, Saturday and Sunday). There's a spacious wooden deck and abundant seafood and drink choices.

BAHIA ITACARÉ

❶ Orientation

Itacaré lies at the mouth of Rio de Contas, where the river meets the sea. A short walk east of the working-class neighborhoods around the fishing port leads to the area known as Pituba, which is essentially one long street, Rua Pedro Longo, lined with pousadas, restaurants and shops. Follow this road east out of town to access Itacaré's prettiest beaches. North of the Pituba strip is known as Condomínio Conchas do Mar, and has higher-end restaurants and pousadas in a more verdant setting. The neighborhood ends at the small beach of Praia da Concha.

❶ Information

There are several exchange offices and an ATM around the main plaza. Internet cafes are plentiful, costing around R$6 per hour. Visit www.itacare.com.br for an overview.

❶ Getting There & Around

Itacaré's **bus station** (☑ 3288-2019) is just out of the center, but it's a bit of a hike from many of the pousadas. A wheelbarrow-pushing *taxista* (R$7 per load of luggage) is helpful for guiding you to your hotel or hostel.

To get to Itacaré, you will most likely need to connect through Itabuna or Ilhéus. **Rota** (☑ 3251-2181) has frequent buses to Ilhéus (R$12, 1½ hours, from 5am to 7:45pm). Several daily buses go to Porto Seguro (R$57 to R$61, eight hours).

Private taxi services like the friendly **Ney Taxi** (☑ 3251-3050; neytaxiitacare@hotmail.com; Praca dos Cachorros) are useful for transfers to Ilheus (R$100 to R$140) and Camamu (R$110), or for do-it-yourself excursions to nearby beaches and waterfalls (round-trip service R$60 to R$100). If you have trouble making arrangements, ask the hotel receptionist to call on your behalf.

Several agencies in town hire cars.

Ilhéus

☑ 0XX73 / POP 220,900

Bright, early-20th-century architecture and oddly angled streets lend a vibrant and rather playful air to slightly rough-around-the-edges Ilhéus. The town's fame comes from its history as a prosperous cocoa port, as well as being the hometown of Jorge Amado, the famous Brazilian novelist, who used it as the setting for one of his best novels, *Gabriela, Cravo e Canela* (Gabriela, Clove and Cinnamon). Though not a primary tourist attraction, the city is worth a quick stopover.

History

Ilhéus was a sleepy place until cacao was introduced into the region from Belém in 1881. With the sugar plantations in the doldrums, impoverished agricultural workers and freed or escaped slaves flocked from all over the Northeast to the hills surrounding Ilhéus to participate in the new boom: cacao, known as the *ouro branco* (white gold) of Brazil.

Sudden, lawless and violent, the scramble to plant cacao displayed all the characteristics of a gold rush. When the dust settled, the land and power belonged to a few ruth-

---

BAHIA'S FAVORITE SON

Nobody is more responsible for bringing Bahian culture to the rest of the world than Jorge Amado, Brazil's most famous romanticist author. Amado's tales have been translated into 49 languages and read the world over.

Born in 1912, Jorge spent his youth in Ilhéus, the scene of many of his later novels. After secondary studies in Salvador, Amado studied law in Rio, but instead of going into practice he decided to become a writer. He surprised critics and the public by publishing his first novel, *O País do Carnaval,* when he was only 19 years old.

An avowed communist, Amado participated in the rebel literary movement of the time, launching two romances set in the cacao zone around Ilhéus: *Cacau* and *Suor*. The first novel was banned by the fascist-leaning Vargas government, which only increased Amado's popularity. Sent to prison several times for his beliefs, Amado was elected a federal deputy for the Brazilian communist party (PCB) in 1945, but he lost his seat after a disagreement with the party several years later. He left Brazil and lived for more than five years in Europe and Asia, finally breaking ties with the communist party after the crimes of Stalin were revealed to the world.

With *Gabriela, Cravo e Canela* (Gabriela, Clove and Cinnamon), published in 1958, he entered a new writing phase, marked by a picturesque style that intimately described the colorful escapades of his Bahian heroes and heroines.

Amado died in Salvador in August 2001, just short of his 89th birthday.

less *coroneis* (so-called 'colonels') and their hired guns. The landless were left to work, and usually live, on the fazendas, where they were subjected to a harsh and paternalistic labor system. This history is graphically told by Amado, who grew up on a cacao plantation, in his book *Terras do Sem Fim* (published in English as *The Violent Land*).

In the early 1990s, the *vassoura de bruxa* (witch's broom) disease left cacao trees shriveled and unable to bear fruit, hurting the area's economy dramatically. Though the disease persists to this day, you can still see cacao *fazendas* and rural workers like those Amado described throughout the lush, tropical hills.

◉ Sights & Activities

The best thing to do in Ilhéus is explore the old streets. The center has several old, gargoyled buildings and pedestrian-only thoroughfares where you can wander.

Casa de Jorge Amado   MUSEUM
(Amado 21; admission R$2; ⊙ 9am-noon & 2-6pm Mon-Fri, 9am-1pm Sat) The Casa de Jorge Amado, where the great writer lived with his parents while working on his first novel, has been restored and turned into a lovely and informative museum honoring Amado's life. Not many writers can boast this sort of recognition while still alive, but he became a national treasure well before his death in 2001.

Catedral de São Sebastião   CHURCH
(Praça Dom Eduardo; ⊙ 10am-8pm) The Catedral de São Sebastião is the city's icon – construction began in 1931 – and is a unique, eclectic mix of architectural styles. For an unforgettable view of the fairy tale–like spires, walk out onto the beach at sunset and look back at the cathedral silhouetted against the clouds.

Igreja de São Jorge   CHURCH
(Praça Rui Barbosa; admission by donation; ⊙ 10am-6pm Tue-Sun) The Igreja de São Jorge is the city's oldest church, dating from 1556, and houses a small sacred-art museum.

Beaches

City beaches aren't the cleanest (though that doesn't stop local surfers from taking to the waves). Your best bet is to head south, but even then you'll find that the area's broad, flat beaches are best for soccer games, and it takes kilometers for the water to lose the muddy color of the river outflow. **Praia dos**

Milionários (7km) has some *barracas* and is popular with locals.

Tours

Trips to a tree-sloth recuperation center, Primavera Fazenda (where you'll be taken through the process of cacao production) and Lagoa Encantada, a state-protected area of Atlantic rain forest with waterfalls and wildlife, can all be arranged through local travel agencies like **Órbita Turismo e Expedições** (☑ 3234-3250; www.orbitaexpedicoes. com.br; Rua Leite Mendes, 71).

✹ Festivals & Events

As any Amado fan would guess, Ilhéus has highly spirited festivals. One of the best is the **Festa de São Sebastião** from January 11 to 19.

⊨ Sleeping

Note that Ilhéus' best hotels, located south of the historic center and the Pontal neighborhood, are convenient only for those traveling by car. Accommodations listed below are within walking distance of downtown sights.

Ilhéus Hotel   HOTEL $
(☑ 3634-4242; www.ilheushotel.com.br; Bastos 144, Centro; s/d with fan R$80/90, with air-con R$145/160; ✹ ☞) This towering 1930s hotel offers faded grandeur and some rooms with views over the bay. If you don't receive a response when trying to book a room through the website, try just showing up in person – this place is somewhat stuck in the past, which is, of course, part of its charm.

Lagoa Encantada II   POUSADA $
(☑ 3632-5675; Italia 156, Pontal; d R$90; ✹ ☞) Located south of the center, near the airport and the beach, this quiet pousada is ideal for budget travelers. During the day, it's pleasant to walk the 5km into the center – mostly along the waterfront. At night, take the bus or a R$25 taxi ride to and from downtown.

Ilhéus Praia Hotel   HOTEL $$
(☑ 2101-2533; www.ilheuspraia.com.br; Praça Dom Eduardo, Centro; s/d with fan R$180/220, with air-con R$200/280; ✹ ☞ ✹) This high-rise hotel is fraying around the edges, but service is good and many rooms have fine views of the cathedral across the plaza. The relatively high prices don't seem in line with these average rooms, but it's extremely convenient for an overnight stay if you're hoping to sightsee in the historic center.

Ilhéus

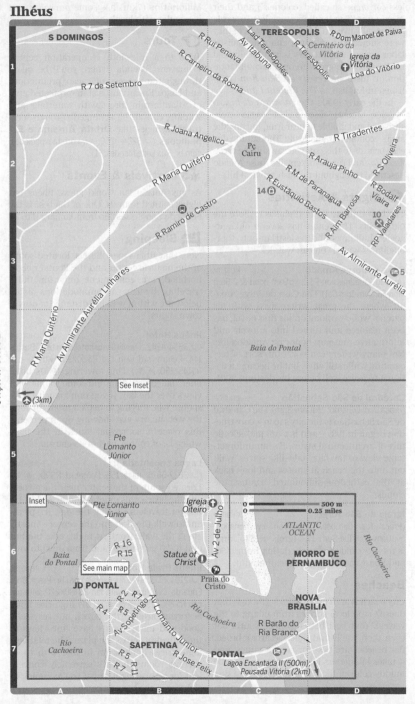

S DOMINGOS

TERESOPOLIS

R Dom Manoel de Paiva

R Rui Penalva

Av Itabuna

Lad Teresópoles

R Teresópolis

R Teresópolis

Cemitério da Vitória

Igreja da Vitória

Loa do Vitório

R Carneiro da Rocha

R 7 de Setembro

R Joana Angelico

R Tiradentes

Pç Cairu

R Araujo Pinho

R S Oliveira

R Maria Quitério

R M de Paranaguá

R Eustáquio Bastos

14

R Bodalf Vieira

R Ramiro de Castro

R Aim Barrosa

10

RP Valadares

Av Almirante Aurélia Linhares

Av Almirante Aurélia

5

R Maria Quitério

Baia do Pontal

See Inset

(3km)

Pte Lomanto Júnior

Inset

Pte Lomanto Júnior

Igreja Oiteiro

Av 2 de Julho

0 — 500 m
0 — 0.25 miles

ATLANTIC OCEAN

Rio Cachoeira

Baia do Pontal

R 16

R 15

See main map

Statue of Christ

MORRO DE PERNAMBUCO

Praia do Cristo

JD PONTAL

R 2

R 7

Av Sopetingo

Av Lomanto Júnior

NOVA BRASILIA

R 4

R 5

Rio Cachoeira

R Barão do Ria Branco

7

Rio Cachoeira

R 5

R 7

R 11

R Jose Felix

SAPETINGA

PONTAL

Lagoa Encantada II (500m);
Pousada Vitória (2km)

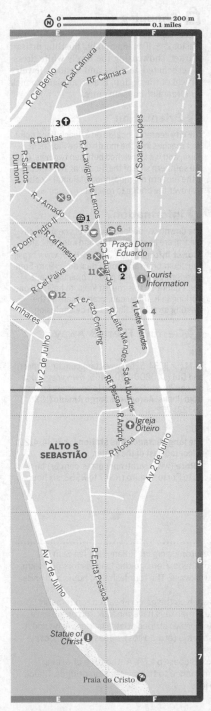

Ilhéus

Pousada Pier do Pontal POUSADA **$$**
(☏ 3221-4000; www.pierdopontal.com.br; Av Lomanto Junior 1650, Pontal; d from R$200; ❊🛜🛌) In a peaceful waterfront location, this contemporary guesthouse has an inviting swimming pool, and colorfully decorated rooms with flat-screen TVs. The on-site sushi bar is open to the public.

✖ Eating & Drinking

For inexpensive sandwiches and cold drinks during daylight hours, try the stands along the pedestrian streets downtown. At night, visit the vendors selling tapioca and other treats across from the cathedral on the waterfront. For a quick pick-me-up, try **Dona Café** (Praça Dom Eduardo; ⊙9am-8pm), the pretty coffee stand on the main square across from the cathedral.

Grão Amado CAFE **$**
(Praça Dom Eduardo; mains R$12-22; ⊙10am-9pm) This stylish new coffee shop offers delicious and beautifully presented pastries, cakes and crepes alongside a thorough coffee menu. It's perfect for breakfast or a late-afternoon snack at one of a few outdoor tables.

Berimbau CAFE **$**
(cnr Paranaguá & Valadares; mains R$12-22; ⊙10am-5pm Mon-Fri) This busy corner cafe serves up

good coffee, sandwiches and pastries to the downtown business crowd. It's the place to soak up a little local culture over lunch.

★ Bar Vesúvio
BAHIAN $$

(☎3634-2164; www.barvesuvio.com; Praça Dom Eduardo; mains R$21-56; ⊙10am-midnight) This landmark bar and restaurant attracts Amado fans (two of his protagonists met here) for *moquecas* and cold beer served at the outdoor tables facing the cathedral, which is beautifully illuminated at night. Start with a few *pasteles arabes*, Arabic-style pastries stuffed with spicy meat.

Barrakítika
BRAZILIAN $$

(☎3231-8300; www.barrakitika.com; Jorge Amado 39; mains R$18-35; ⊙11am-late Mon-Sat) This casual and hugely popular restaurant has outdoor tables, inexpensive set lunches from *feijoada* to *peixe frito* (fried fish), and a full menu with everything from steak to pizza. At night, Barrakítika hosts a lively bar scene; look for live music on weekends.

Bataclan
COCKTAIL BAR

(☎3634-0088; www.bataclan.com.br; Av 2 de Julho 77; ⊙7-11pm Mon-Sat) Once a cabaret frequented by cocoa tycoons (and one of the settings for Amado's *Gabriela*), this colonial building was restored to its original brilliance in 2004. Now it serves as a restaurant, lounge and cultural center staging frequent concerts and art exhibitions. It's best for an evening cocktail, but there's also a full menu of Bahian cuisine (mains R$26 to R$69).

Shopping

Mercado de Artesanato
MARKET

(Bastos 2; ⊙10am-6pm) This bustling artisan market, showcasing the lovely white dresses, crocheted textiles and beaded jewelry typical of the region, is a great place to pick up a few Bahian souvenirs.

ℹ Orientation

The city center is located on a beach-lined point that reaches into the mouth of the Rio Cachoeira, and is sandwiched between two hills. On the southern side of the S-curving river mouth is the modern neighborhood of Pontal – catch a taxi over the bridge to reach it.

ℹ Information

The downtown pedestrian streets near the cathedral are lined with ATMs and internet cafes.

Tourist Information (☎3634-1977; www.brasilheus.com.br; Praça Dom Eduardo; ⊙9am-5pm Mon-Sat) Despite the posted opening hours, don't count on this tourist kiosk to have anyone working in it. If you can, grab a map, as the twisting streets of Ilhéus can be confusing.

ℹ Getting There & Away

AIR

TAM (☎3234-5259; www.tam.com.br; Airport) and **Gol** (☎0800-280-0465; www.voegol.com.br) can fly or connect you to anywhere in Brazil from Ilhéus' **Aeroporto Jorge Amado** (IOS; ☎3231-7629).

BUS

The **long-distance bus station** (☎3634-4121) is located east of the center.

Rota (www.rotatransportes.com.br) buses go to Porto Seguro (R$47 to R$62, six hours,

---

WORTH A TRIP

ECOPARQUE DE UNA

The **Ecoparque de Una** (☎3633-1121; www.ecoparque.org.br; ⊙8am-5pm Tue-Sun) is a lush Atlantic rainforest reserve 60km south of Ilhéus. Here, guides lead visitors on a 2km trail, including four suspended tree-canopy walkways. The tour lasts two hours and ends with a cool pond dip.

Taking refuge in the park are rare species such as the golden-headed lion tamarin (*Leontopithecus chrysomelas*). These unusual monkeys have the look and proud gaze of miniature lions: a blazing yellow, orange and brown striped coat, a golden mane and a long, scruffy tail. If you're lucky you'll also see *tatus* (armadillos), *pacas* (agoutis), capybaras and *veados* (deer), all native to the area.

Visits can be arranged through Órbita Expedições (p437). At the time of writing, the reserve was temporarily closed for maintenance to the suspension bridges. Check Órbita's website for reopening dates and prices.

BAHIA ILHÉUS

four daily), while **Aguia Branca** (www.aguia-branca.com.br) has buses to Salvador (R$49 to R$129, seven to eight hours, seven daily) making a long sweep around the Baía de Todos os Santos, recommended if you are stopping in the *recôncavo* on the way. Otherwise, catch a bus to Bom Despacho on the Ilha de Itaparica, and then a ferry into Salvador.

More frequent connections can be made in Itabuna, which is located 30km inland. Frequent local buses to Itabuna leave from the **local bus terminal** in the town center and also from outside the long-distance bus station (R$5, 40 minutes).

ⓘ Getting Around

The airport is in Pontal, 3.5km from the center. Taxis from the center cost R$20.

Also running along the waterfront between Pontal and the center are bright yellow Via Metro buses (R$2.40).

From the center, buses labeled 'Teotônio Vilela' and 'Salobrinho' pass the bus station. Taxis cost R$18 to R$25.

Olivença

☑ 0XX73

Olivença is a small, charming beach town 16km south of Ilhéus. Sights include a spa, where the waters are believed to have healing powers, and a nearby indigenous village. The grassy town shore has beautiful cove beaches with rock formations and flat sand, powerful waves and a few bars and restaurants. Deserted beaches with calmer water stretch south of Olivença.

Most visitors come here, though, for the great waves just north of town at **Backdoor**, one of Brazil's best surf breaks, and the touristy but family-friendly beachfront complex of **Batuba Beach** (www.batubabeach.com.br; 🔳), where you can do everything from dining on the sand or catching live music to taking a surf lesson. Check the website for more details.

City buses leave every 30 minutes from the Ilhéus bus station (passing the city bus terminal) for Olivença (30 minutes) from 6am to 11pm. The bus travels close to the beaches, so you can hop off when you see one you like. Private transfer can also be arranged through Ilhéus travel agencies (around R$75 for up to four people).

Porto Seguro

☑ 0XX73 / POP 140,000

Historically, Porto Seguro is significant: it's the point where Portuguese sailors first landed in the land now known as Brazil. But apart from its small historic center and colorful colonial houses, the city is rougher than many others in Bahia – not that the hordes of Brazilian and Argentinian package tourists, here for beach action and nightlife, really care. Due to the city's raucous nightlife, the streets are quiet and even rundown during the day, as though the whole city is experiencing a hangover the morning after the party.

History

Pedro Cabral's landing 16km north of Porto Seguro (Safe Port) at Coroa Vermelha is officially considered the first Portuguese landfall in Brazil. The sailors stayed just long enough to stock up on supplies. Three years later Gonçalvo Coelho's expedition arrived and planted a marker in what is now Porto Seguro's Cidade Histórica (Historic City). Jesuits on the same expedition built a church, now in ruins, in Outeiro da Glória. In 1526, a naval outpost, convent and chapel (Igreja NS da Misericórdia) were built in the present-day Cidade Histórica.

The Tupininquin, not the Pataxó, were the indigenous tribe around the site of Porto Seguro when the Portuguese landed. They were rapidly conquered and enslaved by the colonists, but the Aimoré, Pataxó, Cataxó and other inland tribes resisted Portuguese colonization and constantly threatened Porto Seguro. Military outposts were built along the coast in Belmonte, Vila Viçosa, Prado and Alcobaça to defend against both European attacks by sea and *indio* attacks by land.

The *índios* managed to take Porto Seguro twice and, according to colonial documents, reduced Porto Seguro to rubble in 1612 (thus undermining the city's claims to have 16th-century buildings).

◉ Sights & Activities

Motivation is required to climb the stairs to the Cidade Histórica; sweeping views over the coastline make the hike worthwhile. The historic center features the **Museu do Descobrimento** (Museum of Discovery; ☑ 3288-5182; Praça Pero Campos Tourinho; admission R$3, with guide R$16; ◷ 9am-5pm), with exhibits on Brazil's early settlement, the colonial era, and indigenous life. Opposite the museum is

Porto Seguro

N

0 — 400 m
0 — 0.2 miles

1

Aeroporto
Internacional
Porto Seguro

Igreja NS
da Pena

2

Igreja NS da
Misericórdia

CIDADE
HISTÓRICA

Gonçalo Coelho's
Marker Stone

Capela
de São
Benedito

Praia do
Rio da Vila

ATLANTIC
OCEAN

Praia do
Cruzeiro

Steps

Av Adno Musser

Av Beira Mar

Av Beira Mar

Av do Descobrimento

Av dos Navegantes

5

Av 22 de Abril

Bus to
Beaches

Praça
do
Relógio

R 15 de Novembro

Marechal Deodoro

Stadium

R Cova da Moça

R da Faca

R do Cajueiro

R do Golfo

R da Vala

4

3

R Pero Vaz de Caminha

R Itagibá

R 2 de Julho

R São Pedro

Rio Buranhém

Av Getúlio Vargas

R Augusto
Borges

R Oscar
Oliveira

R Armando
Carneiro

Av Portugal

Passarela do Álcool

R do Cáis

9

7

O Beco

Praça
da Bandeira

Praça
Coelho

6

Ferry

8

Praça dos
Pataxós

Ilha dos
Aquários
(600m)

Arraial
d'Ajuda
(400m)

Porto Seguro

Gonçalo Coelho's marker stone, now encased in glass and ringed with a fence. Other reminders of the past are old stone churches like the **Igreja NS da Misericórdia** (1526), the **Igreja NS da Pena** (1772) and the **Capela de São Benedito,** dating from the 16th century. Note that while the area is beautifully illuminated at night, the steps are not safe after dark – it's best to take a taxi.

Back down by the beach, just north of town, the **Memorial da Epopéia do Descobrimento** (☎3268-2586; Av Beira-Mar 800; admission R$6; ⊗8:30am-12:30pm & 1:30-5pm Mon-Sat) is a worthwhile stop. The park features a replica of the Portuguese ship that first landed on Brazilian shores. The surrounding botanical gardens also feature a replica of an indigenous village; the guides are descendants of the Pataxó.

Beaches

North of town is one long bay dotted with *barracas* and clubs with invisible divisions creating **Praia Curuípe** (3km), **Praia Itacimirim** (4km), **Praia Mundaí** (6km) and **Praia de Taperapua** (7km). The sands are white and fluffy, backed by green vegetation lapped by a tranquil sea, dotted with big beach clubs like **Tôa-Tôa** (p444), where MCs and dancers lead Brazilian crowds through popular dances.

☞ Tours

Several travel agencies – try **Pataxó Turismo** (☎3288-1256; www.pataxoturismo.com.br; Shopping Rio Mar, loja 3) – offer tours to Praia do Espelho and Praia do Curuípe (R$50, nine hours) as well as trips to Trancoso and other destinations south. Half-day excur-

sions to the offshore reefs of Recife de Fora and Coroa Alta (R$70), fantastic locales for snorkeling with a wide variety of bright tropical fish, are very popular. Unfortunately, since visitors are encouraged to walk over coral reefs in order to enter internal pools, we don't officially recommend it.

🎉 Festivals & Events

Porto Seguro's **Carnaval,** Bahia's most famous after Salvador's, is relatively small and safe, consisting of a few *trios elétricos* cruising the main drag blasting *axé* music. These days, just as many tourists come for the parties across the way in Arraial d'Ajuda.

🛏 Sleeping

Porto Seguro overflows with hotels but receives a surprisingly high number of visitors on package tours, meaning decent low-cost rooms are difficult to find during high season. Alternatively, you could catch the ferry to Arraial d'Ajuda and stay in a nicer hotel for the same price – transportation between the two towns is quick and easy, but Arraial's accommodations options are superior.

Hotel Estalagem BOUTIQUE HOTEL $
(☎3288-2095; www.hotelestalagem.com.br; Marechal Deodoro 66; d/tr R$90/110; ❄🛜🛏) One of the more stylish options in Porto Seguro, this affordable boutique hotel is housed inside a colonial building dating from 1801 – check out the antique stones, sourced from the coral reef and originally joined together with whale oil, in the entryway. Today, renovated guest rooms are understated and comfortable, with private balconies overlooking the swimming pool below.

Pousada Brisa do Mar POUSADA $
(☎3288-1444; www.brisadomarpousada.com.br; Praça Coelho 188; d/tr/q R$70/100/150; ❄) With spotless rooms and a kind welcome, this long, narrow house is a budget gem. It's close to restaurants, the Passarela do Álcool and the ferry to Arraial – but note that there's no internet access on site.

Hotel Galeão HOTEL $
(☎3288-2122; www.galeaohotel.com.br; Av dos Navegantes 300; d/tr R$80/105; ❄🛏) This tidy guesthouse has trim, inexpensive rooms with tiny balconies, plus a swimming pool.

✕ Eating & Drinking

Most dining and drinking options are found around the Passarela do Álcool (Alcohol

Walkway). At night, the *passarela* has craft stalls and street performers, with live music spilling onto the plazas. Look for fresh-fruit cocktail stands making *capeta* (guaraná, cocoa powder, cinnamon, sweetened condensed milk and vodka) – just the thing to bring a bang to the evening.

★ Portinha
BUFFET $

(☑ 3288-2743; www.portinha.com.br; Saldanha Marinho 32; per kg R$36; ☉ noon-10pm) One of the classiest per-kilo eateries around, Portinha puts out a mouthwatering buffet of gourmet dishes, from pasta with sun-dried tomatoes and basil to fresh fish fillets. Both the leafy patio tables and the stylish rustic interior offer plenty of atmosphere. Look for other locations in Arraial and Trancoso.

O Beco
BRAZILIAN $

(cnr Beco & Rua do Cáis; mains R$12-30; ☉ 5pm-late Tue-Sun) This quaint little open-air galleria, just around the corner from the Passarela do Álcool, is lined with small bistros and cafes where you'll find everything from sushi to crepes to Portuguese-style baked goods.

Tia Nenzinha
BAHIAN $$

(Passarela do Álcool 170; mains for 2 R$35-70) A classic in Porto since 1976, Tia Nenzinha serves a fine assortment of Bahian dishes. Try one of the house specialties, *casquinha de siri* (shredded crab meat) served on a slice of toasted baguette.

☆ Entertainment

Young partiers selling club and party tickets (R$20 to R$60) around the Passarela let you know what's happening on any given night. The major beach clubs all put on weekly nighttime *luaus* (parties); the one at **Barramares** (☑ 3679-2980; www.barramares. com.br; Av Beira Mar, Km 6, Praia de Taperapuã) is the most stunning. It's about 6km north of town, and several other good nightspots are on the way, including **Tôa-Tôa** (☑ 3679-1555; www.portaltoatoa.com.br; Av Beira Mar, Km 5, Praia de Taperapuã). On a river island between Porto Seguro and Arraial, the **Ilha dos Aquarios** (☑ 3268-2828; www.ilhadosaquarios. com.br; Ilha Pacuio; admission R$55; ☉ box office 8pm-5am Tue-Sun, party nights vary) complex usually offers a good party, probably because of the novelty of the aquariums and its setting, reachable by boats from the port on party nights (transportation is included with the entry fee.)

ℹ Information

Banco do Brasil ATM (Av 22 de Abril)

Bradesco ATM (Praça do Relógio) Also on Av dos Navegantes.

Clínica NS d'Ajuda (☑ 3288-1307; Av dos Navegantes 640) Medical service.

Tourist Information Kiosk (Praça dos Pataxós; ☉ 10am-6pm Mon-Sat)

SAFE TRAVEL

It's best to take a taxi (versus walking) on Av Beira Mar at night as muggings are common.

ℹ Getting There & Away

AIR

Gol (☑ 3268-4460; www.voegol.com.br; airport), **Azul** (www.voeazul.com.br; airport) and **TAM** (☑ 3288-3399; www.tam.com.br; airport) can connect you anywhere in Brazil from **Aeroporto Internacional Porto Seguro** (BPS; ☑ 3288-1880), a short drive outside of town. At the time of writing, there were no buses to the airport; taxis cost around R$30.

BUS

The turnoff for Porto Seguro from Hwy BR-101 is at Eunápolis. The **bus station** (☑ 3288-1914) is 1.5km outside town on the road to Eunápolis; taxis cost R$20 to R$30 to the ferry or the center.

Rota Sul (☑ 3288-3065) goes to Ilhéus (R$47 to R$62, six hours, four daily).

São Geraldo (☑ 3288-1198) makes the long haul to São Paulo (R$237, 26 hours, one daily) and Rio de Janeiro (R$171, 16 hours, one daily); purchase tickets through travel agencies in the center. During high season, there are more frequent departures. **Águia Branca** (☑ 3288-1039) goes to Vitória (R$90 to R$129, 10 hours, two daily) and Salvador (R$150, 11 hours, two daily).

For more frequent connections, three companies run buses to Eunápolis (R$10, one hour, every 30 minutes from 5:30am to 10pm).

ℹ Getting Around

If you're heading to beaches north of Porto Seguro, look for Riacho Doce, Alto do Mundaí, Campinho–Barramares or Cabrália buses that pick up passengers at a bus stop on Praça do Relógio, among other places. On the return trip, hop off at the traffic circle if your bus is heading up to the bus station. Taxis are widely available throughout the city.

South of Porto Seguro

South of Porto Seguro, the Bahian coastline is particularly lovely, lined with pristine sands, colorful cliffs and charming beach villages that become increasingly rustic (and less touristy) as you head south.

Arraial d'Ajuda

📍 0XX73 / POP 12,000

Atop a bluff overlooking an enchanting stretch of coastline, Arraial d'Ajuda is a peaceful tourist village with indisputable appeal. Its narrow paved roads and dusty lanes wind beneath large, shady trees, with lovely pousadas and open-air restaurants hidden among the greenery. Solid, brightly painted facades surround its plazas, and the air remains tinged with the scent of tropical vegetation. In the past, Arraial was the playground of the wealthy, which isn't far removed from the upmarket tourists the town tends to attract: the place is an extremely popular vacation spot for well-off Argentincans. More recently, however, a new wave of international backpackers and nouveau hippies have brought a little diversity to the idyllic surroundings.

◉ Sights & Activities

Praia Mucugê is Arraial's main tourist beach and is crowded with *barracas* and blasted by music. As you continue south, **Praia do Parracho** is also built up, but with beach clubs and a few condominium complexes. Both of these beaches are sheltered by offshore reefs. Around the point, beautiful **Praia Pitinga** has red-striped sandstone cliffs, pretty, calm waters and a few *barracas*. South of Pitinga, **Praia da Lagoa Azul** and **Praia Taípe** are backed by tall cliffs, and face stronger waves.

Near the coast, the family-friendly water park **Eco Parque** (📞 3575-8600; www.arraialecoparque.com.br; Estrada da Balsa, Km 4,5; adult/child R$85/50; ⊙10am-5pm; 🚻) has long, twisting waterslides, a wave pool and a 'lazy river' you can float down on rafts. There's also a *tiroleza* (zip line), kayaks for rent and a host of other outdoor activities.

☞ Tours

Several travel agencies, including recommended operators include **Arraial Trip Tur** (📞 3575-2805; www.arraialtriptur.com.br; Mucuge s/n) and **Arco-Iris Turismo** (📞 3575-1672; Mucugê 199), organize day trips to beautiful beach villages south of Arraial. Popular excursions include the trip to **Praias Espelho and Curuípe**, including a stop in Trancoso (R$50), a long day's outing to **Caraíva** (R$65) and a snorkeling trip to the offshore

reef of **Recife de Fora** (R$75). If you're visiting between July and October, ask about humpback whale-watching tours (R$150).

Arraial Trip Tur also rents bikes (per day/hour R$35/10).

🛏 Sleeping

Arraial is home to a large number of lovely pousadas where you'll probably want to stay for a week. You'll see plenty of options on the road from the ferry dock to the center (frequent buses and vans run the route), but most visitors find the village to be more convenient for its access to dining, shopping and nightlife.

Pousada Erva Doce POUSADA $
(📞 3575-1113; www.ervadoce.com.br; cnr Mucugê & Amendoeiras; d R$140; ❄🔊❄) Squarely in the center of the village on a cobblestoned plaza lined with boutiques and cafes, this peaceful guesthouse has spacious, thoughtfully designed rooms. Surrounding the small swimming pool is a leafy tropical garden with an open-air bar and hammocks, ideal for lazing away the afternoon.

Arraial d'Ajuda Hostel HOSTEL $
(📞 3575-1192; www.arraialdajudahostel.com.br; Campo 94; dm/s/d R$53/150/210; ❄@🔊❄) This colorful HI hostel offers well-equipped private rooms as well as dorm-style accommodations in a funky Greco Bahian-style building with a courtyard swimming pool. Travelers like the communal outdoor kitchen and the location near the beach. Air-conditioning is free at night, and R$12 extra (per room) during the day.

Vila do Beco POUSADA $$
(📞 3575-1230; www.viladobeco.com.br; Beco dos Jegues 173; d without/with sea view R$220/290; ❄❄) This tranquil property spreads toward the edge of the bluff – white buildings are spread through lush grounds, ending at a pool with jaw-dropping ocean views. Many guest rooms, outfitted with rustic wood furnishings and romantic mosquito nets, offer two levels and a terrace.

Atmosphera Pousada POUSADA $$
(📞 3575-1954; www.atmospherapousada.com.br; Estrada do Mucugê 735; d from R$200; ❄🔊❄) 🌿 A new favorite in Arraial, this smart and sustainably built pousada is set in a pretty tropical garden just steps from Praia Mucugê. Each of the 14 guest rooms features two rooms, a private balcony with hammock, and a solar-powered shower.

BAHIA SOUTH OF PORTO SEGURO

Pousada Catamarã
POUSADA $$

(cnr Mucugê & Av dos Oitis; s/d from R$145/195) The inviting outdoor pool, festive thatched-roof pool bar, comfortable guest rooms with private verandas, and proximity to the beach make this pousada a top choice. It's located downhill from the village on a side street just before you reach Praia Mucugê.

✕ Eating

Arraial has no shortage of excellent restaurants, many offering atmospheric outdoor seating. For something more casual, head to the main square at night for inexpensive crepes, tapioca, caipirinhas and traditional Bahian plates of rice, beans and grilled steak, or stop at one of the gourmet ice-cream stands along Rua do Mucugê.

★ Piazza del Caffé
CAFE $

(www.piazzadelcaffe.com.br; Mucugê 200; mains R$12-24; ⊗6pm-late) On a picturesque plaza in the center of the village, this adorable cafe turns out delicious espresso and cappuccino, rich chocolate cakes, freshly baked *pão de queijo* (cheese bread) and gourmet sandwiches. Outdoor tables on the veranda are perfectly positioned for people-watching over the village's main thoroughfare.

Portinha
BUFFET $

(www.portinha.com.br; Mucugê s/n; per kg R$36; ⊗11am-9pm) Just by looking, you'd never guess this good-looking eatery is a self-service spot: with elegant outdoor tables and a style-conscious crowd, it looks like any of Arraial's upscale restaurants. Like its sister locations in Porto Seguro and Trancoso, Portinha serves an impressive spread of seafood, salads, stews and grilled meats – all kept hot over a wood fire.

Beco das Cores
BRAZIL $

(cnr Mucugê & Beco das Cores; mains R$15-45; ⊗5pm-late) This lively galleria is a big draw for its atmosphere and variety: you'll find great sushi, crepes, pizza and more elegant fare; there's live music on summer weekend nights, and it's a cozy spot for cocktails on balmy evenings.

Che Empanada
ARGENTINIAN $

(Mucuge 430; mains R$6-12; ⊗11:30am-late) This easygoing spot specializes in Argentinian-style empanadas, pizza and cold beer – sit outside on the small plaza, or get a dozen takeaway empanadas to take to the beach.

Manguti
ITALIAN $$

(☑3575-2270; www.manguti.com.br; Mucugê 99; mains R$25-48; ⊗6-11pm) This Italian classic, housed in a sweet, old-fashioned house on the main drag, is known for its hearty portions of homemade gnocchi. Also are on the menu are excellent grilled fish, prepared virtually any way you like.

Boi nos Aires
STEAKHOUSE $$

(☑3575-2554; Mucugê 200; ⊗5pm-midnight Tue-Sat, 1:30-10:30pm Sun) This sleek *parrilla* (steakhouse) offers a break from Bahia's famous seafood, plus a good wine list; it's often populated by vacationing Argentines homesick for their national cuisine.

Rosa dos Ventos
BRAZILIAN $$

(☑3575-1271; Alameda dos Flamboyants 24; mains R$25-55; ⊗4pm-midnight) Considered by some to be Arraial's finest restaurant, Rosa dos Ventos offers a short menu of exquisite grilled seafood, perfect cocktails and decadent desserts from apple strudel to Italian profiteroles; the candlelit front patio is the ideal place to linger over a bottle of wine. It's on the road that runs parallel to the main drag – walk down Amendoeiras to get here.

Aipim
BRAZILIAN $$

(☑3575-3222; Beco do Jegue 131; mains R$28-50; ⊗6pm-midnight Mon-Sat, plus 5:30pm-1am Sun Jan) This stylish eatery exudes tropical chic with its old-world decor, new-world music, superb grilled seafood and wines by the glass: it's a first-rate locale for a romantic evening out in Arraial.

☆ Entertainment

Arraial has great nightlife throughout the summer, when beach clubs host huge parties (cover R$25 to R$45); you'll see promoters everywhere, and local travel agencies can also provide the latest details. Another popular option for night owls is the Ilha dos Aquarios (p444) nightclub complex on an island between Porto Arraial and Porto Seguro.

Morocha Club
CLUB

(www.morochaclub.com; Mucugê 260; cover generally free; ⊗6pm-late, event times vary) In town, Morocha is ground zero for nightlife, particularly in summer and around Carnaval. A popular local hangout and restaurant, it's relaxed and lounge-like earlier in the evening, then busy with concerts, dancing, DJs and theme parties late at night.

ℹ Information

There are several internet cafes (charging around R$6 per hour) and ATMs around town. For tourist information, stop by the well-stocked kiosk in the main plaza at the top of Rua do Mucugê – the attendants distribute maps and brochures for all of the major excursions and tours from Arraial.

ℹ Getting There & Around

Car and passenger ferries travel almost constantly between Porto Seguro and Arraial d'Ajuda between 7am and midnight, with hourly boats running from midnight through the early morning. Prices vary depending on which way you're going, and which ferry you happen to get on: passengers either travel for free, or pay R$2.50, while cars cost between R$9.50 and R$12. The ride takes 10 to 15 minutes. From the boat dock, jump on a bus or Kombi van to Arraial (R$2.50). It's also possible to walk the 4km along the beach, but be cautious about carrying valuables or walking alone during hours when the beaches are deserted.

If you're arriving into Porto Seguro's airport and coming straight to Arraial, you can also skip the hassle and pay for a taxi (R$120) to take you the whole way to your destination, ferry included.

Bicycles, motorbikes, cars and beach buggies are available to rent from agencies in Arraial. Have a good map before you set out for excursions – when we last visited, our buggy broke down without warning on an unmarked dirt road.

Trancoso

✓ OXX73

Sitting atop a grassy bluff overlooking fantastic beaches, Trancoso embodies a certain rustic sophistication that captivates style-minded travelers – indeed, much of the village looks straight out of a *Travel & Leisure* spread. Trancoso is smaller in scale than Arraial, with a relaxed air, an assortment of pretty guesthouses, a postcard-worthy church overlooking the ocean, and irresistible open-air bars and restaurants surrounding the grassy (and car-free) *quadrado* (square). Though the place caters to rich tourists, the sight of the candlelit *quadrado* at night remains magical.

The beach is a 15-minute walk downhill from the clifftop village: if you're standing in the Quadrado and facing the ocean, the start of the path is located to the right of the church.

🛏 Sleeping

Reservations are a must during January and major holidays.

Café Esmeralda Albergue   GUESTHOUSE $
(*✓* 3668-1527; www.trancosonatural.com; Quadrado; r without/with bathroom from R$100/120; 🛜) The cheapest overnight on the *quadrado* is a friendly multilingual guesthouse with extremely basic, fan-cooled rooms. It's behind the cafe of the same name. Breakfast isn't included.

Pousada Jacaranda   POUSADA $$
(*✓* 3668-1155;   www.pousadajacaranda.com.br; Jovelino Vieira 102; bungalows for 1/2 people from R$140/165; ✳🛜🌡) *✎* This eco-friendly pousada features six freestanding bungalows built with natural, locally sourced materials, plus a lovely swimming pool and art-filled interiors. It's a short walk from both the *quadrado* and the beach, but the quiet location is a benefit if you're looking to relax.

Pousada Quarto Crescente   INN $$
(*✓* 3668-1014; www.quartocrescente.net; Principal s/n; d/tr from R$210/270; ✳🌡) Gardens surround handsomely decorated rooms with thoughtful touches. There's also a well-stocked library, a pool and a fine breakfast spread. It's on the road into town, a short walk from the *quadrado*.

Bom Astral   POUSADA $$
(*✓* 3668-1270;   www.bomastral.net;   Quadrado; d from R$160; ✳🛜) Decent value on the *quadrado,* Bom Astral has pleasant, simple rooms, small but well maintained. Several rooms have air-con and kitchens, but most quarters are fan-cooled only.

Pousada Jequitibá   POUSADA $$
(*✓* 3668-1028;   www.pousadajequitibatrancoso. com.br; Rua do Bosque s/n; d from R$180; ✳) On the grassy plaza to the right of the *quadrado,* Jequitibá has tidy rooms, opening onto a shared veranda, with crisp white canopied beds and pretty decor.

Pousada Porto Bananas   POUSADA $$$
(*✓* 3668-1017; www.portobananas.com.br; Quadrado; d from R$250; ✳) Spread through a towering junglelike garden, Porto Bananas has lovely minimalist rooms with smooth cement floors and bright bathrooms (the shower faces tropical greenery – a great way to start your day).

BAHIA SOUTH OF PORTO SEGURO

Pousada Mundo Verde POUSADA $$$
(☑ 3668-1279; www.pousadamundoverde.com.br; Telegrafo 43; d without/with view from R$300/340; ❋ ☷) Not far from the *quadrado* and set on a quiet bluff overlooking the ocean, stylish Mundo Verde has spacious, airy rooms painted in cheerful colors. There's a pool with a spectacular view.

✖ Eating

In the evening, colorful glowing lanterns illuminate the restaurants around the *quadrado* - each looks prettier than the one before - but the dining scene here is known for high prices and hit-or-miss quality and service. In this town, you're paying first and foremost for the atmosphere. You can find more casual snacks, ice cream and tapioca pastries in the small plaza behind the *quadrado*, where taxis and buses drop off.

★ Portinha BUFFET $$
(www.portinha.com.br; Quadrado; per kg R$47; ☉ noon-10pm) This Trancoso classic woos diners with a sumptuous per kilo buffet (don't miss the dessert spread) and atmospheric seating at tree-shaded turquoise picnic tables on the Quadrado. It's one of the few places open for lunch.

Capim Santo BRAZILIAN $$
(www.capimsanto.com.br; Quadrado; mains R$26-48; ☉ 5-11pm Mon-Sat) Dining on the impossibly quaint porch of this old house - or in the beautifully illuminated garden beside it - makes for a memorable evening. Part of the pousada of the same name, Capim Santo specializes in fresh, innovative juice infusions and traditional Bahian seafood dishes with an international twist.

O Cacau BAHIAN $$$
(www.ocacautrancoso.com.br; Quadrado; mains R$52-85; ☉ 6pm-late) This beautifully appointed eatery is a haven for foodies interested in Bahian cuisine. Look for light, modern takes on classic dishes from *acarajés* to *moqueca* and grilled lobster. O Cacau has a great wine list (especially for Brazil) and to-die-for desserts, with prices to match.

Maritaca ITALIAN $$$
(☑ 3668-1258; Telégrafo 388; mains R$50-80; ☉ 7pm-late) Elegant and airy Maritaca does delicious thin-crust pizzas - the carpaccio is a standout - as well as Italian pastas and rich desserts made with top-end imported ingredients. The prices are lofty for a pizzeria; then again, this is Trancoso.

☆ Entertainment

There's live music somewhere on the *quadrado*. If local legend Elba Ramalho, 'The Queen of Forró,' is giving a show, don't miss it. One venue she has performed at is **Pára-Raio** (www.pararaiotrancoso.com.br; Quadrado; no cover; ☉ 5pm-1am), an ambient restaurant with outdoor tables under massive trees and an enclosed dance space where DJs spin. In summer, there are some happening nighttime beach parties at *barracas* with pumping trance music and psychedelic decor - look for promoters handing out flyers.

ℹ Information

At the small plaza tucked behind the quadrado, find ATMs, a few internet cafes, supermarkets and a taxi stand. There's a tourist office on the plaza, too, offering maps and information, though it was closed when we visited.

ℹ Getting There & Away

Hourly **Aguia Azul** buses connect Trancoso with Arraial d'Ajuda and the ferry dock – some continue to Porto Seguro – and run from 6am to 8:30pm (R$8, one hour). Some buses leave from the *quadrado*, but to catch most of the departures, walk inland from the square towards the main road that runs in and out of town. Kombi vans run the same route for the same price.

It is also possible to walk the entirely beautiful 13km along the beach from Arraial d'Ajuda, but be cautious about walking alone during hours when the beaches are deserted.

Trancoso to Caraíva

Rated among Brazil's top 10 beaches, **Praia do Espelho** is 27km south of Trancoso and 14km north of Caraíva. Protective offshore reefs create calm, warm, transparent waters, while reefs closer to shore create natural pools at low tide. White and orange cliffs divide Espelho from **Praia do Curuípe**, its neighboring beach, which has a collection of top-end pousadas. Tour agencies in Arraial d'Ajuda and Trancoso offer day trips to these beaches (recommended, as the roads are bumpy and arriving on your own is a challenge) or you can catch one of Aguia Azul (p448)'s two to three daily buses between Trancoso and Praia do Espelho.

Caraíva

☑ 0XX73 / POP 5200
Time moves slowly in the remote and beautiful village of Caraíva, where roads

and cars don't exist (neither did electricity before 2007). The easygoing atmosphere has long attracted hippies and those looking for a quiet pace. Today, even though there's cell-phone reception and internet, locals say Caraíva feels like Trancoso did a couple of decades ago. Power outages are common – noisy generators light up the shops and restaurants lining the streets, and importantly, keep the *forró* hopping on Friday night.

The dreamily rustic village is strung along the eastern bank of the mangrove-lined Rio Caraíva and a long-deserted beach kissed by strong waves. Boat trips upriver, south to Parque Nacional de Monte Pascoal or Corumbau, and north to Praia do Espelho and Praia do Curuípe, are easily organized through pousadas (around R$80 per person). Most visitors make the short journey to **Barra Velha**, the indigenous Pataxó village, 6km away from town – you can walk, catch a boat or even hire a horse to get there. When going to the village, bring lots of water and small bills in case you'd like to purchase handicrafts. On the edge of the river, the **Centro Cultural de Tradições Indígenas** (◷10am-6pm Mon-Sat summer) offers exhibits, performances and more information on the Pataxó.

🛏 Sleeping & Eating

Memoan Hostel HOSTEL **$**
(✆61-9275-7649; www.memoanhostel.com.br; dm/d from R$50/130) This brand-new hostel is a welcome addition to Caraíva. The entrance is on the main street of town, and the property is large and wooded, with a rear terrace overlooking the river; features include a communal kitchen, fan-cooled doubles and dorms (one for women only).

THE PATAXÓ

Bahia's largest indigenous group, the Pataxó (pa-ta-*sho*), who number roughly 3000, are among Brazil's many indigenous groups facing an uncertain future. Historically, the Pataxó are survivors. They were a strong tribe who held out against the Portuguese, and up until the 1800s were one of the most feared indigenous groups of the interior. Their resistance hindered frontier expansion, though by the early 19th century their power had waned.

Today, the Pataxó practice subsistence agriculture in the south of Bahia, supplemented by hunting, fishing and gathering. Similar to Amazonian indigenous groups, the Pataxó utilize local plants as their pharmacy, with the rainforests of southern Bahia providing a vital source for traditional medicine. The region boasts incredible biodiversity, with many of its plants and animals found nowhere else on earth. In all, the Pataxó use more than 90 different plant species to treat colds, asthma, fever, toothaches, rheumatism, anemia and dozens of other illnesses.

Despite the wide acceptance of the healer's powers within the community, the Pataxó are struggling to maintain their traditions. As elsewhere in indigenous communities, the youth are not actively embracing the customs of the older generation. Traditional healers *(curandeiros)*, who can be male or female, haven't passed their knowledge down to the next generation. In Barra Velha, the largest Pataxó community (numbering some 1800), all of the healers are over 60, meaning that if nothing changes, their knowledge will be lost within two decades. Today's *curandeiros* may be the final generation of traditional healers in Pataxó culture.

Sadly, the issues of Pataxó health were in the news for a different reason in 2012, when the family of a gravely ill indigenous child fought for treatment in the hospital in Porto Seguro, and then Salvador. Though the child survived, the treatment was delayed due to bureaucratic struggles over who should pay for her healthcare, and the case caught the attention of a large number of Bahians.

In addition to internal struggles, the Pataxó face severe threats from outside. As Bahia's population grows, farmers have pushed them off their lands, leading to violent skirmishes. In 2007, 15 indigenous Pataxó went to Brasília to settle the matter of their land rights. Yet whether the tribe can flourish – and successfully preserve its customs – may be a matter less for government officials to decide than for Pataxó youth, who will be instrumental in ensuring the tribe's longevity.

Camping Caraíva CAMPGROUND $

(☑9992-6324; www.campingcaraiva.com.br; camping per person R$30, cabins per person R$30-130; 🛜) On the main riverside road, this campground has sandy shaded campsites and a few basic but attractive cabins that are ideal for families or groups of friends. There's wi-fi access for all guests in the shared lounge space.

★**Pousada Cores do Mar** POUSADA $$

(☑3668-5090; www.pousadacoresdomarcaraiva. com.br; cottages for 2/3/4 people R$230/275/320; ❋🛜) At this heavenly oceanfront getaway, palm trees tower over freestanding cottages and inviting chaise longues facing the water. Travelers rave about the peaceful interiors, complete with top-end bed linens and private terraces with sea views, and the ample breakfast spread.

Pousada Lagoa POUSADA $$

(☑3668-5059; www.lagoacaraiva.com.br; d/bungalows R$270/315; 🛜) ✔ At this eco-minded pousada (it recycles, composts, and employs local workers), choose between simple but stylish cottages with small verandas, or slightly cheaper suites. The restaurant-bar is a popular nighttime hangout, and open to the public: in addition to fresh fish and homemade bread, the eatery serves produce sourced from the pousada's own garden.

Pousada San Antonio Caraíva POUSADA $$

(☑9962-2123; www.pousadasanantonio.com.br; cabins for 2/4 people from R$200/320; ❋🛜) Overlooking the sea, this popular pousada features freestanding cabins scattered about a grassy lawn and garden. Rooms are bright, comfortable and inviting, as is the outdoor lounge area, ideal for peaceful sunbathing.

Boteco do Pará BAHIAN $$

(mains for 2 R$45-80; ⊙noon-11pm Mon-Sat) One of several casual eateries specializing in fresh seafood, this laid-back spot is a great place to relax by the river and feast on traditional *moqueca* and cold beer.

Mangue Sereno ITALIAN $$

(☑9991-1711; www.manguesereno.blogspot.com.ar; mains R$28-42; ⊙5-10pm Mon-Sat) Homemade pastas and creative seafood dishes are locally famous at this lovely restaurant at the pousada of the same name. Look for specials like pumpkin ravioli and curry shrimp in a romantic, low-key setting.

🛈 Getting There & Away

Two daily buses (three in high season) run by **Aguia Azul** travel between Caraiva and the ferry in Arraial d'Ajuda (R$16, two hours) stopping in Trancoso along the way.

If heading for other destinations north or south, catch the daily bus (R$14, four hours) to Eunápolis via Itabela, both on Hwy BR-101 – at the time of writing, the bus left everyday at 6am. More frequent connections are possible if you're willing to detour through Arraial d'Ajuda.

Parque Nacional de Monte Pascoal

On April 22, 1500, the Portuguese, sailing under the command of Pedro Álvares Cabral, sighted the broad, 536m-high hump of Monte Pascoal (Mt Easter), their first glimpse of the New World. The sailors called the land Terra da Vera Cruz (Land of the True Cross).

The 225-sq-km **national park** (☑3294-1870; www.icmbio.gov.br; admission R$5, tours for groups of up to 10 people R$40) contains a variety of ecosystems: Atlantic rainforest, secondary forests, swamplands and shallows, mangroves, beaches and reefs. Wildlife includes several monkey species, including the endangered spider monkey, two types of sloth, anteaters, rare porcupines, capybara, deer, jaguars and numerous species of bird.

The northeastern corner of the park, below Caraíva, is home to a small number of indigenous Pataxó people, who took over control of the park in 2000. They allow visitors access to two trails while accompanied by a guide (settle fees before setting out), one of which climbs the mountain. The **visitor center** (☑3294-1110), currently undergoing renovations, also offers a small selection of Pataxó handicrafts for sale.

The coastal side of the park is accessible by boat or on foot from Caraíva. Though there are no direct buses to the park, buses run from Porto Seguro to Itamaraju (30km from the park), and from Friday to Monday, buses go from Itamaraju to the park entrance.

Caravelas

☑0XX73 / POP 22,000

Caravelas is a calm fishing town on the banks of the mangrove-lined Rio Caravelas; the primary reason visitors come here is to visit the Parque Nacional Marinho de Abrolhos and other offshore reefs.

◉ Sights & Activities

To get a feel for the town's thriving fishing industry, wander along the riverfront where the fishers return with the day's catch. When the locals go to the beach, most head north for **Praia Grauçá** (7km) or the more isolated **Praia Iemanjá** (20km). Both have calm water colored brown with river silt. Reachable by boat are **Praia Pontal do Sul** (across Rio Caravelas) and the island beach **Coroa da Barra** (30 minutes offshore).

↻ Tours

Travel agencies offer snorkeling day trips to nearby reefs and islands such as Parcel das Paredes, Sebastião Gomes and Coroa Vermelha. Since most tourists head for Abrolhos, these trips rarely meet the minimum number of people required (five) for departure.

🛏 Sleeping & Eating

The restaurants at Praia Grauçá are your best bet for fresh seafood.

Pousada Liberdade POUSADA **$$**
(☎3297-2415; www.pousadaliberdade.com.br; Nogueira 1551; d/tr R$200/216; ✳☀✳) This conveniently located pousada offers accommodations in small cottages with a few creature comforts like televisions and mini-fridges; there's also a pool and trundle beds, making it suitable for families. It's a good place to base yourself while you figure out your plans for heading into the park.

Hotel Marina Porto Abrolhos HOTEL **$$**
(☎3674-1060; www.marinaportoabrolhos.com.br; Rua da Baleia 333, Praia Grauçá; d from R$200; ✳☀✳) The nicest hotel in town is located 7km from Caravelas, and has round, thatched-roof, beachfront chalets surrounding a gigantic pool. There are also tennis courts, a pool bar, gym and library.

Carenagem BRAZILIAN **$$**
(☎3297-1280; Av das Palmeiras 210; mains R$20-32; ☺noon-11pm Mon-Sat) This popular meeting spot has an extensive menu of seafood and meat dishes as well as classic cocktails and live music on weekends. There are several other good dining options on Av das Palmeiras.

ℹ Information

Banco do Brasil (Praça Dr Imbassaí) Has ATMs.

ℹ Getting There & Around

Carvelas and Abrolhos aren't so easy to get to: many travelers find it more convenient to visit with an organized excursion like those run by Porto Seguro's Pataxó Turismo (p443). The one-day (20-hour) trip starts at R$520 per person, including transportation and a scuba outing in Abrolhol, but involves 10 hours of travel; prices for the more appealing two- and three-day excursions vary depending on the size of the group and the accommodations. Contact Pataxó for more information.

Renting a car in the Porto Seguro area and driving to Caravelas/Abrolhos is a popular option; you can also hire a taxi to make the same trip for around R$750 round-trip. Otherwise, you're stuck with the limited bus schedule. **Aguia Branca** (www.aguiabranca.com.br) goes to Salvador (R$120, 16 hours) and Itabuna (R$58, 10½ hours), with more frequent departures in summer and only a few times weekly in low season. Otherwise, access to Caravelas is via Teixeira de Freitas, 74km west. The **bus station** (☎3297-1422) is in the center of town.

Local buses do a round trip between Caravelas and the neighboring village of Barra (providing access to Praia Grauçá), leaving every 30 minutes from 6:30am until 10:30pm.

Parque Nacional Marinho de Abrolhos

It is thought that the name of Brazil's first marine park comes from a sailor's warning: when approaching land, open your eyes (*abre os olhos*). Abrolhos covers an area of 913 sq km, including reefs noted for the variety of colors and a five-island archipelago that Charles Darwin, aboard the HMS *Beagle*, visited in 1832. These days the primary residents of the archipelago are migrating birds and humpback whales (June to October), which come here to rest and give birth. Only the Ilha de Santa Bárbara has a handful of buildings, including a lighthouse built in 1861.

The preservation of the islands is important to Ibama (Instituto Brasileiro do Meio Ambiente e dos Recursos Naturais Renováveis; Brazilian Institute of the Environment and Renewable Natural Resources), so visitor land access is limited to daytime hours on only the Ilha da Siriba. But you didn't come to a marine park for land; you came to snorkel and dive in crystal-clear waters, the visibility of which can reach 20m in the dry season (May to September).

ⓘ Getting There & Around

Abrolhos is located 80km offshore from Caravelas, the primary gateway, where travel agencies offer one- to four-day trips to the park. Day trips start around R$300 per person, depending on availability and what onboard amenities are included. Schooner tours lasting from two to four days, with overnight stays and meals onboard, are offered by small outfitters like **Catamarã Sanuk** (☑ 3297-1344; www.abrolhos.net; Estrelas 80, Caravelas) for R$1050 to R$1890 per person with scuba/snorkeling, or R$682 to R$1176 without. Snorkel-kit rental is R$25 per day.

WEST OF SALVADOR

The great attraction in Bahia's interior is the Parque Nacional da Chapada Diamantina, a verdant area of scenic plateaus, grassy valleys, waterfalls and rushing rivers. Opportunities for trekking and outdoor adventures abound.

In contrast to this verdant area, the rest of this region comprises the bizarre moonscapes of the *sertão*, a vast and parched land on which a struggling people eke out a living raising cattle and tilling the earth. When the periodic tremendous droughts sweep the land, thousands of *sertanejos* (inhabitants of the *sertão*) pile their belongings on their backs and head out in search of jobs.

FOLK ART
....

Bahia has some of Brazil's best artisans, who usually have small shops or sell in the local market. You can buy their folk art in Salvador, but the best place to see or purchase the real stuff is in the town of origin. Feira de Santana is known for its leatherwork. Maragojipinho, Rio Real and Cachoeira produce earthenware. Caldas do Jorro, Caldas de Cipo and Itaparica specialize in straw crafts. Rio de Contas and Muritiba do metalwork. Ilha de Maré is famous for lacework. Jequié, Valença and Feira de Santana are woodworking centers. Santo Antônio de Jesus, Rio de Contas and Monte Santo manufacture goods made of leather and silver.

But with the first hint of rain they return to renew their strong bond with this land.

Feira de Santana
☑ 0XX75 / POP 740,000

After Salvador, Feira de Santana is the second-largest city in Bahia. It's a major cattle-trading center, but not a tourist draw: there's not much to see here. Still, many travelers pass through the bus station on their way to Chapada Diamantina or the *recôncavo*.

✮ Festivals & Events

Feira invented the now widespread concept of **Micareta**, an out-of-season Carnaval. In 1937 a flood caused the city's Carnaval to be celebrated late, a tradition the citizens decided to adopt and rename. In April or early May thousands of spectators fill the city to see Salvador's best *trios elétricos* parade for four days along with local samba schools and folklore groups. For those who missed out on Carnaval in Salvador, this could be the next best thing. Log onto www.micaretafeira.com.br for more information.

🛏 Sleeping & Eating

There are several cheap lodging options near the bus station. Several bars, cafes and restaurants are scattered around town, many with live music and *forró* at night.

Hotel Acalanto   HOTEL $$
(☑ 3612-6700; www.hotelacalanto.com.br; Torres 77; d R$208; ❈ ⊛) This comfortable business hotel, a stone's throw from the bus station, is a solid bet if you have a layover in Feira.

O Picuí   BAHIAN $
(☑ 3221-1018; www.restaurantepicui.com.br; Av Maria Quitéria 2463; mains R$15-33; ☺ 11am-midnight Mon-Sat, to 7pm Sun) A local favorite serving hearty regional dishes from grilled steaks to salmon glazed with *maracuja* (passion-fruit) sauce.

ⓘ Getting There & Away

At the crossroads of three major highways, Feira is a major transportation hub. Frequent buses go to Salvador (R$17, two hours) and Cachoeira (R$7, 1½ hours). Real Expresso buses running between Lençóis and Salvador also pass through Feira de Santana.

Lençóis

OXX75 / POP 10,400

If you want to see a flip side to surf-and-sand Bahia, or have time for only one excursion into the Northeastern interior, this is it. Lençóis is the prettiest of the old diamond-mining towns in the Chapada Diamantina, a mountainous wooded oasis in the dusty *sertão*. While the town itself has charming cobbled streets, brightly painted 19th-century buildings, and appealing outdoor cafés and

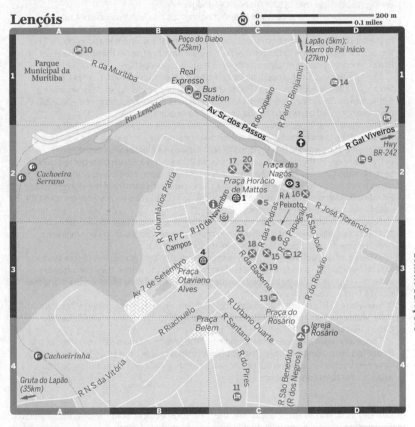

BAHIA LENÇÓIS

Lençóis

GREAT CREATURES OF THE SEA

One of the world's great migratory animals, the humpback whale travels up to 25,000km each year. Massive in scale, adults can reach 17m long and weigh up to 36,000kg. Although they were hunted to near-extinction by the turn of the 20th century, the population is slowly recovering following a moratorium on whale hunting in 1966. Biologists estimate that 30,000 to 60,000 now remain.

Identified by their long pectoral fins, distinct humps and knob-covered heads, the humpbacks feed only during the summer in polar waters on a diet of krill and small fish. In the winter, they migrate from the poles to tropical waters, where mating occurs. Thus, the austral winter (June to September) is the best time to observe them off the coast of Brazil, when they come in large numbers to mate and give birth.

During this time, the humpbacks fast and live off their fat reserves. Competition for females is intense, with groups of two to 20 males (called escorts) sometimes trailing a lone female. To win her over, each male competes to establish dominance – tail slapping, charging and parrying over the course of several hours.

The whale song is perhaps one of the most fascinating and least understood attributes of these mammals. Whales within an area sing the same song – or variations of the same song – while those from different regions sing entirely different songs. Performed only by males, each song lasts 10 to 20 minutes and can be repeated over several hours (some scientists have recorded whales singing continuously for over 24 hours). The songs are staggeringly complex. One research team from the Universidade Estadual de Campinas studied whales off Abrolhos in Bahia one winter and identified 24 note types, organized in five themes.

No one knows the purpose of the song, which changes from year to year, though scientists originally thought it had a role in mating (observations of males singing far from the presence of a female has thrown doubt onto this).

In Bahia, whale watching is a growing tourist industry, with numerous places from which to embark on a seagoing observation trip. During the winter, they can often be observed outside of Salvador, while Parque Nacional Marinho de Abrolhos is among the world's best places to observe them.

Elsewhere in Brazil, other good sighting spots are Praia do Rosa in Santa Catarina state, where mother and calf pairs can come within 30m of the shore, and Arraial do Cabo in Rio state.

Those who want a deeper understanding of the great mammals can volunteer at the **Brazilian Humpback Whale Project** (www.ecobrasil.org.br), based in Praia do Forte. Volunteers spend much time out on the sea, collecting data and contributing to the whale's long-term conservation.

restaurants, the surrounding areas are the real attraction. Caves, waterfalls, idyllic rivers and panoramic plateaus set the stage for some fantastic adventures, with the town of Lençóis serving as a base for treks into the surrounding Parque Nacional da Chapada Diamantina and for sights outside the park.

History

The history of Lençóis epitomizes the story of the diamond boom and subsequent bust. After earlier expeditions by *bandeirantes* (*paulista* explorers and hired guns) proved fruitless, the first diamonds were found in Chapada Velha in 1822. After large strikes in the Rio Mucujê in 1844, a motley collection of prospectors from across Brazil arrived seeking their fortunes.

Miners began searching for diamonds in alluvial deposits. They settled in makeshift tents, which, from the hills above, looked like bedsheets drying in the wind – hence the town's name: Lençóis (sheets). The tents of these diamond prospectors grew into villages: Vila Velha de Palmeiras, Andaraí, Piatã, Igatu and Lençóis. Exaggerated stories of endless riches in the Diamantina mines precipitated mass migrations, but the area proved rich in clouded industrial stones, not display-quality gems.

At the height of the diamond boom, the French – who purchased diamonds and used them to drill the Panama Canal (1881–89), St

Gothard Tunnel and London Underground – built a vice-consulate in Lençóis. French fashions and *bons mots* made their way into town, but with the depletion of diamonds, the fall-off in French demand and the newly discovered South African mines, the boom went bust at the beginning of the 20th century.

Despite these developments, mining held on. Powerful and destructive water pumps were introduced in the 1980s, which increased production until they were finally banned in 1995. The few remaining miners have returned to traditional methods to extract diamonds from the riverbeds. With the establishment of the national park in 1985, the town's economy turned instead to tourism, which continues to be the major industry of Lençóis.

◎ Sights & Activities

You'll notice a few historic buildings during a quick stroll around town. At the 19th-century **French vice-consulate building** (Praça Horácio de Mattos), diamond commerce was negotiated. The lovely **Prefeitura Municipal** (Praça Otaviano Alves), built in 1860, was the mansion of Colonel César Sá – the Neoclassical details were reportedly added to please his wife. The adobe **Igreja Senhor dos Passos** (Av Senhor dos Passos 220; ☺10am-5pm) honors the patron saint of miners – and was built by slaves.

For handicrafts made of local wood and stone, clay soaps, and semi-precious jewelry, stop by the beautiful old **Mercado Cultural** (Praça Aureliano Sá; ☺8am-11pm Mon-Sat). Perched above the river on the main square, the market began construction in the 19th century.

Local agencies offer a wide range of outdoor activities, including hiking, rappelling, climbing, kayaking, mountain biking and horseback riding, in Chapada Diamantina national park. There are far too many to list, but see below for recommended treks and outfitters.

There are also great hikes leaving from town that the adventurous can undertake without a guide. One is a 3km walk out of town, following the Rio Lençóis upstream. You first pass a series of rapids known as **Cachoeira Serrano**; off to the right is the **Salão de Coloridas Areias** (Room of Colored Sands), where artisans gather material for bottled-sand paintings. You then pass **Poço Halley** (Swimming Hole), before seeing **Cachoeirinha** (Little Waterfall) on a tributary to your left. Continuing upriver, **Cachoeira da Primavera** (Spring Waterfall) is on another tributary on your left. (When the water is low, you can start this hike by climbing up the rocky slope on the right side of the stream. When the water is higher, you'll have to cut through the woods – the 'trail,' if you can call it that, should start at the traffic turnaround and run parallel to the river.

Another relaxing 4km hike is to follow Rua São Benedito (known as Rua dos Negros) from Pousada & Camping Lumiar. Continue until the road ends at an upmarket housing development. Continue a short distance, then take a left fork onto a trail that descends and crosses a stream. Keep following the track until you reach a ridge overlooking Rio Ribeirão. At the foot of the ridge is **Ribeirão do Meio**, a series of swimming holes with a natural waterslide (bring shorts or something to slide on). Avoid assured injury by climbing the dry rocks (not the slide's wet ones) before launching off.

For more swimming, catch the morning bus to Seabra and hop off at Mucugêzinho Bar (25km). About 2km downstream is **Poço do Diabo** (Devil's Well), a beautiful swimming hole on the Rio Mucugêzinho with a 25m waterfall.

☞ Tours

The Chapada Diamantina, and the areas surrounding it, are a natural wonderland; unspoiled, in part, because they lack the tourist infrastructure of many national parks. Given the lack of marked trails and public transportation, the easiest way to explore is by going on a tour or a longer trek through a local agency.

Note that most of the major attractions in the park have individual entrance fees of R$15 to R$20 – these days, the fees are often included in the quoted tour price (the same goes for the prices listed below, which also include packed lunches), but ask before committing to anything.

One popular tour (R$160, plus optional R$20 for snorkeling) visits Rio Mucugêzinho and its swimming hole Poço do Diabo, Gruta da Lapa Doce (an 850m-long cave, formed by a subterranean river, with an impressive assortment of stalagmites and stalactites), Gruta da Pratinha (a cave and river with clear, light-blue waters), and Morro do Pai Inácio (an 1120m peak afford-

BAHIA LENÇÓIS

ing an awesome view over a plateau-filled valley).

Tours to Poço Encantado (the Lençóis poster child: a cave filled with stunningly beautiful blue water) and Poço Azul (another rainwater-filled cave you can swim in) are also offered (R$170). Before planning this one, ask the agency about the expected quality of the light; after rains, the water remains murky.

Other popular outings include the trip to Fumaça Waterfall (R$135) and the trip to the Marimbus wetlands (R$160, plus optional R$35 for kayaking).

If you're not interested in going on a formal tour, consider going into the park with a guide: they're affordable (about R$150 per day for groups of up to six people), they're incredibly knowledgeable about local flora and fauna, and they can find the best swimming holes – all priceless in a park with few signs or official trails. For multi-day treks, guides also arrange basic lodging and meals in local homes for the bargain price of around R$60 per person, per day.

The tour agencies listed below are just a small sample of what's available in town – there are many other recommendable outfitters.

Chapada Adventure OUTDOORS
(☑3334-1933; www.chapadaadventure.com; Praça Horácio de Mattos 114; ◷10am-9pm) A friendly agency with multilingual staff.

Fora da Trilha OUTDOORS
(☑3334-1326; www.foradatrilha.com.br; Pedras 202; ◷10am-9pm) Specializes in rock climbing; there's even a climbing wall in the office so you can take a few lessons before heading out into the national park.

H20 Expedições OUTDOORS
(☑3334-1229; www.h2otraveladventures.com; Pousada dos Duendes, Rua do Pires; ◷10am-9pm) Both day trips and treks are offered; the website offers detailed descriptions of each excursion's attractions and level of difficulty.

⚑ Festivals & Events

The week-long **Festa de Senhor dos Passos**, the festival honoring the patron saint of miners, begins on January 23. Celebrated the week of June 23, the lively **Festa de São João** is a huge street party with traditional *forró* dancing, bonfires outside every house, and delicious street food. One of the biggest

cultural events of the year is the **Festival de Lençóis** in September or October – in the past, big-name acts like Gilberto Gil and Gal Costa have performed.

🛏 Sleeping

Lençóis' best pousadas are famous for their fantastic breakfast spreads. Note that most rooms do not have air-conditioning – though most travelers don't notice, as they're off in the national park for most of the day.

★ Pousada Lua de Cristal POUSADA $
(☑3334-1658; www.pousadaluadecristal.com.br; Patriotas 27; d/tr R$110/180, d without bathroom R$80; ☎) Run by an exceptionally kind owner, this charming new pousada offers sweet, simple rooms with antique stained-glass windows, many opening to views over the town. Outdoor breakfast tables are an added bonus.

Pousada da Fonte POUSADA $
(☑3334-1953; www.pousadadafonte.com; Muritiba 3; s/d R$70/120; ☎) With stone walls, outdoor hammocks and an open breakfast porch surrounded by lush forest, this quaint six-room pousada has the feel of a weekend mountain home. It's a short but steep hike uphill from the bus station.

Pousada & Camping Lumiar CAMPGROUND $
(☑3334-1241; lumiar.camping@gmail.com; Praça do Rosário 70; campsites from R$20; ❋) Just off one of the town's main plazas, this is a choice place to pitch your tent. Lumiar features grassy campsites in an attractive, tree-filled setting, hot showers, cooking facilities, even a fishing pond.

Pousada Safira POUSADA $
(☑3334-1443; www.pousadasafira.com; Miguel Calmon 124; d R$100; ☎) This down-to-earth pousada is run by Dona Eulina, something of a local legend for her motherly warmth and hospitality. Basic but cozy, it's a travelers' favorite.

Pousada dos Duendes HOSTEL $
(☑3334-1229; www.pousadadosduendes.com.br; Pires s/n; dm/d R$40/$135, d without bathroom R$115; @☎) ✐ With a relaxed atmosphere, open-air lounge space, a garden with hammocks, and a vegetarian-friendly eatery on site, Duendes is a backpacker institution. You can arrange everything here – park tours, excursions on horseback, kayak trips – and the kitchen will even pack your lunch

on request. It's a five-minute walk outside of town.

Alcino Estalagem & Atelier INN $$
(✆ 3334-1171; www.alcinoestalagem.com; Tomba Surrão 139; d R$280, d without bathroom R$190; ❄ 🛜) This lovely yellow mansion, filled with antiques and hand-painted tiles, was designed and built by a local artist. Peek into his ceramics workshop, peruse the library or relax in the charming interior patio; the extensive breakfast is rightfully famous.

Vila Serrano POUSADA $$
(✆ 3334-1486; www.vilaserrano.com.br; Alto do Bonfim s/n; s/d R$190/250; 🛜) 🍽 In a lush setting, the classy and environmentally conscious Vila Serrano comprises spacious apartments, designed according to the principles of Feng-Shui, with romantic drapery, rustic wooden accents and private verandas where hammocks swing.

Pousada Canto das Águas POUSADA $$$
(✆ 3334-1154; www.lencois.com.br; Av Senhor dos Passos 1; s/d from R$309/345; ❄ 🛜 🛝) 🍽 At the river's edge, this family-friendly, sustainably designed hotel has a sophisticated but earthy look – think stone, hard wood, and large windows facing the trees. There's a swimming pool and a small fitness room; the sound of the river's flowing water fills guest rooms at night. The hotel's excellent coffee shop and restaurant, São Benedito Cafeteria and Azul, respectively, are open to the public.

🍴 Eating

Lençóis has a number of bakeries and basic mini-markets catering to hikers. At night, the town's atmosphere is wonderfully charming as many restaurants on Praça Horácio de Mattos and Rua das Pedras put candlelit tables out on the cobblestone walkways.

Burritos y Taquitos MEXICAN $
(✆ 3334-1083; José Florencio 3; mains R$12-32; ⏰ 5-11pm Tue-Sun) It's a rare chance to get your Mexican fix in rural Bahia: popular with locals, this casual restaurant does reasonably authentic burritos, tacos and guacamole, and has a back patio overlooking the river.

O Bode BUFFET $
(✆ 9913-0722; Beco do Rio; per kg R$24; ⏰ noon-3:30pm) On an open-sided terrace over the river, this pleasant, well-liked per kilo restaurant spreads a small but enticing buffet that includes meats, pasta and salads.

★ Cozinha Aberta FUSION $$
(✆ 3334-1321; www.cozinhaaberta.com.br; Barbosa 42; mains R$28-44; ⏰ 12:30-11pm) This gourmet bistro, specializing in slow food, serves eclectic fusion dishes from Thai noodles to Indian curries and Italian pastas. The setting is charming and homelike, with daily specials spelled out on chalkboards.

Maria Bonita
Casa de Massas ITALIAN $$
(✆ 3334-1850; www.mariabonitalencois.blogspot.com.ar; cnr Pedras & Baderna; mains R$20-35; ⏰ noon-3pm & 5-11pm) Perfectly prepared homemade fettuccine and lasagne are the house specialties at this family-run Italian restaurant; grab a table at this quaint corner spot for hearty Italian food and wines by the glass.

Lampião BRAZILIAN $$
(✆ 3334-1157; Baderna 51; set lunch R$28; ⏰ noon-11pm) This popular new eatery specializes in cuisine from Brazil's Northwest – think grilled meats, fishes and chicken, served at cute al fresco tables for two – and offers a good-value set lunch.

Os Artistas da Massa ITALIAN $$
(✆ 3334-1886; Baderna 49; mains R$19-28; ⏰ 12:30-10:30pm) Fantastically fresh handmade pastas and jazz music are on the menu at this gourmet restaurant.

Bodega PIZZERIA $$
(✆ 3334-1019; Pedras 121; mains R$22-35; ⏰ 5-11pm) This stylish pizzeria and Italian eatery

---

ℹ NAVIGATING LENÇÓIS

At the time of writing, Lençóis was undergoing significant changes: almost all of the town's streets have been officially renamed. The locals, of course, continue to use the original names, causing confusion for tourists. Note that while some businesses have embraced using their new addresses, many have not: you might have trouble when you're asking for directions. Luckily, Lençóis is small and easy to navigate, but if you're arriving at night, you should look at the map so you know where you're going when you arrive at the bus station.

offers prime people-watching, gourmet pies and potent cocktails.

ⓘ Information

The online portal of Guia Lençóis (www.guia-lencois.com.br) is a great resource for tourist information. Another excellent resource – especially for those heading into the park for a few days – is the English-language *Guia Turistico Chapada Diamantina* (R$29, www.guiachapadadiamantina.com.br), an excellent information booklet with color photos, maps and detailed descriptions of area hikes. It's for sale at the tourist office and at businesses around town.

Associação dos Condutores de Visitantes de Lençóis (☑ 3334-1425; cnr Baderna & 7 de Setembro; ⊘ 8am-noon & 2-8pm) Information about tour guides. Guides may also be hired through the town's various outfitters and travel agencies.

Banco do Brasil (Praça Horácio de Mattos 56) Has ATMs.

Post Office (7 de Setembro s/n; ⊘ 9am-5pm Mon-Sat)

ⓘ Getting There & Away

BUS

If coming from the south, the journey, though indirect, will be a lot quicker if you route through Salvador. **Real Expresso** (☑ 3334-1112; www.realexpresso.com.br) buses for Salvador (R$59, seven hours) leave four to five times daily. Buses stop in Feira de Santana, where connections can be made to just about anywhere. Be sure to bring a sweater for the journey: these buses are notorious for blasting the air-conditioning.

CAR

Lençóis is 13km off Hwy BR-242, the main Salvador–Brasília route. There's a gas station 22km east of Lençóis on Hwy BR-242, in Tanquinho. The drive from Salvador to Lencois takes about five hours.

Parque Nacional da Chapada Diamantina

☑ 0XX75

Located within this national park's 1520 sq km boundaries, waterfalls cascade over the Sincora Range's mountains and plateaus, dropping into rivers and streams that wind their way through grassy valleys and clean swimming holes.

A seemingly endless network of walking trails is dotted with cactus and strawflowers in some places, and the philodendrons,

velosiaceas, orchids and other bromeliads that have escaped poaching in others. Several species of monkey swing through trees where *araras* (macaws) perch. *Veados* (deer) pick their way past gaping caves, while *mocós* (native rodents) and *cutia* (agouti) scurry underfoot. Even an *onça pintada* (jaguar) or two sharpens its claws on a towering tree, but you are much more likely to cross paths with a cute *quati* (small, furry carnivore with a brown-and-yellow-ringed tail).

The region's unique natural beauty and the tranquility of its small colonial towns have attracted a steady trickle of Brazilian and foreign travelers for several decades; some have never left. These introduced residents, moved by the degradation of the environment and depletion of the wild-animal population, spearheaded an active ecological movement in direct opposition to the extractive mentality of diamond miners and many locals. After six years of bureaucratic battles, biologist Roy Funch helped convince the government to create the Parque Nacional da Chapada Diamantina in 1985.

The park has very little infrastructure for visitors. Bus service is infrequent and scarce, particularly to the remote parts of the park. However, camping or sleeping in the park's small caves is free and can be done without a permit. You'll want gear such as backpacks, sleeping bags or tents, which can easily be rented in Lençóis, and reasonably warm clothes.

Note that the natural attractions and treks listed on the following pages represent only a fraction of what's available in the sprawling Chapada Diamantina: serious hikers will want to pick up a more detailed guide, available for purchase in Lençóis.

Geology

According to geologists, the diamonds in Chapada Diamantina were formed millions of years ago near present-day Namibia (Bahia was contiguous with Africa before continental drift). The diamonds were mixed with pebbles, swept into the depths of the sea that covered what is now inland Brazil, and imprisoned when the seabed turned to stone. Ultimately this layer of conglomerate stone was elevated, and the forces of erosion released the trapped diamonds, which then came to rest in the riverbeds.

Day Hikes & Trips

The most popular day trip into the park is to the top of Brazil's tallest waterfall, **Cachoeira da Fumaça** (Smoke Waterfall), so named because before it has plummeted the entire 420m, the water evaporates into mist. This 6km hike requires a guide, so contact an agency in Lençóis. Alternatively, you can originate from the closest village, **Capão** (80km west of Lençóis by road), which has a number of pousadas and a few travel agencies. The nearby mystical Vale do Capão, or **Caeté-Açu**, has attracted an international community of folks interested in an alternative, back-to-the-land lifestyle.

Up the road and outside the park, **Palmeiras** (54km west of Lençóis by car) is a drowsy little town with a scenic riverside position. The streets are lined with colorful houses and a couple of budget-friendly pousadas.

Hikers may want to take the trail along Barro Branco between Lençóis and **Morro do Pai Inácio**, an 1120m peak affording a brilliant view over a plateau-filled valley. Allow four or five hours one way for the hike.

Just southwest of Lençóis, upstream from Ribeirão do Meio, is the lovely **Cachoeira do Sossêgo** waterfall, with a deep pool at its base and rock ledges for diving. The 7km hike involves a great deal of stone-hopping along the riverbed and should not be attempted without a guide, or when rain or high water has made the lichen-covered rocks slippery.

Gruta do Lapão is probably the largest sandstone cave in South America and is just a 5km hike north of Lençóis. A guide is required as access is tricky.

'Chapada's Pantanal', or **Marimbus**, is a marshy microregion 94km south of Lençóis where you can canoe or kayak while fishing for *tucunaré* (peacock bass) and keeping a lookout for capybaras and *jacarés* (caimans). H2O Expedições and several other Lençóis agencies offer kayak tours here (from R$80).

Longer Hikes

Navigating the correct routes for these treks can be very difficult, so using a guide is strongly recommended. Treks organized with a guide can last anywhere from two to eight days, and can be custom fitted to the group. They usually involve a combination of camping and staying in local homes and pousadas.

The Base of Fumaça

This extremely beautiful yet tiring 36km trek traverses the park from Lençóis to Capão in three days. Detours to other waterfalls are taken along the way, in addition to reaching the base of **Cachoeira da Fumaça**. An extra day can be added walking back to Lençóis or you can continue with the Grand Circuit. Be forewarned that the area around Fumaça's base gets extremely crowded at times, so you may find yourself sharing your sleeping cave with unexpected companions.

Vale do Patí

Much easier than the Fumaça trek, this recommended hike starts and ends in Vale do Capão, and can last from four to six days depending on detours. You are more likely to have the trails to yourself here, and the views over the plains and Chapada's table mountains are spectacular. Stopping in at a local home for a meal or a night is a possibility: it's much easier to negotiate if you're traveling with a local guide.

Grand Circuit

The Grand Circuit of the park covers about 100km, best done in a counterclockwise direction. It takes about five days, but at least eight days are required to include side trips. Especially if you're not carrying all of your own camping equipment and food, it's best to go with a knowledgeable guide, who can arrange overnight stays and meals in locals' homes along the way.

On the first day, make the hike from Lençóis to Vale do Capão (25km, about seven hours) – on the way, you can take a side trip to the top of **Cachoeira da Fumaça**. In the visitor-friendly Vale do Capão, you can camp or stay at a pousada like the ecominded **Pousada Pé no Mato** (www.penomato.com.br; Ladeira da Vila, 2, Caeté-Açú; dm/s/d from R$50/85/95, cabins for 2/3/4 people R$160/230/300), offering peaceful and affordable dorms, private rooms and freestanding cabins, plus an onsite tour agency that can help you plan almost any adventure in the park.

From the Bomba neighborhood of Vale do Capão, continue on to cross the beautiful plains region of Gerais do Vieira and the Rio

Preto highlands to the **Vale do Patí**. You can camp overnight on the plains; if you're with a guide, you'll probably stay overnight in a local home.

You can power on in one day to Andaraí, or take a recommended day or two to explore the Vale do Patí, checking out the gorgeous waterfall **Cachoeirão** and the **Morro do Castelo** mountain before moving on.

Once in Andaraí, side trips to **Poço Encantado** (56km from Andaraí) and the intriguing diamond-era stone ruins in **Igatu** (12km from Andaraí) are highly recommended. In Andaraí, either camp or check into the cozy **Pousada Sincorá** (☑ 3335-2210; www.sincora.com.br; Paraguaçu 120; s/d/tr R$63/115/145; ❉ 🛜), renowned for its delicious breakfast. You can go for a dip at the nearby river beaches along the **Rio Paraguacu** or take the short hike to **Cachoeira do Ramalho**, a 90m waterfall.

In Igatu, take the two-hour hike along the **Rampa do Caim** for sweeping views over the Vale do Patí. You can spend the night at the charming **Flor de Açucena** (☑ 3335-7003; https://sites.google.com/site/igatur; Nova s/n; campsites per person R$30, s/d from R$80/100; ❉), offering campsites, guest rooms built into the rocky hillside, abundant greenery and striking views, with a trail leading down to the river.

Most choose to drive from Andaraí to Lençóis as the walk is on an uninteresting dirt road. If you decide to walk, allow two days, camping the first night near Rio Roncador.

☞ Tours

Many reputable travel agencies offer group tours into the park.

For multiday trips, an even better option is contracting your own guide, an experience that greatly enhances any trip into the park. In Lençóis, you can find a guide by heading to the Associação dos Condutores de Visitantes de Lençóis or asking at any of the big tour agencies or even at reputable pousadas. The going rate at the time of writing was R$150 per day for a group of up to six travelers, though prices vary. In addition to offering expertise on the park's trails and the local flora, fauna, history and geology, a guide can arrange meals and overnight stays in local homes along the way (around R$60 per person, per day).

Whether or not you take a guide, do not go into the park alone.

Sergipe & Alagoas

POP 5 MILLION

Includes ➡

Best Places to Sleep

➡ Pousada Colonial (p476)

➡ Pousada da Amendoeira (p477)

➡ Pousada Aquarela do Brasil (p469)

➡ Pousada Canto de Yemanjá (p474)

➡ Pousada Olho D'água (p478)

Best Off the Beaten Track

➡ São Miguel Dos Milagres (p477)

➡ Laranjeiras (p467)

➡ Praia Do Francês (p474)

➡ Japaratinga (p477)

➡ Pontal de Coruripe (p474)

Why Go?

Overshadowed by big Bahia to the south, the tiny states of Sergipe and Alagoas have long been overlooked by travelers. But it's a tendency that's changing – in the past few years, the thoroughly likable coastal city of Maceió has emerged as a buzzing vacation destination for Brazilian tourists. Still, despite the influx of ecofriendly pousadas and stylish restaurants, there remain plenty of isolated, paradise-like stretches of white sand, emerald waters, swaying palms and quaint villages along Alagoas' coast. Inland travel appeals to history-minded travelers: Penedo is a charming riverfront town with picturesque colonial churches and hilly cobblestone streets. Further south, Sergipe's provincial capital has fewer attractions of its own, but Aracaju serves as a gateway to more sleepy colonial towns. In these off-the-beaten-path hamlets, historic 17th-century churches attest to the region's prominence in the early days of European settlement in Brazil.

When to Go
Maceio

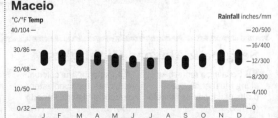

Dec–Feb High season brings crowds of domestic tourists to Maceió and Aracaju.

Mar–Aug Temperatures remain high and rain is possible; hotel prices drop.

Sep–Nov Near-perfect weather and few tourists.

History

During the invasion by the Dutch in 1630, many slaves took advantage of the confusion and escaped to the mountains behind the coasts of northern Alagoas and southern Pernambuco. Where the Alagoan towns of Atalaia, Capela, Viçosa, União dos Palmares and Porto Calvo stand today, virgin forests with fruit and wildlife once provided for colonies of runaway slaves. Palmares, the mightiest republic of escaped slaves, led by the former African king Zumbi, covered present-day Alagoas and Pernambuco. In the 18th and 19th centuries, sugarcane and cotton brought the region prominence; today, sugarcane is still an important crop in the area, alongside

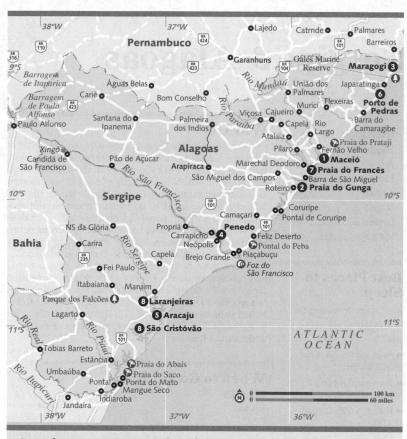

Sergipe & Alagoas Highlights

❶ Pedaling a rental bike along the friendly beach paths of happening **Maceió** (p468).

❷ Boarding a dune buggy for a joyride along the smooth white sands of **Praia do Gunga** (p474).

❸ Snorkeling the colorful coral reefs miles off the shore of **Maragogi** (p478).

❹ Exploring the colonial churches and cobblestone streets of historic **Penedo** (p475).

❺ Feasting on fresh crabs and listening to traditional *forró* music in the open-air eateries of **Aracaju** (p463).

❻ Riding the slow local bus to **Porto de Pedras** (p477)

and the laid-back beach villages north of Maceió.

❼ Sunbathing and playing in the surf in the up-and-coming hot spot of **Praia Do Francês** (p474).

❽ Stepping back in time in Sergipe's colonial gems of **Laranjeiras** (p467) and **São Cristóvão** (p467).

oranges and cassava, though tourism is making inroads in Maceió. Unfortunately, the states are also known for extreme poverty in the interior and rampant corruption.

ℹ Getting There & Away

Hwy BR-101 skirts the coastline of both Sergipe and Alagoas between 25km and 50km inland. It is the main thoroughfare through the region and the chosen route of most long-distance buses. The main airports in the region are in the capital cities, Aracaju and Maceió.

ℹ Getting Around

As is the norm in the Northeast, there is always some form of transportation between where you are and where you need to go – buses, Kombi vans (aka *bestas*), *taxis colectivos* (collective taxis) or moto-taxis (motorcycle taxis). In this area, it pays to be communicative and flexible, as transportation is less formal than in some other areas of Brazil.

SERGIPE

Brazil's smallest state, Sergipe is a land of sugarcane fields with a coastline of swamp, mangrove and sandy shores. In addition to attractive beaches just south of Aracaju, the state capital, Sergipe, is home to the sleepy, picturesque colonial towns of São Cristóvão and Laranjeiras.

Aracaju

📞 079 / POP 571,000

Though Aracaju's coastline attracts Brazilians for weekend getaways, the city isn't much of a draw for international tourists. Still, many travelers spend a night or two here while in transit between Alagoas and Bahia. Apart from the picturesque main square with its towering cathedral, the historic center is slightly run-down. The outlying beaches boast a seemingly endless number of restaurants and hotels to accommodate summertime crowds.

History

The seat of state government was moved from São Cristóvão to Aracaju in 1855, in part because of its good, deep harbor – badly needed to handle large ships transporting sugar to Europe – and because residents of the old capital were on the verge of armed revolt. Within a year, an epidemic broke out and decimated Aracaju's population, which the residents of São Cristóvão naturally saw as an omen that the new capital had a doomed future. The city received a makeover in the early 1900s with the advent of streetcars and other urbanizing elements.

◉ Sights & Activities

Oceanário   AQUARIUM
(📞3243-3214; www.tamar.org.br; Santos Dumont s/n, Atalaia; adult/child R$12/6; ◷9am-9pm Tue-Sun) The Tamar Project's small but interesting Oceanário has tanks with sea turtles, rays and eels as well as examples of specific local freshwater environments and their species.

Mercado Municipal   MARKET
(José do Prado Franco s/n, Centro; ◷6am-6pm Mon-Sat, to noon Sun) At the colorful Mercado Municipal, locals sell and barter a wide range of goods; if you're passing through downtown around lunchtime, stop in for a casual meal and people-watching.

Beaches

With rustling palms and a relative lack of buildings, **Praia Atalaia Nova** (6km across the Rio Sergipe, southeast of the center), is generally calmer than the city beaches to the south, namely **Praia dos Artistas** (7km), **Praia Atalaia** (9km) and **Praia Aruana** (11km). These beaches are heavily developed but are popular with locals; they are also good sources of inexpensive seafood. Further south, **Praia do Refúgio** (18km) is the prettiest and most secluded beach nearby.

☞ Tours

Local travel agencies offer a variety of day tours, including catamaran trips on the Rio São Francisco to the green waters of the canyon of **Xingó**, or to the **Foz do São Francisco**, where the river meets the sea. A tour is also a pretty good way to check out difficult-to-reach **Mangue Seco**, on the border with Bahia. Exotic-bird enthusiasts will enjoy a visit to the **Parque dos Falcões** (www.parquedosfalcoes.com.br), a reserve located 45km from Aracaju; contact Ecotur (📞3224-9115; www.ecotur.tur.br) for details.

Nozes Tur   OUTDOORS
(📞3243-7177; www.nozestur.com.br; Av Santos Dumont 340, Atalaia; ◷9am-7pm) Offers a range of day tours. The office is well located on Atalaia's waterfront; tour reservations are also available online.

✪ Festivals & Events

On January 1 a huge fleet of fishing boats sails along the Rio Sergipe following the image of their patron saint to celebrate **Bom Jesus dos Navegantes**. The largest festival of all is the **Festa de São João**, which runs for the entire month of June and includes live *forró* (a music and dance style of the Northeast) bands and *quadrilha* (a type of square dancing) presentations.

🛏 Sleeping

The majority of Aracaju's hotels are on Atalaia, the waterfront, which is a bit of a trek from the bus station and the center – travelers who are only passing through for a night may find downtown accommodations more convenient. If you're staying on the beach, remember that the coastline is several miles long. Most visitors are happiest staying on the far northern end in the district of Coroa de Meio, or on the far southern side near the Passarela do Caranguejo, though there are plenty of pousadas in between.

Casa da Vovó Guida GUESTHOUSE $
(2 3243-1847; http://casa-da-vovo-guida.blogspot. com; Rua Cel José F Albuquerque 174, Atalaia; s/d R$100/140; ❇ ⓦ 🞅) A top budget pick in Aracaju, this 18-room hotel, a block away from the beach and a five minutes' walk north of Passarela do Caranguejo, is spotlessly clean and family-run. The guesthouse doors close at 10pm – and breakfast isn't included – but the proprietress speaks perfect English.

Pousada Mirante Das Águas POUSADA $
(2 3255-2610; www.mirantedasaguas.com.br; Delmiro Golveia 711, Coroa do Meio; d R$120; ❇ @ ⓦ) Two blocks from the waterfront, the Pousada Mirante das Águas has standard rooms and family friendly amenities, including a game room. The location in Coroa do Meio is about midway between downtown and the Passarela do Caranguejo – access either by a long walk or short bus or taxi ride.

Hotel Jangadeiro HOTEL $
(2 3211-1350; www.jangadeirose.com.br; Santa Luzia 269, Centro; s/d from R$122/145; ❇ ⓦ 🞅) Located a few blocks south of the historic center's main plaza, this business-style hotel is dated but serviceable, good for a quick overnight stay in Aracaju. In-room perks include new bed linens, fluffy pillows and flat-screen TVs.

Pousada Olá POUSADA $$
(2 3243-7045; www.pousadaola.com.br; Niceu Dantas 618, Atalaia; s/d R$133/153; ❇ ⓦ 🞅) This simple, efficiently run pousada is one of several located near the Passarela do Caranguejo, offering easy access to the beach and some of Aracaju's best dining and drinking options. Note that this popular area is about as far away as you can get from the center of Aracaju, which usually means expensive taxi rides to and from the bus station or airport.

Pousada do Sol POUSADA $$
(2 2104-7338; www.hotelpousadadosol.com.br; Eng Francisco Manoel de Costa 43, Atalaia; s/d from R$160/199; ❇ ⓦ 🞅) This well-located pousada, a stone's throw from many of Atalaia's waterfront attractions, is a travelers' favorite. Expect simple, spotless and bright guest rooms, a pleasant swimming pool and terrace, and a children's play area.

Mercure Aracaju del Mar HOTEL $$
(2 2106-9100; www.delmarhotel.com.br; Av Santos Dumont 1500, Atalaia; d from R$290; ❇ ⓦ 🞅) This contemporary high-rise, featuring minimalist interior design, several bars and restaurants, and a large swimming pool complete with waterfalls and a bar, is a slick addition to Atalaia's waterfront; it's usually occupied by business travelers, but it's also family-friendly.

✗ Eating & Drinking

Although Aracaju is hardly a culinary capital, it does offer one particularly succulent dish: fresh, savory crabs. Just south of Atalaia, you'll find the popular Passarela do Caranguejo (Crab Lane), a row of open-sided restaurants facing the waterfront that serve the respected local dish – the locals' favorite is *forró* institution Cariri.

Restaurants and drinking spots stretch out along the waterfront in Atalaia. It's a good spot to stroll at night, when sidewalk stands sell crepes, coconuts and tapioca sweets. During the day, you'll find simple sandwich shops and per-kilo lunch spots on the blocks around downtown's main square. But the center empties out at night and is potentially unsafe for wandering.

★ Cariri SEAFOOD $$
(2 3243-1379; www.cariri-se.com.br; Av Santos Dumont 530, Atalaia; mains R$18-35; ◷ 8pm-late) If you have only one night in Aracaju, Cariri is the place to be for a taste of local culture. This famed Northeastern restaurant on the

VELHO CHICO: THE RIVER OF NATIONAL UNITY

For the *Nordestino* (Northeasterner), it's impossible to speak about the Rio São Francisco without a swelling of pride. There is no river like the São Francisco, which is Brazil's third most important river, after the Amazon and the Paraguay/Paraguai. Those who live along its banks speak of it as a friend – hence the affectionate nickname Velho Chico or Chicão (Chico is a diminutive for Francisco).

The location of the São Francisco gave it great prominence during the colonial history of Brazil. With its headwaters in the Serra da Canastra, 1500m high in Minas Gerais, the Rio São Francisco flows north across the greater part of the Northeast *sertão* (backlands) and completes its 3160km journey at the Atlantic Ocean after slicing through the states of Minas Gerais and Bahia, and delineating the Bahia–Pernambuco and Sergipe–Alagoas state borders.

For three centuries the São Francisco, also referred to as the 'river of national unity,' represented the only connection between the small towns at the extremes of the *sertão* and the coast. 'Discovered' in the 17th century, the river was the best of the few routes available to penetrate the semi-arid Northeastern interior. Thus, the frontier grew along the margins of the river. The economy of these settlements was based on cattle, which provided desperately needed food for the gold miners in Minas Gerais in the 18th century and later fed workers in the *cacao* (cocoa) plantations throughout southern Bahia.

The history of this area is legendary in Brazil: the tough *vaqueiros* (cowboys) who drove the cattle; the commerce in salt (to fatten the cows); the cultivation of rice; the rise in banditry; the battles between the big landowners; and the odd developments, like Canudos, with its strange religious fanaticism (and later its horrific destruction).

The slow waters of the São Francisco have been so vital to Brazil because, in a region with devastating periodic droughts, the river provides one of the only guaranteed water sources. Today the river valley is irrigated to produce a huge amount of produce for local consumption and export.

Owing to its life-sustaining importance, the São Francisco has been the source of much myth-making and storytelling. The *bicho da água* (water beast), for example, is part animal and part human. It walks on the bottom of the river and snores. The crews on the riverboats placate the *bicho da água* by throwing handfuls of tobacco into the water. *Nordestinos* also believe that São Francisco is a gift from God to the people of the *sertão* as recompense for all their suffering in the drought-plagued land.

Passarela do Caranguejo features live *forró* in the traditional style of *pé de serra* (Luis Gonzaga's signature 'foothills' *forró*).

Bada Grill BRAZILIAN $$
(☑ 3223-3664; Av Santos Dumont 526, Atalaia; mains R$25-42; ⊙11:30am-midnight Tue-Thu, to 2am Fri & Sat, to 6pm Sun) Located just north of the Passarela do Caranguejo and across the street from the beach, this casually elegant eatery has a breezy open terrace that's inviting for happy hour drinks and *petiscos* (snacks) like the popular *lambretas gratinadas* (clams baked in cheese).

Maria Flôr BRAZILIAN $$
(☑ 9129-5360; Av Santos Dumont s/n; mains R$25-48; ⊙noon-3pm & 7-11pm Mon-Sat) This stylish new restaurant offers the best dining atmosphere on the beach: the look mixes rustic and elegant, with colorful painted wooden chairs and fine place settings at tables open to the sea breeze. The wide-ranging menu offers everything from coconut risotto and filet mignon to creative pizzas and crepes.

República dos Camarões SEAFOOD $$
(☑ 3255-3361; Av Santos Dumont 10, Coroa do Meio; mains R$25-32, mains for 2 R$50-60; ⊙noon-3pm & 6-11pm Tue-Fri, noon-midnight Sat & Sun) Fresh, creatively prepared shrimp are the specialty at this popular waterfront restaurant, located within easy walking distance of many beachfront pousadas; it's a safe bet for a good seafood dinner.

New Hakata JAPANESE $$
(☑ 3213-1202; www.newhakata.com.br; Av Beira Mar, Anexo ao late Clube, 13 de Julho; mains R$20-65; ⊙11am-late Mon-Sat, to 5pm Sun) This popular Japanese restaurant draws crowds with fresh seafood dishes, all-you-can-eat sushi and live jazz nights. It's next to the Yacht Club.

Point do Coelho BAR

(☑ 9854-9728; Praca Olimpio Campos; ☉ noon-9pm Mon-Fri) If you're in the historic center, this casual outdoor bar and eatery on the main square is your best bet for a cold beer with views of the cathedral. In fact, it's one of the only places that stays open after the downtown business crowd clears out after 5pm.

ℹ Orientation

Aracaju's Centro sits on the Rio Sergipe, guarded from the ocean by a sandy barrier island, the Ilha de Santa Luzia. To the south, past the river mouth, are the city beach neighborhoods of Coroa do Meio, Jardim Atlantico (Praia dos Artistas) and Atalaia, collectively referred to as the orla (waterfront). Most of the action and nightlife is concentrated in these suburban neighborhoods.

ℹ Information

ATMs are plentiful in Aracaju. There are internet cafes downtown, but at the beaches you'll probably have to use wi-fi at your pousada.

TOURIST INFORMATION

Emsetur (www.emsetur.se.gov.br; ☉ 10am-5pm Mon-Fri) Atalaia (www.emsetur.se.gov.br; Praia de Atalaia s/n) Centro (☑ 3214-8848; www.emsetur.se.gov.br; Rua Propriá) Also has an office in Rodoviária Nova (new bus station); the helpful Centro main office of the state tourism authority distributes free maps of Aracaju.

ℹ Getting There & Away

AIR

Gol (☑ 0800-280 0465; www.voegol.com.br) and **TAM** (☑ 3212-8567; www.tam.com.br;

airport) can fly or connect you to other Brazilian cities from Aracaju's **airport** (AJU; ☑ 3212-8500), 11km south of the center.

BUS

Most long-distance buses leave from the **Rodoviária Nova** (New Bus Station; ☑ 3259-2848), 6km east of the center.

Bomfim (☑ 3211-2210; www.bomfim.com.br) runs several daily buses to Salvador (R$50 to R$98, four to six hours). Bomfim buses also go to Maceió (R$43 to R$70, four to five hours, four daily) and Penedo (R$17, three hours, one daily). **Real Alagoas** (☑ 3259-2832; www.realalagoas.com.br) and **Guanabara** (www.expressoguanabara.com.br) also make the journey to Maceió.

For further access to Penedo, catch a pricier but quicker and more direct Kombi van (approximately R$30, four daily) – just ask around to find out where the vans are currently departing from.

ℹ Getting Around

BUS & TAXI

A taxi to the airport from the center costs around R$35, more if you're coming from the beaches. To get to the airport from downtown's Rodoviária Velha, take the Aeroporto city bus.

City buses depart from a large shelter with a series of triangular roofs beside the Rodoviária Nova. For the center, catch any bus going to the Rodoviária Velha, such as Centro or Terminal Rodoviária. The Circular Cidade 02 bus (R$2.80) leaves from the Rodoviária Velha and runs down Av Rio Branco south to Atalaia, terminating at the Terminal Integração Atalaia. From there, change to a Circular Praias 01 bus to reach the southern beaches.

From the beaches to the center, hop on the Santa Tereza/Bairro Industrial bus. Or, if you're

---

MIRACLE MAKERS

In many shrines and churches in the Northeast, visitors come face-to-face with carved wooden heads, arms, feet and other body parts, hung from ceilings or piled in baskets in a special room. A unique mixture of faith and folk art, these ex-votos are called milagres (miracles) and are left by supplicants seeking a cure for a specific ailment such as an injured limb or a congenital deformity. In exchange, the petitioner makes a vow (usually to a particular saint) promising to give up their wicked ways or perhaps make a long pilgrimage – which may even be performed on the knees.

The makers of these ex-votos are often self-taught artisans and their work has a primitive, almost cubist, quality. If the artisans are particularly skilled they may model their work – made of either wood or clay – on the sufferer. No one knows exactly how this custom originated, but the milagre probably has links to old Iberian traditions, mingled with African and indigenous customs. In some communities, there is an element of mysticism to these carved objects, as if they could absorb the ills of the sufferer.

Many churches and shrines in the sertão (backlands) have a casa dos milagres (miracle house), where such objects are displayed. During religious festivals, milagre artisans make the rounds, offering their services for a small fee.

not ready to brave the bus system, take a taxi: fares between the bus station and the center or the beaches run around R$25 to R$30.

CAR HIRE

Find a range of car-rental agencies along Atalaia's waterfront: these agencies do steady business, as many destinations in the region are much easier to visit with your own car than by public transportation.

Laranjeiras

☑ 079 / POP 26,900

Positioned between three grassy, church-topped hills, Laranjeiras is the colonial gem of Sergipe, and together with São Cristóvão, it makes a short and sweet side trip from Aracaju for travelers interested in Sergipe's history.

With a quiet grandeur, Laranjeiras has picturesque cobblestone roads, colonial buildings topped by terracotta roofs and views over the meandering Rio Cotinguiba. The whole town seems unblemished by modern development; the surrounding countryside hides crumbling ruins of old sugar mills and estates.

First settled in 1605, Laranjeiras became the commercial center for its surrounding verdant sugar and cotton fields during the 18th and 19th centuries. At one point there were more than 60 sugar mills in and around Laranjeiras sending sugar down the Rio Cotinguiba to Aracaju for export to Europe.

◉ Sights

Facing the bus station, the **Trapiche** is an imposing 19th-century structure that historically held cargo waiting to be shipped downriver. At the top of Alto do Bonfim (Bonfim Heights) is the picturesque 19th-century **Igreja NS do Bonfim**. Although the church is often closed, the fine views make it worth the climb. Reach it by following the street to the left of Nice's Restaurant.

Upriver 4km from town is the baroque **Igreja de Comandaroba**, constructed by Jesuits in 1734. Unfortunately, the church hasn't been well maintained, and you're unlikely to see inside. A 1km tunnel leads from the church to the **Gruta da Pedra Furada**, a large cave built by the Jesuits to escape their persecutors.

Museu de Arte Sacra   MUSEUM
(Museum of Sacred Art; ☑ 3281-2486; Praça Dr Heráclito Diniz Gonçalves 39; admission R$2;

⊙ 10am-5pm Tue-Fri, 1-5pm Sat & Sun) Built in 1897, this colonial house still has its original wood floors and walls bordered with hand-painted flowers. One room contains life-sized wooden statues of saintly figures, including several used in the town's religious processions. Christ beneath the cross and NS das Dores have real human hair – donated by the faithful for prayers answered.

Museu Afro-Brasileiro   MUSEUM
(☑ 3281-2418; José do Prado Franco 19; admission R$2; ⊙ 10am-5pm Tue-Fri, 1-5pm Sat & Sun) Laranjeiras is considered to be the stronghold of Afro-Brazilian culture in Sergipe. This museum offers displays on sugar production, slave torture methods, Afro-Brazilian religions and Laranjeiras' cultural traditions.

⚝ Festivals & Events

During the last week of January, Laranjeiras hosts the **Festa de Reis** (also called Encontro Cultural), a religious and folklore festival of traditional music and dance. More folklore revelry occurs during **Semana Folclórico** (Folklore Week), usually the second week of August. You can also catch colorful religious processions during **Semana Santa** (Holy Week; the week preceding Easter).

✕ Eating

Nice's Restaurant   BRAZILIAN $
(Praça Dr Heráclito Diniz Gonçalves 4; mains R$12-25; ⊙ 11:30am-10pm Mon-Sat) Though Laranjeiras doesn't have much in the way of tourist services, this casual eatery on the main square is a classic, serving up excellent grilled meats and seafood. Grab a table on the breezy patio.

❶ Getting There & Away

Both Coopertalse and São Pedro buses make the 21km trip between Laranjeiras and Aracaju's Rodoviária Velha (R$2.50, 25 minutes, half-hourly) from 6am to 9:30pm. Unofficial *colectivos* run the same route at the same price.

São Cristóvão

☑ 079 / POP 75,000

Atop a steep hill with expansive views over the countryside, the historic center of São Cristóvão houses a sleepy concentration of 17th- and 18th-century colonial buildings along narrow stone roads and a few wide plazas. Founded in 1590, São Cristóvão was the capital of Sergipe until 1855.

Of particular distinction is **Igreja de Senhor dos Passos** (Praça NS dos Passos; admission by donation), with a ceiling painted by José Teófilo de Jesus. The **Museu Histórico Sergipe** (☑ 3261-1435; www.museuhsergipe.blogspot.com.ar; Praça São Francisco; admission R$2; ◉ 10am-4pm Tue-Sun) is housed in the former Palácio do Governo and features paintings from Carybé and other Northeastern artists, a room for aficionados of the outlaw Lampião, and antique furniture and other relics recalling bygone days.

While in town, stop at one of a few casual bakeries to try *queijadas*, traditional Portuguese cheese pastries considered a local specialty.

Frequent buses make the 28km trip between São Cristóvão and Aracaju's Rodoviária Velha (R$2.80, 45 minutes). The town is 8km off Hwy BR-101.

ALAGOAS

Maceió

☑ 082 / POP 932,750

One of the hot, up-and-coming destinations in the Northeast, Maceió is a navigable modern city set on some truly beautiful beachfront. Maceió may not be well known to international tourists – yet – but Brazilians have rediscovered it as a vacation getaway, and the past few years have seen a boom in domestic tourism. The city has a small but buzzing dining and drinking scene, a new bike-share system, and friendly, laid-back streets that close to traffic for street parties on Sundays; it's also the gateway to wonderfully idyllic shorelines to the north and south. On the city's beaches, vivid, emerald-hued water laps the powdery sands that are lined with palms and brightly painted *jangadas* (traditional sailboats). By night, locals follow the meandering beachside path as it weaves past thatched-roof restaurants and palm-shaded football pitches. Maceió's sights are relatively few, leaving you plenty of time to catch some rays and soak up the relaxed atmosphere.

◉ Sights & Activities

Museu Théo Brandão   MUSEUM
(☑ 3221-2651; Av da Paz 1490; admission R$2; ◉ 9am-5pm Tue-Fri, 2-5pm Sat) Housed in a handsomely renovated colonial building on the seafront, this museum offers excellent exhibits on the state's history and popular culture; the most impressive displays are festival headpieces modeled after churches, which are loaded with mirrors, beads and multicolored ribbons and weigh up to 35kg.

Pedala Maceió   BICYCLE RENTAL
(☑ 9183-9882; www.pedalamaceio.com.br; cnr Dr Antonio Gouveia & JP Filho; bike rental per hr R$12; ◉ 6am-11pm) Grab a bicycle or a three-wheeler to explore Maceió's 20km-long waterfront bikepath. This outfit operates four rental locations along the beaches – there's another convenient branch at the point of Ponta Verde, in front of the old yacht club.

Beaches

Protected by an offshore coral reef, Maceió's ocean waters are calm and a deep emerald color. The most popular and beautiful of the city beaches are **Praia de Ponta Verde** (4km from the city center) and **Jatiúca** – a pair of lounge chairs and a rental umbrella will run you about R$8 for the afternoon. Be forewarned that Praia do Sobral and Praia da Avenida, close to the center, are polluted. **Praia de Pajuçara** and **Praia dos Sete Coqueiros** sometimes suffer from pollution as well.

The nicest beaches north of the city are thought to be **Garça Torta** (14km) and **Pratagi** (17km), but **Jacarecica** (9km), **Guaxuma** (12km) and **Riacho Doce** (17km) are also tropical paradises. The Riacho Doce bus, which can be picked up in several spots along the coastal road, runs up the coast to these northern beaches.

☞ Tours

From Praia de Pajuçara, **jangadas** (R$13) (sailboats) travel 2km offshore at low tide to **natural pools** formed by the reef (R$25). After a short journey aboard one of the delightfully old-fashioned, colorfully painted *jangadas*, you're free to float in the clear water; snorkel mask rental (R$10) is optional. You can arrange trips with any boat captain – stop in early to find out when the boats are sailing or just stroll down the beach and wait for someone to approach you first. The whole trip lasts about two hours.

A plethora of organized day trips are possible from Maceió, including a **beach tour** (R$25 to R$30, taking in Praia do Francês, Barra de São Miguel and Praia do Gunga), a boat trip to **offshore islands** (R$70), an excursion to **Foz do São Francisco** (R$75) and a trip to the **natural pools** off the coast of

Maragogi (R$65, including boat transport). Another popular excursion is the **Nove Ilhas** (Nine Islands) tour (R$70) – in addition to cruising the Lagoa Mundaú, you'll stop at the outlet of the lake into the ocean.

Such excursions are extremely easy to plan in summertime, when travel agencies' representatives camp out around Pajuçara's artisan market, advertising their services to passersby. Outside summertime, plan further ahead, contacting a few travel agencies through their web forms – a minimum number of passengers is required for most tours. Try contacting **Marcão Turismo** (☑ 9981-7896; www.turismomaceio.com.br; Quebrangulo 68, Cruz das Alamas) or **Edvantur Turismo** (☑ 9117-5657; www.edvanqueeuvoualagoas.com.br).

✦✦ Festivals & Events

Carnaval   CARNAVAL
(☉ mid-February) Maceió hosts a small but lively Carnaval with all of the usual trappings: music, food, dancing. The bigger parties happen at beaches outside the city, especially Barra de São Miguel.

Maceió Music Festival   MUSIC
(www.maceiomusicfest; ☉ March) A major music festival occurring in March, the event draws big names in Brazilian music.

Festa Junina   RELIGIOUS
(☉ 2nd half of June) Fifteen days of folk dancing, fireworks, street food, bonfires, costumed revelry and free-flowing beer take over Maceió during Brazil's winter solstice; it's a Portuguese tradition beginning on Saint Anthony's day in mid-June and lasting through Saint Peter's day at the end of the month.

🛏 Sleeping

Several high-rise chain hotels have opened along the waterfront in recent years. In general, Maceió's lodging options are on the pricey side, especially considering that few pousadas offer much in the way of style or character – luckily, you're not going to spend much time in your room in this lively coastal city.

Pousada Hotel Maceio   POUSADA $
(☑ 3316-8645; www.pousadahotelmaceio.com.br; Pompeu de Sarmento 455; d R$150; ✳ 🛜) This simple eight-room pousada is nothing fancy, but the place is clean, well-managed and conveniently located a half-block from the beach action, making it one of the better-value sleeping options in the area.

Maceió Hostel e Pousada   HOSTEL $
(☑ 3231-7762; www.maceiohostel.com.br; Almirante Mascarenhas 85, Pajuçara; dm/d from R$35/120; ✳ 🛜) This attractive hostel is a great budget choice a few blocks from the beach. The place is small – shared quads don't leave much room for your backpack – but friendly and efficiently run; doubles are basic and spotless with good showers and large lockers.

Pousada Praia Verde   POUSADA $
(☑ 3327-4040; www.praiaverdemaceio.com.br; Sandoval Arroxelas 822; s/d from R$120/150; ✳ @ 🛜) Welcoming and well-located near the beach, this efficient pousada has clean, cookie-cutter sea-green rooms with tiled bathrooms; R$10 extra gets you a small balcony with hammock.

Pousada Aquarela do Brasil   POUSADA $$
(☑ 3231-0113; www.pousadaaquareladobrasil.com; Des Almeida Guimaraes 367, Pajuçara; d/tr from R$140/180; ✳ 🛜) Just off the waterfront, this pretty pousada offers simple but (relatively) sophisticated rooms with flat-screen TVs and modern artwork. Ground-level rooms have tiny private patios.

Hotel Praia Bonita   HOTEL $$
(☑ 2121-3700; www.praiabonita.com.br; Dr Antônio Gouveia 943, Pajuçara; s/d from R$140/170; ✳ 🛜 ✳) This small waterfront hotel, dwarfed by the high-rise buildings around it, has an attractive, modern design. Rooms are simple and cheery with sizable windows.

Maceió Mar   HOTEL $$
(☑ 2122-8000; www.maceiomarhotel.com.br; Álvaro Otacílio 2991, Ponta Verde; d from R$300; ✳ 🛜 ✳) This high-rise, beachfront hotel has spacious, brightly lit rooms with floor-to-ceiling windows, all with sea views. With plenty of upscale amenities and a swimming pool, it's suited to both business travelers and families.

Gogó da Ema   POUSADA $$
(☑ 3327-0329; www.hotelgogodaema.com.br; Francisco Laranjeiras 97, Ponta Verde; s/d R$130/160; ✳) On a quiet street near two lovely beaches, Gogó da Ema (named for a famous old palm tree that fell in the city in 1955 and has come to symbolize Maceió itself) is a five-story guesthouse with rather bland, aging rooms. Travelers give mixed reviews, but it's still a decent well-priced option.

Maceió

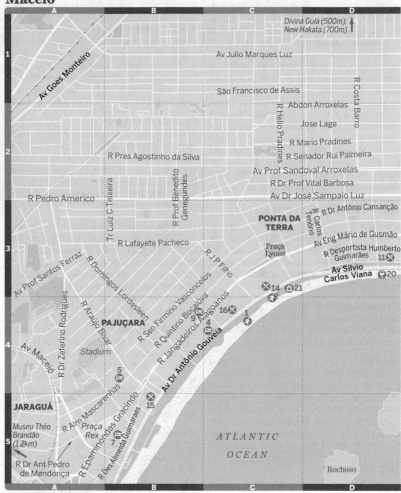

✕ Eating

Maceió offers an impressive selection of eateries, from casual to trendy, with the beachfronts of Pajuçara, Ponta Verde and Jatiúca sprinkled with snack stands and restaurants. Take a stroll before choosing – you'll find everything from casual pizzerias to classy seafood restaurants. If you're more interested in memorable cuisine than beachfront ambience, head to the neighborhood of Jatiúca, where many of the locals' favorites are clustered.

Local seafood specialties worth trying are *sururu* (small mussels) and *maçunim* (shellfish) cooked in coconut sauce, served as main courses or in a *caldo* (soup). Other seafood treats include *peixe agulha* (needlefish) and *siri na casca com coral* (crab in its shell with roe). **Stands** clustered on the Ponta Verde shoreline make the Northeastern specialty *beiju de tapioca* by heating manioc flour until it solidifies, folding it like a taco, then filling it with savory or sweet fillings.

✕ Pajuçara & Ponta Verde

Panificação Alteza   BAKERY $
(☎ 3231-0447; Pitão 1181; prepared foods per kilo R$18-24; ☺ 6am-8pm Mon-Sat)   This gourmet

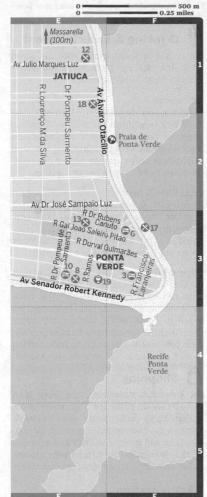

cuisine, ideal for a quick lunch when you need a break from the sun.

Nakaffa   CAFE **$**
(📞 3235-6459; www.nakaffa.com.br; Av Carlos Viana 1785, Ponta Verde; mains R$12-25; ⊘ noon-midnight Mon-Sat, 10am-midnight Sun) This cool, contemporary cafe specializes in frothy cappuccino, light salads, gourmet sandwiches and decadent chocolate desserts. It's your best bet for a beachside cup of coffee after breakfast hours.

Sorveteria Bali   ICE CREAM **$**
(📞 3231-8833; www.sorvetesbali.com.br; Av Gouveia 45, Pajuçara; 1/2 scoops R$4/7) Grab an outdoor table and enjoy Maceió's best ice cream. Favorite flavors include walnut, guava and tapioca.

Kani Mambo   SELF-SERVE **$**
(📞 3377-8000; Av Carlos Viana 2299; buffet per kilo R$37; ⊘ 11:30am-3:30pm) With breezy picnic tables and a full lunch buffet featuring salads, grilled steak, seafood and tropical fruits, this self-service lunch spot, just across the street from the beach, is a welcome refuge from the midday sun.

mini-market, complete with a coffee bar and bakery, is the perfect place to get your caffeine fix while stocking up on fresh bread, tropical fruits, cold cuts, Argentinian wine and chocolate cake for your picnic or hotel room.

Sueca Comedoria   SELF-SERVE **$**
(📞 3327-0359; www.suecacomedoria.com.br; Dr Antônio Gouveia 1103, Pajuçara; per kilo R$35; ⊘ 11:30am-3pm Mon-Fri & 5:30-9pm Mon-Thu, 11:30am-4pm Sat & Sun) Despite the name, this sleek eatery across from the beach doesn't serve Swedish food – it's a family-run self-serve spot offering fresh seafood and regional

Parmegianno
BRAZILIAN $$

(☑ 3313-9555; Av Gouveia 1259; mains for 2 R$32-45; ☺ 11am-midnight Sun-Thu, to 1am Fri-Sat) Brazilian families flock to this popular chain restaurant, just across from the beach, for gourmet pizzas and hearty portions of shrimp, steak, fish, and chicken – accompanied with beans, rice, and salad.

✕ Jatiúca

★Divina Gula
BRAZILIAN $$

(www.divinagula.com.br; Paulo Brandão Nogueira 85, Jatiúca; mains R$29-58; ☺ 11am-11pm; ☑ ☑) A Maceió institution, Divina Gula specializes in the hearty cuisine of Minas Gerais and the Northeast. The *picanha* (steak) is excellent as is the *carne de sol* (grilled salted meat) with plantains, corn and zucchini. It has a children's menu, vegetarian options and a full cocktail list.

Wanchako
PERUVIAN $$

(☑ 3377-6114; www.wanchako.com.br; São Francisco de Assis 93, Jatiúca; mains R$25-55; ☺ noon-4pm Fri, 7-11:30pm Mon-Thu, to 12:30am Fri & Sat) Worth a detour, this highly acclaimed Peruvian restaurant serves excellent seafood in a lovely art-filled setting. On Monday through Thursday, lunch is served in the restaurant's annex, in a cool and casual space called **El Brujo Cebicheria** (☑ 3377-6024; São Francisco de Assis 103; ☺ noon-3pm Mon-Thu).

O Peixarão
SEAFOOD $$

(☑ 3325-7011; www.opeixarao.com.br; Av Dr Júlio Marques Luz 50, Jatiúca; mains R$22-40; ☺ 11am-5pm Mon-Thu, to 10pm Fri-Sun) This casual place is a local favorite for its seafood. Grilled fish with shrimp sauce and *caldeirada* (Portuguese seafood stew) are top picks.

Massarela
ITALIAN $$

(☑ 3325-6000; José Pontes Magalhães 271, Jatiúca; mains R$18-35; ☺ 6-10:30pm Mon-Sat; ☀) This festive cantina is the place for homemade pastas and brick-oven pizzas; Italian pastas are traditionally prepared, and each plate is big enough for two to share. It's especially popular in summer and visitors complain about slow service when things get busy.

New Hakata
JAPANESE $$$

(☑ 3325-6160; www.newhakata.com.br; Paulo B Nogueira 95, Jatiúca; mains R$38-55; ☺ 11am-midnight Sun-Thu, to 2am Fri & Sat) With a spacious outdoor seating area, Maceió's top Japanese restaurant offers a long menu of sushi and sashimi, tempura, noodles and calamari; in the evenings, there are live music, free-flowing caipirinhas and sake cocktails.

🍷 Drinking & Entertainment

For a laid-back caipirinha with an ocean view, just pick any place along the waterfront in Ponta Verde or Pajuçara.

★Lopana
BAR

(www.lopana.com.br; Viana 27; ☺ 11am-late) Maceió's best beachfront bar is always buzzing: when an acoustic guitarist is playing and a good-looking crowd is drinking beer and caipirinhas under the sky-high palm trees, the place looks straight out of a movie.

29.11 Café & Bistro
BAR

(☑ 3317-1325; Guimarães 882, Ponta Verde; ☺ 7-11pm Mon-Thu, to midnight Fri & Sat) With contemporary decor and a garden that's illuminated at night, this bistro is a stylish locale for cocktails, small plates or a nightcap.

Coconut Bar
LIVE MUSIC

(☑ 3325-4884; www.coconutmaceio.com; Av Carlos Viana 2167, Ponta Verde; ☺ 6pm-late) This buzzing open-air music club, just across from the beach in Ponta Verde, features live music every night, from samba to *forró* to pop and rock, plus a varied menu of cocktails and bar food. A good time is practically guaranteed.

🛍 Shopping

On Pajuçara's waterfront, the busy **Mercado Praia de Pajuçara** (Pajuçara waterfront; ☺ 10am-10pm) craft market sells lacework, hammocks, baskets and ceramics. Serious shoppers will prefer the deals and selection at the **Mercado do Artesanato** (Levada; ☺ 7am-6pm Mon-Sat, 7am-noon Sun) downtown.

❶ Orientation

Maceió sits on a jagged peninsula between the Lagoa Mundaú and the ocean. The peninsula features two main headlands: one is the site of the city's port, and the other divides Praia de Pajuçara and Praia dos Sete Coqueiros from the more northern Praia de Ponta Verde and the long Praia de Jatiúca. The Centro is located near the oceanfront, 2km from Pajuçara and 4km from Ponta Verde.

❶ Information

ATMs can be found in commercial areas along the beach, and at the **Bom Preço** grocery store in Pajuçara. Most travelers will access the internet from their pousada, hotel or hostel, though a few internet cafes are also scattered around town.

EMERGENCY

Police (☏190)

Pronto Socorro (ambulance & first aid; ☏3221-5939)

ⓘ Getting There & Away

AIR

Gol (☏3214-4078; www.voegol.com.br; airport) and **TAM** (☏3214-4048; www.tam.com.br; airport) can fly you or connect you to anywhere in Brazil from **Aeroporto Zumbi dos Palmares** (MCZ; ☏3036-5200).

BUS

The **bus station** (☏3221-4615; Av Leste Oeste s/n, Feitosa) is 4km north of the city center.

Bomfim (☏3336-1112; www.bomfim.com. br) buses go to Salvador (R$92 to R$140, 11 hours, four daily) and Aracaju (R$43 to R$70, five hours, four daily). **Real Alagoas** (www. realalagoas.com.br) goes north to Recife (R$30 to R$56, four to five hours, 10 daily) and offers more infrequent service south to Penedo (R$25, 2½ hours).

The quickest way to get to Penedo is on one of the *colectivo* minibuses that departs from the Posto Sobral gas station in the city center. The ride lasts about 2¼ hours and costs R$18; the same route provides access to Coruripe (R$10) and Praia do Gunga (R$8) as well as several small towns along the way. Ask your taxi driver to take you to the departure spot for *colectivos* to Penedo – from Maceió's bus station, the fare is about R$15.

DEF runs meandering buses up the coast to Maragogi and Porto de Pedras, stopping at many of the beach villages along the way. Fares range from R$2.50 (to nearby Paripuera, one hour) to R$12.50 (to Maragogi, 3½ hours). There are four daily departures to Maragogi, and four making the return trip; six daily buses go to and from Porto de Pedras.

The quickest way to get to Maragogi is a taxi *colectivo* (R$30, two hours). These depart from a gas station north of Maceió – again, you'll have to communicate with your taxi driver to get there, asking for 'colectivos a Maragogi.' These shared taxis require four passengers to depart; they're quicker and cooler than the official bus lines.

ⓘ Getting Around

TO/FROM THE AIRPORT

Maceió's airport is 20km north of the center. To reach the center, hop in one of the spiffy taxis operated by the local taxi collective (R$60) – you pay inside the airport and take your ticket to a driver waiting curbside. Buses also run between Ponta Verde and the airport (labeled Aeroporto–Ponta Verde) every 45 minutes or so (R$2.50). The same bus can be picked up in Pajuçara heading north along Rua Jangadeiros Alagoanos – there are several stops along this stretch – look for a bus with 'Aeroporto' on the front.

TO/FROM THE BUS STATION

To reach the center, take the Ouro Prêto bus; for the beaches, catch the Circular 1. A taxi to the center costs R$12 to R$15, and around R$20 to the beaches.

TAKING THE SCENIC ROUTE

When traveling from Penedo to Maceió, throw in an extra two hours and opt for the *pinga litoral* (coastal drip) bus. If constant stops and deviations off the main road don't drive you crazy, you'll get a refreshing glimpse into rural life, passing tiny churches, dusty roads leading off into jungle, and rustic fishing huts, with children waving as the bus rolls by.

From Penedo, the bus travels along the river toward the coast, passing the scattered fishing community in Piaçabuçu, then swings in from the river and north to Pontal do Peba, where it does a U-turn on the beach. From there it passes through Feliz Deserto, which has lots of cowboys and coconuts, one pousada and plenty of seafood. The bus turns off Hwy AL-101 a bit further north at Miaí de Cima, where there are no pousadas, but many locals on the beach on weekends. The next time the bus turns off the main road is into Barreiras and pretty Coruripe before continuing to Pontal de Coruripe.

Next stop is Lagoa do Pau, with shrimp cultivation, weekend homes and a couple of pousadas. Then it's on to Poxim, past sugarcane fields and coconut palms. Approaching Maceió, it stops at the turnoffs for Barra de São Miguel and Praia do Francês. Passing the huge estuaries of the Mundaú and Manguaba lagoons, it's not long before the bus reaches the capital. If you plan to stay at Pajuçara or beaches further north, get off the bus as soon as it turns off the coast road and before it continues into the center of Maceió.

South of Maceió

This stretch of coast is characterized by small, quaint coastal villages – some with amazing beaches – surrounded by wide stretches of coconut plantations. The tourism hot spots on Alagoas' south coast are Praia do Francês and Barra de São Miguel.

Praia do Francês

📞 082

Francês is a surfer's paradise. Given its proximity to Maceió (22km), Praia do Francês has long functioned as a day trip destination: cars and buses roll in on weekend days and clear out by sunset. But this is changing quickly as more travelers fall in love with the beach town, and pousadas have popped up left and right to accommodate the influx of visitors.

The action is concentrated on one end of Francês' fine, white sands, where just-offshore reefs create calm green waters, and a string of restaurants have beer and fried shrimp. Alagoas' best waves are at the southern end – don't despair if you're not traveling with your own equipment, both bodyboards and longboards are available for rent right on the sand. Swimmers opt for the protected reef at the beach's northern end. Walk a few minutes in either direction to escape the crowds.

🛏 Sleeping & Eating

There are several standard Alagoan eateries, pizzerias and self-serve buffets in town and along the beach.

Pousada Ricardinho do Frances   POUSADA $
(📞 3260-1488;   www.pousadaricardinhodofrances.com.br; Arrecifes 10; s/d from R$90/120) An ideal location close to the beach, plus a fantastic breakfast and tidy guest rooms equipped with private balconies and hammocks, make this pousada one of the current favorites in town.

Pousada Aconchego   POUSADA $$
(📞 3260-1193;   www.pousadaaconchego.com.br; Carapeba 159; d from R$150; ❄ ⊛) Aconchego has pleasant rooms set around a lush garden. Hammocks, a pool and friendly service add to the charm.

Pousada Ecos do Mar   POUSADA $$
(📞 3260-1191;   www.pousadaecosdomar.com.br; Carapeba 160; d from R$220) At this popular pousada, colorfully painted guest rooms have flat-screen TVs and mini-fridges, plus access to a pool and a breakfast buffet.

Cesar's Lanches   SANDWICHES $
(mains R$4-6; ⊙ 10am-5pm) This simple sandwich stand, located right on the sand in the middle of the beach action, is famous for its juicy burgers and sandwiches.

ℹ Getting There & Away

From the bus station in Maceió, **Real Alagoas** (📞 3336-6816) runs regular buses (R$3, 35 minutes) to and from Praia do Francês.

Barra de São Miguel

📞 082 / POP 7500

The center of this small village sits on the riverbank, facing **Praia do Gunga**, an idyllic,

---

OFF THE BEATEN TRACK

PONTAL DE CORURIPE

A traditional fishing village that sees few visitors, Pontal de Coruripe lies in an area of verdant coconut plantations, on the edge of a long, deserted beach with beautiful emerald waters. On the peaceful streets of town, women sit in front of their homes gossiping and weaving palm baskets, placemats and handbags, while out at the cove just opposite the lighthouse, fishermen guide their boats across the sunlit sea.

Watch the scenery while dining on fresh seafood at **Peixada da Madalena** (📞 3273-7234; Ladeira do Farol 248; mains R$15-30; ⊙ 10am-6:30pm), one of a few restaurants clustered around the lighthouse. Named for the Candomble goddess of fertility, the lovely **Pousada Canto de Yemanjá** (📞 3273-7316; www.pousadacantodeyemanja.com; Rua da Praia 244; d R$140-180; ❄ 🛜) is worthy of a getaway: the tranquil inn, outfitted with contemporary decor and vibrant colors, is located on the beach, outside town.

Transportation to and from Pontal de Coruripe is frequent but fairly informal. The coastal *pinga litoral* bus heading for Maceió (R$10, two hours) passes through Pontal de Coruripe at least twice daily, with more limited service on Sundays. You can also catch a daily bus to Penedo (R$14, 2½ hours) or frequent collective transport (R$9 to R$18, one hour) to Maceió – just ask around.

white-sand beach that curves to a point at the meeting of the Rio São Miguel and the sea. Indeed, Barra isn't much of a destination in itself: it's better known as the gateway to Praia do Gunga, where the local beaches are protected by a huge offshore reef, leaving the waters calm for bathing or kayaking.

There are pousadas and tourist infrastructure in the area, clustered a few kilometers away from the dock in the neighborhood of Niquin. With an appealing swimming pool and terrace overlooking the ocean, **Hotel Portal Duleste** (☑ 3272-1089; www.hotelportalduleste.com.br; Edison Frazão 108, Niquin; s/d R$156/250; ✴ 🛜 ☒) is a good option. But in general, travelers looking to overnight south of Maceió usually prefer to stay in Praia do Francês.

Boats for Praia do Gunga (R$30) leave in the morning from the town's port. Several open-air restaurants line the harbor, catering to the tourists coming and going from the beach.

During high season on Praia do Gunga, **dune buggies** take tourists on an hour-long adventure: you'll speed along the sands, stop to photograph the rocky dune-lined landscape, and go for a dip in a natural pool.

Note that in Praia do Gunga, dining options are infamously overpriced: be aware that most of the *barracas* insist on a minimum consumption of upwards of R$50 per person. Many beachgoers prefer to bring their own picnic from Maceió, or buy simple snacks and sandwiches from the stands set up around the gigantic parking lot.

ⓘ Getting There & Away

Barra de São Miguel is located 35km from Maceió. Brazilian tourists usually arrive in their own cars, while most foreign tourists visit Praia do Gunga on a day trip with a travel agency in Maceió (the standard 'beach tour' visits Praia do Francês, Barra de São Miguel and Praia do Gunga).

To arrive independently from Maceió, ask your taxi driver to take you to the Texaco petrol station in the southwest of Maceió where the *colectivos* (vans or buses) depart for Barra de São Miguel. Once in Barra, you can catch a *colectivo* taxi to and from Praia do Francês (R$5, 20 minutes).

Marechal Deodoro

☑ 082 / POP 48,000

On the banks of the tranquil Lagoa Manguaba, Marechal Deodoro is a small, peaceful town with pretty churches and a few streets of colonial architecture dating back to early settlement days. Marechal served as capital of Alagoas between 1823 and 1839, and although there's not a lot to see, it's an easy jaunt from Maceió – and if you're heading to the beaches south of Maceió on public transportation, you'll probably pass through anyway. If you have a few minutes, check out the pretty white-and-yellow facade of the **Igreja de NS da Conceição**, located on top of the hill above the lagoon. If you're around on a weekend, the **Saturday market**, held until noon along the waterfront, is particularly lively. Arrive early in the morning to see fishermen working their nets out along the water.

Buses and minibuses for Marechal Deodoro (R$3, 35 minutes) via Praia do Francês depart frequently from a stop behind a Texaco petrol station (Rua Dias Cabral and Zacarias de Azevedo) southwest of Maceió's center. Buses, Kombi vans and *colectivo* taxis leave from Marechal's plaza for Praia do Francês (R$3, 15 minutes) and for Maceió.

Penedo

☑ 082 / POP 60,400

Penedo, known as the capital of the lower São Francisco, is the colonial masterpiece of the state and is almost unaltered by tourism. Attractions include the city's many baroque churches and colonial buildings and the opportunity to travel the sometimes jade-colored waters of the Rio São Francisco. Penedo's downtown bustles with a daily market as people from surrounding villages pour in to do their shopping.

History

Since its founding, Penedo has been a commercial center, owing to its prime position on the Rio São Francisco. The town was founded sometime between 1535 and 1560 by Duarte Coelho Pereira, who descended the Rio São Francisco in pursuit of the indigenous Caetes who were responsible for killing a bishop. Penedo is claimed to be the river's first colonial settlement. It was also the scene of a fierce 17th-century battle between the Dutch and the Portuguese for control of the Northeast. In the 19th century, Penedo was one of the focal points of the abolitionist movement in Alagoas. In the 20th century, the city lost its prominence as a commercial center, which probably saved its colonial buildings from destruction.

◎ Sights & Activities

Penedo has a rich collection of 17th- and 18th-century colonial buildings, including many churches. Unfortunately, regardless of the posted opening hours, these churches are not reliably open to visitors – your best bet is to walk around and see what's open.

Churches & Museums

Convento de São Francisco e Igreja NS dos Anjos   CHURCH

(Praça Rui Barbosa; admission R$2) The Convento de São Francisco e Igreja NS dos Anjos was under construction for nearly 100 years before its completion in 1759, and is considered the finest church in the state. Even Dom Pedro II (Brazil's second and last emperor) paid a visit. Of particular note are the richly colored ceiling, the gold rococo altar and the statue of St Francis to the left of it that was carved by Aleijadinho.

Igreja de NS da Corrente   CHURCH

(Praça 12 de Abril) The Igreja de NS da Corrente, completed in 1765, has some fine Portuguese *azulejos* (tiles), painted in green, purple and gold – colors rarely seen in Brazil, or Portugal for that matter. The Lemos family were big benefactors of the church (their family seal is marked on the floor) and abolitionists; slaves fled to the church for protection – some were even hidden behind panels of the church walls.

Igreja de São Gonçalo Garcia   CHURCH

(Av Floriano Peixoto) The Igreja de São Gonçalo Garcia was built at the end of the 18th century. The small **oratório** (Praça Barão de Penedo) is where the condemned spent their last night praying before being hanged.

Igreja NS do Rosário dos Pretos   CHURCH

(Catedral do Penedo; Praça Marechal Deodoro) The Igreja NS do Rosário dos Pretos was built by slaves.

Museu do Paço Imperial   MUSEUM

(Praça 12 de Abril 9; admission R$4; ◎11am-5pm Tue-Sat, 8am-noon Sun) Occupying the top floor of the house Dom Pedro II once slept in, the Museu do Paço Imperial displays lamps, portraits, furniture and elegant finery from the imperial period (17th and 18th centuries); it's tiny but nicely presented.

River Trips

Regular ferries (R$2) depart from the center for **Neópolis**, a hilltop colonial town with historic buildings and fine crafts for sale. During high season, it may be possible to get in on an organized tour to the **Foz do São Francisco** (R$100 for up to four people), where the river meets the sea at a beach with dunes and natural pools. The most frequent departures for this excursion leave 28km downriver in Piaçabuçu, easily accessible by collective van or bus from Penedo.

✭✭ Festivals & Events

Festa do Senhor Bom Jesus dos Navegantes   RELIGIOUS

(◎from 2nd Sun of Jan) This festival is held over four days, and features an elaborate procession of boats and a sailboat race.

🛏 Sleeping

If you're booking a hotel room online, be sure that you're searching for results in Penedo, Alagoas – otherwise you'll probably be looking at hotels in a Brazilian town in the state of Rio de Janeiro that's also named Penedo.

★ Pousada Colonial   POUSADA $

(☎3551-2355; www.pousadacolonialdepenedo.com.br; 12 de Abril 21; d/t/q R$120/160/200; ❄🛜) To fully soak up the colonial charms of Penedo, book a room at this charming historic house on the waterfront. Dating from 1734, the beautifully restored building has stained wood floors, dramatic high ceilings, antique furniture, and old-fashioned wooden shutters, some of which open to fabulous views over the river. It's located on the main square.

Pousada Central   POUSADA $

(☎3551-2460; www.pousadacentral-al.com.br; Floriano Peixoto 64; d from R$100; ❄) This cheerful pousada, tucked behind the main square on a smaller square presided over by Igreja São Gonçalo, is a solid budget choice in Penedo, with small, basic rooms that are clean, if a little dark.

Hotel São Francisco   HOTEL $$

(☎3551-2273; www.hotelsaofrancisco.tur.br; Floriano Peixoto 237; s/d/t from R$120/157/215; ❄🛜🏊) This 1960s-style hotel – considered an eyesore on the town's scenic skyline by some – has relatively contemporary rooms with satellite TVs and minibars; thanks to its slight elevation over the river, most rooms also have lovely water views.

✕ Eating & Drinking

Several supermarkets, sandwich kiosks and self-service eateries are on the main waterfront plaza; it's also a good place for a cold beer at night, when bars set up plastic tables on the cobblestones.

Boteco Velho Chico   BRAZILIAN $

(☑ 3551-2087; Floriano Peixoto 235; mains R$15-25; ☉ 7-11pm) At night, this bar brings in local foodies. Located next door to the entrance of Hotel São Francisco (p476), it's easy to spot: look for a small crowd clustered at atmospheric sidewalk tables, sampling regional specialties like the bar's famous *caldinhos* (stews) made from shrimp, tripe or pork.

Oratório   BRAZILIAN $$

(Av Beira Rio 301; meals for 2 R$40-58; ☉ 9am-midnight Mon-Fri, to 2am Sat & Sun) This casually elegant riverfront spot is popular throughout the day: come for a breakfast of coffee and fruit, a good-value set lunch, or a dinner of grilled fish and marinated shrimp.

Forte da Rocheira   BRAZILIAN $$

(☑ 3551-3273; Rocheira 2; mains R$28-45; ☉ 11am-4pm daily, 6-10:30pm Fri & Sat) This former Dutch fortification, perhaps better for drinks than dinner, has a splendid view out over the water. The location is slightly out of the way – just follow the signs, as the restaurant is well advertised in town, and try to time your visit with sunset.

NORTH OF MACEIÓ: BEACH TOWNS

Many travelers zip up the coastline from Maceió with one destination in mind: Maragogi, and its spectacular offshore coral reef and snorkeling site. But if you have more than a day or two, it's worthwhile to slow down and explore some of the rustic beach villages along this stretch of Alagoas' northernmost shoreline with its fluffy white sands, green waters and tall coconut palms. These easygoing towns barely have the basics to support tourism – save for a few luxury pousadas – but they offer an authentic look at the local lifestyle, and a chance to truly unplug. Wherever you go, it's advisable to get cash before heading out, as you won't find a bank until you reach Maragogi.

Heading north from Maceió, the first town you'll pass through is **Barra de Santo Antônio**, a mellow fishing village built along the mouth of the Rio Jirituba. Just south of the village is Praia Tabuba, a pretty, tranquil bay with a few bars and a couple of pousadas. There are reef tidal pools off the beach – ask at the bars about a ride there by *jangada* (sailboat). Next is **Barra do Camaragibe**, an idyllic fishing village on the edge of a small, reef-laden bay. *Jangadas* make trips south to Praia do Morro, a deserted beach with cliffs and clear waters.

The stretch from Barra do Camaragibe to Porto de Pedras is a lovely place to treat yourself. **São Miguel dos Milagres** has fine beaches with warm, shallow seas protected by offshore reefs. Splurge on a night or two in a stylish, environmentally conscious bungalow at **Pousada da Amendoeira** (☑ 3295-1213; www.amendoeira.com.br; Praia do Toque 7; d incl half-board R$470-710; ❊ ⎙) ✿, which also has an excellent restaurant specializing in gourmet seafood and organic regional dishes. If you're sticking around for a few days, eco-minded tour outfitter **Gato do Mato** (☑ 3033-1040; www.gatodomato.com) runs highly recommended half-day excursions, ranging from river kayaking to snorkeling to oyster collecting; contact the agency ahead of time, as a minimum number of participants is required for most trips.

Porto de Pedras is a sweet little fishing town and, as it is the most established on this stretch of road, it boasts a few shops, bars and restaurants, plus a hilltop lighthouse offering great views. Further north, in **Japaratinga**, shallow waters are protected by coral reefs, and the beaches are backed by coconut trees and fishing huts. Under the moonlight, you can walk a couple of kilometers into the sea. Kombi vans regularly make the 10km trip north to Maragogi (R$7).

There are a variety of transport options to reach northern destinations. Real Alagoas (p473) runs buses to Porto de Pedras (R$20, 3½ hours, five daily) via Barra do Camaragibe, São Miguel dos Milagres and Porto da Rua from the bus station in Maceió. Similar service by bus line **DEF**, as well as minibuses, *bestas* and *colectivo* taxis traveling the same route, can be caught at the posto Mar Azul at the northern edge of Maceió (ask your taxi driver to take you). Travel between these little towns is extremely easy up until about 7pm.

❶ Information

You'll find a **Bradesco bank** (Av Duque de Caixas 71) with an ATM on the riverfront. Other ATMs are located nearby, around the central square.

❶ Getting There & Away

There are two places to look for transportation options in Penedo: an informal bus stop on the main square, near the ferry dock, sees the arrivals and departures of taxi *colectivos* and vans heading to destinations as far afield as Maceió and Aracaju. A few blocks away along the river, behind the large supermarket, Penedo's small bus station is the place to buy tickets and board larger bus lines like Real Alagoas.

For Maceió, bus options are the *expresso litoral* (R$22, 2½ hours, two daily) and the *pinga litoral* (R$20, four hours, two daily). *Bestas/colectivos* run more frequent services to Maceió (R$17 to R$25, every 30 minutes). Any of these options provide access to Pontal de Coruripe, Barra de São Miguel and Praia do Francês.

Bomfim (www.bomfim.com.br) runs one daily bus to Salvador (R$73, eleven hours) and Aracaju (R$17, four hours). *Topiques* (vans) also go to Aracaju, Propriá and most frequently to Piaçabuçu (R$2, 40 minutes, every 30 minutes from 6am to 6pm). Ask the *topique* drivers hanging out on the riverfront for departure times.

Maragogi

🗹 082 / POP 28,800

Maragogi is a small beach town with a cluster of pousadas and restaurants along its waterfront, old-fashioned sailboats bobbing in the sea, and wide, flat beaches where local kids play soccer every evening at sunset. Though these beaches aren't anything special, Maragogi is one of the most visited destinations in the state, thanks to its major draw: the sandbars and reefs that make up the **Galés marine reserve**, 6km offshore, where the underwater scene is rich with colorful sea life.

Many visitors visit the reserve on day trips from Maceió, but Maragogi is also a friendly destination to spend a night or two. Trips to the reserve (R$65) are easily organized through beachfront restaurants or hotels – the excursion is heavily advertised left and right. The helpful travel agency **Costazul** (🗹 3296-2125; www.costazulturismo.com.br; Francisco Holanda Cavalcante 6) can help arrange excursions and book rooms, too.

On the waterfront, smart-looking **Pousada Olho D'água** (🗹 3296-1263; www.pousadaolhodagua.com; Senador Rui Palmeira 94; d from R$180) offers a terrace overlooking the ocean, comfortable rooms with private balconies (some have views) and a lovely swimming pool. Another excellent option – a five-minute walk north of the plaza in a residential area – is **Pousada Maragolfinho** (🗹 3296-1513; www.pousadamaragolfinho.maragogi.com; Escritor Graciliano Ramos 14; s/d from R$110/140; ✳🛜), with spacious guest rooms, modern showers, nice linens and a big breakfast spread.

Several seafood restaurants on the waterfront offer Bahian food, pizza, fresh juices and cocktails, plus relaxed outdoor seating on the beach. **Restaurante Frutas do Mar** (🗹 3296-1403; Senador Rui Palmeira 876; mains R$20-35; ⏰8am-10pm) is a locals' classic.

Maragogi has a Banco do Brasil with an ATM. For more eating and sleeping options and additional tourist information (including a section in English), log onto www.maragogionline.com.br.

The quickest way to get to Maceió from Maragogi is by taxi *colectivo* (R$30, two hours). Go to Maragogi's main square and look for the taxi stand. Each taxi transports four passengers, so there's often a short delay while the driver waits for other travelers to show up. The trip takes just over two hours, thanks to the race-car-style drivers who weave in and out of traffic along the coastal roads.

DEF has four daily departures from the main square to Maceió (R$12.50, 3½ hours) and the beach villages south of Maragogi.

Travel agencies provide private transfer, but since they charge an exorbitant R$170 for a solo traveler, consider it a last resort.

Pernambuco, Paraíba & Rio Grande do Norte

Best Places to Eat

➡ Oficina do Sabor (p495)

➡ Palhoça da Colina (p507)

➡ Tapas (p522)

➡ Chica Pitanga (p487)

➡ Camarões Potiguar (p518)

Best Places to Stay

➡ Toca da Coruja (p522)

➡ Manary Praia Hotel (p517)

➡ Pousada de São Pedro (p494)

➡ Pousada Ilha do Vento (p524)

➡ Spa da Alma (p521)

Why Go?

The nearly-1000km-long coastline of the three states at Brazil's northeastern corner is one sandy, sunburnt beach after another, backed by dunes, palms or cliffs. It's dotted with villages and small towns that are just perfect for tasty meals and sunset drinks and chilling out in a homey pousada – when you're not dipping, snorkeling, surfing, kitesurfing, windsurfing or diving in the delicious tropical waters. Or racing around the beaches and dunes with the wind in your hair on a beach-buggy ride. The coast is also home to four very different cities – gutsy, historic, cultural Recife; cute, artsy Olinda; appealingly revived João Pessoa; and the holiday playground of Natal. So you need never lack for urban vibes to spice up your beach idylls.

And arguably the region's greatest treasure lies 350km offshore – the Fernando de Noronha archipelago, a tropical-island getaway unrivaled in Brazil for its world-class beaches, diving and scenery.

When to Go
Recife

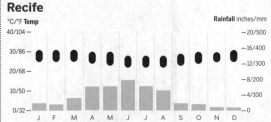

Feb–Mar Head to Recife and Olinda for Carnaval...if you can cope with inflated prices.

Apr–Jul Rainy season; lower prices, lower temperatures, lots of heavy showers.

Dec–Feb High season; the sunniest, driest, busiest, most expensive months.

Pernambuco, Paraíba & Rio Grande do Norte Highlights

1 Dance in the streets and experience the unique culture of artsy **Olinda** (p492) during euphoric Carnaval.

2 Be stunned by the world-class beaches, scenery, diving and snorkeling at crowd-free **Fernando de Noronha** (p499).

3 Enjoy the stylish but unpretentious international beach scene of beautiful **Praia da Pipa** (p519).

4 Immerse yourself in the cultural, culinary and historical attractions of the region's best city, **Recife** (p482).

5 Dig your toes into sands less traveled at **São Miguel do Gostoso** (p523).

6 Feel the wind in your hair on a beach-buggy ride from São Miguel do Gostoso to remote **Galinhos** (p524).

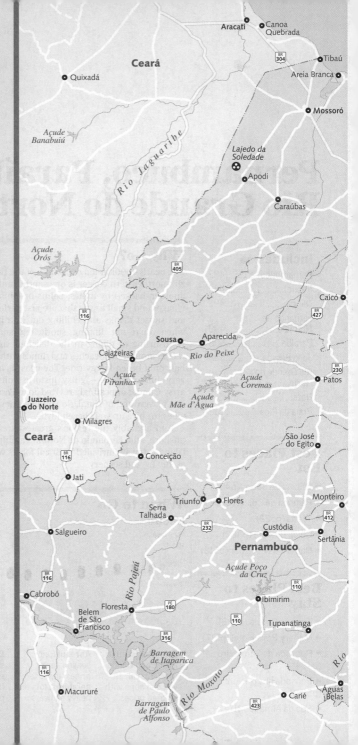

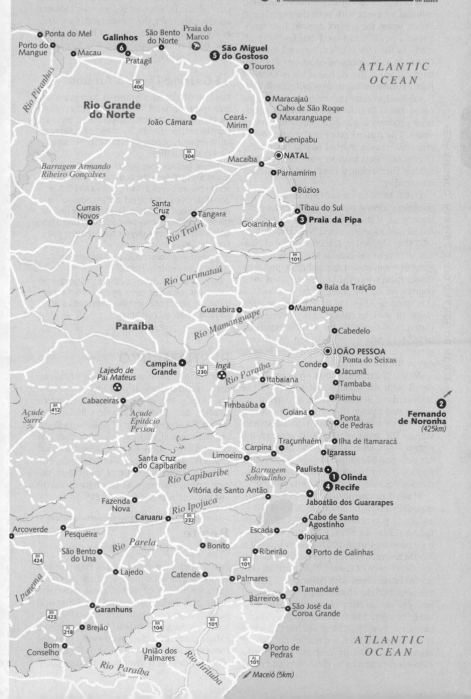

History

This corner of Brazil was a hotly contested colonial property, with both the French and Dutch vying for control against the Portuguese. French brazilwood traders were already in the region when Portugal founded Olinda in 1535 as capital of its new Pernambuco captaincy. Recife began life as Olinda's port. With the indigenous population brutally subdued, coastal Pernambuco quickly became one of Brazil's most important sugarcane producers, using the labor of African slaves. The region's other major cities, Natal and João Pessoa, started out as Portuguese rivermouth forts built to stake out territory against their colonial rivals and their indigenous allies.

Dutch invaders sacked Olinda in 1631 but, doubtless feeling more at home among the waterways of Recife, developed it as the capital of ambitiously named New Holland. In 1637 they shipped in Prince Maurice of Nassau to govern the colony. Maurice's enlightened freedom-of-worship policy helped keep things calm while the Dutch extended their control round the coast as far as São Luís (Maranhão). After the prince was ordered home in 1644, uprisings against Protestant Dutch rule eventually led to their expulsion in 1654. Olinda was rebuilt, but Recife outgrew it to become South America's biggest city in the late 17th century.

As the Northeast's sugar economy floundered with the abolition of slavery in the 19th century, Brazil's balance of population, power and money tipped to the Southeast, and the Northeast declined to backwater status. For most of the 20th century the region – and especially its arid interior, *sertão* – was a Brazilian byword for grinding poverty. Many Northeasterners migrated to the Southeast in search of a better life.

Much has changed in the 21st century, especially since the advent in 2002 of Workers' Party government for Brazil under Luíz Inácio (Lula) da Silva, who was the country's president until 2010. Lula is himself a Northeasterner, born in the backwoods Pernambuco town of Caetés. The Brazilian economic boom along with government aid for the poor and the channeling of government and private investment into the Northeast have brought much better times. Unemployment has dived, and the middle class is growing fast. Even the traditional flow of migration is changing direction, with Northeasterners returning to their roots and some

Southeasterners moving north in search of a better life! Coastal tourism is very much part of this boom, and is a growth industry all the way from the former fishing village of Porto de Galinhas, south of Recife, to still (for now) remote spots like São Miguel do Gostoso, north of Natal.

ⓘ Getting There & Around

Recife and Natal are the region's main gateways, both receiving direct flights from Europe (including Lisbon and other cities), and in Recife's case from Miami, too. Recife, Natal and João Pessoa all have plenty of daily flights from other significant Brazilian cities.

Decent bus services link all major cities and towns along the coasts, both within the region and to places beyond like Fortaleza and Salvador. Main cities have direct bus services to Rio de Janeiro and São Paulo. Smaller, more remote towns and villages may be reached by only a few bus or van services a day (or not even every day in cases like Galinhos).

Fernando de Noronha is reachable only by flights from Recife or Natal.

Rental cars are widely available and worth considering if you will be covering a lot of distance. Rates are reasonable and the main roads are, in general, in decent condition.

PERNAMBUCO

This exciting state is home to two fascinatingly cultural, historic and highly contrasting cities – big, gritty Recife and its much smaller, far cuter neighbour Olinda, both famed for staging some of Brazil's most euphoric, original and participatory Carnaval celebrations – and to the unique tropical getaway destination of Fernando de Noronha, a paradise for divers, snorkelers, nature lovers, surfers and beachgoers 525km out into the Atlantic from Recife.

Recife

⬈ 0XX81 / POP 1.5 MILLION (METROPOLITAN AREA 3.7 MILLION)

Recife ('heh-*see*-fee'), capital of Pernambuco, is the Northeast's most exciting city after Salvador, with a vibrant cultural, entertainment and restaurant scene, an intriguing historic center, an impressive coastal setting, and a fabulous Carnaval. It's a sprawling, urban place of glassy high-rises, crowded commercial areas, thundering traffic and extensive suburbs; if you like your cities gutsy, gritty and proud, Recife is for you. It takes its name from the offshore *recifes* (reefs) that calm the waters of its ports and shoreline.

The charming and far more tranquil historic town of Olinda lies on Recife's northern edge, just 6km from the city center, and many visitors opt to stay in Olinda and visit Recife during the day, or venture into Recife for the animated nightlife.

The city center, a jumble of office blocks, colonial churches and thronged market areas, is spread over several islands and peninsulas at the mouths of the Rio Capibaribe and other rivers, with a dozen bridges crisscrossing the waterways (which often don't smell too great). The main districts of interest here are the historic Recife Antigo on the ocean side, increasingly attractive to visit thanks to an ongoing revival program, and Santo Antônio to its west, with governmental and bustling commercial districts. After dark and on Sunday afternoon many streets in the center (except Recife Antigo) are empty. The high-rise, middle-class, beach suburb Boa Viagem, with the best range of accommodations and restaurants, begins 3km south of the center and extends about 5km along the coast. Recife's airport is at the south end of Boa Viagem, 2km inland; the bus station is a 17km metro ride west of the center.

◉ Sights

◉ Recife Antigo

The narrow streets of Recife Antigo (also called the Bairro do Recife), where the city began, have been revitalized in recent years, and the area is well worth a slice of your time.

Marco Zero   PLAZA
(Map p484; Praça Rio Branco) The Marco Zero, a small 'Km 0' marker in the middle of the broad waterside Praça Rio Branco, marks the place where the Portuguese founded Recife in 1537, and has given its name, unofficially, to the praça and immediate surrounds. Old port warehouses and other buildings are being converted into a series of cultural and other attractions.

The **Centro de Artesanato de Pernambuco** (Map p484; Praça Rio Branco; ◉10am-8pm) displays (and sells) the best of Pernambuco crafts in wood, ceramics, lace, lithographs and other media. To the west, **Caixa Cultural** (Map p484; www.caixacultural.

gov.br; Av Alfredo Lisboa 505; ◉noon-6pm Tue-Fri, 10am-8pm Sat-Sun), **Santander Cultural** (Map p484; www.santandercultural.com.br; Av Rio Branco 23; ◉1-8pm Tue-Sun) and the **Centro Cultural Correios** (Map p484; Av Marquês de Olinda 262; ◉9am-6pm Tue-Fri, noon-6pm Sat-Sun) all host exhibitions and films. More renovation projects including restaurants, shops and the multimedia **Centro Cultural Cais do Sertão Luiz Gonzaga** (Map p484; Av Alfredo Lisboa) – dedicated to *forró* music and Pernambuco culture and the *sertão* in general – were due to be completed by mid-2014.

Praça do Arsenal   PLAZA
(Map p484) This leafy praça is home to the **Paço do Frevo** (Map p484; Praça do Arsenal; ◉9am-8pm Tue-Sun), which houses exhibits, performances and classes of *frevo*, the quintessential dance of the Recife Carnaval. **Rua do Bom Jesus**, to the south, was formerly known as Rua dos Judeos because a number of Jewish businesses opened here during Dutch rule (1630–54).

The oldest synagogue in the Americas, **Sinagoga Kahal Zur Israel** (Map p484; ☑3224-2128; Rua do Bom Jesus 197; admission R$6; ◉9am-4:30pm Tue-Fri, 2-5:30pm Sun), now a Jewish cultural center, has interesting murals (in Portuguese and English) depicting the role of Jews in Recife's development. Two doors down, the **Embaixada dos Bonecos Gigantes** (Map p484; Rua do Bom Jesus 183; admission R$4; ◉8am-6pm) displays some of the giant puppets that feature in the Olinda Carnaval. Bom Jesus is at its best during the Feirinha do Recife Antigo (p489), its colorful Sunday crafts market.

Paço Alfândega   HISTORIC BUILDING
(Map p484; www.pacoalfandega.com.br; Rua da Alfândega 35; ◉10am-10pm Mon-Sat, noon-9pm Sun) This 19th-century customs house has been converted into a glitzy shopping mall – worth dropping in for a coffee or a bite in its food court.

◉ Santo Antônio

This district encompasses both the formal **Praça da República** (Map p484), surrounded by imposing 19th-century governmental buildings at its northern end, and a bustling commercial area further south, where the streets are lined with shops, stalls, fine facades and colonial churches in assorted states of preservation.

PERNAMBUCO, PARAÍBA & RIO GRANDE DO NORTE RECIFE

Central Recife

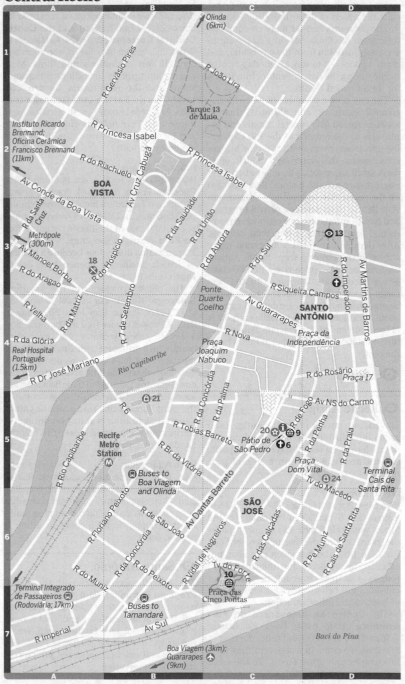

Olinda
(6km)

R Gervásio Pires

R João Lira

Parque 13
de Maio

R Princesa Isabel

R Princesa Isabel

Instituto Ricardo
Brennan;
Oficina Cerâmica
Francisco Brennand
(11km)

R do Riachuelo

R Cruz Cabugá

R da Saudade

R da União

**BOA
VISTA**

Av Conde da Boa Vista

R da Santa
Cruz

Metrópole
(300m)

Av Manoel Borba

R da Aurora

R do Sul

⊙ 13

R do Imperador

Av Martins de Barros

2
✚

R do Aragão

R do Hospício

18 ✗

Ponte
Duarte
Coelho

Av Guararapes

R Siqueira Campos

**SANTO
ANTÔNIO**

R Velha

R da Matriz

R 7 de Setembro

R Nova

Praça da
Independência

R da Glória
Real Hospital
Português
(1.5km)

R Dr José Mariano

Rio Capibaribe

Praça
Joaquim
Nabuco

R do Rosário

Praça 17

🏛 21

R da Concórdia

R da Palma

Av NS do Carmo

R de Fogo

20 ✪

ℹ
🏛 9

R da Penha

R da Praia

**Recife
Metro
Station**
Ⓜ

R Tobias Barreto

R Br da Vitória

Pátio de
São Pedro

✚ 6

🚌 Buses to
Boa Viagem
and Olinda

Praça
Dom Vital

Terminal
Cais de
Santa Rita

R Rio Capibaribe

R 6

Tv do Macedo

🏛 24

R 6

R Floriano Peixoto

R de São João

Av Dantas Barreto

**SÃO
JOSÉ**

R das Calçadas

R Pe Muniz

R Cais de Santa Rita

Terminal Integrado
de Passageiros 🚌
(Rodoviária; 17km)

R do Muniz

R da Concórdia

R do Peixoto

R Vidal de Negreiros

Tv do Forte

10
🏛

Praça das
Cinco Pontas

Buses to
Tamandaré

R Imperial

Av Sul

Baci do Pina

Boa Viagem (3km);
Guararapes ✈
(9km)

Central Recife

◎ Sights

⊗ Eating

⊖ Drinking & Nightlife

⊕ Entertainment

🔒 Shopping

Capela Dourada   CHAPEL

(Golden Chapel; Map p484; Rua do Imperador; admission R$3; ⊗8-11:30am & 2-5pm Mon-Fri, 8-11:30am Sat) Built between 1696 and 1724, this gem of Brazilian baroque, part of the Convento de Santo Antônio, owes its name to the huge quantities of gold covering its elaborately sculpted walls, altars and ceiling.

Pátio de São Pedro   SQUARE

(Map p484) This traffic-free square, lined with bars, restaurants and colorful 19th-century houses, is one of the area's more peaceful spots and a good place to stop for a drink. The 18th-century baroque **Concatedral de São Pedro dos Clérigos** (Map p484; Pátio de São Pedro; ⊗8am-noon & 2-5pm Mon-Fri) contains incredibly fine wood-carvings, while the **Memorial Chico Science** (Map p484; ☎3355-3158; www.recife.pe.gov.br/chicoscience; Pátio de

São Pedro 21; ⊙ 9am-5pm Mon-Fri) **FREE** highlights the revered founder of the *mangue beat* musical movement, who died tragically in a Recife car accident in 1997.

Museu da Cidade do Recife   MUSEUM, FORT
(Map p484; ☑ 3355 3107; Praça das Cinco Pontas; admission R$4; ⊙ 9am-5pm Tue-Fri, 1-5pm Sat & Sun) Recife's City Museum is housed in the Forte das Cinco Pontas (Five-Pointed Fort), built by the Dutch in 1630. It exhibits old maps and historic photos but could be so much more interesting given Recife's fascinating history.

◉ Brennand Workshop & Institute

The ceramics 'workshop' of Francisco Brennand and the art institute of his cousin Ricardo constitute a regional highlight and it's well worth setting aside half a day for the trip out to Várzea, on Recife's western edge, to see them. The only times both places are open simultaneously are Tuesday to Friday afternoons. The easiest way to reach them is a round-trip by taxi (around R$100 from Boa Viagem, with about 1½ hours at each place). The alternative from Boa Viagem is to take a CDU/Caxangá bus to the end of its route on Rua Acadêmico Hélio Ramos, then a taxi round-trip from the bus stop to both sites (around 10km in total) for around R$60.

★ Oficina Cerâmica
Francisco Brennand   MUSEUM
(☑ 3271-2466; www.brennand.com.br; Várzea; admission R$10; ⊙ 8am-5pm Mon-Thu, to 4pm Fri) Francisco Brennand, born in 1927 into an Irish immigrant family and now considered Brazil's greatest ceramicist, revitalized his family's abandoned tile factory to create his own line of decorative ceramic tiles. The expansive indoor and outdoor space is now mostly dedicated to his own enormous and fascinating oeuvre, which ranges over painting, tilework and hundreds of highly original sculptures.

The grounds, set amid thick Atlantic rainforest, include a couple of temples, Moorish arches and all sorts of surreal sculptures including rows of contorted busts and a garden of bizarre sexualized earthworms.

Instituto Ricardo Brennand   MUSEUM
(☑ 2121-0352; www.institutoricardobrennand.org. br; Alameda Antônio Brennand, Várzea; admission R$15; ⊙ 1-5pm Tue-Sun) The scenic Instituto contains a massive collection of European and Brazilian art, swords, armor and historical artifacts in a fake medieval castle on lovely grounds.

★⁂ Festivals & Events

The Recife **Carnaval** (www.carnavaldorecife. com.br) is a hard-to-believe explosion of color, costume, crowds, alcohol, fabulous music and dancing, and infectious happiness that adds up to one of Brazil's most euphoric and folkloric festivals, and has its claims to being the best Carnaval in the country – though it attracts far fewer tourists than Salvador's or Rio's. There are also many hundreds of music and dance events on stages around the city, but this is essentially a participatory event where people don't just sit and watch; they don elaborate costumes and dance for days to most conceivable Brazilian rhythms, but especially to Recife's very own, frenetic *frevo*.

Galo da Madrugada (Cock of the Morning), which is claimed, probably correctly, to be the largest Carnaval *bloco* (parade group) in the world, erects a giant cock on the Ponte Duarte Coelho and pulls over a million people into central Recife for its parade on Carnaval Saturday morning, starting around 8am. Carnaval activity focuses around a number of *polos* (poles) dotted about the city. Recife Antigo (especially Marco Zero, Praça do Arsenal and the Paço Alfândega) and the Pátio de São Pedro are among the best areas to head for. Printed programs are widely available.

Carnaval in Olinda is so close that you could participate in both on the same day, and there is a lot of crossover in the events. Accommodations in both cities hike prices mercilessly and may demand three- to five-night minimum stays; some get booked up months, even a year, in advance.

🛏 Sleeping

Accommodations in the city center are limited and of poor value. The nicer, safer beach suburb Boa Viagem, with options from hostels to five-star hotels, is a much better base.

Cosmopolitan Hostel   HOSTEL **$**
(Map p489; ☑ 3204-0321; www.cosmopolitanhostel.com; Paulo Setúbal 53, Boa Viagem; dm/s/d R$45/130/140; ✸@🛜) This bright, welcoming hostel in a converted family home on a quiet residential street is the best budget bet for ambience, space and location. Private rooms and six-bed dorms (one is women-only) are set around a courtyard with mango and

acerola trees. Amiable bilingual owner Filipe is a fount of local information, and a small family of fluffy rabbits adds to the homey feel.

Albergue Piratas da Praia   HOSTEL $

(Map p489; ☑ 3326-1281; www.piratasdapraia.com; Av Conselheiro Aguiar 2034, Boa Viagem; dm with/without air-con R$50/40, r with/without air-con R$150/140; ✸ @ ☎) You'd never know it was here, but this friendly, highly colorful hostel occupies the 3rd floor of a building named Edificio Barão de Camaçari (entered from Rua Osias Ribeiro). It's a bit like staying in a friend's apartment, with a good clean kitchen, and bicycles and beach volleyballs for rent. Discounts for card-carrying students.

Pousada Casuarinas   POUSADA $$

(Map p489; ☑ 3325-4708; www.pousadacasuarinas.com.br; Antônio Pedro Figueiredo 151, Boa Viagem; s/d R$150/195, with veranda R$160/205; ✸ @ ☎ ✸) A tranquil former family home run by two sisters (one English speaking), Casuarinas is a marvelous retreat from the heat and bustle outside. Spotless rooms are set around a shady courtyard and regional folk art spices up the decor.

Pousada Vitória   POUSADA $$

(☑ 3462-6446; www.pousadavitoriarecife.com.br; Capitão Zuzinha 234, Boa Viagem; s/d R$165/185; ✸ ☎) Aside from having more color and character than any other in this price range, this cute pousada (guesthouse) is a mere 1.5km from the airport, perfectly located for those just passing through. Staff will pick you up for free if you land between 6am and 6pm.

Cult Hotel   HOTEL $$

(☑ 2123-2777; www.culthotel.com.br; Av Conselheiro Aguiar 755, Boa Viagem; d from R$230; ✸ ☎ ✸) Rooms are functional, clean and comfy, staff helpful and the breakfast ample, but what's special here is the art and displays on Pernambuco culture and history that adorn the entire hotel, and the comprehensive city information available from reception and the hotel website.

Hotel Aconchego   HOTEL $$

(Map p489; ☑ 3464-2989; www.hotelaconchego.com.br; Félix de Brito Melo 382, Boa Viagem; r R$240-300; ✸ ☎ ✸) Well-run Aconchego has substantial common areas, an affordable 24-hour poolside restaurant (and bar!) and good, multilingual service. Rooms are spotless though you could expect more space for the price: the best are Nos 203, 206, 303 and 306, upstairs with private verandas.

Recife Palace Hotel   HOTEL $$$

(Map p489; ☑ 3201-8200; www.goldentulipre cifepalace.com; Av Boa Viagem 4070, Boa Viagem; s/d from R$394/446; ✸ ☎ ✸) The mid-1980s beachfront Recife Palace is still one of Boa Viagem's most luxurious hotels. Public areas are all black marble, polished woods and gleaming brass, and the rooms are spacious, staid and very comfortable, nearly all with sea views.

✖ Eating

Recife has great places to eat, from cheerful-and-bustling to refined establishments comparable with Rio's and São Paulo's finest.

✖ Central Recife

Salada Mista   SELF-SERVE $

(Map p484; Rua do Hospício 59, Boa Vista; per kg R$25; ☉ 10:30am 8pm Mon-Fri, to 4pm Sat) One of the best of many per-kilo eateries in the center, Salada Mista has a big range of options in a clean and comfortable setting.

Bistrô & Boteco   BRAZILIAN $$

(Map p484; Av Alfredo Lisboa, Recife Antigo; mains R$23-35, buffet lunch R$38; ☉ 11:30am-1am) A great stop during your explorations of Recife Antigo, Bistrô & Boteco's grills, shrimp and salads are enhanced by its superb harbor views. The *prime rib de leitão* (suckling pig ribs) comes with a *rodízio* of vegetable accompaniments offered by waiters circulating from table to table.

From 3:30pm onwards there are tasty *petiscos* (light dishes) to go with drinks.

✖ Boa Viagem

La Vague   CREPERIE $

(Map p489; ☑ 3465-1654; Rua Rui Batista 120; crepes R$14-23; ☉ 6-11:30pm; ☑) La Vague serves up good-value savory and sweet crepes, and fab salads in a cool, semi-outdoor ambience.

King's Kilo   SELF-SERVE $

(Map p489; Hipermercado Extra, Av Domingos Ferreira 1818, Boa Viagem; per kg R$28.90, after 3:30pm R$17.90; ☉ 11:15am-8pm) This busy place offers up a varied and good-value per-kilo buffet.

★ Chica Pitanga   SELF-SERVE $$

(www.chicapitanga.com.br; Petrolina 19, Boa Viagem; per kg lunch/dinner R$54/47; ☉ 11:30am-3:30pm & 6-10pm; ☑) As near as a per-kilo lunch gets to a gourmet experience, Chica

PERNAMBUCO, PARAÍBA & RIO GRANDE DO NORTE RECIFE

Pitanga offers a different array of diverse dishes every day. The 12 salad options might, for example, include tabouleh salad and carrot mousse, while bacon-wrapped filet mignon and shrimp in Parmesan sauce might appear among the 10 hot dishes. Lighter regional dishes are served in the evenings.

Parraxaxá
SELF-SERVE $$
(www.parraxaxa.com.br; Av Fernando Simões Barbosa 1200, Boa Viagem; per kg R$45; ☉11:30am-11pm;🛜) Festive decor and staff in police and outlaw outfits spice up your meal at this fun Northeast-themed restaurant. The self-serve food is a cornucopia of tasty Northeastern dishes – *carne de sol* (salted beef), *macaxeira* (cassava root), *baião de dois* (a spicy rice, beans and cheese dish) and grilled meats – with good salads, too.

Camarada
SEAFOOD $$$
(Map p489; ☑3325-1786; www.ocamarada.com.br; Baltazar Pereira 130, Boa Viagem; mains for 2 R$67-120; ☉11:45am-1am Mon-Sat, 11:45am-midnight Sun;🛜) Airy, bustling Camarada does shrimp in endlessly creative ways – fondue, salads, beer-marinated, *moquecas* (stews) – but it's also wildly popular for happy hour, as patrons flood the front deck with ice-cold draft beer in hand. If your appetite and budget are on the small side, try the delicious *antepasto Camarada* (R$26).

 Drinking & Entertainment

Recife is justly proud of its nightlife and the variety of music that can be found in the city. You can find somewhere exciting to go every night of the week. Many venues are in Boa Viagem but the streets behind Recife Antigo's Paço Alfândega also have lively bars. Tourist offices hand out useful entertainment guides, and several websites provide good listings, including www.acontecenorecife.com.br (in English as well as Portuguese).

Recifenses are passionate about their football, even though their most successful teams, **Sport** (www.sportrecife.com.br) and **Náutico** (www.nautico-pe.com.br), both have a history of yo-yo-ing between the national Série A and Série B. Náutico plays at the 46,000-seat **Arena Pernambuco** (www.cidadedacopa.com.br), 20km west of the city center in São Lourenço da Mata – a stadium built for the 2014 World Cup, in which it was slated to host five matches, including one round-of-16 game.

Central Recife

Burburinho
BAR
(Map p484; ☑3224-5854; www.facebook.com/barburburinho; Tomazina 106, Recife Antigo; ☉5pm-late Mon-Sat) Frequented by students, journalists and a generally bohemian crowd, Burburinho is nicer inside than it appears and usually has live music at least three times weekly – recently, blues sessions on Monday (10pm), Beatles nights on Wednesday (8pm) and varied bands on Friday (10pm).

Metrópole
GAY
(☑3423-0123; clubemetropole.com.br; Rua das Ninfas 125, Boa Vista; ☉10pm-6am Fri & Sat) Recife's best gay (and GLS) club has multiple spaces from its main DJ-ruled 'NY Street' dance area to an outdoor area with swimming pool. There are frequent theme parties and live shows by big-name artists.

Terça Negra
LIVE MUSIC
(Black Tuesday; Map p484; Pátio de São Pedro; ☉8pm-1am Tue) This great free weekly night of Afro-Brazilian rhythms takes place in the picturesque Pátio de São Pedro. Come ready to dance.

Boa Viagem

Guaiamum Gigante
BAR
(Map p489; ☑3327-1413; Av Boa Viagem, 2° Jardim, Boa Viagem; ☉11:30am-1am Mon-Sat, 11:30am-11pm Sun) An upscale, beach-facing *boteco* (neighborhood bar) that is packed every night. The breezy outdoor patio serves as a decadent drinking den and you can also eat good seafood (dishes for two R$55 to R$98).

UK Pub
LOUNGE
(Map p489; ☑3465-1088; www.ukpub.com.br; Francisco da Cunha 165, Boa Viagem; admission R$12-40; ☉8pm-late Tue-Sat, from 7pm Sun) UK Pub is a sophisticated lounge that draws a sexy Anglophile crowd for proper pints (Guinness, Old Speckled Hen and Newcastle, around R$35 a pint!) and, from Thursday to Sunday, varied live bands and DJs. The Sunday samba nights are a riot. Take your passport for ID.

Dona Carolina
BAR
(Map p489; ☑3466-2743; www.bardonacarolina.com.br; Av Boa Viagem 123, Boa Viagem; women/men R$30/40; ☉8pm-5am Thu-Sat) This sleek, modern bar and restaurant hosts live *brega*

Boa Viagem

on Thursday, *sertaneja* on Friday (both are favorite popular musical styles in Northeast Brazil) and samba on Saturday, with enough hotness to melt Antarctica.

Shopping

Mercado de São José   MARKET
(Map p484; Praça Dom Vital, São José; ⊙6am-5:30pm Mon-Sat, to noon Sun) As well as traditional Pernambuco handicrafts, such as lace and leather goods, palm baskets and clay figurines, this bustling city-center market sells all manner of food, and shelves of medicinal herbs.

Casa da Cultura   HANDICRAFTS
(Map p484; Floriano Peixoto, Santo Antônio; ⊙9am-6pm Mon-Fri, to 5pm Sat, to 2pm Sun) An excellent source of Pernambuco crafts, and a lot of T-shirts: the Casa da Cultura occupies a creepy colonial-era prison where prisoners languished until 1973.

Feirinha do Recife Antigo   ARTS & CRAFTS
(Map p484; Rua do Bom Jesus; ⊙2-8pm Sun) This interesting street market specializing in high-class artisanry – dresses, jewelry, ceramics – brings Recife Antigo to life on Sunday afternoons. Nearby bars open and there's often live music.

Livraria Cultura   BOOKS, MUSIC
(Map p484; Rua da Alfândega; ⊙10am-10pm Mon-Sat, noon-9pm Sun) Probably the best bookstore north of Salvador, with a big English-language selection including Lonely Planet guides, plus music and movies.

ℹ️ Information

DANGERS & ANNOYANCES

Surfing is prohibited at Boa Viagem beach due to the danger of shark attacks. Swimmers there are advised to stay out of the water at high tide and not go beyond the reef at any time. Since 1990, at least 31 shark attacks have been recorded along Recife's shores, most of them at Boa Viagem or the next beach south, Piedade.

Although crime levels have fallen significantly in recent years, Recife still has one of Brazil's highest murder rates. Tourists are more at risk from pickpockets and bag snatchers: stay alert to your surroundings and people around you, and don't walk down unlit streets at night. Boa Viagem is generally safer than the city center though some robberies occur there, too.

EMERGENCY

Police (cnr Av Conselheiro Aguiar & Praça Cidade do Porto, Boa Viagem)

Police (Emergency) (📞190)

Tourist Police (📞3322-4867; ground fl, airport; ⊙24hr)

INTERNET ACCESS

Caravelas Cybercafé (Rua do Bom Jesus 183, Recife Antigo; per hr R$2.50)

Recarga Expressa (Hipermercado Extra, Av Domingos Ferreira 1818, Boa Viagem; per hr R$3.60; ⊙8am-9pm Mon-Sat, 10am-4pm Sun)

MEDICAL SERVICES

Real Hospital Português (📞3416-1122; www. rhp.com.br; Av Agamenon Magalhães 4760) Large, modern, 24-hour private hospital, with a smaller clinic (Av Conselheiro Aguiar 2502) in Boa Viagem also offering 24-hour emergency service.

MONEY

The airport has plenty of ATMs as well as the exchange office **Confidence Câmbio** (📞4004-5700; airport; ⊙24hr).

MUSIC OF RECIFE & OLINDA

In Recife and Olinda you'll hear plenty of that very popular, typically Northeastern country music, *forró*. There is also music from further south in Brazil such as samba, *pagode* and *choro*. But Pernambuco state, and these two cities in particular, is also an exciting music-and-dance world of its own – home to some wonderful original genres mostly bound up with Carnaval, and featuring fabulously exotic costumes and fast-paced, mostly percussion-heavy music.

Top of the list has to be *frevo*, feverishly fast brass-and-percussion music that inspires feverishly energetic dancing. Dancers sport supercolorful shiny costumes and twirl equally colorful mini-umbrellas. *Frevo's* origins are thought to lie in the marching-band music of Carnaval in 19th-century Recife and the capoeira movements of those who cleared the way for the bands. The umbrellas are today's equivalent of the capoeiristas' sticks or knives.

Maracatu nação (also called *maracatu de baque virado*) involves large African-style drum ensembles with dancers dressed as baroque-era Portuguese courtiers – a weird juxtaposition that derives from investiture ceremonies for leaders of the African slave community. *Maracatu rural* (or *maracatu de baque solto*) is rooted in similarly heavy drum rhythms with dancers representing a melange of characters from animals to *baianas* (bouquet ladies in big hooped skirts) and the spectacular *caboclos de lança* (spear-carrying guards with enormous beehive-like headdresses of brilliantly colored tassles).

Then there's *caboclinho*, which has roots in the rituals of Brazil's indigenous *groups*. A set of characters from kings and queens to witch doctors and the *caboclinhos* themselves (*índio*/Euro mixed-race characters wearing fantastic feathered headdresses) dance energetically to the *pífano* flute, maracas and big drums.

Pernambuco is also one of the homes of *afoxé*, an Afro-Brazilian music-and-dance genre based on the rhythms and spirit of Candomblé.

A more recent Recife contribution to Brazilian music is *mangue beat*, which emerged in the 1990s among young bands who combined traditional forms such as *maracatu* with electrified instruments and rhythms of rap, hip-hop and electronica. They did a lot to connect the younger generation with the traditions of their ancestors. Leader of the genre was singer Chico Science with his group Nação Zumbi, whose iconic 1996 album *Afrociberdelia* summed up the *mangue* movement as neatly as one word can. Science died in a car crash in 1997 and is still much mourned: Nação Zumbi plays on.

Banco do Brasil (Av Dantas Barreto 541, Santo Antônio; ☺10am-4pm Mon-Fri, ATMs 6am-10pm daily) Currency exchange and ATMs.

Bompreço (Av Domingos Ferreira 1380, Boa Viagem; ☺7am-midnight Mon-Sat, 7am-8pm Sun) The Banco do Brasil ATM inside this supermarket accepts foreign cards.

Bradesco (Av Conselheiro Aguiar 3256, Boa Viagem; ☺8am-10pm) ATMs accept foreign Visa and MasterCard.

POST

Post Office (Map p489; Hipermercado Extra, Av Domingos Ferreira 1818, Boa Viagem; ☺8:30am-6pm Mon-Fri, 8am-noon Sat)

TOURIST INFORMATION

Most Recife tourist offices, known as Postos de Informação Turística (PITs), have helpful, professional, English-speaking staff and can provide good city maps.

PIT (☑3355-0128; airport; ☺24hr)

PIT (☑3182-8298; Rodoviária; ☺7am-7pm) At the bus station.

PIT (Map p484; ☑3355-3310; Patio de São Pedro, Santo Antônio; ☺9am-5pm Mon-Fri)

PIT (Map p484; ☑3355-3402; Praça do Arsenal, Recife Antigo; ☺8:30am-9pm)

ℹ Getting There & Away

AIR

Recife's **Guararapes Airport** (REC; ☑3322-4353) has direct flights to/from some 20 Brazilian cities on **TAM** (☑3322-4663; www.tam.com.br; airport), **Azul** (www.voeazul.com.br; airport), **GOL** (www.voegol.com.br; airport), **Trip** (☑0800-887-1118; www.voetrip.com.br; airport) or **Avianca** (www.avianca.com). There are also daily flights to/from Lisbon with **TAP Portugal** (☑0300-210-6060; www.flytap.com; airport), and Miami with **American Airlines** (☑0300-789-7778; www.aa.com; airport), and a few flights weekly to/from Frankfurt with **Condor** (www.condor.com), and Panama City with **CopaAirlines** (www.copaair.com).

BUS

Recife's bus station is the large **Terminal Integrado de Passageiros** (TIP; ☑3452-1088), generally known as the Rodoviária, 17km west of the center. TIP handles all interstate buses and many destinations within Pernambuco. You can purchase many bus tickets at agencies in town, or by calling **Disk Rodoviária** (☑3452-1211; www.diskrodoviaria.com.br), a bus-ticket delivery service.

Destinations include Fortaleza (R$123 to R$177, 13 hours, three daily), João Pessoa (R$20, two hours, 27 daily), Maceió (R$34 to R$80, four to five hours, 11 daily), Natal (R$43 to R$62, 4½ hours, nine daily), Rio (R$358,

38 hours, three daily) and Salvador (R$127 to R$160, 12 to 15 hours, three daily).

CAR & MOTORCYCLE

Recommended car-rental agencies with airport offices include **Avis** (☑0800-725-2847, 3322-4016; www.avis.com.br) and **Localiza** (☑3471-7329; www.localiza.com).

ℹ Getting Around

Recife is spread out and some of the buses (R$2.25; R$1.15 on Sunday) take circuitous, confusing routes. A few taxis will save you time and stress. Bus routes and schedules are online at www.granderecife.pe.gov.br (click Serviços then Itinerário).

TO/FROM THE AIRPORT

Prepaid taxis from the airport cost between R$17 and R$26 to Boa Viagem (R$21 to R$32 from 10pm to 6am). During high traffic times, these can be a better-value option then metered taxis.

Air-conditioned bus 042 (R$2.80) from outside the arrivals hall heads to Boa Viagem and the city center but takes a convoluted route which slows it down considerably. At busy times, a better option for Boa Viagem is to walk to the right outside the arrivals hall and catch bus 040 CDU/Boa Viagem/Caxangá (initially heading south) from the stop on busy Av Mascarenhas de Morais opposite a Mercedes Benz dealership.

Going to the airport from Boa Viagem, get any Aeroporto bus on Av Domingos Ferreira; from the center, take a 033 Aeroporto bus from Terminal Cais de Santa Rita.

TO/FROM THE BUS STATION

From the TIP to Boa Viagem, take the metro to Joana Bezerra station, then a Joana Bezerra/Boa Viagem bus from there. A R$2.25 'Integracão A' ticket from the Rodoviária metro station in the TIP covers both rides. From Boa Viagem to the TIP, take a Joana Bezerra bus from Av Conselheiro Aguiar to Joana Bezerra metro station, then a Camaragibe-bound metro train to the Rodoviária.

If you arrive outside metro hours (5am to 11pm), night-time taxis run R$45 to R$55 to Boa Viagem.

TO/FROM BOA VIAGEM

In Boa Viagem, southbound buses run along Av Domingos Ferreira; northbound buses run along Av Conselheiro Aguiar. The 032 Setúbal/Conde da Boa Vista bus runs north to Recife Antigo, Av Guararapes and Av Conde da Boa Vista (westbound) in the center, and back to Boa Viagem. Buses 031 Shopping Center and 033 Aeroporto run north from Boa Viagem to **Terminal Cais de Santa Rita** (Map p484) and back.

From the center to Boa Viagem, you can also take a **Setúbal/Príncipe bus** (Map p484) outside Recife metro station.

A taxi between central Recife and Boa Viagem costs around R$15.

Olinda

🖉 0XX81 / POP 368,000

Picturesque Olinda, set around a tree-covered hill 6km north of Recife, is the artsy, colonial counterpart to the big city's hubbub. It's an artist colony full of creative types and brimming with galleries, artisans' workshops, museums, lovely colonial churches and music in the streets. With twisting streets of colorful old houses and gorgeous vistas over trees, church towers and red-tile roofs, this is one of the best-preserved and prettiest colonial towns in Brazil. The historic center has some lovely pousadas and good restaurants and bars, and makes a much more tranquil base than the bigger neighbor that stands towering in the distance.

Olinda was the original capital of Pernambuco, founded in 1535. Sacked and burnt with all its Catholic churches by the Calvinist Dutch in 1631, it was rebuilt but finally lost its ascendancy when Recife's merchants eclipsed Olinda's sugar barons in a bloody 18th-century feud called the Guerra dos Mascates. Although many Olinda buildings were originally constructed in the 16th century, most of what you see today dates from the 18th century and after. The whole picturesque historic center was declared a Unesco World Heritage site in 1982.

◉ Sights

Olinda's sights are easy and enjoyable to visit on a walking tour, although highly random opening hours make it impossible to look in on everything in one day.

A good place to start is Praça do Carmo, where most buses arrive. The plaza is overlooked by the recently restored **Igreja NS do Carmo** (Praça do Carmo) built in 1580. Up Rua de São Francisco, the large **Convento de São Francisco** (Rua de São Francisco 280; admission R$3; ◉8am-noon & 2-5pm Mon-Fri, 8am-noon Sat) contains the 16th-century **Igreja NS das Neves** and two later chapels, with rich baroque detailing and lovely *azulejos* (Portuguese ceramic tiles).

Climb up to Alto da Sé, which affords superb views of Olinda and Recife. The area is peppered with food, drink and craft stalls.

The imposing **Igreja da Sé** (◉8am-noon & 2-4:30pm), originally built in 1537, was burnt in 1631 and has been reconstructed four times since, most recently from 1974 to 1984 in a Mannerist style that revives the original 16th-century look. Check the touching inscription in simple Portuguese on the wooden door to the left inside the entrance.

Most other churches only open at mass or prayer times. The **Igreja da Misericórdia** (Rua Bispo Coutinho; ◉mass 6:20am Mon-Sat, 7:30am sun, prayers 11:45am-12:20pm Mon-Sat), built in 1540, has fine *azulejos* and gilded carvings. Head down Saldanha Marinho to see the restored 1613 **Igreja NS do Amparo** (◉mass 10am Sun), and then the **Igreja NS do Rosário dos Homens Pretos de Olinda** (Largo do Bonsucesso 45; ◉mass 6:30pm Sat), built by an African brotherhood in the 17th century.

On your way back southwards, the **Museu de Arte Contemporânea** (🖉3184-3153; Rua 13 de Maio 149; admission R$5; ◉9am-5pm Tue-Sun), in an 18th-century Inquisition jail, is recommended for both its permanent and temporary exhibits, while the **Museu do Mamulengo** (🖉3493-2753; Rua São Bento 344; admission R$2; ◉10am-5pm Tue-Sat) boasts a unique 1000-piece collection devoted to the Northeastern popular tradition of traveling puppet shows. The huge **Mosteiro de São Bento** (Rua São Bento; ◉8-11:30am & 2:15-5:30pm Mon-Sat, 8-9:30am & 2:30-5pm Sun), originally built in 1582, has some exceptional woodcarving in its church, where Sunday morning mass (10am) is celebrated complete with Gregorian chants.

⮔ Courses

Angola Mãe   COURSE
(🖉3429-9503; angolamae@hotmail.com; Ilma Cunha 243; per 1½hr class R$15; ◉classes 9am & 7:30pm Mon, Wed & Fri, roda 6:30pm Sun) If you'd like to check out a capoeira school, Angola Mãe teaches the slower and more traditional Angola style. The *roda* is the circular formation within which capoeira is performed.

☞ Tours

While in Olinda you'll no doubt hear the offer '*Guia!*' ('Guide!'). The best guides are those accredited by the local guides association, the **Associação dos Condutores Nativos de Olinda** (ACNO; Av da Liberdade 68). They wear yellow shirts with their names on, and an ACNO tag, and the official charge

FORRÓ FOR ALL

Wherever you go in Northeast Brazil you'll often hear the strains of *forró* (fo-*hoh*), a simple country dance music that began life perhaps two centuries ago and ended up taking the country by storm in the 1990s. Originally played by just three musicians with an accordion, triangle and *zabumba* (a hand-held African drum), *forró* started out as music for popular dances in the Northeast, with simple lyrics speaking of the hard life of the countryside, the tribulations of love and the beauty of dance. The term actually encompasses several different musical styles and the dances that go with them – including the fast-paced *baião*, the even faster *arrasta-pé* and the slower *xote*.

Forró is danced in close couples with the man leading. At its simplest it's just two steps to the left and two to the right, but there are many variations and it's a good idea to take a class or two if you want to enjoy dancing *forró*.

The first icon of *forró* was Luiz Gonzaga (1912–89), from the small Pernambuco town of Exu. Known as O Rei do Baião (King of Baião), he was responsible for taking the sound of Pernambuco to the rest of the country, later influencing some internationally renowned Brazilian musicians. Despite his personal popularity, *forró* continued to be looked down on by the middle classes of São Paulo, Rio de Janeiro and other southern cities, as backwoods Northeastern music. Then in the 1990s some *forró* musicians modernized their sound, adding electric guitars, keyboards and drum sets. Forró became a national craze, filling a void for an upbeat music that's easily danced with a partner. Meanwhile the original accordion, triangle and *zabumba* style of *forró* has now enjoyed a comeback and goes by the name *forró pé-de-serra* (foot-of-the-hills *forró*).

for a tour of about two hours is R$50 for two to four people.

★ Festivals & Events

Olinda's Carnaval (carnaval.olinda.pe.gov.br) celebrations last a full 11 days and have a spontaneity, inclusiveness and great irreverence that you don't get in big-city Carnavals. 'Pre-Carnaval' events get going the Sunday before the normal Carnaval weekend, with the parade of the Virgens do Bairro Novo, a *bloco* of more than 400 'virgins' (men in drag) who are joined by up to 900,000 revellers. They start out at noon from Praça 12 de Março.

There are organized Carnaval events, including balls and gatherings of *maracatu* and *afoxé* dance-and-music groups, but everything else happens in impromptu fashion on the streets, where endless groups of fabulously costumed musicians and dancers work their way through packed throngs of revellers, who often dance along to the rhythms of *frevo*, samba, *maracatu*, *caboclinho* or *afoxé*. The euphoric atmosphere and the sheer fun have to be experienced to be believed. Another famous feature of Olinda's Carnaval is the *bonecos gigantes*, huge puppets representing historical, cultural and other figures. One Carnaval high point is the parade of the top-hatted Homem da Meia-Noite (Man of Midnight) *boneco*, who emerges on Largo do Bonsucesso at midnight on Carnaval Saturday night.

🛏 Sleeping

Book several months ahead for accommodations during Carnaval and be prepared for massive price hikes.

Albergue de Olinda HOSTEL $
(☎ 3429-1592; www.alberguedeolinda.com.br; Rua do Sol 233; dm/s/d R$38/75/100; 🖥 🛜 ⊛) Olinda's excellent HI hostel isn't on a colorful street, but offers modern installations, spotless, no-frills rooms and a sizable garden with a lovely pool, loungers, outdoor kitchen, and a stage where there's sometimes live music.

Pousada Bela Vista POUSADA $
(☎ 3429-3930; www.hotelbelavista.tur.br; Rua do Amparo 215; s R$90, d R$130-150; ⊛ 🛜 ⊛) A large colorful lobby-lounge leads through to three lower floors with 12 rooms and a pool, breakfast area, and terraces with views all the way to Recife. Stone walls lend the place a vaguely castlelike atmosphere. Rooms are decked in bright primary colors and all have air-con but some are small, windowless and claustrophobic.

Olinda

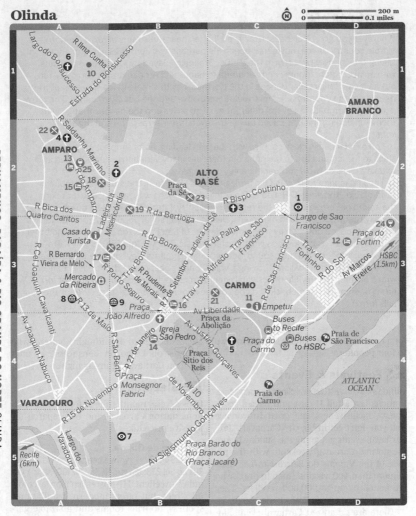

Pousada d'Olinda POUSADA $
(☑3493-6011; www.pousadadolinda.com.br; Praça João Alfredo 178; dm/s/d R$35/80/100, s/d with air-con R$100/115; ❄ 🖥 🕿) The cavernous lone dorm can get noisy, and the private rooms are nothing special, but the friendly management, middle-of-town location, big garden and pool, and R$29/kg self-service lunch make this spot a popular budget travelers' gathering place.

★**Pousada de São Pedro** POUSADA $$
(☑3439-9546; www.pousadapedro.com; Rua 27 de Janeiro 95; s/d/tr R$100/160/190; ❄ 🖥 🕿)

Charming and friendly, the São Pedro occupies a 19th-century house full of art, crafts and antiques and has a lovely pool in the leafy, shady garden. For a treat, request the top-floor *apartamento* (R$250) with picture windows, terrace with gorgeous views, and Jacuzzi bath. English, French and German spoken.

Pousada dos Quatro Cantos POUSADA $$
(☑3429-0220; www.pousada4cantos.com.br; Prudente de Morais 441; s R$222-455, d R$255-523; ❄ 🖥 🕿) High ceilings, tall windows, hardwood floors, lots of attractive art and a nice pool make this 19th-century house a delight-

Olinda

ful place to stay. While the cheapest (standard) rooms are quite acceptable, an extra R$50 will get you a much brighter, more characterful *luxo* abode. English spoken.

Pousada do Amparo POUSADA $$$
(☑ 3439-1749; www.pousadadoamparo.com.br; Rua do Amparo 199; r R$240-460; ❈ ⌖ ❈) The refined Amparo occupies two 18th-century houses with lovely gardens and views back toward Recife. It's full of character, very comfortable, has two excellent restaurants and will give you the full Olinda experience. English is spoken.

✖ Eating

A variety of good restaurants are tucked away among the old town's cobblestone streets. A great way to start an evening is with a tasty tapioca snack and a beer or caipirinha from the **tapioca stands** (Praça da Sé; snacks R$2-7; ◷ approx 6-11pm).

Estação Café CAFE $
(☑ 3429-7575; Prudente de Morais 440; R$9-30; ◷ 10am-10:30pm Tue-Sun) This artsy cafe is a perfect little pit stop for cappuccino, macchiato and light bites such as quiche, salad and crepes. There's free *chorinho* (samba-related instrumental music) at 7:30pm on Saturday.

Maison do Bomfim INTERNATIONAL $$
(☑ 8813-2008; Rua do Bonfim 115; mains R$28-56; ◷ 6pm-midnight Mon, noon-4pm Tue, noon-4pm & 6pm-1am Wed-Sat, noon-9pm Sun) A smart, French-run place that has been around more

than a decade, with nice arty decor and even better filet mignon, fish and prawns (there's pizza, too, but only for dinner). Service is friendly but isn't spawned from the same European gene.

Casa de Noca NORTHEASTERN $$
(Rua da Bertioga 243; mains for 2 R$50; ◷ 11am-11pm) For simple Northeastern food at its best, you can't beat this backyard restaurant which offers just one dish – large chunks of grilled *queijo coalho* (a light cheese) and slabs of surprisingly tender *carne de sol* (salted beef) atop a mountain of steamed *macaxeira*.

Creperia CREPERIE $$
(Praça João Alfredo 168; crepes R$6-32, pizza R$20-30; ☑) A nice spot for crepes, pizza and salads, which you can enjoy on a pleasant outdoor patio under tall bamboo trees.

★ Oficina do Sabor BRAZILIAN $$$
(☑ 3429-3331; www.oficinadosabor.com; Rua do Amparo 335; mains for 2 R$74-130; ◷ noon-4pm & 6pm-midnight Tue-Sat, noon-5pm Sun) With a specialty in baked pumpkin stuffed with assorted fillings – the shrimp, lobster and passion fruit sauce variety is fantastic – this is one of the Northeast's best restaurants, and worth every centavo. It's also great on seafood in general.

Beijupirá SEAFOOD $$$
(www.beijupira.com.br; Saldanha Marinho s/n; mains R$45-87; ◷ noon-midnight Wed-Mon) This romantic spot with views over Olinda's roofs is one of the region's best places for creative

WORTH A TRIP

CARUARU

The big **Festa de São João** (late May to late June; also called Festa Junina) at Caruaru (population 307,000), 137km west of Recife, is claimed to be Brazil's largest *forró* festival – 30 straight days of couples swaying to the accordion and triangle. But Caruaru is worth a visit at any time of year (possible in a long day trip from Recife) for its huge daily market, the **Feira de Caruaru** (Parque 18 de Maio; ⊘6am-5pm) – the biggest in the Northeast – and for the famous ceramic figurines made in Alto de Moura, 6km west of the center. The figurines, of brightly painted little people captured in activities such as dancing, chasing chickens and playing the *pífano* flute, follow in the tradition of Mestre Vitalino (1909–63), Caruaru's original ceramic-figurine genius.

The **Museu do Barro e do Forró** (☑081-3701-2545; Praça José de Vasconcellos; admission R$2; ⊘8am-5pm Tue-Sat, 9am-1pm Sun), in the center, is the best place to see original Mestre Vitalino pieces, and also holds every bit of memorabilia on Luiz Gonzaga, the father of *forró*, that it could get its hands on – including the pajamas he died in.

In Alto de Moura you can browse at dozens of workshops and galleries along Rua Mestre Vitalino: noted artists include Manuel Eudócio, Luiz Galdino and Luiz Antônio da Silva; good pieces sell for anything from R$20 to R$3000. The **Museu Casa do Mestre Vitalino** (☑081-3725-0805; Mestre Vitalino 281; admission free; ⊘8am-5:30pm Mon-Sat, to noon Sun) contains the master's tools, personal effects, and copies of some of his famous pieces. For lunch, head for **Bode Assado do Luciano** (☑081-3722-0413; Mestre Vitalino 511; mains for 2 R$25-40; ⊘11am-4pm Tue-Fri, to 6pm Sat-Sun), justifiably the most famous of the dozens of *churrascarias* (barbecued-meat restaurants) serving Alto de Moura's specialty, roast goat.

If you decide to stay, **Hotel Eduardo de Castro** (☑081-3724-8360; www.hotel-eduardodecastro.com.br; Amélia Maria da Conceição 148, Pinheirópolis; r R$122; ❋🐾🖳), a five-minute walk from Caruaru bus station, is decent value. Staff are friendly and rooms simple but clean, with modern air-conditioning.

Buses run at least hourly to Caruaru from Recife (R$19 to R$25, 1½ to two hours). Caruaru's **bus station** (☑081-3721-1930; Av José Pinheiro dos Santos s/n) is 3km southwest of the center, halfway between the center and Alto do Moura. It's easy to get a taxi, moto-taxi or local bus into town. To reach Alto de Moura from the center, catch a taxi (around R$25) or bus 135 (R$2) from Rua Duque de Caixas (next to the Catedral NS das Dores).

seafood. Try the shrimps in whisky and bechamel sauce with pineapple chunks, or the *beijucastanha* – a filet of the eponymous fish (cobia in English) in a chopped-cashew crust, served with spinach rice.

🍷 Drinking & Entertainment

Alto da Sé gets busy in the evening as locals and visitors buy drinks and snacks from the street vendors, watch capoeira and savor the view and the breeze. There's usually live samba, *chorinho* or other Brazilian rhythms somewhere in Olinda Wednesday to Saturday nights and Sunday afternoons – tourist offices have information. On Friday nights from 9pm strolling musicians make a circuit through town, joined in song by onlookers, in what's known as the *serenata* or *seresta*.

⭐**Bodega de Véio**　　　　　　BAR
(Rua do Amparo 212; ⊘9am-11pm Mon-Sat) Also a small and very eclectic general store, this wonderful little bar serves ice-cold bottled beer, shots of *cachaça* (potent sugarcane liquor) and great charcuterie plates (R$12), and tries its best to manage the crowds of locals and tourists congregating on the street and small terrace at the side. If you're running short of dental floss, spaghetti, catapults or violins, you can do your shopping right here.

A Fábrica Bar　　　　　　　BAR
(www.afabricabar.com; Praça do Fortim; ⊘5pm-4am Tue-Sun) This large, fun, popular, semi-open-air bar near the seafront has music of some kind every night it's open, including live samba from 7pm Wednesday and Friday.

Shopping

Olinda is full of small shops and galleries selling a plethora of art and artisanry such as ceramics, textiles, and wood and stone carvings. Much of the work is incredibly colorful and browsing these places is one of Olinda's great pleasures. The hub of the creative scene is Rua do Amparo, where many of the best artists and artisans have their homes, workshops and galleries.

ℹ Information

DANGERS & ANNOYANCES

Crime (mostly petty) exists, especially during Carnaval. Don't walk alone along deserted streets at night.

EMERGENCY

Tourist Police (☑3439-9696; Av Justino Gonçalves; ⊘24hr) Very helpful, English speaking.

INTERNET ACCESS

Empório do Carnaval (Prudente de Morais 483; per hr R$3.50; ⊘9am-5pm Mon-Sat, 9am-2pm Sun) Fast internet among Carnaval figures.

MONEY

There are no ATMs in the old town. The nearest one without serious clone risk is at **HSBC** (Av Getúlio Vargas 1050, Bairro Novo; ⊘9am-5pm Mon-Fri, ATMs 6am-10pm Mon-Fri), reachable by any 974 Jardim Atlântico bus heading north from the **post office** opposite Praça do Carmo.

TOURIST INFORMATION

Casa do Turista (☑3305-1060; www.olindaturismo.com.br; Prudente de Morais 472; ⊘9am-6pm) The municipal tourist information office has helpful staff, but little English. Its comprehensive website, however, is in English and Portuguese.

Empetur (☑3429-0244; Av da Liberdade s/n; ⊘8am-6pm) The state tourist info office has lovely, English-speaking staff.

ℹ Getting There & Away

Bus 910 Piedade/Rio Doce runs about every half-hour from Boa Viagem (any stop on Av Conselheiro Aguiar) to Olinda and back. The 983 Rio Doce/Princesa Isabel and 992 Pau Amarelo buses run from Terminal Cais de Santa Rita in central Recife to Olinda and back. All cost R$3.45. Olinda's main bus stop is in Praça do Carmo.

From Recife airport, you can take bus 042 outside arrivals to Terminal Cais de Santa Rita, then the 983 or 992 from there. But it's usually quicker to make the five-minute walk to Aeroporto metro station on Rua 10 de Julho (across a busy highway, though a pedestrian overpass was scheduled for 2014), take a 20-minute metro ride to the central Recife station (also called Estação Central; R$1.60), and then a 992 Pau Amarelo bus to Olinda (about every 15 minutes) from Rua Floriano Peixoto outside the station.

From Recife bus station, again take the metro to the central Recife station and then a 992 Pau Amarelo bus.

Taxis to Olinda cost around R$30 from Boa Viagem, R$50 from Recife bus station and R$60 from the airport. Add about 20% between 10pm and 6am.

Beaches South of Recife

South of the big city, the sea is calm, the waters are clear and the beaches are lined with coconut palms. Porto de Galinhas, 70km from Recife, has morphed into one of the most popular resorts in the Northeast. Further south, Tamandaré is less frenetic.

Porto de Galinhas

☑OXX81 / POP 10,000

Twenty years ago, Porto de Galinhas (Port of Chickens) was just another fishing village at the end of a dirt road, with a palm-fringed beach and a few Recifenses' holiday homes. Today it's one of Brazil's booming beach destinations, with several large resort hotels strung along Praia Muro Alto and Praia do Cupe, north of the center, and dense festive crowds flocking here at holiday times. Pedestrianizing the few streets that make up the town center, where the odd restaurant opens right on to the beach, has preserved some village ambience. Beautiful white-sand beaches stretch several kilometers in both directions from the town.

The town gets its name from the period between 1853 and 1888, when the slave trade, but not slavery itself, was illegal in Brazil, and ships would land here loaded with crates of chickens (*galinhas*) as cover for their human cargo. Today, sculptures of brainless-looking chickens dotted round town are a tasteless reminder of the past.

The **tourist information office** (☑3552-1728; Beijupirá; ⊘9am-8pm) and **Banco do Brasil** (Beijupirá; ⊘9am-3pm, ATMs 6am-10pm) sit opposite each other on the inland street Beijupirá.

🏊 Activities

Porto's fisherfolk have mostly given up fishing and now ferry tourists out to the **piscinas naturais** (tide pools) in the coral reefs,

100m in front of the main beach. Clusters of their triangular-sailed *jangadas* (boats) on the aquamarine waters are Porto's main postcard image. Take a snorkel to scrutinize the abundant marine life in these pools. The 45-minute outing costs R$15 per person and you can rent a snorkel and mask from most accommodations for around R$7.

The breezes are often good for windsurfing and kitesurfing off Pontal de Maracaípe, 4km south of town at the far end of Praia de Maracaípe, especially from June to September. Diving is also an option: for professionalism and high safety standards, the PADI Dive Resort **Aicá Diving** (☑3552-1895; www.aicadiving.com.br; Rua Beijupirá 1001; ☻8am-5pm) is recommended. Best visibility is October to March.

🛏 Sleeping

Apart from the many options in town, consider lodging at quieter Praia Maracaípe, a much broader, longer and less crowded beach 3km south.

Hostel Maracabana　　　　　HOSTEL $
(☑3552-2963; hostelmaracabana@gmail.com; Rua Sertânia, Maracaípe; dm/d R$50/150; ✳🎜) Set behind Praia Maracaípe, this new hostel looks and feels like a good hotel. There are spacious common areas including a big roof terrace, spotlessly white private rooms, and air-con dorms with floor rugs and reading lights for each good solid wooden bunk. It provides an excellent breakfast. Another good Maracaípe option is the cozy **Pousada Maleleo** (☑9928-2489; pousadamaleleo@hotmail.com; Praia de Maracaípe; r R$260-280; ✳@🎜).

Pousada A Casa Branca　　　HOSTEL $
(☑3552-2332; www.pousadaacasabranca.com.br; Praça 18, Loteamento Recanto Porto de Galinhas; dm with/without air-con R$50/45, d with/without air-con R$150/140; ✳@🎜) Galinhas' HI hostel is a few hundred meters back from the town beach, but sits on a quiet plaza and is one of the few decent budget options. It's well kept, with separate-sex dorms, and CCTV for security.

Pousada Beira Mar　　　　POUSADA $$
(☑3552-1052; www.pousadabeiramar.com.br; Av Beira Mar 12; r R$190-290; ✳🎜) In a great location right on the beach in the middle of town, comfortable Beira Mar offers worthwhile discounts in the low season. It's Swiss-owned, multilingual, GLS friendly, and has a coffee machine to boot.

🍴 Eating

Famed for its seafood, Porto de Galinhas has several good eateries. The beach bars serve inexpensive, fresh crabs.

Churrasco Gaúcho　　　　SELF-SERVE $
(2nd fl, Rua da Esperança 400; per kg R$23, buffet R$29; ☻10am-11pm) A great-value option for a meaty fill-up, with a large buffet of salad, seafood and more, plus a *rodízio de carne* (waiters come round offering one meat item after another).

Peixe na Telha　　　　　SEAFOOD $$
(☑3552-1323; www.peixenatelha.com.br; Av Beira Mar 40B; mains for 2 R$45-130; ☻10am-4pm & 6:30-10pm) The excellent fish dishes at this longstanding seafooder are served in orange roof tiles *(telhas)* and staff can bring them right down to the sand. There's live music every afternoon.

Munganga Bistrô　　　　SEAFOOD $$$
(☑3552-2480; www.mungangabistro.com.br; Rua Piscinas Naturais 32; mains R$40-109; ☻noon-11pm Tue-Sat, noon-5pm Sun) This creative, part openair, beachside seafood restaurant serves exceptional fish (try the yummy Terra Mar) as well as risottos and paellas for four people.

🍷 Drinking & Nightlife

Luz de Limão　　　　　　LOUNGE
(☑8411-9080; Rua Piscinas Naturais; cocktails R$5.50-16; ☻11am-11pm) Run by Italians, Luz de Limão is a trendy lounge with plush sofas, groovy tunes and Asian-inspired carpets.

Birosca　　　　　　　　CLUB
(☑3552-2699; www.biroscadacachaca.com.br; Rua Beijupirá; ☻10pm-late Mon-Sat) Billing itself a 'dancing bar and *cachaçaria*,' Birosca has been packing in sweat-soaked Pernambucans for over a decade to groove to *brega* (Northeastern pop), funk, techno and other rhythms.

ⓘ Getting There & Around

Bus 195 (R$11, two hours) leaves central Recife's Terminal Cais de Santa Rita hourly from 5:30am to 4:30pm and at 7:30pm and 8:30pm, heading to Porto de Galinhas via Boa Viagem (Av Domingos Ferreira) and Recife airport (outside the arrivals hall). In the other direction, buses leave Porto de Galinhas hourly from 5:10am to 7:10pm, stopping at the airport and along Av Conselheiro Aguiar in Boa Viagem.

Coming from the south, get off your bus at Ipojuca, where buses and vans run to Porto de Galinhas (R$2.20, 45 minutes) about every half-hour.

Buses and vans to Maracaípe (R$2.20, 10 minutes) stop every 15 to 30 minutes at the gas station on the corner of Rua Esperança and highway PE-009 in Porto. You can also take a moto-taxi (R$4), buggy (R$10 to R$15) or taxi (R$20).

Tamandaré

☑ 0XX81 / POP 16,000

Tamandaré, 30km south of Porto de Galinhas (57km by road), is a small, far less hyper beach town boasting a big stretch of coastline – 16km of lovely palm-fringed beaches. Fishing boats will take you out to the tidal pools here for R$15 per person. Eight kilometers north up the beach, fashionable and ultrarelaxed **Praia dos Carneiros** is one of Northeast Brazil's loveliest strands. Never very crowded, it has wonderful calm, clear, shallow waters, fine sand shaded by coconut palms, and tidal pools formed by a rocky bar stretching across the wide mouth of the Rio Formoso.

Tamandaré itself has plenty of places to stay. **Pousada Recanto dos Corais** (☑ 3676-2155; www.pousadarecantodoscorais.com.br; Hermes Samico 317; r R$90-120; ✳ 🛜) is run by a welcoming, German-speaking, southern Brazilian couple and has comfy, spotless little rooms and a good breakfast. There's a two-night minimum stay at weekends. Upping the cutesy quotient is **Pousada Beira Mar** (☑ 3676-1567; www.pousadabeiramartamandare.com; Almirante Tamandaré 140; s R$100, d R$160-180; ✳ 🛜), with bright, design-forward rooms and well-manicured lawn right on the beach. Austrian-run **Quiosque Pimenta Rosa** (☑ 8648-3806; Rua São José 17; items R$3-60; ☺ 8am-late) is the best of the long line of beach kiosks, serving *caldinho* (spicy bean soup) and fresh fish. Italian-owned **Pizzaria do Farol** (☑ 3676-2676; Av Dr Leopoldo Lins; pizza R$12-33; ☺ 7-11pm) serves thin and authentic brick-oven pizza.

Praia dos Carneiros is lined with private coconut groves, and beach access is only via a few fairly expensive beach lodgings and restaurants. Any of the restaurants make a fine base for a day of swimming, snorkeling, snoozing and strolling. **Sítio da Prainha** (☑ 3676-1681; www.sitiodaprainha.com.br; s R$330-410, d R$380-460, incl dinner; ✳ @ ⊠), at the far northern end, where the Rio Ariquindá spills into the Formoso, is a very tranquil choice, with quite luxurious bungalows, a good restaurant and a bar. The two-story chalets of **Pontal dos Carneiros** (☑ 3465-0055; www.pontaldoscarneiros.com.br; d Mon-Fri R$413, Sat-Sun

R$590; ✳ 🛜) are the super-luxury accommodation option, and the area's best restaurant, **Beijupirá** (www.beijupira.com.br; mains R$46-86; ☺ 9am-5pm), is next door. Between Prainha and Pontal, **Bangalôs do Gameleiro** (☑ 3676-1421; www.praiadoscarneiros.com.br; d R$250-400; ✳) is Carneiros' least expensive lodging: its 12 cosy brick-and-tile cottages, most with kitchen, are spaced among the palms.

❶ Getting There & Away

The majority of tourists, especially those without cars, visit Tamandaré on a day trip from Porto de Galinhas. Traveling independently, you need to take a bus from Galinhas to Ipojuca, and another from there to Tamandaré. Approaching Tamandaré, most buses pass the turnings to the accommodations and restaurants along Praia dos Carneiros, 500m to 1km off the road. Some are signposted. **Cruzeiro** (☑ 2101-9000) runs **buses to Tamandaré** (Map p484; R$14 three hours) from southern Av Dantas Barreto in central Recife at 10am and 5:40pm Monday to Saturday, and 7:30am Sunday. They head back from Tamandaré at 5:20am and 2:20pm (4pm on Sunday).

Coming north up Hwy PE-060 from Alagoas, get off your bus at Barreiros, where buses and vans to Tamandaré (R$3.30, 40 minutes) leave about every half-hour till 8pm.

Moto-taxis cost R$7 from Tamandaré to Praia dos Carneiros.

Fernando de Noronha

☑ 0XX81 / POP 2630

While religion, science and philosophy continue to battle out what happens when we die, in Brazil there is little discourse on the subject: heaven plays second fiddle to the 21-island Fernando de Noronha archipelago. Located in the Atlantic, 525km from Recife and 350km from Natal, Noronha's natural beauty holds its own against any tropical locale in the world. With crystal-clear waters, rich marine life and spectacular tropical landscapes, it's in a Brazilian class all by its lonesome. The country's 'Beach bible,' *Guia Quatro Rodas Praias,* awards five stars to just five beaches in the whole country – and one, two and three are right here.

Give yourself plenty of time because Noronha is addictive. It's a great place for doing things both water-based (diving, surfing, snorkeling) and on land (horseback riding, hiking, touring), and the average stay is four to five nights. Thanks mostly to the **Parque Nacional Marinho de Fernando de Noronha**

Fernando De Noronha

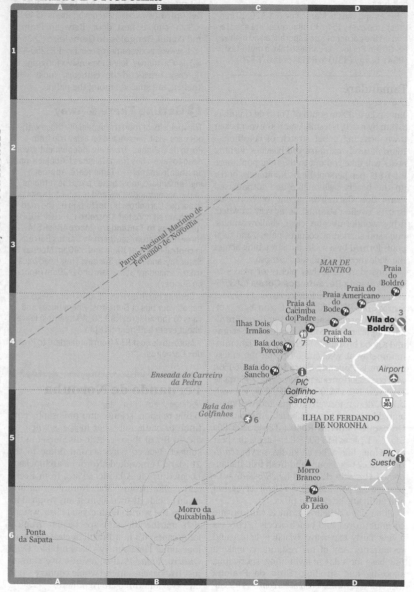

(Fernando de Noronha National Marine Park; www.parnanoronha.com.br) ✐ and conservation projects based here, the marine and coastal environment is tightly regulated: locals joke that it's the island of 'No' – no you can't do this, no you can't do that.

With only about 270 plane seats per day normally available to Noronha, tourism doesn't overwhelm the islands, and it's rarely a problem to find an isolated patch of sand on a dreamy beach, even in high season. However, it's advisable to reserve

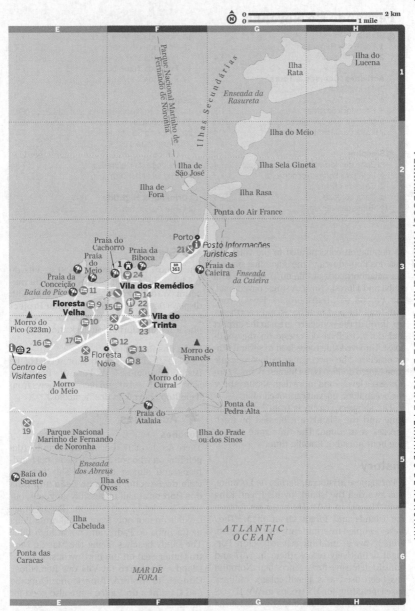

accommodations and flights well ahead for December, January, February, July and August. The week or so either side of New Year can get booked up six months in advance.

Paradise comes at a cost: due to the price of transporting goods from the mainland, prices are surreal and rooms cost about double what you'd pay on the mainland. But as a guaranteed highlight of any trip to Brazil, Fernando de Noronha is worth the expense.

The largest and only inhabited island, Ilha de Fernando de Noronha, is 10km long, with

Fernando De Noronha

its population concentrated in the village of Vila dos Remédios and the adjoining, spread-out neighborhoods of Vila do Trinta, Floresta Velha and Floresta Nova. A single paved road, the BR-363 (or Transnoronha Hwy!), runs 7km from the port near the island's northeast tip, through the populated area, to the airport and down to Baía do Sueste on the south coast. Unpaved side roads lead to several other beaches. The spectacular extinct volcanic cone Morro do Pico is the highest point, 323m above sea level – and more than 4300m above the ocean floor. no, you cannot climb it.

The showery season is from February to June and the islands are blessed by fresh breezes year round. The time zone here is one hour ahead of Brasília time.

History

A Portuguese aristocrat, Fernão de Loronha, was awarded the islands by his friend King Dom Manoel in 1504. He never set foot on the islands and forgot about them. They were occupied intermittently by the English, French (twice) and Dutch (twice) before Portugal definitively retook them in 1737 and built 10 defensive forts. Since then, Noronha has been used as a penal colony, military base (including for US troops in WWII), US missile-tracking station and, now, a tourist destination. A struggle between developers and environmentalists over their future was resolved in 1988 when 75% of the archipelago, including much of the main island and its surrounding waters, was declared a marine national park. It was included on the Unesco World Heritage list in 2002.

⊙ Sights

The Centro de Visitantes (p508) at Vila do Boldró includes a small open-air **turtle museum** (Vila do Boldró; admission free; ⊙24hr) with displays on sea turtles by the **Tamar Project** (☎3619-1171; www.tamar.org.br; Vila do Boldró) ⚑, plus a Tamar information desk and shop.

Forte dos Remédios   FORT
(⊙24hr) FREE Easily the best preserved of the island's Portuguese forts, Forte dos Remédios is well worth a visit and has great views from its hilltop above Vila dos Remédios.

🕺 Activities
Beaches
There are 16 or 17 beaches on Noronha (depending on who you ask), all clean, postcard-ready and almost deserted. The 'five-star' **Baía do Sancho**, **Praia do Leão** and **Baía dos Porcos** are all impossibly gorgeous, but there is a lot of competition. (Porcos is accessible on foot only from neighboring Praia da Cacimba do Padre, and not at high tide.) The sandy beaches facing the Mar de Dentro (Inner Sea) on the northwest side of the island – **Cachorro** (at Vila dos Remédios), **Conceição**, **Boldró**, **Americano**, **Quixaba** and **Cacimba do Padre** – are also good for surfing.

Access to beaches in the national park is closed off from 6:30pm to 8am. **Praia do Atalaia**, which has shallow tide pools great for snorkeling, can only be accessed by a guided hike.

Baía dos Golfinhos is strictly off-limits to swimmers and all watercraft.

Boat Tours

A number of boats make enjoyable daily three-hour tours from the Porto (port), along the main island's northwest coast and back. Spinner dolphins like to swim and perform acrobatics near the boats, and a 40-minute snorkeling stop at Baía do Sancho is normally part of the trip. **Naonda** (☑ 3619-1307; barconaonda@hotmail.com) is a recommended boat, and one of the least expensive at R$100 per person; for R$30 more you can add 30 minutes' *planasub* (snorkeling while being slowly towed along by the boat). For a trip of about four hours with *planasub* and lunch both included (R$150), **Trovão dos Mares II** (☑ 3619-1228) is recommended. Prices include pickup and drop-off at your accommodation.

Diving

With 30m to 40m of visibility (at its very best in October), beautifully warm seas, a well-preserved underwater environment and abundant marine life from iridescent fish to spinner dolphins and giant sea turtles, diving around Noronha is world class. There are 230 fish species, 15 coral varieties and five types of (harmless) shark. For certified divers, a two-tank dive including transfers and all equipment normally costs R$384/404 with cash/credit card. Open Water courses are R$2141/2252 and *batismo* (baptism) dives for first-timers are R$350/368.

★ **Atlantis Divers**   DIVING
(☑ 3206-8840; www.atlantisdivers.com.br; Praça dos Remedios, Vila dos Remédios) 🏄 French-run, highly professional, and a committed member of Abeta, Brazil's only ecotourism and adventure-tourism standards association.

Águas Claras   DIVING
(☑ 3619-1225; www.aguasclaras-fn.com.br; Alameda do Boldró, Vila do Boldró) Friendly PADI National Geographic Dive Center, based near the Centro de Visitantes (p508).

Snorkeling

There are simply hundreds of good places to snorkel on the islands, from the rocks in Baía do Sancho (where harmless lemon sharks are often present) to the tranquil tide pools of Atalaia, or Baía do Sueste where you can swim with turtles at high tide (local guides accompany you for R$30). Snorkel gear can be rented for R$10 to R$20 per day in the village, at the harbor and at Baía do Sueste.

Dolphin Watching

From the cliff-top lookout **Mirante dos Golfinhos** you can watch an average of over 300 spinner dolphins cavorting in Baía dos Golfinhos from 6:30am. Trainee biologists provide Portuguese commentary from Monday to Saturday.

Hiking

Most trails within the national park can only be walked with a local guide. A great one runs from Vila do Trinta to **Praia do Atalaia**, where there's good snorkeling in tidal pools (no flippers or sunscreen allowed) – about two hours there and back. Portuguese-language guides (there are about 100 on the island) charge R$40 to R$60 per person, usually with a two-person minimum, for this trip. With an extension from Atalaia to Praia da Caieira (with more tidal pools and the last 2km on tough volcanic rock) the walk lasts about 4½ hours and costs R$50 to R$80 per person. Fábio from Pirata Passeios (p508) does these walks in English or Italian for R$75 per person (Atalaia only) or R$150 (including Caieira). Another recommended English-speaking guide is biologist **Lisandro de Almeida** (☑ 3619-1539; lisandro@atairubrasil. com.br); he charges R$80 (R$120 including Caieira).

Surfing

Praia da Cacimba do Padre is the most famous surfing beach here and it hosts surf festivals or championships during the December to March season. Waves can reach 5m in height. Other surfing beaches on the Mar de Dentro, including Boldró and Bode, are also good, and in a big swell there are some thrilling waves among the Ilhas Secundárias. **Locadora SolyMar** (Rua São Miguel, Vila dos Remédios; boards per day R$30-50; ⊙ 7am-9pm) rents boards.

🛏 Sleeping

Noronha has around 150 pousadas, from the very basic to very luxurious. Most are in the Remédios/Trinta/Floresta area and only a handful have sea views. It's highly advisable to book ahead, and essential for the dozen or so most-luxurious places (charging R$500-plus) except maybe in May and June. Some places require 100% credit-card prepayment and a scan or photo of your passport. Most places include airport transfers in their rates.

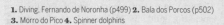

1. Diving, Fernando de Noronha (p499) 2. Baía dos Porcos (p502)
3. Morro do Pico 4. Spinner dolphins

Fernando de Noronha

For many Brazilians a trip to the archipelago, 350km out into the Atlantic from Natal, is the holiday of a lifetime. What is it that makes this former penal colony and military base, comprising one medium-sized and 20 small islands, so magnetic?

The Beauty

Small-scale but majestic, the combination of long sandy strands, lush vegetation, towering rock pinnacles and ocean rollers breaking on dramatic rocky cliffs and islets has few parallels on the planet.

The Conservation

Much of the archipelago's land and sea areas are a strictly regulated national park, so fauna, flora, landscape and the marine environment are protected from the effects of over development. Visitor numbers are restricted so there is always plenty of space, and active conservation organizations zealously protect its dolphin and turtle populations.

The Beaches

The main island's 17 or so sandy bays are some of Brazil's most beautiful, mostly backed by thickly vegetated slopes or cliffs, and all fronted by wonderfully warm, clear waters. Some are protected by promontories or picturesque offshore islands and ideal for swimming and snorkeling; others have sets of ocean breakers rolling in and are a dream for surfers.

The Diving & Snorkeling

With 30m-plus visibility, beautifully warm seas and abundant marine life including big creatures such as turtles, dolphins and (harmless) sharks, the diving around Noronha is Brazil's best. For the same reasons, snorkeling is fantastic too.

Casa do Joab
HOMESTAY **$$**

(☑3619-1267; dricaschmidt@gmail.com; Praia da Conceição; s/d R$200/350; ✳@🖤) Local workhorse Joab and his wife Mônica have slowly turned their simple home into a friendly and tasteful choice that sits steps from Conceição beach – something no other pousada can boast. Three of the four rooms have sea views, and Morro do Pico looms close by. If Mônica happens to whip up her famous *pudim de leite* (sweet condensed-milk flan), you won't even care about the scenery.

Pousada Golfinho
POUSADA **$$**

(☑3619-1837; pousadagolfinhofn.jimdo.com; São Miguel 144, Vila dos Remédios; s/d R$100/160; ✳🖤) This friendly place is the best value-for-money budget pousada. No breakfast but you can use the kitchen and washing machine for free.

Casa de Mirtes
HOMESTAY **$$**

(☑3619-1792; www.facebook.com/casa.demirtes; Antônio Alves Cordeiro 457, Floresta Velha; dm/d R$75/170) Simple, clean accommodation in a welcoming private home. You can use the kitchen and garden barbecue. No English spoken but you can reserve through Your Way (p508).

Beijupirá Lodge Noronha
POUSADA **$$$**

(☑3619-1250; www.beijupiralodgenoronha.com.br; Amaro Preto, Floresta Velha; r R$690-1180; ✳🖤) 🌿 Seven-room Beijupirá has an intimate, comfortable, cottagey feel with all sorts of tasteful art and knick-knacks dotted about. Meals are from the same recipe book as the owners' fine seafood restaurants in Olinda and Porto de Galinhas, and there's a lovely big garden with great Morro do Pico views.

Beco de Noronha
POUSADA **$$$**

(☑3619-1568; www.becodenoronha.com.br; Alameda das Acácias 3, Floresta Nova; r R$522-697; ✳🖤) 🌿 With quaint eco-artisanal touches (like short pathways made of upturned bottles) and charmingly helpful staff, wood-built Beco is a good choice for a comfortable stay in a central location on the island.

Pousada do Vale
POUSADA **$$$**

(☑3619-1293; www.pousadadovale.com; Pescador Sérgio Lino 18, Vila dos Remédios; s R$558-828, d R$792-1026; ✳@🖤) Intimate Vale is one of the friendliest and most service-oriented pousadas on the island. Rooms aren't as high-end as the prices suggest, but are bright and well-appointed with design-forward touches like *mantas nordestinas* (colorful

throws). The free fish barbecue dinner on Thursdays helps keep the camaraderie level high between locals and guests.

Pousada Mar Aberto
POUSADA **$$$**

(☑3619-1178; www.pousadamaraberto.com.br; Alameda das Flores 2, Floresta Nova; s/d R$310/392; ✳🖤) Noronha's 'upscale' neighborhood, Floresta Nova, has plenty of midrange-quality pousadas dotted along its streets. Mar Aberto is one of the best, with English-speaking management, pleasant wood-and-brick rooms with quiet air-con, and a long, airy veranda. Also recommended in this area, and a bit less expensive, are **Pousada Alamoa** (☑3619-1839; www.pousadaalamoa.com; Alameda das Acácias, Floresta Nova; s/d R$22/340; ✳🖤) and the fiercely nonsmoking **Pousada Algas Marinhas** (☑3619-1341; www.pousadaalgasmarinhas.com.br; Alameda das Flores 118, Floresta Nova; r R$280; ✳🖤).

Pousada Teju-açu
POUSADA **$$$**

(☑3619-1277; www.pousadateju.com.br; Estrada da Alamoa, Boldró; r R$1141-1230; ✳@🖤🏊) Almost underneath Morro do Pico, Pousada Teju-Açu is a well managed, fun-designed pousada with a good restaurant, spacious, quite stylish rooms (tiny bathrooms but huge beds) and a pleasant wood-decked pool area.

Pousada Zé Maria
POUSADA **$$$**

(☑3619-1258; www.pousadazemaria.com.br; Nice Cordeiro 1, Floresta Velha; s R$798-1958, d R$838-2418; ✳@🖤🏊) Luxurious Zé Maria boasts a stunning view of the Morro do Pico from its pool and is famed Brazil-wide for its over-the-top, all-you-can-eat R$153 seafood buffet spectacle on Wednesday and Saturday evenings (reservations highly advisable). Owner Zé Maria catches about half the fish himself.

Eating

Açaí e Raízes Noronha
CAFE **$**

(☑3619-0058; BR-363, Floresta Nova; items R$7-22; ⏱8am-11:30pm; 🖤) Locals and tourists people-watch from the veranda of this store that's good for *açaí*, tapiocas and fresh sandwiches. It's one of the best spots to pick up the island's free wi-fi signal.

Pizzaria Namoita
PIZZERIA **$$**

(☑3619-1914; BR-363, Vila do Trinta; pizza R$35-55; ⏱7-11pm Fri-Wed) São Paulo emigré Mauricio Vilela does his best to recreate *pizza paulistana* and does a fine job considering Noronha logistics. Favorites like *cearense* (spicy ground sausage with chillis and moz-

ⓘ NORONHA FEES

Visitors to Fernando de Noronha have to pay two special charges. The state government environmental preservation tax, known as the TPA, is R$45.60 per day for the first four days, then goes up by varying amounts for each extra day: a one-week/two-week/four-week stay costs, in total R$283/752/3226 at 2013 rates. You pay by cash or credit card on arrival at the airport. If you decide to stay longer than planned, go to the airport between 11am and 5pm at least one day before your original departure date and pay for your extra days – otherwise you'll pay double.

The second charge is the national park entry fee (you're almost certain to enter the national park while here). The fee for up to 10 days is R$65 for Brazilians and R$130 for foreigners; you get a plastic card with your name on it to prove you've paid. It can be paid in cash (R$, US$ or euros) or by credit card at a **kiosk** (Bosque Flamboyant, Vila dos Remédios; ⊘8am-10pm) in Vila dos Remédios, or at the Centro de Visitantes (p508) at Vila do Boldró, or at two Postos de Informações e Controle (PICs) at park entrances: **PIC Golfinho-Sancho** (⊘8am-6:30pm) and **PIC Sueste** (⊘8am-6:30pm). Take your passport when you pay. A third PIC is to be built at Praia do Leão. It is possible to buy the card with cash *reais* at the port from 7am to 9am if you are diving or on a boat tour.

zarella) are served in an atmospheric setting under a giant cashew tree in his front yard.

O Pico
FUSION $$

(BR-363, Floresta Velha; dishes R$12-54; ⊘noon-3pm & 6-11pm) Pico serves very tasty light meals such as its felafel wrap, ceviches, burgers and tapiocas, plus wine and other drinks – and it's also an art and crafts shop with original Northeastern wares.

Empório São Miguel
SELF-SERVE $$

(☑3619-1859; Bosque Flamboyant, Vila dos Remédios; per kg R$41.90; ⊘11:30am-4pm) The best of a few per-kilo lunch places in Remédios; it also has some good à la carte fare.

★Palhoça da Colina
SEAFOOD $$$

(☑3619-1473; www.palhocadacolina.com; Estrada da Colina, Vila do Trinta; meals R$100; ⊘from 8:30pm) The single most memorable dining experience on the island: a feast under an atmospheric *palapa* hut with tatami mats and pillows, in the yard of a local home. All-you-can-eat grilled catch of the day (barracuda, tuna, mackerel) is served on banana leaves with great side dishes such as arugula-and-mango salad, and banana *farofa* (sautéed manioc flour). There's a maximum of 20 people per night; reservations are essential, ideally the previous day.

Mergulhão
MEDITERRANEAN $$$

(☑3619-0215; Porto; mains R$47-75; ⊘noon-11pm Mon-Sat; ☑) Mergulhão makes use of its breezy site with stupendous views over the port, while the Mediterranean menu with a Brazilian twist is one of Noronha's most innovative. Try the *peixe crocante* – crispy fish

stuffed with shrimp, cheese and palm hearts – or a vegetarian or seafood risotto or pasta. There's wine, and boutique Colorado beers.

Ekologiku's
SEAFOOD $$$

(☑3619-1807; Antiga Vila DPV; mains for 2 R$110-120; ⊘7-10:30pm) Kitchen staff trained by a sassy Bahian oversees this consistently good seafood restaurant beyond the airport. It serves up superb *moquecas capixabas* (seafood stews made with olive oil instead of palm oil) in a surprisingly tropical-cool space considering its remote location. If you're at least a group of four, they'll send a free transfer; otherwise, taxis are R$25 each way.

🍺 Drinking & Entertainment

Bar do Cachorro
BAR

(Vila dos Remédios; ⊘noon-midnight) The famous open-air Dog Bar is the hub – in fact the only locale – of Noronha nightlife, busy every night but really packed Thursday through Sunday. There's music for dancing from around 10:30pm, including live *forró* on Wednesdays and a good samba group on Saturdays.

Bar Duda Rei
BAR

(Praia da Conceição; ⊘10am-sunset) Noronha's only real beach bar has a fabulous setting beneath a couple of palms, with Morro do Pico towering behind. It serves food, too.

ⓘ Information

INTERNET ACCESS

Noronha has free island-wide wi-fi, but signals vary greatly depending on location, and speeds are painfully slow. Fortunately most pousadas have their own better setups.

Cia da Lua (☑ 3619-1631; Bosque Flamboyant, Vila dos Remédios; wi-fi per 3hr R$15; ⊘ 9am-11pm) A decent signal from a private provider.

INTERNET RESOURCES

Fernando de Noronha (www.noronha.pe.gov. br) The island government site has every detail imaginable.

MEDICAL SERVICES

Hospital São Lucas (☑ 3619-0923; Bosque Flamboyant, Vila dos Remédios)

MONEY

ATMs at the airport and the Centro de Visitantes accept international cards, but they can run out of cash at weekends, so it's best to bring some with you.

TOURIST INFORMATION

National park information is available from the **Centro de Visitantes** (Vila do Boldró; ⊘ 8am-10pm), PIC Golfinho-Sancho (p507) and PIC Sueste (p507).

Posto Informacões Turisticas (Porto; ⊘ 8am-6pm) Pick up a map at this tourist info booth above the port. There's another booth in the airport arrivals hall.

TRAVEL AGENCIES

Pirata Passeios (☑ 9657-6427; piratanoronha@gmail.com; Pousada Aleffawi, BR-363, Vila do Boldró) Friendly Fábio 'Pirata' speaks English and Italian and is an experienced dive instructor. He specializes in hiking, island tours and budget accommodation bookings.

Your Way (☑ 011-99385-7705, 9949-1087; www.yourway.com.br) An indispensable contact on the island, this veteran ecotourism specialist is perfect for independent travelers of all budgets. Fluent English-speaker Adriana will help you find the best-value flights to the island and offers unbiased tips and bookings of accommodations, restaurants and activities – at no additional cost. Contact by email or phone.

ⓘ Getting There & Away

The **airport** (FEN; ☑ 3619-0950) sits in the middle of the main island. **Trip** (www.voetrip.com.br) and **GOL** (www.voegol.com.br) both fly Recife–Noronha–Recife daily; Trip also flies Natal–Noronha–Natal daily. Round-trip fares from either city normally range from R$800 to R$2000. Buy your ticket as early as you can. Your Way (p508) can usually find you the best deal.

GOL seats are available to their Brazil and South America airpass holders, but not to their Northeast Brazil airpass holders.

ⓘ Getting Around

A good bus service (R$3.10) runs the length of the BR-363 between the port, Vila dos Remédios, the airport and Baía do Sueste, about every 30 to 40 minutes from 6:30am to midnight. You'll see bus-stop signs along the road. Hitchhiking is safe and commonplace.

Taxis (some of which are buggies) have fixed rates from R$15 to R$37 depending on distance. The airport to Vila dos Remédios costs R$21.

A popular way to get around is to rent your own buggy. Rates for reliable vehicles are R$150 to R$250 per 24 hours, plus fuel (be aware: there is no insurance on the island for rental vehicles). Pousadas will usually organize a buggy for you, and all renters will deliver the buggy to you. You can also rent motorcycles, if you are licensed for one back home.

PARAÍBA

Sandwiched between Pernambuco and Rio Grande do Norte, the small, sunny state of Paraíba contains the easternmost point of the continent, Ponta do Seixas, where you are closer to Senegal than to southern Brazil. The tranquil, reasonably well-developed coast is this small state's most important economic region, fueled by the farming of sugarcane and pineapples, and some tourism. Cattle-ranching dominates the drought-affected interior, which also harbors some intriguing archaeological sites.

João Pessoa

☑ 0XX83 / POP 721,000

The coastal city of João Pessoa is the capital of Paraíba and the third-oldest city in Brazil. It claims to have more trees than any other capital city, including an Atlantic rainforest preserve, and has a reputation for being friendly and safe. It's an increasingly popular holiday destination for Brazilian families. The 20km-long beachfront is agreeably clean, low-key and low-rise (no buildings above four stories allowed), with the central beach neighborhoods of Tambaú, Manaíra and Cabo Branco being the best areas to base yourself. The historic center, 7km inland, is being steadily spruced up after being declared a National Heritage site in 2007, and makes for an interesting wander. All in all, 'John Person' is a very nice spot to break up a journey.

Central João Pessoa

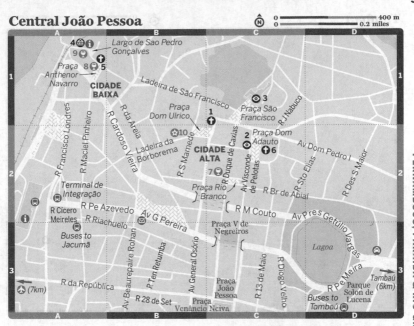

Bus travelers arrive on the western edge of the center, a little over 1km from Parque Solon de Lucena and its lake, called the Lagoa.

History

Founded in 1585, the city was formerly known as Vila de Felipéia de NS das Neves. It was renamed in the 20th century for João Pessoa, a governor of Paraíba who formed an alliance with Getúlio Vargas to run for the Brazilian presidency in 1930. When courted by opposing political parties, João Pessoa uttered a pithy *'nego'* (I refuse), which is now given prominence in all Brazilian history books and emblazoned in bold letters on the Paraíba state flag. The Vargas–Pessoa ticket lost the election, and Pessoa was assassinated a few months later – an event which, ironically, sparked a revolutionary backlash that swept Vargas to power later in 1930.

◉ Sights & Activities

◉ Tambaú & the Coast

Estação Cabo Branco   ARTS CENTER
(☑ 3214-8303; joaopessoa.pb.gov.br/estacaocb; Av João Cirilo Silva s/n; ◷ 9am-9pm Tue-Fri, 10am-9pm Sat & Sun) FREE Inaugurated in 2008, this cultural center 5km southeast of Tam-

Central João Pessoa

baú was designed by famed Brazilian architect Oscar Niemeyer and is more interesting for its space-age architecture than for the exhibits, which are often underwhelming, except for Abelardo da Hora's naked-women sculptures dotted around the grounds. The hexagonal glass main building provides great views from its top-floor terrace. Bus 507 runs here from Av Epitacio Pessoa in Tambaú.

Tambaú

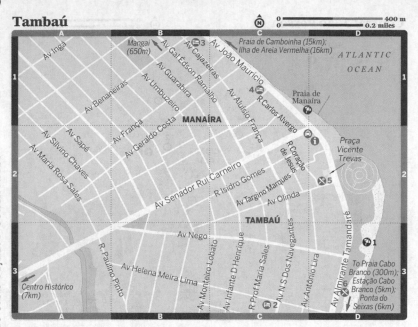

Tambaú

◎ Sights
1 Praia de Tambaú....................................D3

🛏 Sleeping
2 Pousada do Caju.................................C3
3 Slow Hostel..B1
4 Verdegreen Hotel................................C1

✖ Eating
5 Empório Café......................................D2
6 Giramundo...D3

Walk left out of the parking lot at the south end of the complex and down to the beach (two minutes) through the Parque Municipal do Cabo Branco, then head 600m south along the beach and you'll be at **Ponta do Seixas**, the easternmost point of the Americas.

Praia de Tambaú   BEACH
(Map p510) Praia de Tambaú, 7km east of the center, is an urban beach but an enjoyable area to spend time. Bars, restaurants, coconut palms, fig trees and a broad promenade are strung along the seafront. Southward, Praia Cabo Branco, a beautiful stretch of sand, cliffs and palms, curves 5km round to Cabo Branco and Ponta do Seixas.

Ilha de Areia Vermelha   BEACH
Ilha de Areia Vermelha is an island of red sand that emerges off the northern beaches at low tide about half the days in each month. Boats park around the island and the party lasts until the tide comes in. You can catch a boat out there for R$20 to R$25 from Praia de Camboinha, 15km north of Tambaú.

◉ Centro Histórico

Under the wing of Iphan (Brazil's national cultural heritage institute), many parts of João Pessoa's historic center have been attractively renovated, and the area makes for an enjoyable wander, with architectural styles ranging from baroque to art deco. Tourist offices have a useful walking-tour map to hand out. If you have time for only one site, make it the **Centro Cultural São Francisco** (Map p509; ☎ 3218-4505; Praça São Francisco; admission with guided tour R$4; ⊗9am-noon & 2-5pm), one of Brazil's most beautiful monasteries, built over two centuries (1589–1779). Its highlight, especially for the quantity of gold adorning its altars, is the Capela (Chapel) de la Ordem Terceira de São Francisco.

A short distance east of São Francisco, take a look at Praça Dom Adauto, where the beautifully blue-tiled **Casarão dos Azule-**

jos (Map p509; Av Visconde de Pelotas) faces an impressive complex of church buildings with the 16th-century **Igreja NS do Carmo** (Map p509; Praça Dom Adauto; ⊙9:30-11am Mon-Fri) at its center. Nearby Praça Dom Ulrico, with the **Basílica NS das Neves** (Map p509; Praça Dom Ulrico), and **Av General Osório** have some particularly prettily restored buildings. Westward, down in what's called the Cidade Baixa, head for the adjacent squares **Praça Anthenor Navarro** and **Largo de São Pedro Gonçalves**, both lined with pastel-colored buildings and dominated by the large 19th-century **Igreja de São Pedro Gonçalves** (Map p509). The **Hotel Globo** (Map p509; Largo de São Pedro Gonçalves 7; ⊙9am-5pm Mon-Fri, 9am-4pm Sat), built in 1928, houses a small museum and has a lovely rear terrace with views over tile roofs to the river.

✹ Festivals & Events

João Pessoa cuts loose in the **Folia da Rua** (Party in the Streets), the week before Carnaval proper (Friday to Friday), with *blocos* (music and dancing groups) parading through parts of the city, some attracting up to a million revellers.

⤙ Sleeping

★ Slow Hostel   HOSTEL $
(Map p510; ☑ 3021-7218; www.facebook.com/slowhostel; Av Cajazeiras 108, Manaíra; dm R$38-40; ☞) ✒ Excellent hostel with a friendly atmosphere in a spacious house one short block from the beach, run by the charmingly helpful Marina and her family. Most of the rooms (single-sex and mixed dorms and two privates) have private bathroom, common areas are spacious, there are bicycles to rent and optional activities including yoga classes. Marina adores her city and knows everything you could possibly want to ask about it.

Pousada do Caju   POUSADA $$
(Map p510; ☑ 2107-8700; www.grupocaju.com.br; Av Helena Meira Lima 269, Tambaú; s/d R$221/240; ✲☞✲) This professionally run guesthouse is two blocks from the beach and contains a pool, games area and several giant *caju* (cashew) trees. A recent makeover provides rooms with comfy beds and stone-faced walls, while common areas are adorned with all sorts of cute Brazilian accoutrements. Caju has seven other branches of varying quality and price within a few blocks.

Verdegreen Hotel   HOTEL $$$
(Map p510; ☑ 3044-0000; www.verdegreen.com.br; Av João Maurício 255, Manaíra; s R$297-347, d R$330-388; ✲☞✲) ✒ Verdegreen is the eco-conscious choice, with solar-heated showers, reforested wood, half-flush toilets, and LED TVs and lighting throughout. It's all very hip and stylish, too, decked out in soothing greens and beiges with tasteful art and *objets* scattered around. Staff are sweet and helpful, it's fully nonsmoking and has free bicycles for guests.

✗ Eating

Empório Café   CAFE $
(Map p510; ☑ 3247-0110; emporiocafejp.com.br; Coração de Jesus 145, Tambaú; R$7-20; ⊙2pm-last customer; ✐) This retro-indie cafe/bar dishes up great-value salads, sandwiches, quiches, hummus, cheese-and-meat platters – you name it, with loads of veggie options – to a beautiful crowd. As the evening wears on, it packs in more trend and beauty for cocktails and indie tunes.

★ Mangai   NORTHEASTERN $$
(☑ 3226-1615; www.mangai.com.br; Av General Édson Ramalho 696, Manaíra; per kg R$43.90; ⊙11am-10pm) Mangai's spectacular regional buffet is alone worth the stop in João Pessoa. Most items are labeled in English and there's plenty for vegetarians, as well as great meat and seafood dishes. Save room for some of the decadent desserts!

Giramundo   BRAZILIAN, GERMAN $$
(Map p510; ☑ 3226-2324; Av Almirante Tamandaré s/n, Tambaú; mains R$18-27; ⊙6pm-1am Mon-Sat) This wildly popular beach kiosk, a Swiss-Brazilian endeavor, is notable not only for the usual seafood and meat offerings but also for its grilled bratwurst, *kalbsbratwurst* (veal sausage), *schublig* (pork and beef) sausages and Eisenbahn microbrews – none of which are often seen north of Santa Catarina.

♬ Drinking & Entertainment

The historic center has a lively nocturnal scene with some good bars and music venues attracting students, their teachers and an informal, arty crowd. Saturday is the big party day, kicking off with an open-air *chorinho* (instrumental music) session in Praça Rio Branco from around noon to 3pm. Then people move onto a jam session at nearby **Cachaçaria Philipéia** (Map p509; Beco da Philipéia 39; ⊙2-8pm Mon-Sat), an atmospherically old-fashioned little bar serving *caldinho* and many *cachaça* varieties for around R$2 a shot. From here you can head down to the sunset party at **Vila do Porto** (Map p509; ☑ 8791-7786; www.facebook.com/espacoviladoporto; Largo de São Pedro Gonçalves 8; ☉ 11am-11pm Tue-Sat, 3-11pm Sun), a restaurant/bar and courtyard overlooking the river (plus there's samba here every Saturday from 10pm). As evening arrives, a samba session normally runs from about 7pm to 11pm every second Saturday at the **Ateliê Multicultural Elioenai Gomes** (Map p509; www.ateliemulticultural.com.br; Ladeira da Borborema 101). Otherwise, go for a cold beer and conversation at **Espaço Mundo** (Map p509; Praça Anthenor Navarro 53; ☉ 8pm-3am Thu-Sat), or encounter reggae rhythms thumping out from **Casa de Mathilde** (Map p509; ☑ 9688-1477; www.facebook.com/casademathildejp; Praça Anthenor Navarro 39). It's safe to travel to the historic center by bus till late afternoon (or later if you're in a group), but best to take a taxi back later.

Nightlife in Tambaú is centered on and around Rua Coração de Jesus (where Empório Café (p511) is one of the hippest joints) as well as in the seafront kiosks, some of which offer live music.

Bolero at Sunset
LIVE MUSIC

(Praia do Jacaré; ☉ sunset) Almost every Brazilian tourist in João Pessoa goes to the north of the city for sunset to see saxophonist Jurandy play Ravel's Bolero while being paddled up and down the waters of Rio Paraíba in a small canoe. The daily event is a supremely kitschy, classic Brazilian phenomenon, and some people come from Natal and Recife just for this. Taxis from Tambaú (10km) are about R$35 each way.

Four overwater bars play host, charging covers of R$5 to R$7 (try Jacaré Grill for the added bonus of violinist Belle Soares, who plays afterwards). Arrive by 4:30pm (4pm in winter) to get a choice seat and be ready to sit through a pre-Jurandy cacophony of competing bands while you wait.

❶ Information

Banco do Brasil (Av Senador Rui Carneiro 166, Tambaú; ☉ 10am-4pm Mon-Fri, ATMs 7am-10pm daily) There are also Banco do Brasil and Banco 24 Horas ATMs at the bus station.

PBTUR (☑ 3214-8185; www.destinoparaiba.pb.gov.br) The Paraíba tourism department runs helpful, well-informed information offices in the bus station (Map p509; ☑ 3218-6655; Rua Francisco Londres, bus station; ☉ 8am-6pm), Tambaú (Map p510; Centro Turístico Tambaú, Av Almirante Tamandaré 100, Tambaú; ☉ 8am-7pm) and the historic center (Map p509; Hotel Globo, Largo de São Pedro Gonçalves 7; ☉ 9am-5pm Mon-Fri, to 4pm Sat).

❶ Getting There & Away

AIR

Presidente Castro Pinto Airport (☑ 3041-4200), 8km west of the center, has flights to Rio, São Paulo, Brasília and the major cities of the Northeast.

BUS

From the **bus station** (Map p509; ☑ 3221-9611; Rua Francisco Londres) there are services to many destinations, including Fortaleza (R$100 to R$152, 10 hours, two daily), Natal (R$29 to R$40, three hours, eight daily), Recife (R$20, two hours, 27 daily) and Salvador (R$125 to R$189, 16 hours, departing 7pm or 7:30pm except Saturday).

❶ Getting Around

Local buses run from the **Terminal de Integração** (Map p509; Padre Azevedo), across the street from the bus station. **Buses 510 and 513** (Map p509) run frequently to Tambaú (R$2.30, 25 minutes) via Parque Solon de Lucena. Returning from Tambaú, catch them southbound on Av General Édson Ramalho or Rua Maria Sales. A taxi from the bus station to Tambaú is around R$25.

Jacumã & Around
☑ 0XX83 / POP 4500

The string of good beaches and small, spread-out villages from Jacumã to Tambaba, south of João Pessoa, make a relaxed and inexpensive stop on the way to or from Recife, or a day out from João Pessoa.

Jacumã, biggest of the villages, has *forró* bars by night and a thin, 3km-long beach featuring colored sandbars, natural pools and pink cliffs, but other beaches in the area are more enticing. Praia de Carapibus, divided from Praia de Jacumã by small bush-covered headland, is just 500m long, with more low cliffs and pools, and merges into the broader Praia da Tabatinga, which curves nearly 2km south. The most beautiful beach is Praia dos Coqueirinhos, round the headland at the south end of Praia Tabatinga, with coconut palms, high red cliffs, freshwater springs and a dozen *barracas* (stalls), but it can get overly crowded on weekends. **Praia de Tambaba**, 4km further south, is famed as the only official nudist beach in

THE TIMELESS SERTÃO

The interior of the Northeast (sertão) is not all drought-stricken countryside and dirt-poor towns, as its stereotype might have us believe. The sertanejos (sertão residents) are a proud people with a rich popular culture evident in their music, festivals and artisanship. There is also amazing natural beauty out there in the rocky backlands – and fascinating evidence of a history stretching right back to the dinosaurs. The towns of the sertão are equipped with adequate hotels and pousadas and are served well enough by buses. The ideal (greenest and coolest) months to venture there are June and July. Natal-based Cariri Ecotours (p519) specializes in tours to these areas. These are a few highlight destinations to launch your explorations:

Ingá, Paraíba The Pedra do Ingá (pedradoinga.blogspot.com) is a single rock 23m long and nearly 4m high in the middle of the Rio Ingá, covered in beautiful carvings possibly up to 5000 years old. It's 95km west of João Pessoa and 46km short of Campina Grande, a city famed for its huge Festa Junina, a party lasting all June.

Lajedo de Soledade, Rio Grande do Norte Rock paintings up to 10,000 years old (including the world's oldest macaw pictures), ancient ceremonial sites and Ice Age animal fossils are all found here. Guided visits are run from the Museu do Lajedo (084-3333-1017; www.lajedodesoledade.org.br; 8am-noon & 2-5pm Tue-Sun), 75km southwest of Mossoró, near Apodi.

Lajedo da Pai Mateus, Cariri, Paraíba A bizarre, otherworldly, rocky landscape of round boulders, granite blocks, caves and ancient petroglyphs, some 70km west of Campina Grande; several recent Brazilian films were shot here. Excellent accommodations are available at Fazenda Pai Mateus (083-2356-1250; www.paimateus.com.br; r R$250;).

Serra da Capivara, Piauí The earliest evidence of humanity in the Americas and 30,000 rock paintings in a dramatic rocky landscape near São Raimundo Nonato.

the region. Men may only enter the nude section if they are gay couples or accompanied by a woman. The clothing-optional part of Tambaba is also stunning, with a broad swathe of petrified sandstone forming natural tidal pools along the shoreline. Tambaba hosts the one-of-a-kind Open de Surf Naturista (Nude Surfing Festival) in August.

Unless the tide is very high, it's possible to walk this entire coast along the beach.

🛏 Sleeping & Eating

Pousada das Conchas POUSADA **$$**
(3290-1303; www.conchaspousada.com.br; Praia de Tabatinga; s R$190, d R$210-230;) Conchas is a superb option perched on a small rise just above Tabatinga beach. The Swedish owner has jazzed up a rustic-style lodge with her own brightly designed rooms around a well-manicured garden. There's also a breezy restaurant, and staff are very friendly and accommodating.

Pousada Bemtevi POUSADA **$$**
(3290-1334; www.bemtevipousada.com; Hwy PB-008, Tabatinga; s/d R$150/200;) This cleverly designed modern pousada sits beside the road 1km back from Tabatinga beach (but doesn't suffer traffic noise). The 12 lovely, clean-lined rooms all have queen size beds, solar-heated water (so no dodgy electrical shower contraptions) and private sea-view terraces overlooking the attractive garden and pool (romantically lit at night). It's gay friendly, with Dutch and Brazilian co-owners. No children under 12.

Pousada dos Mundos POUSADA **$$**
(3290-1356; www.pousadadosmundos.com.br; Praia de Tabatinga; s/d R$130/160;) Friendly Mundos, 400m back from Tabatinga beach, offers airy rooms with river-facing hammock terraces. The grassy garden contains not only a pool but also a creperia (crepes R$13-20, pizza R$15-40; 8:30am-9pm), which is one of the area's better places to eat. Free kayaks for guests.

Restaurante Tulipas BRAZILIAN **$$**
(3290-1108; Hwy PB-008, Tabatinga; mains for 2 R$40-60; 10am-10pm, to 6pm Mon-Fri Carnaval-Christmas) A Dutch-Brazilian team runs this colorful and discerning restaurant decked out to the sounds of MPB (Música Popular

Brasileira) and the tulip paintings of the co-owner. It's located 1km back from Tabatinga beach; seafood is the specialty but the menu is well-rounded. Don't miss the Jorge Amado caipirinha, a lime and passion-fruit cocktail made with cinnamon and clove-infused *cachaça*.

ⓘ Getting There & Around

Buses run about every 40 minutes to Jacumã (R$5, 45 minutes to 1½ hours) from Rua Cícero Meireles near **João Pessoa bus station** (Map p509). The 5:30am departure (only) continues to Tambaba, and there's one daily bus back from Tambaba, leaving at 5pm. **Shared taxis** (Map p509) also run between João Pessoa and Jacumã charging R$5 per person (or R$20 for the whole car); in João Pessoa you can find them near the Lagoa and near the bus station: ask for 'Jacumã' outside the Terminal de Integração or in Rua Cícero Meireles. Regular taxis charge around R$50 to Jacumã.

Between Jacumã and the other beaches, there are moto-taxis (R$5 to R$10) and taxis.

Slow Hostel (p511) was planning to launch a convenient hop-on/hop-off shuttle service between João Pessoa and the southern beaches, with day tickets costing around R$20. Keep your eyes open for information in hostels and pousadas.

Coming from the south on Hwy BR-101, ask to be dropped off at the turnoff for Conde and Jacumã, and catch a local bus, van or shared taxi there.

RIO GRANDE DO NORTE

Pure air, sun, fine beaches and sand dunes symbolize this small state in Brazil's northeast corner. Rio Grande do Norte has one of the country's most spectacular coastlines, some 500km of beautiful beach after beautiful beach, many of them fronted by reefs with natural pools and backed by tall dunes or cliffs. The locals, known as *potiguares*, are generally friendly and welcoming.

Natal

☑ 0XX84 / POP 804,000

Rio Grande do Norte's capital is a clean, bright and rather bland city that has swelled as a hub for coastal package tourism, much of it catering to Brazilian families. Its main attractions are touristic beaches, buggy rides and other organized excursions, restaurants and nightlife – it won't appeal too much if you seek museums, theater or wild empty strands.

Most visitors stay in the beach neighborhood of Ponta Negra – a striking location, overlooked by fantastic dunes, with steady surf and some lively nightlife. The older part of Natal, including the unexciting city center, Cidade Alta, about 12km northwest of Ponta Negra, is on a peninsula flanked to the west by the Rio Potengi and to the east by Atlantic beaches and reefs.

The bus station is 10km northwest of Ponta Negra and 6km south of the center; the airport is 8km west of Ponta Negra and 15km south of the center. A new, bigger airport, intended to be a hub for the whole Northeast, was due to open in April 2014 at São Gonçalo do Amarante, 11km west of the center, but whether it would be ready on schedule was anybody's guess.

History

An early Portuguese attempt to settle the Natal area in 1535 failed due to the hostility of the indigenous Potiguar people and French brazilwood traders. The Portuguese didn't return until 25 December 1597, when a fleet arrived at the mouth of the Rio Potengi with orders to build a fort to keep the French and Potiguars at bay (hence the name Natal, which is Portuguese for Christmas). On January 6, 1598, the day of the Reis Magos (Three Wise Men), the Portuguese began building the fortress, the Forte dos Reis Magos.

Apart from a period of Dutch occupation (1630–54), Natal remained under Portuguese control thereafter. During WWII its strategic location close to Brazil's northeastern tip prompted Presidents Getúlio Vargas and Franklin D Roosevelt to turn the sleepy city into a supply base for Allied operations in North Africa. Thousands of US military were stationed here and the city became known as the 'Trampoline to Victory.' These days, it's marketed as the Cidade do Sol (Sun City), with good reason.

◎ Sights & Activities

Forte dos Reis Magos　　　　　FORT
(admission R$3; ⊙ 8am-4:30pm) The fort that got Natal started still stands in its original five-point star shape on the reef at the tip of the peninsula at the north end of town. The views of the city, the Ponte Nova bridge and the dunes across the Rio Potengi are fantastic. The fort contains a chapel, a well, cannons and soldiers' quarters – plus the Marco de Touros, a marker stone placed by the Portuguese at Praia do Marco, near São

Central Natal

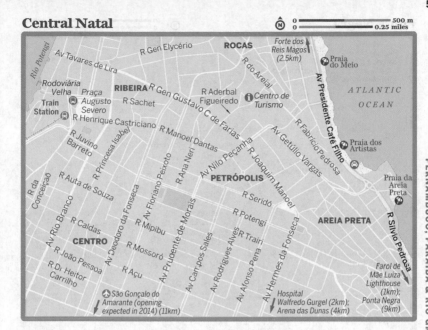

Miguel do Gostoso, in 1501, and thus considered Brazil's oldest historical document. You can try a chocolate-and-pepper ice cream in the snack bar in the old jail. A taxi to the fort from Praia da Areia Preta (reached by bus 56 from Ponta Negra) costs R$12.

Natal's Beaches   BEACH

Natal's northern city beaches, **Praia do Meio** (Map p515), **Praia dos Artistas** (Map p515) and **Praia da Areia Preta**, stretching 5km south from the Forte dos Reis Magos to Farol de Mãe Luiza lighthouse, are unattractive, not very clean urban beaches that get crowded at weekends and holidays. South of the lighthouse, the coast road Via Costeira continues 8km south to Ponta Negra, passing the calm **Praia da Barreira d'Água**, with its resort hotels.

Praia de Ponta Negra, at the far south end of the city, is the nicest beach in Natal – 3km long and full of surfers, sailing boats and beach bars, with the city's best selection of hotels, pousadas and restaurants in the streets behind. The surf here is consistent if small: you can rent boards from a few places for around R$10 per hour.

At the south end of the beach is the **Morro da Careca**, a spectacularly high sand dune with a steep face dropping straight into the sea. Access to the dune has been closed off to prevent further erosion and damage to the primary Atlantic rainforest that covers it.

Dunas de Genipabu   BUGGY TRIP

A number of operators (**Natal Vans** (Map p516; ☎ 3642-1883; www.natalvans.com.br; Duna Barcane Mall, Av Engenheiro Roberto Freire 3112, Ponta Negra) and **Marazul** (Map p516; ☎ 3204-7900; www.passeiodebuggy.com.br; Rua Vereador Manoel Sátiro 75, Ponta Negra) are recommended) offer several fairly standardized out-of-town trips, easily booked through your accommodation. The most popular and exciting outing is to the spectacularly high and steep dunes about 10km north of the city near Genipabu, where you're driven up and down the sand mountains for an hour or so in a beach buggy.

You'll be asked if you want the trip *com ou sem emoção* (with or without excitement), and if you choose *com*, you'll be treated to thrills such as Wall of Death and Vertical Descent.

Operators generally include Genipabu as part of longer day trips (R$300 to R$400 per buggy depending on season) that may involve a 15km beach drive north from Genipabu to Jacumã (with a river crossing by raft), and several other stops for zip lining, dune surfing into lakes and other thrills. Buggies hold up to four passengers: operators can

Ponta Negra

usually put separate individuals together to share the total cost.

If you just want to do the Genipabu dunes without the extras, a round-trip from Natal costs R$200 to R$250 per buggy, plus R$10 per person to enter the dune area. Choose a *bugueiro* (buggy driver) who's authorized by the state tourism authority Setur – check for their Buggy Turismo photo ID card and the vehicle's red license plate and Rio Grande do Norte sunshine-logo stickers (for full details see www.buggyturismo.rn.gov.br).

⚜ Festivals & Events

Natal's out-of-season Carnaval, **Carnatal** (www.carnatal.com.br), takes to the streets of the Lagoa Nova district over four days in early December, with Salvador-style *trios elétricos* (bands playing atop huge trucks) and *blocos* (parade groups) sporting names such as Burro Elétrico (Electric Donkey)

and Cerveja & Coco (Beer & Coconut). It's the wildest out-of-season Carnaval in Brazil and a great substitute for anyone who can't make it to the real deal.

🛏 Sleeping

Options for all budgets abound in Ponta Negra.

Republika Hostel   HOSTEL **$**
(Map p516; ☎3236-2782; www.republikahostel. com.br; Porto das Oficinas 8944; dm/d R$40/100; ❄@☎) Republika's low-lit bar, comfy hammock and TV areas, and big, clean kitchen and eating area create a cozy atmosphere for mingling with fellow travelers. It's housed in a converted family home and run by youthful cousins Sofia and Anderson (he lived for many years in England and Portugal). The dorms and doubles are unexceptional but well priced.

Ponta Negra

Albergue da Costa HOSTEL $
(Map p516; ☑ 3219-0095; www.alberguedacosta.
com.br; Av Praia de Ponta Negra 8932; dm/d
R$50/120; ❄ @ 🛜 ⌨) This super-friendly hos-
tel has comfortable dorms, good breakfasts,
ample common spaces and laid-back management. Other attractions include free use
of bikes and skateboards, surfboard rental
and regular social activities (dance lessons,
live music, barbecues, etc). There's also a
surf and kitesurfing school. English, Italian
and Spanish are spoken.

Casa Grande Apart-Hotel HOTEL $
(Map p516; ☑ 3236-3401; www.aparthotelcasa-
grande.com; Pedro da Fonseca Filho 3050; r R$100-
140, with kitchen R$170-220; ❄ 🛜 ⌨) Casa
Grande offers exceptional rates (especially
in low season, when they nearly halve) for
spacious rooms three blocks from the beach.
Most have hammock-strung balconies and
some have sea views.

Pousada Castanheira POUSADA $$
(☑ 3236-2918; www.pousadacastanheira.com.br;
Rua da Praia 221; r R$329; ❄ @ 🛜 ⌨) It's quite a
surprise to find such a secluded and leafy re-
treat just one short block up from Ponta Ne-
gra beach. Rooms are cool and tile-floored
with bamboo furnishings (three of the 10
have sea views), and there's a good pool area
with a bar, plus a nice, small front garden.
Staff are welcoming and English is spoken.

Pousada Manga Rosa POUSADA $$
(☑ 3219-0508; www.mangarosanatal.com.br;
Erivan França 240; r R$240-250; ❄ 🛜) As close
as you can get to the sea without sleeping on
the beach, Manga Rosa sits right across from
the tree-lined southern end of Praia Ponta
Negra. It has a refreshingly rustic style with
a stone-faced frontage and wooden stair-

ways and balconies, but doesn't cheat on
comfort. The 15 rooms are moderately sized
but bright and attractive, with wood furnishings, paintings and colorful bedspreads. Six
have sea views.

Pousada Caicó POUSADA $$
(Map p516; ☑ 3219-5518; www.pousadacaico.com.
br; Desportista José Leão de Oliveira 9148; s R$120,
d R$160-180; ❄ 🛜) A cute little place steps
from the beach, with just eight small but
spotless and thoughtfully arranged rooms.
The English-speaking owners are very help-
ful and friendly, breakfast is good, and most
rooms will hold three or four people.

⭐**Manary Praia Hotel** BOUTIQUE HOTEL $$$
(Map p516; ☑ 3204-2900; www.manary.com.br; Fran-
cisco Gurgel 9067; s/d from R$527/585; ❄ @ 🛜 ⌨)
One of the Northeast's most charming places
to stay, Manary is decked with the beautiful
nature photos of its late owner and creator, Eduardo Bagnoli, and tasteful artisanal
artifacts from around the world. The detail
is stunning: more thought was put into the
one-room spa than nearly all the other spas
in Brazil combined. To top it off, the poolside
restaurant (Map p516; mains R$40-90; ⏱11am-
4pm & 7-11pm), with creative salads and superb
seafood, is one of Natal's very best.

✗ Eating

Casa de Taipa BRAZILIAN $
(Map p516; ☑ 3219-5798; MA Bezerra de Araújo
130A, Alto de Ponta Negra; dishes R$7-28; ⏱5pm-
midnight; ☑) This hugely popular palm-
thatched eatery specializes in great local
tapioca and couscous creations. The tapiocas comprise a lightly fried tapioca 'pancake'
around fillings ranging from vegetables and
cheeses to *carne de sol* (grilled salted meat)
or prawns. The eight-piece mini-tapioca ap-

petizers *(petiscos)* are a riot. Get there early to avoid waiting for a table.

Tranquilo
SELF-SERVE $
(Map p516; Erivan França 94, Ponta Negra; all-you-can-eat R$12.90; ☺11:30am-4pm & 6-10pm) Excellent all-you-can-eat value on Ponta Negra's beachfront. Load your plate with rice, beans and salads, then flag down a waiter for the main course of your choice (garlic shrimp, beef in onions etc).

★Camarões Potiguar
SEAFOOD $$
(Map p516; www.camaroes.com.br; Pedro da Fonseca Filho 8887, Ponta Negra; mains for 2 R$63-92; ☺11:30am-3:30pm & 6:30pm-midnight, to 11pm Sun) This bright, stylish and creative homage to the shrimp is arguably Natal's finest restaurant, and it's permanently packed. Start with the Caprese salad and follow up with anything from shrimp in a pumpkin to shrimp Thai-style to crispy shrimp with Brie risotto. There are enough fish and meat dishes to satisfy non-crustacean lovers too.

Over a predinner drink in the large bar area you can admire the walls made variously of wine corks, plants, and mud-colored plaster that looks like logs. If the wait looks too long, head to the more traditional, but equally good, original **Camarões Restaurante** (Map p516; ☎3209-2424; Av Engenheiro Roberto Freire 2610, Ponta Negra; mains for 2 R$63-200, for 1 R$45-50; ☺11:30am-3:30pm & 6:30pm-midnight, to 11pm Sun), 400m away.

Cipó Brasil
PIZZERIA $$
(Map p516; ☎3219-5227; Aristides Porpino Filho 3111, Alto de Ponta Negra; pizzas R$23-65; ☺6pm-midnight; ✍) A unanimous favorite with a jungle theme, this is a fun place for sesame-crusted pizza (more than 30 types from shrimp-and-four-cheese to banana-and-chocolate, and both savory and sweet crepes, and is a starting point for evenings out. Get there early to avoid waiting.

🍷 Drinking & Entertainment

The Alto de Ponta Negra neighborhood in the upper part of Ponta Negra, around Rua MA Bezerra de Araújo and Rua Aristides Porpino Filho, is dense with a variety of bars, and packed from Wednesday to Saturday nights. Sex tourism is part of this scene. **Sancho Music Bar** (Map p516; www.sanchomusic.com.br; Aristides Porpino Filho 3163, Ponta Negra; ☺from 10pm Fri-Sun), with live samba, and **Rastapé** (Map p516; rastapecasadeforro.com.br; Aristides Porpino Filho 2198, Ponta Negra; ☺10pm-4am Wed, Fri & Sat), famous for live *forró*, are a couple of the more salubrious spots.

Natal gained the new, 32,000-seat **Arena das Dunas** (Av Salgado Filho), halfway between the city center and Ponta Negra, for its four group-stage matches in the 2014 World Cup. It's expected to be the home of the city's two best teams, **ABC** (www.abcfc.com.br) and **América** (www.americadenatal.com.br), both usually found in national Série B.

Taverna Pub
PUB
(Map p516; ☎3236-3696; MA Bezerra de Araújo 500, Alto de Ponta Negra; cover R$15-45; ☺10pm-4am Mon-Sat) Attached to the Lua Cheia hostel and resembling a pub inside a medieval castle, this ever-popular tavern has different live bands every night, from Brazilian rhythms to '70s disco and blues. No flip-flops.

Pepper's Hall
CLUB
(Map p516; peppershall.com.br; Rua Pedro da Fonseca Filho 3071, Ponta Negra; ☺from 10pm Thu-Sat) Ponta Negra's latest hotspot pulls in an 18-to-35 crowd for its mix of DJs and live rock and *forró*. Entrance is on Rua Fonseca Filho.

Decky
LIVE MUSIC
(Map p516; Av Engenheiro Roberto Freire 9100, Ponta Negra; admission R$10; ☺from 5pm Wed-Sat) One of the most popular spots in Ponta Negra, catering across several age brackets, Decky provides live rock, blues, jazz or MPB every night from 8:30pm. Plop down on the massive, wind-struck patio or inside the spacious main room with air-con.

❶ Information

INTERNET ACCESS
Phone.com (Vilarte, Av Engenheiro Roberto Freire 2107, Ponta Negra; internet per hr R$6; ☺10am-9pm) Also does phone calls, printing, photocopying, scanning and faxing.

INTERNET RESOURCES
Guia Natal (www.guianatal.com.br) Fairly useful tourism site.

MEDICAL SERVICES
Hospital Walfredo Gurgel (☎3232-7500; www.walfredogurgel.rn.gov.br; Av Salgado Filho, Tirol) The main public hospital, with emergency service.

MONEY
The airport, the Centro de Turismo (p519) and the **Vilarte** (Av Engenheiro Roberto Freire 2107, Ponta Negra; ☺9am-10pm Mon-Sat, 10am-9pm Sun), **Praia Shopping** (Av Engenheiro Roberto Freire 8790, Ponta Negra; ☺8am-10pm) and

Natal Shopping (Av das Brancas Dunas, Candelária; ⊙8am-10pm) malls all have ATMs that should accept non-Brazilian cards.

POLICE

Tourist Police can be found at **Praia dos Artistas** (⌨190, 3202-2920; Av Presidente Café Filho, Praia dos Artistas; ⊙8am-11pm) and **Praia Shopping.** (Delegacia do Turista; ⌨3232-7404; Praia Shopping, Av Engenheiro Roberto Freire 8790, Ponta Negra; ⊙24hr).

POST

Post Office (Praia Shopping, Av Engenheiro Roberto Freire 8790, Ponta Negra; ⊙10am-7pm Mon-Fri, 10am-2pm Sat)

TOURIST INFORMATION

There is an intermittently staffed tourist-information desk at the bus station, and supposedly one due to open at the airport.
Centro de Turismo (Map p515; ⌨3211-6149; Aderbal Figueiredo 980, Petrópolis; ⊙8am-7pm Mon-Sat, 8am-6pm Sun; tourist information 8am-noon Mon-Fri) This former jail near the city center now houses a lot of craft and souvenir stalls and a minimally open tourist information center. If you get here, treat yourself to a couple of scrumptious *bolinhos de macaxeira* (cassava patties with shrimp or meat) at the Marenosso Restaurante.

TRAVEL AGENCIES

Cariri Ecotours (⌨9660-1818, 9993-0027; www.caririecotours.com.br; Travessa Joaquim Fagundes 719, Tirol) An experienced agency, recommended for adventurous coastal and inland tours from Natal. It can, for example, take you to Fortaleza along the beach, or to inland destinations like Lajedo de Pai Mateus (p513).

❶ Getting There & Away

AIR
Natal's **Augusto Severo Airport** (⌨3087-1270), at Parnamirim has daily scheduled flights from Lisbon with **TAP Portugal** (www.flytap.com) and weekly charter flights from Amsterdam with **ArkeFly** (www.arkefly.nl), tickets also sold online at www.flybrazil.nl. **Air Italy** (www.meridiana.it) flies weekly from Milan, and from Rome and Torino in the European summer-holiday season. There are flights to many Brazilian cities with **Azul** (www.voeazul.com.br), **GOL** (www.voegol.com.br), **TAM** (www.tam.com.br; airport), **Trip** (www.voetrip.com.br) and **Avianca** (www.avianca.com).

BUS
Long-distance buses go from the **Rodoviária Nova** (New Bus Station; ⌨3205-2931; Av Capitão Mor Gouveia 1237), which received a facelift for the 2014 World Cup. Destinations include Aracati

(near Canoa Quebrada, R$55 to R$60, 6½ hours, six daily), Belém (R$310, 36 hours, at 9:30am), Fortaleza (R$75 to R$110, eight hours, six to eight daily), João Pessoa (R$27 to R$38, three hours, eight daily), Recife (R$43 to R$62, 4½ hours, eight daily), Rio de Janeiro (R$400, 44 hours, 1pm Tuesday and Thursday) and Salvador (R$176 to R$202, 21 hours, two daily). For information on buses to Praia da Pipa, see p519.

CAR & MOTORCYCLE
Car-rental companies with airport desks include **Avis** (⌨3087-1403; www.avis.com.br) and **Localiza** (⌨3643-1557; www.localiza.com).

❶ Getting Around

TO/FROM THE AIRPORT
A new airport at São Gonçalo do Amarante, 11km west of the center, was supposedly being readied for the 2014 World Cup. Meantime, buses marked 'Natal' (R$2.60) run from Augusto Severo airport to the city center (Praça Cívica); for Ponta Negra, get off after about 10km at Via Direta shopping center, cross the footbridge and take bus 26, 46 or 73 (R$2.20). A taxi from Augusto Severo costs about R$43 to Ponta Negra.

TO/FROM THE BUS STATION
For Ponta Negra (Av Engenheiro Roberto Freire), catch bus 66 (R$2.20) from the stop opposite the Petrobras gas station next to the Rodoviária Nova; a taxi is R$30 to R$35. Bus 20 runs between the Rodoviária Nova and the **Rodoviária Velha** (Map p515; Praça Augusto Severo), a local bus terminal in the city center.

BUS
From stops north of Rota do Sol on Av Engenheiro Roberto Freire in Ponta Negra, buses 26, 46 and 73 run north to the Praia Shopping and Via Direta malls; 56 goes along the Via Costeira to Areia Preta then heads inland to the Rodoviária Velha.

Buses 54 and 56 go from the Rodoviária Velha to Ponta Negra.

City bus fares are R$2.20.

Praia da Pipa
⌨0XX84 / POP 6500

Pipa is one of Brazil's magical destinations – pristine beaches backed by tall cliffs, dreamy lagoons, decent surfing, dolphin- and turtle-filled waters, a great selection of pousadas, hostels, global restaurants and good nightlife. Just another small, roadless, fishing village when discovered by surfers in the 1970s, Pipa today rivals Jericoacoara as the Northeast's hippest beach town, attracting partiers from Natal, João Pessoa, Recife and beyond at holidays and weekends, and a slew of international travelers year-round. Its laid-back, independent-traveler and ecological vibe still reigns and, with luck, Pipa may be just too small for that to change, despite the ranks of umbrella'ed tables along the main beaches catering to vanloads of day-trippers from Natal.

Pipa is small but it can be a little hard to get your bearings on arrival. The main, central beach faces north. At its east end the coastline curves southeast to Praia do Amor. To its west, Baía dos Golfinhos and then Praia do Madeiro curve northwest. The narrow main street, Av Baía dos Golfinhos, runs about 2km through town parallelling the main beach and Praia do Amor, with small streets and lanes running off it down to the beach or uphill inland. The inland ones in central Pipa are, from west to east, Céu, Bemte-vis, Gameleira, Mata and Albacora (with Arara branching off Albacora). Full-size public buses and tour vans stop at the west end of Av Baía dos Golfinhos; public minibuses and microbuses terminate on Av Baía dos Golfinhos near the southeast edge of town.

◉ Sights & Activities

The main beach, **Praia da Pipa** (Praia do Centro), about 1.5km long, has fishing boats, numerous bar/restaurants, and rock pools at low tide. **Baía dos Golfinhos**, to its west, is where dolphins come close inshore most mornings: it's backed by cliffs and accessible on foot only from the main beach, within about 2½ hours either side of low tide – during which time you can get cold beer, coconuts and caipirinhas here from enterprising locals. **Praia do Madeiro** curves northward from the headland at the far end of Baía dos Golfinhos and has a few upmarket hotels dotted along its length. It's good for beginner surfers (group classes run R$50 to R$60).

Praia do Amor, the advanced surf beach, is accessed off the eastern part of Av Baía dos Golfinhos. You can rent surfboards here and in town for R$50 to R$60 per day; swimming can be dangerous.

Lagoa de Guaraíras, behind the river mouth at Tibau do Sul, 8km northwest of Pipa, is one of the area's most stunning landscapes, a massive dune- and mangrovebound lagoon, particularly spectacular at sunset. The dockside **Creperia Marinas** (crepes R$8-20; ◷11am-8pm) is a brilliant sunset-viewing spot. **Bicho do Mangue**

(☑9928-1087; bichodomangue@yahoo.com.br; per person R$30) does excellent three-hour guided kayak excursions starting about an hour before high tide (you can book through accommodations in Pipa).

Santuário Ecológico de Pipa
NATURE RESERVE

(☑9982-8044; www.ecopipa.com.br; admission R$10; ◷7am-5pm Mon-Fri, from 8am Sat-Sun) ✔ This small, privately owned reserve, 2km west along the main road from the town center, does a valuable job of protecting at least some of the Pipa coast from development. Well-marked trails lead through secondary forest to impressive lookouts over Baía dos Golfinhos and Praia do Madeiro, from which you can often see large green turtles at high tide.

🛌 Sleeping

Pipa has dozens of pousadas, hostels and hotels, ranging from dumpy to five-star gorgeous. Many accommodations offer good discounts in low season.

★Pousada Xamã
POUSADA $

(☑3246-2267; www.pousadaxama.com.br; Cajueiro 12; s/d R$70/120; ❋@🛜☰) Hidden up a side street near Pipa's southeastern edge is one of the Northeast's best budget pousadas. Ultra-hospitable owner Neuza presides over faultless, pleasantly decorated rooms, most of which open onto a leafy, flower-fringed pool and garden area, with hammocks and hummingbirds. The breakfast is good and it offers Natal airport pickups for R$80 (up to four people).

Media Veronica Hostel
HOSTEL $

(☑9997-7606; mediaveronicahostel.com.br; Albacora 555; without breakfast dm R$30, d R$70-80; @🛜) A labor of love for two Argentine brothers, this hostel impresses with reasonable prices and an emphasis on cleanliness, security and information for guests. The three doubles out back each have their own hammock-slung veranda. Breakfast isn't provided, but guests get special breakfast deals at three nearby eateries.

Sugar Cane Hostel
HOSTEL $

(☑3246-2723; www.sugarcanehostel.com.br; Arara 19; dm/r R$50/120; @🛜) Sugar Cane is popular with Europeans and North Americans and strong on traveler camaraderie, with a bar and hammock-strung terraces that make excellent hang spots. The dorms are fancooled only and can get pretty hot. Other recommended hostels include HI's **Pipa Hostel** (📞3246-2151; www.pipahostel.com.br; Arara 105; dm/d R$50/140; ✳@🛜🏊), and **Hostel do Céu** (📞3246-2235; www.hosteldoceu.jimdo.com; Rua do Céu 153; dm/d R$40/120; 🛜🏊).

Paraíso das Tartarugas POUSADA $
(📞9617-3969, 3246-2020; www.paraisodastartarugas.net; Praia do Amor; s R$80-100, d R$120-150; @) If you've dreamt of staying in a wooden shack inches from the ocean, 'Turtle Paradise' is your place. The six rooms and apartments are rustic but clean and pleasant, and four have decks almost on top of the waves. Amiable owner Bruno runs surf classes on Praia Madeiro for beginners (R$60 per person, 1½ hours), and surf trips to Bahia Formosa.

The pousada is 200m along the shore from the east end of the main beach; take care when the tide's up.

⭐**Spa Da Alma** POUSADA $$
(📞3246-2357; www.spadaalma.tur.br; Rua do Spa 9; d R$270-330; ✳@🛜🏊) On lush, sprawling hilltop grounds, 1.5km beyond the southeast edge of town, this great-value place boasts luxury at midrange prices. The scattered bungalows offer wide bay windows and verandas with wowing views towards the beaches below; there's a gorgeous pool beside the restaurant, and a lovely multiservice garden spa down below. It's stunning, very private and the price is very right.

Pousada Alto da Pipa POUSADA $$
(📞3246 2281; www.pousadaaltodapipa.com.br; Gameleira 555; s/d R$120/180; ✳@🛜🏊) This cute and colorful pousada uphill from the main street has small, clean and pretty pastel-hued rooms, but it's their setting along a lush courtyard-garden, with palm trees and small footbridges over tiny ponds, that makes it a special find. There's 20% off for cash payments.

Pousada Tamanduá POUSADA $$
(📞3246-2734; www.pousadatamanduapipa.com.br; Tamanduá 3; r R$180; ✳🛜🏊) A cute little place with clean, pretty rooms and appeal-

---

BUGGYING THE NORTHEAST

With broad, sandy beaches stretched along much of the 1800km-long coastline from Tamandaré (Pernambuco) to São Luís (Maranhão), the Northeast is Brazil's true beach-buggy paradise. These four-wheel, five-seat contraptions – usually built on a VW Beetle chassis – roar along beaches and up and down dunes the length of the region, with cargoes of happy tourists enjoying off-road trips with the ocean wind in their hair amid fabulous scenery.

If you can cope with the fact that buggies guzzle a liter of gasoline every 5 or 6km and make an unholy racket, a buggy trip is invariably a lot of fun. One passenger sits in front with the driver; up to three sit in the back. Trips can be as short or long as you like, and you can stop wherever you please. The Genipabu dunes make a fun half-day outing from Natal, while the 180km round-trip from São Miguel do Gostoso to Galinhos and back is a fabulous day trip. Even longer trips such as Natal to Fortaleza (700km), Fortaleza to Jericoacoara (nearly 300km), or Jericoacoara to the Lençóis Maranhenses (300km) are quite feasible. The Natal to Fortaleza stretch is one of the most beautiful and least-developed coastlines in Brazil, strung with colored cliffs, rolling dunes, salt flats, reefs, palm-lined beaches, freshwater lagoons, tiny traditional fishing villages and some larger settlements popular with local weekenders. The trip takes three to five days and passes approximately 92 beaches, at a cost of around R$1800 plus accommodations and meals. Make sure you go with an authorized driver (see Dunas de Genipabu, p515)). It's also possible to do the trip more comfortably in Jeeps, with agencies such as Natal's Cariri Ecotours (p519) or **Top Buggy** (📞084-4141-6262; www.topbuggy.com.br), or **Nordeste Off Road** (📞3246-4023; www.nordesteoffroad.com; Sala 202, Av Barão de Studart 2360, Joaquim Távora) in Fortaleza.

For a slightly shorter trip, start from São Miguel do Gostoso, where a buggy, jeep or 4WD pickup to Fortaleza costs around R$1200.

For good environmental reasons and/or consideration for other beach users, local regulations prohibit vehicle traffic on certain beaches and dunes on some or all days, and sometimes you have to duck inland around river mouths, mangrove areas and so on, but there is still plenty of beach to roar along.

ing stone-and-wood stairs and walkways, run by an amiable young couple.

Morada dos Ventos
POUSADA $$

(☑3246-2284; www.moradadosventos.com; Rua dos Colibris 3; d R$170-220, q R$360; ⊘closed May; ❀❀❀) Large rooms in a breezy location, a good restaurant and large garden with pool make this welcoming Brazilian–Scottish operation a dependable choice.

★Toca da Coruja
POUSADA $$$

(☑3246-2226; www.tocadacoruja.com.br; Av Baía dos Golfinhos; r R$580-935; ❀@❀❀) ⚘ One of Brazil's most charming luxury pousadas, Toca da Coruja is an eco- and community-conscious place wrapped in sprawling tropical gardens with monkeys, birds and two gorgeous pools. All rooms are huge, but the deluxe bungalows are gigantic, with breezy wraparound verandas in the style of old Northeast ranch houses.

The pousada is built with some recycled materials and rescued 19th-century farmhouse furniture, and has copper-ionization treatment for the pools. Most of the 70 staff are locals. The superb facilities include a top-class restaurant and a nice garden bar. Children under 10 not permitted.

✖ Eating

Pipa is a wonderful place to eat out, but finding quality is more challenging than cheap.

Dona Branca
SELF-SERVE $

(Av Baía dos Golfinhos; per kg R$10; ⊘noon-11pm) Places like this are a dying breed in popular beach towns like Pipa – take your pick of any two meat items from the grill, then fill your plate with rice, beans, salad and other goodies from the buffet. It's R$2 extra with fish or shrimp, and there's a R$3 fine if you don't finish your plate!

★Tapas
FUSION $$

(☑9414-4675; Bem-te-vis 8; dishes R$7.50-40; ⊘6:30-11pm, closed May-Jun; ⚘) Just up from the main street, Tapas is a culinary godsend, serving large Brazilian tapas peppered with Thai, Indian, French and Italian influences in a casual and artsy space. Sesame-crusted fresh tuna is one specialty, but it's all tasty, including the shrimp with honey and ginger and the arugula, lettuce, mango and Gorgonzola salad.

Pan'e Vino
ITALIAN $$

(Albacora; mains R$12-34; ⊘6:30-11pm Tue-Sun) Real Italian food from well-traveled, Roman-born chef Michele, whose passion for fresh ingredients can be seen in his ever-changing menus – lamb with rosemary, Messina-style fish with capers, olives and white wine – plus homemade pasta, risottos and pots of real Italian basil (seeds smuggled direct from Italy!).

Garagem
SEAFOOD $$

(☑3246-2154; Praia do Centro; mains R$18-38; ⊘10:30am-sunset) With superb views of Pipa's cliffs and dunes, Garagem got its start as a famous bar (and is still good for that) but it's also the best spot in Pipa proper to drop down for a beach lunch (excellent Argentine picanha, fresh fish, sandwiches, salads) and a Bohemia to wash it down. It's the westernmost bar on the main beach. On full-moon nights, there's live music, too.

Rancho da Pipa
CHURRASCARIA $$

(Gameleira 47; mains R$30-40; ⊘6:30-11pm) A brightly lit rival at the foot of the street may snare some tourists, but this is where locals come for a good grilled-meat feed. Try the picanha with or without garlic, or the filet mignon with pepper sauce.

★Cruzeiro do Pescador
SEAFOOD $$$

(☑3246-2026, 9121-6485; cnr Av Baía dos Golfinhos & Concris; mains for 1 R$42-59; ⊘1pm-midnight) It looks like a typical mess of a house, but a closer look reveals a don't-miss culinary experience. Chef Daniel does everything with homegrown finesse from the poetically hand-written menus to the romantic candle-lit setting, not forgetting the products from his own garden and the delicious flavors of his cooking.

Smoked or grilled seafood is a good way to go, but call ahead as some dishes take two hours to prepare, like the Seleção do Mar, a slow-grilled seafood feast of Biblical proportions. It's on the southeast edge of town, about 1.5km from the center.

☕ Drinking & Nightlife

Nightlife focuses on Tribus and Oz bars, opposite each other on Av Baía dos Golfinhos, which are usually pretty full by mid-evening. Other come-and-go options are dotted along the same street and there's often live music in at least one bar.

Boate dos Calangos
CLUB

(www.facebook.com/calangos; Av Baía dos Golfinhos ; ⊘from 1am Fri-Sun) Calangos, a big dance hall at the far end of Av Baía dos Golfinhos, fills for live *forró* on Sunday and Euro-style DJs the other nights.

Shopping

Bookshop   BOOKS
(☑ 8882-7172; Gameleira; ⊙ 5-10pm Wed-Fri, 6:30-10pm Sat-Sun) A good selection of books in a variety of languages, for rent or trade.

Information

Pipa is extraordinarily well endowed with helpful, informative websites. Take your pick from www.pipa.com.br, www.praiadapipa.com.br or www.mapaguiapipa.com.br.

Bring some cash – many places do not accept credit cards and the **Banco do Brasil ATM** (Falésia Galeria, Av Baía dos Golfinhos 369; ⊙ 8am-10pm) at the west end of town (the only one accepting international cards) sometimes runs out of cash.

Calls.Net (Av Baía dos Golfinhos, btwn Bem-te-vis & Céu; internet per hr R$3; ⊙ 10am-10pm Mon-Sat, 2-10pm Sun)

Mandacaru Expedições (☑ 9988-5892; www.mandacaruexpedicoes.com.br) This excellent small Pipa-based agency can arrange any Brazilian travel experience or itinerary without any extra agent's fees, based on its widely traveled owner's personal knowledge, and with an emphasis on high ecotouristic and safety standards.

Pipatour (☑ 3246-2234; www.pipatour.com; Av Baía dos Golfinhos 767; ⊙ 9am-noon & 3-7pm) Helpful agency for flight, bus and tour bookings.

DANGERS & ANNOYANCES
Crime does occur in Pipa, doubtless exacerbated by the crack habit of some people here: don't leave belongings unattended on beaches and don't leave valuables lying around in your room.

❶ Getting There & Away

Oceano (☑ 3311-3333; www.expresso-oceano.com.br) runs 12 daily buses (six on Sunday) from Natal's Rodoviária Nova to Pipa (R$11.50, 2½ hours) and back. Last departure in both directions is 6pm. Going to Pipa from Natal, you can also catch them at the stop on Av Salgado Filho in front of Carrefour in Lagoa Nova (reachable from Ponta Negra by bus 26, 46 or 73), about 10 minutes after they leave the Rodoviária Nova. The 10am, noon and 6pm buses from Pipa Monday to Saturday (but none going out to Pipa) stop at Natal's Augusto Severo airport. **Alternativo Vans** (☑ 9973-0353) runs microbuses from Pipa to the Rodoviária Nova (R$10, 2½ hours), and back, three times daily. Heading into Natal, they'll drop you at Augusto Severo airport for

an extra R$5. Schedules on all these services change frequently, so check in advance.

A taxi between Augusto Severo airport and Pipa should cost R$120. **Pipa Natureza** (www.pipanatureza.com.br; Av Baía dos Golfinhos 654) offers airport transfers for R$45 per person (minimum two) between 8am and 11pm.

If you're coming by bus from the south, get out at Goianinha (1½ hours from João Pessoa), where minibuses run every few minutes to Pipa (R$3.50, 50 minutes, 5am to midnight) from behind the pale-blue church, 250m off the main road.

Pipatour can reserve bus seats from Goianinha to Recife or Salvador for a R$10 fee.

North of Natal

The nearly 400km of coastline between Natal and the Ceará state border (during which the coast veers from east-facing to north-facing) is a growing playground for weekenders and day-trippers from Natal, but there are still dozens of lovely beaches. The further from Natal you go, the more isolated and empty they become.

São Miguel do Gostoso

☑ 0XX84 / POP 4100
'Gostoso,' 110km from Natal, is an increasingly popular weekend and holiday getaway, with excellent pousadas, restaurants and bars, but also with several gorgeous nearby beaches that are mostly near-empty. If you want to go somewhere still undiscovered by package tourism and still be awed by the scenery, go now.

Bradesco and Banco do Brasil ATMs on the main street accept foreign cards, but can be temperamental.

◉ Sights & Activities

The main beaches in town, **Praia do Maceió**, **Praia da Xêpa** and **Praia do Cardeiro**, make up a wide, continuous 2km stretch of relaxing sands, but the true gem is **Praia de Tourinhos**, 8km west at the end of a gravel road. It's a beautiful semicircle bay with just a few kiosks, nothing more. During the week you won't share it with more than a few others. You can walk there along the coast, or take a round-trip by moto-taxi (R$20 per person) or buggy (R$80 for up to four). **Ponta do Santo Cristo**, at the far east end of Cardeiro, catches the wind and is a very popular wind- and kitesurfing spot: **Clube Kauli Seadi** (☑ 9197-1297; Praia do Cardeiro) does classes and equipment rentals.

★**Buggy trips to Galinhos** (R$280/350 one-way/roundtrip for up to 4 people), about three hours each way, are unforgettable wind-blown expeditions along a spectacular 90km sequence of long, empty beaches, dunes and lagoons. Organize through your accommodation.

🛏 Sleeping & Eating

★**Pousada Ilha do Vento**　POUSADA, HOSTEL **$**
(☑3263-4048; www.ilhadovento.com.br; Caraúnas 70; dm R$50, d R$120-160; ❋ ⛶ 🖳) A superb option on a sizable garden property at the east end of town. Dorms and private rooms are spotless, comfy, well designed and pleasingly decorated; breakfast is generous and good; and the well-traveled Italo-Brazilian owners are super-helpful and welcoming.

Pousada Casa de Taipa　POUSADA **$$**
(☑3263-4227; www.pousadacasadetaipa.com.br; Bagre Caia Coco 99; d R$230; ❋ ⛶ 🖳) The owners of this spot, 300m from the beach, are English-speaking and lovely to the core. The property has a Northeastern culture theme and is specially memorable for the artsy endeavors of one of the owners, who has fashioned tables from egg and coconut shells and painted beautiful large murals in each room. It's all set round a nice garden with pool and restaurant.

Esquina Brasil Bistro　CAFE **$**
(☑9156-1920; Av dos Arrecifes 1976; dishes R$6-25; ⊙6pm-midnight Mon-Sat; 🖉) This simple but adorable cafe, towards the west end of the main street, does superb light meals such as tapiocas with many options of savory or sweet fillings, light sandwiches on Indian chapati bread, and fabulous cashew-nut pesto pasta. The greens are organic, and little touches like ground *malagueta* chillies put it a cut above the rest.

Bar do Tico　SEAFOOD **$$**
(Praia do Cardeiro; mains R$15-35; ⊙10am-8:30pm) Just across from wide Cardeiro beach, this simple beach bar does simple fare very well – the *filete de cavala* (mackerel), served with salad, fried potato or *macaxeira* chips, and *farofa*, is a treat with a couple of beers.

❶ Getting There & Away

Expresso Cabral (www.expressocabral.com.br) runs four daily buses from Natal's Rodoviária Nova to Gostoso (R$12.50, 2½ to three hours), and back. Some require switching buses in Touros. Taxis should cost R$160. Returning to Natal, you may be able to find a shared taxi for R$25 per person. Westbound public transportation is nonexistent.

Galos & Galinhos
🗺 0XX84 / POP 2100

On a narrow sandbar between a lagoon and the ocean, 160km northwest of Natal, these two isolated fishing villages are still only emerging as beach destinations. Galinhos, with sandy streets, warm, gentle waters, and the majority of the few accommodations, is a great place to unwind. Pristine beaches and dunes stretch 2km west to the lagoon mouth, and endlessly along the coast to the east. In Galos, 3.5km east up the lagoon, only 400 or so people live in even more peaceful surroundings.

The breezes here can be good for kitesurfing, and boat, buggy, horseback and horsecart excursions are easily arranged. Especially recommended is the *'passeio ecológico'* (R$180 for two people), a four- or five-hour boat excursion on the lagoon in which you catch and eat your own crab or fish lunch.

🛏 Sleeping & Eating

Pousada da Dalva　POUSADA **$**
(☑3552-0046; pousadadadalva@gmail.com; Senador Dinarte Mariz s/n, Galinhos; r without/with aircon R$90/180; ❋) The freshly decorated non-air-con rooms in the back of this beachside pousada are the Galinhos' best budget deal.

Chalé Oásis　POUSADA **$$**
(☑3552-0024; www.oasisgalinhos.com; Beira Rio, Galinhos; s R$150-180, d R$230-290; ❋ ⛶ 🖳) Effervescent, English-speaking, Portuguese Clara, a devotee of primary colors, runs Galinhos' most appealing accommodation, on the lagoon shore. The eight wood-built bungalows are decked with highly original, beachy-style decorations. Facilities include a garden restaurant. Clara's enthusiasm for her adopted home is wholly infectious.

Pousada Peixe-Galo　POUSADA **$$**
(☑3552-2001; www.pousadapeixegalo.com.br; Rua da Candelária 30, Galos; r R$210; ❋ ⛶ 🖳) Galos' only accommodation sits just 5m from the lagoon, flanked by tall palm trees. Rooms, surrounding a nice pool, are comfortable but nothing fancy; service is professional and friendly, and the lookout tower boasts wonderful views over the peninsula, lagoon and ocean. **Restaurante Irene** (buffet lunch R$25, mains for 2 R$25-50; ⊙7am-7pm), next door, serves the area's best meals.

Pousada Brésil Aventure POUSADA **$$**
(📞 3552-0085; www.bresil-aventure.com/aventure-et-nature; Senador Dinarte Maris 123, Galinhos; r R$180-200; ✳🖥❄) This pousada run by a French tour company is the center of attention on Galinhos' beach. The **restaurant** (mains R$18-52; ⏰ 10am-3pm & 7-9:30pm) serves the usual suspects, plus somewhat adventurous additions like stingray *moquecas* (seafood stew); the sunsets are worthy of writing home about.

❶ Getting There & Away

Access to Galos and Galinhos is not particularly easy, which is part of their charm. The most exciting approach is by beach buggy from São Miguel do Gostoso (p523). From Natal's Rodoviária Nova, **Expresso Cabral** (www.expresso-cabral.com.br) runs buses at 6am Sunday, and 6am and noon Monday and Friday to Pratagil

(R$23, three hours), across the lagoon from Galinhos. From Pratagil, boats ferry passengers to Galinhos (per person/whole boat R$2.50/10, 10 minutes) and Galos (per person/whole boat R$4/40, 15 minutes) from approximately 8am to 5pm. Buses to Natal return from Pratagil at 5am Sunday and 9am and 5pm Monday and Friday.

Alternatively, take a Macau-bound Cabral bus (departing Natal every three hours from 6am to 6pm) as far as the Galinhos turnoff *(trevo de Galinhos)* on Hwy BR-406 (R$15, 2½ hours), and then a taxi to Pratigil (R$30; organize through Galinhos/Galos accommodations) .

Another option for returning from Galinhos from Natal is a shared van (R$30) leaving at 6am daily.

If you have a vehicle you can leave it safely parked at Pratagil for free.

Taxis between Natal and Pratagil should cost R$280 (R$350 at night). To Fortaleza it's around R$900.

Ceará, Piauí & Maranhão

POP 19 MILLION

Best Places to Eat

➡ Colher de Pau (p533)

➡ Restaurante Senac (p555)

➡ Pimenta Verde (p543)

➡ Coco Bambu (p533)

➡ Restaurante do Antônio (p561)

Best Places to Stay

➡ Rancho do Buna (p561)

➡ Casa Lavinia (p555)

➡ Pousada Les Alizés (p540)

➡ Vila Kalango (p542)

➡ Sítio do Alemão (p545)

Why Go?

These three Northeastern states stretch along Brazil's only north-facing coast and deep into the arid interior. The main draw for visitors, the beaches of Ceará, are arrayed for hundreds of glorious kilometers either side of Fortaleza, the fun-loving biggest city. These are some of the very best beaches in Brazil, some supporting growing resort towns, others with at most a small, traditional fishing village. The hip travelers' hangout Jericoacoara, uniquely located inside a dune-swept national park, is the jewel of Ceará's gorgeous coastline.

An adventurous coastal route leads west from Jericoacoara to the scenic, wildlife-rich Delta do Parnaíba and the vast expanse of high dunes and clear lagoons known as the Lençóis Maranhenses, one of Brazil's highlights. The Lençóis' beauty will floor you. Further west still are two of Brazil's most picturesque, intriguing colonial gems: half-decayed, half-restored São Luís, with its markedly Afro-Brazilian culture, and its perfect sleepy neighbor Alcântara.

When to Go
Fortaleza

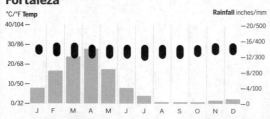

Jun São Luís erupts with color, music and dance in its Bumba Meu Boi festival.

Jul–Aug The Lençóis Maranhenses are at their most spectacular.

Jul–Jan Constant strong breezes make the coast one of the world's premier kitesurfing destinations.

History

The Portuguese were slow off the mark in occupying these distant northern lands, and it was the French who founded São Luís, the capital of Maranhão (in 1612), and the Dutch who founded Fortaleza, capital of Ceará (in 1637). These incursions spurred the Portuguese into action and they expelled both rival colonial powers within a few years. The main settlers in Ceará were from Portugal's Azores islands. Colonial sugar and cotton plantations, worked by slave labor, were developed in both states, but it was cattle ranching that dominated their economies, as it still does to a large extent today. Until 1774 Maranhão was governed together with Pará to its west as a separate entity from the rest of Brazil, with their capital at São Luís. Piauí, between Ceará and Maranhão, was first settled inland by poor cattle herders moving westwards from Ceará and north from São Paulo in the 17th and 18th centuries.

Despite resistance, the indigenous population of all three states was subdued by the 18th century. Once the wars ended, the colonists in the interior were faced with serious droughts. As many as two million people died in droughts in Ceará in the 1870s, with survivors streaming into Fortaleza. Neighboring Piauí was initially landlocked but eventually a land swap was arranged with Ceará in the 19th century so that it could enjoy the benefits of a coastline. Piauí still has the lowest population density of any Brazilian state.

Fortaleza, with its commerce and tourism, is the region's economic powerhouse. Some large industrial projects have been sited near São Luís in recent decades, but all three states are still among Brazil's poorest.

🛈 Getting There & Around

Fortaleza has an international airport with flights from Europe as well as many Brazilian cities. São Luís and Teresina are served by domestic flights.

Fortaleza, Teresina and São Luís have bus connections with Natal and Recife to the east, and cities to the south such as Brasília, Rio and São Paulo. There are also buses from the main cities to Belém at the mouth of the Amazon, but the stretch between São Luís and Belém has a history of bus robberies, so it's an idea to consider flying that stretch – which can in fact be cheaper than buses if booked ahead. In general, flying into or out of the region is often cheaper than a long bus trip.

Buses link pretty much every town and village in this region. Road quality has improved a lot, though access to a few coastal villages including Jericoacoara is partly unpaved. Beach buggies and 4WDs with drivers provide trips along the coasts and dunes. A hire car is useful if you plan to visit some smaller places with limited bus service, but you should research road conditions first as some less-traveled routes require 4WD – notably the stretch between Paulino Neves and Barreirinhas on the route between Parnaíba and the Lençóis Maranhenses. Fortaleza is the easiest place to get a rental vehicle.

CEARÁ

In a country of glorious coastlines, Ceará has one of the most glorious of all – nearly 600km of beautiful and varied beaches, from idyllic little palm-fringed bays to 20km strips washed by ocean breakers. From the busy urban beaches of Fortaleza to hip Jericoacoara to the smallest of fishing villages where people still sail *jangadas* (triangular-sailed fishing boats) and live in thatched-roof homes, Ceará has everything you could wish for in terms of beach ambience. Much of the coast is backed by large expanses of high, white dunes, lending a starkly elemental touch to the landscape, while the waves and winds provide some of the world's best conditions for kitesurfing, surfing and windsurfing.

Fortaleza

📞 085 / POP 2.5 MILLION (METROPOLITAN AREA 3.6 MILLION)

Considering its isolation on the Brazilian map, Fortaleza is a surprisingly large and sprawling place. It's one of Brazil's biggest cities and an economic magnet for people from Ceará and beyond. It's also a magnet for tourists from Brazil and overseas, who come for the beaches, the party atmosphere and the spectacular smaller beach spots, rolling dunes and fishing villages they can get to from here. Some city beaches are reasonably attractive and the nightlife is definitely a lot of fun.

The city stretches 20km along the coast and up to 10km inland. Centro is the oldest part of town and is a lively area to wander round by day, with many busy streets full of small stores, though it lacks any specific attractions of note. The bus station is 4km south of Centro and the airport is 2km further south. The main areas of interest are east

Ceará,
Piauí &
Maranhão
Highlights

1 Surf, chill, party and stare at spectacular sunsets in the remote backpacker village of **Jericoacoara** (p540).

2 Dip into pristine lagoons between endless dunes in Maranhão's surreal **Parque Nacional dos Lençóis Maranhenses** (p559).

3 Enjoy the quirky combo of colonial heritage and Afro-Brazilian culture in **São Luís** (p550).

4 Step back in time at the charmingly crumbling colonial town of **Alcântara** (p558).

5 Have a long, palm-lined curve of beach almost to yourself at **Icaraí de Amontada** (p539).

6 Enjoy the restaurants, nightlife and beach scene of **Fortaleza** (p527).

7 Kitesurf or windsurf some of the world's best breezes almost anywhere along the coast.

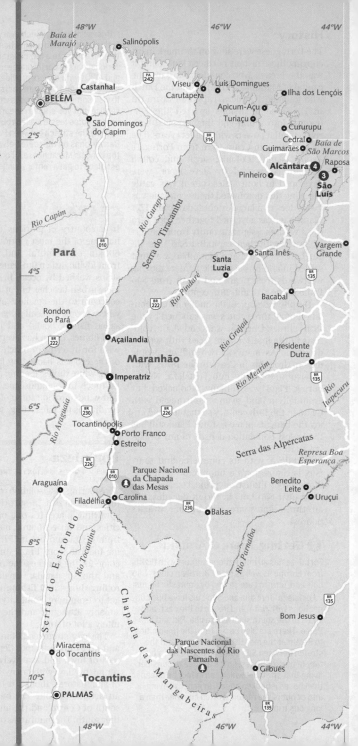

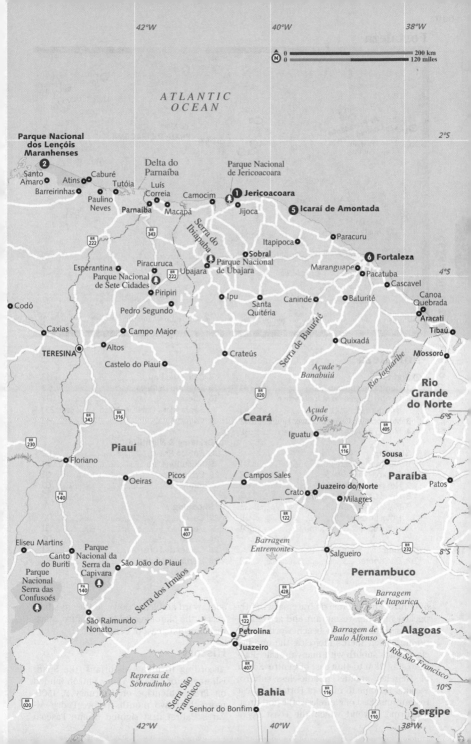

Fortaleza

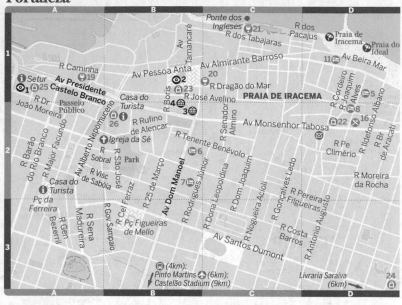

Fortaleza

Sights
1 Centro de Turismo A1
2 Centro Dragão do Mar de Arte e
   Cultura B1
3 Memorial da Cultura Cearense B2
4 Museu de Arte Contemporânea B2

Sleeping
5 Albergaria Hostel D1
6 Backpackers Ceará B2
7 Hostel Terra da Luz B2
8 Hotel Casa de Praia D2
9 Hotel La Maison G3
10 Hotel Luzeiros G2
11 Hotel Sonata de Iracema D1

Eating
12 50 Sabores G2
13 Coco Bambu H3

14 Colher de Pau H3
15 Empório Delitalia G3
16 Gheller D2
   Santa Clara Café Orgânico .... (see 23)
17 Vojnilô H3

Drinking & Nightlife
18 Boteco Praia E2
19 Mucuripe Club A1
20 Órbita C1
21 Pirata Bar C1

Shopping
22 Ceart D2
23 Ceart B1
24 Ceart D3
25 Centro de Turismo A1
26 Mercado Central B2

of Centro. First is Praia de Iracema, a tightly packed nightlife, restaurant and accommodations zone, with no beach worth mentioning. Then there's Meireles, the middle-class beach suburb with many upscale places to stay, 2km to 4km east of Centro. South of Meireles, another middle-class suburb, Varjota, is home to many of Fortaleza's best restaurants. East of Meireles is the port area, Mucuripe, beyond which the coast veers southward and leads down to the city's best beach, the 5km-long Praia do Futuro, starting some 8km east of Centro.

History

According to many historians, the Spanish navigator Vicente Yáñez Pinzón landed on Praia Mucuripe on February 2, 1500, more than two months before Pedro Álvares Cabral first sighted Monte Pascoal

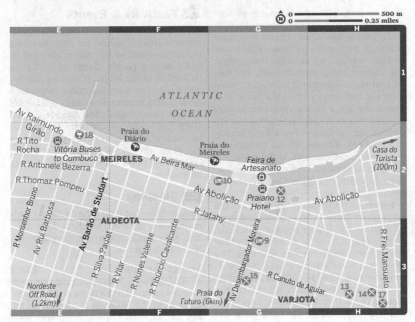

in Bahia (the officially recognized European discovery of Brazil). The first Portuguese attempts to settle here, in the early 17th century, were short-lived, and it was the Dutch who built Fort Schoonenborch in 1637. When the Dutch abandoned their Brazilian possessions in 1654, the Portuguese renamed this fort the Fortaleza de NS da Assunção (Fortress of Our Lady of the Assumption). Around it grew a village, then a town, then a city that came to be called Fortaleza.

Indigenous resistance slowed Portuguese colonization of interior Ceará until the 18th century, but cattle ranchers, and later cotton growers, occupied land. It was cotton exports in the 19th century that made Fortaleza an important town (it had previously played second fiddle to Aracati). Growing commerce and industry in Fortaleza, and droughts in the interior, have since pulled ever more migrants to the city. Since the early 1990s tourism has joined textiles and food among its leading industries.

⊙ Sights & Activities

Centro Dragão do
Mar de Arte e Cultura ARTS CENTER
(☏3488-8600; www.dragaodomar.org.br; Dragão do Mar 81; ⊙8am-midnight) This excellent, extensive complex includes cinemas, performance spaces, a good cafe, a planetarium and two good museums: the **Museu de Arte Contemporânea** (⊙10am-8pm Tue-Sun) **FREE**, and the **Memorial da Cultura Cearense** (⊙10am-8pm Tue-Sun) **FREE** with exhibits on Ceará's traditional way of life and culture. Elevated walkways join blocks on different streets and it all blends well with the surrounding older buildings, many of which have been restored to house bars, restaurants and artisans' workshops. It's a successful social focus for the city, and is very popular with locals.

Centro de Turismo HANDICRAFTS, MUSEUM
(☏3101-5507; Senador Pompeu 350; ⊙8am-6pm Mon-Sat, 8am-noon Sun) The Centro de Turismo, a converted 19th-century jail, houses a lot of craft stalls and, upstairs from the tourist information office, the Museu de Arte e Cultura Popular, with an impressive collection of Ceará crafts.

Beaches
For most tourists, Fortaleza's greatest attractions are its beaches.

Praia do Futuro is a clean length of sand stretching 5km along Fortaleza's east-facing coast. This is easily the best city beach, although far from most accommodations. It's lined by huge restaurants known as *barracas*, serving seafood, beer and cocktails at tables on the sand, and attracts enormous crowds at weekends – fortunately the beach is long enough to accommodate everyone without being overwhelmed. The nicest part starts a couple of kilometers down from the industrial port at the north end. Unless you are a strong swimmer, beware of rough waves. You can reach Praia do Futuro on the 49 Caça e Pesca bus running east on Av Monsenhor Tabosa, Av Historiador Raimundo Girão and Av Beira Mar. Or get a bus to Terminal Papicu then a Papicu–Praia do Futuro or Papicu–Caça e Pesca bus from there.

Fortaleza's north-facing beach, nearer the areas you're likely to be staying in, is lined by a broad and hugely popular pedestrian promenade running 4km from the Ponte dos Ingleses pier to Praia do Mucuripe. The nicest part is the central Praia do Meireles, which with all its high-rise hotels resembles a northeastern Copacabana, but also has numerous beach bars beneath the leafy trees, which are popular places to hang out by day or evening. The water here is less clean than at Praia do Futuro, although that doesn't deter surfers.

Tours

Day trips from Fortaleza to beaches along the coast to the east and west are very popular. Dozens of travel agencies, hotels and pousadas will arrange these for you. Operators will normally come and pick you up from your accommodations. The main destinations (with transport-only prices per person) are Brazil's best water park, Beach Park (R$25), Cumbuco (R$25), Canoa Quebrada (R$40), Lagoinha (R$35) and Mundaú (R$40). The tours are easier than taking public buses and you can use them just one way if you want to stay over.

Some agencies also offer longer-distance 4WD or beach-buggy tours, along Ceará's glorious beaches wherever possible, as far afield as Jericoacoara or even the Lençóis Maranhenses or Natal. With accommodations included, a three-day return trip to Jericoacoara costs from R$650 per person. Try Nordeste Off Road (p521), or Jericoacoara-based **Jeri Off Road** (☎088-3669-2268; www.jeri.tur.br; Pousada Bella Jeri, Travessa da Rua do Forró, Jericoacoara), both members of Abeta, Brazil's only ecotourism and adventure-tourism standards association.

Festivals & Events

Fortal (fortal.com.br), Fortaleza's lively out-of-season Carnaval, is held for four days over the last weekend of July and is attended by half a million people. **Carnaval** itself is at its liveliest in the Praia de Iracema district, which also sees four Saturdays of pre-Carnaval revelry in preceding weeks. Fortaleza's **Parada pela Diversidade Sexual** (Sexual Diversity Parade), on Av Beira Mar on the last Sunday of June, is one of Brazil's biggest gay pride events. **Réveillon** (New Year's) sees a huge fiesta with live bands at Praia de Iracema.

Sleeping

Competition between the many hotels means there are some excellent deals to be had, including some midrange-quality hotels at budget prices.

Albergaria Hostel HOSTEL $
(☎3032-9005; www.albergariahostel.com.br; Antônio Augusto 111, Praia de Iracema; dm R$35-45, d R$90-120; ❄@📶🏊) This cheerful, well located, well-run hostel has very good facilities, including a bar, pizza bar and a backyard with pool, plus a sociable atmosphere helped along by the friendly English-speaking owner. There are separate-sex and mixed four-bed dorms and four good private rooms with bathroom. Breakfast is plentiful.

Hostel Terra da Luz HOSTEL $
(☎3082-2260; www.hostelterradaluz.com; Rodrigues Junior 278; dm R$35-45, d R$100-130; ❄@📶) Installed in a former family home, Terra da Luz has spacious common areas including a cool hammock and sitting area in the backyard, but what makes it special, and helps create the good vibe, is the extremely helpful, welcoming manner of owners and staff. It's in a quietish street a few blocks south of the Dragão do Mar center.

Hotel La Maison HOTEL $
(☎3048-4200; www.hotellamaison.com.br; Av Desembargador Moreira 201, Meireles; r R$110-140; ❄@📶) This excellent-value place in Meireles is just a couple of blocks from the beach, with 25 spotless rooms (those upstairs are generally brighter than downstairs) and bright, colorful common areas. The French owner knows the city very well, speaks English, and can point you in the right direction whatever your needs.

Hotel Casa de Praia   HOTEL **$**
(☑3219-1022;   www.hotelcasadepraia.com.br;
Joaquim Alves 169, Praia de Iracema; s/d R$120/140;
✳@☎☒) For its modest price, this hotel offers many pluses: clean, neat, medium-sized
rooms with ocean views from some (best
from the 3rd floor), efficient and helpful staff,
a shallow rooftop pool, a good breakfast in
a bright dining room and an easy two-block
walk to the seafront. It gets heavily booked, so
it's essential to reserve.

Backpackers Ceará   HOSTEL **$**
(☑3091-8997; www.backpackersce.com.br; Av Dom
Manoel 89; dm R$20, r R$40-60; ☎) The vibe is
super-informal at this basic hostel where
small but prettily decorated rooms line up on
two floors alongside a scrap of garden. There
are ample, open-air, kitchen and hangout
areas (but no breakfast). It's a stone's throw
from the Centro Dragão do Mar.

Hotel Sonata de Iracema   HOTEL **$$**
(☑4006-1600; www.sonatadeiracema.com.br; Av
Beira Mar 848, Praia de Iracema; s/d R$250/274;
✳☎☒) The cute two-story street frontage is
slightly misleading, as most of the hotel is in
the 13-story block behind, but that means all
the tasteful, bright and modern rooms have
sea views. One of Fortaleza's nicest larger
hotels, it has an outdoor pool deck too.

Hotel Luzeiros   HOTEL **$$$**
(☑4006-8585; www.luzeirosfortaleza.com.br; Av
Beira Mar 2600, Meireles; s R$475-850, d R$560-
1000; ✳@☎☒) The designer of Fortaleza's
first design hotel could have been a little
more daring, but the clean-lined, modern
spaces and rooms of this sleek, Portuguese-
owned option, plus probably the best breakfast in Ceará, make it a mainstay with high-
end clientele.

✖ Eating

Santa Clara Café Orgânico   CAFE **$**
(☑3219-6900; Centro Dragão do Mar; items R$3-14;
☺3-10pm Tue-Sun; ✐) ✐ Santa Clara is one
of the city's hot '*Pontos de Encontros,*' which
loosely translated means where hot people go
to mingle (and, here, cool down in the icy air-
con). It's a wonderful little cafe on an upper
level of Dragão do Mar, serving organic coffee,
sandwiches, crepes, omelettes, waffles, tapiocas and a plethora of fancier coffee drinks.

50 Sabores   ICE CREAM **$**
(☑3023-0050; Av Beira Mar 4690, Mucuripe; one/
two scoops R$9/12; ☺9am-11:30pm; ✤) Ice
cream heaven, though with a terribly mis-

leading name: there are actually 100 flavors
here, including caipirinha (made with *cachaça,* sugarcane liquor – you must be 18 to
purchase!), beer, and crispy cheese, among
loads of Brazilian fruits and more classic options. It's absolutely wonderful.

★Colher de Pau   NORTHEASTERN **$$**
(☑3267-6176; Ana Bilhar 1178, Varjota; mains for 1
R$23-95, for 2 R$33-135; ☺11am-midnight) The
large, mostly open-air 'Wooden Spoon' is is
one of the best places in a neighborhood
thronged with popular midrange restau-
rants. It's great for seafood including a su-
perb chunky *peixada* (fish, vegetables and
herbs in coconut sauce) and atmosphere,
and consistently voted among the best in
town for regional cuisine.

★Coco Bambu   BRAZILIAN **$$**
(www.restaurantecocobambu.com.br; Canuto de
Aguiar 1317, Varjota; mains R$25-100; ☺11am-3pm
& 5pm-midnight) This huge, festive eatery is
one of those ridiculous Brazilian restaurants
that does a whole lot of everything and – one
could expect – not a whole lot well. Oh no, not
here. The 14-page menu covers pizza, tapiocas, crepes, sushi and regional mains (as well
as per kilo for lunch) – and everything is excellent, including the tropical-garden setting.

Gheller   SELF-SERVE **$$**
(Av Monsenhor Tabosa 825; buffet lunch/dinner
R$26/22; ☺11am-11pm) Fantastic-value set-
price buffet meals at always-busy Gheller
comprise a 60-item self-serve buffet (with
seafood, sushi, pasta and hot veg dishes as
well as salads) and a 25-item meat *rodízio*
(waiters offering them round the tables),
which includes exotica like *javali* (wild
boar) as well as choice beef cuts like *pi-
canha* and *alcatra*. Enjoy! But remember:
drinks and desserts cost extra.

Empório Delitalia   CAFE, PIZZERIA **$$**
(www.delitalia.com.br; Av Desembargador Moreira
533; breakfast items R$4-20, pizza R$30-55;
☺6:30am-10pm Mon-Sat, 7:30am-10pm Sun)
Consider forgoing breakfast at your accommodation for the great juices, coffees,
waffles, hot filled croissants, omelettes and
tapiocas at this classy cafe. Come anyway for
Fortaleza's best deli and bakery (adjoining)
and one of its best pizzerias (upstairs).

Crocobeach   SELF-SERVE, SEAFOOD **$$**
(www.crocobeach.com.br; Av Zeze Diogo 3125,
Praia do Futuro; buffet per kg R$49.90, mains for
2 R$24-100; ☺8am-6pm; ✤) For the full Praia

CEARÁ, PIAUÍ & MARANHÃO FORTALEZA

do Futuro experience, go to *megabarraca* (mega beach bar) Crocobeach, with its swimming pools and live music on Saturday and Sunday. It's lots of fun and the buffet is excellent.

Vojniló
SEAFOOD $$$

(☑ 3267-3081; www.vojnilo.com; Frederico Borges 409, Varjota; mains R$46-98; ⊙ 5pm-midnight Mon, 1-3pm & 7pm-midnight Tue-Sat, 1-5pm Sun) This stone-walled, subtly maritime-themed restaurant with a confusing Macedonian name regularly wins top seafood accolades in the city. The seafood spaghetti (R$69), topped with two whole *lagostas* (small lobsters), and the house whole fish in caper sauce are both phenomenal. The fish is market-fresh and there's a seven-country wine list too.

🍷 Drinking & Entertainment

Fortaleza is famed for its nightlife and the Dragão do Mar area is one of the best places to go out.

Boteco Praia
BAR

(Av Beira Mar 1680, Meireles; ⊙ 5pm-2am; 🛜) The number-one spot for evening drinks and conversation, Boteco Praia attracts all ages to its long, arcaded hall and its terrace facing the seafront promenade. You do pay for the privilege though – R$6.60 per *chope* (draft beer), and R$15 to R$20 for the tempting portions like *picanha* steak and breaded shrimp offered by the attentive waiters.

Órbita
BAR

(www.orbitabar.com.br; Dragão do Mar 207; admission R$20-25; ⊙ 9pm-4am Thu-Sun) Reminiscent of a college-town rock club (with way better-looking people than your college or ours), this large, black-and-purple Dragão do Mar bar hosts live rock, surf and pop amid snooker tables and a legion of flirtatious upper-class clientele.

Mucuripe Club
CLUB

(mucuripe.com.br; Travessa Maranguape 108; admission R$30-60; ⊙ 10pm-5am Fri & Sat) In addition to being the best and most stylish disco in the Northeast, Mucuripe is a mindblowingly huge, modern, nontouristy venue with a dinner club and five different dance areas where you skirt between DJs and live *forró* (the Northeast's quintessential popular country dance music), *sertaneja* (northeastern country pop), *axé* (Afro-Brazilian pop), rock and more. If you lose a friend in here, they'll see you tomorrow.

Pirata Bar
CLUB

(www.pirata.com.br; Tabajaras 325; admission R$40; ⊙ 8pm-late) The bar and club scene around the Praia de Iracema waterfront area is rather touristy, but the *'Segunda-feira Mais Louca do Mundo'* (Craziest Monday in the World) here is still legendary. Live bands play *forró* and other Brazilian dance rhythms to packed crowds right through the night.

Sports

Fortaleza's Castelão stadium, 9km south of the center, was completely renovated to seat 64,000 fans for the 2014 World Cup, when it was scheduled to host six matches, including one quarter-final and at least one game involving Brazil. The city's two top clubs, Ceará (www.cearasc.com) and Fortaleza (www.fortalezaec.net), play many of their games at the Castelão.

🛍 Shopping

You'll find handicrafts from around Ceará in Fortaleza. Some of the finest work is in delicate lace, a tradition that came with the Portuguese. Artisans also work with *carnaúba*-palm fronds, bamboo, vines and leather.

Ceart
HANDICRAFTS

(Centro Dragão do Mar; ⊙ 9am-6pm Tue-Thu, 2-9pm Fri-Sun) This beautiful state-run craft store sells lace, ceramics, wood carvings, baskets and bags of sisal and *carnaúba*, and textiles. Branches are at Iracema (Av Monsenhor Tabosa 777, Praia de Iracema; ⊙ 8am-6pm Mon-Fri, 8am-5pm Sat) and Aldeota (Av Santos Dumont 1589, Aldeota; ⊙ 9am-6pm Mon-Fri, 9am-3pm Sat)

Mercado Central
MARKET

(www.mercadocentraldefortaleza.com.br; Av Nepomuceno 199; ⊙ 8am-6pm Mon-Fri, 8am-4pm Sat, 8am-noon Sun) Mainly geared to a tourist clientele, the three-story Central Market has good prices at more than 500 stalls selling everything from leather bags and colorful palm baskets to excellent local cashews and a huge variety of *cachaça* – some bottles have fruit salad or crabs pickled inside. You might well find a desirable curio.

Centro de Turismo
HANDICRAFTS

(Senador Pompeu 350; ⊙ 8am-6pm Mon-Sat, 8am-noon Sun) The many stalls here focus on lace and embroidery and you can usually see lace-makers at work.

Laselva Bookstore
BOOKS

(Aeroporto Pinto Martins; ⊙ 24hr) Upstairs in the airport; good for maps and guides.

ℹ️ Information

DANGERS & ANNOYANCES

Beware of pickpocketing in the city center and petty theft on the beaches. Tourists waiting at bus stops to return from Praia do Futuro have been targeted. Empty streets in Centro after dark are best avoided.

EMERGENCY

Ambulance (☑192)
Police (Polícia; ☑190)
Tourist Police (Delegacia de Proteção ao Turista; ☑3101-2488; Av Almirante Barroso 805, Praia de Iracema)

INTERNET ACCESS

Internet C@fé (Loja 16, Polo Comercial 101, cnr Ildefonso Albano & Av Monsenhor Tabosa; internet per hr R$4; ⏲8:30am-7:30pm Mon-Sat) Helpful little place that also does printing, scans, faxes and phone calls.

MEDICAL SERVICES

SAT (☑3261-2220; www.gruposat.com.br) The area's best travel-medicine specialist, with multilingual 24-hour house-call service.

MONEY

ATMs at the airport accept international cards.
Banco do Brasil Meireles (Av Abolição 2308; ⏲10am-4pm Mon-Fri, ATMs 6am-10pm daily); **Praia de Iracema** (Av Monsenhor Tabosa 634; ⏲10am-4pm Mon-Fri, ATMs 8am-7pm daily) These branches also do currency exchange.
HSBC (Av Monsenhor Tabosa 1200, Praia de Iracema; ⏲10am-4pm Mon-Fri, ATMs 24hr)
Confidence (Av Beira Mar, Meireles; ⏲8:30am-8:30pm Mon-Fri, 8:30am-6pm Sat, 8:30am-1:30pm Sun) Changes cash US dollars, euros and British pounds.

TOURIST INFORMATION

Casa do Turista Centro (☑3105-1444; Praça da Ferreira; ⏲9am-5pm Mon-Fri, 8am-noon Sat); **Mucuripe** (☑3105-2670; Av Beira Mar, Mucuripe; ⏲9am-9pm); **Mercado Central** (☑3253-1227; Basement level, Mercado Central, Av Nepomuceno 199; ⏲8am-5pm Mon-Fri, 8am-noon) The city tourism department operates these information booths; staff may or may not speak English.

Setur Centro de Turismo (☑3101-5508; Centro de Turismo, Senador Pompeu 350; ⏲8am-6pm Mon-Fri, 8am-3pm Sat, 8am-noon Sun); **bus station** (☑3230-1111; Rodoviária; ⏲6am-10pm); **airport** (☑3392-1667; airport; ⏲6am-midnight) The Ceará tourism organization has useful information offices, with English-speaking attendants usually available.

Setfor (www.fortaleza.ce.gov.br/turismo) The city tourism site; in Portuguese only but a useful reference.

ℹ️ Getting There & Away

AIR

Pinto Martins airport (☑3392-1200) has daily flights to/from Lisbon with **TAP Portugal** (www.flytap.com), twice-weekly Rome flights with **Alitalia** (www.alitalia.com), weekly Milan flights with **Air Italy** (www.meridiana.it), and weekly Amsterdam flights with **ArkeFly** (www.arkefly.nl). There are flights to many Brazilian cities with **Azul** (www.voeazul.com.br), **GOL** (www.voegol.com.br), **TAM** (www.tam.com.br), **Passaredo** (www.voepassaredo.com.br) and **Avianca** (www.avianca.com).

BUS

You can buy bus tickets in town at agencies including the welcoming, English-speaking **DP Tur** (☑3219-5210; www.diskpassagens.tur.br; Loja 0, Av Monsenhor Tabosa 631, Iracema; ⏲8:30am-noon & 1:30-6pm Mon-Fri, 8:30am-

BUSES FROM FORTALEZA

DESTINATION	FARE (R$)	TIME (HR)	FREQUENCY (DAILY)
Belém	230-234	24-30	3
Natal	75-110	8-9	7
Parnaíba	75-148	8-12	4
Piripiri	50-84	7-8	3
Recife	123-177	12-14	4
Rio de Janeiro	399	48	1-2
Salvador	207	22	1
São Luís	147-157	19	3
Teresina	67-113	9-11	6
Ubajara	31-40	7	5

noon Sat). From the bus station buses run to destinations including the following:

To Jericoacoara, several companies, such as **Girafatur** (☑ 3219-3255; www.girafatur.com.br) and **Enseada** (☑ 3091-2762; www.enseada.tur. br) offer direct door-to-door van transfers from Fortaleza hotels (R$60, six hours) – most accommodations can book these for you. Another option is **Fretcar** (☑ 3402-2222; www.fretcar. com.br), which runs up to three buses daily to Jericoacoara (R$43 to R$58, six to seven hours) from Fortaleza's bus station. The 8am departure (year-round) and usually one afternoon bus (4pm, 6:30pm or 7pm depending on season) also pick up at the airport about 15 minutes after leaving the bus station, and at the **Praiano Hotel** (Av Beira Mar 2800) on Meireles beach about 30 minutes after that. The last part of the Fretcar trip is a one-hour ride in a *jardineira* (open-sided 4WD truck) along sandy tracks and the beach and through dunes from Jijoca to Jericoacoara. You can check Fretcar schedules and buy tickets (advisably a day ahead) at **Beach Point** (☑ 3242-2911; Av Beira Mar 2915, Meireles; ⊙ 8am-10pm). The most exciting way of reaching Jericoacoara is by 4WD along the coast – an option offered by agencies such as Jeri Off Road (p532), which charges R$750 for up to four people.

CAR & MOTORCYCLE

Half a dozen rental agencies have airport desks, including the recommended **Avis** (☑ 3392-1369; www.avis.com.br), **Hertz** (☑ 3477-5055; www.hertz.com) and **Localiza** (www.localiza. com). There's a slew of local rental firms on Av Monsenhor Tabosa in Praia de Iracema, including **Maresia** (www.maresiarentacar.com.br; Av Monsenhor Tabosa 1001; ⊙ 8am-6pm), where some staff speak English.

🚹 Getting Around

Fortaleza has a very extensive city bus system with good frequency on most routes. Fares are mostly R$2.20 and if you have to transfer at a Terminal de Integração (Integration Terminal), such as Papicu or Parangaba, you don't have to pay a second fare.

Taxis are metered. A 4km trip across town from the Centro Dragão do Mar to Varjota, for example, costs about R$15.

TO/FROM THE AIRPORT

A taxi from the airport to Meireles or Praia de Iracema costs R$30 to R$40 depending on traffic. Buses 027 Siqueira/Papicu/Aeroporto, 087 Expresso Siqueira/Papicu and 066 Parangaba/Papicu/Aeroporto all run to Terminal Papicu in the east of the city, where you can change to the 051 Grande Circular 1 for Meireles and Praia de Iracema. Or get an 066 to Terminal Parangaba, and change there to the 077 Parangaba/Mu-

curipe bus, which runs to the Centro Dragão do Mar, Praia de Iracema and Meireles. Or take a 404 Aeroporto Benfica Rodoviária bus to the bus station and then bus 013 Aguanambi I to Av Dom Manuel and the Centro Dragão do Mar.

TO/FROM THE BUS STATION

Bus 013 Aguanambi I outside the bus station runs north up Av Dom Manoel to the Centro Dragão do Mar. For Praia de Iracema and Meireles, walk left outside the bus station, turn right at the traffic signal along Av Borges de Melo and walk to a bus stop about 200m along on the far (south) side of the street. From here buses 073 Siqueira/Praia de Iracema and 078 Siqueira/Mucuripe will take you up Av Dom Manuel to the Centro Dragão do Mar, then to Praia de Iracema and (the 078 only) Meireles.

A taxi from the bus station to Praia de Iracema costs R$25 to R$30.

Canoa Quebrada

☑ 088 / POP 4000

The coast southeast of Fortaleza has many fine beaches, a lot of them backed by dunes, but is increasingly developed and built up. It's not until you reach the environs of Canoa Quebrada, 140km from the city, that the coast starts to regain its natural majesty. Once a tiny village cut off from the world by its huge, pink sand dunes and beloved of early hippie travelers, Canoa Quebrada today has shifted towards a more family-oriented beach spot, and it's a favorite destination of daily van tours from Fortaleza. But the craggy, eroding sand cliffs and the large dune expanses still lend Canoa that elemental, otherworldly feel for which it's famous. With numerous good pousadas and restaurants, and varied outdoor activities easily available, it's an enjoyable spot to relax for a few days.

The main street, Rua Dragão do Mar (Rua Principal), runs west to east along the ridge of the hill from which Canoa slopes down to the beach. The eastern, pedestrianized half of the street, with most of the restaurants and bars, is known as Broadway.

🏃 Activities & Tours

Southeast of Canoa, 30km of beach, backed by colorful cliffs, sweeps round to the headland of **Ponta Grossa**. It's a great **beach-buggy trip** (R$250 for three or four hours round-trip, up to four people) and you can stop for a seafood lunch at beach bars like **Barraca Pantanal** (mains R$20-60; ⊙ 7am-5pm), just before Ponta Grossa – a great spot for lobster in season (July to December).

North of Canoa a large area of high dunes stretches 12km to the mouth of the Rio Jaguaribe: a one-hour **buggy trip** with some exciting steep descents costs around R$140 for up to four people. Pousadas can recommend and organize authorized buggy drivers.

Hugely popular and huge fun if you have a head for heights is tandem paragliding with **Vôo Duplo Jerônimo** (8806-6570; 10-20min flight R$70), where you ride the breezes above Canoa's beaches from their take-off point at the east end of Broadway.

Kitesurfing is best around the mouth of the Rio Jaguaribe, 12km northwest, with its reliable wind and calm waters (the season runs from July to December) – reachable only by buggy (R$25 per person round-trip). **Kite School Canoa Quebrada** (9960-6070; extremekiteschool@hotmail.com.br) and **Kite Flat Water** (3421-7403; www.brasilkiteflatwater.com; Pousada Colibri, Rua do Toquinho) are recommended schools with International Kiteboarding Organization (IKO) instructors. A two-hour discovery course is around R$170, or a complete eight-hour course R$750. Both rent equipment too.

🛏 Sleeping

Pousada California POUSADA $
(3421-7039; www.californiacanoa.com; Nascer do Sol 135; r R$140-200; ❄ 🐾 🛜 🏊) This popular 28-room pousada has a variety of neat, comfortable rooms on two sides of the street, and an attractive courtyard with a sociable bar and pool. Free fruit and coffee are available all day in the breakfast room-cum-TV lounge, a chill hang spot, and there's a new gym. English-owned and Dutch-managed.

Hostel Pousada Ibiza HOSTEL $
(3421-7262; www.hostelpousadaibiza.com; Dragão do Mar 360; dm R$35-40, d R$80-100; ❄ @ 🛜) Dorms and rooms are smallish but brightened by colorful art, and each comes equipped with its own bathroom. But what's best about this hostel is the long, airy, balcony/lounge/bar overlooking the heart of the Broadway action. It shares premises with a pizzeria (downstairs) and has a small guest kitchen. English spoken.

Vila Canoa POUSADA $$
(3421-7183; www.vilacanoa.com; Av Beira Mar 35; r R$190; ❄ 🛜 🏊) Canoa's only beachfront pousada is welcoming, Dutch-run and an excellent choice. Cool, tasteful rooms are dotted around a garden of grass and flagstone pathways that slopes down to the pool, a great sunbathing deck and the pousada's own *barraca* (beach bar/restaurant).

Pousada Dolce Vita POUSADA $$
(3421-7213; www.canoa-quebrada.it; Descida da Praia; r R$180-240; ❄ 🛜 🏊) The Dolce Vita is friendly and relaxed, with its rooms arranged round a garden of palms, flowers and lawns with a beautiful pool at its center. Rooms are spotlessly clean and have more character than your average pousada, each being named for a Fellini film and decorated with movie memorabilia.

🍴 Eating

El Argentino CHURRASCARIA $$
(3421-7123; www.elargentino.com.br; Broadway; mains R$25-45; ⏱11:30am-11:30pm) At the east end of Broadway with picture windows looking down to the beach, Argentino is the best spot for grilled meats and does an all-you-can-eat *rodízio* for R$55.

Bar Evolução PIZZERIA $$
(3421-7291; Eliziário 1060; pizza R$12-30; ⏱7-11pm Thu-Tue) Great little Italian-run place serving up thin-crust, wood-oven pizzas with farm-fresh mozzarella in an atmospheric open-air ambience.

Lazy Days SEAFOOD, INTERNATIONAL $$
(9633-1499; www.lazydaysbrasil.com; Praia; mains R$20-35; ⏱9am-5pm) At the eastern

---

REDONDA

The fishing village of Redonda, 35km southeast of Canoa Quebrada, beyond the headland of Ponta Grossa, is reminiscent of Canoa Quebrada 30 or 40 years ago – a fine place to forget the wider world for a few days – and also a good spot to eat locally caught lobster at lower-than-usual prices (around R$40 to R$50 for a two-person serving). **Pousada O Pescador** (088-3432-3018; Rua Praia 496; r R$70), right on the beach, has simple but good rooms. Slightly fancier but still with a rustic ambience are the brick chalets of **Oh! Linda Pousada** (088-3432-3025; www.ohlindapousada.com.br; Rua da Serra 100; r R$140) up on the clifftop. You can get there from Fortaleza by taking a bus to Aracati (R$13.50, three hours, 10 daily), then a van from Aracati's Igreja Matriz to Redonda.

end of the beach, Lazy Days is the best of the beach *barracas* that rub up against Canoa's picturesque red cliffs. It does excellent BBQ fish, steaks and curries and a bang-up barbecue on Thursday or Saturday nights. And if you want to stay as close to the ocean as you possibly can, it also has a couple of nice upstairs rooms (R$80 to R$100) and a dorm with double beds (per person R$35 to R$50).

Drinking & Nightlife

There's no need to structure your evening, just walk along Broadway and you'll find what's going on. Caverna (Broadway; ⊘from 4pm), towards the beach end of the street (with darts and pool) is usually the center of the action. Friday and Saturday are liveliest.

Reggae parties start every Friday and Sunday night about 1am at Freedom *barraca* on the beach.

Information

Banco do Brasil and Bradesco ATMs and the post office are all in a small shopping plaza near the west end of Rua Dragão do Mar. **Canoa Guide** (www.canoaguide.com) is a useful website.

Getting There & Away

There are five daily buses to/from Fortaleza bus station (R$16.30, 3¼ hours), or you can go by tour van (R$40, 2½ hours) with companies such as **Oceanview** (✆85-3219-1300; www.oceanviewturismo.com.br) or **Lisatur** (✆85-3219-5400; www.lisatur.com.br). The tour vans pick up and drop off at accommodations in Fortaleza, departing there around 8am and starting back from the west end of Rua Dragão do Mar around 3:30pm.

Coming from Rio Grande do Norte, get off your bus at Aracati, 13km southwest of Canoa. From there, with any luck you can catch São Benedito's Fortaleza–Canoa bus (R$2, 8:50am, 11:30am, 1:50pm, 4:20pm or 8:20pm). Otherwise, minibuses (R$3, about every half-hour, 6am to 8pm) depart from the Igreja Matriz in Aracati's center, about 1km from the bus station. Taxis charge R$25 for the quick Aracati–Canoa run.

A new airport at Aracati was expected to be operational by mid-2014, with the first flights expected to be from São Paulo.

Beaches Northwest of Fortaleza

The coast northwest of Fortaleza is strung with beautiful beaches and villages that are great for unwinding and exploring dunes, bays, lakes and rivers. The winds and waves provide some perfect conditions for surfing, windsurfing and kitesurfing.

Cumbuco

Cumbuco, 35km from Fortaleza, has a long beach that's cleaner than Fortaleza's city beaches, and an expanse of dunes and a few lagoons that make it very popular for buggy rides and day tours from Fortaleza. But you'll do better to head to much prettier places further along the coast – unless you are, or want to be, a kitesurfer. Praia de Cumbuco itself and the Lagoa da Barra do Cauipe, 10km west of the town, have some of Brazil's best kitesurfing conditions from July to February. The lagoon's perfect combination of strong winds and gentle waters even means that it can get overcrowded at times. Rental and classes are available. Cumbuco has several hotels and pousadas if you want to stay over. Empresa Vitória (✆085-4011-1299; www.evitoria.com.br) runs minibuses to Cumbuco (R$5.15) from in front of Clube Ideal in Meireles, Fortaleza, at 9am, 11am, 3:50pm and 6:20pm.

Paracuru

✆ 085 / POP 20,500

On a curving bay 95km northwest of Fortaleza with palms and rustic fishing boats, and cobblestone streets behind, Paracuru is a popular weekend retreat from the city. It's pretty quiet during the week and is not a regular destination for Fortaleza tour vans.

Surfing can be good here year-round, and the kitesurfing conditions are generally excellent from August to January, with November and December optimal. What's normally the best kite spot is 4km east of the town center.

There's a Banco do Brasil ATM just south of the central Praça da Matriz. Twelve daily buses run to Paracuru from Fortaleza's bus station (R$9.10, two hours).

Sleeping & Eating

Pousada Sol & Lua POUSADA $
(✆3344-2055; www.pousadaparacuru.com; Izaura Moreira Lima 203; s R$95-130, d R$106-145; ❋❂✉) A pleasing German-owned pousada with 12 brightly decked-out rooms, a bar, a pool and CCTV cameras, in a quiet street 1km east of the center.

Fórmula 1   SEAFOOD, INTERNATIONAL **$$**
(☑ 3344-2048; formula1paracuru.com.br; Praia da Munguba; mains for 2 R$45-70; ⊙ 10am-11pm) On Paracuru's central beach, well-known Fórmula 1 serves a variety of dishes including couscous, fondues, grilled fish and its specialty snails, and is also a fine place to enjoy a cold beer. The French owner also runs **Pousada Fórmula 1** (☑ 3344-2048; formula1paracuru.com.br; Paulo Henrique 100; s R$80-90, d R$100-120; ✳ 🛜 🏊), where good, large, colorful rooms are spread around nice gardens with a good pool, 1.5km back from the beach.

Lagoinha

☑ 085

About 20km along the coast from Paracuru (45km by road), Lagoinha has a beautiful, long beach – with coconut palms and *jangadas* – that extends 15km to the northwest and is one of the prettiest stretches of sand in Ceará (and it has some competition). It's not yet heavily developed (though large constructions have broken ground and Fortaleza tour vans roll in daily) and is a good choice for a short visit from Fortaleza. There are hourly buses from Fortaleza's bus station to Paraipaba (R$8.45, two hours, 6:30am to 8:30pm), from where you need a taxi (R$12) for the final 20km to Lagoinha.

🛏 Sleeping & Eating

Pousada do Sol   POUSADA **$**
(☑ 3363-5092; www.apousadadosol.com; Antônio Cordeiro Filho 10; s/d R$110/140; ✳ 🛜) A neat and friendly little surprise at the village entrance, with small, prettily decorated rooms round a stone-paved courtyard.

Hotel Vivamar   HOTEL **$$**
(☑ 3363-5077; www.vivamarhotel.com.br; Praia; s/d R$140/230; ✳ 🛜 🏊) Lovely bright rooms in warm tones all have ample verandas with views across the garden to the beach. The restaurant has amiable service and a short but good seafood and meat menu (mains for two: R$34 to R$87).

Flecheiras & Mundaú

☑ 085

The end-of-the-road settlements of Flecheiras (136km from Fortaleza and 11km north of the town of Trairi) and Mundaú (142km from Fortaleza and 17km northwest of Trairi) are traditional fishing areas with long, wide stretches of beautiful sand, offshore reefs and dunes. They are still relatively undeveloped – fine places for doing nothing much in a postcard setting.

Little Flecheiras, a favored weekend retreat of well-heeled Fortaleza folk and a good kitesurfing spot (best: August to November), has several pousadas including **Pousada Edmar** (☑ 3351-3069; Rua da Praia 674; s R$45-60, d R$90-120), with neat, simple, well-kept rooms, some looking straight on to the beach, and the more upscale **Pousada Catavento** (☑ 3281-1818; www.pousadacataventoce.com.br; Rua da Praia; s R$150-180, d R$170-200; ✳ 🛜) with pleasant brick-walled rooms facing the beach across the street. A good place to eat, for its quirky English menu translations as well as the fodder itself (fish to burgers to beef), is beachside **Tempero Mineiro** (Praia; mains R$29-50; ⊙ 11am-11pm).

In larger Mundaú, tourism still takes second place to fishing. The **river trip** (per person R$25; ⊙ 10:30am & 4pm, any time if more than 2 people) along the Rio Mundaú is a lovely 1½-hour outing, especially the afternoon one which stops for sunset-viewing from high dunes. Well-run **Estrela de Mundaú Hotel** (☑ 3351-9063; www.estrela.cc; Vila Nova 50; s/d R$90/135; ✳ 🛜) , a few steps from the bus stop on the central *praça* (square), has some rooms with sea views and a big tropical garden with pool. English and German are spoken. Order a couple of hours ahead for the terrific paella at **Pousada Beach House** (☑ 9921-0399; www.mundaubeachhouse.com; Rua da Praia 537, Mundaú; s/d R$80/125, restaurant mains for 2 R$25-60; ⊙ restaurant 11am-3pm & 7-10pm; ✳ @ 🛜), a pousada (with spacious rooms) and beach *barraca* run by an Englishman who spent 10 years in Barcelona.

Six Fretcar (☑ 085-3402-2222; www.fretcar.com.br) buses leave Fortaleza bus station daily for Flecheiras (R$12.75, three hours) and three for Mundaú (R$13, 3¾ hours).

Icaraí de Amontada

☑ 088

Icaraizinho, as it's affectionately known, is the loveliest of the small beach spots between Fortaleza and Jericoacoara. Its wide beach of fine sand sits on a beautiful, palm-lined curve of bay, with a few fishing boats on the water, high dunes rising to the west, and rarely more than a handful of people in sight – reminiscent, some say, of Jericoacoara 25 years ago. It's 190km from Fortaleza (beyond the reach of day-tour buses), has no ATM, and the 24km road linking it to Hwy CE-085 was only paved a few years ago. Icaraí has a selection of excellent pousadas and some good restaurants, and is a top windsurfing and kitesurfing spot (best from July to December). **Club Ventos** (☑3636-3006; www.clubventos.com), at the east end of the beach, gives windsurfing and kitesurfing classes and rents quality equipment, plus surfboards, kayaks and stand-up-paddle (SUP) boards.

One daily Fretcar (p539) bus leaves Fortaleza bus station for Icaraí (R$19.45, 4½ hours) at 2:30pm, starting back at 5:50am (1:20pm Sunday).

🍴 Sleeping & Eating

★ Pousada Les Alizés   POUSADA $$
(☑9697-0880, 3636-3006; www.lesalizes.com.br; s/d fan R$115/150, air-con R$150/178; ❄ 🛜 🏊)
At the eastern end of the bay, Les Alizés has four cute air-con bungalows in its large beachside gardens, and non-air-con rooms in a side block. The excellent breakfast in a breezy pavilion gazing out at the beach is a true delight.

Villa Mango   CHALET $$$
(☑3636-3089; www.villamango.com.br; apt R$250, bungalow R$300-500; ❄ 🛜 🏊) Eight rustic but luxurious wooden stilt chalets (some two-level) stand in a garden sloping down to the west end of the beach. Villa Mango also offers a good restaurant, bar, pool and its own kitesurf club.

Café Zapata   BRAZILIAN $
(☑3636-3084; www.cafezapata.com; Joaquim Alves Parente 94; mains R$14-25; ⊙6:30-10pm) This pretty garden restaurant on a narrow street leading towards the far east end of the beach does everything from pasta to chicken to seafood to salads and sandwiches. It's all pretty good, and so are the prices.

Jericoacoara

☑ 088 / POP 3000

Jericoacoara, known to its many friends simply as 'Jeri,' magnetizes travelers with its perfect combination of hard-to-reach location (access is only by unpaved tracks through the dunes), stunning coastal scenery, exciting activities, good-value pousadas and restaurants, and fun nightlife. The village's sandy streets are wedged between a broad beach, a series of grassy hills and the majestic Pôr do Sol (Sunset) dune, a towering mountain of sand that affords one of South America's most stunning sunsets. It is here each evening that Jeri's allure climaxes: a crowd swells – drinks in hand from an enterprising local with a cocktail cart – to what is allegedly one of the earth's few locations where you can see the rare phenomenon known as the 'Emerald Sunset,' when the tip of the setting sun turns bright green for the final instant before it slides below the horizon. Bring your camera!

Jericoacoara's isolated position, inside a far-flung national park at the top edge of the country, is unique. Hopefully the new Jericoacoara airport, 30km away in Cruz municipality – possibly opening in 2014 – will not lead to a transformation that shatters its otherwordly allure. The airport is at least well outside the national park.

Jeri itself is closed to unauthorized vehicles, though there is still more traffic than there should be. The main streets (of sand) run parallel to each other, westward towards the beach. In the middle is Rua Principal. To the north are Rua do Forró (where buses arrive) and then Rua da Igreja (also called Rua da Matriz); to the south (the dune side) are Rua São Francisco and Rua das Dunas.

🏃 Activities

The steady winds between late June and February make Jericoacoara a top destination for kitesurfing and windsurfing. There are also nightly capoeira classes on the beach and decent waves for surfing. If you are of a calmer demeanor, you can visit the dunes and lakes outside town by buggy, take yoga classes or stroll along the beach to **Pedra Furada**, an arched rock 3km east of town.

Buggy Rides
Organize buggy rides through your pousada or agencies in town or the **Associação dos Bugueiros** (Buggy Drivers' Association; ☑3669-2284; Rua Principal), which has a stand on the central square. The buggies take up to four passengers and prices are for the vehicle (with driver), so if you join with others it's cheaper. Jeri Off Road (p542) is a helpful and environmentally conscious agency that also organizes buggy adventures near and far. An excellent five-hour outing (R$250) is to **Tatajuba**, 24km west, a fishing village with a beach at the mouth of a tidal river, and a large lagoon among the dunes behind the village. There are *barracas* beside the lagoon. One of the

dunes actually overtook the old Tatajuba, which had to be moved to its present site – brick by brick. You can still see evidence of where the church used to be.

Capoeira

Classes (R$25, 1½ hours) are held at 7am or 8am and 4pm every day on the beach, followed (except Sunday) by a sunset *roda de capoeira* (open capoeira performance), which always attracts a crowd.

Surfing

There are good waves for surfing (best from about March to May) right out in front of Jeri beach. Praia Malhada, round the corner to the right, has bigger waves for more advanced surfers. Board rental costs R$20 to R$30 per hour, or around R$60 per day.

Windsurfing

The same winds that make Jeri a kitesurfing mecca work for windsurfing too. July to January are the best months, with fine conditions for experienced riders right in front of Jeri beach. **Ticowind** (✆9662-9291; www.ticowindjeri.com; Vila Kalango, Rua das Dunas 30) is highly popular for its good quality/ price combination (and it's thus sometimes necessary to book ahead for its services): it rents windsurfers for one day/one week/two

KITING JERI & THE NORTHEAST

Steady, strong trade winds blowing across the Atlantic from Africa for the second half of the year place Brazil's northeast coast among the world's very best kitesurfing zones. Lovers of this exciting, physically demanding sport fly in from around the world and have spawned a whole infrastructure of kite schools, kite pousadas and kite safaris. There is a full range of conditions from flat water to waves, and the steady easterly breeze blowing along the whole coast makes for some epic downwinder voyages.

Equipment rentals are widely available, but with rates of around R$150 per day it makes more sense for experienced surfers to bring their own. A rental car is a huge help both for transporting your gear and for reaching the best spots. Beginners can learn the art at almost any kitesurfing destination: a course of nine or 10 hours, usually spread over three days, costs around R$800 to R$900. For proper safety standards and quality teaching, go to a school with instructors certified by the **International Kiteboarding Organization** (IKO; www.ikointl.com).

Jericoacoara is one of the most popular kite locations, thanks to its combination of traveler facilities and winds that blow at an average 23 to 30 knots for eight months of the year. From late June to February the breeze springs up mid-morning and blows till sunset; it's strongest in September and October. The rivermouth waters at Guriú, 12km west of Jeri, and along the shore for several kilometers back towards Jeri, are calm and particularly good for learners. Other good spots are Tatajuba, 12km beyond Guriú, with a flat-water lagoon, and Preá, 12km east of Jeri, with choppier waters.

Jeri has numerous kite schools. Freelance teachers may charge as little as R$600, but it's better to use a school with IKO instructors such as **MH Kiteschool** (✆3669-2268; www.facebook.com/MhKiteschool; Pousada Bella Jeri, Travessa da Rua do Forró), Preá-based **Rancho do Kite** (✆3669-2080; www.ranchodokite.com.br; Rancho do Peixe, Preá), **Jeri Kite School** (✆9693-7343; www.jerikiteschool.net) (also Preá-based, but with a shop in the lane beside Pimenta Verde restaurant), or **Kiteiscool** (✆9670-2330; www.kiteiscool.com; Praça Principal).

The whole coast around Jeri – from Barrinha, 6km east of Preá, to Camocim, 20km west of Tatajuba – is great for downwinders. It's easy to find a buggy for transport; they charge R$120 to R$150 for four or five people from Jeri to Guriú, for example. Much longer downwinders are equally possible, on any stretch of the coast, and can be organized through local pousadas, agencies and kite schools. Jeri Off Road (p542), for example, offers 'kitesurfaris' of several days with 4WD from Canoa Quebrada to Fortaleza (140km), Fortaleza to Jeri (300km), or Jeri to Barra Grande (100km). Another Jeri-based specialist is **Downwind Brazil** (✆3660-3158; www.downwindbrazil.com).

For information on other kitesurfing locations, see this book's sections on Porto de Galinhas, Natal, São Miguel do Gostoso, Galinhos, Canoa Quebrada, Fortaleza, Cumbuco, Flecheras and Icaraí de Amontada.

weeks R$49/249/407, and charges R$300 for a four-hour beginner's course. **Club Ventos** (🖉3669-2288; www.clubventos.com; Praia de Jericoacoara), just east of the foot of Rua do Forró, is also professional and well-equipped, though more expensive. It also rents kayaks, surfboards and stand-up-paddle (SUP) boards.

🖝 Tours

Apart from buggy day-trips you can also take buggy or 4WD trips as far west as Parnaíba, the Lençóis Maranhenses and São Luís, a route known as the Rota das Emoções (Route of the Emotions). A tour is a lot easier though more expensive than public transport: a three-day 4WD expedition to São Luís, including accommodations, transportation, a Delta do Parnaíba boat trip and a Lençóis Maranhenses tour, costs R$3000/3960 for two/four people with **Jeri Off Road** (🖉3669-2268; www.jeri.tur.br; Pousada Bella Jeri, Travessa da Rua do Forró) 🏄.

🛏 Sleeping

There are dozens of pousadas and small hotels in Jericoacoara. Some close during May, the low point of Jeri's low season.

Casa Côco Verde HOSTEL $
(🖉8872-0865; www.casacocoverde.com; Dunas; dm R$40, s/d R$130/150; 🛜) Kitesurfer and world traveler Angela has created an inviting ambience in this sociable hostel with murals, ample breakfasts, equipment storage, hammocks and an open patio shaded by coconut palms. Downstairs dorms and upstairs doubles are cooled by fans and crossbreezes. Angela also offers guided horseback rides, can help organize kitesurfing and other trips and tell you anything you need to know about Jeri.

Pousada Tirol/
Jericoacoara Hostel HOSTEL $
(🖉3669-2006; www.jericoacoarahostel.com.br; São Francisco 202; dm with fan/air-con R$45/55, d R$130; 🛠🛜) Despite its rather basic dorms, this hostel wins huge points for its welcoming atmosphere. The large patio and hammock space with well-stocked 'honor fridge' promote easy socializing, and trilingual manager Gaúcho is constantly assisting guests with travel advice, well-organized information boards and reasonably priced laundry service.

Bella Jeri POUSADA $$
(🖉3669-2268; www.bellajeri.com.br; Travessa da Rua do Forró; s/d R$135/165; 🛠🛜) It has seven cute, tasteful rooms with brick walls, good wood furniture and outside hammocks, plus a nice little garden and breezy roof terrace with views to the dune and the ocean. The breakfast is great, and the English-speaking owners also run Jeri Off Road and MH Kiteschool (p541).

Pousada Papaya POUSADA $$
(🖉3669-2219; www.jeripapaya.com; Dunas 74; s R$145-180, d R$160-180; 🛠🛜) Neat, comfy rooms with colorful check bedspreads, a good breakfast, the pool in the flowery front garden, and attractive common areas inside and out, make the Papaya a deservedly popular little choice.

Pousada Surfing Jeri POUSADA $$
(🖉3669-2260; www.surfingjeri.com.br; São Francisco 150; d R$250-280; 🛠🛜🏊) Solidly constructed rooms and apartments with wood floors and ceilings are set along a green, shady garden with pool, adding up to a solidly sensible choice.

★**Vila Kalango** POUSADA, CHALET $$$
(🖉3669-2291; www.vilakalango.com.br; Dunas 30; r R$350-540; 🛠@🛜🏊) A longtime top-end favorite, Vila Kalango's round brick bungalows are serene escape pods (some are elevated on stilts with driftwood staircases leading the way), with beautiful canopy beds and native wood furniture. The smaller *apartamentos* are equally tasteful and have air-con to offset their lack of breeze. Staff are charming, and the pool deck and restaurant look out onto the beach.

Pousada Jeribá POUSADA $$$
(🖉3669-2206; www.jeriba.com.br; Rua do Ibama; r R$330-572; 🛠🛜🏊) Spacious rooms with gorgeous hardwood verandas and hammock chairs are set in tasteful, exposed-brick bungalows amid colorful grounds draped in lush tropicalia. Rooms 12, 13 and 14 have the best views. The oceanfront patio and lounge is a near-perfect chillout pad with views over Jeri's dunes and prime windsurfing waters, and the classy **restaurant** (🕙noon-10pm) right next to it.

🍴 Eating

Jeri offers a great variety of excellent food for such a small place. Best-value economical eats are the *pratos feitos* (combination dishes) available for R$10 to R$15 at places like **João do Barro** (São Francisco), **Ponta Big** (cnr Principal & Beco do Guaxêlo) and the neat little family-run **Jeri Jú** (Forró).

Café Brasil
CAFE $

(Beco do Guaxêlo 65A; dishes R$5-21; ☺9am-10:30pm) In an alley between Ruas Principal and São Francisco, Café Brasil makes massive, shareable sandwiches with wholegrain breads, salads, burgers, crepes, cakes, coffee, juices and smoothies. Consistently some of the best food in town.

Padaria Santo Antônio
BAKERY $

(São Francisco; ☺2am-7am) A Jericoacoara classic, this bakery opens in the wee hours of the morning to provide coffee and freshly baked goods to party-goers on their way home.

★ Pimenta Verde
INTERNATIONAL, BRAZILIAN $$

(☑9916-0577; São Francisco; mains R$19-47; ☺noon-10:30pm) This delightful little corner restaurant with only a few tables pumps out memorable cuisine from octopus *Provençal* (best dish in Jeri?) to a divine green peppercorn filet. Cute artistic touches round out the culinary happiness.

Tamarindo
BRAZILIAN $$

(☑9937-9057; Farmacia; medium pizza R$17-29, mains R$23-48; ☺6pm-midnight) The most creative dining experience in Jeri, romantically lit under the shadow of a giant tamarind tree. Nearly everything is cooked in the brick oven, which is the norm for the pizza, but not for exquisite gems like the Brazil-nut-crusted filet mignon. From the cocktails (frozen *tangeroskas* with ginger) to the staff and service, it's a class act.

Peixe Brasileiro
SEAFOOD $$

(☑9703-8989; cnr São Francisco & Beco do Guaxêlo; fish/shrimp/lobster per kg R$35/70/100; ☺7-11pm) Some local fisherman got a bright idea: throw some hot coals and nice tables in the sand alley by night and grill whole fresh fish for tourists. Pick your dinner – *pargo* (red snapper), *garoupa* (grouper), *robalo* (sea bass), shrimp and/or *langosta* – right out of the fish cooler, where it arrived only hours ago. An experience!

Pizza Dellacasa
PIZZERIA $$

(☑9962-3640; Principal 595; pizza R$23-39; ☺6-11:30pm Tue-Sun, closed May) Probably the best pizza in town, with medium-thin crusts, and the seafood spaghetti is pretty good too. The frozen drinks in flavors like mango, tangerine and passionfruit are a tropical godsend in this heat.

Club Ventos
SELF-SERVE $$

(Praia de Jericoacoara; per kg R$41.90; ☺noon-5pm) Soak up the spectacular views from the cashew-tree-shaded oceanfront terrace at this per-kilo eatery, then settle into a lounge chair and catch some rays for the rest of the afternoon. Good salads and vegetable options compensate for the limited array of main dishes.

☕ Drinking & Entertainment

Everything starts at the cocktail carts on the beach at the foot of Rua Principal from early evening. Some nights a DJ joins them and everyone dances on the sand till the early hours. From here partiers move on to other entertainments around the village. A few steps up from the beach, **Planeta Jeri** (Principal; ☺8pm-late), playing a mostly electronic soundtrack, is at its best from around 2am to 4am.

The Wednesday, Friday and Saturday *forró* nights with a live band at **Restaurante Dona Amélia** (Forró; ☺11:59pm-4:30am Wed, Fri & Sat) are thronged with swaying couples on the dance floor from around 2:30am till closing at 4:30am. To get the most out of *forró* it helps to learn the dance – especially for men, who must lead. Head to teacher Mel at **Academia Samba Jeri** (☑9678-3665; www.sambajericoacoara.moonfruit.com; Principal, above Padaria Central; 2/4 classes R$25/35) for tuition in forró, samba or other Brazilian dances.

Espaço Cultural Oka (Forró) has a popular live reggae night on Saturday – at its best from 1am or 2am till closing at 4:30am. **Maloca** (Igreja) at the top end of Rua Igreja hosts Jeri's best samba night, from 10pm to 2am on Friday, but there are further good samba sessions at **Tortuga** (São Francisco) from around 11pm Sunday, and by the pool at **Pousada Hippopotamus** (Forró), Tuesday from 10pm to 2am.

Places and events change frequently, so ask around.

ℹ Information

Many pousadas and restaurants will accept Visa or MasterCard, but Jeri has no international-friendly ATM. You can stock up with cash before arriving, at **Banco do Brasil** in **Jijoca** (Av Manoel Teixeira 139, Jijoca; ☺9am-2pm Mon-Fri, ATMs 7am-6pm daily), 23 km southeast, or **Camocim** (José de Alencar 54, Camocim; ☺9am-2pm Mon-Fri, ATM 6am-8pm daily), 45km west.

Boa Viagem Câmbio (Principal; ☺10am-noon & 4-10pm) Exchanges cash US dollars and euros.

Cyber Jeri Café (São Francisco; internet per hr R$2; ◷9:30am-10:30pm) You can also print and photocopy here.

Global Connection (◲9900-2109; Forró; internet per hr R$2.50; ◷7:30am-10:30pm) Sells bus tickets from Jeri to Fortaleza and many other regional routes, plus air tickets; also offers internet and phone calls.

Rota das Emoções (www.rotadasemocoes. com.br) Good website on the whole route from Jericoacoara to Parnaíba and the Lençóis Maranhenses.

Tem de Tudo (Principal; ◷7am-midnight) This supermarket can usually give cash back, with a 10% charge for debit cards and 15% for credit cards.

❶ Getting There & Away

Construction of Jericoacoara airport, some 30km southeast of town, has been an on-off affair, but at the time of writing a 2014 opening was on the cards, so it may soon be possible to fly there from Brazilian cities and even other countries.

Fretcar's service to Fortaleza (R$43 to R$58, six to seven hours) leaves at 3pm (and 8am and/or 10:30pm depending on season and day of the week). You go by *jardineira* (open-sided 4WD truck) as far as Jijoca, then by bus. The *jardineira* starts from Global Connection, which also sells tickets for this and other regional bus services.

You can also travel to Fortaleza in the tour vans of companies such as **Girafatur** (◲085-3219-3255; www.girafatur.com.br), which drop off at Fortaleza hotels (R$60, six hours). Most accommodations can book these for you. The vans usually leave about 9am and some stop 2½ hours at Lagoa Paraíso, near Jijoca, en route.

The most frequent transportation between Jeri and Jijoca is by *camionetes* (4WD passenger trucks; R$8 to R$10 one way), which leave whenever they fill with passengers – most frequently between about 6am and 9am. A good place to find one in Jeri is in front of Padaria Jeripan on Rua São Francisco. If you can't find one, a buggy costs around R$50 for up to four people. From Jijoca there are up to eight Fretcar buses to Fortaleza (R$25 to R$35, five to six hours) and up to four to Camocim (R$8 to R$10, 1½ to 2¼ hours).

If you are coming to Jeri by car, it's best to leave it in Jijoca, where there are safe parking lots for R$7 to R$10 per day, then get a *camionete* or buggy on to Jeri.

TO/FROM THE LENÇÓIS MARANHENSES

Moving on westward towards the Lençóis Maranhenses, the direct coastal route includes a 40km 4WD-only stretch from Paulino Neves to Barreirinhas, so travelers by regular bus have to go almost to São Luís before heading 200km back east to Barreirinhas.

For the coastal route, the easiest and costliest options are a straight one-day 4WD transfer from Jeri (around R$1200 to Barreirinhas for up to four people), or a tour, which can take in the Delta do Parnaíba en route. The best combination of speed and economy (available in its entirety Monday to Friday only) starts with a 4WD truck for 45km along the coast to the fishing and market town of Camocim (R$35, 1½ to three hours), leaving Jeri about 7am Monday to Saturday. The truck connects with a minibus from Camocim, Monday to Friday only, reaching Parnaíba about 1:30pm (combined tickets for these two legs cost R$75 – book through Jeri accommodations). Take the 2pm Viação Coimbra bus from Parnaíba to the village of Paulino Neves (R$21, 3½ hours, Monday to Saturday), stay the night in Paulino Neves, then take a 4WD truck along the rough track through the dunes to Barreirinhas (R$20, 2½ hours) at 4am, 9am or noon (times variable). The 4am truck enables you to fit in a Lençóis tour from Barreirinhas the same day and move on to São Luís by late afternoon.

If you're not hell-bent on speed, there are also options using regular buses from Jijoca to Camocim and the daily 4:15pm Guanabara bus from Camocim to Parnaíba (R$18, 2¾ hours), plus different possibilities from Parnaíba.

Coming to Jeri from the Lençóis, transportation schedules along the coastal route are less convenient, so a direct 4WD transfer is worth considering.

Parque Nacional de Ubajara

◲ 088

The entrance to this **national park** (admission with guide R$5; ◷8am-4pm Tue-Sun) 🚶 is 3km east from the center of the small town of Ubajara, 325km west of Fortaleza. The main attractions are giant caves, the cable car down to them, and walks in the surrounding forest. Atop a thickly forested escarpment 850m above sea level, Ubajara offers some spectacular vistas over the *sertão* below, and relatively cool temperatures that provide a welcome respite from the *sertão's* searing heat. **Portal Ubajara** (www.portalubajara.com.br) is a useful website.

◉ Sights

Caves

Nine chambers with strange limestone formations extend more than 500m into the side of a mountain. The main formations seen inside the **caves** (guide R$5) are **Pedra do Sino** (Bell Stone), **Salas da Rosa** (Rose Rooms), **Sala do Cavalo** (Horse Room) and

Sala dos Retratos (Portrait Room). A cable car (per person 1 way R$4; ⏰9am-2:30pm Tue-Sun) makes the descent from the park entrance to the cave quick and easy. Last entry to the cave is at 2pm, and the last cable car up leaves when the last group leaves the caves around 3pm. But if you fancy a beautiful hike, take the 7km trail down to the caves via two waterfalls and a lookout point. Hikers must be accompanied by a park guide, leaving from the entrance at 8am, 9am and 10am. Wear sturdy footwear and take enough to drink. You can catch the cable car back up.

🛏 Sleeping & Eating

★ Sítio do Alemão   CHALET $

(☑9961-4645; www.sitio-do-alemao.20fr.com; Sítio Santana; s R$40-60, d R$60-100; ❄◎🛜) ⟋ There are wonderful panoramas from this German-run property, 4.5km from Ubajara center and 1.5km from the park entrance (fork right just past Pousada de Neblina coming from town). The rustic but cosy chalets are tucked away on lushly vegetated grounds frequently visited by a troupe of capuchin monkeys, and you'll take your excellent breakfast in a pavilion among the trees.

Your host is a mine of information on the area including several excellent walks starting right here, and he offers half-day trips to another area highlight, the beautiful Cachoeira do Frade (a series of waterfalls in a canyon 30km away), for R$130/160 per two/four people (less if you have your own car).

Pousada Gruta   POUSADA $

(☑3634-1375; pousadagruta@hotmail.com; Sítio Amazonas; s/d R$70/100, restaurant mains for 2 R$25-35; ⏰restaurant 11:30am-3pm; 🛜) ⟋ This small pousada 200m from the park entrance offers cool, clean, simple rooms, but the difference here is the owner's special attention to local history, plants, foods and drinks, including coffee roasted on the premises with *rapadura* (dried sugarcane juice) and served with sugarcane honey, and his potent invention, the *maracuchaça*, a delicious cocktail made with liquors of *maracujá* (passion fruit) and other seasonal fruits.

Nevoar   NORTHEASTERN, SUSHI $

(☑3634-1312; Av Mons Gonçalo Eufrásio 171; mains for 2 R$18-40; ⏰10:30am-11pm) The best restaurant in town offers good regional fish and meat dishes, a wildly varied, world-savvy wine list and respectable sushi.

ℹ Getting There & Around

Buses leave Ubajara for Fortaleza (R$31 to R$40, 6½ to nine hours, six daily), and for Piripiri (R$16, 2½ hours) and Teresina (R$38, five hours) at 10am. There are more connections from Tianguá, on Hwy BR-222 17km north of Ubajara. Frequent minibuses link Tianguá to Ubajara (R$2.05).

You can get here from Jericoacoara in under six hours using the 12:30pm Fretcar bus from Jijoca to Granja (R$6, one hour), then the 2:25pm Gontijo bus from Granja to Ubajara (R$9.85, 2¼ hours). Or get from Jeri to Camocim and take the same Gontijo bus at 2pm in Camocim. From Ubajara to Jeri, take the 9:30am Gontijo bus to Granja then the noon or 4:30pm Fretcar from Granja to Jijoca.

To reach the park entrance from Ubajara, either walk or take a taxi (R$15) or mototaxi (R$4).

PIAUÍ

Piauí, one of the largest states in the Northeast, boasts several fantastic natural attractions, including the Delta do Parnaíba, the Parque Nacional de Sete Cidades and the Parque Nacional da Serra da Capivara (one of the top prehistoric sites in South America). Colonial settlement in Piauí began in the arid southern *sertão* and gradually moved north toward the coast, creating an oddly shaped territory with underdeveloped infrastructure. Today, Piauí is Brazil's poorest state.

Teresina

TRANSPORT HUB
POP 768,000

Teresina, the flat, orderly capital of Piauí, is famed as the hottest city in Brazil. Founded in 1852, it was Brazil's first planned city. If time is on your hands, take a look in the city center at the Central de Artesanato (☑086-3222-5772; Praça Dom Pedro II; ⏰8am-6pm Mon-Fri, 9am-3pm Sat), which has a sculpture-enlivened courtyard of shops offering intriguing crafts from all over Piauí.

🛏 Sleeping & Eating

Hotel Teresinha   HOTEL $

(☑086-3211-0919; www.hotelteresinha.com.br; Av Getúlio Vargas 2885; s/d R$55/75; ❄🛜) A simple but well-kept and welcoming place right opposite the bus station.

CEARÁ, PIAUÍ & MARANHÃO TERESINA

Life's a Beach

In a country famed for its fabulous beaches, the shoreline of Ceará, Piauí and Maranhão has both hands on the supreme crown. The 1000km from Ceara's southeastern limits to São Luís is a rarely-interrupted succession of long, sweeping, dune-backed strands and smaller palm-lined bays with a few fishing boats riding at anchor.

Jericoacoara

Set inside a national park with no paved roads (only sandy tracks), this hip, ultra-laid-back travelers' hangout (p540) just about has it all. Majestic dunescapes, world-class winds for kite- and windsurfers, a nightly party scene on the beach and in the music joints, good restaurants and dozens of good-value pousadas.

Atins

For that true end-of-the-road feeling, head down the jungle-clad Rio Preguiças to tiny Atins (p560), with a scattering of pousadas along its sandy streets, and the incredible expanse of high dunes and fresh water lagoons that is the Lençóis Maranhenses beginning a short walk away.

Icaraí de Amontada

Little Icaraí (p539), just far enough from Fortaleza to preserve its tranquility, spreads round a gorgeous curve of palm-lined sand with a few fishing boats bobbing in the surf and rarely more than a handful of people in sight. A few surprisingly good pousadas and restaurants cater to those in the know.

Canoa Quebrada

A budget backpackers' destination that is transitioning into a more family-friendly spot, Canoa (p536) sits on an endless beach lined by pink cliffs on one side and high dunes on the other, and is full of fun things to do from tandem paragliding to beach reggae parties.

2

1. Parachuting, Canoa Quebrada (p536) 2. Praia de Ponta Negra (p515), Natal 3. Beach football, Atins (560) 4. Windsurfing, Jericoacoara (p540)

4

Luxor Piauí Hotel
HOTEL $$

(☑086-3131-3000; reservas@luxorpiaui.com.br; Praça Marechal Deodoro 310; s R$231-256, d R$278-307; ✱☎❄) This stylish contemporary place faces a leafy park in the center, and its restaurant, **Forno e Fogão** (buffet R$32; ☺noon-3pm), does a great-value regional lunch buffet.

Coco Bambu
NORTHEASTERN $$

(Profesor Joca Vieira 1227; mains for 2 R$50-130; ☺11:30am-midnight) Most of the best restaurants cluster in the Jóquei district east of the Rio Poti. Coco Bambu has a bright atmosphere and some great fish dishes (try the specialty *sirigado*), plus crepes, tapiocas and a whole page of desserts.

❶ Getting There & Around

Teresina's **airport** (☑086-3133-6270; Av Centenário), 6km north of the center, has direct flights to Fortaleza, São Luís, Brasília, Goiânia and São Paulo.

The **bus station** (☑086-3218-1761; csi.ati.pi.gov.br/rodoviaria; Hwy BR-343) is 6km southeast of the center. Destinations include Belém (R$125 to R$140, 14 to 18 hours, 11 daily), Fortaleza (R$46 to R$113, nine to 12 hours, 19 daily), Parnaíba (R$59 to R$87, five to six hours, 12 daily), Piripiri (R$18 to R$42, three hours, 20 daily), São Luís (R$55 to R$68, seven to nine hours, 11 daily), São Raimundo Nonato (R$76, nine to 10 hours, four daily) and Ubajara (R$38, five hours, 11am).

Any 'João Luiz' bus (R$2.10), across the road outside the bus station, will take you to the city center. 'Rodoviária' buses from the central Praça João Luiz go out to the bus station. Taxis cost around R$20 in light traffic.

Parnaíba

☑ 086 / POP 138,000

Parnaíba was a major port until its river silted up and its *carnaúba*-palm wax industry died when artificial waxes were invented for cosmetics and car polish. Today it soldiers on as a market town and transit point for the new port at nearby Luís Correia. For travelers, it's a stepping stone on the coastal route from Jericoacoara to the Lençóis Maranhenses, and the starting point for trips into the beautiful Delta do Parnaíba.

Visitors gravitate to **Porto das Barcas** on the Rio Igaraçú waterfront, a small complex of craft shops, restaurants and travel agencies in converted 18th- and 19th-century warehouses. The main street, Av Presidente Vargas, runs 1km east from here; the bus station is 5km southeast.

⊨ Sleeping

Pousada Porto das Barcas
POUSADA $

(☑3321-2275; www.pousadaportodasbarcas.com; Rua da Praia 100; d R$60-80, air-con R$90-120; ✱☎) Set in a converted ex-port-warehouse in the Porto das Barcas complex, this pousada sports a courtyard decked out with lots of colorful art and crafts, and quite cute little rooms with flagstone floors and small bathrooms. The owner speaks English.

Residencial Pousada
POUSADA $

(☑3322-2931; www.residencialpousada.com.br; Almirante Sampaio 375; s/d R$50/65, air-con R$60/85; ✱@☎) This budget spot in a neat, cottagelike building is good value and, one block north of Av Presidente Vargas, well located. The rooms, around a grassy garden, are large and high-ceilinged.

Pousada Vila Parnaíba
POUSADA $$

(☑3323-2781; www.pousadavilaparnaiba.com.br; Monsenhor Joaquim Lopes 500; s R$110-150, d R$140-175; ✱☎❄) Professionally run with some English-speaking staff, Vila Parnaíba is easily the nicest central choice. Rooms are colorful and medium-sized, with good modern bathrooms, and the verdant garden (with pool) and patio are decked out with all sorts of regional crafts and historical curios. It's one block north of Av Presidente Vargas, two blocks back from Porto das Barcas.

✗ Eating

Caranguejo Expresso
SEAFOOD $$

(☑3323-9653; Quentinha Pires 64; mains for 2 R$25-45; ☺6-11pm) Locally famous for its enormous and delicious *torta de caranguejo* (crab omelette). Don't expect *expresso* service but do expect it to be worth the wait. Take mosquito repellent in the evening.

Comilão
PIZZERIA $$

(Rua da Praia; medium pizza R$29, pasta R$12-30; ☺from 6pm) OK pizza in a pretty setting, on a cobblestone street in the Porto das Barcas.

La Barca
SEAFOOD $$$

(Av Nações Unidas 200; mains R$35-55; ☺10am-midnight) This large, half-open-air, half-air-con restaurant, facing a bend of the river 600m north of Av Presidente Vargas, is a nice place to dine on fish or crab helped down by an Antarctica Original beer.

❶ Information

Banco do Brasil (Praça da Graça 340; ☺9am-2pm Mon-Fri, ATMs 7:30am-8:15pm) On the

WORTH A TRIP

DELTA DO PARNAÍBA
....

The **Delta of the Rio Parnaíba** (sometimes called the Delta das Américas) is a 2700-sq-km expanse of islands, beaches, lagoons, channels, high sand dunes and dense mangrove forest full of wildlife. Around 65% of its area is in the state of Maranhão, but the easiest access is from Parnaíba in Piauí. Agencies around Parnaíba's Porto das Barcas offer several half-day and day tours into the delta in fast motor launches or big party boats, starting from Porto dos Tatus, 14km north of Parnaíba. A better option if you're interested in peace, quiet and nature is boatman **José Ribamar** (☑ 086-3323-0201, 086-9924-5598; Rua da Gloria 900, Centro Ilha Grande) ✎, who uses traditional and quiet wooden boats and can pick you up in Parnaíba. José speaks only Portuguese but a multilingual guide is available, and you can make arrangements through José's German business partner **Anne Knapp** (www.deltaparnaiba.com). One of their day trips, known as **Micro-Macro** (R$320 for up to five people), will take you to the Morro Branco dunes, Pontal where you can swim at a meeting point of freshwater and ocean, a fishing village, and then by motorized canoe into mangrove channels where you can hope to see plenty of wildlife such as howler and capuchin monkeys, caimans, iguanas, snakes and birds. Other options include a six- to seven-hour one-way tour through the delta to Tutoia (R$450 for up to eight people), and overnight trips.

Clip, the largest agency, does four-hour afternoon-and-evening wildlife-spotting trips to the **Igarape do Guirindó** (R$300 for up to five people) using a motorized canoe, on which you also get to try your hand at piranha fishing. Other Clip options use fast motor launches: the five-hour **Revoada dos Guarás** trip (R$400 for up to four people), available afternoons in the second half of the year only, treats you to the sight of flocks of *guarás* (red ibis) flying into their evening roosts, as well as visiting dunes and a beach.

main central square. There's also a 24-hour Banco do Brasil ATM in the bus station.

Clip (☑ 3322-3129; www.clipecoturismo.com.br; Av Presidente Vargas 274; ☺ 7:30am-noon & 2-6pm Mon-Fri, 7:30am-noon Sat) The major provider of Delta do Parnaíba trips; also offers tours and travel agency services throughout the region.

EcoAdventure Tour (☑ 3323-9595; www.ecoadventure.tur.br; Av Presidente Vargas 26; ☺ 7am-8pm) Organized, experienced agency offering a range of tours in the region from Fortaleza to São Luís.

ℹ Getting There & Around

From the **bus station** (☑ 3323-7300; Av Pinheiro Machado 2318) there are services to Fortaleza (R$39 to R$124, 7½ to 11 hours, five daily), Camocim (R$18, 2¼ hours, 7:15am), São Luís (R$60 to R$74, eight to nine hours, three daily) and Teresina (R$59 to R$87, five to seven hours, seven daily via Piripiri). You can buy tickets for these destinations at Clip (p549).

Any city bus (R$1.20) outside the bus station will take you to Av Presidente Vargas. A taxi is R$15 to R$20. Going back, catch buses to the bus station by Bradesco bank at Av Presidente Vargas 403.

TO/FROM THE LENÇÓIS MARANHENSES

The adventurous and fun direct route to the Lençóis Maranhenses involves getting to Tutoia, 65km west of Parnaíba, and then to Paulino

Neves village, 34km beyond Tutoia, then via a rough track to Barreirinhas or along the beach to Caburé (each 40km). To Tutoia, the options are bus (R$16, three hours, four or more daily) or a chartered boat through the delta (R$600 for up to four people, four hours) organized through travel agencies. From Tutoia, passenger trucks (R$5 to R$10) and taxis (R$40 to R$70) run to Paulino Neves, and from there 4WD trucks head to Barreirinhas (R$20, 2½ hours) at 4am, 9am or noon (times variable). There is also a direct Viação Coimbra bus at 2pm (except Sunday) from Parnaíba bus station to Paulino Neves (R$21, 3½ hours). Either way you would be lucky to get through from Parnaíba to Barreirinhas in one day, but both Tutoia and Paulino Neves have a handful of adequate pousadas. Alternatively, Parnaíba agencies offer 4WD trips direct to Barreirinhas or Caburé for R$600 to R$800 per vehicle (up to four passengers).

Parque Nacional de Sete Cidades

☑ 086

Sete Cidades is a small, 62-sq-km **national park** (☑ 3343-1342; admission R$3; ☺ 8am-5pm) ✎ with bizarre rock formations that some have claimed are *sete cidades* (seven cities) left behind by some mysterious long-departed culture (aliens, Vikings etc). The place doesn't need such fantasies to make it worth visiting. The rock formations are indeed fantastic – some look like giant turtle shells, others resemble a castle, an elephant, a map of Brazil or the head of emperor Dom Pedro II – and there are also superb vistas over a landscape that combines caatinga (semi-arid land) and cerrado (savanna) vegetation. There are 1500 intriguing rock paintings between 3000 and 5000 years old, wildlife that includes marmosets, small rodents called *mocós* (cavies) that like to pose for photos, tarantulas and (we're told) rattlesnakes, and two delectable natural bathing pools.

The park entrance is 190km northeast of Teresina, 24km northeast of the small town of Piripiri and 8km north by paved road off Hwy BR-222. From the entrance it's another 5km (unpaved) to the visitors center. Obligatory guides cost R$60 for a three-hour tour of the seven 'cities' by vehicle, or R$80 for a five-hour walking tour (up to six people), or R$60 for a three-hour circuit by bicycle (up to 10 people, plus R$10 for each bike you rent). Shorter, cheaper tours of fewer 'cities' are also available and staff at the visitors center will explain the options. Bring insect repellent, water, a hat and sunscreen.

🛏 Sleeping & Eating

Califórnia Hotel HOTEL **$**
(☑ 3276-1645; jesus-holanda@hotmail.com; Antenor Freitas 546, Piripiri; s/d R$60/80; ❊ 🛜) This big-value, modern hotel is the place to stay in Piripiri, with well-kept rooms, wi-fi and cheap rates. It's 700m from the bus station and two blocks off the central square.

Pizzaria Julio's PIZZERIA **$**
(☑ 3276-1912; Praça da Bandeira 542; medium pizza R$14-17, grilled meat per half-kg R$18-28; ☺ 6pm-2am; 🛜) On the main square, Julio's has four outlets in São Paulo and one in Piripiri – odd – but the grilled meats or 62 pizzas here are your best bet for sustenance. The pizzas have inventive names like 'Scottish' – with *catupiry* cheese, which we're pretty sure isn't common in Scotland.

❶ Getting There & Around

A taxi from Piripiri costs R$50 to or from the park, or R$110 round-trip including a two-hour park driving tour. Alternatively, you can try to catch the free park staff bus at 7am in Piripiri's main plaza, returning at 5pm, providing there's space available.

From **Piripiri bus station** (☑ 3276-2333) there are buses to Fortaleza (R$50 to R$84, seven to nine hours, five daily via Tianguá),

Parnaíba (R$29 to R$45, 2½ to five hours, six daily), São Luís (R$90, 10 to 12 hours, two daily), Teresina (R$30 to R$43, three hours, 16 daily) and Ubajara (R$16, 2½ hours, 1:30pm).

MARANHÃO

The atmosphere-laden colonial city of São Luís, its tranquil but gorgeous neighbor, Alcântara and the wild natural beauty of the Parque Nacional dos Lençóis Maranhenses have put the Northeast's furthest-flung state firmly on the travel map. The coastal route from Jericoacoara (Ceará) to the Lençóis Maranhenses is an adventure in itself.

Southern and eastern Maranhão are characterized by vast expanses of *babaçu* (palms) and typical *sertão* landscapes, but the state's western and northwestern regions merge into humid Amazon rainforests.

São Luís

☑ 098 / POP 956,000

The World Heritage-listed historic center of São Luís is an enchanting neighborhood of steamy cobbled streets and pastel-colored colonial mansions, some handsomely restored, many still deep in tropical decay. It's a charming area with a unique atmosphere and one of the best concentrations of museums, galleries and craft stores in the Northeast; but unfortunately, a general sketchiness pervades some of these streets after dark. The city as a whole has a markedly Afro-Brazilian tinge to its culture, from its lively reggae scene to its highly colorful and unusual Bumba Meu Boi festivities. The trip across Baía de São Marcos to Alcântara, an impressive historic town slumbering in regal decay, is an added reason to put São Luís on your itinerary.

São Luís sits at the northwest corner of the 50km-long Ilha de São Luís, which is separated from the mainland only by narrow channels. The city itself is divided by the Rio Anil. South of the Anil, the Centro Histórico's street grid rambles up and down over hilly terrain, with its heart in the lower area known as Praia Grande. North of the Anil are the more modern suburbs, as well as the city's beaches stretched along the island's north coast. The bus station is 9km southeast of the center and the airport 3km further southeast.

São Luís

São Luís

⊗ Eating
1 Cabana do Sol D1
2 Maracangalha B1

❖ Entertainment
3 Chama Maré A2

🛍 Shopping
4 Ceprama B4

The widely available *Roteiro e Mapa Turístico São Luís* (R$7) is an excellent map and information guide to the historic center, but be forewarned: many street names will not match the street signs – it seems each new mayor likes to rename the streets to their liking.

History

São Luís is the only city in Brazil that was founded by the French. In 1612 three French ships sailed for Maranhão to try to commandeer a piece of South America. Once established at São Luís, the French used the local indigenous population, the Tupinambá, to assail tribes around the mouth of the Amazon to try to expand their foothold in the region. But come the inevitable Portuguese attack in 1614, the French fled within a year and before long the Portuguese had 'pacified' the Tupinambá.

After a brief Dutch occupation between 1641 and 1644, São Luís developed gradually as a port for exporting sugar, and later, cotton. The plantation owners prospered and by the early 19th century São Luís was one of the wealthiest cities in Brazil, on the back of the labor of African slaves. Today the city has the third-highest Afro-Brazilian population in the country (after Rio and Salvador).

When demand for São Luís' crops slackened later in the 19th century, the city

Central São Luís

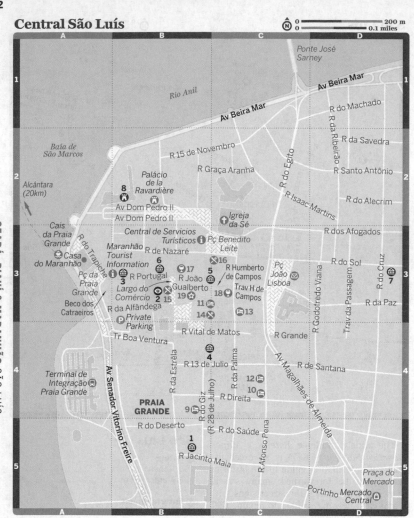

CEARÁ, PIAUÍ & MARANHÃO SÃO LUÍS

went into a long decline, but the economy has been stimulated by several megaprojects in recent decades. In the 1980s a big port complex was constructed at Itaqui, just west of São Luís, to export the mineral riches of the Carajás in neighboring Pará state, and Alcoa constructed an enormous aluminum-processing plant on the highway south of the city – both of which remain key to the city's economy today. Thanks to the restoration of many of São Luís' beautiful old buildings, tourism is now also important.

◉ Sights & Activities

The center of São Luís is the best-preserved colonial neighborhood in the Northeast, full of 18th- and 19th-century mansions covered in colorful 19th-century European *azulejos* (decorative ceramic tiles, often blue or blue-and-white). The tiles provided a durable means of protecting walls from São Luís' ever-present humidity and heat. The historic center has been under piecemeal restoration under Projeto Reviver (Project Revival) since the late 1980s, after many decades of neglect and decay. Many of the restored buildings house interesting museums, galleries, craft

Central São Luís

shops and restaurants, though much still needs to be restored.

Casa de Nhôzinho
MUSEUM

(Portugal 185; ⊙ 9am-6pm Tue-Sun) FREE At the eclectic and fascinating Casa do Nhôzinho, you can see a collection of ingenious fish traps, rooms of Maranhão indigenous artisanry, and hosts of colorful, delicate Bumba Meu Boi figurines made by the 20th-century master artisan Mestre Nhôzinho.

Centro de Cultura Popular Domingos Vieira Filho
MUSEUM

(☑ 3218-9925; Rua do Giz 221; ⊙ 9am-6pm Tue-Sun) FREE An impressive 19th-century mansion houses three fascinating floors of exhibits on São Luís' festivals – Carnaval, Bumba Meu Boi and Divino Espírito Santo – and its Afro-Brazilian cults such as Umbanda and *tambor de mina*. Staff will show you round and explain, but speakers of English or other non-Portuguese languages may or may not be available.

Museu Histórico e Artístico do Estado de Maranhão
MUSEUM

(☑ 3218-9922; Rua do Sol 302; admission R$5; ⊙ 9am-5pm Tue-Sun) In a restored 1836 mansion, the Museu Histórico e Artístico is set out as it might have been in days of yore, displaying all the furnishings, valuables and everyday belongings of an upper-class 19th-century family – including a private theater. It's very well done.

Casa das Tulhas
MARKET

(Largo do Comércio; ⊙ 6am-8pm Mon-Fri, 6am-6pm Sat, 6am-1pm Sun) This 19th-century market building now trades in an interesting variety of typical Maranhão crafts and foods, from dried prawns and Brazil nuts to an artificially colored purple cassava liquor called *tiquira*. It also has a couple of bars that get animated in late afternoon.

Museu de Artes Visuais
MUSEUM

(☑ 3218-9938; Portugal 273; admission R$2; ⊙ 9am-6pm Tue-Fri, 9am-4pm Sat & Sun) There's a fine collection of old *azulejos*, engravings, sculptures and paintings at the Visual Arts Museum.

Cafua das Mercês
MUSEUM

(Jacinto Maia 43; admission R$2; ⊙ 9am-5pm Mon-Fri) In a building that was once a 'holding facility' for slaves newly arrived from Africa, this museum has a small but interesting exhibition on slavery, the slave trade and Afro-Brazilian culture. It's in a sketchy part of the historic center, so ask advice before going there.

Exhibits include a replica whipping-post and a striking collection of modern wood carvings and statuettes from the parts of West Africa where the origins of many of São Luís' Afro-Brazilian population lie.

Centro de História Natural e Arqueologia do Maranhão
MUSEUM

(www.cultura.ma.gov.br/portal/cphna; Rua do Giz 59; ⊙ 9am-noon & 2-6pm Mon-Fri) FREE Interesting exhibits of artifacts from Maranhão's indigenous cultures past and present, from contemporary feather adornments to ancient ax-heads, plus models of megafauna that roamed Maranhão around 95 million years ago.

Palácio dos Leões   PALACE
(🕿 3232-9789; Av Dom Pedro II; ⊘ 2-5pm Wed-Sun) FREE The Palácio dos Leões is the state governor's palace, built in the 18th century on the site of the original French fort; it contains a wealth of valuable antique furnishings and art, mostly French from the 18th and 19th centuries. Next along the handsome plaza is the **Palácio de la Ravardière**, dating back to 1689 and now the Prefeitura (City Hall). A bust of São Luís' French founder, Daniel de la Touche, stands before it.

Beaches

The city's beaches are along the north-facing ocean coast, beginning about 4km north of the historic center. They can be busy and fun, but are far from Brazil's finest and a distinct smell pervades most of the city's water. Beware of rough surf, tides and pollution.

OFF THE BEATEN TRACK

ARCHAEOLOGICAL TREASURES: THE SERRA DA CAPIVARA

In the south of Piauí, the dramatic rocky landscape of the 1300-sq-km **Parque Nacional da Serra da Capivara** (Brazilian/foreigner R$11/22; ⊘ 6am-6pm) 🏊, a Unesco World Heritage site, contains 40,000 prehistoric rock paintings – claimed to be the greatest concentration on the planet. Entered 35km north of the small town of São Raimundo Nonato, the park has 800 archaeological sites and has yielded what's considered to be the oldest evidence of human presence in the Americas, at least 50,000 years ago, predating previous 'earliest' finds by about 30,000 years. The rock art is mostly 6000 to 12,000 years old and includes depictions of deer and caimans, and people dancing, hunting and having sex.

Over R$50 million has been spent on developing the park's facilities and the museum in São Raimundo, and a surprising number of visitors do find their way to these distant parts. The park has wooden walkways, disabled access to many sites, good vehicle tracks, walking trails, a visitors' center, lookout points and helpful bilingual signs.

Over 170 sites are open to the public, organized into four main driving circuits and several walking trails helping visitors appreciate the landscape, geology, vegetation and wildlife as well as the evidence of ancient humanity. You should give yourself two days or more, as some of the circuits and trails require a whole day. Outstanding sites include the **Boqueirão da Pedro Furada**, where remains of cooking fires provided evidence of human presence 50,000 years ago (this site is equipped with illumination for night visits); and the **Baixão do Sítio do Meio** and **Desfiladero da Capivara**, both with wealths of rock art.

A local guide is obligatory for visiting the park, costing R$75 per day for up to eight people – best organized through your accommodations in São Raimundo Nonato. Round-trip transport options, including wait times and/or touring, are moto-taxi (R$60) and taxi (R$150). It's best to start at the modernized **Museu do Homem Americano** (🕿 089-3582-1612; www.fumdham.org.br; Bairro Campestre; admission R$8; ⊘ 9am-6pm Tue-Sun) on the outskirts of São Raimundo, with excellent English info on what you will see in the park. It also exhibits the oldest human skull found in the Americas, dated nearly 10,000 years old.

Another attraction of the area is the appealing ceramics decorated with designs from Capivara rock art, produced by the villagers of Barreirinho just outside the park.

Of São Raimundo's half-dozen hotels and pousadas, the best option overall is the 20-year-old **Hotel Serra da Capivara** (🕿 089-3582-1389; hotelserradacapivarra@firme.com.br; Km 0, Hwy PI-140, Santa Luzia; d R$115-145; ❄🛜🏊), 2km north of the center on Hwy PI-140. Staff are welcoming and the 18 rooms are simple and mostly well kept, though it's a good idea to look at the one you're offered before deciding. The hotel has a restaurant and can organize park guides for you.

Four daily buses make the 500km odyssey from Teresina to São Raimundo Nonato (R$76, nine to 10 hours) and back. Another approach is via Petrolina in Pernambuco, 280km east, to which you can fly from Recife, Salvador or São Paulo. A **Gontijo** (www.gontijo.com.br) bus leaves Petrolina for São Raimundo (R$49, six hours) at 2:15pm.

Praia Ponta d'Areia is the closest beach to the center, and the busiest, with bars and restaurants for beach food. It can be polluted. Two kilometers further along, Praia de São Marcos is frequented by younger groups and surfers. The best local beach, Praia de Calhau, is broad and attractive, with hard-packed sand perfect for football games. It is 9km from the center and popular on weekends. The large *barracas* lining the beach cater to late-night partiers throughout the week.

You can reach Ponta d'Areia, São Marcos and Calhau on bus 403 Calhau/Litorânea (R$2.10) from the Terminal de Integração Praia Grande (p558).

✴ Festivals & Events

São Luís has one of Brazil's richest folkloric traditions, evident in its many festivals including Carnaval. For two to three weeks between early May and early June the city celebrates the Festa do Divino Espírito Santo with a uniquely strong Afro-Brazilian influence. São Luís' famous festival Bumba Meu Boi lasts through the second half of June. The Tambor de Mina festivals in July are important events for followers of the Afro-Brazilian religions.

🛏 Sleeping

Pousada Colonial POUSADA $
(✆3232-2834; www.hotelpousadacolonial.com.br; Afonso Pena 112; s/d R$115/141; ❋@☎) A certain colonial charm pervades this refurbished old-town mansion with its interior patio and unique raised *azulejos* inside and out. The rooms don't quite live up to the ambience, some having no natural light, others having cardboard-thin mattresses, but they have crisp sheets and, in a few cases, views over the old town rooftops.

Solar das Pedras HOSTEL $
(✆3232-6694; www.ajsolardaspedras.com.br; Rua da Palma 127; dm/d R$35/80; ☎) This HI hostel in a restored 19th-century home has acceptable and clean facilities including a sizable sitting area, though the rooms are rather dark and poorly ventilated, and the kitchen small. Overall, it's the best backpacker option. Discounts for HI members.

Pousada Vitória POUSADA $
(✆3231-2816; pousadavitoria@hotmail.com; Afonso Pena 98; s/d/tr/q with fan R$45/90/135/180, s/d air-con R$50/100; ❋☎) Perky little dogs and a family atmosphere, albeit somewhat dour, combine with ample but basic rooms, with bathrooms built into the corners, along an inner patio.

★**Casa Lavinia** B&B $$
(✆8103-1842; www.casalavinia.com; Rua do Giz 380; d/tr/q R$220/240/260; ❋☎) The Italian owners have achieved a truly gorgeous conversion of this 19th-century mansion. The four big and beautiful rooms boast four-poster beds, polished-wood floors and stylish, uncluttered decor and furnishings from Africa, Italy, Brazil and elsewhere. In the Padronal suite the bathroom alone is as big as three rooms in your average pousada. An excellent breakfast is served in a cool courtyard dining area.

It's highly recommended to reserve ahead by email.

Pousada Portas da Amazônia POUSADA $$
(✆3182-8787; www.portasdaamazonia.com.br; Rua do Giz 129; s R$139-189, d R$189-249; ❋☎) Rambling corridors in this restored mansion lead around two patio-gardens to attractive, spacious and comfortable rooms, with excellent mattresses and modern air-con. You can take the good buffet breakfast in one of the courtyards.

🍴 Eating

Maranhense cuisine mixes Portuguese, African and indigenous influences and much of the best of it comes from the sea. Regional specialties include *casquinha de caranguejo* (stuffed crab), *caldeirada de camarão* (shrimp stew) and the city's specialty, *arroz de cuxá* (rice with shrimp, toasted sesame and the slightly bitter herb *vinagreira*). Unfortunately, the culinary scene in the Centro Histórico is rather sparse (and almost nonexistent on Sundays), and foodies must head out to the northern beaches for most of the best options.

★**Restaurante Senac** SELF-SERVE $$
(Rua de Nazaré 242; lunch buffet R$30, dinner mains for 2 R$61-119; ☉noon-3pm Mon-Sat, 7-11pm Thu & Fri) Showpiece for the São Luis branch of Brazil's best-known cooking school, this place gets packed at lunchtime for its superb all-you-can-eat buffet, which includes a big salad bar and eight or 10 hot meat and seafood dishes, plus rice, vegetables and yummy desserts.

Pizzeria del Centro PIZZERIA $$
(Rua da Estrela 180; mains R$18-30; ☉5pm-midnight or later Mon-Sat) With Italian owners and an Italian *pizzaiolo*, the pizzas here live up

to expectations – and the caipirinhas far exceed them! The *isca de peixe* (breaded fish cubes) is a delicious starter. There's different live music every night too.

Dom Francisco
BRAZILIAN $$
(Rua do Giz 155; lunch per kg R$26.90, mains R$20-25; ⊘11:30am-4pm & 6-11pm Mon-Sat) An excellent buffet that doesn't try to do every dish ever known to Maranhão, but rather a select repertoire of meals that are all wonderful. It's open at night for à la carte dining.

Maracangalha
NORTHEASTERN $$$
(⊘3235-9305; Mearim 3, Quadra 13, Ponta do Farol; mains for 2 R$45-150; ⊘noon-midnight Mon-Sat, 11:30am-5pm Sun) Chef/owner Melchíades Dantas turns out creative seafood and meat dishes that match the artsy atmosphere in flair and presentation (the *caldeirada maranhense* – a seafood stew – is excellent). The staff is impeccably on point. If there's a flaw, it's the noise-hugging space that can swell with kids.

Cabana do Sol
NORTHEASTERN $$$
(⊘3227-5467; Av Litorânea 10, Calhau; mains for 2 R$76-126; ⊘11am-midnight) This huge, two-story, picture-windowed 'cabin' is a memorable spot for *maranhense* cuisine. It's pricey, but the irresponsibly enormous portions for two can serve four with gusto. The specialty is *carne de sol* (tastily grilled salted meat) – the *picanha* (steak) version is superb – but there's a wealth of chicken and seafood dishes, too.

Drinking & Entertainment

Live bands playing a variety of rhythms – samba, *chorinho*, jazz, blues, bossa nova, MPB – compete for your eardrums at several bars and restaurants on and around Largo do Comércio, in the heart of the Centro Histórico, from around 8pm every evening Monday to Saturday. Especially popular are the sidewalk tables of **Cafofinho da Tia Dica** (Beco da Alfândega).

The *barracas* along Ponta d'Areia, São Marcos and Calhau beaches are also popular drinking spots, with the added attraction of a sea breeze and, in the evenings, especially at Calhau, live music.

São Luís is the reggae capital of Brazil, and many bars and clubs have reggae nights, sometimes live, other times with DJs and vast banks of speakers. Being Brazilians, locals like to dance reggae in couples. It's worth asking locals or tourist offices about what's hot – check kamaleao.com/saoluis. There is also a vibrant GLBT scene here.

Chez Moi
CLUB
(⊘3221-5877; barchezmoi.com; Rua da Estrela 143; admission R$15-30; ⊘10pm-late Fri, from 7pm Sun) A frenetically popular club in the Centro Histórico. The downstairs operates as a disco with DJs from all over Brazil (and occasionally overseas), while live pop, rock, samba, reggae and *forró* happen in another dance area upstairs. Sunday evenings are dedicated to live rock.

Roots Bar
BAR
(Rua da Palma 86; ⊘6pm-2am Wed-Fri) A good old-town spot for DJ reggae on Friday from around 8pm.

Bar do Nelson
LIVE MUSIC
(⊘3226-4191; Av Litorânea 135 , Calhau; admission R$5-20; ⊘4pm-3am Tue-Sun) With its shanty clubhouse feel, Bar do Nelson is the most famous reggae spot in town and is good for live music and dancing, especially Thursday to Saturday from around 9pm.

Chama Maré
LIVE MUSIC
(Av São Marcos 8, Ponta d'Areia; ⊘from 5pm Sun) This beachside bar has a wonderful Sunday reggae night. People drift in off the beach for sunset and the music starts around 7pm.

Shopping

São Luís is the place for Maranhão handicrafts such as painted tiles, wood carving, basketry, lace, ceramics and leather work. The large **Ceprama** (Centro de Produção de Artesanato do Maranhão; Rua de São Pantaleão 1232, Madre de Deus; ⊘9am-6pm Mon-Sat), 2km southeast of the center, functions as an exhibition hall and major sales outlet. There are also plenty of shops around Rua Portugal and Rua da Estrela in the historic center.

ℹ Information

INTERNET ACCESS
Cybercafé Praia Grande (João Vital 48; per hr R$2.50; ⊘10am-8pm) Air-conditioned.

MEDICAL SERVICES
UDI Hospital (⊘3216-7979; Av Carlos Cunha 2000, Jacarati) Private hospital with emergency service.

MONEY
Praça Deodoro, 800m east from Praça João Lisboa along Rua da Paz, has the only Banco do Brasil branch offering currency exchange.
Banco do Brasil Av Dom Pedro II (Av Dom Pedro II 78; ⊘10am-4pm Mon-Fri, ATMs 6am-8pm daily); Travessa Boa Ventura (Travessa

BUMBA MEU BOI

São Luís is famous for its Bumba Meu Boi – a fascinating, wild folkloric festival. Derived from African, indigenous and Portuguese influences that mingled in colonial times, it's a rich mixture of music, dance and theater, with fantastic and colorful costumes and masks. In a Carnavalesque atmosphere, participants dance, sing, act and tell the story of the death and resurrection of the bull – with plenty of room for improvisation. It happens all over Maranhão, and in São Luís alone some 400 groups take to the streets every June. New songs, dances, costumes and poetry are created every year.

The story and its portrayal differ throughout the Northeast, but the general plot is as follows: Catrina, goddaughter of the local farm-owner, is pregnant and feels a craving to eat the tongue of the best *boi* (bull) on the farm. She cajoles her husband, Chico, into killing the beast. When the dead bull is discovered, several characters (caricatures drawn from all levels of society) track down the perpetrator of the crime. Chico is brought to trial, but the bull is resuscitated by magic incantations and tunes. A pardon is granted, and the story reaches its happy ending when Chico is reunited with Catrina.

Groups traditionally start rehearsing on Easter Saturday in preparation for the 'baptism' of their *boi* on June 13, the feast of Santo Antônio, or June 23 (São João). Many rehearsals are open to the public and some groups begin months before Easter (check with tourist offices or your accommodations for schedules). During the festival, several groups perform in different places in the city every night from June 13 to 30. The more commercial performances may last only one hour, while local community celebrations can go on all night. Things get especially lively on the nights of June 23–24 and 29–30.

The Bumba Meu Boi period is also a good time to catch other Afro-Brazilian cultural manifestations such as the Tambor de Crioula dance by women.

Boa Ventura; ⊙10am-4pm Mon-Fri, ATMs 6am-10pm daily); Praça Deodoro (Av Gomes de Castro 46; ⊙10am-4pm Mon-Fri)

TOURIST INFORMATION

São Luís' information offices usually have helpful, English-speaking attendants.

Central de Servicios Turísticos (☑3212-6211; Praça Benedito Leite; ⊙8am-7pm Mon-Fri, 8am-1pm Sat-Sun) The main information office of Setur, the city tourism department.

Maranhão (www.turismo.ma.gov.br) Maranhão's official bilingual tourism site has helpful descriptions.

Maranhão Tourist Information (☑3244-4500; airport; ⊙24hr)

Maranhão Tourist Information (☑3249-4500; bus station; ⊙8am-7pm)

Maranhão Tourist Information (☑3231-4696; Portugal 165; ⊙8am-7pm Mon-Fri, 9am-6pm Sat, 9am-1pm Sun)

São Luís (www.visitesaoluis.com) The site of the São Luís Convention & Visitors Bureau, with some interesting material.

TRAVEL AGENCIES

Riberão Turismo (☑3231-1621; Rua do Sol 141; ⊙8am-6pm Mon-Fri, 8am-noon Sat) A useful agency for air tickets, and bus tickets to points east and south.

Terra Nordeste (☑8857-7408; www.terra-nordeste.com; Rua do Giz 380; ⊙9am-6pm

Mon-Fri all year, 9am-1pm Sat Jun-Sep) This excellent, ecotourism-focused, Northeast Brazil specialist is friendly, French-owned and multilingual, and can organize any trip you fancy from two days to a month or more – including treks across the Lençóis Maranhenses.

🛈 Getting There & Away

AIR

From the **airport** (☑3217-6100; Av dos Libaneses, Tirirical) there are direct flights to main destinations in the Amazon and Northeast, as well as Rio de Janeiro and São Paulo, with **Azul** (www.voeazul.com.br), **GOL** (www.voegol.com.br; airport), **TAM** (www.tam.com.br) or **Trip** (www.voetrip.com.br).

BUS

The **bus station** (☑3243-1305; Av dos Franceses, Santo Antônio) has departures to many destinations including Belém (R$120 to R$276, 13 hours, four buses daily), Brasília (R$270 to R$337, 33 hours, 5pm), Fortaleza (R$147 to R$156, 18 to 21 hours, three daily), Parnaíba (R$60 to R$74, eight to 10 hours, three daily) and Teresina (R$54 to R$94, seven to 8½ hours, eight daily).

Night buses to Belém have a history of being robbed, so consider flying, which can be cheaper in any case (advance-booking fares with TAM start at R$111).

❶ Getting Around

A taxi to the Centro Histórico costs R$30 from the bus station and R$40 from the airport. Traffic on the main roads in and out of São Luís is so heavy that this takes between one and two hours. The 'São Cristóvão Aeroporto' bus runs between the airport, the bus station and the **Terminal de Integração Praia Grande** (Av Senador Vitorino Freire), an urban bus terminal on the edge of the Centro Histórico. Between the bus station and the Terminal Praia Grande you can also use the Socorrão Rodoviária bus. Bus fares are R$2.10.

Alcântara

☑ 098 / POP 6400

Across the Baía de São Marcos from São Luís is the colonial town of Alcântara. Built between the 17th and 19th centuries with slave labor, Alcântara was the preferred residence of Maranhão's rich plantation owners. In decline since the latter half of the 19th century, Alcântara today is an atmospheric amalgam of ruined, maintained and restored mansions, houses and churches set along streets of artistic crisscrossed cobblestones. With a population no bigger today than 150 years ago, it is one of the country's most tranquil, authentic and stunningly beautiful historic sites. Keep an eye out for *guarás*, beautiful red ibises that are unusually plentiful around here and add yet another wonderful element to an Alcântara trip.

Since 1990 Centro de Lançamento de Alcântara (CLA), the rocket-launching facility for the Brazilian space program, has operated nearby. It is an odd juxtaposition: rockets alongside a slumbering colonial town.

There is a small tourist information booth, open according to boat arrival times, beside the ferry ticket office near the dock. You may be lucky enough to find the excellent guide-map *Alcântara Roteiro e Mapa Turístico* on sale here.

◉ Sights

Don't miss the broad, hilltop **Praça da Matriz**, where the best-preserved **pelourinho** (whipping post) in Brazil stands beside the shell of the 17th-century **Igreja de São Matias**. Two 18th-century mansions on the praça's west side have been turned into museums – **Museu Histórico de Alcântara** (admission R$2; ◷9am-3pm Tue-Fri, 9am-1pm Sat-Sun) and the **Casa Histórica** (admission R$2; ◷9:30am-4:30pm Tue-Fri, 9:30am-2:30pm Sat-Sun) **FREE** – exhibiting the lifestyle of Alcântara's privileged families of yore, with a wealth of period furnishings and memorabilia. Visits are guided in Portuguese, and if you can manage only one, go for the Museu Histórico, which has more impressive collections.

Moving north along Rua Grande, with its beautiful row of two-story houses, you can look round the intriguing **Casa do Divino** (Rua Grande; admission R$1; ◷9am-3pm Tue-Sun), the main center of activities during Alcântara's famous Festa do Divino, before reaching the pretty, two-towered **Igreja de NS do Carmo** (admission R$2; ◷9am-1pm), built in 1665 and recently restored, with a ruined convent beside it. In front of and opposite the church stand the ruined **1° and 2° Palácios do Imperador** (First and Second Palaces of the Emperor), built for a visit by the 19th-century emperor Dom Pedro II that never actually happened.

✨ Festivals & Events

Alcântara's **Festa do Divino Espírito Santo**, a 12-day festival culminating on the first Sunday after Ascension Day (usually in May), is one of the most colorful annual events in Maranhão. It represents a fusion of African and Catholic elements and features two children dressed as emperor and empress and a series of complex rituals focused on the Casa do Divino, which is decked out like a palace. Colorful musical parades are part of the program.

🛏 Sleeping & Eating

Alcântara is a straightforward day trip from São Luís, but an overnight stay here is enjoyable and allows more time for exploring and for excursions to colonies of red ibis.

Pousada Bela Vista　　　　　　POUSADA **$**
(☑3337-1569; www.belavistapousada.com; Vila Jerico; s R$60-80, d R$130-150; ❋ 🖥 ❀) A wonderful option with eight simple, clean rooms (five have sea views), a good patio restaurant adorned with antique knickknacks and art, a pool with stunning views across to São Luís, and an inviting lookout tower that encourages lazy afternoons of doing a whole lot of nothing. It's run by the family of one of Alcântara's most famous local guides, locally born and raised Dannilo, who doesn't speak English but offers excellent tours and nature trails just the same.

It's about a 30-minute walk or R$4 mototaxi ride from the dock. It's advisable to call ahead to check it has vacancies.

Pousada do Sossego POUSADA $
(☎ 3337-1261, 9147-8261; Rua do Sossego; r without/with air-con R$50/80; ❇) Run by the amiable Hamilton ('*como Lewis Hamilton, Fórmula Um*'), this friendly pousada in town has large, bare, fan-cooled rooms in its main, streetside building, and comfier air-con ones in the green garden behind.

Bururú Barará BRAZILIAN $$
(Rua Silva Maia; dishes R$12-30; ☺ 6pm-midnight) A lively spot for pizza, burgers, tapiocas or good *carne de sol* in the evenings, sometimes with live music on Wednesday or Thursday.

❶ Getting There & Away

Two or three boats to Alcântara (R$12, 1¼ hours) leave daily from the **Cais da Praia Grande** (☎ 3232-0692; Av Senador Vitorino Freire) in São Luís. Times vary with tides but there are usually two departures between 7am and 9am and one later. It's a good idea to check times and buy your ticket the day before. Two boats start back from Alcântara around 4pm or 5pm and one in the early morning. Seasickness sufferers will be happier on the larger boats *Bahia Star* and *Diamantina* than the catamaran *Lua Nova*.

Parque Nacional dos Lençóis Maranhenses

☑ 098

The name of this 1550-sq-km national park refers to its immense expanses of dunes, which look like *lençóis* (bed sheets) strewn across the landscape and stretch 70km along the coast and up to 25km inland. Halfway between São Luís and the Piauí border, it is a spectacularly unique place, especially from about March to September when rain that has filtered through the sand forms thousands of crystal-clear pools and lakes between the dunes. The lagoons are at their best in July and August. The park also includes beaches, mangroves, lagoons and some interesting fauna, especially turtles and migratory birds.

The main base for visiting the park is the not particularly charming town of **Barreirinhas** on the Rio Preguiças near the park's southeast corner, 260km from São Luís. Other access points – well worth the effort of getting to if you have at least two nights to spend in the area – are the remote villages of **Atins**, where the Preguiças meets the ocean, and **Santo Amaro** on the park's western border, where the dunes come right to the edge of the village and there are sandy river beaches where you can bathe even when the lagoons among the dunes are dry.

Barreirinhas' main street has a branch of **Banco do Brasil** (Av Joaquim Soeiro de Carvalho, Barreirinhas; ☺ ATMs 6am-10pm), whose ATM (when not malfunctioning) dispenses cash to international Visa cardholders, and an internet cafe, **Netpoint** (Av Joaquim Soeiro de Carvalho 693, Barreirinhas; internet per hr R$2; ☺ 8am-10pm Mon-Fri, 8am-1pm & 3-10pm Sat, 6-10pm Sun).

⫶ Activities

Several agencies in Barreirinhas offer daily half-day trips to **Lagoa Azul** (R$50 per person) and **Lagoa Bonita** (R$60), two of the park's biggest lagoons, northwest of town, in open-sided 4WD buses. You can also take a wonderful seven-hour **boat tour** (R$60) down the Rio Preguiças, between jungle, mangroves and dunes, to Mandacuru lighthouse (with great panoramas), the ocean beach at Caburé (with restaurants for lunch), and Atins at the river mouth. Both excursions are absolute don't-misses if you are using Barreirinhas as your base. Recommended Barreirinhas agencies that follow strict safety and environmental standards include **São Paulo Ecoturismo** (☎ 3349-0079; saopauloecoturismo.com.br; Av Brasília 108, Barreirinhas) and **Tropical Adventure Expedições** (☎ 3349-1987; www.tropicaladventure.com.br; Av 31 de Março 15, Barreirinhas), but agencies pool together, so it often won't matter which you choose.

From Atins, half-day 4WD-plus-walking trips to lagoons such as **Lagoa Verde** and **Lagoa Guajiru** cost R$200 for up to four people, plus R$50 per extra person, through Rancho do Buna (p561). Atins is also the base of one of the Lençóis' most experienced, knowledgeable and multilingual guides, Bernard de Laroche of **Sandwalkers** (☎ 8864-0526; sandwalkers.ma@gmail.com); you can ask for him at the cafe and informal information center **Baratins** (Rua Principal, Atins; ☺ 11am-11pm) on Atins' main street.

From Santo Amaro, again with a combination of 4WD and walking, you can reach the little visited **Lagoa Gaivota** and **Lagoa Betánia**.

A wonderful way to experience the Lençóis is to trek across them. It takes three or four days to cross from west to east or vice-versa, sleeping in hammocks or fishers' huts in the few tiny, poor villages along the way. A locally arranged guide should cost around R$120 per day. If you go east to west, you'll have the prevailing wind behind you. The most magical way of all is to trek by night under the full moon.

São Luís–based Terra Nordeste (p557) arranges well-organized trans-Lençóis hikes: a four-day return trip from São Luís with three days of trekking costs R$3000 to R$4000 for two people including transfers, meals, nights and an English-speaking guide.

🛏 Sleeping & Eating

🛏 Barreirinhas

Barreirinhas has plenty of accommodations. The Rio Preguiças meanders elaborately round the west, north and east of town, giving it at least four separate riverfronts. The most important one, a few steps from the main street, Av Joaquim Soeiro de Carvalho, is pedestrianized Av Beira Rio, which has several restaurants and is the main boat-departure point.

Pousada d'Areia POUSADA $
(☑ 3349-0550; www.pousadadareia.com.br; Av Joaquim Soeiro de Carvalho 888, Barreirinhas; s R$70-104, d R$100-150; ✹) Friendly staff, a good breakfast and a convenient location (the south end of the main street) make the Areia a solid choice – if you opt for the more expensive rooms at the rear, which are bright and new, with hammock-strung verandas. The cheaper rooms are smaller and much more enclosed.

Pousada do Porto POUSADA $
(☑ 3349-0654; Anacleto de Carvalho 20, Barreirinhas; s/d R$50/80, with air-con R$70/120; ✹) Just upriver from the Cisne Branco bus stop, Pousada do Porto's best-value rooms are its fan- and breeze-cooled upstairs units with river views.

Encantes do Nordeste CHALET $$
(☑ 3349-0288; www.encantesdonordeste.com.br; Rua Boa Vista s/n, Barreirinhas; s R$209-254, d R$280-336; ✹ ☎ ☒) ✐ This ecofriendly pousada is a little gem of comfort outside the hubbub, 3.5km east of Barreirinhas' center. The sloping plot leads down past cosy chalets to a beautiful garden with pool, from which it's just 200m to its lovely riverside restaurant, Bambaê. The pousada's own travel agency can arrange all excursions.

Pousada Sossego do Cantinho POUSADA $$
(☑ 3349-0753; www.sossego-do-cantinho.com; Rua Principal 2, Povoado Cantinho; d/tr/q R$215/275/300; ✹ ☎) On the riverbank 1.5km north of town, Swiss-owned Sossego is a perfect haven for resting a couple of days, or a relaxed base for excursions. The four large bungalows have big beds with lots of pillows, and there's a white-sand river beach at the foot of the gardens. Call to organise a boat pick-up from Barreirinhas.

A Canoa BRAZILIAN, PIZZERIA $$
(Av Beira Rio 300, Barreirinhas; mains R$19-35) For grilled fish, wood-fired pizza, river breezes and live music nightly, head for this spot on the pedestrianized riverside strip.

🛏 Caburé

This handful of rustic pousadas and restaurants sits on a beautiful, isolated sand peninsula between the lower Rio Preguiças and the Atlantic. It exists solely to serve tourists (mostly those who are on day trips from Barreirinhas), and while it's a nice enough place for lunch, you're much better off sleeping in funkier Atins, a 15-minute boat ride away at the mouth of the river. A good choice for fresh grilled fish or *caldeirada de camarão* in Caburé is **Restaurante Península do Caburé** (mains for 2 R$40-80; ⊙ 11am-9pm).

🛏 Atins

Atins is a small village of sandy streets amid dune vegetation at the mouth of the Rio Preguiças, with an ocean beach, a sizable foreign population and a surprising number of pousadas scattered among its scattered dwellings. It's a good base for visiting some of the more isolated parts of the park – you can have many gorgeous dunes and lagoons all to yourself.

Pousada do Irmão POUSADA $
(☑ 3349-5013; pousadairmaoatins.blogspot.com. br; Rua Principal, Atins; s R$60, d R$90-110) This attractive, new, locally owned place offers clean and colorful rooms sporting verandas strung with hammocks, and bathrooms walled with hundreds of seashells, set along a strip of grassy garden. Good fish, chicken and shrimp dishes (R$18 to R$27) are served in the shell-floored dining area under a big *palapa* roof.

Pousada da Rita
POUSADA $

(📞 9993-7537; Rua Principal, Atins; s/d R$35/60) Lovely clean rooms in a lovely clean family home.

★ Rancho do Buna
POUSADA $$

(Rancho Pousada; 📞 9616-9646; www.ranchodo-buna.com; Atins; s/d/tr/q R$110/168/195/224; 🗷)

🍴 This is easily the best pousada, despite the large property's chickens, guinea fowl, peacocks, ducks, dogs and cats wailing a dawn chorus from 5am. The comfortable brick chalets (built using many recycled materials), a fascinating common area, expansive grounds (with pool and duckpond), and well-prepared food (mains for two R$18 to R$56 and the breakfast tapiocas are world-class) are all long on charm.

It offers wonderful excursions to the dunes and lakes of the national park, and can arrange transportation by boat or 4WD. English is spoken.

★ Restaurante do Antônio
SEAFOOD $$

(Restaurante Canto dos Lençóis; Canto de Atins; per person R$25; ⊘ approx 10am-8pm) Get there by foot, horseback, car, boat or ox cart (ask at your pousada), but get yourself somehow to the wonderful fish or shrimp barbecue at this rustic culinary destination 7km west of Atins. The location, isolated between the dunes (600m away) and the sea (1.5km at low tide), is travel-memory fodder at its finest. Rancho do Buna will bring you in its 4WD for R$40 per person roundtrip (minimum R$150), or you can make a half-day trip of it by visiting some lagoons before lunch here – or you can walk here after breakfast (it takes about two hours), enjoy a leisurely lunch, and walk back late afternoon.

🛏 Santo Amaro

Ciamat Camp
CHALET $

(📞 9604-5824; www.ciamatcamp.com; Santo Amaro; s/d R$140/185) This Brazilian–Italian operation has just four comfortable wooden chalets scattered around its lovely and luxuriant riverside garden, across the Rio Alegre from the village. The operators will ferry you back and forth. Meals available.

❶ Getting There & Around

A good paved road, Hwy MA-402, runs east to Barreirinhas from Hwy BR-135, south of São Luís. **Cisne Branco** (www.cisnebrancoturismo.com.br; Anacleto de Carvalho 623, Barreirinhas) runs four daily buses from São Luís to Barreirinhas (R$28, 4½ hours), and back, but they start and finish at São Luís' bus station, way out of the city center. More convenient are the 'vans' (minibuses) of **BRTur** (📞 3236-6056; R$40); they take 4½ hours and will pick you up from your accommodation in São Luís around 5am or 7am, and start back from Barreirinhas at 4pm or 5pm. Accommodations in São Luís and Barreirinhas will book this for you.

To get to Atins from Barreirinhas, you can either take the Rio Preguiças boat tour (R$60), with its lunch stop in Caburé, and disembark at Atins about 2pm; or hire a boat in Barreirinhas for a direct transfer (R$250 to R$300 for up to five people, 1½ hours); or take a Toyota 4WD (R$20, two hours) leaving around 9am (and sometimes 10am) from Rua Monsenhor Gentil (opposite Lojas Vitória). The Toyotas head back from Atins to Barreirinhas at 4am or 4:30am (and 1pm some days).

For Santo Amaro, get a Cisne Branco bus or BRTur van as far as Sangue on Hwy MA-402, then a prearranged 4WD along the 36km sandy track north to Santo Amaro (R$45 to R$50). Either BRTur or your accommodations in Santo Amaro can organize the 4WD connection.

Heading on east from Barreirinhas towards Parnaíba and Jericoacoara, 4WD trucks leave for Paulino Neves (R$20, 2½ hours) at 8am daily, and usually 8:30am and 2pm Monday to Saturday, from opposite Banco do Brasil on Av Joaquim Soeiro de Carvalho. From Paulino Neves take a taxi (R$40 to R$70) or another truck (R$5 to R$10 per person) to Tutoia. From Tutoia there are a few daily buses, including at 3.30pm to Parnaíba (R$16, 2½ hours). There is also a bus from Paulino Neves to Parnaíba (R$21, 3½ hours) at 6am Monday to Saturday. A 4WD from Parnaíba to Jeri costs around R$500 (ask at the travel agencies in Parnaíba bus station). Otherwise, there's a daily 7:15am Guanabara bus from Parnaíba to Camocim (R$18, 2¼ hours). In Camocim you can catch 4WD trucks to Jericoacoara from the Mercado Central Monday through Saturday (R$35, 1½ to three hours, usually 11am to noon, or take a buggy (an exciting ride costing around R$200 to R$220 for up to four people). There are also four daily Fretcar buses (including one at 11:30am) from Camocim to Jijoca (R$8 to R$10, 1½ hours), from which 4WD trucks head to Jeri for R$10.

A direct 4WD transfer from Barreirinhas costs around R$600 for up to five people to Parnaíba, or R$1200 all the way to Jericoacoara.

For information on approaching Barreirinhas from the east (Jericoacoara and Parnaíba), see p544. To reach Caburé from the east without going via Barreirinhas, you need 4WD transport that can make it along the beach for the final stretch from Paulino Neves.

Paulino Neves

☎ 098

This small fishing and farming community between Barreirinhas and Tutoia – a staging post on the route between Barreirinhas and Parnaíba – is a tranquil place where the dune fields of the Pequenos Lençóis (effectively an extension of those in the national park to the west) are within a 20-minute walk of the village. Comfortable **Pousada Oásis dos Lençóis** (☎ 3487-1012; São Francisco 50; s/d with fan R$40/60, with air-con R$50/80; ❄) has a garden running down to the Rio Novo, and Dona Mazé cooks a fabulous *moqueca* or *mariscada* (seafood stew). **Pousada Rota dos Lençóis** (☎ 3487-1307; suz.reis@hotmail.com; Av Rio Novo 35; s/d with fan R$50/60, with air-con R$60/80; ❄ 🛜), also good, is close to the bridge and the departure point for trucks to Barreirinhas.

Tutoia

☎ 098 / POP 18,700

Tutoia is a relatively large yet somewhat underdeveloped market town at the western end of the Delta do Parnaíba. A boat ride through the delta from Parnaíba to Tutoia is a nice way to start a trip to the Lençóis Maranhenses. There are also several daily buses from Parnaíba to Tutoia (R$16, 2½ hours), the first at 5:30am and the last at 4:30pm. Taxis and 4WD trucks provide transportation between Tutoia and Paulino Neves, 34km west.

Pousada Jagatá POUSADA $$
(☎ 3479-1551; www.pousadajagata.com.br; Av Beira Mar 1000; s R$105-115, d R$130-175; ❄ 🛜 ☀) If you'd like nothing but the best, Pousada Jagatá is it, with simple but well-kept rooms and a pretty garden looking over the delta. It's about 1.5km from the central Praça Tremembés. Grab a moto-taxi.

The Amazon

POP 15.8 MILLION

Includes ➡

Best Nature Reserves

➡ Reserva de Desenvolvimento Sustentável Mamirauá (p626)

➡ Xixuaú-Xipariná (p623)

➡ Floresta Nacional (FLONA) do Tapajós (p590)

➡ Parque Nacional do Jaú (p623)

➡ Parque Estadual do Jalapão (p600)

Best Places to Stay

➡ Local family's home in Floresta Nacional (FLONA) do Tapajós (p590)

➡ Pousada Pico da Neblina (p623)

➡ Hotel Casarão da Amazônia (p586)

Why Go?

Named after female warriors of Greek mythology, the Amazon is itself a place of nearly mythical status. What traveler hasn't imagined a trip to the Amazon, not only to admire the towering trees and awesome river, but to enter, in a real sense, the very life spring of the planet, the source of so much of the air we breath, the water we drink and the weather we rely on. To be sure, expecting a Discovery Channel–like experience (jaguars in every tree, spear-toting *indios* around every bend) is a recipe for disappointment. In fact, the Amazon's quintessential experiences are more sublime than superlative: canoeing through a flooded forest, dozing in a hammock on a boat chugging upriver, waking to the otherworldly cry of howler monkeys. On a river whose size is legendary, it's actually the little things that make it special. Give it some time, forget your expectations, and the Amazon cannot fail to impress.

When to Go
Manaus

°C/°F **Temp**   **Rainfall** inches/mm

May The world-famous Amazonas Opera Festival is held in Manaus.	**Jun** The rain eases, but the river is still high and the forest flooded.	**Oct** Hot dry weather makes for good hiking.

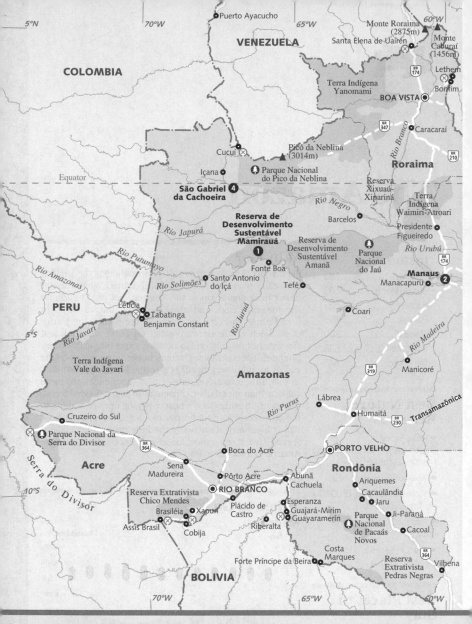

The Amazon Highlights

1 Glide through the flooded forest at **Reserva de Desenvolvimento Sustentável Mamirauá** (p626), in search of the shaggy-coated uakari monkey.

2 Soak up night sounds and river life on **jungle tours** (p610) outside Manaus.

3 Rough it with rubber-tappers in **Floresta Nacional do Tapajós** (p590), outside Alter do Chão.

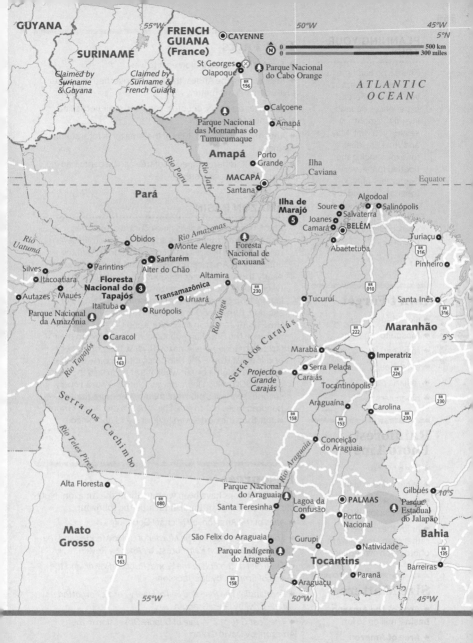

④ Hike through remote primary forest and indigenous lands outside **São Gabriel da Cachoeira** (p614).

⑤ Ply the windy Atlantic beaches at **Ilha de Marajó** (p583) — on foot or on the back of a water buffalo!

PLANNING YOUR TRIP

There's no bad time to visit the Amazon, but you'll have different experiences depending on the month or season you visit. May and June are ideal for experiencing the flooded forest, while September and October are hot and dry and good for hiking. As for how long to stay, a week is plenty for any one area.

Don't Forget

➜ closed-toe shoes

➜ mosquito repellant

➜ rain gear

➜ plastic bags

➜ malaria pills

➜ binoculars

Rainforest Photo Tips

➜ use a tripod

➜ avoid using a flash

➜ learn how to set your camera to a low ISO

➜ enjoy the moment rather than struggling to photograph everything

Size Matters

➜ **Area of the Amazon basin** 7 million sq km

➜ **Area of Amazon rainforest** 5.5 million sq km

➜ **Area of Amazon rainforest in Brazil** 3.3 million sq km

Fast Facts

➜ The Amazon used to flow east to west.

➜ After leaving the Andes, the Amazon riverbed descends just 1.5cm per kilometer.

➜ Pink river dolphins, or *botos*, can bend their necks and shrug their shoulders.

➜ Ants make up 10% to 30% of the Amazon's total animal biomass.

➜ Up to 1000 different species of tree can be contained in 1 sq km of Amazon rainforest.

AMAZON BASIN

The Amazon Basin spans nine countries and three standard time zones. It has an area of more than seven million square kilometers, accounting for 40% of the entire South American continent. The Amazon Basin is nearly the size of the contiguous USA and more than twice that of India. The Amazon rainforest is the world's largest tropical rainforest, and despite rampant deforestation, remains 80% intact and untouched. (By contrast, many forests in Asia, Africa and Central America, and even the Brazilian Atlantic coast, are down to their last 5% to 10%.) The Amazon River is the world's second-longest river – the Nile beats it by a hair – but the biggest in volume by far: when it's at its fullest, the river dumps 300 million liters of water into the ocean every second, sending a plume of fresh water more than a hundred miles out to sea. The Amazon discharges more water than the next seven biggest rivers combined.

Resources

Countless books have been written about the Amazon. Notable ones available in English include the following:

➜ *Atlas of the Amazon*, by Michael Goulding

➜ *The Burning Season: The Murder of Chico Mendes and the Fight for the Amazon Rain Forest*, by Andrew Revkin

➜ *The Thief at the End of the World: Rubber, Power, and the Seeds of Empire*, by Joe Jackson

➜ *Fordlandia: The Rise and Fall of Henry Ford's Forgotten Jungle City*, by Greg Grandin

➜ *The Lost City of Z: A Tale of Deadly Obsession in the Amazon*, by David Grann

➜ *The Last of the Tribe: The Epic Quest to Save a Lone Man in the Amazon*, by Monte Reel

➜ *The River of Doubt: Theodore Roosevelt's Darkest Journey*, by Candice Millard

History

The Amazon Basin has been inhabited for at least 10,000 years, possibly longer. Its earliest inhabitants lived in hundreds of far-flung tribes, some tiny, others numbering in the tens of thousands. Early researchers believed the rainforest was simply too inhospitable to support large populations, though recent studies have challenged that notion, suggesting up to five million people may have lived in the Amazon by the time of European contact. That occurred in 1541, after a Spanish expedition led by Gonzalo Pizarro in present-day Peru ran short of supplies; Pizarro's cousin, Francisco de Orellana, and 60 men ostensibly went in search of supplies, but ended up floating down the entire length of the Amazon. The expedition suffered numerous attacks by indigenous groups, including women, they reported, like the Amazons of Greek mythology. Thus the world's greatest river got its name. No one made a serious effort to claim this sweaty territory, however, until the Portuguese built a fort near the mouth of the river at Belém in 1616, and sent Pedro Teixeira up the river to Quito and back between 1637 and 1639. During the 17th and 18th centuries, Portuguese fortune-seekers penetrated ever further into the rainforest in pursuit of gold and *índio* slaves, exploring as far as present-day Rondônia.

Amazonian *índios* had long used the sap from rubber trees to make waterproof bags and other items, but the material proved difficult to work with outside the warm humid rainforest. But once American Charles Goodyear developed vulcanization (which made natural rubber durable) in 1842, there soon was an unquenchable demand for rubber in the recently industrialized USA and Europe. As the price for Brazilian rubber soared, so did exploitation of the *seringueiros* (rubber-tappers) who were lured into the Amazon, mostly from the drought-stricken Northeast, by the promise of prosperity only to be locked into a cruel system of indentured labor.

In 1876, a Briton named Henry Wickham smuggled 70,000 rubber-tree seeds from the Amazon to London, and before long, rubber trees were growing in neat and efficient groves in the British colonies of Ceylon and Malaya. The price of latex plummeted, and by the 1920s Brazil's rubber boom was over.

Fearful of foreign annexation of the Amazon, Brazil embarked on a development and settlement program embodied by the 1970s slogan *'Integrar para não entregar'* (essentially, 'Use it or lose it'). The effort proved disastrous for the rainforest. Roads meant to facilitate settlement of the interior became arteries from which rampant destruction of the Amazon rainforest was – and still is – fed. In Rondônia, the population leaped from 111,000 in 1970 to 1.13 million in 1991, and 20% of the state's primary forest was cut down. The rate of deforestation in the 1980s was equivalent to more than a football field a minute, for a whole decade.

In December 1988, Chico Mendes, an internationally recognized union and environmental leader from Acre state, was gunned down on his back porch by ranchers angry about his efforts to stop clear-cutting. The attack, by no means the first of its kind, but remarkable for its brazenness, focused worldwide attention on deforestation in the Amazon. (American nun Dorothy Stang was murdered under similar circumstances in 2005.) Fortunately, Brazil's efforts to stem the destruction including strict burning and cutting regulations, and use of publicly available real-time satellite monitoring – has proved remarkably successful, and deforestation has dropped to its lowest recorded rates.

The effects of global climate change on the Amazon continue unabated, however. Since 2005, the Amazon has been whiplashed by a series of extreme droughts and floods, each breaking the record set by the previous. The flood of 2012 was the latest record-breaker, with water levels rising nearly 30m, more than double the 'normal' seasonal rise. Meanwhile, the Amazon's population continues to grow well above the national average, threatening to undo the considerable progress made combating pollution and deforestation in this vibrant, invaluable and embattled ecosystem.

ⓘ Getting There & Away

Manaus and Belém are the major transportation hubs of the Amazon. Most travelers arrive by air – Manaus receives the bulk of international flights, including direct flights from Miami and Buenos Aires, while both cities have frequent domestic air service. Manaus has limited bus service, while Belém has buses arriving and departing from all over Brazil. Some travelers enter the Brazilian Amazon by boat from Peru or Colombia, crossing at what is known as the Triple Frontier; others arrive overland from Venezuela or Guyana, which have bus services to Manaus, or from Bolivia, at the border towns of

Guajará-Mirim or Brasiléia. Those coming from the interior of Brazil, including Brasília or the Pantanal, can enter the Amazon via Porto Velho, where they catch a plane or riverboat to Manaus, or via Palmas in the state of Tocantins, connecting by bus to Belém.

ℹ️ Getting Around

Virtually every major town along the Amazon, Solimões, and Madeira rivers has both a port and an airstrip – but no roads in or out – so travel is limited to plane or boat. Choosing between flying and boating is really a matter of time, money and preference. Boat travel is certainly an experience, and most travelers cover at least one or two legs by water. But the distances are enormous and the boats very slow, especially going upstream. Flying gives you more time to do the fun stuff (hiking, canoeing etc) and frequent promotions can make the cost of flying surprisingly close to that of taking a boat. Bus services are available in states along the edges of the rainforest, such as Pará, Tocantins, and Rondônia. Highway conditions are improving, and there are more deluxe and direct options available, which help make the invariably long bus routes a bit less taxing.

PARÁ

Pará doesn't have the name 'Amazonas' like the state next door, so it might be easy to think it's not part of 'the Amazon' either. In fact, Pará has some terrific Amazonian destinations: The national forest along the Rio Tapajós has monster trees and a fascinating living history of rubber boom and bust, and is reachable via the laid-back beach town of Alter do Chão. The capital city, Belém, is lively and pleasant, and you can wander deserted beaches on the islands of Algodoal and Marajó.

Travelers understandably see Pará as 'not deep enough' into the Amazon to warrant an extended visit, and extensive deforestation in the state certainly doesn't help. But it doesn't take long to see that Pará has plenty of authentic Amazonia, and those who give it a chance are rarely disappointed.

Belém

𝄃 091 / POP 1.4 MILLION

Belém is a surprisingly rewarding city, with streets and parks shaded by mango trees, and a number of fascinating monuments and museums. The sloping central park is quiet during the week and bustling on weekends, when locals come out en masse for free performances and tasty street food. Nightlife tends toward the bohemian intellectual sort: art-house theaters, small music venues, heady cafe-bars. From Belém you can take overnight trips to Algodoal and Ilha de Marajó, both appealing coastal destinations, and it's a logical launchpad for journeys up the Rio Amazonas (Amazon River). The Amazon is not known for its cities, and Belém can't compete with places such as São Luis or Salvador for charm or urban flair. But, given time to explore, most find Belém is not nearly as rough around the edges as they expected.

History

Belém was one of the first Portuguese settlements on the Amazon River, founded in 1616. It prospered for over two centuries, relying on enslaved *índios* (and later enslaved Africans) for finding and harvesting Amazonian treasures such as cacao, indigo and animal skins, all for export to Europe. But it was a fragile success, and an economic downturn in the early 19th century helped spark a popular uprising and bloody civil war.

The rubber boom at the turn of the century sent Belém's population rocketing, from 40,000 in 1875 to more than 100,000 in 1900. The city suddenly had electricity, telephones, streetcars and a distinctly European feel. Officials erected a few grand monuments such as the Teatro da Paz, earning the city the nickname 'the tropical Paris.'

Rubber eventually crashed, but the ports built during the boom remained active. Today some 800,000 tons of cargo pass through Belém, mostly timber and soy beans, but also fish, shrimp, Brazil nuts and palm hearts.

◎ Sights & Activities

◉ Central Area

★**Estação das Docas** ⠀⠀⠀⠀⠀MARKET
(www.estacaodasdocas.com.br; Blvd Castilho França; ⊙9am-1am) An ambitious renovation project converted three down-at-heel riverfront warehouses into a popular gathering spot, with restaurants, bars, shops and even an art-house theater. There are nice river views and displays about Belém's history, plus a post office and numerous ATMs. Enjoy live music most nights, performed from a moving platform in the rafters, rolling slowly the length of the dining area.

Teatro da Paz
HISTORIC BUILDING

(Praça da República; admission R$4, Wed free; ☺ guided visits every hr 9am-noon & 2-5pm Tue-Fri, 9am-noon Sat-Sun) Overlooking Praça da República, the Teatro da Paz is one of Belém's finest buildings. Completed in 1874 and built in neoclassical style, the architecture has all the sumptuous trappings of the rubber-boom era: columns, busts, crystal mirrors and an interior decorated in Italian theatrical style. Half-hour tours are a mildly interesting trip to the city's former glory years.

Mercado Ver-o-Peso
MARKET

(Blvd Castilhos França; ☺ 7:30am-6pm Mon-Sat, to 1pm Sun) The name of this waterfront market, with its iconic four-turreted structure, comes from colonial times, when the Portuguese would *ver o peso* (check the weight) of merchandise in order to impose taxes. The display of fruits, animals, medicinal plants and more is fascinating; go early to see fishing boats unloading their catch.

Some stands sell souvenirs, but be alert for pickpockets and avoid going after 5pm.

Valeverde
BOAT TOUR

(☎ 3213-3388; www.valeverdeturismo.com.br; Estação das Docas) Offers a variety of short tours on the river (per person R$30 to R$100), including sunrise bird-watching tours and pleasant evening cruises. Valeverde has an office and daily schedule at the pier at Estação das Docas; in most cases you can simply show up.

◉ Cidade Velha

The 'Old City' has most of the city's museums and galleries, fronting the river and four nearly adjoining plazas. The area is safe during the day, with plenty of people about, but it is tucked below the Comercio neighborhood, which gets seedy at night. Take a taxi if you're there late.

Forte do Presépio
FORTRESS

(Praça Fr Brandão; admission R$2; ☺ 10am-6pm Tue-Fri, to 2pm Sat & Sun) The city of Belém was founded in 1616 with the construction of this imposing fort, which was intended to protect Portuguese interests upriver against incursions by the French and Dutch. Today it houses a small but excellent museum, primarily about Pará's indigenous communities (displays in Portuguese only), and has great river and city views from atop its thick stone walls.

Palácio Antonio Lemos & MABE
MUSEUM, HISTORICAL BUILDING

(MABE; ☎ 3283-4665; Praça Dom Pedro II; ☺ 10am-5pm Tue-Fri, 9am-1pm Sat) FREE This rubber-boom palace served as city hall in the late 1800s, and now houses, on the 2nd floor, the Museu de Arte de Belém. The museum has gorgeous wood floors – cloth slippers are provided – and a fine collection of statuettes, antiques and Brazilian 20th-century paintings, such as Theodoro Braga's 1908 oil *Fundação da Cidade de Belém*.

Museu do Estado do Pará
MUSEUM

(Pará State Museum; ☎ 3225-2414; Praça Dom Pedro II; admission R$4, free Tue; ☺ 10am-6pm Tue-Fri, to 2pm Sat & Sun) This grand building, Palácio Lauro Sodré, was the residence of Portugal's royal representatives in Belém and later of various governors of Pará. One governor, Ernesto Lobo, was killed on the staircase during the Cabanagem Rebellion in 1835. Today it's the home of the Museu do Estado do Pará, a mildly interesting collection on the founding and growth of Belém and Pará.

Casa das Onze Janelas
MUSEUM

(Praça Frei Brandão; admission R$1; ☺ 10am-6pm Tue-Fri, to 2pm Sat & Sun) Once the home of a sugar baron, then a military hospital, the Casa das Onze Janelas now houses an excellent art gallery and one of Belém's finest restaurants, Boteco das Onze (p574). The medium-sized gallery contains a mix of classical and modern artwork, plus a good photography exhibit upstairs. The cafe in back has a view of the Rio Guamá.

Museu de Arte Sacra
MUSEUM

(Praça Frei Brandão; admission R$4; ☺ 10am-6pm Tue-Fri, to 2pm Sat & Sun) This museum has two parts: the impressive Igreja do Santo Alexandre and the adjoining Palâcio Episcopal (Bishop's Palace). Santo Alexandre was Belém's first church, founded by Jesuits in the early 17th century, and contains incredible cedar and plaster detailing. The rambling Bishop's Palace has a decent collection of modern art, though was closed for renovation at the time of research.

Museo do Círio
MUSEUM

(Jóao Alfredo; adult/student R$2/1, Tue free; ☺ 10am-6pm Tue-Fri, to 2pm Sat & Sun) The many idiosyncrasies of Belém's famous religious festival, the Círio de Nazaré, are explained in this handsome museum, from the discovery of a tiny statue of Mary in a riverbank in

Belém

Rio Guajará

37

Porto de Belém

31

Paratur

Praça Waldemar Henrique

Av Marechal Hermes

Estação das Docas 28 1
36

Blvd Castilho França

11

R Gaspar Viana

R S Antônio 25 24

Tv Frei Gil de Vila Nova
R 28 de Setembro

Av Pres Vargas

19 15

COMÉRCIO

Praça do Pescador

Tv 1 de Março

Tv Padre Prudêncio

R Aristides Lobo

5

Blvd Castilho França

R 15 de Novembro

R João Alfredo

7 de Setembro

R 13 de Maio

Tv Frutuoso Guimarães

Tv Campos Sales

R Sen Barata

R Riachuelo

Praça do Relógio

Av Portugal

Praça da Bandeira

23

4

6

2 Praça Fr Brandão 7

Praça Dom Pedro II

35

18

3

8

9

Praça Felipe Patron

R João Diogo

Palácio Lauro Sodré (Museo do Estado do Pará)

Siqueira Mendes

R Aver Rocha

R Távora

Praça do Carmo

Dr Malcher

CIDADE VELHA

Av Tamandaré

Tv São Pedro

Av 16 de Novembro

Dr Assis

Tv Gurupá

Tv São Francisco

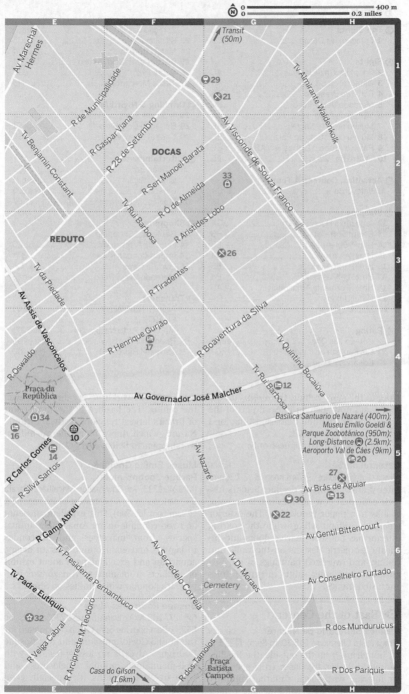

Belém

1700, to the story behind the 400m, 1000lb rope that's now such an integral part of the procession, the faithful masses jostling for a chance to touch or pull it.

Explanations in Portuguese only.

Catedral da Sé CHURCH
(Praça Frei Brandão; ☉7am-noon & 2-7:30pm) After years of slow, sad decline, Belém's historic cathedral now radiates inside and out, thanks to a major renovation. The exterior gleams a brilliant white, while the soaring interior has polished marble floors and intricate geometric designs on the walls and ceiling, and oversized paintings of the Virgin Mary and other saints in ornate gold-encrusted frames.

◎ East of the Center

Basílica Santuario de Nazaré CHURCH
(Praça Justo Chermont; ☉5:30am-8pm) **FREE** A bit humdrum from the outside, the Basílica Santuario de Nazaré has a truly spectacular interior, with soaring marble columns, brilliant stained-glass windows and ornate wood and tile work in every direction, even the ceiling. The basilica is the focal point of Brazil's largest religious festival, Círio de Nazaré, which draws more than a million worshippers to Belém every October.

Museu Emílio Goeldi & Parque Zoobotánico ZOO
(☎3249-1233; Av Governador Magalhães Barata 376; park, aquarium & permanent exhibit each R$2; ☉9am-5pm Tue-Sun) This excellent museum and zoo contains many Amazonian animal species, from manatees and anacondas to jaguars and giant otters, plus an aviary, aquarium and excellent permanent exhibit of artifacts from ancient Amazonian peoples. It's popular with families on Sundays.

Bosque Rodrigues Alves ZOO
(☎3277-1112; Av Almirante Barroso 2305; admission R$2; ☉9am-5pm Tue-Sun) Often overlooked for the Emílio Goeldi museum and zoo, Bosque Rodrigues Alves is no less appealing, with well-maintained animal enclosures and wide, tree-shaded paths. It's especially good for families, with huge, curious structures

including a castle and replica grotto. From the center, take any 'Alm. Borroso' bus, and get off when you see the park's long yellow exterior wall.

✨ Festivals & Events

Every year on the morning of the second Sunday of October, Belém explodes with the sounds of hymns, bells and fireworks. Started in 1793, the **Círio de Nazaré** is Brazil's biggest religious festival. People from all over the country flock to Belém, and even camp in the streets, to participate in the grand event.

The diminutive image of Nossa Senhora de Nazaré (Our Lady of Nazareth) is believed to have been sculpted in Nazareth (Galilee) and to have performed miracles in medieval Portugal before getting lost in Brazil. It was rediscovered in 1700 by a humble cattleman on the site of the basilica, to which it later returned of its own accord after being moved away several times.

The day before the main annual event, the little statue, having previously been taken 23km north to Icoaraci, is carried in a river procession back to the cathedral in Belém. On the Sunday itself, well over a million people fill the streets to accompany the image from the Catedral da Sé to the Basílica Santuario de Nazaré. The image is placed on a flower-bedecked carriage, and thousands squirm and grope in an emotional frenzy to get a hand on the 400m rope pulling the carriage. Five hours and just 3.5km from the cathedral, the Virgin reaches the basilica, where she remains for the duration of the festivities.

🛏 Sleeping

Hotel Unidos　　　　　　　　　HOTEL **$**
(☏ 3224-0660; www.hotelunidos.com.br; Ó de Almeida 545; s/d/tr R$93/105/135; ✻@🕸) One of Belém's best values, the Unidos has large spotless rooms and competent, welcoming staff. The decor is admittedly plain, but the rates here are lower than comparably equipped alternatives, even without the 15% cash discount. Just a half-block off Av Presidente Vargas, it's walking distance to many restaurants and sights, and close to the bus stops for everything else.

Hotel Le Massilia　　　　　　　HOTEL **$**
(☏ 3222 2834; www.massilia.com.br; Henrique Gurjão 236; s/d standard R$130/145, d/tr superior R$170/185; ✻🕸❄) This French-run hotel

near Praça da República has a guesthouse atmosphere, small swimming pool and recommended French restaurant. Rooms open onto a long leafy garden and have homey details like beanbag chairs and writing tables; superiors have lofts and can sleep up to four, albeit somewhat cozily. A dip in the pool is a nice way to end the day.

Amazônia Hostel Belém　　　HOSTEL **$**
(☏ 4008-4800; www.amazoniahostel.com.br; Av Governador José Malcher 592; s/d R$58, s/d R$85/115, s/d with shared bathroom R$65/105, with HI card discount R$10; ✻@🕸) A century-old rubber-baron mansion in a safe area is the perfect home for Belém's only youth hostel. Smallish dorms have solid bunks and large lockers, plus 4m ceilings and gorgeous wood floors. Internet, kitchen and laundry are welcome features. Prices are high for a hostel, and management is oddly stingy with breakfast and linens, but it's still a nice spot.

Hotel Grão Pará　　　　　　　HOTEL **$**
(☏ 3221-2121; www.hotelgraopara.com.br; Av Presidente Vargas 718; s/d R$100/120; ✻🕸) A reliable if rather charmless high-rise hotel, with midsized rooms and updates like glass showers and marble counters, but older beds and air conditioners. Rooms facing the street have views of Praça da República, but can be noisy – ask for a high floor. Service is friendly if somewhat uneven, but you can definitely count on a hearty breakfast and strong wi-fi signal.

Hotel Amazônia　　　　　　　HOTEL **$**
(☏ 3222-8456; www.hotelamazoniabelem.com.br; Ó de Almeida 548; dm R$20, r with fan/air-con R$50/60; ✻@🕸) Not to be confused with the hostel of nearly the same name, this cramped grim hotel has a good location and rock-bottom rates, but precious little in the way of atmosphere. One small dorm room and several thin-walled private rooms will do in a pinch. The kitchen and common TV room are more tolerable; breakfast is not included.

★ Manacá Hotel　　　　　　　HOTEL **$$**
(☏ 3222-9224; www.manacahotel.com.br; Travessa Quintino Bocaiúva 1645; s/d R$180/210; ✻🕸❄) Rooms in this boutique hotel are cozy yet up to date, while the common areas have beautiful wood and stone floors, and creative artwork, including the original wooden front door hanging like a painting in the hallway. The neighborhood is equally appealing, with

stylish shops and restaurants, and the Basílica Nazaré and zoo a short walk away. Small swimming pool.

Hotel Portas da Amazônia HOTEL $$
(☑ 3222-9952; Dr Malcher 14; s R$110, d R$140-160; ✳ 🛜) A former mansion with a gorgeous tile facade, this attractive boutique-ish hotel has just nine rooms and is close enough to the main cathedral that you'll think the bells are being rung next door. Huge front rooms have large windows overlooking Praça Brandão, while rear rooms have less light, but high ceilings and exposed brick. The surrounding area can get a bit dodgy late at night.

Belem Soft Hotel HOTEL $$
(www.belemsofthotel.com.br; Av Braz de Aguiar 612; s/d R$130/150) This no-frills hotel is located in a pleasant neighborhood, near to several sights and restaurants, and removed from the hustle and bustle around Praça da República. A recent renovation means the rooms are modern and comfortable (albeit with old-school air conditioners), though quite bare in terms of decor. Overall, practical and affordable, if not particularly inspiring,

Hilton Belém HOTEL $$$
(☑ 4006-7000, toll free 0800-728-0888; www.hilton.com; Av Presidente Vargas 882; s R$470-790, d R$500-820; ✳ @ 🛜 ☲) One of Belém's largest and most upscale hotels has a central location, opposite Praça da República, and offers all the expected services, including a business center, exercise room, lobby bar and swimming pool. Rooms are spacious and reasonably modern. The rest of the hotel could really use an update, though, especially its gaudy fabrics and aging furniture.

Eating

✕ Center

Restaurante Belo Centro SELF-SERVE $
(☑ 3241-8677; 2nd fl, Santo Antônio 264; per kg R$30; ☺ lunch Mon-Fri) This friendly, airy restaurant cooks up tasty self-serve, with plenty of options for vegetarians and carnivores. It's located on the 2nd floor in the middle of a busy commercial zone; look for the large vinyl sign hanging from the balcony and a narrow stairway leading up from the street.

Mãe Natureza VEGETARIAN $
(Sen Manoel Barata 889; per kg R$39; ☺ lunch Mon-Sat; ✎) The sterile dining room doesn't do justice to the unique vegan lunch buffet,

though the air-con will have you ahh-ing even before you get to the food. Mãe Natureza – the name is Portuguese for 'Mother Nature' – uses only fresh veggies and ingredients (even raw sugar) and makes its own soy milk.

★ Estação das Docas RESTAURANTS $$
(www.estacaodasdocas.com.br; Blvd Castilho França; ☺ 10am-midnight Sun-Wed, to 3am Thu-Sat) One of the best places in Belém to eat no matter what you're hungry for. The bustling complex has almost a dozen restaurants, most with indoor and outdoor seating and open for lunch, dinner and late-night feasting. Favorites include Lá em Casa, serving pricey but outstanding regional food, and Amazon Beer, with tasty pub grub to accompany its artisanal beer.

K'Delícias IV SELF-SERVE $$
(Carlos Gomes 237; per kg R$38, Sun R$45; ☺ lunch) Its extensive and smartly displayed spread makes this one of the center's best per-kilo spots, and with air-con blasting, one of the most comfortable too. One of the few eateries open on Sunday.

✕ Outside the Center

★ Tasca Mercado SANDWICHES $
(Travessa Quintino Bocaiúva 1696; sandwiches & salads R$4-20; ☺ 6:30am-11pm) Fresh-baked baguettes, focaccia and other breads serve as the basis for a variety of tasty sandwiches at this high-ceilinged, trendy cafe, from humble *misto quente* (ham and cheese) to more refined options with ingredients like garlic eggplant, caramelized onions, smoked salmon, roasted peppers, Parma ham or fresh herbs. Salads, quiches, bruschettas, pizzas and *petiscos* (snacks) round out the menu.

Cosanostra Caffé BRAZILIAN $
(Travessa Benjamin Constant 1499; mains R$7-20; ☺ noon-1am) The dim lighting and unmarked entrance lend a certain *Goodfellas* ambience, and Frank Sinatra happened to be playing when we visited, but the beefy guys at the bar are mostly businesspeople on a break. Lunch specials include a main dish, side dish and soda for R$15, or order larger plates off the menu. The bar is open late, and there's live music after 11pm.

Boteco das Onze BRAZILIAN $$
(Praça Frei Brandão; mains R$21-63; ☺ noon-midnight Tue-Sun, 5pm-midnight Mon) Part of

SURF THE POROROCA!

Every month or so, when alignment of the sun and moon makes tides their strongest, powerful waves can form at the mouth of certain rivers and barrel upstream with tremendous force. The phenomenon – which occurs when the tide briefly overpowers the force of the river – is technically a 'tidal bore' but in Brazil is better known as the *pororoca*, an indigenous word for 'mighty noise.' And no wonder: the waves can reach heights of 4m and speeds of 30km/h, and can rip full-sized trees off the bank with their force.

All of which is music to the ears of extreme surfers (and wave-surfing kayakers) in search of the mythic 'endless wave.' The record for the longest ride is 37 minutes, covering nearly 13km. Surfers generally report the *pororoca* to be stronger than a like-sized ocean wave, and it constantly changes size and speed according to the river's contours. What's more, the water is loaded with debris that's been swept off the shore and river bottom, including tree trunks and abandoned canoes. (At least the caimans tend to stay away.)

The National Pororoca Surfing Championship has been held at the town of São Domingos do Capim, 120km east of Belém on the Rio Guamá, since 1999. (A related competition is held on the Rio Araguari in Amapá.) The event usually takes place in March, on the full moon nearest the spring equinox, when the *pororoca* is strongest. The bash draws top-ranked surfers and includes street fairs, cultural performances, even a Miss Pororoca competition. A paved road makes getting there easier, though there still is no direct service; from Belém, go to Castanhal and transfer. Alternatively, Amazon Star Turismo, a travel agency in Belém, organizes *pororoca* packages.

Casa das Onze Janelas gallery, this is one of the city's best restaurant-bars. It has an indoor dining room with modern art on the walls and a breezy back patio overlooking the river. Meals include *moqueca de filhote,* a tasty stew prepared with catfish, shrimp and lobster. Live music most nights.

Santa Pizza
PIZZERIA $$

(☑ 3409-6450; Travessa Quintino Bocaiúva 945; mains R$15-40; ⊙ 6pm-1am Fri & Sat) Sharp decor, hip music and mood lighting make Santa Pizza, between Travessa Tiradentes and Rua Boaventura da Silva, feel more like a lounge bar than a pizzeria, which is precisely the point. The outdoor tables are especially nice on warm evenings.

Cia Paulista de Pizza
PIZZERIA $$

(☑ 3212-2200; Av Visconde de Souza Franco 559; dishes R$18-35; ⊙ 10am-1am Sun-Thu, 10am-4am Fri & Sat) You wouldn't know from the dining room that this is actually a chain restaurant, as the wineglasses, tablecloths, attentive waiters and recorded jazz create a unique and classy ambience. Prices are quite affordable, and the pizza and pasta excellent.

🍷 Drinking & Nightlife

Av Visconde de Souza Franco has several bars and clubs, where you can simply follow the music to find the current hot spot.

Amazon Beer
BEER HALL

(www.amazonbeer.com.br; Av Marechal Hermes, Estação das Docas; ⊙ 5pm-1am) As much as Brazilians love beer, it's remarkably difficult to find anything darker or more complex than a pilsner. This popular boutique brewery is an exception, with an amber ale, a Dutch *witbier,* an IPA, even a unique açaí stout (plus several lighter beers) all brewed on the premises. It has indoor and outdoor seating, and a full menu.

Capital Lounge Bar
BAR

(www.capitalbarlounge.com; Av Brás de Aguiar 420; ⊙ 7pm-3am Wed-Sat) A huge Union Jack and other flags from around the world suggest an old-school English pub, but the sleek booths, creative cocktails and pulsing DJ-mixed music give this much more of a club vibe. There's restaurant service but the real action gets started long after dinner time. Popular with Belém's jetset.

Bohêmio Cervejaria
BAR

(Av Visconde de Souza Franco; ⊙ 6pm-3am Mon-Fri, noon-3am Sat & Sun) Cool, laid-back bar with dark wood tables and a huge bank of beer bottles as modern art against the back wall (pray for no earthquakes). There's live music most nights – and a R$3 to R$4 cover when there is – varying from rock to pop to MPB (Música Popular Brasileira).

Transit
BAR

(cnr Rua 28 de Setembro & Travessa Almirante Waldenkolk; ☺5pm-2am Thu-Sat) The crowd is usually young and down to earth at this lively open-air bar and club. There's a kitchen service and a stage for live music, with performances Thursday to Sunday nights ranging from rock to bossa nova.

☆ Entertainment

Teatro da Paz holds a variety of theatrical events, from plays to symphonies to international dance performances. Most events have same-day tickets available.

Casa do Gilson
LIVE MUSIC

(☑3272-7306; Travessa Padre Eutíquio 3172; ☺8pm-3am Fri, noon-3am Sat & Sun) Come here for Belém's best live music. Opened in 1987, Gilson's draws intellectuals and hipsters alike with first-rate samba, *choro* (improvised samba-like music) and other music, and terrific food and atmosphere to boot. It's between Ruas Nova and Tambés.

African Bar
SAMBA, DANCE

(☑3241-1085; cnr Av Marechal Hermes & Travessa da Piedade) Across from the state tourist office, this longtime club often stages samba groups on Saturday nights. Check the posters by the door for upcoming events.

Cine Estação
CINEMA

(☑3212-5615; www.estacaodasdocas.com.br; Estação das Docas; admission R$8) Cine Estação has month-long runs of Brazilian and international art films, typically with screenings twice-nightly on three or four days per week.

Cinépolis
CINEMA

(Av Visconde de Souza Franco, Boulevard Shopping) Cinépolis is a megatheater located in a megamall, with seven screens, including one for 3D films, and supercomfy stadium seating. Weekends can be extremely crowded.

Moviecom Cinémas
CINEMA

(www.moviecom.com.br; Travessa Padre Eutíquio) Moviecom Cinemas shows mostly Hollywood films at its top-floor location in Shopping Pátio Belém, an upscale mall.

🛍 Shopping

Feira de Artesanato
MARKET

(Praça da República; ☺Fri-Sun) A large crafts fair that has the city's biggest range of attractive artwork, and a lot of it is homemade. It's especially busy on Sundays.

Mercado Ver-o-Peso
MARKET

(Av Castilho França; ☺5am-6pm) This is Belém's most interesting place to shop, whether for long pants, dried piranha or anything in between. Pará has gained national attention with *technobrega* music, a defiantly from-the-streets genre whose best collections aren't sold in stores but on amateur CDs in Ver-o-Peso (and on YouTube). Be wary of pickpockets in the early and late hours.

Boulevard Shopping
MALL

(Av Visconde de Souza Franco 776) Belém's latest, biggest mall is a modern cement, steel-glass structure, brilliantly lit at night, and boasting top-tier clothing, electronics and department stores as well as a cinema complex.

Clio
BOOKS

(☑3210-6368, 3210-6369; airport; ☺24hr) Belém's best English-language selection, including guidebooks.

Livraría Newstime
BOOKS

(☑3212-3298; Estação das Docas; ☺noon-midnight Mon-Fri, 10am-midnight Sat & Sun) Fairly large bookstore with a handful of English titles, plus maps, CDs and more.

Imperador das Redes
OUTDOOR EQUIPMENT

(Padre Eutício at Riachuelo; ☺7:30am-5pm Mon-Fri, to 2pm Sat) Large hammock store, with everything from light, simple hammocks to deluxe matrimonial ones with lace fringe (R$40 to $120).

ℹ Orientation

Belém's central park is called Praça da República, a quiet leafy spot. West of there, and closer to the water, is Comércio, a busy commercial district whose narrow streets have a gritty vitality during the day, but turn lonely and dodgy at night. Further south is Cidade Velha (Old City), where Belém's best museums are located. East of the center is an upscale neighborhood called Nazaré, with cafes, a few hotels and the Basílica Santuario de Nazaré, Belém's most important church.

ℹ Information

DANGERS & ANNOYANCES

Pickpocketing can be a problem in Mercado Ver-o-Peso and the Comercio districts; take care during the day and avoid altogether at night. The narrow streets between Av Assis de Vasconcelos and Av Visconde de Souza Franco are known for prostitution and drug activity at night; take a cab if you're returning late from bars or the movies.

EMERGENCY
Police (☎190)
Tourist Police (CIPTUR) Central station (☎3222-2602; Rua 28 de Setembro, Central station); Paratur office (☎3212-0948; Praça Waldemar Henrique s/n, Paratur Office).

INTERNET ACCESS
Equilibrium (Ó de Almeida; per hr R$3; ⊘8am-6pm Mon-Fri)
Hilton Belém (Av Presidente Vargas 882; per min R$0.10, per hr R$6; ⊘8am-10:30pm)

LAUNDRY
Most hotels do laundry for guests, albeit at higher per-piece rates. Laundromats can usually do same-day service if you drop off early.
Lav & Lev (☎3223-7247; Travessa Dr Moraes 576; ⊘8am-6pm Mon-Sat) R$10 per wash cycle, R$10 per dry cycle (large loads may require more than one), R$10 service charge. Seven kilogram maximum per load.
Lava Na Hora (Av Serzedelo Correia 141 Altos; wash, dry & fold up to 5kg R$25; ⊘8am-6pm) Look for a narrow stairway leading to the 2nd floor. The owners live on-site, so knock (several times if necessary) if the door is closed during business hours.

MEDICAL SERVICES
Hospital Adventista de Belém (☎3084-8686; www.hab.org.br; Av Barroso 1758) One of the better private hospitals.

MONEY
Bradesco (Av Presidente Vargas 988; ⊘10am-1pm & 2-4pm Mon-Fri) Changes Amex traveler's checks on the 4th floor in the morning only; passport required.
Estação das Docas (Blvd Castilhos França) Has numerous cash machines in a secure setting.
HSBC (Av Presidente Vargas 670; ⊘10am-5pm Mon-Sat)
Turvicam (☎3201-5465; www.turvicam.com.br; Av Presidente Vargas 636; ⊘8am-6:30pm Mon-Fri, to 1pm Sat) Busy travel agency has currency exchange in rear.

POST
Main Post Office (☎3211-3147; Av Presidente Vargas 498; ⊘9am-5pm Mon-Fri)

TOURIST INFORMATION
Paratur (☎3212-0575; www.paraturismo.pa.gov.br; Praça Waldemar Henrique; ⊘8am-2pm Mon-Fri) Reasonably helpful state tourism agency.

TRAVEL AGENCIES
Amazon Star Turismo (☎9982-7911, 3212-6244; www.amazonstar.com.br; Henrique Gurjão 210; ⊘8am-6pm Mon-Fri, to noon Sat)

Offers free booking service for long-distance boat and plane tickets to and from Belém – easier and more reliable than booking directly. Also offers day trips around Belém, including bird-watching, nature walks, and city tours (per person R$150 to R$300), plus overnight tours combining the above options, and multiday packages to Ilha de Marajó. Skilled, multilingual service.
Turvicam (☎3201-5465; www.turvicam.com.br; Av Presidente Vargas 636; ⊘8am-6:30pm Mon-Fri, to 1pm Sat) Sells plane tickets.

ⓘ Getting There & Away

AIR
Belém's Aeroporto Val de Cães is a hub for international, domestic and regional flights.
Air France (☎0800-888-9955, 4003-9955; www.airfrance.com)
Azul-TRIP (☎0800-887-1118, 4003-1118; www.voeazul.com.br)
Gol (☎0300-115-2121, 3210-6312; www.voegol.com.br)
Surinam Airways (☎3210-6436; www.slm.nl)
TAM (☎3212-2166; www.tam.com.br; Av Assis de Vasconcelos 265)
TAP (☎0300-210-6060; www.flytap.com)

BOAT
All long-distance boats leave Belém from the **Terminal Hidroviária** (Av Marechal Hermes). You can purchase tickets from the booths inside the terminal, but an easier and more reliable option is to contact **Amazon Star Turismo** (☎3212-6244; www.amazonstar.com.br; Henrique Gurjão 210), whose multilingual staff can book boat tickets, including over the phone or internet, for trips to or from Belém, for no extra cost. It's a great service if you don't speak Portuguese, or want to make onward arrangements well in advance (recommended in high season).

Marques Pinto Navigação (☎3272-3847) and **ENART** (☎3224-1225) offer boat service to and from Manaus, and most points along the way. At last check, boats to Manaus left Wednesday and Friday, plus every other Tuesday, at 6pm with stops at Monte Alegre (hammock/cabin R$150/750, two days), Santarém (R$230/800, 2½ days), Parintins (R$330/950, four days), and Manaus (R$370/1000, five days). Keep in mind that cabin rates are for two people; all cabins have air-conditioning, and some have en suite bathrooms and TVs. Some boats have an air-conditioned hammock area. Meals are not included, but you can purchase buffet service (R$5 to R$13 per meal) or buy hamburgers and snacks from the boat's on-board grill.

Arapari Navegação (☎3241-4977) and **Rodofluvial BANAV** (☎3269-4494, 8047-2440) alternate service to Ilha de Marajó, with daily ferries from Belém to Camará, (R$19 standard, R$30 with air-con and airplane-style seating, three hours) at 6:30am and 2:30pm Monday to Saturday, and 10am on Sunday.

BUS

Belém's long-distance bus station is 3km east of the town center. Major destinations may be served by several lines, while *leito* and *semi-leito* (overnight sleeper) seats are available on some longer routes. Note that there have been a number of accounts of roadside robberies of buses coming to and from São Luís. If possible, flying is recommended.

Itaperim (☎3226-3382; www.itaperim.com.br) Serves Fortaleza (R$233, 24 hours, once daily), Salvador (R$313, 33 hours, three departures weekly) and Rio de Janeiro (R$498, 53 hours, four departures weekly).

Rápido Excelsior (☎3249-6365) Has service to Marudá (R$19, four hours, four departures daily, five on Friday and Saturday, including 6am and 9am).

Sinprovan (☎3226-5872) Also has van service to Marudá (R$17, 3½ hours, direct at 5:45am and 8am, otherwise transfer in Cantanhal).

Transbrasilia (☎3226-1942) Serves dozens of cities, near and far, including São Luís (R$111, 10 hours, one departure daily), Rio de Janeiro (R$399, 50 hours, four departures weekly), and Paraíso do Tocantins (R$133, 17 hours, three times daily).

❶ Getting Around

Aeroporto Val de Cães is 8km north of the center on Av Júlio César. The 'Pratinha – Pres Vargas' bus (638) runs between the airport and Av Presidente Vargas (R$2.20, 40 minutes); the 'E Marex' bus also goes there, but you may have to change buses at the depot (no charge). Arriving by plane, turn left as you leave the terminal; buses stop at the traffic circle about 50m past the end of the terminal. A taxi between the airport and center is a fixed R$45 when booked inside the terminal; you can catch one for less at the bus stop (R$30), though they pass somewhat infrequently.

The long-distance bus station is on the corner of Av Almirante Barroso and Av Governador José Malcher, 3km east of the city center. Going into town, catch almost any westbound bus on Av Governador José Malcher or cross to the far side of Av Almirante Barroso and catch any bus saying 'Aero Club' or 'P Vargas' – both can drop you at Praça de República. Going out to the bus station, take any 'Guama – P Vargas' bus (316) from Av Presidente Vargas.

Algodoal

☎091 / POP 1350

The small fishing village of Algodoal on Ilha de Maiandeua, 180km northeast of Belém, attracts younger Belenenses and a few foreign travelers. It's an attractive natural retreat with firm, windswept beaches and a sometimes turbulent sea.

The island's name comes from an indigenous word meaning 'uncountable riches beneath the sea.' Legend has it that an enchanted city is submerged off the island's northern tip; it emerges occasionally and is visible from Praia da Princesa, which was named for the city's royal daughter.

◉ Sights & Activities

Praia do Farol is the broad attractive beach across a tidal canal from town. You can wade there at low tide or catch a canoe (R$2). Past a rocky outcropping is **Praia da Princesa** with a cluster of beach restaurants and 7km of beautiful white sand. Across an even stronger canal is **Praia do Mupéua**, which extends another 7km to Fortalezinha village.

⚐ Tours

Algodoal has various options for guided and do-it-yourself excursions. You can canoe up the canal at Praia do Farol to spot birds and sometimes monkeys (best at sunset); visit Lago de Princesa (best April to June), walk or boat to the village of Fortalezinha, or even walk around the island.

Sunset is the best time to spot birds and wildlife, including the timid but radiant guará (scarlet ibis). However, high tide is when the canals are deepest and canoes can penetrate the furthest. Ideally, you'll be visiting when sunset and high tide happen to coincide! At high tide, you can canoe clear to **Praia do Mupéua** on the other side of the island (and from there walk back to town, about 7km) or else return along another canal to Porto do Mamede, Algodoal's main dock.

Partway up the canal from Praia do Farol, a path cuts through the forest and low sand dunes to **Lago da Princesa** and onward to **Praia da Princesa** (2km to 3km total). Boatmen can drop you at the path, and you can visit the lake, then return by foot along the beach (4km). The lake is just a small lagoon, and worth visiting only when full (April to June).

Around Belém

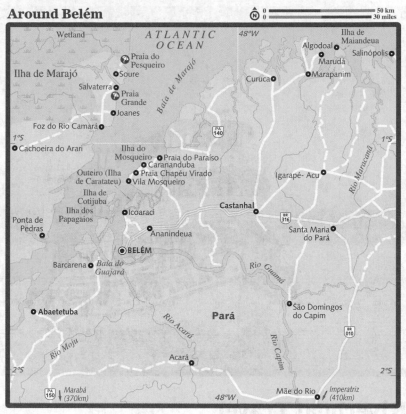

Another option is visiting **Fortalezinha**, a small village on the other side of the island, where you can walk the beach and grab lunch at one of several small restaurants. The boat ride from Algodoal to Fortalezinha is scenic but pricey (R$80 one way); alternatively, you can catch a canoe from Porto do Mamede to the nearby community of Camboinha (R$3 per person) and follow well-marked paths from there.

From Fortalezinha it's possible to walk counter-clockwise back to Algodoal. (The reverse is much less pleasant, as you'll be walking against the wind.) It's a long (14km) but scenic walk. However, there's a powerful *furo* (tidal inlet) about halfway around, that should never be crossed on foot. Wait for a fisherman to ferry you across or else turn back.

On any trip, be sure to bring mosquito repellant, water and sun protection.

Guided trips range from R$30 to R$150 per person, depending on what you do. For simple trips, boatmen can be hired at the mouth of the canal at Praia do Farol. Pousada da Chilena and Pousada Marhesias have more in-depth information (including simple maps of the island) and recommended guides.

🛏 Sleeping

Pousada da Chilena POUSADA **$**
(☎ 3744-1415; jgapmaga@hotmail.com; Bertoldo Costa; dm with hammock R$20, camping per person R$20, r R$40) A delightful place with simple boho-style rooms with fan, and a covered patio area for hammocks (R$5 off if you have your own hammock). Campers can set up tents in the tree-filled garden. The namesake Chilena is a helpful and knowledgable host, and can help organize excursions around the island. Breakfast can be purchased for R$5 to R$10.

Riverboat Travel

Rivers are roads in the Amazon and riverboat trips are a uniquely Amazonian experience. Trips are long and languid, measured in days instead of hours. Much of the time is spent on the boat's upper deck, watching the scenery glide by, knocking back beers, talking and laughing over the ever-blasting music. The middle deck is where hammocks are slung, a place to read, nap or practice Portuguese with your neighbor. Night falls quickly and decisively, and night skies on the river can be spectacular.

For most people a two- to three-day trip is plenty. For all its romantic appeal, riverboat travel can get rather tedious, especially with the constant pounding of the music and engine. There's virtually no chance of seeing wildlife and a boat typically travels far from shore. Consider taking a boat for one leg, and flying the others; air and boat fares can be surprisingly comparable, and you'll have more time for tours and other activities.

The two-day boat trip between Belém and Santarém is an interesting one, passing through the tidal zone around Belém, the narrows of Breves, the high bluffs around Monte Alegre and finally the main channel near Santarém. (The Santarém–Manaus leg, by contrast, follows the main channel only.) The Rio Negro, especially the upper regions, has little boat traffic and winds through massive archipelagos. Porto Velho to Manaus, along the Rio Madeira, is another good choice, a scenic backdoor route to the Amazon.

➤ You'll need a hammock and rope, and a light sheet in case the temperature drops. Most boats have a few private

1. Amazon boat travel
2. Travelers playing cards to pass time
3. Hammocks

cabins, with bunks, private bathrooms and air-conditioning, though for the price you may as well fly.

➡ Get to the boat early to secure a good hammock spot. Away from the restrooms is best.

➡ Buffet-style meals are sold (or included) on all boats, but are notoriously unsanitary. Instead, stick with made-to-order burgers and sandwiches sold from the boat's grill.

➡ Bring water, dry snacks and extra toilet paper.

➡ Theft isn't rampant, but foreigners make tempting targets. Be especially alert when the boat stops in port, which can be in the middle of the night.

➡ Never leave cameras, cell phones or other valuables unattended in your hammock, and keep your backpack zipped and locked.

➡ Make friends with the passengers around you, as they can keep an eye on your gear.

➡ Bring a thin cable and lock to secure your bag to one of the boat's center poles. Some thieves will snatch a promising piece of luggage and jump overboard; an accomplice waiting in a motorboat fishes thief and bag from the river and zips away to salvage whatever's not waterlogged. Victims can't jump in after them and captains will not stop or turn around.

★ **Pousada Marhesias** POUSADA $
(☑ 9112-3461, 3854-1129; www.marhesias-algodoal.com; Bertoldo Costa 47; s/d/suite R$100/130/170; ❋ ☎) A friendly well-run hotel with attractive guestrooms, all with air-con and TV, opening onto a large leafy garden and sitting area; suites are larger, with two beds and a minifridge. A covered kiosk is used for painting classes, massage, yoga and more. Located at the far end of town, closest to the Praia do Farol. Free wi-fi at reception.

Pousada Ponta do Boiador HOTEL $
(☑ 3279-0060; www.boiador.com; Bertoldo Costa; d with air-con R$120, with air-con & hot water R$140; ❋ ☎) Rooms here are tiny, but the all-wood construction lends a clean, dry air, and small patios with hammocks have nice sea views. Even better, it's the only hotel with direct beach access, as well as a large waterfront deck with basic lunch and dinner service, and tall chilly beers.

Pousada Bela-Mar POUSADA $
(☑ 3854-1128; www.belamar.hpgvip.com.br; Magalhães Barata; s/d without bathroom R$30/55, with bathroom & fan R$45/70, with air-con & minibar R$75/100; ❋) A clean, reliable choice, this is the first hotel you reach from the boat drop-off. Fifteen tidy rooms are arranged around a pretty central garden, all with high ceilings and attractive decor. An ample breakfast spread is served in the hotel's spacious restaurant.

 Eating

Some hotel restaurants serve only their own guests, for some or all meals, especially in low season. Just ask the waiter when you walk in.

Restaurante La Izla BRAZILIAN $$
(Bertolda Costa; mains R$15-30; ☺ 11am-11pm) Friendly family-run eatery with a few tables on a sunny patio and a few more inside the owners' clapboard home. The menu is painted on the wall and consists of Brazilian basics: choice of fried fish, chicken or beef, plus rice, *feijão* and *farofa* (manioc flour sautéed with butter).

Pousada Marhesias BRAZILIAN, ITALIAN $$
(Bertoldo Costa 47; mains R$8-40; ☺ noon-10pm, bar service till late) Serving a little of everything, from fish and seafood to pasta and pizza, all freshly made and served in a large 2nd-floor dining area with views across the channel to Praia do Farol. You can count on

hearing some great jazz over your meal – it's all they play.

Pousada Kakurí BRAZILIAN $$
(mains R$9-25; ☺ noon-11pm) The dining area consists of a few tables set up on the porch, but that's all you need to enjoy the kitchen's tasty creations – mostly fresh fish, grilled or fried, with veggies and rice – and a couple of cold beers. Usually has great music playing, too.

ⓘ Orientation

Algodoal village is on the island's west coast. The streets are unpaved – some dirt, others grass – and have no street signs. A tidal canal marks the northern end of town; across it are Praia do Farol and, beyond that, Praia da Princesa. Around the island are three more small communities: Fortalezinha, Mocoóca and Camboinha.

ⓘ Information

There is no ATM on the island or even in Marudá, and not all hotels accept credit cards. Best to bring cash from Belém. There's free community wi-fi, but finding a strong signal can be tough. Pousada da Chilena (p579) is near the tower, and so has a stronger signal, and nonguests are welcome to set up in the dining area. **Farmacias Kadosh** (☺ 7:30am-8pm Mon-Thu, 7:30am-9pm Fri & Sat, 7:30am-7pm Sun) is a small pharmacy selling sunscreen, bug spray, condoms, medicines etc.

Check out www.algodoal.com for info on the island's news, history, hotels and activities.

DANGERS & ANNOYANCES
The island has several tidal channels (known as *furos*, or 'punctures,' in Portuguese) that connect inland lagoons to the ocean. They rise and fall, and even change direction, according to the tide. The one between Praia do Farol and Praia da Princesa (known as Furo Velho) is especially treacherous and should never be crossed on foot. Fishermen are usually around and can ferry you across.

ⓘ Getting There & Around

Access to Algodoal is via the mainland village of Marudá. Boats leave there for Algodoal (R$6, 40 minutes) at 9am, 11am, 1:30pm and 5pm Monday to Thursday, and at 9am, 10:30am, 12:30pm, 2:30pm and 5pm Friday to Sunday, and Friday at 8:30pm too; departure may be delayed if there aren't enough people. Buses from Belém drop off (and pick up) passengers at the port, but vans only go as far as the bus station, which is five long blocks away, or R$7 in a taxi.

Arriving at Algodoal, the boat drops you at the beach, where a slew of donkey-cart drivers will vie for the chance to take you to your hotel (per person R$7). Some drivers will try to convince you to go to certain hotels where they earn a commission; always insist on going to the one of your choosing.

Boats return to the mainland at 6am, 8am, 10:30am and 1:30pm Monday to Thursday, and at 6am, 8am, 10:30am, 1:30pm, 3pm and 5pm Friday to Sunday. Buses for Belém leave Marudá's bus station at 6am, 7am, noon and 3pm Monday to Saturday, and at 6am, noon, 3pm and 5pm Sunday.

Ilha de Marajó

☑ 091 / POP 43,200

The 50,000-sq-km Ilha de Marajó, slightly larger than Switzerland, lies at the mouths of the Amazonas and Tocantins rivers. It was the ancient home of the Marajoaras indigenous culture, notable for their large ceramic burial urns. Today, Marajó's friendly residents live in a few towns and villages and on the many *fazendas* (ranches) spread across the island. This is a world apart, where bicycles outnumber cars and water buffalo graze around town. Legend has it the buffalo are descended from animals that swam ashore from a French ship that sank while en route from India to French Guiana. The island is well known for its buffalo cheese, buffalo steaks and buffalo-mounted police force.

Only the island's eastern shore is easily accessible to tourists. It has three small sleepy towns: Joanes is the smallest of the three, with a decent beach and small hotel (and not much else); Salvaterra has the island's best and largest beach but the town itself is a bit lacking; and Soure has the most in terms of hotels, services and overall ambience, though the beaches are a bit harder to reach. Much of the island's interior is wetland, and is home to tens of thousands of birds, including the graceful *guará*, with its scarlet plumage and long, curved beak.

Services are slowly improving on Marajó; there are two ATMs in Soure, and more hotels accept credit cards. That said, it's not a bad idea to bring extra cash from Belém. Also be aware that Marajó is very wet from January to June, with almost-daily rain.

❶ Getting There & Away

Arapari Navigação (p578) and Rodofluvial BA-NAV (p578) (R$19 standard, R$30 with air-con and airplane-style seating, three hours) leave Belém's main boat terminal at 6:30am and 2:30pm Monday to Saturday and 10am on Sunday, arriving at a port south of Joanes called Foz do Rio Camará, or Camará for short. They return from the same port at 6:30am and 3pm Monday to Saturday, and 3pm Sunday.

❶ Getting Around

Buses and minivans meet ferries arriving from Belém and at Camará, Marajó's main port. Each has a sign to its destination; simply look for the place you're going to and get on. It's R$6 to Joanes, Salvaterra, or the ferry port, or R$9 to R$12 to Soure, including the barge across the river and drop-off at your hotel. (The full-sized buses don't do hotel drop-offs.)

Moto-taxis are common in all three towns, and cost R$4 around town, R$4 to R$7 to outlying beaches and R$15 between Joanes and Salvaterra.

Salvaterra and Soare are separated by the wide mouth of the Rio Paracauari. In Salvaterra, boats leave from a pier at the end of Salvaterra's main road; in Soure, they leave from a pier at the end of Travessa 14 (R$2, 15 minutes, 7am to 6pm); you can bring bicycles on board. Boats also go from Soare to the car-ferry pier (8km from Salvaterra, R$1) or you can hop on the ferry itself for free.

Joanes

Head to sleepy Joanes for total isolation. It's got an appealing hotel and beach, the remains of a 17th-century Jesuit church, and hardly a soul in sight.

There are no services in Joanes, and getting to and from there can take awhile. Shuttles from the ferry port cost R$6; moto-taxis are an easy way to get elsewhere around the island (R$30 to Salvaterra).

🛏 Sleeping & Eating

Pousada Ventania do Rio-Mar   POUSADA $
(☑ 3646-2067; www.pousadaventania.com; Quarta Rua; s/d R$85/105) Atop a breezy headland overlooking the shore. Large rooms have whimsical decor and oversized paintings, bathrooms (but no TV or air-con), and open onto a large patio. The beach is just steps away, and the staff can arrange a variety of excursions, including canoeing and fishing with local guides.

Jacaré   SEAFOOD $
(On the beach; mains R$12-25; ⊙ 7am-10pm) One of a handful of beach restaurants serving the Marajoana favorites of grilled fish and buffalo steaks.

Salvaterra

POP 20,200

Eighteen kilometers north from Joanes, Salvaterra has the island's best and longest beach, the aptly named Praia Grande, a short walk outside town. Salvaterra isn't as big as Soure, but is more compact, so it can feel busier.

◉ Sights

Praia Grande is a big beach, a long wide swathe of golden-brown sand about 500m south of Salvaterra proper. A slew of beach restaurants perched on stilts overlook the first section of the beach, but the far end is virtually deserted, save one large resort.

As everywhere on Ilha de Marajó, stingrays are common and they pack a nasty sting. Always try to enter and leave the water where other people have done so, as the rays have likely been scared off. Otherwise, shuffle your feet or use a stick to poke the sand in front of you to avoid stepping on a ray.

🛏 Sleeping & Eating

There are many beach restaurants on Praia Grande, where you can fill up for R$12 to R$40.

Hotel Beira Mar   HOTEL $

(☑ 3765-1400; Rua 5, at Travessa 2; r with fan/aircon R$40/60; ❄) A short walk from the center and Praia Grande; rooms are of the large and plain variety, with graying tile floors, TV, and thin mattresses and linens. Laundry service is R$1 per piece. No wi-fi, but there's an internet cafe around the corner.

Pousada Bosque dos Aruãs   POUSADA $

(☑ 3765-1115; Segunda Rua; s/d R$75/85; ❄ 🛜) On an oceanfront lot shaded by mango trees, long wood cabins have two guestrooms apiece, each with small private patio, bright interior paint, TV and air-con. Two standalone suites are larger with slightly nicer amenities, like glass showers, and are nearest the water. Somewhat shabby overall, but very peaceful. Praia Grande is a 10-minute walk away. Great restaurant.

Restaurante Umuarama   SEAFOOD, PIZZA $

(cnr Travessa 2 & Rua 6; mains R$10-25; ⊘ 11am-3pm, 7-10:30pm) Serves up shrimp, fish and buffalo dishes during the daytime, and pizza at night, in a low-key open-air dining area. Located a short walk from Praia Grande, this is a popular and less expensive alternative to restaurants right on the beach.

PREHISTORIC AMAZONIA

Most researchers agree that human occupation of the Amazon Basin began 10,000-15,000 years ago, based in part on studies of ancient cave paintings near Monte Alegre, in Pará state, by archaeologist Anna Roosevelt, a great-grandaughter of Theodore Roosevelt. Around 6000 years ago, the Tapajoara people, living near present-day Santarém, started creating simple clay urns, the oldest known pottery in the Americas, and other indigenous Amazonians began mastering rudimentary agriculture.

By the last few centuries of the pre-Christian era, the Amazon was home to numerous cohesive communities, numbering in the thousands and led by chiefs. They produced good-quality pottery and cultivated maize and manioc intensively. It was in this time that the techniques of itinerate agriculture still used today were first developed, including selective burning, crop rotation, and allowing the land periodic 'rest periods' to regenerate.

The Marajoara were among the most sophisticated pre-colonial Christian-era Amazonians, flourishing between AD 400 and AD 1350 on the wetlands of present-day Ilha de Marajó. They built massive earth platforms called *aterros* – the largest were 6m high and 250m long – to escape the annual floods and buried their dead in elaborate urns, considered to be the most sophisticated ceramics produced in pre-colonial Brazil.

Interestingly, early human occupation of the Amazon has emerged as a proxy for today's environmental debates. Conservationists have long argued that the prehistorical record proves a healthy rainforest is incompatible with large-scale occupation and development. However, recent research suggesting the early Amazon may have been far more populated than previously thought has been used by some to argue that greater exploitation of the rainforest is not only harmless, but has been part of its history for millennia.

Pousada Bosque dos Aruãs BRAZILIAN $$
(mains R$21-$35; ☺ noon-3pm, 6-10pm) Salvaterra's best hotel also has its best lunch and dinner menu. True, dishes like fish with shrimp sauce or breaded buffalo steak can be had anywhere on the island, but the food and presentation here are surprisingly refined, and well worth the somewhat higher prices. Open to guests and nonguests alike, with service on the hotel's small wooden patio.

ℹ Orientation

The main street through town is Av Victor Engelhard, which dead-ends at the town pier. The cross streets are numbered starting at the pier – 1a Rua, 2a Rua etc – though few people refer to them as such. Praia Grande is about 500m south of town.

ℹ Information

Along the main drag is the **post office** (☺ 8am-noon & 2-5pm Mon-Fri) and an internet cafe **Cyber Marajó Online** (per hr R$2; ☺ 8am-noon, 3-7pm Mon-Sat). Hotel Beira Mar (p584) offers laundry service (per item R$1) for guests and nonguests alike. **BANAV** (☐ 3269-4494; ☺ 8-11am) sells ferry tickets from its office on the main street; otherwise, buy tickets on the shuttle or at the port.

Soure

POP 23,000

The 'Capital of Marajó,' Soure is on the far side of the Rio Paracauari and is the biggest town on the island. It's a charming, convenient place to base yourself, with water buffalo grazing on the soccer fields and double-wide streets, many of them dirt or grass with just a bike track weaving down the middle.

A bicycle is a great way to get around Soure. Operating out of his house (it's the one with a stone facade, next to a hardware shop), a guy named **Bimba** (Rua 4 btwn Travessas 18 & 19; per hour/day R$2/12) has the island's lowest rates. Pousada O Canto do Francês and Hotel Casarão da Amazônia have bikes available for their guests.

Beaches

The beaches near Soure, which have a mix of salt- and freshwater, are often covered with fantastic seeds washed down from the Amazonian forests. But beware of stingrays, which have an extremely painful sting. Try to swim during high tide, and avoid the mouth of streams, especially in late afternoon. Enter and exit the water only where other people have recently done so. If the beach is deserted, shuffle your feet as you enter the water to scare away any hiding rays.

Praia do Pesqueiro is Soure's most popular beach, a broad swath of soft beige sand, backed by thatch-roofed restaurants with tables set up in the sand. Pesqueiro is further from town (about 12km) than the other beaches, but along the way you can spot buffaloes wallowing in marshes and catch a glimpse of Marajó's lush interior. A moto-taxi runs R$10 each way, while cabs charge R$30 for up to four people.

Praia Barra Velha and **Praia de Araruna** are narrow beaches edged by thick mangrove stands and separated from each other by a wide tidal channel. Barra Velho has several small restaurants, while Praia de Araruna is virtually deserted. High tide can reduce both shorelines to a thin strip of sand, but otherwise they're pleasant, and easy to reach by foot, bike, or taxi. To get there, follow Travessa 14 out of town for about 4.5km to a fork in the road; to the right is a walkway leading to Praia Barra Velha, while to the left and a short distance further is a footbridge across the channel to Praia de Araruna.

Praia Garrote is a completely undeveloped beach at the mouth of the Rio Paracauari. To get there, follow Travessa 9 east out of town; the road makes a sharp right-hand turn and continues to a tidal inlet; fishermen there can ferry you across, and the beach is a short distance further.

☞ Tours

Three nearby *fazendas* (ranches) make for interesting half-day trips. **Fazenda Bom Jesus**, **Fazenda São Jerônimo**, and **Fazenda Araruna** offer the same basic activities, including riding water buffaloes, visiting mangroves and beaches, and spotting birds, monkeys and other animals. Bom Jesus is the most adventurous of the three – the grounds look more like a nature preserve than a ranch – though at São Jerônimo you can ride your buffalo in the surf.

Morning boat rides up Rio Paracauari can also be arranged, including passing through a mangrove 'tunnel' and a chance to see birds and pink dolphins. There are also city tours, with visits to local artisans, and beach-hopping tours.

Hotel Casarão da Amazônia and Pousada O Canto do Francês can provide additional details and make reservations. Prices average R$40 to $100 per person, with transport.

✱ Festivals & Events

On the second Sunday in November, Soure has its own **Círio de Nazaré** with a beautiful procession. Hotels can be booked up at this time.

🛏 Sleeping & Eating

Hotel Araruna   HOTEL $

(☎8793-2481; nelsonmarajo@hotmail.com; Travessa 14 btwn Ruas 7 & 8; s/d R$60/80) Large simple rooms open onto breezy corridors. The rooms show their age, but are reasonably clean. Quiet and convenient location, next to the tall Cosampa water towers, on the same road that leads to Praia de Araruna and Praia Barra Velha.

Pousada Restaurante Ilha Bela   POUSADA $

(☎3741-1313; pousadailhabelasore@gmail.com; Rua 1 at Travessa 13; s/d/q R$80/100/170) A short distance from Soare's ferry dock, this reliable pousada-restaurant has eight spotless rooms with updated amenities and a tasty breakfast served in the airy ground-level eatery. Quads have patios with views of the river. Festivals, celebrations and other events are held in the plaza directly in front, and could make sleeping tough if you happen to visit then.

Pousada O Canto do Francês   POUSADA $

(☎3741-1298; http://ocantodofrances.blogspot.com.br; cnr Rua 6 & Travessa 8; s/d/tr R$110/130/160; ❄🌐) Nine attractive suites have whitewashed walls, fine woodwork and comfortable beds. Breakfast is served in the hotel's welcoming foyer or a patio overlooking a huge private grassy yard. Quite removed from the center, but the hotel rents bikes and arranges recommended excursions. Discount of 10% for paying in cash.

★ Hotel Casarão da Amazônia   HOTEL $

(☎3741-1988; www.hotelcasaraoamazonia.blogspot.com.br; cnr Rua 4 & Travessa 9; s/d/q 110/130/240; ❄🌐🍴) Occupying a beautifully restored 19th-century *casarão* (mansion), rooms here have high ceilings, flat-screen TVs and small but stylish bathrooms; some units are oddly narrow, but still comfortable. A newer garden annex has slightly larger rooms, with patios and hammocks. The hotel's large pool is heaven on a hot day, and the attentive owner organizes island tours. Bike rentals, good restaurant.

Pousada Restaurante Ilha Bela   BRAZILIAN $

(Rua 1 at Travessa 13; R$13-25; ⏱7am-3pm, 6-11:30pm, closed Tue) Fresh typical *marajoara*

fare, including fried fish and buffalo steak, served in an breezy corner dining area. There's live music on Friday evenings.

Restaurante Patú Anu   BRAZILIAN $

(☎3741-1359; cnr Rua 2 & Travessa 14; mains R$15-25; ⏱7:30am-10pm Mon-Sat, to 3pm Sun) A simple, reliable menu and a convenient location make this a popular eatery among locals, first-timers and repeat visitors alike. Large servings of chicken, beef, fish or shrimp, plus rice and beans.

Café Soare   BRAZILIAN, FRENCH $$

(Rua 3 btwn Tv 14 & 15; mains R$15-45; ⏱6:30pm-10pm Mon-Sat) Run by an earnest French expat, this small but excellent restaurant has just a few tables in its attractive dining area and a few more on the sidewalk. The buffalo steak with Gorgonzola cream sauce is a favorite, plus tasty crepes and mixed salads.

🛍 Shopping

Cerâmica Mbara-yo   CERAMICS

(Travessa 20 btwn Ruas 3 & 4) This is the modest shop of ceramicist Carlos Amaral, who combines traditional Aruã and *marajoara* ceramic traditions with award-winning results. You can have a short tour of the workshop to see how the pieces are made. Numerous small, affordable pieces are for sale, and each has a particular tale or significance behind it.

ℹ Orientation

The streets running parallel to the river are Ruas (with Rua 1 closest to the Rio Paracauari). The perpendicular streets are Travessas, with Travessa 1 closest to the seashore. The main bus and passenger ferry deposits near the corner of Travessa 11 and Rua 1. Motorized canoes shuttle to downtown Salvaterra (R$2) and to the passenger ferry dock (R$1), leaving Soare from a long pier at Travessa 14 and Rua 1.

ℹ Information

Banco do Brasil (Rua 3 btwn Travessas 17 & 18; ⏱10am-3pm Mon-Fri) ATM usually accepts foreign cards.

Bradesco (Rua 2 at Travessa 16; ⏱9am-2pm Mon-Fri) Reliable ATM.

Cyber Gigabyte (Travessa 15 at Rua 2; per hr R$2; ⏱8:30am-noon & 3-8:30pm Mon-Sat)

Drogaria Big Farm (Rua 4 at Travessa 16; ⏱7am-9pm Mon-Sat, 8am-noon Sun) Pharmacy and minimart.

Post Office (Rua 1; ⏱9am-noon & 2-5pm Mon-Fri) Between Travessas 13 and 14.

ZERO IMPACT BRAZIL

Big Tree Adventure Tours (www.bigtreeadventuretours.com) is the eco-tour arm of Zero Impact Brazil, an American-owned company that gathers and sells the leftover parts of trees cut down in the Amazon, mainly by timber, mining and development companies. (Prohibited from burning excess tree parts, developers often bury them.) ZIB supplies rare and beautiful woods, with names like 'purpleheart' and 'tigerwood,' to anyone who can make use of small and sometimes oblong pieces; clients include sculptors, pool cue and knife-handle makers, and high-end guitar designers. ZIB's founder Rick Paid also owns 1000 hectares of primary forest across the highway from FLONA do Tapajós, one of ever-fewer plots of private land along that corridor that hasn't been cleared for soy farming.

Big Tree Adventure Tours offers fascinating all-day tours that begin in ZIB's sawmill in Santarem, where you can learn about the myriad types and properties of Amazonian wood (and snag a few samples). The tour then heads south by car or van, winding through soy plantations – a macabre yet arresting sight – to the private forest for a guided hike, lunch with a local family, and a refreshing swim; additional options, such as canoeing, mountain biking, and overnight stays, were in the works at the time of research. The whole operation is new, so expect some kinks, but it's a unique and engaging glimpse into both the natural and commercial aspects of Amazonia.

❶ Getting There & Away

Edgar Transporte BUS
(☑ 9634-0722, 3741-1763; edgar-transporte@hot mail.com; Travessa 15 No 935 btwn Ruas 6 & 7; per person R$12) For transport between Camará and Soare, this professionally run shuttle service has modern, air-conditioned shuttles and confirmed reservations for just slightly more than standard service. Boat tickets, including VIP, can be purchased on the shuttle. Reserve one to three days in advance.

Santarém

☑ 093 / POP 281,000

Santarém has two distinct personalities, befitting its location at the confluence of the creamy brown Amazon river and the much darker Rio Tapajós. On one hand, it's a reasonably pleasant city, with river breezes and a wide waterfront promenade, popular with families, joggers and even cruise-ship passengers. On the other hand, it's also a gritty port town – through which vast quantities of soy are funneled onto huge cargo ships – and host to an odd mix of port workers, businessmen, ship crews and hangers-on. Passenger boats between Belém and Manaus stop here, and it's a great place to get off and break up the journey. You can also hop on a bus to Alter do Chão, a cool little town 35km away with white-sand river beaches and a laid-back backpacker vibe. Both Santarém and Alter do Chão provide easy access to

the Floresta Nacional (FLONA) do Tapajós, a beautiful national forest where you can hike, canoe and stay the night with rubber-tapper families.

History

The Santarém region has been a center of human settlement for many thousands of years. In 1661, more than 20 years after Pedro Teixeira's expedition first contacted the local Tupaiu indigenous people, a Jesuit mission was established at the meeting of the Tapajós and Amazon rivers, and officially named Santarém in 1758.

The later history of Santarém was marked by the rubber boom and bust, and a series of gold rushes that started in the 1950s. The economy today is based mainly on soy and hardwoods and, increasingly, on gold and bauxite mining, whose severe enviornmental impact make them controversial.

❍ Sights

Museu de Santarém MUSEUM
(Rua do Imperador, Praça Barão de Santarém; admission by donation; ⊙ 8am-5pm Mon-Fri, 8am-1pm Sat) Housed in a large yellow waterfront mansion, the Museu de Santarém is also known as the Centro Cultural João Fona, after the Pará artist who painted the frescoes on its interior walls. It features, among other things, an excellent collection of stone and clay artifacts from the Tapajoara culture that flourished in this area more than 6000 years ago.

Santarém

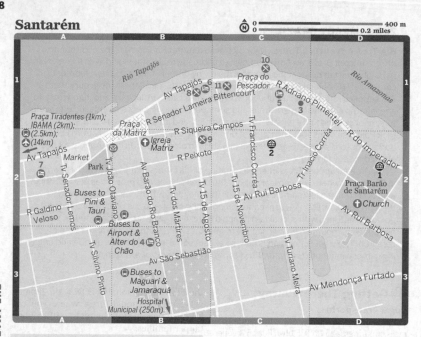

0   400 m
0   0.2 miles

Santarém

◎ Sights
1 Museu de Santarém.............................D2
2 Museu Dica Frazão...............................C2

◎ Activities, Courses & Tours
3 Gil Serique..C1

◎ Sleeping
4 Barão Center Hotel...............................B3
5 Brisa Hotel...C1
6 Central Hotel..B1
7 Hotel Encontro das Aguas..................A2

◎ Eating
8 Cantinha do Marguita..........................B1
9 Delicias Caseiras..................................B2
10 Massabor..C1
11 Restaurante O Mascote.......................C1

Museu Dica Frazão   MUSEUM
(Peixoto 281; admission by donation; ◎8am-6pm Mon-Sat) Dona Dica Frazão has spent more than 50 years making clothing and fabrics from natural fibers, including grasses and wood pulp. Ninety years old and counting, she still guides guests through the display room of her creations, including a dress made for a Belgian queen, a tablecloth for a Pope and costumes for the Boi-Bumbá festival.

Waterfront Promenade   WATERFRONT
The Nova Orla Fluvial promenade follows Av Tapajós. A nice stroll starts at Praça da Matriz, heading west, passing colorful boats, a busy fish market, and ending in the shadow of the massive Cargill facility, a symbol of Brazil's burgeoning soy trade.

✴ Festivals

The patron saint of fisherfolk, São Pedro, is honored on June 29, when boats decorated with flags and flowers sail in procession before the city.

🛏 Sleeping

Brisa Hotel   HOTEL $
(☏3522-1018; brisahotel@hotmail.com; Bittencourt 5; s/d R$60/80; ❄) The Brisa changes color every time we pass through, but the rooms remain the same: simple, clean, a bit claustrophobic, but overall a decent value. The location is ideal, with restaurants and the waterfront promenade right in front.

Central Hotel   HOTEL $
(☏3522-4920; Tapajós 258; s/d R$70/90; ❄🖥) Yes, this hotel is faded, and the interior rooms are claustrophobic, but the air-con works and the location at the heart of Santarém's waterfront can't be beat.

Hotel Encontro das Aguas HOTEL **$**
(☎3522-1287; encontrodasaguashotel@hotmail.
com; 24 de Octubro 808; s/d 75/90, d/tr with view
R$120/130) Large spotless rooms with mod-
ern bathrooms and firm beds are an oasis
of class in Santarém's gritty waterfront area
west of the market. Rooms with river views
have large windows and nice natural light.
Often full with visiting businessmen, but
worth checking for its value and comfort.

Barão Center Hotel HOTEL **$$**
(☎3064-9950; www.baraocenterhotel.com; Av
Barão do Rio Branco; r R$254-268; ✱@🛜)
Santarém's best hotel and a favorite for busi-
nesspeople connected to the massive soy
and timber river ports just outside town. The
rooms are comfortable and well equipped
(flat-screen TV, mini splits, key-card entry),
though curiously lacking in windows. Fortu-
nately, you can always escape to the rooftop
restaurant, which has a terrific view of the
city and river.

✕ Eating

★Massabor PIZZERIA **$**
(☎3522-0509; Av Tapajós; pizza & pasta R$7-30;
⊙5-11pm) Occupying a raised pier perched
high over the water, this popular open-air
restaurant opposite Praça do Pescador has
nice breezes and views of the river, where
you can often spot dolphins. The menu has
mostly pizza and pasta.

Cantinha do Marguita BRAZILIAN **$**
(Av Tapajós at Travessa 15 de Agosto; mains R$9-
20; ⊙9am-11pm) A bright breezy dining area
right on Av Tapajós makes this a convenient
choice, with friendly service and excellent
food too. The *prato feito* is R$9, with choice
of entree and a plateful of sides. Run by the
same friendly English-speaking family from
Amazon Star's Cyber, a few doors down, so
it's a good place for info too.

Delicias Caseiras SELF-SERVICE **$**
(Travessa 15 de Agosto; dishes R$10; ⊙lunch Mon-
Sat) Budget travelers rejoice: for just R$10,
you can pile as much grub on your plate as
humanly possible. Alas, some of the special-
ty items are doled out by hairnetted ladies
behind the warming trays, but portions are
still generous and they often include some
less-common options like tongue and chick-
en patties. Air-con is intermittent.

Restaurante O Mascote BUFFET, SEAFOOD **$$**
(Praça do Pescador; selve-serve per kg R$35, mains
R$23-50; ⊙11am-11pm) The lunch buffet is

tasty and good value, and the air-cooled dining room is a welcome respite on a hot day.
The outdoor patio is ideal for dinner, which
ranges from sandwiches and pizza to well-
prepared fish plates, the house specialty.

ℹ Information

EMERGENCY
Ambulance (☎192)
Police (☎190)

INTERNET ACCESS
Amazon's Star Cyber (☎3522-3648; Av
Tapajós; per hr R$4; ⊙8am-8pm Mon-Fri,
9am-6pm Sat)
Upgrade Cyber Café (São Sebastian near
Barão do Rio Branco; per hr R$3; ⊙8am-6pm
Mon-Fri) Fast connection and Skype-enabled
computers.

LAUNDRY
Lavandería Estoril (☎3523-1329; Travessa
Turiano Meira 167; wash and dry per kg R$12,
plus iron per kg R$21; ⊙8am-6pm Mon-Sat)
Same-day service if you drop off clothes in the
morning.

MEDICAL SERVICES
Hospital Municipal (cnr Av Presidente Vargas
& Av Barão do Rio Branco) Has an emergency
room.

MONEY
Bradesco (Av Rui Barbosa; ⊙9am-3pm Mon-
Fri) Reliable ATMs; near Travessa 15 de Agosto.
HSBC (Av Rui Barbosa; ⊙9am-3pm Mon-Fri)
Reliable ATMs; near Travessa 15 de Novembro.

POST
Main Post Office (Siqueira Campos; ⊙9am-
5pm Mon-Fri)

TRAVEL AGENCIES
Santarém Tur (☎3522-4847; www.santarem
tur.com.br; Adriano Pimentel 44; ⊙8am-6pm
Mon-Fri, to noon Sat) Plane tickets and tour
packages, including city tours, day trips to Alter
do Chão by boat or car, and overnight riverboat
tours to FLONA. Friendly and helpful staff.

ℹ Getting There & Away

AIR
All flights go through Manaus or Belém.
Azul-TRIP (☎4003-1118; www.voeazul.com.br;
at airport only)
Gol (☎0300-115-2121, 3522-3386; www.
voegol.com.br; at airport only)
TAM (☎3529-2201, 0800-570-5700; www.
tam.com.br; Mendonça Furtado 3551; ⊙10am-
10pm Mon-Sat, 2-8pm Sun)

BOAT

There are two ports for passenger boats. The main one, Docas do Pará, is located 2.5km west of the center and is the one most travelers use. There you can catch a *recreo* (slow boat) to Belém (hammock R$180, double cabin $800, 48 hours, 11am Friday to Sunday), which stops at Monte Alegre (hammock R$50, five to seven hours) along the way; or to Manaus (hammock R$150, double cabin R$400, 40 to 48 hours, noon Monday to Saturday), with a stop at Parantins (hammock R$70, 20 hours). Meals are not included, but can be purchased on board. Buy your ticket in advance, especially in high season, to be sure you get a spot. Be aware you can only board during designated time slots: 6am to 7am, 10am to 10:30am, noon to 12:15pm, and 1pm to 2pm.

Praça Tiradentes, located 1km west of the center on Av Tapajós, is used for boats to less-common destinations, including Macapá (hammock R$140 including meals, 36 hours, 6pm daily), Monte Alegre (hammock R$30, six hours; take Macapá boat), and Alenquer (hammock R$25, seven hours, 8am daily).

Viação Tapajós (📞 93-9184-8781; www.viacaotapajos.com.br; Av Tapajós, 500m west of center; R$40; ⏰7am-7pm Mon-Sat, 7:30am-4:30pm) has daily speedboat service to and from Monte Alegre (R$40, three hours) leaving Santarém at 4pm and returning at 5:45am. It also has service to Alenquer, Óidos and elsewhere.

BUS

The **bus station** (📞 3523-4940) is 2.5km west of town. However, departures from there – primarily to Rurópolis, Itaituba, Cuiabá, and Marabá – are unreliable in the rainy season, and can be dangerous year-round due to highway robberies.

Buses to Alter do Chão (R$2.50, 60 minutes) stop on Av Rui Barbosa near Av Barão do Rio Branco roughly every hour between 5am and 6:30pm.

ℹ Getting Around

The airport is 14km west of the city center. Buses (R$1.90, 30 minutes) run to the city every hour or so between 5:30am and 11:30am, and every 90 minutes from 2:55pm to 5:30pm. Service is reduced on Sundays; ask at the airport info kiosk for the next departure time. The bus stop is to the right leaving the terminal doors. Taxis into town officially cost R$53, but you can get a better price by walking to the bus stop and waiting for an empty cab to pass. Going to the airport, catch the 'Aeroporto' (but not 'Aeroporto Velho') on Av Rui Barbosa near Av Barão do Rio Branco, between 5am and 5:30pm. There are no buses from the airport to Alter do Chão; a taxi there costs R$80.

If arriving by boat, 'Orla Fluvial' minibuses (R$1.90) shuttle between the city center and Docas do Pará every 20 to 30 minutes until 7pm. A taxi makes the same trip for R$15, and moto-taxis for R$6. It's possible to catch the bus to Alter do Chão by walking three long blocks straight from Docas do Pará to Av São Sebastião, though the bus is sometimes full by the time it reaches that stop; otherwise, catch the bus in town.

Moto-taxis are the best way, beyond walking, to get around town. Most trips cost R$3 to R$4.

Around Santarém

Floresta Nacional (FLONA) do Tapajós

Behemoth *samaúma* trees, with trunks too big for even 20 people to stretch their arms around, are a highlight of this 5440-sq-km reserve on the east side of the Rio Tapajós. Within the reserve, numerous small communities live primarily by rubber tapping, fishing and gathering Brazil nuts. Several now have modest ecotourism initiatives too, and a trip here is a unique way to experience not just the forest, but also village life within it.

The side-by-side villages of **Maguarí** and **Jamaraquá** have been hosting travelers the longest, and remain the preferred choices for most visitors. Maguarí has a well-maintained trail (9km each way) that weaves past a number of impressive trees, including a cluster of jawdropping *samaúmas* at the end. On the way back, you can visit families that use natural rubber to make toys, flip-flops, even stylish bags and purses.

Jamaraquá is smaller than Maguarí but is located near a lovely *igarapé* (inlet) with great canoeing and animal-spotting when the water is high. Jamaraquá also has a hiking trail, about 7.5km each way, which passes impressive trees.

Other communities with ecotourism projects include **Pini, Tauri, Prainha, Paraíso**, and **Itapuama**. Canoeing, fishing and even snorkeling are the highlights, so it's best to visit when the water levels are high.

Lodging and meals are with local families. Let the bus driver know which town you'd like to visit, and he'll drop you at the home of the main host family there. You'll pay the *taxa comunitaria* (community tax, R$10 per person per day) to the family, along with R$45 to $50 per person per day for meals and a place to hang your hammock.

Around Santarém

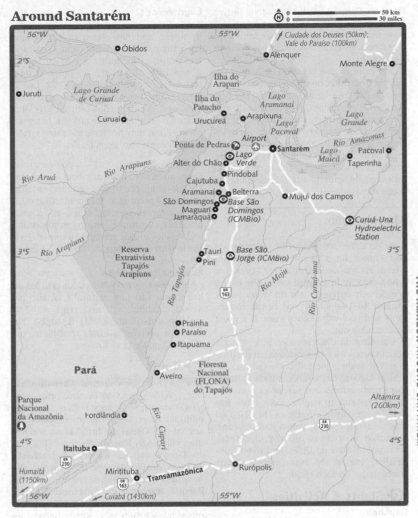

Your hosts can help arrange outings, too; the standard fee is R$50 for one to two people, paid directly to the guide. Be sure to bring mosquito repellent, flashlight, and cash in small bills; a hammock and extra bottled water is recommended too, but not usually essential. Needless to say, a friendly, go-with-the-flow attitude also helps.

A small fee and authorization from **ICM Bio** (🗹 3523-2964; www.icmbio.gov.br; Av Tapajós 2267, Santarém; ⊘ 8am-noon, 2-6pm Mon-Fri) (a division of IBAMA, and the government agency that oversees federal protected areas) is required for visiting Floresta Nacional (FLONA) do Tapajós. An ICMBio base station in the São Domingos, a neighboring village, handles fees and authorizations for visitors to Maguarí or Jamaraquá. For less-visited spots, it's a good idea to get permission and pay the fee at the ICMBio/IBAMA office in Santarém beforehand. If you go with a tour, the operator typically arranges the permissions.

You can visit FLONA by bus from Santarém, or boat from Alter do Chão.

Buses to Maguarí and Jamaraquá (R$8, three to four hours, 11am Monday to Saturday) depart from downtown Santarém.

Buses to Tauri and Pini (R$15, four to five hours, daily except Thursday and Sunday) leave from a different stop. Buses from both areas pass through the villages at 3am to 4am (ouch!).

You can get also get to FLONA by boat, leaving from Alter do Chão. Freelance boatmen do day trips for around R$100 per person, but it's a tiring three hours each way in a small motorized canoe, and does not include guide service. The tour agencies charge R$180 to R$200 per person, including a local guide and using faster and more comfortable motorboats. The agencies also do overnight trips to FLONA, sleeping on board the river boat.

Alter do Chão

☑ 093 / POP 7800

Alter do Chão, 33km west of Santarém, is best known for a picturesque white-sand island, known as Ilha do Amor (Island of Love), directly in front of town. The island is especially striking when the water is low (August to December) and beach restaurants and cool calm water make it a great place to chill out.

But Alter do Chão is much more than a beach town – it's a true Amazonian destination. The town is located at the entrance to a huge lagoon, Lago Verde, which is home to myriad animals and can be explored by canoe or stand-up paddle. Even more impressive are Floresta Nacional (FLONA) do Tapajós and the lesser-known Rio Arapiuns, reachable on tours of one day or several, arranged in Alter do Chão. And don't miss Arariba, one of the best indigenous art stores in the Amazon region.

◎ Sights & Activities

Beaches

When the water is low, you can wade from the waterfront to Ilha do Amor. Otherwise, rowboats will take you across for R$3 per person. A bevy of shacks serve food and drinks year-round, and have chairs set up along the water's edge. Walk a few blocks west on the waterfront promenade to reach **Praia do Cajueiro**, another nice beach, wrapping clear around to the Tapajós river. Beaches further afield are best reached in a car or on a beach-hopping tour, including **Pindobal** (8km), **Cajutuba** (16km), **Aramanai** (26km) and **Ponta de Pedras** (28km).

Lago Verde

This huge three-fingered lake is surrounded by forest, and has places to swim, snorkel with ornamental fish, and spot birds and animals (including a resident family of monkeys). Tour agencies do good **boat tours** (per person R$50 to R$75, two to three hours, two to six people) or you can hire one of the yellow-shirted freelance boatmen on the waterfront; the latter are cheaper, but may not have the same service or equipment that agencies do.

Ponta de Cururú   DOLPHIN WATCHING

Every afternoon, large numbers of pink and grey dolphins congregate just offshore from this sandy point near the mouth of the Rio Tapajós for an evening snack. It's a great place to go for sunsets and dolphin-spotting, and many guides combine tours of Lago Verde with a stop here.

Espaço Alter do Chão   ADVENTURE SPORTS

(☑ 9122-9643; ⊙ vary) Better known for its live music, this new cultural spot also has a rock-climbing wall and rents stand-up paddleboards (half-/full-day R$40/75). The owner, a friendly *paulista* transplant, can also arrange for tree-climbing.

☞ Tours

Besides short trips around Alter do Chão (Lago Verde, Ponta do Cururú, beach-hopping) there are some great options for longer multiday tours. These include canoeing the animal-rich **Canal do Jarí**, hiking and visiting villages in Floresta Nacional (FLONA) do Tapajós and the **Reserva Extrativista Tapajós Arapiuns**, river trips up the **Rio Arapiuns** and adventure routes into the **Parque Nacional da Amazônia**. Discuss details with tour agencies in town; prices range from R$160 to R$450 per person per day, all-inclusive.

Areia Branca Ecotour   ECOTOUR

(☑ 9121-5646, 3527-1317; www.areiabrancaecotour.com.br; Orla Fluvial; ⊙ 8am-noon & 2-7pm Mon-Fri) Located on the waterfront walkway a short distance from the plaza, this small competent agency is run by friendly multilingual siblings from Alter do Chão.

Mãe Natureza   ECOTOUR

(☑ 3527-1264, 9131-9870; www.maenaturezaecoturismo.com.br; Praça 7 de Setembro; ⊙ 8:30am-1pm, 4-10pm) A reliable, experienced agency run by Jorge Bassi and Claudio Chena.

Gil Serique ECOTOUR
(☑ 9115-8111; www.gilserique.com; Av Copacabana 45 at PA-457; per person R$120-150) Gil is a lithe and groovy guy, a teller of tales, a cheerful hedonist and one of the area's top naturalists. Born and raised nearby, Gil's tours are part history, ecology, family lore and personal conquest. He does mostly day trips in and around FLONA, but can overnight in the forest too. His waterfront home doubles as a backpacker crash pad.

From the bus dropoff, walk down to the plaza and bear right along the waterfront. It's the house at the end, painted with travel-related logos.

✨ Festivals

The **Festa do Çairé** in the second week of September is the major folkloric event in western Pará. The Çairé is a standard held aloft to lead a flower-bedecked procession;

its origins may go back to symbols used by early missionaries to help convert *índios*.

🛏 Sleeping

⭐ **Pousada do Tapajós Hostel** HOSTEL, INN **$**
(☑ 9210-2166; www.hosteltapajos.com.br; Sodré 100; dm R$45, s/q R$115/195, HI member discount R$10-15; ✳ 🐾 🛜) Five blocks west of the town square, this very welcome addition to Alter do Chão's budget-travel landscape opened in mid-2012. With its friendly staff, ultra-clean rooms (dorms, doubles and quads), spacious common area and kitchen, big grassy backyard with hammock space and well-organized information boards, it's a cut above the other budget options in town.

Albergue da Floresta HOSTEL, POUSADA **$**
(☑ 9132-7910; www.alberguedafloresta-alterdochao. blogspot.com; Travessa Antônio Pedrosa s/n; hammock R$25-35, shared bathroom per person $40, cabin s R$100, d R$150-170) This backpacker

---

THE BELO MONTE DAM

Construction officially began in 2011 on the Belo Monte Dam on the Rio Xingu in southern Pará, but the fight over the controversial project seems far from over. If completed, the dam (actually a trio of dams) would be the world's third-largest hydroelectric complex, reportedly capable of generating 11,000 megawatts, or enough to power 23 million homes. But critics point out that fluctuations in river flow mean the dam is unlikely to average more than 40% capacity, and could drop to under 10%. (The solution to uneven flow is to build even more dams upstream, something opponents say Belo Monte's planners have quietly anticipated all along.) Subtracting from that the energy lost in the thousands of kilometers of transmission lines, and the fact that dams in the Amazon are notorious for actually emitting methane (due to decomposition of flooded rainforest) and Belo Monte could well rank as the world's most inefficient power-generating dam.

Then there's the impact on the forest, the river, and the people living there: at least 12,000 people would be displaced by the project and 450 sq km of forest would be flooded. Both figures would rise dramatically if secondary dams are required further upstream. A 100km stretch of the mighty Xingu River would essentially dry up, including the part that runs alongside the Paquiçamba territory, home of the Juruna indigenous group. And experts say draining the river would threaten dozens of fish and other species, including many found nowhere else in the world.

The Brazilian environmental agency (IBAMA) says the current plan is an improvement on those proposed in the 1970s and again in the 1990s, and shelved amid international uproar. Among other things, the flooded area has been reduced by two-thirds (albeit with the construction of twin feeder canals, each 500m wide and 12km long) and contractors will be required to pony up nearly US$2 billion on resettlement and environmental protection projects. And even at reduced efficiency, the dam would produce the energy equivalent of burning 1.4 billion barrels of oil, enough to power the entire state of Pará.

Wrangling over the project has moved into the courts, and the project has been halted and restarted several times following decisions by various federal judges. Large public protests have acompanied every stage, from indigenous leaders decamped from the rainforest to international celebrities like Sting and *Avatar* director James Cameron.

> ### ⓘ WATCH YOUR STEP
> ....
> Stingrays are a concern around Ilha do Amor, Lago Verde and Tapajós river, especially in the afternoon and evening. Fortunately they're very skittish, so it's safe to swim and wade where other people are doing the same. Otherwise, get in the habit of shuffling your feet when entering and exiting the water – this will kick up a cloud of sand in front of you and scare rays away.

favorite has a spacious hammock area, dorms, and colorful wood cabins with fans and private bathrooms; breakfast isn't provided, but there's an outdoor kitchen. The hostel is nestled in the trees east of the center; follow the signs past Espaço Alter do Chão and up a tree-lined dirt road. Capoira classes, bike and kayak rental, but no wi-fi.

Pousada do Mingote   HOTEL $
(☑ 3527-1158; www.pousadadomingote.com.br; Travessa Antônio A Lobato s/n; s R$100-110, d R$130-150; ✳) Standard rooms at this long-time hotel are plain and rather dark, with old-school TVs and air-conditioners, but still a decent value. Superior rooms have mini-splits, basin sinks and generally more space and light. Either way, the location can't be beat, just a half-block down from the bus stop, and a half-block up from the plaza.

Pousada Tupaiulândia   INN $
(☑ 3527-1157; pousadatupaiulandia@hotmail.com; Teixeira 300; s/d $60/90; ✳) The suites here occupy two circular buildings, making for curving walls and uncommon angles. No matter, the units are spacious and clean, all with TV, minibar and air-conditioning. Decor is rather bare, but the shellacked brick interior walls make up for it. Good value.

Mirante da Ilha   HOTEL $$
(☑ 3527-1268; www.hotelmirantedailha.com.br; Rua Lauro Sodré 369; s/d R$153/177, d/tr with river view R$200/250; ✳ @ ⓢ) Only a handful of rooms at this big boxy hotel have, as the name suggests, a view (in this case, of Ilha do Amor), but they're worth the higher rate. All rooms are clean and modern, and the hotel's staff is friendly and professional. Be sure to check out the rooftop patio for outstanding views.

Beloalter Hotel   HOTEL $$
(☑ 3527-1230; www.beloalter.com.br; end of Rua Pedro Teixeira; r R$200-275, 2-room ste R$505;

✳ ⓢ ✳) Alter do Chão's most upscale hotel is near Lago Verde, about 500m east of the highway down a shady dirt road. Standard rooms are spacious with modern decor, while split-level 'ecological' rooms have wood interiors, shutter windows and, in at least one case, a huge tree trunk angling through the room. Private beach, clean swimming pool.

🍴 Eating & Drinking

Tribal   BRAZILIAN $
(Travessa Antônio Lobato; dishes R$10-36; ⊙ 11am-11pm) Churrasco plates come with a spear of steak, sausage, chicken and tongue, while well-prepared fish dishes serve two easily, with potato salad to spare. This spacious two-floor open-air dining area is located a block and a half up from the plaza, on the opposite side of Rua Dom Macedo.

Mãe Natureza   INTERNATIONAL $
(☑ 3527-1264; www.maenaturezaecoturismo.com.br; Praça 7 de Setembro; mains R$10-45; ⊙ meals 6pm-midnight Thu-Sun, bar open daily) An eco-tourism agency by day, bar and restaurant by night. The eclectic international menu ranges from Indian to Greek to Mexican, served at tables set up facing the plaza. Live *carimbó* music on Friday and Saturday nights starting at 9pm. It's one of three side-by-side restaurants on the plaza, all open late, making this a fun gathering spot.

★ Candeeiro   BRAZILIAN, INTERNATIONAL $$
(☑ 9156-4994; Center; mains R$16-40) Run by a German-Brazilian couple, the food here is exceptional, created within the tenets of the slow-food movement and utilizing the freshest possible ingredients. The menu changes frequently, but includes items like patê of pea, fish curry over rice, and pineapple-ginger drinks. It was changing locations at the time of research, but surely won't be hard to find.

Farol da Ilha   BRAZILIAN $$
(Orla Fluvial s/n; dishes R$17-30; ⊙ 11am-5pm Mon, to 10pm Thu-Sun, closed Tue & Wed) Travelers tend to miss this low-key waterfront restaurant, despite it having first-rate fish meals and outstanding river and island vistas from its 2nd-floor dining area. Most dishes serve two people, and are priced accordingly. Solo diners can order cheaper chicken dishes or just come for drinks and the view.

★ **Epaço Alter do Chão**   LIVE MUSIC
(☑ 9122-9643; www.espacoalter.com.br; cover R$5-10; ☺ 7:30pm-1am Tue-Sat) Events and hours vary, but there's always something worth seeing at this cool music and cultural space at the east end of the waterfront promenade. There's live *carimbó* on Saturday starting at 11pm, and guest bands play rock, *forró*, samba and more most other nights. Occasional classes range from yoga to juggling. Check Facebook or the chalk board out front for the latest.

🛍 Shopping

★ **Araribá Cultura Indígena**   HANDICRAFTS
(☑ 3527-1324; www.araribah.com.br; Travessa Antônio Lobato; ☺ 9am-9pm) Arguably the best indigenous art store in the Amazon, with items ranging from inexpensive necklaces to museum-quality masks and ceremonial costumes, and representing communities throughout the Amazon basin. Shipping available; credit cards accepted.

ℹ Orientation

Entering Alter do Chão, the bus stops on the corner of Rua Dom Macedo Costa and Travessa Antônio A Lobato, kitty-corner from Araribá Cultura Indígena store. It's a good place to get off – pretty much everyone does – just a block from Praça 7 de Setembro, the main square, and within walking distance of most lodging options.

ℹ Information

A **Banco do Brasil** (inside Mini-Center Mingote, Praça 7 de Setembro; ☺ 6:30am-8:30pm Mon-Sat, to 7:30pm Sun) ATM is located inside the large grocery store facing the main plaza. The **post office** (PA-457 at Rua Dom Macedo Costa; ☺ 9am-noon, 2-5pm Mon-Fri) and **pharmacy** (☑ 3527-1105; PA-457; ☺ 9am-8pm Mon-Fri, to noon Sat) are on PA-457, the main road into town, a few blocks up from where it deadends at the waterfront. There's free wi-fi in the main plaza, and many hotels have wi-fi for their guests. Some hotels accept credit cards, but not all.

ℹ Getting There & Away

Buses from Alter do Chão to Santarém (R$2.50, one hour) depart hourly from 6am to 7:20pm, except on Sunday, when service ends around 6pm. Catch the bus a block up from Praça 7 de Setembro, at the corner of Rua Dom Macedo Costa and Travessa Antônio A Lobato. There is no bus to the airport from Alter do Chão, unfortunately. It's possible to take the bus as far as the airport turnoff, and wait for the airport bus from Santarém to pass, usually within 30 to 60 minutes. Otherwise, a taxi to the airport (or to Santarém or the riverboat ports) costs a painful R$70.

TOCANTINS

The state of Tocantins was created in 1989 from what was previously the northern half of Goiás. It's in a transition zone between the Amazon rainforest to the north and the *cerrado* (savanna) in the southeast. This makes for plenty of outdoor opportunities, and the state is making a concerted effort to portray itself as Brazil's next ecotourism hot spot. It certainly has the potential, from easy-to-reach hiking and waterfalls around Taquarussú to vast protected areas like Parque Estadual do Jalapão and Ilha do Bananal, a Pantanal-like wetland.

Palmas
☑ 063 / POP 228,300
Twenty five years ago, the broad valley bisected by the Rio Tocantins held just a scattering of rural *fazendas*. Starting in 1989, a new state capital was built from scratch, and construction, state government and economic incentives brought thousands of Brazilians to this unlikely landscape, 1000km north of Brasília and 1600km south of Belém. The city itself is sure to strike most first-timers as sterile and shadeless, but it has a way of growing on you, with a number of good outdoorsy options nearby.

◎ Sights & Activities

Most of the sights of interest are in **Praça Girossóis**, purportedly the second-largest municipal square in the world after the Red Square in Moscow.

Palacio Araguaia   PALACE
(☑ 3218-1000; ☺ 8am-6pm) FREE Built on the only hill in town, the Palacio Araguaia, the state capitol building, looks over the plaza and Palmas itself. The lobby has huge colorful mosaics and, in one corner, an impressive scale model of Praça Girossóis. No shorts or tank tops; 2nd floor closed on weekends.

Memorial Coluna Prestes   MEMORIAL
(Praça Girossóis; ☺ 8am-6pm Tue-Sun) FREE Housed in a curious white, tubular structure near Palacio Araguaia, the Memorial Coluna

Palmas

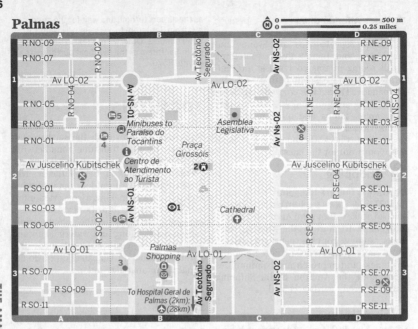

THE AMAZON PALMAS

Prestes tells the life story of Captain Luis Carlos Prestes, who led 1500 rebel soldiers against the military dictatorship in 1924. The march lasted three years and covered 25,000km, and is credited with helping bring democracy to Brazil, especially its long-isolated interior.

🧭 Tours

Bananal Ecotour ECOTOUR
(☑ 3028-4200; www.bananalecotour.com.br; Quadra 103 Sul, cnr Av NS-01 & Rua SO-07) Offers tours to the Ilha Bananal and Jalapão areas, and operates a well-recommended ecolodge near Taquaruçu.

🛏 Sleeping

Hotel Serra Azul HOTEL $
(☑ 3215-1505; Rua NO-03; s/d R$75/95; 🅿🕸🛜) Clean rooms, affordable prices and convenient location make this Palmas' best budget option. Rooms are small with few frills, but face onto a sunny courtyard with a quaint dining room where breakfast is served. Close to the bus stop for those who don't have a car, and offering secure parking for those who do.

Eduardu's Palace Hotel HOTEL $$
(☑ 3215-9300; www.eduardosphotel.com.br; cnr Ruas NO-01 & NO-02; s/d standard R$149/195,

deluxe R$195/248; 🕸🛜🏊) Whatever you do, don't miss the rooftop pool and patio, which have a terrific view of the city and lake. Large rooms have fresh paint and modern appointments; deluxe rooms are larger, but standards have balconies. Street parking only.

Pousada dos Girassóis HOTEL $$
(☑ 3219-4500; www.pousadadosgirassois.com. br; Av NS-01; r R$320; 🕸🛜🏊) Rooms at Palmas' best hotel are small, but have details like modern paintings, glass showers and a writing desk with a leather chair. Large windows and private verandas make some units feel more spacious. The pool area is oddly small and uninviting.

🍴 Eating

Restaurante Seara SELF-SERVICE $
(Rua NE-03 btwn Av NS-02 and Rua NE-02; per kg R$27; ⊙ 11am-3pm Mon-Sat) Large bustling per-kilo place that's popular with workers at nearby government offices. Friendly service and well-prepared food, but best of all it's open until 3pm, when it seems every other self-service restaurant is dead and gone by 2pm.

★ **Pizzería Paço do Pão** PIZZERIA $$
(☑ 3215-5665; Av Juscelino Kubitschek; mains R$18-25; ⊙ 5-11pm, closed Tue) The pizza menu at this popular eatery runs into the dozens,

Palmas

with a house special that comes loaded with three types of meat, plus corn, heart of palm, olives and a thick layer of cheese. Outdoor seating makes it a great place for lingering over a pie and cold Skol.

Trattoria Toscana ITALIAN $$
(☑3218-2795; Quadra 104 Sul, cnr Av NS-04 at Rua SE-09; mains R$16-$45; ☺11am-3pm Sat & Sun, 5-10pm Mon-Sat) The gnocchi, ravioli and lasagna are all made in-house, and served in hefty portions. For dessert, splurge on the divine *petit gateau di cioccolato* (petite chocolate cake; R$10).

❶ Orientation

Palmas' layout is highly logical, but still confuses most first-time visitors. All *quadras* (blocks) are numbered, and the main avenues are named for their direction: 'NS' for *norte–sul* (north–south) and 'LO' for *leste–oeste* (east–west). Smaller *ruas* (roads) are named according to their quadrant – like 'NO' for the northwest or 'SE' for southeast – in relation to Praça Girassóis, the center of the city. Only Palmas' two main thoroughfares have regular names: Av Juscelino Kubitschek (known as Av JK) and Av Teotônio Segurado.

❶ Information

There are cash machines located at Palmas Shopping, a small busy mall on the south side of Praça Girossóis.

EMERGENCY
Ambulance (☑192)
Police (☑190)

INTERNET ACCESS
MSD Inform@tica (☑3215-8562; Quadra 103 Nte, Rua NO-03; per hr R$2; ☺9am-10pm

Mon-Sat, noon-10pm Sun) Fast, inexpensive internet service.

LAUNDRY
Quality Lavandería (☑3215-5060; cnr Av NS-01 & Av LO-01; wash/dry per kg R$8.50, plus ironing per kg R$14; ☺8am-6:30pm Mon-Fri, 9am-1pm Sat) Can do your laundry the same day if you drop it off early, and will deliver loads of 2kg or more to your hotel.

MEDICAL
Droganita (☑3228-5804; ☺24hr) One of several pharmacies in Galeria Bela Palma.
Hospital Geral de Palmas (☑3218-7802; Quadra 201 Sul, Av LO-5) Between Av Teotônio Segurado and Av NS-01, this is the city's main public hospital; 24-hour emergency room.
Hospital Oswaldo Cruz (☑3219-9000; Quadra 501 Sul, Av NS-01) Between Av LO-09 & Av LO-11, this recommended private hospital is in Palmas's medical district; 24hr emergency room.

MONEY
Banco do Brasil (Quadra 103-Sul, cnr Av Juscelino Kubitschek & Av NS-01) Handy to a lot of hotels.
Bradesco (Quadra 104 Nte, cnr Av Juscelino Kubitschek & Av NS-02) Across the plaza from Banco do Brasil; ATM.
HSBC (Av Juscelino Kubitschek) Reliable ATM; near Av NS-02.

POST OFFICE
Post Office (Palmas Shopping; ☺10am-9pm Mon-Fri, 10am-1pm Sat) There's another post office on Av Juscelino Kubitschek between Rua SE-04 and Av NS-04.

TOURIST INFORMATION
Centro de Atendimento ao Turista (CATUR; ☑2111-0213; Quadra 103, Av NS-01 at Av Juscelino Kubitschek; ☺8am-4pm Mon-Fri) Conveniently located and reasonably helpful.

TRAVEL AGENCIES
Viagem & Cia (☑3215-2085; www.viagemecia. com.br; Quadra 104 Nte, Av NS-02) Sells plane tickets.

❶ Getting There & Around

AIR
GOL (☑3218 3738; airport only) and **TAM** (☑3219 3777; airport only) are the primary airlines serving Palmas. All flights go via Brasília.

The airport is located 26km south of the city center. A taxi from the airport to the hotel area costs R$50 to R$55, and the same to return. Alternatively, catch the red bus 75 at the airport curb (hourly from 7am to 7pm) to the 'Terminal,' where you can switch to bus 20 (hourly from

MONTE ALEGRE

The sandstone hills behind Monte Alegre (pop 55,450), about 120km downstream from Santarém, are dotted with caves and bizarre rock outcroppings. They, in turn, are adorned with dozens of rock paintings believed to be around 11,000 years old, the oldest known human creations in Amazonia and possibly Brazil. Most are in red and yellow, and depict human and animal figures, plus geometric designs and handprints of the painters themselves. Some are clustered tightly together, others appear to be isolated doodling. Tour agencies in Santarém and Alter do Chão arrange trips to Monte Alegre. To do it yourself, contact **Nelsí Sadeck** (☑ 93-3533-1430; nelsi@netsan.com.br; Rua do Jaquara 320), a local teacher and engineer who bears much of the credit for the conservation of the paintings, and is the go-to guide for visiting them. You'll need to stay at least one night; **Hotel Panorámica** (☑ 93-3533-1282; s/d R$60/75; ❊) is a reliable option. Viação Tapajós (p590) has daily speedboat service to and from Santarém.

7:35am to 7:35pm), which passes Galeria Bela Palma in the center. Do the reverse to get back. In either direction, the first leg is R$2.40; the second leg is free.

BUS

Most long-distance buses do not enter Palmas, stopping instead in the highway-side town of Paraíso do Tocantins, 15km west of Palmas; note that departures listed here are from Paraíso. To get between Paraíso and Palmas, minibuses operated by **Tocantinsense** (☑ 3228-5652) loop around 30 to 60 minutes (R$9, 25 minutes) from roughly 5:45am to 7:30pm, with reduced service on weekends. Catch inbound shuttles at the Paraíso bus station, outbound ones at the bus stop in front of Galeria Bela in Palmas.

Transbrasiliana (☑ in Palmas 3217-5604, in Paraíso 3361-2475) has service to Belém (R$156, 18 hours, 9:50am, 2pm and 8pm), Brasília (R$100, 13 hours, 2pm, 7pm and 8:30pm) and São Paulo (R$223, 25 hours, 5:30am).

For Taquarussú, take bus 90 from Praça Girossóis in front of Galeria Bela Palma.

CAR

Car-rental agencies include **Avis** (☑ 3215-3336, airport 3219-3802; cnr Rua SO-03 & Rua SO-04), **Hertz** (☑ 3215-1900; Av LO-02 at Av NS-01) and **Localiza** (☑ 9978-9995, toll-free 0800-979-2020)

Around Palmas

Taquarussú

This cozy town is nestled in the green Serra do Carmo hills, 30km southeast of Palmas, in an area studded with waterfalls and blanketed in forest. The state and local tourism boards have dedicated themselves to making Taquarussú an ecotourism mec-

ca, with modest success. Guides are needed for most outings, some of whom have cars. Most do not, though, so consider renting a car from Palmas to really enjoy the area's attractions.

ℹ Orientation & Information

The **Centro de Atendimento ao Turista** (CATUR; ☑ 3554-1515; Rua 20-A; ☺ 8am-noon & 2-6pm Mon-Fri, to 4pm Sat & Sun), near the plaza, is the best place for information about the area, and to hire a guide to visit the falls. There's a Banco do Brasil cash machine next to CATUR, and a small **clinic** (☺ 24hr) on the road toward Fazenda Encantada.

🏃 Activities

There are 80 identified waterfalls, caves and pools in the area, of which 10 to 15 are open and accessible to the public during most of the year. The tourist office encourages visitors to use guides for all the sites, though several of the most popular ones are easy to visit on your own. **Cachoeira de Roncadeira** is the tallest waterfall in the area (70m), and **Cachoeira Escorrega Macaco**, just 100m away, is nearly as tall (60m). Both tumble picturesquely down sheer rust-brown cliffs, fringed by green vegetation, into small pools good for wading and swimming. The falls are located 1.5km down a well-marked trail; follow signs toward Hotel Fazenda Encantada and look for a large turnoff and parking area as the road ascends just out of town. **Cachoeira Taquaruçu** is a beefy cascade with a choppy swimming hole that can get crowded on hot summer weekends. Look for the large roadside parking area along the highway from Palmas, about 4.5km before reaching Taquarussú; the falls are a 150m

Around Palmas

walk from there. A R$4 per person trail fee applies if you come without a guide.

Other popular spots that are best visited with a guide include the **Cachoeira do Rappel**, on the Fazenda Encantada grounds and used for rappelling (naturally), and **Vale do Vai-Quem-Quer**, a broad valley with a series of falls and good swimming spots. Before setting out, discuss with your guide what type of falls you'd like to see, how much hiking and driving you want, and whether the car you have is adequate for all sites (some require 4WD, especially in the rainy season).

🛏 Sleeping & Eating

Pousada Lokau   POUSADA **$**
(☑ 3554-1238; 3a Av; r per person R$40) Part art gallery, part pousada, the Lokau has five clean, comfortable rooms opening onto a pleasant garden. They can be a bit musty at first, but high ceilings and stand-up fans

help. To get here, turn left after the plaza, right just before Restaurante Mandala, and left at the roundabout. The pousada is at the next corner on your left.

Pousada Catarse   GUESTHOUSE **$**
(☑ 3554-1237; Rua 20; s R$50-60, d R$80-90) This place, two blocks from CATUR, is very homey, with a common kitchen and small TV room, complete with aquarium. One room has a bathroom, while the other two share one in the hallway; all have ceiling fans and simple cozy decor. Usually open on weekends only; call ahead if you'll be visiting during the week.

Restaurante Mandala   BRAZILIAN **$**
(Av Belo Horizonte; R$9-20; ⏱ lunch daily, dinner Wed-Sun) Right around the corner from the plaza, on the road toward Fazenda Encantada. The fixed-plate lunch comes with pasta, rice, beans, salad, *farofa* and a choice of meat, all for R$9.

ℹ Getting There & Away

From Palmas by car, take Hwy TO-010 past the bus station and follow the signs, passing first through the town of Taquaralto.

From Palmas, take any bus (including Bus 90 in front of Galeria Bela, R$2.40) to the *terminal urbano*, where you transfer to a bus for Taquarussú.

Parque Estadual do Jalapão

Jalapão state park is a unique 34,000-sq-km area in far eastern Tocantins, combining cerrado vegetation, hills, caves, crystalline rivers and springs, 40m-high sand dunes, waterfalls, freshwater bathing spots, odd rock formations, quite a range of wildlife – including anteaters, armadillos, macaws and rheas – and very few people. Bananal Ecotour (p596) arranges multiday tours of the park, including transport, hotels, food and guide services. The best season to explore Jalapão is the dry season from May to September.

Ilha do Bananal

Ilha do Bananal is arguably the world's biggest river island – only Ilha do Marajó in Pará state is bigger, and some say Marajó doesn't qualify since part of it faces the ocean. Bananal covers 19,000 sq km, slightly less than the size of Israel, and is formed where the Rio Javaés splits from the Rio Araguaia and rejoins it 350km downstream. Three ecosystems converge here – rainforest, cerrado and wetland – and the island teems with plant and animal life, especially birds. Bananal Ecotour (p596) arranges all-inclusive tours to Ilha do Bananal, including to Lagoa da Confuão, a large lake east of the island. Available June to October only.

AMAZONAS

Amazonas is Brazil's largest state, spanning almost 1.6 million sq km. You could fit four Germanys within its borders with room left over for, say, Greece. It is here that the massive Solimões, Negro and Madeira rivers converge to form the Rio Amazonas, the granddaddy of them all. Manaus is the state capital and, with nearly two million people, the largest city in the Amazon region. Manaus is easy to reach by air, and the vast majority of travelers arrive here first. Tour operators in Manaus specialize in three- to six-day jungle tours. You can also book riverboat tours here, and the city itself has some worthwhile sights. Manaus is also a good jumping-off point for jungle trips further up the Rio Solimões, including Tefé and the outstanding Mamirauá reserve, or for the remote regions of the Rio Negro.

Manaus

🖉 092 / POP 1.9 MILLION

Manaus is the Amazon's largest city, an incongruous pocket of urbanity in the middle of the jungle, a major port for ocean vessels that's 1500km from the ocean. The rainforest has a population density half that of Mongolia's, but the journey there invariably begins in (or passes through) this bustling city. Don't be surprised if you feel a little out of whack.

The city itself has some genuinely rewarding sights, including a leafy zoo with as many animals out of the cages as in them, and a beach-and-museum combo that gets you out of the city center. It's a place to stock up on anything you forgot to pack, or to refill your tank with beer and internet after a week in the forest. Manaus will be a host city for the 2014 FIFA World Cup, and the city is bustling with construction and improvement projects.

Manaus is where most Amazon tour operators are based; plenty are honest professionals, ranging from budget to upscale, but the city is also full of scammers. Be smart and avoid touts like the plague: the tours they sell are miserable, occasionally dangerous, and cheaper only because they cut corners on basics like food and transport.

⊙ Sights

CITY CENTER

★ Teatro Amazonas   THEATER

(🖉 3232-1768; Praça São Sebastião; guided tour R$10; ⊙ 9am-5pm, tours hourly until 4pm) This gorgeous theater was built at the height of the rubber boom, using European designers, decorators, even raw materials. The original driveway was Brazilian, though, made of Amazonian rubber to soften the clatter of late-arriving carriages. The theater's performance schedule includes an excellent opera festival in April and May. Guided tours offer an up-close look at the theater's opulent construction.

Centro Cultural Usina Chaminé   MUSEUM

(🖉 3633-3026; Av Beira Rio at José Paranaguá; ⊙ 10am-4pm Tue-Fri, 5-8pm Sun) **FREE** Also

JUNGLE TRIPPING

The top priority for most foreign visitors to Manaus is a jungle trip. While anything's possible, the most common trip is three to five days based at a jungle lodge or on a riverboat, with daytrips for hiking, canoeing, fishing for piranha, spotting caiman at night and visiting local villages. Spending a night or two in the forest is usually possible, but not required. Many operators also offer 'survival tours,' which are spent mostly or entirely in forest camps.

Thinking carefully about what sort of trip you want can help determine which operator is best for you. How much do you want to rough it? Do you want a bed or a hammock? What about sleeping aboard a boat? Private bathroom, shared or pit toilet? Do you want to spend a night or two in the forest or do day trips from the lodge? How much do mosquitoes bother you? Do you prefer hiking or canoeing? There is no shame in choosing more or less comfort – you are there to enjoy yourself, after all.

There are also a few questions to ask the tour operator: does the guide speak English (or a language you understand)? How long will you spend getting there? What is the trip itinerary? How much hiking and/or canoeing will you do? Ask to see recent pictures of the accommodations and activities, and a guest comment book.

And talk to other travelers! Virtually every foreigner you see in Manaus is planning a trip or returning from one, and they are the best source of honest, up-to-date info.

The Amazon is teeming with animals, but seeing them can be quite hard. (It's a much better place to be wowed by the flora and the river itself, rather than wildlife.) On a typical trip, you are virtually guaranteed to see pink and grey dolphins and a slew of birds, including herons, parrots and possibly macaws. Monkeys, sloths and caimans are relatively common, but seeing them is no sure thing. River otters and tapirs are even more elusive, and you're almost sure *not* to see jaguars, manatees or anacondas – they are extremely hard to spot. White-water areas tend to have more animals, but they also have more mosquitoes and thicker vegetation, inhibiting even the keenest observer. State and national reserves have more (and less skittish) wildlife. The biggest factor in seeing animals is luck, followed by the quality of the forest and the diligence of your guide. Trips should leave punctually and last the allotted time, and guests should refrain from chatting unnecessarily.

Bring closed shoes or boots for hiking, sandals for around the lodge, long-sleeved shirt and pants, mosquito repellent, a hat and sunscreen, rain gear, flashlight, roll of toilet paper, daypack and a water bottle. Your own binoculars are much recommended, as few operators have them to rent or borrow. Plastic bags, including a heavy-duty one large enough for your entire pack, are useful for rainstorms and leaky boats. Most hotels in Manaus offer secure luggage storage for whatever you don't bring along.

known as the Museu dos Cinco Sentidos (Museum of the Five Senses), this innovative museum uses the five senses to evoke and illustrate indigenous and *coboclo* life and culture. You can hear recordings of native languages, smell Amazonian spices, admire indigenous folk art and more, as you pass from room to room.

Museu Amazônico　　　　　　　MUSEUM
(☑ 3234-3242; www.museuamazonico.ufam.edu.br; Ramos Ferreira; ☺ 8am-noon & 2-5pm Mon-Fri) **FREE** Housed in a converted mansion, the Museu Amazônico has a small but excellent collection of indigenous items and artifacts from around the Amazon, many from ongoing archaeological studies in Amazonas

state. Highlights include Matis and Maku hunting tools, and terrific masks and costumes used in Yanomami and Ticuna rituals. The 1st floor is used for temporary art and educational exhibits.

Palacete Provincial　　　　　　MUSEUM
(Praça da Polícia; ☺ 9am-5pm Tue & Wed, 9am-7pm Thu-Sat, 4-8pm Sun) **FREE** The 'Image and Sound' center at this handsome cultural complex has a huge collection of films, including century-old documentaries by Portuguese filmmaker Silvino Santos, some of the earliest recordings of Amazonian native people. The art gallery is decent, too, but the police and archaeology displays are snoozers. Young eager docents are available for guided tours.

Manaus

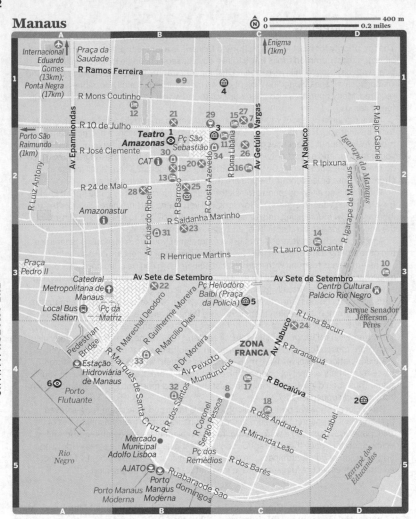

THE AMAZON MANAUS

Galeria do Largo
GALLERY

(Costa Azevedo; ⊙ 5-9pm Tue-Sun) FREE Right on Praça São Sebastião, Galeria do Largo has a modern-minded rotation of art exhibits, from contemporary paintings to innovative sculpture. The attached cafe serves unique snacks and drinks at tables set up on the plaza.

Porto Flutuante
FERRY TERMINAL

(Estação Hidroviária de Manaus) FREE Inaugurated in 1902, Manaus' 'floating port' was a technical marvel of its day, able to adjust 15m or more to seasonal water levels. (Look for high water marks on a wall facing the river.) There's a busy indoor-outdoor shopping and eating area, with nice river views. From Praça da Matriz, an elevated bridge leads to the main terminal area.

OUTSIDE THE CITY CENTER

Centro Cultural dos Povos da Amazônia
MUSEUM

(☎ 2123-5301; www.povosdamazonia.am.gov.br; Praça Francisco Pereira da Silva s/n; ⊙ 9am-5pm Mon-Fri) FREE At the heart of this massive cultural complex is the excellent Museu do Homem do Norte (Museum of Northern Man), which contains an incredible array of

Manaus

artifacts and multimedia exhibits on Amazonian indigenous groups. From the center, buses 625, 711, and 705 all pass by, or ask a taxi to take you to the 'Bola da Suframa.'

Elsewhere in the complex are a well-stocked film-screening room, a replica *maloca* (large traditional indigenous structure), an outstanding collection of life-like statues of indigenous people by Peruvian sculptor Felipe Lettersten, and a huge arena used for, among other things, a major Amazonian dance festival held every June.

Bosque da Ciência (INPA)   ZOO
(Forest of Science; http://bosque.inpa.gov.br/prin cipal.htm; Av Cabral; admission R$5; ⊙ 9am-noon & 2-5pm Tue-Fri, 9am-4pm Sat & Sun) Occupying a lush forest plot within the city, Bosque da Ciência (aka INPA, for the research institution that runs it) has enclosures for rescued manatees, giant otters and more, and many smaller animals simply roaming around, such as squirrel monkeys, sloths and anteaters. It also has a small nature museum and an excellent restaurant. Located in Petrópolis district, 5km northeast of the center.

To get there from Praça da Matriz, the 810 'Especial' minibus (R$2.65) stops right outside the gates, while bus 519 (R$2.20) stops a half-block away. A taxi costs R$30.

**Jardim Botânico
Adolpho Ducke**   PARK
(⊙ 8am-5pm Tue-Fri, 8am-4pm Sat & Sun) `FREE` Spanning over 100 sq km, this 'garden' is actually the world's largest urban forest. There's a network of five short trails (guides required, two to three hours, free), and three open-air exhibits on Amazonian flora and fauna. From Praça da Matriz, take bus 448 'Ciudad de Deus' to the end of the line (R$2.20, one hour); taxis run R$50 to R$60. Closed shoes recommended.

Museu do Seringal Vila Paraíso   MUSEUM
(Rubber Museum; admission R$5; ⊙ 8am-4pm Wed-Sun) Located on the grounds of a former rubber-baron estate, this unique museum includes tours of the grand historic townhouse, a replica rubber-tapper shack and smokehouse, and a leafy trail showing how rubber trees are tapped. Sounds gimmicky, but still intriguing. Consider combining it with a stop at Praia da Lua, Manaus' best beach.

Boats to the museum (R$8, 25 minutes, via Praia da Lua) leave frequently from Marina Davi, just past the Hotel Tropical in Ponta Negra. From the center, take bus 011, 012, or 120 (R$2.20, 20 minutes) to the end of the line, then walk or catch a free 'Especial' bus to the marina.

THE AMAZON MANAUS

Praia da Lua BEACH

Manaus's best beach has fine white sand and tea-colored water, and can be coupled with a visit to the Museu do Seringal for a nice city escape. Like all river beaches, Lua is biggest when the water is low (September to December). Beach shacks serve fish and beer at tables set up along the water. The big drawback: no toilets.

Catch a boat to Praia da Lua (R$5, 10 minutes) from Marina Davi, just past Ponta Negra. Take bus 011, 012, or 120 (R$2.40, 20 minutes) to the turnaround and wait for the free 'Especial' bus to the marina.

Encontro das Águas RIVER

Just beyond Manaus, the warm, dark Rio Negro pours into the cool creamy Rio Solimões, but because of differences in temperature, speed and especially density (the Solimões carries eight times more sediment than the Negro) their waters don't mix, instead flowing side by side for several kilometers. The bi-color phenomenon occurs throughout the Amazon, but nowhere as dramatically as here.

You're almost certain to pass the meeting of the waters en route to a jungle lodge (or, better yet, see it from the plane). You can also book a day trip with Amazon Explorers, which combines a stop there with a visit to touristy Parque Ecológico Janauary.

🎊 Festivals & Events

Inaugurated in 1997, the annual **Manaus Opera Festival** brings high-quality opera deep into the rainforest at the Teatro Amazonas (p600). The three-week gala usually takes place in late April and early May, and audience apparel ranges from tuxedos and ballroom gowns to jeans and T-shirts that have obviously done duty in the jungle (they do draw the line at shorts, tank tops and flip-flops, however). Tickets (R$5 to R$60) are available at the Teatro Amazonas several weeks before the festival opens.

In November, the ever-more-popular **Amazon Film Festival** screens dozens of films related in some way to the Amazon, from rare Brazilian features filmed in Manaus to foreign documentaries about destruction of the rainforest. Headliners are shown in Teatro Amazonas, but you can see films every night of the week for free at a large outdoor screen set up right in the Praça São Sebastião.

The June **Festival Folclórico do Amazonas** features a wide variety of regional folklore performan8ces, including rehearsals of the Parintins Boi-Bumbá teams. The festival culminates on June 29 with the Procissão Fluvial de São Pedro (St Peter River Procession), when hundreds of riverboats parade on the Rio Negro before Manaus to honor the patron saint of fishers.

🛏 Sleeping

There are also jungle trips and lodges outside the city.

★Hostel Manaus HOSTEL $

(📞3233-4545; www.hostelmanaus.com; Cavalcante 231; dm with fan/air-con R$27/30, s/d with fan & shared bathroom R$60/66, with fan & private bathroom R$70/76, with air-con & private bathroom R$80/86; ❄@🛜) Manaus' first hostel is still its best: HI-registered and Australian-operated, with comfortable dorms, tidy private rooms, and a rooftop patio with great city views. It's a bit removed from the center, but a recommended tour operator is based here, and the hostel owner has info on visiting São Gabriel da Cachoeira, way up the Rio Negro.

Gol Backpackers Manaus HOSTEL $

(📞3304-5805; www.golbackpackers.com; Barroso 365; dm R$25-30, r R$70; ❄🛜🏊) Being a half-block from Teatro Amazonas is the best reason to stay at this five-room hostel. Other amenities sound good – the small backyard pool, for example – but in reality the rooms are only so-so and the common spaces rather uninviting. A longtime tour operator has a desk here and sometimes has hostel discounts for booking a trip.

Big Hostel Brasil HOSTEL $

(📞3086-3083; www.bighostel.com.br; Av Sete de Setembro 1653; dm R$38, s/d with shared bathroom R$55/110; ❄🛜) Friendly and family-run, with two floors of spacious air-cooled dorms opening onto long breezy corridors. There are a couple of private rooms, and a rear patio was being built when we visited. Daily cleaning, laundry service, and guests can use the small kitchen. The main drawback here is the location – a long walk through a somewhat dodgy area, especially at night.

Hotel Ideal HOTEL $

(📞3622-0038; www.hotelidealmanaus.com.br; Rua dos Andradas 491; s/d R$46/59, with air-con R$59/73, with TV & minibar R$73/87; ❄🛜) A multistory block of plain but adequate rooms coated in gray and white high-gloss paint. The owner and staff are friendly and honest, though the area has gotten a bit sketchy; be especially wary at night, and beware freelance guides peddling cut-rate tours on the sidewalk.

Hotel Brasil
HOTEL $

(☎2101-5000; www.hotelbrasil.tur.br; Av Getúlio Vargas 657; s/d R$90/110; ❋🛜) This non descript eight-story hotel on busy and safe Av Getúlio Vargas is actually a very solid value and a great location. Rooms on the lower level have been renovated and are far superior to the old-school air-conditioners and itty-bitty bathrooms upstairs. The breakfast spread is ample, and buses to and from the airport and bus station stop a half-block away.

Hotel Colonial Manaus
HOTEL $

(☎3233-3216; www.hotelcolonialmanaus.com; Quintino Bocaiúva 462; s/d/tr $70/90/110; 🛜) A classy comfortable hotel in an area that's known for pretty much the opposite. Built in a renovated colonial home, spacious rooms have high ceilings with crown molding and rich wood floors. Most are clustered around the lobby, and voices and noises echo throughout, but somehow it's part of the charm. Friendly helpful owners, ample breakfast.

Hotel 10 de Julho
HOTEL $$

(☎3232-6280; www.hoteldezdejulho.com; Rua 10 de Julho 679; s/d R$75/90, with hot water & minibar R$90/105; ❋🛜) Rooms in this large rambling hotel are spacious and clean, somewhat sterile perhaps, but a good value. The breakfast spread is huge and the location ideal, near Teatro Amazonas and several recommended restaurants. The guys hanging around in front look like touts but they aren't really: they work with the three (yes, three) different tour offices in the lobby.

★ Boutique Hotel
Casa Teatro
HOTEL $$

(☎3633-8381; www.casateatro.com.br; Rua 10 de Julho 632; s/d superior R$185/210, standard R$140/160; ❋🛜) Rooms here are gorgeous but really tiny. The cheaper ones even have shared bathrooms and bunks instead of a bed, as if you're on a boutique ocean liner. En suite rooms are a better value: still small, but quite lovely. Common space includes two cozy sitting rooms and a rooftop patio with views of the opera house.

Go Inn
HOTEL $$

(☎3306-2600; www.atlanticahotels.com.br; Monsenhor Coutinho 560; s/d R$165/185; ❋❋🛜) A bit plasticky, perhaps, but still a welcome oasis of business-class comfort amid Manaus's mostly gritty downtown options. Rooms are small but spotless, with modern bathrooms and flat-screen TVs. It has a large restaurant and business area off the lobby, even a small fitness room. No swimming pool, alas, but a reliable choice in every way.

Chez les Rois
POUSADA $$

(☎3584-3549; www.chezlesrois.com.br; Conjunto Manauense Q/G 01, Barrio Vieiralves; s/d R$138/165; ❋@🛜❋) Occupying an attractive colonial home in a swanky neighborhood, Chez les Rois has great common areas, with wood floors and many little nooks where you can read a book or soak up the sun, plus a welcoming little pool. The guestrooms are less inspired (and rather small) but the service and overall ambience are worth a few bumped elbows.

Park Suites Manaus
HOTEL $$$

(☎0800 55 5855, 3306-4500; www.atlantica hotels.com.br; Coronel Teixeira; s/d R$335/375, ste R$475-915) Located in Ponta Negra, a short distance from the fading star Hotel Tropical, Park Suites is Manaus' top commercial hotel for tourists and businesspeople alike. Enjoy bracing views of the Rio Negro from your room and the hotel's gorgeous infinity pool. Rooms are large and fairly modern, and the staff is friendly. Ponta Negra makes for pleasant exploring (including the city's best nightlife) while downtown Manaus is a 20-minute cab ride away.

✖ Eating

Skina dos Sucos
JUICE BAR $

(cnr Av Eduardo Ribeiro & Rua 24 de Maio; juices R$4-8, snacks R$4-12; ⊘7am-8pm Mon-Sat) Stake out some counter space at this busy eatery, where you can order filling snacks and sandwiches to go along with large *sucos* (fresh juices) made from Amazonian fruits, including guaraná (a tropical berry thought to have numerous medicinal properties), *cupuaçú* (sweet cousin of the cacao fruit) and *graviola* (custard apple).

Kibe da Irene
FAST FOOD $

(Barroso, at Rua Saldanha Marinho; snacks R$2-10) Pretty much devoid of character, but a great choice for travelers on a budget. At lunchtime, fill up on a *prato feito* (plate of the day) for just R$7, or come anytime for cheap snacks; the namesake *kibes* (deep-fried cracked wheat stuffed with spiced meat) are kinda tough, but the rest, including breaded chicken legs and *bolinhas* (fried cheese balls) is plenty good. Look for a narrow stairway off the street.

★ Casa do Pensador   PIZZERIA, BRAZILIAN $
(Praça São Sebastião; mains R$13-28; ⊙ 4-11pm) Simple wood tables set up on the plaza facing Teatro Amazonas make this an easy low-key place for dinner and a beer. The menu is equally low-key, mostly pizza (including a couple of veggie options) and standard rice-beans-meat dishes.

Delícias Caseiras   BRAZILIAN, SELF-SERVICE $
(Rua 10 de Julho; lunch per kg R$20, mains R$15-40; ⊙ 11am-10pm Mon-Sat, to 3pm Sun) The tables are crammed together and the fans are blowing full blast to accommodate the scads of loyal clients at this great hole-in-the-wall eatery just off Praça São Sebastião. Lunch self-serve is outstanding, especially for the price, but it's also open for dinner, serving homestyle classics.

Casa da Pamonha   VEGETARIAN $
(Barroso 375; per kg R$34; ⊙ 7am-7pm Mon-Fri, to 2pm Sat; 🖉) Cool and friendly, this vegetarian place has art exhibitions, soy burgers, Spanish tortillas, fresh juices and tasty cakes served all day, and a creative, flavorful lunch buffet.

Scarola Pizzaria   PIZZERIA, BRAZILIAN $
(🖉 3234-8542; Rua 10 de Julho 739; mains R$10-30, per kg R$20-22; ⊙ lunch & dinner) Good food, good service and good *chope* (draft beer) make for a varied clientele, from backpackers back from jungle trips to professionals pontificating on the latest opera performance. The affordable lunch spread has all the standards, including fresh grilled meats, while pizza is the dinner of choice. One of the few places around that's open late, even on Sunday.

Filosóphicus   SELF-SERVICE $
(3rd fl, Av Sete de Setembro 752; self-service per kg R$27; ⊙ 11am-3pm Mon-Fri; 🖉) Vegetarians should head to this small upstairs restaurant, serving a creative, genuinely meat-free lunch buffet. A bit hard to find, and not exactly bursting with atmosphere, but worth the effort all the same.

Restaurante Castelinho   SELF-SERVICE $$
(🖉 3633-3111; www.restaurantecastelinho.com.br; Barroso 317; per kg R$35; ⊙ 11am-3pm Mon-Sat)

The food and service at this popular per-kilo place are perfectly good, but the highlight has to be the building itself: a rubber-era mansion that served as a private residence, doctor's office and foreign consulate before being converted into a restaurant. With high ceilings, gleaming wood floors, ornate crown molding, it's a real beauty.

★ Rancho Búfalo   CHURRASCARIA $$
(🖉 3633-3733; Av Joaquim Nabuco 628; weekday/weekend per kg R$47/51, all-you-can-eat R$35/40; ⊙ 11am-3pm Mon-Fri, to 3:30pm Sat & Sun) A cadre of white-jacketed chefs man the large grill, wielding skewers of perfectly prepared meat which they'll slice right onto your plate. Many say it's got the best meat in the city, and you'll find no argument here. Add to that a huge salad and sides bar, and there's no chance of leaving here hungry.

Restaurante Giratório   BRAZILIAN, INTERNATIONAL $$
(🖉 3627-3737; tajmahal@internext.com.br; Taj Mahal Continental Hotel, Av Getúlio Vargas 741; dishes R$25-50; ⊙ lunch & dinner) She's starting to creak a bit, but the revolving restaurant atop the Taj Majal hotel still offers unbeatable views and better-than-average meals. Snag a table just upstream from the view of Teatro Amazonas so you're sure to get at least two passes. The menu is pricey, but not outrageously so; try the *tucanaré* in *cupuaçu* sauce (a tart, tropical fruit).

🍸 Drinking & Entertainment

There are a few quiet bars in town, but for more of a party scene, you should head to Ponta Negra.

Bar do Armando   BAR
(Rua 10 de Julho 593; ⊙ 5pm-1am) Near the opera house, this is a traditional rendezvous place for Manaus' intellectual and bohemian types, but all sorts of people crowd around the outdoor tables for beers and conversation.

Laranjinha Bar   BAR
(Ponta Negra; ⊙ from 9pm Mon-Sat) On the waterfront in Ponta Negra, Laranjinha's was closed during research because of renovations to the area for the soccer World Cup, but will reportedly reopen. It's a good place to start your night, with beer and burgers. Live performances are held most nights at the bar's large outdoor stage.

Enigma CLUB

(☎ 3234 7985; Silva Ramos 1054; ⊙ 11pm-late Thu-Sat) A mixed gay-lesbian-straight *boate* (nightclub) about 1km north of the center, with beat music and dancing.

★ **Porão do Alemão** LIVE MUSIC

(www.poraodoalemao.com.br; Estrada da Ponta Negra 1986; ⊙ 9pm-late Wed-Sat) Porão do Alemão and Coração Blue are both located on Estrada de Ponta Negra, and are lively, safe bars frequented by tourists and locals alike.

 Shopping

Galeria Amazônica HANDICRAFTS

(☎ 3233-4521; www.galeriamazonica.org.br; Costa Azevedo 272) Right on Praça São Sebastião, this is Manaus's top shop for genuine-article Amazonian handiwork, including gorgeous basketwork, pottery and folk art. Prices are on the high side, but so is the quality.

Artesanato da Amazônia HANDICRAFTS

(☎ 3232-3979; José Clemente 500; ⊙ 9am-6:30pm Mon-Fri, 9am-3pm Sat) Once a terrific store for folk art, but the good stuff here is getting buried by a growing amount of predictable kitsch. But you can still find some quality items, especially indigenous masks and handmade weapons.

Comercial São Bento OUTDOOR GEAR

(Miranda Leão 133; ⊙ 8am-6pm Mon-Fri, to 4pm Sat) The best of several *casas de redes* (hammock shops) clustered on and around this corner, with a monster selection and friendly service. For riverboat trips, suitable cloth hammocks start at R$25, while larger, prettier, more durable ones go for R$60 to R$120. If you'll be sleeping in the jungle, consider getting a mosquito net (R$14 to R$30) as well.

Carrefour DEPARTMENT STORE

(Av Eduardo Ribeiro; ⊙ 7am-8pm Mon-Sat, to 4pm Sun) The best downtown supermarket, and

---

JUNGLE TRIP SCAMS

Manaus is teeming with scammers and touts. Most peddle cut-rate tours that turn out to be woefully uninspired: awful accommodations, surly guides and sad, damaged forest with no wildlife. Tourists have been seriously injured, and even a few killed, on tours with unscrupulous or inexperienced guides. Mainly, though, they simply get duped: swindled out of their time, money and what is probably their only chance to experience the Amazon.

There are some simple ways to avoid getting scammed. Chief among them: don't be naive. The smooth-talking guy who approaches you on the street, or snags you at the door of your hostel, with promises of an epic adventure at a rock-bottom price is scamming you, plain and simple. Here are some more tips to avoid falling victim:

Never pay for a tour anywhere except at the agency's main office in town Touts often pretend they are with a legitimate agency but steer you to a cafe or airport bench to make the deal. They even make phony phone calls to convince you the main office is closed, or that you must commit right away to get the best price or the 'last seat on the boat.' These are all scams.

Firmly turn down anyone who approaches you at the airport, or outside your hostel, about booking a tour Legitimate agencies have offices where you can get legitimate information and tours. If you've reserved ahead of time and are being picked up at the airport, look for a sign with your name on it.

Do not tell touts what hotel or agency you're interested in, nor accept help locating them They're only trying to squeeze a commission out of the owners, which of course gets passed on to you. If a persistent tout follows you into a hotel or tour office, make it clear you arrived on your own.

Confirm the agency is registered with the state tourism authority Go to www.visitamazonas.am.gov.br, select the Portuguese version (it's more up-to-date than the English one), then *Agências de Turismo*.

Above all, don't risk your life to save a little time or money In the end, the reason there are so many scammers is because travelers keep booking with them. There are legitimate agencies with low-cost tours; take the time to find one that works for you.

a good place to buy batteries, rain ponchos and any toiletries you may need. It's also the only place in the center to buy Havaianas flip-flops.

Crafts Stands

SOUVENIRS

(⊗9am-6pm Mon-Sat) Numerous crafts stands sell mostly identical souvenir-type items in Praça Tenreiro Aranha.

ⓘ Information

EMERGENCY

Ambulance (☑192)

State Police (☑190) A police station is located across from the bus station on Praça da Matriz.

Tourist Police (☑3231-1998; Av Eduardo Ribeiro) At the Centro de Atendimento ao Turista.

INTERNET ACCESS

GDM Informática (Getúlio Vargas at Lauro Cavalcante; per hr R\$3; ⊗9am-6pm Mon-Fri, to noon Sat) Set back from street, next to an ice-cream shop.

Juliana Cyber Café (Nabuco at Bocaiúva; per hr R\$2; ⊗8am-11pm Mon-Sat, from 9am Sun) Internet access.

Rede Cyber (Porto Flutuante; per hr R\$3.60; ⊗8am-8pm Mon-Fri, 9am-9pm Sat) Cool, clean reliable internet café inside the main port. Charges by the minute.

Selva Net (Joaquim Sarmento; per hr R\$5; ⊗7am-7pm Mon-Fri, to 6pm Sat)

Top Cyber (Av Getúlio Vargas at Rua 10 de Julho; per hr R\$2.50; ⊗8am-10pm Mon-Fri, 9am-9pm Sat)

LAUNDRY

Most hotels offer laundry service to guests at per-piece rates.

Lavandería Paradise (☑3633-6092; Quintino Bocaiúva; per kg R\$10; ⊗7am-5pm Mon-Fri, to noon Sat) Most hotels also offer laundry service to guests.

LEFT LUGGAGE

Most hotels have luggage storage, as do the airport and long-distance bus station.

MEDICAL SERVICES

Fundação de Medicina Tropical (Tropical Medicine Foundation; ☑2127-3555; Av Pedro Teixeira 25) Also known as Hospital de Doenças Tropicais, this well-regarded hospital specializes in tropical diseases. It also provides free yellow fever vaccines, which are required for entering Brazil and many South American countries by land or sea. Keep in mind the vaccine is not effective until 10 days after administration.

Unimed (☑3633-4431; Av Japurá 241) One of the best private hospitals in the city.

MONEY

Banco do Brasil (Guilherme Moreira 315; ⊗9am-3pm Mon-Fri) ATMs in front; exchange office on the 2nd floor open weekdays from 9am to 11am only.

Bradesco (Av Eduardo Ribeiro 475) Reliable ATMs.

HSBC Rua Dr Moreira 226 (Rua Dr Moreira 226; ⊗9am-3pm Mon-Fri); Rua 24 de Maio (Rua 24 de Maio; cnr Rua 24 de Maio & Rua Costa Azevedo; ⊗9am-3pm Mon-Fri).

POST

Post Office (Barroso 220; ⊗8am-4pm Mon-Fri, 8am-noon Sat) Also a branch at the airport.

TELEPHONE

Embratel cards, available at the post office, are best for making international calls from payphones (per minute R\$0.50 to R\$1). Most internet cafés have Skype-ready computers.

TOURIST INFORMATION

CAT (☑3182-6250; www.visitamazonas. am.gov.br; Av Eduardo Ribeiro 666 ; ⊗8am-5pm Mon-Fri, 8am-noon Sat & Sun) Amazonastur, the state tourism agency, maintains this tourist-assistance center at the corner of Av Eduardo Ribeiro and Rua José Clemente, while the administrative office is on Rua Saldanha Marinho near Rua Lobo D'Almada.

TRAVEL AGENCIES

Paradise Turismo (☑3633-8301; Av Eduardo Ribeiro 656; ⊗8am-6pm Mon-Fri, 8:30am-noon Sat)

RBS Viagens & Turismo (☑3233-4070; www. rbsturismo.com.br; Getúlio Vargas 188; ⊗8am-6pm Mon-Fri, 9am-1pm Sat) Sells plane tickets.

ⓘ Getting There & Away

AIR

The **Aeroporto Internacional Eduardo Gomes** (☑3652 1210; Av Santos Dumont 1350) is 13km north of the city center. Smaller regional airlines may use a separate terminal (known as 'Eduardinho'), about 600m east of the main one. The large modern airport terminal has a tourism office, cash machines, luggage lockers and wi-fi.

Azul-TRIP (☑4003-1118, 3215-3741; www. voeazul.com.br; cnr Costa Azevedo & Rua 24 de Maio; ⊗8am-5pm Mon-Fri)

Copa/Continental (☑3622-1381; www. copaair.com; Av Eduardo Ribeiro 654)

Delta (☑0800-881-2121, 4003-2121; www. delta.com)

Gol (☎ 3652-1601, 3652-1593; www.voegol.
com.br)

LAN (☎ 0300-788-0045; www.lan.com)

TAM (☎ 4002-5700, 3652-1300; www.tam.
com.br)

TAP (☎ 0300-210-6060; www.flytap.com)

BOAT

Large passenger boats plying the Rio Solimões
use the **Estação Hidroviária de Manaus** (Porto
Flutuante). Speedboats to Tefé, Tabatinga and
Parintins use the **Porto Manaus Moderna**
(behind Mercado Municipal Adolfo Lisboa).
Porto São Raimundo, a seedy port about 1.5km
northwest of the center, is used for slow and fast
boats headed up the Rio Negro.

A small **ticket office** (☎ 3088-5764, 3233-
7061; Marquês de Santa Cruz; ⊙ 6am-6pm)
outside the boat terminal sells passage on long-
distance riverboats. Boats going downstream
to Belém usually make stops in Itacoatiara,
Parintins, Santarém and Monte Alegre. Up the
Rio Solimões, boats call at Tefé, Benjamin Constant and Tabatinga. Boats to Porto Velho, along
the Rio Madeira, make stops at Manicoré and
Humaitá. It's not recommended to buy tickets
from the men with desks along the sidewalk
in front of the boat terminal; although they're
slightly cheaper, you're the first to be bumped if
the boat is full.

AJATO (☎ 3622-6047; http://terminalajato.
com.br; Porto Manaus Moderna; ⊙ 8am-5pm
Mon-Fri, 8am-noon Sat) operates comfortable
speedboats upstream to Tefé (R$220, 13 hours,
daily except Tuesday at 6am or 7am) and to
Tabatinga (R$500, 36 hours, Friday at 6am and
Sunday at 7am) and downstream to Parintins
(R$160, eight hours, four times weekly at 7am).
There's also service up the Rio Madeira as far
as Manicoré (R$170, 14 hours, five times weekly
at 6am).

Slow boats going up the Rio Negro use the
rather seedy Porto São Raimundo, 1.5km northwest of the center. Departures for Barcelos
(hammock R$100, d cabin R$280, 26 to 32
hours) are on Tuesday, Wednesday and Friday
at 6pm and for São Gabriel (hammock R$270,
d cabin $790, 72 hours) at 6pm Friday. Boat
companies **Azevedo** (☎ 9143-1223, 3625-6984;
Porto São Raimundo) and **Vencedor** (☎ 9117-
8757, 9463-2255; Porto São Raimundo) serve
Barcelos, while **Gênesis** (☎ 97-9152-3444,
92-8171-4442) and **Tanaka** (☎ in Manaus 9239-
8024, in São Gabriel ca Cachoeira 97-3471 1730;
Porto São Raimundo) serve São Gabriel.

Speedboats serve the same stops in about half
the time. The *Diamantina Express* operated by
Tanaka, leaves for Barcelos (R$170, 12 hours)
and São Gabriel ($330, 24 hours) every Tuesday
and Friday at 3pm. Bring a camping pad if you've
got one: many passengers lie in the aisle to get
some sleep.

Slow boats along the Rio Solimões do not
include meals, but those along the Rio Negro do.
Speedboats always include meals.

BUS

Manaus' **long-distance bus station** (Rua Recife
2784) is rather small and dumpy, probably a
consequence of the fact that there aren't many
places you can get to by bus. It's 6km north of
town, in the same direction as the airport.

Eucatur (☎ 3301-5800; www.eucatur.com.
br) has service to Boa Vista (R$120, 11 to 12
hours, 6pm, 7pm and 8pm). If you plan to continue directly to Venezuela, take the 6pm bus
from Manaus in order to have the best chance
of catching the one and only bus to the border,
which leaves Boa Vista at 7am.

Aruanã (☎ 3236-8305) has a bus service to
Presidente Figueiredo (R$22, two hours, 6am,
10am, 12:30pm, 5pm and 9:20pm) and to Itacoatiara (R$37, four hours, 6am, 7am, 10:30am,
1pm, 2pm and 7pm).

CAR

Few travelers rent cars in Manaus, but if you feel
the need, there are several agencies at the airport that can put you behind a wheel in no time.
They include **Localiza** (☎ 3652-1176), **Unidas**
(☎ 3652-1327), **Avis** (☎ 3652-1579) and **Hertz**
(☎ 3652-1421).

🛈 Getting Around

Bus fare is R$2.25 on most routes. Taxis are
plentiful, but rather expensive – from R$15
within the center, more for destinations beyond
that or if you get mired in traffic.

RIVERBOATS FROM MANAUS (ESTAÇÃO HIDROVIÁRIA)

DESTINATION	DAYS	TIME	UPPER DECK (R$)	CABIN, 2 PAX (R$)
Belém	Wed & Fri; 11am	4 days	300	1200
Porto Velho	Tue, some Fri; noon	4 days	177, incl meals	550
Santarém	Tue-Sat; 8-9am	3 days	159	590-800
Tabatinga	Wed, Fri & Sat; 11am	7 days	350	1300
Tefé	daily exc Mon; 5-6am	3 days	135, incl meals	590

TO/FROM THE AIRPORT

Buses 306 'Aeroporto' (R$2.25) and 813 'Aeroporto-Ejecutivo' (R$4.65) run about every half-hour between the airport and Praça da Matriz in the center of town; the latter is air-conditioned, less crowded, and definitely worth the extra reais. At the airport, turn right out of the main doors and walk to the bus stop at the end of the terminal. In town, the most convenient stops are Praça da Matriz and on Av Getúlio Vargas near Rua José Clemente.

Taxis at the airport charge a fixed R$60 for the 20-minute ride into town, while the return trip costs around R$50. In either case, be sure to agree on a price before setting off.

TO/FROM THE BUS STATION

Buses 306 and 813 (the same ones you take to the airport) also pass the bus station; get on either at Praça da Matriz or on Av Gétulio Vargas. The bus station is small and easy to miss, so be sure to tell the driver where you're headed and keep your eyes peeled. It's the second stop after the stadium on the left.

You can catch the same buses back into town. Leaving the bus station, use the pedestrian bridge to cross Rua Recife and turn left along the busy street on the far side of the gas station there. The bus stop is 100m further along, on the far side of the street.

A taxi between the bus station and the center costs R$25 to R$30.

Around Manaus

Jungle Trips

Most agencies have a small lodge or jungle camp where guests stay, and from which activities such as canoeing, hiking and fishing are launched. Many have amenities such as electricity and flush toilets, but not all. Prices usually include meals, lodging, transport and guides, and average R$180 to R$250 per person per day (including the time it takes to get to and from the lodge, not just the time you're actually there). Prices vary primarily by the type of accommodations: hammocks with shared toilets are the cheapest option, followed by dorms and private rooms, then riverboats and specialized tours.

Amazon Antonio Jungle Tours   ECOTOUR
(☑9961-8314, 3234-1294; www.antonio-jungle-tours.com) On the scenic (and mosquito free!) Rio Urubú, northwest of Manaus, Amazon Antonio's lodge has dorms, private rooms, chalets, even a two-bedroom cabin across the lake and an observation tower. Over-night hikes journey deep into primary forest, and unlike elsewhere, you can stay after your tour is over, relaxing, canoeing, and soaking up the views. Pricier, but worth it.

Amazon Gero Tours   ECOTOUR
(☑9983-6273; www.amazongero.com; Rua 10 de Julho 695) Gero Mesquita, an effusive and all-round good guy, runs a popular lodge in the Juma-Mamori area with comfortable dorms and private rooms, and a cadre of skilled guides (several former guides have opened agencies of their own). Besides standard tours, Gero arranges multiday treks into untouched forest and offers 'social sustainability' programs where travelers work on needed community projects.

Malocas Jungle Lodge   ECOTOUR
(☑3648-0119, 9128-4741; www.malocas.com) Tranquility prevails at this simple jungle lodge, located on a quiet bend of the Rio Preto da Eva and run completely on solar power. The rooms, occupying a large circular *maloca*, are a bit downtrodden, but the tours and overall vibe are great, including hiking, canoeing and swimming in the area's many small waterfalls. Operated by a friendly French-Brazilian couple.

Dolphin Lodge   ECOTOUR
(☑3663-0392, 8806-4777; www.dolphinlodge.tur.br) For years this was the preferred lodge of an agency selling upscale group packages. But it's operating independently now, so regular guidebook-toting travelers can enjoy the lodge's comfortable rooms and unblemished views from its perch atop a high riverbank in the Mamori-Juma area. The friendly owner ably runs the lodge and tours, while the booking system is steadily improving.

There was no tour office in Manaus at the time of research, so take extra care to be sure you're dealing directly with lodge's owners when booking.

Amazonas Indian Turismo   ECOTOUR
(☑9198-3575;   amazonasindian@hotmail.com; Andradas 311) This longtime budget agency has a rustic camp on the Rio Urubú, with latrine toilets and no electricity. You won't spend much time there, though, as the operator specializes in multiday hikes through the forest, sleeping in makeshift camps, hammocks slung between two trees. Notable for being indigenous owned and operated; most guides are Wapixano, and all speak English.

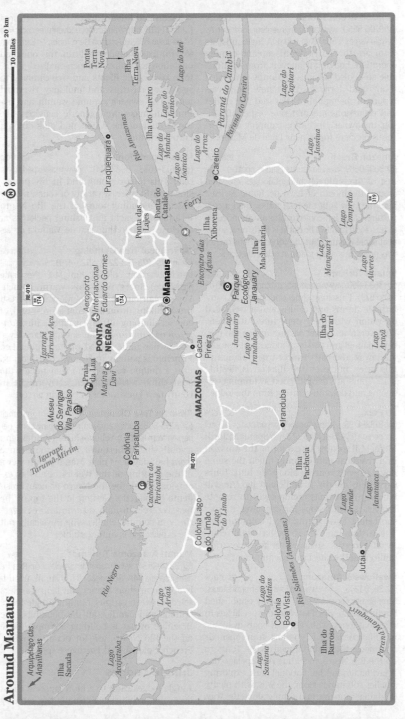

Around Manaus

N

10 miles
20 km

Arquipélago das
Anavilhanas

Ilha
Sacada

Lago
Acajatuba

Rio Negro

Igarapé
Tarumã-Mirim

Museu
do Seringal
Vila Paraíso

Colônia
Paricatuba

Cachoeira do
Paricatuba

Igarapé
Tarumã-Açu

RE-010
BR
174

Aeroporto
Internacional
Eduardo Gomes

BR
174

PONTA
NEGRA

Praia
da Lua

Marina
Davi

Manaus

Puraquequara

Rio Amazonas

Ponta das
Lajes

Ponta Terra
Nova

Ilha
Terra Nova

Lago do Rei

Ilha do Careiro

Lago do Careiro

Lago do
Mandi

Lago do
Janio

Lago do
Arroz

Paraná do Crambix

Paraná do Careiro

Lago do
Capituri

Lago
Jassua

BR
319

Lago
Comprido

Lago
Atveres

Lago
Manguari

Lago do
Joanico

Ponta do
Catalão

Careiro

Ferry

Encontro das
Águas

Ilha
Xiborena

Ilha
Machantaria

Parque
Ecológico
Janauary

Lago
Janauary

Lago do
Iranduba

Cacau
Pireira

AMAZONAS

RE-070

Colônia
Lago do Limão

Lago
do Limão

Lago
Ariaú

Colônia
Boa Vista

Lago do
Matias

Lago
Santana

Ilha do
Barroso

Rio Solimões (Amazonas)

Iranduba

Ilha
Paciência

Ilha do
Curari

Lago
Grande

Lago
Jamanaca

Lago
Aruçá

Jutaí

Paraná à Mamaguri

RE-010
BR
174

Amazon Green Tours ECOTOUR
(☑ 9106-5650; www.amazongreentour.com; cnr Av Getúlio Vargas & Rua 10 de Julho) A husband-wife team are the heart of this up-and-coming operation. Lodging is uneven, from comfortable air-cooled cabanas to dumpy fan-cooled rooms and dorm space. (A new lodge was reportedly being built.) That said, the guides and excursions are first rate (especially Elson, the owner), including camping in a gorgeous patch of forest near Lago de Mamori.

Amazon Brasil ECOTOUR
(☑ 3087-0689; www.amazonjungletours.com.br) The best of three (three!) budget lodges crowded around the mouth of Lago de Juma. At least here the view is of the lake rather than a cow pasture. Large fan-cooled cabins are attended by a stern local family. The outfit is fairly new, so expect some hiccups, but the conscientious owner was previously a top guide at other agencies.

Iguana Turismo ECOTOUR
(☑ 3633-6507; www.amazonbrasil.com.br; Rua 10 de Julho 679) This long-time operator has comfortable dorms and cabins and a well-oiled operation with daily departures. It suffers, however, from a cow pasture across the narrow channel and two rival lodges just a stone-toss away. You can't expect true isolation at this price, but even the illusion is fleeting here. Tours are decent; good swimming, canoeing and dolphin-spotting from the lodge.

Lo Peix ECOTOUR
(☑ 8182-4793; http://lopeix.typepad.com; all-incl per person R$435-1680, 3-12 days) Spaniard Jordi Miguel Gil spent years exploring the Amazon in a riverboat and is doing much the same now but with tourists alongside him. Tours vary from nearby Arquipélago das Anavilhanas (Anavilhanas archipelago) to remote Rio Araca, with stops for canoeing, hiking, snorkeling and visiting local communities. The custom-built riverboat has small comfortable berths, solar power for max tranquility and the latest safety equipment.

Swallows & Amazons ECOTOUR
(☑ 3622-1246; www.swallowsandamazonstours.com; Ramos Ferreira 922) This long-established South African–Brazilian agency specializes in riverboat tours, with different boats available for different levels of comfort, from open-air hammocks to air-conditioned cabins. Tours go up the Rio Negro, including Arquipélago das Anavilhanas and Jaú national park, exploring smaller tributaries along the way, with plenty of hiking, canoeing and fishing along the way.

Amazon Eco Adventures ECOTOUR
(☑ 8831-1011; http://amazonecoadventures.com; Rua 10 de Julho 695, at Amazon Gero Tours; ⊙ 8am-5pm Mon-Fri) Exceptionally well-run, this one-man operation specializes in personalized tours, from panoramic flights and tree-climbing to speedboat daytrips and multiday riverboat tours. The owner's genuine warmth and enthusiasm make even generic activities like the Meeting of the Waters and pink dolphin encounters fun.

Maia Expeditions ECOTOUR
(☑ 3613-4683, 9983-7141; www.maiaexpeditions.com) This long-running and highly professional outfit offers a variety of tours, mostly upscale, including tours of the Rio Negro in a modern yacht and fishing packages at a deluxe lodge in the Lago de Mamori area.

★ Tropical Tree Climbing ECOTOUR
(☑ in US 973-783-2277, 2123-4791; www.tropicaltreeclimbing.com; BR-178 Km 144, Presidente Figueiredo) Tours with this warm French-Venezuelan operation include garden-fresh meals, hiking through verdant forest and, of course, climbing a tree – usually a huge *angelim* or *samaúma* – for spectacular views. The owner-guide (noted photographer Leo Principe) is patient and knowledgeable, and uses a unique rope system that makes the 50m climb reasonably easy. Overnight in comfy new guestrooms or even in a tree!

Amazon Tree Climbing ECOTOUR
(☑ 8195-8585; www.amazontreeclimbing.com; per person from R$220) Yellow-shirted guides lend a youth vibe to this outfit, whose tours range from half-day trips near Manaus with views of the Meeting of the Waters to all-day excursions along the Rio Negro or near Presidente Figueiredo. Getting to the top of the massive trees, usually a *samaúma* or *angelim*, can be quite challenging physically, but the experience is unforgettable.

Manati Amazônia Turismo TRAVEL
(☑ 3234-2534; www.manatiamazonia.com; Rua Independência 44A, Redenção) This small, friendly and competent agency can help travelers select between various tour and jungle-lodge options and handles all the bookings. The Brazilian owner is building a simple lodge on the Rio Negro; ask for details. English, French, Spanish and Portugese spoken.

Jungle Lodges

Jungle lodges cater to a more upscale client base; the activities are usually the same as those offered by operators in Manaus, but the lodging, food and service tend to be somewhat more refined (and the prices substantially higher).

Anavilhanas Jungle Lodge
LODGE $$

(☑ 3622-8996; www.anavilhanaslodge.com; per person per day all-inclusive from R$250; ❋) This well-run lodge is located on a secluded bend of the Rio Negro, yet is accessible by paved road. That cuts your transfer time considerably. The cabins have electric lighting, private bathrooms, even air-conditioning, yet guests have direct access to pristine forest and waterways, including the namesake Arquipélago das Anavilhanas.

Amazon Eco Lodge
LODGE $$$

(☑ 3308-8393; http://www.amazonlodgeamazonas.com.br; 3-night packages per person R$1300-1800) A homey floating lodge in a secluded corner of the long Juma lake. Standard rooms are small but comfortable, while larger end-suites have private outdoor showers; none have private toilets, however.

Juma Lodge
LODGE $$$

(☑ 3232-2707; www.jumalodge.com; all-inclusive packages from 3 days/2 nights s/d jungle view R$1900/2700, lake view US$2000/3000) The deluxe lakefront cabins here stand dramatically on 15m stilts, connected by wood walkways, with huge screened windows and private patios. West-facing units can get hot in the late afternoon, but that's when you might be sipping a caipirinha in the lodge's shady deck or spacious communal dining area. Tours make use of comfortable motorized canoes, though groups can be large.

Rio Negro Basin

The Upper Rio Negro is one of the most beautiful and unusual regions of Brazilian Amazonia. There are three major towns, including Barcelos (closest to Manaus) and São Gabriel da Cachoeira (the furthest). Barcelos is adjacent to Mariuá Archipelago, the largest fluvial archipelago in the world with over 750 islands. It's a known fishing destination, but still off the beaten path for independent travelers. Even fewer tourists make it to São Gabriel da Cachoeira, a pleasant town surrounded by forest and beckoning peaks. São Gabriel has some nascent ecotourism options, and is a backdoor adventure route to Colombia or Venezuela.

Barcelos

Barcelos is no secret to fishermen, foreign and Brazilian alike, who flock to the small town for *tucanaré* (peacock bass) package tours. Fleets of yachts and riverboats serve eager khaki-clad anglers, and locals earn good money as guides and boat crew. Nonfishing tourism, however, is relatively rare, though not for lack of potential. Barcelos provides access to the world's largest river archipelago and Brazil's highest waterfall, though established tours to both are still in the making. Barcelos holds a lively ornamental fish festival each January, complete with rival camps, the Discs and the Cardinals.

◉ Sights & Activities

Praia Grande
BEACH

This is Barcelos' biggest and most accessible beach. It's on an island directly opposite town, and is a short R$2 boat ride from the main dock. Shacks serve hot meals and cold drinks, especially on summer weekends. There are many smaller, more secluded beaches a bit further away, where boatmen can drop you off for a few hours.

Serra do Aracá State Park
WATERFALL, PARK

Although this state park was established in 1990 to preserve the unique canyonlands carved out by the Rio Aracá, it wasn't until recently that the massive waterfall at its heart was officially measured and certified. Turns out, Cachoeira do El Dorado is Brazil's highest waterfall, plunging 353m over a sandstone cliff into a mist-swept pool below.

It's possible to reach the falls – a two- to three-day journey by boat and on foot, and by all acounts gorgeous – but there were no established excursions there at the time of research. Ask at Hostel Barcelos about arranging a trip.

☞ Tours

Amazonas Mataverde
ECOTUR

(☑ 9185-6071; www.barcelosecotur.com; per person per day R$100-120, food & lodging only R$60) Four hours by motorized canoe from Barcelos, this simple camp has good hiking and even better canoeing, exploring the islands and waterways of the labyrinthine Mariuá archipelago, with a chance to see birds, turtles, dolphins, even river otters. Operated by a young Spaniard and his Brazilian wife, who grew up in a nearby village; contact directly or through Hostel Barcelos.

WORTH A TRIP

PARINTINS

Tens of thousands of people descend on Parantins on the last weekend of June for the **Boi-Bumbá festival**, an Amazonian version of the Northeast's Bumba Meu Boi, and one of the Amazon's largest parties. The festival centers around a rivalry between two 'clans,' the Caprichoso, who dress all in blue, and Garantido, who dress in red. Parintins' hotels are booked months in advance, but travelers can usually score hammock space on one of the hundreds of riverboats that head there from Manaus and elsewhere. A five-night boat trip east from Manaus including transportation to and from Parantins and lodging aboard the boat (but no meals) costs around R$700.

Rates include transport, food, lodging (hammocks or private cabin) and guided tours. However, guests are welcome to hang out at the lodge, taking just one tour per day or none at all, for around R$60 per person per day.

🛏 Sleeping & Eating

Hostel Barcelos　　　　　　　　HOSTEL $
(☑ 9179-7657; http://hostelbarcelos.com; Anauali 46; hammock per person R$10, private rooms per person R$20; 🛜) Comfortable rooms, a swimming pool and a hands-on Lithuanian expat owner who serves a mean lime-passionfruit-vodka cocktail all make this the go-to spot for travelers arriving in Barcelos. Located near the airport; free wi-fi, but no TV or air-conditioning. Reservations essential.

Hotel Rio Negro　　　　　　　　HOTEL $
(☑ 3321-1260; hotelrionegrobarcelos@hotmail.com; s/d R$70/100) An attractive and reliable choice that has large clean rooms with TV and air-conditioning; rear units have views of the river. The hotel also has its own pier and can arrange short fishing trips for people not interested in the big multiday packages.

Camaleón Beach Grill　　　　　BRAZILIAN $
(mains R$5-25) This popular eatery is just off the main plaza, but you can't see it from there, as it's partway down the steep river embankment. A wooden stairway leads to platforms where umbrella-shaded tables have views overlooking moored boats, the river and Praia Grande beyond. Grilled fish and meats are served with standard sides.

ℹ Information

Bradesco (Av Mariuá s/n) Bank.
Megastar (Av Mariuá s/n; per hr R$3; ⏱8am-midnight Mon-Sat) Internet.
Tourist Office (Av Mariuá s/n)

São Gabriel da Cachoeira

São Gabriel da Cachoeira is the Upper Rio Negro's largest city, and the nearest to the Colombian and Venezuelan borders, but you'd never guess either from the town's pleasant laid-back vibe. (The large army base is a clue, however.) The town sits on a lovely bend of the Rio Negro, with a long series of rapids stumbling picturesquely by, and sandy beaches lapped by the Negro's blood-orange water. Outside town, several buttes jut up from the rainforest, including a three-peaked mountain known as Bela Adormecida (Sleeping Beauty). São Gabriel has long been the jumping-off point for 10-day journeys up Brazil's highest peak, Pico da Neblina (2994m/9823ft), a rocky wedge awhirl in freezing fog, though the beaurocratic challenges of getting a permit to do so deter all but a few mountaineers. Most of the forest around São Gabriel is Yanomami indigenous land and makes for great hiking and boating, provided you obtain the proper permission. A word of warning: think twice before booking tours to this area with agencies in Manaus. Very few are able to obtain authorization to enter the region's indigenous territories (despite claims to the contrary) and tourists without proper permits have been detained by the Federal Police. Better to make your way to São Gabriel and make arrangements with operators and authorities there.

⊙ Sights & Activities

Pousada Pico da Neblina (p623) is the best place to start for excursions of all kinds. The Australian owner has long-standing contacts with Yanomami tribal leaders, and can obtain guides and necessary permissions, plus arrange for boats and other gear.

(Continued on page 623)

Amazon Wildlife

A huge variety of animals call the Amazon home: piranha and pink dolphins ply the waters, macaws fill the air in squawking flight, squirrel monkeys dart through the trees, and tarantulas and poison dart frogs lurk in the underbrush. The lush rainforest and murky water can make spotting animals quite hard, but all the more rewarding when you do.

Contents
➡ **Land Mammals**
➡ **Birds**
➡ **Aquatic Animals**
➡ **Reptiles, Insects & Amphibians**

Above Squirrel monkey

1. Howler monkey **2.** Three-toed sloth **3.** Tapir **4.** Giant anteater

Land Mammals

➡ **Jaguar** Jaguars are the Americas' largest cat, though Amazonian jaguars are smaller than those elsewhere. During flooding season, they can live for months entirely in the tree tops, munching mainly on sloths. Where to see: Mamirauá, FLONA Tapajós, Upper Rio Negro

➡ **Margay** Small cat that's a master climber with paws that can rotate 180-degrees. Where to see: Mamirauá, Upper Rio Negro

➡ **Three-toed sloth** A fairly common sight, sloths (or *preguiça* in Portuguese) are a favorite prey of jaguars and harpy eagles. Where to see: everywhere

➡ **Squirrel Monkey** Aptly named, squirrel monkey are tiny and agile, living in clans numbering into the hundreds. Where to see: everywhere

➡ **Capuchin Monkey** Early explorers thought this small monkey's brown fur looked like the hooded cape of Capuchin friars. Where to see: everywhere

➡ **Howler Monkey** The male howler monkey's deathly cry can be heard for miles, though spotting the brown or black tree-dwellers can be tough. Where to see: Mamirauá, around Manaus

➡ **Coati** Related to raccoons and similarly clever, coati have long tails and long sensitive noses, which they use to forage for insects, lizards and other small prey. Where to see: everywhere

➡ **Giant Anteater** Distantly related to sloths, Amazonian giant anteaters are skilled climbers, useful for feeding on insect nests built in tree trunks. Where to see: everywhere, but difficult to spot

➡ **Brazilian Tapir** Up to a meter tall and weighing over 200kg, tapirs are a prized but challenging prey for jaguars, caiman, even anaconda, and of course humans. Where to see: everywhere, but difficult to spot

➡ **Spider Monkey** The largest and most intelligent of Amazon monkeys, spider monkeys are also among the most sensitive to human intrusion. Where to see: primary forest areas

Birds

> **Toucan** Its long colorful beak allows the toucan to crack hard nuts, but makes long flight difficult. Its distinctive whistle lets you know one's near. Where to see: everywhere

> **Ibis** With long curved beaks, the brilliant scarlet ibis, or *guará*, prefers mangroves and estuaries, while the larger green ibis is common further inland. Where to see: Algodoal, Ilha Marajó, around Manaus, Mamirauá

> **Macaw** Known as *araras*, Amazonian macaws can be scarlet, green or blue. Macaws mate for life, and pairs can be seen (and heard) in long squawking flights in the morning and evening. Where to see: everywhere

> **Amazon Parrot** Catch-all name for various closely-related species of parrots, mostly green with splashes of red, yellow or blue, and highly adept at mimicking human speech. Where to see: everywhere

> **Harpy Eagle** Over a meter tall, harpy eagles are the Americas' largest raptors, known to snatch monkeys and sloths right out of trees. Where to see: everywhere, but difficult to spot

> **Hoatzin** This pheasant-like bird may be a living link between dinosaurs and modern birds, with its reptilian appearance, poor flying, and claws on its chicks' wings. Where to see: FLONA Tapajós, around Manaus, Upper Rio Negro, Mamirauá

> **Yellow-Rumped Cacique** This talkative yellow-and-black bird is one of the most commonly seen birds in the Amazon, known for building its dangling bag-like nests near active wasps nests. Where to see: everywhere

> **Wattled Jacana** A common bird with a loud urgent call, found in wetlands throughout the Amazon. Male jacanas incubate the eggs, while females may maintain up to four active partners. Where to see: everywhere

1. Harpy eagle 2. Scarlet ibis 3. Macaws 4. Hoatzin

Aquatic Animals

KEVIN SCHAFER/MINDEN PICTURES / CORBIS ©

KEVIN SCHAFER / GETTY IMAGES ©

1. Boto **2.** Piranha **3.** Giant otter

➡ **Giant Otter** Up to 6ft long, giant otters are playful and social, though hunting and trapping (for their soft, extremely dense pelt) has reduced their numbers to critical levels. Where to see: Xixuaú-Xiparina Reserve; Upper Rio Negro

➡ **Boto** The Amazon's famous pink dolphins are easy to spot, occurring in large numbers throughout the river system. Unlike other dolphins, botos can bend their necks and paddle backward, adaptions that help them navigate the flooded forest without getting stuck. Where to see: everywhere

➡ **Tucuxi** The Amazon's 'other' dolphin looks and behaves much like a bottlenose dolphin, but growing to just 1.5m (5ft). Unlike botos, tucuxi do not venture into the flooded forest to feed. Where to see: everywhere

➡ **Amazon Manatee** Although they grow to nearly 3m (10ft) and up to 450kg (1000lb), manatees are extremely difficult to spot in the wild and their precise numbers are unknown. Manatees gorge on aquatic plants during the flood season, and may fast for several months when the water is low. Where to see: Mamirau

➡ **Pirarucú** The world's largest scaled fish, pirarucú (also known as arapaima, outside the Amazon) can grow to 3m (10ft) and 220kg (480lb) and breathe air from the surface. Where to see: around Manaus, Mamirauá

➡ **Sting Ray** Most Amazonian rays have distinctive spots and a nasty sting if you step on them. They are more closely related to Pacific rays than Atlantic ones, one of the clues that the Amazon originally flowed east to west. Where to see: everywhere

➡ **Piranha** The Amazon's most famous fish is found through the river system, and range from 14cm to 26cm (5.5in to 10in). There are at least 30 species of piranha, including the small but aggressive red-bellied piranha. Contrary to myth, piranha rarely bite humans. Where to see: everywhere

Blue poison dart frog

Reptiles, Insects & Amphibians

➡ **Caiman** Caiman are related to alligators and live throughout the Amazon. The largest, black caiman, can grow to 6m, but most are 2m or less. Where to see: Everywhere

➡ **Anaconda** The world's largest snake is known to grow up to 37ft and weigh more than 500lb, though stories of much larger ones abound. They live mostly in swamps and river channels, and eat fish, turtles, and occasionally caiman or land animals such as deer and rodents. Where to see: around Manaus, Mamirauá, but difficult

➡ **Tarantula** The Amazon has several species of huge hairy arachnids, including one with a leg span of more than 33cm (13in). Most tarantulas live in burrows, and hunt insects, frogs, even small birds. Where to see: everywhere

➡ **Morpho Butterfly** The brilliant metallic blue wings of the morpho butterfly have a way of brightening up any forest path. They can grow up to 20cm (8in) across, though most are somewhat smaller. Where to see: everywhere

➡ **Ants** A single acre of Amazonian rainforest can have more than 3.5 million ants, and collectively ants make up 10% to 30% of the Amazon's total animal biomass. There are dozens of species, including leaf-cutter ants and aggressive bullet ants. Where to see: everywhere

➡ **Poison Dart Frog** Most poison dart frogs are tiny (around 1.5cm) and brightly colored. Some secrete a powerful toxin, which indigenous Amazonians used to make their blow darts even more potent. Where to see: everywhere, but difficult

(Continued from page 614)

Climbing Bela Adormecida (four to five days, R$175 per person per day, two person minimum) is the most popular option, and includes motoring up the ink-black Rio Curicuriari, with its picturesque rapids and rock formations; visiting Yanomami villages; and hiking through towering rainforest to reach the thousand-meter peaks.

Ilha do Sol is a long sandy island in the middle of the river opposite Barrio Praias. Boats ferry beach-goers from the shore to the island (R$2, five minutes), where you'll find a small restaurant and great swimming. Sundays are especially busy.

🛏 Sleeping & Eating

★Pousada Pico da Neblina   POUSADA $
(☑9168-0047; www.pousadapicodaneblina.com; Rua Capitão Euclides, Barrio da Praia; camping per person R$10, dm with fan R$23, s/d with air-con R$45/70) Occupying a grand old mansion with views of São Gabriel's best beach, Pico da Neblina has comfortable, newly renovated private rooms and dorms (which come with breakfast) and space for hammocks and tents in the garden and exterior passageways. Free wi-fi and community kitchen for all, and the Australian owner, who also owns Hostel Manaus in Manaus, arranges excellent tours.

Hotel Deus Me Deu   HOTEL $
(☑3471-1395; Av Presidente Castelo Branco 313; s/d R$55/100) The 2nd-floor reception area has a sunny patio with tables and chairs, overlooking the street. Rooms in the rear are clean, basic and perfectly acceptable; some with mini-split air-conditioners. No wi-fi, but there's an internet cafe directly below, and most other services are within a couple blocks. Run by a friendly family that lives on-site.

Restaurante Dina   SELF-SERVICE $
(☑3471-1552; 31 de Março s/n; per kg $30; ☺7am-3pm, closed Mon) Popular self-service spot located two long blocks from the soccer field.

ℹ Information

Banco do Brasil (Av Presidente Castelo Branco s/n; ☺8am-1pm Mon-Fri) ATMs.

Bradesco (Av Presidente Castelo Branco s/n; ☺8am-1pm Mon-Fri) Bank.

Maraska Net (Av Presidente Castelo Branco s/n; per hr R$3; ☺9am-9pm Mon-Fri) Internet access below the Hotel Deus Me Deu.

Post Office (Rua 31 de Março; ☺7:30am-noon, 1:30-4pm Mon-Fri)

Xixuaú-Xipariná

This gorgeous but little-visited area includes a vast swath of pristine rainforest along the Rio Jauaperí in southern Roraima state, some 500km (35 to 40 hours by boat) from Manaus. It is one of the best places in the Amazon to see giant river otters, not to mention monkeys, dolphins, wild boars and caimans. (Although not technically part of the Upper Rio Negro, or even the state of Amazonas, you access it via there.)

There's an ecolodge founded by a Scottish transplant named Cris Clark (who still lives there full time), but technically owned and operated by Asociação Amazônia (www.amazoniabr.org), an organization of local residents. A large *maloca*-style lodge has common dining and hammock areas, while smaller cabins have double beds, bathroom, and verandas. The nearby community has a public telephone and even satellite internet. Tours are led by local guides, while Clark helps manage the lodge and arrange your visit. The lodge is open year-round, though April and May see extremely heavy rain.

Visits start at €120 per person per day, including transportation, with a week being the minimum, considering you burn up almost three days just getting there and back.

Parque Nacional do Jaú

Spanning nearly 23,000 sq km, Jaú is Brazil's second-biggest national park, and one of the largest tracts of protected tropical rainforest in the world. It stretches west from the Rio Negro along the Jaú and Carabinani rivers, and is rich in flora and fauna. The park was designated a Unesco World Heritage listing in 2000.

There are no lodges in the park, so it's best to visit with a tour outfit that specializes in riverboat tours, such as Swallows & Amazons (p612) or Lo Peix (p612), both in Manaus. Booking is essential, as the operator must obtain special permission to enter the park.

Tefé

☑097 / POP 61,000
A gritty bustling town, Tefé sits on the shores of the massive Lago Tefé, with good opportunities for hiking, boating and visiting local indigenous villages. Tefé is best known as the jumping-off point to Reserva

de Desenvolvimento Sustentável Mamirauá (Mamirauá Reserve), one of the best overall eco-destinations in the Amazon. But Tefé's leaders have worked mightily to convince Mamiraua-bound tourists to budget time for exploring Tefé too. New tourism projects, combined with improved air and boat transport options, are slowly but surely making Tefé a destination unto itself.

Sights & Activities

Tefé's tourism infrastructure is still in its infancy. For now, the best way to explore the area is to contact Bettine Robers, the Dutch owner of Pousada Multicultura (p624), who arranges a variety of day trips (and was recently appointed Tefé's Secretary of Tourism).

Set on high riverbank bluffs a short distance downriver from Tefé, three side-by-side **indigenous villages** make for an interesting day trip. Villagers are assimilated (that is, wear Western clothes and speak Portuguese) but come from three different native groups and maintain certain traditions. Trips here typically include boating to the furthest village and backtracking on foot, visiting local homes along the way.

Nearer to Tefé, **As Misões** (The Missions) was founded in 1897 and remains a working seminary, with a well-kept garden, a huge church, and a cemetery full of former missionaries. It's also a vocational training center, where many of Tefé's masons, metalworkers and other tradesmen got their start.

Tefé has a small **Encontro das Aguas** (Meeting of the Waters), where an offshoot of the creamy brown Solimões merges with the red-black water pouring out of Lago de Tefé. It's an excellent place to spot pink dolphins.

Pousada Multicultura has a large plot of land outside Tefé that's part forest, part fruit plantation, with a stream and rustic cabin. It's a good place to spot monkeys and various tree species; Robers' Brazilian husband leads short hikes there, customized to guests' time and interests.

Sleeping & Eating

★**Pousada Multicultura**   POUSADA $
(☑ 3343-6632; www.pousadamulticultura.com; Rua 15 de Junho 136; dm R$40, s/d R$55/80, s with lake view R$80-100, d with lake view R$110-130; ✴ ☎) Tefé's best lodging for a bunch of reasons: rooms are comfortable and affordable, all with air-conditioning. The

hillside perch makes for outstanding views of the lake and beyond. And the friendly multilingual Dutch-Brazilian owners are the best source of pretty much everything you may need, including daytrips around Tefé, restaurant recommendations, information on Mamirauá, and even plane and boat reservations.

Egas Hotel   HOTEL $
(☑ 3343-6299; egashotel@hotmail.com; cnr Ruas Getúlio Vargas & Daniel Servalho; s R$90, d R$120-150, tr R$180; ✴ ☎) Large clean rooms, most opening onto breezy corridors, and a convenient location near both parks and opposite a bank and internet cafe. You'll be greeted with friendly service.

Hotel Patricia   HOTEL $
(☑ 3343-2541; Praça Tulio Azevêdo; s/d R$40/70; ✴) The best of Tefé's cheap hotels is run like a guesthouse by a friendly grandma figure. Rooms with windows onto the street are tolerable, others grimy and unpleasant; all have air-con, TV, and wi-fi.

Restaurant Ki-Papo   SELF-SERVE, BRAZILIAN $
(Rua Juruá; per kg R$25; ☺11am-3pm) Friendly low-key per-kilo place with good food and an amazing panoramic view of Lago de Tefé. A short walk east of the center, but well worth it.

Restaurante Stylo   BRAZILIAN $
(Floriano Peixoto 190; mains R$8-35; ☺10am-10pm Mon-Sat) The most reliable eatery in the center, with hefty, well-prepared dishes served at outdoor tables right on the street corner. The menu includes all the standard fish, meat and chicken dishes, plus a few less-common ones, such as *lingua na brasa* (grilled tongue).

Pizzaria Varandas   PIZZERIA $
(pizza R$15-40; ☺3-11pm Tue-Sun) Bright welcoming pizzeria, with red, white and green table settings, both inside and along the sidewalk. You can order up to three different topping combinations on a single pizza, including dessert toppings, like banana with condensed milk.

Drinking

Barzinho   BAR
(Rua Olavo Bilac) Perched on a small rise above one of Tefé's main drags – with a tree growing through the floor and out the roof – this is a cool little spot to have a beer or two and listen to live music, mostly of the singer-songwriter variety.

PRESIDENTE FIGUEIREDO

Self-named the 'Terra de Cachoeiras' (Land of Waterfalls), this dusty little town is surrounded by dozens of waterfalls and caves. Among the most impressive are Iracema, Cachoeira da Onza, Caverna do Maroaga, Gruta Judéia, Santuario, Asaframa and Pedra Furada (the most distant of the falls, 60km from town). You need a vehicle to visit the waterfalls here; you can rent a car from Manaus (125km south), or take the bus and hire a guide in Presidente Figueiredo; there's a tourist kiosk a short distance from the bus station. Several agencies in Manaus offer tours in this area, too, notably Amazon Eco Adventures (p612) and Tropical Tree Climbing (p612). Be aware that this is the only leisure spot easily accessible by road from Manaus, and so it gets obscenely packed most weekends.

Banzarê BAR
(☑ 3343-4448; Duque de Caixias 35; ☺ 3pm-3am Wed-Sun) One of several roadside restaurant-bars in a mango-tree-shaded spot known as Muralha, located just off Tefé's main drag, with open-air tables and nice river views. Food and drink service.

ℹ Orientation

Most of the main hotels, restaurants and services are within a block or two of Tefé's two central plazas. The main plaza – not because it's larger, but because it has the church – is Praça Santa Tereza, a long tapered wedge running roughly east–west, with the church on the western end. A block north is Praça Tulio Azevêdo, a more traditional square with trees, benches and newsstands. Beyond that is the municipal market and the waterfront. Both plazas are bordered by busy streets, down which flows a constant stream of scooters and moto-taxis.

ℹ Information

EMERGENCY
Ambulance (☑ 192)
Hospital São Miguel (☑ 3343-2469; Rua Marechal Deodoro 66)
Police (☑ 190)

INTERNET ACCESS
Eganet (Rua Gétulio Vargas; per hr R$3; ☺ 8am-10:30pm Mon-Sat) Opposite the Egas Hotel.

LAUNDRY
Lavandería do Paulo (Daniel Servalho 345; per item R$0.50-2; ☺ 7am-5:30pm Mon-Fri, to noon Sat)

MONEY
Banco do Brasil (Rua Olavo Bilac at Praça Tulio Azevêdo; ☺ 9am-2pm Mon-Fri)
Bradesco (cnr Ruas Getúlio Vargas & Daniel Servalho)

POST
Post Office (Estrada Aeroporto; ☺ 8am-4pm Mon-Fri)

TRAVEL AGENCIES
Pousada Multicultura (☑ 3343 6632; www.pousadamulticultura.com; Rua 15 de Junho 136) The multilingual owners can purchase boat and plane tickets to and from Tefé, and even email you a printable ticket in some cases; service fee is 15% of the ticket price. They also offer highly informative tours to local sights, natural areas and indigenous villages.

ℹ Getting There & Away

AIR
TRIP (☑ 4003-1118; www.voeazul.com.br) has two daily flights daily to and from Manaus, and two flights per week to and from Tabatinga.
Amazonaves (☑ in Manaus 92-3654 5555; www.amazonaves.com.br; Terminal Eduardinho, Manaus) has one flight daily to and from Manaus, using small propeller planes. TRIP is certainly more comfortable but can be pricey if tickets aren't bought well in advance.

BOAT
Slow boats between Manaus and Tefé (hammock R$135, d cabin R$400 to R$590, 36 hours) depart in both directions six days per week. Boats to and from Tabatinga (R$140, 40 to 48 hours) don't dock in Tefé proper; instead, take a boat to the village of Nogueira and taxi from there to Alvarães. Do the reverse if arriving from Tabatinga, but be aware that taxis and boats are available only during the daytime.

AJATO (☑ in Manaus 92-3622-6047, in Tefe 3343-5306; ajatonavegacao@r7.com) has comfortable speedboat service to and from Manaus (R$220, 13 hours), with departures six to seven days per week at 7am, and to and from Tabatinga ($380, 24 hours), with departures twice weekly.

Advance reservations are recommended, especially for speed boats. Pousada Multicultura (p625) has up-to-date transport information and can book tickets for a small fee.

BLACK & WHITE

There are three types of rivers in the Amazon Basin: *negro* (black), *branco* (white) and *claro* (clear). White rivers (actually more a creamy beige) come from the Andes, and get their color from sediment eroded from those 'young' mountains. These rivers – including the Solimões and Madeira – are loaded with nutrients and can support more plants and animals along their path.

Black rivers, such as the Rio Negro and Rio Urubú, originate in northern Amazonia and flow over much older land, long swept clean of sediment. Black rivers tend to be slower and warmer than white ones (which start as snowpack in the Andes, after all) and the vegetation in them has time to rot, releasing organic acids. Those acids turn the water 'black,' actually a tealike color. The same acids kill mosquito larvae, meaning black-water areas have amazingly few mosquitoes and a low incidence of malaria and other diseases.

Clear rivers have neither the sediment nor the organic acids that would make them white or black. The massive Tapajós and Arapiuns rivers are clear, and small tributaries in predominantly white or black water areas can be clear if their course happens to allow it.

Both white and black water rivers flood seasonally, but the result is not the same, at least in name. Forest flooded with black water is referred to as *igapó*, while forest flooded with white water is called *várzea*.

Reserva de Desenvolvimento Sustentável Mamirauá

By many accounts the Amazon's best eco-tourism operation, the Mamirauá Sustainable Development Reserve offers the visitor pristine rainforest, comfortable lodging and an excellent guide service, yet is just 1½ hours by boat from a large town with reliable air and boat service. The price can be prohibitive for some, but with so many places claiming to be eco-this and eco-that, Mamirauá is one of few places in the Amazon that really does it right.

Mamirauá is Brazil's last large area of *várzea* (forests seasonally flooded with sediment-rich 'white water'). It covers 12,400 sq km northwest of Tefé between the Solimões and Japurá rivers. The park's eastern edge merges with the Amanã reserve, which in turn borders Jaú national park. Together the three reserves span 57,000 sq km, making up the second-largest block of protected tropical rainforest in the world.

Mamirauá was Brazil's first sustainable development reserve (there are now 20). Its purpose is to combine nature conservation and scientific research, while promoting sustainable practices and improved opportunities for the local population. There are numerous small communities within the Mamirauá reserve; many residents work part time as tour guides, cooks and boat drivers while continuing traditional work such as fishing, planting and hunting under a mutually agreed sustainable-use plan.

The reserve is ably managed by the **Instituto Mamirauá** (☏ 3343-4160; www.mamiraua.org.br; Rua Brasil 197; ⊘ 8am-noon & 2-6pm Mon-Fri, 8am-noon Sat). Packages are coordinated with the Manaus–Tefé flight schedule, and priced according to the length of stay: R$1350 per person for four days/three nights (Friday to Monday); US$1650 per person for five days/four nights (Monday to Friday); and US$2250 per person for eight days/seven nights; single rooms carry a R$100 per night surcharge in the peak season. Accommodations are in the **Pousada Uacari** (www.pousadauacari.com.br), an excellent floating lodge with spacious, comfortable bungalow-style units, each with hot-water bathrooms, solar energy and a small patio with hammock. The lodge has a large common area where generous meals are served.

Tours include food, lodging, guides and boat transfer to and from Tefé, plus pick-up and drop-off at airport or speedboat port. Visitors to Mamirauá can be reasonably assured of seeing sloths, caimans and dolphins, and dozens of birds, such as macaws and toucans. There are five species of monkeys, including howlers, capuchins and the highly elusive white uakari, an endemic species that's notable for its crimson face and shaggy white coat. Manatees, anacondas, margays, and jaguars also live in the reserve but are extremely difficult to spot.

You'll also visit a local village and one of the reserve's ongoing research projects.

Both can be fascinating, and you'll likely see dolphins, birds and even monkeys along the way. A new option is a night in the 'tree house,' a one-room cabin on 5m stilts a short way into the forest with great early-morning bird-watching. An English-speaking naturalist is at the main lodge at all times (and accompanies some excursions) but most guides speak Portuguese only.

High water here is in June and July, when the forest is completely flooded and you glide through the water in canoes. (This is not to be confused with rainy season, which runs from December to May). This is when monkeys and sloths are most visible, and tends to be the busiest time. In low water, roughly October and November, hiking is possible and aquatic animals, especially fish and caimans, are more concentrated.

The Triple Frontier

The Brazilian town of Tabatinga and the Colombian town of Leticia lie side by side on the eastern bank of the Amazon River, about 1100km west of Manaus, while the far bank belongs to Peru. A logical travel hub, the 'triple frontier' also happens to be a good area for taking jungle trips, particularly to remote areas up the Rio Javari (the Brazil–Peru border) and further up the Amazon in Colombia.

Most travelers stay in Leticia, which is more pleasant and better equipped than Tabatinga or the small villages on the Peruvian side.

Tabatinga
097 / POP 52,250

Tabatinga is most notable as the place where the Amazon River enters Brazil; otherwise, it's a nondescript border town. Boats headed down to Manaus and up to Iquitos in Peru depart from Tabatinga's two ports, and its airport serves Brazilian and Peruvian destinations.

🛏 Sleeping & Eating

Hotel Restaurant Te Contei?　　HOTEL $
(3412-4548; Av da Amizade 1813; s/d R$50/70; ❄) Large rooms with air-conditioning off a breezy upstairs patio and corridor. The back rooms have less street noise, and there's a popular self-serve restaurant (per kg $25) on the ground floor.

Pousada Takanás　　HOTEL $
(3412-3557; Oswaldo Cruz 970; s/d R$88/118, ste R$140/160; ❄🛜) Tabatinga's best hotel has

The Triple Frontier

reasonably modern rooms, with hot water, air-conditioning, TV and minibar, plus a lush central courtyard. A bit removed from the main drag, but that's not necessarily a bad thing. Suites are larger and have king-size beds.

Restaurante Tres Fronteiras do Amazonas　　BRAZILIAN $
(3412-2341; Rua Rui Barbosa; mains R$9-20; ⊙breakfast, lunch & dinner) Try the *peixe tres fronteiras,* a fish fillet with spices from Peru, Brazil and Colombia, served on a large banana leaf. Wash it down with a beer or caipirinha. Located 200m west of Av da Amizade.

Churrascaria Tia Helena　　BRAZILIAN $
(3412-2165; Marechal Mallet 12; all-you-can-eat per person R$28; ⊙lunch) Waiters bring skewered meats directly from the grill and carve it at the table in classic *churrascaria* fashion. Decor is austere (think cement floors and fluorescent lights), but the food is good and the ambience cheerful.

ⓘ Orientation

Tabatinga's main artery is Av da Amizade (aka Av Principal), which runs parallel to the river for 3km from Tabatinga's airport to Leticia and the international border. The most useful cross streets include Rua Marechal Rondon (250m south of the border), Rua Rui Barbosa (650m), Av Marechal Mallet (900m), Rua Santos Dumont (1.2km) and Rua Duarte Coelho (1.7km). Rua Santos Dumont leads to Porto da Feira, Tabatinga's small-boat port; you can also get there by going down Av Marechal Mallet, turning left at the end and passing the market. Porto Fluvial, where boats for Manaus dock, is at the end of Rua Duarte Coelho.

❶ Information

CONSULATES
Colombian Consulate (☑097-3412-2104; Sampaio 623)

EMERGENCY
Hospital Militar (☑3412-2117, 3412-2403, 192; Rua Duarte Coelho, at Av da Amizade)
Police (☑190)

IMMIGRATION
Polícia Federal (☑3412-2180; Av da Amizade 26; ⊙8am-6pm) One hundred meters south of Rua Duarte Coelho.

INTERNET ACCESS
Digital Net (☑3412-3505; Pedro Teixera 397; per hr R$2; ⊙8am-noon & 2-10pm Mon-Sat) On the street parallel to Av Marechal Mallet, one block south.

MONEY
Bradesco (Av da Amizade, at Av Marechal Mallet)

POST
Post Office (Av da Amizade s/n; ⊙8am-5pm Mon-Fri) Located 300m north of the federal police station.

TRAVEL AGENCIES
CNM Câmbio e Turismo (☑3412-3281; Av da Amizade 2017) Also exchanges money.

❶ Getting There & Away

AIR
The airport is 4km south of Tabatinga; coming from Leticia, catch one of the *colectivos* marked 'Comara.'

Trip-AZUL (☑reservations 0300-789-8747; www.voeazul.com.br) has two to three flights daily between Manaus and Tabatinga, and twice-weekly to and from Tefé. Prices vary widely, and advanced booking is always recommended.

BOAT
Slow boats to Manaus (hammock R$350; seven days) leave from the Porto Fluvial every Wednesday and Saturday, plus some Tuesdays, between 8am and noon. Arrive early to stake out good hammock space, as boats can be quite crowded.

Speedboats operated by **AJATO** (☑in Porto Manaus Moderna 3622-6047, in Tabatinga 3412-2227; ⊙8am-5pm Mon-Fri, 8am-noon Sat) leave Tabatinga for Manaus (R$500, 35 hours) on Sunday and Tuesday at 6am and Friday at 8am.

To get to Tefé, the Sunday and Tuesday speedboats to Manaus now make a stop in Tefé proper (R$380, 22 to 24 hours). Otherwise, take a Manaus-bound slow boat as far as the town of Alvarães (R$140, 44 to 48 hours) where you can catch a shared taxi to the village Nogueira (R$6, 20 minutes) and then a motor boat (R$6, 20 minutes) into Tefé; note that taxis and local boats only operate during the day time.

TO/FROM COLOMBIA
The international border is marked by nothing more than a few moneychangers on the Brazilian side and a Colombian police officer directing traffic on the other side. You are free to move between Tabatinga and Leticia as much as you like, but if you plan to travel onward, even to Amacayacu national park, you should clear immigration for both countries – DAS in Colombia, the Polícia Federal in Brazil – before leaving

---

UP RIVER, DOWN RIVER

From the time South America and Africa went their separate ways, and for some 150 million years after that, the Amazon actually flowed east to west, the opposite direction to the way it flows today. That's why Amazonian stingrays are more closely related to Pacific species than Atlantic ones, and how telltale sediment from eastern South America ended up in the middle of the rainforest. It was only 15 to 20 million years ago that the Andes shot up and blocked the water's westward exit. Around the same time, a smaller ridge of land, now called the Purus Arch, rose like a spine in the middle of the continent.

East of the Purus Arch the river started draining into the Atlantic Ocean, but west of there, the water was trapped and a huge inland sea formed. Eventually the water poured over the Purus Arch, gouging a deep channel near present-day Parantins – still the narrowest and deepest part of the river – and the Amazon returned to being a river, but now flowing west to east.

town. If you need it, there's a Colombian consulate in Tabatinga.

TO/FROM PERU

Transtur (☑ 3412-2945; www.portaltabatinga. com.br/transtur.htm) runs high-speed passenger boats – known in Portuguese as *rápidos* – from Tabatinga and Iquitos (US$65, nine to 10 hours, two meals served). Boats depart Tabatinga's Porto da Feira on Wednesday, Friday and Sunday at 5am (boarding begins at 4am). Be sure to get a Brazilian exit stamp the day before; you'll stop at the island community of Santa Rosa, where the Policía Internacional Peruviano (PIP) handles Peruvian border control.

If you just want to get to Santa Rosa, small motorboats go back and forth frequently from Porto da Feria (R$2, five minutes) from around 6am to 6pm.

There is a Peruvian consulate in Leticia, Colombia, as well.

❶ Getting Around

For a *colectivo* (minibus) from the airport to town (R$1.50), walk to the left outside the airport terminal and down the approach road to the corner of the main road. Some continue into Leticia. Taxis and moto-taxis are ubiquitous and inexpensive.

A taxi from the airport costs R$15 to hotels in Tabatinga and R$20 to those in Leticia. Moto-taxis are ubiquitous and cheap (R$2 to R$5) but most cannot cross the international border.

Leticia (Colombia)

☑ 8 / POP 39,700

Leticia is a remarkably spruce little town, with brightly painted houses, pleasant outdoor eateries and well-maintained parks and streets. For travelers, it's got hotels in all price categories, regularly scheduled flights to and from Bogota, and a long-standing military presence that keeps the city and surrounding region safe. It's also the starting point for trips to the Colombia's Parque Nacional Natural Amacayacu, and up the Rio Javari into Peru.

There are no border checkpoints between Tabatinga and Leticia, and you're free to pass back and forth provided you stay within either town. However, do clear immigration if you plan to go any further into Colombia or Peru, even on short-term jungle trips.

◎ Sights

Museo Etnográfico
Amazónico   MUSEUM
(☑ 592-7729; Carrera 11 No 9-43; ☺ 8:30-11:30am & 1:30-5pm Mon-Fri, 9am-1pm Sat) Museo Etnográ-

fico Amazónico has a small collection of *índio* artifacts and implements. Located inside the Banco de la República.

Reserva Tanimboca   NATURE RESERVE
(☑ 310-791-7570; www.tanimboca.com; Km 11, Via Tarapacá; zip-lining COP$60,000, kayaking COP$35,000; hammock/bed per person COP$20,000/25,000; ☺ 8am-4pm) ✎ Visitors can monkey around atop 35m-high trees, then slide 80m along zip lines from one tree to another through the beautiful forest canopy (COP$60,000); and visit the small serpentario (COP$7000). There's also kayaking (COP$35,000). Or splurge for an overnight stay in a treehouse (per person including breakfast COP$99,000), which includes a nocturnal jungle hike.

🛏 Sleeping

Unlike in Brazil, hotels do not commonly offer free breakfast.

Mahatu Jungle Hostel   HOSTEL $
(☑ 311-539-1265; www.mahatu.org; Calle 7 No 1-40; dm COP$20,000-25,000, s/d COP$50,000/60,000; @ 🛜 🌊) An urban jungle in the heart of Leticia, this hostel sits on 5 hectares, complete with duck- and geese-filled ponds, throngs of parrots and loads of exotic fruit trees – cashew, *asaí*, *cananguche* and *copasú* among them. Rooms are very simple, but it has a pool and a community kitchen.

Hospedaje Los Delfines   GUESTHOUSE $$
(☑ 592-7488; losdelfinesleticia@hotmail.com; Carrera 11 No 12-81; s/d COP$40,000/70,000; 🛜) A 10-minute walk from the town center, this small, family-run place has eight spacious if basic rooms with beds and hammocks, surrounding a gorgeously landscaped courtyard filled with flowers and fruit. Good value here (if you manage to get a toilet seat).

Hotel Yurupary   HOTEL $$
(☑ 592-4741; www.hotelyurupary.com; Calle 8 No 7-26; s/d incl breakfast COP$69,000/98,000; ❋ 🛜 🌊) This moderately priced favorite has large, recently refurbished rooms with private bathroom and TV. The outside courtyard features a refreshing swimming pool, garden, bar and restaurant.

🍴 Eating

Food in Leticia is generally good and reasonably priced. The local specialty is fish, including *gamitana* and *pirarucú*.

Leticia (Colombia)

La Casa del Pan BAKERY $
(Calle 11 No 10-20; breakfast COP$4500) Facing Parque Santander, the rickety outdoor tables at this bright, bustling bakery are sensitive – sneeze and you'll spill your coffee. But it's an atmospheric spot for breakfast (eggs, bread and coffee for COP$4500).

Restaurante El Sabor COLOMBIAN $
(Calle 8 No 9-25; set meals COP$7000, mains COP$15,000; ☺6am-11pm Mon-Sat) Leticia's best budget option serves set meals, vegetarian burgers, and fruit salads, plus unlimited free fruit juice with your meal. The banana pancakes are excellent.

ℹ Information

CONSULATES

Brazilian Consulate (☑592-7530; Calle 10 No 9-104; ☺8am-2pm) Citizens of some countries, including the USA, need a visa to enter Brazil. Bring a passport photo and yellow-fever vaccination certificate to the Brazilian Consulate; processing can take up to three days.

Peruvian Consulate (☑592-7204; Calle 11 No 5-32; ☺8am-1pm & 3-6pm Mon-Fri) If you're coming from or going to Iquitos, get your entry or exit stamp at the Peruvian Consulate.

EMERGENCY

Hospital San Rafael de Leticia (☑592-7075; Av Vásquez Cobo 13-78) Has a 24-hour emergency room and pharmacy.

Police (☑112; Carrera 11) Between Calles 12 and 13.

IMMIGRATION

Migración Colombia (☑592-7189; www.migra cioncolombia. gov.co; Leticia Airport; ☺7am-6pm Mon-Fri, 7am-4pm & 7pm-10pm Sat & Sun) Go to the airport for entry/exit stamps.

INTERNET ACCESS

Centro de Negocios (Carrera 10 No 8-96) Has a good selection of terminals in an air-conditioned premises.

LAUNDRY
Lavandería Aseo Total (📞592 6051; Calle 9 No 9-85; wash & dry per lb COP$2700; ⊗7am-9pm Mon-Sat, 8am-1pm Sun)

MONEY
Most businesses in Leticia accept Brazilian reais as well as Colombian pesos. Always check online for the current exchange rate. Banks have ATMs.
Banco de Bogotá (cnr Carrera 10 & Calle 7) ATM.
BBVA Banco Ganadero (cnr Calle 7 & Carrera 10; ⊗8-11:30am & 2-4:30pm)
Casas de Cambio (cnr Calle 8 & Carrera 11) To exchange Colombian, Brazilian, Peruvian, US or European currency.

TOURIST INFORMATION
City Tourist Office (Secretaría de Turismo y Fronteras; 📞592-7569; Calle 8 No 9-75; ⊗8am-noon & 2-5pm Mon-Fri)

⊙ Getting There & Away

AIR
All foreigners must pay COP$19,000 tourist tax upon arrival at Leticia's airport, Aeropuerto Internacional Alfredo Vásquez Cobo. **Copa** (www.copaairlines.com) and **LAN** (www.lan.com) fly from Leticia to Bogotá daily. **Trip** (www.voetrip.com.br) and **TAM** (www.tam.com.br) fly from Tabatinga International Airport to Manaus.

BOAT
Passenger boats headed to and from Iquitos, Peru, stop at the small island community and border post of Isla Santa Rosa, the third part of the 'triple frontier.' Everything is located along the single paved footpath through town, including the office of the Policía Internacional Peruviano (PIP), where you get your passport stamped. Water taxis (COP$3000) ply the Leticia–Santa Rosa route from dawn to dusk.

⊙ Getting Around
The main mode of public transport is moto-taxi, charging COP$1000 for most trips in town, or COP$2000 to Tabatinga. *Colectivos* to Tabatinga wait at the corner of Carrera 10 and Calle 8 (COP$2500) – in Tabatinga, they pass Porto da Feria, the turnoff for Porto Fluvial, the Policía Federal post and the airport, before turning back.

A taxi to Leticia's airport runs COP$7000; there's a stand on Carrera 10 between Calles 7 and 8. *Colectivos* to Leticia's airport leave from Parque Orellana (COP$1000).

To get to Puerto Nariño and Parque Nacional Amacayacu, buy tickets for the fast boat from Transportes Fluviales near the market in Leticia. Boats leave at 8am, 9am and 2pm, take 2½ hours and cost COP$29,000.

Puerto Nariño (Colombia)
📶8 / POP 2000

The tiny Amazonian village of Puerto Nariño, 75km upriver from Leticia, has taken the concept of green living and turned it into an art form. Motorized vehicles are banned. Rainwater is collected in cisterns for washing and gardening. Electricity comes from the town's energy-efficient generator, but only runs until midnight. It's also a great base from which to visit the pink dolphins of Lago Tarapoto by kayak, explore the nearby Amacayacu National Park (PNN Amacayacu), or simply chill out in a hammock, enjoying the sights and sounds of the Amazon.

The majority of Puerto Nariño's residents are indigenous Tikuna, Kokoma, and Yagua peoples.

⊙ Sights & Activities
You can **hike** to several nearby indigenous villages including **San Martín** (three hours) and **20 de Julio** (30 minutes) by following the sidewalks leading out of town. For a bird's-eye view of the village, climb the **Mirador Naipata** observation tower (COP$7000, 6am-6pm) located at the top of Calle 4.

Centro de Interpretación
Natütama   MUSEUM
(www.natutama.org; admission COP$5000; ⊗8am-12:30pm & 2-5pm Wed-Mon) The **Centro de Interpretación Natütama** has a fascinating museum with nearly 100 life-sized wood carvings of Amazonian flora and fauna. There's also a small turtle hatchery outside.

Lago Tarapoto
Lago Tarapoto, 10km west of Puerto Nariño, is a beautiful jungle lake that is home to pink dolphins, manatees and massive Victoria Regia waterlilies. A half-day trip to the lake in a *peque-peque* (motorized canoe) can be organized from Puerto Nariño (COP$50,000 for up to four people). You can organize similar outings to **Parque Nacional Natural Amacayacu**, located a short distance downstream.

🛏 Sleeping & Eating
Alto del Águila   POUSADA $
(📞311-502-8592; altodelaguila@hotmail.com; r per person COP$20,000) A 20-minute walk from town, this magical hilltop retreat with basic rooms is run by a genial and eccentric holy man, accompanied by monkeys and macaws he keeps as pets. It's possible to

arrange cheap excursions into the jungle and nearby communities. Call (or ask around at the dock) when you arrive to arrange a boat pick-up.

Malocas Napu HOTEL $
(☑310-488-0998; olgabeco@yahoo.com; Calle 4 No 5-72; hammocks COP$15,000, r per person with/without balcony COP$30,000/25,000) The rooms are simple but comfortable, with basic furnishings, fan and shared bathrooms. Try for rooms 7 and 8 at the back of the building, which share a balcony with hammocks overlooking the courtyard garden and jungle. Friendly owners.

Casa Selva HOTEL $$
(☑in Bogota 315-333-2796; casaselvahotel@yahoo.es; Carrera 6 No 6-78; s/d/tr COP$112,000/134,000/186,000) A tall, handsome wood building two blocks up from the dock is the most luxurious option in town. The 12 tasteful rooms have bathroom, fan and balcony, surrounding a two-story courtyard and restaurant.

Las Margaritas COLOMBIAN, AMAZONIAN $$
(Calle 6 No 6-80; set meals COP$15,000) Beneath a huge *palapa* (thatched roof), Las Margaritas has excellent home-cooked meals, served buffet-style from traditional clay cookware. Breakfast doesn't stand out as much as lunch and dinner, but it's all shockingly tasty.

ℹ Information

There are no banks or ATMs in Puerto Nariño, and credit cards are not accepted anywhere. Bring plenty of cash from Leticia.

Hospital (cnr Carrera 4 & Calle 5)

Tourist Office (☑313-235-3687; cnr Carrera 7 & Calle 5; ⊘closed Sun) Located inside the town hall.

ℹ Getting There & Away

High-speed boats to Puerto Nariño depart from Leticia's dock at 8am, 10am and 2pm daily (COP$29,000, two hours); return boats to Leticia depart at 7am, 11am and 4pm.

Purchase tickets at **Transportes Fluviales** (☑592-6752; Calle 8 No 11) near the riverfront in Leticia. Boats can get very full, so buy your tickets early or the day before.

Rio Javari

The meandering Rio Javari provides Brazil and Peru with a border, and travelers with excellent opportunities to see the Amazon rainforest up close and undisturbed. A handful of jungle lodges offer accommodations and activities similar to those found elsewhere in the Amazon Basin, including forest walks, fishing, nighttime caiman-spotting, birdwatching and dolphin-watching. It's also possible to visit indigenous settlements (though be forewarned they are not the 'uncontacted' sort many travelers imagine). Petru Popescu's book *Amazon Beaming* relates photographer Loren McIntyre's extraordinary experiences among one of the indigenous groups here. Prices vary according to the number of days and types of activities you schedule, as well as the season. In general, expect to pay US$75 to US$125 per day per person.

Operated by Amazon Jungle Trips, **Zacambú Lodge** (☑57-592-7377; amazonjungletrips@yahoo.com; Av Internacional 6-25, Leticia) is on Lake Zacambú, in a lake region on the Peruvian side of the Javari river. It's the closest of the lodges to the triple frontier – about 70km from Tabatinga, or three hours by motorboat. Accommodations are simple but comfortable, in hammocks or small rooms, with shared toilets. Most excursions are made by motorboat or canoe, for obvious reasons – the bird-watching is excellent.

★**Reserva Natural Palmari** (☑in Bogotá 57-610-3154; www.palmari.org) ✐ is another 20km upstream on the south bank of the river, overlooking a bend where pink and gray dolphins are often seen. A slew of activities and outings are possible, from trekking and canoeing to sport fishing and zip-lines up in the canopy. The lodge receives a number of large groups; you may want to ask how many people will be at the lodge when you are (and adjust your schedule accordingly).

Even further still, **Reserva Natural Heliconia** (☑311-508 5666; www.amazonheliconia.com; Calle 13 No 11-74, Leticia, Colombia) provides room and board in thatch-covered cabins, plus tours via boat or foot of the river, creeks and jungle. There are also organized visits to indigenous villages and special tours devoted to bird-watching and dolphin-watching.

RORAIMA

The tropical rainforest that blankets Roraima's southern half (bisected by the equator) gives way to broad savanna in the middle of the state, and remote and beautiful mountains in the north. It includes most of the Brazilian territories of the Yanomami, one of the country's largest surviving indigenous peoples. The state capital, Boa Vista, still doesn't make the itinerary of most travelers, but has better and better tour options every year. Roraima is home to Monte Roraima (2875m), but this intriguing flat-topped mountain sits on the Brazil–Venezuela–Guyana border, and the best way up is from the Venezuelan side.

Boa Vista

095 / POP 297,000

The state capital, a planned city on the banks of the Rio Branco, is home to more than half of Roraima's population. While not without some attractions of its own, Boa Vista serves mostly as a transfer point for travelers headed to Guyana or to Venezuela's beautiful high plains, just three hours north.

Sights

Praia Grande   BEACH

A tawny sandbar beach emerges on the far bank of the Rio Branco, opposite Boa Vista, during low water, roughly December to April. Known as Praia Grande, it is indeed big and beachy, and makes for a pleasant afternoon visit. Its transitory existence means there is no shade – bring an umbrella or consider waiting until the afternoon. **Porto do Babazinho** (3624-8382; Av Major Williams 1) offers ferry service for R$4 round trip, and can provide food and drinks. Be alert for stingrays.

Activities & Tours

Porto do Babazinho   ADVENTURE TOUR

(9111-3511; babarinhorr@yahoo.com; Av Major Williams 1) Porto do Babazinho is home-base for longtime local guide Sebastião de Souza e Silva (aka 'Babazinho'), who leads and arranges a variety of adventuresome outings, from windsurfing lessons and rentals to daylong and multiday hiking, canoeing and animal-spotting excursions, all at reasonable rates.

Roraima Adventures   TOUR

(3624-9611; www.roraima-brasil.com.br; Coronel Pinto 86; 8am-noon & 2-6pm Mon-Fri, 8am-noon Sat) Roraima Adventures offers professional multiday camping tours all over Roraima, including Serra do Tepequém and Mt Roraima in Venezuela, and even into the Yanoma-

mi reserve (provided the proper permissions can be secured).

Sleeping

Hotel Ideal   HOTEL $

(3224-6342; Araújo Filho 481; s/d R$60/70;) Boa Vista's best budget option, the Ideal's bright lobby and dining area give way to tidy rooms with high ceilings, TV and air-conditioning. Decor is quite sparse, but the friendly service and convenient location more than make up for it.

Hotel Euzébio's   HOTEL $

(2121-0300; www.hoteleuzebios.com.br; Cecília Brasil 1517; s/d standard R$80/110, superior R$100/120;) Standard rooms are clean but small; superiors are bigger, more cheerful and come with hot water and minibar. All rooms have air-con and TV, and the swimming pool is a treat. A bit removed from the center, but closer to the appealing walkways and nighttime restaurants in the center of Av Capitan Ene Garcez. There's a 10% to 15% discount for paying in cash.

Uiramutam Palace   HOTEL $

(3624-4700; www.uiramutam.com.br; Av Capitan Ene Garcez 427; s/d/tr standard R$70/100/120, deluxe R$120/160/180;) Standard rooms here are awfully plain for the price, but the deluxe units are larger and cheerier, with spiffy bathrooms (think porcelain sinks and glass showers), flat-screen TVs, and a 20% cash discount to boot. The pool is a welcome midafternoon diversion, notwithstanding the huge satellite dish peering up from one corner of the pool area.

Eating

La Gondola   SELF-SERVE $

(Av Benjamin Constant 35 W; self-service per kg R$25; lunch) Facing the plaza across a busy intersection, this small per-kilo place offers outdoor, fan-cooled or air-con dining areas, in addition to the typical per-kilo options: pasta, potatoes, roast chicken, grilled beef, rice, beans etc.

Open-Air Food Court   BRAZILIAN $

(mains R$5-20; 5pm-midnight) A busy open-air food court occupies part of the long narrow park between the split lanes of Av Capitan Ene Garcez. A slew of mom-and-pop restaurants have tables set up under a high awning, serving cheap tasty Brazilian fare. There's occasionally live music, but the lively, family-friendly ambience is the real draw here.

Boa Vista

Boa Vista

🌀 Activities, Courses & Tours
1 Roraima Adventures D3

🛏 Sleeping
2 Hotel Euzébio's A2
3 Hotel Ideal..B3
4 Uiramutam Palace..............................A2

🍴 Eating
5 La Gondola..C3
6 Open-Air Food Court...........................A1
7 Peixada Tropical A2

🛍 Shopping
8 Mercado Turístico C3

Peixada Tropical   SEAFOOD $$
(cnr Ajuricaba & Pedro Rodrigues; dishes for 2 R$35-50; ⏱11am-10pm) Another popular open-air lunch spot serving fish in every way imaginable.

🛍 Shopping

Mercado Turístico   MARKET
(☑3623-1615; Av Sebastião Diniz; ⏱8am-6pm Mon-Sat) Two city blocks have been designated as pedestrian only, and are lined with stalls selling everything from handicrafts to cashew nuts.

ℹ Information

CONSULATES

Venezuelan Consulate (☑3623-9285; Av Benjamin Constant 968) Travelers of many nations, including USA, Canada, Australia and most EU countries, need to obtain a Venezuelan tourist card before entering Venezuela by land. The process can be completed in Boa Vista and takes about a half-hour; you'll need to present a passport photo, and copies of your passport data page, your Brazilian entry stamp, and the front and back of your Brazilian tourist slip and yellow fever vaccination certificate.

Photos are available at booths in Boa Vista's main plaza, and there's a copy shop around the corner from the consulate. Be aware that the consulate is open weekdays until noon only, and Venezuelan border control is not as lax as it used to be. At the time of research, Israeli citizens were not allowed to enter Venezuela unless they had a confirmed international plane ticket out of the country, and even then were permitted to stay for 72 hours only.

EMERGENCY

Ambulance (☎192)
Police (☎190)

INTERNET ACCESS

Nobel (☎3621-3422; Av Glaycon de Paiva 789A; per hr R$3; ☺9am-7pm Mon-Sat)
Red Zone (cnr Araújo Filho & Av Benjamin Constant; per hr R$2; ☺9am-midnight)

MEDICAL SERVICES

Hospital Geral (☎3236-0326; Recife 1581) Boa Vista's main public hospital, located 2km from the center of town toward the airport. It has a 24-hour emergency room.

MONEY

Banco do Brasil (Av Glaycon de Paiva 56; ☺8am-2pm Mon-Fri) Changes euros and US dollars.
Bradesco (cnr Av Sebastão Diniz & Inácio Magalhães) Reliable ATMs.

POST

Main Post Office (☎3621-3535; cnr Av Amazonas and Av NS da Consolata; ☺8am-4:30pm Mon-Fri, 8am-noon Sat)

TRAVEL AGENCIES

Timbo Turismo (☎3224-4077; timbotur@osite.com.br; Av Benjamin Constant, at Rua Araújo Filho; ☺8am-noon & 2-6pm Mon-Fri, 8am-noon Sat) Sells plane and bus tickets.

❶ Getting There & Away

AIR

Frequent promotions mean flying is often only slightly more expensive than the bus.
Gol (☎3224-5824; www.voegol.com.br; ☺11:30am-5:30pm & 10pm-4am)
Meta (☎3224-7490; www.voemeta.com.br; ☺8am-6pm Mon-Fri) Flights to Guyana and Suriname twice weekly.
TAM (☎3623-0049; www.tamairlines.com.br; ☺8am-10pm Mon-Fri, 8am-6pm Sat & Sun)

BUS

Eucatur (☎3623-1318) has five daily buses to Manaus (R$119, 10 to 12 hours, 9am, 6pm, 7pm, 8pm and 9pm); the 7pm and 9pm are direct. To get to Venezuela, there's one daily bus to the border town of Pacaraíma (R$22, three hours, 7am) or you can take a collective taxi to Pacaraíma, which costs R$40 but makes the trip in under three hours.

Amatur (☎3224-0004) operates daily buses to Bonfim on the Guyana border (R$15, 1½ hours, 7am, 10am, 2pm and 4:30pm). From there, you cross the border to Lethem, and catch a bus to Georgetown (R$95 from Boa Vista; 15 to 16 hours, Monday, Tuesday, Thursday, Friday and Sunday).

❶ Getting Around

Around town, taxis marked 'Lotação' operate like buses, following fixed routes and carrying up to four passengers. The fare is R$2, or R$4 if the driver veers off the route to drop you at a given spot. Private cabs use meters, and can be pricey.

The airport is 3.5km northwest of the city center. To get there, you can take a 'Carana-Aeroporto' bus 206 (R$2) from the *rodoviária urbano* (municipal bus terminal) on Av Dr Silvio Botelho or across from the *mini-terminal urbano* at the top of Praça do Centro Cívico. Buses depart roughly every 30 to 90 minutes from 6am until 11:15pm; the schedule is reduced on weekends. Taxis to/from the airport and center charge R$25.

The **bus station** (Av das Guianas, Bairro São Vicente) is 2.5km southwest of the center. Several buses go there to/from the *rodoviária urbano* and the *mini-terminal urbano,* including '214-Jockei Clube' and '215-Nova Ciudad' (all R$2, every 20 to 30 minutes). Catch any of the same buses back to the center; buses run from 5:30am to midnight every day. A private taxi from the center to the bus station costs about R$10, a *lotação* cab is R$2.50.

Around Boa Vista

Bonfim & Lethem (Guyana)

The small town of Bonfim (☎095 / pop 11,000), 125km northeast of Boa Vista, is the stepping stone to Guyana. The Guyanese town of Lethem (☎072 / pop 900) is about 5km west across the Rio Tacutu. Neither Bonfim nor Lethem is exactly pleasant, but Lethem is the better of the two; both have hotels in case you get stuck.

A Brazilian-built bridge – with a cool lane-crossing system that switches from Guyana's left-hand driving to Brazil's right-hand driving – straddles the river; customs and immigration for both countries are on their

THE YANOMAMI

The Yanomami are one of the most populous indigenous peoples of Amazonia, their lands spanning much of northen Amazônia, including across the Venezuelan border. Despite their numbers – estimated at around 15,000 – they remained relatively unmolested until the 1970s. That's when the Brazilian government decided to build Hwy BR-210, abruptly exposing the Yanomami to hundreds of construction workers and other outsiders. Predictably, the Yanomami began dying of measles, influenza and venereal diseases; several villages were wiped out entirely.

A decade later, a gold rush sent some 40,000 miners swarming into Yanomami territory, polluting rivers and destroying the forest anew. In 1988 the government attempted to strip the Yanomami of 70% of their traditional territory in order to open it to mining. National and international uproar forced the government to back off, but the plight of the Yanomami remained dire. Nearly a fifth of the group's population died between 1986 and 1993, mostly of disease.

In 1991 the Venezuelan government officially recognized its portion of the Yanomami territory as a special indigenous reserve. Brazil followed suit a month later, creating the 96,650-sq-km **Terra Indígena Yanomami**, Brazil's largest single *índio* territory.

The Yanomami are a slight people, with typical Amerindian features. The focal point of each community is the *yano*, a large round timber-and-thatch structure where each family has its own section facing onto an open central area used for communal dance and ceremony. Each family arranges its own area by slinging hammocks around a constantly burning fire that forms the center of family life.

Their traditional diet includes monkey, tapir, wild pig and a variety of insects, plus fruits, yams, bananas and manioc. The Yanomami hold elaborate ceremonies and rituals and place great emphasis on intertribal alliances, primarily to minimize feuds. When nearby soil and hunting grounds are exhausted, the *yano* is dismantled and the village moves to a new site.

Disease is cured with shaman dances, healing hands and various herbs, including *yakoana* (a hallucinogenic herbal powder). When a tribe member dies, the body is hung from a tree until dry, then burned to ashes. The ashes are mixed with bananas, which are then eaten by friends and family of the deceased to incorporate and preserve the spirit.

Anthropologist Napoleon Chagnon lived with the Yanomami off and on for three decades and described them in his best-selling book *The Fierce People* as aggressive and living in a state of 'chronic warfare.' He received acclaim when the book was published in 1968, but his methods and findings have come under increased scrutiny over the years, including accusations that he knowingly exacerbated a measles outbreak and that he greatly exaggerated the degree of violence within the community. The controversy highlighted the ethical dilemmas inherent in studying isolated indigenous groups and the importance, above all, of emphasizing nuance over grand (and usually Western-centric) proclamations.

respective sides. Money changers abound – you can't miss 'em.

Takutu Hotel (☑ 772-2094; www.takutuhotel.com; Takutu Dr; d from G$5000;) is the best option in Lethem, with options ranging from air-cooled doubles and suites to a place to sling your hammock. **Pousada Fronteira** (☑ 3552-1294; Rua Aluísio de Menezes 2, Bonfim; s/d US$27/35) is one of various not-so-good options in Bonfim, with basic rooms and OK bathrooms.

Santa Elena de Uairén (Venezuela)

☑ 0289 / POP 30,000

Santa Elena de Uairén (Santa Elena) is a dusty town located a few kilometers north of the only land-border crossing between Brazil and Venezuela. The town is higher and cooler than Boa Vista, and provides access to Venezuela's vast and beautiful Gran Sabana. The region is dotted with waterfalls and curious flat-topped mountains called *tepuis*; the largest and most famous *tepui* is Mt Roraima, a spectacular natural monument and the spot where Brazil, Venezuela and Guyana meet.

Brazilian and Venezuelan immigration procedures are all dealt with at the border, locally known as La Línea, 15km south of Santa Elena (and about 1km apart from each other). Most travelers no longer need an advance visa to enter Venezuela – it can be issued on the spot at the border. Returning to Brazil, you'll need to show a valid yellow-fever vaccination card.

◉ Sights & Activities

GRAN SABANA

Santa Elena is at the southern tip of the massive Parque Nacional Canaima (30,000 sq km). At its heart is the Gran Sabana, a high savanna dotted with stark flat-topped mountains called *tepuis,* and crisscrossed by rivers. Trips here include great vista points, swimming in natural pools and visiting spectacular waterfalls, including the 100m Salto Aponwao. Other options include rafting and visiting the town/region of El Pauji, a combination of natural attractions and counterculture community.

MT RORAIMA

The largest and highest of the *tepuis* is 2810m Mt Roraima, and climbing it is the reason most people come to Santa Elena. The standard trip is six days, including three spent exploring the wild 60-sq-km moonscape on top. Highlights up there include La Ventana with terrific views; El Foso, a round deep sinkhole with interior arches; and a series of freezing quartz-lined ponds called the Jacuzzis. If a tour doesn't appeal, you can hire a guide and porters in the towns of San Francisco de Yuruaní (66km north of Santa Elena) or Paraitepui (26km east). Reaching the top requires no technical climbing, but you definitely should be in good shape. Mt Roraima straddles Venezuela, Brazil and Guyana, but this is the only nonvertical route to the top.

☞ Tours

All Santa Elena tour agencies run one-, two- or three-day jeep tours around the Gran Sabana, with visits to the most interesting sights, mostly waterfalls. Budget between 300BsF to 800BsF per person per day, depending on group size and whether it includes just guide and transportation or food and accommodation as well.

For most visitors, the main attraction is a Roraima tour, generally offered as an all-inclusive six-day package for 3200BsF to 3500BsF (you get what you pay for). The operators who organize this tour usually also rent out camping equipment and can provide transportation to Paraitepui, the starting point for the Roraima trek, for about 1800BsF per jeep each way for up to six people. Check on specifics, including group size, hiker-to-guide ratio and equipment quality before signing up for any Roraima tour. Most agencies also sell Salto Ángel and Orinoco Delta tours.

Adrenaline Expeditions   EXTREME SPORTS
(☑ 0414-886-7209, 0426-894-8143; www.adrenalin expeditions.com) Ricardo handles the Gran Sabana with great passion and knowledge, offering all manner of tours, with an emphasis on extreme sports.

Backpacker Tours   TOUR
(☑ 995-1430; www.backpacker-tours.com; Urdaneta) The local powerhouse, it has the most organized, best-equipped and most expensive tours of Roraima and the region. Also rents mountain bikes.

Mystic Tours   TOUR
(☑ 414-5696; www.mystictours.com.ve; Urdaneta) Some of the least expensive tours to Roraima, and local tours with a new-age bent.

Ruta Salvaje   EXTREME SPORTS
(☑ 995-1134; www.rutasalvaje.com; Av Mariscal Sucre) The standard tours, plus rafting trips and paragliding.

🛏 Sleeping

Posada Michelle   GUESTHOUSE $
(☑ 995-2017; hotelmichelle@cantv.net; Urdaneta; s/d/tr BsF80/120/180) The undisputed backpacker headquarters, this clean and surprisingly quiet pousada has 25 rooms with fans, hot water and a basic kitchen downstairs. Sweat-caked Roraima hikers can take advantage of half-day rest-and-shower (80BsF per room) or shower-only (20BsF) rates before taking the night bus out. Bulletin boards announce upcoming trips, if you're looking to join or fill out a group.

Posada Backpacker Tours   GUESTHOUSE $
(☑ 995-1415; www.backpacker-tours.com; Urdaneta; dm/s/d/tr BsF60/80/120/180; @ 🗢) Affiliated with the recommended tour operator

of the same name; rooms here are reasonably clean and comfortable, and there's a popular outdoor restaurant and internet cafe on-site.

Hotel Lucrecia
GUESTHOUSE $$

(☎ 995-1105; www.hotellucrecia.com.ve; Av Perimetral; r/tr BsF250/300 ; ❀ @ ☎) Slightly removed from the central hubbub, Lucrecia has 15 bright hot-water rooms arranged around a lush garden veranda. Breakfast and dinner are available upon request.

✗ Eating

Alfredo's Restaurant
ITALIAN $$

(☎ 995-1628; Av Perimetral; mains BsF50-110; ☻11am-3pm & 6-10pm Tue-Sun; ☞) One of the best restaurants in town, Alfredo's has a lengthy menu, gourmet meals and tortellini with ricotta and spinach that melts in your mouth.

ServeKilo Nova Opção
BRAZILIAN, BUFFET $

(Av Perimetral; buffet per kg BsF80; ☻11am-3pm; ☞) You'll think you're back in Brazil at this popular lunch spot. The large spread includes dishes from both sides of the border, including grilled meats and a few vegetarian options. When the heat drives you to drink, revitalize with a freshly blended juice.

ⓘ Orientation

Calle Bolívar is Santa Elena's main drag, with hotels, internet and shops. Where it intersects with Calle Urdaneta is called Cuatro Esquinas (Four Corners); this is the spot where money-changers typically hang out. Turn right on Calle Urdaneta and you hit Plaza Bolívar, the town's central square; turn left and in a couple blocks you'll pass backpacker central – a cluster of hotels, eateries, and tour operators. At the end of the block is Av Perimetral, which runs along the edge of town.

ⓘ Information

EMERGENCY
Ambulance, Fire, Police (☎171)

MONEY
Money changers (for US dollars and euros) work the corner of Bolívar and Urdaneta, popularly known as Cuatro Esquinas. This is the safest place in the country to delve into the black market, with the best rates – though it's technically illegal.

Banco Caroni (Plaza Bolívar)
Banco Industrial de Venezuela (Calle Bolívar)

POST
Ipostel (Urdaneta) Between Calles Bolívar and Roscio.

ⓘ Getting There & Away

AIR
The tiny airport is 7km southwest of town, off the road to the Brazilian border. There's no public transportation; take a taxi. With enough passengers, Rutaca flies five-seater Cessnas to Ciudad Bolívar via Canaima (BsF1500). The flight from Canaima offers spectacular *tepui* and winding river views. LTA has infrequent weekly flights from Puerto Ordaz.

BUS
The bus terminal is on the Ciudad Guayana Hwy, about 2km east of the town's center. There are no buses – catch a taxi or get a ride from a tour operator. Ten buses depart daily to Ciudad Bolívar (BsF115 to BsF172, 10 to 12 hours), all stopping at Ciudad Guayana. Some continue to Caracas (BsF280 to BsF311, 20 hours). From Icabarú, two to three jeeps leave for the counter-culture artisan community of El Paují (BsF50, two to three hours) in the morning.

There is no direct service from Santa Elena into Brazil. Instead, take a taxi across the border to the Pacaraíma bus terminal. From there, comfortable and frequent minivan taxis go to Boa Vista (R$25, 2½ hours); Eucatur (www.eucatur.com.br) runs three buses (R$16.50) Monday through Friday and two on Saturday and Sunday.

Both Venezuelan and Brazilian passport formalities are done at the border itself, locally known as *La Línea*, 15km south of Santa Elena de Uairén. *Por puestos* from Icabarú travel to the bus station in the Brazilian border town of Pacaraima, but you have to commandeer the whole taxi (BsF60) or they won't wait for you while you have your passport stamped at the Venezuelan and Brazilian immigration offices at *La Línea*. There's no departure tax here.

RONDÔNIA

In 1943 President Getúlio Vargas created the Territory of Guaporé from chunks of Amazonas and Mato Grosso. In 1981 it became the state of Rondônia, named for Marechal Cândido Rondon, the enlightened and humane soldier who 'tamed' this region in the 1920s when he constructed a telegraph line linking it to the rest of Brazil. Rondon also founded the Serviço de Proteção ao Índio (SPI), predecessor of Funai (Fundação Na-

UNCONTACTED

The idea of indigenous groups living deep in the rainforest, yet to be contacted by the outside world, is not as illusory as you might think. In fact, such groups exist all around the world, with the greatest number in the Brazilian Amazon. A 2007 report by Funai, Brazil's indigenous-affairs agency, estimates there are 67 uncontacted tribes (or 'isolated peoples') in the country, up from the previous estimate of 40.

Arriving at that number, and estimating how many people belong to each group, is obviously difficult, but not impossible. Contacted tribes often tell of uncontacted families living in remote areas of their territories. Occasionally members of an uncontacted group will emerge from the jungle, having left or been expelled from their land. Funai studied footprints, abandoned huts and other clues in its recent study. Experts believe most uncontacted groups have seen or even encountered non-*índios* – and have probably seen and heard airplanes – but choose to remain hidden.

Several uncontacted groups are believed to live in Rondônia, including at least three in the Uru-eu-Wau-Wau indigenous reserve, in the center of the state. The reserve suffers rampant illegal mining and logging, and uncontacted groups have retreated ever deeper into the forest. Rondônia also is home to an indigenous man believed to be the last member of an unknown tribe. He has refused all contact, despite being surrounded by pastures and plantations. When Funai arranged for a woman from a nearby tribe to meet him, and possibly reproduce, he chased away the would-be bride with bow and arrows. He is called the 'man in the hole' because he has a hole in his hut, protected by sharp spikes, where he hides when outsiders approach. For the complete account, pick up a copy of Monte Reel's excellent book *The Last of the Tribe* (2010).

cional do Indio; government *índio* agency). He exhorted SPI agents to '*Morrer, se preciso for, matar nunca!*' ('Die, if necessary, but never kill!').

Policies later in the century were not so forward-thinking. In 1981 the Brazilian government, with help from the World Bank, launched an initiative to distribute land to poor settlers. Called Polonoreste, the project spawned a land rush, and Rondônia's population leapt from 111,000 in 1970 to 1.13 million in 1991. Environmental safeguards were flimsy, and about one-fifth of the state's primary virgin forest was cut down to make farmland. The rate of deforestation in the 1980s was equivalent to more than a football field a minute, for a whole decade.

Rondônia is a transition zone between dense Amazonian forests and cerrado (savanna), and despite its sad environmental past, it still has a rich diversity of fauna and flora.

Deforestation in Rondônia has dropped considerably from those highs, accounting for less than 10% of overall cutting in the Amazon, down from more than 15% in past years. However, in 2010, a Dutch study conducted in Rondônia showed that that small-time farmers, not medium or large-scale op-erations, are now the driving force behind deforestation in the state (and, presumably, the rest of the Amazon). Federal law stipulates that no more than 20% of any land grant may be cleared for farming or ranching; corporate farms have proved easier to police than smaller ones, who, the study found, clear as much as 50% of their forest plots. And while political pressure has proved effective against large argo-business, changing the practices of small-time farmers will require a far more nimble bureaucracy – never Brazil's strong point, especially in the Amazon.

Porto Velho

☏ 069 / POP 442.700

Porto Velho is a vital link in Brazil's agricultural economy, as soybeans and other products are shipped on huge barges from here up the Rio Madeira and transferred directly to ocean liners headed abroad. That same ride – albeit on a boat not a barge – draws some travelers up from Cuiabá and the Pantanal on the slow route to Manaus and the Amazon. The city itself has a few bright spots, but mostly serves as a transfer point.

Porto Velho

THE AMAZON PORTO VELHO

⊙ Sights & Activities

**Estrada de Ferro
Madeira-Mamoré** HISTORICAL SITE

(Madeira-Mamoré Railway Museum; cnr Avs Sete de Setembro & Farquhar) Several large warehouse-like structures that once served as a railway station have been undergoing major renovation for several years now. Right on the waterfront, the project includes plans for a railroad museum, river tours, shops and restaurants, and plenty of open space, not unlike Belém's excellent Estação das Docas. Hopefully it'll be done by the time you read this.

River Trips
The broad Rio Madeira forms the western boundary of Porto Velho. Formed in the Bolivian Andes, it's 3200km long and has a peak average flow of 1.4 billion liters a minute – the sixth-largest river in the world. It enters the Amazon River 150km downstream from Manaus.

From about 9am to 7pm daily, riverboats make 45-minute cruises along the Rio Madeira from the dock in front of the Madeira-Mamoré train station (R$12 per person). While not exactly thrilling, this is a reasonable way to idle away an hour or so – with luck you'll see a few pink dolphins. You can buy snacks and drinks on board.

🛏 Sleeping

Hotel Samaúma
HOTEL $
(☎ 3224 5300; www.hotelsamauma.com.br; Rua Dom Pedro II No. 1038; s/d R$90/110) A charming, affordable – and very welcome – addition to Porto Velho's otherwise uninspired hotel scene. A pair of two-story brick buildings have exterior corridors and an airy, almost outdoorsy feel; rooms are small, but have flat-screen TVs, modern bathrooms, and warm wood furniture. Good breakfast spread, and within walking distance of restaurants and bars on Av Pinheiro Machado.

Vitória Palace Hotel
HOTEL $
(☎ 3221-9232; Duque de Caxias 745; s/d R$50/60; ❄) Rooms here are simple and tidy, though showing their age. Too much furniture makes them feel smaller than they are, but high ceilings help. Bathrooms have hot water and there's a pleasant guesthouse atmosphere. Consider asking for a back room, as the front ones open onto the dining area.

Hotel Central
HOTEL $$
(☎ 2181-2500; www.hotelcentral-ro.com.br; Tenreiro Aranha 2472; s/d R$160/200; ❄🛜) This classy modern hotel has large bright spotless rooms, with glass showers (but, oddly, still sports the old air conditioners and televisions). Service is prompt and professional, partly because there never seems to be more than a handful of guests. Discount of 20% for paying with cash.

Hotel Vila Rica
HOTEL $$$
(☎ 3224-3433; www.hotelvilarica.com.br; Av Carlos Gomes 1616; s/d R$245/390; ❄@🛜🏊) Porto Velho's finest hotel has a spacious lobby, comfortable rooms, and views from the top floors. A business center and swimming pool make this suitable for work or pleasure. On Saturdays, the hotel hosts a popular lunch buffet, *Feijoada do Vila* (per plate R$35).

🍴 Eating

Caffé Restaurante
SELF-SERVE $
(☎ 3224-3176; Av Carlos Gomes 1097; per kg R$28; ☺11am-3pm Mon-Sat) The excellent buffet includes a wide selection of mains – from shepherds pie to fried fish – and a slew of sides and a refrigerated case full of succulent desserts are served in a nice and cool dining area. Popular with professionals, but still reasonably priced.

Fiorela
PIZZERIA $
(Pinheiro Machado at Campos Sales; dishes R$20; ☺6pm-midnight, closed Mon.) *Rodízio* restaurants usually have a smorgasbord of skewered meat but the concept works just as well with Italian food: waiters at this loud, glaring, family-favorite eatery rotate around with platters of pasta and pizza, including chocolate and banana varieties for dessert.

O Rei do Peixe
SEAFOOD $
(Rua Rogério Weber at Sete de Setembro; mains R$10-35; ☺11am-11pm) One of several open-air restaurants across from the plaza popular with local workers and families. R$10 lunch plates include an entree and sides; add a pitcher of fresh juice for a great cheap meal. As the name suggests, fish is the specialty here, but there's also beef and chicken. At night, this area can be a bit edgier.

Food Stalls
BRAZILIAN $
(cnr Av Sete de Setembro & Rogerio Weber; ☺8am-11pm) A handful of kiosks in the lower part of the plaza serve hot sandwiches, fresh juices and other light fare at street-cart prices.

Remanso do Tucunaré
BRAZILIAN $$
(☎ 3221-2353; Av Brasília 1506; dishes R$16-40; ☺11am-10pm) The good fish dishes serve two easily; try a delicious *caldeirada de tucunaré* (river-fish stew) or *tambaquí* – big fish chunks boiled with onion and tomatoes in a soup-like sauce, accompanied by rice. Decor is decidedly downmarket, but that's part of the charm. Popular with locals.

🍷 Drinking & Entertainment

The corner of Av Pinheiro Machado and Av Presidente Dutra is the epicenter of Porto Velho's nightlife. Bars like **Emporium, Confraria**, and **Dom Pedro** – all clustered within a half-block – serve beer, mixed drinks and a cool, bohemian-ish atmosphere that draws a mixed-age crowd. Weekends are busiest and occasionally feature live music.

Cine Rio
CINEMA
(2nd fl, Rio Shopping, Av Carlos Gomes; tickets R$12) Cine Rio is a one-screen theater located on the 2nd floor of Rio Shopping, a small mall on Av Carlos Gomes, between Rua Joaquim

Nabuco and Av Brasília; at least five people are required to run the movie, and some nights a quorum is not to be had.

ℹ Information

EMERGENCY

Ambulance (☎192)
Emergency Room (☎3224-5225; Julio de Castiho 149, Hospital Central)
Police (☎190)

INTERNET ACCESS

Amazon House (Av Pinheiro Machado 753; per hr R$3)
PortoNet (per hr R$2.50; �)8am-10:30pm Mon-Sat, 5-10:30pm Sun)

LAUNDRY

Lavandería Mamoré (☎3221-3266; Av Pinheiro Machado 1455; per piece R$1.50-6; ☉8am-6pm Mon-Sat) Quick and professional, but prices are ridiculously high. You can save a bit by forgoing ironing.

MEDICAL SERVICES

Drogaria Natal (Av Pinheiro Machado, at Julio de Castiho; ☉7am-1am) Large pharmacy and convenience store.
Hospital Central (☎3224-5225; Julio de Castiho 149) Public hospital.
UNIMED (☎3216-6800; Rio Madeira 1618) Private hospital.

MONEY

Bradesco has reliable ATMs on Av Carlos Gomes and Av Sete de Setembro.

POST

Post Office (☎3217-3667; cnr Av Presidente Dutra & Av Sete de Setembro; ☉8am-5pm Mon-Fri, 9am-noon Sat)

TRAVEL AGENCIES

Nossa Viagens e Turismo (☎3224-4777; Tenreiro Aranha 2125) Sells plane tickets; one of many agencies around town.

ℹ Getting There & Away

AIR

Porto Velho airport is 7km north of town. There are daily direct flights to and from Rio Branco, Manaus, Cuiabá, and Brasília, with onward connections from there. The airport was undergoing renovation at the time of research.
Avianca (☎4004-4040; www.avianca.com.br)
Gol (☎3219-7491; www.voegol.com.br)
TAM (☎3219-7508; www.tam.com.br)
Azul-TRIP (☎4003-1118; www.voeazul.com.br)

BOAT

Slow boats down the Rio Madeira to Manaus (R$200 hammock, R$500 to R$600 double cabin, 2½ days) leave twice weekly from Porto Cai n'Água at the end of Rua 13 de Maio. Departures are on Tuesdays and Saturdays at 6pm. You'll need your own hammock, and meals are available for purchase. Buy tickets at **Agencia Moreira** (☎9211-4987, 9235-2525; Porto Cai n'Água; ☉8am-6pm Mon-Sat) or one of the other kiosks at the port. You can claim a spot and sleep on board two to three days before departure.

BUS

The **bus station** (cnr Av Jorge Teixeira & Av Carlos Gomes) is 2km east of the center.

Real Norte (☎3225-2891) runs four daily buses to Rio Branco (R$65, eight hours) departing at 7am, noon, 9pm and 11:30pm; the 9pm departure is direct. It also has service to Guajará-Mirim (R$51, six hours) at 6:30am, 10am, 2pm, 3pm, 6pm, 11:30pm and 1am. Collective taxis also serve Guajará-Mirim (per person R$70) and are much faster, usually around four hours. The price is based on a minimum of four passengers, so you may have to wait for a quorum.

Eucatur (☎3222-2233) also serves Rio Branco (R$65, eight hours, 10:30pm only) and provides long-distance service to destinations like Cuiabá and Brasília.

ℹ Getting Around

Buses with signs reading 'Almirante' or 'Hospital de Base via Aeroporto' run between the city center and the bus station and the airport, passing each every 30 minutes (every hour on weekends). Pick it up at the bus station or airport terminal (in both cases, the stop is to your right as you leave the main doorways), or along Av Sete de Setembro. A taxi between the bus station and town costs R$15; to or from the airport is R$35.

Guajará-Mirim

☎069 / POP 42,200

This low-key town on the Rio Mamoré came into existence as the southern terminus of the Madeira-Mamoré railway. Both Guajará-Mirim and Bolivian Guayaramerín across the river are free-trade zones with a steady stream of shopping tourists. For travelers, it's mainly a border-crossing point.

◉ Sights & Activities

Museu Histórico Municipal   MUSEUM
(cnr Avs Constituição & 15 de Novembro) **FREE**
This sad little museum was under renovation when we passed through; with any luck

Guajará-Mirim

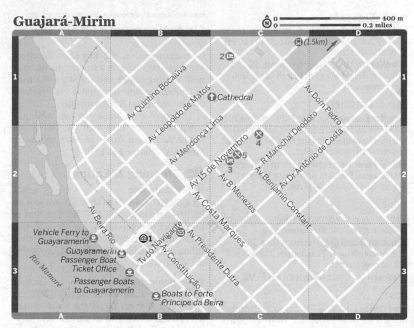

they'll do away with the amateur taxidermy and deformed animals in formaldehyde and focus on the one thing that's actually historic here: the Madeira-Mamoré railroad, which used this very building as a station during its short existence.

🛏 Sleeping & Eating

Hotel Mine-Estrela   HOTEL $
(☑ 3541-1206; Av 15 de Novembro 460; s/d R$50/80; ❄ 🛜) Offers large basic rooms with cable TV, internet, a location that's convenient to restaurants and passing taxis for getting to the port or bus station. By no means luxurious, but a reliable budget choice, especially if you're just passing through.

Hotel Jamaica   HOTEL $
(☑ 3541-3722; Av Leopoldo de Matos 755; s/d R$80/140; ❄ 🛜) Near the cathedral, the Jamaica has excellent service and large comfortable rooms arranged along an internal corridor and lobby. Rooms vary in size; those in front are larger, but the rear units get less hallway traffic. All have a flat-screen TV and include a well-supplied breakfast.

Lanchonete e Pizzaria Pit Stop   PIZZA $
(☑ 3541-4213; Av 15 de Novembro 620; dishes US$4-6; ⏰5-10pm) A popular if somewhat sterile eatery serving decent pizzas. It has a huge

Guajará-Mirim

◎ **Sights**
  1 Museu Histórico Municipal.................B3

🛏 **Sleeping**
  2 Hotel Jamaica...............................C1
  3 Hotel Mine-Estrela.........................C2

🍽 **Eating**
  4 Lanchonete e Pizzaria Pit Stop..........C2
  5 Restaurante Oásis..........................C2

wide-screen TV, so you're sure not to miss a moment of the latest *novela* or soccer game.

Restaurante Oásis   SELF-SERVICE $
(☑ 3541-1621; Av 15 de Novembro 460; self-service per kg R$30; ⏰11am-3pm except Tue) This long-time favorite in Guajará-Mirim can be counted on for a tasty, well-prepared lunch buffet, including fresh grilled meats. The airy dining area gets some street noise, but is still a pleasant and convenient place for a midday break.

ℹ Information

EMERGENCY
Emergency Room (☑192; Hospital Regional, cnr Marechal Deodoro & Av Costa Marques; ⏰24hr)
Police (☑190)

THE AMAZON GUAJARÁ-MIRIM

INTERNET ACCESS

Lan House Center (Av 15 de Novembro; per hr R$2; ☻9am-10pm Mon-Sat) Across the street from the bus station.

TriboNet (Av 15 de Novembro; per hr R$1.75; ☻8am-midnight Mon-Fri, 1-11pm Sat & Sun) Fast connection.

MEDICAL SERVICES

Hospital Regional (☏3541-7129, toll-free 192; cnr Marechal Deodoro & Av Costa Marques) You may have to wait a long time for service at this crowded public hospital.

Yellow-Fever Vaccinations (Hospital Regional, cnr Marechal Deodoro & Av Costa Marques; ☻8am-1pm Mon-Fri; ♿) Free.

MONEY

There are numerous moneychangers at the port in Guayaramerín, on the Bolivian side.

Banco do Brasil (Av Mendonça Lima 388; ☻9am-2pm Mon-Fri) Exchanges US cash but not traveler's checks.

Bradesco (Av Costa Marques 430) ATMs.

POST

Post Office (☏3541-2777; cnr Av Presidente Dutra & Marechal Deodoro; ☻8am-4pm Mon-Fri, from 9am Tue)

ⓘ Getting There & Around

Bus Station (Av 15 de Novembro) Taxis from the bus station into town cost R$15 to R$25; moto-taxis are R$10.

Real Norte (☏3541-2302) runs six daily buses to Porto Velho (R$51, six to seven hours) at 6:30am, 10am, 1pm, 2pm, 6pm and 11:55pm; the 1pm and 11:55pm departures are direct and about an hour quicker. There's just one bus to Rio Branco (R$55, nine hours, noon).

TO/FROM BOLIVIA

Motorboats ferry passengers across the Rio Mamoré between Guajará-Mirim and Guayaramerín, Bolivia (R$5 or B$20, 10 minutes). A minimum of 10 passengers is usually required, but it's rare to wait more than 30 minutes. The port and **ticket office** (☏3541-7221; ☻24hr) in Guajará-Mirim are on Av Beira Rio.

Bolivian Consulate (☏069-3541-8620; Beira Rio 50; ☻7am-3pm Mon-Fri) Look for a Bolivian flag on the 2nd floor; the door is partway down a narrow passageway on the south side of the building.

Polícia Federal (☏3541-0200; cnr Avs Presidente Dutra & Bocaiúva; ☻7am-9pm) The immigration office is an unmarked door on Av Presidente Dutra, but you can use the main entrance on Av Quintino Bocaiúva after hours and on weekends.

Guayaramerín (Bolivia)

☏0855 / POP 36,000

Guayaramerín, on the Rio Mamoré opposite Guajará-Mirim, is a frontier town, river port, trading center and the start of a road to La Paz, the Bolivian capital, via Riberalta (90km away) and Rurrenabaque.

The town is so small you can walk just about anywhere, except to the bus terminal (2.5km south from the ferry terminal). Moto-taxis charge B$1 to B$3.

🛏 Sleeping & Eating

Hotel Santa Ana HOTEL $
(☏855-3900; Calle 25 de Mayo 611; s/d with fan B$70/140, d with air-con B$150; ✳) The best of the cluster of hotels on this corner, with spacious, often air-conditioned rooms and some suites. Reasonable value, though be sure to avoid the windowless rooms.

Hotel Balneario San Carlos HOTEL $$
(☏855-3555; Calle 6 de Agosto 347; s/d B$190/260; ✳☎⬚) By far the most upmarket place in town, with an attitude and parking area full of SUVs to prove it. Guests can make use of a pool, restaurant and billiards table; rooms are a bit disappointing for the price, but still a step above the competition.

Snack Bar Antonella FAST FOOD $
(main plaza; mains B$15-30) Pleasant place for a beer and a snack as you watch the world go round the plaza.

ⓘ Information

Hospital Guayaramerín (☏885-3008, 885-3007, 112; Calle Mamoré s/n) Basic medical services.

Internet M@s@s (Calle 25 de Mayo; per hr B$5; ☻9:30am-midnight) Internet.

Moneychangers (Guayaramerín port) Change US, Bolivian and Brazilian cash.

Police (☏110; cnr Av Mariscal Santa Cruz & Calle 6 de Agosto)

Post Office (Av Mariscal Santa Cruz s/n; ☻8am-noon & 2-5pm Mon-Fri, 8am-noon Sat)

ⓘ Getting There & Away

AIR

Guayaramerín's small airport is on the eastern edge of town, and the airline offices are on the nearby Av 16 de Julio, around the corner with Calle 25 de Mayo. **AeroCon** (☏855-5025; Calle 25 de Mayo, near Beni) runs daily flights to Trinidad with onward connections to other cities. **TAM** (☑855-3924; Av 16 de Julio) flies to Riberalta on Sunday mornings (B$130, 20 minutes) and has a daily flight to Trinidad (B$523, 50 minutes), except Tuesday and Thursday. **Amaszonas** (www.amaszonas.com) connects Guayaramerín with Riberalta and Trinidad most days, though there is no office in town. Flights to Cobija via Riberalta (per person B$600) are by private rental *avioneta* (light aircraft) and must be full (five people) to depart. Call **Avionetta Ariel** (☑852-3774) or **El Capitán** (☑7686-2742) at least a day in advance.

BOAT

Motorboats zip back and forth between Guayamerín and Guajará-Mirim (R$5, five minutes). Cargo boats up the Río Mamoré to Trinidad (around without/with food B$250/350) leave very irregularly and take six days. Ask at the port captain's office for the latest info.

BUS & TAXI

Think twice about taking long-distance buses here, especially in the rainy season (roughly from November to April). Flooded roads and bridges can triple the estimated travel time, and two-, three- and even five-day epics are not uncommon. Most locals either fly or wait for the roads to clear.

The bus terminal is 2.5km from the river along Av Federico Román. A taxi to the terminal will cost you B$5.

TO/FROM BRAZIL

For most travelers, both Brazil and Bolivia offer 90-day tourist visas for free and on the spot. Americans, Canadians and Australians, however, must obtain a five-year multi-entry visa, which costs US$130 in both countries; the Brazilian consulate claims it processes them in one to two days, while the Bolivians can take two weeks or more. You'll also need passport-sized photos, yellow-fever vaccine and other items; needless to say, you're much better off having handled all this before arrival. Officials on both sides look for the other's exit stamp, so be sure to get one before crossing the river.

Bolivian Immigration (☑855-4413, after hours 7395-2902; cnr Av Costañera & Calle Mariscal Santa Cruz; ⊗8am-8pm Mon-Fri, 8am-noon Sat & Sun)

Brazilian Consulate (☑855-3766; Avs Beni & 24 de Septiembre; ⊗9am-5pm Mon-Sat)

ACRE

Present-day Acre was originally part of Bolivia, but by the end of the 19th century it was mostly populated by Brazilian *seringueiros* (rubber-tappers), spreading south from the Amazonas. In August 1902, Bolivia sent its army to assert control and was met by fierce resistance from the *seringueiros* in what is known here, a bit melodramatically, as the 'Acrean Revolution.' Bolivia eventually ceded the territory to Brazil in exchange for two million British pounds and a promise to build a railroad from the border to Porto Velho to facilitate Bolivian exports. (The railroad was never completed and some in Bolivia say the money was never paid.) The Brazilian government, however, had never really supported the upstart Acreans and refused to name Acre a state, designating it the nation's first 'federal territory' instead. Thus the 'autonomist' movement was born, a sometimes-armed conflict that culminated, 60 years later, in Acre winning full statehood.

Acre is the home state of martyred union and environmental leader Chico Mendes, and was a key battleground for the conflict over deforestation. Hundreds of union leaders, activists and ordinary workers died in the conflicts, including Mendes, who was assassinated in 1988. But thanks to those struggles, today a full third of the state is under environmental protection or designated as indigenous lands.

Rio Branco

☑068 / POP 348,300

Rio Branco, the capital of Acre, was founded in 1882 by rubber-tappers on the banks of the Rio Acre. Once a brash, uneasy town, Rio Branco has transformed itself into a genuinely pleasant place, with several excellent cultural outlets and easy access to some interesting sites, including Xapuri, the hometown of the environmentalist Chico Mendes. Unfortunately for Rio Branco, few travelers make it here for the simple reason that it's not on the way to or from anywhere travelers commonly go.

◉ Sights

Palacio Rio Branco   HISTORIC BUILDING
(Praça Povos da Floresta; ⊗8am-6pm Tue-Fri, 4-8pm Sat) Acre's first capital building, the imposing Palacio Rio Branco is now mostly a tourist attraction. A maze of interconnected rooms contain interesting and well-done displays on prehistoric artifacts, indigenous communities, Chico Mendes and the Acrean Revolution. Docents are available for free guided tours, though you'll have to understand Portuguese. (Same goes for the displays.)

Rio Branco

Rio Branco

◉ Sights

⊜ Sleeping

⊗ Eating

✪ Entertainment

Memorial dos Autonomistas MEMORIAL
(Autonomists Memorial; ☎3224-2133; Praça Eurico Dutra; ⊗8am-6pm Tue-Fri, 4-8pm Sat) FREE
In its spiffy home on the main plaza, the Memorial dos Autonomistas has a permanent display on Acre's battle for statehood, plus space for rotating art exhibits. It's also where José Guiomard dos Santos is buried; though not Acrean by birth, Guiomard served as federal administrator of the region and later, as Senator, helped pass legislation giving Acre its statehood.

Museu da Borracha MUSEUM
(Rubber Museum; Av Ceará 1441; ⊗8am-6pm Tue-Fri, 4-8pm Sat) FREE Cramped but fascinating, the Museu da Borracha traces the history of rubber tapping in Acre. Its three small rooms have displays ranging from how tappers learned to extract the milky sap without killing the tree (a tool called a *cabrita*, or 'little goat', was key) to the life and work

of Chico Mendes and the Rural Workers Union. In Portuguese only.

Mercado Velho MARKET
(Praça Bandeira) FREE Not only a great place for a meal or that late-afternoon beer, Rio Branco's refurbished riverside Mercado Velho is a favorite spot for city-sponsored cultural events, including live music, dance performances, poetry readings and comedy troupes, usually held evenings and weekends.

🛏 Sleeping

Be aware that hotels in Rio Branco are required to record the passport and visa information of all guests, as part of an effort by the federal police to stem illicit cross-border activity.

Hotel do Papai HOTEL $
(☑3223-2044; Floriano Peixoto 849; s/d R$70/110; ❄🛜) A strange but reliable budget choice, the Papai's huge reception area and pimped-out business center (leather sofas, flat-screen TV, computers) give way to cleanish rooms with ancient TVs and air-conditioners and not much natural light, but also fresh paint, high ceilings and scenes of Amazônia painted on the walls. The friendly elderly owner tends the desk.

AFA Hotel HOTEL $
(☑3224-1396; www.afabistro.com.br; Ribeiro 109; s/d R$92/138; ❄🛜) Service is friendly and the rooms are cozy at this small centrally located hotel. Decor is sparse, but large windows allow for good natural light. Modern air conditioners, old school TVs. There's a 5% discount for paying in cash and guests get 10% off at the hotel restaurant, one of the best per-kilo restaurants in town.

Hotel Guapindaia Centro HOTEL $$
(☑3223-5747; www.hoteisguapindaia.com.br; Floriano Peixoto 550; s/d R$100/165; P❄🛜) Don't let the busy street-corner location turn you off to this friendly midrange hotel; the price is reasonable and the city's main sights are just a block away. Clean crisp rooms, albeit a bit small, have sage-colored walls, updated bathrooms and quiet air-conditioners, and include a huge breakfast spread.

Hotel Guapindaia Praça Business HOTEL $$
(☑3224-7677; www.hoteisguapinda.com.br; Rui Barbosa 354; s/d R$130/190; P❄🛜🖥) Rooms are pretty tiny at this business-friendly hotel, though you can't beat the location, a block from a leafy plaza and the city's narrow central park. The large air-conditioned lobby and professional service are a breath of fresh air, and guestrooms are spotless, if not spacious.

🍴 Eating

Café do Theatro BRAZILIAN $$
(☑3223-5862; cnr Av Brasil & Av Getúlio Vargas; dishes R$17-28; ⏰noon-11pm Mon-Sat) Attached to the Memorial dos Autonomistas (but operated separately) this classy resturant-cafe attracts a mostly professional crowd, with its sunny patio, artsy air-cooled dining room, and creative menu, including items like roast beef in banana leaves and grilled fish with capers. There also is an extensive drink menu and fresh desserts.

Mercado Velho MARKET $
(Praça Bandeira; pratos feitos from R$6; ⏰7am-10pm) Dubbed the 'Old Market', this is actually part of a recent and highly successful urban-renewal effort. An old port building was transformed into an attractive food market where you can order anything from grilled comfort foods to complete entrees, served at indoor booths or at tables overlooking a riverfront plaza. Especially popular in the evenings, when there's live music.

Churrascaria Triângulo BRAZILIAN $$
(☑3224-9265; Hotel Triângulo, Floriano Peixoto 727, per kg R$33, rodízio R$30; ⏰11am-3pm daily, 7-10pm Mon-Sat) True, the ambience here is rather lacking, but if you're famished and in the mood for meat, you're sure to leave satisfied. The *rodízio* is especially filling: an all-you-can-eat meat buffet where waiters pass by your table with skewers of fresh-grilled meats and includes all the self-serve side dishes you like.

AFA Bistrô D'Amazônia SELF-SERVE $$
(Ribeiro 99; per kg R$41.50, R$50 Sun; ⏰11am-2:30pm) This unassuming bistro is easily the best per-kilo lunch spot in town, and arguably in all Amazônia. The city's professional classes pack in for fresh and original salad combinations, tender meat and fish dishes, and irresistible desserts. Sundays feature *frutas do mar* (seafood).

☆ Entertainment

Mercado Velho LIVE MUSIC
(Praça Bandeira; ⏰5-11pm) Many of the eateries in this attractive riverfront market have evening and nighttime service, from cool

beers to full meals. It's a popular and pleasant place to while away a few hours, listening to music (there's usually at least one singer-guittarist plying his trade before a low-key amplifier) and contemplating the pedestrian bridge, bathed in a hypnotic blue light.

Cine Araujo   CINEMA
(www.cinearaujo.com.br; Shopping Via Verde, Estrada da Floresta; R$18) Large modern cinema in a large modern shopping center 6km west of the center, showing mostly dubbed Hollywood flicks and the odd Brazilian production. A taxi will cost R$30, or catch the 'Shopping' or 'Floresta' bus at the city terminal.

❶ Information

EMERGENCY
Emergency Room (☏3223-3080, 192; Hospital Geral, cnr Av Nações Unidos & Hugo Carneiro)
Police (☏190)

INTERNET ACCESS
Viper.net (Av Ceará; per hr R$2; ⊙7am-8:30pm Mon-Sat, noon-8:30pm Sun)

MONEY
Banco do Brasil (Porta Leal 85)
Bradesco (Porto Leal 83)
HSBC (cnr Rui Barbosa & Marechal Deodoro)

POST
Post Office (Epaminondas Jácome 447; ⊙7am-4pm Mon-Fri, 8am-noon Sat)

TOURIST INFORMATION
Centro de Atendimento ao Turista (Praça Povos da Floresta; ⊙8am-5:30pm Mon-Sat, 5-8pm Sun) Not terribly helpful, but a good place to start.

TRAVEL AGENCIES
Discovery Viagens (☏9238-9495; www.discoveryviagens.com; AFA Hotel, Ribeiro 109; ⊙8am-5pm Mon-Fri) Local tour operator offering guided excursions of all sorts, including bike tours in Xapuri and visits to the Yawanawá indigenous community and Serra do Divisor national park. There's an info desk in the lobby of the AFA Hotel.

❶ Getting There & Away

Highway BR-364 is paved and well maintained between Rio Branco and Porto Velho, and as far as Sena Madureira, 170km west of Rio Branco. Likewise, the road from Rio Branco to Brasiléia (235km) and Assis Brasil on the Peruvian border is also paved, and has year-round bus service. Beyond those corridors, however, most of Acre's roads are unpaved, and can be difficult or impassable during the rainy season, usually October to May (most of the year, that is). Boat and plane may be the only options during those times.

CHICO MENDES & HIS LEGACY

In the mid-1970s an ambitious military-government plan to tame the Amazon attracted a flood of developers, ranchers, logging companies and settlers into Acre, who clear-cut rubber and Brazil trees to make room for ranches. Francisco Alves Mendes Filho, better known as Chico Mendes, was a 30-something rubber-tapper, but one of the few who could read and write, and had long taken an interest in improving the lives of fellow rubber-tappers, or *seringueiros*. In 1977, he cofounded the Sindicato dos Trabalhadores Rurais de Xapuri (Xapuri Rural Workers' Union) to defy the violent intimidation and dispossession practiced by the newcomers.

Mendes organized *empates* (stoppages), nonviolent human blockades to stop the clear-cutting. But Mendes was not initially an environmentalist – his motivation was to help rubber-tappers, whose livelihood happened to depend on a healthy, intact forest. Likewise, the environmental movement (largely based in the USA at the time) was focused on preserving 'virgin' forest, which it assumed to be empty of humans save a few *índio* tribes.

The joining of those groups – rubber-tappers and US environmentalists – was one of Mendes' key accomplishments. He convinced rubber-tappers to see themselves as stewards of the forest and allies of indigenous peoples. And he helped conceive of 'extractive reserves,' to this day an important means of protecting land and people there. He won numerous international awards in the process, including election to the UN Environment Organization's Global 500 Honor Roll in 1987.

Mendes' fame abroad made life increasingly dangerous at home. Killings of rural workers and activists, including priests and lawyers, jumped from single digits in the 1960s, to over a hundred in 1980, to nearly 500 between 1985 and 1987, according to Amnesty International.

In December 1988 he moved to establish his birthplace, Seringal Cachoeira, as an extractive reserve, defying a local rancher and strongman, Darly Alves da Silva, who claimed

AIR

Rio Branco's small airport has daily flights to Porto Velho and Brasília (and onward connections from there), plus seasonal service to Cruzeiro do Sul.

Gol (☑0300-115-2121; www.voegol.com.br; airport)

TAM (☑4002-5700; www.tam.com.br; airport)

Azul-TRIP (☑4003-1118; www.voeazul.com. br; airport)

BOAT

The Rio Acre is navigable all the way to the Peruvian border at Assis Brasil but there's little river traffic (and none that follows a schedule). Headed the other direction, it's possible to catch a boat down the Rio Purus from the town of Boca do Acre, north of Rio Branco, theoretically all the way to Manaus. That said, if Manaus is your destination, there's much more frequent and reliable boat service on the Rio Madeiro, leaving from Porto Velho.

BUS

Long distance buses leave from the **Rodoviária Internacional de Rio Branco** (☑3221-3693; www.rodoviariainternacional.com; Km 125, Hwy 364), a sleek new bus terminal located 8km southwest of town. **Real Norte** (☑3221-2428, toll-free 0800-647-6666; www.realnorte.com. br) has service to Xapuri (R$26, 3½ hours, 6am and 1:45pm), Brasiléia (R$30, four hours, 6am,

6:30am, noon, 3pm and 6pm), Assis Brasil (R$40, six hours, 6am and noon), Guajará-Mirim (R$56, seven to eight hours, 10:30am only) and Porto Velho (R$66, seven to eight hours, 7am, 11am, 9pm, 10pm and 11pm). The road to Cruzeiro do Sol ($92, nine hours) is now passable year round.

Eucatur (☑3224-2233; www.eucatur.com. br) and **Transacreana** (☑3224-6669) also have service from this bus terminal.

ⓘ Getting Around

At Rio Branco's bustling **terminal urbano** (City Bus Terminal; Rua Sergipe btwn Av Ceará & Rua Benjamin Constant) you pay your fare at a bank of turnstiles and buses come and go from clearly marked platforms.

The airport is located 22km west of town, on Hwy 364. A taxi to or from town costs an eye-popping R$80 to R$90; definitely ask fellow passengers about sharing a ride. Alternatively, bus 304, signed as 'Custódio Freire' runs between the airport and town about once an hour (R$2.40, 45 minutes, 5am to 10:30pm).

At least three different city buses run between the downtown terminal and the Rodoviária Internacional; they are marked either 'Norte-Sul,' 'Parque Industrial' or 'Jacarandá' (R$2.40, 20 to 30 minutes, every 15 minutes). A taxi to or from the city center costs R$25, a moto-taxi costs R$10.

---

the land. Mendes had already denounced Silva to the police for threatening his life and for the murder of a union representative earlier that year. Mendes received innumerable death threats, but resisted the urging of colleagues to flee Acre state. On December 22, 1988, Mendes stepped onto the back porch of his home in Xapuri and was shot at close range by men hiding in the bushes. He staggered into the house, where his wife and children were watching TV, and bled to death.

Mendes' was the first of hundreds of murders to be thoroughly investigated and prosecuted, owing to the massive international reaction to his killing. Darly Alves da Silva and his son Darci Pereira da Silva were sentenced to 19 years in prison for ordering and committing the crime. Both da Silvas escaped from jail in 1993, apparently just walking free, suggesting complicity among the guards, but were recaptured in 1996, after another outcry, and returned to jail. The men completed their sentences in 2009; Darci reportedly lives in the Pantanal area, but Darly has remained in the area, and can be seen around Xapuri to this day.

Mendes' life and death brought unprecedented international attention to the environmental crisis in the Amazon. But activism on behalf of the forest and people who live there remains a dangerous undertaking. On February 12, 2005, a US-born nun named Dorothy Stang was gunned down in the small town of Anapú, in the soy and cattle country of Pará state. She was killed by men acting on the orders of a rancher Stang had accused of illegally clearing land. The rancher who ordered her killing was convicted in 2007 and sentenced to 30 years in prison. However, he is only the fourth such 'mastermind' to have been held to account for scores of murders that have taken place there, even since the assassination of Chico Mendes.

Xapuri

🏃 068 / POP 16.600

This tidy little town of neat wooden houses along broad streets was home to environmental and labor hero Chico Mendes. It lies about 12km northwest of Hwy BR-317, the main road between Rio Branco (241km away) and Brasiléia (74km away).

◎ Sights & Activities

Casa Chico Mendes   HISTORIC BUILDING
(www.chicomendes.org.br; Batista de Moraes 494) This simple wood house is where Chico Mendes lived with his family until his murder on the back steps in 1988. Tours include a graphic description of the moment he was shot, with bloodstains still on the walls. Across the street, the Chico Mendes Foundation center has poster-sized photos of Mendes and a collection of personal items and international awards.

Museu do Xapuri   MUSEUM
(Rua C Brandão; ⊘ 8am-6pm Tue-Fri, 8:30am-5:30pm Sat, 9am-1pm Sun) FREE This small but interesting museum tells how Xapuri, located at the confluence of two rivers, was once a major transport hub for rubber, nuts, wood and other products, and a favorite of Middle Eastern merchants peddling everything from shovels to perfume. Housed in an attractive mansion that served as the city hall from 1929 to 2000.

Pousada Ecológica
Seringal Cachoeira   ECOTOUR
(🖉 9947-8399; 32km from Xapuri; per person R$50-70) The *seringal* where Chico Mendes first worked tapping rubber is still operating, and now has an ecolodge offering interesting tours. One popular outing leaves at 4am for a real-life look at how workers collect latex and Brazil nuts, with good opportunities to spot wildlife too. There's also a canopy tour, with 500m of rope bridges and ziplines.

🛏 Sleeping

Pousada das Chapurys   POUSADA $
(🖉 3542-2253; pousada _chapurys@hotmail.com; Sadala Koury 1385; s/d/tr R$50/80/110; 🕸🤶) A short walk from the bus terminal, this is the old standby of Xapuri's hotels, and still a pleasant place to stay. The friendly owners were friends of Chico Mendes, and have photos and memorabilia in the dining area (and some fascinating stories). Rooms are large and comfy, though showing their age.

Pousada Villa Verde   POUSADA $
(🖉 3542-3012; pousada-villaverde@hotmail.com; Nogueira 500; s/d R$75/100; 🕸🤶🖤) A 200m walk from the bus terminal, the Villa Verde has a huge leafy garden and just eight cozy rooms, all with air-con and comfortable beds, some with private patios. There's a small clean pool for cooling off.

★ Pousada Ecológica
Seringal Cachoeira   LODGE $
(🖉 9947-8399; dm R$60, d R$130-190; 🕸) Thirty-two kilometers outside Xapuri is Seringal Cachoeira, where martyred union leader Chico Mendes first tapped rubber trees and collected Brazil nuts. It's still a working rubber forest, but a new lodge offers visitors cozy accommodations and excellent guided hikes. Lodging is in large dorms or comfortable stand-alone 'chalets,' while meals are served in the spacious main building.

On Hwy BR-317, look for a turnoff 4km south of the Xapuri junction; from there it's another 16km by well-maintained dirt road to the lodge. A taxi from Xapuri costs R$100.

🍴 Eating & Drinking

Pizzaria Tribos   PIZZERIA $
(🖉 3542 2531; Rua C Branbão; mains R$15-25; ⊘ dinner) One of a handful of kiosks in a small park a block off the main plaza, Tribos serves up tasty pizzas at small outdoor tables and gets kudos for playing a nice mix of international rock.

Bebum   BAR
(Rua C Branbão) In a park off the main plaza, this kiosk is a popular watering hole for Xapuri's young and restless.

ℹ Information

Banco da Amazona (Rua C Bradão) Next to the gas station.
Tourist Information Kiosk (⊘ 7am-noon & 2-5pm Mon-Fri) Opposite the bus station, this place has more handicrafts than tourist information, but does have friendly attendants and a handy brochure about Xapuri.

ℹ Getting There & Away

Real Norte (🖉 3542-2384, toll-free 0800-647-6666; www.realnorte.com.br) has bus service from Xapuri to Rio Branco (R$26, 3½ hours) twice daily at 6am and 3:20pm. There's only one bus from Xapuri to Brasiléia (R$10, two hours) at 10am. Or, you can catch a cab to the *trocamento* (junction) on Hwy BR-317 (R$15) and catch a passing Rio Branco or Brasiléia bus there.

Brasiléia

068 / POP 22,300

The border town of Brasiléia is separated from Cobija, Bolivia, by the Rio Acre and Igarapé Bahia. There's little to do here, unless you're in the market for a computer or DVD player – for that, you can join the crowds crossing into Cobija to take advantage of the lower prices and a duty-free border.

Sleeping & Eating

Pousada
Las Palmeras   POUSADA $
(3546-3284; Pratagi at Geny Assis; s/d R$60/80;) Brasiléia's most appealing hotel has a variety of rooms, from narrow singles to spacious doubles, all with air-con, TV, minibar and hot water; the breakfast is excellent. Newer units are spotless, older ones have less tile and more character, but also creak and complain more.

Saborella   BRAZILIAN $
(Rua Odilon Pratagi s/n; mains R$9-28; 11am 3pm daily, 5-10pm Tue-Sun) Daily specials make ordering easy at this small restaurant, one of few genuinely agreeable places in town. It's half a block from the bus station, and about 300m from the internet cafe.

Orientation

Hwy BR-317 from Rio Branco approaches Brasiléia from the southeast, through the adjacent but independent town of Epitáciolândia. The Brasiléia bus station is just across a small bridge; from there it's a 300m walk (or R$6 taxi ride) to the center of town. If you do walk, bear right out of the bus terminal, and follow Rua Odilon Pratagi to Av Prefeito R Moreira, where most of the main listings are located.

A bridge over the Igarapé Bahia connects Epitáciolândia to Cobija, and is the official border crossing, with immigration offices for both countries nearby. A smaller, more convenient bridge spans the Rio Acre, making it possible to walk from one downtown to the other in just a few minutes. The smaller bridge – which is dedicated to Wilson Pinheiro, a rubber-tapper union president and friend of Chico Mendes who was assassinated in July 1980 – is at the end of Av Prefeito R Moriera; there is a customs post there, but no immigration officers.

Information

Banco do Brasil (Av Prefeito R Moreira No 470) Has an ATM.

No-Name Internet Café (Rua Odilon Pratagi; per hr R$3; 8:30am-10pm) Two blocks from Pousada Las Palmeras.
Police (3546-3207, 190; Av Prefeito R Moreira No 456; 24hr) Police
Post Office (Av Prefeito R Moreira btwn Banco das Amazonas & tourist information kiosk; 8am-noon & 2-5pm Mon-Fri)

Getting There & Away

BUS

The bus station is 500m from most of the hotels and the main commercial strip; a taxi in either direction costs R$5. **Real Norte** (3546-3257; www.realnorte.com.br) has five daily departures to Rio Branco (R$30, four hours) plus service to Xapuri (R$10, two hours) and Assis Brasil (R$10, two hours). You can usually catch a collective taxi to any of the above as well, which are pricer but much quicker.

TO/FROM PERU

Access to Peru is through the village of Assis Brasil, 110km west of Brasiléia. Once an adventure route, the road is now paved and has daily bus services. Complete Brazilian immigration procedures in Brasiléia, and Peruvian immigration at the border town of Iñapari.

Real Norte has bus services to Assis Brasil to/from Rio Branco and Brasiléia.

TO/FROM COBIJA (BOLIVIA)

You are free to cross back and forth between Cobija and Brasiléia without passing immigration, provided you're going for a short period. If you plan to continue inland, or stay longer than a couple of days, you ought to clear immigration officially.

Bolivian immigration (9am-5pm Mon-Fri) is on the main international bridge. In Brazil, the **Polícia Federal** (3546-3204; 8am-7pm) handle immigration procedures; the office is in Epitáciolândia, just across the main international bridge. In Cobija, the **Brazilian consulate** (842-2110; Av René Barrientos; 8.30am-12.30pm Mon-Fri) is a half-block from the main plaza, on Av General Rene Barrientos, next to the Banco Mercantil de Bolivia.

Remember that both Bolivia and Brazil have made visa requirements much stricter for US citizens, charging US$130 and taking a week or more to process the application. Most non-US travelers are issued with 90-day tourist visas on the spot, free of charge. Both countries require proof of yellow-fever vaccinations.

A Brazilian taxi from Brasiléia into Bolivia, with brief stops at the immigration offices, costs R$10 to R$15. A Bolivian cab charges R$5 for the same trip back.

Cobija (Bolivia)

☑ 03 / POP 22,300

The capital of Bolivia's Pando department is the wettest spot in Bolivia, with 1770mm of precipitation annually. It is a hilly town on the banks of the Rio Acre, with a pleasant enough plaza but a somewhat gritty atmosphere. You can use Brazilian reais to pay for just about everything.

🍽 Sleeping & Eating

It is not customary in Bolivia to include free breakfast in room rates.

Hotel Nanijo's   HOTEL $$
(☑842-2230; 6 de Agosto 147; s/d B$200/350; ❋ ❋) A large, modern hotel, with the best facilities in town. All rooms have tiled floors and cable TV and the courtyard splash pool is welcome in the sticky heat.

Esquina de la Abuela   INTERNATIONAL $$$
(Molina near Sucre; mains B$40-65) This is Cobija's nicest eatery with alfresco tables and fresh, well-cooked chicken and meat dishes served under a gigantic *palapa* wigwam.

❶ Orientation

Crossing the smaller bridge from Brasiléia, turn left after the military base and make your way up to Cobija's main plaza, at the top of the hill. Coming from the main international bridge, Av Internacional extends 600m to Av 9 de Febrero. Turn right, and follow Av 9 de Febrero about 1.5km to the center of town.

❶ Information

Police (☑110) Police
Post Office (ECOBOL; main plaza; ⊙8am-noon & 3-7pm Mon-Fri, 9am-noon Sat)
Prodem (Plaza Principal 186) In addition to giving cash advances on Visa and MasterCard and changing US dollars, Prodem has an ATM.

❶ Getting There & Away

AIR

Flights arrive and depart from Aeropuerto Anibal Arab (CIJ), 5km from the center at the top end of Av 9 de Febrero. A taxi to/from the town center is B$20; moto-taxis charge B$10. Alternatively, hop on Micro A (B$2.50), which shuttles between the airport and the market. Flights in June, July, August, December and January get heavily booked, and advance reservations are almost always required in those months.

Amazonas (www.amaszonas.com; no office in town) and **AeroCon** (☑842-4575; Leoncio Justiniano 43) between them have at least daily flights to Trinidad. **TAM** (☑842-4145; Av 9 de Febrero 59) flies daily to La Paz (B$746, two hours), except Sunday. Flights to Guayaramerín via Riberalta are in *avionetas*; ask at the airport or call ☑7621-0035.

BUS

Bus companies cluster at Km 2 of the road to the airport, just past the turnoff for Av Internacional and the main bridge to Brazil. Bus travel in this part of Bolivia is never deluxe, and can be arduous during the rainy season (November to April). The roads are unpaved and there are numerous river crossings (four on the Cobija–Riberalta stretch alone). Travel times can easily double or triple due to mud and flooding. There's daily service on various buslines to **Riberalta** (B$70, 16 hours) and **Guayaramerín** (B$70, 16 hours) and one tortuous service to **La Paz** via Rurrenabaque runs by La Yungueña (B$280, 35 to 60 hours), but if you are smart, you'll take a flight.

TO/FROM BRASILÉIA

You are free to make short trips back and forth between Cobija and Brasiléia, without passing immigration. For longer stays, it's a good idea to get your passport stamped; remember that you will be required to show a valid yellow-fever vaccination in order to enter (or re-enter) Brazil.

A taxi from Cobija into Brasiléia costs B$20 or R$8, including stops at both countries' immigration offices. Moto-taxis charge the same around town, but are not allowed to carry passengers into Brazil. A taxi from Brazil into Bolivia costs R$20.

Understand Brazil

Brazil Today

With a burgeoning middle-class and a booming economy, the promising future so long delayed for Latin America's giant has finally arrived. Since winning the rights to host both the 2014 World Cup and the 2016 Summer Olympics, Brazil has set to work, investing millions in building stadiums and improving infrastructure. Big challenges remain however, including combating social problems, corruption and endemic environmental threats.

Best on Film

Cidade de Deus (City of God, 2002) Brutality and hope in a Rio favela by award-winning director Fernando Meirelles.

Orfeu Negro (Black Orpheus, 1959) Retelling of a classic myth, set during Carnaval with a bossa nova soundtrack.

Central do Brasil (Central Station, 1998) Walter Salles' moving tale of a homeless boy and an older woman on a road trip across Brazil.

Best in Print

Brazil on the Rise (Larry Rohter, 2010) Insightful portrait of the politics, culture and challenges of the South American nation.

The Lost City of Z (David Grann, 2009) Gripping journey into the Amazon to retrace the steps of lost explorer Colonel Fawcett.

Gabriela, Clove and Cinnamon (Jorge Amado, 1958) Hilarious story of seduction and betrayal set in 1920s Bahia, written by one of Brazil's best writers.

Boom Times

Blessed with abundant natural resources, Brazil has seen its fortunes rise over the past generation on an economic boom fueled by a wide range of sectors, including agriculture, mining, petroleum, hydroelectric energy, manufacturing and biofuels. Brazil's GDP has grown tremendously since the turn of the millennium and, as of 2013, Brazil had become the world's seventh-largest economy. Unemployment has reached historic lows and the once vast disparity between rich and poor has declined for each of the last 14 years.

Much of the credit for the good times has been given to former president Lula, who grew bilateral trade to US$25 billion and lifted some 40 million Brazilians out of poverty through the innovative Bolsa Familia (Family Allowance) program. The anti-poverty scheme provides conditional cash transfers to Brazil's poorest families, providing children stay in school and receive vaccinations. In 2012, it reached some 13.7 million families.

A New President

Riding Lula's coattails, fellow party member Dilma Rousseff was elected Brazil's first ever female president in 2010. A former Marxist guerilla, Dilma was imprisoned for nearly three years (and allegedly tortured) during the military regime. Her former radicalism has proved an appropriate résumé for her administration's hard line on corruption. During her first year in office, six of her government ministers lost their positions due to their involvement in corruption scandals. President Rousseff's tough, no-nonsense approach to governing has boosted her approval ratings, which stood at more than 70% after her first year in office. Brazil's economic growth appeared to be slowing under Rousseff's watch (GDP grew a paltry 1.3% in 2012) and the rising cost of living continues to spark public-sector strikes.

The High Cost of the Games

In the run-up to the World Cup and Summer Olympics, Brazil has invested billions in the games – with most of the money going toward stadium construction (Rio's Maracanã football stadium upgrade alone cost nearly R$1 billion). The staggering amounts being spent on these sporting events was one of the catalysts that led to mass protests in 2013, when Brazilians gathered by the tens of thousands in São Paulo, Rio, Brasília and other major cities. It was a historic moment, being the first time in more than 20 years Brazilians took to the streets. What started out as a protest over a bus-fare increase in São Paulo, led to a release of pent-up anger nationwide over a host of other issues – rising inflation, corruption and the amount of tax-payer dollars being spent on sporting arenas that protesters argue could be better utilized on public services. Brazilians pay the highest taxes of any nation outside the developed world (over 35% of their GDP), and many feel they get very little in return.

Environmental & Social Issues

Threats to the Amazon and Brazil's other extraordinary ecosystems continue to come in many forms – cutting down rainforest to raise cattle or grow soybeans along with illegal logging chief among them. The good news is that the rate of deforestation has declined, from nearly 13,000 sq km in 2008 to around 5000 sq km in 2012. Development is also taking a toll on the rainforest. The most controversial project of the moment is the Belo Monte Dam on the Xinguriver in Pará. At an estimated cost of US$16 billion, the dam would have a projected operating capacity of more than 11,000 megawatts of clean, renewable hydroelectricity. The dam's creation, however, would flood 400 sq km of rainforest and displace some 20,000 indigenous people, which has led to vocal protests both within Brazil and in the international community.

On other fronts, Brazil continues to break new ground. In 2013, a judicial decision helped pave the way for gay marriage by stating that government offices have no standing to reject gay civil unions. Meanwhile, a same-sex marriage bill being debated in congress faces fierce opposition from conservatives in the world's largest Catholic country.

POPULATION: **201 MILLION**

GDP: **R$5 TRILLION**

INFLATION RATE: **5.5%**

MONTHLY MINIMUM WAGE: **R$675**

INFANT MORTALITY PER 1000 LIVE BIRTHS: **21 (USA: 6)**

UNEMPLOYMENT: **5.8% (USA: 7.5%)**

if Brazil were 100 people

54 would be white
38 would be mulatto (mixed white and black)
6 would be black
2 would be other

belief system
(% of population)

| Roman Catholic | Protestant | Spiritualist |
| 74 | 15 | 1.5 |

| Candomblé | Other | None |
| 0.5 | 2 | 7 |

population per sq km

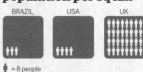

BRAZIL   USA   UK

≈ 8 people

History

Brazil's population, the fifth biggest in the world, reached its lands from Africa, Asia, Europe and other parts of the Americas – diverse origins that have created one of the planet's most racially mixed societies. How they came, intermingled and developed the unique Brazilian identity that charms visitors today is a rough-and-tumble story of courage, greed, endurance and cruelty, eventually yielding a fitful progress towards the democracy the country now enjoys.

French philosopher Jean-Jacques Rousseau based his optimistic view of human nature (the noble savage) in part on early Portuguese descriptions of natives who were 'innocent, mild and peace-loving'.

Before the Portuguese

By the time the Portuguese rolled up in AD 1500, what is now Brazil had already been populated for as long as 12,000 years. But unlike the Incas, Brazil's early inhabitants never developed a highly advanced civilization and they left few clues for archaeologists to follow.

It's generally believed that the early inhabitants of the Americas arrived from Siberia in waves between about 12,000 and 8000 BC, crossing land now submerged beneath the Bering Strait, then gradually spreading southward over many millennia. Researchers in the remote Serra da Capivara in the Northeastern state of Piauí have found some of Brazil's earliest evidence of human presence. The oldest traces of human life in the Amazon region can be seen on a detour from a river trip between Santarém and Belém: a series of rock paintings estimated to be 12,000 years old near Monte Alegre.

By the time the Portuguese arrived, there were probably between two and four million people in what's now Brazil.

Cabral & Chums

The course of Brazilian history was changed forever in 1500, when a fleet of 12 Portuguese ships carrying nearly 1200 men arrived near what is today Porto Seguro. When they arrived, their indigenous reception committee was ready and waiting.

'There were 18 or 20 men,' marveled scribe Pero Vaz de Caminha in a letter back to the Portuguese king. 'They were brown-skinned, all of them

TIMELINE	c 12,000 BC	AD 1500	1549
	Early inhabitants of the Americas arrive from Siberia from 12,000 to 8000 BC, crossing land now submerged beneath the Bering Strait.	Portuguese explorer Pedro Álvares Cabral makes landfall around present-day Porto Seguro and claims possession of the land – believed at first to be an island – for the Portuguese crown.	Tomé de Sousa is named Brazil's first governor. He centralizes authority and founds the city of Salvador, which will remain Brazil's capital for more than two centuries.

naked, without anything at all to cover their private parts. In their hands they carried bows and arrows.'

The festivities didn't last long. Having erected a cross and held Mass in the land they baptized Terra da Vera Cruz (Land of the True Cross), the Portuguese took to the waves once again. With lucrative spice, ivory and diamond markets in Asia and Africa to exploit, Portugal had bigger fish to fry elsewhere. It wasn't till 1531 that the first Portuguese settlers arrived in Brazil.

Brazil's Indigenous People

For Brazil's *índios* (indigenous people), April 22, 1500 marked the first chapter in their gradual extermination. Sixteenth-century European explorers along the Amazon encountered large, widespread populations; some were practicing agriculture while others were nomadic hunter-gatherers. Coastal peoples fell into three main groups: the Guarani (south of São Paulo and in the Paraguai and Paraná basins inland), the Tupi or Tupinambá (along most of the rest of the coast) and the Tapuia (peoples inhabiting shorter stretches of coast in among the Tupi and Guarani). The Tupi and Guarani had much in common in language and culture. A European adaptation of the Tupi-Guarani language later spread throughout colonial Brazil and is still spoken by some people in Amazonia.

Over the following centuries a four-front war was waged on the indigenous way of life. It was a cultural war, as well as a physical, territorial and biological one. Many *índios* fell victim to the *bandeirantes* – groups of roaming adventurers who spent the 17th and 18th centuries exploring Brazil's interior, pillaging *índio* settlements as they went. Those who escaped such a fate were struck down by the illnesses shipped in from Europe, to which they had no natural resistance. Others were worked to death on sugar plantations.

Sugar & Slavery

Brazil didn't boast the ivory and spices of Africa and the East Indies, and the only thing that had interested the Portuguese in the early years after they had found it was a rock-hard tree known as *pau brazil* (brazilwood), which yielded a valuable red dye. Merchants began sending a few ships each year to harvest brazilwood and take it back to Europe, and the colony changed its name to Brazil in tribute to the tree. Alas, the most accessible trees were rapidly depleted, and the *índios* soon stopped volunteering their labor. But after colonization in 1531, the settlers soon worked out that Brazil was a place where sugarcane grew well. Sugar came to Brazil in 1532 and hasn't left since. It was coveted by a hungry European market, which used it for medicinal purposes, to flavor foods and even in wine.

Quilombo (directed by Cacá Diegues) is an epic history flick in which the vast Palmares *quilombo* – a community of runaway slaves led by the legendary Zumbi – is reconstructed in Rio's Baixada Fluminense

HISTORY BRAZIL'S INDIGENOUS PEOPLE

1550	1621	1644–54	1650s
Facing a shortage of labor (as *indios* die from introduced European diseases), Portugal turns to the African slave trade; open-air slave markets flourish in the slowly growing colony.	The Dutch West India Company sets up shop in Northeastern Brazil, heralding the beginning of the Dutch presence in Brazil. Its goal: to wrest control of the colony from Portugal.	Over a decade, the Portuguese wage war against Holland's presence in Brazil, pushing the Dutch back to Recife; they surrender in 1654, ending Holland's presence in Brazil.	Communities of runaway slaves, *quilombos*, flourish in the countryside, eventually becoming targets by *bandeirantes*. Hundreds of informal communities become towns following abolition in the late 1800s.

Perhaps envisaging Brazil's sugarcoated future, the colonists turned to this new industry. They lacked just one thing: a workforce.

The Slave Trade

African slaves started to pour into Brazil's slave markets from about 1550. They were torn from a variety of tribes in Angola, Mozambique and Guinea, as well as the Sudan and Congo. Whatever their origins and cultures, their destinations were identical: slave markets such as Salvador's Pelourinho or Belém's Mercado Ver-o-Peso. By the time slavery was abolished in Brazil in 1888, around 3.6 million Africans had been shipped to Brazil – nearly 40% of the total that came to the New World.

Africans were seen as better workers and less susceptible to the European diseases that had proved the undoing of so many *índios*. In short, they were a better investment. Yet the Portuguese didn't go out of their way to protect this investment. Slaves were brought to Brazil in subhuman conditions: taken from their families and packed into squalid ships for the month-long journey to Brazil.

Masters & Slaves

For those who survived such ordeals, arrival in Brazil meant only continued suffering. A slave's existence was one of brutality and humiliation. Kind masters were the exception, not the rule, and labor on the plantations was relentless. Slaves were required to work as many as 17 hours each day, before retiring to the squalid *senzala* (slave quarters), and with as many as 200 slaves packed into each dwelling, hygiene was a concept as remote as the distant coasts of Africa. Dysentery, typhus, yellow fever, malaria, tuberculosis and scurvy were rife; malnutrition a fact of life. Syphilis also plagued a slave population sexually exploited by its masters.

Sexual relations between masters and slaves were so common that a large mixed-race population soon emerged. Off the plantations there was a shortage of white women, so many poorer white settlers lived with black or indigenous women. Brazil was already famous for its sexual permissiveness by the beginning of the 18th century.

Resistance & the Quilombos

Resistance to slavery took many forms. Documents of the period refer to the desperation of the slaves who starved themselves to death, killed their babies or fled. Sabotage and theft were frequent, as were work slowdowns, stoppages and revolts.

Other slaves sought solace in African religion and culture. The mix of Catholicism (made compulsory by slave masters) and African traditions spawned a syncretic religion on the sugar plantations, known today as Candomblé. The slaves masked illegal customs with a facade of Catholic

CHICO REI

One of Brazil's great folk heroes is Chico Rei, an African king enslaved and brought to work in the mines, but who managed to buy his freedom and later the freedom of his tribe.

1695	1696	1750	1750s
Palmares, the largest *quilombo* in Brazil's Northeast – and home to more than 20,000 inhabitants – is finally destroyed following decades of attacks by Portuguese troops.	News of the discovery of gold in Brazil reaches Lisbon. In ensuing years, tens of thousands of migrants will stream into present-day Minas Gerais, Mato Grosso, Goiás and southern Bahia.	The Spanish concede to the Portuguese the Treaty of Madrid, which hands over 6 million sq km to the Portuguese and puts Brazil's western borders largely where they are today.	Gold (and later diamonds) begin to define the colonial economy. In Minas Gerais the population explodes from 30,000 in 1710 to 500,000 by the end of the century.

BRAZIL'S ÍNDIOS TODAY

When the Portuguese arrived in 1500, there were, by the most common estimates, between two and four million *índios* (indigenous people) already living in Brazil, in over 1000 different tribes. Five centuries later there are an estimated 700,000 *índios* left, living in a little over 200 tribes. Slavery, diseases, armed conflict and loss of territory all took a savage toll on Brazil's native peoples, to the point where in the 1980s *índio* numbers were under 300,000 and it was feared they might die out completely. Since then there has been a marked recovery in the indigenous population, partly thanks to international concern about groups such as the Yanomami, who were threatened with extermination by disease and violence from an influx of gold prospectors into their lands. Government policy has become more benign and huge areas of Brazil are now Terra Indígena (Indigenous Land). Just over 1 million sq km – more than 12% of the whole country – is now either officially registered as Indigenous Land or in the process of registration

Unsurprisingly, there are those who think that 12% of national territory reserved for 0.25% of the national population is too much and fail to respect *índio* rights to these lands. Disputes between indigenous groups and loggers, miners, homesteaders, hunters, road builders and reservoir constructors are still common, and sometimes violent.

It's thought there may still be more than 60 uncontacted tribes, mostly small groups in the Amazon forests – home to about 60% of Brazil's *índios* (and almost all of the existing Indigenous Lands).

Most of Brazil's *índios* still live traditional lifestyles, hunting (some still with blowpipes and poisoned arrows) and gathering and growing plants for food, medicine and utensils. Their homes are usually made of natural materials such as wood or grass. Ritual activity is strong, body- and face-painting is prevalent, and most indigenous people are skilled in making pottery, basketry, masks, headdresses, musical instruments and other artisanry with their hands. None of those known to the outside world are truly nomadic. Indigenous Lands generally have an exemplary record of environmental conservation because their inhabitants continue to live sustainable lifestyles.

saints and rituals. The martial art capoeira also grew out of the slave communities.

Many slaves escaped from their masters to form *quilombos,* communities of runaway slaves that quickly spread across the countryside. The most famous, the Republic of Palmares, which survived through much of the 17th century, was home to some 20,000 people, before it was destroyed by federal troops.

As abolitionist sentiment grew in the 19th century, many (unsuccessful) slave rebellions were staged, the *quilombos* received more support and ever-greater numbers of slaves fled the plantations. Only abolition itself, in 1888, stopped the growth of *quilombos.*

1763	1789	1807	1815
With gold flowing from Minas Gerais through Rio de Janeiro, the city grows in wealth and population; the Portuguese court transfers the capital of Brazil from Salvador to Rio.	The first organized independence movement springs to life. Tiradentes and 11 other conspirators organize the Inconfidência Mineira to overthrow the Portuguese. The plot fails, however, and Tiradentes is executed.	Napoleon invades Portugal and the Portuguese prince regent (later known as Dom João VI) and his entire court of 15,000 flee for Brazil. The royal coffers shower wealth upon Rio.	Dom João VI declares Rio the capital of the United Kingdom of Portugal and Brazil. The same year, a mounting financial crisis forces the king to return to Portugal.

The Bandeirantes & the Gold Rush

The group known as *bandeirantes* were keen to make inroads into Brazil. These bands of explorers roamed Brazil's interior in search of indigenous slaves, mapping out undiscovered territory and bumping off the odd indigenous community along the way.

The *bandeirantes* took their name from the trademark flag-bearer who would front their expeditions. During the 17th and 18th centuries, group after group of *bandeirantes* set out from São Paulo. The majority were bilingual in Portuguese and Tupi-Guarani, born of Portuguese fathers and indigenous mothers. They benefited from both indigenous survival techniques and European weaponry.

By the mid-17th century they had journeyed as far as the peaks of the Peruvian Andes and the Amazon lowlands. It was the exploits of these discoverers that stretched Brazil's borders to their current extent. In 1750, after four years of negotiations with the Spanish, their conquests were secured. The Treaty of Madrid handed more than 6 million sq km to the Portuguese and put Brazil's western borders more or less where they are today.

The *bandeirantes* were known for more than just their colorful flags. Protected from *índio* arrows by heavily padded cotton jackets, they waged an all-out war on Brazil's natives, despite the fact that many of them had indigenous mothers. Huge numbers of *índios* fled inland, searching for shelter in the Jesuit missions. But there were few hiding places – it is thought the *bandeirantes* killed or enslaved well in excess of 500,000 *índios*.

A book about the relationship between slaves and masters on Pernambuco's sugar plantations, Gilberto Freyre's *The Masters and the Slaves* (1933), revolutionized Brazilian thinking about the African contribution to Brazilian society.

Gold

'As yet we have no way of knowing whether there might be gold, or silver or any kind of metal or iron [here],' reported Pero Vaz de Caminha to his king in 1500.

Though it wasn't discovered until nearly two centuries later, there certainly was gold in Brazil. Unsurprisingly, it was the *bandeirantes* who, in between decapitating *índios*, discovered it in the Serra do Espinhaço in Minas Gerais.

For part of the 18th century Brazil became the world's greatest gold 'producer,' unearthing wealth that helped to build many of Minas Gerais' historic cities. The full title of Ouro Prêto, one of the principal beneficiaries of the gold boom, is actually Vila Rica de Ouro Prêto (Rich Town of Black Gold).

Other wild boom towns such as Sabará, Mariana and São João del Rei sprang up in the mountain valleys. Wealthy merchants built opulent

1822
Left in charge of Brazil after his father Dom João VI returns to Portugal, the prince regent Dom Pedro I declares independence from Portugal and crowns himself 'emperor' of Brazil.

1831
Brazil's first home-grown monarch, Dom Pedro, proves incompetent and abdicates the throne. His son Pedro II takes power in 1840 and ushers in a long period of growth and stability.

DEA PICTURE LIBRARY / GETTY IMAGES ©

➜ Dom Pedro's acclamation as first constitutional emperor

mansions and bankrolled stunning baroque churches, many of which remain to this day.

Gold produced a major shift in Brazil's population from the Northeast to the Southeast. When gold was first discovered, there were no white settlers in the territory of Minas Gerais. By 1710 the population had reached 30,000, and by the end of the 18th century it was 500,000. An estimated one-third of the two million slaves brought to Brazil in the 18th century were sent to the goldfields, where their lives were often worse than in the sugar fields.

But the gold boom didn't last. By 1750 the mining regions were in decline and coastal Brazil was returning to center stage. Many of the gold-hunters ended up in Rio de Janeiro, which grew rapidly as a result.

Dom João Vi

Brazil became a temporary sanctuary to the Portuguese royal family in 1807. Running scared from Napoleon, whose army was at that moment advancing on Lisbon, some 15,000 court members fled to Rio de Janeiro, led by the prince regent, Dom João.

Like so many *estrangeiros* (foreigners) arriving in Brazil, the regent fell in love with the place and granted himself the privilege of becoming the country's ruler. He opened Rio's Jardim Botânico (Botanical Gardens) to the public in 1822, and they remain there to this day in the upmarket Jardim Botânico neighborhood.

Even after Napoleon's defeat at Waterloo in 1815, Dom João showed no sign of abandoning Brazil. When his mother, Dona Maria I, died the following year, he became king and declared Rio the capital of the United Kingdom of Portugal and Brazil. Brazil became the only New World colony ever to have a European monarch ruling on its soil.

Independence

Independence eventually came in 1822, 30 years after the Inconfidência Mineira. Legend has it that, on the banks of São Paulo's Ipiranga river, Brazil's then regent, Dom João's son Pedro, pulled out his sword, bellowing, '*Independência ou morte!*' (Independence or death!). With the same breath he declared himself Emperor Dom Pedro I.

The Portuguese quickly gave in to the idea of a Brazilian empire. Without a single shot being fired, Dom Pedro I became the first emperor of an independent Brazil. The *povo brasileiro* (Brazilian people), however, were not as keen on Pedro as he was about their newly born nation. From all accounts he was a blundering incompetent, whose sexual exploits (and resulting string of love children) horrified even the most permissive of Brazilians. After nine years of womanizing he was forced to abdicate, leaving his five-year-old son, Dom Pedro II, to take over.

'Order and Progress,' the slogan on Brazil's flag, comes from French philosopher Auguste de Comte (1797–1857), whose elevation of reason and scientific knowledge over traditional religious beliefs was influential on the young Brazilian republic.

mid-1830s	1835	1865	1888
The coffee bush, which flourishes in Rio de Janeiro province, plays a major role in the colony's economy. *Fazendas* (ranches) spring up as Brazil becomes a major coffee exporter.	Inspired by the successful Haitian Revolution some years earlier, Brazilian slaves in Salvador stage an uprising – Brazil's last big slave revolt – which narrowly fails.	Brazil, allied with Uruguay and Argentina, wages the 'War of the Triple Alliance' on Paraguay. South America's bloodiest conflict leaves untold thousands dead, and wipes out half of Paraguay's population.	Slavery is abolished in Brazil, the last country in the New World to do so. The law is signed by Princesa Isabel, admired by many blacks as their benefactress.

A period of crisis followed: the heir to the throne was, after all, just a child. Between 1831 and 1840 Brazil was governed by so-called *regências* (regencies), a time of political turmoil and widespread rebellions. The only solution was the return of the monarchy and a law was passed to declare Dom Pedro II an adult, well before his 18th birthday.

Aged just 15, Dom Pedro II received the title of Emperor and Perpetual Defender of Brazil, precipitating one of the most prosperous spells in the country's history, barring the war with Paraguay in 1865. Invaded by its neighbor, Brazil teamed up with Argentina and Uruguay and thrashed the Paraguayans back across the border.

Paraguay was left crippled – its population slashed to just 200,000, of whom around 180,000 were women. Brazil, too, suffered heavily: around 100,000 men died, many of them slaves sent to war in the place of wealthier Brazilians.

Abolition & the Republic

Since the 16th century, slavery had formed the backbone of a brutally unequal society in Brazil. 'Every dimension of our social existence is contaminated,' lamented abolitionist Joaquim Nabuco in 1880.

To undo something so ingrained into the Brazilian way of life was never likely to be easy. Brazil prevaricated for nearly 60 years before any resolution. The 19th century was punctuated by halfhearted legislative attempts to lay the slave industry to rest. Repeatedly, such laws failed.

Slave trafficking to Brazil was banned in 1850, but continued clandestinely. Another law, in 1885, freed all slaves over the age of 65. The lawmakers had obviously forgotten that the average life expectancy for a slave at this time was 45. Not until May 13, 1888 – 80 years after Britain had freed its slaves – was slavery itself officially banned in Brazil. Unsurprisingly, this didn't make a huge immediate difference to the welfare of the 800,000 freed slaves, who were largely illiterate and unskilled. Thousands were cast onto the streets without any kind of infrastructure to support them. Many died, while others flooded to Brazil's urban centers, adding to the cities' first slums. Still today, blacks overall remain among the poorest and worst-educated groups in the country.

Not far out of the door behind slavery was the Império Brasileiro. In 1889 a military coup, supported by Brazil's wealthy coffee farmers, decapitated the old Brazilian empire and the republic was born. The emperor went into exile, where he died a couple of years later.

A military clique ruled Brazil for the next four years until elections were held, but because of ignorance, corruption, and land and literacy requirements, only about 2% of the adult population voted. Little changed, except that the power of the military and the now-influential coffee growers increased, while it diminished for the sugar barons.

Brazil is the only country in the New World that was both the seat of an empire (when the Portuguese king came here) and an independent monarchy (when Dom Pedro I declared independence).

1889	1890s	1920	1930
A military coup, supported by Brazil's wealthy coffee farmers, overthrows Pedro II. The monarchy is abolished and the Brazilian Republic is born. Pedro II goes into exile in Paris.	With slavery abolished, Brazil opens its borders to meet its labor needs. Over the next four decades, millions arrived from Italy, Portugal, Spain, Germany and later Japan and other countries.	The rubber boom goes bust as the Dutch and English plant their own rubber trees in the East Indies. Brazil's monopoly on the world rubber market deflates.	Getúlio Vargas comes into power. Inspired by European fascists, President Vargas presides over an authoritarian state, playing a major role in Brazilian politics until his fall from power in 1951.

Open Borders

In the final decade of the 19th century, Brazil opened its borders. Millions of immigrants – from Italy, Japan, Spain, Germany, Portugal and elsewhere – streamed into Brazil to work on the coffee *fazendas,* and to make new lives in the rapidly growing cities, especially Rio and São Paulo, adding further textures to Brazil's ethnic mixture and confirming the shift of Brazil's economic center of gravity from the Northeast to the Southeast.

Over the next century, immigrants continued to flood into Brazil. The country became a haven for Jews fleeing persecution at the hands of the Nazis, as well as Nazis looking to avoid being put on trial for war crimes. Arabs, universally known as *turcos* by the Brazilians, also joined the influx of newcomers. Many of the traders you'll meet at Rio de Janeiro's Rua Uruguaiana flea market hail from the Middle East.

History Books

Brazil: Five Centuries of Change (2009), Thomas E Skidmore

The History of Brazil (1999), Robert Levine

A Concise History of Brazil (1999), Boris Fausto

Getúlio Vargas, Populist Dictator

The Vargas era began in 1930 when members of the newly formed Liberal Alliance party decided to fight back after the defeat of their candidate, Getúlio Vargas, in the presidential elections. The revolution kicked off on October 3 in Rio Grande do Sul and spread rapidly through other states. Twenty-one days later President Júlio Prestes was deposed and on November 3 Vargas became Brazil's new 'provisional' president.

The formation of the Estado Novo (New State) in November 1937 made Vargas the first Brazilian president to wield absolute power. Inspired by the fascist governments of Salazar in Portugal and Mussolini in Italy, Vargas banned political parties, imprisoned political opponents and censored artists and the press.

Despite this, many liked Vargas. The 'father' of Brazil's workers, he introduced new labor laws, and remained popular throughout his tenure. In 1951 he was elected president – this time democratically. But Vargas' new administration was plagued by the hallmark of Brazilian politics – corruption. Amid calls from the military for his resignation, Vargas responded dramatically. He penned a note saying 'I leave this life to enter into history,' and on the following morning, August 24, 1954, fired a single bullet through his own heart.

A masterpiece of Brazilian literature, *Rebellion in the Backlands* vividly describes the Canudos massacre. Author Euclides de Cunha witnessed the end of Canudos as a correspondent for a São Paulo newspaper.

The Generals Take Over

In 1964 the left-leaning president João Goulart was overthrown in a so-called *revolução* (revolution) – really a military coup, believed by many Brazilians to have received backing from the US government. President Lyndon Johnson did nothing to dampen such theories when he immediately cabled his warmest wishes to the new Brazilian administration.

1937	1942	1950	1954
Getúlio Vargas announces a new constitution for what he calls the 'Estado Novo' (New State); he passes minimum wage laws in 1938, expands the military and centralizes power.	Initially maintaining neutrality, Brazil enters WWII on the side of the Allies, providing raw materials, plus 25,000 troops (the only Latin American nation to do so).	Newly constructed Maracanã Stadium in Rio plays center stage in the FIFA World Cup. Brazil dominates until the final, when before 200,000 fans, it suffers a stunning loss to Uruguay.	Following an explosive political scandal, the military calls for the resignation of President Getúlio Vargas. He pens a melodramatic letter then shoots himself through the heart at his Rio palace.

WORLD CUP DREAMS

Bringing the World Cup back to Brazil has long been a dream of the football-crazed nation. In 2007, the dream became reality when FIFA announced that Brazil had won the rights to host the World Cup in 2014. The South American giant last staged the big sporting event in 1950, when Brazil lost in the dramatic final against Uruguay before 200,000 fans in Rio's Maracanã Stadium (which has since been modified to hold smaller crowds). The unforgettable day of infamy was later called 'maracanazo' and is still in common parlance.

Brazil, the most successful football nation in the history of the games (with five World Cup victories), becomes the fifth country to host the event twice. Unlike in 1950, when games were largely held in the South and Southeast, the 2014 World Cup event will be staged all across the country in 12 different cities: Belo Horizonte, Brasília, Cuiabá, Curitiba, Fortaleza, Manaus, Natal, Porto Alegre, Recife, Rio de Janeiro, Salvador and São Paulo. Normally host nations hold the event in only eight to 10 cities, but because of Brazil's great size and its number of significant cities, FIFA granted an exemption.

To prepare for the event, Brazil has invested more than US$12 billion in the event. Huge sums were earmarked for stadium construction and remodeling, along infrastructure projects, including upgrading ports, highways and 10 of the host cities' airports (most importantly Rio's and São Paulo's) to cope with the huge influx of fans – an estimated 500,000 visitors.

Rio for its part will play a starring role in the 2014 World Cup, hosting both the opening match and the final; it will play an even bigger role two years later when it hosts the Summer Olympics.

Brazil's military regime was not as brutal as those of Chile or Argentina – a reality that led to the somewhat unkind saying, 'Brazil couldn't even organize a dictatorship properly.' Yet for the best part of 20 years, freedom of speech was an unknown concept and political parties were banned.

The Brazilian economy flourished. Year after year in the late 1960s and early 1970s, the economy grew by over 10%, as Brazil's rulers borrowed heavily from international banks. But in the absence of rural land reform, millions moved to the cities, where favelas filled up the open spaces.

During this time, Brazil's obsession with 'megaprojects' was born. Under the quick-spending regime, construction began on numerous colossal (and mostly ill-fated) plans, including the Transamazônica highway, the Rio-Niterói Bridge and the Ilha do Fundão, which was to house Rio's Federal University.

1956	1958	1960	1964
Juscelino Kubitschek de Oliveira (better known as JK), is elected president, and builds a new capital – Brasília. JK had to borrow heavily to finance the project, leading to inflation that would dog the economy for decades.	Brazil wins its first football World Cup. The team catapults to victory over Sweden, largely on the skills of a precocious 17-year-old unknown by the name of Pelé.	President Juscelino Kubitschek spearheads the creation of a new capital. Architects Oscar Niemeyer and Lúcio Costa play a starring role in building hypermodern Brasília from scratch in just 41 months.	President Goulart is overthrown by a military coup – with strong evidence of US involvement. So begins the era of dictatorship, with generals running the show for the next 20 years.

The Workers Organize

By the late 1970s, the economic boom was dying and opposition to the regime began to spread from the educated middle class to the working class. A series of strikes in the São Paulo car industry signaled the intent of the militant new workers' movement. At the helm was Luíz Inácio 'Lula' da Silva, who famously lost one *dedo* (finger) in a factory accident but made up in charisma for what he lacked in the finger department.

The Partido dos Trabalhadores (PT; Workers' Party), Brazil's first-ever mass political party to speak for the poor, grew out of these strikes, and helped pave the way toward *abertura* (opening), a cautious return to civilian rule between 1979 and 1985. With popular opposition gathering force, the military announced gradual moves toward a democratic Brazil.

Democracy & Debt

In 1985 a presidential election took place, though the only voters were members of the national congress. Unexpectedly, Tancredo Neves, opposing the military candidate, came out on top, and millions of Brazilians took to the streets to celebrate the end of military rule.

Immediately a spanner was thrown in the works: Neves died from heart failure before he could assume the presidency. His vice-presidential candidate, the whiskered José Sarney, took over. Sarney – who had supported the military until 1984 – held office until 1989, a period in which runaway inflation helped Brazil rack up a gargantuan foreign debt. By 1990 the external debt stood at a crippling US$115 billion.

In the 1989 direct presidential election it was a Northeastern political climber by the name of Collor who was victorious, beating Lula, the PT's candidate, by the smallest of margins.

A Troubled Administration

Fernando Collor de Mello, former governor of the small state of Alagoas, revolutionized consumer laws. 'Sell by' dates, however, couldn't save him from disgrace. An ever-lengthening list of scandals involving Collor and his intimate associate PC Farias – alleged corruption on a vast scale, alleged drug deals, family feuds – led to a congressional inquiry, huge student protests and eventually the president's impeachment.

Though out of office, 'Fernandinho' managed to avoid a prison sentence, receiving little more than an eight-year ban from politics. Found not guilty of 'passive corruption' by the Supreme Court in 1994, he moved to Miami, where he remained for five years. In 1998 Collor returned to Brazil, and after several unsuccessful attempts to re-enter Brazilian politics was elected to congress as a senator for Alagoas.

BARRETO

Set during the military dictatorship, Bruno Barreto's film *Four Days in September* (1998) is based on the 1969 kidnapping of the US ambassador to Brazil by leftist guerrillas.

From 1980 to 1994, Brazilians suffered devastating hyperinflation, that peaked above 2000% several years. At this rate, rent doubled every 10 weeks, credit cards charged 25% a month interest and food and clothes went up 40% a month.

1968	1968	1972	1979–80
The government passes the repressive Ato Institutional 5 law, which purges opposition legislators, judges and mayors from public office; most political parties are banned. Protests erupt nationwide.	The Brazilian economy booms, averaging an incredible 10% growth for the next six years. Rapid income growth continues into the 1970s.	The era of megaprojects and skyrocketing deficits begins, with the opening of the 5300km Trans-Amazonian highway. It cost nearly US$1 billion, but never achieved its goal of colonizing the Amazon.	The consistent decline of workers' wages leads to strikes across the country. Unions call for justice and young workers join with intellectuals and activists to form Brazil's Workers' Party (PT).

Brazil's Boom Days

The first favela (slum or shantytown) appeared on Rio's landscape in 1897, but it wasn't until 1994 that the communities (which today number over 600) were included on maps.

Following Collor's impeachment, Vice-President Itamar Franco found himself in the hot seat. Despite his reputation as an eccentric, his administration was credited with competence and integrity. Franco's greatest achievement was to stabilize Brazil's violently erratic economy, introducing a new currency, the real. Pegged to the US dollar, the real caused inflation to plummet from a rate of over 5000% in late 1993 to under 10% in 1994.

The Plano Real sparked an economic boom that continues to this day, though it was his successor, former finance minister Fernando Henrique Cardoso, who presided through the mid-1990s over a growing economy and record foreign investment. He is often credited with laying the groundwork that put Brazil's hyperinflation to bed, though often at the neglect of social problems.

THE ORIGINS OF THE FAVELA

In the 1870s and '80s, terrible droughts coupled with the decline of the sugar industry, brought economic devastation. Offering a vision of hope, messianic movements became popular among Brazil's poor. The most famous was that of Canudos, led by an itinerant preacher Antônio Conselheiro (Antônio the Counselor), who wandered for years through the backlands preaching and prophesying the appearance of the Antichrist and the end of the world. He railed against the new republican government and in 1893 eventually settled with his followers at Canudos, in the interior of northern Bahia. Within 1½ years Canudos had grown to a city of 35,000.

The republican government sensed plots in Canudos to return Brazil to the monarchy, although it took them several attempts, a federal force of 8000 well-supplied soldiers – many of whom hailed from Rio – eventually took Canudos after vicious, hand-to-hand, house-to-house fighting. It was a war of extermination that nearly wiped out every man, woman and child from Canudos; the settlement was then burned to the ground to erase it from the nation's memory.

The surviving soldiers and their wives returned to Rio, where they were promised land in exchange for their victory. The government, however, reneged on the promise, and the soldiers occupied the nearby hillside of Morro da Providência. Oddly enough, as the first tenants put up makeshift shelter and settled in, they came across the same hardy shrub they found in the arid lands surrounding Canudos. Called 'favela,' this plant caused skin irritations to all who come in contact with it – according to some accounts, the protective shrub even helped repel the army's initial invasions. Soon hillside residents began calling their new home the Morro da Favela, and the name caught on. Soon the word favela was used to describe the ever-increasing number of informal communities appearing around Rio, which quickly gathered a mix of former slaves and poverty-stricken inhabitants from the interior, who came to the city seeking a better life.

1984	1985	1988	1994
The Movimento Sem Terra (MST; Landless Workers' Movement) – an organization calling for land reform – is founded. The fringe organization of 6000 families grows to more than 1.5 million today.	Brazil holds an indirect presidential election. Tancredo Neves wins, but dies of heart failure before taking office. Vice-president José Sarney fails to tame the huge debt left by his predecessors.	Amazonia rubber-tappers' leader and environmentalist Chico Mendes is murdered by a local rancher and his son. The public outcry following Mendes' death forces the government to create extractive reserves.	The Favela-Bairro project is unveiled in Rio. Over the next decade, US$180 million will be spent providing neglected communities with access to decent sanitation, health clinics and public transportation.

Come the 2002 election, Lula, at the fourth time of asking, toned down his socialist rhetoric, and promised to repay Brazil's international debts. This, and the PT's corruption-free reputation, won over enough of the electorate's middle ground to give Lula a convincing victory over the center-right candidate Jose Serra. For the first time ever, Brazil had a government on the left of the political spectrum and a president who really knew what poverty was like. One of 22 children born to a dirt-poor illiterate farm-worker from Brazil's stricken Northeast, Lula had worked as a shoeshine boy, then a mechanic, then a trade-union leader.

His accession initially alarmed investors, who had envisioned a left-leaning renegade running the economy amok. In fact, he surprised friends and foes alike with one of the most financially prudent administrations in years, while still addressing Brazil's egregious social problems.

When Lula left office in 2010, Brazil's economic prosperity was clear. Brazil became a net foreign creditor (as opposed to debtor) for the first time in 2008 and the country weathered the economic recession at the end of the decade better than any other developing country. He also helped achieved notable success in anti-poverty measures, and helped millions enter the middle class – all of which helps explain why Lula was rated Brazil's most popular president in history; in his final months in office his approval rating was above 80%.

The Accidental President of Brazil, by Fernando Henrique Cardoso, is an elucidating memoir by one of Brazil's most popular presidents, a former sociology professor vaulted into power.

HISTORY BRAZIL'S BOOM DAYS

2002	2011	2014
After four unsuccessful attempts, Luíz Inácio 'Lula' da Silva is elected president. The former union leader serves a moderate first term, despite upper-class fears of radical agendas.	Dilma Rousseff is sworn in as president of Brazil, becoming the first woman ever to hold the office. As Lula's handpicked successor, she largely continues the policies of her predecessor.	Brazil hosts the 2014 FIFA World Cup, spending US$12 billion in preparation for the event, which is staged at 12 different cities across the country.

JON FEINGERSH / GETTY IMAGES ©

→ Football fans

Life in Brazil

Brazil is a nation of astounding diversity, forged from African, European and indigenous influences, along with the tens of millions of immigrants who flooded into the country in the late 19th and early 20th centuries. Brazilians of today represent a complicated portrait of colors and creeds and hail from a wide range of socioeconomic backgrounds. The lifestyle is no less diverse – not surprising for a country that's home to both age-old indigenous cultures and modern metropolises.

Dozens of uncontacted indigenous groups still live in the Amazon. In 2007, 89 Metyktire suddenly emerged in a village in Pará, the first time this particular group (feared dead) had been encountered since 1950.

Multiculturalism

Brazilian identity has been shaped not only by the Portuguese, who provided its language and main religion, but also by native *índios*, Africans and the many immigrants over the years from Europe, the Middle East and Asia.

Indigenous culture, though often ignored or denigrated by urban Brazilians, has helped shape modern Brazil and its legends, dance and music. Many indigenous foods and beverages, such as tapioca, manioc (cassava), potatoes, maté and guaraná (a shrub whose berry is a stimulant; also a popular soft drink) have become staples.

The influence of African culture is also evident, especially in the Northeast. The slaves imported by the Portuguese brought with them their religion, music and cuisine, all of which have become a part of Brazilian identity.

Brazil had several waves of voluntary immigration. After the end of slavery in 1888, millions of Europeans were recruited to work in the coffee fields. The largest contingent was from Italy (some one million arrived between 1890 and 1920), but there were also many Portuguese and Spaniards, and smaller groups of Germans and Russians.

Immigration is only part of the picture when considering Brazil's diversity. Brazilians are just as likely to mention regional types, often accompanied by their own colorful stereotypes. Caboclos, who are descendents of the *índio*, live along the rivers in the Amazon region and keep alive the traditions and stories of their ancestors. *Gaúchos* populate Rio Grande do Sul, speak a Spanish-inflected Portuguese and can't quite shake the reputation for being rough-edged cowboys. By contrast, *baianos*, descendents of the first Africans in Brazil, are stereotyped for being the most extroverted and celebratory of Brazilians. *Mineiros* (residents of Minas Gerais state) are considered more serious and reserved than Brazil's coastal dwellers, while *Sertanejos* (residents of the backlands – called *sertão* – of the Northeast) are dubbed tough-skinned individuals with strong folk traditions. *Cariocas* (residents of Rio city) are superficial beach bums according to *paulistanos* (residents of São Paulo city), who are often denigrated as being workaholics with no zeal for life – a rivalry that anyone who's lived in LA or New York can understand.

Today there are dozens of terms to describe Brazilians' various racial compositions, and it is not uncommon for apparently white Brazilians to have a mix of European, African and indigenous ancestors. Yet, despite appearances of integration and racial harmony, underneath is a brutal reality. Although blacks and mulattoes account for 45% of the population, they are sorely underrepresented in government and business, and often see little hope of rising out of poverty. The indigenous are even more openly discriminated against, continuing a cycle that began with the genocidal policies of the first Europeans.

Population

Brazil is the world's fifth most populous country, but it also has one of the smallest population densities, with around 24 people per sq km. Most of Brazil's population lives along the coast, particularly in the South and Southeast, home to 75% of the country's inhabitants. Until the mid-20th century, Brazil was largely a rural country – today, its population is more than 80% urban. The population in cities has exploded in the last half-century, though growth is slowing.

The Northeast has the highest concentration of Afro-Brazilians, with Salvador as its cultural capital. In the Amazon live Caboclos (literally 'copper-colored'), the mixed descendants of indigenous peoples and the Portuguese. In the South is the most European of the Brazilian population, descendants of Italian and German immigrants.

While there is much more mixing between races, Brazil is a long way from being a color-blind society. Afro-Brazilians make up the bulk of low-paid workers, and are far more likely to live in favelas than in middle-class neighborhoods. More than 40% of Afro-Brazilians live in poverty (twice the rate of whites). Afro-Brazilians die younger than whites, earn less and have a greater risk of going to prison. Barely 2% of Afro-Brazilians attend university – though a new quota system (approved by the supreme court in 2012) aims to address the longstanding racial imbalance. Black political representatives and even high-ranking black employees are rarities – clear examples of the lack of opportunities for blacks in Brazil.

How to Be a Carioca, by Priscilla Ann Goslin, is a humorous portrait of the Rio dweller, with tongue-in-cheek riffs on beach-going, driving, soap operas, football and *carioca* slang.

WOMEN IN BRAZIL

Brazil had one of the earliest feminist movements in Latin America, and women were among the first in the region to gain the right to vote, in 1932. Today there is a growing number of feminist NGOs, dedicated to educating women about their legal rights and family planning, while also training police how to handle cases of domestic violence. In Brasília there's even a feminist lobby. More importantly, Brazil's head of state is a woman. Dilma Rousseff, who became Brazil's first female president in 2011, serves as a major icon for breaking down barriers for women.

In spite of advances, many *machista* (chauvinist) stereotypes persist, and women are still sorely underrepresented in positions of power. Only about 16% of senators and 9% of deputies in the lower house are women, which is one of the lowest figures in Latin America (where women on average make up around 20% of the legislature).

In other spheres, women represent 45% of the workforce – a huge leap from decades past but still below the average in Latin America (where women comprise 53% of the workforce). Unfortunately, the wage gap remains high, with men earning 30% more than women of the same age and income level.

Instances of domestic abuse are frighteningly common (one report stated that every 24 seconds a woman is beaten in Brazil, and that 10 women a day die from domestic violence). In response, the first women's police station opened in 1990 specifically to handle violence against women. Today there are more than 300 women's police stations, largely staffed by female police officers.

Women receive 120 days of paid maternity leave (men receive five days of paternity leave). Abortions are still illegal in Brazil (except in cases of rape and maternal health risks), and an estimated one million are performed each year, often with substantial health risks. More than 200,000 women each year are hospitalized from clandestine abortions.

The indigenous population today numbers more than 700,000, comprising 200 tribes. Although this is a fraction of the estimated two million or more in Brazil at the time of European arrival, the indigenous population has shown a remarkable resurgence in recent years – the population has tripled since 1970. Customs and beliefs vary widely from tribe to tribe – as do the strengths of these traditions in the face of expulsion from traditional lands, declining numbers, missionary activity and other influences.

After centuries of genocidal attacks, slavery, dispossession and death from imported diseases, Brazil's indigenous population is growing again but still faces a host of problems. Most of them live in the Amazon rainforest, and therefore the threats that the rainforest faces – logging, mining, ranching, farming, roads, settlements, dams, hydroelectric schemes – also threaten the indigenous whose way of life depends on it.

> Japanese immigration began in 1908, and today São Paulo has the world's largest Japanese community outside of Japan.

Lifestyles

Constructing a portrait of the typical Brazilian is a complicated task, given the wide mix of social, cultural and economic factors in play. One thing that everyone agrees on is the huge chasm separating rich from poor.

The country's middle and upper classes live in comfortable apartments or houses, with all the trappings of the first world, including good health care in private clinics, cars, vacation homes and easy access to the latest gadgets and trends (though prices for luxury goods are much higher here, eg 16GB iPhones without a plan cost R$1850). The wealthiest send their children to private schools and abroad to university. Maids are common – even among middle-class Brazilians – and some families have chauffeurs and cooks. Depending on where one lives in the country, crime is likely to be of high concern. Those who can take extra precautions, opting for high-security buildings or even hiring bodyguards.

Somewhere below the elite are working-class folks struggling to put food on the table and pay the rent; the children tend to live at home until they are married. Couples tend to marry younger.

At the bottom of the socioeconomic ladder are *favelados* (slum dwellers), who live in self-constructed housing (usually boxy concrete or brick dwellings) in crowded makeshift communities. Ranging in size from a few thousand inhabitants to over 70,000, favelas are found in nearly every urban area in Brazil. Most residents have electricity and running water, though open sewers run through many favelas. Access to education, adequate health care, transportation and other essential infrastructure can often be limited, though this is slowly changing under government-funded favela improvement schemes.

> DOMESTICAS
>
> *Domesticas* (Maids), the first film by Fernando Meirelles, delves into the lives of five women who work as *domesticas*, creating a compelling portrait of Brazil's often overlooked underclass.

In the countryside, conditions for the poor can be even worse. Unequal land distribution dating back to the colonial era means that thousands of homeless rural families are left to squat on vacant land or work long hours as itinerant laborers for low wages.

Regardless of socioeconomic background, most Brazilians have a healthy appreciation for a a good party (Carnaval is but one manifestation). This joie de vivre can be seen in football matches, on the beaches, in the samba clubs and on the streets. The flip side of this trait is *saudade*, that woeful manifestation of longing or deep regret, given much play on old bossa nova records.

Brazilian Rhythms

Shaped by the mixing of varied influences from three continents, Brazilian popular music has always been characterized by great diversity. The samba canção (samba song), for example, is a mixture of Spanish bolero with the cadences and rhythms of African music. Bossa nova was influenced by samba and North American music, particularly jazz. Tropicália mixed influences ranging from bossa nova and Italian ballads to blues and North American rock. Brazil is still creating new and original musical forms today.

Samba & Choro

The birth of modern Brazilian music essentially began with the birth of samba, first heard in the early 20th century in a Rio neighborhood near present-day Praça Onze. Here, Bahian immigrants formed a tightly knit community in which traditional African customs thrived – music, dance and the Candomblé religion. Such an atmosphere nurtured the likes of Pixinguinha, one of samba's founding fathers, as well as Donga, one of the composers of 'Pelo Telefone,' the first recorded samba song (in 1917) and an enormous success at the then-fledgling Carnaval.

Samba continued to evolve in the homes and *botequims* (bars with table service) around Rio. The 1930s are known as the golden age of samba. Sophisticated lyricists such as Dorival Caymmi, Ary Barroso and Noel Rosa popularized samba *canção*, melody-driven samba laid over African percussion. Songs in this style featured sentimental lyrics and an emphasis on melody (rather than rhythm), foreshadowing the later advent of cool bossa nova.

The 1930s were also the golden age of samba songwriting for Carnaval. *Escolas de samba* (samba schools or clubs), which first emerged in 1928, soon became a vehicle for samba songwriting, and by the 1930s samba and Carnaval would be forever linked.

Great *sambistas* (samba singers) continued to emerge in Brazil over the next few decades, although other emerging musical styles diluted their popularity. Artists such as Cartola, Nelson Cavaquinho and Clementina de Jesus made substantial contributions to both samba and styles of music that followed from samba.

Traditional samba went through a rebirth a little over a decade ago with the opening of old-style *gafieiras* (dance halls) in Lapa. Today, Rio is once again awash with great *sambistas*. Classic *sambistas* such as Alcione and Beth Carvalho still perform, while rising stars such as Teresa Christina and Grupo Semente are intimately linked to Lapa's rebirth. Other talents include Diogo Nogueira, the deep-voiced samba son of legendary singer João Nogueira, and Mart'nália, daughter of samba icon Martinho da Vila.

Another popular artist still active in Rio is Maria Rita, the talented singer and songwriter whose voice is remarkably similar to that of her late mother, Elis Regina – one of Brazil's all-time greats. Rita's album *Samba Meu Samba Meu* is still one of her best.

Choro is a relative of samba. Characterized by its jazzy sound, melodic leaps and sometimes rapid-fire tempo, choro is mostly instrumental

The Brazilian Sound, by Chris McGowan and Ricardo Pessanha, is a well-illustrated, readable introduction to Brazilian music, with insight into regional styles and musicians (big-name and obscure). Useful discography included.

music and highly improvisational. It's played on the *cavaquinho* or guitar alongside a recorder or flute. The flutist Pixinguinha (1898–1973) is one of the great legends of choro.

Bossa Nova

In the 1950s came bossa nova (literally, 'new wave'), sparking a new era of Brazilian music. Bossa nova's founders – songwriter and composer Antônio Carlos (Tom) Jobim and guitarist João Gilberto, in association with the lyricist-poet Vinícius de Moraes – slowed down and altered the basic samba rhythm to create a more intimate, harmonic style. This initiated a new style of playing instruments and of singing.

Bossa Nova: The Story of the Brazilian Music that Seduced the World, by Ruy Castro, is an excellent book that captures the vibrant music and its backdrop of 1950s Rio.

Bossa nova's seductive melodies were very much linked to Rio's Zona Sul, where most bossa musicians lived. Songs such as Jobim's 'Corcovado' and Roberto Menescal's 'Rio' evoked an almost nostalgic portrait of the city with their quiet lyricism. Bossa nova was also associated with the new class of university-educated Brazilians, and its lyrics reflected the optimistic mood of the middle class in the 1950s.

By the 1960s bossa nova had become a huge international success. Bossa nova classics were adopted, adapted and recorded by such musical luminaries as Frank Sinatra, Ella Fitzgerald and Stan Getz, among others.

In addition to the founding members, other great Brazilian bossa nova musicians include Marcos Valle, Luiz Bonfá and Baden Powell. Bands from the 1960s such as Sergio Mendes & Brasil '66 were also quite influenced by bossa nova, as were other artists who fled the repressive military dictatorship to live and play abroad. More recent interpreters of the seductive bossa sound include the Bahian-born Rosa Passos and *carioca* Paula Morelenbaum.

Tropicália

One of Brazil's unique artistic movements, emerging in the late 1960s, *tropicália* was a direct response to the dictatorship that held power from 1964 to 1984. Leading the movement were Caetano Veloso and Gilberto Gil, making waves with songs of protest against the national regime. In addition to penning defiant lyrics, *tropicalistas* introduced the public to electric instruments, fragmentary melodies and wildly divergent musical styles.

Tropical Truth: A Story of Music and Revolution in Brazil, by Caetano Veloso, describes the great artistic experiment of *tropicália* in 1960s Brazil. Although digressive at times, Veloso captures the era's music and politics.

Important figures linked to *tropicália* include Gal Costa, Jorge Ben Jor, Maria Bethânia, Os Mutantes and Tom Zé. Although *tropicália* wasn't initially embraced by the public, who objected to the electric and rock elements (in fact, Veloso was booed off the stage on several occasions), by the 1970s its radical ideas had been absorbed and accepted, and lyrics of protest were ubiquitous in songwriting of the time.

While 'pure' *tropicália* bands aren't around any more, the influence can still be heard in the music of groups such as AfroReggae, one of Rio's leading funk bands.

Música Popular Brasileira (MPB)

Música Popular Brasileira (MPB) is a catchphrase to describe all popular Brazilian music after bossa nova. It includes *tropicália, pagode,* and Brazilian pop and rock. All Brazilian music has roots in samba; even in Brazilian rock, heavy metal, disco or pop, the samba sound is often present.

MPB first emerged in the 1970s along with talented musicians such as Edu Lobo, Milton Nascimento, Elis Regina, Djavan and dozens of others, many of whom wrote protest songs not unlike the *tropicalistas*. Chico Buarque is one of the first big names from this epoch, and is one of Brazil's best songwriters. His music career began in 1968 and spanned a time during which many of his songs were banned by the military dictatorship – in fact his music became a symbol of protest during that era.

Jorge Ben Jor is another singer whose career, which began in the 1960s, has survived up to the present day. Highly addictive rhythms are omnipresent in Ben Jor's songs, as he incorporates African beats and elements of funk, samba and blues in his eclectic repertoire. The celebratory album *África Brasil* and his debut album, *Samba Esquema Novo* (with recognizable hits such as 'Mas, Que Nada!'), are among his best.

Carlinhos Brown continues to make immeasurable contributions to Brazilian music, particularly in the realm of Afro-Brazilian rhythms. Born in Bahia, Brown has influences that range from *merengue* (fast-paced dancehall music originating in the Dominican Republic) to Candomblé music to straight-up funk in the style of James Brown (the US artist from whom Carlinhos took his stage name). In addition to creating the popular percussion ensemble Timbalada, he has a number of excellent albums of his own (notably *Alfagamabetizado*). Involved in many diverse projects, Brown was even nominated for an Oscar in 2012 for best original song ('Real in Rio' for the film *Rio*), which he and Sergio Mendes composed.

Brazilian Rock, Pop & Hip-Hop

MPB tends to bleed into other genres, particularly into rock and pop. One artist who moves comfortably between genres is Bebel Gilberto (the daughter of João Gilberto), who blends bossa nova with modern beats on jazz-inflected bilingual albums like *All in One* (2009). Another heiress of Brazilian traditions is the Rio-born Marisa Monte, popular at home and abroad for her fine singing and songwriting. Mixing samba, *forró* (traditional, fast-paced music from the northeast), pop and rock, Marisa has created a number of fine solo albums (*Barulinho Bom* – A Great Noise in English – is one of her best) and has performed on many others. Her brief collaboration with Arnaldo Antunes and Carlinhos Brown resulted in the superb album *Tribalistas* (2003). Other notable young singers who hail from a bossa line include Roberta Sá, whose most recent album, *Segunda Pele* (2012), features elements of bossa, jazz and even reggae; and Fernanda Porto, whose music is often described as drum 'n' bossa, a blend of electronica and bossa grooves – check out her 2009 album *Auto-Retrato*.

The expat singer-songwriter and performance artist Cibelle incorporates a mix of pop, folk and Brazilian sounds in her lush (mainly English-language) recordings like those on *The Shine of Dried Electric Leaves*

SEIXAS

Raul Seixas (1945–89) is often called 'the father of Brazilian rock.' Many of his wild rock anthems are well known, and it's not uncommon to hear shouts of 'toca Raul!' (play Raul!) at concerts. Curiously, Paulo Coelho (future best-selling author of new-age novels) co-wrote many of his songs.

CANNIBALISM, BRAZILIAN STYLE

The eating of human flesh, as practiced by at least a few pre-Colombian tribes, contributed to some notion of Brazilian identity. In the 1920s, the intellectual movement of anthropophagy (a fancy word for cannibalism) came to denote Brazil's lust for new ideas and culture from abroad that would be consumed, digested and then transformed into something uniquely Brazilian.

In music, bossa nova incorporated (ingested) American jazz, blues and classical music, but created something entirely new. A few years later, along came the *tropicalistas*, who were open admirers of Oswald de Andrade's 1928 *Manifesto Antropofágico* (Cannibalistic Manifesto). *Tropicália* devoured elements of American rock and roll, blues, jazz and British psychedelic styles, as well as samba and even bossa nova, and produced a powerful new sound entirely Brazilian in its construction.

This notion of cultural cannibalism has been used to explain the prodigious output of Brazil not only in music, but also in fiction, painting and even filmmaking. As Caetano Veloso described, 'Antropofagia is a Brazilian state of being.'

(2006). She came to prominence as the main vocalist on Suba's noteworthy album *São Paulo Confessions* (1999). With a host of Grammy nominations to her name, Céu has many fans both at home and abroad. She has recorded three albums over the last seven years, creating dreamlike melodies with elements of *tropicália*, samba, reggae and jazz. Her latest, *Caravana Sereia Bloom* (2012), is a colorful work with songs inspired by a road trip across Brazil.

Brazilian hip-hop emerged from the favelas of Rio sometime in the 1980s, and has been steadily attracting followers ever since. Big names such as Racionais MCs first emerged out of São Paulo, but Rio has its share of more recent success stories. One of the best on the scene is Marcelo D2 (formerly of Planet Hemp), earning accolades for albums like *A Procura da Batida Perfeita* (2003) and *A Arte do Barulho* (2008).

Better known to international audiences is Seu Jorge, who starred in the film *Cidade de Deus* and performed brilliant Portuguese versions of Bowie songs on Wes Anderson's film *The Life Aquatic*. His best solo work is *Cru* (2005), an inventive hybrid of hip-hop and ballads, with politically charged beats.

Most of today's hip-hop artists hail from São Paulo. A few names to look out for include Emicida, a youthful rapper admired for his cutting improvisational rhymes. Check out his funk-laden single 'Triunfo,' one of his early breakthrough hits. Rael de Rima is a fast-rapping lyricist with a strong sense of musicality, often performing with guitar and a full back-up band (a rarity for many hip-hop artists). MC Criolo, whose

THE IPOD 20: SOUNDS FROM BRAZIL

One of the world's great music cultures, Brazil has an astounding array of talented musicians. A list of our favorite songs could fill a small book, but we've limited our highly subjective pick to 20 songs from 20 different artists.

➡ 'Sampa' – Caetano Veloso

➡ 'Alvorado' – Cartola

➡ 'Calice' – Chico Buarque & Milton Nascimento

➡ 'Aguas de Março' – Elis Regina (written by Tom Jobim)

➡ 'Hoje é Dia da Festa' – Elza Soares

➡ 'Namorinho de Portão' – Gal Costa

➡ 'Quilombo, o El Dorado Negro' – Gilberto Gil

➡ 'Desafinado' – João Gilberto

➡ 'Mas, Que Nada!' – Jorge Ben Jor

➡ 'A Procura da Batida Perfeita' – Marcelo D2

➡ 'Novo Amor' – Maria Rita

➡ 'Carinhoso' – Marisa Monte (written by Pixinguinha)

➡ 'Besta é Tu' – Novos Baianos

➡ 'Panis et Circenses' – Os Mutantes

➡ 'Beira Mar' – Raimundo Fagner and Zeca Baleiro

➡ 'Funk Baby' – Seu Jorge

➡ 'Acenda o Farol' – Tim Maia

➡ 'Garota de Ipanema' – Tom Jobim

➡ 'Não me deixe só' – Vanessa da Mata

➡ 'Felicidade' – Vinícius de Moraes

songs tackle urban violence, police brutality and racism, has become a huge hit in the favelas.

Brazil gets its share of mega-rockers on world tours. It also has a few homegrown talents. The group Legião Urbana from Brasília remains one of the all-time greats among rock lovers. The band (which folded shortly after the death of lead singer Renato Russo in 1996) enjoyed enormous success in the 1980s and early 1990s, and has sold over 15 million records. Raul Seixas, Skank, O Rappa, Paralamas Sucesso and the Rio-based Barão Vermelho are other essential names. The versatile and original Ed Motta, from Rio, injects soul, jazz and traditional Brazilian music into rock.

In other genres, indie-rock favorites Los Hermanos were a top band that created catchy albums before breaking up in 2007. Check out *Ventura* (2003) or *Bloco do Eu Souzinho* (2001), one of the seminal pop-rock albums of its time. Vanguart, fitting somewhere in the folk-rock genre, are also a group to watch. Their self-titled debut album (2007) channels samba, blues and classic rock. Other breakout successes include the saucy girl-band Cansei de Ser Sexy (Tired of Being Sexy), who blend '80s new wave and electro-pop with irreverent lyrics (sung in English) and up-tempo beats.

Regional Music

The Northeast has perhaps the most regional musical and dance styles. The most important is *forró*, a lively, syncopated music centered on the accordion and the *zabumba* (an African drum). Although a few artists, such as Luiz Gonzaga and Jackson do Pandeiro, have achieved national status, *forró* was long dismissed by urbanites as unsophisticated. The film *Eu, Tu, Eles* (Me, You, Them) brought down-home *forró* to center stage, aided in part by Gilberto Gil singing the hit 'Esperando na Janela.'

The *trio elétrico*, also called *frevo baiano*, began more as a result of a change in technology rather than in music. It started as a joke when, during Carnaval in Salvador in the 1950s, a group of musicians spearheaded by innovative musical talents Dodo and Osmar (aka Adolfo Nascimento and Osmar Alvares Macedo) got on top of a truck and played *frevo* with electric guitars. The *trio elétrico* is not necessarily a trio, but it's still the backbone of Salvador's Carnaval, when trucks piled high with speakers – with musicians perched on top – drive through the city surrounded by dancing mobs. Another important element of Carnaval on the streets of Salvador is the *bloco afro* (Afro-Brazilian percussion group). Filhos de Gandhi and Grupo Olodum are the most famous of these – Filhos has deep African roots and is strongly influenced by Candomblé; Olodum invented samba-reggae.

Mangue beat (also known as *mangue bit*), from Recife, combines folkloric and regional styles with international influences as diverse as hip-hop, neo-psychedelic and *tejano* (instrumental folk music with roots in northern Mexico and southern Texas). The early leaders of the genre were Chico Science and Nação Zumbi – the title of whose 1996 masterpiece, *Afrociberdelia,* kind of summed up what its music was about.

Axé is a label for the profuse samba-pop-rock-reggae-funk-Caribbean fusion music that emerged from Salvador in the 1990s. Taking its cue from Salvador's older Carnaval forms, *axé* was popularized by the powerful, flamboyant Daniela Mercury. Other exponents include the groups Ara Ketu and Chiclete com Banana. At its best it's great, superenergetic music – hear Daniela sing 'Toda Menina Baiana' (Every Bahian Girl) – but some bands overcommercialized it at the end of the '90s.

The influence of Brazilian indigenous music was absorbed and diluted, as was so much that derived from Brazil's indigenous cultures. The *carimbó* music of the Amazon region (where the majority of *índios* live today) is influenced primarily by the blacks of the coastal zones.

Top Music Sites & Blogs

The Saudade Project (www. saudadeproject. com)

Slipcue (www. slipcue.com/ music/brazil/ brazillist.html)

Jungle (jungle-drumsonline.com)

Brazilian Music Day (brazilianmusic day.org)

The Beautiful Game

Brazilians, quite simply, are football mad. No one goes to work on big international game days, with everyone packing into neighborhood bars or on the sidewalks out front to watch the game. After a big win, the whole country erupts with a rowdy night of partying. And should the team lose, the sadness in the air is palpable. Everyone cheers for the national team but, for most of the year, the local club team is the one that matters most.

The last time Brazil hosted the World Cup, in 1950, the national team lost in a dramatic final against Uruguay before some 200,000 fans in Rio's Maracanã stadium. The unforgettable day of infamy was later called 'maracanaço' and is still in common parlance.

The Game, the Fans

Most of the world generally acknowledges that Brazilians play the world's most creative, artistic and thrilling style of football. They are also generally known as lousy defenders, but no one seems to mind since they make the attack so exciting. The fans, too, are no less fun to watch. Skillful moves and adroit dribbling past an opponent receives a Spanish bullfight-style 'olé!' while fans do their best to rev up the action by pounding drums (or the backs of chairs), waving huge flags, setting off fireworks and smoke bombs and sometimes launching nefarious liquids over the grandstands of opposing fans.

Legends of the Sport

Brazil has raised many world-famous players through its ranks, from the Afro-Brazilian player Leonidas da Silva – who helped break down racial barriers (and scored the only bicycle kick goal ever in World Cup history in 1938) – to Romario, a powerful striker who scored more than 900 goals during his career. The greatest of all though is Pelé, sometimes referred to simply as 'O Rei' (the king). Throughout a 22-year career, the teams he played on won 53 titles, including three World Cups (the first, in Sweden in 1958, when he was just 17 years old). By the time he retired in the 1970s, he had played in 1366 games and scored more than 1200 goals, making him one of the world's greatest all-time goal scorers.

European Vacation

Until recently, most of the best players left Brazil for more lucrative contracts with European clubs. Over the last decade, however, many Brazilian stars have returned home to play for more adoring fans and not insubstantial contracts. The strengthening of the real against the euro, along with Brazil's economic boom, have allowed top Brazilian clubs to offer salaries near to the wages Brazilian players earn in Europe. TV rights and corporate sponsorships have also helped deepen the pockets of Brazilian clubs. The return of more players to Brazil, coupled with the ongoing growth of new talent in the big clubs could help transform Brazil into one of the world's footballing giants – on the club level as well as the international level.

The Clubs

Brazil has a staggering number of league teams – more than 400 according to the Brazilian Football Confederation (CBF) – with 20 top-level pro teams (part of the so-called Campeonato Brasileiro Série A). Apart from a couple of short breaks for the Christmas–New Year holiday and Carnaval, professional club competitions go on all year. There are a bewildering number of competitions throughout the year with hotly contested state championships – particularly in Rio (the Campeonata Carioca) and São Paulo (the Campeonata Paulista). Expect intense and bitter matches, especially when historic hometown rivals match-up such as Flamengo versus Fluminense in Rio; Palmeiras versus Corinthians in São Paulo; Atlético Mineiro (led by Ronaldinho) versus Cruzeiro in Belo Horizonte; and Grêmio (Gisele Bündchen's favorite team) versus Internacional in Porto Alegre. Here's a run-down of the top four club teams in Brazil:

Flamengo

The most successful among Rio's big four, Flamengo has an enormous fan base both in Rio and around the world – an estimated 36 million followers, which makes them the most popular football club in Brazil. Flamengo certainly does not lack for cash flow, with annual revenue of over R$120 million. Famous players who have donned the iconic red-and-black jerseys include Zico, often hailed as the best player never to win a World Cup; Leonidas, leading scorer at the 1938 World Cup; Beheto, Mario Zagallo and Romario.

> For insight into what's happening in the Brazilian football scene – from player news to upcoming matches – visit www.sambafoot.com.

Fluminense

Founded by sons of the elite in Rio back in 1902, Fluminense has contributed a number of top players to the national team. It has also been hailed as the 'champion of the century,' for winning the largest number of Campeonato Carioca titles in the 20th century (28 in all). Current stars include Fred (aka Frederico Chaves Guedes), who scored the fastest goal in Brazilian history (finding the net 3.17 seconds after the game's start). Like Flamengo, Fluminense plays its home games in the newly upgraded Maracanã stadium.

Santos

This port city 80km southeast of São Paulo has a legendary footballing reputation. Santos has won eight national championships and has nurtured

......

BRAZILIAN FOOTBALL: THE CLUBS

If you get a chance, see a game live; there's no experience quite like it. Many stadiums have gone through upgrades in preparation for the World Cup. Here's a short list of top teams to catch.

CLUB	HOME CITY	STADIUM (CAPACITY)	JERSEYS
Bahia	Salvador	Fonte Nova (57,000)	white
Botafogo	Rio de Janeiro	João Havelange (47,000)	black & white stripes
Corinthians	São Paulo	Arena Corinthians (68,000)	white; black collar
Cruzeiro	Belo Horizonte	Mineirão (65,000)	blue
Flamengo	Rio de Janeiro	Maracanã (80,000)	red; black hoops
Fluminense	Rio de Janeiro	Maracanã (80,000)	red, green & white stripes
Grêmio	Porto Alegre	Arena do Grêmio (61,000)	blue, black & white stripes
Internacional	Porto Alegre	Beira-Rio (60,000)	red
Náutico Capibaribe	Recife	Arena Pernambuco (46,000)	red & white stripes
Palmeiras	São Paulo	Arena Palestra Itália (60,000)	green
Santos	Santos	Vila Belmiro (26,000)	white
São Paulo	São Paulo	Morumbi (67,000)	white; red & black hoops
Vasco da Gama	Rio de Janeiro	São Januário (35,000)	white; black slash

FUTEBOL

Futebol, by Alex Bellos (2002) is a fascinating and humorous look at the culture behind Brazil's nationwide obsession, with stories of the legendary players and the way that football has shaped Brazilian society.

the talents of some of Brazil's all-time greats, including Pelé, who played on the team from 1957 to 1974. On the World Cup teams of 1962 and 1970, eight of the 11 starting players came from Santos. Its top player today is Neymar, whose youth (he scored his 100th goal as a professional in 2012 at age 20) and skill has earned him comparisons to Lionel Messi and Pelé. In both 2011 and 2012, Neymar won the South American Footballer of the Year award. Unable to resist bigger fame (and income) abroad, Neymar signed a five-year contract with FC Barcelona in 2013.

Corinthians

The most popular of São Paulo's three big teams, Corinthians is also Brazil's most valuable club team with an estimated worth of over US$350 million. The team vaulted to fame in 2012, winning both the Copa Libertadores and the FIFA Club World Cup (defeating English superpower Chelsea 1-0 in the final). Their arch-rivals are Palmeiras, a team they face (and often defeat) in the legendary Derby Paulista. Fans are noted for their diehard loyalty. Over 30,000 supporters made the trip to Japan in the 2012 Club World Cup final.

The World Cup

Brazil, the most successful football nation in the history of the games (with five World Cup victories), becomes the fifth country to host the World Cup twice. Aside from Rio, where the opener and final take place, 11 other cities across the country will stage games. Brazil spent more than R$27 billion in preparation for the 2014 event, including stadium construction, upgrades to airports, roads and other infrastructure.

Cinema & Literature

Brazil has a flourishing film industry, though many productions don't see screen time beyond the country's borders. Key periods in Brazilian cinema include the avant-garde Cinema Novo movement of the 1960s and hard-hitting socially conscious films of the last decade, with a new crop of talented directors emerging on the scene. In the realm of literature, Brazil has produced a handful of great writers, including the Bahian legend Jorge Amado and the brilliant modernist Clarice Lispector.

Cinema

In the 1960s the Cinema Novo movement emerged in Brazil, focusing on the country's bleak social problems. Young filmmakers, influenced by Italian neorealism and the French new wave, set about making a series of experimental films embracing the avant-garde filming techniques of the time. One of the great films made during this epoch was Anselmo Duarte's 1962 *O Pagador de Promessas* (The Payer of Vows), a poetic story about a man who keeps his promise to carry a cross after the healing of his donkey. It won the Palme d'Or at the Cannes film festival. Another great pioneer of Cinema Novo is the director Glauber Rocha. In *Deus é o Diabo na Terra do Sol* (Black God, White Devil; 1963), Rocha explored the struggle, fanaticism and poverty of Northeastern Brazil. It's one of the great films of the period.

The 1964 military coup stymied much creative expression in the country, and Cinema Novo died out just as its filmmakers were entering their prime. The first significant film to be made after the 1960s was Carlos Diegues' *Bye Bye Brasil* (1980). It chronicles the adventures of a theater troupe as it tours the country, witnessing the profound changes in Brazilian society in the second half of the 20th century.

In the 1980s, Hector Babenco emerged as one of Brazil's rising stars. In *Pixote* (1981), Babenco brought to life the yawning chasm between haves and have-nots in a story about a homeless child who gets swept from innocent waif to criminal by the currents of the underworld. Two decades later, his film *Carandiru* (2003) offered an inside look at São Paulo's hellish state penitentiary of the same name.

Fernando Meirelles earned his credibility with *Cidade de Deus* (City of God), the 2002 film based on a true story by Paolo Lins. The film, which showed brutality and hope coexisting in a Rio favela, earned four Oscar nominations. More importantly, it brought much attention to the urban poor in Brazil.

Set in 1970 during the height of the military dictatorship, *O Ano em Que Meus Pais Saíram de Férias* (The Year My Parents Went on Vacation; 2006), directed by Cao Hamburger, is a poignant coming-of-age story. Brazil's official Oscar entry for best foreign film in 2007 tackles complex issues with sensitivity in the story of one young boy left adrift in a working-class neighborhood of São Paulo. Political repression, the World Cup of 1970 and Jewish culture all form the backdrop of Hamburger's remarkably well-made film.

Brazilian Cinema, edited by Randal Johnson and Robert Stam, provides a fascinating overview of the great movements that have shaped the industry, exploring Cinema Novo, tropicalism, anthropophagy and other important influences.

TOP FILMS

● ●

➡ *O Som ao Redor* (Neighboring Sounds, 2012), by Kleber Mendonça Filho

➡ *Tropa de Elite* (Elite Squad, 2007), by José Padilha

➡ *Casa de Areia* (House of Sand, 2005), by Andrucha Waddington

➡ *Carandiru* (2003), by Hector Babenco

➡ *Cidade de Deus* (City of God, 2002), by Fernando Meirelles

➡ *Madame Satã* (2002), by Karim Aïnouz

➡ *Central do Brasil* (Central Station, 1998), by Walter Salles

➡ *O Que é Isso Companheiro* (Four Days in September, 1998), by Bruno Barreto

➡ *Pixote* (1981), by Hector Babenco

➡ *Bye Bye Brasil* (1980), by Carlos Diegues

➡ *O Pagador de Promessas* (The Payer of Vows, 1962), by Glauber Rocha.

➡ *Orfeu Negro* (Black Orpheus, 1959), by Marcel Camus

One of the most talked-about films of recent years is the 2007 *Tropa de Elite* (Elite Squad), which depicts police brutality in the favelas; it also makes a very clear link between middle-class college kids who buy drugs and the deaths of young children in the favelas who are recruited by drug lords to help meet the demand for cocaine and other substances. It was made by José Padilha, the acclaimed director of the disturbing documentary *Bus 174* (2002), which depicts a high-profile bus hijacking that took place in Rio de Janeiro in 2000.

Walter Salles is Brazil's best-known director, whose Oscar award-winning *Central do Brasil* (Central Station; 1998) should be in every serious Brazilianist's film library. The central character is an elderly woman who works in the main train station in Rio writing letters for illiterates with families far away. A chance encounter with a young homeless boy leads her to accompany him into the real, unglamorized Brazil on a search for his father. Salles' film *Diarios de Motocicleta* (The Motorcycle Diaries; 2004) chronicles the historic journey of Che Guevara and Alberto Granada across South America, while *On the Road* (2012) is a colorful adaptation of the Jack Kerouac classic. Some of Salles' best works came earlier. His first feature film, *Terra Estrangeiro* (Foreign Land, 1995) holds an important place in the renaissance of Brazilian cinema.

Literature

An Anthology of Twentieth-Century Brazilian Poetry (1972) is a fine introduction to Brazilian poets. It's edited by American poet Elizabeth Bishop, who planned a short trip to Santos and ended up staying 15 years.

Brazil's most famous writer is Jorge Amado, who died in August 2001. Born near Ilhéus in 1912, and a longtime resident of Salvador, Amado wrote colorful romances about Bahia's people and places. His early work was strongly influenced by communism. His later books are lighter in subject, but more picturesque and intimate in style. The two most acclaimed are *Gabriela, Clove and Cinnamon*, which is set in Ilhéus, and *Dona Flor and Her Two Husbands*, set in Salvador. *Tent of Miracles* explores race relations in Brazil, and *Pen, Sword and Camisole* laughs its way through the petty worlds of military and academic politics. *The Violent Land* is an early Amado classic.

Clarice Lispector (1920–77), one of Latin America's great 20th-century novelists, is little known outside the country. Her existentialism-influenced writings focus on human isolation, alienation and moral doubt, and convey a deep understanding of women's feelings. The short-story collections *Family Ties* and *Soulstorm* are among her best works.

Flavors of Brazil

Brazilian cuisine is as syncretic as the country itself. The most basic 'Brazilian' meal can include Portuguese olive oil, native manioc, Japanese sushi, African okra, Italian pasta, German sausage and Lebanese tabbouleh.

Regional flavors add to the culinary variety, with seafood and coconut *moqueca*, sundried beef, and pork-and-black bean *feijoada* among the classics. Sizzling steaks, tender Amazonian fish, fresh tropical juices, decadent snacks, refreshing cocktails and heavenly desserts are also key elements of the Brazilian dining experience.

Staples & Regional Specialties

Brazilian cuisine varies from region to region, but there are a few dishes you'll find across the country. *Arroz e feijão* (rice and beans), is a staple of

Above Chicken and shrimp dish with caiprinha (p684)

the Brazilian diet. On top of the beans, Brazilians often sprinkle *farofa* – manioc flour sautéed in butter, perhaps with bits of egg or bacon.

Grilled meats, known as *churrasco* or *grelhadas,* are the meal's crowning glory: chicken, beef or pork is dredged in salt and grilled over an open fire. A green salad or sautéed or steamed vegetables round out the main course.

Bahia & the Northeast

Bahian cuisine developed in the kitchens of the region's slave-based sugar plantations, and its African origins reveal themselves in dishes such as *moqueca*, a delicious seafood stew with coconut milk; spicy *malagueta* peppers; and *dendê* (palm) oil. On the streets of Bahia you can't escape the smell of *acarajé* – fritters made with brown beans and shrimp fried in *dendê* oil.

By contrast, drier inland areas of the Northeast known as the Sertão produce *carne seca* or *carne de sol,* beef that has been salted and dried. Squash, which manages to survive in difficult growing conditions, is also very popular.

Eat Smart in Brazil, by Joan and David Peterson, provides an excellent introduction to Brazil's culinary history, some classic recipes and an extensive and very useful glossary.

FOOD GLOSSARY

Main Dishes

barreado ba·rre·a·do A mixture of meats and spices cooked in a sealed clay pot for 24 hours and served with banana and *farofa*; the state dish of Paraná

bobó de camarão bo·bo de ka·ma·*rowng* Manioc paste flavored with dried shrimp, coconut milk and cashew nuts

carne de sol *kar*·ne de sol Tasty, salted meat, grilled and served with beans, rice and vegetables

casquinha de siri kas·*kee*·nya de see·*ree* Stuffed crab

cozido ko·*zee*·do A meat stew heavy on vegetables

feijoada fay·zho·a·da Bean-and-meat stew served with rice and orange slices, traditionally eaten for Saturday lunch

moqueca mo·*ke*·ka Bahian fish stew cooked in a clay pot with *dendê* oil, coconut milk and spicy peppers

pato no tucupí *pa*·to no too·koo·*pee* Roast duck flavored with garlic, juice of the manioc plant and *jambú*; a favorite in Pará

picanha pee·*kah*·nya Brazil's favorite cut of beef comes from the cow's rump

pirarucu ao forno pee·ra·oo·*koo* ow *forr*·no Delicious Amazonian fish, oven cooked with lemon and other seasonings

tutu á mineira too·*too* a mee·*nay*·ra Savory black-bean mash typical of Minas Gerais

vatapá va·ta·*pa* a Seafood dish of African origins with a thick sauce of manioc paste, coconut and *dendê* oil

Snacks

acarajé a·ka·ra·*zhe* Bahian fritters made of brown beans and dried shrimp fried in *dendê* oil

empadão eng·pa·*downg* A tasty pie, typical of Goiás, made from meat, vegetables, olives and eggs

pão de queijo powng de *kay*·zho Balls of cheese-stuffed tapioca bread

pastel pas·*tel* Thin square of dough stuffed with meat, cheese or fish, then fried

quibe *kee*·be Cracked wheat stuffed with spiced meat then deep-fried

Comida mineira (food from Minas Gerais; p168)

The Amazon

Amazonian cuisine is strongly influenced by the region's native Tupi people, who live largely on manioc, freshwater fish, yams and beans, and exotic fruit. *Caldeirada* is a popular fish stew not unlike bouillabaisse, and *pato no tucupí* is a regional favorite made with duck, garlic, liptingling *jambú* leaves and the juice of both lemons and manioc roots. *Jacaré* (caiman meat) is another delicacy.

The Central West

Occupying the prairie-like cerrado, the Central West is dominated by sprawling *fazendas* (ranches) that produce pork and beef, as well as staples such as corn, rice, kale and manioc. The region's rivers offer up the meaty *dourado* fish, the *pintado* (a type of catfish) and the infamous piranha.

Rio, São Paulo & the Southeast

In the mountainous state of Minas Gerais, pork is popular, as is the kale-like *couve,* which is sautéed in oil with garlic and onions. *Frango ao molho pardo* (chicken stewed in its own blood with vegetables) sounds gruesome but tastes delicious.

São Paulo, the gastronomic capital of Brazil, has both five-star dining rooms and humble ethnic restaurants that reflect the city's many immigrant communities. You'll find outstanding Japanese, Lebanese and Italian food, and the wood oven–baked pizza is world-class.

Rio offers excellent food from every region. *Feijoada,* a bean-and-meat stew served with rice, *farofa,* kale and sliced orange, is the city's contribution to the national cuisine. It is traditionally served on Saturday.

GUARANÁ

The indigenous Maué so revere guaraná – an Amazonian fruit whose caffeine-packed seed resembles the human eye – that its plant is said to have given birth to the tribe's founder.

The South

Italian and German food rules the day in the South. Expect to see lots of sausage and sauerkraut in the German enclaves of Joinville and Blumenau. Brazilian wine, whose quality improves year by year, comes from grapes lovingly imported from Italy and planted in the accommodating soil of Rio Grande do Sul.

The far south is *gaúcho* (Brazilian cowboy) country, and grilled beef restaurants are excellent here. The region preserves another cowboy tradition – *erva maté* tea.

Maria-Brazil.org (www.maria-brazil.org) has a very good section on Brazilian food, including easy-to-follow recipes and a guide to shopping in the country's supermarkets and street fairs.

Pan-Brazilian Fusion

Like much of the world, Brazil has undergone a kind of culinary renaissance in the last decade. One result has been a new pan-Brazilian fusion cuisine, which fuses native ingredients from the Amazonian fruits of the north to the grass-fed beef of the south.

Drinks

Juices

Brazilian *sucos* (juices) are divine. Staples include known quantities such as mango, orange, papaya, banana, passionfruit, watermelon and avocado. Then there are the Amazonian fruits like *açaí, graviola, cupuaçu* and *fruta do conde*.

Fresh *agua de côco* (coconut juice) is available across the country and is highly recommended.

Beer

Brazilians enjoy their beer served *bem gelada* (icy cold). Bohemia and Original are among the best national brands, though there are a growing number of (better) microbrews, including Devassa from Rio, Colorado from São Paulo and Eisenbahn from Santa Catarina.

Chope (*shope*-ee) is a pale-blond pilsner draft that's lighter and generally superior to canned or bottled beer.

Cookbooks

....

The Brazilian Table, by Yara Roberts

....

The Brazilian Kitchen, by Leticia Moreinos Schwartz

....

The Food and Cooking of Brazil, by Fernando Farah

Caiprinhas

The caipirinha is the unofficial Brazilian national drink. Ingredients are simple – *cachaça* (a high-proof sugarcane alcohol) with crushed lime, sugar and ice – but the results are sublime. You can replace the *cachaça* with vodka (to make a *caipirosca*) or sake (to create *caipisakes*) and the lime with a variety of fruit, including passion fruit, pineapple, mango, kiwi or the cherry-like *pitanga*.

Where to Eat & Drink

Eating out in Brazil can mean fried treats at the corner *lanchonete* (snack bar or greasy spoon); a lunchtime *prato feito* (ready-to-eat hot meal including rice, beans, a meat dish and salad) at a *bar* (pub) or *botequim* (working man's restaurant); a gorge session at a sit-down *rodízio* (all-you-can-eat) restaurant; or à la carte dining on white linen.

To eat quickly and well, head to a *por-kilo* restaurant, which serves food by weight, and costs from R$35 to R$60 per kilogram. Offerings generally include fresh salads and veggies, rice, beans, grilled meat and fish, plus regional specialties.

Churrascarias are generally *rodízio*-style and include a salad bar, plus meat that's brought from the grill to your table and carved for you. Prices vary wildly, from R$35 to R$100 for the all-the-meat-you-can-eat experience. *Rodízio* restaurants serving pizza and *massa* (pasta) are also popular and meals cost between R$18 and R$30.

The Natural World

Home to the world's largest rainforest, as well as some of the greatest wetlands, Brazil boasts some of the most astounding plant and animal life on earth. More known species of plants, freshwater fish, amphibians and mammals are found in Brazil than in any other country in the world. Unfortunately, Brazil is also renowned for the destruction of its natural environment. Conservation remains a hot topic, and protecting Brazil's natural wonders is increasingly seen as pivotal for Brazil's future.

The Land

Brazil is the planet's fifth-largest country. Its 8.5 million sq km occupy almost half of South America. It contains five principal biomes (major regional plant and animal groupings): Amazonia, Atlantic rainforest, caatinga (semiarid land), cerrado (the central savanna) and the Pantanal wetlands.

Above Morpho caterpillars (p622)

Amazonia

Covering over 4 million sq km – almost half the country – Brazilian Amazonia incorporates 30% of the world's tropical forest. It's home to around 45,000 plant species (some 20% of the world total), 311 mammals (about 10% of the world total), 1000 bird species (15%), 1800 types of butterfly and around 2000 species of fish (in contrast, Europe has about 200). The forest still keeps many of its secrets: to this day, major tributaries of the Amazon River remain unexplored, thousands of species have not yet been classified and dozens of human communities have eluded contact with the outside world.

Including a further 2 million sq km in neighboring countries, the entire Amazon Basin holds 20% of the world's freshwater and produces 20% of the world's oxygen.

Seasonal rainfall patterns mean that the water levels of the Amazon River and its tributaries rise and fall at different times of the year. This produces dramatic alterations in the region's geography. Water levels routinely vary by 10m to 15m between low and high marks; during high-water periods, areas totaling at least 150,000 sq km (about the size of England and Wales together) are flooded.

The Iguaçu Falls, along with other scenic Brazilian locations, featured in the James Bond movie *Moonraker* (1979) and the Oscar-winning *The Mission* (1986) with Robert de Niro and Jeremy Irons.

Forest Layers

The rainforest is stratified into layers of plant and animal life. Most of the animal activity takes place in the canopy layer, 20m to 30m above ground, where trees compete for sunshine, and butterflies, sloths and the majority of birds and monkeys live. Here hummingbirds hover for pollen, and macaws and parrots seek out nuts and tender shoots. A few tall trees reaching up to 40m, even 50m, poke above the canopy and dominate the forest skyline. These 'emergent trees' are inhabited by birds such as the harpy eagle and toucan and, unlike most other rainforest plants, disperse their seeds by wind.

The dense foliage of the canopy layer blots out sunlight at lower levels. Below the canopy is the understory. Epiphytes (air plants) hang at midlevels, and below them are bushes, saplings and shrubs growing up to 5m in height. Last is a ground cover of ferns, seedlings and herbs – plants adapted to very little light. Down here live ants and termites, the so-called social insects. The *saubas* (leaf-cutter ants) use leaves to build underground nests for raising fungus gardens, while army ants swarm through the jungle in huge masses, eating everything in their path. Insects, fungi and roots fight for access to nutrients, keeping the forest floor quite tidy.

The forest's soils are typically shallow. Many trees have buttress roots that spread over wide patches of ground to gather more nutrients.

The Amazon on Film

Amazon: Land of the Flooded Forest, National Geographic

Amazon – River of the Future, Jacques Cousteau

Amazon – Journey to a Thousand Rivers, Jacques Cousteau

The Burning Season: The Chico Mendes Story, by John Frankenheimer

Atlantic Rainforest

Brazil's 'other' tropical rainforest, the Mata Atlântica (Atlantic rainforest), is actually older than the Amazon forest and evolved independently. It once extended along the country's southeast-facing coast, from Rio Grande do Norte to Rio Grande do Sul. Today, three-quarters of Brazil's population and all its main industrial cities are located in what used to be the Mata Atlântica, and only 7% of the original forest remains.

Along the coast, there are still long stretches of this luxuriant forest. Some areas boast what may be the highest biodiversity levels on earth. It also contains many unique species – 21 of its 26 primate types are found only here, as are more than 900 of its 2000-plus kinds of butterflies, and many of its 600-plus bird species. Unsurprisingly, many of these species are endangered, including the four types of lion tamarin and the two woolly spider monkeys (the largest primates in the Americas).

The pirarucu has gills, but they are basically useless. It breathes with lungs instead and has to surface for air about every 10 minutes or it will drown.

Anaconda (p622)

Pantanal

The Pantanal is a vast swampy wetland in the center of South America, about half the size of France – some 210,000 sq km spread across Brazil, Bolivia and Paraguay. It's the largest inland wetland on earth, and 140,000 sq km of it lies in Brazil, in the states of Mato Grosso and Mato Grosso do Sul.

During the wet season, from October to March, the waters from the higher surrounding lands run into the Pantanal, inundating as much as two-thirds of it for half the year. The Pantanal, though 2000km upstream from the Atlantic Ocean, is only 100m to 200m above sea level and drains very slowly.

This seasonal flooding has made systematic farming impossible, severely limiting human impact on the area, and it creates an enormously rich feeding ground for wildlife. It is the best area to head in all Brazil if you want to see wildlife, boasting greater visible numbers of animals and at least as much variety of creatures as Amazonia, with which it shares many species. The Pantanal supports numerous species, including iconic creatures like the giant anaconda, the jaguar, the puma, the giant anteater, the hyacinth macaw, the giant otter, and the black howler and brown capuchin monkeys – and millions of caimans. The most visible mammal is the capybara, the world's largest rodent, which is often seen in family groups or even large herds.

Wildlife

Brazil's teeming flora and fauna make it one of the planet's best destinations for nature lovers.

Amazon Books

Tree of Rivers, John Hemming

The Smithsonian Atlas of the Amazon, Michael Goulding

The Last Forest, Mark London and Brian Kelly

One River, Wade Davis

The Lost Amazon, Isabel Kuhl

Humpback whale (p454)

Mammals

Anteaters & Sloths

The giant anteater (up to 2m long) lives off termites and ants. Its meat is prized in some areas of Brazil, and it's a threatened species. The collared or lesser anteater, up to 1.4m long, is yellow and black, mainly nocturnal, and often climbs trees.

Sloths have strong arms and legs, and spend most of their time hidden (and sleeping) in trees. You have a good chance of seeing some if you get a bit off the beaten track in Amazonia: from a moderate distance they look like clumps of vegetation high in trees. The species you're most likely to see is the brown-throated three-toed sloth.

The giant ground sloth, which grew to the size of an elephant, once inhabited much of Brazil. It was easy prey for prehistoric hunters and was presumably hunted to extinction 10,000 years ago.

Dolphins, Manatees & Whales

On many rivers in the Amazon Basin you should catch glimpses of the pink dolphin. It's most often seen where tributaries meet larger rivers, and is most active in the early morning and late afternoon. Sightings are tantalizing – and getting good photos virtually impossible – as the dolphin surfaces unpredictably, for just a second or so at a time, to breathe. Often it won't even lift its head above the surface. The pink dolphin has a lumpy forehead, a long beak and no dorsal fin (just a ridge). Adults are 1.8m to 2.5m long, weighing 85kg to 160kg.

Amazonian rivers are also home to the gray dolphin, a bit smaller than the pink and often found together with it. Unlike the pink dolphin, the gray also inhabits the sea, in coastal waters from Florianópolis to Panama. When it surfaces it usually lifts its head and part of its body out of the water.

Larger than the dolphin is the Amazon manatee, a slow-moving vegetarian that is illegally hunted for its meat and is in danger of extinction.

Prospects are even poorer for the marine West Indian manatee, of which there are just 500 left in coastal waters from Alagoas northward.

Seven whale species occur off Brazil's coasts, with good sightings off Praia do Rosa between June and October. The rare humpback whale breeds in the same months in the Parque Nacional Marinho de Abrolhos, off the coast of southern Bahia.

Felines

Many visitors dream of sighting a wild jaguar, but few have the luck of seeing one in the wild. The elusive and splendid jaguar is widely but thinly distributed in Brazil, occurring in Amazonia and the Pantanal among other regions. Jaguars hunt at night, covering large distances. They prey on a wide variety of animals, in trees, in water and on the ground, including sloths, monkeys, fish, deer, tapirs, capybaras and agoutis – but rarely people.

The puma, almost as big as the jaguar and similarly elusive, is the same beast as North America's cougar or mountain lion. As well as preying on deer, it sometimes attacks herds of domestic animals, such as sheep or goats.

Monkeys

About 80 of the world's approximately 300 primate species (which also include marmosets and tamarins) are found in Brazil, many of them unique to the country. Southeast Brazil's two species of woolly spider monkey, the southern *muriqui* and northern *muriqui*, with their thick brown fur, are the largest primates in the Americas and both are endangered, the northern species critically so and down to a population of under 300.

Howler monkeys are known for their distinctive roar. They live in groups of up to 20 that are led by a single male. In Amazonia you're most likely to encounter the red howler monkey. Further south, including in the Pantanal, the black howler monkey is the local species. The brown howler monkey inhabits the small remaining areas of the Mata Atlântica.

The two types of uakari monkey, the black-headed and the bald, inhabit Amazonian flooded forest. The bald uakari has a red or pink bald head and thick, shaggy body fur ranging from chestnut-red to white (giving rise to the popular names red uakari and white uakari).

Birds

With its diverse habitats and extraordinary number of species, Brazil is a major hot spot for bird-watchers.

MAN BITES PIRANHA

Why are people scared of piranhas? The fish should be frightened of us, as humans eat piranhas a billion times more often than piranhas eat people. They're tasty, if a bit small and bony. A standard activity on an Amazon jungle trip is catching a piranha lunch.

A piranha is not just a piranha, of course. It could be any of about 40 species of the *Serrasalmo* genus. Piranhas are found in the basins of the Amazon, Orinoco, Paraguay and São Francisco Rivers and in the rivers of the Guianas. Some live on seeds and fruits, some on other fish, and only a handful of species are potentially a risk to larger creatures. These types are most dangerous when stuck in tributaries, meanders or lakes that get cut off from main rivers in the dry season. When they have eaten all the other fish, the piranhas will attack more or less anything, including wounded mammals entering their waters. The scent of blood or bodily fluids in the water can whip a shoal into a feeding frenzy. Confirmed accounts of human fatalities caused by piranhas are extremely few, but plenty of Amazonian river folks have scars or missing fingers to testify just how sharp and vicious those little triangular teeth can be.

Top Toucan (p618)
Bottom Caracara

THE NATURAL WORLD WILDLIFE

Macaw (p618)

Hummingbirds beat their wings up to 80 times a second, allowing them to hover while extracting pollen from flowers – making a light humming noise as they do.

Birds of Prey

Much like great cats, birds of prey command respect and are always an object of fascination. Brazil has around 40 species of eagle, hawk, falcon, kite, caracara and kestrel, some quite common, and they're not very easy to tell apart.

The largest bird of prey in the Americas is the ferocious harpy eagle, with claws bigger than human hands. It eats sizable mammals (including monkeys) and nests at least 25m above the ground in large jungle trees. Although a few harpies still inhabit Mata Atlântica, the bird is found chiefly in Amazonia.

Parrots

These are the kinds of bird that have come to symbolize tropical rainforests, and people travel from all over the world to see some of Brazil's dozens of species.

The name scarlet macaw is given to two large, gloriously colored species – *Ara chloroptera,* also called the red-and-green macaw, which grows up to 95cm long, with blue-and-green wings and a red-striped face; and *Ara macao,* which is a bit smaller with blue-and-yellow wings. The latter bird is restricted to Amazonia, but the red-and-green macaw also inhabits the Pantanal, cerrado and even caatinga. The blue-and-yellow macaw, about 85cm long, is also widely distributed. The yellow covers its underside, the blue its upper parts.

Toucans

Among the most colorful groups of Latin American birds are toucans, which despite their large beaks are able to fly with a surprising agility. Toucans live at forest treetop level and are often best seen from boats.

Field Guides

Birds of Brazil, Ber van Perlo

Medicinal and Useful Plants of the Upper Amazon, James L Castner

Neotropical Rainforest Mammals, Louise Emmons

A Neotropical Companion, John Kricher

Brazil: Amazon and Pantanal, David L Pearson and Les Beletsky

Pantanal wetlands (p694)

Brazil's biggest is the toco toucan, whose habitat ranges from Amazonia to the cerrado to the Pantanal. Around 55cm long, including its bright orange beak, the plumage is black except for a white neck area. In Amazonia you may see the white-throated toucan or the yellow-ridged toucan. Both are fairly large birds, with black beaks.

Waterfowl

Highly visible birds in the Pantanal and Amazonia include herons, egrets, storks, ibises, spoonbills and their relatives. The tiger heron, with its brown and black stripes, is particularly distinctive. The sight of hundreds of snowy egrets gathering in a waterside rookery looks like a sudden blooming of white flowers in the treetops.

Of the storks, one of the most striking is the tall black-headed and scarlet-necked jabiru found in the Pantanal and Amazonia. In the Pantanal, also look for the similarly sized maguari stork, which is mainly white with a pinkish face, and the smaller wood stork, with its black head and beak with a curved end. The beautiful pink roseate spoonbill is another Pantanal resident. The spectacular scarlet ibis lives in flocks along the Northeast coast.

For 15 years Mark Plotkin devotedly tracked down Amazonian shamans to understand some of their encyclopedic knowledge of medicinal plants. His *Tales of a Shaman's Apprentice* is both travelogue and adventure story.

Plants

The last ice age did not reach Brazil and the rainforests have never suffered long droughts, so the area has had an unusually long period of time to develop plant species that are found nowhere else in the world.

Though estimates run at around 45,000, it would be impossible to determine an exact number of plant species in the Amazon, let alone in the whole of Brazil, as new plants are being discovered all the time and, unfortunately, others are disappearing with frightening frequency. The

TOP RESERVES & NATIONAL PARKS

➡ **Fernando de Noronha archipelago** (p504) Fabulous marine park of islands, 350km from Natal.

➡ **Floresta Nacional do Tapajós** (p590) Lush Amazonian rainforest preserve.

➡ **Ilha de Marajó** (p583) Huge river island in the mouth of the Amazon.

➡ **Ilha Grande** (p121) Hilly island covered by virgin Atlantic rainforest, a few hours from Rio.

➡ **Mamirauá Reserve** (p626) Amazonian floodplain reserve teeming with wildlife; excellent ecotourism program.

➡ **Pantanal** (p685) Vast wetlands that are one of Brazil's best places to see wildlife.

➡ **Parque Estadual da Pedra Azul** (p214) Dramatic 1822m blue-tinged rock formation with natural pools and forest.

➡ **Parque Estadual de Itaúnas** (p208) Sand dunes, beaches, sea-turtle preserve.

➡ **Parque Nacional da Chapada Diamantina** (p458) Large mountainous park in Bahia with stunning scenery, waterfalls and rivers.

➡ **Parque Nacional da Chapada dos Guimarães** (p367) Waterfalls, canyons, bizarre rock formations.

➡ **Parque Nacional da Chapada dos Veadeiros** (p354) High-altitude cerrado with picturesque landscapes near Brasília.

➡ **Parque Nacional da Serra da Capivara** (p554) Park in southern Piauí with thousands of prehistoric paintings and unique rock formations.

➡ **Parque Nacional do Itatiaia** (p138) Ruggedly beautiful mountainous park, 150km from Rio.

➡ **Parque Nacional do Iguaçu** (p281) Brazilian side of the spectacular waterfalls.

➡ **Parque Nacional dos Lençóis Maranhenses** (p559) Enormous expanse of sand dunes and clear rain pools.

➡ **Praia da Rosa** (p306) Beach town in Santa Catarina that's a famed whale sanctuary.

great majority of the plants in Brazil's rainforests are trees – estimated at some 70% of the total vegetation. Many rainforest trees look similar even though they are of different species, but a trained eye can distinguish more than 400 species of tree per hectare in some areas.

National Parks & Protected Areas

Much of Brazil is, officially at least, under environmental protection. Over 1000 areas, covering some 1.3 million sq km (around 15% of the whole country), are protected. Some of these are run by the federal government, some by state governments and some by private individuals or nongovernmental organizations (NGOs).

Terras Indígena (Indigenous Lands) occupy about 12% of Brazilian territory, nearly all in the Amazon. Though they are not explicitly dedicated to nature conservation, their inhabitants tend to use them with minimal environmental impact.

Environmental Issues

Sadly, Brazil is as renowned for its forests as it is for destroying them. At last count more than one-fifth of the Brazilian Amazon rainforest had been completely destroyed. Cutting down forests for cattle ranches and to grow crops (namely soybeans) and illegal logging are among the chief threats to the Amazon. The good news is that the rate of deforestation has slowed in recent years, falling year-on-year from nearly 13,000 sq km in 2008 to under 5000 sq km in 2012.

Big development projects are also affecting the Amazon. The government has some 30 large hydroelectric dams in the works for the Amazon region. The biggest is the massive Belo Monte dam on the Rio Xingu in Pará, which will affect 1500 sq km of rainforest, and displace some 20,000 people, including thousands of indigenous people who have resided along the river for centuries. As of 2013, construction was about to get under way, though vigorous protests continue.

The Pantanal wetlands also face serious threats, including the rapid spread of intensive soy, cotton and sugarcane farming on Brazil's central plains, which are the source of most of the Pantanal's water. The sugarcane is the raw material of ethanol motor fuel, whose international growth has led to the creation of dozens of new ethanol distilleries in Mato Grosso do Sul. Herbicides, fertilizers and other chemicals from the plantations drizzle their way into Pantanal waters, and forest clearance on the plains leads to erosion and consequent silting of Pantanal rivers. The growing cities around the Pantanal (many of which lack adequate waste-treatment plants) and ongoing industrial development also pose serious risks to this region.

On Brazil's coasts, growth of cities and burgeoning tourism developments threaten many delicate coastal marine ecosystems despite the creation of protected areas on extensive tracts of land and sea.

The greatest number of different tree species ever found in 1 hectare (10,000 sq meters) was 476, recorded in an area of Atlantic rainforest in the hills of Espírito Santo state.

Survival Guide

Directory A–Z

Accommodations

Brazilian accommodations range from battered, windowless cells to sumptuous, seaside guesthouses, with many possibilities in between. Nearly every pousada (guesthouse), hostel and hotel serves some form of café da manhã (breakfast). Private rooms with communal bathrooms are called quartos. Rooms with a private bathroom are apartamentos.

At the bottom end of the price scale, you'll find cheap hotel rooms outside of major cities and resort areas. Expect a bare room with nothing but a bed and maybe a fan.

Midrange listings are usually comfortable but not stylish, with decent beds, air-conditioning, hot-water bathrooms and cable TV. The top end offers more spacious digs, with maybe a veranda, a pool and other amenities. Many midrange and top-end hotels have safes in the rooms for storing valuables.

Reservations

In tourist centers, especially Rio, it's wise to make reservations during July (school holidays) and from Christmas to Carnaval. The same holds for any vacation mecca (eg Búzios, Ilha Bela, Morro de São Paulo) on weekends, and anywhere during major festivals. For prime peak times (eg Carnaval), make contact months ahead.

Hostels

Youth hostels in Brazil are called albergues da juventude. The HI-affiliated **Federação Brasileira de Albergues da Juventude** (www.hostel.org.br) has more than 90 hostels in the country, most with links on the website. There are also scores of private hostels. Rio is by far the country's hostel capital, with over 100 at last count. Quality varies considerably, but they're generally good places to meet Brazilian and foreign travelers.

A dorm bed in a hostel costs between R$40 and R$75 (up to R$100 in Rio).

Hotels

Brazil's hotels range from the good, modern and luxurious, to shabby and moldy. At the more expensive places, taxes of 15% are often added to the price. Prices typically rise by about 30% during the high season, and room rates double or even triple during Carnaval and around New Year's Eve. Hotels in business-oriented cities such as São Paulo, Curitiba, Porto Alegre and Brasília usually give discounts for stays on weekends.

Jungle Lodges

One popular type of remote-area accommodations is the jungle lodge, which caters to tourists in or on the edge of the forest. Though sometimes pricey, you're paying for the experience of lodging in the rainforest, rather than amenities – which are midrange at best. The largest number of jungle lodges are found outside of Manaus.

Pousadas

A pousada typically means a small family-owned guesthouse, though some hotels call themselves 'pousadas' to improve their charm quotient. Rustic pousadas can cost as little as R$80/120 per single/double and as much as R$500 for a lavish double.

BOOK YOUR STAY ONLINE

For more accommodations reviews by Lonely Planet authors, check out http://lonelyplanet.com/hotels. You'll find independent reviews, as well as recommendations on the best places to stay. Best of all, you can book online.

DIRECTORY A–Z CUSTOMS REGULATIONS

Rental Accommodations

It's possible to rent holiday, short- or long-term apartments through a number of sources. Real estate agencies in most large cities will be able to provide information on rentals for foreigners. The best bet is to speak to other foreigners in Brazil to get an idea of current prices, which vary from city to city. **Air BnB** (www.airbnb.com) has thousands of listings across Brazil for finding rooms or apartment rentals.

Customs Regulations

Travelers entering Brazil can bring in 2L of alcohol, 400 cigarettes, and one personal computer, video camera and still camera. Newly purchased goods worth up to US$500 are permitted duty-free. Meat and cheese products are not allowed.

Electricity

110V/220Hz/60Hz

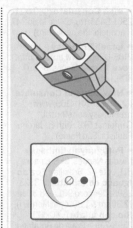

110V/220Hz/60Hz

Embassies & Consulates

The embassies are all in Brasília, but many countries have consulates in Rio and São Paulo, and often other cities as well. For addresses in Brasília, SES stands for Setor de Embaixadas Sul.

➡ **Argentine Embassy** (☑0xx61-3364-7600; www.brasil.embajada-argentina.gov.ar; Casa 19, SHIS Quadra 2, Conj 01, Lago Sul, Brasília); **Foz do Iguaçu consulate** (☑3574-2969; www.mrecic.gov.ar; Travessia Bianchi 26; ◷10am-3pm Mon-Fri); **Porto Alegre consulate** (☑0xx51-3321-1360; Rua Coronel Bordini 1033); **Rio**

consulate (☑0xx21-2553-1646; Praia de Botafogo 228, Room 201, Botafogo); **São Paulo consulate** (☑0xx11-3897-9522; www.sanpablo.argentinaconsul.ar; Av Paulista 2313, Consolação)

➡ **Australian Embassy** (☑0xx61-3226-3111; www.brazil.embassy.gov.au; Av das Nações, SES, Q 801, Conj K, Lota 7, Brasília); **Rio consulate** (☑0xx21-3824-4624; www.dfat.gov.au/missions/countries/brri.html; 23rd fl, Av Presidente Wilson 231)

➡ **Bolivian Consulate** (☑0xx61-3364-3362; Casa 06, SHIS, Q L-10, Conj 01, Lago Sul, Brasília); **Brasiléia consulate** (☑0xx61-3366-3432; Casa 19 , SHIS, QL 19, Conj 13; ◷8am-noon Mon-Fri); **Corumbá consulate** (☑3231-5605; coliviancorumbams@hotmail.com; Porto Carrero 1650; ◷8am-12:30pm & 2-4:30pm Mon-Fri); **Guajará-Mirim consulate** (☑069-3541-8620; Beira Rio 50; ◷7am-3pm Mon-Fri); **Rio consulate** (☑0xx21-2552-5490; www.consuladodeboliviaenrio.org.br; No 101, Av Rui Barbosa 664)

➡ **Canadian Embassy** (☑0xx61-3424 5400; www.canadainternational.gc.ca; Av das Nações, SES, Q 803, Lote 16, Brasília); **Rio consulate** (☑2543-3004; www.brasil.gc.ca; 5th fl, Av Atlântica 1130, Copacabana); **São Paulo consulate** (☑0xx11-5509-4321; www.canadainternational.gc.ca; 16th Fl, Torre Norte, Itaim Bibi, Av das Nações Unidas 12901)

SLEEPING PRICE RANGES

The following price ranges refer to a double room with bathroom in high season (December to March). Unless otherwise stated, breakfast is included in the price.

$ less than R$150
$$ R$150–350
$$$ more than R$350

The price range for Rio is higher:

$ less than R$200
$$ R$200–500
$$$ more than R$500

➡ **Colombian Embassy**
(☎0xx61-3226-8897; www.
embcol.org.br; Av das Nações,
SES, Q 803, Lote 10, Brasília);
Rio consulate (☎0xx21-
2552-6248; Room 101, Praia do
Flamengo 284); **Tabatinga
consulate** (☎097-3412-2104;
Sampaio 623)

➡ **Dutch Embassy** (☎0xx61-
3961-3200; www.mfa.nl; Av das
Nações, SES, Quadra 801, Lote
05, Brasília); **Rio consulate**
(☎0xx21-2157-5400; www.
riodejaneiro.nlconsulaat.org;
10th fl, Praia de Botafogo 242)

➡ **French Embassy** (☎0xx61-
3222-3999; www.ambafrance-
br.org; Av das Nações, SES,
Q 801, Lote 04, Brasília); **Rio
consulate** (☎3974-6699;
http://riodejaneiro.ambafrance-
br.org; 6th fl, Av Presidente
Antônio Carlos 58, Centro)

➡ **German Embassy**
(☎0xx61-3442-7000; www.
brasilia.diplo.de; Av das Nações,
SES, Q 807, Lote 25, Brasília);
Rio consulate (☎0xx21-
2554-0004; www.rio-de-janeiro.
diplo.de; Carlos de Campos 417)

➡ **Guyanese Embassy**
(☎0xx61-3248-0874; Casa 24,
SHIS Quadra 5, Conj 19, Brasília)

➡ **Irish Consulate** (☎0xx21-
2501-8455; Rua 24 de Maio 347,
Riachuelo, Rio de Janeiro)

➡ **Israeli Embassy** (☎0xx61-
2105-0500; www.brasilia.mfa.
gov.il; Av das Nações, SES, Q
809, Lote 38, Brasília)

➡ **New Zealand Consulate**
(☎0xx11-3141-4169; www.
nzembassy.com/brazil;
Campinas 579, 15th Fl, Jardim
Paulista, São Paulo)

➡ **Paraguayan Embassy**
(Av das Nações, SES, Quadra
811, Lote 42, Brasília); **Foz do
Iguaçu consulate** (☎3523-
2898; Deodoro 901; ☺8:30am-
12:30pm & 1:30-4pm Mon-Fri);
Rio consulate (☎0xx21-
2553-2294; Praia de Botafogo
24, 2nd fl, Rio de Janeiro)

➡ **Peruvian Embassy**
(☎0xx61-3242-9933; www.
embperu.org.br; Av das Nações,
SES, Quadra 811, Lote 43,
Brasília); **Rio consulate**
(☎0xx21-2551-9596; 2nd fl, Av
Rui Barbosa 314, Flamengo)

➡ **Spanish Embassy**
(☎0xx61-3244 2121; Av das
Nações, SES, Quadra 811, Lote
44, Brasília); **Rio consulate**
(☎0xx21-2543-3200; Rooms

1601 & 1612, Torre Rio Sul, Rua
Lauro Müller 116, Botafogo)

➡ **UK Embassy** (☎0xx61-
3329-2300; www.reinounido.
org.br; Av das Nações, SES,
Quadra 801, Conj K, Lote 08,
Brasília); **Rio consulate**
(☎2555-9600; www.
reinounido.org.br; 2nd fl, Praia
do Flamengo 284 , Flamengo);
São Paulo consulate
(☎0xx11-3094-2700; www.
ukinbrazil.fco.gov.uk; Fereira
de Arauja 741, 2nd fl, Pinheiros,
São Paulo)

➡ **Uruguayan Embassy**
(☎0xx61-3322-1200; www.
emburuguai.org.br; Av das
Nações, SES, Quadra 803,
Lote 14, Brasília); **Porto
Alegre consulate** (☎0xx51-
3224-3499; Rua Siqueira
Campos 1171); **Rio consulate**
(☎0xx21-2553-6030; www.
emburuguai.org.br; 6th fl, Praia
de Botafogo 242)

➡ **US Embassy** (☎0xx61-
3312-7000; www.embaixada-
americana.org.br; Av das
Nações, SES, Quadra 801, Lote
3, Brasília); **Rio consulate**
(☎3823-2000; www.
embaixadaamericana.org.
br; Av Presidente Wilson 147,
Centro); **Salvador consulate**
(☎0xx71-3113-2090; Room
1401, Salvador Trade Center,
Torre Sul, Av Tancredo Neves
1632); **São Paulo consulate**
(☎0xx11-5186-7000; http://
saopaulo.usconsulate.gov;
Henri Dunant 500, Chácara
Santo Antônio)

➡ **Venezuelan Embassy**
(☎0xx61-3322-1011; Av das
Nações, SES, Quadra 803,
Lote 13, Brasília); **Boa Vista
consulate** (☎3623-9285;
Av Benjamin Constant 968);
Manaus consulate (☎0xx92-
3233-6006; Río Jatai 839); **Rio
consulate** (☎0xx21-2554-
6134; 5th fl, Praia de Botafogo
242 , Botafogo)

Gay & Lesbian Travelers

Brazilians are pretty laid-
back when it comes to most
sexual issues, and homo-
sexuality is more accepted

PRACTICALITIES

➡ The biggest Portuguese-language daily newspapers
are **Jornal do Brasil** (www.jbonline.com.br) and **O Globo**
(www.globo.com.br), both from Rio, and *O Estado de São
Paulo* and *Folha de São Paulo,* out of São Paulo. The
weekly *Veja* is a current-affairs magazine, and in Rio and
São Paulo it comes with a good pullout guide to what's
happening locally. For English-language news in Rio,
check out the **Rio Times** (www.riotimesonline.com).

➡ TV programming revolves around sports, comedy
shows and the nightly *telenovelas* (soap operas). *O
Globo* is the largest nationwide TV network.

➡ Brazil uses the PAL system for video/DVD.

➡ The electrical current is not standardized in Brazil
and can be almost anywhere between 110V and 220V.
The most common power points have two sockets,
and most will take both round and flat prongs. Carry
a converter and use a surge protector with electrical
equipment.

➡ Brazilians use the metric system for weights and
measures.

here than in any other part of Latin America. That said, the degree to which you can be out in Brazil varies greatly by region, and in some smaller towns discrimination is prevalent.

Rio is the gay capital of Latin America, though São Paulo and to a lesser extent Salvador also have lively scenes. Gay bars in Brazil are all-welcome affairs attended by GLS (Gays, Lesbians e Simpatizantes), a mixed heterosexual and homosexual crowd far more concerned with dancing and having a good time than anything else.

There is no law against homosexuality in Brazil, and the age of consent is 18, the same as for heterosexuals.

Gay Travel Brasil
(☑️0xx21-3415-3126; www.gaytravelbrasil.com; Rua Sergipe 57, Rio de Janeiro), a gay-owned travel agency in Rio and São Paulo, arranges customized trips, language instruction and cruises; staff also work with gay-owned and gay-friendly guesthouses and properties throughout Brazil.

The **Rio Gay Guide** (www.riogayguide.com) is an excellent resource for gay and lesbian travelers in Rio.

Health

For an ambulance in Brazil, call 192, or an emergency number.

Good medical care is available in the larger cities but may be difficult to find in rural areas. Medical care in Brazil may be extremely expensive.

Each Brazilian pharmacy has a licensed pharmacist. Most are well supplied.

Infectious Diseases

The diseases of most concern are mosquito-borne infections, including malaria, yellow fever and dengue fever, which are not a significant concern in temperate regions.

DENGUE

Found throughout Brazil, dengue is transmitted by Aedes mosquitoes, which bite preferentially during the daytime and are more common in densely populated, urban environments.

Dengue usually causes flu-like symptoms, including fever, muscle aches, headaches, nausea and vomiting, often followed by a rash. There is no vaccine or treatment for dengue fever except to take analgesics such as acetaminophen/paracetamol and to drink plenty of fluids.

MALARIA

Malaria is transmitted by mosquito bites, usually between dusk and dawn. The main symptoms are high spiking fevers, which may be accompanied by chills, sweats, headache, body aches, weakness, vomiting or diarrhea. Severe cases may involve the central nervous system and lead to seizures, confusion, coma and death.

Taking prophylaxis (malaria pills) is strongly recommended for forested areas within the nine states of the Amazonia region.

If you develop a fever after returning home, see a physician, as malaria symptoms may not occur for months.

TYPHOID

Typhoid fever is caused by ingestion of food or water contaminated by a species of salmonella known as *Salmonella typhi*. Fever occurs in virtually all cases. Other symptoms may include headache, malaise, muscle aches, dizziness, loss of appetite, nausea and abdominal pain. Either diarrhea or constipation may occur.

Unless you expect to take all your meals in major hotels and restaurants, typhoid vaccine is a good idea.

YELLOW FEVER

Yellow fever is a life-threatening viral infection transmitted by mosquitoes in forested

areas. The illness begins with flu-like symptoms, which may include fever, chills, headache, muscle aches, backache, loss of appetite, nausea and vomiting. These symptoms usually subside in a few days, but one person in six enters a second, toxic phase characterized by recurrent fever, vomiting, listlessness, jaundice, kidney failure, and hemorrhage, leading to death in up to half of the cases. There is no treatment.

The yellow-fever vaccine is recommended for all travelers to Brazil, except those visiting only Rio, São Paulo and the coastal areas south of São Luís. Proof of vaccination is required from all travelers arriving from a yellow fever–infected country in Africa or the Americas.

Water Quality

Tap water in Brazilian cities such as Rio and São Paulo is generally safe to drink, but it tastes awful. In remote areas, tap water may be suspect. Many hotels and guesthouses filter their water – be sure to inquire about the status where you're staying. Vigorous boiling for one minute is the most effective means of water purification, though you can also use a water filter, ultraviolet light (such as a steripen) or iodine pills.

Insurance

A travel-insurance policy to cover theft, loss and medical problems is a good idea. The policies handled by STA Travel and other student-travel organizations are usually good value. Some policies offer lower and higher medical-expense options; the higher ones are chiefly for countries such as the USA that have extremely high medical costs. There is a wide variety of policies available, so check the fine print.

Some policies specifically exclude 'dangerous activities,' which can include scuba diving, motorcycling and even hiking.

You may prefer a policy that pays doctors or hospitals directly rather than your having to pay on the spot and claim later. If you have to claim later, make sure you keep all documentation.

Check that the policy covers ambulances or an emergency flight home.

Worldwide travel insurance is available at www.lonelyplanet.com/travel_services. You can buy, extend and claim online any time – even if you're already on the road.

Internet Access

Many hostels and hotels, as well as some cafes and restaurants, provide wi-fi access (indicated in this book with the icon 🛜). It's usually free, although pricier hotels sometimes charge for it.

Internet cafes are slowly disappearing, though you can usually find at least one in most destinations. Most places charge between R$5 and R$10 an hour.

Legal Matters

If something is stolen from you, you can report it to the police. No big investigation is going to occur, but you will get a police report to give to your insurance company.

In recent years, Brazil has gotten quite strict about drink driving. Police checkpoints stop cars at random.

The penalties for drug possession are harsh, and you don't want to end up in a Brazilian prison. Some police checkpoints are set up outside nightclubs to stop taxis and give the full pat down to club-goers on their way home (hint: don't carry anything!). Police along the coastal drive from Rio to Búzios and Rio to São Paulo are notorious for hassling young people and foreigners. Border areas are also a danger, particularly around the Bolivian border.

If you are arrested, know that you have the right to remain silent, and that you are innocent until proven guilty. You also have a right to be visited by your lawyer or a family member.

A large amount of cocaine is smuggled out of Bolivia and Peru through Brazil. Be very careful with drugs. If you're going to buy, don't buy from strangers and don't carry anything around with you.

Marijuana is plentiful in Brazil and very illegal. Nevertheless, it's widely used, and, like many other things in Brazil, everyone except the military and the police has a rather tolerant attitude towards it. Bahia seems to have the most open climate.

If you're coming from one of the Andean countries and have been chewing coca leaves, be especially careful to clean out your pack before arriving in Brazil. Sentences are stiff even for possession of coca leaves.

Because of the harsh penalties involved with possession or apparent possession, it's wise to stay away from drugs in any form.

Maps

The best maps in Brazil are the Quatro Rodas series. These good regional maps (Norte, Nordeste etc) are available throughout Brazil. It also publishes the *Atlas Rodoviário* road atlas, useful if you're driving, as well as excellent street atlases for the main cities.

In the USA, **Omni Resources** (www.omnimap.com) is a good source of Brazil maps, publishing both paper maps as well as downloadable road maps for GPS. You can order online.

Good topographical maps are published by the **IBGE** (www.ibge.gov.br), the govern-

---

FRAUD WARNING

Credit-card and ATM fraud is widespread in Brazil, especially in the Northeast. Card cloning (*clonagem* in Portuguese) is the preferred method: an entrepreneurial opportunist sticks a false card reader into an ATM that copies your card and steals the PIN when you come along and withdraw money. Shazam! A few hours later, $1500 disappears from your account in Recife while you and your card are safe and sound sipping caipirinhas on the beach in Natal!

To combat fraud, restaurants will bring the credit-card machine to your table or ask you to accompany them to the cashier to run a credit-card transaction. Never let someone walk off with your card. Other tips:

➡ Use high-traffic ATMs inside banks during banking hours only.

➡ Always cover the ATM keypad when entering personal codes.

➡ Avoid self-standing ATMs whenever possible and never use an ATM that looks tampered with.

ment geographical service, and the DSG, the army geographical service. Availability is erratic, but IBGE offices in most state capitals sell IBGE maps. Office locations can be found on the IBGE website.

Money

Brazil's currency is the real (hay-*ow;* often written R$); the plural is reais (hay-*ice*). One real is made up of 100 centavos.

Banknotes are easy to distinguish from each other as they come in different colors with a different animal featured on each. There's a green one-real note (hummingbird), a blue two (hawksbill turtle), a violet five (egret), a scarlet 10 (macaw), a yellow 20 (lion-faced monkey), a golden-brown 50 (jaguar) and a blue 100 (grouper fish).

ATMs

ATMs are the easiest way of getting cash in big cities and are common. In many smaller towns, ATMs exist but don't always work for non-Brazilian cards. Make sure you have a four-digit PIN (longer PINs may not work). In general HSBC, Citibank, Banco do Brasil and Bradesco are the best ATMs to try (HSBC currently charges the lowest transaction fees). Look for the stickers on the machines that say Cirrus, Visa, or whatever system your card uses – though this may not mean the machine will necessarily work.

Bargaining

A little bargaining for hotel rooms should become second nature. Before you agree to take a room, ask for a better price. '*Tem desconto?*' (Is there a discount?) and '*Pode fazer um melhor preço?*' (Can you give a better price?) are the phrases to use. There's sometimes a discount for paying *à vista* (cash).

You should also bargain when shopping in markets, and if you're about to ride in unmetered taxis arrange the price before departing.

Cash

It might be handy to keep cash in reserve, though you'll want to be exceptionally cautious when traveling with it. Cash should be in US dollars or euros.

Credit Cards

You can use credit cards for many purchases and to make cash withdrawals from ATMs and banks. Visa is the most widely accepted card, followed by MasterCard. Amex and Diners Club cards are less useful. Visa cash advances are widely available, even in small towns with no other currency-exchange facilities; you'll need your passport, and the process can be time consuming, especially at the ubiquitous but bureaucratic Banco do Brasil.

Credit-card fraud is extremely common in Brazil. Keep your card in sight at all times, especially in restaurants. Have them bring the portable machine to your table – don't give them your card.

Tipping

Workers in most services get tipped 10%. In restaurants the service charge will usually be included in the bill and is mandatory. If a waitperson is friendly and helpful you can give more. When the service charge is not included, a 10% tip is customary.

On jungle trips, it's customary to tip your guide at the end, and certainly appreciated if you can give a little to the assistant or boat operator(s).

Tipping is also optional for low-wage earners such as hotel housekeepers, juice-bar baristas, beach vendors, hair stylists and shoe shiners.

Parking assistants receive no wages and are dependent on tips, usually R$2 or more.

Most people round up taxi fares to the nearest real, but tipping is not expected.

Opening Hours

→ Banks: 9am to 3pm Monday to Friday

→ Bars: 7pm to 2am

→ Juice bars and cafes: 8am to 10pm

→ Malls: 10am to 9pm Monday to Saturday, 3pm to 10pm Sunday

→ Restaurants: noon to 2:30pm and 6pm to 10pm

→ Shops: 9am to 6pm Monday to Friday and 9am to 1pm Saturday

Public Holidays

April 19, the Dia do Índio (Indigenous Day), is not a national holiday but is nevertheless marked by festivities in indigenous villages around the country.

→ New Year's Day: January 1

→ Carnaval: February/March, the two days before Ash Wednesday

→ Good Friday & Easter Sunday: March/April

→ Tiradentes Day: April 21

→ May Day/Labor Day: May 1

→ Corpus Christi: late May/June – 60 days after Easter Sunday

→ Independence Day: September 7

→ Day of NS de Aparecida: October 12

→ All Souls' Day: November 2

→ Proclamation of the Republic: November 15

→ Christmas Day: December 25

Safe Travel

Brazil receives a lot of bad press about its violence and high crime rate. Use common sense and take general precautions applicable throughout South America:

➜ Carry only the minimum cash needed plus a fat-looking wad to hand over to would-be thieves.

➜ Dress down, leave the jewelry at home and don't walk around flashing iPhones, iPads and other expensive electronics.

➜ Be alert and walk purposefully. Criminals home in on dopey, hesitant, disoriented-looking individuals.

➜ Use ATMs inside buildings. Before doing so, be very aware of your surroundings. Thieves case ATMs and exchange bureaus.

➜ Check windows and doors of your room for security, and don't leave anything valuable lying around.

➜ Don't take anything unnecessary to city beaches (bathing suit, towel, small amount of cash – nothing else!).

➜ After dark, don't ever walk along empty streets, in deserted parks or on urban beaches.

➜ Especially in Rio, only take radio taxis. Never get into an unofficial taxi.

Scams & Robbery Techniques

Distraction is a common tactic employed by street thieves. The aim is to throw potential victims off guard so that they're easier prey. It may be something as simple as asking you for a cigarette or a light so that you slow down and take your attention off other people around you.

There have also been reports of druggings, including spiked drinks. While you're temporarily unconscious or semiconscious as a result of some noxious substance being slipped into your beverage, you're powerless to resist thieves. If you start to feel unaccountably dizzy, disoriented, fatigued or just mentally vacant not long after imbibing, your drink may have been spiked. If you suspect this to be the case, call for help, quickly extricate yourself from the situation and get to a safe place – your hotel room.

Exercise *extreme* caution when someone you don't know and trust offers you a drink of *any* kind or even cigarettes, sweets etc. If it make you suspicious, the offer can be tactfully refused by claiming stomach or other medical problems.

Cut-Rate Tour Operators & Touts

In Manaus, Cuiabá and other parts of the Amazon and the Pantanal, there's a major problem with freelancers and shady operators selling cut-rate tours that turn out to be ecologically unsound, awful and/or unsafe. As a rule never book a tour (or even accept help) from someone who approaches you unsolicited at the airport or on the street. Go directly to the offices in town, or book on websites ahead of time.

Shopping

Handicrafts, artwork and CDs all make fine souvenirs. Try to buy arts and crafts directly from the artist or artisan.

Glitzy, air-conditioned shopping malls – imaginatively called *shoppings* – are in every self-respecting medium-size city and often contain decent music stores (and amazing food courts).

For genuine indigenous arts and crafts, have a look in the Artíndia stores of Funai (the government indigenous agency) and museum gift shops.

Artisans in the Northeast produce a rich assortment of artistic items. Salvador and nearby Cachoeira are most notable for their rough-hewn wood sculptures. Ceará specializes in fine lace. The interior of Pernambuco, in particular Caruaru, is famous for wildly imaginative ceramic figurines.

Candomblé stores are a good source of curios, ranging from magical incense guaranteed to increase sexual allure, wisdom and health, to amulets and ceramic figurines of Afro-Brazilian gods.

Telephone

Domestic Calls

You can make domestic calls – intercity or local – from normal card pay phones on the street and in telephone offices. The phone cards you need are sold in denominations of 20 to 100 units (costing between R$5 and R$20) by vendors and at newsstands and anywhere you see advertising *cartões telefônicos*.

For calls within the city you're in, just slide the card into the phone, then check the readout to see if it's given you proper credit, and dial the eight-digit number. Local fixed-line phone calls cost only a few units.

For calls to other cities, you need to precede the number with 0, then the code of your selected carrier, then the two or three digits representing the city area code. City codes are therefore usually given in the format ☎0xx-digit-digit, with the 'xx' representing the carrier code. A long-distance call usually eats up between five and 10 phonecard units per minute.

Include the city code (☎0xx-digit-digit) when calling to another city even if it has the same city code as the one you're calling from

To make a *chamada a cobrar* (intercity collect) call, stick a 9 in front of the 0xx. To make a local collect call, dial ☎9090 and then the number. A recorded message in Portuguese will ask you to say your name and the name of the state where you're calling from, after the beep.

International Calls

Brazil's country code is ☎55. When calling internationally to Brazil, omit the initial 0xx of the area code.

International landline-to-landline calls from Brazil using Embratel start from R$0.66 a minute to the USA, R$1.42 to Europe and R$1.42 to Australia.

Orelhãos are of little use for international calls unless you have an international calling card or are calling collect. Most pay telephones are restricted to domestic calls, and even if they aren't, a 30-unit Brazilian phone card may last less than a minute internationally.

Without an international calling card, your best option is Skype. For international *a cobrar* (collect) calls, secure a Brazilian international operator by dialing ☎0800-703-2111 (Embratel).

Cell (Mobile) Phones

Brazil uses the GSM 850/900/1800/1900 net-

work, which is compatible with North America, Europe and Australia, but the country's 4G LTE network runs on 2500/2690 (for now), which is not compatible with many North American and European smartphones, including initial releases of the iPhone 5. *Celular* (cell) phones have eight-digit numbers (nine-digit numbers in São Paulo) starting with 6, 7, 8 or 9. Calls to mobiles are more expensive than calls to landlines. Mobiles have city codes, just like landlines, and if you're calling from another city, you have to use them.

Tim (www.tim.com.br), **Claro** (www.claro.com.br), **Oi** (www.oi.com.br) and **Vivo** (www.vivo.com.br) are the major operators. As of late 2012, foreigners can purchase a local SIM with a passport instead of needing a Brazilian CPF (tax ID number) – a major bureaucratic roadblock dismantled.

Time

Brazil has four time zones. Brasília time, which is GMT/ UTC minus three hours, covers the whole of the Southeast (including Rio and São Paulo), South and Northeast regions, plus, in the Central West section, Distrito Federal (including Brasília) and the state of Goiás, and, in the Amazon, the states of Tocantins, Amapá and the eastern half of Pará.

The remainder of the Central West (Mato Grosso and Mato Grosso do Sul states) and the rest of the Amazon are one hour behind Brasília time (GMT/UTC minus four hours). The Fernando de Noronha archipelago, out in the Atlantic Ocean, 350km off Natal, is one hour *ahead* of Brasília time (GMT/UTC minus two hours).

Thus, when it's noon in London and 7am in New York, it should be 9am in most of Brazil, but 10am in Fernando de Noronha and 8am in Mato Grosso and the Amazon. We say 'should be' because daylight saving means that it usually isn't. Brazilian daylight-saving time runs from mid-October to mid-February, during which period clocks are advanced

---

BRAZILIAN CITY CODES & CARRIERS

Brazil has several rival long-distance telephone carriers. When making a long-distance call (either between cities or internationally), you have to select a carrier and include its two-digit *código de prestadora* (code) in the number you dial. Brazilian city codes are commonly quoted with an xx representing the carrier code, eg ☎0xx21 for Rio de Janeiro or ☎0xx71 for Salvador.

This construction may look complicated, but in practice it's straightforward. For one thing, you can use the main carriers, **Embratel** (☎21) or **Oi Telemar** (☎31) for any call; for another, other major carriers usually have their names and codes widely displayed in their localities, particularly on public phones.

For example, to call from Rio de Janeiro to Fortaleza (city code ☎0xx85), in the state of Ceará, you dial 0 followed by 21, 23, 31 or 85 (the codes of the four carriers that cover both Rio and Ceará), followed by 85 for Fortaleza, followed by the number.

For an international call, dial 00 followed by either 21, 23 or 31 (the international carriers), followed by the country code, city code and number.

one hour – but only in the Southeast, South and Central West and the states of Bahia and Tocantins! And of course northern hemisphere daylight saving happens in the other half of the year, so in reality the time difference between Rio and New York is three hours in December and one hour in July. And the time difference between Rio and Manaus is three hours from October to February but two hours otherwise.

Toilets

Public toilets are not common but can be found at every bus station and airport in most cities and towns; there's usually a charge of around R$0.50 to R$1. People will generally let you use the toilets in restaurants and bars. As in other Latin American countries, toilet paper isn't flushed. There's usually a basket next to the toilet to put waste in.

Tourist Information

Tourist offices in Brazil are a mixed bag. Some offices have dedicated, knowledgeable staff, and others have little interest in helping tourists.

Embratur (www.visitbrasil. com), the Brazilian tourism institute, provides limited online resources.

Travelers with Disabilities

Travelers in wheelchairs don't have an easy time in Brazil, but in the large cities there is a concerted effort to keep people mobile. Problems you'll encounter include immensely crowded public buses, and restaurants with entrance steps. It pays to plan your trip through contact with some of the relevant organizations.

Rio is probably the most accessible city in Brazil for disabled travelers to get around in, but that doesn't mean it's always easy. The metro system has electronic wheelchair lifts, but these aren't always operational. The streets and sidewalks along the main beaches have curb cuts and are wheelchair accessible, but most other areas do not have cuts. Many restaurants also have entrance steps. For transport around Rio, contact **Coop Taxi** (🕿3295-9606).

Most of the newer hotels have wheelchair-accessible rooms, and some cable TV is closed captioned.

Useful Organizations

The **Centro de Vida Independente** (🕿2512-1088; www.cvi-rio.org.br; Rua Marquês de São Vicente 225, Gávea) can provide advice for those with disabilities about travel in Brazil.

Those in the USA may like to contact the **Society for Accessible Travel & Hospitality** (🕿212-447 7284; www.sath.org), whose website is a resource for travelers with disabilities. Another website to check out is www. access-able.com.

Visas

Citizens of the USA, Australia and Canada need a visa; citizens of the United Kingdom, France, Germany and New Zealand do not. Tourist visas are valid for arrival in Brazil within 90 days of issue and then for a 90-day stay. The fee and length depends on your nationality; it's usually between US$20 and US$65, though US citizens are hit with a whopping US$160 reciprocal bill. Processing times vary from five to 10 business days, sometimes less depending on nationality and consulate efficiency. Brazilian consulates will never provide expedited visa services under any circumstances, so plan ahead. You'll generally need to present one passport photograph, proof of onward travel and a valid passport.

People under 18 years of age who wish to travel to Brazil without a parent or legal guardian must present a notarized Visa Consent Form from the nontraveling parent/guardian or from a court. Check with a Brazilian consulate well in advance about this.

If you decide to return to Brazil, your visa is valid for five years.

Entry/Exit Cards

On entering Brazil, all tourists must fill out a *cartão de entrada/saída* (entry/exit card); immigration officials will keep half, you keep the other. They will also stamp your passport and, if for some reason they are not granting you the usual 90-day stay in Brazil, the number of days you are

---

MOBILE PHONE NUMBERS

Brazil's expanding middle class means the country finds itself with a mobile phone problem. As a result, Rio-based mobile numbers in this book received an extra '9' on the front end as of late 2013, following São Paulo's lead in 2012. As this plan is said to eventually affect the entire country over the lifespan of this guide, if the mobile number published in this edition isn't working, try adding a '9' in front of our published number. So, 'xxxx-xxxx' becomes '9xxxx-xxxx' and so on. This change is for mobile phones only.

allowed to stay will be written in your passport.

When you leave Brazil, the second half of the entry/exit card will be taken by immigration officials. Don't lose your card while in Brazil, as it could cause hassles and needless delays when you leave.

EXTENSIONS TO ENTRY/ EXIT CARDS & VISAS

Brazil's Polícia Federal, which has offices in the state capitals and border towns, handles visa extensions. You must apply no fewer than five days before your entry/ exit card or visa lapses. The convoluted process:

➡ Fill out and print the form 'Requerimento de Prorrogação de Prazo' found in the 'Estrangeiros' section under the subheading 'Prorrogar Prazo do Estada de Turista e Viajante a Negócios (Temporário II)' from the Polícia Federal website (www.dpf.gov.br).

➡ Generate a government tax collection form, called a GRU (Guia de Recolhimento da União), found by clicking through from the same heading to 'GRU - FUNAPOL,' then 'Pessoas e Entidades Estrangeiras.'

➡ In that GRU form, fill out your personal info; enter code '140090' under 'Código da Receita STN;' choose the Polícia Federal office nearest you under the drop-down menu 'Unidade Arrecadadora;' and enter R$67 under 'Valor Total R$.'

➡ Click 'Gerar Guia' to generate the barcoded form. Take it to any bank, post office or lottery point and pay the R$67 fee.

➡ Head to the nearest Polícia Federal office with all in hand as well as your passport and original entry card. When you go, dress nicely! Some Fed stations don't take kindly to people in shorts. The extension is at the discretion of the officer you deal with and you may be asked to provide a ticket out

of the country and proof of sufficient funds. If you get the maximum 90-day extension and then leave the country before the end of that period, you cannot return until the full 90 days has elapsed.

Passports

By law you must carry a passport with you at all times, but many travelers opt to carry a photocopy (preferably certified) when traveling about town and to leave their passport securely locked up at their hotel.

Volunteering

RíoVoluntário (📞0xx21-2262-1110; www.riovoluntario. org.br), headquartered in Rio de Janeiro, supports several hundred volunteer organizations involved in social work, the environment and health care. It's an excellent resource for finding volunteer work.

One notable organization you can get involved with is Rio-based **Iko Poran** (📞0xx21-2205-1365; www. ikoporan.org), which links the diverse talents of volunteers with needy organizations. Previous volunteers have worked as dance, music, art and language instructors, among other things. Iko Poran also provides housing for volunteers.

Elsewhere in Rio state, **Regua** (www.regua.co.uk; Reserva Ecológica de Guapi Assu) accepts volunteers from all over the world for reforestation and other conservation work.

The UK-based **Task Brasil** (www.taskbrasil.org. uk) is another organization that places volunteers in Rio. Here, you'll have to make arrangements in advance and pay a fee that will go toward Task Brasil projects and your expenses as a volunteer.

The best website for browsing volunteer opportunities is **Action Without Borders** (www.idealist.org).

A little doorknocking can help you find volunteer work

in Brazil. There's plenty of need, and many local welfare organizations will gladly find you some rewarding work. Ask around at churches and community centers.

International NGOs (nongovernmental organizations) work in all sorts of fields in Brazil, including environmental, medical and social-welfare projects. If you have some particular interest or skill, try contacting relevant organizations to volunteer your services.

Women Travelers

Depending on where they travel in Brazil, women traveling alone will experience a range of responses. In São Paulo, for example, where there are many people of European ancestry, foreign women without traveling companions will scarcely be given a sideways glance. In the more traditional rural areas of the Northeast, where a large percentage of the population is of ethnically mixed origin, blonde-haired and light-skinned women, especially those without male escorts, will certainly arouse curiosity.

Flirtation – often exaggerated – is a prominent element in Brazilian male-female relations. It goes both ways and is nearly always regarded as amusingly innocent banter; no sense of insult, exploitation or serious intent should be assumed.

Work

Visitors who enter the country as tourists are not legally allowed to take jobs. It's not unusual for foreigners to find English-teaching work in language schools, though. It's always helpful to speak some Portuguese, although some schools insist that only English be spoken in class. Private language tutoring may pay a little more, but you'll have to do some legwork to get students.

Transportation

GETTING THERE & AWAY

Most travelers start their Brazilian odyssey by flying into Rio, but the country has several other gateway airports as well as land borders with every country in South America except Chile and Ecuador.

Flights and tours can be booked online at lonelyplanet.com/bookings.

Entering the Country

Immigration and customs formalities are fairly straightforward, though you'll want to be sure to have your visa in order if you're from a country (like the USA, Canada or Australia) that needs it.

Air

Airports & Airlines

The most popular international gateways are Aero-porto Galeão (GIG) in Rio de Janeiro and São Paulo's Aeroporto Guarulhos (GRU). From both, connecting flights leave regularly to airports throughout the country. Salvador (SSA) and Recife (REC) receive a few direct scheduled flights from Europe.

TAM is Brazil's main international carrier, with flights to New York (USA), Miami (USA), Paris (France), London (UK), Lisbon (Portugal) and seven South American cities. The US Federal Aviation Administration has assessed TAM as Category 1, which means it is in compliance with international aviation standards.

Tickets

For high-season travel, roughly between mid-December and the end of February, tickets to Brazil cost about US$300 more than they do during the rest of the year.

INTERNATIONAL AIR PASSES

If you're combining travel in Brazil with other countries in southern South America, air passes can be decent value if you're covering a lot of ground in 30 days and don't mind a fixed itinerary. The TAM South America Airpass is valid for flights within Argentina, Bolivia, Brazil, Chile (except Easter Island), Paraguay, Peru, Uruguay and Venezuela. The cost is based on the number of standard air kilometers/miles you want to cover (prices range from US$399 to US$1500 for 3040km/1900 miles to 13,200km/8200 miles).

The Visit South America air pass offered by airlines of the **Oneworld Alliance** (www.oneworld.com) allows stops in more than 30 cities in 10 South American countries. Prices are calculated on a per-flight, per-distance basis. Sample fares include US$222 Rio de Janeiro to Lima (Peru), US$167 from

CLIMATE CHANGE & TRAVEL

Every form of transport that relies on carbon-based fuel generates CO_2, the main cause of human-induced climate change. Modern travel is dependent on airplanes, which might use less fuel per kilometer per person than most cars but travel much greater distances. The altitude at which aircraft emit gases (including CO_2) and particles also contributes to their climate change impact. Many websites offer 'carbon calculators' that allow people to estimate the carbon emissions generated by their journey and, for those who wish to do so, to offset the impact of the greenhouse gases emitted with contributions to portfolios of climate-friendly initiatives throughout the world. Lonely Planet offsets the carbon footprint of all staff and author travel.

São Paulo to Buenos Aires (Argentina) and US$160 from Santiago (Chile) to Lima (Peru).

The Gol Mercosul air pass is valid for travel on Gol's network, including routes between Brazil and Chile, Argentina, Paraguay, Uruguay, Peru and Bolivia. Fares are US$682 plus tax for four flights, US$822 for five flights; each additional flight is US$120.

BOLIVIAN ENTRY REQUIREMENTS

Any US citizen entering Bolivia is required to have a visa, which costs US$135. Citizens from most other nations receive free 30-day entry. Although technically it's possible to obtain a visa at the border, it's wise to secure this beforehand – particularly if arriving overland, as long delays are likely. Bolivian Immigration has a whole host of other requirements, including a certificate of yellow-fever vaccine, proof of financial solvency, and more. Visit www.bolivia-usa.org for the latest.

Land

There's direct land access to Brazil from nine countries. Several border towns can also be reached by river from Bolivia or Peru. If arriving overland from Colombia or Venezuela, you'll need to have a certificate of a yellow-fever vaccine to enter Brazil (not to mention a visa!).

Border Crossings

ARGENTINA

The main border point used by travelers is Puerto Iguazú–Foz do Iguaçu, a 20-hour bus ride from Buenos Aires. Further south, you can cross from Paso de los Libres (Argentina) to Uruguaiana (Brazil), which is also served by buses from Buenos Aires.

Direct buses run between Buenos Aires and Porto Alegre (R$195, 18 hours) and Rio de Janeiro (R$260, 42 hours). Other destinations include Florianópolis (R$283, 25 hours), Curitiba (R$322, 34 hours) and São Paulo (R$325, 36 hours).

BOLIVIA

Brazil's longest border runs through remote wetlands and forests, and is much used by smugglers. The main crossings are at Corumbá, Cáceres, Guajará-Mirim and Brasiléia.

The busiest crossing is between Quijarro (Bolivia) and Corumbá (Brazil), which is a good access point for the Pantanal. Quijarro has a daily train link with Santa Cruz (Bolivia). Corumbá has

bus connections with Bonito, Campo Grande, São Paulo, Rio de Janeiro and southern Brazil.

Cáceres, in Mato Grosso (Brazil), has a daily bus link with Santa Cruz (Bolivia) via the Bolivian border town of San Matías.

Guajará-Mirim (Brazil) is a short river crossing from Guayaramerín (Bolivia). Both towns have onward bus links into their respective countries (Guayaramerín also has flights), but from late December to late February heavy rains can make the northern Bolivian roads a very difficult proposition.

Brasiléia (Brazil), a 4½-hour bus ride from Rio Branco, stands opposite Cobija (Bolivia), which has bus and plane connections into Bolivia. Bolivian buses confront the same wet-season difficulties.

CHILE

Although there is no border with Chile, direct buses run via Argentina between Santiago and Brazilian cities such as Porto Alegre (R$367, 36 hours), Curitiba (R$373, 54 hours), São Paulo (R$360, 54 hours) and Rio de Janeiro (R$388, 62 hours).

COLOMBIA

Leticia, on the Rio Amazonas in far southeast Colombia, is contiguous with Tabatinga (Brazil). You can cross the border on foot or by Kombi van or taxi. From within Colombia, Leticia is only really accessible by air. Tabatinga is a quick flight (or a several-

day Amazon boat ride) from Manaus or Tefé.

FRENCH GUIANA

The Brazilian town of Oiapoque, a rugged 560km bus ride from Macapá (R$90, 12 to 15 hours), stands across the Rio Oiapoque from St Georges (French Guiana). A road connects St Georges to the French Guiana capital, Cayenne, with minibuses shuttling between the two. (Get there early in the morning to catch one.)

GUYANA & SURINAME

From Boa Vista, there are daily buses to Bonfim, Roraima (R$18.50, 1½ hours), on the Guyanese border, a short motorized-canoe ride from Lethem (R$3; southwest Guyana).

Overland travel between Suriname and Brazil involves first passing through either French Guiana or Guyana.

PARAGUAY

The two major border crossings are Ciudad del Este (Paraguay)–Foz do Iguaçu (Brazil) and Pedro Juan Caballero (Paraguay)–Ponta Porã (Brazil). Direct buses run between Asunción and Brazilian cities such as Florianópolis (R$167, 20 hours), Curitiba (R$129, 14 hours), São Paulo (R$159, 20 hours) and Foz do Iguaçu (R$40, five hours).

PERU

There is at least one daily bus connecting Rio Branco (Brazil) to Puerto Maldonado

(Peru) via the border at Assis (Brazil)–Iñapari (Peru) on the new US$2.75-billion Interoceanic Hwy. You can also reach Assis on daily buses from Epitáciolândia (R$13, two hours) and cross the Rio Acre to Iñapari.

URUGUAY

The crossing most used by travelers is at Chuy (Uruguay)–Chuí (Brazil). This is actually one town, with the international border running down the middle of its main street. Other crossings are Río Branco (Uruguay)–Jaguarão (Brazil), Isidoro Noblia (Uruguay)–Aceguá (Brazil), Rivera (Uruguay)–Santana do Livramento (Brazil), Artigas (Uruguay)–Quaraí (Brazil) and Bella Unión (Uruguay)–Barra do Quaraí (Brazil). Buses run between Montevideo and Brazilian cities such as Porto Alegre (R$162, 12 hours), Florianópolis (R$209, 18 hours) and São Paulo (R$310, 32 hours).

VENEZUELA

From Manaus; five daily buses run to Boa Vista (R$96, 12 hours), from where you can connect on to Puerto La Cruz (Venezuela; R$130, 20 hours) for access to Caracas or Isla Margarita.

Bus

International buses travel between Brazil and Argentina, Paraguay and Uruguay, along decent roads. Prices of bus tickets between countries are substantially more than you'd pay if you took a bus to the border, crossed on foot and caught another on the other side, but you'll lose a lot of time that way. If arriving by bus, make sure your papers are in order.

Car & Motorcycle

If you plan to take a vehicle into Brazil, be informed about essential documents, road rules and info on fuel and spare parts. At the border you will be asked to sign a bond called a *termo de responsabilidade*, which lists

the owner's identification details and home address, your destination, and a description of the vehicle (make, model, year, serial number, color and tag number). You will also be asked to pay a bank guarantee (the amount to be determined by customs) and sign a statement agreeing that if you stay for more than 90 days, you will contact customs in the area where the entry was registered to apply for an extension for the permit. This must be presented to customs at the time of departure. If your vehicle overstays its permitted time in Brazil, it is liable to be seized and the bank guarantee forfeited. It's illegal to sell the vehicle in Brazil.

River

Bolivia

From Trinidad in Bolivia you can reach Brazil by a boat trip of about five days down the Río Mamoré to Guayaramerín, opposite the Brazilian town of Guajará-Mirim.

Peru

Fast passenger boats make the 400km trip (around US$90, eight to 10 hours) along the Amazon River between Iquitos (Peru) and Tabatinga (Brazil). From Tabatinga you can continue 3000km down the river to its mouth.

GETTING AROUND

Air

Because of the great distances in Brazil, the occasional flight can be a necessity, and may not cost much more than a long-haul bus journey. If you intend to take more than just a couple of flights, a Brazil Airpass will probably save you money. Book ahead if traveling during busy travel times – from Christmas to Carnaval, around Easter,

and July and August. Always reconfirm your flights, as schedules frequently change.

Airlines in Brazil

Brazil has two major national carriers, Gol and TAM, and a handful of smaller regional airlines. Brazil's main carriers:

Avianca (AV; ☑0300-789-8160; www.avianca.com)

Azul (☑0800-887-1118; www.voeazul.com.br)

Gol (☑0300-115-2121; www.voegol.com.br)

TAM (☑0800-570-5700; www.tam.com.br)

Air Passes

A Brazil Airpass is a good investment if you're planning on covering a lot of ground in 30 days or less. Gol offers an air pass involving four/five domestic flights anywhere on its extensive network for USS$582/722, plus taxes; each additional flight costs US$140. Gol also has a Northeast air pass, which costs US$440, plus tax, for three flights. TAM's air pass gives you four/five flights for US$582/772 (US$532/672 if you fly TAM to Brazil). Additional flights cost U$170 each (US$120 if you fly TAM to Brazil).

Either of these passes must be purchased before you go to Brazil, and you have to book your air-pass itinerary at the time you buy it – or possibly pay penalties for changing reservations. Many travel agents sell the air pass, as does the Brazilian travel specialist **Brol** (www.brol.com).

If for any reason you do not fly on an air-pass flight you have reserved, you should reconfirm all your other flights. Travelers have sometimes found that all their air-pass reservations had been scrubbed from the computer after they missed, or were bumped from, one flight.

Air Taxis

Many areas, especially Amazonia, feature air-taxi companies that will fly you anywhere

Domestic Air Routes

their small planes can reach. You need to book the whole plane, and costs are high. Unfortunately, these planes and the runways they land on aren't always maintained. You might think twice before booking one of these flights.

Bicycle

You don't see many long-distance cyclists in Brazil. Among the hazards are crazy drivers who only respect vehicles larger than themselves, lots of trucks on the main roads spewing out unfiltered exhaust fumes, roads without shoulder room, long distances and the threat of theft. Given the many real dangers, long-distance cycling in Brazil is not recommended.

If you're determined to tackle Brazil by bike, go over your bike with a fine-tooth comb before leaving home and fill your repair kit with every imaginable spare part. There are several decent bike shops in Rio for buying equipment and gear as well as renting bikes (which average R$50 per day).

Boat

The Amazon region is one of the last great bastions of passenger river travel in the world. Rivers still perform the function of highways throughout much of Amazonia, with vessels of many shapes and sizes putt-putting up and down every river and creek that has anyone living near it.

Boats are also essential for getting around parts of the Pantanal and accessing islands and beaches along the Atlantic coast.

Bus

Bus services in Brazil are generally excellent. Departure times are usually strictly adhered to, and most of the buses are clean, comfortable and well-serviced Mercedes, Volvo and Scania vehicles.

All major cities are linked by frequent buses – one leaves every 15 minutes from Rio to São Paulo during peak hours – and there is a surprising number of long-distance buses. Every big city, and most small ones, has at least one main long-distance bus station, known as a *rodoviária* (pronounced ho-do-vi-*ah*-ree-ya).

Bus service and road conditions vary by region. The South has the most and the best roads. Coastal highways are usually good, while the roads of Amazonia and the *sertão* (backlands of the Northeast) are quite bad. The Quatro Rodas *Atlas Rodoviário*, a very useful road atlas for any traveler, helpfully marks the worst stretches of road with lines of large Xs and classifies them as *estradas precárias*.

Brazil has numerous bus companies and the larger cities have several dozen rival agencies. **Itapemirim** (www.itapemirim.com.br) and **Cometa** (www.viacaocometa. com.br) are two of the best and biggest companies. The easiest resource to search national bus routes is **Busca Ônibus** (www.buscaonibus. com.br).

Classes

There are three main classes of long-distance bus. The ordinary *convencional* or *comum* is indeed the most common. It's fairly comfortable and usually has a toilet on board. An *executivo* is more comfortable (often with reclining seats), costs about 25% more and stops less often. A *leito* (overnight sleeper) can cost twice as much as a *comum* and is exceptionally comfortable. It has spacious, fully reclining seats with blankets and pillows, air-con and, more often than not, an attendant serving sandwiches, coffee, soda and *água mineral* (mineral water). If you don't mind missing the scenery, a *leito* can get you there in comfort and save you the additional cost of a hotel room.

With or without toilets, buses generally make pit stops every three or four hours. These stops are great places to meet other passengers, buy bizarre memorabilia and load up on greasy plates of food.

Air-con on buses is sometimes strong; carry a light sweater or jacket to keep warm.

Costs

Bus travel throughout Brazil can be expensive; *convencional* fares average around R$8 to R$10 per hour. Sample fares from Rio:

➡ Belém R$400 to R$505 *convencional*, 52 hours

➡ Florianópolis R$197 *convencional*, 18 hours

➡ Foz do Iguaçu R$252 *convencional*, 22 hours

➡ Salvador R$240 to R$260 *convencional*, 25 hours

➡ São Paulo R$76/91/119 *convencional/executivo/ leito*, six hours

Reservations

Usually you can go down to the bus station and buy a ticket for the next departing bus. In general, though, it's a good idea to buy a ticket at least a few hours in advance or, if it's convenient, the day before leaving. On weekends, holidays and from December to February, advance purchase is always a good idea. It's sometimes possible to buy bus tickets from travel agencies. Although they tack on a small commission, it will save you an extra trip out to the station. Ask at local tourist offices for agencies that sell bus tickets.

Car & Motorcycle

Especially in Rio, the anarchic side of the Brazilian personality emerges from behind the driver's wheel as lane dividers, one-way streets, sidewalks and pedestrians are disregarded.

Bringing Your Own Vehicle

All vehicles in Brazil must carry the registration document and proof of insurance. To take a vehicle into or out of Brazil, you might be asked for a *carnet de passage en douane*, which is kind of vehicle passport, or a *libreta de pasos por aduana*, which is a booklet of customs passes; in practice these are not often required. Contact your local automobile association for details about all documentation.

Driver's License

Your home-country driver's license is valid in Brazil, but because local authorities probably won't be familiar with it, it's a good idea to carry an International Driving Permit (IDP) as well. This gives police less scope for claiming that you are not driving with a legal license. IDPs are issued by your national motoring association and usually cost the equivalent of about US$10. It is illegal for foreigners to drive motorbikes in Brazil unless they have a Brazilian license.

Fuel & Spare Parts

Ordinary gasoline (called *combustível* or *gasolina*) costs around R$3 per liter. Travelers taking their own vehicles need to check in advance what spare parts and gasoline are likely to be available.

Hire

A small four-door car with insurance and unlimited kilometers costs around R$100 a day (R$130 with air-con). You can sometimes get discounts for longer rentals.

To rent a car you must be 25 years old (21 with some rental firms, including Avis), have a credit card in your name and a valid driver's license from your home country (not just an IDP).

Minimum insurance coverage is always tacked onto the cost of renting, though you can get extra protection (a wise idea) for another R$20 to R$40.

In Brazil, 4WD vehicles are hard to come by and can be quite expensive (over R$200 per day). Motorbike rental is even harder to find. Riders planning a long trip might have better luck purchasing a bike in Brazil and reselling it at the end of the trip.

Road Rules & Hazards

Brazil is a dangerous place to drive, with over 35,000 people killed in automobile accidents each year. Some roads are especially hazardous, such as the busy highways between Rio and São Paulo. The cult of speed is insatiable.

Owing to the danger of robbery, at night many motorists don't stop at red lights but merely slow down. This is particularly common in São Paulo. In big cities, keep your windows closed and doors locked when stationary.

Driving at night is particularly hazardous; other drivers are more likely to be drunk and, at least in the Northeast and the interior, the roads are often poor and unreliable. Poorly banked turns are the norm. To save a bit of fuel, some motorists drive at night with their headlights turned to low beam or turned off completely.

Brazilian speed bumps are quite prevalent. Always slow down as you enter a town.

Further headaches for drivers in Brazil are posed by poor signposting, impossible one-way systems, tropical rainstorms, drivers overtaking on blind corners, flat tires, all common, but there are *borracheiros* (tire repairers) stationed at frequent intervals along the roads – and, of course, the police pulling you over for bogus moving violations.

For security, choose hotels with off-street parking; most midrange and top-end places offer this option.

Hitchhiking

Hitchhiking is never entirely safe in any country, and is not recommended. Travel-

ers who decide to hitchhike should understand that they are taking a small but potentially serious risk. People who do choose to hitchhike will be safer if they travel in pairs and let someone know where they are planning to go.

Hitchhiking in Brazil, with the possible exception of the Pantanal and several other areas where it's commonplace among locals, is difficult. The Portuguese word for 'lift' is *carona*, so ask '*Pode dar carona?*' (Can you give us a lift?). The best way to hitchhike – practically the only way if you want rides – is to ask drivers when they're not in their vehicles; for example, by waiting at a gas station or truck stop. But even this can be difficult. It's polite to offer to pay for your share of the gas in return for your lift.

Local Transportation

Bus

Jumping on a local bus is one of the best ways to get to know a city. With a map and a few dollars you can get an overview of the town.

Local bus services tend to be decent. Since most Brazilians take the bus to work, municipal buses are usually frequent and their network of routes comprehensive. Fares range from R$2 to R$3.

In most city buses, you get on at the front and exit from the back, though occasionally the reverse is true. Usually there's a money collector sitting at a turnstile just inside the entrance.

Crime can be a problem: don't take valuables onto the buses, and think twice about taking minibuses, which have seen a recent increase in attacks.

Metro

Both Rio and São Paulo have excellent metro systems, with Rio's system being expanded for the 2016 Olympic Games. These metros are a safe, cheap and efficient way of exploring the cities. One-way fares are R$3.50 in Rio and R$3 in São Paulo.

Taxi

Taxi rides are reasonably priced, and a taxi is the best option for getting around cities at night. Taxis in cities usually have meters that start at R$4.80 and rise by something like R$2 per kilometer (more at night and on weekends). Occasionally, the driver will refer to a chart and revise slightly upwards. This reflects recent official hikes in taxi rates that the meter does not yet reflect.

In small towns, taxis often don't have meters, and you'll have to arrange a price – beforehand.

Some airports and bus stations have a system for you to purchase a fixed-price taxi ticket from a *bilheteria* (ticket office). At a few such places it's cheaper to go onto the street outside and find a cab that will take you for the meter fare or sometimes even less. If carrying valuables, however, the special airport taxi, or a radio taxi, can be a worthwhile investment.

If possible, orient yourself before taking a taxi, and keep a map handy in case you find yourself being taken on a wild detour. The worst place to get a cab is where the tourists are. In particular, don't get a cab near one of the expensive hotels. In Rio, for example, walk a block away from the beach at Copacabana to flag down a cab.

Moto-taxis (involving a ride on the back of a motorcycle) are another means of short-distance travel in places such as Rio.

Train

Brazil's passenger-train services have been scaled down to almost nothing, though there are a few journeys well worth taking. One outstanding trip goes from Curitiba to Paranaguá, descending the coastal mountain range with memorable views. The Belo Horizonte–Vitória run, via Santa Bárbara and Sabará, is also scenic.

Steam trains are affectionately known as Marias Fumaça (Smoking Marys), and several still run as tourist attractions. There's a 13km ride from São João del Rei to Tiradentes in Minas Gerais. Another pleasant short trip, this time by elec-

tric train, is the ride through the Serra da Mantiqueira of São Paulo state from Campos do Jordão to Santo Antônio do Pinhal, the highest stretch of track in the country.

Language

Portuguese is spoken by around 190 million people worldwide, 90% of whom live in Brazil. Brazilian Portuguese today differs from European Portuguese in approximately the same way that British English differs from American English. European and Brazilian Portuguese show some differences in spelling, pronunciation and, to some extent, vocabulary. For example, in Portugal, the word for 'train' is *comboio* and in Brazil you'd say *trem*.

Most sounds in Portuguese are also found in English. The exceptions are the nasal vowels (represented in our coloured pronunciation guides by ng after the vowel), which are pronounced as if you're trying to make the sound through your nose; and the strongly rolled r (represented by rr in our pronunciation guides). Also note that the zh sounds like the 's' in 'pleasure'. The stressed syllables (generally the second-last syllable of a word) are indicated with italics. If you keep these few points in mind and read our pronunciation guides as if they were English, you'll have no problems being understood.

BASICS

Hello.	*Olá.*	o·*laa*
Goodbye.	*Tchau.*	tee·*show*
How are you?	*Como vai?*	ko·mo vai
Fine, and you?	*Bem, e você?*	beng e vo·*se*
Excuse me.	*Com licença.*	kong lee·*seng*·saa
Sorry.	*Desculpa.*	des·*kool*·paa

WANT MORE?

For in-depth language information and handy phrases, check out Lonely Planet's *Brazilian Portuguese Phrasebook*. You'll find it at **shop.lonelyplanet.com**, or you can buy Lonely Planet's iPhone phrasebooks at the Apple App Store.

Please.	*Por favor.*	por faa·*vorr*
Thank you.	*Obrigado.*	o·bree·*gaa*·do (m)
	Obrigada.	o·bree·*gaa*·daa (f)
You're welcome.	*De nada.*	de naa·daa
Yes.	*Sim.*	seeng
No.	*Não.*	nowng

What's your name?
Qual é o seu nome?   kwow e o se·oo no·me

My name is ...
Meu nome é ...   me·oo no·me e ...

Do you speak English?
Você fala inglês?   vo·se faa·laa eeng·gles

I don't understand.
Não entendo.   nowng eng·teng·do

ACCOMMODATIONS

Do you have a ... room?	*Tem um quarto de ...?*	teng oom kwaarr·to de ...
double	*casal*	kaa·zow
single	*solteiro*	sol·tay·ro
twin	*duplo*	doo·plo

How much is it per night/person?
Quanto custa por noite/pessoa?   kwang·to koos·taa porr noy·te/pe·so·aa

Can I see it?
Posso ver?   po·so verr

campsite	*local para acampamento*	lo·kow paa·raa aa·kang·paa·meng·to
guesthouse	*hospedaria*	os·pe·daa·ree·a
hotel	*hotel*	o·tel
youth hostel	*albergue da juventude*	ow·berr·ge daa zhoo·veng·too·de

DIRECTIONS

Where is ...?
Onde fica ...?   *ong·de fee·kaa ...*

What's the address?
Qual é o endereço?   *kwow e o eng·de·re·so*

Could you please write it down?
Você poderia escrever   *vo·se po·de·ree·aa es·kre·verr*
num papel, por favor?   *noom paa·pel porr faa·vorr*

Can you show me (on the map)?
Você poderia me   *vo·se po·de·ree·aa me*
mostrar (no mapa)?   *mos·traarr (no maa·paa)*

at the corner	*na esquina*	*na es·kee·naa*
at the traffic lights	*no sinal de trânsito*	*no see·now de trang·zee·to*
behind ...	*atrás ...*	*aa·traaz ...*
in front of ...	*na frente de ...*	*naa freng·te de ...*
left	*esquerda*	*es·kerr·daa*
next to ...	*ao lado de ...*	*ow laa·do de ...*
opposite	*do lado oposto ...*	*do laa·do o·pos·to ...*
right	*direita*	*dee·ray·taa*
straight ahead	*em frente*	*eng freng·te*

EATING & DRINKING

What would you recommend?
O que você recomenda?   *oo ke vo·se he·ko·meng·daa*

What's in that dish?
O que tem neste prato?   *o ke teng nes·te praa·to*

I don't eat ...
Eu não como ...   *e·oo nowng ko·mo ...*

Cheers!
Saúde!   *sa·oo·de*

That was delicious.
Estava delicioso.   *es·taa·vaa de·lee·see·o·zo*

Bring the bill/check, please.
Por favor traga   *porr faa·vorr traa·gaa*
a conta.   *aa kong·taa*

I'd like to reserve a table for ...	*Eu gostaria de reservar uma mesa para ...*	*e·oo gos·taa·ree·aa de he·zer·vaarr oo·maa me·zaa paa·raa ...*
(eight) o'clock	*(às oito) horas*	*(aas oy·to) aw·raas*
(two) people	*(duas) pessoas*	*(doo·aas) pe·so·aas*

Key Words

bottle	*garrafa*	*gaa·haa·faa*
breakfast	*café da manha*	*ka·fe daa ma·nyang*

KEY PATTERNS

To get by in Portuguese, mix and match these simple patterns with words of your choice:

When's (the next flight)?
Quando é (o   *kwaang·do e (o*
próximo vôo)?   *pro·see·mo vo·o)*

Where's (the tourist office)?
Onde fica (a   *ong·de fee·kaa (aa*
secretaria de   *se·kre·taa·ree·aa de*
turismo)?   *too·rees·mo)*

I'm looking for (a hotel).
Estou procurando   *es·to pro·koorr·ang·do*
(um hotel).   *(oom o·tel)*

Do you have (a map)?
Você tem (um   *vo·se teng (oom*
mapa)?   *maa·paa)*

Is there (a toilet)?
Tem (banheiro)?   *teng (ba·nyay·ro)*

I'd like (a coffee).
Eu gostaria de   *e·oo gos·taa·ree·aa de*
(um café).   *(oom kaa·fe)*

I'd like to (hire a car).
Eu gostaria de   *e·oo gos·taa·ree·aa de*
(alugar um carro).   *(aa·loo·gaarr oom kaa·ho)*

Can I (enter)?
Posso (entrar)?   *po·so (eng·traarr)*

Could you please (help me)?
Você poderia   *vo·se po·de·ree·aa*
me (ajudar),   *me (aa·zhoo·daarr)*
por favor?   *por faa·vorr*

Do I have to (get a visa)?
Necessito   *ne·se·see·to*
(obter visto)?   *(o·bee·terr vees·to)*

cold	*frio*	*free·o*
cup	*xícara*	*shee·kaa·raa*
dessert	*sobremesa*	*so·bre·me·zaa*
dinner	*jantar*	*zhang·taarr*
drink	*bebida*	*be·bee·daa*
entree	*entrada*	*eng·traa·daa*
fork	*garfo*	*gaarr·fo*
glass	*copo*	*ko·po*
hot (warm)	*quente*	*keng·te*
knife	*faca*	*faa·kaa*
lunch	*almoço*	*ow·mo·so*
market	*mercado*	*merr·kaa·do*
menu	*cardápio*	*kaar·da·pyo*
plate	*prato*	*praa·to*
restaurant	*restaurante*	*hes·tow·rang·te*
spicy	*apimentado*	*aa·pee·meng·taa·do*
spoon	*colher*	*ko·lyerr*

Useful Telephone Phrases

I'd like to make an international call to...
Quero fazer uma ke·ro faa·zerr oo·maa
ligação inter- lee·gaa·sowng eeng·terr·
nacional para... naa·syo·now paa·raa ...

I'd like to reverse the charges.
Quero fazê-la ke·ro faa·ze·la
a cobrar. aa ko·braarr

I'm calling from a public/private phone in ...
Estou falando dum es·to faa·laan·do doom
telefone público/ te·le·fo·ne poo·blee·ko/
particular no ... paarr·tee·koo·laarr no ...

The area code/number is...
O código/ o ko·dee·go/
número é... noo·me·ro e ...

Meat & Fish

beef	carne de vaca	kaar·ne de vaa·kaa
chicken	frango	frang·go
crab	siri	see·ree
fish	peixe	pay·she
lamb	carneiro	karr·nay·ro
meat	carne	kaar·ne
oyster	ostra	os·traa
pork	porco	porr·ko
seafood	frutos do mar	froo·tos do maarr
shrimp	camarão	ka·ma·rowng
tuna	atum	aa·toong
veal	bezerro	be·ze·ho

Fruit & Vegetables

apple	maçã	maa·sang
apricot	damasco	daa·maas·ko
avocado	abacate	aa·baa·kaa·te
cabbage	repolho	he·po·lyo
capsicum	pimentão	pee·meng·towng
carrot	cenoura	se·no·raa
cherry	cereja	se·re·zhaa
corn	milho	mee·lyo
cucumber	pepino	pe·pee·no
grapes	uvas	oo·vaas
lemon	limão	lee·mowng
lettuce	alface	ow·faa·se
mushroom	cogumelo	ko·goo·me·lo
onion	cebola	se·bo·laa
orange	laranja	laa·rang·zhaa
peach	pêssego	pe·se·go
pineapple	abacaxí	aa·baa·kaa·shee
potato	batata	baa·taa·taa

spinach	espinafre	es·pee·naa·fre
strawberry	morango	mo·rang·go
tomato	tomate	to·maa·te
watermelon	melancia	me·lang·see·aa

Other

bread	pão	powng
cake	bolo	bo·lo
cheese	queijo	kay·zho
chilli	pimenta	pee·meng·taa
eggs	ovos	o·vos
honey	mel	mel
ice cream	sorvete	sorr·ve·te
jam	geléia	zhe·le·yaa
lentil	lentilha	leng·tee·lyaa
olive oil	azeite	a·zay·te
pepper	pimenta	pee·meng·taa

Drinks

rice	arroz	a·hoz
salt	sal	sow
sauce	molho	mo·lyo
sugar	açúcar	aa·soo·kaarr
beer	cerveja	serr·ve·zhaa

CARIOCA SLANG

Cariocas (inhabitants of Rio de Janeiro) pepper their language with lots of interesting oaths and expressions.

Oi!	Hello!
Tudo bem?	Everything OK?
Tudo bom.	Everything's OK.
Chocante!	That's great!/Cool!
Merda!	That's bad!/Shit!
Ta ótimo!/Ta legal!	Great!/Cool!/OK!
Meu deus!	My God!
Ta louco!	It's/You're crazy!
Nossa!	Gosh! (lit: Our Lady)
Opa!	Whoops!
Oba!	Wow!
Falou!	You said it!
Eu estou chateado com ...	I'm mad at ...
Tem jeito?	Is there a way?
Sempre tem jeito.	There's always a way.

Signs

Banheiro	Toilet
Entrada	Entrance
Não Tem Vaga	No Vacancy
Pronto Socorro	Emergency Department
Saída	Exit
Tem Vaga	Vacancy

coffee	café	kaa·fe
fruit juice	suco de frutas	soo·ko de froo·taas
milk	leite	lay·te
red wine	vinho tinto	vee·nyo teeng·to
soft drink	refrigerante	he·free·zhe·rang·te
tea	chá	shaa
(mineral) water	água (mineral)	aa·gwaa (mee·ne·row)
white wine	vinho branco	vee·nyo brang·ko

EMERGENCIES

Help!	Socorro!	so·ko·ho
Leave me alone!	Me deixe em paz!	me day·she eng paas

Call ...!	Chame ...!	sha·me ...
a doctor	um médico	oom me·dee·ko
the police	a polícia	aa po·lee·syaa

It's an emergency.
É uma emergência.	e oo·maa e·merr·zheng·see·aa

I'm lost.
Estou perdido.	es·to perr·dee·do (m)
Estou perdida.	es·to perr·dee·daa (f)

I'm ill.
Estou doente.	es·to do·eng·te

It hurts here.
Aqui dói.	a·kee doy

I'm allergic to (antibiotics).
Tenho alergia à (antibióticos).	te·nyo aa·lerr·zhee·aa aa (ang·tee·bee·o·tee·kos)

Where are the toilets?
Onde tem um banheiro?	on·de teng oom ba·nyay·ro

SHOPPING & SERVICES

I'd like to buy ...
Gostaria de comprar ...	gos·taa·ree·aa de kong·praarr ...

I'm just looking.
Estou só olhando.	es·to so o·lyang·do

Can I look at it?
Posso ver?	po·so verr

How much is it?
Quanto custa?	kwang·to koos·taa

It's too expensive.
Está muito caro.	es·taa mweeng·to kaa·ro

Can you lower the price?
Pode baixar o preço?	po·de bai·shaarr o pre·so

There's a mistake in the bill.
Houve um erro na conta.	o·ve oom e·ho naa kong·taa

ATM	caixa automático	kai·shaa ow·too·maa·tee·ko
credit card	cartão de crédito	kaarr·towng de kre·dee·to
post office	correio	ko·hay·o
tourist office	escritório de turismo	es·kree·to·ryo de too·rees·mo

TIME & DATES

What time is it?
Que horas são?	kee aw·raas sowng

It's (10) o'clock.
São (dez) horas.	sowng (des) aw·raas

Half past (10).
(Dez) e meia.	(des) e may·aa

morning	manhã	ma·nyang
afternoon	tarde	taar·de
evening	noite	noy·te

yesterday	ontem	ong·teng
today	hoje	o·zhe
tomorrow	amanhã	aa·ma·nyang

Monday	segunda-feira	se·goong·daa·fay·ra
Tuesday	terça-feira	terr·saa·fay·raa
Wednesday	quarta-feira	kwaarr·taa·fay·raa
Thursday	quinta-feira	keeng·taa·fay·raa
Friday	sexta-feira	ses·taa·fay·raa
Saturday	sábado	saa·baa·do
Sunday	domingo	do·meeng·go

Question Words

How?	Como é que?	ko·mo e ke
What?	Que?	ke
When?	Quando?	kwang·do
Where?	Onde?	ong·de
Which?	Qual?/Quais? (sg/pl)	kwow/kais
Who?	Quem?	keng
Why?	Por que?	porr ke

January	janeiro	zha·nay·ro
February	fevereiro	fe·ve·ray·ro
March	março	marr·so
April	abril	aa·bree·oo
May	maio	maa·yo
June	junho	zhoo·nyo
July	julho	zhoo·lyo
August	agosto	aa·gos·to
September	setembro	se·teng·bro
October	outubro	o·too·bro
November	novembro	no·veng·bro
December	dezembro	de·zeng·bro

TRANSPORT

Public Transport

boat	barco	baarr·ko
bus	ônibus	o·nee·boos
plane	avião	aa·vee·owng
train	trem	treng

When's the ... (bus)?	Quando sai o ... (ônibus)?	kwang·do sai o ... (o·nee·boos)
first	primeiro	pree·may·ro
last	último	ool·tee·mo
next	próximo	pro·see·mo

a ... ticket	uma passagem de ...	oo·maa paa·sa·zheng de ...
1st-class	primeira classe	pree·may·raa klaa·se
2nd-class	segunda classe	se·goom·daa klaa·se
one-way	ida	ee·daa
return	ida e volta	ee·daa e vol·taa

What time does it leave/arrive?
A que horas sai/chega? aa ke aw·raas sai/she·gaa

Does it stop at ...?
Ele para em ...? e·le paa·raa eng ...

Please stop here.
Por favor pare aqui. poor faa·vorr paa·re aa·kee

bus stop	ponto de ônibus	pong·to de o·nee·boos
ticket office	bilheteria	bee·lye·te·ree·aa
timetable	horário	o·raa·ryo
train station	estação de trem	es·taa·sowng de treng

Numbers

1	um	oom
2	dois	doys
3	três	tres
4	quatro	kwaa·tro
5	cinco	seeng·ko
6	seis	says
7	sete	se·te
8	oito	oy·to
9	nove	naw·ve
10	dez	dez
20	vinte	veeng·te
30	trinta	treeng·taa
40	quarenta	kwaa·reng·taa
50	cinquenta	seen·kweng·taa
60	sessenta	se·seng·taa
70	setenta	se·teng·taa
80	oitenta	oy·teng·taa
90	noventa	no·veng·taa
100	cem	seng
1000	mil	mee·oo

Driving & Cycling

I'd like to hire a ...	Gostaria de alugar ...	gos·taa·ree·aa de aa·loo·gaarr ...
bicycle	uma bicicleta	oo·maa bee·see·kle·taa
car	um carro	oom kaa·ho
motorcycle	uma motocicleta	oo·maa mo·to·see·kle·ta

bicycle pump	bomba de bicicleta	bong·baa de bee·see·kle·taa
helmet	capacete	kaa·paa·se·te
mechanic	mecânico	me·ka·nee·ko
petrol/gas	gasolina	gaa·zo·lee·naa
service station	posto de gasolina	pos·to de gaa·zo·lee·naa

Is this the road to ...?
Esta é a estrada para ...? es·taa e aa es·traa·daa paa·raa ...

(How long) Can I park here?
(Quanto tempo) Posso estacionar aqui? (kwang·to teng·po) po·so es·taa·syo·naarr aa·kee

I have a flat tyre.
Meu pneu furou. me·oo pee·ne·oo foo·ro

I've run out of petrol.
Estou sem gasolina. es·to seng ga·zoo·lee·naa

GLOSSARY

afoxé – music of Bahia, which has strong African rhythms and close ties to Candomblé

albergue – lodging house or hostel

albergue da juventude – youth hostel

aldeia – originally a village built by Jesuits to convert índios to Christianity; now the term for any small, usually indigenous, village

andar – walk; also a floor of a multistory building

apartamento – hotel room with a private bathroom

apelido – nickname

arara – macaw

artesanato – handcrafted workmanship

ayahuasca – hallucinogenic drink

azulejos – Portuguese ceramic tiles with a distinctive blue glaze, often seen in churches

babaçu – versatile palm tree that is the basis of the rural economy in Maranhão

bairro – district

bandeirantes – bands of 17th- and 18th-century roaming adventurers who explored the vast Brazilian interior while searching for gold and indios to enslave; typically born of an indio mother and a Portuguese father

barraca – any stall or hut, including food and drink stands common at beaches, parks etc

bateria – rhythm section of a band, including the enormous ones in samba parades

beija-flor – literally 'flower kisser'; hummingbird; also the name of Rio's most famous samba school

berimbau – musical instrument that accompanies capoeira

bilheteria – ticket office

bloco – large group, usually numbering in the hundreds, of singing or drumming Carnaval revelers in costume, organized around a neighborhood or theme

boate – nightclub with a dance floor, sometimes featuring strippers; also boîte

bonde – cable car, tram or trolley

bossa nova – music that mixes North American jazz with Brazilian influences

boteco – small, open-air bar

boto – freshwater dolphin of the Amazon

Bumba Meu Boi – the most important festival in Maranhão, a rich folkloric event that revolves around a Carnavalesque dance/procession

bunda – African word for buttocks

caatinga – scrub vegetation of the sertão

Caboclo – literally 'copper-colored'; person of mixed Caucasian and indio ancestry

cachoeira – waterfall

camisinha – condom

Candomblé – Afro-Brazilian religion of Bahia

cangaceiros – legendary bandits of the sertão

capivara – capybara; the world's largest rodent, which looks like a large guinea pig and lives in the Pantanal

Capixaba – resident of Espírito Santo state

capoeira – martial art/dance developed by the slaves of Bahia

Carioca – resident of Rio de Janeiro

cartão telefônico – phonecard

casa de câmbio – money-exchange office

casa grande – big house or plantation owner's mansion

casal – married couple; double bed

chapada – tableland or plateau that divides a river basin

churrascaria – restaurant featuring barbecued meat

cidades históricas – historic colonial towns

Círio de Nazaré – Brazil's largest religious festival, which takes place in Belém

cobra – any snake

coronel – literally 'colonel'; rural landowner who typically controlled the local political, judicial and

police systems; any powerful person

correio – post office

delegacia de polícia – police station

Embratur – Brazilian Tourist Board

engenho – sugar mill or sugar plantation

escolas de samba – large samba clubs that compete in the annual Carnaval parade

estalagem – inn

estrangeiro – foreigner

Exú – spirit that serves as messenger between the gods and humans in Afro-Brazilian religions

fantasia – Carnavalesque costume

favela – slum, shantytown

favelado – resident of a favela

fazenda – ranch or farm, usually a large landholding; also cloth, fabric

fazendeiro – estate owner

feira – produce market

ferroviária – train station

festa – party

Filhos de Gandhi – Bahia's most famous Carnaval bloco

fio dental – literally 'dental floss'; Brazil's famous skimpy bikini

Flamengo – Rio's most popular football team; also one of Rio's most populated areas

Fluminense – native of Rio state; also the football team that is Flamengo's main rival

forró – popular music of the Northeast, recently enjoying a wave of nationwide popularity

frevo – fast-paced, popular music from Pernambuco

frigobar – minibar

Funai – Fundação Nacional do Indio; government indio agency

Fusca – Volkswagen Beetle, Brazil's most popular car

futebol – football

futevôlei – volleyball played without hands

gafieira – dance hall

garimpeiro – prospector or miner; originally an illegal diamond prospector

garimpo – mining camp

gaúcho – cowboy of southern Brazil

gringo – foreigner or person with light hair and complexion; can even refer to light-skinned Brazilians

gruta – grotto or cavern

hidrovia – aquatic freeway

hidroviária – boat terminal

hospedagem – cheap boardinghouse used by locals

Iemanjá – Afro-Brazilian goddess of the sea

igapó – flooded Amazon forest

igarapé – creek or small river in Amazonia

igreja – church

ilha – island

índio – indigenous person; translates as 'Indian'

jacaré – caiman

jangada – beautiful sailboat of the Northeast

jangadeiros – crews who use jangadas

jeito/jeitinho – possibly the most Brazilian expression, both a feeling and a form of action; from dar um jeito, meaning 'to find a way to get something done,' no matter how seemingly impossible, even if the solution may not be completely orthodox or legal

leito – sleeping berth

literatura de cordel – literally 'string literature'; popular literature of the Northeast

litoral – coastal region

machista – male chauvinist

mãe de santo – female Afro-Brazilian spiritual leader

malandro do morro – vagabond; scoundrel from the hills; a popular figure in Rio's mythology

maloca – indio dwelling

Maracanã – soccer stadium in Rio

mercado – market

mestiço – a person of mixed indio and European parentage

Mineiro – resident of Minas Gerais

moço/a – waiter or other service industry worker

morro – hill; a person or culture of the favelas

mulato/a – person of mixed black and white parentage

novela – soap opera; Brazil's most popular TV shows

NS – Nosso Senhor (Our Lord) or Nossa Senhora (Our Lady)

orixá – deity of the Afro-Brazilian religions

pagode – popular samba music

pai de santo – male spiritual leader in Afro-Brazilian religions

palácio – palace or large government building

palafita – stilt or a house built on stilts

pampas – grassy plains of the interior of southern Brazil

parque nacional – national park

pau brasil – now-scarce brazilwood tree; a red dye made from the tree that was the colony's first commodity

Paulista – resident of São Paulo state

Paulistano – resident of São Paulo city

PCB – Communist Party of Brazil

pensão – guesthouse

posta restante – poste restante

posto – post; lifeguard posts along Rio de Janeiro's beaches, used as names for different sections of beach

posto de gasolina – a gas (petrol) station

posto telefônico – telephone office

pousada – guesthouse

praça – plaza or town square

praia – beach

PT – Partido dos Trabalhadores (Worker's Party); Brazil's newest and most radical political party

quarto – hotel room without a bathroom

quente – hot

quilombo – community of runaway slaves

Quimbanda – black magic

rápido – fast

real – Brazil's unit of currency since 1994; plural reais

rio – river

rodoferroviária – bus and train station

rodoviária – bus station

s/n – abbreviation for sem número (without number), used in some street addresses

sambista – samba composer or dancer

sambódromo – street with tiers of seating built for samba parades

senzala – slave quarters

serra – mountain range

Sertanejo – resident of the sertão

sertão – the drought-prone backlands of the Northeast

telefonista internacional – international telephone operator

Terra da Vera Cruz – Land of the True Cross; the original Portuguese name for Brazil

terreiro – Afro-Brazilian house of worship

travessa – lane

travesti – transvestite; a popular figure throughout Brazil, considered by some to be the national symbol

trem – train

trio elétrico – three-pronged electrical outlet; electrically amplified bands that play atop trucks

tropicalismo – important cultural movement centered in Bahia in the late 1960s

Tupi – indigenous people and language that predominated along the coast at the time of the European invasion

Umbanda – white magic, a mixture of Candomblé and spiritism

vaqueiro – cowboy of the Northeast

várzea – Amazonian floodplain

zona da mata – bushland just inside the litoral in the Northeastern states

Behind the Scenes

SEND US YOUR FEEDBACK

We love to hear from travelers – your comments keep us on our toes and help make our books better. Our well-traveled team reads every word on what you loved or loathed about this book. Although we cannot reply individually to postal submissions, we always guarantee that your feedback goes straight to the appropriate authors, in time for the next edition. Each person who sends us information is thanked in the next edition – the most useful submissions are rewarded with a selection of digital PDF chapters.

Visit **lonelyplanet.com/contact** to submit your updates and suggestions or to ask for help. Our award-winning website also features inspirational travel stories, news and discussions.

Note: We may edit, reproduce and incorporate your comments in Lonely Planet products such as guidebooks, websites and digital products, so let us know if you don't want your comments reproduced or your name acknowledged. For a copy of our privacy policy visit lonelyplanet.com/privacy.

OUR READERS

Many thanks to the travelers who used the last edition and wrote to us with helpful hints, useful advice and interesting anecdotes:

Steve Agnew, Ariel Albrecht, George Balleste, Jorge Balleste, Sats Bleeker, Inka Blumensaat, Marcelo Boratto Peixoto Do Vale, Ella Bowen, Jean Bowen-brooks, Frank Boyce, Debora S Carvalho, Marcelo Castro, Adriana Caznoch Kürten, Caio Cesar S Araujo, Tom Cookson, Imma Cortes, Machiel Crielaard, Birute Curran, Christophe Dang, Nadia De Matos Barros, Zé Do Rock, Aldo Domingo, Sarina Eliyakim, Laura Erickson-schroth, Justin Fisch, Sarah Fisher, Nghe Francheokie, Alessandra Furlan, Noel Gallivan, Pierre Gaspart, Katie Gelbart, Thomas Georgiadis, Susanne Halbmayer-watzina, Jennifer Hammer, Martin Hämmerle, Oliver Herzog, Manuela Hirt, Stephen Hodes, Miriam Hofmann, Richard Howard, Flemming Jensen, Fernanda Junqueira, Janina Kaese, David Karp, Margot Kaszap, Tess Kelley, Greg Kondrak, Theresa Kuhles, Stefanie Ley, Albert London, Joanne Louis, Nina Mardell, Louis Martins, Carolina Menna, Lonny Miller, Adela Minae, Danilo Ortiz Ribeiro, Geneviève Pagé, Lucas Paio, Elena Pedrini, Matt Pepe, David Peterson, Karsten Pohl, Lisa Rausch, Diederik Ravesloot, Analy Ribeiro, James Robinson, Gustavo Rosa, Jill Sanguinetti, Francesca San-toro, Marc Schillgalies, Stefanie Schwarz, Henk Segaert, Francesco Segoni, Wanda Serkowska, Gitanjali Seth, Paul Soerensen, Silvia Spitta, Tobias Stoltze, Wolfram Stolz, James Sullivan, Helmer Svensson, Julia Tchikhatcheva, Joshua Telser & Esther Tryban, Bas Van Der Sluis, Kate Vyborny, Anne Waak, Elizabeth Wei, Phelia Wenzel, Zoe Wick, Sian Williams, Ronald Wolff, Rosemary Zakrzewski.

AUTHOR THANKS

Regis St Louis

Many thanks to new and old friends who helped with tips and advice. In particular I'd like to thank Cristiano Nogueira, Jakki Saysell, Marcelo Esteves, Michael Waller, Thiago Mourão, Ian Papareskos, Eduardo Cruxen, Carina Jallad, Sophie Lewis and the folks at Riotur. Also a big thank you to my hardworking co-authors on Brazil. At home I'd like to thank Cassandra, Magdalena and Genevieve for their continued love and support.

Gary Chandler

At Lonely Planet, thank you to Kathleen, Regis, Bruce, and Alison for their kind and capable support. In Brazil, I'm especially grateful to Alex, Gerard, Bettine, Christophan and Pedro. And my sincere thanks to Suegro, Suegrita, Dad and Elyse for their help and generosity; to troopers Eva and Leo; and to Liza, who I love and admire a million Amazons over.

Gregor Clark

Thanks as always to the countless Brazilians whose thumbs-ups and warm smiles lighted my way. In particular, *um grande abraço* to Bia, Bete and John in Tiradentes, Paula in São João del Rei, Alex and Maira in Diamantina, Lena and Ricardo in Ouro Preto, Dinho and Lidia on Ilha Grande, Antônio in Caratinga, Margarida in Paraty and Bixão in Itaúnas. Lastly, enormous *muriqui*-style hugs to Gaen, Meigan and Chloe, who always make coming home the best part of the trip.

Bridget Gleeson

Thanks to all the friendly Brazilians who helped me, a solo female traveler, along the way – your advice and good cheer made all the difference. Thanks to Daniel for joining me on the road, and to my co-workers at Lonely Planet for their ongoing support.

John Noble

Special thanks to Anna Lazareva, Adriana Schmidt, Roberta Rodrigues, Kevin Raub, Patrick and Ana Muller, Angela Hofer, Marina Prado, Steven Joynson, David (Canoa), Mônica (Atins), Juliane Lähnert, Herbert Klein, Carlos Macedo and Gregor Clark.

Kevin Raub

Thanks to my wife, Adriana Schmidt Raub, who always manages to smooth over my clashes with Brazilian culture by doing the cultural sensitivity dance. At Lonely Planet, Kathleen Munnelly and my partners-in-crime, especially Regis St Louis, John Noble and Gregor Clark. On the road, Marcos Nogueira, Nick Orosz, Kely Zimuth, Mario Saraiva, Cânion Turismo, Carlos Bertolazzi, Isabella Raposeiras, Gabriel Prieto, Isabella Daelli, Clara Padron, Carlos Bertolazzi, Patricia Moll Novaes, Monique Paoletti, Thais Gagliardi, Juliana Bichir and *pizza paulistana* – I adore you.

Paul Smith

Thanks to everybody who offered their expert advice on the road, particularly Ailton Lara. Kathleen, the other authors and the rest of the team were the usual solid support network. Carol and Shawn always make sure that coming home is even more fun than traveling. Mum, Dad, Margie, Joe and Tom this is another one is for you. Miss you loads!

ACKNOWLEDGMENTS

Cover photograph: Cristo Redentor, Rio de Janeiro/SA Team/Foto Natura/Corbis

BEHIND THE SCENES

THIS BOOK

This 9th edition of Lonely Planet's *Brazil* guidebook was researched and written by Regis St Louis (coordinating author), Gary Chandler, Gregor Clark, Bridget Gleeson, John Noble, Kevin Raub and Paul Smith. Regis St Louis also coordinated the previous three editions, and the other authors have all worked on at least one previous edition.

This guidebook was commissioned in Lonely Planet's Oakland office, and produced by the following:

Commissioning Editor Kathleen Munnelly

Coordinating Editor Justin Flynn

Senior Cartographers Mark Griffiths, Alison Lyall

Coordinating Layout Designer Virginia Moreno

Managing Editors Sasha Baskett, Bruce Evans, Martine Power

Managing Layout Designer Jane Hart

Assisting Editors Sarah Bailey, Kate Daly, Katie O'Connell, Monique Perrin, Erin Richards, Jeanette Wall, Simon Williamson

Assisting Cartographers Mick Garrett, Rachel Imeson, James Leversha

Cover Research Naomi Parker

Internal Image Research Kylie McLaughlin

Language Content Branislava Vladisavljevic

Thanks to Anita Banh, Laura Crawford, Ryan Evans, Larissa Frost, Genesys India, Jouve India, Catherine Naghten, Trent Paton, Dianne Schallmeiner, Kerrianne Southway, Gerard Walker

Index

Map Legend

Sights

- Beach
- Bird Sanctuary
- Buddhist
- Castle/Palace
- Christian
- Confucian
- Hindu
- Islamic
- Jain
- Jewish
- Monument
- Museum/Gallery/Historic Building
- Ruin
- Sento Hot Baths/Onsen
- Shinto
- Sikh
- Taoist
- Winery/Vineyard
- Zoo/Wildlife Sanctuary
- Other Sight

Activities, Courses & Tours

- Bodysurfing
- Diving/Snorkelling
- Canoeing/Kayaking
- Course/Tour
- Skiing
- Snorkelling
- Surfing
- Swimming/Pool
- Walking
- Windsurfing
- Other Activity

Sleeping

- Sleeping
- Camping

Eating

- Eating

Drinking & Nightlife

- Drinking & Nightlife
- Cafe

Entertainment

- Entertainment

Shopping

- Shopping

Information

- Bank
- Embassy/Consulate
- Hospital/Medical
- @ Internet
- Police
- Post Office
- Telephone
- Toilet
- Tourist Information
- Other Information

Geographic

- Beach
- Hut/Shelter
- Lighthouse
- Lookout
- Mountain/Volcano
- Oasis
- Park
-)(Pass
- Picnic Area
- Waterfall

Population

- Capital (National)
- Capital (State/Province)
- City/Large Town
- Town/Village

Transport

- Airport
- Border crossing
- Bus
- Cable car/Funicular
- Cycling
- Ferry
- Metro station
- Monorail
- Parking
- Petrol station
- Subway station
- Taxi
- Train station/Railway
- Tram
- Underground station
- Other Transport

Note: Not all symbols displayed above appear on the maps in this book

Routes

- Tollway
- Freeway
- Primary
- Secondary
- Tertiary
- Lane
- Unsealed road
- Road under construction
- Plaza/Mall
- Steps
- Tunnel
- Pedestrian overpass
- Walking Tour
- Walking Tour detour
- Path/Walking Trail

Boundaries

- International
- State/Province
- Disputed
- Regional/Suburb
- Marine Park
- Cliff
- Wall

Hydrography

- River, Creek
- Intermittent River
- Canal
- Water
- Dry/Salt/Intermittent Lake
- Reef

Areas

- Airport/Runway
- Beach/Desert
- Cemetery (Christian)
- Cemetery (Other)
- Glacier
- Mudflat
- Park/Forest
- Sight (Building)
- Sportsground
- Swamp/Mangrove

John Noble

Pernambuco, Paraíba & Rio Grande do Norte; Ceará, Piauí & Maranhão John's second expedition from Recife to São Luís for this title confirmed his conviction that nowhere else on earth has real beaches. An author on around 80 Lonely Planet titles over nearly three decades, John is from the UK and ranks Brazil among his very favorite countries for, among other things, its musical and footballing genius, the scarcely believable euphoria of Carnaval, the beautiful Brazilian Portuguese language – and above all the Brazilian people's innate sense of what makes life good.

Kevin Raub

São Paulo State; Paraná; Santa Catarina; Rio Grande do Sul Kevin grew up in Atlanta and started his career as a music journalist in New York, working for *Men's Journal* and *Rolling Stone* magazines. He ditched the rock 'n' roll lifestyle for travel writing and moved to Brazil. His trek through the South involved way too many encounters with chicken hearts (In pasta? On pizza? No, thanks!) but disappointingly too few with the region's amazing microbrews. This is Kevin's 25th Lonely Planet guide. Find him at www.kevinraub.net.

Paul Smith

Brasília & Goiás; Mato Grosso & Mato Grosso do Sul From an early age, and with a vague and naive ambition to be the next David Attenborough, Paul dreamed of exploring the remotest areas of the globe in search of wildlife. Then Lonely Planet offered him a more realistic way of doing it. While researching this edition Paul hit Carnaval in Piri, stared into the bowels of the earth at the Nascente Azul and burnt his ears on an eternal flame in Brasília.

OUR STORY

A beat-up old car, a few dollars in the pocket and a sense of adventure. In 1972 that's all Tony and Maureen Wheeler needed for the trip of a lifetime – across Europe and Asia overland to Australia. It took several months, and at the end – broke but inspired – they sat at their kitchen table writing and stapling together their first travel guide, *Across Asia on the Cheap*. Within a week they'd sold 1500 copies. Lonely Planet was born.

Today, Lonely Planet has offices in Melbourne, London and Oakland, with more than 600 staff and writers. We share Tony's belief that 'a great guidebook should do three things: inform, educate and amuse'.

OUR WRITERS

Regis St Louis

Coordinating Author; Rio de Janeiro Regis first visited Brazil back in 2003, and he fell hard for Rio de Janeiro: its stunning landscapes, dynamic music scene, and the open and celebratory spirit of the *cariocas*. Since then he's traveled all across the country, celebrating Carnaval in Bahia, Ouro Preto and Rio, watching wildlife in the Pantanal, hunting for the perfect beach in Santa Catarina and traveling the length of the Brazilian Amazon. Regis' articles on Rio and South America have appeared in the *Chicago Tribune*, the *LA Times*, on BBC.com and elsewhere. He is also the coordinating author of Lonely Planet's *Rio de Janeiro* guide and *South America on a Shoestring*. He splits his time between New York City and the tropics.

Gary Chandler

The Amazon Gary Chandler has covered the Amazon for Lonely Planet for a decade, and has contributed to more than 20 guidebooks to Mexico and the Americas. Few assignments compare to the Amazon for sheer size and variety, from climbing 50m *samaúma* trees outside Manaus to trekking in indigenous lands 500 miles up the Rio Negro. Gary studied Ethnic Studies at UC Berkeley and journalism at Columbia University. He lives in Colorado with his wife and fellow travel writer Liza Prado, and their two children.

Gregor Clark

Rio de Janeiro State; Espírito Santo & Minas Gerais Gregor's love of all things Brazilian began with his first Portuguese class at age 19. In a quarter century of Brazilian travel, he's visited virtually every state from the Amazon to the Uruguayan border. Highlights of this research trip include watching *muriquis* cavort and rediscovering three favorite off-the-beaten-track destinations: Visconde de Mauá, Vale do Matutu and Sao Gonçalo. Gregor contributes regularly to Lonely Planet's European and South American titles. He lives in Vermont (USA) with his wife and two daughters.

Bridget Gleeson

Bahia; Sergipe & Alagoas After years of living in Argentina, the dream of coconuts and coral reefs finally lured Bridget over the Brazilian border, where she promptly fell in love with the Northeast. She writes about Latin American food, wine, art and culture for *Afar*, *Budget Travel*, *Wine Enthusiast*, *BBC Travel* and *Jetsetter*.

OVER MORE
PAGE WRITERS

Published by Lonely Planet Publications Pty Ltd
ABN 36 005 607 983
9th edition – Nov 2013
ISBN 978 1 74220 060 6
© Lonely Planet 2013   Photographs © as indicated 2013
10 9 8 7 6 5 4 3 2 1
Printed in China